# MASTERPIECES
# OF WESTERN ART

Edited by Ingo F. Walther

# MASTERPIECES OF WESTERN ART

## A history of art in 900 individual studies
## From the Gothic to the Present Day

PART I

## From the Gothic to Neoclassicism

by Robert Suckale, Manfred Wundram,
Andreas Prater, Hermann Bauer,
Eva-Gesine Baur

BARNES
&NOBLE
BOOKS
NEW YORK

*Page 2:*
**Titian**
Flora, c. 1514
Oil on canvas, 80 x 63.5 cm
Florence, Galleria degli Uffizi

This work was originally published in two volumes.

This edition published by Barnes & Noble, Inc.,
by arrangement with Benedikt Taschen Verlag GmbH

2000 Barnes & Noble Books

M 10 9 8 7 6 5 4 3 2 1

© 1995 Benedikt Taschen Verlag GmbH
Hohenzollernring 53, D-50672 Köln
© 1995 for the illustrations: VG Bild-Kunst, Bonn,
artist's heirs and artists
Editing and production: Ingo F. Walther, Alling
Cover design: Angelika Taschen, Cologne
English translation: Karen Williams, High Warden;
Ishbel Flett, Frankfurt/M.

Printed in Italy
ISBN 0-7607-2294-3

# Contents

Robert Suckale

# GOTHIC

## The rebirth of art

The Gothic era opens a new chapter in the history of art, one which marks the transition from the Middle Ages to the Renaissance and the beginning of secular painting.

In contrast to the Middle Ages, whose imagery remained rooted exclusively in the realms of the hereafter, the artists of the Gothic era drew their inspiration from life itself and in so doing found a new truth. Their discovery of a new, physical world simultaneously led them to a more joyful vision of reality which placed greater emphasis upon feeling.

With the development of court society and the rise of civic culture, the Gothic style blossomed. Art was infused with a new sophistication and elegance. Loving attention to detail, animated use of line, a luminous palette and a refined technique were typical features of the new style which would quickly take Europe by storm.

Gothic art reached its high point in the frescos and panel paintings of Giotto, Duccio, the Lorenzetti brothers, Simone Martini and Fra Angelico in Florence and Siena, in the exquisite illuminations executed by the Limburg brothers and other manuscript artists in France and the Netherlands, in the panels produced by Bohemian painters at the Prague court, and in the "soft" style of the North German masters and the graceful works of Stefan Lochner.

Giorgio Vasari (1511–1574), a Florentine painter from the school of Michelangelo (1475–1564), was the first historian of Italian art and thereby a pioneering figure in art historiography as a whole. Writing in his *Lives of the Artists*, first published in 1550, Vasari pays tribute to Giotto (c. 1266–1337) as the artist who initiated the rebirth in art. Vasari's words are no less valid today, and it is with Giotto, indeed, that we shall open our own discussion of the Gothic age. Two things should thereby be borne in mind, however. Giotto's innovations were limited solely to painting, and do not apply to sculpture or architecture. Secondly, the great Sienese painters must also be ranked alongside Giotto at the forefront of this new development.

By a rebirth of art, Vasari did not mean a return to perfect mastery of artistic means and flawless imitation of nature as in the art of Ancient Greece and Rome. For this we use the term Renaissance. This is not, however, a term we may apply to art between 1300 and 1430, as will be explained below. In the case of the Gothic era, we can speak of a rebirth neither of the art of classical antiquity nor even of painting. It is true that, in the works of classical art known to us today, we can recognize much that would later prove characteristic of the 14th and 15th century: the study of nature, and in particular the structure and movements of the human body, for example, together with the depiction of landscape and space, and a differentiated use of colour. The 13th century, however, had no first-hand knowledge of the paintings of antiquity; such works were known only from historical writings.

Artists did, however, have access to the mosaics and faded frescos of Rome's basilicas from early Christian times. Indeed, painters in Rome in the 13th century who were engaged on the restoration of these wall paintings – today entirely lost – appear to have drawn from them inspiration for their own work. The heritage of classical antiquity was also handed down in manuscript illumination, although it only started to filter through to contemporary illustrators in the 15th century. For earlier artists, however, such classical sources might simply not have existed.

Works from other fields of Greek and Roman art were, of course, to be seen in plenty. These included gems and coins, statues and sarcophogi reliefs, and the imposing remains of classical architecture, many of which abounded more than today. But although they were studied, such works formed neither a point of artistic departure nor an example to be emulated.

**Giotto di Bondone**
The Devils Cast out of Arezzo (detail), c. 1296–1297
Fresco. Assisi, San Francesco, Upper Church

## The historical role of France

As a patriotic Florentine, Vasari was no more willing to concede a leading role to his neighbouring rival city of Siena than, as an Italian, he was willing to acknowledge the contribution made by France to the emergence and development of European and Italian art in the 14th century. His contemporaries, such as Dante Alighieri (1265–1321), and Petrarch (1304–1374), who spent some years living in France, saw things differently. France was the land of knights and chivalry. The French monarchy, moreover, enjoyed enormous prestige. Louis IX, the Pious (1226–1270), was the most revered ruler in Europe and was considered the ideal king. France was not simply the birthplace of the great religious orders of the 11th and 12th century – the Clunaics, Carthusians, Cistercians and Premonstratensians – but was also the seat of colleges of learning attached to churches and cathedrals and home to the first proper university, based in Paris. Here the scientific and philosophical system of Scholasticism was conceived and developed. It married the study of classical philosophers, which for the first time included Aristotle, with a new rationalism of thought and soberness of observation. While classical antiquity represented one of its essential components, Scholasticism was nevertheless something entirely new.

Something similar might also be said of the Gothic architecture which arose in France. For while its motifs can be traced genetically to those of antiquity, what is more striking, in our view, is the independence demonstrated by its construction and planning, its mathematics and design. The spread of the new French art was of course helped by France's prestige. But we should not overlook the fact that France was also a political power of the first order. Lower Italy was ruled by the French dynasty of Anjou, which had many partisans in the country as a whole, including Florence and Siena. In 1309 the French king had forced the pope to leave Rome and establish his Curia in Avignon. Until the mid–14th century, no country commanded a comparable degree of power and respect.

Both the start and the subsequent years of the Gothic era were thus profoundly influenced by the situation in France. Wilhelm Pinder (1878–1947) was correct in describing the period after 1300 as "the rise of the age of painting"; by 1430 painting was the leading genre in Europe. But its beginnings were nevertheless modest. They were determined by architecture, which soared above all the arts, and sculpture, which had acquired a new prominence in sacred buildings. Even goldsmithery was more important. It was only with the rise of art in Italy that painting was to "grow up" to be anything.

## The Gothic architect as leading artist

The architect of the Gothic era was more of a technician and engineer than his forerunners. Even in their own day, the great master builders of the 13th century were being compared with Daedalus, the inventor of Greek legend who could actually fly – and who lost his son in so doing. Experimentation in things technical was a characteristic of the entire epoch, including the fine arts.

Large and ever larger cathedral projects demanded new planning techniques. Scale drawings first appeared in about 1200, and the work of the architect began to concentrate itself around the drawing board. The design process was intellectualized. In tandem with an innovative basic approach, design increasingly became a matter of "invention", as it was then termed. Artists' training, too, appears to have become more thorough and went beyond a simple practical apprenticeship. What we now know as a formal academic training assumed its earliest form in the guilds of cathedral stonemasons. So that building should no longer be considered a lowly "mechanical art", architects made an intensive study of geometry, one of the so-called liberal arts. They thereby reflected the contemporary view which saw God as the architect of the world.

Working with basic geometric forms and standard measurements became an automatic part of architectural design and a feature of the Gothic mentality. The geometric ornament of tracery was an artistic leitmotif of the entire era. In seeming contradiction to this stood a love of decorative elements drawn from the realm of nature, including foliage rendered in the most accurate detail. The relegation of such decoration to "subservient", secondary architectural components, however, and its combination with tracery, clearly show that geometry was understood as nature's most ideal form. It was precisely this understanding of geometry as something "natural", coupled with the desire for constant change, that led to ever more complex mathematical figurations and to the additional introduction of non-geometric components. These intricate patterns of forms were considered rational, although they may no longer seem so; to us they appear fantastical, since we do not recognize the perception of reality behind them.

As architects rose in social standing and commanded growing fame, with some of them even being knighted, so gradually other artists began to rise to prominence in their wake. An architect was not simply in charge of planning, but was himself an artist, first and foremost a sculptor, but sometimes also a designer of stained glass and a painter of decorations. The school of architecture embraced sculpture and all the arts.

## The cathedral portal: a new challenge for sculpture

Between the architects who initiated the Gothic era and the painters who brought it to its climax lay the sculptors. They introduced into the fine arts not simply the new techniques of design, but also the underlying understanding of reality and their own independent powers of invention. They made use of drawing. Painters needed only to refer to these designs and pattern books. The main task assigned to cathedral stonemasons was to carve the figurative decoration of the portals. As a new challenge for which they could draw on almost no tradition, this offered an opportunity for greater creative freedom.

The great portals and their sculptural schemes played an obvious role as publicly visible works of art. The 12th and 13th centuries were a time of economic and social upheaval. National monarchies assumed an importance equal to and even greater than the Holy Roman Empire. We see the first appearance of the powerful merchant classes and the accompanying money economy. Western Europe entered a phase of change and innovation.

Although this situation, which we recognize today as one of transition from the Middle Ages to the Renaissance, was perceived in a similar light by some contemporaries, it was viewed by others as one of serious crisis and danger, as an era of the destruction of the old, indeed even as the end of the world and the ruin of Church and State. The Church in particular was fundamentally challenged by a spate of rapidly expanding heretical movements.

One of the chief purposes of cathedral portals was to present the teachings of the Church in a solid and clear form. If the Cathars, for example, were questioning the human nature of Christ, how better to evidence that nature than through the medium of art? How better to refute doubts about the connection between the Old and the New Testament than by revealing their parallels in the symmetrical antitheses and stepped arrangements of the figures in the portals? The fascination exerted by such painted, three-dimensional sculptures, simulating the presence of those they depicted, was used to advantage. For the sculptors, this made it important, indeed imperative, to portray their characters and objects with the greatest possible expressiveness and fidelity to life.

Their sources thereby included the highly regarded sculpture of classical antiquity, together with ivories, small bronzes, fragments of statues and sarcophagi reliefs. By studying these, artists gained greater confidence in their treatment of the human body, its position when standing and its movements. They discovered the creative possibilities of drapery and the portrayal of emotion through facial expression and body language. Since one of the main aims of the new art was to achieve an emotional effect, however, the French Gothic sculptors infused the static Antique motifs with a new dynamism. Expressions were exaggerated. Drapery, too, attracted particular attention. Never totally improbable, it nevertheless changed the figures, increased their expressiveness and at the same time heightened their distance from the spectator.

From about 1250/60 onwards, there began in France a trend towards an increasing systemization of forms and standardization of types, a process which was concluded towards the end of the 13th century. Sculptors and other artists nevertheless retained something of their newly won freedom, as they were required to vary these set formulae in their own way in order to avoid producing works that all looked alike. From now on, artists strove for greater freedom and for greater sophistication of form. The zest of a work now lay less in its overall scheme than in the elaboration of its detail.

This Gothic "orthodoxy" led to paralysis in the advanced artistic forces in France and at the same time made art too academic in structure – although, at the same time, art now became more "learnable". Meanwhile, however, the "new art" had also established a foothold beyond the borders of France. Italy, in particular, was growing in importance. Here sculptors such as Nicola Pisano (c. 1220–before 1278), his son Giovanni (c. 1245–after 1314) and his pupil Arnolfo di Cambio (c. 1254–c. 1302) were heightening yet further the expressive powers of Gothic sculpture and were making the portrayal of the body once again the aim of art.

## Painting in France in the 13th century

The chief tasks required of the French painters of the 13th century were neither as new nor as unusual as those of the cathedral stonemasons. Their spheres of activity included stained glass, which occupied an important position within the decorative schemes planned for churches, and manuscript illumination. For fresco painters, however, the almost unbroken fenestration of walls left increasingly little scope for their art, which survived only in side rooms or spandrels.

None of these fields attracted the public attention granted to the church portal, however. Painting was considered of secondary importance; much of it, furthermore, was mass-produced. This was true both of the thousands of stained-glass windows and of the illuminations that were painted, in a largely routine manner and by means of extensive division of labour, in countless numbers and often in a very similar style into the same types of manuscript. Even in the case of books destined for the royal court, emphasis was placed less on the uniqueness of the individual page than on the overall homogeneity of the complete cycle. Although we may recognize analogous instances in sculpture, in the great cycles of Chartres and Amiens for example, sculptors were never dominated by the almost serial production methods of book illuminators and stained-glass painters.

## Books of Hours as a new sphere of activity

From the middle of the 13th century onwards, the growing participation of the laity in church practices fuelled the rise of the Book of Hours. Such books combined sections of the breviary with the prayer-book used by the lay congregation.

A commonly practised form of religious contemplation in those days was to meditate upon certain aspects of a scene selected according to one's personal preference. Individual elements were correspondingly elaborated in rich illustrations which allowed the pictures to be read like a text. At the same time, Books of Hours had to satisfy demands as to their aesthetic quality and indeed their entertainment value. This led not only to some fantastic ornamentation; it also meant that these books became costly and decorative objects. In their colours and forms, religious illuminations increasingly came to resemble the sophisticated luxury arts of the day. Thus they assumed the qualities of ivories and precious silks, and above all of works crafted out of gold and studded with translucent enamels in broken hues. Manuscript illumination itself became a luxury art. The illuminator came to rival other artist craftsmen. Alongside technical ability, sophistication and original invention were increasingly in demand.

## The influence of Byzantine painting

Unlike sculptors, the painters of the 13th century could look back on a well-established tradition: Byzantine painting and its older Western forms. Byzantine influence can be recognized more clearly in French painting than in sculpture (cf. ill. p. 27). This orientation towards Eastern art was even more pronounced in other countries and indeed increased over the course of the 13th century. In Venice, officially a Byzantine duchy, this was understandable – Byzantine art remained dominant here even into the 15th century. This makes it all the more surprising, however, that the main portal of St Mark's cathedral, so richly decorated with mosaics in the Byzantine style, should also bear sculptures which undoubtedly owe their origins to the latest forms of the French Gothic and even contain echoes of classical antiquity.

In Tuscany, too, which had boasted its own school of painting in the 12th century, painters took up what Vasari would later despise as the *maniera greca* and made it their own. One commonly cited reason for this development was the conquest of Constantinople by the Crusaders, with Venetian support, in 1204. But this cannot have been the sole deciding factor since, in addition to several earlier Crusades, Tuscany had already had other contacts with the East. More important was the fact that, both thematically and in its portrayal of pious contemplation, Byzantine panel painting offered something which Western painting lacked. The receptiveness towards Byzantine art coincided with a growth in popular religious movements. As the birthplace of these movements, Italy was also the country where the influence of Byzantine art was felt most deeply.

## The altarpiece: a major new genre in Italy

Church interiors in earlier times were dominated by their large altarpieces. It is hard to imagine that, for the 13th century, such paintings were something new. The story of their origins is so complicated, however, that we shall here simply describe the situation as it stood in Italy in 1300. For Italy was at that time the country in which a painted panel rested on virtually every altar. From here the altarpiece spread northwards, eventually replacing even the stone retable.

The inspiration for the altarpiece came from Byzantine iconostases and icons, while its raison d'être was born out of changes in the liturgy and in church practices. Whereas priests had previously celebrated Mass facing the congregation, it now became the custom for them to face in the opposite direction, at side altars as before, with their backs to the faithful. The priest was now seen as the leader of a procession to God.

The mendicant orders called for greater numbers of religious images to increase the devoutness of the people. This was accompanied more generally by a growing desire for greater visual immediacy. Corpus Christi, the festival celebrated in honour of the Eucharist, was only introduced in 1264. At this time it became common for the priest to lift up the Host during the sacrifice of the Mass. It was during this same period that monstrances and ostensoria were designed in which the holy sacraments could actually be seen. The altarpiece can only be understood in the light of this desire for greater visibility. For the faithful, it placed the priest visually against a sublime backdrop. The painted altarpiece also replaced the mosaics and frescos in the apses and supplanted costly golden antependia and centrepieces. Although the main panel was always solemn and splendid, other sections of the altarpiece often abounded with up to fifty different scenes portrayed in separate compartments, as in the *Maestà* by Duccio (c. 1250/60–1318). The altarpiece, and no longer the church portal, became the most important element of a church's decoration.

This shift is best illustrated in an example. On the altar of their cathedral, the Sienese worshipped the so-called *Madonna con gli occhi grossi* (Madonna with the Large Eyes), a modest work of the early 13th century to which they attributed their great victory over the Florentines in 1260. But not even fifty years after this miracle, the altarpiece was "deposed". It was replaced by Duccio's *Maestà*, a painting praised by contemporaries as "bigger, more beautiful and more pious". On the day that Duccio's panel was taken from his workshop to the cathedral in 1311, the shops stayed shut; everyone was out on the streets to accompany the new portrait of the city's patroness on its ceremonial procession to the cathedral.

### Devotional images

In the longer term, devotional paintings became almost more important than altarpieces. Not only were they more richly varied, but they also formed the focus of private worship and hence the genre of painting in which personal taste was first able to come to the fore. Devotional pictures looked back to the Byzantine icon as their model. Their spread was fuelled by the trend in the 13th century towards the practise of religion in settings other than church. In France this trend produced the Book of Hours, in Italy the painted panel. With their large format, larger even than altar retables, devotional images served religious confraternities as a focal point of worship which at the same time publicly identified their respective patron saints. As icons, whether half-length or in other formats, they could be found in various parts of the church, for example in the sacristy or over doors, as well as in chapels and private homes. A number of different types of private devotional picture gradually emerged, such as pictures for the bedroom or for journeys, in the form of diptychs or in imitation of an altar.

Byzantine subjects such as the Man of Sorrows and Our Lady of Sorrows, and the many paintings of the Virgin portraying the tender or dolorous relationship between Mother and Child, were joined by new themes and motifs and by ever new pictorial inventions. Most remarkable of all, however, is the composition of these works. Since they could be painted relatively free from liturgical and other ecclesiastical constraints, their content and form could be infused with a very personal interpretation, one either warmer and deeper in human terms, or alternatively more splendid and superficial. Good pictures of this kind are rarely schematic; rather, the genre inspired the most individual and unusual solutions.

### Giotto and fresco painting in Central Italy

Giotto was a fresco painter by nature. In order to understand his historical importance, we need to take a closer look at this – to us, now unfamiliar – branch of painting. Earlier fresco painting in Italy was a flourishing genre little bounded by traditions or rules. In the 13th century it received a fresh boost in Rome, as artists working on the restoration of early Christian frescos, such as those in San Paolo fuori le mura, assimilated the influence of these much older works into their own style.

Florentine fresco painters profited from this stimulus from Rome, in particular during the decoration of the Upper Church of San Francesco in Assisi, the most important commission of the period. With the exception of Duccio, all of the great artists of the day were active in Assisi between 1270 and 1340. Previously, wall painting had often been viewed as simply a cheap substitute for more expensive mosaics. Through the work of Giotto, however, it earned a reputation so great that it was now considered worthy even of wealthy palace chapels. Apart from Venice and some papal buildings, mosaics were now almost completely supplanted.

### The fresco technique

The word *fresco* (It. "fresh") is derived from the technique of applying paint to plaster that is still damp, as opposed to painting on a dry ground (*a secco*), a technique which was common in the northern countries. Frescos were painted in sections corresponding to a day's work, usually from top to bottom. The artist was required to work fast, if the painting was not to perish. Only the preparatory work was free from time pressure. A monochrome sketch (*sinopia*) of the composition was drawn onto the raw plaster ground; if necessary, a second could be outlined on a new layer of plaster. These underlying sketches were gradually covered as the fresco was executed. Such sketches are frequently revealed when frescos are removed today for conservation reasons. A final layer of plaster was then applied to the section to be painted that day, and the main elements of the composition were once more scored or lightly painted onto its surface. Artists needed a trained hand since it was virtually impossible to make corrections. Only blues and the finer details of ornamentation and gilding were added later.

Unfortunately, these were often precisely the areas that were the first to perish and peel off (cf. ill. p. 31). As a result, the overall appearance of older frescos is often very misleading. In the case of the *Annunciation* by Fra Angelico (c. 1395/1400–1455) in San Marco in Florence (ill. p. 59), for example, only a pale pink shadow remains of the red gold brocade worn by the Virgin Mary, originally the strongest colour accent in the entire composition. We can clearly see in this fresco which sections interested the artist the most – the capitals, for example, which he has tried to render as accurately as possible. The fact that the Virgin's robe has undergone several alterations since the preliminary drawing also points to the artist's ongoing efforts to perfect the main figure. In this fresco, as in many others, it is also possible to identify a number of different hands. Less important areas such as the grassy area on the left were entrusted to assistants.

### Giotto's rationalism

In the case of large-scale projects such as the decoration of entire churches, good organization and a sensible division of labour were needed, together with properly trained assistants and easy-to-grasp formulae for the painting of faces, clothing and gestures. Giotto's talents included all of these. Tautness and clarity of composition were also fundamental characteristics of his art. In his *Life of St Francis* in Assisi, the frescos have been arranged into groups of three, and their ordering principle has been determined both by a uniform architecture with a single focal point, and by the composition itself. The scenes are thus presented both as strictly framed pictures and at the same time as part of a carefully structured wall.

This clarity was part of the legacy of French Gothic architecture. A comparison of the thrones in two panels by Cimabue (c. 1240–after 1302) and Giotto (ills. pp. 28 and 29) clearly reveals what French architecture had to teach about clarity (and at the same time rhythm) in the organization of forms. But Giotto went far beyond all that had gone before. In the Arena Chapel in Padua, his masterpiece, the painter became the designer of space, walls and vault – he placed

**Giotto di Bondone**
Crucifixion (detail), 1303–1305
Fresco. Padua, Arena Chapel (Cappella degli Scrovegni all'Arena)

himself in the position of architect. But he also thought like an architect: his scenes and architectural details are painted as if illuminated by a single light source, one identical with the main window in the west wall.

There is something paradoxical about the changes which Giotto wrought vis-à-vis the painting of the past. Figures in earlier frescos appeared distanced and unfamiliar, lined up as if in a shop window with no real eye contact or interaction. Giotto was the first to logically develop dramatic narrative. Always bearing in mind the precise location of the viewer, he abandoned popular conventions such as the three-quarter view of head and body, and presented his figures from behind, from the side, or turning round, just as the story demanded. In no way, however, is the content of the scene thereby obscured. On the contrary: Giotto uses such means

**Giotto di Bondone**
The Marriage Procession of the Virgin,
1303–1305
Fresco. Padua, Arena Chapel (Cappella
degli Scrovegni all'Arena)

to heighten the expressiveness of the whole, as in his *Lamentation of Christ* in Padua (ill. p. 32).

### Giotto's depiction of real life
Giotto was a painter of fact, not fiction. The innovations which he introduced into his art were never mere whimsy. There is nothing artifical about them. Each narrative is divided into main and subsidiary themes, with main and subsidiary characters presented either individually or in groups, according to their varying importance for the story. Giotto's compositions are born less of artistic tradition than of the desire to capture the essence of the scene in hand and to lend it the authenticity of real life. Movement and expression are restrained.

It is hard to imagine today just how astonished Giotto's contemporaries must have been by the – in comparison to earlier frescos – almost ordinary world he portrayed. Giotto's "naturalness" was lauded over and over again. But we should not mistake him for a forerunner of the Dutch genre painters of the 17th century. His figures remain severe; their actions are measured and dignified. His paintings create an overall impression of nobleness and monumentality. Giotto thereby renounced much that had characterized frescos in the past. Thus the abundant folds of drapery which had for the most part resembled abstract swathes of fabric are reduced to a small number of somewhat tectonic forms. He also diminished the lavish quantities of ornamentation and gold paint. Landscape, setting and objects are rendered with the greatest economy.

### The imitation of nature
Modern-day viewers of Giotto's works will find it hard to agree with Giovanni Boccaccio (1313–1375), writing in his *Decameron* (1348–1353), that Giotto "was a genius so sublime that there was nothing produced by Nature [...] that he could not depict to the life, whether his implement was a stylus, a pen or a paintbrush: his depiction looked not like a copy but the real thing, so that more often than not the viewer's eye was deceived, convinced that it was looking at the real object and not his depiction of it." But nor is such praise, heard repeatedly over the centuries, merely empty words. We should bear in mind that in using terms such as "nature", "naturalness" and "illusion", we assign to them our own meanings, without stopping to ask ourselves if they were perhaps understood differently in earlier times. Nor do we consider the widely differing ways in which individual aspects of reality can be reproduced in a manner "close to nature". Photography, for example, offers us the naturalism of the imitation of materials and the precise reproduction of surfaces. Yet we no longer have much of what earlier periods took for granted: the accurate feeling for the body and the rendering of its different ways of standing and resting, movements and expressions. We must learn to see that Giotto is first and foremost a figure painter. Buildings and landscape are simply accompanying features which occupy a secondary position. Giotto distinguishes between type and social class in his characters; he shows their reactions, but pays less attention to their individual peculiarities.

## The social status of Giotto and art

Something of the rationalism of the Florentine merchants and bankers with whom Giotto was acquainted, and from whom he received commissions, is recognizable in his art. This alone does not explain the processes by which it arose, however. Although Giotto painted for princes and cardinals, Franciscans and churches, he was neither a court painter in the proper sense nor the painter of just one social class. He never went beyond the demands of good painting to satisfy the tastes of his patrons or their wishes as to how they should be portrayed. The artist retained the republican freedom of his home city of Florence.

Giotto's self-confident approach to his commissions was undoubtedly helped by his healthy financial position. At the same time, however, there was a growing belief in Italy that it was better to own an important work of art than to engage the services of a great artist merely as a partisan or lackey. Thus the first known work by Duccio is a large panel painting for a Florentine confraternity – a commission awarded the Sienese artist over local competition. Thus, too, the Pisan artist Giovanni Pisano worked in his rival city of Siena. Robert of Anjou (c. 1275–1343) employed both Giotto and Simone Martini (c. 1280/85–1344), and Cardinal Orsini (d. 1343) issued commissions to Simone Martini and Pietro Lorenzetti (c. 1280/90–c. 1348). Such patrons demonstrated the philosophy of the "collector" of art. Although this philosophy was by no means in evidence throughout the era, it became very important for the development of an independent art.

The influence which Giotto exerted on artistic activity in his home city was not always inspirational, however. Thus the themes he avoided were similarly ignored by Florentine artists, who only began to expore the genre of the small-format domestic altar and devotional picture – a genre which Giotto apparently disliked – as a consequence of impulses from Siena. It seems that Giotto's workshop contemporaries, for all their own talents, never perceived themselves as anything more than his lesser imitators, and hence remained entrenched in the same set formulae and standard canon of figures, heads and gestures.

## The singularity of Duccio's art

If many aspects of Giotto's art seem distant to us today, that of Duccio, his artistic peer and the founder of what would come to be known as the Sienese school of painting, seems positively foreign. The reasons for this lie not so much in Duccio's proximity to the Byzantine style, but in the singularity of his art. Giotto's painting has the momentum and clarity of a confidently delivered speech; Duccio's art is that of absorption and a slow, gentle penetration of things; it is a meditative manner of painting. Hence as Giotto's field was chiefly the fresco, Duccio's was the panel painting. Hence, too, his best works show signs of constant reworking going

far beyond what might be dismissed as pentimenti (formal changes made in the course of painting). To the modern-day viewer, accustomed to simple pictorial signals, Duccio's delicate linear rhythms and finely gradated hues therefore offer a particularly difficult challenge.

For many art historians, however, Duccio's openness to outside stimuli undermines the value of his art and makes him, in their eyes, insufficiently original. There was hardly a contemporary painter so intimately indebted to Eastern art as Duccio. He also, undoubtedly, admired the work of the Florentine Cimabue, and his late masterpiece, the *Maestà* in the Cathedral Museum in Siena, also testifies to his assimilation of Giotto.

## Duccio, a painter of devotional pictures

To call Duccio an eclectic, however, is certainly not the right way to understand his work. If we look more closely at the few surviving paintings from his hand, it becomes clear that Duccio devoted himself first and foremost not simply to panel painting but, more specifically, to the genre of the domestic devotional picture. Whereas we may recognize in Giotto an inner affinity with the large-scale altarpiece, the singularity of Duccio's art arises out of the traditions and requirements of devotional works.

In the case of the devotional picture, as we have seen, it was not so much a matter of following rules and conventions or of imitating traditional types (although this might be the case in a painting executed for a more conservative-minded

**Duccio di Buoninsegna**
The Temptation of Christ on the Mountain, c. 1308–1311
Tempera on wood, 43.2 x 46 cm
New York, The Frick Collection

**Cimabue**
Maestà, c. 1270 (?)
(Madonna Enthroned)
Tempera on wood, 427 x 280 cm
Paris, Musée National du Louvre

patron); rather, it was a question of personal interpretation, wealth of variety, inventiveness and the ability to find solutions for widely differing subjects and clients. This must be seen as a protracted process having a transformational influence upon art which lasted into the 16th century. At first, however, the more relaxed requirements of devotional pictures stood at the opposite end of the spectrum to the stylistically tight-knit schools of the day and their insistence upon adherence to convention. As the awareness of the separateness of the individual increased and the genre of portraiture rose, however, the wish to own a personally conceived and composed devotional image grew ever stronger. It no longer sufficed for a family to commission a single Madonna for the home. Those who could afford it now wanted a picture for themselves alone or even – as in the case of collectors – a new one at regular intervals.

This also gave rise to new demands. It was no longer sufficient for artist and client to discuss the latter's personal wishes as regards subject. The painters themselves had to take part in this process of individualization. Only then could they truly personalize their art, could they become more varied and inventive. One means to this end was to introduce additional details into their paintings: carpets, flowers, precious vases. But this path failed to lead very far, and often proved a dead end.

Duccio showed that the only meaningful response to this new challenge was the adoption of more sophisticated means of composition and technique and an artistically richer design, stimulated amongst other things by the assimilation of foreign models.

### Duccio's Madonna of the Franciscans
Duccio's innovative approach to the devotional painting can be demonstrated in the example of his *Madonna of the Franciscans* (ill. p. 33). The picture portrays the enthroned Madonna of the Protective Mantle, a type derived from Byzantine art. Three Franciscans are seen kneeling at the Virgin's feet, their passionate plea for intercession expressed in the repetition and intensification of their imploring gestures. A differentiated contrast is provided by Mary's face which, infused with grace and protectiveness, appears gentle and tender. The picture is held in a multi-layered tension of symmetry and asymmetry. The Madonna is seated in the central axis, emphasized by a large nimbus. She is looking not at the Franciscans, but out of the picture at the viewer. Her head is both the centre of the composition and at the same time a calm and concentrated focal point of devotion. The picture is reminiscent of a cult image and provides a centrepiece for prayer. Since it was designed, in line with earlier religious practice, to be viewed and contemplated for a long time, it is filled with a host of small additional narrative details: angels, the childish figure of Christ, his gesture of blessing and his grip on his mother's finger. Above all, however, it is the style of artistic representation which captivates and holds the viewer's attention in thrall.

The finely undulating gold lines of the hem of the Madonna's mantle are derived from older painting, although they are also seen in Giotto. They are not merely decorative forms, but also – as can be seen on the hem of the right arm – vehicles of expression and a guide for the eye. They combine and further develop French Gothic and Byzantine motifs, and are used by the artist as a means both of direct description and ornate circumscription, and of formulating delicate or hard movements. They introduce restlessness and variety into the picture, so that the eye never tires of looking at it.

This is a new response to the demands imposed by the devotional picture. Duccio's palette can be explained in a similar way. As a general rule, he avoids covering garments entirely with gold Byzantine herringbone patterns. Hems and seams, painted in costly gold, stand isolated on the colour plane. Their value is thereby heightened and they appear all the more sumptuous. This is almost paradoxical, however, for in Duccio's day it was blue –obtained in a laborious process from the semi-precious stone lapis lazuli – which in material terms was more expensive than gold. The manner in which it is applied, however, makes the gold appear more precious, in line with its luminosity and symbolic meaning.

While Duccio did not work exclusively with the purest and most expensive colours, it was by using gradated and mixed hues that he drew conscious attention to their superior status. Around the central characters and components of the composition, portrayed in pure colours, are grouped a rich sequence of delicate shades. The already emotionally profound impact of the pure colours is thereby amplified, without obscuring their monetary value.

### Duccio's innovative use of different styles

For a painter of devotional images, the idea of a break with the past of the sort ventured by Giotto was unthinkable. Byzantine art had left too deep an impression and was not to be deposed. At the same time, however, contemporary tastes were calling for modernization. Here Duccio took French art as his model, employing French Gothic motifs in their pure form for individual standing figures, who thereby assume an expression of elegant animation. The Byzantine style nevertheless remained a valid alternative, and was used for particularly solemn subjects such as the *Transfiguration* and Christ's appearances after his death on the rear of the *Maestà*, as well as for parts of the main front.

Nowhere does Duccio reveal signs of the pattern-book mentality of older artists. He looked to existing styles as an opportunity to enrich his own means of expression and representation. These not only inspired him, but also encouraged in him – and perhaps even gave birth to – a tendency towards differentiation and innovation. It was this which enabled him to become the true pioneer of the devotional picture as a forum for artistic achievement.

Duccio thereby fuelled the metamorphosis and renewal of art. At the same time, his openness to outside sources made him the founder of a distinct Sienese school of painting. In contrast to Giotto's followers, rarely able to break away from the substance of their master's art, the great Sienese artists Simone Martini and the Lorenzetti brothers made Duccio's flexibility the principle of their own work. Duccio himself suffered the consequences of this when, during his own lifetime and just four years after the completion of his acclaimed *Maestà*, the commission for a *Maestà* fresco in Siena Town Hall was awarded to Simone Martini (ill. p. 18). The fame of the teacher was already overshadowed by that of his pupil.

**Duccio di Buoninsegna**
Rucellai Madonna (Maestà), c. 1285
Tempera on wood, 450 x 290 cm
Florence, Galleria degli Uffizi

### Simone Martini – the first court painter

Simone was the only painter to be as famous amongst his contemporaries as Giotto. In contrast to the latter, however, he was the first example of the new breed of court painter. He shaped court taste in painting right up to the early 15th century, and his influence, both inside and outside Italy, cannot be overestimated. He worked chiefly in the service of the French royal house of Anjou and for its courtiers and supporters, and towards the end of his life for the Curia in Avignon. In 1317 Simone was raised to the nobility and thereby became the first recorded artist in a long line of European painters and sculptors to be rewarded for his services at court.

Like Duccio, Simone's painting shows him processing different sources. This characteristic mix can be clearly seen in his own *Maestà* of 1315/16 in Siena Town Hall. The composition owes its basic organization, and in particular the ordering of its secondary figures, to Duccio. The pair of kneeling

**Simone Martini**
Maestà, 1315/16
Fresco (detail), 10.58 x 9.77 m (total size)
Siena, Palazzo Pubblico, Museo Civico

angels takes up a motif from Giotto's *Ognissanti Madonna* (ill. p. 29), while the use of coloured molten metals in the fresco indicates a knowledge of Roman artistic practices. The focal point of the picture, however, the Madonna enthroned, is French.

### Simone's assimilation of French Gothic

Simone was particularly drawn to French art, more so than any other painter in Italy. French art and French courtly culture provided the models for the regal and dignified representation of the Madonna in his *Maestà*. A richly ornate throne employing forms from Gothic architecture provides a royal seat for the Virgin, who is clad in a silk fabric of subtle beauty, patterned in gold and decorated with jewels. The saints making up her band of courtiers hold a large textile canopy over her as if in a procession. Mother and Child appear truly regal.

There are French aspects to other elements of the composition. The drapery is borrowed from Parisian sculpture from the second half of the 13th century (and not from contempor-

ary 14th-century sculpture). This style of drapery is complex · and hence difficult to interpret. It both alienates and lends shape to the body, neither denying it nor itself becoming unnatural. But while it is studied from nature, it is consciously stylized and reworked. The folds have plastic volume, yet appear predominantly linear and rhythmical in effect. In the hands of the artists of the day, these drapery systems became expressive or decorative, full of pathos or ornamental. Duccio had also discovered them for himself.

Simone emphasizes the aesthetic side of his painting even more than his French forerunners, stylizing both faces and clothes more strongly. Everything appears deliberately beautiful, but also cooler and more distant. The sense of unapproachability exuded by his figures must have greatly pleased the members of the court. At the same time, however, he is much more concrete than the French: courtiers would have been able to recognize themselves in Simone's distanced, nonchalant and elegant figures. More still, they would have found confirmed in them the comtemporary ideals of pose and gesture.

Simone's representation of the real society of the day extended to what we may call "costume realism", i.e. the precise observation of fabrics, dress and accessories. We can take his paintings unreservedly as faithful records of the culture of their day. His contemporaries, meanwhile, would have been able to recognize how many florins per ell each fabric cost. No French artist, it may be said, had ever ventured this before. Simone thereby breached the bounds of convention in French sacred art. Only one who had visited France, but had not completed his training there, could paint in this way.

### Painting and luxury art

It is clear from the antependia and retables of the 12th and 13th century that they were often simply a cheap substitute for the works wrought in gold that belonged more properly to the altar, but which were often prohibitively expensive. Imitation was thereby carried to such a point that painters would ornament their gold grounds using the instruments and techniques of goldsmithery, often also incorporating the latter's motifs and decorative forms.

Manuscript illumination in the late 13th century in France also became, as we have seen, a luxury art – decorative, costly and delicate. It had a striking affinity with the textile arts, ivory carving and goldwork. It would be a long time before painting could compete. Only panel painting started from a position of slight advantage, thanks to its more refined techniques.

First, however, it should be remembered that the goldsmith's art was held in extraordinarily high esteem in the Middle Ages. In the 12th century it was the leading branch of fine art. The prestige enjoyed by goldsmiths arose both out of the technical skills which their craft demanded and out of the great monetary and symbolic value of their materials, which took pride of place within churches and which served rulers for their insignia.

In the 13th century, the social rank of goldsmiths was no longer quite so exclusive, but it was still predominantly they who shaped the contemporary taste for things fine, hard and pointed, and the preference for works of great artifice. They explored in their pieces the sophisticated interplay of light and shadow and treated their surfaces in varying ways in order to subdue or heighten effects of light. Different ways of setting precious stones, together with innovations in enamelling techniques, gave birth to exquisite combinations of colour and light.

In the face of the rivalry between the goldsmith's art and painting, Giotto chose total abstinence and restricted himself solely to the media and techniques proper to painting. So too did Duccio. In the field of the devotional picture, however, it seems that artists were in the long term unable to withstand the pressures of contemporary taste and the expectations of their clients. People's delight in costliness was too great for them not to want something similar in painting.

### Simone's technical innovations

Simone took up the gauntlet and surpassed the goldsmith's art with its own means. In so doing, however, he made painting at least indirectly dependent upon luxury art. Although this dependency helped panel painting to success in its own right in the 13th century, in the years around 1400 in particular it occasionally produced hermaphroditic pictures which lay closer to goldsmithery than to painting. Seen in this light, it is easy to understand why, in his book on painting, the first art theoretician of the Renaissance, Leon Battista Alberti (1404–1472), recommended using no gold whatsoever, but urged artists to portray the effects of light exclusively through the media of painting. It was better, he argued, to depict even metals themselves with paint.

Simone attained a particularly high degree of perfection in his treatment of gold surfaces. His saints are given not simply ordinary nimbuses, but richly embossed disks or even glorioles made up of a number of engraved rays of varying lengths. Under the right light they begin to glitter and shine.

Other areas of Simone's gold grounds are chased or deadened, whereby the artist partly employed the tools of the goldsmith. He also had various dies and embossing hammers made for his workshop use, featuring small suns, leaves, pointed arches and over a dozen other patterns. Such a wealth of forms and rich variation of light effects cannot be found amongst his goldsmith contemporaries. These, for their part, were now obliged to look to painters for instruction.

They thereby rapidly came up against the limits of what was technically possible. The goldsmith was unable to imitate Simone's luminous colour technique, for example. Although this technique, which involved applying thin glazes of colour over a sheet of silver or gold, was inspired by that of translucent silver enamel, enamel itself was fragile and soon fell off. The number of enamel pigments, too, was limited. The painter, on the other hand, could mix his colours as he pleased. Above all, the surfaces thus treated could also be engraved or overpainted with further layers of varying degrees of transparency.

Simone Martini may also be credited with pioneering an iridescent palette in which, for example, green is transformed into red within the same plane. He employed this new technique even in fresco, a medium in which it is almost impossible (cf. ill. p. 35). Overall, it may be said that in his attempts to achieve differing degrees of luminosity and transparency by means of sophisticated colouring, he showed up for the first time the limits of the traditional tempera technique. It was not until the end of the 14th century that this technique was itself improved. Experimentation with new binding agents eventually led to the oil painting of the brothers Hubert (d. 1426) and Jan van Eyck (c. 1390–1441), who nevertheless retained tempera for the layers of the underpainting.

It is clear even from such a brief look at Simone's technical innovations why, from this point in time onwards, painting became prince of the arts in the courts of Europe. It would be its powers of representation, however, that would ensure its enduring supremacy over the luxury arts.

### Backward-looking modernists: the Lorenzetti brothers

In the manner of their Sienese predecessors, Pietro and Ambrogio Lorenzetti (c. 1290–c. 1348?) both drew upon the heritage of older traditions and were at the same time independent, self-confident and highly original. Particularly unusual were their studies of nature, which extended to things not previously considered worthy of attention. In this respect their art went beyond the mere recording of topographical background and must properly speaking be called landscape painting. They observed such details as time of day and season of the year, colour reflections and the shadows cast against the wall by a fire. In their narrative paintings, they introduced many secondary figures and individual features borrowed from real life and their daily environment, in part anticipating later genre-style painting. Sometimes, however, their pictures thereby came slightly "unstuck", as in the case of some of Pietro's frescos in the Lower Church in Assisi, in which he attempted to portray Duccio-type figures with the physical solidity of those by Giotto – and to place them in a realistic setting to boot.

The Lorenzetti brothers' study of nature went hand in hand with the expansion and improvement of their artistic means. Their observation of spaces and buildings led not only to early forms of architectural fantasy (ill. p. 38), but also to original solutions with regard to the relationship between figure and setting and to a clearer structuring of the pictorial composition. They were similarly purposeful in their first attempts at centralized perspective. Colour, too, became the subject of new exploration, as evidenced in Ambrogio's highly individual combinations of expressive colours and Pietro's finely gradated sequences of greens and greys. In their urge to train their vision more closely upon objects and people, and at the same time upon art itself, the Lorenzetti brothers went so far as to execute studies of classical art with a clarity never previously seen in painting.

### The Tuscans: artistic giants of the 14th century

The reason why we have discussed the Florentine and Sienese painters in such depth is because they were recognized, both during their own lifetimes and all the more so afterwards, as great artists whose example was to be emulated. Their special position within the era demands appropriate recognition. Together with the somewhat earlier sculptors Nicola and Giovanni Pisano and Arnolfo di Cambio, they were the first truly individual artist personalities in Italy. Their standing was also acknowledged north of the Alps. But whereas central Europe was in some ways still a developing country with respect to art, the widespread impact of Italian art in France, a country with its own established traditions, is indeed astonishing, and cannot be explained simply by the exile of the papal court to Avignon.

As can be seen in the case of the greatest master known to us from this era, Jean Pucelle (active c. 1319–1335), Italian influences were directly embraced by the French painters themselves, who assimilated them into their work with a maximum degree of independence and freedom. As with the younger of the great Sienese masters, Pucelle may be said to have studied his great predecessors (above all Duccio) not out of dependency, but in order to enrich his own art.

Pucelle's grisaille miniatures should thus be understood less as a gesture of modesty than as a demonstration, analogous to the art of Simone Martini, of the superiority of painting over the luxury arts. The precious and expensive materials of ivory and marble are here replaced by the artistry of the painter. Just as the elegant paleness of such materials, so highly prized in aristocratic and court circles, was further underlined by contrasting them with gems, enamels, or a coloured or gold setting, so Pucelle's greys are ennobled by the introduction of two or three chromatic colours on either side.

Only in Bohemia, and even then not until the mid–14th century, would Italian influence be assimilated into painting in a similarly independent and far-reaching manner.

### The great plague of 1347–1350 and its consequences

All these developments were interrupted by an event on a European scale, the Black Death, which between 1347 and 1350 carried off over one third of the population, and in some places, such as Siena, even more. Both historically and psychologically, it was a major turning point – something clearly reflected in art. Although it made less of an impact upon the political situation – for example upon one of the kingdoms or systems of government – the plague nevertheless produced significant social shifts which would eventually express themselves in a change in the balance of power.

The plague led to a concentration of wealth in the hands of those who had survived. This in itself would not have been particularly significant, were it not for the fact that the Black Death had changed people's attitudes to money. In his memorable description of the epidemic in Florence, Boccaccio highlights the opposite reactions it prompted. While some saw the disaster as a reason for repentance and good works, others took it as an excuse to let their hair down and live it up while they still could. With the end of the plague, this sense of wanting to live life to the full came to predominate, although without suppressing asceticism altogether. The consequence for art was an unexpected boom in the market for luxury goods, an increased demand for the things that made life beautiful and served human pleasure.

Due to the periodic return of the plague, population levels failed to recover from their sudden and dramatic drop (only in the 18th century did cities again attain the average population figures of the period before 1347). This had its own consequences. The declining number of customers brought about a crisis in such traditional centres of the textile industry as Flanders and Florence. Some cities never recovered economically and succumbed to a concentration of political power, such as Siena and Pisa. The number of urban centres in Italy shrank.

The reduction in the population also brought about an agricultural crisis which dealt a devastating blow across the whole of Europe. The price of grain and many other crops fell, while the price of hand-made goods generally rose. Since farming had accounted for a good 90 per cent of the economy of the old Europe, this agricultural crisis became a decisive factor in the economic demise of all those deriving their income from the land and its produce: the nobility, the land-owning monasteries and above all the clergy.

### Reactions in art

The repercussions for art were many and varied. The decline of the urban centres in Tuscany, the continued exile of the papacy in Avignon and other factors led to a shift in the political, economic and hence also artistic balance in Upper Italy. The rise of cities north of the Alps was accelerated, as was the expansion of some of the principalities, above all Bohemia. Flanders, like the other provinces of the Netherlands, became a principality. The large monasteries played an ever dwindling role as patrons of art, as did the lesser nobility. Into their places stepped the middle classes and courtiers, with very different demands and expectations. In central

**Duccio di Buoninsegna**
Christ Entering Jerusalem, 1308–1311
(from the back of the Maestà, formerly on the
high altar of Siena cathedral)
Tempera on wood, 100 x 57 cm
Siena, Museo dell'Opera del Duomo

flowering of the International Gothic, which began to un-
dergo radical upheaval after about 1410.

An immediate consequence of the plague was an increasing number of paintings of Christ's Passion. Although the
subject is found prior to the years of the Black Death, it now
began to be treated on an especially large scale and often in
an exaggerated manner, as in the grotesque caricatured
Pietàs produced in Germany.

Another characteristic feature of these years are the many
Byzantine-style panel paintings which they brought forth.
It seems that neither the new painting of the first half of the
14th century nor the very secular style of images after the
plague were considered appropriate for sacred representations of the heavenly sphere. The gap between religious and
artistic content widened, leading amongst other things to
the outburst of Hussite iconoclasm at the end of this era.

Such internal contradictions are clearly apparent in the art
of Tommaso da Modena (c. 1325/26–1379), whose fresco
cycle of the *Legend of St Ursula* was effectively a secular society piece (ill. p.46). Were it not for her nimbus, there
would be nothing to make St Ursula holier than her equally
chubby-cheeked, chattering companions. The contemporary
fashion for close-fitting dresses, whose cording granted a sensual emphasis to breast and hips, aptly matches the artist's
thoroughly physical, this-worldly vision. Both share the
same very earthly vitality.

### Patrons in a changing set of circumstances

Such contradictions in art are clear pointers to the tensions
inherent within the age. A striking feature of this era is its
retrospective tendency. The reasons for Byzantine-style icons
in religious circles were not the same, however, as those
which prompted the Benedictines to turn to their past and
copy works from the early Middle Ages. Charles V of France
(1338–1380) looked back to the reign of Louis the Pious,
under whom French art was considered to have reached its
greatest flowering. His uncle Charles IV (1316–1378), on
the other hand, based in his new capital of Prague, cham-
pioned everything that would help legitimize his fabricated
claims to power. He thereby drew not only upon the architecture and sculpture of the 13th century, but also upon even
older styles such as pre-Carolingian Irish manuscript illumination. He collected and integrated almost all kinds of antiquities, especially those that could simultaneously serve as re-
liquaries.

The nobility, the class which had suffered the most in the
agricultural crisis, also revealed backward-looking tendencies in what art it could still afford. The world of chivalry
saw a first revival; the old romances were newly transcribed,
richly illustrated and read. Courts entertained themselves
with masquerades and – from a practical point of view, superfluous – tournaments. It was not the knights themselves
who dressed up as such, but the princes and their house-

Europe, however, the influence of the middle classes would
only become prominent in the 15th century. The second half
of the 14th century was still dominated by the princes and
their courts.

Nevertheless, the epoch was neither chronologically, geographically nor socially uniform. Nor was this be to expected
in a time of such rapidly accelerating change. It can be
divided instead into two halves: a first phase lasting up till
around 1370/80 and comprising a diverse series of regional
developments, and subsequently the more homogeneous

holds, who although nobles by descent had long since ceased to be knights in real life, and who now simply played at their roles. These were elite circles who created their own world with symbolic colours, mottos and devices understood only by fellow initiates.

There was nevertheless an astonishing structural uniformity in the contradictoriness of the era, particularly towards the end of the century. Contributing towards this homogeneity was the fact that the ruling families were all closely related by marriage. The princes of Bavaria, Bohemia, Milan and France were intimately allied, often at several levels. Gifts were exchanged and even court painters were dispatched on visits.

The art of this epoch has become known as the International Gothic. International is a word that could also be applied to the art of a century earlier. The situation at that time was nevertheless different; dominant around 1300 was French art (with the weighty exception of Giotto). Around 1400, however, a number of more or less equally important and creative centres existed alongside each other: Upper Italy, the Franco-Flemish region, Bohemia, as well as other cities and provinces. Stimuli were mutually exchanged. One might say there was a basic structure to the epoch, although this should not automatically be assumed to imply something stable. Everything was shifting, albeit at first in a similar direction.

## Collectors

The analogous conditions reigning throughout Europe produced a similar philosophy of life, a related attitude towards the world, to possessions, and to art. Naturally, art continued to serve a range of specific functions; traditions were by no means severed. But tastes were changing. Commissions intended for public purposes and display now increasingly gave way to art destined for the private sphere. This process intensified between 1370 and 1400: whereas the Holy Roman Emperor Charles IV had built a cathedral in Prague in which much was created for public effect, his son and successor King Wenceslas IV (1361–1419) commissioned works almost solely for his personal use.

Commissions during this era came from a new source, the art collector. The most prominent representative of this new breed of patron was Duke Jean de Berry (1340–1416), younger brother of Charles V, who took over the regency from his nephew Charles VI (1368–1422) when he went mad, and who used his position for his personal enrichment. From the estate of his royal relatives he took precious manuscripts, such as the Book of Hours of Jeanne d'Evreux, illuminated by Jean Pucelle (ill. p. 43). The scope of Jean de Berry's passion for collecting is perhaps best illustrated in the fact that it even extended to dogs (in 1388 he owned approximately 1500 of them), bears, swans and other exotic animals. He also collected jewels and re-

liquaries. All these objects were for his entertainment and were precious to him.

It was, however, art, and above all manuscript illumination, which took pride of place. Jean de Berry was a true connoisseur; the works of art which he owned were more than just another facet of his personal wealth. He had both a sense of artistic value and an appreciation of great art. He was constantly on the look-out for new talent, stealing artists from others or – as in the case of the brothers Paul, Jean and Herman Limburg (after 1385–c. 1416) – seizing upon them after the death of his brother and taking them into his own employ. As well as supporting his artists financially, he encouraged them artistically. It is for this reason that the manuscript illuminations in his collection are so outstanding. By taking artists into his own service and paying them well, the Duke bypassed the market for book illumination – a market which was oriented towards mass production and in which, although abilities were great, powers of invention were limited and execution often schematic.

## The rise of individuality

Collectors are individualists, at least when compared to the more traditional type of patron who prefers to follow established conventions so that his commissions will impress the outside world. This individualistic element is particularly striking in the case of the French king and his brothers. King Charles V mostly supported semi-official trends in art, although he also favoured the Early Netherlandish realists such as his court painter Jean Bondol (active 1368–1381). Louis of Anjou (1339–1384) demonstrated Italian preferences, although it was also he who commissioned the most remarkable tapestry cycle of his day, the *Apocalypse* in Angers. Meanwhile, the youngest brother – Philip the Bold, duke of Burgundy and Flanders (1342–1404) – concentrated on sculpture and panel painting. In favouring the realistic tendencies of his age, he was the most influential in hastening the advent of the modern Netherlandish painting of the 15th century.

In the case of the Duc de Berry, however, the emphasis upon individuality clearly grew over the years. The works he commissioned were initially conventional; his first painter, Jean Le Noir (c. 1335–1380) was not an independent artist in the true sense, but a painter in the style of Pucelle. This was to change. The Limburg brothers were unmistakably original and within just a few years grew all the more so.

It would be wrong to consider the attitude of the patron as the sole explanation for the increasingly pronounced indi-

**Fra Angelico**
St Lawrence Receiving the Church Treasures,
c. 1447–1450
Fresco, 271 x 205 cm
Rome, Vatican, Cappella Niccoliana

viduality of the artist – the processes are too complex for that. It would be equally mistaken, however, to think that individuality is something which happens by itself, or is some sort of "force of nature". Historical experience suggests that it is a delicate flower which can only grow in the right conditions. Collectors (and with them other patrons infected with the same passion) wanted something special, and not just the conventional, however skilfully executed. They therefore had to allow creative individuality the opportunity to develop, above all by granting their artists greater freedom.

The position of court artist, which we tend to see as a gilded cage, in fact offered decisive advantages for the artists themselves. True, their job was frequently that of an elevated theatre painter, as when they had to provide the decorations and sets for lavish feasts and splendid processions or even to produce pennants for the princely fleet, a task which fell to the Netherlandish artist Melchior Broederlam (active 1381–1409). But this was outweighed by the freedom the position carried from the burdens and constraints imposed by the guilds, with their many rules and regulations. For manuscript illuminators, for example, it offered a means of release from the mechanisms of the market and from the need to satisfy the – on the whole rather mediocre – tastes of the general public. Royal employ was also the vital key to greater fame and a larger income.

Private commissions for princes allowed artists unparalleled freedom in their choice of subject and design. As long as they had the backing of their patrons, they were able to experiment and to explore new approaches. In the public sphere, on the other hand, any such experimentation was out of the question from the start. This also explains why civic art remained conventional during this era, for all the power of the middle classes. The ordinary citizen could not and would not take the risk of abandoning the rules of etiquette in the same way as a prince might do.

Thus it might be said that, as from the late 13th century, the step from artisan to artist was also completed north of the Alps. The painter's social status was finally superior to that of the craftsman. The higher pretensions to which the artist now laid claim were amongst the driving forces behind the changes in art in the 15th and 16th century.

From the end of the 14th century, artists began to adopt a new philosophy and a new approach to their profession. An important element of this was what has been called the switch from pattern book to sketch book. Motifs were not simply copied from other sources, but were studied directly from nature. Moreover, artists began to take pride in their own powers of invention. Their approach to the world and to art was indeed that of inventors and discoverers – this was an epoch of technical innovations and other experiments. The empirical age of Leonardo da Vinci and Albrecht Dürer was dawning.

## The predominance of the private commission

To reverse Pinder's phrase, "Form is mentality", it might be said that a mentality such as that of princely collectors around 1400 also had its form. And since collectors all over Europe shared similar preferences, the predominance of the private commission lent the art of around 1400 certain common characteristics.

The rise of the private commission should not be seen as a structural development precipitated by collectors, however, but must be viewed in its historical context. In view of the Great Schism of 1378, the major economic and social upheavals of the age, its bloody battles and civil wars and the general state of political confusion, it becomes apparent that art was a consciously created pendant to a gloomy exterior situation. It stressed the harmony and beauty of the world. In the face of historical reality, however, this should sooner be termed harmonization. The city palaces in Paris resembled heavily-defended fortresses on the outside; examples here include Charles V's old Louvre building and the Bastille. Inside their walls, however, lay artistic paradises of tapestries, paintings, manuscripts and other collector's items.

The contradictions of the age can be recognized within its pictures. The tension between beauty and realism was growing. Overall, however, a characteristic feature of this art remained the fact that it granted predominance or conscious emphasis to the beautiful, the harmonious and the precious.

The model was thereby undoubtedly Simone Martini, with his exquisite colours and the luxury character of his technique, which led to the integration and assimilation of luxury art into painting. The graceful movements of his figures, the delicacy of his line and the sophistication of his narrative details were also perceived as ideals of beauty.

But there were noticeable deviations from Simone Martini, too; the period around 1400 was by no means one of mere slavish copying. At the same time, there was exaggeration, as the trend turned towards smaller formats. The fact that manuscript illumination could regain the tremendous importance it enjoyed at the hands of the Limburg brothers, despite its more limited technical possibilities (in comparison to panel painting), can only be explained in this light.

## Costliness and beauty

The sumptuous nature of Simone's art was now carried to new heights. The greatest passion of the princes of the day was collecting precious stones, not as a form of financial investment but because of the combined charm of their costliness, beauty, magical powers and light effects. Most prized of all were the pale types of ruby and sapphire, together with milky pearls in combination with diamonds. Collectors took pleasure in their colours and light effects alone. Thus even when painting had long since surpassed the goldsmith's art in terms of artistic value, gems and similar treasures remained the models towards which it aspired. Towards the end of the

14th century, painters intensified their efforts to refine their effects of colour and light. Their constant experimentation is witnessed by the fact that almost all of the pictures which have survived into the present employ a different technique. Oil binders were borrowed from sculpture painting, but were used for only some of the many layers of a painting – depending on the degree of transparency and luminosity desired. The physical process of painting a picture was thereby slowed down significantly; it also became more secretive and technically more individual. It was these processes, however, that produced the extraordinary brilliance and costliness of colour which we admire so greatly in Early Netherlandish painting.

Increasingly sophisticated tastes demanded an increasingly high degree of artistic quality. The years around 1400 may be said to have brought a flowering of the fine arts. Painting in particular was held in the highest regard, and with it painters. It is noticeable that the works from this era are regularly described in the literature as "beautiful". The beauty of this art is much more concrete and sensual than Simone's art, however. Painters and sculptors indulge in all types of aesthetic pleasure, wallowing in beautiful forms that are tender and soft, delicate and rich. Lavish folds of drapery and daintily curled locks of hair often seem to be painted purely for their beautiful effect – sometimes at the expense of content, which often simply becomes a peg for artistic preferences.

Beauty was not introduced at the expense of realism, however. While sumptuous costumes, animals and many other elements originally made their way into painting as the collector's items and luxury objects of the wealthy, they also served to expand the conventional vocabulary of composition and created variety in an art which, for all the beauty of its forms and colours, was still in danger of growing dull.

Above all, however, it should be remembered that the people of this epoch were aware of more than just the seamy side of life, which they saw before them every day and long sought to repress; they had, too, an equally well-developed sense of realism. The striving towards an idealizing style of painting would thus have been perfectly reconcilable with the emergence of the individual portrait, which saw a first flowering after 1350. The discovery and portrayal of the beauty of objects themselves, of animals and plants, of the daily and seasonal changes in the landscape, was just another short step away.

Ultimately, however, the growing interest in reality and its all-embracing rather than selective portrayal, coupled with greater artistic freedom and an increasingly serious train of thought, served to upset the balance of the International Gothic, weighted so one-sidedly in favour of the beautiful. In the long term, the idealized world it presented proved merely a fiction. Thus the style contained within itself the very forces that would in the end destroy it.

## The crisis in Bohemia

Following the accession to power of Charles IV, Bohemia had enjoyed a significant political and economic upswing. By 1340 the arts, too, were flowering, a process lent wings above all by the assimilation of Italian influences. Even so, Bohemian artists were producing important works in their own right from a very early stage.

The rapid economic changes created a divide between the mostly German merchant classes and the Bohemian nobility and peasant classes – a divide almost impossible to bridge. Prague had also become a melting pot of nationalities on a scale greater than any other city north of the Alps. Up to 10,000 students were recorded as being in Prague at any one time, and over 1200 clerics, most of them only poorly provided for. Reasons for tension abounded.

**Master Theoderich**
St Gregory, c. 1360–1365
(from the Chapel of the Holy Cross, Karlstein Castle)
Tempera on wood, 113 x 105 cm
Prague, Národni Galeri

Charles had been introduced to the use of art as a means of influencing the people and public opinion both in France and Italy, and he now applied his knowledge logically and systematically. During his lifetime Bohemian art attained a high level of aesthetic quality, higher than anywhere else in central Europe, and its powers of persuasion were correspondingly great. Its somewhat gloomy, Byzantine-influenced palette, the intensity of its expression and the great beauty of its outer form remain impressive even today.

But these practices were too new, too obviously steered and managed from above, and they drew forth criticism and rejection. In the early Middle Ages at least, there had always been a current of opinion opposed to paintings – in the universities and the stricter monastri orders, for example. But the vehement criticism of the cult of images which set in during Charles IV's reign was altogether more radical. By way of response, as it were, paintings of particularly great fascination were created and propagated, in part as devotional images attributed with miraculous powers. Although such paintings carried the fame of Prague art to even greater heights, they were unable to prevent the outbreak of religious unrest, beneath which lay social, national and political grudges. When the religious reformer John Hus (c. 1369–1415) was burned as a heretic in Constance in 1415, the wave of protest which followed culminated in uprisings and eventually the Hussite wars, during which vast quantities of art works fell victim to a wave of iconoclasm which destroyed paintings and monasteries. It is only thanks to the resistance of some of the noble families of southern Bohemia and Moravia, who remained Catholic and withstood the Hussite attacks, that anything of Bohemian art has survived at all.

One of the aspects of Bohemian painting that came under critical attack were the subtle techniques employed to tap the willingness of the pious to make sacrifices. Artists were also denounced as liars for painting something they had never seen, and because, in the name of the saints, they portrayed handsome men and women who inspired "sinful desires" in the viewer. How could they show Christ and the Apostles in fine robes when everyone knew they were poor? True faith and art seemed irreconcilable. But this was just the initial, most severe reaction. Fine art was not rejected lock, stock and barrel. The Hussites themselves made use of pictures, in which the life of Christ was emphatically contrasted with the Roman Catholic church, the church of the Antichrist. They demanded that the substance of religion should be treated with much greater seriousness – a demand which would also have aesthetic consequences.

Between the radical Hussites and the supporters of the old church lay other, more conciliatory trends. It was clear, however, that in the Bohemian territories after 1410, art could no longer remain the same, even in Catholic circles. It was partly the painters themselves (a surprising number of whom were Hussites) who, of their own volition, demanded a re-thinking of art and its role, and partly their patrons. The surviving results, however, are characterized less by new aesthetic departures than by a renunciation of rich form, sensual design, ornament and colour.

### The end of the International Gothic

Events in Bohemia paralleled events in Europe, where similar upheavals were taking place. Yet all of these changes took a different form, occurred for different reasons and had different aims. The astonishing uniformity of the aims and means of the International Gothic had gone. What was enacted in revolution by the Hussites is found in the Master of the Rohan Book of Hours as expressionistic pathos (ill. p. 65), in the van Eycks as a sensitive study of nature and light, and in the Florentines as a new seriousness, a study of classical art and an awareness of the new science of perspective. They all share the same point of the departure. None of their elements is fundamentally new. But the one-sidedness evinced by the International Gothic in its combination of beauty and realism, stylization and nature study could no longer be maintained.

As at earlier points in the history of science, we may speak here of a change of paradigm. This must be qualified, however, by reminding ourselves that there can be no distinction in art between the "wrong" old and the "right" new. While the painters who clung to the old ideals even after 1450 may be called conservative, that does not by any means make them bad artists.

Painters such as Fra Angelico and Stefan Lochner (c. 1400–1451) are evidence that the old stylistic ideals remained potential tools for use with certain subjects, certain types of commissions and certain stylistic situations. Even after 1500, the idealizing formulae of the International Gothic were still held in respect and served as the models for a number of innovative modernizing tendencies.

## FRENCH MASTER

C. 1213

The magnificent psalter commissioned for the private use of Queen Ingeborg, probably by her husband Philippe Auguste, is the most important French illuminated manuscript to survive from the 13th century. At the time the psalter was executed, the sculpture cycle at Chartres cathedral was well on the way to completion and that of Reims already begun, and the west portals of Notre-Dame in Paris were being built. Its compositions and many of its motifs nevertheless follow the Byzantine tradition, as represented by the great mosaic cycles in Sicily, for example, while the gold ground and the border look ahead to later 13th-century developments.

The Paris artist restricts himself to the generally muted colours of Eastern art. In imitation of classical models, however, he moderates the severity of his forms through the use of more softly moulded draperies, without thereby reverting to earlier, ornamental styles. The figures are shown in calm poses even in the most dramatic situations. The picture is kept two-dimensional and provided with the barest of backgrounds. The figures remain the yardstick, obscuring unimportant details. Their severity and dignity recall the greater monumentality being sought by contemporary sculptors. In embracing such a style, however, the workshop would also have reflected the tastes of the French royal court.

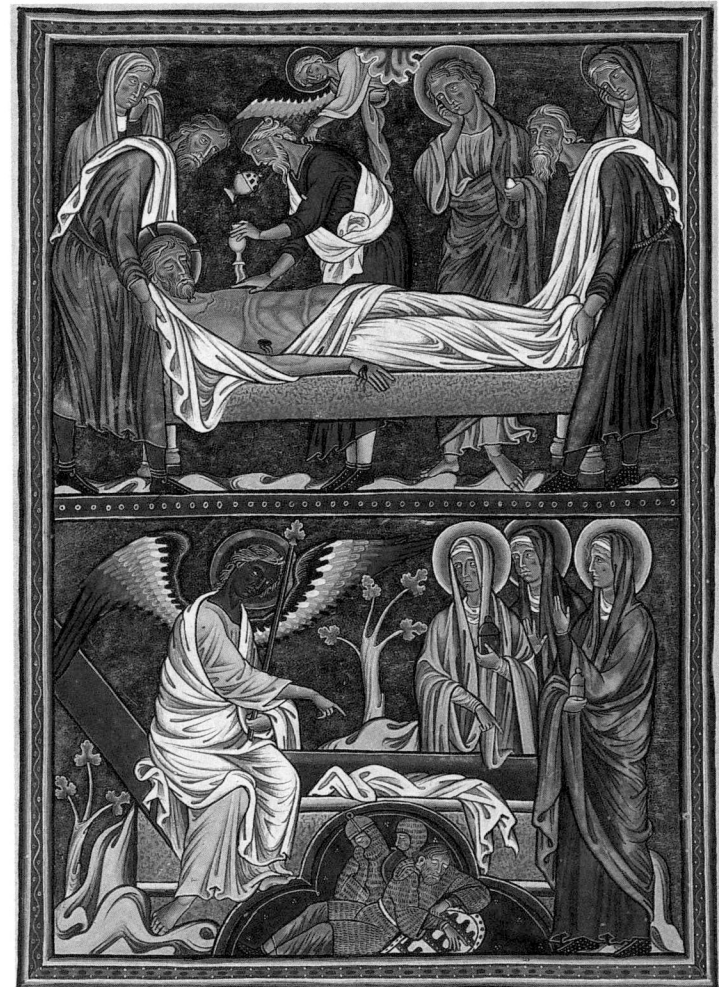

**Workshop of the Ingeborg Psalter**
Embalming of the Body of Christ and The Three Marys at the Empty Tomb. From the Psalter of Queen Ingeborg of Denmark, c. 1213
Manuscript illumination,
30.4 x 20.4 cm
Ms. 1695, fol. 28 v
Chantilly, Musée Condé

## FRENCH MASTER

BETWEEN 1258 AND 1270

This exquisite manuscript was produced for King Louis the Pious of France. A series of 78 full-page miniatures of scenes from the first books of the Old Testament, presented in pairs, precede the actual text of the psalter. The background architecture with its prominent rose windows, cites the Gothic style of church architecture of which Louis was a major patron. Its function is ornamental rather than representational, and the painter uses it to divide the narrative into two halves.

On the left we see Joshua commanding the sun and the moon to stand still until the decisive battle against the Amorite kings is won. On the right we see the enemy being chased back into their cities. Although the events have been brought forward into the contemporary setting of the 13th century, much remains unreal: the reds and blues presented in an alternating succession of pure and diluted tones against a gold ground do not designate the actual colours of the objects they describe, but are a form of costly decoration comparable to the dazzling stained-glass windows of Chartres. The slender figures of Joshua and the soldiers hardly call to mind a patriarch and one of the greatest miracles in Israel's early history, but rather illustrate the new ideal of the perfect courtier. The refined style of this art is almost an end in itself, and its very sophistication a source of pleasure for the reader.

**Workshop of the Louis Psalter**
Joshua Stops the Sun and Moon. From the psalter of Louis IX of France, c. 1258–1270
Manuscript illumination,
21 x 14.5 cm
Ms. lat. 10525, fol. 46 r
Paris, Bibliothèque Nationale

Bonaventura Berlinghieri
St Francis and Scenes from
his Life, 1235
Tempera on wood,
160 x 123 cm
Pescia, San Francesco

## BONAVENTURA BERLINGHIERI

C. 1205/10 – AFTER 1274

To his contemporaries, Francis of Assis (1183–
1226) appeared to be a second Christ, but one
whose presence was much more vital and immediate than the ascended Son of God. Such
was his reputation that the visits he paid to
places were commemorated in paintings, as for
example in Subiaco. Yet just nine years after
his death and seven after his canonization, he
was being portrayed in this work from Pescia
as an aged stylite from a wall of Byzantine
icons. Its severity and frontality cannot be explained by the fact that it is a retable. There
was, in fact, much resistance to the foundation
and running of the Franciscan order of poverty
and lay mission. This is probably the reason
why St Francis is presented as a heavenly and
hence unchallengeable authority.

This is also underlined by the smaller
scenes on either side. Presented in unchrono-
logical order, they show, top left, Francis receiving the stigmata, the seal of his similarity
to Christ; next his sermon to the birds, as an illustration of the fact that the animal kingdom
immediately recognized Francis as sent by
God, and also of the saint's great love for nature. Miracles which he performed during his
lifetime or which took place at his tomb serve
to confirm his divine powers (bottom left: Cur-
ing a crippled child; right from top: Healing
cripples, healing the lame man, driving out demons from the possessed).

Cimabue
Madonna and Child Enthroned with
Angels and Prophets (Maestà), after 1285
(from Santa Trinità, Florence)
Tempera on wood, 385 x 223 cm
Florence, Galleria degli Uffizi

## CIMABUE

C. 1240 – AFTER 1302

This Madonna was originally an altar retable,
at that time a new type of commission, but one
which rapidly became popular. The presence of
Christ evoked by the painting was intended to
make the sacrifice of the Mass appear more concrete and at the same time to reinforce the divine authority of the priest taking the service.

The painter was required to create a work
which combined solemn, monumental effect
with an image that was easy to read. The
plinth-like arrangement of the prophets indicates that, both chronologically and theologically, they provide the steps which lead up to
Mary and Christ. Their banderoles refer to Mary's virginity and Christ's role as Saviour. The
organization of the painting, with its central
emphasis, symmetry and balanced sides, is
beautifully clear. The artist only deviates from
this order in the figure of the Virgin, who is
seen at a slight angle and who thereby focuses
more attention upon her son.

The composition of the painting is clear
and simple, the drawing precise. The seated
and standing poses are nevertheless strangely
removed from reality and lack tectonic cohesion. The individual motifs betray Byzantine
sources. Apparent in the execution are certain
traits of the fresco painter, with little attention
paid to finer details. The panel has been unan-
imously attributed to Cimabue ever since its
first mention by Vasari (1568).

# GIOTTO DI BONDONE
1266 (?)–1337

This panel by Giotto, which hangs in the same room in the Uffizi as Cimabue's painting opposite, clearly demonstrates the significant distance separating Giotto from all that had gone before. Giotto's painting, perhaps just twenty years the younger, has the same function and subject as Cimabue's, is almost the same size and employs a similarly symmetrical composition. There is a greater three-dimensional conviction to Giotto's throne, however: it is not be understood as having descended from Heaven – as Cimabue unconvincingly attempts to portray it – but rests on two stone steps decorated with slabs of marble and colourful inlay. It is roofed by an ornamental canopy in Gothic forms which replaces a built architectural setting. The steps serve both to raise up the Madonna just as a plinth elevates a statue, and at the same time to create an empty space at the bottom of the composition corresponding to the area obscured by the officiating priest and the altar cross.

The accompanying figures are crowded into the sides of the painting, their heads lower than that of the Child. All eyes are turned towards the Virgin, with a reverence further heightened by the introduction of two kneeling angels in the foreground. She alone looks out of the picture at the worshipper/spectator; it is to her that we must turn. Mary's role as intercessor is thus more clearly illustrated here than in Cimabue. The weight of her seated body is clearly palpable, even as she draws herself up and presents her son. She is indeed the Seat of Wisdom.

Giotto does not pattern her robes with the gold weave of Byzantine fabrics, the formula conventionally used to identify heavenly beings; nor does he employ colours solely of diamond-like purity and sumptuousness, but includes broken tones, as seen in the green of the two angels standing on either side. His palette thereby appears to belong more to this world (the blue of the Virgin's mantle has greatly deepened and is too flat). Dress is portrayed just as it would appear in real life. In line with 13th-century sculpture, however, it nevertheless also serves a compositional purpose: the clear silhouette of the Madonna's cloak emphasizes the block-like nature of the central group. Its width reinforces the Virgin's monumentality, while the folds of the drapery lend her structure and at the same time guide the viewer's gaze to the infant Christ.

Giotto portrays the Virgin by selecting the most dignified and the most beautiful of human features and heightening them to a sublime degree. Despite this exaggeration of the norm, the Madonna does not seem alien. Instead, she is a vision of regal might. By contrast, Cimabue's Madonna appears distanced, an impression fuelled by the tall, narrow format of the painting and Mary's elevated position. The structure of Giotto's composition is easier to read. The top line of the plinth demarcates the bottom quarter of the painting, the front edge of the seat its middle. The panel is one of the few works whose attribution to Giotto is unchallenged.

Giotto di Bondone
Enthroned Madonna with Saints (Ognissanti Madonna), c. 1305–1310
(from Ognissanti church, Florence)
Tempera on wood, 325 x 204 cm
Florence, Galleria degli Uffizi

**Giotto di Bondone**
Joachim Takes Refuge in the Wilderness,
c. 1303–1305
Fresco, c. 185 x 200 cm
Padua, Arena Chapel (Cappella degli Scrovegni
all'Arena)

# GIOTTO DI BONDONE
1266 (?)–1337

This fresco might perhaps more accurately be called "Joachim Downcast". Joachim, the future father of Mary, has been to the Temple, where his sacrifice was refused. Bitter and ashamed (owing to the disgrace of being childless), he returns not to his home, but to the solitude of his flocks. He approaches slowly, sunk deep in thought; he sees neither the dog who greets him joyfully nor the shepherds before him, whose sympathy for him is plain to see. The rocks behind provide an almost architectural backdrop which concludes the group and subtly paraphrases the composition. An impression of three-dimensional space is created by the depth and rounding of the figures

and the staggered organization of the three men. Indeed, such is his sense of spatial depth that Giotto even treats Joachim's nimbus in three-dimensional terms.

The scene is one of maximum simplicity and at the same time maximum effectiveness. In contrast to other subjects from the New Testament, Giotto could allow himself much greater freedom in his treatment of episodes from the lives of Joachim and Anna, which were taken from apocryphal biblical writings and legends and were governed by virtually no iconographical traditions. The two frescos shown here were the first that he painted for the chapel which Enrico Scrovegni had built in the so-called Arena, a former Roman amphitheatre. Giotto executed them largely single-handed, and they are rightly considered the masterpieces of the cycle as a whole.

One day, while out in the fields, Joachim is visited by an angel who told him of the future birth of his daughter Mary and of the important role she would play in the salvation of humankind. An angel also appeared to Anna, Joachim's wife, in Jerusalem. Joachim immediately returned to the city. Here we see husband and wife meeting at the Golden Gate, where they joyfully embrace each other.

In contrast to the previous fresco, in which Giotto expresses Joachim's sadness through a small number of isolated and calm figures, this scene is presented as a festive procession. The elderly Joachim, arriving at a more measured pace, has halted on the left-hand side of the composition, his companion cut off by the edge. The viewer is thus skilfully informed that the two have been frozen in mid-movement. Anna, on the other hand, has already passed under the gate, accompanied by a train of four women.

Giotto translates this group of women into contemporary life. In order to prevent their general expressions of joy from devolving into monotony, and to underline the caesura between Anna and her companions, he introduces a woman shrouded in a dark cape, as if to show that even such an occasion for celebration contains an element of future sadness.

It is apparent in this fresco that areas of blue, which were applied in a second stage of painting, often failed to adhere for long. The same is true of other sections painted *a secco*, such as the ornamentation of the Golden Gate and the gold braid on the clothes. This loss is partly compensated, however, by the fact that we are better able to study the underpainting and hence the overall design process.

**Giotto di Bondone**
Anna and Joachim Meet at the Golden Gate, 1303–1305
Fresco, c. 185 x 200 cm
Padua, Arena Chapel (Cappella degli Scrovegni all'Arena)

**Giotto di Bondone**
The Lamentation of Christ, 1303–1305
Fresco, c. 185 x 200 cm
Padua, Arena Chapel (Cappella degli Scrovegni all'Arena)

**Giotto di Bondone** and assistants
St Francis Giving his Cloak to a Poor Man, between 1296 and 1299
Fresco, 270 x 230 cm. Assisi, San Francesco, Upper Church

# GIOTTO DI BONDONE
## 1266 (?)–1337

The *Lamentation of Christ* is located two rows beneath the story of Joachim and Anna and on the opposite, well-lit wall of the Arena Chapel, in the immediate proximity of the visitor. Giotto's figures and narratives are typically characterized by a subdued degree of animation. This means that the scope for intensifying their expressiveness is correspondingly large. The most powerful outbursts of feeling within the entire cycle are demonstrated here by the figures in the *Lamentation*. They are not caught up in a single wave of pain, however; instead, each individual conveys a different set of emotions. In the foreground, two block-like women sit numb and frozen. By obscuring part of Christ's corpse, they concentrate the viewer's attention upon the central group of mother and son. Composed in her anguish, Mary embraces the body of Christ in farewell. Mary Magdalene, at Christ's feet, bows her head in silent grief. The woman in the middle, in a tender and original motif, raises Christ's arms as if to pull him to his feet, but simultaneously abandons the attempt upon catching sight of his wounds. John, in great distress, has flung back his arms, in a similar fashion to the angels in the sky. In line with their advanced years, Joseph of Arimathaea and Nicodemus on the right react in a more restrained but nevertheless individual fashion. Even nature is caught up in the mourning. The tree on the right has died, and the landscape is barren. Particularly effective is Giotto's decision to locate the main focus of the scene low down in the far left-hand corner, and to draw down the landscape in the background in a diagonal towards the head of Christ.

This scene from the life of St Francis illustrates the compassion and love which Francis felt for the poor, even before his conversion. The wealthy son of a cloth merchant, he meets a nobleman who has fallen on hard times and spontaneously gives him his cloak. While the nobleman is not shown in rags, he nevertheless lacks a cloak in keeping with his class. There is thus only a vague parallel between this story and the famous tale of St Martin, who cut his cloak in two in order to give one half to a beggar. In view of the somewhat puzzling and one-sided selection of scenes making up the St Francis cycle in the Upper Church, one might even ask whether the present fresco was intended to show that the Franciscan ideal of poverty was not aimed against the social order *per se*. Francis is not captured in an act of spontaneous giving, but is presented in hierarchical fashion in the central axis of the composition. The figures are lined up in a row at the front of the picture, without appearing to have anything of substance to stand on. The dimensions of the pictorial surface and the proportions of the format are only poorly mastered, while the treatment of the bodies and the handling of spatial depth are artistically far removed from the first frescos in the chapel. In view of both its execution and its design, the fresco is thus considered to be the work of one of Giotto's assistants.

# DUCCIO DI BUONINSEGNA
## C. 1255–C. 1319

Mary is presented in the central axis and looks out at the viewer/worshipper. Behind her, four angels hold up a silk, gold-bordered cloth of honour, which together with her throne identifies her as the Queen of Heaven and the Seat of Wisdom. Christ is holding her fingers, symbolizing the mystic marriage between Son and Mother of God. The mantle spread around three Franciscan monks is a motif which identifies the Madonna as the Virgin of the Protecting Cloak. This small devotional panel is the painted pendant to a hymn to the Virgin.

The artist clearly changed his mind in several places, deviating from the preliminary sketch scored in outline onto the surface. He frequently painted over the previously applied gold ground, something which not only demonstrates a carefree attitude to cost but which also explains why much of the paint has since peeled off. The throne, too, has been painted on top of the curtain of the ground, in order to emphasize the kneeling Franciscan monks more strongly. This highly unusual, ongoing experimentation is evidence that Duccio carried out his commissions in neither a routine nor a coolly calculated manner. Unfortunately, the delicacy of his modelling is also to blame for the fact that nothing has survived of what was formerly, no doubt, the very rich decoration of the Virgin's clothing. The painting today appears more two-dimensional and hence more severe that originally intended. There may have been two wings attached to this small panel, allowing it to be closed to view. Even these are unlikely to have contained any more details about the donor, however. The three monks cannot be interpreted as identifiable individuals; they kneel here in witness to the Franciscan veneration of the Mother of God.

This panel was originally part of the predella, since broken up, of the high altar retable in Siena cathedral. Its poor condition is a result of its low location. It was originally framed by individual portraits of the prophets, including a picture of King Solomon. Destined as it was for the front of a hieratic altarpiece, even this small scene is strict and dignified in its composition.

The centre is emphasized by the architecture of the background, and in particular the triangular gable. The figures are presented in strict relief. Characteristic motifs include the group of horses in classical style, borrowed from the Three Kings relief by Nicola and Giovanni Pisano on the pulpit in Siena cathedral, and the Virgin's throne. The palette concentrates upon the pure triad of blue, red and gold, as found in French court art and as commonly employed by Duccio for his highest-ranking figures, at least on the altar front. Within this strict framework there are many subtleties: the shift from red as the main colour accent on the left to blue on the right, for example, the use of contour and the cave roof to emphasize the Mother and Child group, and the manner in which the composition takes up the panel's frame.

**Duccio di Buoninsegna**
Madonna of the Franciscans,
c. 1300
Tempera on wood, 24 x 16cm
Siena, Pinacoteca Nazionale

*Below:*
**Duccio di Buoninsegna**
Adoration of the Magi,
1308–1311
(detail of the predella of the
Maestà)
Tempera on wood, 42.5 x 44cm
Siena, Museo dell'Opera del
Duomo

## DUCCIO DI BUONINSEGNA
### C. 1255–C. 1319

What is surprising about this panel is the way in which Duccio has taken two separate events from the Bible (albeit unfolding in the same building) and made them into one picture.

Above we see Christ before Annas, the high priest to whom he was taken after his arrest and who now seeks a reason to convict him. The scene shows Christ's interrogation and, more particularly, the false evidence being offered against him by different people. Below, in what is presented as the courtyard of the high priest's palace, Peter is seated in a circle of the priest's men, warming his feet at the fire. Viewers contemplating the rear of Duccio's *Maestà* would have known, from the order of the pictures, to read the panel from bottom to top. They would thus have understood the *Denial* as the first scene and *Christ Before the High Priest Annas* as the second. This sequence is affirmed both by the figure of the servant girl, seen from behind in the act of turning to mount the stairs, and by the stairs themselves. Indeed, the pose of the servant girl is a stroke of artistic genius. Her outstretched arm may be understood both as gripping the railing and simultaneously as pointing at Peter. Her isolated position at the left-hand edge of the composition immediately identifies her as an important figure playing an explanatory role, yet one who is not amongst the main characters.

A rich network of relationships is interwoven between the lower and the upper scenes, partly through analogy and partly through contrast. The spatial relationship between the servant girl and Peter is similar to that between Annas and Christ. The theme introduced in the lower half is taken up and amplified above: Christ stands alone in front of the soldiers, distinguished from them by the style and colour of his dress. Peter, on the other hand, has mingled with Annas' men and is hard to pick out from the group. He is sitting down and taking it easy, warming his feet by the fire, while his similarly barefoot master suffers. Whereas the figures in the lower scene form an almost complete circle, those above are presented more frontally. The architecture below is portrayed in some detail and includes a succession of receding planes, whereas the events above take place parallel to the pictorial plane, on a shallow stage whose wings and backdrop are provided by a symmetrical fake architecture. The ceiling lines vanish towards the centre, emphasizing Christ. There are many more such comparisons to be made, but we should mention in particular the intensification of colour which accompanies the progression from bottom to top, not just in the main characters. A striking feature from an art-historical point of view is the fact that the panel combines design principles which we would normally date to different epochs. Thus the flatter, symmetrical upper scene would usually be considered older, and the more plastic lower scene, with its greater spatial depth reminiscent of Giotto, more recent. Duccio here employs both in order to distinguish between the solemnity and importance of the two events.

**Duccio di Buoninsegna**
Peter's First Denial of Christ and Christ Before the High Priest Annas, 1308–1311
(from the back of the Maestà formerly on the high altar of Siena cathedral)
Tempera on wood, 99 x 53.5 cm. Siena, Museo dell'Opera del Duomo

# SIMONE MARTINI

c. 1280/85–1344

Simone's fresco is located in the Sala del Map-pamondo on the wall opposite his other mas-terpiece, the *Maestà* (ill. p. 18). It was painted in honour of the military commander Guido-riccio da Fogliano and shows a topographical view of the besieged town of Montemassi on the left and the Sienese fortress on the right. The siege took place in 1328, following the end of Ludwig of Bavaria's Italian campaign, when the papal party – which included Siena – sought to turn the Emperor's imminent defeat to their advantage. The rider and the location are treated as two separate entities. The com-mander is not shown engaged in actual battle. The location is almost abstract, although prob-ably based on a study from nature. The eques-trian portrait of the commander is projected like a monument against the landscape.

Men like Guidoriccio were a phenomenon of the 14th century and were born of the rise of mercenary armies over civilian forces. Ac-cording to Jacob Burckhardt, these condottieri developed something of a right to an official portrait, and the state a duty to provide it. In the figure of Guidoriccio, Simone portrays a military type rather than an individual, but nevertheless pays precise attention to his splen-did appearance, heightened by the large dia-mond patterns on a gold ground which adorn the horse's caparison and the rider's magnifi-cent cloak like the tails of kites.

The decoration of the Lower Church in Assisi was funded by a donation from a Franciscan cardinal who died in 1312. The cardinal had been an ardent supporter of the house of Anjou, in whose service he had helped with the acquisition of Hungary. The cycle com-prises ten scenes from the life of St Martin, starting with the episode in which he divides his cloak with the beggar and finishing with his death. Despite its church setting, the cycle is a work of court art; painted by Simone Mar-tini, himself ennobled while in Anjou service, it glorifies the French ruling house through the figure of St Martin, who was both French and Hungarian. It thereby gave implicit bless-ing to French dominion over the kingdom of Hungary and lent support to the Anjou party all over Italy and in its struggle for the im-perial crown. But while the episode in which St Martin is dubbed a knight belongs to the chivalric and secular world, not so Simone's painting.

Although the detail reproduced here shows a group of musicians – their faces by no means noble – in colourful dress, they are fully ab-sorbed in their music-making. This is particu-larly true of the singers. The severity of the line, the stylization, and the limited scope of movement and space within Simone's composi-tion distance the scene from the viewer. The fresco is recognizably the work of a panel painter. Simone's attempt to create an iri-descent effect by superimposing two different colours within the brim of the recorder-players's hat, and his focus upon fine details, show him applying the techniques of panel painting to the medium of fresco.

**Simone Martini**
Guidoriccio da Fogliano, c. 1328
Fresco (detail), 340 x 968cm (total size)
Siena, Palazzo Pubblico

**Simone Martini**
Musicians. Detail from: St Martin is dubbed
a Knight, between 1317 and 1319
Fresco, 265 x 200cm (total size)
Assisi, San Franceso, Lower Church

**Simone Martini**
The Road to Calvary, c. 1315 (or later)
(part of the Orsini Polyptych)
Tempera on wood, 29.5 x 20.5 cm
Paris, Musée National du Louvre

**Simone Martini**
The Deposition, c. 1315 (or later)
(part of the Orsini Polyptych)
Tempera on wood, 29.7 x 20.5 cm
Antwerpen, Koninklijk Museum voor
Schone Kunsten

## SIMONE MARTINI
### c. 1280/85–1344

These two panels originally formed part of the same polyptych, painted for Cardinal Orsini. The four other panels are currently housed in Antwerp (*Annunciation* and *Crucifixion*) and Berlin (*Entombment*). In these small-scale devotional pictures, Simone reveals a very different side to his art. The personal nature of these paintings, which were intended for private worship, demanded an approach and a treatment different to the fresco or the altarpiece. These are small, almost miniature-like pictures full of figures. Particularly striking is their impassioned movement: here, a stream of people is flowing out of the city of Jerusalem in the directions indicated by the arms of the cross. But this is no narrative in the conventional sense: although Christ is shown walking, he nevertheless appears frozen in mid-step like a statue, inviting the viewer to reflect upon his tragic fate. Of secondary importance, but clearly established, is the relationship between Christ and his mother. Mary raises her arms as if wanting to help carry the cross in a gesture which is simultaneously one of lamentation. But she can neither help her son nor stop the procession to Calvary; the captain who will recognize Christ's divinity beneath the cross braces his shield against her. Looking back, Christ takes his leave of his mother. Our eyes are also drawn to Mary Magdalene, dressed in crimson with her arms raised in despair above her head. Simone's introduction of new narrative details, his deviation from the conventional norm and his compositional mastery of both serve to demonstrate his great artistry.

As the donor of the polyptych, Cardinal Orsini did not have himself portrayed at the foot of the cross in the *Crucifixion* panel as was usually done, but rather in the *Deposition*. The striking, steep diagonal of the ladder establishes the chief axis of the composition. The main group of figures is at the extreme left. In retaining the wooden cross as the centre, the painter pays reverence to this most sacred of holy relics. Mary throws herself towards her son, while John attempts to restrain her. Like Mary, the entire main group faces towards the dead Christ, including the donor; indeed, even the brush strokes of the ground lead in this direction. A visual caesura to the right of the cross ensures that this single wave of motion is not weakened. The faces and gestures of the figures on the right also point towards Christ, in particular the emphatically visible figure of Mary Magdalene. Beside her, a woman holds two nails from the cross in her cloaked hands (a sign of respect) – a further reference to the cult of relics from Christ's Passion. The same figures appear repeatedly in the polyptych, fusing the individual scenes into a cyclical whole. Each panel nevertheless remains an original and unique devotional picture. With their jewel-like luminosity, their finely gradated nuances of colour and their delicate execution, however, they simultaneously provide an inexhaustible source of delight for the eye which would undoubtedly have corresponded to the donor's wishes.

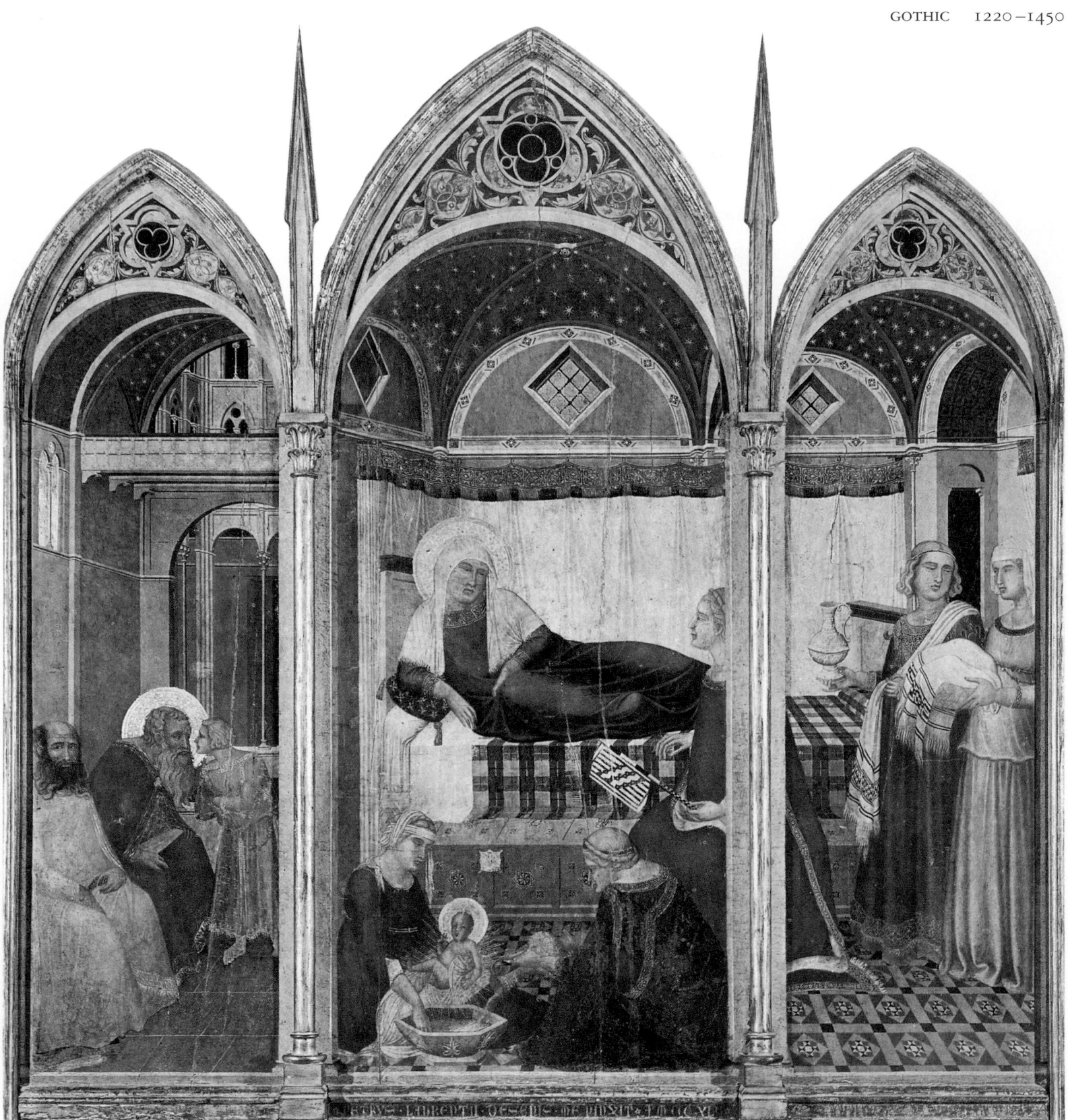

## PIETRO LORENZETTI

C. 1280/90–1348 (?)

The scene is set within an illusionistic architecture. Through open arches, which also frame the painting, we glimpse two rooms of different size. In the centre and on the right we see a group of women, and on the left Joachim and his companions. The curtain around the bed has been pulled back so that Anna, whose broad and heavy figure is reminiscent of Giotto, can be seen. The painted starry vault simulta-

neously lends the room a sacred character. Clearly framed at the centre of the composition, Anna is immediately identified as its focal point. Contrary to the convention of the day, whereby paintings were read from left to right, this work must be decoded in the opposite direction. The artist thereby took into account the fact that the altar on which it was destined to stand could only be approached from the right. For this reason, too, only the room on the left opens further inward. The precise execution of the interior and scene is just as innovative as the artistic concept underpinning the whole.

Pietro Lorenzetti
Birth of the Virgin, 1342
(from Siena cathedral)
Tempera on wood, 188 x 183 cm
Siena, Museo dell'Opera del Duomo

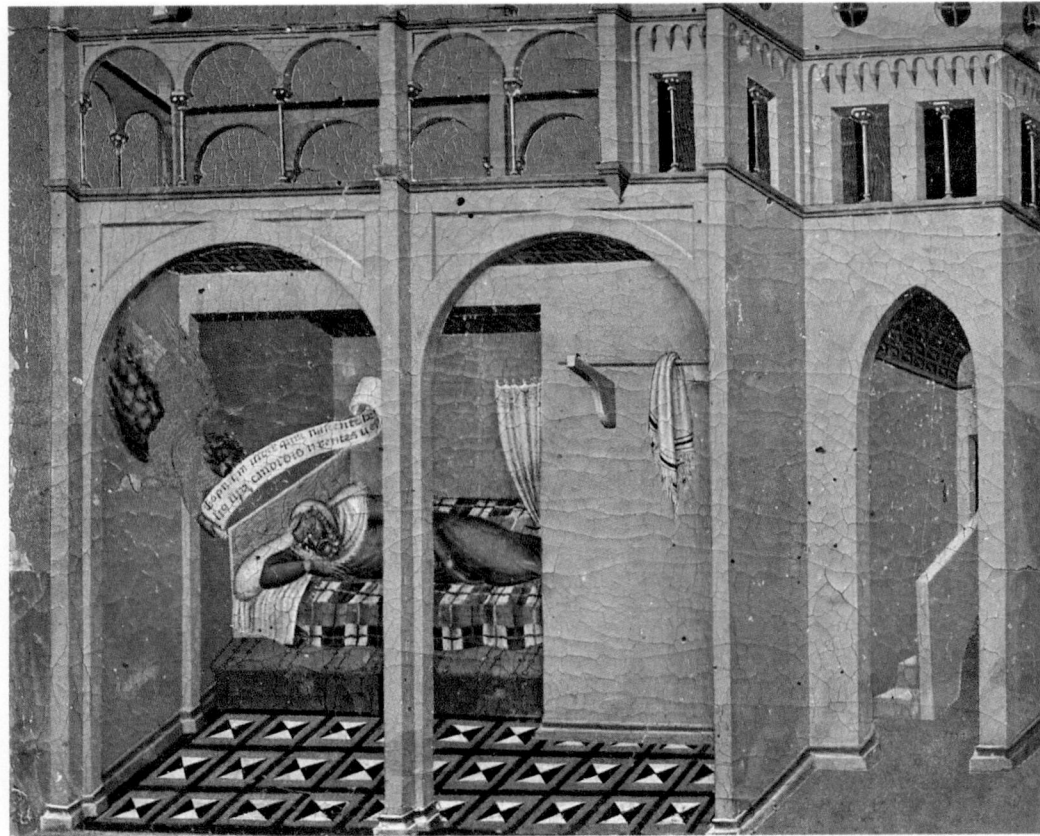

**Pietro Lorenzetti**
Sobach's Dream, 1329
(from the predella of the high altar of Santa Maria
del Carmine, Siena)
Tempera on wood, 37 x 44 cm
Siena, Pinacoteca Nazionale

**Pietro Lorenzetti**
The Deposition, c. 1320–1330
Fresco, 232 x 377 cm
Assisi, San Francesco, Lower Church

## PIETRO LORENZETTI
c. 1280/90–1348 (?)

In 1327/28 Lorenzetti was commissioned to paint a winged altar for the Carmelite church in Siena. He only handed the finished work over to the Carmelites once they had paid his fee – 150 gold florins – in full. In the present scene, an angel appears in a dream to the father of the prophet Elijah and tells him that his son will be the founder of the Carmelite order.

While altarpieces obeyed a strict and hierarchical format in line with their function, artists enjoyed much greater freedom in the design of predelle. Pietro was one of the first to exploit this. He thereby indulged his personal preferences – for large and boldly patterned surfaces, for example, seen here in the blanket and the floor tiles, which also reflect the painter's remarkable feel for the qualities of materials. The palette is also very much Lorenzetti's own, dominated by greeny greys and tonal sequences in rich gradations. What appears to be subjectivism also opens up new and advantageous ways of treating the main theme, a dream: the dreamer is thrust not to the very front of the picture, as one might customarily expect, but into the depths of the room. The remaining areas of the picture are given over not to a continuous gold ground, but to a complex architecture which is neither drawn from real life nor even possible. The picture is an architectural fantasy of an unusually modern kind and as such alludes to the mysterious nature of the world of dreams.

Of all his fellow Sienese painters, Pietro Lorenzetti made the most intense study of Giotto's design principles. In his Passiontide cycle for the Lower Chapel in Assisi, which he executed in several stages between 1320 and 1330, in part with the aid of assistants, his style assumed an increasing simplicity as his richly animated use of line gave way to powerfully expressive, unbroken curves. In the *Deposition*, undoubtedly executed by Lorenzetti himself, this development reaches a high point. Only the slenderly proportioned body of Christ, its limbs indicating a number of contrasting directions, betrays the Sienese origins of the artist. Spatial depth is established primarily by the three-dimensional grouping of modelled figures. Individual figures can thereby be traced directly back to Giotto: Mary Magdalene, for example, who is seen kneeling at the foot of the cross, is based on the figure of Joachim making his sacrifice in the Arena Chapel in Padua.

Rather than portraying a specific moment during the Deposition, Lorenzetti suggests a chronological sequence of events. The oblique traced by Christ's body is reinforced by the line of bowed heads and upper bodies which descends from the head of Joseph of Arimathaea down to the figure in the bottom right-hand corner, Nicodemus, who is pulling out the nails from Christ's feet with a pair of pliers. This same line seems to continue into the *Entombment* on the opposite side of the end wall of the Orsini Chapel.

# AMBROGIO LORENZETTI

c. 1290– c. 1348 (?)

This small domestic altar, cropped and in poor condition, originally featured two wings and would have been more differentiated in its palette and in its modelling of the draperies. It was probably executed for a member of the clergy with a special interest in its compositional structure, which follows that of an altarpiece, and its theological patrons (Pope Clemens and Gregory the Great, two holy bishops and the saints, Dorothy and Catherine). The references to altar painting are nevertheless only faint: Mary sits not on a throne but on a folding chair as she clasps her son – who is pointing to a verse from the Lord's Prayer ("Thy will be done") on a banderole – in a maternal embrace. Overall, too, the fine details of the execution and the wealth of objects on display place the panel firmly in the sphere of the private devotional picture.

In a bold compositional device, the saints and angels are grouped in the shape of a mandorla around the aureoled Madonna. This clear basic form reveals a complexity of its own: the figures are staggered both in height and depth around the throne. The kneeling figures of the popes, seen almost from behind, direct the eye to the centre in a movement taken up by the stripes of the carpet. The bishops kneeling behind and slightly above them are seen in profile. The female saints, meanwhile, stand above the foreground figures but behind the Virgin. The angels are painted on top of the gold ground, lending them luminosity and the appearance of floating above and behind the Madonna like celestial beings.

The stripes of the oriental carpet and the rising steps of the throne establish a tangible, earthly foreground which vanishes into the dazzling light of a heavenly, rationally no longer comprehensible dimension beyond. Blue and red, together with gold, make up a pure triad of colour which is echoed in a succession of ever paler hues, and which also serves a compositional function. Just as the blue of Dorothy's robe is lighter than Mary's, so too her facial expression is softer: her beauty belongs more to this earth than the Madonna, who continues to embody the more severe type favoured by tradition.

The sumptuous carpets, brocades and silks and the oriental gold vase are ornamental extras, further enhanced by the delicacy and detail of their execution. In his treatment of the gold grounds and fabrics, Lorenzetti draws upon the most sophisticated aesthetic effects of Simone Martini. Although the carnations and roses in the vase carry a symbolic significance, it is evident from devotional pictures of this kind that they provided an early forum for artists to explore their love of art for art's sake.

In the emphasis which it places upon the popes, and in its subtle variations upon the French royal colours of gold, blue and red, the painting may also be seen as covertly approving the alliance between the papacy, at that time based in Avignon on the Rhône, and France; Siena at that time supported the French house of Anjou which ruled Italy and remained loyal to the pope.

**Ambrogio Lorenzetti**
Madonna and Child Enthroned, with Angels and Saints, c. 1340
Tempera on wood, 50.5 x 34.5 cm
Siena, Pinacoteca Nazionale

## AMBROGIO LORENZETTI

C. 1290 – C. 1348 (?)

We tend to see Gothic art as something reserved exclusively for churches, and there can be no doubt that the development of new artistic techniques and media was primarily fuelled by ecclesiastical commissions. There is nevertheless evidence that a large and important body of secular art was also created between the 13th and 15th centuries. Historical sources document commissions for paintings, almost none of which have survived into the present. Examples include portraits of traitors, debtors and political opponents, ofen suspended by their legs in disgrace. Large fresco cycles were also common both in city palaces and in houses. There are descriptions of pictures of bathhouses, gardens, castles and illustrated chivalric romances. While frescos painted outdoors have long since weathered away, others were lost for more complex reasons.

In the 17th and 18th centuries there was generally little sense of the artistic value of earlier art. Age continued to count only in the Church: the frescos in San Francesco in Assisi, for example, were virtually equal to holy relics.

The Church was essentially concerned with continuity and did not know the fluctuations experienced by systems of government. In the sphere of secular art, on the other hand, every change in ruler, in party and even in day-to-day politics (such as a switch of allegiance) threatened any paintings created to champion the ideas and teachings of those previously in power. In short, secular art was destroyed more thoroughly than religious art. This is why the present set of frescos, located in Siena's Town Hall, are so precious. They give us an idea of what we have lost.

At the time when they were painted, Siena had a republican constitution, but was *de facto* an oligarchy controlled by the merchant classes. Lorenzetti's frescos adorned the Sala dei Nove, the council chamber housing the meetings of the so-called "Nine", Siena's highest decision-making body. Since members of the public were probably admitted to the chamber at times, the cycle would also have served as a form of propaganda. The scenes illustrated here form part of a comprehensive intellectual programme expressed in artistic (allegorical) terms.

The central theme is stated on the end wall opposite the window. The large figure right of centre is the personification of Good Govern-

**Ambrogio Lorenzetti**
Allegory of Good Government, c. 1337–1340
Fresco (detail), 296 x 1398 cm (total size)
Top right: Allegorical personifications of Faith, Charity and Hope
Left: Peace, Fortitude, Prudence
Middle: Good Government
Right: Magnanimity, Temperance, Justice
Siena, Palazzo Pubblico, Sala dei Nove

ment, representing both the city of Siena and the public weal. On the far left we see Justice with her scales, guided by Wisdom (Sapientia) above. To her right is Concordia, who holds a rope in a play upon her name (*corda* = rope). This rope is held by the 24 city councillors below, some of them clearly portraits.

Lorenzetti has orchestrated the cycle in such a way that, upon entering the chamber, the spectator is presented first with the gruesome personifications of Bad Government, and then, on turning to the right, with the figure of Justice as its counterpart. The procession of city councillors then leads the eye to the main group composed of Good Government and the cardinal virtues. The right-hand wall bears the large fresco of *The Effects of Good Government*. Lorenzetti's cycle should be read not simply horizontally from left to right, however, but also vertically, and above all with regard to its intellectual axes. One such axis can be identified on the *Good Government* wall in the classical-style figure of Peace (*Pax*) portrayed in a semi-reclining pose between the personifications of Justice and Good Government. Not without reason is this room frequently referred to in older sources as the Peace Chamber.

In the fresco on the wall on the right, undoubtedly the most impressive part of the cycle today, the effects of Peace and Good Government are spread out in detail. Ambrogio offers us a view of Siena as if seen over the city wall. The figures in the foreground are clearly larger than those further back, and the buildings in front are similarly taller than those beyond. Even if the figures are still not exactly the right size in relation to the architecture, Lorenzetti nevertheless applies the rules of perspective with an accuracy previously unseen. His pictorial space thereby appears not just deeper but altogether more real. A few anomalies nevertheless creep in: the buildings behind and to the left of the ring of dancers are lit from the right, for example, while those to the right are lit from the left. The general direction of movement of the figures also changes at this point. The richly dressed, disproportionately tall dancers might be called the main axis of this portrayal of the city and the activities of the people living in it. The group are seen performing the steps of a circle dance in a demonstration of Ambrogio's mastery of space and rhythm.

In concentrating his artistic efforts upon this group of dancers, Lorenzetti has a deliberate aim in mind. For this same group also contains the key to the meaning of the fresco, summarized in the words of St Bernard of Siena: *la pace e allegrezza* – peace is joy.

The right-hand section of the fresco echoes this theme in its evocative depiction of the Tuscan countryside, showing people hunting, riding and working in the fields. It also introduces a second theme, namely the security brought by peace, represented in the personification of Securitas (above left). No one has any fears, everyone works for the good of the city or brings his wares to market. The frescos were only given their present titles by Achille Lanzi in 1792; as Lorenzo Ghiberti (1378–1455) testifies in his *Commentarii*, they were previously known as *Peace and War*.

Ambrogio Lorenzetti
Life in the City
From: The Effects of Good Government, c. 1337–1340
Fresco (detail). Siena, Palazzo Pubblico, Sala dei Nove

Ambrogio Lorenzetti
Life in the Country
From: The Effects of Good Government, c. 1337–1340
Fresco (detail). Siena, Palazzo Pubblico, Sala dei Nove

**Ambrogio Lorenzetti**
Nursing Madonna, c. 1320–1330
Tempera on wood, 90 x 48 cm
Siena, Pontificio Seminario Regionale

## AMBROGIO LORENZETTI
### C. 1290– C. 1348 (?)

This is an example of a type of painting widespread in Italian art, namely the large Madonna icon. It perpetuated an older, Byzantine tradition in a relatively unadulterated form, but served a wider range of functions. Big enough to stand on side altars, such panels could also be added to more sizeable altarpieces, hung in a prominent place in a chapel or in a larger room in the home. They were less suitable for close-up viewing, however. They thus occupy a niche between large, more formal altarpieces and private devotional images.

The motif of this panel nevertheless belongs to the sphere of private worship: Mary is nursing her child while standing up – a representative pose taken from older icon painting. With a serious expression on her face, she looks at her son, not at the viewer. Such is the curiosity of the infant Jesus, however, that he almost forgets his thirst. His left leg is raised in a kick. He is a healthy baby, his body more solid than that of his mother, and he is cradled in the Madonna's veil – a successful motif which would be reused by later artists (cf. ill. p. 71).

The veil serves to emphasize the child and conclude the bottom of the painting. The tender harmony of mother and child is typical of Ambrogio's sweet and contemplative art.

## MASO DI BANCO
### ACTIVE 1320–1350

This fresco is the lowest and hence most easily visible of a cycle devoted to the life of St Silvester, the pope who converted Empress Helena to Christianity and baptized Emperor Constantine. The cycle, which is located in the Bardi di Vernio burial chapel, represents Maso di Banco's most important piece of work and earned high praise from Ghiberti. Pope Silvester is here seen, on the left, taming a dragon which had made its home in the Forum Romanum in Rome and which had already poisoned numerous people with its foul breath. The narrative then switches direction, and the Pope reappears in the centre, in the act of resurrecting two of the dragon's victims. Emperor Constantine and a group of companions are shown standing on the right.

Maso offers his own version of the historical ruins of the Forum, using its walls and arches to structure his composition. Thus the wall behind the central figure of the Pope is interrupted by a gap, creating a caesura which is further emphasized by the arch in the background. The architecture subdivides the scene, reinforces the directions in which the characters are looking and the narrative is unfolding, and furthermore lends the picture a severe, two-dimensional character. The individual bodies and objects are also rendered in a precise, almost crystalline fashion, albeit lacking in plasticity or movement.

**Maso di Banco**
St Sylvester Sealing the Dragon's Mouth, between 1340 and 1350
Fresco, 535 cm (total width)
Florence, Santa Croce, Cappella Bardi di Vernio

## JEAN PUCELLE
ACTIVE C. 1319–1335

The Book of Hours which Jean Pucelle illustrated for Jeanne d'Evreux marks the climax of Parisian court painting. It was a gift from King Charles IV to his wife, who was one of the most cultured and active patrons of art of her day. Along with a number of other women at court, she thereby played an influential role in shaping contemporary French taste in art.

In the initial D beneath a scene of the Annunciation, the queen is shown reading at her prie-dieu. The manuscript was evidently intended to surprise its recipient, and it is indeed surprising in both its small format and its widespread renunciation of colour. Pucelle executed every aspect of the work himself, something rare and remarkable in itself. Scenes from Jesus' childhood and Passion are organized in pairs in front of each section of the book. The borders are inventively ornamented, here with children's and party games, together with grotesque figures and beings, partly to amuse the reader and partly in witty allusion to the main illustrations.

Both the compositions and the portrayal of space are derived from Duccio's *Maestà* (ills. pp. 33, 34), but are enriched with the addition of imaginative details and inventions (such as the angel captured in flight below and to the right of the Virgin), making this Book of Hours a collection of miniature works of art.

Jean Pucelle
The Betrayal of Christ and The Annunciation, between 1325 and 1328
(from the Book of Hours of Jeanne d'Evreux; fol. 15 v and 16 r)
Manuscript illumination, 9.4 x 6.4 cm (dimensions of page)
New York, The Metropolitan Museum of Art, The Cloisters

## FRENCH MASTER
C. 1350–1355

This miniature introduces the *Tale of the Lion* by Guillaume de Machaut. The author describes a garden from which he is separated by a river. He nevertheless succeeds in gaining access to the garden, where he meets numerous animals, and in particular a lion, who symbolizes the fidelity of the lover and who eventually leads him to the beloved. The landscape is described – and illustrated – as an unreal idyll, in no recognizable location and with no indication of time of day or year. Landscapes of this kind had a literary tradition going back to classical antiquity, but no similar history in painting.

The magical garden is pictured in the form of a small panel at the start of the text. More or less conventional in its treatment of individual details, the overall effect is nevertheless astonishing. The trees are painted in standard formulae extending both to their shapes and colours. The distribution of blue and yellow flowers obeys decorative convention, as does the gold patterning of the blue background.

The animals are portrayed with greater animation and closer to life, indicative of a society which loved hunting and animal enclosures. The garden as a whole, however, becomes an enchanted park, painted in a naïve style, but full of fascination and charm for the viewer even today.

Master of Guillaume de Machaut
The Tale of the Lion: The Secret Garden, c. 1350–1355
Manuscript illumination, 30 x 21 cm (dimensions of page)
Ms. fr. 1586, fol. 103 r
Paris, Bibliothèque Nationale

**Master of the Berlin Nativity**
Nativity, c. 1330–1340
Tempera on wood, 33 x 24 cm
Berlin, Gemäldegalerie, Staatliche Museen zu Berlin – Preußischer Kulturbesitz

## BAVARIAN MASTER
C. 1330–1340

The Berlin *Nativity* forms one half of a diptych (the other half, a *Crucifixion*, is located in the Bührle Collection, Zurich). It bears a *Man of Sorrows* on the reverse (the back of the *Crucifixion* features a *vera icon*). Diptychs, which consist of a hinged pair of panels, were a major type of private devotional picture and their small and handy format made them particularly suitable as travelling altars.

In contrast to the *Crucifixion,* in which motifs from Sienese painting predominate, the present panel copies Giotto's fresco of c. 1303/05 in the Arena Chapel in Padua. As a comparison between the two clearly shows, however, the German artist sought to avoid the bold overlapping demonstrated by Giotto's figures and therefore made a few alterations to the composition. Particularly significant is the change in the mother-child relationship: instead of lifting her son out of the crib as in Giotto's fresco, Mary is now shown clasping him closely to her – a motif belonging to the sphere of the devotional picture. Indeed, the artist appears to have taken a scene from monumental painting and translated it into a small format without a second thought. Giotto's powerful figures are replaced by small genre motifs, particularly in the background, where a bear and a deer, a boar and a weasel populate the landscape for the entertainment of the spectator.

## BOHEMIAN MASTER
C. 1350

This painting is part of a larger altarpiece comprising nine panels in three rows of three. It was donated by one of the lords of Rosenberg. The family owned large tracts of southern Bohemia and also played a leading role in court society in Prague. Thanks to their later refusal to join the Hussite movement, a small number of older works of art in their possession have survived intact, giving us an idea of the rich flowering of Prague painting between 1330 and 1410. The Hohenfurth Altar itself, however, is rather a mediocre work. A typical feature of Bohemian art during this era is its combination of certain Byzantine or Upper Italian-Byzantine stylistic elements, such as flesh colouring and facial type, with calligraphic drawing and motifs of Western art.

It is most improbable that the artist had made a first-hand study of Italian art. His starting-point was more likely a local Prague synthesis of the various trends in European painting which Charles IV had brought with him to his new capital. The stylistic differences between these sources have not been ironed out, as is evident from the contrast between the Mount of Olives, which is thoroughly unrealistic in character, and the highly accurate renditions of the birds, which might have been taken from the pattern book of an Upper Italian painter.

**Hohenfurth Master**
The Agony in the Garden, c. 1350 (panel from the Hohenfurth Altar)
Tempera on canvas on wood, 100 x 92 cm. Prague, Národni Galeri

# BOHEMIAN MASTER

C. 1340

The importance of Passiontide in the Italian religious calendar and the corresponding popularity of the Crucifixion as a motif in art rapidly spread north of the Alps. The master of the present *Crucifixion* seems to have been inspired by Italian models in his rich use of embossing and in certain aspects of his technique, such as the different coloured ground given to the faces. Unlike the Master of the Berlin Nativity, however, the artist here equals the skill and ability of his Italian counterparts. He is unafraid to let his figures be sliced by the edges of the frame.

This Bohemian master also employs foreshortening of the most difficult kind, such as profil perdu. But he remains an artist who thinks entirely for himself. He has clearly invented a number of figures and motifs: the two thieves crucified to the right and left of Christ are barely conceivable in Italian art, for example. Other elements of the scene have been reinterpreted in an original way, such as the dice player sprawled at the foot of the cross. Particularly distinctive is the artist's palette. He does not subscribe to a hierarchy of colour in which pure, strong colours carry greater symbolic weight than broken and diluted tones, which serve to indicate lesser importance. By preferring lighter shades for the foreground and darker colours for the background, however, he establishes an innovative transition from light to dark.

**Master of the Kaufmann Crucifixion**
The Crucifixion of Christ, c. 1340
Tempera on wood, 76 x 29.5 cm
Berlin, Gemäldegalerie, Staatliche Museen
zu Berlin – Preußischer Kulturbesitz

*Below:*
**Master of the Eichhorn Madonna**
Eichhorn Madonna (from Eichhorn,
Moravia), c. 1350
Tempera on wood, 79 x 63 cm
Prague, Národni Galeri

# BOHEMIAN MASTER

C. 1350

The genre of the large-format Italian-Byzantine Madonna icon was introduced into Bohemia by Charles IV, King of Bohemia and Holy Roman Emperor, who also greatly furthered its cult. The severity and devoutness of Byzantine motifs, the enamel-like brilliance of its palette, the exquisite beauty of its forms and its use of a gold ground strewn with engraved and embossed ornament were both foreign and fascinating. These types of pictures underwent several changes in Bohemia. Thus the Madonna was given a crown, and often a gold coronet and other items of jewellery. Her face was made as beautiful as possible. The success of these panels was extraordinary. Never before in central Europe had pictures occupied such a focal position in religious worship. Many were attributed with miraculous powers and even became the object of pilgrimages. Unlike other types of icon, however, the Madonna icon did not come to assume a standardized format. Astonishing features of the regal *Eichhorn Madonna* are its monumental composition, extending to all four sides of the frame, and in particular the figure of Christ, highly serious in expression and not at all childlike. In his right hand he clutches a goldfinch (a symbol of the Passion); with his left he grasps the Virgin's veil, which will one day serve as his loincloth on the cross and of which Prague cathedral boasted a large piece amongst its holy relics.

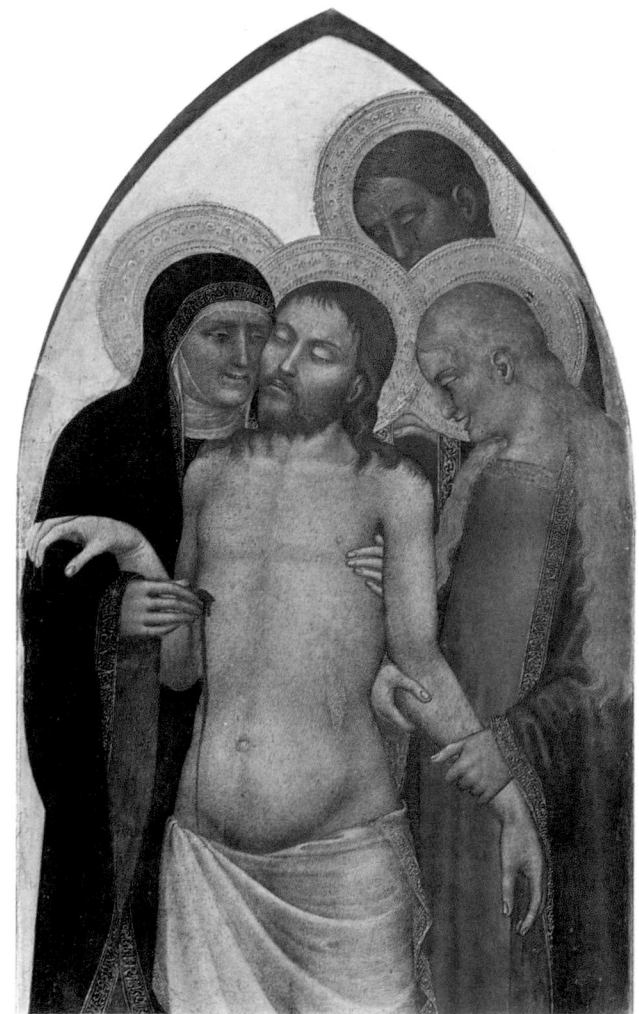

**Giovanni da Milano**
Pietà, 1365
(from San Girolamo della Costa, Florence)
Tempera on wood, 122 x 58 cm
Florence, Galleria dell'Accademia

## GIOVANNI DA MILANO
### ACTIVE 1346–1369

Is it a Pietà, or is it a Deposition? This is far from being a narrative painting. It is clear from the way in which Mary clasps her son and moves her right arm, that she is not meant to be seen as holding his full weight. She is tenderly saying her last farewell, and thereby pointing to the wound in his side so greatly venerated in 14th-century religious practice: it was through this wound that Christ's heart was pierced, releasing a stream of water and blood which, according to earlier theological thinking, signified the moment of the birth of the Church and the establishment of the sacraments of baptism and the Eucharist. As a sign of God's love for humankind, the wound was an object of devotion not just in the specific context of the Sacred Heart.

Correspondingly, the starting-point of the present panel is not a narrative genre of painting, but rather the half-length devotional image of the Man of Sorrows, a Byzantine icon widespread in western Europe since the 13th century as the embodiment of the Passion and its re-enactment in the sacrifice of the Mass. Such was the degree of freedom granted the artist in this type of picture that he was at liberty to narrow, widen or modify its scope. Giovanni has only placed it within a narrative context, thereby lending it the physical realism and animation in line with the religious trends of his day.

**Tommaso da Modena**
The Departure of St Ursula, c. 1355–1358
(from the cycle in the choir of the Augustinian anchorite church of Santa Margherita)
Fresco (detail), 233.5 x 220 cm (total size). Treviso, Museo Civico

## TOMMASO DA MODENA
### 1325/26–1379

In a cycle of twelve large frescos, Tommaso relates the legend of St Ursula, daughter of the king of Brittany, and her 11,000 virgins, their journey to Rome and their martyrdom at the hands of the Huns in Cologne. As so often the case, the cycle was commissioned following the acquisition of a holy relic. Were we ignorant of the religious nature of its content, we might easily mistake the present fresco – whose colours are no longer seen in their full glory owing to the loss of most of the *a secco* painting – for a scene from the world of court society.

The figures are clad in the latest fashions: tight-fitting clothes emphasize the bodies of both the women and the men. Where forms are not sufficiently rounded, they are improved upon by the artist. The shortness of the men's tunics is underlined by their long sleeves.

Tommaso's artistic approach is similarly inspired by the real world. He has taken his characters from the well-fed middle classes and religious circles of Treviso, portraying them more as individuals than as types. Despite the large numbers of figures involved, he nevertheless groups them in a successful manner. It was this unaffected view of reality more than the study of older Tuscan art that led to the flowering of painting in Upper Italy from the mid-14th century.

# BARNABA DA MODENA

ACTIVE 1361–1383

In comparison to works by Tommaso, also from Modena, this panel may at first sight appear something of an anachronism. Its broad, richly decorated gold ground and the Madonna's mantle, covered with Byzantine-style gold ornament, seem to look even further back than the first half of the 13th century.

On the other hand, the Byzantine herringbone pattern is undeniably given a modern linear roundness. The standing Christ is also a contemporary type. His face clearly betrays the influence of child paintings by Ambrogio Lorenzetti.

To dismiss Barnaba's art as simply an imitation of the Venetian-Byzantine style, however, would be to ignore the historical situation. For the plague years of 1347/48 had prompted two reactions: the resolution to enjoy life to the full, and a renewed embrace of religion. Even the pious severity of older art now seemed too profane, to say nothing of Tommaso's worldly visions. A new, retrospective style was now expressly sought for devotional images. Artists thus spoke two languages, depending on the commission in hand; similar works in the "devout style" from the hand of Tommaso are also extant.

Barnaba da Modena
Madonna and Child, 1370
Tempera on wood,
101 x 69 cm
Turin, Galleria Sabauda

*Below:*
**Altichiero da Zevio**
The Beheading of St George, c. 1382
(from a fresco cycle of scenes from the
life of Christ and SS Lucy, Catherine
and George)
Fresco (detail)
Padua, Oratorio di San Giorgio

# ALTICHIERO DA ZEVIO

C. 1320/30 – C. 1385/90

We know almost nothing about this Veronese painter, but his frescos show him to be one of the great narrators of the 14th century and an artist who deserved greater fame. He does not use the martyrdom of St George as an opportunity to portray a scene of great commotion. Instead, he concentrates upon the tension preceding the execution. The saint kneels in humble resignation. His executioner is scrutinizing his victim before taking aim with his sword. His assistant holds a cloth ready. The heathen priest – betraying the greatest animation of any of the characters – is still attempting to convert George, but all the onlookers sense that his words will fall on deaf ears. The commander is therefore already issuing the order to proceed. Aware of the terrible scene that is about to be enacted, an anxious father moves to lead his young son away.

A number of distinct but close moments in time are here brought together and interpreted in terms of different emotional reactions. The tension in the air is heightened by the threatening phalanx of soldiers and their lances, and indeed even by the steep cliffs looming in the background. With a keen eye for individual and social behaviour, Altichiero brings this execution scene to life, without forgetting that it concerns the martyrdom of a saint which took place long ago in a distant land.

**Michelino da Besozzo**
The Christ Child crowns the Duke, c. 1402/03
(illustration to P. da Castelletto's obituary for
Giangaleazzo Visconti)
Manuscript illumination, 37.5 x 25 cm. Ms. lat. 5888, fol. 1 r
Paris, Bibliothèque Nationale

**Michelino da Besozzo**
The Mystic Marriage
of St Catherine,
c. 1410–1420
Tempera on wood,
75 x 58 cm
Siena, Pinacoteca
Nazionale

## MICHELINO DA BESOZZO
### ACTIVE 1388–1442

The court artist Michelino was also a miniaturist, a panel painter and an architect employed on Milan cathedral. His patron, Duke Giangaleazzo Visconti, was the most powerful despot of his day and ruled almost the whole of Upper Italy up till his death. He was brother-in-law both to the French King Charles V and his brothers Duke Jean de Berry and Philip the Bold, and to Emperor Wenceslas of Bohemia. In the Italian principalities, which were ruled efficiently and energetically, art too had a permanent place. At a public level it was a form of propaganda and lavish display, but it also served to satisfy more sophisticated aesthetic needs.

This illumination testifies to the presumptuous settings in which ruling figures liked to be portrayed. Giangaleazzo has been taken up to Heaven. He has not even had to knock at St Peter's gate, but is seen here being crowned by the infant Christ. The crown itself is modelled on imperial crowns of late antiquity – a clever, ambiguous motif which can signify both the Duke's claim to be king of Italy and the crown of heavenly bliss. The central group, here attended by the twelve virtues, obeys the typical and familiar arrangement employed in paintings of the Coronation of the Virgin. The angels are portrayed as court pages presenting the Duke's arms, jousting helmets and alliances.

The whole is painted using the polished means of Sienese sacred art, with its gradated colours and gold ornament. The border is richly decorated with prophets, whose words refer both to the Duke and Christ alike. This is followed by a genealogy tracing the descent of the Visconti from Aeneas and his mother Venus. It is no contradiction, however, that the same duke should also sponsor realistic studies of animals and plants, for which Michelino was famous.

In this (poorly preserved) panel the artist strikes a different note. It is true that the gold is skilfully worked, the throne given a fine matt finish, and the nimbuses and signature (beneath Mary) worked in relief; originally, the crowns were even studded with precious stones. But such lavishness was nothing out of the ordinary. It is clear from the composition of the main group that the artist has given much greater thought to his subject that in the case of the miniature. The Virgin gently pushes the shy Catherine towards the infant Christ, whose helplessness is very accurately studied. Catherine cautiously holds out her hand to receive the ring.

Animated form is one of the main aims of Michelino's art – in the contours of the throne, in the scoop of the draperies and their undulating hems, even in his brush strokes. The result is not mere ornament, however, but an enrichment of the expressiveness of the whole. Michelino's position as court artist allowed him to be original. Counter to prevailing convention, he thus makes no attempt to convey spatial depth or to distinguish between the gold ground and the floor.

## GIOVANNINO DE' GRASSI (?)

#### DOCUMENTED FROM 1389, D. 1398

The *Tacuinum Sanitatis* (Book of Health) owes its origins to an 11th-century Arab treatise which was translated for the Hohenstaufen king Manfred in the 13th century and which in the 14th century onwards assumed the form of an illuminated manuscript with explanatory texts. In the present picture, a peasant is digging onions and a woman is collecting them in her lap. A net full of the vegetables is already hanging from the tree. The text underneath describes the best onions as white and juicy and credits onions with the beneficial properties of assisting urine formation and increasing virility, as well as with the possible disadvantage of causing headaches, which can be relieved with vinegar and milk.

It is striking that the plants discussed in the *Tacuinum Sanitatis* are presented not in isolation and in botanical detail, but in the context of their harvest or use. Since the seasons and the ground are also observed and depicted with great accuracy, these illuminations contain the beginnings of a new, objective approach to landscape. They also detail social differences in physiognomy, dress and pose which would not have escaped the reader. This realistic style of portrayal was a phenomenon of court culture and arose in the courts of the Upper Italian condottieri, with their lack of tradition and their sober, objective attitude towards their environment.

Circle of **Giovannino de' Grassi**
Onions. From the herbal *Tacuinum Sanitatis*, c. 1380–1390
Manuscript illumination,
32.3 x 25 cm (dimensions of page)
(from the collection of the wife of Duke Leopold III of Austria, née Visconti)
Ms. nouv. acq. Iat. 1673, fol. 24 v
Paris, Bibliothèque Nationale

## STEFANO DI GIOVANNI

#### C. 1374/75 – AFTER 1438

Presented with this panel, we begin to wonder whether it is indeed painted or in fact fashioned in gold. The distribution of blue and red across the surface recalls the manner in which goldsmiths studded their works with sapphires and rubies. The colours are applied with the brilliance of enamel. By dulling and glazing the areas of gold in a highly varied manner, the artist makes them glitter and shine in ever different ways. In the years around 1400, the subject of the *Virgin of the Rose Garden* was to be found not only in painting, but also in goldsmithery, as for example in the so-called *Golden Horse* in Altötting, one of the best examples of French court goldwork of the epoch. The contemporary taste for gems and gem-like qualities, and the poetic treatment given to holy objects, thereby led each medium to accommodate aspects of the other: goldsmiths sought to imitate the colours and the scenic dimension of painting, while painters sought to recreate the effects of light and sophisticated luxury of metalwork. Virtuosity and originality, however, were expected of every artist of the day. Stefano gives of his best above all in the gracefully animated figures of the angels and in the accurate reproduction of the birds, in emulation of his model Michelino da Besozzo. Alongside drawings, numerous frescos have also survived from Stefano's hand, the majority of them in and around Verona.

Stefano di Giovanni
(Stefano da Verona)
The Virgin of the Rose Garden, c. 1425
Tempera on wood,
129 x 95 cm. Verona,
Museo di Castelvecchio

# PISANELLO
## BEFORE 1395-1455

According to legend, Eustace was a Roman knight. While out hunting one day, he came across a large stag and set off on its trail. After a long chase, the animal leapt up onto a steep cliff and stood still. Between its antlers there appeared a crucifix, which spoke to the huntsman and called upon him to convert to Christianity. In the 14th century, saints were traditionally portrayed as half or full-length figures identified by their attributes, or in a narrative cycle of several paintings. The present work is undoubtedly a single-figure portrait, yet it is neither a narrative nor an altarpiece, nor even a devotional picture. Nor, however, it is simply a painting of the hunt.

This enigmatic picture has many layers. The huntsman is dressed in contemporary fashion with a turban-like head-dress and a long, fur-trimmed tunic, but without the usual colourfulness. The gold, with its dark glaze, recalls both the magnificence of court dress and the gold of religious art. Indeed, the entire painting is plunged into a semi-darkness which can be explained neither by pigment discoloration nor by the lighting of the forest. The half-light infuses the picture with a mysterious atmosphere.

Hunters amongst the spectators would have enjoyed identifying the various different breeds of hunting dogs which Pisanello has included, each studied carefully and reproduced true to life. The dogs are not there merely to entertain the viewer, however, but are directly caught up in the events of the scene. Only the greyhound on the right, chasing a hare, has not yet noticed that his master has encountered something extraordinary. The other animals and the landscape impart a rich internal frame and backdrop to the miraculous scene, whereby even the landscape is simply "accompanying" the main figures. Pisanello studies the animals in much greater depth. His treatment of nature is not "naturalistic" on principle. Rather, he creates the overall impression of a paradise into which the hunter has disruptively intruded.

Unlike some of his older colleagues, Pisanello has here used a religious scene not merely as the vehicle for something else, nor as an excuse for cynical self-aggrandizement in the manner of the Visconti. In training his sights on the real world, he was not simply exploring new and attractive surface structures or satisfying his curiosity. He was too interested in animals and objects in their own right, and not just in their external appearance. The seriousness of Tuscan painting had given rise to a new intellectual and monumental approach which was also embraced by the artists of Upper Italy.

Pisanello
The Vision of St Eustace, c. 1435
Tempera on wood, 55 x 65 cm
London, National Gallery

**Pisanello**
Portrait of Lionello d'Este, 1441 (?)
Tempera on wood, 28 x 19 cm
Bergamo, Accademia Carrara

**Pisanello**
The Virgin and Child with the
Saints George and Anthony Abbot, c. 1445
Tempera on wood, 47 x 29 cm
London, National Gallery

# PISANELLO
## BEFORE 1395—1455

Pisanello, who had well mastered the complexities of spatial depth and three-dimensional representation as can be seen below, here creates an emphatically two-dimensional portrait. The prince is shown in strict profile, set in sharp relief against a dark background. Even the modelling of his head remains flat, while the chest is presented as a solid but only weakly three-dimensional base. To suggest that the panel represents a design for a coin is insufficient to explain these features. Pisanello was certainly the greatest medallist of his time and inspired a renaissance in the genre. He liked the strict framework and simple forms of relief work. But severity of external form was also a feature of contemporary taste and extended to hairstyles and clothing, as can be seen here. With its dark blue ground and luminous rose blossoms, however, the overall mood of the portrait is softened and infused with a fairy-tale character.

The panel below documents the approach which Pisanello adopted towards the traditional genre of domestic devotional picture during the last years of his career. In its tripartite division and symmetry, it recalls an altarpiece. Beneath a dazzling vision of the Virgin and Child, stand, on the left, St Anthony Abbot, protector against the plague and leprosy, and on the right, St George, the model of knightly virtue. The relationship between the two men is purely formal. For we surely cannot suppose that the stooping hermit with his grumpy expression and clanging handbell is gesturing at St George, nor that the aristocratic pose of the knight is directed at the old man.

In his portrayal of the two saints, Pisanello forgets the religious nature of his commission. In shape and material, George's fashionable hat is a beautiful display of artistry – but it cannot replace a halo. We can admire the figure of George for the accuracy with which the rounded volumes of his armour are drawn, and for the light effects on the metal, but not as a convincing portrayal of saintliness.

We might easily make do with the explanation that the artist simply had a different aim in mind. Things are not that simple, however. The hardness characterizing the two saints is set against the atmospheric backdrop of a forest. In a similar fashion to the portrait above, the overall character of the composition is thereby fundamentally altered. An even greater contrast, however, is provided by the visionary apparition of the Madonna. The gold radiates its celestial light both above the dark ground and over the clear daylight in which the figures stand. The Virgin is not dressed in true-to-life contemporary style but in the colours and forms of the International Gothic of around 1415. Just as Duccio cited older, strictly speaking, outdated Byzantine art when he wanted a figure to appear particularly dignified, so Pisanello here takes up a device invented by the Limburg brothers (d. 1416)!

# GENTILE DA FABRIANO

### c. 1370–1427

The last surviving work by Gentile da Fabriano documents, in this pilgrimage scene, an interesting chapter in the history of religion. It shows the viewer the pilgrimage to the tomb of St Nicholas in Bari, the popularity of the pilgrimage site, and also, in the figure of the man front left, an instance of miraculous healing. At the same time, it is sober and objective in its view, cataloguing the different forms of religious zeal and containing no indication of the presence of the heavenly spheres or of any divine intervention. With astonishing historical fidelity, Gentile depicts a 12th-century mosaic in the apse of the church, and beneath it – in what appears to be an old-fashioned style – the very five scenes from the life of St Nicholas which can be seen on the predella of the Quaratesi altarpiece. The gloomy lighting inside the old church is rendered with the same fidelity as, for example, the Madonna icon on the side wall of the left apse. The growing awareness of historical change, one of the great achievements of the humanistic 15th century, was thus something of which Gentile was fully a part. It was during this time that proof emerged that Emperor Constantine had not, after all, bestowed the Papal States upon the pope. A clearer line began to be drawn between epochs – one of the conditions which would permit a conscious return to classical antiquity.

The present scene, part of the same predella, illustrates the legendary episode in which Nicholas saved three impoverished girls from prostitution by tossing three gold balls through their window one night. It is conceived in quite different terms to the panel above. It was long considered to be a work by Masaccio – an understandable error which shows that there is no firm break between the Gothic and the Renaissance, but at best a change of paradigm whose advent is announced sometimes clearly, sometimes less obviously in advance.

The panel offers us a view into a simple bedroom, in which four people are preparing to go to bed. (The use of just one bed by the entire family, and by both sexes and all ages, shows how poor they are.) Gentile draws upon the genre of family painting in composing the scene: we see the father smiling kindly at his daughter's efforts to assist him, and there is no suggestion of the threat that hangs over their existence. For the artist, however, the most interesting challenge was probably to portray the figures in complex and highly fore-shortened poses: one daughter binding her hair in a scarf as she apparently catches sight of the saint at the window, the other in the process of pulling off her dress. Gentile, a foreign painter of the older generation, thereby offered the city of Florence – where a new generation of artists was in the process of making Florentine art the foremost in Italy – a deliberate demonstration of his skill and talent.

According to an inscription now lost, the altar, praised by Vasari as Gentile's greatest work, was completed in May 1425.

**Gentile da Fabriano**
A Miracle of St Nicholas, 1425
(part of the predella of the Quaratesi triptych from San Niccolò, Florence)
Tempera on wood, 35 x 36cm
Washington, National Gallery of Art

**Gentile da Fabriano**
St Nicholas and the Three Gold Balls, 1425
(part of the predella of the Quaratesi triptych from San Niccolò, Florence)
Tempera on wood, 36 x 36cm
Rome, Musei Vaticani, Pinacoteca Vaticana

**Gentile da Fabriano**
Adoration of the Magi, 1423
(from the Strozzi Chapel in Santa Trinità, Florence;
the right-hand predella panel is a copy)
Tempera on wood, 303 x 282 cm (incl. frame)
Florence, Galleria degli Uffizi

## GENTILE DA FABRIANO

C. 1370–1427

This panel for the Strozzi family chapel in Florence is not a private altarpiece but a public demonstration. The predella scenes of the Nativity, the *Flight to Egypt* and the *Presentation in the Temple* are prize examples of precision painting and pay particular attention to effects of light. The *Adoration of the Magi* uses exactly the same setting as the *Nativity* on the predella, but transforms it into a scene of royal splendour. The Strozzi thereby place themselves on a par with the princes of Italy. Not only are the figures arrayed in sumptuous fabrics, but these are rendered with supreme skill in a wide range of gilding, engraving and painting techniques. But Gentile also acts as a master of ceremonies: the characters are strictly ordered according to the richness of their dress, documenting the hierarchy of dress and court protocol. The falcons, hunting leopards and monkeys appear to be added, however, for the amusement of all the members of the court.

# SASSETTA

## C. 1392–1450

Sassetta was the most important painter in Siena in the early 15th century. The city had lost its former political and economic status and was unwillingly forced to recognize the superiority of Florence. Artists, however, showed themselves no more open to Florentine trends than before. On the contrary: the ties between the Sienese and Florentine painters were less close now than they had been in the first half of the 14th century, during the most intense period of rivalry between the two cities. Both camps had since turned their attention largely back to their artistic pasts. Sassetta is an illustration, however, of how this could nevertheless produce significant results.

The panel illustrated here was once part of a winged altarpiece whose components were separated at the start of the 19th century. It was originally painted for the Franciscan church in Borgo San Sepolcro. It tells the story of how, on a broad plain between Campiglia and San Quirico not far from Siena, St Francis encountered three poor women who were identical in age, stature and appearance. They greeted him with the words "Welcome Lady Poverty" and then disappeared. Bonaventura, who relates the tale, interprets the three women as Poverty, Chastity and Obedience. The painting is thus both an allegory and a highly dramatic narrative. Sassetta has elaborated somewhat upon the story. The three women are no longer identical in dress, for example: Poverty wears Franciscan brown, Chastity white (the colour of the lily) and Obedience burgundy red. Nor are we simply shown a meeting, but the mystic marriage of St Francis to Poverty – a motif from the frescos by the school of Giotto in the Lower Church of San Francesco in Assisi. The true magic of this painting lies in its background. The sweeping plain is seen in the clear but still subdued light of early morning. The landscape, with its mountains seen in sharp silhouette in the background and its monochrome colours, is reminiscent of Simone Martini, albeit viewed through Sassetta's eyes: it incorporates both the rectangular fields of the Tuscan countryside and trees dotted irregularly across the hillsides. The entire palette is oriented towards the Franciscan brown. Although the towns and castles scattered across the countryside are Tuscan in their cubic architectural style, they nevertheless appear unreal.

This *Procession of the Magi* is just a fragment in which Sassetta, inspired by the sumptuous compositions of Lombard painters, shows the Three Kings on their way to Bethlehem. The landscape is wintery and parched, in keeping with the season of Christ's birth, and immersed in a cold, bright light. The blue of the sky intensifies towards the top of the painting. A line of stylized birds of passage is seen overhead. In the background we can identify a gate in the style of the Porta Romana in Siena. The choice and use of colour recall the art of Fra Angelico, whose painting in Cortona had impressed Sassetta. But Sassetta's paintings are of a more austere and rigorous beauty.

Sassetta
The Mystic Marriage of St Francis,
1437–1444
(from the back of the Borgo San
Sepolcro altarpiece)
Tempera on wood, 95 x 58 cm
Chantilly, Musée Condé

Sassetta
The Procession of the Magi, c. 1432–1436
(fragment of a picture showing the Adoration of the Magi)
Tempera on wood, 21.3 x 29 cm
New York, The Metropolitan Museum of Art

**Lorenzo Monaco**
The Annunciation,
c. 1410–1415
(detail of an altar in the
Badia, Florence)
Tempera on wood,
130 x 230 cm (total size)
Florence, Galleria
dell'Accademia

**Lorenzo Monaco** Adoration of the Magi, 1421/22
Tempera on wood, 144 x 177 cm. Florence, Galleria degli Uffizi

# LORENZO MONACO

### C. 1370 – C. 1425

The model for this painting, in which an Annunciation takes the place of the usual enthroned Madonna as the centre of the altarpiece, was provided by Simone Martini's *Annunciation* of 1333 in Siena cathedral. It was from here that Lorenzo adopted the motif of the Virgin surprised by the angel, albeit in a modified form. Building upon Simone's sophisticated technical skills, Lorenzo embosses and engraves the various different areas of gold leaf and gloss paint and thereby makes the gold sparkle and shine. He uses the least worldly colours of yellow, red/violet and blue for his palette, which he lightens to such an extent that they acquire a brightness similar to the gleam of gold. Rhythmical curves, just one of the formal tools of older Sienese painting, are here adopted as the chief design principle. Bodily actions are translated into a sequence of folds and curving contours, thereby softening the violence of Mary's reaction.

At the same time, her pose is enriched as it dissolves into a wealth of movements and countermovements. Above all, by carrying the lightness of his palette and the fluidity of his line to such extremes, the painter succeeds in convincing the viewer that the Archangel Gabriel is indeed floating on a cloud of light inside the room.

In the late 15th century, in keeping with the taste of the day, this panel was given a rectangular frame and an Annunciation and prophets were added to its spandrels. It probably originally featured a predella. The *Adoration of the Magi* was at that time a very popular subject. The homage offered by the Three Kings, one from each of the three known continents and representing the three stages of man, to the "new-born King of the Jews" underlined Christ's status as the king of kings. Hence, too, the name Epiphany for the festival on 6 January (epiphany = the appearance of a divinity). The oldest king, Caspar, represents Asia, considered the noblest continent since it was here that Jerusalem, the centre of the world, was to be found. Caspar brings gold, a symbol of Christ's power. The second, middle-aged king, Melchior, symbolizes Europe and bears frankincense as a token of Christ's priesthood. Balthasar, the youngest, represents Africa and presents myrrh as a symbol of Christ's Passion and sacrifice on the cross.

In the years around 1400, this subject was prized as an opportunity to mount a display of courtly pomp, to paint a party of travellers, and also to portray exotic peoples in a fashion true to life. Thus the present panel includes Africans, Turks and Mongols each wearing their own distinctive dress and, in particular, striking hats. There is even a camel behind the mounted figures on the right. The composition incorporates several different moments in time: on the right, the figures are watching the star of Bethlehem, i.e. the comet, that led them to the stable, while in the middle and on the left we see the procession and the Adoration.

# FRA ANGELICO

C. 1395/1400–1455

The precise origins of this large Florentine altarpiece are unknown. Since Cosmas and Damian – the patron saints of the house of Medici, doctors and apothecaries – occupy positions of honour on either side of the Virgin's throne, it is thought that the painting may have been commissioned by the elder Cosimo de' Medici.

Florentine artists after 1400 took the rigid assembly of saints around the Madonna traditionally found in older styles of altar painting and transformed them into a lively group. The saints are now all related in different ways to the centre of the composition, whether through their gestures (pointing, instructing) or their expressions, (reverent, contemplative

or enraptured). The typical frontality of the altarpiece is nevertheless retained, as is the use of sumptuous gold brocade and the rich decoration of the background, so that the solemn spendour of the altarpiece is preserved. The Madonna is magnified in size and her appearance amplified by the steps (inlaid with precious materials) and the throne, with its scalloped niche and artfully curved arms. Certain features of the painted architecture, such as the garlands of fruit and flowers with their pomegranates, testify to Fra Angelico's interest in the Renaissance architecture being developed by Filippo Brunelleschi and his colleagues on the basis of their studies of classical antiquity. In the robed figures, however, the artist-monk sticks closer to Gothic tradition.

Fra Angelico bathes the group in a gentle light. Shadows are clearly visible on the throne. The light nevertheless intensifies to-

**Fra Angelico**
Annalena Panel, c. 1445
The Virgin and Child enthroned with SS
Peter the Martyr, Cosmas and Damian (left),
John the Baptist, Lawrence and Francis (right)
Tempera on wood, 180 x 202 cm
Florence, Museo di San Marco

wards the centre of the composition. More luminous even than the Virgin's dress, whose gloss colours lend it a powerful sheen, is the polished gold leaf of the engraved and embossed nimbuses.

**Fra Angelico**
The Lamentation of Christ, 1436
(from the church of the Confraternity of the Madonna of the Cross, Florence)
Tempera on wood, 108 x 165 cm
Florence, Museo di San Marco

**Fra Angelico**
Entombment, 1438–1443
(from the predella of the high altar of San Marco, Florence)
Tempera on wood, 37.9 x 46.4 cm
Munich, Bayerische Staatsgemäldesammlungen, Alte Pinakothek

# FRA ANGELICO
## C. 1395/1400–1455

The *Lamentation* is a painting which offers us a rather one-sided view of Fra Angelico's art. It nevertheless occupies an important position in his œuvre. In this work for a religious Florentine confraternity, Fra Angelico took an earlier 14th-century genre as his basis, as if the tradition embodied in the older model were a guarantee of devout sentiment. The new painting thereby also took on the quality of a meditation. The raising of the dead Christ's arms is a motif invented by Giotto to express ardent concern. The similarity to Giotto is purely external, however, for the motif here serves a very different purpose. John and the saints in the foreground hold up Christ's arms in order to contemplate his countless welts and wounds – and thereby urge the viewer to do the same. Other details within the painting are similarly isolated and presented for individual meditation, with the result that the persons in the scene remain unrelated to one other, united only in their contemplation of Christ. Hence the artist had no difficulty introducing the figures of St Catherine and a 14th-century beatified woman on the right, and St Dominic on the left. This is in no sense a narrative painting, but one with a general mood rather than a central compositional focus. Its atmospheric quality is emphasized by the empty and pallid landscape and the stern city wall.

The *Entombment* is part of the high altarpiece installed in the convent church of San Marco in 1440. It formed the centre of a five-part predella bearing scenes from the lives of the saints Cosmas and Damian (patron saints of the Medici, who donated the altar). It is this picture which the priest officiating at the altar would have had before him. Christ's dead body is held up like the Host. The picture is saying: Christ, sacrificed for our salvation, is (like) the Host sacrificed in the Mass. This is why the scene shows the Entombment rather than the Deposition. For according to earlier thinking, Christ's tomb was essentially the same as the vessels or the tabernacle in which the Host was kept. Like the painting by Giovanni da Milano (ill. p.46), it is an expanded version of a Man of Sorrows. It is conceived as a devotional picture, as is clear from the reverence which the Virgin and John are showing to Christ's wounds. The dark ground of the tomb establishes an inner field – almost a picture within a picture – in which the most important theological elements are highlighted. It thereby cites an earlier genre of paintings attributed with miraculous powers. Fra Angelico breathes subtle life into the strict symmetry and emphatic central axis, however: Christ is closer to Mary and leans towards her, underlining her special importance as the Mother of God, while Mary bends even more obviously towards her son. Christ's frontal and spatial position on the door of the tomb nevertheless serves to isolate him. The painting is both austere and animated, logical and full of feeling. The landscape and the rock form a dark foil against which the light – and within it the figure of Christ – appears luminous.

Although its mood shares the devout piety of the previous two panels, the fresco of the *Annunciation* is nevertheless conceived in a different manner. Fra Angelico painted it for his fellow brothers in the Dominican monastery. It is situated at the end of the stairs leading to the monks' cells, and invites the viewer to linger and – as its inscription says – to pray. The *Annunciation* cites a painting in the neighbouring Servite church which was greatly venerated for its miraculous powers, and thereby itself assumes such powers. The divine protection it offered the monastery was nevertheless just one aspect of its function. Addressed to educated monks, it also operates at a more profound intellectual level. It deals with the dogma of the incarnation of Christ, his "entry" into earthly life – hence its setting in front of a doorway. The Annunciation takes place in the porch of the Temple in Jerusalem. The enclosed garden on the left is a reference to Mary's virginity. It also contains a cypress, which was equated with the cedar of Lebanon, another popular symbol for the Virgin. In the background we can see a cell resembling the monks' cells in the Convent of San Marco. Since Mary lived in the Temple like a nun, she was a model of monastic life.

The cell has another, higher meaning, however: it illustrates the idea that Mary is the nuptial chamber, the vessel in which God is made man on earth. By taking up the familiar arcades of the monastery, Fra Angelico places the Annunciation firmly in the present. The clear and strict order of Michelozzo's architecture and the purity of its forms imprint themselves upon the scene, which despite its multi-layered content remains a whole. The perspective composition makes clear, however, what can also be read in the different intensity with which the two figures are treated: namely, that the two halves of the fresco have a differing significance. The central focus of the painting is the Virgin, as emphasized by the red gold brocade of her dress (now peeled off). She is also an example of humility, which was considered the highest of all monastic virtues.

The *Coronation of the Virgin* was a triumphal subject which was excellently suited for an altarpiece. It was believed that, at the moment of the consecration of the Host on the altar, the heavens opened and the community of Heaven, i.e. the Church triumphant, took part in the sacrifice of the Mass. Since theology taught that the Church was, in a mystic fashion, identical with Mary, the Mother and simultaneously the Bride of Christ, this painting of Mary's coronation is also a metaphorical picture of the triumph of the Church.

This idea was particularly welcome to the Dominicans, who had made it their goal to strengthen papal power and defend it against all critics and deviationists. This also explains why many members and patrons of the order of the Black Friars are portrayed amongst the saints in this celestial gathering. One of the scenes on the predella underneath shows St Dominic supporting the walls of the church against collapse, illustrating the order's understanding of its role.

**Fra Angelico** The Annunciation, c. 1450
Fresco, 216 x 321 cm
Florence, Convent of San Marco

**Fra Angelico**
The Coronation of the Virgin,
c. 1430–1435 (from the convent
church of San Domenico, Fiesole)
Tempera on wood, 209 x 206 cm
Paris, Musée National du Louvre

**Jean Bondol of Bruges**
Title page of the Bible of Jean
de Vaudetar:
The Donor presents the Bible to
King Charles V of France, Paris,
1371
Manuscript illumination,
29.5 x 21.5 cm
Ms. 10 B 23, fol. 2 r
The Hague, Museum Meer-
manno-Westreenianum

## JEAN BONDOL
### ACTIVE 1368–1381

Knowing that Charles V (the Wise) was a
great lover of books, his counsellor commissioned a bible decorated with 269 beautiful
illuminations. The king had a title page inserted in which Jean Bondol of Bruges, his
court painter, shows him being presented with
the book.

This is the only surviving work from the
hand of the Flemish artist. Evocative of a
panel painting, it nevertheless takes up the
conventions of court manuscript illumination
in the grisaille of the clothing (cf. ill. p. 43).
In so doing, it simultaneously highlights the
most important element of the composition:
the two portraits. The artist offers us a merciless, far from regal picture of the 35-year-old
king, with his overly large head and long nose,
his pale face – he was a scholar rather than a
military man – and the stoop of his weakly
built body.

While this "natural" objectivity apparently
pleased the king, it contrasts strongly with the
rich heraldic décor of the background. Other
outstanding features include the artist's rendition of light and shade and the accuracy with
which he portrays objects and materials, such
as the wood of the royal chair, the delicate
weave of the king's cap and the structure of
the stone tracery. This illumination represents
the earliest example of Early Netherlandish
realism.

**Master of the Antwerp
Polyptych**
Nativity, c. 1400
Tempera on wood, 33 x 21 cm
Antwerpen, Museum Mayer
van den Bergh

## NETHERLANDISH MASTER
### C. 1400

This panel, the wing of a domestic altar, illustrates the way in which artists in northern
Europe approached the private devotional picture in the period around 1400 – namely, with a
strange mix of the other-worldly and ideal with
the familiar and genre-like. Mary reclines on a
golden silk cloth which forms a sort of aureole
around her. This delicate cloth, however, is itself
lying on sheafs of corn. The family is so poor
that Joseph has to cut a nappy for the baby out
of one of the legs of his trousers. Yet the wet
nurse, seen placing the naked infant Jesus in the
crib, wears a brocade dress and an apron, which
would surely make a much better nappy.

We should not question the inconsistencies
within the picture, however. Certain motifs
have their own explanation: around 1400, for
example, a tradition of pilgrimage sprang up
in Aachen around the holy relic of Joseph's
trousers. The ears of corn, too, are symbolic of
the bread of the Eucharist. But this does not
remove the contradictions within the painting. The background has an icon-like unnaturalness – yet the reverse of the panel bears a
relatively successful landscape. There is clearly
a large need for ornament. While the figure of
Mary is noble and dignified, other elements
seem to have been taken from a doll's house,
such as the animals and the little table bearing
items of crockery. This was what patrons and
donors wanted.

# MELCHIOR BROEDERLAM
## ACTIVE 1381–1409

The carved middle section of the altar retable to which this wing belongs is lavishly gilded. The eye, however, is involuntarily drawn to the painted panels on either side which, strictly speaking, occupy a subordinate position. The reason for this lies in the beauty of their colours and in their wealth of detail. The artist reinterprets the traditionally austere and solemn character of the altarpiece and spreads a colourful world before us. True, the *Presentation in the Temple* making up the left half of this wing recalls Ambrogio Lorenzetti's famous panel painting of 1342, but the hieratic composition is here further embellished with a host of details, an exquisitely slender architecture and an even more sumptuous palette. In the *Flight to Egypt* on the right, meanwhile, Broederlam goes far beyond the conventional limits of altarpiece painting. The richness of his landscape, and his use of genre motifs sooner belong to the realms of manuscript illumination and art destined for the private sphere. In his fidelity to nature and finely graded palette, however, Broederlam far surpasses contemporary illuminators. He pays loving attention to the donkey's coat, and to the miraculous well from which Holy Family were able to drink in the desert. The multi-layered, innovative and contradictory nature of the International Gothic around 1400 are all visible within this one picture.

**Melchior Broederlam**
The Presentation in the Temple and The Flight to Egypt, 1394–1399
(left-hand wing of the Chartreuse de Champmol Altar)
Tempera on wood, 167 x 130 cm. Dijon, Musée des Beaux-Arts

# JACQUES IVERNY
## ACTIVE 1411–1435

The Marchese Tommaso II of Saluzzo, the father of the man who commissioned this fresco, had spent some time at the French court, where he had written the allegorical tale of the *Straying Knight*. This chivalric romance brings together all the themes which fascinated aristocratic society at the time, including the story of the Nine Heroes and Nine Heroines. Tommaso's son subsequently commissioned a cycle of frescos depicting these figures, accompanied by corresponding verses from the romance, for the hall of his castle.

Five of the heroines are seen here. They are all exotic and legendary figures from the past, such as Queen Semiramis (second from the right) and the Amazon Penthesilea. Although almost all of them bear weapons, they are presented as court ladies rather than as heroines. They are standing on a carpet-like meadow bedecked with flowers. Shields hanging from the trees on their right bear fantasy coats of arms. The women are dressed in contemporary court fashions of the costliest kind, composed of gold brocades, ermines, jewels, gold crowns and floral wreaths. These elaborate costumes serve in themselves to reinforce the element of fantasy within the composition. The cycle is a rare example of secular art and at the same time a document of French court culture in the early 15th century, far removed from reality and cocooned in its own imaginary world.

**Jacques Iverny**
Five Heroines, c. 1420
Fresco (detail) in the hall of La Manta castle, wall height 5 m
La Manta castle near Saluzzo, Piemont

Paul, Jean and Herman Limburg
Miniature accompanying the prayer
Before setting out on a journey,
after 1410
(from the Petites Heures)
Manuscript illumination,
21.5 x 14.5 cm
Ms. lat. 18014, fol. 288 v
Paris, Bibliothèque Nationale

## LIMBURG BROTHERS
### AFTER 1385 – C. 1416

This illumination was added by the Limburg
brothers to the first of the sumptuous Books of
Hours commissioned by the Duc de Berry. The
book was originally begun by Jean Noir, a pupil
of Pucelle, who worked on it between 1372–
1375. A few years later it was taken up again by
the new court painter Jacquemart de Hesdin.
Although the Duc de Berry's tastes were constantly changing and he regularly took new artists into his employ, he continued to attach
great value to this manuscript, as witnessed by
the late addition of the Limburg illumination.

The Limburg brothers oriented themselves
in part towards the existing illustrations, as in
the case of the tendril border. A notable feature of this scene is the fact that the guardian
angel to whom the prayer is addressed is relegated to a secondary position in the lunette at
the top, while the main part of the picture is
dominated by a portrait of the Duke dressed
for a journey, accompanied by his Lord Marshal and attendants. Charles V, the Duc de Berry's eldest brother, frequently had himself depicted in manuscript illuminations and on
church portals, whereby his image signified
not just the person, but also the office of king.
The inclusion of the Duc de Berry in the present miniature, however, is a pure instance of
self-portraiture. It is a conspicuous fact that
the Duke liked to have himself portrayed – as
here – several times within one book.

This miniature was probably included by the
brothers on their own initiative, since it treats
a subject not normally found in Books of
Hours. The Fall nevertheless represents a thoroughly appropriate antithesis to the Annunciation scene which follows. On the left we see
Eve being tempted by the serpent; in the
middle, Eve offers Adam the apple; to the
right, God the Father pronounces judgement
on the unhappy pair, and on the far right
Adam and Eve are expelled from the Garden
of Eden by a seraphim. The setting is equally
original: Paradise is conceived as a visionary
plateau in the mountains above the clouds,
and appears as a symbolic ring. There is no attempt to portray the figures in correct proportion to the environment. Seen from another
angle, the picture might also be described as a
large item of goldsmith's work decorated with
rich enamel painting. The well in the Garden
of Eden might easily serve as a table fountain
fit for a prince. But this neither removes nor
explains the contradictions within the picture.
In the naked figure of Eve, standing opposite
God the Father in his celestial robe, we see a
female body corresponding to the erotic ideal
of the time. Artistic virtuosity has clearly
become one of the main themes of this miniature. Seen in this light, the other illuminations in the manuscript may also be understood in a new way. Artificiality of this kind
was only possible – even during such an era of
transition – in manuscript illumination and
only for a small handful of patrons. Yet it is
precisely such magnificent illuminations
which point up the contradictions inherent in
this seemingly so harmonious style.

Paul, Jean and Herman
Limburg
The Expulsion from
Paradise, 1414–1416
(from the Très Riches
Heures),
Manuscript illumination,
29 x 21 cm
Ms. 65, fol. 25 v
Chantilly, Musée Condé

Calendar illuminations for the month of January usually portrayed the double-headed god Janus banqueting at table in a small medallion. In this last and most important Book of Hours, commissioned by the Duc de Berry at the age of about 75, the calendar illustrations become the central focus. The conventionally somewhat token indications of the seasons and the labours of the months here give way to full-page illuminations, in which the typical activities associated with each month are set in a seasonal landscape featuring one of the castles belonging to the Duke or the French king in the background. In the arches above, we see the ruling planetary divinity and the astrological sign of the month.

In this picture of *January*, the Duc de Berry has himself portrayed at a banquet in an allusion to Janus. He is seated on a bench draped in a blue cloth. At a respectful distance further along the bench sits one other man, probably the Bishop of Chartres, one of the Duke's favoured advisors. Rather than flaunting the symbols of his rule, the artists highlight the Duke's special status through artistic means. Thus the yellow screen ostensibly designed to protect him from the heat of the open fire takes the form of a nimbus, and at the same time provides an effective foil against which the Duke's blue robe (painted with the most expensive lapis lazuli) stands out clearly. This section of the painting is further emphasized by the red baldachin above, decorated with the fleur-de-lys coats of arms and the two heraldic animals of the swan and the bear. On the table beside the Duke stands an elaborately crafted piece of gold tableware, the most striking in the entire room: this is the Gold Salt Ship, detailed in the Duke's inventories. Beneath the inscription "approche, approche", the chamberlain to the left of the Duke invites the guests to present themselves. Two pages in the foreground divide the long table into two unequal halves, whereby the direction in which they are facing and gesturing lends greater weight to the half occupied by the Duke. The Limburg brothers thereby demonstrate the ease with which they handle compositional devices which were still so new in Giotto's *Lamentation of Christ* (ill. p. 32). In a display of skill, the artists show the Duke – in compositional terms the central focus of the picture – facing the other guests and thus captured in what appears a realistic and candid moment of the banquet. The Duke's attention is directed not solely to his neighbour on the bench, but also to the strangers approaching from behind and being invited to draw nearer by the chamberlain.

In this picture we learn a great deal not just about life at court and the protocol of the day, but also about lifestyles. The furniture is crudely built, but hidden beneath sumptuous cloths. The large fireplace forms the focal point of the room, near which everything takes place. The walls are hung with tapestries; like a picture within a picture, and in a play upon the different levels of reality, these show battle scenes from the Trojan War, yet feature knights dressed in contemporary armour and a non-Antique manner of composition. Displayed on the table on the left is a selection from the Duke's valuable collection of gold and silverware, in a demonstration of luxury and wealth.

**Paul, Jean and Herman Limburg**
Calendar of the months: January, 1414–1416
(from the Très Riches Heures)
Manuscript illumination, 29 x 21 cm
Ms. 65, fol. 1 v
Chantilly, Musée Condé

# LIMBURG BROTHERS
## AFTER 1385 – C. 1416

This picture introduces the readings for the first Sunday in Lent. In it, the Limburg brothers offer a rare depiction of the third of the temptations to which Christ was exposed after his 40-day fast in the wilderness. Satan takes Christ to the top of a high mountain, shows him all the kingdoms of the world and promises to give them to him if Christ will worship him. We are presented with a sweeping landscape of mountains, cities, rivers and oceans – an attempt to go beyond symbolism and give an impression of the true size of the world. This "global" perspective was a feature of the Renaissance and would be found right up to Pieter Bruegel the Elder (cf. ill. p.206). The present miniature only acquires its inner tension, however, from the presence of the Duke de Berry's favourite château of Méhun-sur-Yèvre. We see the Duke's swans swimming in the moat and, on the right, a bear which has climbed up into a tree to escape a lion – perhaps an allusion to the serious political crises of the day. Are these the earthly riches that Christ did not want? Are they those of the devil? Is the castle a symbol of the ephemerality of all things? Only court artists enjoying the full trust of their patron could risk posing such questions.

In the case of the château of Méhun-sur-Yèvre in the previous miniature, bird's-eye and worm's-eye views of the various components of the architecture are abruptly juxtaposed. Here, however, the buildings in the background are presented with topographical accuracy and in a convincing perspective. On the left we see the many-turreted Palais de la Cité in Paris, the residence of the king, and on the right the Sainte-Chapelle. This astonishing heterogeneity within one and the same Book of Hours is also paralleled in the landscape: the global landscape of the *Temptation of Christ* appears fantastical compared to the objective portrayal of this meadow. We must therefore conclude that the Limburg brothers adopted a different approach depending on their subject. So accurate are their powers of observation in this illustration to the month of June, for example, that they may be seen as the forerunners to the van Eyck brothers. Thus they capture the various different greens of the meadow and the dried hay. They cannot simply be called naturalists, however, since their miniature clearly aims at another effect: it is first and foremost intended to provide a welcome change for the eye of the spoiled collector.

Every ruler at some point develops a yearning for the simple life. The peasants portrayed here are seen through the eyes of the non-labouring classes – to whom the Limburg brothers, in their privileged position as court artists, also belonged. These are not the faces of peasants nor the wearied bodies of those who toil in the fields. And yet a sense of two opposite worlds nevertheless emerges from the contrast between the life of aristocratic society (ill. p.63) and that of the peasant, marking a step in the direction of greater artistic freedom and a more objective portrayal of reality.

**Paul, Jean and Herman Limburg**
The Temptation of Christ (showing Méhun-sur-Yèvre castle), 1414–1416 (from the Très Riches Heures)
Manuscript illumination, 29 x 21 cm
Ms. 65, fol. 161 v
Chantilly, Musée Condé

**Paul, Jean and Herman Limburg**
Calendar of the months: June (showing the Palace de la Cité and Sainte-Chapelle in Paris), 1414–1416 (from the Très Riches Heures)
Manuscript illumination, 29 x 21 cm. Ms. 65. fol. 6 v. Chantilly, Musée Condé

# ANDRÉ BEAUNEVEU

## 1335– BEFORE 1413

This illumination represents the left half of a diptych-style sheet which introduced a sumptuous manuscript by Jacquemart de Hesdin. It is the work of a sculptor, although in terms of its composition and background more of a panel painting on vellum. The other half shows a nursing Madonna enthroned.

The Duke is as large as his patron saints. This is far more than simply a matter of consistency of scale, but implies that the living person is as important as the saints. Strictly speaking, the Duke is even more important, since he occupies the centre of the composition; John the Baptist and St Andrew are merely assisting him. Nothing similar is to be found in panel painting for the next thirty years.

The clothing of all the figures is painted in the subdued grisaille which we saw in Bondol (ill. p.60). The palette is dominated by red, blue and gold, the same triad as found in the psalter for Louis IX (ill. p.27). Here, however, gold is used with greater restraint. The same three colours are seen in the background, which does not consist of the usual tendrils scrolling beyond the bounds of the miniature, but which incorporates small decorative forms with the Duke's coat of arms, together with garlands of flowers sheltering butterflies and birds.

André Beauneveu
The Duc de Berry between his Patron Saints Andrew and John the Baptist, c. 1390
(preface page to the Très Belles Heures)
Manuscript illumination,
27.5 x 18.5 cm
Ms. 11060–61, fol. 1
Brussels, Bibliothèque Royale

# FRENCH MASTER

## C. 1420–1430

The work of the Limburg brothers inspired two extreme reactions amongst the artists who followed. Stated simplistically, these were naturalism, in the shape of the van Eyck brothers, and expressionism, in the figure of the Master of the Rohan Book of Hours. In the case of the present picture, we are initially tempted to ask what possible connection it could have with the Limburg brothers. But the manuscript reveals that its painter had both the *Belles Heures* and the *Très Riches Heures* before him as he worked. His response, was renunciation of beautiful colours, of sensual bodies, and of the portrayal of space and nature. Even careful technique, that professional imperative, is lacking in the decoration of the nimbuses, for example. The painter feels a revulsion for the beauties of the International Gothic. Christ lies on the ground, his naked body distorted by rigor mortis. Mary flings herself over him and is only just caught by John. Even God the Father, who usually remains distanced on his throne above the clouds, is looking down at his son with an expression of great sorrow. The figural group is extremely simple: situated left of the cross, it breaks out of the frame. The sky is the blue of a dark night. All the compositional means employed in this miniature derive from earlier French and Italian painting. And yet together they offer the most abrupt possible rejection of the old art.

Master of the Rohan Book of Hours
Lamentation, c. 1420–1427
(from the Book of Hours of Jolanthe of Aragon)
Manuscript illumination,
29 x 21 cm
Ms. lat. 9471, fol. 135 r.
Paris, Bibliothèque Nationale

Jean Malouel
Pietà (La grande Pietà ronde), c. 1400
Tempera on wood, diameter 64.5 cm
Paris, Musée National du Louvre

Henri Bellechose
The Last Communion and Martyrdom of St Denis, c. 1416 (altar retable)
Tempera on wood on canvas, 162 x 211 cm. Paris, Musée National du Louvre

## JEAN MALOUEL

D. 1415

Malouel was one of the many Netherlandish artists working for the French princes and their courts. He was an uncle of the Limburg brothers. As court painter to the dukes of Burgundy in Dijon, he was employed on the decoration of the Carthusian monastery at Champmol and also worked in Paris. The present panel bears the Burgundy coat of arms on the reverse and was clearly painted at the commission of the ducal family. The circular shape of this devotional painting is derived from that of the Italian tondo. It combines and condenses a number of different themes. Thus the notion of the Trinity as portrayed in the image of the Throne of Grace is here fused with the lamentation of the dead Christ by Mary and John. Similarly, the wounds of Christ – and in particular the heart wound, pointing to the transubstantiation of the wine of the Eucharist into the blood of Christ and to the heart wound as the origin of the sacraments – are combined with a Pietà, i.e. the presentation of Christ's body, which is also a symbol of the Host. The finely modelled body is treated with supreme delicacy. The paint is applied extremely thinly in places. Other transparent varnishes and new binders are also employed – an indication that the panel was painted during an era of technical transition which would reach its first high point in the art of the van Eycks just a few years later.

## HENRI BELLECHOSE

C. 1380 – C. 1440/44

Like his teacher Malouel, whom he succeeded as court painter, Bellechose came from the Netherlands. The centre of this painting is occupied by a large figure of the crucified, bleeding Christ. Above him, the presence of God the Father and the dove of the Holy Ghost surrounded by angelic hosts simultaneously makes the work a picture of the Trinity and of redemption. By contrast, the scenes taking place on either side at first appear somewhat inappropriate: on the left we see the last communion of St Denis, and on the right his martyrdom on Montmartre hill in Paris. St Denis, the legendary first bishop of Paris, was the national patron of France and the special patron saint of the French royal house, to which the Burgundian dukes also belonged. The blue and gold of the liturgical robes in this picture refer to the colours of the royal fleur-de-lys. St Denis was believed to have been a disciple of St Paul. According to legend, Christ appeared to St Denis in prison in order to give him the Last Communion in person. This episode underlined his particular closeness to Christ and hence his preferential status amongst the church saints. His martyrdom, however, may be seen as the highest form of imitation of Christ, and as drawing the closest possible parallel between saint, kneeling humbly at Christ's feet, and Saviour.

# GIRARD D'ORLÉANS (?)

ACTIVE 1344–1361

This painting of King John II is one of the earliest surviving autonomous portraits in European art. It is true that there had been portraits of rulers ever since classical antiquity – the importance of such models is reflected in the choice of pure profile in the present work, a pose typical of Antique coins and medals. Medieval portraits, however, did not show a king's individual traits, but rather his ideal and typical characteristics.

It was only with the major change in thinking ushered in towards the end of the 13th century that individuality began to be recognized, in a reversal of the previous belief that ideas were the higher, true reality, and individuals merely their imperfect expression. From now on, the individual was real, while ideas and concepts were simply "names". As a consequence, increasing value came to be attached to experience (empiricism), and less to philosophical thinking (theory). This nominalism came from Italy, as did a new genre of portrait painting which emphasized the empirical. Certain elements of the ideal and typical lingered on, however: here, in line with an earlier convention, the king is given the red hair considered most suitable for a ruler, together with a Roman nose. Rather than appearing with his royal insignia, the king is shown wearing a collar similar to those worn by scholars, in order to underline his wisdom.

Girard d'Orléans (?)
Portrait of John II "The Good",
King of France, c. 1349
Tempera on canvas on wood,
59.8 x 44.6 cm
Paris, Musée National du Louvre

# ENGLISH MASTER

ACTIVE C. 1390–1395

This is a more modern, more courtly form of the diptych. In the left-hand panel, the English king is being presented by his patron saints to the Madonna and Child, seen surrounded by a ring of angels in the right-hand panel, and with whom he appears to enjoy almost equal status. The diptych thus serves both as a devotional painting and as a staged piece of self-promotion for the king. The reproduction opposite can convey only an imperfect idea of the painting's highly sophisticated technique. Thus, for example, a tiny picture of the British Isles with a white castle can be found on the globe above the flag. The flowers beneath the Virgin's feet are portrayed in the greatest of detail, as are the small stags on the angels' robes and the brocade patterns on the clothes worn by the aristocratic figures on the left, with their folds and other decorative features, in part embossed and engraved as well as painted. The diptych was probably executed by an English master, but one who was thoroughly acquainted with the art being practised at the French courts. He was clearly equally familiar with the Bohemian type of the beautiful Madonna (cf. ill. p. 71) – Richard II's first marriage had been to a Bohemian royal princess. A distinctive feature of this work in the aptly-named International Gothic style is its use of foreshortening, whereby the artist borrows Italian motifs in a demonstration of his virtuosity.

Master of the Wilton Diptych
The Wilton Diptych
Left: King Richard II of England with his patron saints Edward the Confessor, Edmund and John the Baptist.
Right: Virgin and Child with angels, c. 1395 (or later)
Tempera on wood, each 45.7 x 29.2 cm. London, National Gallery

## MASTER THEODERICH
### ACTIVE FROM 1359, D. C. 1381

Circle of
**Master Theoderich**
The Crucifixion, c. 1370
(from the Na Slovanech Em-
maus monastery, Prague)
Tempera on wood,
132 x 98 cm
Prague, Národni Galeri

*Below:*
**Master Theoderich**
St Jerome, c. 1360–1365
(from the Chapel of the
Holy Cross, Karlstein castle)
Tempera on wood,
113 x 105 cm
Prague, Národni Galeri

Master Theoderich represents an innovative trend in Bohemian art after 1360 whose sources are not immediately to be found in the painting of other countries. Rather, the artists of his circle took their inspiration from southern German sculpture. Even group paintings are composed out of monumental individual figures. This *Crucifixion* might more accurately be called the "Crucified Christ between Mary and the Captain". Stretched out on the cross, Christ occupies the entire height and width of the panel. His body is solid, even massive. There is a sense of cramped oppression amongst the figures, who also seem to harry the viewer. Just as the painter pays scant regard to anatomical accuracy, so he shows little interest in drapery: robes simply veil the figures and heighten their already block-like character. There is an innovative understanding of light: the colours of the figures are brighter at the front, darker at the sides; line as boundary is absent. The figures are not illuminated from one side, but appear to emit light themselves: the captain a glowing red, Mary a luminous pallor, Christ a waxy transparency. This is directly related to the underlying theme of the composition: we are presented not with the drama of Christ's death on the cross, but with the calm contained in his words: "It is finished".

This picture was originally painted for the Chapel of the Holy Cross in Karlstein castle, designated by Emperor Charles IV to house the imperial treasures, which included a large piece of the True Cross, the Holy Lance and the Holy Nail, and other holy relics of note. The gilt ceiling of the chapel was decorated with stars made out of gilded glass, representing Heaven, and with frescos. The walls were adorned with 133 panel paintings presenting a hierarchical "host" of saints. The impression of being not simply in front of a representation of Heaven, but of being in Heaven itself, was reinforced by the semi-precious stones studding the walls. 550 candles filled the dark chamber with light. Their flickering flames not only emphasized the glitter of the gilded décor but also made the colours sparkle. Within this chapel, so the emperor desired, the churches of Heaven and earth were to meet; it was to demonstrate both his imperial might and its divine legitimation. Master Theoderich, who played a major role in the decoration of the chapel, deliberately created the paintings as wall panels. In their restriction to head and hands, however, they also have something of an icon-like quality. They deliberately lack spatial depth. Their attributes, such as the book held by St Jerome in the present example, are disproportionately large. The saints portrayed were lent a potency above and beyond their artistic presence by the fact that each of their frames contained a relic associated with them.

Whether this panel stems from the hand of Master Theoderich himself, or whether it is the work of one of his assistants, is a question which remains unanswered.

## BOHEMIAN MASTER
c. 1380–1390

The retable which once stood on the high altar of the Augustinian Canons' church in Trebon today survives only in fragments. It is nevertheless clear that the two panels on this page, formerly visible on the weekday side of the retable, are the works of a master of European standing. A comparison with the Hohenfurth Master's *Agony in the Garden* (ill. p.44) reveals just how far Bohemian art had advanced in thirty years. The present version is more homogeneous and concentrates upon portraying its theme in an appropriate manner: Christ in mortal fear, the sleeping disciples and – on the left – Judas approaching with his henchmen.

The landscape, which the artist creates to suit his own requirements, thereby serves as a useful compositional device. The serpentine figure of Christ is powerfully expressive; drops of bloody sweat have formed on his brow. Instead of the usual formula of blue and red, the painter clothes him in grey. The penumbral mood of the palette suggests the darkness of night. The intensity with which the artist has re-thought and re-interpreted his subject is also clear in his *Resurrection*. The risen Christ has floated through and out of the closed and sealed tomb. We are shown not the moment of resurrection, but the state of being resurrected. The painter presents the event as a true miracle. The watchmen fix their eyes on the apparition as if entranced.

While *The Agony in the Garden* takes place in twilight, the light in the *Resurrection* is more vibrant. The painter displays a feel for the expressive powers of objects; never before have weapons appeared sharper or shields more spiked. But he has a feel, too, for beautiful rhythmical forms, as can be seen in the sequence of curves in Peter's robe. This delight in softly undulating lines is by no means in conflict with the artist's more profound approach to his theme. Studied in depth, these two panels yield a wealth of detail which extends not only to individual members of the natural world, such as the many birds, but to much more besides. Striking features include the looseness of the brushwork and the varying treatment of the surfaces. Helmets and nimbuses are painted in different layers of glaze, as if the artist was already acquainted with the techniques of oil painting. Effects of light and colour are richly gradated. Looking closely, too, we can see that the artist has frequently deviated from his own preliminary sketches, scored into the ground and still clearly visible. It is evident that this painter, even as he established the types which others would copy, did not approach his composition with fixed ideas, but continued to rework his subject even in the final stages of execution. A notable exception is the figure of the resurrected Christ, in which he clearly cites an older, more static and two-dimensional type in the manner of the Master of the Hohenfurth *Crucifixion*. The composition of *The Agony in the Garden* is as unusual as it is skilful: the diagonal wall of rock slices the picture into two halves, the left-hand side dominated by the figure of Christ, the right-hand side by the disciples.

**Master of Trebon**
The Agony in the Garden,
c. 1380–1390
(from the altar of the Augustinian
Canons' church of St Aegidius)
Tempera on wood,
132 x 92 cm
Prague, Národni Galeri

**Master of Trebon**
The Resurrection, c. 1380–1390
(from the altar of the Augustinian
Canons' church of St Aegidius)
Tempera on wood, 132 x 92 cm
Prague, Národni Galeri

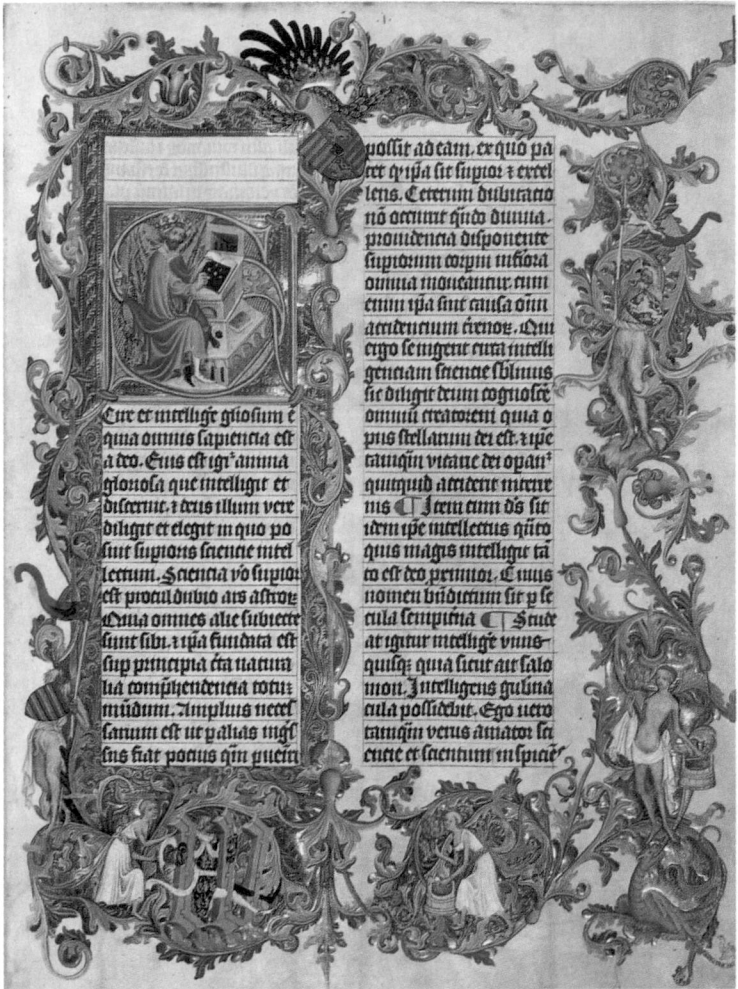

**Workshop of the
Wenceslas Bible**
Title illustration to Ptolemy's
Quadripartitus, c. 1395–1400
Manuscript illumination,
41 x 30.5 cm
Cod. 2271, fol. 1 r
Vienna, Nationalbibliothek

## BOHEMIAN MASTER

C. 1395–1400

In the initial on the title page of Ptolemy's
major work of classical astronomy, the *Quadripartitus*, Emperor Wenceslas is shown as an
astronomer seated at his desk. He is entering
numbers into the tables on a tablet. Astronomy, which in those days also included astrology, dominated the thinking of the epoch and
in particular Wenceslas' own mentality: his belief that all events were predetermined by the
stars both corresponded to and fed his in-
ability to make decisions. Wenceslas was one
of the greatest book-lovers of the era around
1400. He exerted a direct influence upon the
style in which his manuscripts were illustrated, florid decoration being something he
liked. He and his favourites (who probably
formed a secret society) also thought up the
symbolism behind the illuminations, such as
the young women seen here freeing the emperor from the "W" in which he is trapped as
if in a pillory. They represent Venus – or Wenceslas' wife – in allegorical disguise. The
knotted scarves, or love knots as they were
known, which they wear around their necks
and hips are a symbol of Wenceslas' fidelity to
his wife Sophie. The wild men stand for the
wildness of the forces of nature and at the
same time for Wenceslas. This symbolism also
has a very real, erotically sensual side, which is
further heightened by the artist's treatment of
his motifs and his lavish use of gold leaf.

## BOHEMIAN MASTER

C. 1400

This work was probably painted for the altar
of a prince's chapel. While the crucified Christ
filling the central panel follows on from the
*Crucifixion* by Master Theoderich (ill. p. 68),
the composition here feels less crowded and
the figures to either side have more room to
move. Colour and form are developed with a
subtlety of the highest aesthetic order. The
gold ground is decorated with embossed reliefs together with the delicate, barely visible
engraved figures of angels.

The muted reds and blues of the central
panel strike a different note to the grisaille-
like grey and beige of John the Baptist and
the brown of St Barbara, the most fashionable
colour around 1400.

In the design of the figures, too, there are
differences between the central panel and the
wings. Mary's silhouette is severe, yet of almost Nazarene sweetness. Her profile view
highlights her gesture of holding up a blood-
stained veil, a motif taken from Byzantine
tradition. By contrast, John the Evangelist is
almost as static in expression and pose as the
Virgin in Master Theoderich's *Crucifixion*. The
draperies of the saints in the two wings, on the
other hand, are both richer and more beautiful
in their composition.

The Pähl Altar transforms the more passionate style of the Master of Trebon into an
art which is noble and calm.

**Master of the Pähl Altar**
The Crucifixion of Christ between John the
Baptist and St Barbara, c. 1400
(altar retable from the chapel of Pähl Castle)
Tempera on wood, 103.5 x 68 (central panel)
and 103.5 x 28.5 cm (wings)
Munich, Bayerisches Nationalmuseum

# BOHEMIAN MASTER

C. 1390/1400

This panel has a frame (not shown) lavishly ornamented with a dozen free-standing wood reliefs portraying saints, angels and a donor. Precious stones would originally have been mounted between the figures. This frame alone lends the panel an aura of extraordinary rarity, something extending both the beauty of the Madonna and the beauty of the painting. Mary, according to theological thinking the most beautiful of all women, is also portrayed as such, with a sweet mouth, golden hair, serene countenance and unblemished features. At the same time, however, she comes so close to the feminine ideal of the time that one can understand why Bohemia's iconoclasts accused such paintings of the Virgin as showing nothing more than beautiful women.

To portray Mary as the humble wife of Joseph the carpenter and at the same time as Queen of Heaven was always an impossible challenge. Here, the sacred ideal crosses over into the sphere of the profane. There is affectation in the position of Mary's hands, while her fingers sink into the soft body of the child. Although her dress covers her body so thoroughly that we barely suspect it is there, and in so doing removes something of the painting's sensuality, the wealth of forms and the play of red and blue draperies are clearly pursued as ends in themselves. They are not means of expression, but a feast for the eye.

Master of the St Vitus
Madonna
Madonna, c. 1390-1400
(from St Vitus, Prague)
Tempera on wood,
89 x 77 cm (incl. frame)
Prague, Národni Galeri

# BOHEMIAN MASTER

C. 1400

The *St Vitus Madonna* was revered as a painting possessing miraculous powers and existed in numerous copies. The work itself, however, is only a copy of an older picture. It was derived from the Italian Madonna icon (cf. ill. p. 42), a genre which appears to have arisen in Bologna around 1340 and which – according to the inscription on another, similar panel – is descended from a portrait of the Virgin painted by St Luke. Such paintings could easily be expanded into full-length figures or portraits of the Madonna enthroned, or could be added to an Adoration of the Magi. They also existed in the form of sculpture. Indeed, it was sculptors who first lent them the sensual and physical qualities to which the Master of the St Vitus Madonna aspired. He thereby gave the Madonna type the sweetness and radiance which led to the increase in its veneration and its widespread copying.

In the *Neuhaus Madonna*, the same pictorial type has been translated into a domestic devotional panel. Mary is enthroned in glory, yet appears even more sweet and doll-like. The child is as winsome as a real baby. The veil covering his body is a charming idea, visually attractive and at the same time accenting and underlining the child's significance. The draperies, the palette and the childlike charm of the figures all recall the manuscript illumination of the day.

Master of the Neuhaus
Madonna
Madonna, c. 1400
Tempera on wood,
25 x 19 cm
Prague, Národni Galeri

Workshop of the
**Gerona Martyrology**
The Story of Creation, c. 1415
Frontispiece to the Boskovic
Bible
Manuscript illumination,
41.5 x 28.5 cm. M III 3
Olomouc, University Library

## BOHEMIAN MASTER

C. 1405–1425

This miniature is representative of a group of
outstanding manuscripts from the period
around 1405–1425, which must have corresponded to panel paintings no longer extant.
The artist uses gloss paints on gold and silver –
a highly unusual technique for this genre, and
a very complicated process both at the sketching stage and in the actual execution.

The quality of the art and the sophistication of the design are also correspondingly
high. The top medallion is both the first and
last in the series, showing God the Father enthroned and at the same time representing the
seventh day, on which God rested. The days of
Creation are arranged in order from top to bottom on the left and from bottom to top on the
right.

The chaos in the background gradually
evolves – more and more clearly from medallion to medallion – into landscapes filled with
plants, animals and people, whereby the
curved horizon in each case lies only just
below the upper edge of the picture. God the
Father is portrayed in all seven medallions,
each time in a new and highly convincing
pose. His changing position within the frame
nevertheless obeys the requirements of each
composition. This manuscript illumination is
more than simply an exalted form of decorative art; the workshop is a Bohemian parallel to the Limburg brothers.

**Master of the Raigern Road to Calvary**
The Road to Calvary, c. 1415–1420
(panel from the Raigern Altar)
Tempera on wood, 99 x 147 cm
Brno, Moravské Museum

## BOHEMIAN MASTER

C. 1415–1430

In comparing the *Gerona Martyrology* with the
art of the Limburg brothers, it must also be
said that Bohemia went on to produce no van
Eyck, nor indeed could it have done. Hussite
criticism of the use of images led to the virtual
cessation of artistic production, and above all
to contempt for all art aimed at a sensually
beautiful effect.

Although the donors of this work were
probably not followers of Hus, they were
nevertheless influenced by his ideas; it is striking in itself that the feastday side of this retable should be made up of a *Road to Calvary*
and a *Crucifixion*, one above the other. Nor is
there anything festive about their appearance:
on the contrary, they are dominated by soldiers
and henchmen. In the top right-hand corner of
the present panel, Calvary is brutally portrayed as a hill of skulls; the stench of rotting
bodies forces bypassers to hold their nose. The
colours are dull and gloomy or, in the case of
the red, burning; they are never deliberately
beautiful. The figures are grouped not in an
artful and organized fashion but in a jostling
throng. The unpleasant side of the Passion is
deliberately emphasized. The chief interest is
in the content; from an artistic point of view,
the panel simply reworks old motifs, such as
Simone Martini's Mary Magdalene with arms
upraised (cf. ill. p. 36) on the left, and has a
limited range of existing pictorial means.

## AUSTRIAN MASTER

C. 1420

This small panel may be seen as the Austrian counterpart to Fra Angelico's *Entombment* in San Marco, Florence, from the years 1438–1443 (ill. p. 58). It, too, expands upon the Man of Sorrows theme in a highly personal and unique manner.

Christ has been taken down from the cross and rests slumped against its foot. He does not have the stiffness of a corpse, however, but appears almost alive, in a pose of resignation. The seated figures of Mary and John appear to be lost in meditation rather than preparing to lay the body in the tomb, visible in the rock on the left. None of the other assistants, such as Nicodemus and Joseph of Arimathaea, are present.

This private, devotional panel serves a number of different purposes. On the one hand, it is a meditation upon the Passion and upon the individual instruments of Christ's martyrdom, which are leaned up against the cross. At the same time, however, meditation is itself a theme of the painting: Mary and Joseph are models with whom the viewer can identify. Unlike older Passion panels of this kind, however, the scene is not set somewhere outside time and space. This is Calvary, immersed in the gloom of an almost night-time sky against an empty landscape and a stark city wall – details conveying the essential mood of the painting.

Master of the Offerings
Christ at the Foot of the Cross with Mary and John,
c. 1420
Mixed media on wood, 25 x 34 cm
Berlin, Gemäldegalerie, Staatliche Museen zu Berlin –
Preußischer Kulturbesitz

## AUSTRIAN MASTER

C. 1420–1440

This panel only makes full sense when seen in conjunction with the two groups of donors who appear beneath the Madonna kneeling on a patch of grass against a gold background, accompanied by their patron saints. Mary is thus to be understood as a heavenly apparition. At the same time, however, she recalls the woman clothed with the sun and pursued by a dragon described in Revelations (and who was theologically associated with the Mother of God), as well as the vision of the Virgin seen by St Anthony Abbot on the day of Christ's birth (the so-called Madonna Aracoeli; cf. ill. p. 52), and the Virgin who has ascended into Heaven. None of these are contradicted by the fact that she has the infant Christ on her lap: this is a picture of Mary in her role as eternal mother and – even more importantly in the context of a votive panel – intercessor.

The blue of the Virgin's mantle is gently graded from dark to light, lending it a luminous quality such as we have already seen in Bohemian painting.

The golden glory and the vibrant red aureole with its angels compose, together with this blue, a powerful triad of intensely radiating colour reminiscent of older paintings. Mary thereby appears as the truly celestial Queen of Heaven, crowned by angels.

Master of the London Throne of Grace Madonna, c. 1420
(fragment of a votive panel from the Benedictine foundation of St Lambrecht,
Styria). Tempera on wood, 58 x 55.5 cm. Graz, Landesmuseum

**Master of the Paradise Garden**
Garden of Paradise (Virgin in Hortus conclusus with Saints), c. 1410
Mixed media on wood, 26 x 33 cm
Frankfurt am Main, Städelsches Kunstinstitut

## UPPER RHENISH MASTER
### C. 1410

Perhaps intended for a canoness or abbess, this panel offers an original variation upon the theme of the Virgin of the Rose Garden. Although Mary, reading a book in the upper half of the picture, is recognizably the most important figure in the composition, contrary to the conventions of the day she is neither the central focus of events nor even the central axis of the composition. At her feet, St Catherine is playing with Christ; to her left, St Dorothy is picking cherries, and in the bottom left-hand corner St Barbara is ladling water out of the well. Seated on the right are St Michael, with the devil at his feet, and St George with a small dragon; the legendary figure of St Oswald is leaning against the trunk of the tree.

There is a deliberateness and reflectiveness to all the activities taking place. Nowhere is the tenderness of the mood disturbed. Our eye wanders across the picture, stopping to contemplate each figure and natural detail in isolation. The painting as a whole is infused with Marian symbolism: the enclosed garden protected within its solid walls, is an image of Mary's intact virginity. At the same time, it establishes an internal frame within the composition. With its delight in details this type of devotional painting renders harmless such elements as the dragon accompanying St George and opens the door to more subjective interpretations of traditional themes of painting.

**Master of St Veronica**
St Veronica with the Sudarium, c. 1420
(probably from St Severin, Cologne)
Mixed media on wood, covered with canvas,
78.1 x 48.2 cm
Munich, Bayerische Staatsgemäldesammlungen, Alte Pinakothek

## MASTER OF ST VERONICA
### C. 1400–1420

Veronica is a creation of legend. She arose out of the *vera icon*, the supposedly "true image" of Christ which variously took the form of panel paintings, shrouds (as in Turin) and painted cloths. The story of St Veronica is associated with one such piece of cloth, known as the sudarium. According to legend, Veronica offered Christ her veil as he passed her on the way to Calvary. After he had wiped his brow, his image remained miraculously imprinted upon it. The popularity of the subject in art was fuelled by the fact that the sudarium was one of the main objects of pilgrimages to Rome in the Middle Ages, and that veneration of such pictures earned many indulgences. Furthermore, many Christians hopefully believed that the vision of this miraculous picture warded off the threat of sudden death.

Thus the sudarium bearing the "true image" of Christ is both the real subject and the centre of this panel. The much smaller figure of Veronica holds up the cloth with an expression of devotion. The two groups of small angels contemplate in the sudarium both the mystery and the entirety of the Passion. These angels are painted in the most delicate of colours and with a highly sophisticated technique, and testify to the great skill and sensitivity of the artist – something to which Goethe would draw admiring attention in 1815.

## KONRAD OF SOEST

C. 1370 – AFTER 1422

This panel by Konrad of Soest is one of many which the great Westphalian painter produced for the parish church of St Nikolaus in Bad Wildungen.

In this instance he was required to create an image worthy of the high altar retable, yet which was also suitable for devotional contemplation. In accordance with the conventions of devotional painting of the day, it was thereby to extend wherever possible to additional details and narrative features.

The artist has cleverly fulfilled this multiple challenge: mother and child are fittingly highlighted as the only figures with nimbuses, and are framed by the architecture of the stable (the upright which separates off the angel appearing to the shepherds on the right was added at a later date). A gloriole of angels in red and gold is visible behind the Virgin's head.

Mother and child are nevertheless shown in the tenderest of poses, as familiar from Pisanello (cf. ill. p. 52), and which can undoubtedly be traced back to a Netherlandish Madonna type. Taken in isolation, the half-length group could serve equally well as a complete (devotional) picture in itself. At the same time, however, the remainder of the composition is richly garnished with domestic details, and in the figure of Joseph cooking over the fire we see a portrait of the loving father.

Konrad of Soest
The Nativity, 1403
Mixed media on wood,
73 x 56 cm
Bad Wildungen,
St Nikolaus

## MASTER FRANCKE

C. 1380 – C. 1436

This panel is one of a cycle devoted to the legend of St Barbara in Turku cathedral (Finland). It shows the episode in which Barbara's father, in angry pursuit of his daughter, finds his path blocked by a wall which has suddenly and miraculously materialized. The father, in sumptuous oriental dress, rushes in from the left with his fist clenched and his sword drawn.

The wall passes diagonally across the picture from top left to bottom right and completely bars the way ahead. It becomes an image of insurmountability. To the viewer, the wall is like a piece of theatrical scenery. It does not obstruct our view of the saint in the background. The falling diagonal of the top of the wall becomes a rising diagonal in the silhouette of the hills behind, where space is opened up rather than blocked. Spatial depth is not an end in itself in Franke's art, but a vehicle of his narrative; it remains subordinate to the figures and – as a means of setting the scene – to the composition as whole.

A striking feature of the panel is its twilight atmosphere. The artist thereby attaches greater importance to achieving a rich gradation of light than simply to contrasting strong planes of colour. In this he shows himself to belong to a younger generation of painters influenced by the new art coming out of the Netherlands.

Master Francke
The Miracle of the Wall, 1414
(from the St Barbara Altar, Turku)
Mixed media on wood, 91.5 x 54 cm
Helsinki, Kansallismuseo

**Stefan Lochner**
Adoration of the Child, 1445
(part of a domestic altar or diptych)
Mixed media on wood, 37.5 x 23.6cm
Munich, Bayerische Staatsgemälde-
sammlungen, Alte Pinakothek

**Stefan Lochner**
The Presentation in the Temple, 1447
(from the high altar retable in St Katharina, Cologne)
Mixed media on wood, 139 x 126cm
Darmstadt, Hessisches Landesmuseum

# STEFAN LOCHNER

## C. 1400–1451

When assessing Lochner's historical significance, it is important to bear in mind that all
his works arose after the death of van Eyck and
Masaccio. But this is not to conclude that
Lochner was an old-fashioned or even provincial painter. When it came to technique, he
ranked amongst the best Netherlandish masters. He worked largely in oils, applying his
paints in wafer-thin layers. Thus the luminosity of Mary's mantle is achieved not by mixing
the blue with white, but by allowing the
white ground to shine through. Just as he
painted no shadows, but rather shading, so he
also disliked radiant lustre and glittering
light. He loved the matt shimmer of pearl and
similar mild shades, avoided earth colours, and
glazed his gold in order to subdue and modulate its gleam. In terms of technique, he was
one of the greatest masters of the century.

His attitude towards the art of his Netherlandish contemporaries, who were primarily
concerned with the faithful reproduction of
reality, is stated in the large altarpiece which
he executed for Cologne cathedral. The outer
wings portray objects and space in a naturalistic style and take up the broken drapery
motifs of the new painting of Robert Campin.
The interior, however, reiterates the soft, solemn forms of the International Gothic. We
sense that, for Lochner, these older compositional means and motifs represent not simply
a stylistic ideal but an ideal way of life. He is
drawn only to the gentle and sweet aspects of
religion – we find no representations of the
Passion in his art. Yet Lochner is never monotonous, but responds with appropriate solutions to each new commission and subject.
Thus the *Adoration of the Child*, a simple, small-
format domestic altar modestly executed without a gold ground, restricts itself to the Virgin
and the Child, who is laid on a communion
cloth like the Host. The background lacks virtually all spatial depth, its details merely
grouped around the figure of Mary dominating the pictorial plane. By contrast, the *Presentation in the Temple*, painted for a high altar, is
much richer, more complex and more ostenta-
tiously splendid.

Lochner displayed his greatest delicacy and
sensitivity in his painting of *The Virgin of the
Rose Garden*. In contrast to other versions of
the subject, there is nothing here to distract attention from the person of Mary. The panel is
primarily a statement of the Virgin's humility
and apotheosis, and only secondly a portrayal
of her characteristics (the flowers as symbols of
her virtues, the unicorn brooch as a token of
her virginity, the crown as a sign of her royal
rank). Lochner employs the entire spectrum of
his artistic means to express the purity, lightness and sweetness of his subject.

**Stefan Lochner**
The Virgin of the Rose Garden, c. 1448
Mixed media on wood, 51 x 40cm
Cologne, Wallraf-Richartz-Museum

**Lukas Moser**
Magdalene Altar, 1432
Mixed media on wood, c. 300 x 240 cm
Tiefenbronn, S. Maria Magdalena

Pediment: Feast in the house of Simon
From left: Mary Magdalene, Martha, Lazarus,
Maximinus and Sidonius voyage by sea;
the Saints Sidonius, Maximinus, Lazarus and
Martha asleep; Mary Magdalene appears to the
prince and his wife in a dream (above); Last
Communion of Mary Magdalene

# LUKAS MOSER

C. 1390 – AFTER 1434

Of all the artists of his generation, Moser was
probably the most modern and the closest to
the new realism issuing from the Netherlands. The main front of the Magdalene Altar

is divided into three scenes, all obeying the
same perspective and lit from a single source.
The landscape and architecture create an astonishing impression of depth and are observed with a keen eye: the sea is partly under-
laid with a sheet of metal foil to make it look
more watery.

The painted retable covers a fresco, but one

hardly notices that the middle section of the
altarpiece conceals a sculpture of the ascension
of Mary Magdalene. The painter is not interested in making a distinction between a weekday and a feastday side of the altar – he simply
wants to create a homogeneous, permanently
visible panel of the kind with which he was
familiar from Italy.

Manfred Wundram

# EARLY RENAISSANCE

## European painting in the 15th century

During the Early Renaissance, painting rose to a position of primacy amongst its fellow disciplines for the first time in the history of Western art. A new relationship was born between the work of art and the spectator: the painting no longer sought merely to fulfil a function, but issued its own challenge to the person before it.

Amongst the great innovations of this new era were the exploration of perspective and proportion, a new understanding of portraiture as the likeness of an individual, and the beginnings of landscape painting.

Artists increasingly trod a path away from superficial "naturalness" in their works and towards a more profound understanding of the natural world, a trend seen in Italy in Masaccio, Uccello, Piero della Francesca, Botticelli and Mantegna and in Germany in Multscher and Witz. In the Netherlands, meanwhile, panel painting flowered at the hands of the van Eyck brothers, Rogier van der Weyden, Hugo van der Goes, Memling, and in the mysterious spectral world of Hieronymus Bosch.

In Venice in the late 15th century, Antonello da Messina and Giovanni Bellini in particular spearheaded a revolution in painting whose impact would reverberate beyond the High Renaissance and into the 16th century.

## Early Renaissance and Late Gothic

The major stylistic epochs into which we like to divide Western art – Pre-Romanesque, Romanesque, Gothic, Renaissance and Baroque – are no more than pointers offering us a primitive means of orientation. They are approximations within a development which, while often driven by artistic innovation, might equally well imply the revival of earlier design principles; a development characterized less by clear breaks than by ongoing evolution. And even within this evolution, phase displacements must be taken into account which challenge the validity of any single definition of the epoch. Thus while the Early Gothic was emerging and unfolding in northern France in the 12th century, the Romanesque style was reaching its peak in the southern reaches of France and in Germany and Italy.

Since fine art is simply a means of expression of our general cultural and intellectual history, so historical, religio-historical, sociological and cultural-geographical conditions play a decisive role in shaping the art forms and artistic developments of each era. Without placing in question the value of interpreting a painting purely from an aesthetic point of view, it should be borne in mind that these neighbouring disciplines can provide vital clues to understanding a work of art – just as a work of art can shed light on other, broader cultural issues. In seeking to adopt an interdisciplinary approach, however, we should not forget that works of fine art can communicate their information only via the eye, and hence rely on the accuracy of our powers of observation. Any interpretation for which there is no visual evidence must remain in the realms of speculation.

There can be few other epochs in our European past which so stubbornly refuse to fit under a generalized heading than the 15th century. While in Italy around 1400 the dawn of the Early Renaissance was heralding a new age in art – the competition for the two bronze doors for the Baptistery in Florence in 1401 is seen as a pivotal event in this development – the countries north of the Alps were experiencing an unparalleled flowering of what is termed the Late Gothic. The Renaissance is generally perceived to have arrived here only one hundred years later, in particular in the wake of the two trips which Albrecht Dürer (1471–1528) made to Italy in 1496 and 1506/07.

It has for a long time been clear, however, that this polarization into Early Renaissance and Late Gothic frequently

fails to describe the forms adopted by art in the 15th century. The introduction of the terms "Early German" and "Early Netherlandish" for painting north of the Alps in order to distinguish it from Gothic art simply postponed the problem. Similarly, the term "Sondergotik" (special Gothic) coined by Kurt Gerstenberg in 1917 to describe 15th-century German architecture is merely a means of demarcating the latter from the Late Gothic, without clearly identifying its character. Is it possible, then, to find other categories for the art – and specifically the painting – of the century from 1400 to 1500 which more aptly describe its different and common traits?

## Florence and the advent of the Early Renaissance

Let us turn first to Italy, seemingly the most "progressive" region of Europe in the early 15th century. Florence, a centre of moderate political but large economic importance, was emerging as the cradle of a new development in art which, in the eyes of the historians of the 19th century and in particular Jacob Burckhardt (1818–1897), was comparable only to Athens in the 5th century BC. At the chronological forefront of this new trend stood a number of outstanding sculptors, amongst them Lorenzo Ghiberti (1378–1455), Nanni di Banco (c. 1375–1421) and Donatello (c. 1382/86–1466). They replaced the drapery-clad statuary of the Middle Ages with the figure sculpture of the Renaissance, developed out of the organic structure of the human body, and created a style of relief which permitted them to carve highly naturalistic multi-figural scenes with a spatial depth previously unknown. A similar development took place in architecture around 1420, in the early works of the architect Filippo Brunelleschi (1377–1446) – the Foundling Hospital, the Old Sacristy at San Lorenzo and the church of San Lorenzo itself. Here, Gothic architecture was replaced by a new style whose dimensions were reduced to a humanly comprehensible scale and which adopted individual elements from the architecture of Ancient Rome. Finally, starting in 1424 and within a rapid space of just five years, there followed the works of the painter Masaccio (1401–1428), whose portrayal of perspective and anatomy pointed the way forward for the entire century.

Classical antiquity thereby served as a source of inspiration to all three branches of art. The statues of Donatello and Nanni di Banco revived the contrapposto figure sculpture, whereby the figure stands poised with most of its weight on one leg and with the other leg relaxed. Such references to the past were made doubly clear in other details, such as the reappearance of the Roman toga. This revival of late Antique and early Christian forms was most apparent of all in architecture. Meanwhile, as Emil Maurer has shown in the case of the fresco of the *Tribute Money* (ill. pp. 94/95), Masaccio was probably familiar with the early Christian mosaics in San Paolo fuori le mura in Rome.

**Benozzo Gozzoli**
Procession of the Magi, 1459–1461
Fresco (detail), width c. 750 cm
Florence, Palazzo Medici-Riccardi
Four members of the Medici family can be identified amongst the riders: Cosimo the Elder (with the reins in both hands) and, to the right, his sons Giovanni and Piero di Cosimo, together with Cosimo's illegitimate son Carlo (at the top, with the tall red hat)

**Masaccio**
Adoration of the Magi, 1426
(panel from the predella of the Pisa Polyptych)
Tempera on wood, 21 x 61 cm
Berlin, Gemäldegalerie, Staatliche Museen zu Berlin – Preußischer Kulturbesitz

Is it therefore true that, as art-historical tradition has long maintained, the Florentine Early Renaissance represented a revival of sculpture, architecture and painting in the spirit of classical antiquity? The body of art surviving from the period before 1400 quite clearly proves the opposite. In Tuscan architecture of the late 11th and early 12th century, which Burckhardt has described as "Proto-Renaissance", we find the same classicizing decorative forms and the same harmoniously balanced organization of interiors and walls employed by Brunelleschi in his early works. The Baptistery and the façade of San Miniato in Florence are the most important surviving examples of this Renaissance movement, which can also be seen less explicitly in the Tuscan Gothic. The heritage of antiquity thus runs throughout like an unbroken thread, more or less close to the surface. If we remember that Brunelleschi, according to his biographer Antonio Manetti (1423–1491), held the Baptistery to be an original Antique building, we are justified in seeing his work as part of a home-grown tradition, and not as something conditional upon a study of the ancient monuments in Rome.

A similar situation applied to sculpture. Here, too, the important influence of late Antique and early Christian models was never questioned. Nicola Pisano (c. 1220–before 1287), his son Giovanni (c. 1245–after 1314) and his pupil Arnolfo di Cambio (c. 1254–c. 1302) indeed revived sculpture in the spirit of classical antiquity; both in their own creations and in other outstanding works by Florentine cathedral stonemasons dating from the latter decades of the 14th century, classical models were copied on a scale which, after 1400, was found only in exceptional instances. Without wishing to dispute the fact that this exploration of antiquity was continued by the Early Renaissance, it may be said that classical

antiquity was not the decisive force which propelled Western art across the threshhold from the Middle Ages into the Renaissance.

This conclusion is reinforced by the origins of the term "Renaissance". In his *Lives of the Artists*, first published in 1550 and subsequently reprinted in an expanded edition in 1568, Vasari was the first to speak of the *rinascità*, the rebirth of art. By that, however, he did not mean a rediscovery of antiquity, but rather the *rinascità* of "good art", something in his eyes synonymous with a renunciation of the art of the Middle Ages, with its formal vocabulary abstracted from nature, and in particular of the severe linear style derived from Byzantine art, which he termed the *maniera greca*. For Vasari, a – if not *the* – decisive chapter in Italian art began with the painting of around 1300, represented above all by Giotto (1266?–1337). More recent research, not least in neighbouring disciplines within the humanities, has itself pondered the question of whether the transition from the 13th to the 14th century was not indeed more profound than that from the 14th to the 15th. The new experience of reality which was reflected particularly in painting as from 1300 made an enduring impression both upon contemporary observers and on subsequent generations, as the following extract from the *Decameron* (1348–1353) by Giovanni Boccaccio (1313–1375) reveals: "The other, whose name was Giotto, was a genius so sublime that there was nothing produced by Nature, mother and mover of all things in the course of the seasons, that he could not depict to the life, whether his implement was a stylus, a pen or a paintbrush: his depiction looked not like a copy but the real thing, so that more often than not the viewer's eye was deceived, convinced that it was looking at the real object and not his depiction of it."

Thus the "rediscovery of the world and of man" postulated by Burckhardt as the prime mover of the Early Renaissance had its roots in the 14th century. Amongst Giotto's successors, and in particular the great Sienese painters Simone Martini (c. 1280/85–1344), Ambrogio (c. 1290–c. 1348) and Pietro Lorenzetti (c. 1280/90–1348 ?), this exploration of the phenomena of here-and-now reality was pursued to an astonishing degree. The focus in Giotto's era upon the large, summarized form was thereby both enriched and at the same time replaced by the precise study of details.

We can therefore state the following: firstly, it was not classical antiquity but the entry into art of the real world of human experience – the reproduction of figure, space and landscape – which laid the foundations for the Early Renaissance. Secondly, the years around 1400 represent a major stage, but not an abrupt break in this development. The Early Renaissance was not an artistic revolution, but the end of an evolution. Just how great the continuity between the 14th and 15th centuries was, and just how little contemporaries were conscious of living in an era of great change, is evidenced many times over in Florentine art. Thus the formal design and even the angle of the vault of the dome of Florence cathedral, for example, widely viewed as the first great example of Early Renaissance architecture, was already largely determined before Brunelleschi took over the project. And in 1401, when a competition was held for a new set of bronze doors for the Baptistery, the artists were required to orient the general organization and framework of their designs towards the older bronze doors executed by Andrea Pisano (c. 1295–after 1349) in 1330–1336.

What is it then which entitles us to see in the 15th century a new chapter in Western culture? Vasari once again provides a clue to the answer. While in Giotto he praised the naturalness of the painter's style, in the leading artists of the Early Renaissance he admired the perfect imitation of nature. For him, Giotto and Masaccio represented the first and second stages in the *rinascità*; in terms of fidelity to nature, Masaccio was a Giotto on a higher level, so to speak. To see things in this light, however, is an inadmissible simplification of the truth.

It is true that Leonardo da Vinci (1452–1519) also praised Masaccio for his faithful study of nature; offering an important insight into the epoch, however, he also added that nature should not simply be copied, but shown in all its perfection. "Painting preserves that harmony of corresponding parts which nature, with all its powers, is unable to maintain. It keeps alive the image of a divine beauty whose natural model is soon destroyed by time and death."

It is thus the search for the ideal norms underlying the outer face of nature which distinguishes the 15th from the 14th century. The inner kinship between classical antiquity and the Early Renaissance lies in this interpenetration of the real and the ideal, and not in the sphere of outer similarity.

**Piero della Francesca**
Senigallia Madonna, c. 1460–1475
Tempera on wood, 61 x 53.3 cm
Urbino, Galleria Nazionale

The fact that artists nevertheless looked back to their classical heritage was conditioned by their search for "natural" forms – in accordance with the maxim of Denis Diderot (1713–1784): "Il faut étudier l'antiquité pour voir la nature" (one must study antiquity to see nature). Cause and effect are here stood on their head: it was not the wish to copy antiquity that led artists to adopt naturalistic forms, but the desire to reproduce natural forms that opened their eyes to antiquity.

There is a second, no less important factor distinguishing the 15th from the 14th century. While the portrayal of space and the human figure during the 14th century was based largely on pragmatical values, from about 1420 it began to assume a mathematical dimension. Perspective and the theory of proportion, especially, were discussed and investigated from a scientific point of view. This was the consequence of a philosophical awareness arising from man's new conception of his status within Creation. The new value attached to the individual, unknown in the Middle Ages, was reflected in the fine arts in the emergence of a new genre: portraiture in the modern sense of the word, i.e. the picture of a unique, unmistakable personality. The portrayal of donors changed for the same reason; having been accorded only diminutive stature in medieval art in line with their perceived insignificance, they now assumed the same size as saints and other figures from religious history.

Up till now we have only discussed the concept of the Renaissance in terms of Florence. To what extent is it justifiable to speak of a pan-Italian Early Renaissance after 1400? In seeking a reply, we are immediately confronted with the difficulty of agreeing upon a single definition for the 15th century. Traditions and developments in northern Tuscany were different to those even in southern Tuscany, such as the Siena region, where many characteristics of painting remained indebted throughout the century to the innovations of the previous century. The "modern" vocabulary of form only filtered through gradually and in isolated details.

## The art centres of Upper Italy

A comparison of Florence with the art-producing regions of Upper Italy, and in particular Lombardy and Venice, spotlights a number of positively contradictory phenomena. Lombardy and Venice were, alongside Tuscany, the most important centres of Italian art; following the return of the papacy from Avignon (1376) and the Great Schism (1378–1417) which followed, Rome had been relegated for the time being to artistic obscurity. During the opening decades of the 15th century, Milan remained entirely under the spell of the International Gothic, while the Venetian art of the same period developed strictly along lines established in the 14th century. Where Renaissance forms were adopted at all, they were simply added onto Gothic structures. The artistic disparities between Florence, Lombardy and Venice can be

partly explained by the undoubtedly very different traditions prevalent in each region. Lombardy, owing to its geographical position and trade links, had always had closer ties with northern Europe than central Italy, while Venice remained strongly influenced by the Byzantine sphere due to its economic orientation towards the East. More important factors in the equation, however, were the very different social conditions reigning in each of the three centres.

Alongside the Church, the major patrons of art in Lombardy remained the dukes of the house of Visconti and, after 1447, those from the Sforza line. Giangaleazzo Visconti (1351–1402) planned to establish a united kingdom of Italy under his own rule – an ambitious scheme which came to nought following his early death in 1402. Venice, although nominally a republic, was *de facto* the most glittering feudal state south of the Alps. Florence, on the other hand, had been governed by its citizens since the 12th century. All major official commissions were issued by the city council. There is no more typical example of this than the new cathedral, whose founding charter of 1296 announced that the work was to be built to the glory of the city and the Virgin Mary. In 1331 responsibility for the continuation of its construction was transferred to the Arte di Lane – the wool weavers' guild. The supervisory committees were made up of experts, citizens and just one representative of the cathedral chapter. The list of similar examples goes on.

In contrast, therefore, to the art centres of Upper Italy, we find in Florence a culture shaped by civic requirements. The middle classes towards the close of the Middle Ages had only partly established their own artistic traditions, however. Having risen to prosperity and political influence, they began in the years around 1400 to create their own forms of expression – forms which could draw upon tradition but were not bound to it. Church and nobility, on the other hand, had always claimed their legitimacy through tradition and were eager that this should be perpetuated into the future. For them, holding on to the forms of the past was a natural desire.

Furthermore, bankers, wool weavers and cloth merchants would have felt a much closer intellectual affinity with the phenomena of the real world than art patrons from the spheres of the Church and the nobility. The roots of the Early Renaissance may thus be seen to lie in a movement instigated first and foremost by the middle classes – their first great cultural achievement. In the new forms of artistic expression adopted as a result, we simultaneously find a drawing up of "demarcation lines" separating the new from the old.

## Early 15th-century painting north of the Alps

What positions did the fine arts, and in particular painting, occupy in the early 15th century north of the Alps? Can we still speak of a polarization of Early Renaissance and Late

**Giovanni Bellini**
St Francis in the Wilderness, c. 1480
Tempera and oil on wood, 124.4 x 141.9 cm
New York, The Frick Collection

Gothic? How great were their fundamental differences? To what degree might it also be possible to draw parallels between them?

Since the 1430s – corresponding surprisingly closely, in other words, with Masaccio's chief phase of activity – a series of outstanding masters had emerged in Flanders and in the southwest of the German-speaking region. These artists addressed themselves to the portrayal of space, figure and landscape with the same passion as their Italian contemporaries. The Ghent Altar (ill. p.125) was begun at some point before 1426, the year of the death of its main artist, identified in its inscription as Hubert van Eyck (c. 1370–1426). It was completed in 1432 by Jan van Eyck (c. 1390–1441). During this same period Robert Campin (c. 1380–1444) produced the first of his mature works. The Magdalene Altar (ill. p.78) by Lukas Moser (c. 1390–after 1434), the *Mirror of Salvation* altarpiece by Konrad Witz (c. 1400–1445) in Basle (ill. p.142), Campin's Werl Altar (ill. p.126) and the Wurzach Altar (ill. p.143) by Hans Multscher (c. 1390–c. 1467) all date from between 1430 and 1440.

These and the works of numerous other masters took as their themes, with varying degrees of emphasis, the representation of foreshortened space, the three-dimensional figure modelled to appear like a statue, and the natural landscape. Their artistic goals thus directly paralleled those of Masaccio, Paolo Uccello (c. 1397–1475) and Andrea del Castagno (c. 1421/23–1457). In the case of Witz and Castagno, it even led to identical ends, insofar as both perfected in their art the free-standing polychrome statue to the degree that painting and sculpture became interchangeable. In this case, the north even had the chronological edge over the south.

## Painting and sculpture

In the north as in the south, therefore, a close relationship existed between the two main branches of fine art. It was now sculpture, however, which exercised a direct influence on painting – a reversal of the situation in the early 14th century, when Giotto and his followers had provided important stimuli for sculpture. We have already briefly mentioned that the Tuscan painters of the Early Renaissance had their most important teachers in the great sculptors and bronze founders. Significantly, the situation north of the Alps was the same. The works which the Netherlands sculptor Claus Sluter (c. 1355–1406), appointed to the court of Philip the Bold in Dijon, produced for the Carthusian monastery at Champmol near Dijon – the portal figures, the so-called *Well of Moses* (begun in 1395) and the Duke's tomb – are regularly cited as important stylistic sources for Campin, Witz and the Master of the Annunciation Altar in Aix-en-Provence (active c. 1442–1450). Indeed, the links are in places so close that the painters may be assumed to have studied the sculptures.

**Andrea Mantegna**
Portrait of Cardinal Lodovico Trevisano, c. 1459–1469
Tempera on wood, 44 x 33 cm
Berlin, Gemäldegalerie, Staatliche Museen
zu Berlin – Preußischer Kulturbesitz

The influence of sculptors on painters in the early 15th century demands closer examination. One figure deserving greater attention in this regard is Madern Gerthner (c. 1360–1430/31), about whom still too little is known. And in Multscher's workshop, it is possible that painter and sculptor were one and the same person: either the most important German sculptor and carver of the first half of the 15th century was also one of the leading painters of his day, or first-rate painters employed by him assimilated the sculptural types of the workshop to the extent that they became identical with their art.

This close relationship between painting and sculpture was not the only characteristic linking the north and the south at the start of the Early Renaissance; another was the chronological order in which the two disciplines appeared. Just as, south of the Alps, the painting of the Early Renaissance arrived on the scene almost a generation later than sculpture, so in the north sculpture preceded painting. Sluter produced his authenticated works in the last decade of the 14th century and the first decade of the 15th; Gerthner

**Robert Campin**
Annunciation, undated
Tempera on wood, 61 x 63 cm
Brussels, Musées Royaux des Beaux-Arts

belonged to the generation born around 1365. Since the portrayal of the human body was the central theme of both disciplines, we need to find an explanation for the time lag between their respective embracing of the empirical world. The very attempt to search for a solution must surely bring us closer to a comprehensive definition of the 15th century.

It is important to be aware of the differing degrees of reality present in the various disciplines of art. The three-dimensional work of sculpture, and above all the statue, possesses by its very nature the highest degree of reality – it comes closest to being identical with the object it represents. In his *Ästhetik oder Wissenschaft des Schönen* (Aesthetics or Science of Beauty), published in 1846–1857, Friedrich Theodor Vischer (1807–1887) distinguished between the necessity of indirect idealization in painting versus the necessity of direct idealization in sculpture. In other words, idealization in painting is a two-stage process: the object to be portrayed first has to be translated into a two-dimensional medium which inevitably robs it of its immediacy. Only then – if it is not to remain simply a naturalistic copy – can it be idealized. In the three-dimensional medium of sculpture, on the other hand, the object retains its palpability and can be idealized in a single step. Where idealization is not introduced, sculpture simply remains identical to the object it portrays, in the sense of a perfect optical illusion such as achieved in the Pop Art of George Segal (*1924) and Andy Warhol (1928–1987). In view of the fact that sculpture, as the branch of art related most closely to

the object it portrays, was chronologically the first to manifest the forms of the Early Renaissance, we are once again tempted to conclude that the driving force behind the Renaissance was not classical antiquity, but a new artistic confrontation – unknown in the Middle Ages – with the phenomena of the real world.

## Similarities and differences

In attempting to find a common denominator for the painting of the early 15th century north and south of the Alps and hence to arrive at a definition applicable to the epoch as a whole, we must take into account both the differences as well as the similarities in the styles being produced. In this context we may take a closer look at the Ghent Altar executed by the van Eyck brothers. Both in its dimensions and wealth of compositional devices and with regard to its outstanding artistic quality, the Ghent Altar was as important for painting north of the Alps as Masaccio's works for the beginnings of the Early Renaissance in Italy. Despite the differences in their techniques – Masaccio worked predominantly in fresco, the van Eycks in oil tempera –, a comparison between them becomes all the more compelling when we consider that all were working at the same time.

In its closed position, the Ghent Altar features an *Annunciation* in the top section and the donors venerating John the Baptist and John the Evangelist in the lower section. It thereby employs compositional solutions which can be directly compared with those in Masaccio's frescos. The Virgin and the Angel in the *Annunciation* are presented in a perspectivally foreshortened interior whose wealth of vanishing lines suggests extraordinary volume – we are given the impression of looking through the open front of a deep box. The figures are powerfully modelled, so that anatomical volume and perspective space intensify and augment each other. But while closely related to Masaccio's artistic principles up to this point, in other areas the Ghent Altar also reveals profound differences. These may be laid at the door of tradition rather than style, however. While Masaccio, in his fresco of the *Trinity* in Santa Maria Novella (ill. p.93), for example, establishes spatial depth with precisely calculated perspectival means, the van Eyck brothers work from their intuition; they create space using pragmatical values which are derived from accurate observation but which are not subjected to mathematical processing. Correspondingly, the three-dimensional modelling of their figures appears absolutely convincing at first sight, but upon closer inspection reveals a lack of understanding of the organic structure of the body beneath the draperies. Masaccio's figures, on the other hand, make clear their "natural" proportions even through their robes.

At the same time, however, many of the compositional principles employed in the lower section of the Ghent Altar come remarkably close to those of the Italian Early Renaissance. The donors, Jodocus Vyd and his wife, are the same size as the saints with whom they appear. This move away from the portrayal of donors on a diminutive scale testifies to the same shift in contemporary consciousness documented in Masaccio's donor figures. More still, the Vyds are both given such unmistakably individual features that there can be no doubt that these are portraits. The larger scale assumed by donor figures and the emergence of the portrait characterized the painting of the early 15th century in both the south and the north at the same time and to the same degree. The donors are portrayed in colour, underlining the immediacy of their presence; in contrast, the two Johns are rendered in shades of white and grey, distinguishing them from the donors and at the same time rendering them timeless. We are presented here with "painted sculptures".

Other aspects of the Ghent Altar differ profoundly from Masaccio, however. While the Italian subordinated detail to the larger form, the Flemish painters composed the larger form out of a wealth of accurately observed details. The same is true of the composition as a whole, irrespective of its different function as an altarpiece rather than as part of a fresco cycle. Although the top and bottom, sides and centre of the Ghent Altar are convincingly linked by colour correspondences between the *Annunciation* and the two Johns, in contrast to Masaccio – whose compositions are conceived first and foremost as a whole – the individual panels establish their own independence.

While fully aware of the dangers of generalization, it may thus be said that in their confrontation with reality, Masaccio and the van Eyck brothers were all, and to the same degree, representatives of a new phase of development which we may call the Early Renaissance. The differences between them were the same as those characterizing both the preceding and all future stylistic epochs: individualization in the north versus idealization in the south, or in other words subjectivity in the north, and the striving for objectivity in the south, and finally – no less important – intellectualization of artistic phenomena south of the Alps, and intuition based on feeling north of the Alps.

## "Detail realism" and new techniques

As the north increasingly endeavoured to portray the individual as faithfully as possible, so the detail – whether in portraits, in the representation of interiors and landscapes, or in the reproduction of fabrics and trimmings – acquired a significance never attained (because never sought) in the south. The term "detail realism" has been specially coined to describe Netherlandish painting in the 15th century. It is here that several of the genres of panel painting which would emerge in the 16th and above all 17th century have their roots, namely the still life, the landscape, and the domestic interior. Efforts to render details with the greatest possible realism demanded new techniques and media. As throughout the history of art, it was not new technical "inventions"

which led to new artistic solutions, but artists facing new compositional challenges who developed for themselves the practical means best suited to their ends.

Netherlandish painting of the early 15th century marked the start of a decisive new chapter in the history of colour in European painting. According to Vasari (1550), Jan van Eyck "invented" oil painting. While we may dispute the absoluteness of this claim, it undoubtedly contains a kernel of truth. The tempera techniques of previous centuries had already used oil as a binder, although other non-transparent substances, such as fig-tree juice and egg yolk, were more common. Such binders produced a colour that was absolutely opaque. Gradations were subsequently achieved by "heightening" forms with different or slightly varied shades of colour. In the age of the van Eyck brothers, oil – a transparent binder – assumed increasing importance in tempera painting, since it allowed several translucent layers of colour to be applied on top of each other. The paint surface thereby acquired a previously unknown depth and luminosity, which in turn lent the fabrics, jewellery and flowers portrayed in the new medium a naturalness touching the border between

Jan van Eyck
Portrait of Cardinal Nicola Albergati, c. 1432
Oil on wood, 34 x 26 cm
Vienna, Kunsthistorisches Museum

they developed out of the traditions of the 14th century. Thus space, figure and their mutual interpenetration had already been central themes of the workshop of sculptor Peter Parler (c. 1354–1387/88). The series of busts which he began shortly after 1370 for the triforium in the choir of Prague cathedral represent, moreover, a milestone in the evolution of the "modern" portrait. Also in the second half of the 14th century, painting in Bohemia, under the guidance of Master Theoderich (fl. 1359–1381), relinquished its previous emphasis upon boundary and contour line in favour of colour modulation. And we may already suspect a greater proportion of oil in the panels by the Master of Trebon (active c. 1380–1390) dating from the end of the century, which seem to contain an inner radiance (cf. ill. p. 69). Perspective effects, meanwhile, increasingly became the goal of painters in the latter third of the century, as seen for example in the work of Master Bertram of Minden (c. 1340–1414/15), albeit only in "localized" form. Above all, however, it was Flemish-Burgundian manuscript illumination which, in its rendering of architecture and landscape, prepared the ground for the new illusionistic character of Early Renaissance painting. As was the case south of the Alps, the new sense of realism erupting at the beginning of the 15th century in the fine arts was not a revolution, but the end of an evolution.

## Regional differences

A third parallel between north and south sheds further vital light on artistic developments in the 15th century. Campin, the van Eyck brothers, Rogier van der Weyden (c. 1400–1464), Moser, Multscher, Witz and the Master of the Aix Annunciation all grew up in an intellectual climate which was strongly influenced by a civic patriciate. Internationally famed as centres of trade and industry, Ghent and Bruges, Rottweil, Ulm and Basle were free of a past shaped by a dominant ecclesiastical or feudal authority. The forms assumed by painting here were very different to those in cities where the course of the arts had been steered for centuries by the Church and powerful family dynasties, such as Cologne, or which remained closely tied to religious institutions, such as Hamburg. Thus it was possible for the Ghent Altar to arise during a period which, in Hamburg, saw Master Francke (c. 1380–c. 1436) painting his St Thomas Altarpiece with its predominantly spiritual character, and which in Cologne saw the rise of a school of painting which, in the tradition of the 14th century, held firm to gold grounds, figures whose corporeality is only hinted at, and settings intended for identification purposes only. "Modern" design principles only reached the Lower Rhine with the arrival from the Lake Constance area of Stefan Lochner, mistakenly seen as the embodiment of Cologne painting. Lochner fused the heritage of his Swabian home with Cologne tradition in a highly sensitive way.

**Rogier van der Weyden**
Crucifixion in a Church, c. 1445
(central section of the Altar of the Seven Sacraments)
Tempera on wood, 200 x 97 cm
Antwerp, Koninklijk Museum voor Schone Kunsten

reality and reproduction and rapidly admired throughout the whole of Europe. The feastday side of the Ghent Altar marks a first climax in this development.

The artistic innovations north of the Alps no more implied a "revolutionary" new beginning than in Italy; rather,

Regional differences were thus as pronounced north of the Alps as they were in Italy. Here, as there, they arose out of different social conditions. "Progressive", or in other words "Renaissance" trends issued from the sphere of the middle classes. The thesis that the Early Renaissance was the first great cultural achievement of the middle classes is thus confirmed in the north. The polarization of Early Renaissance and Late Gothic thereby naturally appears in a very different light. There was no fundamental difference between Italy and the art centres north of the Alps, but rather a distinct line drawn between tradition and "progress", one which cannot be expressed in geographical terms since it was largely determined by patrons' wishes.

### The importance of the sacred and the secular

One question that inevitably arises out of the discussion so far, and which goes far beyond the bounds of art history, is this: Did the trend which would belong to the future, here described as the Early Renaissance in the strict sense of the term, imply a secularization of art? The answer is frequently given as yes. Seemingly correctly. The Early Renaissance was indeed a decisive step along the path leading away from a theocentric world picture, i.e. one in which God is the prime concern, towards an anthropocentric world picture in which man is the measure of all things. If it had been the task of medieval art to communicate a message of salvation which went beyond that which could be experienced with the senses, painting and sculpture were now determined by direct sensory perception. Although the symbol was not replaced by the illustration, the symbolic was now expressed through the illustrative.

The thesis that art underwent a secularization in the age of the Early Renaissance is nevertheless one to be vigorously refuted. In terms purely of volume, for one, there was little growth in secular painting over previous centuries. It is all too easy here to draw the wrong conclusion from the corpus of surviving works. Secular painting in the Middle Ages was chiefly limited to frescos. We know that castles, palaces and wealthy town houses were decorated with large-scale fresco cycles. Fresco painters in the Middle Ages employed an *a secco* technique which involved painting onto a layer of plaster which had already dried. Works executed in this manner were not very durable and offered little resistance to weathering. Thus the entire body of medieval fresco painting, sacred as well as secular, has today been reduced to a fraction of its original size. Furthermore, we can also place the number of secular frescos deliberately destroyed as higher than those in church interiors suffering the same fate.

Other points, admittedly, are more important. We may speak not of a trend towards secularization in the realm of sacred art, but rather of a shift of emphasis in the understanding of what actually was sacred. Thus the "rediscovery" of nature as worthy of representation had important roots in

Jean Hay (Master of Moulins)
The Virgin in Glory, surrounded by Angels, c. 1489–1499
(central section of the triptych in Moulins cathedral)
Tempera on wood, 157 x 133 cm
Moulins, Notre Dame

the Franciscan movement. When St Francis sang the praises of Brother Sun and Sister Moon, when he glorified God's creation in birds and plants, he directly pointed art in the direction of new pastures. This link has long been acknowledged. In 1885 Henry Thode (1857–1920) published his great work on *Franz von Assisi und die Anfänge der Kunst der Renaissance in Italien* (Francis of Assisi and the Beginnings of the Art of the Renaissance in Italy). And the Franciscan call for *compassio*, compassion, signified a new appreciation of the value of the individual, who thereby began to emerge as separate from the "collective" of the church.

Not as directly tangible, but indirectly of no less significance, was the theology of the German Dominicans, and in particular mysticism. When Master Eckhart (c. 1260–1328) and his contemporaries spoke of the "inner man", and when Johannes Tauler (b. before 1300 in Strasburg of patrician parents; d. 1361) wrote: "For on this depends all: on an unfathomable relinquishing of existence in an unfathomable nothingness", they were challenging not only the worldliness of the Hohenstaufen era but also the legitimacy of illustrative qualities in art.

The painting and sculpture of the early 14th century north of the Alps reflected this concept of a "relinquishing of

**Sandro Botticelli**
Pallas and the Centaur, c. 1482
Tempera on canvas, 207 x 148 cm
Florence, Galleria degli Uffizi

underlying reasons for Eckhart's excommunication, however, were his thesis of the dignity and responsibility before God of the individual, who thus no longer necessarily needed the mediation of the Church, and his rejection of legalism, something which anticipated Protestant thinking.

Mutually related changes in religious thought and in society thus led to a new appreciation both of the individual and of God's creation as experienced via the senses. This process was reflected in the art of the 14th century and found a provisional conclusion in the Early Renaissance. The aim was not to identify an independent aesthetic value in the world of empirical experience, but to explore – in the areas of perspective and proportion, for example – the order of the God-created cosmos.

### Interaction between north and south

Parallel lines of development and related artistic phenomena raise the question of possible interaction between the north and the south. To what extent were there direct exchanges across the Alps in the 15th century? The problem deserves to be discussed in greater depth than has been the case up till now, since a closer examination of the situation might significantly broaden our understanding of Early Renaissance art.

There is no reason to suggest that it was fundamentally uncommon, in the Middle Ages and the early years of the Renaissance, for sculptors and painters who had completed their apprenticeships to spend a few years as travelling journeymen. The fact that the historical records remain silent on the matter should not tempt us to draw hasty conclusions. In the sketchbook of Villard de Honnecourt (active c. 1230–1235), for example, we possess the priceless testimony of a travelling architect. We also know that Jean Fouquet (c. 1415/20 – c. 1480) and Rogier van der Weyden made trips to Italy around the middle of the century, and that Joos van Gent (c. 1435 – after 1480) was active at the Urbino court from 1472 to 1475. Written records, too, tell us that Francesco Sforza (1401–1466), Duke of Milan, sent the painter Zanetto Bugatto (d. 1476) to train under van der Weyden for three years; the letter of thanks which the Duchess wrote to Rogier in 1463 has survived for posterity.

To dismiss such instances of artists travelling from the north to the south and vice versa as exceptions to the rule goes against the generally accepted, stylistically widely demonstrable influence which the Netherlands exerted upon the German-speaking realm. This influence extended not just to those regions geographically the closest to the Netherlandish border, but also to southern Germany. First-hand knowledge of Netherlands art was an essential part of the "education" of every good painter in the second half of the century, and may be taken as read in the case of the outstanding artists of the Early Renaissance. Remembering, however, that the mobility of Europeans remained unchanged up to

existence", of "withdrawing from the world of appearances" (Goethe) in many different ways. Yet in speaking of the individual, the representatives of mysticism revealed a different, extremely "modern" side to their religion: on the one hand, it preached a renunciation of worldly pleasures, and thereby appeared thoroughly medieval; on the other hand, however, it was characterized by an individualism unknown in the Middle Ages. This is seen particularly clearly in the case of Master Eckhart. In 1339, the year of his death, he received a bull of excommunication from the pope in Avignon, on the grounds that 28 of his doctrines were heresies. According to doctrine 11, for example: "Everything in human nature that God the Father gave to his only begotten Son He has also given to me. From this I except nothing, neither the unity nor the holiness…". Doctrine 18 states: "Let us not bring forth outer works which do not make us good, but inner works performed and effected by the Father dwelling within us". On the surface this was suggestive of blasphemy, an arrogant inflation of the status and role of the individual. The

the time of Goethe and beyond, we are justified in asking whether this lively artistic exchange followed an east-west direction rather than north-south.

Awareness of the latest innovations was undoubtedly transmitted through the import and export of art works. We know that Netherlandish masterpieces were collected in Venice, in Urbino, and above all in the Aragonese court in Naples. The Portinari Altar (ill. p.133) by Hugo van der Goes (c. 1440/45–1482), installed in Florence in 1478, also influenced Tuscan painting of the late 15th century. Written records bear witness to the fact that Italians were informed about the art of the north, and in particular about its high quality. In his *De viribus illustris* (Illustrious Men), written between 1455 and 1457, the Neapolitan Bartolomeo Facio (c. 1405–1457) named Gentile da Fabriano (c. 1370–1427), Pisanello (1395–1455), Jan van Eyck and "Rogerius Gallicus" (i.e. Rogier van der Weyden) as the four most famous painters in the world. Facio thus accorded north and south proportionally equal importance, although he strikingly makes no mention of the masters who, for us, were the founders of the Early Renaissance in Italy. A few years later, Giovanni Santi (c. 1435–1494), father of Raphael (1483–1520), also named Jan van Eyck and Rogier van der Weyden as amongst the most important artists of the century – albeit alongside a host of Italian masters.

In the north, no comparable written records have survived. We should thereby remember that a "modern" sense of history emerged earlier in Italy than north of the Alps, and that archive material was also better preserved in the south during the following centuries. We may confidently assume, however, that Italian Early Renaissance paintings would have been collected by the big Tuscan business houses and banks and displayed in their Netherlands offices, where they would have been accessible to local artists.

We may take our enquiry one – albeit tentative – step further. Did an artist such as Domenico Veneziano (c. 1410–1461), about whose training and early years we know next to nothing but whose painting demonstrates a mastery of light and atmosphere previously unseen in Italian art, develop his new technique simply from studying individual works by Netherlands artists, or could it be that he actually spent time in the north? Did the Florentine Alessio Baldovinetti (1425–1499) absorb the strong Netherlandish influences which characterize in particular his landscapes in the very country of their origin? And asking the same question in the opposite geographical direction: had the founders of the Early Renaissance in the north – Campin, the van Eyck brothers, Moser, Witz – seen Italy with their own eyes? To assume the possibility of such lively and immediate exchanges would be to lend flesh and blood to the simultaneously homogeneous and heterogeneous nature of the 15th century, something which we have here sought to explain not primarily in terms of the difference between northern

and southern Europe, but as a consequence of the diversity of cultural and socio-political developments across the whole of what was then the West.

## Stylistic change after 1450

The course of European art in the first half of the 15th century might encourage us to expect a continuous development towards the High Renaissance, the period around 1500. This expectation is fulfilled neither south nor north of the Alps. After the middle of the century, a stylistic change took place in all the artistic displines which might be termed a "Gothic revival", and which was characterized by a return to earlier traditions and in particular the International Gothic. The fact that this process took place in equal measure in the north and the south once again confirms the fundamental homogeneity of the epoch. The artistic and

Domenico Veneziano
Portrait of a Young Woman, c. 1465
Tempera on wood, 52.5 x 36.5 cm
Berlin, Gemäldegalerie, Staatliche Museen
zu Berlin – Preußischer Kulturbesitz

philosophical reasons for this stylistic change have been the subject of frequent debate, and developments within the Church have been regularly offered as an explanation. It is doubtful, however, whether such developments alone, or even on a significant scale, can explain the phenomenon. Without claiming to offer a definitive solution to the problem, we shall discuss the inner logic of the stylistic change after 1450 from two points of view.

In historical terms, stylistic development in the second half of the 15th century appears thoroughly consistent. The major achievement of the first decades – the convincing portrayal of human figure, spatial depth and landscape in their overall combination – was followed both in the north and the south by a concentration upon finer details, with a view to "correctly" mastering anatomy, foreshortening, and the built or natural environment. The most suitable means of describing details is not the modelling of large forms, however, but the line. Van der Weyden had already begun to tread this path in the Netherlands; the same trend can be seen in Multscher's workshop in south-west Germany in the evolution from the Wurzach Altar (1437) to the Sterzinger Altar (1457/58).

In Italy, Sandro Botticelli (1445–1510), Filippino Lippi (c. 1475–1504) and Luca Signorelli (c. 1450–1523) were all protagonists of this development. This new path led away from the overall whole and towards the individual component – a trend which has numerous parallels in the history of Western art. The Italian painting of the generations after Giotto is a particularly illuminating example, and even the art of the 16th century which followed the short-lived peak of the High Renaissance would, for all its stylistic diversity, demonstrate related tendencies.

If we assume, however, for the purposes of this brief overview of the painting of the 15th century, that developments in art history are driven not simply by their own dynamic, but are conditioned by and reflect larger cultural movements, so we must widen our vision to include the broader historical context. There was very clearly a change of attitude amongst the middle classes around the 1450s. Having played a decisive role in the early 15th century in the shaping of the Early Renaissance, as a means of carving out for themselves an identity distinct from tradition and traditional patrons of art, the middle classes now began to display a very different tendency. With their increasing wealth, which simultaneously signified power, they began to exhibit a desire for the glittering pomp of court society. The story of the house of Medici is an outstanding example of this development, and the frescos by Benozzo Gozzoli (1420–1497) in the chapel of the Palazzo Medici-Riccardi are the most significant art works illustrating this turnabout (ills. pp. 80, 102). We may assume that a similar change of sentiment took place in Ghent and Bruges, Cologne and Nuremberg, Ulm and, later, Augsburg, to name just a few. It was reflected not only in painting, sculpture and carving, but also in architecture. The choir of the church of St Lorenz in Nuremberg, for example, and the Town Hall in Löwen testify to the same civic desire for aristocratic display. The urge to create a separate identity in the first half of the century was succeeded after 1450 by the urge to merge. Economic and social history can here contribute much to our understanding of artistic developments.

During this same period, too, the major courts began to adapt the achievements of the Early Renaissance, a fact that served to defuse the antagonism between the art of the middle classes on the one hand, and that of the Church and feudal society on the other. For all its backward-looking tendencies, however, the stylistic change which followed 1450 should not be misunderstood as a retrograde step. There is nothing in art history which is either a pure step "forward" or a pure step "back". The relinquishing of territory that has been won is invariably counterbalanced by the conquest of new terrain.

The sum of the diverse and complex developments of the 15th century would be totalled up around 1500 by the High Renaissance, in the words of Heinrich Wölfflin (1864–1945) the "classic art" of the Renaissance. The High Renaissance would fuse the large-scale vision suggestive of reality embraced by the early 15th century with the realistic detail of the later 15th century, once again in a lively exchange between north and south.

# MASACCIO

1401–1428

Masaccio's *Trinity* fresco, painted for a Florentine patrician family yet to be definitively
identified, is one of the founding works of Renaissance painting. Here, for the first time,
three-dimensional space is projected onto the
two-dimensional plane with the aid of the linear perspective newly rediscovered by Filippo
Brunelleschi. Solid wall truly appears to have
been breached – the foundation of all later "illusionistic" painting in which reality and appearance are rendered indistinguishable to the
eye, and above all that of Mannerism and the
Baroque.

Masaccio enables the viewer to identify directly with the painted world of the fresco by
portraying the figures in life size and by calculating the perspective from the very position
of the onlooker in real space. While the forms
of the architecture are borrowed from antiquity, they are also to be found in the first
works of Early Renaissance architecture, such
as San Lorenzo by Brunelleschi and the sculp-
tured tabernacle in Orsanmichele by Andrea
Orcagna – references through which the artist
again lends his fresco an overwhelming degree
of realism.

*The Trinity* should be appreciated not simply for its revolutionary illusionistic qualities,
however, but also for the highly intelligent organization of its figures. The donors kneeling
in front of the framing pilasters lend depth to
the foreground and reinforce the connection
between the viewer and the fresco. At the
same time, the grouping of all the figures into
a steep-sided triangle – a geometric form – acknowledges the frontality of the plane.

This fresco, unfortunately damaged during the
construction of the Baroque altar, is located on
the lower right-hand side of the window in
the Brancacci Chapel. It shows a scene from
the Acts of the Apostles. Peter had exhorted
the early Christians to give up all their
worldly possessions and to share them evenly
amongst the community. As Peter was distributing the goods, Ananias – who had secretly
kept back a part of his wealth – fell dead.

Here again, Masaccio offers a dramatic contrast to the older International Gothic style
still flourishing on Florentine soil, of which
Gentile da Fabriano's more or less contemporary *Adoration of the Magi* (ill. p. 54) is a particularly potent example. Masaccio's figures are
conceived as polychrome statues and stand in a
staggered arrangement whose depth is emphasized by contrasts of light and shade.

The impression of receding space is heightened by the crosswise architecture and the
view of a mountainous landscape behind, probably inspired by the hills around Florence. (Is
the merloned palazzo in the background the
Villa Torre di Gallo?). It is not Masaccio's intention to reproduce a recognizable scene, however. In contrast to the numerous elements
opening up the background, the foreground
figures – and in particular the body of the
dead Ananias – are positioned parallel to the
pictorial plane.

Masaccio
The Trinity, 1425/26
Fresco, 667 x 317 cm
Florence, Santa Maria Novella

Masaccio
St Peter distributes the Goods of
the Community and The Death
of Ananias, c. 1426/27
Fresco, 230 x 162 cm
Florence, Santa Maria del Carmine, Brancacci Chapel

## MASACCIO

1401–1428

Around 1424 Masaccio and his older colleague Masolino embarked upon the decoration of the Brancacci Chapel, which was dedicated to St Peter. Recent research has disproved the former thesis that Masolino was Masaccio's teacher and originally began the cycle on his own. The first areas of the frescos to be painted were the backgrounds, and since these are entirely indebted to Early Renaissance architecture, they can only have been executed by the artist who also painted the *Trinity*-fresco in Santa Maria Novella.

All Masaccio's pictorial means are concentrated in the scene of the *Tribute Money*. Despite the elongated format and the division of the narrative into three scenes, Masaccio achieves a compositional homogeneity which the viewer unquestioningly accepts. In the centre we see Christ instructing Peter to go and catch a fish, saying that he will find a coin in its mouth; on the left we see Peter obeying Christ's command, and on the right rendering the tribute money to the tax collector. Rather than dividing the pictorial plane into three symmetrical fields and thereby threatening the lively animation of the whole, Masaccio presents the scenes in a seemingly loose relationship. The various groups are nevertheless linked by a large number of differentiated means: by "complementary figures" such as the tax collector, for example, who is seen in rear view in the centre and frontally on the right, and by the disciple on the right-hand edge of the main group and the pointing figure of Peter. A similar purpose is served by correlations of colour and, most emphatically of all, by the artistic but nevertheless natural rhythm established by the facial expressions

worn by the figures and the directions in which they are standing and looking. Here we may recognize early aspects of the "stage management" which would culminate in Leonardo's *Last Supper* (ill. p. 161). Landscape and architecture are also designed to serve the homogeneity of the overall picture. The mountain ranges "pin" the scene together, and the vanishing lines of the architecture converge in Christ's head.

Where do the sources of Masaccio's art lie? The painting of the previous generation offers little in the way of an answer. Rather, the sculptural qualities of Masaccio's figural style suggest that he was profoundly influenced by the early works of Donatello and the statues of

Nanni di Banco. His "statuary" approach thereby places him in a long line of Florentine painters reaching from Giotto to Michelangelo. And in Giotto we find the second point of reference for Masaccio's work. For Masaccio was the true heir to Giotto, albeit with a new degree of naturalism. He shared with Giotto the concept of the three-dimensional figure, the reduction of details to the absolute minimum required by the narrative, and finally the use of architecture and landscape as integral components of the composition.

Having lost much of their brightness over the course of the centuries, the frescos have recently been cleaned and restored to their original glory.

**Masaccio**
The Tribute Money, 1426/27
Fresco, 255 x 598 cm
Florence, Santa Maria del Carmine, Brancacci Chapel

**Paolo Uccello**
Equestrian Portrait of Sir John
Hawkwood, 1436
Fresco, transferred to canvas,
732 x 404 cm. Florence, Duomo

# PAOLO UCCELLO

## C. 1397–1475

Behind this work, signed and dated 1436, lies a lengthy history. Sir John Hawkwood was an English mercenary leader known in Florence as Giovanni Acuto. An original plan to honour his distinguished name with a marble tomb was shelved, for reasons of cost, in favour of an equestrian portrait, duly painted by Agnolo Gaddi. Deemed old-fashioned in 1433, this was replaced by the present work, in which Uccello uses the new means of foreshortening and three-dimensional figure representation to create a "painted sculpture".

The base appears to project out of the wall on three consoles. The view of the coffered underside creates a sense of tangible three-dimensionality which is reinforced by the muted palette. In light of the numerous preliminary studies for stereometric bodies surviving from Uccello's hand, we may assume that here, too, the foreshortening of the individual architectural elements was precisely calculated in advance.

So important did Uccello consider the brilliant rendition of the three-quarter view and underside of the base that he was willing to compromise the integrity of the perspective system governing the overall composition. Thus base and rider are in fact seen from different angles – the base from below and the rider in strict profile from the side.

It would be wrong to deduce from this that Uccello changed his mind half-way through. There could be no question of a worm's-eye view for the heraldic figure of the rider, and in Uccello's eyes the bravura composition of the base made up for the break in perspective. Horse and rider, powerfully modelled, stand out forcefully against the dark background. The influence of sculpture first felt in Masaccio's painting ten years earlier now fully determines Uccello's figural style.

Uccello's *St George and the Dragon* is a prime example of his late work. The heroic monumentality of his large-scale frescos and battle scenes has here given way, in accordance with the changing tastes of the times, to a more narrative phase. For all its deliberate drama, the scene might be an illustration taken from a book of fairy-tales. The slender princess holds the already conquered dragon, its wings patterned in different colours, on a delicate lead, while the knight appears to be charging in from the right. The grey belongs to the breed of powerfully modelled horses in Uccello's battle paintings. The large, gloomy cavern on the left is echoed on the right in the swirling storm clouds behind St George.

The division of the landscape into geometric lots is also something continued from Uccello's battle paintings (right). Here, however, pictorial space opens up continuously from the foreground, across the middle ground, to the background. A second version of this composition is housed in the Musée Jacquemart-André in Paris.

**Paolo Uccello**
St George and the Dragon, c. 1455
Tempera on canvas, 57 x 74 cm
London, National Gallery

The three-part painting of the *Battle of San Romano* was probably executed for the city palace of the Medici; it is certainly mentioned there in an inventory of 1491. It depicts a famous episode from recent Florentine history. On 1 June 1432 the mercenary leader Niccolò da Tolentino, commemorated in the equestrian portrait of 1456 by Andrea del Castagno in Florence cathedral, routed the Sienese in a surprise raid near San Romano. At a time when the Medici were already on their way to feudal supremacy, this celebration of an event from Florence's republican past was probably a piece of political calculation. There were clearly some who wanted to veil the truth, at least to the outside world, about the actual balance of power.

The three panels form a cyclical composition. On the left-hand side (housed in London), Niccolò da Tolentino, depicted in the centre on a grey charger with his commander's baton pointing the way forward, heads the attack on San Romano. In the middle panel (housed in Florence), Bernadino della Carda, the leader of the Sienese mercenaries, is knocked from his horse by a blow from a lance. Uccello thus portrays the decisive moment in the battle at the centre of the entire composition, although avoiding any semblance of rigid symmetry by shifting the figure of Bernadino della Carda slightly right of the central axis. The right-hand panel (housed in Paris) shows Niccolò da Tolentino coming to the aid of the mercenaries of the Florentine condottiere Michelotto da Cotignola and forcing the Sienese to defend themselves on two fronts.

The composition only makes full sense when the three panels are seen together. Uccello establishes a movement which travels simultaneously from the groups of riders on the left-hand edge of the London picture and the right-hand edge of the Paris painting, passes through the two equestrian figures at the centre of each of these panels, and culminates in the middle of the Florence panel. The groupings of lances similarly play an important role in linking together the frieze-like composition. The repeated obliques of these lances serve to emphasize the pictorial surface and at the same time are characteristic of Uccello's style, which is determined by a certain process of abstraction. Thus the silhouettes of horses and riders are simplified in favour of powerful plastic volumes – one may compare here the horses in Gentile da Fabriano's *Adoration of the Magi* (ill. p. 54), which Uccello would have studied – while side views predominate over Uccello's admittedly masterly foreshortenings. The landscape, which echoes the rising backgrounds in Ambrogio Lorenzetti's *The Effects of Good Government* (ill. p. 41) in Siena Town Hall, is parcelled into geometric lots.

Interestingly, Uccello would prove a notable source of inspiration for the early 20th-century tendency within Italian painting grouped around the magazine *Valori Plastici* (Plastic Values), leading to a re-appraisal of his importance within the history of art.

*Top:*
**Paolo Uccello**
Battle of San Romano, c. 1456
(left panel)
Tempera on wood, 182 x 317 cm
London, National Gallery

*Middle:*
**Paolo Uccello**
Battle of San Romano, c. 1456
(middle panel)
Tempera on wood, 182 x 323 cm
Florence, Galleria degli Uffizi

*Bottom:*
**Paolo Uccello**
Battle of San Romano, c. 1456
(right panel)
Tempera on wood, 180 x 316 cm
Paris, Musée National du Louvre

**Andrea del Castagno**
Farinata degli Uberti, c. 1450
(from the series of Uomini famosi in
the Villa Pandolfini, Legnaia)
Fresco, 245 x 165 cm
Florence, Galleria degli Uffizi

## ANDREA DEL CASTAGNO
c. 1421/23–1457

Around 1450 Andrea del Castagno executed a
fresco cycle of *Uomini famosi* in a room in the
Villa Pandolfini in Legnaia, near Florence.
Larger than life in size, these "Famous Men
and Women" comprise a mixture of figures
from history, mythology and art, in line with
the thinking of early humanism.

Alongside the mercenary leaders Niccolò
Acciaiuoli, Farinata and Pippo Spano, they include the poets Dante, Petrarch and Boccaccio, the Cumaean Sibyl, and queens Esther and
Tomyris. The theme of the cycle dated back to
Petrarch and the early 14th century. During
the Early Renaissance, however, it assumed a
particular relevance: in the celebration of great
individuals lay the roots of the Renaissance
cult of genius.

Not until Michelangelo's Sistine ceiling
would the painted sculpture – a challenge so
variously interpreted – find a more convincing
form. The suggestion of the interchangeability
of painting and sculpture is heightened by the
manner in which the figures appear to project
forward out of the mock architecture. Sufficient fragments of the background, itself a virtuoso display of perspective, have survived to
enable us to reconstruct its original appearance. The figures appear to cross the threshold
between pictorial and real space.

**Domenico Veneziano**
Madonna and Child with Saints (St Lucy Altarpiece), c. 1442–1448
Oil on wood, 209 x 213 cm. Florence, Galleria degli Uffizi

## DOMENICO VENEZIANO
c. 1410–1461

This altarpiece, showing the Virgin enthroned
between the saints Francis and John the Baptist on the left and the saints Zenobius and
Lucy on the right, ranks amongst the most important works of the Italian Early Renaissance
on two counts. It dealt a major blow to the
polyptych, a genre still lingering on far into
the 15th century, in which the Virgin and accompanying saints were traditionally
presented on individually framed, hinged
panels. Domenico here links the figures
within a single panel, firstly by means of his
architecture, whose charming mix of classical
and Gothic forms may reflect the influence of
Ghiberti, and secondly by arranging them in a
concave semicircle. His palette, moreover,
must also have made a revolutionary impact
on his contemporaries.

In contrast to the strong local colours
preferred by Florentine painters, Domenico
achieves a wealth of delicate nuances by adding a greater proportion of oil to his tempera
as a binder. For the first time in Renaissance
painting, sunlight is rendered with paint
rather than with gold, as was previously
usually the case. In this, Domenico prepared
the ground for the subsequent achievements of
his pupil Piero della Francesca.

# PIERO DELLA FRANCESCA

C. 1420–1492

Piero's *Baptism of Christ* was originally painted as an altarpiece for a church, demolished in the 19th century, in the town of Borgo San Sepolcro. It was subsequently incorporated into a triptych on an altar in the town's cathedral, flanked by two outer wings – still housed in the cathedral today – by the Sienese artist Matteo di Giovanni. In contrast to contemporary works of Florentine painting, the landscape is rich and differentiated in design and flooded with light. Piero here continues along the path signposted by Domenico Veneziano in the St Lucy altarpiece. In his figural style, Piero thereby begins to move away from the ideals of the Florentine Early Renaissance. He is no longer quite so interested in establishing the three-dimensional solidity of his characters, for all their powerful modelling; outlines have become noticeably simpler, and so too the details of the draperies.

The landscape reveals Piero as a master of spatial depth, as evidenced in the river Jordan winding its way into the background and mirroring the landscape around it. At the same time, however, Piero honours the shallowness of the plane in the relief-like arrangement of his characters, whereby the grouping of two figures at right angles to each other plays an important role. The constellation of Christ and the tree, and the planimetric superimposition of Christ, the baptism bowl, John's hand, the dove and the tree-top, also serve to emphasize the flatness of the pictorial plane.

The angels have been linked to the caryatids on the Acropolis, but Piero could not have known these at first hand.

In choosing to portray his sitters in strict profile – a pose influenced by the art of medal engraving and involving a greater degree of idealization than the three-quarter views preferred by Flemish painters, with their obsessive love of individual detail – Piero is fully in line with Italian Early Renaissance tradition. Entirely without precedent in Italian painting, on the other hand, is his presentation of the figures at a pronounced height above the background landscape, which appears as a sweeping expanse below. It must be assumed that Piero was here assimilating influences from Netherlandish painting, ultimately deriving from Jan van Eyck's *Virgin of Chancellor Rolin* (ill. p. 123).

What in the Netherlands artist, however, was the consequence of a theological programme has here become an exercise in composition. Piero had the opportunity of studying Netherlandish painting at the Urbino court, both in the Duke's collection and in the person of Joos van Gent. Flemish influence is also visible in his technique. In the delicate oil glazes with which he renders the jewellery worn by Battista Sforza, for example, Piero achieves a realism comparable in contemporary Italian painting only to that of Antonello da Messina.

On the reverse of the dipytch, the ducal couple are shown in a triumphal procession in Antique style.

**Piero della Francesca**
The Baptism of Christ,
c. 1440–1450
Tempera on wood, 168 x 116cm
London, National Gallery

**Piero della Francesca**
Double portrait of Federigo da Montefeltro and his wife Battista Sforza, c. 1470
(front of a diptych)
Tempera on panel, each 47 x 33cm
Florence, Galleria degli Uffizi

## PIERO DELLA FRANCESCA

C. 1420-1492

The cycle of frescos in the choir of San Francesco was originally commissioned by the richest family in Arezzo, the Bacci, who had decided as early as 1416 to decorate the main choir chapel. Bicci di Lorenzo, a Florentine painter working in the Late Gothic style, eventually started on the vault in 1447, but died in 1452. Piero della Francesca probably took over the cycle immediately after this. On the end wall and two side walls of the choir, he proceeded to illustrate the legend of the True Cross as related in the *Legenda aurea* (Golden Legend) by Jacobus da Voragine (1230-1298/99) – a subject which, although not new in Franciscan iconography (Agnolo Gaddi had also painted a cycle on the same legend in the choir of Santa Croce in Florence in 1380), had assumed a new relevance in the mid-15th century.

During this period, Pope Pius II sought for the last time in Western history to rouse the princes of Europe to launch a Crusade against the Turks, who appeared to be heading for inevitable victory in Jerusalem. The fresco cycle in Arezzo may well be a form of propaganda for the Crusades: it is surely indicative of wishful thinking that episodes from Voragine are supplemented here by scenes drawn

from another source, showing the defeat of the Persian king Chosroes, who had stolen the True Cross from Jerusalem, at the hands of Emperor Heraclius, and the subsequent return of the Cross to Jerusalem.

Piero approached the two windowless side walls of the choir as a compositional unity. In each case, a central fresco in an architectural setting is sandwiched above and below between scenes in an open landscape. In each fresco, the grouping of the figures establishes a division between left and right which, while remaining free and unconstrained, plays an important role in structuring the whole. Piero also spans subtle stays across the width of the choir, whereby he links the two walls from a purely artistic point of view, without regard to the literary chronology of the legend.

In the lowest position on both walls are the two battle scenes. They are followed at mid-height by the frescos set in a built environment, whereby the main verticals established by the painted architecture are in both cases shifted slightly out of the central axis, injecting a rhythmic impulse into the pictorial plane. Finally, the landscapes in the lunettes at the top represent, respectively, the start and the close of the cycles to which they belong,

with each seemingly the pendant of the other
in the relationship between the distribution of
the figures and the accentuation provided by
the trees.

The fresco illustrated here forms the central
field on the right-hand wall and combines two
scenes. On her way to King Solomon's palace,
the Queen of Sheba reaches a bridge across a
stream. She recognizes the wood from which
the bridge is made as that which will later provide the material for Christ's cross, and she
kneels before it in prayer. On the right we
see the Queen meeting King Solomon in his
palace.

Piero's painting reaches full maturity in
this cycle. The landscape on the left reveals
the same sense of sweeping space and – even
in its present, sadly damaged state – the abundant light that we encountered in the *Baptism
of Christ* (ill. p.99). In the arrangement of the
figures and in the hills running from left to
right in the background, Piero thereby deliberately compromises spatial depth in favour of
reconciliation with the two-dimensionality of
the plane.

This can be seen even more clearly in the
columned hall of Solomon's palace. Drawing
for its details upon classical architecture, the

interior evokes a suggestive impression of spatial depth. According to Paolo Uccello, Piero
was the greatest theoretician and practitioner
of perspective of the Early Renaissance.
Rather than seeking to show off his skills,
however, Piero chooses to balance the vanishing lines of his architecture with emphatic
horizontals.

Piero's significance for the monumental
painting of the Early Renaissance is seen nowhere more clearly than here. Whereas the
first decades of the century had been devoted
to the exploration of spatial depth and the illusionistic breaching of solid walls, Piero reaf-
firmed the validity of the plane. In integrating
three-dimensional space and a two-dimensional plane within his effortless mastery of
perspective, he secured himself a key position
in European fresco painting between Masaccio
and Raphael.

Piero's execution of detail is characterized
by a further simplification of outlines and contours, which here assume an almost archaizing
severity. The faces resemble abstract portraits,
while the architecture is reduced to elementary stereometric forms. Thanks to the painted
light with which they are flooded, the frescos
nevertheless exude a festive, joyful atmosphere.

**Piero della Francesca**
The Discovery of the Wood of the True Cross
and The Meeting of Solomon and the Queen
of Sheba, after 1452
Fresco, 360 x 750 cm
Arezzo, San Francesco

**Fra Filippo Lippi**
The Feast of Herod
Salome's Dance, c. 1460–1464
Fresco, width c. 880 cm
Prato, Duomo, Cappella Maggiore

## FRA FILIPPO LIPPI
### c. 1406–1469

Salome, asked by her mother Herodias for the head of John the Baptist, requested that her father Herod should grant her a wish, which he promised to do if she would dance for him at dinner. Using the pictorial device of continuous representation (whereby two or more episodes from a narrative are combined in a single image), Fra Filippo Lippi shows Salome dancing on the left and the head of John the Baptist being delivered on a platter on the right.

The composition has its roots in representations of the Last Supper. Filippo Lippi would have known Andrea del Castagno's fresco in the refectory of Santa Apollonia in Florence; here, however, he seeks to establish greater spatial depth by arranging the tables in a pronounced horseshoe and by foreshortening the tiled floor.

From this point of view, the fresco represents an important forerunner to Domenico Ghirlandaio's *Last Supper* in the convent of San Marco in Florence (ill. p. 108). Insofar as the present composition appears to be seen from varying heights, Filippo is not yet attempting to fuse pictorial space with real space. Filippo's late style is characterized by a tendency towards affected movements and a decorative drapery style, both of which are seen in the present fresco, executed between 1460 and 1464.

**Benozzo Gozzoli**
Procession of the Magi, 1459–1461
Fresco (detail), wall width c. 750 cm
Florence, Palazzo Medici-Riccardi

## BENOZZO GOZZOLI
### 1420–1497

The present detail is taken from a continuous fresco of the *Procession of the Magi* covering three walls of a small chapel in the Palazzo Medici-Riccardi. Barely a decade after the frescos of Uccello and Castagno had broken new ground in the portrayal of space and figures, Gozzoli presents us with an extraordinary work in which the spirit of the International Gothic seems to breathe again. An extravagant pageant of figures, sumptuous robes and costly trappings is portrayed in front of and passing through a magnificent mountain landscape. The composition seems to draw its inspiration from Gentile da Fabriano's *Adoration of the Magi* painted a generation earlier. With its rich selection of portraits, such as the young Lorenzo the Magnificent seen here on horseback, and its almost inexhaustible wealth of contemporary styles of dress, the fresco must have seemed a mirror of the present.

Benozzo's narrative skills, his love of detail – inherited from his days as a goldsmith's apprentice under Ghiberti – and his fresh palette here combine to maximum effect. The rocky landscape which rises from bottom to top of the pictorial plane points to Gozzoli's first-hand exposure to Ghiberti's "Gates of Paradise" doors for the Baptistery in Florence. The painter builds on the achievements of the preceding generation and adds to them his own artistry as an enchanting story-teller.

## ANTONIO DEL POLLAIUOLO
### 1432–1498

Chiefly active as a sculptor of bronzes, Pollaiuolo addressed himself more than any of his contemporaries to the portrayal of animated figures designed to be seen from different angles. He takes up the same challenge in his paintings, amongst which the present *Martyrdom of St Sebastian* – probably executed with the assistance of his younger brother Piero – takes pride of place. The subject, involving more than just the isolated single figure of sculpture, must have particularly appealed to his temperament, which leaned toward dramatic intensity. The archers, portrayed in highly diverse poses, resemble small bronzes, translated into the medium of painting. In the main group, compositional freedom and discipline are combined in admirable fashion: St Sebastian, lashed high above the ground to the stump of a tree, is surrounded by a circle of archers whose animated poses at first appear freely composed, but which on closer inspection reveal themselves to be precisely calculated, each a counterweight to the other. Like the unusual view of the saint, presented against the horizon in the top half of the picture, so too we are offered an unusual view of the landscape stretching far into the distance, executed with great precision in a delicate gradation of tones. Here Pollaiuolo reflects his knowledge of Antonello, who may have passed through Florence on his way to Venice.

Antonio del Pollaiuolo
The Martyrdom of St Sebastian, 1475
Tempera on wood, 292 x 203 cm
London, National Gallery

*Below:*
**Melozzo da Forlì**
Sixtus IV, his Nephews, and his Librarian Palatina, c. 1480
Fresco, transferred to canvas, 370 x 315 cm. Rome, Musei Vaticani, Pinacoteca Vaticana

## MELOZZO DA FORLÌ
### 1438–1494

In the monumentality of its perspective setting, constructed with great confidence, in the calm dignity of its powerfully modelled figures, and in its two groups of three subtly animated figures, Melozzo's Vatican Library fresco anticipates the achievements of the High Renaissance more than any other painting of its day. The clear, simple outlines of the figures point to the influence of Piero della Francesca. But while Piero always sought the type behind the individual, Melozzo reveals himself to be a portraitist of great psychological sensitivity. His architecture combines a knowledge of classical buildings with a sophisticated taste in decorative detail. A skilful play upon the boundary between painted and real space reveals itself in individual elements: the corner pilasters, for example, seem to project outwards towards the viewer, an impression reinforced by the concave moulding of the plinth on the left, while the hem of the robe worn by the kneeling Platina spills over the edge of the inscribed tablet.

The painter clearly took into account the natural light source of the fresco's original, unknown location: the pillars on the left are in shade, while those on the right are fully lit. Fra Angelico's fresco of the *Ordination of St Lawrence* (ill. p. 23) may have provided the model for this composition.

## SANDRO BOTTICELLI

1445–1510

This panel is one of the most potent witnesses to the changes taking place in Florentine painting in the latter half of the 15th century – changes reflecting the development from an emphatically civic culture to a court culture.

In 1439 the Council of Union, which was intended to re-unite the Western and Orthodox Churches, was transferred from Ferrara to Florence at the wish of the Medici – a clear display of Medici influence and the family's claim to power. The Byzantines brought with them a series of writers and philosophers who gave new impetus to Florentine humanist interests.

A display of pomp on a princely scale was seen twenty years later in the banquet which Piero de' Medici held for Pope Pius II and Galeazzo Sforza, Duke of Milan. The Medici thereby placed themselves on a par with the most powerful figures in Italy. Benozzo Gozzoli's frescos for the Medici chapel in the Palazzo Medici-Riccardi (ills. pp. 80, 102) not only documented the pageantry of the festiv-

ities but provided an exemplary illustration of the structural shift in Florentine society after 1450.

It is against this historical backdrop that Botticelli's panel must be seen. Mars, the God of War, has been conquered by Venus, the Goddess of Love. Reclining upon the ground, the handsome youth has fallen asleep. Naked and robbed of all his weapons, which are now in the hands of the fauns in the middle ground, he embodies a beautiful ideal from whose mind all thoughts of war are banished. Venus, on the other hand, richly dressed like a young woman from a distinguished family and thereby removed from the context of eroticism, remains alert and in this way symbolizes the permanence of peace.

Botticelli's reinterpretation of this mythological love scene can only be understood with reference to the Platonic Academy which, planned by Cosimo de' Medici, blossomed during the era of Lorenzo the Magnificent. Its

leading spirit was the poet and philosopher Marsilio Ficino and its thinking was influenced first and foremost by Plato. Seen in this light, Botticelli's painting takes on a new meaning: love, understood in the Platonic sense as a chiefly spiritual power, has conquered the horrors of war and violence. Classical philosophy here meets Christianity under what would become known as neo-Platonism.

Through the brilliant ingenuity of his composition, Botticelli overcomes the limitations of what might be considered an unfortunately long and narrow format within which to portray such a small number of figures. Equally balanced, Venus and Mars are virtually mirror images of each other. They establish the shape of an inverted triangle which is concluded at the top by the three fauns with the lance. Although expressions and poses are allowed to unfold freely in three-dimensional space, the geometric figure of the triangle informs all the details with the constraints of the plane.

Activity and passivity are exquisitely balanced in the two main figures: from a literary point of view, the alert figure of Venus, her upper body held upright, represents the active part of the scene, while the sleeping figure of Mars, his head leant back, represents the passive part. Within the syntax of the plane, however, their roles are reversed. The line of Venus' body falls in a slant from top left to bottom right, signifying repose – an impression reinforced by her self-contained silhouette. Mars, on the other hand, traces an oblique which rises from bottom left to top right, implying activeness, while his splayed limbs are indicative of movement. Botticelli thus creates a fascinating tension between his thematic motifs and their artistic expression.

The figure of Mars may be seen as an immediate forerunner to Adam in Michelangelo's *Creation of Adam* on the Sistine ceiling (cf. ill. pp. 168/169), painted some thirty years later (c. 1510).

**Sandro Botticelli**
Venus and Mars, c. 1480
Tempera on wood, 69 x 174 cm
London, National Gallery

# SANDRO BOTTICELLI

## 1445–1510

**Sandro Botticelli**
Madonna del Magnificat, c. 1481/82
Tempera on wood, diameter 115 cm
Florence, Galleria degli Uffizi

This panel of the Madonna and Child surrounded by angels takes its name from the open book in which Mary appears to be writing the text of the Magnificat. Painted shortly after 1480, it continues the trends already introduced in Botticelli's *Primavera*. The composition is hallmarked by delicate, flowing contours and a supremely sensitive treatment of the draperies. Details – decorative hems, hair, billowing veil, crown with glory – are executed with a precision and care that point to Botticelli's apprenticeship in a goldsmith's workshop. The incorporation of the figural group into the circular format of the tondo is mastered with an ease and assurance unprecedented in earlier painting. Not until 1515 would Raphael perfect this compositional principle once again in his *Madonna della Sedia*. Botticelli here pays what is for him unusual attention to the landscape in the background. The figures are grouped in a staggered arrangement which lends depth to the foreground and thereby connects them to the landscape opening up behind. The overall impression is thus not dissimilar to looking into a hemisphere.

In his late work, Botticelli moved away from the ideals of perspective and anatomy. He thereby aligned himself with an international trend which followed on from the powerful rendition of reality of the first half of the 15th century.

The type of Pietà reduced solely to the figures of the Virgin Mary and Christ never established itself in central Italy. In contrast to Venetian painting, which leaned more strongly towards contemplative themes and in which the Pietà in a landscape setting rose – particularly through Giovanni Bellini – to become a popular subject, the Florentine temperament tended towards discussion and dramatic intensification, and demanded multifigural compositions in which the nature of the event taking place is reflected in the faces and gestures of those attending it. The setting of Botticelli's scene in front of the rocky tomb lends it an additional dimension: the devotional Pietà so popular north of the Alps here becomes a station between Deposition and Entombment. The work, probably executed with the help of assistants, illustrates Botticelli's last stage of development. The silhouettes and contours of the figures and the rocks are sharply drawn. Pain is directly embodied in the – at times – almost harsh contrasts of colour, and above all in the dramatic contrasts of expression and movement. The panel may thereby reflect the influence not only of Netherlandish painting, but also of the general cultural climate in Florence at the turn of the century, following the end of the glittering epoch of Lorenzo de' Medici (called *il Magnifico*, the Magnificent) and after the public burning of Girolamo Savonarola (1498).

**Sandro Botticelli**
Pietà, after 1490
Tempera on wood, 140 x 207 cm
Munich, Bayerische Staatsgemäldesammlungen, Alte Pinakothek

Probably executed in 1477/78 for Pierfrancesco de' Medici's villa in Castello, this panel combines a monumental format (including life-size figures) with a technique reminiscent of miniature painting. Like the *Birth of Venus*, it testifies to the change in artistic thinking which took place in Florence after 1450. While the literature of classical antiquity continued to provide a source of thematic inspiration, its formal influence became virtually insignificant.

The encoded content of the *Primavera* can be unravelled with the help of a poem by Angelo Poliziano, who himself drew upon Ovid. The figure standing in the centre is Flora; on the far left, Mercury is scattering fog, while on the far right a wind god is chasing a fleeing nymph. Perspective and anatomy are no longer central themes of the composition, which is dominated instead by a sensitive handling of line and elongated proportions. The pale figures, some dressed in transparent robes, stand out against the dark background. In contrast to the strong colours which characterized the early years of the century, Botticelli's palette is restrained and muted. Where he appears to cite classical motifs, as in the case of the Three Graces on the left, he draws not upon antiquity directly, but on Ghiberti's bronze doors for the Baptistery in Florence (specifically, upon the group of serving maids in the relief of Jacob and Esau).

The view expressed in recent research that the *Birth of Venus* was painted at the same time and as a counterpart to the *Primavera* can be countered on a number of points. Firstly, the two paintings employ formats of considerably different size; secondly, they may be considered to represent different phases in the artist's development; and thirdly, they differ in terms of technique. The composition of the *Birth of Venus* is more rigorous in structure — it has been related to the traditional Baptism of Christ — and is infused with a harmony of line and movement. The additive principle which governs the *Primavera* has been overcome. The central figure of Venus standing on the scallop, her pose infused with a momentum that is ultimately still Gothic, is indebted to an ideal of beauty which Botticelli used in various forms, for example in *The Calumny of Apelles* (Florence, Galleria degli Uffizi) probably painted a few years later. Whether his model was Simonetta Vespucci, extolled in Poliziano's verses, is a question which must remain unanswered. A striking feature of the *Birth of Venus*, and indeed of Botticelli's œuvre as a whole, is his lack of interest in landscape, something to which he openly admitted in a conversation recorded by Leonardo da Vinci.

The art historian Jan Lauts has shown that the *Birth of Venus*, on the surface a composition whose content is self-evident, in fact reflects some of the complex thinking of the Platonic Academy which met regularly in the Medicean Villa Careggi under the guidance of Marsilio Ficino.

Sandro Botticelli
La Primavera, c. 1477/78
Tempera on wood, 203 x 314 cm
Florence, Galleria degli Uffizi

Sandro Botticelli
The Birth of Venus, c. 1485
Tempera on canvas, 172.5 x 278.5 cm
Florence, Galleria degli Uffizi

## DOMENICO GHIRLANDAIO
### 1449–1494

**Domenico Ghirlandaio**
Last Supper, 1480
Fresco, total width 812 cm
Florence, Convent of San Marco, Refectory

This fresco marks the most important stage between the Last Suppers of Andrea del Castagno and Leonardo (ill. p. 161). While Domenico Ghirlandaio, with his regular disposition of calm figures around the table, may not achieve the same expressive power as Castagno, he goes significantly beyond him in his efforts to merge real and pictorial space. For the first time, the perspectival composition is calculated from the actual height of the spectator's eye, so that the viewer indeed feels himself to be looking down on the painted marble floor.

The fact that the figures are also life size and that the vaulted ceiling of the refectory appears to pass uninterrupted into the fresco heightens the impression that we are looking into a real podium. The sense of spatial depth is reinforced by the painted view of the monastery garden behind.

Domenico Ghirlandaio endeavours to render details – the tablecloth with its pleats and patterned border, the objects on the table, the trees and birds in the background – with the greatest possible fidelity to nature. Here the influence of Netherlandish painting is clearly visible.

The fact that this *Last Supper* is, in all but a few details, an exact copy of one which Ghirlandaio had completed shortly beforehand in the refectory of Ognissanti shows just how closely his style matched contemporary taste.

**Domenico Ghirlandaio**
Old Man and Young Boy, 1488
Tempera on wood, 62 x 46 cm
Paris, Musée National du
Louvre

This panel occupies a special position in Florentine portraiture of the Early Renaissance. Never before in the name of realism had such careful attention been paid to ugly, even disfiguring detail. From here the path lay clear to the physiognomical studies by Leonardo, who also sought to record abnormalities. Both artists reflect the enduring influence of the Portinari Altar (ill. p. 133); only by looking closely at the heads of Hugo van der Goes' kneeling shepherds can we begin to understand Ghirlandaio's portrait.

Although a slight questionmark still hovers over the attribution of this panel, a number of features link it closely to Ghirlandaio's late work. His frescos for the choir of Santa Maria Novella include numerous portrait busts of elderly men which similarly make no attempt to idealize the characteristics of old age. The head of the child, too, with his gleaming hair heightened with gold, recalls the heads of youths in other panels by Ghirlandaio.

The relationship between grandfather and grandson is vividly brought to life in the kindly, thoughtful expression worn by the old man and the trusting, beseeching look in the child's eyes.

In its precise detailing of every element, yet its deliberately unspecified location, the landscape falls fully in line with Florentine tradition. In the contrast between the solid wall and the view through the window, the artist may be referring on the one hand to the old life that is almost over, and on the other to the young life with so much before it.

## ANDREA DEL VERROCCHIO

### C. 1435–1488

The fact that the artist who painted this composition was also a sculptor is apparent in the carefully pondered poses of the standing figures and in the precise rendition of their anatomical details.

In line with his personal artistic temperament, Andrea del Verrocchio lends a dramatic intensity to the scene: Christ is no longer portrayed strictly frontally as in Piero della Francesco, but turns towards John the Baptist who, captured in mid-step, appears to be entering the picture from the right. Here Verrocchio anticipates some of the compositional principles which would shortly afterwards inform his bronze group of *Christ and St Thomas*.

The main foreground scene is stylistically dominated by line: robes and exposed parts of the body are traced with an almost graphic sharpness, and the individual layers of rock and stones stand out from one other with a similar clarity. Not so, however, the two angels and the river landscape behind: here, line gives way to colour modulation as the chief means of composition. Outlines increasingly lose their focus and colours lighten as they recede into the distance.

Leonardo, at that time active in Verrocchio's workshop, clearly assisted his master on this painting.

Andrea del Verrocchio The Baptism of Christ, c. 1475
Tempera on wood, 177 x 151 cm. Florence, Galleria degli Uffizi

## FILIPPINO LIPPI

### C. 1457–1504

Dating from around 1486, this painting marks the first high point in Lippi's development. The formative influence of his great teacher Botticelli is clearly visible in the pose and expressions of the figures, the sensitive drawing of the heads and the rich movements of the draperies. The restless multiplicity of the composition, on the other hand, looks ahead to Filippino's large fresco cycles, in particular in Santa Maria Novella (Florence, 1501).

Filippino sets the main foreground group against a rocky outcrop which rises to a peak behind the Virgin and St Bernard. Further back on the right we seen scenes from the lives of Franciscan monks. The motif of the truncated donor figure serves to suggest that the scene is simply an excerpt taken at random from a larger whole, and was probably derived from Donatello. The painting exudes an overall impression of seemingly spontaneous arrangement rather than calculated composition. A comparison between Filippino's work and Perugino's treatment of the same subject (ill. p. 111) is particularly illuminating in this respect. In contrast to the sense of permanence and stability in the Perugino, Filippino's Virgin seems to have materialized before St Bernard just an instant ago.

It is evident from the powerful luminosity of the palette that Filippino employed a large proportion of oil in his tempera binder.

Filippino Lippi
The Vision of St Bernard, c. 1486
Tempera on wood, 210 x 195 cm. Florence, Badia Fiorentina

Luca Signorelli
Portrait of a Lawyer, c. 1490–1500
Oil on wood, 50 x 32 cm
Berlin, Gemäldegalerie, Staatliche
Museen zu Berlin – Preußischer
Kulturbesitz

Luca Signorelli
The Damned Cast into Hell, 1499–1503
Fresco (detail), total width c. 670 cm
Orvieto, Duomo, Cappella di San Brizio

# LUCA SIGNORELLI
## C. 1450–1523

Whereas Italian portraiture in the first half of
the 15th century had been dominated by the
strict profile familiar from coins and medals,
Signorelli – like his contemporaries – adopted
the three-quarter view developed in Netherlandish painting, which allowed a greater degree of individualization. In line with his artistic temperament, Signorelli reveals himself as
a cool observer in this portrait of an unidentified man. Despite the small format, he
achieves a remarkable sense of monumentality
through his use of simplified, unbroken outlines and the homogeneous red of the man's
tunic and hat. The facial features, and in particular the furrows around the eyes, nose and
mouth, might almost have been chiselled and
confirm Signorelli's affinity with sculpture –
something also evident in the middle ground
and background.

The painter renounces landscape in the
proper sense of the word in favour of animated figures and classical-style architecture,
portrayed on a much smaller scale far behind
the foreground plane. Of particular interest is
the group of two naked men on the right, inspired by classical sculpture; frequently employed by Signorelli as staffage, they are also
the forerunners of the ephebes in Michelangelo's *Doni Tondo* (ill. p. 167). The triumphal
arch on the right-hand edge of the painting
is the most prominent feature of the background. The narrow side facing the viewer
bears a relief of figures fighting. Rather than
modulating his palette, Signorelli employs
clear contours and strong local colours. The
painting is dominated by the red of the sitter's clothes and the stone-like hues of the
background.

Fra Angelico and Benozzo Gozzoli had originally started decorating the San Brizio Chapel
in 1447, but the commission was only revived
at the end of the century. Signorelli here
reaches the peak of his development, with a
portrayal of the Last Judgement and the story
of the Antichrist on a scale more ambitious
than any previously seen in Western painting.
He reduces the landscape background to a
bare minimum and concentrates on human
figures in dramatic poses. Not until Michelangelo would the sculptural approach at the
heart of Tuscan painting come so clearly to the
fore as in this cycle.

Colour serves exclusively to describe objects
and, more important still, to heighten their
plastic qualities through contrasts of light and
shade. Line is the chief means of composition,
establishing hard contours and clear-cut silhouettes.

Signorelli displays an inexhaustible inventiveness in the positions and angles of his
figures. While echoing the 14th-century Last
Judgement reliefs on the façade of Orvieto cathedral, they are more closely related still to
the genre of the small bronze emerging in the
late 15th century. Signorelli's Orvieto frescos
represent the most important forerunners to
Michelangelo's *Last Judgement*.

# PIETRO PERUGINO

## C. 1448–1523

In the fresco cycle decorating the lower section of the lateral walls of the Sistine Chapel, Perugino's *Christ giving the Keys to St Peter* stands out above all the rest. The painter of expressive and atmospheric altarpieces here proves himself a master of large form and compositional organization. The descending diagonal running from Christ to the kneeling figure of Peter instantly draws our eye to the central event, which is accented further by the octagonal building in the centre background. Piero weights the accompanying groups of figures freely and evenly on either side. While the triumphal arches in classical Roman style in the background are symmetrically positioned on the left and right-hand edges of the fresco, we see them as if set against each other at a slight angle.

The origins of Perugino's art are clearly apparent. In his confident use of perspective, his emphasis upon pictorial zones running parallel to the plane, and the solemn mood of the composition, the influence of Piero della Francesca is unmistakable. The structure of his figures and the modelling of the draperies, on the other hand, reflect the impact of Perugino's first extended stay in Florence, where he is known to have resided as from 1472 and where he worked in Verrocchio's studio. A carefully balanced composition and a tendency towards expansive, as it were soundless backgrounds are stylistic features inherited from Perugino's Umbrian roots, and characterize his entire œuvre.

Executed for the church of Santa Maria Maddalena dei Pazzi in Florence, this panel marks one of the high points of European painting in the late 15th century. It depicts the Virgin Mary appearing in a vision to St Bernard of Siena. The confidence with which Perugino constructs the multi-aisled columned hall and composes his standing figures reflects the fruits of his years spent studying and working in Florence.

In terms of expression, admittedly, Perugino could hardly be more different to contemporary Tuscan masters: his figures appear to be caught up in a dream. Within their balanced grouping, reinforced by the square format, Perugino nevertheless introduces a certain animation: St Bernard's prie-dieu stands slightly to one side of the central axis, while Mary has stepped out of the line of pillars in an indication of her approach. The colours are powerful and luminous, but do not sound the frequently "loud" chord found in the work of Florentine artists. Similarly Umbrian is the loving treatment of the landscape, which unfolds into the distance at the very centre of the composition and serves as a vehicle for the overall mood. Echoes of Umbrian sacred buildings, too, may be heard in the lofty arcades of the architecture.

All the elements of the composition are in perfect harmony. With just a gentle nudge, the spell would be broken and the holy company aroused from its dream – and the threshold to the High Renaissance would be crossed.

**Pietro Perugino**
Christ giving the Keys to St Peter, c. 1482
Fresco, 335 x 550 cm
Rome, Vatican, Sistine Chapel

**Pietro Perugino**
The Vision of St Bernard, 1489
(from Santa Maria Maddalena dei Pazzi, Florence)
Tempera on wood, 173 x 170 cm
Munich, Bayerische Staatsgemäldesammlungen,
Alte Pinakothek

Carlo Crivelli
Annunciation with St Emidius,
1486
(from Santa Annunziata,
Ascoli Piceno)
Oil on canvas, transferred to
wood, 207 x 147 cm
London, National Gallery

## CARLO CRIVELLI
### C. 1430/35 – C. 1500

This panel of 1486 is a prime example of Crivelli's late style. The ostensible subject of the painting, the Annunciation, takes up a surprisingly small space.

There is no direct contact between the small figures of Gabriel and the Virgin, who are separated by the wall of the palace. Their relationship is further interrupted by the figure of St Emidius carrying a model of the town of Ascoli. We have the impression that the angel is talking to the saint.

The eye is drawn instead to the architecture, with its bold perspective features and lavish decoration. Typical of Crivelli is the manner in which his compositions are compiled from copious individual details. Elements borrowed from classical architecture are heaped together without their original character being able to shine through.

Details from the sphere of the still life, such as the peacock on the cornice in the upper foreground, the expensive-looking carpet billowing in the wind and held down by a flower pot, and the two men standing on the parapet in the background, recall Antonello da Messina's painting *St Sebastian* from around 1476 (ill. p. 117).

Crivelli, here still signing himself a Venetian (his signature can be seen at the base of the front pilaster), may have painted this panel during a trip to Venice.

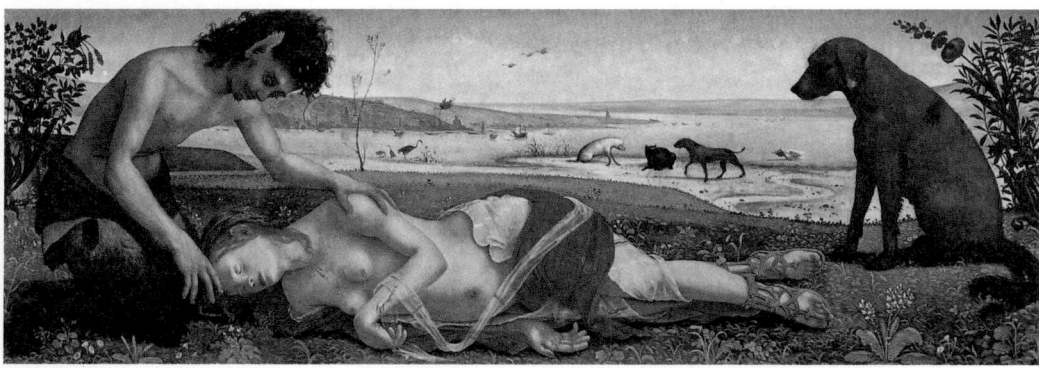

*Above:*
Piero di Cosimo
Death of Procris, c. 1510
Oil on wood, 65 x 183 cm
London, National Gallery

*Below:*
Piero di Cosimo
Venus and Mars, c. 1498
Oil on wood, 72 x 182 cm
London, National Gallery

## PIERO DI COSIMO
### 1462–1521

Despite the different datings they have been given, these two panels may have formed part of a cycle illustrating themes from ancient mythology. Considering that they stem from the hand of a Florentine artist, both demonstrate an unusual interest in landscape. The progression towards lighter colours in the background and the accompanying softening of focus reflect Leonardo da Vinci's new theories of colour.

The upper panel shows the death of Procris, killed by mistake, while out hunting, by a javelin thrown by her husband Cephalos – a javelin which Procris had been given by King Minos and which never missed its mark. The dog on the right was also a gift from Minos.

*Venus and Mars* invites comparison with Botticelli's version of the same subject (ill. pp. 104/105). Both paintings arose out of the philosophical thinking of the Medicean Platonic Academy: the conquest of war by love. Piero's version is much richer in entertaining, narrative detail, and at the same time more sensual: both figures are naked. Here, too, Mars has been robbed of his weapons, and the pair of doves in the foreground symbolize peace. Venus holds the boyish Cupid beneath her left arm, while a hare – a symbol of *voluptas*, or lustfulness – peeps up over her hip.

# FRANCESCO DEL COSSA

## 1436 – C. 1477/78

The scholarly programme for the decoration of the large banqueting hall in the Palazzo Schifanoia was drawn up by Pellegrino Prisciani, a professor of astrology. Twelve fields, extending from a painted plinth right up to the ceiling, were each assigned to one month of the year. Each field is divided horizontally into three zones. The top zones show the astrological rulers of the month in triumphal procession. The narrower middle zones feature the signs of the zodiac and astrological demons. Finally, the bottom zones – twice as high as the middle fields – are devoted to a scene from court life linked to the month in question. The cycle was carried out by Cossa and Cosmè Tura between 1460 and 1470. Only the frescos on the east wall, showing March, April and May, have survived relatively intact. They mark the pinnacle of Cossa's artistic development.

From the freshness of the palette and the relaxed and entertaining narrative style, the impartial observer would never guess that the frescos were based on a strict theoretical programme. Cossa's hunting parties and tournaments are characterized by powerfully modelled figures, confidently foreshortened architecture and numerous quotations from antiquity. In the case of certain details, we must assume that Cossa drew his inspiration from his contact with miniature painting, at that time flowering at the Ferrara court.

Francesco del Cossa
Allegory of the Month of April (overall view), 1470
Fresco. Ferrara, Palazzo Schifanoia, Sala dei Mesi

*Below:*
Cosmè Tura
St George and the Dragon and The Princess,
c. 1470
Tempera on canvas,
413 x 339 cm
Ferrara, Museo del Duomo

# COSMÈ TURA

## C. 1430–1495

These two panels form the outside of a pair of organ shutters which Cosmè Tura, the founder of Ferrarese Renaissance painting, executed for Ferrara cathedral. They open out to reveal an *Annunciation* on the reverse. Their style is typical of a specific school of Ferrarese painting, as distinct from Tuscany as it was from Venice, in which "modern" Renaissance elements are combined with almost medieval qualities in a highly original fashion. St George's battle with the dragon, dramatically intensified by the spiralling sweep of the composition, and the king's fleeing daughter are set against an imaginary, utterly unreal landscape. The figure of the princess is reminiscent of Etruscan models. The nervous lines of the draperies frequently give rise to abstract, inorganic ornament.

The palette is dominated by dark tones; where light values appear, as in St George's steed, they emit a pallid gleam. The overall impression is nevertheless one of costliness, resulting both from the decorative quality of the draperies and, above all, from the artist's inclusion of copious ornamental elements and his rich use of gold leaf.

**Andrea Mantegna**
Agony in the Garden, c. 1460
Tempera on wood, 63 x 80 cm
London, National Gallery

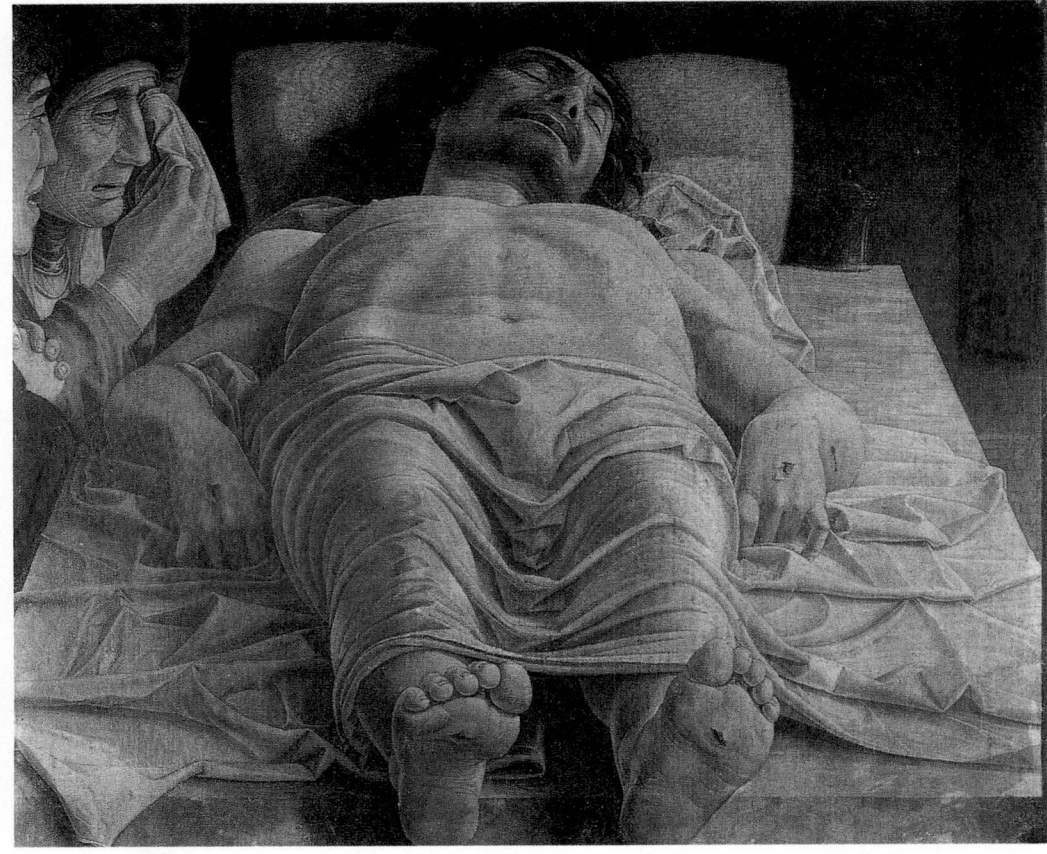

**Andrea Mantegna**
Dead Christ, c. 1480
Tempera on canvas, 66 x 81 cm
Milan, Pinacoteca di Brera

# ANDREA MANTEGNA
## 1431–1506

Mantegna's painting, which although signed is not dated, has been variously assigned to very different phases of his œuvre. The graphic sharpness with which both landscape and draperies are etched suggests a date of around 1460, a period during which Mantegna was still processing the influence of Donatello's Paduan works. The additive nature of the composition, made up of multiple parts, also places the work amongst those produced during Mantegna's early maturity.

The expressive power of the figure of Christ, who faces towards the group of angels in the top left-hand corner, is amplified by the staggered elevation of the landscape in the foreground and background, the upthrusting silhouette of the town and the soldiers seen approaching from the right in the middle ground.

In aligning the main scene along a diagonal descending from top left to bottom right, Mantegna underlines the inescapability of Christ's fate, whereby the disciples sleeping beneath the fissured rock seem to allude to the Entombment. Is the plank which continues the diagonal across the stream intended as a reference to the wood from which Christ's cross would be made?

The mountains in the background and the portrayal of Jerusalem are pure figments of the artist's imagination and show no evidence of having been studied from nature. The panel nevertheless testifies to the antiquarian interests which Mantegna developed during his time in Padua, insofar as the townscape cites individual motifs from ancient and medieval Rome: the Colosseum, Trajan's Column, and the Torre delle Milizie tower.

Already famed in the 16th century as the *Cristo in scurto*, this painting was for a long time admired first and foremost for its extraordinary display of perspective virtuosity. And indeed, a figure presented in drastic foreshortening had never before been seen in Western painting. If we compare this dead Christ with the nearest of the disciples in the panel above, we can see the extent to which Mantegna had perfected his artistic skills. The two works would appear to be separated by almost a whole generation.

To concentrate solely on the technical mastery exhibited in the *Dead Christ* would be to miss its expressive content, however. The wounds seen from above in Christ's hands and feet, the helplessness suggested by his foreshortened upper body, and our oblique view of his slightly tilted head give visual expression to the finality of death in a previously unknown manner. The palette, which borders on grisaille, reinforces the impression of desolateness. The composition seems to exclude all hope of a Resurrection.

The figures of Mary and John, sliced by the edge of the canvas, are painted in a surprisingly coarse fashion and appear clumsily inserted into the scene. Could it be that they were added at a later date?

In 1460 Mantegna was appointed painter to the Gonzaga court in Mantua. Amongst his most important commissions was the decoration of the Reggia, the ducal apartments in the Castello di San Giorgio. Only the frescos in the Camera degli Sposi – the bedroom of Lodovico Gonzaga and his wife – have survived. The loss of the cycles in the other rooms is a reminder of the fragmentary and chance nature of our knowledge of the art and culture of the Early Renaissance.

Mantegna's frescos represent the boldest example of "illusionism" found anywhere in the entire 15th century. Two walls of the room are painted with pilasters and curtains, while the other two depict a contemporary event: the meeting between Cardinal Francesco Gonzaga and his parents in 1472. To understand the significance of the subject in its own day, it should be remembered that Francesco's elevation to the high ecclesiastical rank of Cardinal represented an enormous honour for a family which had only relatively recently risen from being landowners and condottieri to becoming lords of Mantua.

On the entrance wall (not shown), Marchese Lodovico is seen meeting his son Francesco, whereby the life-size figures are lent the physiognomic characteristics of portraits in masterly fashion. They are presented against a mountainous landscape, incorporating a

walled city which – like the Jerusalem in *Agony in the Garden* – is entirely fictitious, but which includes numerous quotations from classical architecture.

The fireplace wall from which the present detail is taken depicts the Gonzaga family in contemporary costume, something which would have made their presence all the more immediate to the spectator. The portrayal of the figures as powerfully modelled "statues" was probably influenced by the work of Andrea del Castagno and his *Uomini famosi* (ill. p. 98): Mantegna was in Florence in 1466 and 1468, and would have been able to study the latest developments in Early Renaissance painting there at first hand. His integration of real and painted architecture is also derived from Castagno.

In Mantegna's frescos, too, individual characters appear to stand in front of the painted architectural features structuring the wall. But Mantegna goes a step further, insofar as certain figures appear to be climbing up into and down out of the picture via a flight of steps leading from the mantlepiece.

Here Mantegna anticipates the playful manipulation of the "aesthetic boundary" (E. Michalski), i.e. the dividing-line between real and painted space, which would become a central compositional feature of Mannerism and the Baroque.

Andrea Mantegna
The Gonzaga Family and Retinue,
finished 1474
Fresco (detail), 600 x 807 cm
Mantua, Palazzo Ducale, Camera degli Sposi

Antonello da Messina
St Jerome in His Study,
c. 1456
Tempera on wood,
46 x 36 cm
London, National Gallery

Antonello da Messina
Virgin Annunciate, c. 1475
Oil on wood, 45 x 34.5 cm
Palermo, Galleria Nazionale
della Sicilia

## ANTONELLO DA MESSINA
### C. 1430–1479

This small panel, executed after Antonello's departure from Messina, shows his close dependence upon Netherlandish painting. In its virtuoso mastery of foreshortening, however, it
simultaneously demonstrates the artist's assimilation of the achievements of the Early Renaissance.

   The painted arch which frames the scene is
a motif taken from Flemish painting and particularly familiar since Rogier van der
Weyden. Gothic architectural elements and
small details from the world of the still life –
the bowl on the front step, the floor tiles, the
view of the landscape beyond – also point to a
study of Netherlandish artists. It was above all
his adaptation of a Netherlandish oil technique, however, which enabled Antonello to
achieve an effect previously unknown in Italy.
By increasing the proportion of oil in his tempera, he was able to apply several layers of
paint, or glazes, on top of each other and
thereby to lend depth and luminosity to his
colours.

   Antonello's panel nevertheless differs from
contemporary Netherlandish works in the disposition of the study, inserted like a monument into the architectural framework, and in
its incorporation of numerous carefully calculated views in what almost amounts to a demonstration of the different possibilities of perspective.

The *Virgin Annunciate* is an iconographically
unusual subject which Antonello painted on
several occasions. The distance separating the
early *St Jerome in his Study* from the present
panel, in which Mary is seen half-length and
without the angel Gabriel, is extraordinary.
What was previously composed of multiple
small details has here given way to a large,
closed form. The figure is contained within a
triangular shape, a geometric tendency emphasized by the folds of the drapery. The composition nevertheless avoids the severity of an
icon. Offset slightly left of the central axis,
Mary appears to be making a cautious
counter-movement with her shoulder and
head. Her eyes are not directed at the spectator but are averted slightly leftwards. Spatial
depth is indicated by several diagonals in the
table, lectern and manuscript, which recede
rightwards into the painting.  Particularly admirable is the "language" spoken by Mary's
hands in the interaction between her extended right hand, its palm in shadow, and
her brightly-lit left hand pointing inwards.
Did Leonardo da Vinci know these hands and
did he vary them in his *Madonna of the Rocks*
in the hand of the Virgin held out over the infant Christ (ill. p. 162)?
   The *Virgin Annunciate* has been called the
chief example of the "severe style" (J. Lauts) in
Messina's œuvre. The delicate glazes making
up the blue of the Virgin's cloak and the differentiation between areas of light and shade,
particularly in the hands and face, date the
panel to the artist's Venetian period. Its closest
parallel is found in the *Sacra Conversazione* (ill.
p. 117).

The works which Antonello produced during a short stay in Venice in 1475/76 mark the culmination of his artistic development. They testify to his encounter with a second, equally important source of inspiration alongside Netherlandish painting: a study of the works of Piero della Francesca.

St Sebastian became a popular subject of altarpieces in the latter years of the 15th century. The reason for this lay not simply in his patronage against the plague, but also because he offered artists an opportunity to portray a male nude in an ecclesiastical context. Antonello's Sebastian is "a Christian Apollo" whose sharp silhouette and sculptural physique, composed of precisely defined, almost stereometric forms, can be traced back to Piero's influence. The buildings lining the square in the background are also resolutely cubic. These sculptural forces seem to crystallize out in the cylindrical section of column lying on the ground – a symbol of the heathenism conquered by the martyr's steadfastness. Here too, the close-up focus and the multi-component structure of Antonello's early works have yielded to the large form.

The artist nevertheless retains his gifted eye for still-life detail: the "contemporary" architectural setting, with the carpets hanging over the parapet of the loggia, and the views glimpsed through the arches beneath are amongst the most exquisite in all 15th-century Italian painting. Antonello also carried his treatment of light a step further in his *St Sebastian* panel, a development again reflecting his exposure to Piero.

Antonello's *Sacra Conversazione*, painted in 1475/76 for San Cassiano in Venice, would establish the pattern of all subsequent Venetian versions of the subject right up to Titian. Sadly, the panel was sawn up in the 17th century and its parts lost or scattered amongst various collections. On the basis of the three fragments which have survived in Vienna, together with other visual sources, it is nevertheless possible to reconstruct the original composition. In the barrel-vaulted apse of a domed church, the Virgin and Child are enthroned on a high pedestal, surrounded by eight saints below. The confident handling of perspective and the balanced but not rigidly symmetrical grouping of the figures recall the *Madonna and Child with Six Saints* of c. 1472–1474 which Piero della Francesca painted for Federigo da Montefeltro. The richness with which Antonello renders the materials and lavishly ornamented costumes is counterbalanced by the strictly geometrical organization governing both overall composition and details, as seen for example in the dominant triangular shapes making up the lower section of the Virgin's robe.

Although there is still argument as to whether Antonello's panel preceded Giovanni Bellini's *Pala di San Giobbe* of c. 1487/88 (ill. p. 120), it seems likely to be the case. It was only after 1475, having been exposed to the depth and luminosity of Antonello's palette, that Bellini entered the new phase of development that would determine his entire future œuvre.

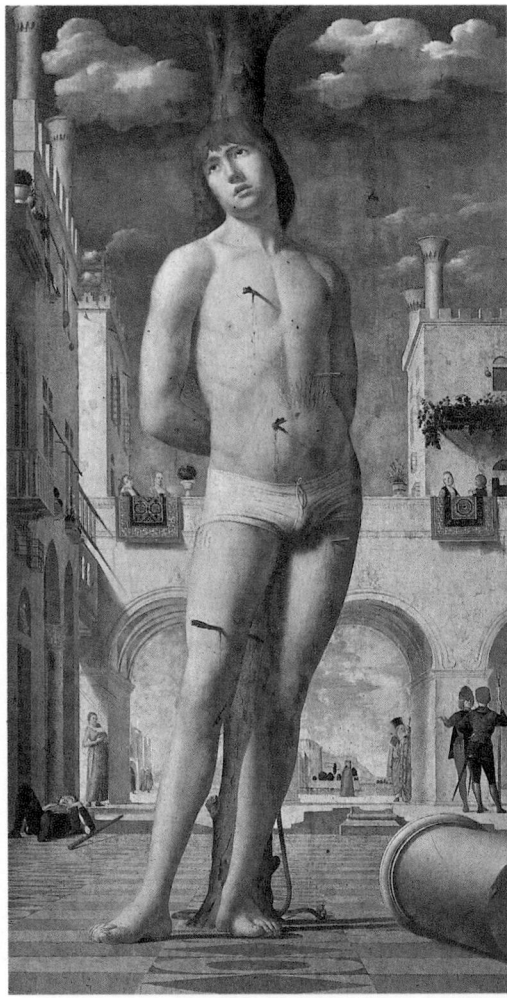

Antonello da Messina
St Sebastian, c. 1476
Tempera on wood, transferred to canvas, 171 x 86 cm
Dresden, Gemäldegalerie Alte Meister

Antonello da Messina
Sacra Conversazione, 1475/76 (from San Cassiano, Venice)
Tempera on wood (fragment). Saints Nicholas and Anastasia, 56 x 35 cm
Virgin and Child, 115 x 63 cm; Saints Dominic and Ursula, 57 x 36 cm
Vienna, Kunsthistorisches Museum

## GENTILE BELLINI

1429–1507

Gentile Bellini, eldest son of Jacopo Bellini and Mantegna's brother-in-law, was official artist to the Venetian government and was ennobled by Emperor Frederick III in 1479.

Towards the end of the 15th century, Gentile painted a series of large-format canvases showing scenes from the legend of the True Cross, commissioned by the Scuola di San Evangelista. The cycle clearly testifies to the legacy of his father Jacopo, but while the elder artist conjured landscapes and buildings out of

his imagination, the younger painted them directly from true life. His fidelity to detail was rooted in the sober distance which he maintained from the object, which thus remained uncoloured by emotional response – an approach well suited for large-scale history paintings.

The procession across St Mark's Square is a visual document of the first order. With his precise eye for detail, the painter shows us just how the piazza looked in the late 15th cen-

tury, before the offices housing the Venetian adminstration were extended. Such is the historical accuracy of the painting that we may take it as a record of the medieval mosaics on the façade of San Marco. Its huge format is lent a systematic structure by the architectural backdrop and by a geometrical stage-managing of the figural groups. For all its fidelity to external detail, however, Gentile's cycle lacks the "holistic" vision underpinning the altarpieces painted during this same period by

his brother Giovanni and marking the transition to the High Renaissance. In its descriptive character, the cycle heralds the birth of the genre of *vedutà* painting which would later become a Venetian speciality, one which would flower at the hands of Canaletto and Guardi in the 18th century.

**Gentile Bellini**
Procession in St Mark's Square, 1496
Tempera on canvas, 367 x 745 cm
Venice, Galleria dell'Accademia

Giovanni Bellini
Sacra Conversazione (Pala di San
Giobbe), c. 1487/88
Tempera on wood, 468 x 255 cm
Venice, Galleria dell'Accademia

Giovanni Bellini
Transfiguration of Christ, c. 1460
Tempera on wood, 134 x 68 cm
Venice, Civico Museo Correr

# GIOVANNI BELLINI
## c. 1430–1516

This monumental panel with its almost life-size figures was probably painted in 1487/88 for San Giobbe church, where its magnificent marble surround can still be found. This surround originally served to integrate the altarpiece into its setting, insofar as it amplified the spatial depth created within the painting (whose upper edge has since been altered) and at the same time established a fascinating interplay between reality and illusion.

The Virgin, Child and saints are here gathered together beneath a coffered barrel vault terminating in an apse. There is no longer any need to structure the enormous panel from without. Even though the poses adopted by individual figures are characterized by a maximum freedom from constraint (e.g. St Sebastian), the composition is underpinned by an overall artistic concept in which each element has its fixed place. This stability is created from inside out, as it were, via correspondences of colour, movement and expression which extend across the pictorial surface and beyond. The trio of angels at the foot of the throne repeats the pyramid formed by the main figures, while the strains of their music seem echoed in the harmony of the composition.

While the luminosity of the palette and the supremacy of colour modulation over drawing point to the influence of Antonello da Messina, they simultaneously place Giovanni Bellini at the forefront of a development which, in the Venetian painting of the 16th century, would grant colour a new role as a compositional means in its own right.

This panel is highly typical of a phase in Bellini's œuvre during which he was assimilating the important influence of Andrea Mantegna. Bellini establishes compositional depth via the receding planes indicated by the foreground, the rocky plateau, and the summit of Mount Tabor with the transfigured Christ between the prophets Elijah and Moses. Since each of these planes also appears above the next, Bellini thereby neatly lends visual height to the mountain.

The disciples, seen asleep or awaking with a start, are portrayed in complex foreshortened poses which testify to the artist's new interest in depicting anatomy beneath draperies.

Bellini's debt to Andrea Mantegna – and hence indirectly also to Donatello's Paduan bronzes – is visible above all, however, in the almost calligraphic incisiveness of his line. This is equally evident in the drawing of the rocks and in the folds of the draperies, which might almost be cast in metal. The palette is correspondingly characterized by strong local colours serving an emphatically representational function.

It is probable that the top of this panel was originally arched and that it featured the figure of God the Father surrounded by cherubim. For unknown reasons, however, it was cut off before 1780.

The new genre of portraiture taking root in Tuscan and Flemish painting in the early 1400s failed to establish itself in Venice to the same degree. Only in the late 15th century, not least under the influence of Antonello da Messina, was the freedom to paint the individual finally won.

This late work by Bellini, dating from the opening years of the 16th century, marks the high point reached by Venetian portraiture at the gateway from the Early to the High Renaissance. The artist demonstrates equal mastery in his treatment of physiognomical detail and of fabrics and decorative detail. Modelling arises exclusively from the interplay of light and shade. There is no attempt to employ conventional means of perspective; the fact that the doge's head is slightly turned is indicated by the strings falling from his hat.

Something of an icon-like quality lingers on in Bellini's portrait in the unspecified nature of the doge's setting, his appearance reminiscent of a marble bust, and his distant expression.

It is difficult to decipher the subject-matter of this scene, which numbers amongst the chief works of Bellini's mature period. Although certain figures – including St Sebastian, St Paul dressed in red and wielding a sword, and the Virgin enthroned – can be directly identified, they provide no clues to the meaning of the whole.

The panel inaugurates a series of partly Christian, partly mythological scenes, the key to which probably lies buried in the corpus of 15th-century theological humanist literature. The present panel is possibly one known to have been painted in response to a commission from Isabella d'Este for a Nativity; unwilling to fulfil the wishes of his noble patroness, Bellini executed a different panel in line with his own ideas.

Attempts to decode this painting have been further complicated by subsequent alterations to the composition. The oriental man at the left-hand edge is a clear addition, since the grass over which he has been painted is visible through his robes. Meanwhile, the figures of Sebastian and Job (or Jerome?) on the right do not share the same quality of modelling.

Bellini shows himself in full possession of his compositional skills in every area. His easy mastery of perspective is demonstrated in the terrace in the foreground, its marble slabs arranged in an artistic and complex pattern, while the qualities of the different materials are evoked in an almost illusionistic fashion. Above all, however, Bellini reveals himself here to be the great Italian landscape painter of the late 15th century. He thereby achieves his spatial depth not with linear perspective but with colour modulation. Following in the footsteps of Antonello da Messina, Bellini arrives at a rich gradation of light which looks forward to the painting of Giorgione.

**Giovanni Bellini**
Portrait of Doge Leonardo Loredan, c. 1501–1505
Tempera on wood, 62 x 45 cm
London, National Gallery

**Giovanni Bellini**
Christian Allegory, c. 1490
Tempera on wood, 73 x 119 cm
Florence, Galleria degli Uffizi

Vittore Carpaccio
Scenes from the Life of St Ursula:
The Pilgrims are met by Pope Cyriacus
in front of the Walls of Rome, c. 1491
(from the Scuola di Santa Orsola, Venice)
Tempera on canvas, 281 x 307 cm
Venice, Galleria dell'Accademia

# VITTORE CARPACCIO

## c. 1455/65–1526

Alongside Hans Memling's *Martyrdom of St Ursula* (ill. p. 131), the nine large canvases which Carpaccio executed for the confraternity of St Ursula in Venice represent the most detailed treatment of the legend of St Ursula in Early Renaissance painting. Carpaccio's approach to history painting is directly related to that of his teacher Gentile Bellini, although without the absolute fidelity to background setting and architecture. While Bellini painted his native city of Venice, Carpaccio had to portray the various stops along the pilgrimage from England to Rome made by St Ursula and her betrothed, none of which he knew at first hand. Although the present scene, in

which the couple are met by the Pope, takes place against the backdrop of the Castel Sant'Angelo, the latter is set amidst the hills of the Venetian mainland. The artist would have seen the castle in drawings or engravings of Roman monuments.

Carpaccio creates order within his large canvas using similar compositional means as his teacher: the main group of figures in the foreground, aligned parallel to the plane, is bounded to the left and right by other groups leading into the background. The solid block of the Castel Sant'Angelo is linked to the foreground by the row of flags, which simultaneously connect the front and rear, top and bottom of the canvas. In contrast to the severe style of Bellini the painter-chronicler, Carpaccio treats details with an imaginative flair and employs a cheerful palette.

# JAN VAN EYCK

C. 1390–1441

Jan van Eyck painted this wedding portrait of Giovanni Arnolfini, a merchant from Lucca who was based in Flanders, in 1434. The painter clearly attended the marriage celebration, since an inscription on the back wall between the chandelier and the mirror reads: "Johannes de eyck fuit hic 1434" (Jan van Eyck was here 1434). The convex mirror, which is framed by small medallions depicting scenes from the Passion, shows the two main figures from behind and two smaller male figures from the front – an ingenious way of reflecting the spectator's side of the room into the painting.

The composition is symmetrical in layout, with the central axis emphasized by the chandelier, the mirror, the couple's joined hands and the dog in the foreground. Spatial depth is created less by vanishing lines than by the way in which figures and objects overlap. The foreshortened side walls are repeatedly reinterpreted in verticals.

The faces of the two figures, who are wearing contemporary dress, are surprisingly lacking in the individuality associated with portraiture. By contrast, smaller details exude all the more "personality": the shimmering chandelier in which a single wedding candle is still burning, for example, together with the mirror, the clothes, the rug, and the window at the left, with its glimpse of the world beyond. Jan van Eyck thereby lends his materials – fur, velvet, silk, linen head-dress, dog's coat – an almost tangible quality.

Nicolas Rodin, Chancellor of Burgundy and Brabant and employed by Philip the Good as from 1422, commissioned this panel for the collegiate church in Autun. The donor is the same size as the Virgin before whom he kneels in supplication. His face is clearly a portrait and he is dressed in a brocade coat rendered in highly naturalistic detail. The room in which the scene takes place appears to be located in a tower and is decorated with princely splendour. The artist largely renounces vanishing lines and instead organizes the foreground figures and arches parallel to the plane. Two figures seen from behind on the crenellated parapet outside lead the eye to a lower-lying landscape, through which a river meanders away towards a distant range of hills. This type of landscape, seen from a superior vantage point, forms one of the roots of the "global landscape" which developed as from the early 15th century.

The modern viewer must guard against explaining these features purely in terms of a new approach to reality, however. Van Eyck's painting clearly draws upon 12th-century treatises on the Virgin Mary and the Song of Solomon by Honorius Augustodunensis, which provided the literary source of such details as the setting in a tower overlooking the town, the crenellated battlement, the course of the river, the snow-capped mountains in the background and even the activities of the town's inhabitants. Artistic innovation and iconographical tradition cannot be seen as independent of each other.

**Jan van Eyck** ✔
Giovanni Arnolfini and His Wife Giovanna Cenami (The Arnolfini Marriage), 1434
Tempera on wood, 82 x 60 cm
London, National Gallery

*Below:*
**Jan van Eyck**
The Virgin of Chancellor Rolin, 1434–1436
Oil on wood, 66 x 62 cm
Paris, Musée National du Louvre

# JAN VAN EYCK
## C. 1390–1441

Jan or Hubert van Eyck
Madonna in a Church, c. 1437–1439
Oil on wood, 31 x 14 cm
Berlin, Gemäldegalerie, Staatliche Museen
zu Berlin – Preußischer Kulturbesitz

*Below:*
Jan van Eyck
The Virgin and Child in a Church, 1437
(central section of a portable altar)
Oil on wood, 27.5 x 21 cm
Dresden, Gemäldegalerie Alte Meister

While the modelling and the serpentine pose of the Madonna are indebted to the International Gothic, the church interior is characterized by an extraordinary wealth of keenly observed detail. Despite certain inconsistencies within the perspective system – Mary is portrayed on a disproportionately large scale – the painter creates a powerful impression of space, not least by positioning the outsized figure of the Virgin in the middle of the nave. The interior clearly belongs to the sphere of the Burgundian Gothic. In contrast to Italy, the northern artist's interest in individual detail is clearly apparent.

The panel below, once the central section of a portable altar, demonstrates a new freedom in its handling of space. The Virgin is portrayed deep inside the church interior, its depth emphasized by the receding flight of different-coloured columns. In comparison to the *Madonna in a Church*, the size ratio between architecture and figures is more natural, while the architecture itself belongs to a more advanced style. Purely Gothic forms have given way to Renaissance elements: the plinths and pillars now have a base, shaft and capital; the rounded has replaced the pointed arch; and the horizontals over the arcades are emphasized. In his rendering of the material qualities of the carpets, canopy and ornament, Jan van Eyck reaches the pinnacle of his abilities.

The Ghent Altar represents the founding work of Netherlandish Early Renaissance painting. In its open position, the central section shows the approximately life-size figure of Christ (or God the Father?) between Mary, intercessor for humankind at the Last Judgement, and John. Underneath we see the inhabitants of the City of God adoring the Lamb. Common to all four panels are their exquisitely luminous colours and their painstaking reproduction of details – sumptuous robes, sparkling jewels, and individual facets of the landscape and architecture. In terms of its artistic qualities, the Ghent Altar is without rival in painting around 1430.

The altarpiece is unusual, however, in its arrangement of large single figures above a scene smaller in scale and of much greater complexity. Equally surprising is the contrast between the setting in the upper three panels – restricted to a tiled floor – and the sweeping landscape below. Have two different projects here been combined into a single altarpiece? Has the uncertainty surrounding the identity of the central enthroned figure (Christ or God the Father?) in fact arisen out of the belated superimposition of the Holy Ghost and God the Father above the Lamb (i.e. Christ), lending the whole the nature of a Trinity?

Jan van Eyck
Ghent Altar (central section), 1432
Oil on wood. Virgin and John the Baptist: each
167 x 72 cm; Christ: 210 x 80 cm; Adoration of
the Lamb, 134 x 237 cm. Ghent, St Bavon

**Robert Campin**
St Barbara, 1438
(right wing of a triptych)
Tempera on wood, 101 x 47 cm
Madrid, Museo del Prado

**Robert Campin**
Portrait of a Man, c. 1435
Tempera on wood, 41 x 28 cm
London, National Gallery

# ROBERT CAMPIN
## C. 1380–1444

While not all doubt has been finally removed, the painter long known as the Master of Flémalle is now generally accepted to have been Robert Campin, Rogier van der Weyden's teacher. No other Netherlandish painter of the early 15th century dedicated himself so passionately to the perspective study of receding interiors. The composition of the present painting, which forms the right-hand wing of a triptych, is deliberately oriented towards the central panel to its left. A host of vanishing lines leads from the right-hand foreground to the window rear left, whereby the tiled floor, the fireplace, the sideboard, the open shutters, the ceiling beams and, in particular, the unusually long bench with its eye-catching red cushions all combine to draw the eye into the depths. The figure of St Barbara, ostensibly the main theme of the painting, is thereby relegated to second place: the true subject of this panel is space itself!

Unlike his Italian contemporaries, however, Robert Campin bases his perspective system not on mathematical calculations but on "personal" experience. Thus the floor and the ceiling, for example, have very different vanishing points. The room nevertheless seems to accelerate away into the depths of the composition in what has been graphically described as a "precipitous" fashion.

The artist strikingly omits all reference to feudal or sacred architecture. St Barbara is presented in a purely middle-class interior, whereby the painter's painstaking attention to detail is directed towards everyday objects, not the trappings of court life.

The winged altar, painted in 1438, is also known as the Werl Altar after its donor, and is the only dated work by Campin. The central panel is today lost; the left-hand wing shows the donor, Heinrich von Werl, kneeling beside John the Baptist.

Alongside Jan van Eyck, Robert Campin embraced the new genre of portraiture with a fervour matched by no other painter north of the Alps at the beginning of the 15th century. Campin thereby respected the opportunity it offered for capturing an individual likeness (even by the time of Rogier van der Weyden, a certain degree of stylization had begun to set in.)

The present portrait is characterized by a tendency towards three-dimensional modelling and by the observation of even the smallest detail, typically illustrated in the differentiated treatment of the eyes and the mouth. It is thereby conceived in relation to a female pendant also housed in London,

While the palette is limited to a small number of dominant hues, the artist nevertheless achieves a range of extremely delicate nuances through the use of light and shade. The treatment of the different textures of skin, fabric and fur collar renders them almost tangible.

A surprising feature of this portrait is the manner in which the half-length figure is firmly held between all four edges of the panel, whereby his red head-dress extends beyond the top and the right-hand side of the composition.

# ROGIER VAN DER WEYDEN
c. 1400–1464

This *Sacra Conversazione* may have been painted in 1450, the year in which Rogier visited Rome. Iconographical details indicate that it was probably commissioned by the Medici family (Saints Cosmas and Damian on the left were the Medici's patron saints, and a modified Florentine lily appears in the coat of arms).

The composition, in which the figures are grouped in a stepped, semicircular arrangement whose gentle curve is restated in the upper arch of the frame, may have been inspired by Domenico Veneziano's St Lucy altarpiece (ill. p. 98). A comparison of the two works nevertheless also reveals the fundamental differences between Flemish and Florentine painting around the middle of the 15th century. Rogier's figures stand close together; in comparison to Domenico's distinctly separate figures, Peter and John here appear directly connected. Their proportions are elongated (compare, for example, the two Johns) and they are given solidity more by the outlines of their robes than by the organic structure of their bodies.

In the precision and texturing of his details, on the other hand, as seen in the plants and vase in the foreground, the glass bottle in St Cosmas' hand, and the sumptuous damask inside the tent-like baldachin, Rogier introduced his Florentine contemporaries to what must have been a whole new experience of painting.

Rogier van der Weyden
Madonna with Four Saints
(Medici Madonna), c. 1450
Tempera on wood, 53 x 38 cm
Frankfurt am Main, Städelsches
Kunstinstitut

Rogier was clearly thinking of an altar shrine with carved figures when he painted this panel, something evidenced not simply by the background with the flat moulding and ornamental tracery in its upper corners, but also by the composition of the figures as if in high relief.

Rogier's artistic temperament, so fundamentally different to that of Jan van Eyck, is here illustrated in exemplary fashion. In contrast to van Eyck's intuitive style of composition, Rogier adopts an intellectual approach in which everything is thought through to a remarkable degree. The pictorial plane is structured by means of corresponding or complementary lines of movement and direction, as illustrated in the figures of John on the far left and Mary Magdalene on the far right – mutually corresponding for all the differences in their expression and modelling – and in the repetition of the dead Christ's pose in the fainting figure of the Virgin Mary. Christ and Mary's arms directly trace the two directions governing the composition.

In comparison to the powerfully modelled but, beneath their draperies, relatively undifferentiated figures of van Eyck, Rogier renders his figures in greater detail and allows their anatomical structure to emerge more clearly despite their elongated proportions.

Rogier van der Weyden
Descent from the Cross,
c. 1435–1440
(central section of a triptych)
Tempera on wood, 220 x 262 cm
Madrid, Museo del Prado

Rogier van der Weyden
Adoration of the Magi, c. 1455
(central section of the St Columba Altar) from
St Columba, Cologne
Tempera on wood, 138 x 153 cm
Munich, Bayerische Staatsgemäldesammlungen,
Alte Pinakothek

# ROGIER VAN DER WEYDEN

## C. 1400–1464

Rogier was at the height of his artistic powers when, in around 1455, he painted the *Adoration of the Magi* altarpiece for the church of St Columba in Cologne. He had by now fully assimilated the impressions left by his trip to Italy ten years earlier. The central panel of the *Adoration* is flanked on the left by an *Annunciation* and on the right by the *Presentation of Christ in the Temple*.

The composition of the present panel demonstrates a masterly balance between freedom and discipline. The Virgin and Child are shifted slightly to the left of the middle axis, which appears to run through the central pillar and down into the hat of the kneeling king. In fact, however, even these two details lie slightly left of centre. This left-hand bias is compensated by the figures of the second kneeling king and the third, youngest king, visually strongly accented by his expansively angled pose. The asymmetrical ruins of the stable correspond precisely to the composition of the main group. Insofar as Rogier arranges his figures from left to right in the style of a relief and orients his architecture parallel to the pictorial plane, he remains true to the principles underlying his *Descent from the Cross*. Here, however, he displays a more sovereign mastery of the organic structuring of the human figure and the partial creation of spatial depth.

The central panel of the Braque triptych shows Christ between the Virgin Mary and the half-length figure of John the Evangelist; the left-hand wing portrays John the Baptist, and the right-hand wing Mary Magdalene. The exterior, today in poor condition, bears the coat of arms of the donor and the names Braque and Barban. Since Jehan Braque, a Tournai knight, died in 1452, and since "un tableau à cinq ymaiges" is mentioned in the estate of his wife Cathérine de Brabant, this altarpiece can probably be dated to 1452 or thereabouts. Triptychs featuring half-length figures were previously unknown north of the Alps, although they had been familiar in Italy since the 13th century. In this respect, the Braque altarpiece reflects another of the influences to which Rogier was exposed during his visit to Italy.

Rogier describes the figure of Mary Magdalene in unbroken contours which emphasize the various components of her body. The three-quarter view must be seen in conjunction with the other two panels. In place of complex folds of drapery, we are struck by the ornamental pattern decorating the red and gold fabric of her sleeve.

The collected, introspective expression on Mary Magdalene's face matches the calm mood of the landscape stretching far into the distance. On the right-hand edge of the panel rises a steep rock; corresponding to the head of the figure, it also serves to conclude the triptych as a whole.

Rogier van der Weyden
Mary Magdalene, c. 1452
(right wing of the so-called Braque Altar)
Oil on wood, 41 x 34 cm
Paris, Musée National du Louvre

Rogier's *Entombment* was originally housed in the Medici family's Villa Careggi and was therefore probably executed around 1450 in Florence. Once again, it bears witness to the painter's confrontation with Italian art. The composition is based on a predella panel by Fra Angelico from the former high altar of San Marco in Florence (ill. p. 58), from where Rogier borrows the upright figure of Christ – a pose not commonly found in conventional treatments of the subject – between the Virgin Mary and John, and the tomb inside the rock behind. Rogier nevertheless counters the taut, almost geometric arrangement of Fra Angelico's panel with a freer composition involving a larger number of figures. Christ has been released from the rigorous confines of the central axis. The kneeling figure of Mary Magdalene leads our eye into the picture and, through her connection with John the Evangelist stepping forward on the left, initiates a sequence of movement which is underlined by the oblique angle of the door of the tomb. The angled position of Christ's body, in combination with the three crosses on Calvary hill behind and the shroud spilling forward across the tombstone at Christ's feet, suggests that Rogier is sharing with us a scene in the events somewhere between the Deposition and the Entombment. In comparison to Fra Angelico, the individual detail everywhere supplants the typical – in the physiognomies, expressions and landscape features. As Cyriacus of Ancona noted of one of Rogier's paintings in 1449: "The faces that the painter wanted to show as living we see breathing, and the departed as perfectly resembling a corpse."

Rogier van der Weyden
Entombment, c. 1450
Oil on panel, 110 x 96 cm
Florence, Galleria degli Uffizi

**Dieric Bouts**
The Empress's Ordeal by Fire in front of Emperor
Otto III, c. 1470–1475
Tempera on wood, 324 x 182 cm
Brussels, Musées Royaux des Beaux-Arts

*Below:*
**Dieric Bouts**
Last Supper (central section of an altarpiece),
1464–1467
Tempera on wood, 180 x 150 cm
Louvain, Sankt Peter

# DIERIC BOUTS
## c. 1410/20–1475

In 1468 Bouts was commissioned to paint four
panels, their subjects serving as an exhortation
to justice, for the courtroom of the city of Louvain. By the time he died, however, he had
only finished one painting, with a second in
progress. His work is said to have been admired by Hugo van der Goes.

The episode related in the present panel
concerns calumny. The Empress is denouncing
the innocent Count, whom she attempted to
seduce, to Otto III. She is subjected to an ordeal by fire which proves the Count's innocence. The story is derived from the Biblical
tale of Potiphar's wife, who tried to seduce Joseph in Egypt and who levelled false accusations at him when he refused her. Bouts may
have taken his inspiration from Rogier van der
Weyden, who painted similar subjects for the
Town Hall in Brussels in 1436; these were destroyed in 1695, however.

In contrast to the *Last Supper* below, the
composition is dominated by an extreme tendency towards the vertical, something already
established by the format. The figures are
strikingly elongated; those at the edges of the
picture, especially, serve to visually restate the
lateral sides of the frame and almost seem to
fulfil the function of architectural elements.
Physical volume is thereby entirely negated.
Although an expansive landscape opens up in
the background, the eye is primarily led not
into the depths of the painting, but to the top.
Within Netherlandish painting, Bouts' Justice
panels designate the most advanced point
reached by the Gothic revivalist tendencies
characteristic of larger towns and cities in the
second half of the 15th century.

This *Last Supper* from Sankt Peter in Louvain
forms the central panel of a winged altarpiece
commissioned by the confraternity of the Holy
Sacrament. The painter was bound by contract
to execute the work himself and thereby to follow the directions of two professors of theology.

For the first time, we are shown not the moment when Christ announces his impending
betrayal, but the establishment of the Host.
By its very nature, therefore, it is not a scene
of intense drama – something which clearly
suited the artist's temperament. In comparison
to the masters of the early 15th century, Bouts
undoubtedly creates a spacious setting, but
one which feels more "empty" than solid. The
impression of depth is countered by the verticals typical of the period after 1450, as seen in
the portrait format, the almost bird's-eye view
of the floor, and the many perpendicular elements in the side walls.

The severity of the composition makes the
whole seem less lifelike and distances us from
the scene. The skilfully emphasized central
axis is also the axis of symmetry. The corporeality of the figures is sharply reduced, and the
disciples seen from the rear in front of the
table almost resemble flat planes of drapery
folds. Overall, the panel contrasts sharply with
the sensual wealth so characteristic of the 15th
century.

# HANS MEMLING
C. 1430/40–1494

The carved and gilded shrine in the form of a small church containing the relics of St Ursula is decorated with paintings on all four sides. The two lateral sides each feature three scenes from the life of St Ursula, while the two narrower ends show the saints and the 11,000 virgins, the Virgin and Child and the donors. The decoration of the shrine occupies a central position in Hans Memling's wide-ranging œuvre and demonstrates both his outstanding qualities and his limitations as an artist. His energies are devoted above all to the portrayal of single figures in graceful poses, to the realistic observation of detail, and to an exquisite palette which is often reminiscent of miniature painting. Although Memling is a narrator, dramatic climax is foreign to his temperament even in a scene of martyrdom. He lacks depth of expression and the ability to convincingly "stage-manage" crowd scenes. Instead, he provides a wealth of inexhaustibly varied details which together "add up" into the overall composition. A comparison with Carpaccio's more or less contemporaneous treatment of the St Ursula legend (ill. p. 122) is particularly illuminating.

Memling was clearly familiar with Cologne at first hand, as demonstrated by his accurate portrayal of the city skyline in the background, showing the unfinished cathedral, the distinctive tower of Great St Martin's church and, on the left, the church of St Cunibert.

This portrait is a typical example of the genre and its stage of development within late 15th-century Netherlandish painting. While the variegated marble pillar in the background indicates a rather grander setting than, for example, the architecture of Robert Campin (cf. ill. p. 126), the location in fact plays only a secondary role. Perspective details are lacking, and the distance between the front edge of the picture and the parapet draped with the carpet behind appears to be extremely short. The half-length figure of the genteel young man is correspondingly lacking in physical depth; although seen in a three-quarter view which incorporates the room beyond, the positioning of his hands and the elements of his costume convert three-dimensional space into two-dimensional plane. In place of powerful sculptural volumes and a balancing of horizontal and vertical values, we find here an emphasis upon the perpendicular and a precise observation of detail, both in the figure and the clothing, as evidenced by the differentiated modelling of the eyes, the sensitive, slightly asymmetrical drawing of the lips, and above all by the almost photographic rendering of the fingers. Memling displays the same painstaking care in his treatment of the richly trimmed sleeves.

In providing a glimpse of landscape in the right-hand corner, Memling obeys a convention which was common in Early Renaissance portraiture and which would remain popular even into the 16th century. In keeping our view into the outdoors narrow, he neither distracts our attention from the sitter nor influences the mood of the scene.

**Hans Memling**
The Martyrdom of St Ursula's Companions and
The Martyrdom of St Ursula
From the Shrine of St Ursula, consecrated in 1489
Oil on wood, each 35 x 25 cm
Bruges, Sint Janshospitaal

**Hans Memling**
Portrait of a Praying Man,
c. 1480–1485
Oil on wood,
29.2 x 22.5 cm
Castagnola, Sammlung
Thyssen-Bornemisza,
Schloss Rohoncz

**Hugo van der Goes**
The Fall of Adam, before 1470
(left side of a diptych)
Oil on wood, 34 x 23 cm
Vienna, Kunsthistorisches Museum

**Hugo van der Goes**
Adoration of the Magi, c. 1470
(centre panel of the Monforte Altar; from the
Monforte de Lemos cloister, Spain)
Oil on wood, 147 x 242 cm
Berlin, Gemäldegalerie, Staatliche Museen
zu Berlin – Preußischer Kulturbesitz

# HUGO VAN DER GOES
## C. 1440/45–1482

This panel is one of the earliest surviving works by Hugo van der Goes. The figures of Adam and Eve look back to the Ghent Altar by Jan van Eyck. In his development of anatomical detail, however, Goes goes beyond the older master, whereby he models his figures less with the aid of line and contour and more by means of colour modulation.

The composition is still largely governed by the laws of the plane: Adam, Eve and the serpent, here with a human head, are presented side by side, very close to the front edge of the picture. Together with the Tree of Knowledge, they form a sort of relief layer, set against the foil of the landscape behind. The shady middle ground plays a minor role in visual terms. Only on the right are we offered a glimpse into the far distance.

The miniature-like format is matched by the artist's precise execution of detail: the grasses, flowers and leaves in the foreground are each treated as independent and distinct. The irises, one of which points to Eve's womb, may also refer symbolically to the Virgin Mary. It is interesting that Goes chooses the blue iris rather than the white lily, a traditional symbol of purity in Annunciations, for example.

Although Hugo van der Goes' artistic development can only be traced over a short period of time, it nevertheless spans a wide stylistic range. The Berlin *Adoration* thereby represents the painter's mature phase, and the Portinari Altar his late period. The present panel was originally flanked by two wings showing the *Nativity* and the *Presentation in the Temple*. It is also missing most of the top section which once extended above the figure of the kneeling king, and in which a circle of angels floating in the sky provided a harmonious conclusion to the composition.

In comparison to *The Fall of Adam*, the figures have gained in volume, the spatial organization in freedom, and the composition in inner stability. So, for example, while the three main figures are positioned at different distances from the front edge of the picture, they are planimetrically contained within a triangle. The youngest king standing on the right provides the composition with its internal conclusion. The architecture running at a slant away from the spectator leads the eye into the picture and at the same time lends rhythm to the main group.

The most convincing explanation for this astonishing artistic development would be that Hugo van der Goes made a trip to Italy. In view of the lively trade which flourished between Flanders and Florence, and in particular in view of the personal links between Hugo van der Goes and the Portinari family, such a direct exposure to Italian stimuli seems more than likely.

The *Adoration of the Shepherds*, the most important work by the greatest Netherlandish
painter of the late 15th century, has a unique
historical and artistic significance. The altar
was donated to the Florentine church of San
Egidio by Tommaso Portinari, who since
1465 had been living in princely style in
Bruges as manager of the Medici family's commercial interests. The central panel is flanked
by two wings depicting other members of the
Portinari family and the family's patron
saints, with a grisaille *Annunciation* on their
reverse.

From an artistic point of view, the differences between this work and those of the
preceding generation, and indeed earlier paintings by the same master, are astounding.
While space and anatomy are easily mastered,
they are no longer major themes of the composition. The infant Jesus lies within an aureole
in an outdoor square, surrounded by his parents, clusters of angels and the worshipping
shepherds. The more or less circular arrange-

ment of the figures can be perceived equally in
three-dimensional and two-dimensional terms.
While the figures may have lost volume in
comparison to the Monforte Altar, their faces
and gestures have gained in expressiveness. A
certain impression of spatial depth is suggested by the figures' varying distances from
the front of the picture and by the oblique line
running from the Antique-style column
beside Joseph in the left-hand foreground,
through the manger with the ox and ass, and
on through the buildings in the middle
ground. Its logic is overthrown, however, as
the artist reverts to the medieval system in
which figures are portrayed on a scale directly
related to their importance. Thus the angels in
the foreground are surprisingly small in comparison to Mary and Joseph – a contrast repeated in the sizes of the donors and saints
portrayed in the wings.

Details such as the angels in their copes
and the still life of flowers in the foreground
are executed with an exquisite delicacy unsur-

Hugo van der Goes
Adoration of the Shepherds,
1476–1478
(central section of the Portinari
Altar)
Oil on wood, 253 x 304 cm
Florence, Galleria degli Uffzi

passed in the entire painting of the Early Renaissance.

The influence of the Portinari Altar, which
was erected in Florence in 1478, was felt by
many of the Florentine painters and is reflected in particular in the works of Ghirlandaio and Leonardo.

**Petrus Christus**
Portrait of a Lady, c. 1470
Oil on wood, 28 x 21 cm
Berlin, Gemäldegalerie,
Staatliche Museen zu
Berlin – Preußischer
Kulturbesitz

## PETRUS CHRISTUS
C. 1410/20 – C. 1472/73

This portrait of a young woman denotes a new stage of development in Netherlandish portraiture. The sitter is no longer set against the foil of a neutral, impersonal ground, but is now placed in an actual physical context: it appears to be a room. Direct contact is established between the spectator and the subject in her own environment.

The work bears witness to a stylistic change which took place after the middle of the 15th century. The emphasis upon volume encountered in the portraits of Roger Campin and Jan van Eyck is here sharply reduced. The elongation evident in the proportions of the narrow upper body and head is heightened by the V-shaped neckline of the ermine collar and the cylindrical hat.

The middle-class realism embraced by the generation of artists at the start of the 15th century is here replaced by an element of aristocratic sophistication. The strip of moulding separating the wood panelling on the lower back wall from the plaster above divides the painting exactly in half; with its emphatic horizontal, it provides a harmonious counterbalance to the vertical format and as such forms an essential component of the composition. In the delicate execution and almost tangible textures of the costume, trimmings and jewellery, Christus reveals himself a pupil of Jan van Eyck.

**Geertgen tot Sint Jans**
St John the Baptist in the
Wilderness, c. 1485–1490
Oil on wood, 42 x 28 cm
Berlin, Gemäldegalerie, Staatliche
Museen zu Berlin – Preußischer
Kulturbesitz

## GEERTGEN TOT SINT JANS
C. 1460/65 – BEFORE 1495

Although Geertgen's early death, and the many gaps in his poorly documented œuvre, make it difficult to assess his role within the Netherlandish painting of the 15th century, this small panel, hardly bigger than the page of a large book, gives us some idea as to his importance.

St John the Baptist, sunk in thought, is positioned close to the front edge of the picture, to which he is directly linked by the tumbling folds of his cloak. His figure, although here small, could easily be translated into monumental scale.

The sense of introspection is reinforced by the muted palette of blue and purple. The background setting, one of the most beautiful of the 15th century, appears little more than "tacked on", although it matches the saint's mood in its tranquility and expansiveness; one is tempted to describe it as one of the earliest examples of a mood landscape.

Its extension across the entire picture is a typical feature of the Haarlem School, as is the precise execution of details such as the plants in the foreground, trees and birds. The suggestion of depth contained in the view of the distant city and hills, and reinforced by the paler hues and increasingly blurred outlines of the background, recalls contemporary works by Bosch and also Leonardo's new theories of colour.

## HIERONYMUS BOSCH

C. 1450–1516

Like the *Haywain* triptych (Madrid, Prado) and the *Last Judgement* (Vienna, Gemälde-galerie der Akademie der Bildenden Künste), the so-called *Garden of Delights* defies conventional iconographical categorization. *The Garden of Delights* is the largest, most complex and probably the last to be painted of Bosch's great triptychs and may be called his most important work. Its title dates right back to the 16th century: when it was brought to El Escorial on 3 July 1593, it was described as "una pintura de variedad del Mundo".

The familiar world of Christian art is encountered only in the left-hand wing. In the foreground, God the Father unites Adam and Eve so that they may live in harmony with nature and all its creatures. The Garden of Eden is made up of gentle hills, meadows, hedges and a lake, and is populated by animals and plants, including a number of strikingly exotic varieties. Only the bizarre silhouettes of the rocky mountains in the background seem to point to the possible disruption of this peaceful co-existence. Whether the strange, pinnacle-like structure rising from the surface of the water should be interpreted as a phallic symbol, pointing to the physical delights so openly enjoyed in the central section of the triptych, is a question that must remain open.

Whatever the case, the central panel shows humankind giving itself entirely to the pleasures of the flesh, portrayed in inexhaustible variations which reveal themselves only upon closer inspection. In the middle ground we see

a pond filled with bathers. Its circular shape is emphasized by a train of riders, almost all of them naked, processing in a ring around it. Is this the fountain of eternal youth, a popular subject of 16th-century painting, or a body of water in which the bathers want to cleanse themselves of their sins? In the right-hand wing, Bosch portrays the torments of Hell to which all of humankind is subjected. There are no just and no damned as in versions of the Last Judgement, but only sinners with no hope of salvation. Was Bosch, under the influence of the unrest in the Church and with a premonition that the centuries-old belief in the truth of salvation was about to collapse, giving vent to a profound sense of pessimism? Whatever the case, he paints a demonic, oppressive, nightmarish world of torments beyond number. Below right, for example, a man must endure being embraced by a pig. In the middle we see a monstrous, deformed figure; his body is hollow and he wears a disc on his head, on which small monsters are dancing. His legs, resembling dead tree stumps, stand on two boats. At the right-hand edge of the picture a ghoulish figure is swallowing people, only to disgorge them again straight away.

In our efforts to decipher the content of Bosch's triptych, we should not overlook its artistic qualities. Despite being made up of many parts and small details, the underlying composition of the triptych is nevertheless carefully planned. Paradise and earth are linked by their bright palette and their landscape, sharing the same horizon. The slender stone form in the centre of the lake in the Garden of Eden also reappears in the middle panel – in five different variations. In conjunction with the

Hieronymus Bosch
The Garden of Delights (triptych), c. 1510
Oil on wood, 220 x 389 cm
Left: The Garden of Eden, 220 x 97 cm
Middle: The Garden of Delights,
220 x 195 cm
Right: Hell, 220 x 97 cm
Madrid, Museo del Prado

circle of water and riders, these forms lend a certain degree of order to the initially seemingly impenetrable mass of figures. Hell, on the other hand, bears no relation to the other two panels; in this world of darkness, there is no hope of any glimmer of light. The luminous palette of the left wing and central section has been compared to Persian miniatures (L. v. Puyvelde), while the grandiose portrayal of night in the upper part of *Hell* looks forward to the night scenes of 16th and 17th-century painting.

**Hieronymus Bosch** The Ship of Fools, after 1490
Oil on wood, 57.8 x 32.5 cm. Paris, Musée National du Louvre

## HIERONYMUS BOSCH
### C. 1450–1516

Towards 1500, the foolishness of the world, the vanity of a life of luxury and the secularization of the Church were themes preoccupying art, literature, philosophy and theology alike. A potent illustration of these trends can be seen in the rigorism with which, in 1494, following the death of Lorenzo the Magnificent, Savonarola sought to end the heyday of the arts in Florence. Within the literary sphere, 1494 also saw the publication of Sebastian Brant's satirical portrait of the follies of the world, *Das Narrenschiff* (The Ship of Fools).

Bosch here offers a literal pictorial interpretation of Brant's *Ship of Fools*. People are drinking, eating and making music in a boat. Seated at the centre of the company, significantly, are a monk and a nun. Other figures are calling for yet more wine and food. No one has noticed, however, the devil's mask looking out from the centre of the treetop above the gaily fluttering pennant. The meaning of the scene is encapsulated in the figure of the man dressed in typical fool's costume perched on a rotten bough. The loose technique and in particular the pastel colours of the landscape and sky place this panel amongst Bosch's late works.

Bosch here applies his eerie imagination to the depiction of a saint whom the 15th century generally tended to portray as a contemplative writer in his study. The lion (left) and cardinal's hat (bottom right) simply serve as accessories, as St Jerome himself lies prone with his hands clasped in seemingly vain prayer, surrounded by elements from Hell. Plants, trees and rocks assume anthropomorphic forms. Its nightmarish apparitions, which also incorporate sexual symbols, align the painting with representations of *The Temptation of St Anthony*. The saint's small size reinforces the impression of his helplessness as he is overtaken by the powers of darkness. The religious unrest spreading in the Netherlands in the late 15th century would have exerted a profound influence on Bosch's haunted world.

Opening up in the background is a landscape of the highest artistic quality, which bears no direct relationship to the main foreground scene. There is no continuous development of space from the front edge of the picture into the depths; instead, the eye is led from the main scene over a sharp drop to a plain, which in terms both of composition and colour forms the link between the foreground and the background. Bosch uses a technique not unlike stippling to paint the hills bordering the lake. Contours, too, are softened and dissolved, and the palette lightens towards the horizon.

**Hieronymus Bosch**
St Jerome, c. 1500
Oil on wood, 77 x 59 cm
Ghent, Musée des Beaux-Arts

**Pedro Berruguete**
Court of Inquisition chaired by St Dominic,
c. 1500
Tempera on wood, 154 x 92 cm
Madrid, Museo del Prado

## PEDRO BERRUGUETE
### C. 1450/55 – C. 1504

In Castille in the 15th century, Netherlandish and Italian influences mingled with local traditions, not least as a result of the royal family's passion for art collecting. This late work by Berruguete is astonishing in the extent to which it points the way forward to the 16th century.

We are presented with a richly populated scene viewed at an oblique angle running from front right to rear left. Compositional balance is nevertheless preserved through the use of precisely calculated artistic means: St Dominic, as the main figure, is shifted to the right of the central axis, while the illuminated front of the canopy and the fluttering pennant are presented virtually parallel to the pictorial plane.

While the overall composition may look ahead to the future, it remains indebted in its details to the trends of the late 15th century and even bears certain late-medieval traits. Thus the individual figures and figural groups in the foreground are conjoined in an additive fashion.

The medieval "scale of importance" also continues to dominate over the logical construction of space: the two condemned heretics in the foreground are relatively small compared to the bailiffs, for example, and appear all the smaller in comparison to St Dominic and the members of the court.

**Jaume Huguet**
Last Supper, after 1450
Tempera on wood, 162 x 170 cm
Barcelona, Museu d'Art de Catalunya

## JUAME HUGUET
### C. 1414–1492

The profound social and political differences which existed between Spain's art centres in the 15th century gave rise to a broad range of styles. The present panel by Huguet thereby lies at the opposite end of the spectrum to that by Berruguete above. Catalonia remained indebted to the Middle Ages to a degree unique within the Early Renaissance. In Huguet's altar retables, importance is attached not to the mastery of space or anatomy, but solely to the hieratic representation of the religious subject.

This *Last Supper*, showing the disciples grouped around the table, employs a compositional format dating from the 14th century, in which different levels of height are used as a substitute for linear perspective as a means of indicating spatial depth. Only the foreshortened tiles of the floor, which we see from above, lead the eye some distance into the painting.

The emphatically frontal figure of Christ occupies the central axis and is set against a gold ground richly ornamented with relief. The disciples are organized into equally balanced and almost symmetrical groups. Judas, second from the left in the foreground, is identified as a traitor by the fact that he has no nimbus. We are shown not the tense moment in which Christ announces his impending betrayal, but the establishment of the Host: the cup, the Host and Christ's gesture of blessing make up the central subject of the painting.

# ENGUERRAND QUARTON
## C. 1410–1461 (?)

This unusual combination of the Coronation of the Virgin with a Crucifixion and Last Judgement follows the most exhaustive written programme to survive for a 15th-century painting. The donor, Canon Jean de Montagnac, prescribed its every detail for the painter, including the parity of God the Father and Christ (which probably goes back to a resolution by the Council of Union which met in Florence in 1439), the names of the members of the heavenly host, the portrayal of the cities of Rome and Jerusalem, the vision of Moses in front of the Mass of St Gregory (bottom left), and the inclusion of the resurrected and the dead as the basis of the entire composition. Beneath the cross in the central axis, the donor is seen kneeling in prayer, wearing his Carthusian habit.

Despite the complexity of the commission, the painter succeeds in establishing an overwhelming sense of unity. This is achieved above all by the sweeping robes of luminous red, blue and gold worn by the three main figures, who are grouped almost into a circle. This circle corresponds to the dark, crescent-shaped segment which stands out against the gold ground and which is probably intended to represent the earth. The central axis is firmly established by the crucifix, the exquisitely painted cope of the Virgin and the dove of the Holy Ghost.

In the almost crass differences in scale employed in the various zones, Quarton reveals himself still thoroughly indebted to the Middle Ages. In his treatment of detail, on the other hand, his pronounced delight in realistic reproduction surges to the fore. This is especially true of the small figures in the Last Judgement scene at the bottom of the panel and of the city views above them: Quarton, who had never been to Rome or Jerusalem, uses buildings which can still be seen in Avignon and Villeneuve.

This *Pietà* has only very recently been identified as another of Quarton's major works. It, too, is likely to have been commissioned by Jean de Montagnac, whose portrait appears in the kneeling figure of the donor on the left.

In contrast to the court art of such painters as Jean Fouquet, this important master represented a different school of thought, one still medieval in character, in which figure and space simply served as the visual means through which to deliver a message beyond the rational grasp of the senses. The silent lamentation of the beloved disciple John, the Virgin Mary with her hands clasped in prayer, and the weeping Mary Magdalene holding the jar of ointment are portrayed with the minimum of physical detail. The extensive gold ground, the reduction of landscape to a mere suggestion and the silhouette of Jerusalem appearing like a vision in the background (the domed building has been identified as Hagia Sophia) all combine to detach the scene entirely from this earthly life. The subtly varied expressions of pain on the faces of the three main figures are heightened by the contrasting directions established by the Virgin and Christ.

Enguerrand Quarton
Coronation of the Virgin, 1453/54
Tempera on wood, 183 x 220 cm
Villeneuve-lès-Avignon, Musée de l'Hospice

Enguerrand Quarton
Pietà, c. 1460
(from the Carthusian monastery of
Villeneuve-lès-Avignon)
Tempera on panel, 162 x 217 cm
Paris, Musée National du Louvre

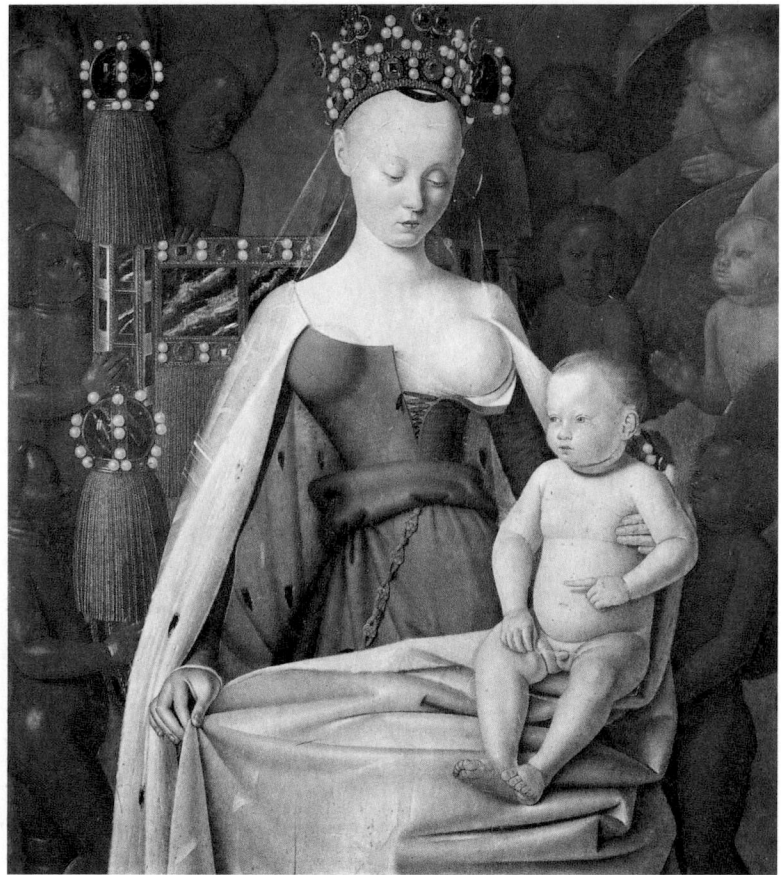

Jean Fouquet
Madonna and Child, c. 1450
(left half of the Melun Diptych)
Tempera on wood, 91 x 81 cm
Antwerp, Koninklijk Museum voor Schone Kunsten

Jean Fouquet
Portrait of Guillaume
Jouvenel des Ursins, c. 1460
Oil on wood, 92 x 74 cm
Paris, Musée du Louvre

## JEAN FOUQUET
### C. 1415/20 – C. 1480

This panel forms the left-hand side of the Melun Diptych commissioned for the tomb of Etienne Chevalier, treasurer to King Charles VIII of France. The right-hand panel (Berlin) shows the figure of the donor being recommended to the Virgin by a saint.

Although the outwardly sacred character of the subject is emphasized by the presence of the angels, the panel nevertheless seems to cross the border into the sphere of the profane. This impression is reinforced by the portrait-like features of the Madonna – the model for whom is traditionally said to have been Agnes Sorel, the King's mistress – and by the exposure and modelling of her breast, a motif not demanded by the subject but possessing an erotic value in its own right.

Here we see a prime example of a work of art hallmarked by the conventions of its social background. Fouquet, court painter to the king, accorded aristocratic sophistication – indeed, affectation – a significance unique in the painting of the mid–15th century. Even the unreal contrast of red and blue in the angels fails to erase the panel's sense of worldliness. The painter shows no interest in the logical composition of spatial depth. Colours are strongly contrasted. In his execution of the ornamental details of the crown and throne, however, Fouquet displays a high degree of sensitivity, evidence that he was familiar with early 15th-century Netherlandish art.

In Fouquet's work, the Italian and French art of the Early Renaissance forge their closest links. The portrait of Jouvenal des Ursins thereby represents the most compelling illustration of this symbiosis.

In contrast to the Madonna in the Melun Diptych, the volume of the present figure has dramatically increased and is reinforced by the oblique angle of his pose – a development which may be traced to the trip which Fouquet made to Italy in the 1440s. On the other hand, Fouquet elaborates his details with an enthusiasm demonstrated by none of his Italian contemporaries. The portrait, which in line with Netherlandish tradition adopts the three-quarter view, shows the artist at pains to render every facial wrinkle and bulge as realistically as possible. The textural qualities of the fur collar and cuffs and the richly ornamented purse hanging down from the belt are also treated in a naturalistic fashion – another reflection of Netherlandish influence.

The thoroughly secular nature of the portrait is emphasized by the gilt architecture of the background, incorporating pilasters, a classical-style entablature and slabs of imitation marble. But while every detail documents the artist's knowledge of Italian ornament, the basic architectural structure is ultimately lost under the web of decoration.

A preliminary drawing for this portrait is housed in the Kupferstichkabinett in Berlin.

# NICOLAS FROMENT

C. 1430 – C. 1485

The present panel forms the central section of Froment's most important work, a triptych commissioned by King René. The wings show the king and his wife accompanied by their patron saints. In line with an iconographical tradition dating back to the Middle Ages, the figure of God who appeared to Moses in the burning bush in the Old Testament version of the story is here replaced by a vision of the Madonna and Child. The fact that the bush remains unconsumed by the flames may be a symbolic reference to Mary's virginity. In the motif of the Madonna and Child the artist takes up the theme of the Virgin of the Rose Garden. At the same time, the angel entering from the left represents a play upon the Annunciation. Various thematic motifs thus come together within this composition.

In comparison to his earlier work, Froment's narrative skills in this panel have developed considerably. The angel turns towards Moses with a lively gesture, while Moses is in the process of removing his second shoe – not a genre motif, but a gesture of humility and respect. In his treatment of details, the Provençale artist betrays the lingering influence of Netherlandish painting; the angel, for example, is one of the most beautiful figures since Rogier van der Weyden. The view of the distant landscape, on the other hand, is a reminder that Froment had also visited Tuscany.

Nicolas Froment
Moses and the Burning Bush, 1476
(central section of a triptych)
Tempera on wood, 410 x 305 cm
Aix-en-Provence, Cathédrale
Saint-Sauveur

# MASTER OF MOULINS

ACTIVE C. 1480 – AFTER 1504

Jean Rolin, son of the Chancellor painted by Jan van Eyck (cf. ill. p. 123), commissioned this altarpiece in 1480 for the cathedral in his home town. While the painting reveals an evident knowledge of Netherlandish art, it is also characterized by certain features belonging specifically to a French Early Renaissance. It is just as far removed from the relief-like composition of paintings by Rogier van der Weyden as from the continuously receding backgrounds found in contemporary Italian works. Instead, the Master of Moulins – only recently identified as Jean Hay (or Hey) – places Mary and Joseph behind the crib and the kneeling angels, with the large-format figure of the donor even further back. The stable area is concluded at the rear by a fence running parallel to the plane, while the landscape beyond is similarly developed primarily from left to right, giving rise to a succession of internal zones arranged one behind the other, yet each acknowledging the two-dimensionality of the pictorial plane.

Verticals dominate, as evident in the details of clothing, stable walls and fence. The overall composition is based on an orthogonal system, giving the painting a "classical" touch. The subtlety of the palette ensures that coolness is avoided, however, with delicate glazes lending the colours a radiant luminosity in an echo of the lessons of Netherlandish painting.

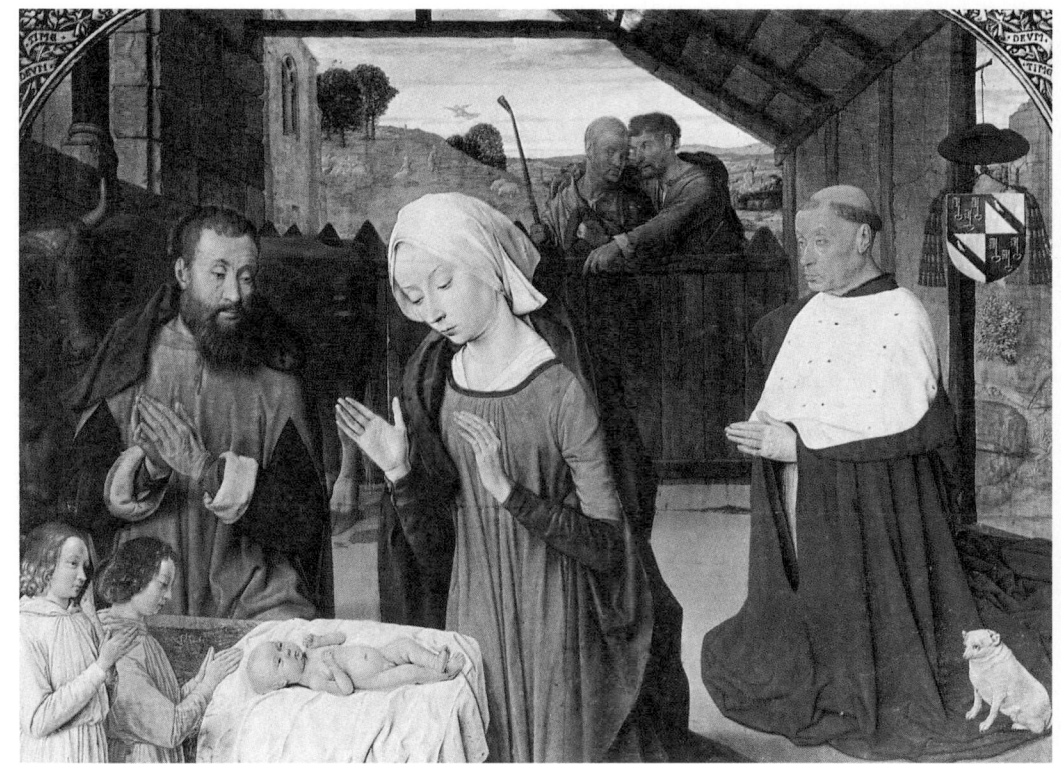

Master of Moulins (Jean Hay)
The Nativity of Cardinal Jean Rolin,
c. 1480
Tempera on wood, 55 x 73 cm
Autun, Musée Rolin

Konrad Witz
Sabobai and Benaiah,
c. 1435
(wing from the
Mirror of Salvation
altarpiece from St
Leonhard, Basle)
Tempera on wood,
102 x 78 cm
Basle, Öffentliche
Kunstsammlung
Basel, Kunstmuseum

Konrad Witz
The Miraculous Draught of Fishes, 1444
Tempera on wood, 132 x 154 cm
Geneva, Musée d'Art et d'Histoire

# KONRAD WITZ

## C. 1400–1445

This panel originally formed part of an altarpiece which Witz executed for St Leonhard's church in Basle. Although the altarpiece, which comprised several such panels, has not survived intact, it can be largely reconstructed. The subjects are drawn from a medieval devotional, the *Speculum humanae salvationis* (Mirror of Salvation), in which scenes from the Old and New Testament are juxtaposed. The events taken from the Old Testament thereby prefigure those in the New.

The present panel with the two knights must be read in conjunction with the panel immediately to its left, which shows Abishai kneeling before David. Together, Sabobai, Benaiah and Abishai are bringing David water from the Bethlehem cistern. The scene was considered the Old Testament counterpart to the Adoration of the Magi. In presenting the painted figure in terms of sculpture, the *Mirror of Salvation* altarpiece was as important for painting north of the Alps as Andrea del Castagno's cycle of *Uomini famosi* (ill. p. 98) for Italy. If this sculptural treatment of his figures suggests that Witz had previously travelled to Italy, the remarkable realism of the different materials of armour, clothes and gold brocade also points to a knowledge of Netherlandish art.

In his representation of these "polychrome statues", however, Witz goes significantly beyond his Italian (Masaccio) and Netherlandish (van Eyck) contemporaries; so much so, in fact, that it has occasionally been suggested that he was also active as a wood carver. No conclusive evidence for this has yet been found, however.

*The Miraculous Draught of Fishes*, the left wing of an altarpiece dedicated to St Peter, ranks amongst the milestones of Early Renaissance painting. For the first time in Western art we are shown a clearly identifiable landscape, namely the shores of Lake Geneva. The distinctive silhouette of the mountain behind Christ's head is that of the Dôle. The fundamental similarities and differences between painting north and south of the Alps can be seen here with particular clarity. While both are devoted with equal fervour to rendering the human body, spatial depth and landscape "correctly", the northerner devotes himself to the individual detail, the southerner to the principle behind the whole.

The powerful robed statue of Christ, and the delicate glaze technique creating the masterly reflections on the surface of the water, point to the influence of Jan van Eyck. The contrast between the animated poses of the disciples and the monumental figure of Christ serves to isolate the latter from his immediate context and thereby emphasizes the miraculous nature of the events taking place.

The heads, damaged in a wave of iconoclasm in 1529, are the result of two restorations. The frame bears the inscription: "Hoc opus pinxit magister conradus sapientis de basilea 1444" ("This work was painted by Master Konrad Witz of Basle 1444").

# HANS MULTSCHER

C. 1390 – C. 1467

The present panel, executed by "hansen muolt-scheren von richenhofen burg ze ulm" (Hans Multscher of Burg Richenhofen near Ulm), forms part of the Wurzach Altar, so-called after the last location in which it was housed. Alongside the works by Konrad Witz, it represents the most important example of a specifically German Early Renaissance style. The reconstruction of the altar, predella and frame remains provisional. Two wings of the altarpiece survive, each with two panels on its front and rear.

The painter here attempts to take reality by storm, not without a certain violence, and with no fear of ugliness or even vulgarity. The prime focus of his interest is the human figure, to which he gives powerful volume. Beneath draperies and clothing, the bodies are modelled with a three-dimensional plasticity which suggests that the artist was a sculptor as well as a painter.

Multscher employs the same forcefulness in establishing the setting. The tomb is angled into the depths of the painting, while the circular group formed by the sleeping watchmen is taken up in the curves of the wooden fence and the trees in the background. Despite a few lingering Gothic references – in the rocky arrête derived from Byzantine painting and the gold ground in the upper section of the painting –, the overwhelming impression is one of realism.

Hans Multscher
Resurrection, 1437
Tempera on wood, 148 x 140 cm
Berlin, Gemäldegalerie, Staatliche Museen
zu Berlin – Preußischer Kulturbesitz

# MARTIN SCHONGAUER

C. 1450–1491

Despite the late year in which it was painted (on its back the panel is dated 1473), Schongauer's masterpiece belongs to the tradition of the International Gothic. On its insertion into its splendidly carved frame in the early 16th century, the panel was trimmed all round, but a smaller-scale copy in Boston gives us an idea of what the original composition must have looked like. It is estimated that the panel formerly stood some 2.5 m tall.

Even though its appearance would thus have been somewhat larger than it is today, the overall impression would still have been dominated by the multiple details subdividing the pictorial plane. Figures, garden seat and rose bower, plants, flowers and birds are woven together into a tapestry, while the gold ground removes all suggestion of a real setting.

Stefan Lochner, in his treatment of the same subject a generation earlier, had placed much greater emphasis on spatial depth and the human body (ill. p. 77). Schongauer instead chooses to concentrate upon the detailed execution of the rose hedge and the ornamental details of the crown – an echo of his study of Netherlandish painting. In the restless, billowing robes of the angels we may recognize something more akin to the contemporary style represented south of the Alps by Botticelli, for example.

Martin Schongauer
Madonna of the Rose Bower, 1473
Tempera on wood, 200 x 115 cm
Colmar, Eglise Saint-Martin

Michael Pacher
The Resurrection of
Lazarus. From the
St Wolfgang Altar,
1471–1481
Tempera on wood,
175 x 130 cm
St Wolfgang, high altar
of St Wolfgang

*Below:*
Michael Pacher
St Augustine and
St Gregory, c. 1480
(cental section of the
Church Fathers' Altar)
Oil on wood, each
212 x 100 cm
Munich, Bayerische
Staatsgemäldesammlun-
gen, Alte Pinakothek

# MICHAEL PACHER
## C. 1435–1498

*The Resurrection of Lazarus* deviates from iconographical tradition in a number of respects.
Firstly, the scene is moved into an indoor setting whose architecture reveals an astonishing
mixture of contemporary forms borrowed from
both the sacred and the secular spheres. Secondly, the narrative unfolds not from left to
right, but from foreground to background. It
is true that Lazarus' sisters are kneeling parallel to the pictorial plane in the foreground,
and that Christ is gesturing in the same direction, but Lazarus himself is seen from behind
and foreshortened towards the rear. The main
lines of the composition reinforce this inward
movement – the vaulted canopy above the
tomb, for example, the arrangement of the
figures into lines resembling a guard of honour, and finally the view through the arch in
the central axis out into the distant landscape.
The New Testament subject is effectively obliged to take second place in this demonstration of the painter's supreme mastery of perspective.

Pacher must undoubtedly have studied the
works of Andrea Mantegna, and the figure of
Lazarus almost seems to anticipate the latter's
*Dead Christ* (ill. p. 114). The principle underlying Pacher's composition points even further
into the future, however, insofar as the vanishing lines converge not upon one central object
or figure, but rather allow the eye to escape, as
it were, out into the open countryside.

Executed for Neustift monastery near Bressa-
none, this altarpiece translates the subject of a
carved shrine into panel painting. It thereby
follows on from Rogier van der Weyden's *Descent from the Cross* (ill. p. 127), but goes far beyond the earlier painting in its optical mixing
of the two genres.

The altarpiece is a depiction of the four
great Fathers of the Church, of whom the second and third are seen here. On the far left,
Jerome is portrayed as a cardinal with the lion
from whose paw he drew the thorn. Next
comes Augustine, accompanied by a child in a
reference to one of the legends surrounding his
life: one day, while walking by the sea sunk in
thought, the saint came across a child scoop-
ing up water with a spoon. In reply to his enquiry as to the sense in this activity, the child
replied that it was just as pointless as Augustine's own attempts to understand the holy essence of the Trinity with his rational mind.
Third comes Pope Gregory the Great, who is
seen delivering Emperor Trajan from purga-
tory, and finally, on the far right, the archbishop Ambrose, busy writing. The dove of
the Holy Ghost appears beside all four saints
as a symbol of their divine inspiration.

The foreshortened floor tiles combine with
the apparently projecting baldachins to confuse the eye, as real and pictorial space seem to
overlap. The virtuosity of the foreshortening is
not matched by the modelling of the figures,
however, who acquire their volume primarily
from the suggestive power of the vaulted canopy above them.

Manfred Wundram

# RENAISSANCE AND MANNERISM

## European painting in the 16th century

In the painting of the Renaissance, Western art reached its absolute zenith. The new intellectual horizons opened up by the natural sciences and the great voyages of discovery, together with the religious tensions of the era and its political and social unrest – all were reflected in painting. The real and the ideal, the secular and the sacred, ecstatic absorption and cool scepticism flourished side by side.

It was Leonardo da Vinci who took the decisive step by abandoning the balance which had previously been maintained between colour and line, and choosing instead to modulate his contours by means of colour. Raphael and Michelangelo followed his example and created forms which would set the standard for the whole of Europe. At almost the same time, Giorgione, Titian, Tintoretto and Veronese in Venice were crafting a new artistic vision in which man and nature were combined into a single unity.

In Germany, painting saw an unprecedented flowering at the hands of Dürer and Grünewald, Altdorfer, Holbein and Lucas Cranach. While in the Netherlands the creative genius of Pieter Brueghel outshone all else, the epoch found its final voice in the religious visions of El Greco.

## The 16th century: an epoch and its names

The era in European art which we call the age of the Renaissance, namely the two centuries between 1400 and 1600, reached its supreme peak in the decades around 1500. It is this brief period that we may term the High Renaissance. In every branch of art, the many and varied means of expression that had developed over the course of the 15th century were now integrated within a single, unifying concept. In the latter years of his life, Burckhardt sought to define this phenomenon. On 18 December 1895 he wrote to Wölfflin that only at the beginning of the 16th century had there been one glorious moment when "simplification and greater economy" had risen to replace "realistic individualization". One year later he again remarked to the Wölfflin: "…you will note – perhaps for the hundredth time – the renunciation of the manifold (even where this was very beautiful) in favour of the monumental and especially the animated." For Burckhardt, the High Renaissance – and in particular the work of Raphael – was the only epoch in recent art on a par with classical Greece. In 1898, his pupil Wölfflin subsequently formulated the term "classic art" to describe the development in Italian art which took place in the years around 1500.

And indeed, at no other time before or since has art come so close to classical antiquity. Its aim was thereby not to imitate the past; that would have led not to "classic" art but to "classicism", as in the late 18th and early 19th century. Rather, it strove to reveal the ideal which lay behind the natural model.

Typical of the High Renaissance, as of all classic art, is its perfect balancing of contradictory – and hence seemingly mutually exclusive – artistic positions. Real and ideal, secular and sacred, movement and rest, freedom and law, space and plane, line and colour are thereby reconciled in a happy harmony.

By its very nature, such a perfect equilibrium of all opposing forces leaves no room for further dramatic development. It can only lead either to stagnation or to its own abolition by the artist. European, and in particular Italian, art took the latter path. It was the very protagonists of the High Renaissance – and above all Leonardo da Vinci, Michelangelo and Raphael – who thereby opened the door to new artistic possibilities. In the sense that its elements can almost all be traced back to the High Renaissance, the subsequent phase in art from around 1520 to 1600 may thus aptly be termed the Late Renaissance. It must be said, however, that High Renaissance ideas were employed by the subsequent gener-

Leonardo da Vinci
Virgin and Child with St Anne and St John the Baptist, c. 1495
Charcoal, heightened with white, on cardboard, 141.5 x 104 cm
London, National Gallery

ations, at times in an entirely new context: the vocabulary was adopted, so to speak, but the grammar was new. Against a backdrop of far-reaching cultural changes, "anti-classic" tendencies thereby began to spread which have more recently been described under the heading of Mannerism rather than Late Renaissance. In attempting to identify binding stylistic categories for the art of the 16th century, the question of an appropriate name for the epoch will need to be constantly rethought.

## Painting around 1500 in Italy

Florence was undoubtedly the centre of the revival in the arts which took place during the 15th century. It was here, between 1400 and 1450, that the Early Renaissance in the narrower sense of the term first arose, and it was from here after 1450 that decisive stimuli went out to the other art centres of Italy. This should not blind us to the fact that the preliminary steps towards "classic art" were nevertheless taken outside Tuscany. Piero della Francesca (c. 1420–1492), who for all his virtuoso handling of perspective was profoundly convinced of the fundamental importance of the plane, and whose "atmospheric lighting" was at the same time highly significant for the history of colour in European painting, is thereby no less important than his fellow Umbrian Pietro Perugino (c. 1448–1523). Perugino's work was unfairly overshadowed by that of his greatest pupil, Raphael, who nevertheless owed him a very great deal. Perugino's importance lay not in his portrayal of expressive figures, but in his specifically Umbrian tendency towards spaciousness, his emphasis upon landscape, his shift away from line in favour of modulated transitions, and above all his understanding of pictorial and mural surfaces as organic wholes which, although they might not yet achieve the fluency of the works of Raphael, marked a vital stage along the path to ever greater fluidity of movement.

In a very similar fashion, albeit with more differentiated means, the Venetian Giovanni Bellini (c. 1430–1516) was treading his own path towards the High Renaissance; in his late works, indeed, he became the only one of the great 15th-century painters to cross the threshold from the Early to the High Renaissance. According to Erich Hubala, Bellini "had been working his way towards the High Renaissance ever since birth… Bellini was born with his compass needle pointing to classicism".

It was not by chance that, around 1500, the emphasis in Italian art shifted to Rome and Venice, and Florence had to relinquish its leading role. The reasons for this were undoubtedly rooted first and foremost in political and social changes. The collapse of Medici rule in 1494 and the rise to prominence of Girolamo Savonarola (1452–1498), a Dominican monk preaching an eschatological vision, brought an abrupt end to the flowering in the arts that had reached its high point under Lorenzo the Magnificent (1449–1492). After Sa-

**Leonardo da Vinci**
Mona Lisa, c. 1503–1505
Oil on wood, 77 x 53 cm
Paris, Musée National du Louvre

vonarola was burnt at the stake in 1498, Florence became the political football of rival forces until the return of the Medici from exile in 1512. During precisely those twenty years in which "classic art" produced its most important works, therefore, Florence was without major patrons of the arts. Venice, on the other hand, passed from the 15th to the 16th century with its feudal ruling class still politically and economically intact, and hence with its market for art uninterrupted. Above all, however, it was the papacy which, having re-consolidated its power over the course of the Early Renaissance, now renewed its efforts to establish Rome as the cultural centre of the Western world. The appointment of Donato Bramante (c. 1444–1514) as architect of the new St Peter's in 1504, the commissioning of Pope Julius II's tomb to Michelangelo in 1505, and Raphael's move to Rome in 1509 set the seal on the city's pre-eminent position in Italian art.

We may nevertheless wonder whether, under different historical circumstances, Florence would in fact have proved

capable of leading the Renaissance to its climax. However inexhaustible the wealth of new artistic forms which it developed over the centuries, Tuscany lacked the aptitude for classical equilibrium; at the heart of all the supreme achievements of Florentine art lay the dialectic principle of reason and emotion, and hence a constant layer of tension. It was no coincidence that, as "anti-classic" tendencies began to assert themselves, so Tuscany would once more return to the limelight.

In the awareness that any attempt at a broad definition inevitably involves simplification and thus approximation, we may say that the High Renaissance in Rome was concerned primarily with form, and in Venice with colour. In the sphere of painting, Leonardo was the only artist who married both at the highest level. At the same time as carrying the realistic tendencies of the 15th century to an extreme degree, he granted the geometry of the two-dimensional plane and the stereometry of three-dimensional space an importance unknown to the previous generation. Leonardo's *Last Supper* in the refectory of Santa Maria della Grazie in Milan (ill. p. 161) overwhelms the viewer with its apparent immediacy. In fact, however, the different perspective systems of real and painted space, the ideality informing even the very smallest detail of the composition, and the monumental scale of the figures ensure that we remain distanced from it. In his panel paintings, Leonardo combines these structural features with a revolutionary new use of colour. Going far beyond Piero della Francesca, Perugino and Giovanni Bellini, he increasingly replaces circumscribing, isolating line – i.e. drawing – with colour modulation. The transitions between figures and objects become fluid. Space is no longer established primarily through mathematical perspective, but by a lightening of the palette and a gradual dissolving of outlines.

Leonardo was the perfect embodiment of the ideal of the universal artist, active in every branch of art and at the same time educated in every field. Yet neither in Florence nor in Rome was he awarded the recognition he deserved. His departure for Upper Italy, ostensibly explained by his many important commissions for Francesco Sforza (1401–1466), Duke of Milan, may ultimately have been prompted by a different, inner logic: he would both be able to further his own development and influence others in the neighbouring art centre of Venice. When, in the work of Giorgione (c. 1477/78–1510) and the young Titian (c. 1473/90–1576), Venetian painting stepped fully into its very own speciality, colour, it was the culmination of a development which would have been unthinkable without the influence of Leonardo.

The other aspect of Leonardo's art, the ideality of form, was taken up in central Italy. In architecture, the centralized building – i.e. one which unfolds regularly on all sides around a static centre – had been increasingly perfected over the course of the 15th century. Its counterparts in painting were symmetrical pictorial formats such as the square and the circle (tondo). The concept of centralized construction dominated not only the architecture of the High Renaissance – the plans by Bramante and Michelangelo for the new St Peter's included pure centralized buildings, possibly in a symbolic allusion to Rome as the centre of Christendom –, but also determined the thinking of painters. Since only a small number of the major building projects of the period around 1500 were actually executed, our knowledge of High Renaissance architecture is largely based on the "background scenery" found in pictures, which we can take as a direct reflection of contemporary building styles. More important however, is the fact that centralizing laws of architecture indirectly came to govern the pictorial composition as a whole: sphere and circle and their mutual interpenetration thereby serve to establish an inner kinship between the construction of the painting and that of the centralized building. In this context, the works of Raphael's mature period, and in particular his frescos in the Stanza della Segnatura in the Vatican, represent the pinnacle of High Renaissance painting.

## Painting around 1500 north of the Alps

Towards the end of the 15th century, with civic culture flourishing at its peak, painting in Germany rose to heights unseen since the miniatures illuminating the magnificent manuscripts of Ottonian and Salian times. In contrast to the earlier part of the century, when German artists were overshadowed by the ground-breaking achievements of their Early Netherlandish contemporaries, the situation was suddenly and astonishingly reversed in an manner which has yet to be explained either in terms of art or cultural history. Did the creative unrest brewing in Germany in the period leading up to the Reformation release new forces in the country's centres of art?

Within this development, the figure of Albrecht Dürer (1471–1528) was of outstanding importance both in artistic and historical terms. Dürer initially remained indebted to the traditions of his teachers, using line as his primary means of expression, and his early work is correspondingly dominated by woodcuts and copper engravings. In 1496 and 1506/07, however, he made two trips to Italy that would decisively influence his art. Like Johann Wolfgang von Goethe (1749–1832) three centuries later, Dürer experienced in Italian art the holistic, organic approach to composition which lay at the opposite end of the spectrum to the art north of the Alps, where painting continued to be understood as the additive combination of individual elements. From the Venetians, and above all from Giovanni Bellini, he learned about modulating contours with colour. Finally, too, he recognized the necessity of a sound theoretical approach to the representation of objects which went beyond mere intuition. His

*Madonna of the Rose Garlands* (Prague, Národni Galeri), *Adoration of the Trinity* (ill. p. 188) – counterpart to Raphael's *Disputà* in the Vatican Stanze – and his *Four Apostles* (ill. p. 187) are outstanding examples of the fusion of the German and Italian feeling for form.

German painting around 1500 spanned an extraordinary breadth. If Dürer started primarily from line, Matthias Grünewald (c. 1470/80–1528) focused on composition with colour. His Isenheim Altar (ill. p. 190), begun around 1512, represents German art's most important contribution to the history of colour. The extent to which Grünewald drew upon the new colour theories of Leonardo and the works of Giorgione is something that deserves closer investigation.

Colour modulation was also the starting-point for the painters of the so-called Danube School, and in particular the young Lucas Cranach (1472–1553), Albrecht Altdorfer (c. 1480–1538) and Wolf Huber (c. 1485–1553), at whose hands landscape painting assumed an importance previously unknown north of the Alps. Confronted with the atmospheric landscapes produced by the Danube School, one

**Albrecht Dürer**
Portrait of Hieronymus Holzschuher, 1526
Oil on wood, 48 x 36cm
Berlin, Gemäldegalerie, Staatliche Museen
zu Berlin – Preußischer Kulturbesitz

is tempted to speak of a first phase of "Romanticism" in German art.

Independent of direct contact with Italian art, meanwhile, a common tendency towards large, balanced form and towards the integration of the real and the ideal was also making itself felt elsewhere in Europe, as evidenced in the mature works of the Netherlandish artist Gerard David (c. 1460–1523), for example. David's works do not open up new avenues for the future, however, but look back to Jan van Eyck in their understanding of the human figure as a powerfully modelled volume.

## Exchanges between north and south

The lively exchanges between the great art centres of Europe are generally considered to have begun with Dürer's Italian trips, whereby the north is widely seen as taking, and the south as giving. This view needs to be modified for two reasons. Firstly, we must assume that such exchanges would have already been taking place in the 14th and 15th centuries, via the heavily-plied trade routes from north to south and vice versa. We know that works by the great 15th-century Netherlandish artists were known and collected in Milan, Venice, Florence, Urbino and Naples. We also know that Rogier van der Weyden travelled across the Alps in

School of Fontainebleau
Gabrielle d'Estrées and One of her Sisters in the Bath, c. 1594–1599
Oil on wood, 96 x 125 cm
Paris, Musée National du Louvre

1450, that Joos van Gent was employed at the Urbino court from 1473 to 1480, and that artists living in the Alps, such as Michael Pacher (c. 1435–1498), established links with Upper Italy. The influence of Netherlandish painting is demonstrable in many examples of Italian Early Renaissance art. We do not know, on the other hand, whether the Italian masters of the 15th century also travelled north. When the

Venetian-born painter and engraver Jacopo de' Barbari (c. 1440/50–c. 1516) settled in Germany in around 1500, and later moved to the southern Netherlands, was he really the first to do so? It is a question which, together with the entire issue of possible Italian influence on art north of the Alps, needs more detailed investigation.

In addition to the migration both of works of art and of individual artists, from the middle of the 15th century there emerged another means of artistic exchange. At approximately the same time on both sides of the Alps, two printing techniques developed into artistic genres in their own right: the woodcut, which developed north of the Alps in the early 15th century, and – more important still – the copper engraving, whose origins probably also lay in the early 15th century in southern German art. The first dated example bears the year 1446. The earliest Italian copper engravings stemmed from the workshops of Andrea Mantegna (1431–1506) and Antonio Pollaiuolo (1432–1498). Prints provided an entirely new means of spreading artistic ideas into even the furthermost corners of Europe. The woodcut and the copper engraving thereby marked the beginning of the development of modern visual mass media.

By around 1500, it may be assumed that prints were available on a wide scale – so much so, in fact, that it frequently becomes hard to judge whether an artist has appropriated a new language of form into his own work as the result of direct or indirect confrontation with its source. Did the Augsburg artist Hans Burgkmair (1473–1531), for example, actually have to travel to Italy, as is generally supposed, in order to paint his *Crucifixion Altar* of 1519 (Augsburg, Bayerische Staatsgemäldesammlungen)? Or might he simply have encountered the holistic compositional approach of Italian art in prints, as recent research convincingly argues? The same question might be asked of Altdorfer. By the same token, we should not underestimate the extent of Italian artists' knowledge of Dürer's graphic works in the early 16th century.

Furthermore, a new, historically documented trend set in as from about 1510 which involved artists moving in both directions. Following the departure of Jan Gossaert (c. 1478/88–1533/36) for Rome in 1508, a trip to Italy became a standard part of every artist's training. This was particularly true for the so-called Romanists of the southern Netherlands. The spread of the Italian Renaissance north of the Alps was in turn encouraged by a number of important Italian painters who spent time abroad, in particular at the French court. Leonardo, who accepted an invitation from Francis I (1494–1547) to live in France in 1516, was followed in 1530 by Rosso Fiorentino (1494–1540) and one year later by Francesco Primaticcio (1504–1570) from Bologna. Rosso Fiorentino and Primaticcio's joint decoration of Fontainebleau palace would subsequently exert a profound influence even beyond the borders of France.

By the time European art began to experience this process of internationalization, however, the unity of the High Renaissance was already dissolving in a whirl of countercurrents.

## Begin of the Late Renaissance

The great works of the Renaissance – Leonardo's *Last Supper* (ill. p. 161), Raphael's *School of Athens* (ill. p. 172), Giorgione's *Sleeping Venus* and Dürer's *Adoration of the Trinity* (ill. p. 188) and *Four Apostles* (ill. p. 187), for example – give the impression that they are definitive and complete in themselves, leaving no room for further development. It would be a misunderstanding, however, to view their progression as a more or less static line rather than as a sweeping curve. All these outstanding masters grew out of the traditions of the late 15th century, orchestrated their pictorial forces into a "classic" harmony and ultimately paved the way towards a new era in art. Their greatness lies not least in their power to transform, enabling them to confront and resolve ever new problems of composition.

For the twenty brief years of his artistic career, Raphael – whose work may be seen as the purest embodiment of the ideals of the High Renaissance – trod a path which took him, with an absolute inner logic, through a succession of entirely different landscapes. Having carried the High Renaissance to its supreme peak and defined it for all time in his frescos for the Stanza della Segnatura in the Vatican, he immediately proceeded to explore entirely new avenues in the neighbouring Stanza dell'Eliodoro. Compare, for example, the *School of Athens* with the *Expulsion of Heliodorus*: although their underlying compositional principles are related, the two scenes can only be described in downright contradictory terms, whereby we should not overlook the very different dramatic character of the events they depict. In the *Expulsion of Heliodorus*, we are immediately struck by Raphael's renunciation of harmoniously calculated proportions approximated to correspond with the semicircular format. Above all, however, the artist abandons the central point of focus towards which, in the *School of Athens*, all lines lead, and replaces it with a centrifugal composition which creates a powerful suggestion of recession in the perpendicular middle axis. The previously equal balance between plane and space is now tipped in favour of the third dimension.

The movement from foreground to background is accelerated by rapid switches between light and shade, whereby the harmony of line and colour simultaneously begins to yield to painterly effect. *The Release of St Peter*, also in the Stanza dell'Eliodoro, explores the same direction. For the first time in the history of the subject in art, Raphael takes the words of the Acts of the Apostles literally: "And all at once an angel of the Lord stood there, and the cell was ablaze with light... [Peter] followed him out, with no idea that the angel's intervention was real: he thought it was just a vision." Reality and supernatural experience here part com-

**Raphael**
Pope Leo X with Cardinals Giulio de' Medici
and Luigi de' Rossi, 1518/19
Oil on wood, 154 x 119 cm
Florence, Galleria degli Uffizi

pany, and the representation of painted light originating from within the picture marks a turning-point in the development of colour in Italian painting.

Raphael's journey culminated both logically and chronologically in his last work, *The Transfiguration* (ill. p. 172). The balanced weighting of the *School of Athens* here gives way to asymmetrical arrangement, while highly dynamic gestures and movements create a new form of pictorial unity which the spectator must actively assimilate. Raphael distinguishes between the two different planes of reality – that of the miracle and that of the earthly zone below – in the treatment of his figures and in the handling of his pictorial means. In the language of Wölfflin, there takes place in Raphael's œuvre a development from closed to open form, from plane to recession, from unity to multiplicity.

With the exception of the sculptures produced when he was barely thirty, such as the *David* (1501–1504), the œuvre of Michelangelo is the hardest to correlate with the normative ideals of the High Renaissance. Michelangelo was already overstepping the bounds of the High Renaissance in his frescos for the ceiling of the Sistine Chapel in the Vatican

(1508–1512). Contrary to first impressions, the enormous cycle does not obey a single system of perspective, but is composed "multi-perspectivally" with individual sections each obeying their own laws. The striking contrasts in scale evident between the Sibyls and Prophets, the ignudi (the naked young men), and the figures in the story of Creation remove any impression of a closed order. The boundaries between architecture, sculpture and painting have become transparent. In the figures of the ignudi, Michelangelo liberates himself from the constraints of iconographical tradition both in terms of form and content. In the urgently increasing freedom which he grants to pose and movement, Michelangelo's future path lies revealed: the representation of the human figure as a statement of personal experience and suffering.

Leonardo, the oldest member of the great triumvirate of the Italian Renaissance, also crossed the border from the High to the Late Renaissance in his last works, insofar as he allowed his figures and objects to recede as if behind a veil – a technique which Vasari called *sfumato* (It. *sfumare* = to soften, shade off). In this Leonardo contradicted a fundamental principle of the High Renaissance that he had himself helped to establish: "classic art" was characterized not least by daylight clarity and tangibility.

North of the Alps, a tendency towards cool distance and scepticism, especially in portraiture, began to emerge amongst the younger members of Dürer's generation, in particular Hans Holbein (c. 1497/98–1543) and Hans Baldung Grien (c. 1484/85–1545), as well as in Altdorfer's late works. Hand in hand with this trend went a growing interest in secular subjects – Holbein's *Madonna of Mercy* (ill. p. 195) of 1528/29 would be his last religious painting! Erotic scenes, foreign neither to the Early Renaissance nor to the Middle Ages, assumed a previously unknown importance, particularly since they were frequently treated outside the mythological context to which they had traditionally been confined – another indication of the crack in the holistic vision which had been one of the foundations of the High Renaissance.

## Mannerism: a name and a misnomer

The term Mannerism which is today widely used to describe the art of the Late Renaissance can be traced back, like the terms Gothic and Renaissance, to Vasari's *Lives of the Artists*, a selection of biographies of Italian artists from Cimabue to Vasari's own times, first published in 1550 and reprinted in a second, expanded edition in 1568. In his book Vasari wrote of Michelangelo's *maniera*, by which he simply meant "manner" in the sense of "style". Understood in this light, Michelangelo's *maniera* can indeed to be said to have influenced not just the 16th century but much of the Baroque era, too. Having a similar sound but a different meaning was the concept of *manière* which had existed in the history of French literature since the late Middle Ages. *Manière* denoted behaviour in accordance with one's social standing, and thus lay at the root of our own phrase "to have good manners".

Both words thus started out with thoroughly positive connotations. During the transition from the late Baroque era to early Neoclassicism in the second half of the 18th century, however, they came to be used in a derogatory sense to imply behaviour that was "mannered", in other words artificial, exaggerated and even peculiar. In the late 19th century, art historians adopted "Mannerism" as a pejorative term for the trends in art from around 1520 to 1600 which, from the standpoint of a classicist aesthetic, were perceived as corruptions of the High Renaissance. Since the opening years of the 20th century, however, recognition of the profound artistic innovations wrought by Mannerism has led the term once again to be used in an increasingly positive sense.

As a name for a stylistic phenomenon in European art, Mannerism nevertheless remains problematical. The common foundation of the art of the 16th century was the High Renaissance, even if its ideals and standards were frequently exceeded or even destroyed. In this respect, it was an era which virtually made contradiction one of its principles. It is nevertheless impossible to formulate a succinct definition of Mannerism – unless it be within a very general framework, reduced to the common denominator of contradiction or the self-contradictory. Rather than use the term Mannerism, we might more cautiously speak of a broad range of "mannerisms" in the art of the years between 1520 and 1600, whereby it should be remembered that the centre of European art in the 16th century, Venice, and its most important representative, Titian, both largely defy such categorization.

## Forms of the Late Renaissance

By its very nature, representational art can capture either just one specific moment or, in what is known as continuous representation, several moments occurring in chronological succession. For the first time in the history of Western art, however, the painting and sculpture of the 16th century made the visual suggestion of movement their primary challenge. In painting, this particularly affected subjects involving the dimension of time, such as Ascensions of Christ or the Virgin, Depositions and Entombments. This development began during a period generally still identified as the High Renaissance. Its grandiose beginnings were provided by Titian's *Assumption of the Virgin* painted for Santa Maria Gloriosa dei Frari in Venice in 1516–1518, and Raphael's contemporaneous *Transfiguration* of 1517–1520.

Michelangelo Buonarroti
Damned soul descending into Hell
Detail from the Last Judgement, 1536–1541
Fresco, 1375 x 1220 cm (total size)
Rome, Vatican, Sistine Chapel

**Titian**
Portrait of a Bearded Man ("Ariosto"), c. 1512
Oil on canvas, 81.2 x 66.3 cm
London, National Gallery

Just how strongly the painting of the 16th century was gripped by the desire to render movement visible is demonstrated by the fact that it introduced a chronological dimension even into those pictorial themes which, by their very nature, seemed destined to remain static and still. This can be seen, for example, in *Sacra Conversazione* paintings of the Virgin and Child surrounded by saints. The *Madonna della Arpie* (1517; Florence, Galleria degli Uffizi) by Andrea del Sarto (1486–1530), Titian's *Pesaro Madonna* (1519–1526; Venice, Santa Maria Gloriosa dei Frari) and, already bordering on the eccentric, the *Madonna di San Gerolamo* (c. 1530; Parma, Pinacoteca) by Correggio (c. 1489–1534) herald the start of a development in which figures, while retaining their traditional air of introspective contemplation, are grouped within a dynamic circular or ascending compositional structure.

Florence now once again assumed a leading role. Returned to political stability and freed from the demand for classical equilibrium, the dialectic Florentine nature rose to the challenge of creating an art in which the contradictory was no longer integrated, but exposed in all its tensions. Under the leadership of Pontormo (1494–1556) and Rosso Fiorentino, Florentine Mannerism would make its influence felt far beyond the borders of Tuscany. In his *Visitation* (c. 1530;

Carmignano church, near Florence), Pontormo transformed a traditionally stately theme into an incessantly turning "roundelay" which, for all its stylistic differences, is closely related in its basic organization to Titian's *Christ Crowned with Thorns* (ill. p.178) of 1576.

Closely related to the challenge of rendering movement visible was the 16th century's new approach to space. Both in architecture and painting, the Early and High Renaissance had established clear, defined space; in contrast to the diaphanous – i.e. largely dematerialized and transparent – wall systems employed in the Gothic era, the limits of space were experienced as finite and provided the viewer with a secure framework and a fixed point. In the course of the 16th century, however, the nature of pictorial space underwent a profound transformation. The two opposite poles of this development can be seen in Leonardo's *Last Supper* of 1496–1498 and the version which Tintoretto (1518–1594) painted a century later (1592–1594; Venice, San Giorgio Maggiore).

For all his virtuoso handling of perspective, Leonardo always keeps in sight the conditions imposed by the two-dimensional plane; Tintoretto, on the other hand, not only allows his space to recede into depths which the eye can no longer clearly grasp, but at the same time removes its lateral boundaries: space loses all rationally comprehensible dimension.

This development can be broken down into a series of chronological stages. In the first step, the balance between plane and space is relinquished in favour of the dominance of space. In a second stage, pictorial space is expanded seemingly to infinity; in many cases, the eye is drawn with confusing speed along a straight line in the central axis far into the depths of the painting. Instead of alighting upon a final "goal", however, it is left to lose itself in the distance. (Just how close painting can come to architecture in this respect is revealed by a comparison of Tintoretto's scenes from the legend of St Mark in Venice and the Uffizi in Florence, begun by Vasari in 1560.) Finally, not only is pictorial space granted unlimited depth, but its lateral boundaries are made permeable.

Painters north of the Alps used different means to create the impression of infinite space, since they did not have at their disposal the various methods of foreshortening which had been increasingly refined in Italy over the course of the 15th century. They developed instead a type of "global landscape" viewed from a bird's-eye perspective – a genre which must be seen as closely related to the history of the map. Netherlandish painting after Joachim Patinir (c. 1480–1524), in particular, took up this new landscape form. Dagobert Frey (1883–1962) summed up the situation in his recognition that the "representation of infinity" had become the new issue of art.

Just as portrayal of movement and infinity are mutually

interdependent, so the 16th century's new approach to space must be seen in causal relation to the desire to remove the barrier between art and reality, and between the different branches of art. Crossing what has been aptly decribed as the "aesthetic boundary" (E. Michalski) between artificial space and real space was something which had already been attempted by the Early Renaissance. It was thereby possible either to make real space appear to extend into the picture, as in Domenico Ghirlandaio's *Last Supper* in Florence (ill. p. 108), or to make elements or figures appear to extend out of the painting and into the space occupied by the spectator, as in Mantegna's frescos in the Camera degli Sposi in Mantua (ill. p. 115). We might speak here of actively or passively crossing the aesthetic boundary. The High Renaissance avoided such blurring of boundaries by giving painted space its own system of perspective no longer oriented to the viewer's eye level; Leonardo's *Last Supper* and Raphael's frescos in the Stanza della Segnatura are outstanding examples of this.

The 16th century, on the other hand, carried the principle of the fusion of real and artificial space far beyond the Early Renaissance. In the decorations which the Sienese artist Baldassare Peruzzi (1481–1536) carried out in 1508–1511 in the Sala delle Prospettive (Room of Perspectives) in the Villa Farnesina in Rome, painted architecture appears to open out onto a view of the surrounding Trastevere district. Vasari, too, plays upon spatial boundaries in his frescos for the main room of the Palazzo della Cancelleria in Rome, called the Sala dei Cento Giorni (Room of the Hundred Days) because the time it took him to paint it. The

**Pontormo**
Joseph in Egypt, c. 1515
Oil on wood, 96.5 x 109.5 cm
London, National Gallery

**Tintoretto**
The Origin of the Milky Way, c. 1575–1580 (?)
Oil on canvas, 148 x 165.1 cm
London, National Gallery

eye is thoroughly confused as walls appear to open up outwards even as stairs and figures appear to penetrate the real interior of the room. Paolo Veronese (1528–1588) would take this to an extreme in his decorative scheme for the Villa Barbaro in Maser, near Treviso, begun in 1561 (ill. p. 184), in which landscape views are combined with *trompe l'œil* architecture and figures created with purely painterly means.

Veronese is also an illustration of the blurring of boundaries of a different kind, namely those between the individual branches of art. The replacement of one genre by another – of sculpture by painting, for example, or of architecture by sculpture – was something that dated back to the late Middle Ages. Following the rise of grisaille (Fr. *gris* = grey) in Cistercian glass painting during the 12th century, sculpture was frequently imitated by painting. In the Early Renaissance, painted figures often resembled polychrome statues. Not until the 16th century, however, did this trend towards the interchangeability of the arts reach its fullest expression. In his work on the Sistine ceiling, Michelangelo drew increasingly closer to the category of the free-standing figure. In his decoration of the Camera di San Paolo in the convent of the same name in 1518/19, Correggio not only abolished fixed visual boundaries for the ceiling but used painting to suggest the presence of sculptures and architectural elements. It was Veronese in the Villa Barbaro, however, who once again went furthest towards dissolving the barriers between architecture, sculpture and painting

But boundaries were also being crossed in contexts which verged on the "abnormal": in the architecture taking the form of figural sculptures in the Giardino della Monstre (Garden of Monsters) in Bomarzo near Orvieto, for example, in which it becomes possible to walk into sculpture, and in the sculptures in the park at Pratolino near Florence, which appear to grow directly out of nature and at the same time become nature.

The representation of movement and infinity, and the erasure of the boundaries between work of art and spectator and between the individual branches of art, represented ways of turning away from the idealized imagery of the High Renaissance. In the process, the foundations were laid for a new approach to the portrayal of the supernatural employing innovative means of composition.

Medieval painting communicated its vision of a heavenly world beyond our own in its combination of a generous gold ground with figures lacking in plasticity and a setting lacking in spatial depth. In the age of the High Renaissance, on the other hand, with the "rediscovery of the world and of man" (Burckhardt), Biblical events, miracles, visions, and everything that belonged to the spiritual sphere was subjugated to the three-dimensional systems of temporal space and figural representation. The miracle became "a process like

**Paolo Veronese**
Allegory of Vice and Virtue (The Choice of Hercules), c. 1580
Oil on canvas, 219 x 169.5 cm
New York, The Frick Collection

any other earthly event" (Frey), as the High Renaissance imposed the same artistic conditions on the sacred and secular sphere alike. In Raphael's *Disputà*, for example, the earthly and heavenly zones are treated with the same degree of realism.

The painting of the 16th century, on the other hand, developed new methods of making a visual distinction between the events of this world and the next. Here, "the spiritual breaks into the temporal" (Frey). This was made possible by a new philosophy of painting. A hundred years earlier, the Early Renaissance had been characterized by the dominance of line over colour. Line fixes an object on the plane and allows it to appear tangible and hence real. The renunciation of line in favour of colour modulation subsequently introduced by Leonardo liberated objects from their "tangibility" Furthermore, while line addresses itself primarily to the rational mind, colour speaks first and foremost to the emotions. Through this emotional force of colour, it thus now became possible for the spectator to be "overwhelmed" by the miracle portrayed in a painting.

In all its forms considered so far, the Mannerist art of the 16th century rejected the norms of the High Renaissance. Mannerism was fundamentally "anti-normative", albeit not yet "manneristic" in the modern sense of the world. "Mannered", on the other hand, is a term which can be applied to a series of phenomena which up till now have served to overly colour our opinion of the era.

The most important of these is the deformation of the ideal human figure, frequently as a means of heightening expressiveness. Thus Rosso Fiorentino, who undoubtedly studied the work of Michelangelo, transposed the latter's Herculean image of man into figures of seemingly arbitrary proportions and into forms whose details are often generously condensed. In Florentine painting especially, figures frequently possess elongated bodies with relatively small heads. This principle, which would be taken up by El Greco (c. 1541–1614) at the end of the century, was first exploited to particular effect by Pontormo.

In the *Self-Portrait in a Convex Mirror* (Vienna, Kunsthistorisches Museum) which he painted in 1523, Parmigianino (1503–1540) made the distortion of the human ideal cultivated by the High Renaissance his overt theme. The Milan painter Giuseppe Arcimboldo (c. 1527–1593) came close to surrealism in the heads which he composed entirely out of plant life (ill. p. 157) or which he placed in unreal, dreamlike settings.

Last but not least, this distortion of the human and natural image extended to anti-classic, unnatural colour combinations, as found in particular in 16th-century Florentine painting, and to the use of non-uniform systems of perspective and scale to subvert the logic of the whole.

To generalize, and hence inevitably to simplify, we may identify in the art of the Renaissance three successive stages in the portrayal of the human figure. The ideal of the Early Renaissance was man in his natural image. The ideal of the High Renaissance was the idealization of that natural image, the portrayal of man in the state of full harmonious development which in real life he is prevented from attaining. The "ideal" of Mannerism was go beyond and in part to distort man's natural image in favour of heightened expression.

**Forces behind the stylistic changes in the 16th century**
The shift from the High to the Late Renaissance was a reflection of far-reaching religious, social and scientific developments. Unlike the reformist and "heretical" movements of the Middle Ages, which had never seriously threatened the power of Rome, when Martin Luther (1483–1546) nailed his famous theses to the door of Wittenberg church in 1517, he publicly signalled the start of a religious revolution which would fundamentally challenge the validity of the Catholic Church. The latter retaliated in the mid–16th century with the reforms of the Council of Trent and, by summoning all its forces, restored religious life in wide areas of Europe. But the underlying damage had been done: the unquestioning acceptance with which the Church had formerly been greeted could never be restored. The 16th century was thus filled with extraordinary religious tensions which would destroy the balance between the secular and the sacred sphere, between the real and the ideal, that had so characterized the High Renaissance. These same tensions helped to fuel the unrest in painting which expressed itself in movement.

For the arts in Germany, the schism remained a constant source of conflict throughout the following centuries. Luther's doctrine of the "freedom of the Christian", who is granted responsibility for himself, undoubtedly represents one of the greatest achievements in the history of German thought. In two respects, however, it also harboured dangers which would prove catastrophic on several occasions in the future. Firstly, Luther's doctine overestimated the moral quality of humankind, a reflection of the fact that Protestantism itself required an educated mentality in order to be properly understood. Secondly, it restricted itself to man's inner freedom, while continuing to demand strict obedience to secular power. In this way Protestantism encouraged an acceptance of political authoritarianism which would prevent the development of democracy for many centuries.

Luther himself experienced the negative consequences of the Reformation. Following earlier demands by rebels for greater freedoms for the peasant classes, by 1526 the Peasants' War was raging. Influenced by the new teachings, the peasants wanted a role in state life and called for the abolition of serfdom and the secular dominion of the Church. After initial successes, the rebels were crushed, primarily for lack of a leader to co-ordinate their efforts. Luther initially

**Giuseppe Arcimboldo**
Spring, 1563
Oil on wood, 66.7 x 50.4 cm
Madrid, Real Academia de Bellas Artes de San Fernando

sought to act as mediator between the opposing sides but then came down clearly on the side of authority.

The denunciation of image worship, voiced most vociferously by John Calvin (1509–1564), led in Germany and the Netherlands to a violent wave of iconoclasm, comparable only with the burning of Byzantine paintings in the 8th century. The scale of the damage would only be surpassed by the devastation wrought by the air raids of the Second World War.

The religious conflicts which lasted throughout the 16th century would also have an enduring consequence for German culture right up to the 20th century, as described by Golo Mann (1909–1994): "Germany, which had previously shared in all of Europe's major experiences – Romanization and Christianity, feudalism and crusades, monasteries and universities, cities and the middle classes, Renaissance and Reformation – now failed to share the greatest experience of all: the burgeoning Europeanization of the world. Her ships plied neither the Atlantic nor the Indian Ocean. Her trading activities dwindled, her cities grew poorer, her middle classes fossilized. The invaluable education signified by colonization and the battle for the colonies, its broadening of horizons and its material enrichment and intensification of life – in all these things Germany took little part." In other words, the Reformation ushered into German culture a cer-

**Lorenzo Lotto**
Portrait of a Young Man, c. 1506–1508
Oil on canvas, 53.3 x 42.3 cm
Vienna, Kunsthistorisches Museum

tain provincialism which it would be unable to shake off for centuries. The lack of major patrons was painfully evident. It was not by chance that Germany's greatest painter since Dürer, Hans Holbein, spent a large part of his life in England. Cranach, having been one of the most imaginatively talented artists around the turn of the century, descended into a cool, artificial aestheticism as court painter to Frederick the Wise of Saxony (1482–1532). The formal vocabulary of the Renaissance was explored predominantly in the ornamental sphere, whereby it was not even received directly from its Italian source, but only through the indirect channel of Netherlandish art.

Alongside religious upheavals, Italy also underwent sensitive political changes in the 1520s. In 1527, and thus at approximately the same time as the Peasants' War in Germany, Italy was profoundly shaken by the sack of Rome by the mercenary armies of Emperor Charles V (1500–1558). The event was widely seen as a chastisement for the relaxation in the country's moral standards and its indulgence in luxurious lifestyles. If Italy's suffering would appease the wrath of God, wrote Jacopo Sadoleto (1477–1547), bishop of Carpentras since 1517, in a letter to Pope Clemens VII (1478–1534) dated 1 September 1527, "if these terrible punish-

ments clear the ground for a return to better morals and laws, then perhaps our misfortune has not been of the greatest". Whatever the case, people's faith in the glittering face of secular power was profoundly shaken, all the more so as broad sections of Italy remained under Spanish rule.

The "crisis in the High Renaissance" was not only rooted in historical, religious and social changes, however, but was also, and in equal measure, the consequence of a new world picture. In 1492 Christopher Columbus (1451–1506) discovered America while attempting to reach India. Between 1497 and 1504, the Florentine explorer Amerigo Vespucci (1451–1512) mounted four voyages of discovery to Honduras and South America; his first name gave the "new" continent its name. In 1497/98 Vasco da Gama (c. 1460–1524) succeeded in sailing round the southern tip of Africa and in finally establishing the sea route to India. Amongst the new territories discovered by others charting the same course were southern China in 1517, New Guinea in 1526 and Japan in 1542. In 1519–1522 an expedition captained by Ferdinand Magellan (c. 1480–1521) embarked upon the first circumnavigation of the world – an astonishing achievement and an important milestone in the history of geography. It was finally proved that the earth was indeed round, as suspected since early Christian times. The vast new continent of America was explored in greater depth in the 1520s and 1530s; as from 1528, the Spaniards penetrated deep into North America from their outposts in Mexico, and in 1534 the French occupied parts of Canada.

In this respect, the 16th century was the era of a quite literally changing world view. The self-contained Old World was now obliged to recognize its relativity to the whole. It no longer ranked as the centre of the world fringed by a few more or less exotic outskirts, but simply as a comparatively small area within a large, for the most part unexplored horizon. The multiplicity of these newly-discovered landscapes, peoples and cultures cast into question the validity of Europe and its outlying regions as the measure of all things.

It was only logical, therefore, that a new definition should be required for the concept of virtually immeasurable dimensions, of infinity. It is undoubtedly here that we find the roots of the new approach to space demonstrated in the art of the epoch.

The world picture would also take a turn in another direction in the early 16th century when, following on from work already carried out by the German astronomer Regiomontanus (1436–1476), Nicolaus Copernicus (1473–1543) began to formulate his revised theory of planetary motion. The heavenly bodies revolved not around the earth, he argued, but around the sun; the earth, too, revolved round the sun and at the same time spun on its own axis. Some one hundred years later, in 1633, Galileo Galilei (1564–1642) would be forced to recant his belief in this heliocentric world picture!

## The development of artistic theory

The stylistic transition from the High to the Late Renaissance was closely accompanied by a widening in the field of theoretical enquiry – a development which we can only touch upon briefly here. The Early Renaissance in Italy had chiefly studied the theory behind practical aspects of the representation of "reality", such as perspective, proportion, and anatomy. In the 16th century, this emphasis shifted towards questions of an aesthetic nature. The debate was dominated by the question of which should be given precedence: line or colour? While Florence argued passionately for the primacy of line, Venice equally vigorously defended the importance of colour as the supreme means of painting. The discussion that ensued would culminate in the 17th century in the heated disputes at the French Academy between the "Rubenists" and the "Poussinists", and would linger on in the tension between Neoclassicism and Romanticism in the 18th and early 19th century.

Closely related to the argument surrounding colour and line was the question of the order of importance of the various branches of art. Here, too, Florence and Venice represented the two opposite poles of opinion. Florence had always held sculpture to be the greatest of all the arts; from Giotto and Masaccio to Michelangelo, its major artistic achievements in all areas of art had been determined by sculptural thinking. Venice, on the other hand, which lent a "pictorial" emphasis even to its architecture and sculpture, saw painting as the supreme expression of all artistic endeavour.

An anecdote related by Paolo Pino (fl. 1534–1565) in his *Dialogo di pittura* (Dialogue on Painting, Venice 1548) makes these different attitudes clear. While engaged in conversation with a group of sculptors, the attempt was made to convince Giorgione of the superiority of sculpture by arguing that sculpture could show the human figure from all sides, whereas painting could only show it from one. Giorgione subsequently proceeded to paint a now vanished *St George* which astounded the sculptors. The knight was shown in armour, holding his lance, beside the waters of a spring in which his entire figure was reflected; leaning against a tree trunk further away was a mirror offering a full view of the saint from one rear side. A second mirror on the opposite edge of the painting reflected his other rear side. Giorgione thereby wanted to demonstrate that a painter could render a figure visible from all sides at once, whereas someone looking at a sculpture would first have to walk around it before they could appreciate it as a whole.

There will always be a temptation to explain the differences between the art centres of Florence and Venice in literal terms of their contrasting topographies. Surely the mountainous region of Tuscany, with its stereometric forms and its contours incisively modelled by light and shade, is primarily an incitement to sculpture, whereas the colours of the Venetian landscape, refracted in the waters of the lagoon, appeal first and foremost to the painter's eye rather than to the sense of touch?

Theoretical debates on the arts assumed various forms over the course of the 16th century. Giovanni Paolo Lomazzo (1538–1600) offers us a key to the understanding of the Late Renaissance – and the distance separating it from the High Renaissance – in his *Idea del tempio della pittura* (Idea of the Temple of Painting) of 1590, in which he discusses the relationship between the creative idea formulated by the artist (the *concetto*) and the natural model.

## The "rediscovery" of Mannerism in the 20th century

Art history has so far made only limited study of the ways in which historical epochs and individual artists have been received and evaluated by theoreticians and practitioners of art. This largely unexplored field nevertheless promises to open up a wealth of new perspectives. Assessing the achievements of the past not only opens our eyes to facts previously unrecognized or perhaps not considered important, but contributes in equal measure to understanding the present. Both in the sphere of art history and art theory, the respective standpoint of the viewer can be shown in numerous cases

**Agnolo Bronzino**
Eleonora of Toledo and her Son Giovanni, c. 1545
Oil on wood, 115 x 96 cm
Florence, Galleria degli Uffizi

to have been influenced – whether consciously or unconsciously – by the artistic trends of the viewer's own day.

The re-appraisal of the "Mannerist" tendencies in the art of the 16th century by early Modernism in the 20th century is a typical example. The older writer Burckhardt, in his *Randglossen zur Skulptur der Renaissance* (Notes on Renaissance Sculpture) of 1894/95, spoke not without gentle irony of the "naïvety in Quattrocentro art which has recently come to be admired", and noted with regard to the Late Renaissance: "Those advanced enough in years, however, will already have seen opinions change in this fashion, and would not be altogether suprised to see a similar swing back in favour of Mannerist works, should the hunger for beauty transfer itself to the gleanings left behind after the harvest has long been taken in". This swing would indeed take place just ten years later.

In Mannerism's distortion and simplification of the natural model, Expressionism and Cubism recognized essential features of their own philosophy of art. Its abolition of rational, logical structures and its exploration of dream-like, subconscious levels of human emotion must similarly have struck a profound chord both with Surrealism and psychoanalysis. Its efforts to render sequences of movement visible to the eye were directly taken up by Italian Futurism between approximately 1900 and 1912.

Filippo Tommaso Marinetti (1876–1944) defined the goals of the movement in his *First Futurist Manifesto* of 1909: the formal reproduction of the *dinamismo* of modern technology and civilization, the dissolution of the static image, and the capturing of "the beauty of speed". When he continues: "We reject the right angle as devoid of passion. We desire the shock of the acute angle, the dynamic arabesque; the oblique lines which rain down on the viewer's senses like arrows coming out of the sky", he seems to be referring directly to the principles of artistic design found in the painting of the 16th century.

## Late Renaissance and Baroque

In fact, however, the historical importance of the art of the 16th century had long ago become apparent with the transition to the Early Baroque. Its central concepts were taken up and developed further by the 17th century. Michelangelo da Caravaggio (1537–1610), for example, took his use of colour from the great Venetians, emphasized the miraculous dimension of his New Testament subjects for all their naturalistic details, and carried the suggestion of dynamic movement even further than his 16th-century predecessors (*Crucifixion of St Peter*, 1601, Rome, Santa Maria del Popolo, Cesari Chapel; *Deposition*, 1602–1604, Rome, Pinacoteca Vaticana). In 1600 the 23-year-old Peter Paul Rubens (1577–1640) made a trip to Italy, during which he was able to study at first hand the heritage of the 16th century; his assimilation and transformation of the influences he encountered would have profound consequences for the development of the Northern European Baroque. Neither the blurring of the boundaries between the different genres which took place in Baroque art nor its removal of the barrier between real and artificial space are conceivable without the achievements of the 16th century.

Every new development is characterized by the tension between profit and loss. The potential gains thereby offered by the painting of the 16th century lay above all in the dynamic means of composition with which it repealed the static laws of the High Renaissance. From a number of points of view, the Baroque era which began around 1600 can be seen as a synthesis of these means with the norms of the High Renaissance, whereby animated harmony was now replaced with harmonious movement.

In view of the wealth and scope of the developments which led from the High Renaissance to the Baroque, we would do better to abandon the largely misleading term of Mannerism and to call the art of the 16th century by its former name: the Late Renaissance.

# LEONARDO DA VINCI

1452–1519

No other work in Western art has come to so typify its subject as Leonardo's *Last Supper*. Building upon the versions by Castagno and Ghirlandaio (ill. p. 108), Leonardo arrives at an entirely new and definitive solution. With its masterly creation of depth, the fresco initially gives the impression of being a real extension to the refectory; but the discrepancy in height between the point of station from which its perspective system is calculated and the viewer's eye, together with the monumental size of the figures, immediately re-establish its distance. The painted architecture of the background, almost austere in its simplicity, serves a single compositional function: all the vanishing lines meet in the seated figure of Christ, whose central thematic significance is additionally emphasized by the wider window and crescent-shaped moulding behind.

In a departure from his preliminary drawings for the fresco, which show Judas on the near side of the table in line with pictorial convention, Leonardo places him in the final version amongst the rest of the disciples. We are thereby shown a different moment in the events. Christ has just announced his impending betrayal, and the shocked disciples are reacting with the question: "Lord, is it I?". On either side of the triangular figure of Christ, further isolated within the composition by his red and blue robes, the apostles are grouped in threes. The range of their responses is reflected in their various movements and gestures – in line with Leonardo's insistence that a painter should express his subjects' thoughts not in their faces but in their poses and movements. As a result, the fresco – despite the poor condition in which it survives today – has lost none of its expressive power.

Despite the fact that only its underpainting was executed, Leonardo's *Adoration of the Magi* heralds the dawn of the High Renaissance. Its square format dictates the grouping of the figures: the kneeling kings form a triangle with the figure of Mary, whose head is both the apex of the triangle and the centre of the panel. The twisted, almost contrapposto pose of the Virgin and Child mediates between left and right in an unconstrained fashion – Mary might be described as the point of articulation at the heart of the pictorial organism as a whole. The powerful facial expressions recall the Portinari Altar by Hugo van der Goes (ill. p. 133), which had been installed in Florence a few years earlier, probably in 1478.

Why Leonardo never finished the painting is a question that remains unanswered. We do know, however, that in 1496 Filippino Lippi painted a new version of the same subject (today also in the Uffizi) for the same patron and the same destination (San Donato a Scopeto monastery, near Florence). Perhaps the graphic precision demanded by the jousting scene in the background could no longer be reconciled with Leonardo's theories of colour, according to which outlines and contours grow increasingly less sharp the further away they appear.

Leonardo da Vinci
Last Supper, 1495–1498
Oil tempera on plaster, 460 x 880 cm
Milan, Santa Maria delle Grazie, Refectory

Leonardo da Vinci
Adoration of the Magi, c. 1481
Oil and bistre on wood, 240 x 246 cm
Florence, Galleria degli Uffizi

Leonardo da Vinci
Virgin of the Rocks, c. 1483
Oil on wood, transferred to canvas,
199 x 122 cm
Paris, Musée National du Louvre

Leonardo da Vinci
Virgin of the Rocks, completed c. 1506
Oil on wood, 190 x 120 cm
London, National Gallery

# LEONARDO DA VINCI
## 1452–1519

The *Virgin of the Rocks* has a number of icono-graphical roots: the Adoration of the Child by Mary and the young St John the Baptist; the Nativity, which in Byzantine pictorial tradi-tion took place in a rocky grotto; and finally a powerful dream of walking through caves re-corded by Leonardo himself.

The composition is determined by the triangle formed by the foreground group, whereby any impression of rigid geometry is avoided via asymmetries and a subtle stagger-ing of the figures. Leonardo employs a highly differentiated range of means to link space and plane, the most important of which is the ana-tomically elongated arm of the angel, a motif which Leonardo studied in great detail in a preliminary drawing. The head of the young Jesus, the pointing hand of the angel and Ma-ry's protective hand are together aligned into a vertical running parallel to the pictorial plane. The significance of this detail for the composi-tion as a whole is made clear when we com-pare this painting with the later verson (below), in which the angel's gesture is omitted.

Leonardo's palette reflects his new theories of colour. The most brilliant draughtsman of his day here renounces all use of linear definition. In the distant background landscape, the colours grow lighter as the contours grow in-creasingly hazy.

We can only guess at the reasons why Leo-nardo should wish to follow his earlier version of the subject with the present panel. The figures have now acquired haloes; John the Baptist is more clearly identified by his cross, and the omission of the angel's pointing hand allows Christ to emerge more strongly as the main figure. What the London version loses in compositional ideality, it gains in iconographi-cal clarity.

Leonardo's *Virgin and St Anne* may be seen in several respects as the counterpart to Michel-angelo's *Doni Tondo* (ill. p. 167). In both cases, three figures characterized by extremely com-plex and largely contrary movements are com-bined into a single group. But while Michel-angelo is concerned above all with portraying the third dimension, Leonardo binds the ges-tures and poses of his figures into the geome-tric forms governing the composition.

Even more striking are the contrasts be-tween the two artists' techniques. Whereas Mi-chelangelo works primarily with line, leaving colour to play simply a descriptive role, Leo-nardo models both silhouettes and inner con-tours purely out of colour – in this respect already looking forward to the late works of -Titian. He also employs colour to link the foreground figures with the fantastical land-scape behind.

Leonardo da Vinci
The Virgin and St Anne, c. 1508
Oil on wood, 168 x 130 cm
Paris, Musée National du Louvre

**Giorgione**
Virgin and Child with SS Francis and Liberalis (Madonna di Castelfranco), c. 1504/05
Oil on wood. 200 x 152 cm
Castelfranco Veneto, San Liberale

**Giorgione**
Concert Champêtre, c. 1510/11
Oil on canvas, 110 x 138 cm
Paris, Musée National du Louvre

## GIORGIONE
### C. 1477/78–1510

Giorgione's earliest authenticated work marks a new stage in the evolution of the Venetian *Sacra Conversazione*. Firstly, the Virgin is seated above the saints on a throne too high to be mounted in real life; secondly, she is portrayed against a view of the landscape. The figures are thereby staggered both in height and depth.

The composition contains echoes of the "crystalline" style of Antonello da Messina. In the grouping of the figures, triangle and parallelogram overlap and thereby connect space, confidently and logically constructed with perspective means, back to the plane. Antonello's influence can also be seen in the sumptuous fabrics and, on the base of the throne, the coat of arms of the Costanzo family for whose private chapel the panel was painted.

Line and colour modulation are still evenly balanced, although indications of Giorgione's future development are already present in the knight's gleaming armour and in the diminishing focus of the receding landscape. It should thereby be remembered that Leonardo was in Venice in 1501.

Precisely by whom and for whom this canvas, so greatly admired by the French artists of the 19th century, was actually painted are questions that have yet to be satisfactorily answered. Are we looking at the last known work by Giorgione? Was it a collaborative effort by Giorgione and Titian? Or did the painting spring chiefly from Titian's brush? The uncertainty surrounding the attribution of this work is itself proof of the stylistic continuity characterizing the development from Giorgione to Titian, and the importance of the former for the œuvre of the greatest European painter of the Late Renaissance.

The blending of figures and landscape is continued into the storm clouds, whereby the sound of the music being played in the foreground seems to find visual expression in the background.

Insofar as figures in contemporary dress are combined with female nudes, the artist offers us a view of nakedness taken out of its traditionally mythological context and brought fully into the present. Unlike Manet's much later painting *Déjeuner sur l'herbe* (ill. p. 491), a direct descendant of this *Concert Champêtre*, none of the figures seek to establish eye contact with the viewer. The closed nature of the world inside the painting is thereby preserved.

The allegorical meaning of the subject on the right has yet to be deciphered. It was described in around 1530 as a "Landscape on canvas with storm, gypsy woman and soldier". Efforts to interpret the painting were further complicated when X-rays revealed that the artist originally intended a second nude in place of the soldier, and that the work was executed in a number of stages – typical of the Venetian artist's spontaneous and emotional approach to the painting process, so different to that of his more reflective Florentine colleagues.

This is undoubtedly one of Giorgione's last works. The relationship between figure and landscape is developed in pronounced favour of the latter, colour modulation almost entirely replaces line, and the literary subject is of secondary interest. In this respect there is good justification for the painting's present title, which dates back to the 16th century: the representation of a natural event was certainly one of Giorgione's main concerns.

The fascinating way in which the artist dissolves fixed line into forcefully expressive colour, as seen in the soldier's clothing and the sky, for example, already looks beyond Titian's early work to the paintings of his mature years.

**Giorgione**
La Tempesta, c. 1510
Oil on canvas, 78 x 72 cm
Venice, Galleria dell'Accademia

**Fra Bartolommeo**
Annunciation, c. 1500
Oil tempera on wood, each wing 20 x 10 cm
Florence, Galleria degli Uffizi

## FRA BARTOLOMMEO
### 1472–1517

These two small panels number amongst the works which Bartolommeo executed before entering the convent of San Marco. The wings of a domestic altarpiece for Piero del Pugliese, they show the Nativity and Circumcision of Christ on their reverse and flank a relief of the Virgin by Donatello. Both panels were later cut down on all sides, upsetting the original relationship between the two figures, as established in particular by the angel's gesture of blessing, and restricting the view through the open door in the wall behind. The portrayal of the *Annunciation* in grisaille (grey monochrome) would have derived from a study of Netherlandish works (Bartolommeo knew the Portinari Altar by van der Goes, installed in Florence in 1478). In his approach to figures and space, however, the young artist is more strongly influenced by Perugino. Between the front edge of the painting and the rear wall running parallel to the plane, he creates a clearly defined "stage"; here, with the aid of sculptural draperies, he establishes the three-dimensional nature of his figures and allows them to unfold in free and unconstrained gestures. In establishing the sequence of their movement from left to right, Bartolommeo nevertheless respects the conditions of the two-dimensional plane, which also underlie the prieu-dieu at which Mary is kneeling, and which takes up the lines of the surrounding frame.

**Andrea del Sarto**
Pietà, c. 1519/20
Oil on wood, 99 x 120 cm
Vienna, Kunsthistorisches Museum

## ANDREA DEL SARTO
### 1486–1530

In reducing the number of bystanders traditionally serving to reflect the event taking place, Andrea del Sarto creates a new type of Pietà in Florentine painting, in which he concentrates solely on the Virgin Mary and the dead Christ accompanied by two angels. The centre is dominated by Mary, her face wearing an expression of anguish. There is no longer a direct connection between mother and son, since Christ is lying on a bier in the foreground and seems to have overcome the suffering of death.

On the one hand, Sarto observes the norms of a "classic" composition: the figures are arranged one behind the other as if in two layers of relief and thereby confirm the laws of the plane, while the composition is equally weighted on the left and right without descending into rigid symmetry.

At the same time, however, the artist introduces a pulsating sense of unrest via the contrast between angular folds of drapery and soft modulations of colour in which contours are dissolved. The right-hand angel holding the instruments of Christ's Passion, in particular, gives the impression of constantly changing his pose and the direction of his gaze. The sweeping, abstract brushwork of the background is typical of Sarto's late works. The proportions and expressions of the faces reflect the influence of Pontormo.

## MICHELANGELO BUONAROTTI
1475–1564

The only panel painting attributed beyond doubt to Michelangelo has frequently been criticized for the artificiality of its figural composition. The three main figures are combined into an extraordinarily complex group in which their natural proportions are of necessity distorted – something which would be copied by the Mannerists of the succeeding generation. But to dismiss the tondo simply as a feat of artistry would be to do it a grave injustice on several counts. Firstly, Michelangelo is here concerned with overcoming the static in favour of the transitory moment. Secondly, he is attempting – as the outstanding sculptural talent in Western art – to portray the group in three-dimensional terms; the geometric triangle so beloved of High Renaissance painting is here replaced by the stereometric pyramid. And thirdly, the way in which Mary lifts Jesus up may symbolize her acceptance of his future sacrifice on the cross and his resurrection. This is also implied by the figure of the young John the Baptist on the right who, separated from his playmate by a wall, will go out into the world to announce the coming of Christ.

Nor should the line of breathtaking male nudes in the background – recalling tondi by Luca Signorelli – be seen as a secularization of the subject, or as a reflection of the sculptor's delight in plastic form, but as symbolizing the sphere of the Old Testament.

The panel, which was probably painted to mark the marriage of Agnolo Doni and Maddalena Strozzi, has become known in the literature as the Doni Tondo.

In his cycle of Sibyls and Prophets in the Sistine Chapel, Michelangelo undergoes a stylistic evolution which leads from the relief to the free-standing figure. Zechariah above the entrance wall and Jonah above the altar wall mark the two poles of this development, which goes hand in hand with an increase in the scale of the figures.

Although the *Delphic Sibyl* was painted during the first stage of the decoration of the Sistine ceiling, it already clearly reveals this trend towards increasing liberation from painted architecture. The Sibyl turns rightwards on her own bodily axis, while her left arm, holding the scroll, reaches across leftwards. A motif from the Doni Tondo is here used to indicate a more powerful crossing of space.

This effect is reinforced by the two putti in the background, who no longer stand side by side but at an oblique angle leading into the picture, thereby helping to release the figure from its architectural context. The relatively cool palette also lends the Sibyl the character of a painted marble sculpture. Never before had painting been so dominated by sculptural thinking as in Michelangelo's Sistine ceiling.

*Above:*
**Michelangelo Buonarroti**
Holy Family (Doni Tondo),
c. 1504/05
Oil tempera on wood,
diameter 120 cm
Florence, Galleria degli
Uffizi

**Michelangelo Buonarroti**
Delphic Sibyl,
c. 1506–1509
Fresco, c. 350 x 380 cm
Rome, Vatican, Sistine
Chapel

## MICHELANGELO BUONAROTTI

1475–1564

In the entry for 2 December 1786 in his *Italienische Reise* (translated as *Letters from Italy*, 1901), Goethe wrote: "On the 28th [of November] we paid a second visit to the Sistine Chapel... all ... is fully compensated by the sight of the great masterpiece of art. And at this moment I am so taken with Michelangelo, that after him I have no taste even for nature herself, especially as I am unable to contemplate her with the same eye of genius that he did." Goethe here recognizes a fundamental phenomenon of the High Renaissance: its relationship to the portrayal of nature in the sense

of the "idea" behind every natural object. In its fusion of natural beauty with ideal beauty, Western painting finds itself for a brief moment in direct proximity to the art of Ancient Greece.

In chronological terms, *The Creation of Adam* probably marks the mid-way point in the Sistine ceiling. By now Michelangelo was increasingly enlarging the scale of his figures and abandoning scenic and landscape detail. For the first time in the history of this subject in painting, God the Father is horizontal, mirroring the reclining figure of Adam. Michel-

angelo thereby takes the words of the Bible literally: "So God created Man in his own image" (Genesis 1:27). The youthful Adam seems the definitive embodiment of the ideal male body. The precise observation of anatomical detail is not an end in itself as in the case of Luca Signorelli (cf. ill. p. 110), but serves to demonstrate the supreme harmony residing in the body's proportions. Maximum naturalness is combined with maximum artistic calculation: despite their wealth of movement in space, the main figures remain bound through their gestures to the plane. This is seen par-

ticularly clearly in the combination of Adam's gaze, left arm and raised knee.

Ground and clouds repeat in more abstract form the silhouettes of Adam and God the Father, whose two outstretched arms are set against a white background comparable in its charged atmosphere to an electric field.

"Nowhere else in the entire sphere of art is the metaphysical so brilliantly expressed in a physical moment of such utter clarity and forcefulness" (Jacob Burckhardt).

**Michelangelo Buonarroti**
The Creation of Adam, c. 1510
Fresco, c. 280 x 570 cm
Rome, Vatican, Sistine Chapel

# RAPHAEL
## 1483–1520

Over the course of his Florentine years, Raphael painted a number of versions of the Virgin with Christ and the young John the Baptist in a landscape. He thereby confronted the latest compositional problems relating to the portrayal of figures and space. The strongly contrasting directions combined within the pose of the present Madonna suggest the influence of Leonardo, in particular his studies for *The Virgin with St Anne*. The freedom of the figures in their relationship to space and plane is effortlessly combined with a precisely calculated composition. The two children in front of the Madonna are positioned to the left of centre, but are incorporated within the almost equilateral triangle describing the group as a whole.

Raphael's *Sposalizio* is a pictorial document of the first order, marking his transition from the Early to the High Renaissance. Although he adopts the overall composition and many of its details from a version of the same subject, also dating from 1504, by his teacher Perugino, the latter merely serves as the foil against which Raphael proves himself the representative of a new generation. The central group is clearly emphasized at the expense of the accompanying figures, and a previous episode in the events – the Virgin's rejection of other suitors – is more forcefully indicated in the young man in the right-hand foreground. Above all, however, Raphael frees himself from the older master's principle of building up his composition in layers of relief. The figures in the foreground are grouped in a concave semicircle which must be seen in conjunction with the landscape in the background, the dome of the building behind and the arching upper edge of the panel. The figures behind, on the other hand, curve towards the interior of the painting; they thereby correspond to the temple rotunda and combine with the landscape to trace the outline of a circle.

In the composition of the *Madonna di Foligno*, Raphael translates into panel painting the principle realized in the frescos of the Stanza della Segnatura, namely the perfect marriage of external format and inner content. The figures in the earthly zone take up the rounded top of the picture, complete the circle and simultaneously project it, through their own staggered positions within the foreground, into the third dimension. The shape of the circle is also taken up in the aureole around Mary and by the rainbow over the landscape. Despite the astonishing homogeneity of the composition, Raphael assigns different degrees of reality to the terrestrial and celestial zones. Through its increase in colour modulation and its wealth of painted light, the heavenly sphere seems to be placed beyond our earthly reach. In this respect, the panel represents a milestone in the history of Western painting.

**Raphael**
Madonna of the Meadows, 1505/06
Oil tempera on wood, 113 x 88cm
Vienna, Kunsthistorisches Museum

**Raphael**
Marriage of the Virgin
(Sposalizio della Vergine), 1504
Oil tempera on wood,
170 x 117cm
Milan, Pinacoteca di Brera

**Raphael**
Madonna di Foligno, c. 1512
Oil on wood, transferred to
canvas, 301 x 198cm
Rome, Musei Vaticani,
Pinacoteca Vaticana

**Raphael**
The Transfiguration, c. 1517–1520
Oil on canvas, 405 x 278 cm
Rome, Musei Vaticani,
Pinacoteca Vaticana

**Raphael**
The School of Athens, 1511/12
Fresco, width c. 800 cm
Rome, Musei Vaticani,
Stanza della Segnatura

# RAPHAEL
## 1483–1520

Raphael's last work is a summation of his entire artistic development and at the same time heralds the dawn of a new age. He treats his subject in a new fashion. In the top half of the picture, the transfigured Christ appears between the prophets Moses and Elijah above the rocky summit of Mount Tabor. The frightened disciples have flung themselves onto the ground beneath Christ's feet. In the lower zone, an epilectic boy is being presented by his distraught parents to the disciples, who can do nothing. Two events related in the Gospels as occurring in chronological succession are here combined into a single scene: Christ is rendered visible in his divine form as the only one who can offer help, whereby salvation is made a certainty. Raphael further amplifies the distinction between the earthly and the heavenly zone. The sculptural modelling and powerful colour harmonies of the lower half of the painting offer a pronounced contrast to the less solid figures of the Transfiguration scene, united by their paler hues.

Raphael nevertheless succeeds in establishing a visual connection between the two halves. Top and bottom are linked by the overall circle into which the figures above and below are grouped, by the numerous upward-pointing gestures made by those below, and above all by the dynamic slant which rises from bottom left to top right in the shadow cast by the rocky cliff. Members of Raphael's workshop, and in particular Guilio Romano, would have been involved in the completion of the lower half of the painting.

Between 1509 and 1512, on the walls of one of Pope Julius II's private rooms, Raphael depicted the four classical faculties, thereby exhibiting a large degree of intellectual freedom. The personification of ancient Philosophy is located on the wall directly opposite the *Disputà* (Theology), showing the veneration of the Holy Sacrament. In the centre of a large vaulted hall, its design indicating a knowledge of the architecture of Roman baths, stand Plato and Aristotle, considered the chief representatives of Greek philosophy throughout the entire Middle Ages. The figure of Socrates can be seen in profile on the left, while Diogenes reclines on the steps in an expression of his absence of material wants. In the left-hand foreground, a boy holds the tablet of musical harmony in front of Pythagorus. In the opposite corner, Euclid is drawing a geometric figure before a group of young men; the figure with the globe seen from behind is probably Ptolemy, with Zarathustra facing him with the sphere. The figure leaning on the block of marble (Heraclitus? Michelangelo?) is a later addition. Presented with this expansive composition, the spectator almost forgets that he is actually standing in an acute-angled, poorly lit room. Raphael does not lead the eye out into infinity, however, but yokes his pictorial space to the laws of the plane. The figures are arranged from left to right, while the recession of the architecture in the central axis is regularly checked by walls coming in from either side.

# PALMA VECCHIO
1480–1528

This painting shows Diana bathing with her companions. The figure at the left-hand edge of the panel has been interpreted as Callisto, whose affair with Zeus – who is later supposed to have transformed her into a bear – has been discovered by Diana. Palma's entire œuvre was heavily influenced by Giorgione. The landscape occupies a significant proportion of the canvas; in the quality of its execution and the subtly differentiated colours of its trees and mountain ranges, it captivates the eye more strongly than the figures. Contours yield to delicate modulations of colour. Unlike Giorgione, however, the composition remains loose and the figures, in places grouped into twos and threes, are distributed freely across the pictorial plane. This may be partly explained by the fact that Palma drew a number of his figures from existing sources. The seated nymph combing her hair can be traced to an engraving by Raimondi while the figure of Callisto is seen as a variation upon the Aphrodite Kallipygos in Naples, and the figure viewed from the rear on the right as a modification of the Aphrodite of Melos. The work offers an interesting contrast to Titian, who always places his figures near the front edge of the painting and who only incorporates the background into the action to a much lesser degree. The substantial modelling of the female nudes places the painting amongst Palma's later works.

Palma Vecchio
Diana discovers Callisto's Misdemeanour, c. 1525
Oil on canvas on wood, 77.5 x 124 cm
Vienna, Kunsthistorisches Museum

# SEBASTIANO DEL PIOMBO
C. 1485–1547

The portrait of Cardinal Carondelet, probably painted at the beginning of Sebastiano's stay in Rome, is an exemplary illustration both of the talents and the limitations of this Venetian-born artist. In an allusion to Raphael, with whom he was briefly acquainted, Sebastiano expands his subject into a group portrait by including the Cardinal's secretary on the right and an unidentified figure on the left. The table and the Cardinal's right arm establish a strict boundary between the spectator outside and the scene inside the painting. The sitter's cool, almost expressionless, soberly observed physiognomy may be seen as a reflection of the atmosphere within the Curia before the Sack of Rome, namely one strongly characterized by secular interests. Pronouncedly secular, too, is the background setting: the colonnade seen in masterly foreshortening could be taken from a nobleman's palace in High Renaissance Rome.

At the same time, however, the technique used to paint the ermine-trimmed robes, together with the contrast between light and shade, are a reminder of the painter's apprenticeship in Venice. The view of the landscape behind the secretary is both a variation upon the landscapes also found on the right-hand side of works by Giorgione, with whom Sebastiano worked in Venice, and upon the landscapes found in the early works of Titian.

Sebastiano del Piombo
Cardinal Carondelet and his Secretary, c. 1512–1515
Oil on wood, 112.5 x 87 cm
Madrid, Museo Thyssen-Bornemisza

**Correggio**
Zeus and Antiope, c. 1524/25
Oil on canvas, 188 x 125 cm
Paris, Musée National du Louvre

**Correggio**
Leda and the Swan, c. 1531/32
Oil on canvas, 152 x 191 cm
Berlin, Gemäldegalerie, Staatliche Museen
zu Berlin – Preußischer Kulturbesitz

## CORREGGIO
### c. 1489–1534

Zeus, disguised as a satyr, approaches Antiope, the daughter of Nycteus, regent of Thebes (according to another version of the myth, Antiope was the daughter of the river god Asopos). The sleeping Cupid signifies the union that is about to take place.

Correggio replaces the classical equilibrium of High Renaissance composition with asymmetry and portrays his figures in extremely complex poses. He nevertheless establishes a stable system of reference within the painting by means of the parallel lines at which the main characters are angled. Correggio's palette is developed out of his confrontation with Leonardo and the Venetian painters of the early 16th century, above all Giorgione. In place of colour contours, Correggio works exclusively with colour modulation, which together with the light infuses the figures with a distinct sense of weightlessness.

Correggio's portrayal of Leda, receiving Zeus in the shape of a swan, demands direct comparison with Michelangelo's versions of the same subject, which survive only in copies. While Michelangelo concentrates exclusively on the figural group, Correggio sets the scene in a wooded landscape and embellishes it with bathing nymphs, Cupid playing his harp, and putti.

By presenting Leda in a complex, twisting pose from the front, the artist grants the spectator the clearest possible view of her union with the swan, yet without approaching obscenity. The accompanying figures – some bathing, others holding their clothes, others again making music – play an important role in this regard. Above all, however, it is the landscape which, painted in the most delicate *sfumato*, lends the scene a thoroughly idyllic character.

The composition, which at first sight appears entirely improvised with its unrestrained sense of movement and free distribution of figures, is in fact carefully crafted. Leda is accentuated by the large tree trunk behind, slightly offset to the left of the central axis. Nymphs, Cupid and putti are arranged in a semicircle around the central group of trees and thereby lead the eye into the depths of the landscape, which is itself treated with a high degree of freedom in its renunciation of emphatic detail.

In *Io* and *Ganymede*, Correggio reaches the height of his artistic powers. The union of Zeus and the nymph Io, daughter of the river god Iachus, goes back in its present form to Ovid's *Metamorphoses*. Io flees before Zeus until the latter "casts darkness over the whole domain, checks the maiden's flight and conquers her modesty". While in Ovid's version Zeus makes himself invisible in the darkness, Correggio turns him into a cloud.

The artist thereby establishes a powerful contrast between the dark clouds filling the sky and the luminous figure of Io. Despite her animated pose, Io remains bound to the plane via her up-turned head and the position

of her left arm and leg. The background, on the other hand, dissolves into indefinite depths through its rich, almost "proto-Impressionist" modulation – a removal of boundaries similar to that which Correggio had achieved shortly beforehand in his cupola frescos in Parma.

The two canvases were undoubtedly de-signed to be seen juxtaposed. The figure of Io anticipates that of the ascending Ganymede. The dog looking upwards at the handsome youth, together with the many verticals contained within the rocks, reinforce this sugges-tion of skyward movement, for which the ex-tremely tall and narrow formats are ideally suited.

**Correggio**
Zeus and Io, c. 1531/32
Oil on canvas, 163.5 x 74 cm
Vienna, Kunsthistorisches Museum

**Correggio**
The Abduction of Ganymede, c. 1531/32
Oil on canvas, 163.5 x 70.5 cm
Vienna, Kunsthistorisches Museum

Titian
Venus of Urbino, c. 1538
Oil on canvas, 119 x 165 cm
Florence, Galleria degli Uffizi

Titian
Bacchanalia (The Andrians), c. 1519/20
Oil on canvas, 175 x 193 cm
Madrid, Museo del Prado

# TITIAN

BETWEEN 1473 AND 1490–1576

Titian's painting invites comparison with Giorgione's earlier *Sleeping Venus* (Dresden). The similarity in the poses extends right into the details, and Titian also adopts from Giorgione the contrast of red and white in the couch. Yet their very similarities also make the differences between the two works all the more evident. The replacement of the landscape background by the view of an interior re-establishes the connection with reality. Most significantly, however, Titian's figure is not seen sleeping, but turns her head to look out of the picture with an alert gaze. A direct relationship is thus established between the figure in the painting and the spectator. The ring on the little finger of Venus' left hand, the roses unfolding between the fingers of her right hand and the bracelet on her right wrist all reinforce the impression that this young woman belongs to the real world. The name Venus in fact arose out of a misunderstanding; this is the portrait of a beautiful courtesan, whose clothes are being laid out by the women in the background. Whereas Giorgione fuses figure and background, Titian's composition contrasts the two. Thus the foreground space is enclosed on the left and open on the right. The pale body and linen are set against the dark wall and curtain. The two paintings differ, too, in the relationship which they establish between the compositional means of line and colour. Whereas Giorgione maintained the two in balance, Titian uses colour modulation to delimit the individual elements of his picture.

The subject and composition of the *Bacchanalia* recall Giovanni Bellini's *Feast of the Gods* of 1514. Compared to his teacher's work, Titian's canvas seeks to infuse a new dynamism into the movements of the revellers and into the ascending line traced from left to right by the landscape and figures and terminating in the sleeping old man on the hill on the far right. The sensuality of the – in part, unaffectedly naked – figures is also lent far more direct expression. Insofar as none of the characters seek eye contact with the viewer, the self-contained nature of the world within the picture is nevertheless maintained. The deliberation with which Titian approached his composition is demonstrated by, amongst other things, the variation upon the motif of Venus seen in the sleeping woman in the bottom right-hand foreground, who serves to consolidate the internal boundaries of the composition.

With its harmonious proportions and natural expression, Titian's portrait of this unknown beauty still belongs to the tradition of the High Renaissance. The clear compositional structure is accompanied by a fine, rhythmical animation of space and surface. The magical nature of Titian's subtly gradated palette places *La Bella* amongst the most beautiful portraits of his mature years.

Titian La Bella, c. 1536
Oil on canvas, 100 x 75 cm
Florence, Galleria Pitti

Titian
Christ Crowned with Thorns, c. 1576
Oil on canvas, 280 x 182 cm
Munich, Bayerische Staatsgemälde-
sammlungen, Alte Pinakothek

*Below:*
Titian
Pietà, c. 1573–1576
Oil on canvas, 351 x 389 cm
Venice, Galleria dell'Accademia

# TITIAN
## BETWEEN 1473 AND 1490–1576

Although Titian remained indebted throughout his lengthy career to the compositional
and figural ideals of the High Renaissance, he
also succeeded in overcoming the static element in composition. Here, the animated gestures of the soldiers link them into a circle
around the "axis" of Christ. The impression of
constant movement is further heightened by
the fact that this axis itself seems to be rotat-
ing. The figures appear to be captured in mid-
action – their poses, momentarily frozen on
the canvas, must change in the next instant.
This destabilization is only made possible by
the artist's complete renunciation of fixating
line in his late works – the goal of a development which he followed consistently throughout the some seventy years of his career as a
painter.

In *Christ Crowned with Thorns*, composition
out of pure colour culminates in almost pre-
Impressionistic effects, which are further amplified by the unfinished state of the painting.
In this regard, it is significant to note that the
young Manet would later study and even copy
Titian's works in the Louvre.

Titian's last work, painted for the altar over his
tomb, was completed by Jacopo Palma the
Younger. In the bottom right-hand corner, beneath the Hellespont sibyl, we are shown a votive panel featuring the painter and his son
Orazio.

An apse filled with golden light, framed by
two columns made up of blocks of stone and a
broken pediment, establish the static element
of the composition. Against this foil, the
movements of the figures appear all the more
dynamic. On the far left and right stand the
painted statues of Moses with the tables of the
law and the Hellespont sibyl with the cross.

A diagonal descends from Moses to the
kneeling Nicodemus. The Lamentation theme
is thereby overlaid with a reference to the impending Entombment. The body of Christ, on
the other hand, initiates an opposite line of
movement leading upwards to the right, activ-
ating the putto with the torch and continuing
on to the sibyl with the raised cross – a corresponding reference to the coming Resurrection.

The pale, luminous body of Christ takes
up the stone-like colours of Moses and the
sibyl, while simultaneously contrasting with
the warm, dark reddish hues dominating the
other figures, and thus appears already
removed from this earthly life. Never before
had a Pietà illustrated the death of the Saviour and his conquest of death in such a profound manner.

The mood of the painting is essentially
characterized by the light and the palette,
whereby drawing gives way entirely to colour
modulation, as can be seen in Christ's right
arm, for example.

# LORENZO LOTTO

C. 1480–1556

According to Roman legend, Lucretia, who was the wife of Lucius Tarquinius Collatinus, was raped by the son of the Roman king – a dishonour which subsequently resulted in her suicide. The event is supposed to have precipitated the collapse of the Etruscan royal line (510 BC) and thus to have led to the founding of the Roman Republic.

In the 16th and 17th century Lucretia was frequently portrayed as a symbol of purity. Lotto presents us with the three-quarter view of a woman dressed in fine, richly trimmed clothes. Turned slightly away from the viewer, in her left hand she holds a drawing of the naked Lucretia about to stab herself in the heart. An inscription in Latin on the sheet on the table reads: "Following Lucretia's example, no dishonoured woman should continue to live".

In the exquisiteness of its palette, the painting ranks amongst Lotto's greatest works. While the subject's face follows on from the tradition of Giorgione, the contrast between her brightly lit shoulders and the richly graded reds and greens of her dress is worthy of a Titian. The costly pendant suspended from the gold chain, its precious stones refracting the light, is virtually without equal in 16th-century Venetian painting.

Lorenzo Lotto
Portrait of a Lady as Lucretia, c. 1530
Oil on canvas, 96 x 111 cm. London, National Gallery

# JACOPO BASSANO

C. 1517/18–1592

This work belongs to the first phase of the painter's career. The figures crowd towards the front edge of the canvas. Landscape and sky are indicated only briefly in the background, at the top of the composition. There is as yet no sign of the bold perspective views of architecture and landscape found in so many of Bassano's later works. Out of the heaving mass of figures, some of them seen in twisted poses and lively foreshortening, Christ and Veronica emerge as the central focus, the shared direction of their movement establishing them as a closed group. Christ looks back towards Veronica, who holds out her veil to him with an expression of compassion and devotion.

The powerful pull towards the left is offset within the composition by the almost square format, the arms of the cross, and the line of heads rising to the right, terminating in the figures in the top right-hand corner. The soldier seen from behind in the centre of the canvas forms a sort of fulcrum, mediating between the opposing lines of movement within the composition. The handling of colour, particularly in the robes of Christ and Veronica, reflects the young artist's first exposure to Venetian painting.

Jacopo Bassano
The Procession to Calvary, c. 1540
Oil on canvas, 145 x 133 cm
London, National Gallery

**Parmigianino**
Madonna of the Long Neck,
c. 1534–1540
(from the Servite church in Parma)
Oil on wood, 216 x 132 cm
Florence, Galleria degli Uffizi

# PARMIGIANINO

1503–1540

This panel, whose right-hand side remains incomplete, represents one of the most important examples of the anti-High Renaissance tendencies which have become known as Mannerism. The very subject itself remains ultimately undecided between a Virgin and Child enthroned and a Pietà.

The complicated, in places almost affected movements of the figures are combined with the anatomical distortions to which the painting owes its title. The Madonna's robes have a decorative value independent of the structure of her body. In the absence of any solid throne, she appears half-way between sitting and floating.

The sense of "alienation" introduced by the anatomy of the figures is echoed in the illogical composition of space. Just as the precise locality of the foreground angels is itself unclear, so the eye is utterly confused by the discrepancies in scale between the main foreground group, the small figure of the prophet announcing the coming of Christ on the right-hand edge of the panel, and the (unfinished) columns towering behind.

It would be wrong, however, to see Parmigianino's deviation from the norms of the High Renaissance as purely formal in nature; rather, he is here exploring a new means of rendering visible a dimension beyond that of earthly reality.

**Agnolo Bronzino**
An Allegory (Venus,
Cupid, Time and
Folly), before 1545
Oil on wood,
146 x 116 cm
London, National
Gallery

# AGNOLO BRONZINO

1503–1572

Agnolo Bronzino here portrays an elaborate allegory of the pleasures and pains of love. In the foreground, the spiralling figure of Cupid embraces Venus, whose upright figure is turned frontally towards the spectator. A boy arriving from the right is scattering roses. In the background, meanwhile, we can identify the figures of Old Age, Jealousy and Deceit.

The composition is almost stilted in its artificiality: Venus' arms and legs run parallel to the edges of the panel, while the background assumes the staggered character of a relief. The anatomically elongated arm of the old man completes the figuration, which calls to mind Theodor Hetzer's concept of "pictorial ornament".

The palette, too, is artificial. Bronzino creates a smooth, enamel-like surface, for which his choice of a wood panel is clearly more suitable than canvas. In its cool eroticism, the painting bears witness to a specifically French style of court art whose roots go back to Jean Fouquet and the 15th century. As court painter to the Medici, Bronzino executed large numbers of portraits characterized by a formal severity, a minute attention to detail and a cool sophistication.

Since Bronzino painted the present panel for King Francis I of France, it must have been executed before 1545.

## ROSSO FIORENTINO

1494–1540

This large altarpiece is one of the most typical and most important examples of so-called Florentine Early Mannerism. Rosso's early panel turns away from the norms of the High Renaissance, which were based on the reproduction of idealized nature. There is no logical spatial connection between the figures, the cross and the ladders; the size of the figures appears arbitrarily chosen, and their elongated bodies and overly small heads offer a distortion of "classical" proportions. Light and shade cannot be explained in terms of a single light source.

In addition, Rosso used boldly abbreviated forms tending towards geometric planes, both in the draperies (as in the case of Mary Magdalene and John in the right-hand corner) and in the modelling of the naked body (e.g. the figure seen from the rear on the ladder). Finally, the powerful local colours of the High Renaissance are replaced by a cool palette.

To assess Rosso's stylistic principles solely from the point of view of their formal qualities would be to misunderstand them. The poses of Mary Magdalene and John the Evangelist are visual statements of profound anguish and despair. Insofar as the viewer is no longer able to identify with the figures in the painting, the emotions they express emerge with all the greater purity, something that has lent Rosso's work a new relevance in our own century.

Rosso Fiorentino
Deposition, 1521
(from Volterra cathedral)
Oil on wood, 333 x 195 cm
Volterra, Pinacoteca Comunale

## PONTORMO

1494–1556

Like Rosso's panel, Pontormo's *Deposition* represents the pioneering vehicle of an anti-classical style of painting. Even the subject is difficult to determine: for a Deposition, it lacks a cross, for an Entombment a grave, and for a Pietà or Lamentation the direct relationship between the Virgin Mary and Christ. Painting, by its very nature, can normally only capture a single moment. Pontormo fascinatingly attempts to overcome this limitation and to portray instead a sequence of movements. It is as if we see the individual stages of a Deposition combining themselves into the suggestion of a continuous downward motion. The figures are grouped into a large, serpentine curve whose descending path is lent particular emphasis via the figure of the Virgin Mary and the falling diagonal in the bottom right-hand corner.

The composition is devoid of stabilizing elements, unstructured either by architecture or landscape. It might be described as a skilful fusion of "unstable equilibria". The transparent and modulating palette, undoubtedly influenced by Rosso, robs the figures of their gravitational weight and distances them from reality.

Pontormo
Deposition, c. 1526–1528
Oil on wood, 313 x 192 cm
Florence, Santa Felicità, Cappella Bardori

Tintoretto
St George and the Dragon, c. 1550–1560
Oil on canvas, 157 x 100 cm
London, National Gallery

Tintoretto
Christ with Mary and Martha,
c. 1580
Oil on canvas, 200 x 132 cm
Munich, Bayerische Staats-
gemäldesammlungen,
Alte Pinakothek

# TINTORETTO
## 1518–1594

This canvas dates from the start of Tintoretto's mature period, in which he finally relinquishes his ties to the plane in favour of a bold use of perspective. The eye is led from the figure of the fleeing princess, across the main group of St George and the dragon and the receding bulwarks of the castle, to the distant horizon of the sea. The striking differences in scale between the figures serve to accelerate this progression from front to rear.

Tintoretto thereby infuses his scene with a greater sense of drama than ever before in the history of the subject. The two different directions indicated by the princess in the bottom right-hand corner of the painting, fleeing towards the spectator, and the landscape leading into the depths behind, provide an exemplary demonstration of the principles of centrifugal composition, diametrically opposed to the classical mode of the High Renaissance. In his precipitous charge towards the left, we see the knight drawing upon all his forces to slay the dragon.

The corpse in the middle ground introduces a new iconographical element pointing to a previous episode in the story. The importance which Tintoretto attached to this figure is evidenced by a carefully executed study in the Louvre. The position of the body, lying on the ground with its arms outstretched, prompts associations with the figure of the crucified Christ. Is St George presented here as the vanquisher of evil in a parallel with Christ?

Tintoretto's palette shifts away from a Titianesque luminosity towards broken hues. Effects of light play a dominant role and lend a visionary character to the heavenly apparition in the light-filled clouds.

While Tintoretto demonstrated the principles of Mannerism most emphatically of all the great Venetian painters of the 16th century, in his late works he frequently moved beyond them towards a style closer to the dawning age of the Baroque.

Numerous other contemporary renditions of the present subject, especially in Netherlandish painting, show the kitchen in the foreground and the main events taking place on a miniature scale in the doorway behind. Here, by contrast, the monumentality of the three main figures ensures that the central theme is directly apparent. While Christ and the two sisters are individually developed, they are also mutually integrated in a fashion which appears as spontaneous as it is skilful. A significant role is thereby played by the correlating colours of their clothing.

Tintoretto nevertheless remains true to his principle of composition, based on often dramatic foreshortening. The line passing from Christ, across the table top, and on to the open doorway and the kitchen in the background draws the eye irresistibly into the depths of the painting – another visual expression of movement, as also suggested by the circle formed by the heads of the main figures.

In the painting of the 16th century, the relationship between Venus and Mars – portrayed by Botticelli in idealized, neo-Platonic terms – assumed a strongly erotic flavour. It is typical of Tintoretto, with his preference for drama, that he should choose to portray the moment not of the lovers' union, but of their discovery by Vulcan, Venus' ageing husband. Vulcan, still in mid-step, lays bare Venus' sex, while Mars hides under the bed.

The room recedes at an angle from front left to rear right. Its pronounced asymmetry is established by the foreshortened wall on the left, reinforced in the figure of Cupid, and by the tiles leading into the neighbouring chamber beyond. A similar extension of space is suggested by the mirror, which simultaneously aligns itself with the main figures into another diagonal. The mirror also serves a second important funtion: it transforms the figure of Vulcan, already rendered substantial by his animated pose, into a "sculpture" visible from all sides at once – an impression further reinforced by his muscular modelling, based on studies by Michelangelo. The nude Venus, probably inspired by Titian's *Andromeda*, appears almost boyishly demure by contrast. Venus provides the compositional counterweight to the powerful diagonal recession into the depths.

The Berlin Kupferstichkabinett houses a preliminary study for this painting in the shape of an ink drawing of great spontaneity, unique in Tintoretto's œuvre in its technique and its exploration of the background. The figures of the reclining Venus and of Mars under the bed are missing, however.

**Tintoretto**
Vulcan surprises Venus and Mars, c. 1555
Oil on canvas, 135 x 198 cm
Munich, Bayerische Staatsgemäldesammlungen,
Alte Pinakothek

Ignoring the moralizing tendencies of other interpretations of this subject, with their emphasis, for example, on the punishment meted out to the two lecherous old men, Tintoretto concentrates exclusively on the erotic nature of the scene. The brightly lit, naked figure of Susanna, a young woman ripened to full maturity, is the chief focus of the composition and the point to which the eye is constantly returned. Unconstrained in her pose and modelled with powerful plasticity, she may be seen in stylistic terms as the link between Michelangelo and Rubens.

The toilet articles, items of jewellery and reflections in the water are rendered with a precision unusual in Tintoretto's œuvre. The painter thereby almost creates a still life between Susanna and the hedge.

Even in this painting, however, Tintoretto remains true to his almost manic desire to guide the eye into the compositional depths, if not indeed into infinity. The edge of the bath, the rose hedge, the abrupt difference in scale between the two old men and the view into the distant park landscape combine to propel the pictorial surface into the third dimension in as many ways as possible.

**Tintoretto**
Susanna at her Bath, c. 1565
Oil on canvas, 147 x 194 cm
Vienna, Kunsthistorisches Museum

**Paolo Veronese**
Giustiana Barbaro and her Nurse, c. 1561/62
Fresco (detail)
Maser (Treviso), Villa Barbaro

**Paolo Veronese**
Allegory of Love: Unfaithfulness, c. 1575–1580
Oil on canvas, 189 x 189 cm
London, National Gallery

## PAOLO VERONESE
### 1528–1588

In Veronese's frescos for the Villa Barbaro completed by Palladio in 1559, the boundaries between appearance and reality are erased to a degree unsurpassed either in the 16th century or even by the Baroque. Seemingly tangible architecture and sculptures are just as much creations of paint as views into neighbouring rooms and into the surrounding parkland. This is equally true of the balconies in the Hall of Olympus. Behind a skilfully foreshortened balustrade, whose individual members are additionally modelled by light and shade, stands a young, well-dressed woman – traditionally identified as the mistress of the house – and her nurse, whose dark skin and simpler style of dress clearly assign her to a different social class. The life-size scale of the two women makes it all the easier for the viewer to accept them as real.

Despite the fact that the fresco technique required him to work at speed, Veronese achieves a fascinating wealth of colour gradations and painted effects of light.

*Unfaithfulness* is one of a cycle of *Four Allegories of Love* probably commissioned by Emperor Rudolf II in around 1580. Veronese places the woman, seen in rear view, at the centre of the composition. While she restrains her husband with her right arm, she turns her face and body towards her lover on the left. The arching line traced by the figures within the pictorial plane is simultaneously projected into their crescent-shaped arrangement in space. As always in Veronese, the landscape elements serve not merely to describe the setting, but also to reinforce the lines of movement within the scene – here emphasized by the directions indicated by the tree trunks and branches.

Rarely has *The Finding of Moses* received such a festive treatment as here. In growing fear of the constantly increasing numbers of Israelites, the Pharaoh ordered all new-born sons to be put to death – the Old Testament counterpart to the slaying of the infants of Bethlehem by Herod. Moses' mother hid her baby in a bulrush cradle amongst the reeds of the Nile, where he was found by the Pharaoh's daughter and adopted as her own child. The composition combines movement of the most natural and unselfconscious kind with the ordered arrangement established by the harmonious relationship between the figures and the landscape. Particularly important in this respect are the two foreground trees, whose diverging V-shape echoes the poses of the main figures. In the delicate luminosity and subtle gradations of its rich palette, the painting occupies a unique position in Veronese's œuvre and seems to look forward to Velázquez.

**Paolo Veronese**
The Finding of Moses, c. 1570–1575
Oil on canvas, 50 x 43 cm
Madrid, Museo del Prado

1498
Das malt ich nach meiner gestalt
Ich war sex und zwenzig Jor alt
Albrecht Dürer

# ALBRECHT DÜRER

1471–1528

Dürer was the first painter in Western art to regularly depict himself in self-portraits, providing us with an invaluable record of his personal development over the years.

In his Prado self-portrait in elegant dress, reminiscent of that of a nobleman, and with carefully coiffured hair and beard, the 26-year-old shows himself striving to rise above the status of artisan. We are reminded of a letter which he wrote to his friend Willibald Pirckheimer seven years later from Venice: "Here I am a master, at home a parasite."

Although seen in three-quarter view – a position reinforced by the view of the landscape on the right –, Dürer ties the figure to the plane by means of the right arm resting on the ledge, the plaited cord of the cloak and the unforeshortened folds of the left sleeve above the sitter's hands. The frame-like setting of the portrait corresponds to Italian models.

In comparison to the self-portrait of seven years earlier, Dürer has here become much freer in the handling of his pictorial means – a result of the influence of Venetian painting. The angle of the young woman's pose is uniformly indicated by the head and shoulders, while the proportions of the head and body are also more natural. Aided by the use of delicate glazes, colour modulation plays an equal role within the composition alongside precisely-observed drawing.

The two panels portraying the apostles John, Peter, Paul and Mark signify both the climax and the conclusion of Dürer's work in oils. The monumental format is combined with a sculptural approach to the figures, and together with the composition, in which colour modulation dominates over drawing, reflects the artist's assimilation of Venetian influences. Although, contrary to former opinion, Dürer's panels were probably never planned as the wings of a triptych, their immediate models can be seen in the two wings of Giovanni Bellini's triptych of 1488 for the Frari church in Venice. At the same time, however, Dürer demonstrates his northern heritage in the richly varied expressions of the faces and in his love of detail.

According to one interpretation, the four figures embody the four humours: in the left-hand panel, John is sanguine and Peter phlegmatic, and in the right-hand panel Mark choleric and Paul melancholy.

Dürer probably dedicated the panels to his native city as an admonition to hold steadfastly to the true Lutheran faith.

**Albrecht Dürer**
Portrait of a Young
Venetian Woman, 1505
Oil on wood, 35 x 26 cm
Vienna, Kunsthistorisches
Museum

**Albrecht Dürer**
Self-portrait, 1498
Oil on wood, 52 x 41 cm
Madrid, Museo del Prado

**Albrecht Dürer**
Four Apostles (John, Peter,
Paul and Mark), 1526
Oil on wood, 215.5 x 76
and 214.5 x 76 cm
Munich, Bayerische Staats-
gemäldesammlungen, Alte
Pinakothek

Albrecht Dürer
The Nativity,
c. 1502–1504
(central section of the
Paumgartner Altar)
Tempera on wood,
155 x 126cm
Munich, Bayerische
Staatsgemälde-
sammlungen, Alte
Pinakothek

*Below:*
Albrecht Dürer
The Adoration of the
Trinity, 1511
Oil tempera on wood,
135 x 123cm
Vienna, Kunsthistorisches
Museum

## ALBRECHT DÜRER
### 1471–1528

The Paumgartner Altar, a triptych, was probably commissioned around 1497 for St Catherine's church in Nuremberg. The central panel is flanked by two wings showing St George and St Eustace – probably portraits of members of the Paumgartner family. Although the two saints turn towards the Nativity scene in the central panel, the differences in their scale and in the composition of the ground and background leave the viewer with the overall impression of three independent paintings. This impression is reinforced by the contrast between the statuesque saints and the lively narrative style of the central Nativity.

In compositional terms, the central panel remains the additive sum of its parts, namely the figures and the various components of the landscape and architecture. In this regard Dürer still falls fully in line with 15th-century tradition, something he would not leave behind until works such as the *Adoration of the Trinity* below, in which he embraces a new holistic approach to composition. In the grouping of the figures in the present panel, however, he continues to employ the medieval scale according to which size indicates significance. The hand of the great draughtsman and graphic artist is betrayed in the precision of the drawing, which reinforces the separateness of the individual elements, even though the different parts of the composition are fused together by the arches in the background ruins and by perspective means.

Matthäus Landauer commissioned this panel for the Trinity chapel in the House of the Twelve Brethren which he had founded in Nuremberg in 1501. The institution was intended to provide accommodation for twelve elderly craftsmen who through no fault of their own had fallen upon hard times.

A preliminary sketch showing the magnificent frame which originally contained the panel is dated 1508 (Chantilly, Musée Condé). Clearly, therefore, the commission had already been awarded by that time and the chief elements of the composition had already been planned. The original frame is today housed in the Germanisches Nationalmuseum in Nuremberg.

The panel portrays the Holy Trinity – God the Father, Christ, and the dove of the Holy Ghost – being worshipped by the *civitas dei* (the inhabitants of the kingdom of God on earth). Both the subject and the composition recall Raphael's *Disputà* in the Stanza della Segnatura in the Vatican, which Dürer nevertheless could not have known, since it was only begun in 1509. Rather, Dürer's panel is part of an international trend towards "classic" form, albeit one inconceivable north of the Alps without the influence of Italy.

The isolated treatment of individual elements in Dürer's earlier paintings is here overcome through the means of colour modulation and, above all, composition. In a similar fashion to Raphael, circular – i.e. geometric – and spherical – i.e. stereometric – segments mutually overlap. At the same time, the top, arched edge of the painting is incorporated into the internal composition.

## HANS BURGKMAIR The Elder

1473–1531

There is scarcely a more impressive portrayal in the whole of German painting of St John writing the Book of Revelations while receiving his visions. The monumentality and pathos of the figure each heighten the other. The fragmented detail characterizing Burgkmair's earlier works here gives way to the large, homogeneous form.

The dramatic train of movement established by the contrasting directions indicated by John's leg, gestures and head must have been inspired at least indirectly by Italian models. The powerful tree trunks serve as framing elements which lend stability to the composition, while their leaning branches place visual emphasis upon the message issuing from the angel appearing in the clouds above left.

Although Burgkmair's inclusion of palms and exotic birds is an allusion to the Greek island setting, he nevertheless betrays a romantic awareness of landscape which can be traced back to the Danube School. He probably based the tropical vegetation on plant studies made in the gardens of the Augsburg Fugger family.

The panel forms the central section of a triptych, whose wings when open depict St Erasmus and St Martin.

Hans Burgkmair the Elder
John the Evangelist on Patmos, 1518
(central section of the St John Altar)
Oil on wood, 153.1 x 127.2 cm
Munich, Bayerische Staatsgemälde-
sammlungen, Alte Pinakothek

## HANS BALDUNG

C. 1484/85–1545

By electing to portray the main figures simply and quietly at the back of the stable, Baldung draws the eye first to the ruined architecture and the ox and ass seen in larger scale on the left. His construction of the interior embraces the opposite poles of precise foreshortening – as in the incisively drawn plinth in the foreground – and perspective uncertainty, something heightened by the differences in scale between the animals and the figures. Viewer irritation and Mannerist alienation are quite clearly not the artist's aims, however.

With the help of painted light, whose source seems to lie beyond the natural world, Baldung portrays the miracle of the Holy Night with what is for him an unusual depth of feeling. The infant Jesus, held in his swaddling bands by putti, seems to radiate light onto Joseph's red coat and Mary's hands and face. Through the brick archway in the cracked, plastered wall, we glimpse a second miraculous vision: an angel encircled by a radiant glory is appearing to a shepherd watching his flock. The fusion of light and shade and the soft modulation of the contours suggest that Baldung may have come into contact with the Danube School.

Hans Baldung (Grien)
The Nativity, 1520
Oil on wood, 105.5 x 70.4 cm
Munich, Bayerische Staatsgemälde-
sammlungen, Alte Pinakothek

Matthias Grünewald
The Mocking of Christ, c. 1503
Oil tempera on wood, 109 x 73.5 cm
Munich, Bayerische Staatsgemälde-
sammlungen, Alte Pinakothek

Matthias Grünewald
Crucifixion, 1512–1516 (central section of the Isenheim Altar)
Oil on wood, 269 x 307 cm. Colmar, Musée d'Unterlinden

# MATTHIAS GRÜNEWALD
## C. 1470/80–1528

In *The Mocking of Christ*, the first work that can be definitely attributed to Grünewald, the painter gives vent to the primeval force of emotion dominating his art and thereby carries the scene to previously unseen heights of dramatic intensity. Christ, his hands and arms tied and his eyes bound, is helplessly exposed to the blows of the soldiers, whose faces are an expression of pure brutality unmitigated by any trace of human sympathy. The hatred portrayed here is emphasized almost to the point of caricature. Parallels have justifiably been drawn with Hieronymus Bosch and the physiognomic studies of Leonardo.

The composition already looks ahead to Grünewald's later development. While careful attention is still paid to the rendering of individual details, large-area use of colour is already giving way to iridescent transitions and softly flowing contours.

The famous *Crucifixion* from the Isenheim Altar portrays the agony of Christ with a penetrating forcefulness seen neither before nor since. The tortured body, with its bowed head and skin almost grey in pallor, its strained sinews and muscles and its fingers seemingly frozen rigid in cramp, bears witness to Christ's suffering. The slight sag in the arms of the cross reinforces the impression that the body is hanging heavily downwards. The terrible nature of the scene is reflected in the stormy night landscape and the intense expressions and poses of the Virgin Mary, John and Mary Magdalene.

Unique in the expressive force of its poses and gestures, Grünewald's panel acquires its "overwhelming" character first and foremost from the eruptive power of colour and colour contrasts. None of the great German painters of Dürer's era matched Grünewald in evoking the emotions of the spectator through colour rather than through drawing.

This solemn and stately panel occupies a unique position within Grünewald's œuvre. The two main figures dominating the foreground resemble polychrome statues. By avoiding any emphasis upon the central axis, Grünewald overcomes the danger of a static composition; instead, the Moorish saint appears to have just arrived from the right.

Through the smaller scale and less clearly defined contours of the figures behind, Grünewald creates an impression of rapidly receding depth. The painterly execution of the bishop's robe and the knight's armour ranks amongst the supreme achievements of German art in the age of Dürer.

Matthias Grünewald
The Meeting of St Erasmus and St Maurice,
c. 1520–1524
Oil on wood, 226 x 176 cm
Munich, Bayerische Staatsgemäldesammlungen,
Alte Pinakothek

## ALBRECHT ALTDORFER
### c. 1480–1538

In the landscapes portrayed in the panels of the St Florian Altar, the "romantic" characteristics of the Danube School reach their high point. The present scene is set in a fantastical rocky landscape whose burning red sky casts an emphatically unnatural light. Christ kneels humbly behind the group of sleeping disciples and seems unaware of the angel holding out the cup in front of him.

The main lines of the composition – indicated by the row of disciples and the diagonal running from the approaching soldiers, through the figure of Christ, to the angel – rise from left to right and hence upwards in the direction of the light. They thereby point beyond the approaching Passion to Christ's future resurrection and ascension, as reinforced by the luminous yellow above Christ's head.

**Albrecht Altdorfer**
The Agony in the Garden,
c. 1515
(panel from the St Florian
Altar)
Oil on wood, 128 x 95 cm
St Florian, Augustiner-
Chorherrenstift

The story of the two lecherous old men who spied on Susanna while she was bathing and who were subsequently punished by stoning (as seen on the terrace in the right-hand side of the picture) is here lent the atmosphere of a fairy-tale seen in the colours of a dream. The fact that Altdorfer succeeds in maintaining compositional unity despite the multiplicity of figural, architectural and landscape details can be traced back to the intensive series of preliminary studies which he made for the panel. The palace complex, with its ostentatious display of the artist's perspective skills, may have been inspired by Upper Italian, probably Venetian, influences.

No history painting had ever before attempted to suggest such a seemingly infinite number of soldiers and thereby to give the impression of a real battlefield. Altdorfer's talent as an artist lay not least in his ability to combine such a wealth of minutely-executed detail into a homogeneous composition. Most significant of all is the setting: from an elevated viewpoint, we look across a landscape which has been convincingly interpreted as a representation of the entire Mediterranean region. In the middle ground we see the eastern Mediterranean with Cyprus; beyond the isthmus the Red Sea; beside it on the right Egypt and the Nile, whose delta is accurately shown with seven arms; left the Gulf of Persia; and in the needle-like mountain beneath, the Tower of Babylon.

In contrast to the fixed boundaries of High Renaissance space, Altdorfer here seeks to portray infinity in a "global landscape". His combination of precision of line with richness of colour modulation identifies him as one of the greatest masters in the history of German painting.

**Albrecht Altdorfer**
Susanna at her Bath and
The Stoning of the Old
Men, 1526
Oil on wood,
74.8 x 61.2 cm
Munich, Bayerische
Staatsgemäldesammlun-
gen, Alte Pinakothek

**Albrecht Altdorfer**
Alexander's Victory (The Battle on the Issus),
1529
Oil tempera on wood, 158.4 x 120.3 cm
Munich, Bayerische Staatsgemäldesammlungen,
Alte Pinakothek

**Hans Holbein the Younger**
The Ambassadors (Jean de Dinteville and
Georges de Selve), 1533
Tempera on wood, 207 x 209.5 cm
London, National Gallery

## HANS HOLBEIN The Younger

C. 1497/98–1543

This panel was probably painted in April
1533, while bishop Georges de Selve (right)
was in London visiting his friend Jean de Dinteville, French ambassador to England.

The square format which Holbein chose for
his painting was one popular in the High Renaissance. Here it forms the starting-point for
a carefully structured composition. The two
men assume a framing function within the picture. Right and left, top and bottom are
linked by means of verticals and horizontals,

whereby the few diagonals present introduce a
certain element of relaxation. The objects on
the shelf and table incorporate themselves into
this overall structure, each charged with a specific symbolism which in some cases has yet to
be understood. There is clear preference for objects from the world of geometry and astrology. The distorting mirror in the foreground
and the broken string of the mandolin are references to death. The open book shows an extract from Johann Walter's *Geystliche Gesänge*
(Sacred Songs) published in Wittenberg in
1524 – an allusion to the mediating position
which the two noblemen occupied between
Catholicism and Protestantism.

This panel marks the last of Holbein's religious commissions. It shows Jakob Meyer, mayor of Basle, and his family under the protection of the Virgin, and was executed for the donor's private chapel. Sadly, we have no information regarding its original frame. Was the monumental, painted scalloped niche continued in a carved or sculpted frame, so that – in a similar fashion to the Venetian *Sacra Conversazione* – pictorial space was extended into real space? And what was the original function of the background views of vegetation and sky on the left and right?

Holbein's composition is precisely calculated. The diagonal leading out of the picture, indicated by the group on the left, is balanced by the position of the Madonna, who is turning towards the right. Here, the group of women provide the composition with a stable conclusion. The motif of the Virgin's protective mantle is taken up in the projecting volutes which in turn enfold the figures.

An astonishing feature of the present panel, when compared to Holbein's earlier *Solothurn Madonna*, for example, is the condensed arrangement of the figures. Space exists only insofar as it is created by the statue-like modelling of the figures. This has led some to suspect that Holbein studied sculpture (including works by Michel Colombe, for example) during his stay in France. In addition, there are echoes of Leonardo in the faces of the Virgin and the donor's elder son. Holbein establishes a deliberate contrast between the idealized figure of the Virgin and the pronouncedly individual faces of the members of the donor's family.

This portrait shows Holbein at the height of his powers. The dominating figure of the sitter, silhouetted by means of just a few clear lines, forms the central focus of an interior filled with a seemingly random arrangement of objects. The angled table and the position of the sitter, turned slightly inwards, are combined into a skilful spatial composition. Holbein observes his model with the same cool, searching gaze with which the sitter looks at us.

The objects on the table reflect an enduring delight in the portrayal of still-life detail – something which Holbein inherited not just from the German painting of the 15th century, but more especially from the Netherlands.

While the individual objects – the vase of flowers, the cashbox, the items carved of wood, the books and the writing implements – may not reveal the warm luminosity so characteristic of Early Netherlandish artists from Jan van Eyck to Hugo van der Goes, Holbein nevertheless demonstrates supreme sophistication in his use of colour. This can be seen not least in the iridescent white heightening on the sitter's red sleeves, in the elaborate, almost palpable weave of the tablecloth, and in the shimmering glass vase.

Here as in his other portraits, Holbein combines the monumentality of Italian form with the "detail realism" of the style of painting north of the Alps. The painting must be counted amongst the most outstanding works to be found in German portraiture.

**Hans Holbein the Younger**
Madonna of Mercy and the Family of Jakob Meyer zum Hasen (Darmstadt Madonna), c. 1528/29
Gum tempera on wood, 144 x 101 cm. Darmstadt, Großherzogliches Schloß

*Below:*
**Hans Holbein the Younger**
Portrait of the Merchant Georg Gisze, 1532
Oil on wood, 96 x 86 cm
Berlin, Gemäldegalerie, Staatliche Museen zu Berlin – Preußischer Kulturbesitz

# LUCAS CRANACH The Elder
## 1472–1553

Executed shortly before the artist was appointed court painter at Wittenberg, the panel shows Lucas Cranach at the height of his creative powers. The composition combines clarity with uncoerced organization. The figures are grouped in a loose triangle whose vertical middle axis is accentuated by Joseph and the tree behind, but whose slightly offset position avoids any introduction of geometric rigidity. The backdrop of nearby trees on the left is harmoniously complemented by the unimpeded view of the distant landscape on the right.

Cranach demonstrates an astonishing freedom in the handling of his compositional means, whereby the dominant role played by colour modulation in the landscape evokes a romantic mood as characteristic of the Danube School.

Whether *Rest on the Flight to Egypt* is indeed an accurate title for this panel is a question that must remain open. Are we not in fact looking at a Holy Family surrounded by angels making music and playing games, their fairy-tale character echoed in the appearance of the landscape?

Whatever the case, Cranach includes neither a donkey nor baggage; the only indication that this might be a stop on a journey is the stick in Joseph's hand. The scene is set with the greatest candour in a mountainous Southern German landscape.

**Lucas Cranach the Elder**
Rest on the Flight to Egypt,
1504
Oil tempera on wood,
69 x 51 cm
Berlin, Gemäldegalerie,
Staatliche Museen zu Berlin –
Preußischer Kulturbesitz

This painting occupies a unique position within Cranach's artistic development. The dignified and stately style demanded of a court painter is here combined for one last time with the stormy spontaneity of the young master.

Far removed from the donors of medieval painting, the Cardinal is the largest figure in the composition, his emphatically red robes filling virtually the entire foreground. Kneeling in a pose of worship, he turns not towards the crucified Christ but looks diagonally out of the picture. Cranach here presents the masterly portrait of a Renaissance man who is ultimately devoted not to the spiritual life but to the pleasures of the world.

The contrast presented by the thin, outstretched body of Christ, who resembles a carved crucifix from the Late Gothic era, could not be more extreme. His unbroken silhouette might in other circumstances evoke a certain sense of calm, were it not for the arms of the cross and the fluttering loincloth pointing to the events behind. Like the wan colours of the barren mound of Calvary, the thunder-black sky – alongside Grünewald's Crucifixions, the most dramatic portrayal of a storm in German Renaissance painting – charge the scene with expression. Once again Cranach proves himself the great master of the Danube School, whereby his landscape and figures have now become the vehicles of separate and different emotions.

**Lucas Cranach the Elder**
Cardinal Albrecht of Brandenburg before the Crucified
Christ, c. 1520–1530
Oil on wood, 158 x 112 cm
Munich, Bayerische Staatsgemäldesammlungen, Alte
Pinakothek

In order to be cured of a serious illness, Hercules was instructed by the Delphic Oracle to sell himself into slavery for three years. While in the service of Omphale, Queen of Lydia, he performed great deeds, killing and capturing the Cercopes, killing the exiled Syleus and his daughter, destroying the city of the Itons and finally killing the great snake. According to various Roman authors, during his enslavement in Lydia Hercules was obliged to wear women's clothing, play musical instruments and sing in order to please his mistress.

The renunciation of a scenic representation in favour of a "group portrait" is a characteristic feature of Cranach's late work. In this case, he chooses a genre-like situation in which Hercules is seen at the distaff while ladies of the court tie a scarf around his head. Like Niklaus Manuel (cf. ill. p. 198), Cranach transposes a subject from Greek mythology into a contemporary setting north of the Alps. Cranach demonstrates less originality than Manuel, however – an indication that his powers of imagination, formerly so impulsive, were now fading. As an upright German citizen "dressed up" by Omphale's ladies-in-waiting, Hercules verges on caricature. Ophale herself appears in the figure of the richly dressed woman in the upper right-hand corner.

Faces and gestures are affected and in places almost laboured. The panel's quality lies in the execution of its details – the still life of the birds on the left, the clothes, and above all the finery and hat worn by Omphale.

**Lucas Cranach the Elder**
Hercules and Omphale, 1537
Oil tempera on wood, 82 x 119cm
Braunschweig, Herzog-Anton-Ulrich-Museum

Whether this panel should be attributed to the elder or the younger Cranach is still the subject of debate – something which demonstrates the stylistic continuity between the two. The landscape prompts associations with the early œuvre of Cranach the Elder as one of the chief representatives of the Danube School. The fact that the overall composition is essentially "totalled up" out of numerous individual elements, however, together with a certain clumsiness in the portrayal of the figures, points to a weaker hand. It is possible that both father and son collaborated on the picture.

The painting draws upon the mythical belief in the purifying and revitalizing properties of water for its subject, and upon medieval bathing scenes for its formal composition. It is striking that all those bathing are female. The elderly women being brought to the pool in wheelbarrows and carts on the left can be seen emerging from the water rejuvenated on the right, where they are directed by a nobleman into tents in order to dress. In the middle ground on the right we are shown the youthful pleasures of food, music and love. Coming off badly out of all of this are the men who have not been rejuvenated, and who must now watch from a distance as their foolish desires are punished.

The direction in which the events unfold from left to right is countered by the foreshortened pool, which leads the eye into the far landscape. Anecdotal detail dominates over overall form.

The erotic atmosphere exuded by the panel is characteristic of Cranach's late work and the somewhat decadent tastes of his noble patrons.

**Lucas Cranach the Elder** or
**Lucas Cranach the Younger**
The Fountain of Youth, 1546
Oil on wood, 121 x 184cm
Berlin, Gemäldegalerie, Staatliche Museen
zu Berlin – Preußischer Kulturbesitz

## JÖRG RATGEB
### c. 1480–1526

The Herrenberg Altar reflects the religious and social unrest of its day with a directness unequalled in any other work of German painting. Here, at an early point in time, the harmony of the High Renaissance has been destroyed in every respect. The panels of the altar, which is signed 1519, depict scenes from the childhood and Passion of Christ. A fantastical rotunda provides the architectural framework not just for the Flagellation in the centre, but also for Christ's crowning with thorns (front right), presentation to the populace (on the steps in the background) and interrogation by Pilate (on the top storey).

With no knowledge of Italian art, the artist takes up some of the fundamental principles of Florentine Early Mannerism: the disruption of logical spatial relationships through the use of drastic foreshortening and enormous differences in scale between the figures; an asymmetrical composition combined with an emphatic spiralling movement around the central pillar; the distortion of natural proportions to heighten expressiveness; and finally a bright, iridescent palette.

With its manifold foreshortenings, vistas and staggered levels, the complex architecture might be seen as a distant forerunner of the visionary, surreal interiors of Giovanni Battista Piranesi's *Carceri d'invenzione* (Imaginary Prisons).

**Jörg Ratgeb**
The Flagellation of Christ, 1518/19
(wing of the Herrenberg Altar in
Herrenberg parish church)
Oil tempera on wood, 262 x 143 cm
Stuttgart, Staatsgalerie Stuttgart

## NIKLAUS MANUEL
### c. 1484–1530

This scene from Greek mythology is transported in a highly personal fashion to a German forest with contemporary figures. Paris appears as a Swiss country gentleman who has just presented Venus with the apple as her prize. Juno and Minerva have turned aside following their defeat.

Juno corresponds with Paris in the colours of her clothes, while Minerva is similarly related to Venus. From a branch of the tree, blindfolded Cupid – a symbol of love, which blinds – shoots an arrow at Paris. The two coats of arms hanging from the boughs belong to the family of Benedicht Brunner, a councillor of Berne, who in all probability commissioned the painting.

There is a strange discrepancy between the classical theme and the thoroughly anti-classical female ideal represented by the women, whose curved bellies can be traced back to Dürer. Manuel compensates for his difficulties with anatomy in the extreme delicacy with which he draws the faces.

Employing the unusual technique of tempera on canvas, Manuel invokes a pastel-like palette of great charm. In details such as Venus' diaphanous dress he demonstrates the sophistication of his art. The composition, in which the figures are arranged as if in relief against the shadowy background of a wood, recalls Gobelin tapestries.

**Niklaus Manuel (Deutsch)**
The Judgement of Paris,
c. 1517/18
Tempera on canvas,
223 x 160 cm
Basle, Öffentliche
Kunstsammlung Basel,
Kunstmuseum

# GERARD DAVID

C. 1460–1523

Comparable with Italian *Sacra Conversazione* compositions from around 1500, David's panel is characterized by a happy balance between stillness and movement, between space and plane, and between the overall homogeneity of the composition and the careful execution of its details.

The starting-point for the present picture was probably Jan van Eyck's *Virgin and Child and Canon van der Paele*. Here, however, the arrangement of the figures in a concave curve is freer, the anatomical detail more animated. The kneeling donor, with his powerful plastic modelling and portrait-like features, is set against the aristocratically refined figures of the saints. The facial types employed for the women recall Hans Memling, whose leading position in Bruges painting was inherited by David.

The painter renounces virtually all movement. St Catherine, identified as a princess by her crown, turns shyly towards Christ, who places a ring on her finger. The exquisite execution of details – accessories, clothes, the carpet hanging behind the Virgin and the still lifes of flowers on either side of the throne – once again points to the influence of Jan van Eyck. A tendency towards multiplicity and diversity is evinced by the townscape seen over the city wall, where secular buildings are combined with grandiose civic architecture in what were then modern architectural forms. The lower storeys of the tower possibly contain a reference to the belfry in Bruges.

The *Baptism of Christ* forms the central section of a triptych commissioned by the treasurer of the city of Bruges, Jean Trompes. The wings show the donor's family and patron saints on the inside, and the Virgin and Child and the donor's second wife with St Elizabeth on the outside. Nowhere does the artist demonstrate more clearly both his talents and his limitations. The present scene contains virtually no action. The kneeling figures of John the Baptist and the angel dressed in a sumptuous cope reveal a mutual correspondence in their approximate symmetry and subtly differentiated positions. The panel's central axis is strongly emphasized by the figure of Christ, the dove of the Holy Ghost and the apparition of God the Father.

The painting's charm lies first and foremost in its broad landscape, interspersed with scenes from the life of the Baptist. The still life of flowers in the foreground is characterized by a dazzling wealth of minute detail. "Gentle, luminous colours infuse this rich, beautiful world of landscapes, figures and objects with a silver shimmer which transports the viewer to a different reality. Filled with a calm grandeur, the elements combine into solemn harmonies. Human warmth infuses the dignified tone." (Wolfgang Schöne)

Gerard David
The Mystic Marriage of St Catherine, c. 1505–1510
Oil tempera on wood, 106 x 144 cm
London, National Gallery

Gerard David
The Baptism of Christ,
c. 1505
(central section of a
triptych)
Oil on wood, 128 x 97 cm
Bruges, Groeningemuseum

**Quentin Massys**
The Money-changer and his Wife, 1514
Oil on wood, 70 x 67 cm
Paris, Musée National du Louvre

**Quentin Massys**
Portrait of a Canon, c. 1510–1520 (?)
Oil on wood, 60 x 73 cm
Vaduz, Collection of the Prince of Liechtenstein

# QUENTIN MASSYS
## c. 1465/66–1530

To a certain degree in opposition to the Romanists amongst his contemporaries, Massys held fast to the traditions established by Early Netherlandish art. Italian influences, to which he was only indirectly exposed, nevertheless make themselves felt in the monumentalization of his figures

*The Money-changer and his Wife* is an early example of the genre painting which would flourish in Flanders and the northern Netherlands over the course of the 16th century. Seated behind the table, and each sliced on one side by the frame, the figures are set back from the front edge of the painting. Although sophisticated in their nuances of colour, the faces wear an expression of relative indifference. Full of their own life, on the other hand, are the still-life details – the lavishly illuminated codex through which the wife is leafing, the angled mirror, which reflects the outer world into the picture in masterly foreshortening, and the glass, accessories and coins gleaming on the table and on the shelves against the far wall. In the dominant role which it grants to these objects, the painting marks an important step along the path towards the pure still life.

By inserting his own likeness into the painting – reflected in the convex mirror – Massys recalls the use of this device by Jan van Eyck in *The Arnolfini Marriage* (ill. p. 123) of 1434.

In contrast to the painting above, Massys here demonstrates his confident abilities as a portrait painter. The canon calmly surveys the outside world, but his thoughts seem to be turned inwards. Sebastiano del Piombo's more or less contemporaneous portrait of *Cardinal Carondelet and his Secretary* (ill. p. 173) offers an interesting comparison in this respect. The Cardinal observes the external world with cool, calculating eyes, but without the kindliness suggested by Massys' canon. The secularity of Carondelet and his setting is diametrically opposed to the personality of the canon, rooted in the Christian faith.

In his composition, Massys achieves a homogeneity and grandeur only rarely paralleled in his œuvre. The half-length figure is contained within the approximate volume of a pyramid, dominating the pictorial field. Massys avoids any sense of ridigity, however, by slightly offsetting the sitter to the left of the central axis and by showing his head slightly turned.

The sensitive handling of paint evidenced in the iridescent hues of the cape and in the light and shade which model the head is on an equal par with contemporary Venetian painting, which Massys would probably not have known. There is a melodious harmony, too, in the relationship between figure and landscape. From a slightly elevated standpoint, we look out across a broad expanse of hills and meadows towards the hazy distant mountains. Nature is filled with the same quiet calm as the canon himself.

# JOACHIM PATINIR
C. 1480–1524

As in the majority of his works, Joachim Patinir uses a narrative event as a pretext to portray a landscape seen from an elevated standpoint. This is an early example of the genre in Netherlandish painting known as the "global landscape", whose roots can be traced back to the first half of the 15th century and Jan van Eyck's *Virgin of Chancellor Rolin*, for example (ill. p. 123). An outstanding example in German painting is Albrecht Altdorfer's *Alexander's Victory* (ill. p. 193).

In a curious mixture of Christian iconography (the angel apparently standing guard on the left bank; the underworld portrayed as Hell on the right) and classical mythology (Charon and the bark in which he ferries the dead across to Hades), Patinir seeks to communicate the gloomy nature of events through the mood of the landscape. The river extends into the depths of the picture and beyond the visible horizon and thereby points to the spherical shape of the earth and at the same time to infinity.

The gathering storm clouds become one with the smoke billowing from the fiery furnaces of the underworld. The influence of Hieronymus Bosch can be seen not just in the ghostly apparitions of Hell, but more particularly in the stylistic treatment of silhouettes and contours, which grow increasingly hazier towards the background.

Joachim Patinir
Landscape with Charon's Bark, c. 1521
Oil on wood, 64 x 103 cm
Madrid, Museo del Prado

# JAN GOSSAERT
C. 1478/88 – C. 1533/36

Depicted is the semi-naked figure of Danaë receiving Zeus in the form of a golden shower, as recounted in Greek legend. The columned niche with its numerous Renaissance elements reflects the influences to which Gossaert was exposed during his trip to Rome. Echoes of Italy are also evident in some of the buildings in the city behind. Gossaert nevertheless draws no closer to the archeologically faithful rendition of Roman architecture so typical of his countryman Maerten van Heemskerck than to the holistic compositional approach of Italian High Renaissance painting. He simply employs individual details like words whose context he has failed to understand. As a consequence, the overall composition remains the additive sum of its parts.

The clarity of the drawing, the cool smoothness of the painting and the restrained palette are all typical features of Gossaert's œuvre. Danaë's draperies, however, veil a flawed mastery of anatomy, while the integration of her plastic volume within the perspective construction of the interior and background lacks conviction. The panel also lacks the erotic tension introduced so masterfully into similar subjects by painters such as Correggio and Titian.

Jan Gossaert, called Mabuse Danae, 1527
Oil tempera on wood, 113.5 x 95 cm
Munich, Bayerische Staatsgemäldesammlungen, Alte Pinakothek

Lucas van Leyden
Lot and his Daughters, c. 1520
Oil on wood, 48 x 34 cm
Paris, Musée National du Louvre

*Below:*
**Bernaert van Orley**
Holy Family, 1522
Oil tempera on wood,
90 x 74 cm
Madrid, Museo del Prado

## LUCAS VAN LEYDEN
### 1494–1533

The story of the destruction of Sodom, Lot's escape, and his subsequent seduction by his two
daughters is told in Genesis. Lot and his family were allowed to leave the city on condition
that they did not look back. Lot's wife dis-
obeyed the instruction and was turned into a
pillar of salt. Lot continued on with his
daughters. Since their husbands had not fled
with them, the daughters said to each other:
"Our father is old and there is not a man in
the country to come to us in the usual way.
Come now, let us make our father drink wine
and then lie with him and in this way keep
the family alive through our father." The sons
born of this union subsequently founded the
tribes of the Moabites and the Ammonites.

   Both as a strongly erotic group painting
and as a history painting, the subject was a
popular one in the 16th and 17th century.
This painting, whose attribution to van
Leyden – said to have executed his first commission at the age of twelve – is not altogether
certain, falls into the second category. Alongside the group in the foreground, the destruction of Sodom seen in the left-hand background establishes a second point of focus. Influenced by Patenier, the painter portrays a
kind of "global landscape" extending from the
front left-hand corner into the depths of the
composition. He thereby devotes particular
care to the execution of the landscape details.

## BERNAERT VAN ORLEY
### C. 1488–1542

The infant running to his mother initiates a diagonal train of movement which leads through
Mary to the kindly, ageing Joseph behind. The
grouping of the main figures thus introduces
both asymmetry and depth to the pictorial
plane. With great artistic intelligence, Orley
balances this on the left by means of the two
angels parallel to the plane, one approaching
with a wicker basket of flowers and one hovering overhead and bearing a golden crown.
Christ serves to link together the various elements of the painting. His left hand reaches
up to his mother's shoulder, his eyes are raised
towards the crown with which he will one day
make Mary Queen of Heaven, while his right
arm gestures towards the apple in Joseph's
hand – a symbol of the sin which Jesus has
come to conquer.

   Orley can here be seen as a painter mediating between two stylistic eras. While lovingly
executed details of material and texture remain the prominent focus of his interest, he
also acknowledges the masters of the High Renaissance in his skilful balancing of depth and
plane and in his delicate gradation of colour in
the receding landscape. Orley is known both
as a painter of large altarpieces and as a portraitist.

# JAN VAN SCOREL

## 1495–1562

Scorel was influenced more strongly than his contemporaries by the time he spent in Italy: under the Netherlandish pope Adrian VI, he succeeded Raphael as superintendant of the Vatican collection of antiquities, a post he held until 1524. Italian influence is evident here in both the formal composition and the artist's use of colour. As a means of enlivening the composition, Mary Magdalene is seated slightly to the right of the perpendicular middle axis. Balance is established within the pictorial plane by the tree on the right whose branches extend across the upper half of the canvas, almost reaching the rocky outcrop which provides a solid conclusion to the composition on the left. Mary Magdalene's shoulders are turned slightly in the opposite direction to her head. Her left arm and the jar of ointment round off the balanced relationship between space and plane.

Scorel's familiarity with Venetian painting finds its echo in the delicately gradated hues of the landscape, in which drawing increasingly yields to colour modulation as the background recedes. The confident composition and virtuoso handling of paint are unable to disguise a certain secular element within the subject. Were it not for the exquisite jar of ointment identifying her as Mary Magdalene, the sitter might well be mistaken for the portrait of a young lady from a well-to-do household.

Jan van Scorel
Mary Magdalene, 1529
Oil on canvas, 67 x 76.5 cm
Amsterdam, Rijksmuseum

# MAERTEN VAN HEEMSKERCK

## 1498–1574

This painting of an unknown family is one of the most important works of portraiture in 16th-century Netherlandish art. It also provides an exemplary illustration of the possibilities offered by the combination of Early Netherlandish tradition, Italian influences and creative talent.

The clear compositional structure, stabilized by its "corner posts" of father and mother yet with no sense of rigidity, reflects both the influences with which Heemskerck was confronted in Rome and his own endeavours to lend plastic conviction to his figures and objects. The richly decked table, on the other hand, with its carefully executed tableware and food, takes up the love of detail so characteristic of Early Netherlandish painting. It is but a short step from here to the emergence of the still life as a genre in its own right.

While the different ages of the three children are accurately characterized, the figures nevertheless remain coolly distanced from the spectator. The inner world of the painting remains hermetically sealed, an impression reinforced by the technique employed for the background, whereby the paint is applied in thin, smooth layers in pale forms which seem to be abstracted from clouds.

Heemskerck's *Family Portrait*, one of his greatest works, was for a long time attributed to his fellow Dutchman Jan van Scorel.

Maerten van Heemskerck
Family Portrait, c. 1530
Oil on wood, 118 x 140 cm
Cassel, Staatliche Gemäldegalerie

**Pieter Brueghel the Elder**
Netherlandish Proverbs, 1559
Oil on wood, 117 x 163 cm
Berlin, Gemäldegalerie, Staatliche Museen
zu Berlin – Preußischer Kulturbesitz

# PIETER BRUEGHEL The Elder

## c. 1525/30–1569

The follies of humankind were amongst Brueghel's favourite subjects in painting. He treated them both singly, as in *The Fall of the Blind* (1568; Naples, Museo Nazionale di Capodimonte), and in densely-populated compositions combining several at once, in what might be called cyclical form. Brueghel thereby directly takes up the tradition of Hieronymus Bosch. It is quite safe to assume that the content of his pictures would have been immediately obvious to his contemporaries.

Brueghel probably made no more use of a specific source for his *Netherlandish Proverbs* than for his *Children's Games* (1560), *The Fight between Carnival and Lent* (1559; both Vienna, Kunsthistorisches Museum) and *Dulle Griet* (*Mad Meg*, c. 1562; Antwerp, Museum Meyer van den Bergh), which were painted around the same time and which – in view of their similar scales – perhaps form part of a cycle. Rather, he drew upon contemporary thinking and translated it into paint.

The present panel is distinguished by the admirable homogeneity of its composition, which embraces a wealth of small and complex

detail. Brueghel achieves this homogeneity first and foremost by organizing the scene along a powerful diagonal running from bottom left to top right. The warm, luminous palette, dominated by browns of every shade, also serves to establish a harmonious atmosphere in which figures, buildings and landscape are integrated.

Some one hundred proverbs have been identified in the picture, all of them related to the concept of the "The World Turned Upside Down", as the painting is also sometimes known. This is directly illustrated in the globe and cross hanging upside-down above the entrance to the large house on the left. In the bottom right-hand foreground, a man is trying to crawl through another globe (a man must "bow and scrape" if he is to "get on in the world"). On top of the crenellated tower in the rear of the picture, a man is "trimming his sails to the wind". Out in the bay in the top right-hand corner, a small boat is demonstrating the advantages of "sailing with the wind", while on the peninsula to the left, one blind man is leading two others (a miniature interpretation of the later *Fall of the Blind*). In focusing on the painting's content, we should not overlook the high degree of artistry with which Brueghel treats even the smallest details.

The story of the Tower of Babel, told in Genesis 11, took place at a time when everyone on earth spoke just one language. The people decided to build a new and magnificent city and at its centre would be a mighty tower which would reach up to Heaven. Angered by their arrogance, Yahweh, the God of the Old Testament, punished the people by confusing their language so that they were no longer able to understand one another's speech. He then scattered them all over the world. The tower itself remained unfinished. The story is first found illustrated in 6th-century manuscript illuminations. In the 16th century the Tower of Babel became a popular subject of panel painting, functioning as a warning both to the secular and the sacred authorities not to fall victim to haughtiness and pride.

Brueghel bases his composition, whose details are executed with the greatest of care, on that of the "global landscape" seen from an elevated standpoint. Respect for the large form is upheld in the tower, whose various stages of construction are nevertheless portrayed in great detail. The cut-away view into the exposed top part of the tower reflects a knowledge of Roman architecture, such as the Colosseum, while the use of brick masonry clad on the outside with finished stone is also adopted from Rome. The cloud encircling the left-hand side of the uppermost storeys serves to indicate that the tower is indeed reaching up to Heaven.

Buildings of this type are known to have existed amongst the early cultures of the Mediterranean region. One such was the *ziggurat* (temple tower) dedicated to the moon god Nanna in Ur (2250–2233 BC), whose lower storeys are still preserved today.

**Pieter Brueghel the Elder**
The Tower of Babel, 1563
Oil on wood, 114 x 154 cm
Vienna, Kunsthistorisches
Museum

This panel belongs to the group of allegorical subjects in which Brueghel castigates the follies and excesses of the world. In contrast to his earlier *Proverb* paintings, however, Brueghel employs in his later works a monumental scale which almost seems to burst out of the confines of the small format. The main "actors" here are three stout men lying either asleep or incapacitated at the foot of a table, on which can be seen the remains of a meal and an overturned flagon. Clearly identified by their clothing as belonging to different classes (knight, peasant and scholar or cleric), the boldly foreshortened figures are grouped like the spokes of a wheel. Brueghel thereby creates a sense of rotation around an axis, a sequence of movement which recalls the compositional principles employed by Italian Mannerism.

Anecdotal details such as the empty egg on two legs, the roast sucking pig and the gingerbread house should not lead us to overlook the skilfulness of the composition and the technical sophistication of its execution. We may admire, for example, the almost tangible texture of the fur-lined coat spread out beneath the refined and – as indicated by his book – learned man on the right.

The precipitous drop down to the lake in the background may be an allusion to the destiny of a humankind devoted solely to material pleasures. Hans Sachs' comic story, *Schlaraffenland* (The Land of Cockaigne), published in 1530, probably provided the literary source for this painting.

**Pieter Brueghel the Elder**
The Land of Cockaigne, 1567
Oil on wood, 52 x 78 cm
Munich, Bayerische Staatsgemäldesammlungen,
Alte Pinakothek

## PIETER BRUEGHEL The Elder
### C. 1525/30–1569

**Pieter Brueghel the Elder**
The Corn Harvest, 1565
(the month of August from the cycle Paintings of the Months)
Oil on wood, 118 x 161 cm
New York, The Metropolitan Museum of Art

Brueghel, in the past nicknamed "Peasant Brueghel" in a profound misunderstanding of his historical importance, for he was the greatest European landscape painter of the 16th century. However much landscape was being cultivated in Venetian painting, it nevertheless remained merely the backdrop to the main scene. In Brueghel, the reverse is true: it is the figures who are the props within the landscapes forming one of the central themes of the painter's œuvre.

In his *Schilderboek* (Book of Painting) of 1604, Carel van Mander describes the profound impact which the Alps made on Brueghel during his trip to Italy in 1554: "As he crossed the Alps, he swallowed up all the mountains and rocks, which he then spat out again in panels after his return home."

*The Corn Harvest* illustrates August in a cycle of *Months* which also includes *Hunters in the Snow* (January), *The Gloomy Day* (February), *The Return of the Herd* (October or November; all in the Kunsthistorisches Museum, Vienna) and *Haymaking* (July; Národni Galeri, Prague).

In an achievement which fits none of the categories of Mannerist painting, Brueghel succeeded in replacing the multiple, small-scale elements of the "global landscape" so popular in the Netherlands with monumental forms. In this respect, his landscapes represent an important preliminary stage in the evolution of Baroque painting, in particular the landscapes of Rubens.

**Pieter Brueghel the Elder**
The Hunters in the Snow, 1565
(the month of January from the cycle Paintings of the Months)
Oil on wood, 117 x 162 cm
Vienna, Kunsthistorisches Museum

As in *The Corn Harvest*, the main subject of the present panel is the landscape, with the scenic elements – the hunters setting off with their pack of hounds, the skaters – simply providing supplementary details. Even without any figures in the picture at all, the spectator would associate the snow-covered fields and mountains, frozen stretches of water and bare trees with winter.

With the same technique that he uses elsewhere to portray sunlight, Brueghel here evokes the overwhelming impression of frost. The landscape unfolds in a similar fashion to that of *The Corn Harvest*: from an elevated foreground, the eye is led over an abrupt drop and across lower-lying fields to the hills rising in the background. Not until the Baroque era would landscape be continuously developed from the front edge of the picture rearwards in a smooth fusion of foreground, middle ground and background.

A grid of vertical and diagonally descending and ascending lines provides the composition with a stable basic framework. The dominant axis is the emphatic diagonal leading from the pack of hounds bottom left to the mountain range top right. In a masterly demonstration of Brueghel's feeling for pictorial space, the landscape – which, for all its detail, seems empty – is lent depth by the bird in mid-flight.

## JEAN CLOUET
C. 1475 – C. 1540/41

Although Clouet left not a single signed work after his death, his authorship of the present portrait is relatively certain, particularly in view of the close links which he enjoyed with the French court.

While the expression on the sitter's face remains little more than flat, his dress and golden chain are executed with careful attention to detail. The sumptuous colours of his clothes, alternating between gold and brown, stand out in all their splendour against the red brocade of the background, decorated with the royal insignia. There is no depth to the composition other than the space occupied by the figure himself between the parapet and the neutral foil of the tapestry.

Clouet was undoubtedly influenced by the School of Fontainebleau. The luminosity of the palette and the unnatural relationship between the relatively small proportions of the head and the monumental trunk are inconceivable without a knowledge of the Italian Mannerists working for the French court around this time.

Clouet probably painted several other portraits of the French royal family, such as the *Equestrian Portrait of Francis I* (Florence, Galleria degli Uffizi), the portrait of the *Dauphin François* (Antwerp, Koninklijk Museum) and the portrait of Francis I's daughter, *Charlotte* (Chicago, Epstein Collection).

Jean Clouet
Portrait of Francis I,
King of France, c. 1535
Oil on wood, 96 x 74 cm
Paris, Musée National
du Louvre

## FRANCOIS CLOUET
C. 1505/10–1572

In seeking to establish a tension between erotic appeal and cool distance, Clouet clearly reflects the influence of Italian painters such as Bronzino. The almost square format becomes the starting-point for an emphatically asymmetrical composition, in which the main figure is located in the front right-hand corner and further accentuated by a large gap in the red curtains. Just as a tension is thereby created between pictorial format and composition, so the same tension arises between plane and space. The beautiful woman in the foreground turns towards the viewer in such a way that her lower and upper arms repeat the horizontal and vertical sides of the frame. The outlines of the curtains further serve to bind the composition to the plane. In diametric opposition to this, however, the eye is drawn almost forcefully into the depths on the left, whereby the distance suggested by the smaller scale of the seated woman in the background is not supported by the perspective construction.

Contradiction is also the keynote of the palette, as seen in the brightly lit nude set against a shadowy ground. Although lagging behind his father Jean in terms of technique, François Clouet surpassed him in artistic invention. Diane de Poitiers, the mistress of Henri II, probably provided the model for the bathing woman.

François Clouet
Lady in her Bath (Diane de Poitiers?), c. 1570
Oil on wood, 92 x 81 cm
Washington, National Gallery of Art

**Corneille de Lyon**
Portrait of
Gabrielle de Roche-
chouart, c. 1574
Oil on wood,
16.5 x 14 cm
Chantilly, Musée
Condé

## CORNEILLE DE LYON

C. 1500/10 – AFTER 1574

While its attribution is not undisputed, this portrait is closely related to a group of miniature-like portraits ascribed to Corneille. Typical features include the neutral, somewhat iridescent grey-green background and the slight turn in the upper body and head, whose connection to the plane is re-established by the fall of the veil.

The cool, distanced expression on the noblewoman's face, the precise drawing of her eyes, nose and lips, and the smooth planes of her forehead and cheeks assign this panel to the sphere of French court painting. Yet there is a contradiction in the loving execution of the details of her clothes. Are we seeing here a reflection of the artist's Netherlandish heritage (Corneille de Lyon was born in The Hague)? This tendency towards "detail realism" nevertheless draws upon new technical means. The pale, puffy elements protruding from the sleeves of the dark dress are daubed on in an "Impressionistic" style, richly modulated and without clear boundaries.

Was the artist, whose work is still surrounded by many unanswered questions, familiar with Venetian painting? Whatever the case, a contemporary source tells us that Corneille painted the entire court and that he rose to become "Peintre et Valet de Chambre du Roi", the highest post that a painter could attain at court.

**Jean Cousin the Elder**
St Mammès and Duke Alexander, 1541
Tapestry, 440 x 450 cm. Paris, Musée National du Louvre

## JEAN COUSIN The Elder

C. 1490/1500 – C. 1560

According to legend, St Mammès was martyred under Emperor Aurelian in Cappadocia in around 275. He was highly revered in Asia Minor in early Christian times and described as a "great martyr". In the 8th century his relics were taken to Langres in France and he became patron saint of Langres cathedral.

In around 1540 eight tapestries depicting scenes from his life were woven for the chancel. Three still survive, two in Langres and one in the Louvre. After the saint had addressed the wild animals (the subject of one of the two tapestries in Langres), he went on, accompanied by a lion, to visit Duke Alexander (according to the inscription woven into the bottom of the present tapestry; strictly speaking, however, it should be Aurelian), who condemned him to death. The saint's execution can be seen in the temple-like building in the middle ground.

The expansive landscape, the confident handling of perspective and the classicizing architecture all point to Italian influences, which may have come from the School of Fontainebleau. This is also suggested by the decorative embellishment of the buildings and the rich ornamentation of the frame. Its astonishing wealth of nuances of colour lead the tapestry to resemble a painting on canvas.

## SCHOOL OF FONTAINEBLEAU
### C. 1530 – C. 1570

As with the *Landscape with Threshers* below, precisely who executed this painting remains unknown. The slender proportions of the figure, with its small head and its extremely complex pose, point to the influence of the first School of Fontainebleau surrounding Rosso Fiorentino and Primaticcio. While Diana is effectively seen in profile, walking from right to left, this side view is skilfully manipulated. Thus the slight twist of her shoulders in the opposite direction to her step allows us to see her spine, while her head is turned in the opposite direction to her shoulders.

Typically Mannerist is the contrasting intensity of the movements made by Diana and the dog beside her. In the juxtaposition of the goddess's slow step and the bounding hound, two different rhythms are captured in the same instant.

The group of trees in the background and the view of the landscape are executed in the same generous, sweeping style as the *Landscape with Threshers* – a distinctive feature of the second School of Fontainebleau and something which would form one of the foundations of the French landscape painting of the 17th century.

The delicate, cool eroticism evident in *Diana the Huntress* is characteristic of many of the works by the School of Fontainebleau and fell fully in line with French tastes of the day.

School of Fontainebleau
Diana the Huntress, c. 1550
Oil on wood, transferred to
canvas, 191 x 132 cm
Paris, Musée National du
Louvre

This canvas occupies a position of outstanding importance within the landscape painting of the 16th century. Up till now, however, no one has even come close to solving the problem of its authorship. The suggestion that it should be attributed to Niccolò dell'Abbate is refuted by a comparison with the latter's known works (*The Finding of Moses*, Paris, Louvre; *Aristaeus and Eurydice*, London, National Gallery). It is hard to believe that his son Guilio Camillo could have produced a work of such artistic quality, while the Frenchman Etienne Delaune is known to us chiefly as a copperplate engraver.

The most useful comparison is offered by Brueghel's more or less contemporaneous cycle of *Paintings of the Months* (cf. ills. p. 206). Here as there, the figures serve merely as props; here as there, the eye is led from an elevated standpoint overlooking the foreground, across a valley, and on to mountains behind. Unlike the diagonals favoured by Brueghel, however, the present artist adopts a centralized composition. The hay stack forms the approximate axis around which the figures and landscape elements rotate. The triangle of figures on the left reappears inverted in the right-hand middle ground. The artist is also more successful in integrating the different pictorial grounds, something he achieves using a "pseudo-Impressionist" technique which is unique in 16th-century painting. The painted light looks forward to Claude Lorraine. Without wishing to venture an attribution, one is tempted to think of the execution of the backgrounds in the portraits of Corneille de Lyon.

School of Fontainebleau
Landscape with Threshers, c. 1555–1565
Oil on canvas, 85 x 112 cm
Fontainebleau, Musée National du Château

**El Greco**
The Despoiling of Christ
(El Espolio), c. 1590–1600
Oil on canvas, 165 x 99 cm
Munich, Bayerische Staatsgemälde-
sammlungen, Alte Pinakothek

**El Greco**
The Agony in the Garden, c. 1595
Oil on canvas, 102 x 114 cm
Toledo (OH), Toledo Museum of Art

## EL GRECO
### C. 1541–1614

The present canvas with its larger than life-size figures is one of three versions which El Greco painted of the subject. The impressions of the artist's Venetian years, and particularly the works of Titian, can still be felt in the strictly centralized composition, in the relatively plastic modelling of the figures, and above all in the sophistication of the palette. The way in which the figures below left are sliced by the frame, and the slight foreshortening employed in the figure of Christ, who appears to be leaning backwards into the picture, suggest that the canvas was destined to be hung at some height. If we consider in this regard the luminous red of Christ's robe, by which he is made to stand out from the crowd, and the multiple verticals of the figures and lances, the painting seems to point beyond its immediate subject to the coming ascension.

When compared to *The Despoiling of Christ*, *The Agony in the Garden* testifies to an astonishing artistic development. The Italian influences recede to the same degree as El Greco frees himself from his obligation to nature. The figures lose their sense of substance, while their expressiveness is amplified by the unreal shapes assumed by the landscape. Thus Christ is literally heightened by the rock behind him, while the disciples are seen in a sheltering cave as a symbol of sleep. The figures are absolved from logical relationships of scale. The falling diagonal which leads from the angel, through Christ, to the soldiers on the right-hand edge of the painting is a visual statement of the inevitability of Christ's fate. Such departures from the natural model, also evident in the visionary apparition of the moon, were one of the major reasons for the revival of interest in El Greco's work around 1900.

The inscription beneath this altarpiece describes the legendary events taking place. During the burial of the devout Count Orgaz in the first half of the 13th century, St Stephen and St Augustine are supposed to have come down from Heaven and placed the body in the tomb themselves.
El Greco paints a fascinating vision in which the earthly and heavenly worlds are both contrasted and at the same time unified. Surrounded by clergy and nobles, the two saints lower the body into the grave. A boy in the left-hand foreground – El Greco's son? – looks out at the spectator and points to the events taking place. All spatial depth and background detail is renounced. This enables the heavens to open directly overhead, revealing Christ seated in judgement with Mary and John the Baptist as intercessors for humanity. The upward train of movement indicated in the celestial sphere complements the lowering movement of the main group on the ground: death and resurrection are simultaneously portrayed.

**El Greco**
The Burial of Count Orgaz, c. 1586
Oil on canvas, 488 x 360 cm. Toledo, Santo Tomé

**El Greco**
The Holy Family with St Anne and
the young St John Baptist,
c. 1594–1604
Oil on canvas, 107 x 69 cm
Madrid, Museo del Prado

*Below:*
**El Greco**
View of Toledo, c. 1604–1614
Oil on canvas, 121 x 109 cm
New York, The Metropolitan
Museum of Art

# EL GRECO
## c. 1541–1614

El Greco painted the Holy Family with St
Anne on a number of occasions. Whereas the
version in the Hospital di San Juan Bautista in
Toledo, probably executed some ten years earlier, employs a bright, almost cheerful palette,
the present canvas is strikingly darker in
colour, its effects of light suggestive of a
storm. The inclusion of the young John the
Baptist, pointing heavenwards with the index
finger of his left hand, allows the painting to
be seen as a vision of the future Passion.

The five figures in this painting are
grouped closely together, however, the spatial
relationships between them are of a complicated nature. St Anne, her daughter's arm
lying around her shoulders, is bending down
over the infant Jesus lying in his mother's lap –
a reminder of Pietà representations and thus
again of the Passion of Christ. Joseph, complementary to St Anne, looks towards Christ
from behind. By avoiding all direct eye contact between the figures, El Greco evokes a
strangely unreal, dream-like atmosphere.

El Greco renounces all detail in his description of objects. The robes are treated broadly,
while contours and outlines are blurred –
something particularly apparent in the modelling of the two children. El Greco is already
moving towards the style of his late work, in
which he would increasingly turn away from
the portrayal of idealized nature.

Towards the end of his career, El Greco
painted his chosen home of Toledo in what is
the only example of pure landscape painting
in his entire œuvre. From a low standpoint,
the eye is led up the hill to the city centre,
dominated by the Alcazar and the cathedral.
The dynamic train of movement from bottom
to top and from foreground to background is
joined by a diagonal which runs from the left-
hand edge of the canvas, across the bridge
spanning the Tajo valley, along the city wall
and up to the cathedral spire.

Unconcerned with representational detail,
El Greco blurs the transitions between trees,
meadows and distant mountains. The individual monuments of the cityscape thereby stand
out all the more sharply in their ghostly light.
The broad expanse of the sky, in which clouds
and buildings are interwoven, corresponds to
the free, increasingly abstract style of his late
works.

The painting is both a "landscape portrait"
and at the same time an interpretive study
filled with tremendous natural forces.
Thunderclouds as black as night are gathering
over the cathedral and the fortress, the sacred
and secular centres of the city. Whether the
artist thereby intended to deliver a specific
message is something on which history is silent.

El Greco's *View of Toledo* was greeted as a
revelation by the painters of Expressionism
and Surrealism.

Andreas Prater

# BAROQUE

## The painting of the 17th century in Italy, France, England, Germany and Spain

The age of the Baroque, between absolutism and the Enlightenment, is acknowledged as the last all-European style. Long regarded as merely an eccentric offshoot of the Renaissance, Baroque presents a complex and dynamic variety of form and expression in stark contrast to the controlled moderation of Neoclassicism.

Worldly joys and sensuality, religious spirituality and stringent asceticism, wide formal diversity and strict regulation all went hand in hand. At the same time, theatricality and stagelike settings entered the world of art with the advent of illusionism. Pageantry, pomp and courtly ceremony were not simply an expression of Baroque exuberance, but also an artistic device in the portrayal of crowd scenes.

In Rome, Caravaggio succeeded in achieving a decisive breakthrough with his dramatic use of chiaroscuro, while in Bologna it was the Carracci who established the Baroque style of painting. French art was dominated by the heroic landscapes of Poussin, the night pieces of La Tour, and Claude Lorrain's lyrical handling of light. In Spain, we find the warm colority of Murillo, the contemplative piety of Ribera and Zurbarán and the forcefully expressive court portraits by Velázquez, while Germany's contribution to Baroque painting reached its zenith in the delicate landscapes of Adam Elsheimer.

## The naming of an era

No other period in the history of European art has proved so difficult to pin down in terms of academic and scholarly definition, in describing its characteristic phenomena, in specifying its time span and in exploring its spiritual and intellectual background. Ever since scholars turned their attention to the Baroque age a century ago, their research has been marked by contradiction and controversy to an extent paralleled only by Mannerism, itself a term coined at a fairly late stage in academic research in order to classify the transition between Renaissance and Baroque.

At the time, such questions of period and epoch were unknown, and the term "baroque" as we know it was unheard of. Neither the patrons nor the painters themselves, nor the theoreticians of art, of whom there were many, actually used this term to describe artistic procedures and achievements. Unlike Rococo, which adopted the expression *goût rococo* for itself, the style we wish to examine here was described, at most, by its contemporaries as *grand goût* in keeping with the absolutist world view of the 17th century and the patrons' desire for prestige and pomp. Only in the workshops and studios do we find the word "baroque" used to describe the curving lines of furniture and the dissolution of firm contours in painting. In the satirical and burlesque literature of Italy, we find the word "barocco" in use from around 1570 to describe an odd or witty idea.

It was the rationalist art critics of the mid-18th century who began employing the term to describe a style they saw as a florid, bizarre and thoroughly tasteless travesty of all the rules of art. Adherents of the new classicist doctrine were well aware of the key role played by certain masters of the previous era, amongst them Gianlorenzo Bernini (1598–1680), whom they held responsible for nothing less than a general decline in artistic standards – an evil whose roots they traced back to Michelangelo. By around the end of the 18th century and the beginning of the 19th, the term had already entered common usage in a thoroughly pejorative sense and, with that, its transformation from polemical insult to accepted stylistic epithet was virtually inevitable, following the same time-honoured pattern by which Gothic, to name but one other similar example, also became an accepted and neutral term. In fact, it was the avantgarde artists of the 19th century who eventually established a more positive attitude to what had hitherto been regarded as the "style of decadence". The works of Diego Velázquez (1599–1660), Rubens, Rembrandt (1606–1669) and Frans Hals (1591–1656) possessed specific painterly qualities in which the Impressionists, at any rate, took a keen interest.

**Caravaggio**
The young Bacchus, c. 1591–1593
Oil on canvas, 66 x 53 cm
Rome, Galleria Borghese

The major monographic work on Diego Velázquez and his century published in Bonn in 1888 by the German art historian Carl Justi (1832–1912) applied a new approach to the era, seen through the eyes of a generation already influenced by the Impressionist sensitivity for light, colority and tone which had begun to permit a revaluation of the Baroque. The emergence of this more positive historical reception was to culminate in the work of the Swiss art historian Heinrich Wölfflin (1864–1945) and the Austrian art historian Alois Riegl (1858–1905), to name but two. Rome was designated the cradle and capital of Baroque and the stylistic characteristics of the period were distinguished systematically and normatively from those of the Renaissance.

## Constant factors

Renaissance and Mannerism are widely regarded as the direct stylistic precursors of the Baroque. Indeed, there is much to be said for the art historical view that the period from the Early Renaissance of the 15th century through to the Neoclassicism of the late 18th century constituted a single and continuous cultural development. In terms of content and theme, there are a number of constant factors which, for all their modal and aesthetic differences, certainly indicate an undeniable homogeneity. The principle of illusionism, for instance, creating a sense of spatial expansion in which monumental mural and ceiling painting transcends the bounds of real architecture into illusory celestial realms, is just one example of a leitmotif that first emerged in the Early Renaissance and was then taken to its full artistic and theoretical flowering in Baroque art.

The theme of column orders, for example, dominated the formal architectural syntax of the day. Even such radical innovators as Michelangelo in the 16th century or Bernini and Francesco Borromini (1599–1667) in the 17th century merely elaborated on their stylistic potential without ever actually questioning the underlying principle. The same is true of the portrayal of ancient gods and mythological heroes in paintings that were neither objects of some neo-heathen worship nor purely decorative designs, but mythologically charged bearers of meaning capable of elevating a contemporary event to a higher plane of historical and mythological reality.

Other variables in painting include the use of chiaroscuro and the triad of cardinal colours, the juxtaposition of the primaries – red, yellow and blue – which are blended to create all other colours. As a counterpoint to this colorism, we find the non-coloured chiaroscuro with its extremes of black and white which modifies the palette of the artist to provide countless possibilities. The awareness that chiaroscuro provides a means of portraying light and darkness as elementary factors in the overall structure and texture of the painting rather than as a means of depicting specific lighting conditions is still relatively new at this stage.

A further constant factor is the use of allegory and, with that, the humanistic love of coded statements which were regarded as evidence of the potential significance inherent in all things as bearers of coded and decipherable messages. 15th century hieroglyphics, heraldry and Baroque iconology are all documented in an extraordinary wealth of publications, bearing witness to a profound belief in the fundamental kinship of word and image that forms the basis for an imperturbable faith in the universal legibility of all natural and man-made signs.

## The ephemeral monument

These otherwise constant factors were to play a new and unique role in Baroque art, primarily because of the era's hitherto unparalleled capacity for synthesis which is so powerfully manifested in the Baroque "grand scheme" which not only sought a fusion of architecture, sculpture, painting and ornamentation such as we may find in churches and palaces, but also arranged festivities and celebrations to unite the arts in a spiritual and worldly ceremony, enriching them with music, poetry and dance. Today, all we tend to see of the Baroque grand scheme is the shell, magnificent as it may be, which served as a lavish setting for those temporary festivities that breathed life and cohesion into the *Gesamtkunstwerk* or total work of art. This pursuit of ceremony and ephemeral pageantry may be regarded as a specific characteristic of the Baroque era. The dynamic movement so frequently associated with Baroque art can be found in its exuberant facades and interiors, in the soaring figures that whirl through teeming ceiling paintings as though propelled by some supernatural force, and in the emotional expression of their faces and gestures; it is aimed at breaking down the contradiction between transience and permanence in a way that could be achieved only symbolically within the scope of pompous ceremony. No other era was so keenly aware of the fragility of earthly bonds. It is no coincidence that enormous intellectual and material investments were made time and time again in temporary structures, visual programmes and decorations for triumphal processions and ceremonies, *trionfi* and *entrées solennelles* as well as for the *castra doloris* structures built for funeral services.

This seeming paradox of what might best be described as "ephemeral monuments" reached its zenith in the Baroque love of firework displays. Unlike today's firework displays, these were distinctly pictorial, and their planners and designers enjoyed as much esteem as the best and most highly regarded artists. The people of the Baroque age would have made no distinction between "art" and the magnificent artifice of a firework display, for the purist 19th century notion of art that was to break the *Gesamtkunstwerk* down into its individual component parts was still a long way off.

## New pictorial themes

Any attempt to determine the specific differences – apart from individual stylistic criteria – between Baroque art and the eras that went before it must take into account the great widening of thematic fields that occurred at that time. Unlike Mannerism, Baroque painting achieved some genuine innovations. The things that Baroque artists found worthy of portraying were no longer restricted to religious and secular history, portraiture and allegory – all of which focused on a classical concept of the liberty and greatness of man. The visual world of the Baroque explored new areas: apotheosis and state portrait, landscape, genre and still life, caricature and anamorphosis (deliberate distortion or elongation of figures).

None of these tasks was entirely new in itself, and all of them had forerunners. What was new, however, was that what had once been the extreme had now become the accepted form of an era. A common feature is that, although all are based retrospectively on the humanist visual concepts of the Renaissance with its anthropocentric principles, they nevertheless invariably point beyond these. For example, *The Apotheosis of St Ignatius* by Baciccio (1639–1709) is not so much a glorification of the saint himself as a glorification of the Jesuit order; and when Charles Le Brun (1619–1690) portrays chancellor Séguir in a ceremonial procession in the full regalia of his office, it is not the person of the chancellor who is manifested in this state portrait, but the concept of the absolutist state as such. The landscapes of Annibale Carracci (1560–1609) or Nicolas Poussin (c. 1593/94–1665) may not be entirely devoid of human life, but they are innovative in that they present a landscape untamed by human hand and one that seems to possess an independence and autonomy far beyond the scope of its pictorial role as the mere setting for an event. In many ways, the genre painting also goes beyond the boundaries of the individual. The art critics of the 19th century quite rightly referred to this as a "social portrait" and the findings of more recent art historiography confirm that interpretation in revealing the moral or universal significance behind the scenes of everyday life. The same applies to the highly popular still life painting which expressly excludes all human participation and whose frequently edifying significance is cloaked in a veritable cult of sensuality. The Renaissance notion of the great and beautiful human individual is decisively countered by the Baroque love of anamorphosis and caricature, whose "invention" and dissemination originated in the school of the Carracci. The comic and the ridiculous have remained a legitimate and inalienable aspect of art ever since.

Finally, there is a singular phenomenon of Italian and German Late Baroque that deserves mention here: the *bozzetto* as an independent work of art. A bozzetto is generally a small painting sketchily executed as a draft in preparation for a mural or ceiling painting and often used as the basis for a contract between patron and painter. One example of this is

**Nicolas Poussin**
Triumph of Neptune and
Amphitrite, 1634
Oil on canvas, 114.5 x 146.6cm
Philadelphia (PA), Philadelphia
Museum of Art

Baciccio's *bozzetto* of *The Apotheosis of St Ignatius* (ill. p.239). Yet from these rather humble and entirely functional beginnings, the bozzetto gradually took on an independent value, becoming a collectors' item and a gallery object in its own right. A kind of interim zone was thus created – neither fresco nor panel painting – without encroaching upon any of the intentions, aims or functions of painting in other areas. In this respect, the bozzetto is an independent creation in which the widely divergent intentions of the Baroque meet and merge: the monumental and the intimate, the sketchy drawing with its fleeting brushwork and the richly coloured texture of the completed fresco, the transportable framed panel painting and the vision of celestial expanses. It combines the ephemeral and the permanent, the fluid and the firm, immutability and metamorphosis. The bozzetto is a painting in the making, its very state of work-in-progress constituting a form in its own right, and imbued with an inherent potential that epitomizes a highly specific aspect of Baroque visuality.

## New imagery

Whereas Renaissance artists concentrated on the problem of imagery in terms of the problem of portraying God's creation of man after his own image, the artists of the Baroque era sought to transcend the natural world with the aid of certain artifices, dramatic and extroverted pathos and illusionism on the one hand and extreme close-up, internalization, alienation and distortion of reality on the other hand. The illusionism of *trompe-l'œil* the artifice of sophisticated technical innovations and the miraculous world of the stage set with its mechanical devices were as much a part of these means as the notion of transposing the whole life of a ruler such as Louis XIV (1638–1715), his palace, his court and the entire state into another, allegorical reality – that of the sun-state and the sun-king.

An essential and fundamental element of Baroque visual concepts is the allegory. Baroque allegory involves rather more than mere personification in the sense of visualizing an abstract concept or situation by endowing a human figure with certain attributes. Indeed, one might say that the extension of allegorical functions into the fields of landscape, genre, still life and caricature are all part of the iconological style of the Baroque. Allegorically conceived figures, scenes and metaphors were used as components of pictorial programmes of great complexity, varying from country to country in accordance with the respective needs and projections of the various nations. which were beginning to emerge more distinctly than ever before in the 17th century.

A particularly fine example of this is the ceiling fresco by Pietro da Cortona (1596–1669) for the great hall of the Palazzo Barberini in Rome (1633–1639), which has come to be regarded as a work that opened a new chapter in Baroque decoration. Its portrayal of the fame of the Barberini as a gift of Divine Providence is the centre and focal point of this large-scale composition. The entire picture is an allegory glorifying the pontificate of the Barberini pope Urban VIII.

**Domenichino**
The Assumption of Mary Magdalen into Heaven, c. 1617–1621
Oil on canvas, 129 x 100cm
St Petersburg, Hermitage

Painted architectural elements, ornaments and painted sculptures form an organizational structure within which the secondary elements of the programme designed by the Barberini court poet Francesco Bracciolini (1566–1645) are distributed. The fresco includes every form of painting: allegory and history, myth, landscape and even still life.

Another noteworthy example is the ceiling fresco in the collegiate library of the monastry of St Florian near Linz in Austria, painted in 1747 by Bartholomäus Altomonte (1702–1783). The creator of his *concetto*, or thematic concept, was Daniel Gran (1694–1757), a *pictor doctus* or scholarly painter. The centre of the ceiling presents the main allegory: the marriage (*connubium*) of science and virtue through religion. The system of placing the key concept at the centre of a large allegorical structure was widely adopted.

### New visuality

The great synthesizing power of the Baroque visual concept is expressed not only in the iconography of such allegorical "marriages", but is also immediately and sensually palpable in the relationship between the disciplines. Architecture and painting were united in a new overall visual concept. In the Renaissance, paintings were either integrated into an architectural framework that strictly respected the architectural

boundaries or else they were conceived perspectively as views through a window. Certainly, there were already inherent similarities: painting had adopted architectonic, sculptural and decorative elements. The Baroque, however, brought a mutual interaction between painting and architecture, with light being handled in such a way as to create a smoothly continuous transition from built environment to illusionistic space. In the Baroque era, architecture itself became highly pictorial, and can indeed be best appreciated with this in mind. Admittedly, this is only one of the possibilities opened up by Baroque painting, for at the same time the process of pictorial autonomy, one of the most far-reaching innovations of the Renaissance, was being pursued even more radically. It was not until the Baroque age that the works so aptly described as "cabinet paintings" became widespread. These cabinet paintings had no specific cult or propaganda function and were sought solely as works of art for collection. Indeed – and it is this that is new – this was the sole purpose for which they were produced.

The great Roman collections of the 17th century, those of the Giustiniani or the Barberini, indicate that paintings were not purchased and grouped according to motif and content, but coveted instead for their artistic value, their rarity and the fame of their creators. The early collection history of a painting by Caravaggio, who played a major role in the emergence of the early independent gallery painting, illustrates this well. Joachim von Sandrart (1609–1688), the widely travelled painter and art critic, reported in his *Teutsche Academie* of the advice he had given to Marchese Vincenzo Giustiniani (died 1637), an extraordinarily ambitious patron and art collector, with regard to Caravaggio's *Amor Vincit* (now in Berlin, Gemäldegalerie): "He (Caravaggio) painted for the patron Marchese Justinian a life-size cupid in the form of a boy of about twelve, sitting on the globe and holding his bow above him in his right hand, with all manner of art instruments to his left, including books for study and a laurel wreath upon the books; cupid was painted with large brown eagle wings, altogether drawn in correctura with strong colority, clean and rounded as in life. This work was to be seen publicly in a room with a hundred and twenty others painted by the finest artists but at my advice it was covered with a dark green silken curtain and shown last of all when everything else had been perused to satisfaction for otherwise it would have made all the other rarities pale in comparison so that this work may justifiably be described as an eclipse of all paintings."

### Rome as the capital of the Baroque

This newfound possibility of regarding art primarily as art for its own sake opened up a whole new dimension of further and predominantly aesthetic potential for synthesis involving conscious references to other artists and their styles. In the early stages of the Baroque, Rome was the place where the decisive structures of a "Renaissance of the Renaissance" began to take shape. The fact that the Baroque emerged in Rome remains a valid tenet in the history of stylistic development. Yet whereas architecture developed along more or less continuous and uniform lines – the architectural history of St Peter's or Il Gesù springs to mind – early Baroque painting ran a considerably more dramatic and incalculable course. Annibale Carracci, with his studio of family members and academic artists, and Caravaggio, tend to be regarded if not as rivals, then at least as opposites in terms of artistic thesis and anti-thesis. Indeed, anyone who has visited the Cerasi chapel in Santa Maria del Popolo and has seen Caravaggio's *Crucifixion of St Peter* and his *Conversion of Saul* together with Annibale Carracci's *Assumption of the Virgin* immediately realizes that one of the most exciting challeges taken up by the subsequent generation of painters must surely have been the quest to unite the dramatic "tenebroso" of the artist from Lombardy with the Neoclassical grace of the artists from Bologna.

Annibale's decoration of the Galleria Farnese (ill. p. 227) was to be of seminal importance to Roman and Baroque monumental painting. The return to monumentality played a decisive role in itself. On the other hand, Caravaggio's handling of great themes with humility was equally significant. The heightened realism of the large-scale work went hand in hand with the increasing realism invested in exploring the trivial, the everyday and the ordinary. Different as these two starting points may be, both are based on compositional inventions of the high Renaissance. Giorgione, Titian, Raphael, Michelangelo and Correggio are the names that must be mentioned here as "forefathers" of the Baroque. Yet it was Rubens, perhaps the most universal visual thinker of the Baroque age, who was the first to succeed in drawing all these sources together in a true synthesis and establishing them throughout the courts of Europe.

It is frequently and quite rightly stressed that a general weariness and dissatisfaction with late Mannerist formal conventions may well have contributed towards certain reforms. Early Baroque in Rome may justifiably be described as anti-Mannerist. One key concept – the rediscovery of an idealistic natural portrayal based on High Renaissance art – could already be found in the work of Francesco Barocci (c. 1535–1612) of Urbino, even before the Carracci studio adopted it as the mainstay of their artistic programme. Caravaggio's rigorous realism, on the other hand, is programmatic in the sense that he broke with the classical ideals which Mannerism had stripped of meaning; the ideals of "buon costume", of "invenzione", of "disegno", of "decoro" and of "scienza" (invention and draftsmanship, pleasing decor and scholarship) as Caravaggio's most vehement critic, Giovanni Pietro Bellori (c. 1615–1696) claimed.

It was in Rome, however, that the paths of Italian, French, German and Netherlandish artists were to cross. National characteristics were more clearly articulated in the Baroque era than ever before. Only the city whose cosmopolitan open-mindedness and generous patronage had captivated so many artists failed to create its own local style of painting; the international talents who lived in Rome and fuelled its role as myth, topos and idea were far too diverse and independent for that.

### Stylistic pluralism in the early Baroque

These artists closely studied the latest contemporary trends whose sheer diversity called for synthesis, as embodied in the didactic concept of the Carracci studio and in the roughshod maverick approach of Caravaggio. Rome was not a historically transfigured city of dreams echoing with the plaintive cry of its ruins, but a vibrant metropolis where temporal and spiritual patrons of almost decadent liberality set the tone and whose individuality made any attempt at establishing a single early Baroque style impossible. To divide the artists of the day into the followers of Caravaggio on the one hand and the followers of the Carraccis on the other, would be all too simplistic and quite misleading.

Though the Carracci students Francesco Albani (1578–1660) and Domenichino (1581–1641), and the Caravaggio-influenced artists Carlo Saraceni (c. 1580/85–1620) and Guercino (1591–1666) often tend to be played off against each other, such comparisons merely outline a very general trend. After all, not only was there a degree of mutual esteem between these artists, but their successors also found a lasting and fertile source of inspiration for the development of Baroque painterly form in a combination of their extraordinarily innovatory achievements. Indeed, the very notion that it is impossible to unite idealists and naturalists is a doctrine that emerged relatively late and one that has remained beyond the bounds of artistic practice. Even in the œuvre of such an archetypal classicist as Guido Reni (1575–1642) there is a considerable body of evidence bearing witness to the intensity with which he studied the work of his "opponents".

Only for a very few highly independent talents such as Adam Elsheimer (1578–1610) or Velázquez did the question of association with one particular school or certain dominant influences play no role at all. The same is true of Pietro da Cortona, that master of Roman fresco painting who was also a distinguished architect and an experienced sculptor. It was a combination of these talents that enabled him to tackle such vast spaces as the ceiling of the Palazzo Barberini. He was a decorative painter of the highest stature: not only did he apply architectural and sculptural elements as painterly elements, but he even combined painterly and sculptural components, as we can see in some of the ceiling paintings of the Palazzo Pitti – a system that was to be of enormous significance for the future possibilities of Baroque interior decor.

While it is undoubtedly true to maintain that specifically national schools did not emerge until the Baroque, we can also say with some justification that the international exchange of ideas and fluctuation of artists had never been so intense. This intellectual climate made it possible, to cite just one example, for the German painter Johann Liss (c. 1595– c. 1629/30) to represent the Venetian painting of his day with a standard of quality and temperament no local artist could match. It was a time of expanding horizons, assisted by the spread of printed reproductions which made a number of pictorial inventions – admittedly without colour – more rapidly accessible and available to a broader public. Rubens employed engraving studios which made his compositions famous throughout Europe. Many painters also began exploring the possibilities of printing, using it to create their own independent pictorial compositions, resulting in new inventions such as mezzotint and aquatint which soon found a place alongside more current techniques of engraving and etching.

It seems as though this internationalization of European painting in the Baroque, triggered by all these factors, also led to a distinct articulation of national schools, for it was only now that artists had the possibility of choosing from a huge range of old and modern art. The choice of an inspirational model may well have been the decisive factor that kept both the microcosm and the macrocosm of Baroque art in perpetual motion. It is the constant topic of all academic and educational reflections – from the Accademia degli Incaminati of the Carracci to the Parisian Académie Royale where a vehement debate raged between "Rubenists" and "Poussinists" regarding the predominance of colour or line. For the individual artist, this choice was as existential and decisive as it was for the commune or the prince who determined prevailing taste through his patronage and who frequently sealed the fate, overnight, of artists who had fallen out of favour.

Few nations famed for their distinctive artistic culture are so unequivocally indebted to the importation of foreign influences – in this case Italian and Flemish – as France. Yet what could be more French than the timeless landscapes of Claude Lorrain (1600–1682), the heroic harmony of man and nature in the work of Poussin, the crisp portraiture of Philippe de Champaigne (1602–1674) or the mathematical clarity in the still lifes of Lubin Baugin (c. 1610/12–1663)? Their origins in the work of Domenichino and in the art of Flanders and Holland may be proven, but it is not the decisive factor. It was the power of transformation that breathed life into the very substance of art and shaped the face of French Baroque.

The incredible capacity for metamorphosis that astounded his contemporaries in the work of Sébastien Bourdon (1616–1671), an artist who could fool even the connoisseur with his paintings in the style of Poussin, the Le Nain brothers, or an Italian or Dutch painter, is a phenomenon of crucial importance not only in terms of an individual artist's personal choice of role model but also in terms of France's position with regard to the sources of Baroque painting. It certainly sheds some light on this aspect of the era. The purist cult of genius we have inherited from the 19th century has given us a tendency to disparage such phenomena as mere eclecticism, hampering our understanding of the complex processes that informed the stylistic creation of the Baroque. In order to reassess it, we must first seek to understand the Baroque attitude to imitation.

## Counter-Reformation and absolutism

Of all the explanations offered in an interpretation of Baroque history, there are two which have become firmly established, both for good reason. The first regards Baroque as the style of the Counter-Reformation. As long as the forms of Protestant Baroque are not ignored and as long as the Counter-Reformation is not regarded as the seminal principle from which a certain style emerged, but which wilingly adopted that style as a convenient instrument of religious propaganda, this interpretation is acceptable. It is, after all, remarkable that such influential figures as the reform popes Pius V (1504–1572), Gregor XIII (1502–1585) and Sixtus V (1521–1590) as well as the great founders of religious orders Thomas Cajetanus (1469–1534, Ignatius of Loyola (1491–1556), Filippo Neri (1515–1595) and Carl Borromäus (1538–1584) seem to have lacked any artistic policy pointing specifically towards the Baroque.

The second political theory is similarly flawed. It regards Baroque art as the perfect expression of absolutist claims to power in the state. This functional equation is also acceptable as long as we bear in mind that the early absolutist states – such as Florence under Cosimo I de' Medici (1519–1574) in the second half of the 16th century – were not actually centres of early Baroque art, and that the origins of this style are to be sought instead in Bologna and Rome, far from the ideals of the absolutist sovereign and the absolutist state of the 17th century.

## France

A classic example of Baroque art in the service of absolutism can be found in France under the reign of Louis XIV. For the early Baroque period of the first half of the 17th century, developments in France were of little significance. The French sun did not rise until the second half of the century and, when it did, it shone with a brilliance and exemplary power that dazzled the aristocracy of Europe. It is tempting to surmise that it was only through the example of France that Baroque became the absolutist style – that is, if it can be described as a style at all. Though it was by no means new for art, and indeed all the arts, to be used as a vehicle for political ideals, never before had this purpose been organized to such perfection through institutions and directors wielding so much power nor through projects on such a grand scale.

When Louis took the reins of power in 1661 following the death of the French prime minister Cardinal Jules Mazarin (1602–1661), thereby reuniting monarch and state in one person, he chose Jean-Baptiste Colbert (1619–1683) as his advisor in matters of art. Colbert began in 1663 with the reorganization of the Manufacture Royale des Meubles de la Couronne, which was entrusted with producing all manner of luxury furnishing and decoration, including tapestries. At the same time, Colbert acted as the political head of the Académie Royale de Peinture et de Sculpture, founded in 1648, whose artistic director was Le Brun, and in doing so he made the academy an instrument of royal artistic policy. Appointed *surintendant des bâtiments* from 1664, Colbert founded the Académie Royale d'Architecture in 1671 and was henceforth in charge of supervising all architectural projects and training new architects. In 1666, this process of centralization culminated in the creation of the Académie de France in Rome, a move that distinctly curbed the freedom of artistic life in the eternal city by exercising greater control over the French students there. At the same time, however, this same institution gave Paris a firm foothold in the promised land of art, on which it subsequently based its claim to a role as the "second Rome" in matters of art. Bernini's failure in Paris is also to be regarded in the light of this particular situation.

Baroque art is inextricably linked with the concept of the academy, and consequently with academic theory and debate, even to the point of pursuing theory as an independent discipline without necessarily requiring that it should have any effect on actual art policy. One example of this can be found in the famous debate, mentioned above, between the Rubenists and the Poussinists (in reference to their respective symbolic figureheads Rubens and Poussin) regarding the superiority of colour or line in painting. The key factor in this respect – a feature of the Baroque in general, as it were – is in fact the principle of polarity, along very much the same lines as the rivalry that had previously erupted between the "eclectic" followers of the Carracci and the "naturalistic" followers of Caravaggio in Rome, albeit under somewhat different circumstances.

Whether a colourist such as Jean-Antoine Watteau (1684–1721) may seriously be considered in terms of this theoretical debate and the triumph of colour over line must remain an open question. Although he may have been the only French painter to have seen in the works of Rubens an inherent coloristic kinship-by-choice, whereas a Rubenist like Pierre Mignard (1612–1695) went no further than superficial adaptation, his ground-breaking work had already begun to pave the way towards a new era that found itself weary of the "grand goût".

Simon Vouet
The Toilet of Venus, c. 1628–1639
Oil on canvas, 183.8 x 153 cm
Cincinnati (OH), Cincinnati Art Museum

As regards the equation of Baroque and absolutism mentioned above – which, while not entirely incorrect, is certainly not unproblematic – it cannot be denied, particularly in the case of Louis XIII, Colbert and Le Brun, that a significant proportion of French painters went their own way, ignoring centralized art policies. Ironically, the very artist who was seminally important to the Neoclassical doctrine, Poussin himself, the epitome of French painting during the 17th century – a century which the French often refer to as their "golden age" of painting – was so deeply disappointed by Paris (to which he had been summoned as court painter by Louis XIII) that he returned within the space of just eighteen months to Rome, the city that had also become the chosen home of Claude Lorrain. Nevertheless, even at such a distance, both these artists were to exert an influence on the spirit of French painting that would prove to be more lasting and profound than any of their colleagues residing in Paris, including Le Brun himself.

Independent, but no less highly esteemed, were the Le Nain brothers Antoine (c. 1588–1648), Louis (c. 1593–1648) and Mathieu (1607–1677), Georges de La Tour (1593–1652) and last but not least, the great engraver Jacques Callot (c. 1592/93–1635), whose cycle *The Horrors of*

*War* produced in 1632/33 held up the cracked mirror of negative counter-image against the sovereign claim to the glorification of politics through art.

The non-academic tendencies in French painting were powerful indeed. Their realism, inspired by Caravaggio, enjoyed not only bourgeois approval, but occasionally gained royal acceptance as well. Louis XIV even had all the paintings removed from his room and replaced by a single work: Georges La Tour's *St Sebastian* (ill. p. 243). In his bedroom, he had five works by Valentin de Boulogne (1594–1632) and what is more, the king had also purchased paintings by Caravaggio.

**Diego Velázquez**
Portrait of Philip IV of Spain in Brown and Silver, 1631–1632
Oil on canvas, 199.5 x 113cm
London, National Gallery

## Naples

In considering these two very different centres of Baroque painting – Rome and Paris – we should not forget the third major centre, Naples. The city had only recently taken on such a role. Before the 17th century, the painting here had barely achieved European stature; the city had no independent artistic tradition that might have triggered a new movement in the way the High Renaissance had emerged in Rome. It is for this reason that Neapolitan Baroque painting also lacks the harmonizing classical touch that might have moderated its tendency towards audacious non-conformity. An important aspect is the fact that Caravaggio spent some time in this city, where he created the masterpieces of his later style. His chiaroscuro and his earthy realism were to pave the way for the entire century. It is interesting to note that although Domenichino and Giovanni Lanfranco (1582–1647) also spent some time in Naples, this seems to have had no particular influence.

A unique feature of Neapolitan art of the period is the dissolution of pictorial structure into a pattern of daubs of colours referred to as "macchia", for which its exponents are described as "macchiettista". This sketchy style of painting, sometimes erroneously referred to as "impressionistic", is the stylistic instrument of an improvizational and virtuoso painting which does not concern itself with iconographic content, but concentrates instead on presenting cavaliers in battle, bawdy "bambocciata" and genre scenes from the lives of soldiers and vagabonds. The leading representative of this style is the painter and poet Salvator Rosa (1615–1673) who was a brilliant master of all thematic fields and whose particular speciality was battle scenes. Of all the painters of the era, he may certainly be described as the one with the most flamboyant imagination. He has left us as his heritage the unforeseen, fickle and unpredictable stroke of the imagination that has come to be known as the "capriccio". Since Salvator Rosa, it is impossible to think of Baroque painting without the capriccio.

The most popular representatives of Neapolitan Baroque painting have always been Mattia Preti (1613–1699) and Luca Giordano (1634–1705), known to his contemporaries as "fa presto" in reference to the prodigious speed at which he is said to have painted. Giordano is acknowledged as a great Neapolitan fresco painter who went beyond the scope of local style, exploring Roman influences, especially that of Pietro da Cortona.

The importance of Naples in the field of Baroque painting is further enhanced by a curious circumstance: the city's position as a Spanish dominion. Naples would play an influential role in the development of Spanish Baroque painting and would be an important source of inspiration for its painters. A key figure in this respect is the Naples-based Spanish artist Jusepe de Ribera (1591–1652), the main exponent of Neapolitan Caravaggism.

## Spain

Certain external factors have to be taken into consideration when addressing the subject of Spanish Baroque painting. First of all, we should bear in mind the extremely low social status of painters, a situation against which the generation of Spanish artists following El Greco still continued to struggle. Much of our information about their lot comes from El Greco's own no longer fully extant writings on architecture, sculpture and painting, together with the modest 17th century contributions of Francisco Pacheco (1564–1654), Vincente Carducho (c. 1576–1638) and Juan Bautista Martínez del Mazo (1612–1667), whose writings were also aimed at enhancing the social stature of artists – an aim that had already borne fruit in Italy a full two centuries previously.

Dependent as Spanish painters were on outside contacts in order to keep pace with artistic developments in Italy and the Netherlands, they themselves had very little influence on the rest of Europe until the 19th century. This is due to the circumstances which also shaped the specific physiognomy of Spanish Baroque. Its "golden age" coincided with the Spanish government's progressive loss of power and prestige. Such events as the defeat of the Armada by the English, dealing a fatal blow to Spain's marine power, the ceasefire negotiated with Protestant Holland in 1609 after a long and wearing struggle, and the eventual recognition of this small country's independence in 1648, are only the most spectacular outward signs of the decline and fatigue that had gripped the country as the result of decades of aggressive power politics.

The Spanish court under Philipp II (1527–1598) had few commissions to award that would have been attractive to foreign artists. Though Rubens did produce a number of works in Madrid, we should remember that this Flemish artist was working in the service of the crown as a Spanish subject and a diplomat.

Apart from representative, prestigious and diplomatic portraits, the only works commissioned by the Spanish court were the cycles of battle paintings for the Salon de Reinos, Francisco de Zurbarán's (1598–1664) *Hercules* cycle, and the mythologies for the royal hunting lodge of Torre de la Parada executed by the Rubens studio. This lack of courtly commissions and the low social status of artists in Spain are two important factors which were further exacerbated by an absence of aristocratic and bourgeois patronage. The Spanish nobility led a distinctly Don Quixotic life and the repertory of Baroque themes held little appeal for them as they tilted at windmills to escape the reality of their own insignificance. Only the church felt an increased need for paintings, and welcomed the stylistic devices that had emerged in the Roman Counter-Reformation. Cloyingly sweet Immaculadas – an iconographic speciality since El Greco – the delicate portrayals of the infant Jesus by Bartolomé Esteban Murillo (c. 1617/18–1682) and the austere, enigmatic portraits of

**Bartolomé Esteban Murillo**
The Pie Eater, c. 1662–1672
Oil on canvas, 124 x 102 cm
Munich, Bayerische Staatsgemäldesammlungen,
Alte Pinakothek

saints by Zurbarán represent the extremes of Spanish religious painting in this era.

The advent of Caravaggism also acted as an important stimulus on Spanish art, where it fell on the fertile soil of a local chiaroscuro technique based on Netherlandish and late Mannerist painting. In Seville, home to what was probably the leading Spanish school of painting in the 17th century, this produced a highly distinctive variation of earthy, brown-toned painting in which the colour structure of a canvas was reduced to its bare essentials, at times even paring it down to little or no colour so that each hue seemed to take on the function of a light intimately merged with the very substance of the paint itself. In Zurbarán's *The Ecstasy of St Francis* (ill. p. 264) it is no longer a sudden and glaring burst of light from some outside source that heightens the sense of supernatural emotional excitement as an accompanying rhetorical gesture; nor is there any natural source of light of the kind employed by the followers of Caravaggio to create their unnatural light effects. Zurbarán's chiaroscuro is inherent within the colours themselves, and the surfaces of his objects are bathed in it. In this merging of light, that most immaterial of all things, with the clay-like hues of the very humblest of all materials – to be found in the earthy tones of so many portraits, still lifes and genre scenes – Spanish Baroque painting possesses a spiritual quality that lends it a unique position in European art.

Velázquez, in his early period, is also a highly original representative of this Spanish tenebroso. In an early work such as *The Water Seller of Seville* (London, Wellington Museum), he undertakes to transform a simple glass of water, ennobled by the cool and silvery breaking of the light, into an enigmatic and precious object and to reflect this in the sphere of experience of the characters. Velázquez turned briefly to the genre pieces of kitchens and cellars known as "bodegones", but he never specialized in any direction and went on to expand his repertory beyond the routine commissions of court, portraiture, children's portraits, equestrian portraits, to such an extent that, apart from mural and ceiling painting, which played only a minor role in Baroque Spain anyway, his œuvre covers all the major thematic fields of the time. It includes the female nude in the form of the *Rokeby Venus* (ill. p. 272), the only surviving example of four portrayals of Venus – an extremely rare subject matter in Spanish painting – as well as mythological and sacred history paintings and the great allegories of painting which he integrated into his *Weavers* (Madrid, Prado) and into his famous portrait of the family of Philipp IV known as *Las Meninas* (ill. p. 272). In his time, Velázquez was a contemplative painter, a man of ideas and a thinker who upheld the value of human dignity as none had done before. His great painting of the *Surrender of Breda* (ill. p. 270) is not a picture of subjection, but of conciliation. Even in his portraits, so popular at court, of the dwarves, fools and idiots who were regarded at the time as living caricatures, Velázquez imbues these individuals with an undeniable dignity that brooks no mockery. In spite of these achievements, or perhaps precisely because of the personal qualities that produced them, Velázquez was nevertheless one of those artistic personalities who could not create a following or a school of painting.

## Germany

Whereas it was unusual for Spanish painters to travel to Rome and Italy (Ribera was the exception, and he never returned from Naples), it was common practice for German Baroque painters to spend as much as several years abroad in the Netherlands, Italy or even in both these countries. Leaving aside the greatest and most decisive intervention in early Baroque artistic development in Germany, the Thirty Years War, we find the most important reason for the fluctuation of artists is their lack of a territorial centre of their own in the Holy Roman Empire of the German Nation which, as a capital city, might have been able to establish certain stylistic standards, creating some uniformity in German Baroque painting.

The German love affair with Venice begins with Hans Rottenhammer (1564–1625), who settled in that city in 1589. The Frankfurt artist Adam Elsheimer joined him there and in 1600 both these artists were to find their chosen home in Rome. Venice was also the destination of the Holstein artist Johann Liss (d. 1629) and the Munich artist Johann Carl Loth (1632–1698). Whereas Loth combined the Roman tenebroso of Caravaggio with a Venetian handling of colour, Liss brought Netherlandish elements with him from Amsterdam and Haarlem, integrating them into Venetian painting, of which these two German artists were regarded as the leading representatives in the 17th century. Their influence on German painting, at least in the case of Liss, was limited.

Other artists, such as Johann Heinrich Schönfeld (1609–1682), who passed on his Roman and Neapolitan experience on his return, had a more widespread impact as mediators of foreign schools of painting. One of the most significant results of this propensity for travel was Sandrart's "Teutsche Academie der edlen Bau-, Bild- und Mahlerey-Künste" published in Nuremberg in 1675–1679. It is an invaluable source of theoretical and historical documents comparable to Vasari's *Lives of the Artists* and may be regarded as a fundamental work of German art historiography.

Sandrart, a highly esteemed artist and a respected authority, had founded an academy in 1662. At his initiative, it was situated in Nuremberg, but it was barely able to fulfil its intended function of an influential centre of art that could set standards. In the light of overall developments in Europe, and given the role played by the academies in other countries during this period, it came a little too late.

# ANNIBALE CARRACCI
## 1560—1609

The interest taken by artists and art buyers in worldly images of "humble" everyday life has always been of particular socio-cultural significance. Initial forays in this direction led to the evolution of the so-called "genre" scene, already evident in Franco-Flemish tapestries of the 15th century and in the works of Pieter Aertsen and Willem Beuckelaer in the mid-16th century. Without their example, its emergence in early Italian Baroque would probably have been quite unthinkable. The Northern Italian schools, in particular, which had always been receptive to Flemish influences, for example, showed a keen interest in the realism of the genre.

A simple peasant or farm labourer is sitting down to a meal. With a wooden spoon, he greedily scoops white beans from a bowl. Onions, bread, a plate of vegetable pie, a glass half full of wine and a brightly striped earthenware jug are standing on the table. Everything in the picture is homely and simple. The food, the man, his clothing, his loud table manners and his furtive, and hardly inviting, glance towards the spectator. None of this would be particularly striking in comparison with the examples of other painters.

What is truly new and quite astonishing, however, is the fact that Annibale's painterly technique and artistic approach are entirely in keeping with the rough and ready subject matter. Matt, earthy colours are applied to the canvas in thick and rugged brushstrokes. The compositional simplicity makes no attempt at sophisticated perspective or spatial structure, and the simple alignment of objects on the table is portrayed in almost clumsy foreshortening. What is revolutionary about this painting, of which several prelimin-ary studies exist, is the deliberate lack of artifice or skill — an approach that actually makes it all the more compelling.

This tale from the life of St Peter is recorded in the collection of legends written down by Jacobus a Voragine in the 13th century. It tells how the apostle, having triumphed over Simon Magus, was persuaded by the Christians of Rome to leave town. Jacobus a Voragine relates how Peter encountered Christ on the Appian way and asked "Quo vadis domine" (Whither goest thou, master?), to which Christ replied "To Rome, to be crucified anew."

This apocryphal legend is in fact the beginning of Peter's own martyrdom. This would certainly explain the vigorous movements in Carracci's painting, with the apostle recoiling in terror. It is not the unexpected encounter with the risen Christ that has taken the apostle aback, but his awareness of his own human frailty. Annibale's magnificent rhetoric reminds the spectator of Christ's call to turn back.

**Annibale Carracci**
The Beaneater, c. 1580—1590
Oil on canvas, 57 x 68 cm
Rome, Galleria Colonna

**Annibale Carracci**
"Domine, quo vadis?"
(Christ appearing to St Peter
on the Appian Way),
c. 1601/02
Oil on panel, 77.4 x 56.3 cm
London, National Gallery

**Annibale Carracci**
The Martyrdom of St Stephen, c. 1603/04
Oil on canvas, 51 x 68 cm
Paris, Musée National du Louvre

**Annibale Carracci**
The Lamentation of Christ, 1606
Oil on canvas, 92.8 x 103.2 cm
London, National Gallery

## ANNIBALE CARRACCI
### 1560–1609

This small panel showing the martyrdom of St Stephen reveals a very different side of Annibale's art, and one that fully confirms his consummate skill in applying the stylistic means appropriate to the theme.

Before the walls of the city, a group of men has gathered to execute Stephen, a deacon of Christian faith. The martyr is already on his knees and bleeding. He pays no heed to the stones being brandished menacingly against him, for already an angel is floating towards him bearing the crown and palm frond of the martyr. It is a celestial messenger from the golden realms of heaven which can be seen beyond the parted clouds, revealing a glimpse of God and Christ, who – visible only to the saint – have appeared to witness his martyrdom. A number of individual movements over a broad area have been skilfully drawn together against a sweeping landscape background.

The great finesse of of this painting with its meticulous draughtsmanship and its strong yet delicate colority reveals a mastery of compositional organization capable of lending superb form to a dramatic event.

In this *Lamentation*, a late work executed in 1606, Carracci has achieved a degree of monumentality in his narration of an episode from the Passion of Christ that certainly bears comparison with Caravaggio's *Entombment* in the Vatican. As in the work of the Lombard artist, it is a profound sense of gravity that determines the character of the composition here. None of the figures, not even the woman standing in the centre, is fully upright. Stooping, she stretches her arms out towards Mary, who has fallen backwards in a swoon. The composition is structured by the portrayal of reclining, crouching, bent and stooping positions and by the unusual motif of the three figures in staggered graduation behind one another. The upper edge of the painting seems to be drawn down low so that not one of the figures is able to stand in an upright full-length position. All of this contributes towards conveying the gravity and heaviness of the dead Christ, not only physically, but also psychologically: the view of Christ's dead body does not call for an upright statuary figure as in a memorial, but seeks an equivalent to the deep sense of melancholy, as expressed in the gestures and body language of the grieving women.

Other compositional devices would also suggest that the artist intended to trigger a similar mood in the spectator. The grouping of the figures can hardly be called beautiful or harmonious. A deep rift has been torn between the two Marys with the dead Christ and the two mourners, and although the body of Christ is the common bond between the mourning women, he is also presented as an isolated figure in the eyes of the spectator. The pallor of his body stands out against the full and heavy colority of the robes and the gloomy silhouette of the tomb.

As the 16th century drew to a close, a certain weariness of the forms of late Mannerism, which dominated the entire European art scene by the second half of the century, was becoming evident. In this respect, the early Baroque in Italy may also be regarded as a conscious and critically motivated phase of reform in every field of art.

The school of the Bolognese artists Lodovico, Agostino and Annibale Carracci formulated this approach clearly by founding an academy. A masterpiece of this reform movement was the huge cycle of paintings commissioned to decorate the Galleria Farnese in Rome, created under the auspices of Annibale Carracci, who was responsible for its planning and execution.

The grand mythological programme representing the power of love by way of example of the Olympian gods went hand in hand with an aesthetic concept that was to be of fundamental importance for all subsequent Baroque fresco painting. The underlying motivation of the academy is clearly evident in this

major work; it is aimed at a revival of the natural ideal once embodied by the art of the High Renaissance.

Bernini, master of Roman Baroque, expressed this aim in his assessment of Annibale, who, he claimed, had "combined all that is good, fusing the grace and drawing of Raphael, the knowledge and anatomy of Michelangelo, the nobility and manner of Correggio, the colour of Titian and the invention of Giulio Romano and Mantegna".

The result of this approach based on synthesis was not a work of stale eclecticism, but a visual world of enormous vitality in which it was possible to develop a single programme – based on Ovid's Metamorphoses – over a vast area while at the same time jettisoning the more esoteric elements of Mannerism in order to convey the heady eroticism and physicality of the myths with greater immediacy.

In the bridal procession of Bacchus and Ariadne, which fills the central area of the ceiling, these qualities merge to the most highly condensed composition of the Farnese Gallery.

**Annibale Carracci**
Triumph of Bacchus and Ariadne, c. 1595–1605
Ceiling painting (detail)
Rome, Palazzo Farnese

Orazio Gentileschi
The Lute Player, c. 1626
Oil on canvas, 144 x 130 cm
Washington, National Gallery of Art

## ORAZIO GENTILESCHI
### 1563– c. 1639/40

Of all the major followers of Caravaggio in Italy, Gentileschi is surely the strongest personality. Yet it was not so much the tenebroso and the dramatic handling of light in the middle and later period of the Lombard artists, but the clear and cool colority of Caravaggio's early work that he has taken up and adopted with great originality.

*The Lute Player*, produced around the time of his emigration to England, is one of Gentileschi's most famous works. A young girl in a lemon-yellow dress is seated with her back to the spectator at a table on which a violin, a shawm and two music scores are lying. Listening intently, the girl has lifted the lute to her ear, and is concentrating her entire attention on the chord that the fingers of her left hand are strumming on the broad body of the instrument.

It is not easy to interpret this painting, particularly as it was created in a period when allegorical messages tended to be conveyed through seemingly everyday genre scenes. The fact that she is listening so intently would certainly suggest an allegory of hearing, but it is just as possible that this is intended as a portrayal of Harmonia, the pleasing combination of different parts, as suggested by the nineteen strings of the double lute the girl is playing.

Caravaggio
Basket of Fruit, c. 1596
Oil on canvas, 46 x 64 cm
Milan, Biblioteca Ambrosiana

## CARAVAGGIO
### 1573–1610

Caravaggio is reported to have claimed that he put as much effort into painting a vase of flowers as he did into painting human figures. Such an attitude not only calls into question the hierarchy of pictorial genres that had prevailed since Alberti, but also marks the beginning of a tradition of European still life painting that was to develop continuously from then on.

Whereas, until then, there had only been occasional cases of "pure" object paintings – one by Carpaccio, a hunting trophy by Barbari and a message (1506) about one Antonio da Crevalcore, who is said to have made a "painting full of fruit" – from Caravaggio onwards, still life was to be the most popular of genres. It is a response to the increase of private art collections and their demand for profane and virtuoso painting.

Caravaggio compensated for the apparent loss of contentual gravity in an astonishing way. The basket is at eye level and juts out over the edge of the table into the real space of the spectator.

In this formal exaggeration and with a viewpoint liberated from all attributive connotations, the otherwise trivial object takes on an unheard of monumentality that renders the secret lives of objects, the play of light on their surfaces and the variety of their textures worthy of such painting.

With *The Fortune Teller (La Zingara)*, Caravaggio introduced, around 1594/95, a subject into Italian painting that was known, if at all, only in Netherlandish paintings: the so-called genre, depicting scenes of everyday life, but with a hidden or underlying meaning intended for the edification of the observant spectator.

A foppishly dressed young man, a milksop with no experience of life, gives his right hand to a young girl whose expression is difficult to define, in order to have his future read. His ideas about his future are effectively influenced by the astute young gypsy girl, whose gentle caress in tracing the lines of his hand captivates the handsome young fool so completely that he fails to notice his ring being drawn from his finger. This anecdotal narrative could be further embroidered, and indeed the painting invites us to do so as much through the plot it portrays as through what it tells us of the two characters by way of their clothing. The feathered hat, the gloves and the showy, oversized dagger immediately tell us who we are dealing with here. Similarly, the gypsy girl with her light linen shirt and her exotic wrap is intended as a "type" rather than as an individual person.

This means, of course, that what we have here is not an anecdote of two specific people, but an everyday tale. No specification of place or time detracts our attention from the point of the story, which gives the spectator a sense of complacent superiority as well as aesthetic pleasure.

Caravaggio
The Fortune Teller (La Zingara),
c. 1594/95
Oil on canvas, 99 x 131 cm
Paris, Musée National du Louvre

The gospel according to St Luke (24:13–32) tells of the meeting of two apostles with the resurrected Christ. It is only during the meal that his companions recognize him in the way he blesses and breaks the bread. But with that, the vision of Christ vanishes. In the gospel according to St Mark (16:12) he is said to have appeared to them "in an other form" which is why Caravaggio did not paint him with a beard at the age of his crucifixion, but as a youth.

The host seems interested but somewhat confused at the surprise and emotion shown by the apostles. The light falling sharply from the top left to illuminate the scene has all the suddenness of the moment of recognition. It captures the climax of the story, the moment at which seeing becomes recognizing. In other words, the lighting in the painting is not merely illumination, but also an allegory. It models the objects, makes them visible to the eye and is at the same time a spiritual portrayal of the revelation, the vision, that will be gone in an instant.

Caravaggio has offset the transience of this fleeting moment in the tranquility of his still life on the table. On the surfaces of the glasses, crockery, bread and fruit, poultry and vine leaves, he unfurls all the sensual magic of textural portrayal in a manner hitherto unprecedented in Italian painting.

The realism with which Caravaggio treated even religious subjects – apostles who look like labourers, the plump and slightly feminine figure of Christ – met with the vehement disapproval of the clergy.

Caravaggio
The Supper at Emmaus, c. 1596–1602
Oil on canvas, 140 x 197 cm
London, National Gallery

**Caravaggio**
Bacchus, c. 1598
Oil on canvas, 98 x 85 cm
Florence, Galleria degli Uffizi

# CARAVAGGIO

1573–1610

In order to understand the historical position of Caravaggio's art, we have to be aware of his peerless and revolutionary handling of subject matter. This is true not only of his religious themes, but also of his secular themes. His Bacchus no longer appears to us like an ancient god, or the Olympian vision of the High Renaissance and Mannerism. Instead, Caravaggio paints a rather vulgar and effeminately preened youth, who turns his plump face towards us and offers us wine from a goblet held by pertly cocked fingers with grimy nails. This is not Bacchus himself, but some perfectly ordinary individual dressed up as Bacchus, who looks at us rather wearily and yet alertly.

On the one hand, by turning this heathen figure into a somewhat ambiguous purveyor of pleasures, Caravaggio is certainly the great realist he is always claimed to be. On the other hand, however, the sensual lyricism of his painting is so overwhelming that any suspicion of caricature or travesty would be inappropriate.

Something similar can be found in the *Crucifixion of St Peter* in the church of Santa Maria del Popolo, where it is one of two paintings in the Cerasi chapel. Three shady characters, their faces hidden or turned away, are pulling, dragging and pushing the cross to which Peter has been nailed by the feet with his head down.

Caravaggio's St Peter is not a heroic martyr, nor a Herculean hero in the manner of Michelangelo, but an old man suffering pain and in fear of death. The scene, set on some stoney field, is grim. The dark, impenetrable background draws the spectator's gaze back again to the sharply illuminated figures who remind us, through the banal ugliness of their actions and movements – note the yellow rear and filthy feet of the lower figure – that the death of the apostle was not a heroic drama, but a wretched and humiliating execution.

Of all Caravaggio's paintings, *The Entombment* is probably the most monumental. A strictly symmetrical group is built up from the slab of stone that juts diagonally out of the background.

The painting is from the altar of the Chiesa Nuova in Rome, which is dedicated to the Pietà. The enbalming of the corpse and the entombment are actually secondary to the the Mourning of Mary which is the focal point of the lamentation.

Nothing distinguished Caravaggio's history paintings more strongly from the art of the Renaissance than his refusal to portray the human individual as sublime, beautiful and heroic. His figures are bowed, bent, cowering, reclining or stooped. The self-confident and the statuesque have been replaced by humility and subjection.

Caravaggio
The Crucifixion of
St Peter, 1601
Oil on canvas,
230 x 175 cm
Rome, Santa Maria
del Popolo

Caravaggio
The Entombment, c. 1602–1604
Oil on canvas, 300 x 203 cm
Rome, Musei Vaticani, Pinacoteca
Vaticana

Guido Reni
The Massacre of the Innocents, 1611
Oil on canvas, 268 x 170 cm
Bologna, Pinacoteca Nazionale

Guido Reni
The Baptism of Christ, c. 1623
Oil on canvas, 263.5 x 186.5 cm
Vienna, Kunsthistorisches Museum

## GUIDO RENI
### 1575–1642

Though the historical significance of Caravaggio and his enormous influence on Baroque painting cannot be overlooked, we should not ignore the the fact that there was considerable resistance against the more extreme tendencies in his art, such as the loss of the heroic sphere, or the presentation of the everyday and the ordinary. His greatest rival, whose influence was to extend far beyond that of Caravaggio well into the 18th and 19th centuries, was undoubtedly the Bolognese artist Guido Reni. An early work such as *The Massacre of the Innocents* bears clear traces of his initial links with Caravaggio and, at the same time, already reveals the most important arguments against him.

Before a landscape bathed in light, but set with dark and heavy architecture, a group of eight adults and eight children (including the putti distributing the palm fronds of victory) has been skilfully arranged. The unusual vertical format, rarely used for this theme, and above all the symmetrical structure of figural counterparts indicate that Reni was particularly interested in a specific problem of composition: that of achieving a balance between centripedal and centrifugal movement while combining them in a static pictorial structure. Reni also seeks to achieve this equilibrium in his expression of effects and in the distribution of colour accents.

Reni's *Baptism of Christ*, created in the mid 1620s as a major masterpiece of his mature style, is based on principles of composition similar to those applied in *The Massacre of the Innocents*. The painting is built up into three clearly distinct planes. At the very front, Christ bows beneath the baptismal cup, which John the Baptist pours over him with his raised right hand. The Baptist is standing or, rather, slightly kneeling over Christ on the banks of the Jordan. Below the arc formed by these two figures facing each other in humility, we see two angels who, together with a third figure at the outside left, are holding Christ's robes in readiness. Behind that, the trees, clouds and deep blue sky combine to create a sense of indefinable distance from which the Holy Spirit floats down in the form of a dove.

The entire scene, in its structure and colority, is of overwhelming simplicity. The act of baptism itself is entirely void of bright colours. The matt and shimmering flesh tones of the two nude figures stand out clearly against the middle ground and background, where everything is dominated by the solemn purity of the three primary colours red, yellow and blue. On another level, however, all the figures are closely linked in that expression of complete spiritual devotion that Reni could convey like no other artist.

Reni was able to create a balance of strictly disciplined compositional form and profound sentiment that his many imitators failed to achieve.

# CHRISTOFANO ALLORI
## 1577–1621

Christofano Allori trained in the school of his father and his grandfather, the leading Florentine Mannerist Agnolo Allori, known as Bronzino. Even if Christofano may be regarded as an artist who broke with late Mannerist tendencies and went on to become an express proponent of early Baroque reform ideas, he nevertheless continues to borrow certain traits of "Mannerist physiognomy" in order to heighten the effect of a picture. In his most famous painting, *Judith with the Head of Holofernes*, the extreme contrast between the dark and bearded head of Holofernes and the angelic face of his murderess owes much to the Mannerist school in which he was trained.

Allori is said to have created a portrait of his mistress Mazzafirra in the figure of Judith and her mother in the figure of the elderly servant woman. The head of Holofernes may be a self-portrait. If this is true, the picture would certainly be a classic example of the so-called "portrait historié" in which real figures are presented as figures from history. Whether or not this is true, the significance of this painting lies predominantly in the enormous erotic tension that emanates not only from the faces of Judith and Holofernes, but also from the sensuality with which the Old Testament heroine is portrayed. This major theme of triumph over tyranny had never before been presented from this point of view.

Cristofano Allori
Judith with
the Head of
Holofernes, 1613
Oil on canvas,
139 x 116 cm
Florence, Galleria
Pitti

# FRANCESCO ALBANI
## 1578–1660

Albani is a typical representative of the reform movement introduced by Carracci. As a student of the Bolognese artists and a colleague of Annibale who collaborated on the decoration of the Aldobrandini lunettes, he had developed a degree of confidence in his choice and application of stylistic means that allowed him not only to handle large wall areas, but also to create small and intimate devotional pictures.

In his *Sacra Famiglia* or *Holy Family* Albani finds that characteristic blend of sovereign grace and delicacy that today's spectator may find slightly disturbing. Those of us who regard such emotional emphasis and charm with some suspicion tend to forget the specific tasks and needs these pictures were intended to fulfil in order to satisfy a highly educated and cultivated group of buyers. The usual setting for pictures on this theme was a niche in the bedroom of a patrician house or palace intended for devotional purposes. This function also explains some of the typical traits of such a picture: the intimacy of a family gathering, framed by fragments of great architecture, the gestures of devotion of the two angels and the meditative attitude of the elderly Joseph – all signals with which the contemporary spectator would have been able to identify clearly.

Francesco Albani
Sacra Famiglia (The Holy
Family), c. 1630–1635
Oil on canvas, 57 x 43 cm
Florence, Galleria Pitti

Domenichino
The Maiden and the Unicorn, c. 1602
Fresco. Rome, Palazzo Farnese

## DOMENICHINO
### 1581–1641

*The Maiden and the Unicorn* is part of the decor commissioned for the Galleria Farnese under the artistic directorship of Annibale Carracci. The fresco above the south-east wall was identified at an early stage as the work of his student Domenichino, yet scholars still disagree as to the extent to which it was executed alone.

Whatever aspects of this painting may be comparable with Annibale's own compositions, this work betrays a very different temperament indeed. The strict avoidance of dynamic spatial diagonals and the grouping of unicorn and maiden parallel to the picture plane correspond much more closely to Domenichino's "classicistic" orientation and his preference for the art of the Renaissance, including the paintings of Raphael. Psychologically, too, much speaks for this painting's entire execution by Domenichino. The unicorn is not merely an attribute of the virgin. In the tradition of this allegory of chastity, the unicorn seeks refuge in the lap of a virgin. Domenichino emphasizes the shyness of these two sensitive creatures who have moved out of the centre of the picture towards the edge of the woods. Instead of the full-blooded sensuality of Annibale's figures in the Galleria Farnese, Domenichino conveys an expression of quiet and gentle introversion.

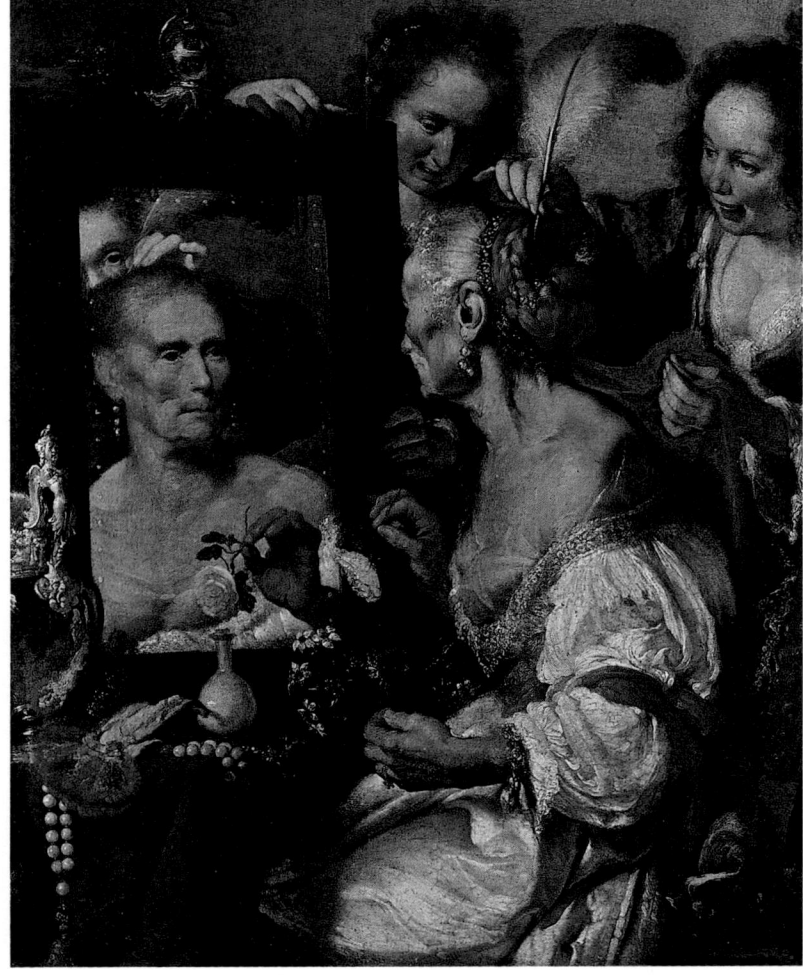

Bernardo Strozzi
Vanitas Allegory,
c. 1635
Oil on canvas,
132 x 108cm
Bologna, Private
collection

## BERNARDO STROZZI
### 1581–1644

Shortly after completing his apprenticeship, Strozzi entered the capuchin convent of Santa Barbara in Genoa. Although he was to leave the convent later as a lay preacher, his ascetic inner attitude is evident throughout his œuvre. Here, he portrays an old woman with jaded skin and white hair who is denying herself the dignity of old age. She is having her hair sumptuously styled and ornamented with ribbons and feathers, is wearing a youthful, low-cut dress and admiring herself with pleasure in the mirror.

The theme of this painting has a long tradition: the old woman who has not learned to give her life any other meaning but that of ornament and vanity, and who is unable to see the truth or recognize her true self in the mirror. Strozzi's formulation, however, is both individual and new. It makes the most of the surface values, deliberately contrasting the wrinkled skin of the old woman with the fresh complexion of her servant and juxtaposing the firm and rounded forms of youth with the withered slackness of old age. He reveals in the mirror that the old woman's red cheeks are painted with rouge, and he places a blossoming, scented rose in her wrinkled hand. He also shows us the uncriticizing complacency on her face, leaving it up to the spectator to deduce a sense of embarrassment, emptiness, transparent illusion and moral warning.

# GIOVANNI LANFRANCO
## 1582–1647

Sarah, Abraham's childless wife, brought her Egyptian maid Hagar to him so that he would produce an heir with her. However, when she herself bore Isaac, she demanded of her husband: "Cast out this bondwoman and her son: for the son of this bondwoman shall not be heir with my son, even with Isaac." (Genesis 21:10) Hagar and Ismael wandered in the wilderness, dying of thirst. Yet God heard the lamentations of the mother and sent her an angel who showed her the way to a spring and prophesied that her son would be the founder of a great nation.

In the painting, Hagar, who has been crying, is just lifting her head to look up at the angel in astonishment; her child, half hidden behind her shoulder, is also looking up incredulously at the kindly angel who has taken Hagar by the arm and is showing her the way to the water. It is the handling of colour, in particular, that highlights the unexpected aspect of the occurrence so clearly: against the gloomy brown of the wasteland, the sumptuous red and midnight-blue of Hagar's robes radiate like a lamentation of pathos. Her pale, exhausted face is turned towards the shining figure of the angel that seems to have brought light with it. Light bathes the figure, and radiates from the angel towards Hagar, rising in a pale cloud behind the angel and enflaming the orange of his hair and robe.

Giovanni Lanfranco
Hagar in the Wilderness,
undated
Oil on canvas, 138 x 159 cm
Paris, Musée National du Louvre

# DOMENICO FETTI
## c. 1589–1623

Melancholy quite literally means "black bile" – indicating the origins of this concept based on the ancient theory of the four body fluids that were believed to determine an individual's temperament.

According to this theory, the emotions and personality traits could be explained by specific physical attributes and were associated with certain qualities: in this case all things dry, cold and heavy. Accordingly, melancholy is associated with the element of earth, the season of winter, the astronomical constellation of Saturn, the leaden star.

Fetti portrays all this in his painting: the head of the woman lies heavy in her hand, her flesh is heavy, her eyelids heavy. The setting is a gloomy landscape of ruins, with no green shoots of spring and without the fruits of summer. Brown tones dominate.

Yet the philosophical temperament of melancholy, rediscovered by the Neoplatonic philosophers in Florence, is already evident. The deep contemplation of the skull, the abandoned tools (plane, palette, brush and plaster model of a torso), the unused attributes of science (astrolabe, book and geometric theory) show that melancholy is not simply a creature helpless against fits of depression, but also a talented and knowing creature, whose inaction stems only from an awareness of insoluble problems.

Domenico Fetti
Melancholy, c. 1620
Oil on canvas,
168 x 128 cm
Paris, Musée National
du Louvre

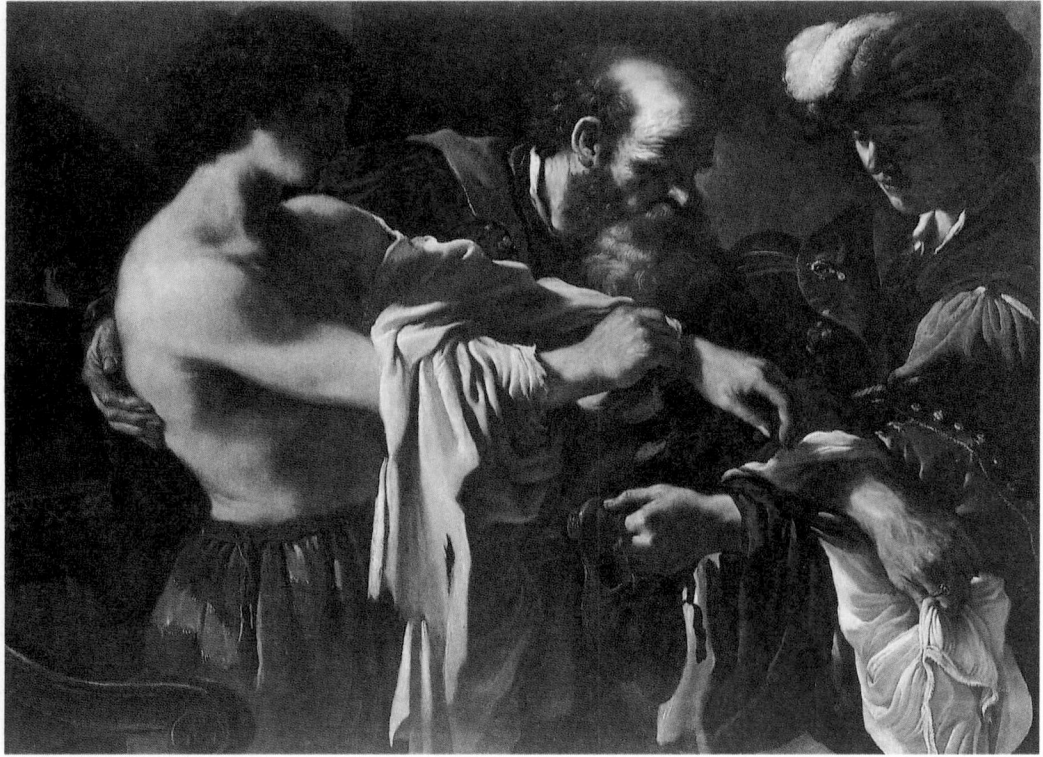

**Guercino**
The Return of the Prodigal Son, 1619
Oil on canvas, 106.5 x 143.5 cm
Vienna, Kunsthistorisches Museum

# GUERCINO
## 1591–1666

This work is from Guercino's early period, when he was beginning to achieve some initial fame and was already familiar with both the main trends of early Italian Baroque, Caravaggism and the Bolognese reform of the Annibale Carracci school. His decision to use the approach of Caravaggio may have something to do with the choice of subject matter, contrasting the humility of human existence and the possibilities of costume as disguise – a concept formulated by Caravaggio in his paintings for San Luigi and frequently taken up by his followers.

Guercino does not portray the return of the prodigal son as a scene of recognition or joy, choosing instead to depict a more tranquil motif from the biblical parable – the moment when he is given fine robes to wear. On the left in the painting, the young man has stood up and is removing the rags of the swineherd, while an old man, presumably his father, places a hand on his shoulder and takes a clean shirt from the other, foppishly dressed young man who is holding new clothes over his outstretched arm and new shoes in his hand. By using light and shade to divide the group, Guercino lends a singular autonomy to the dynamics of the outstretched and grasping hands, thereby intensifying the narrative in a most unusual way.

**Pietro da Cortona**
Holy Family Resting on
the Flight to Egypt,
c. 1643
Oil on copper, 48 x 39 cm
Munich, Bayerische Staats-
gemäldesammlungen,
Alte Pinakothek

# PIETRO DA CORTONA
## 1596–1669

This small painting of the Madonna by the great fresco artist and architect Cortona, founder of Roman High Baroque, may be regarded as the very epitome of a Baroque devotional picture. It shows the Holy Family resting on the flight to Egypt. Joseph is approaching in the background, while in the foreground an angel is offering fruit to refresh the child.

Yet the expression "devotional picture" should be used with caution, for the question of specific types in this genre is still the subject of lively debate and much research remains to be conducted into the eras after the Middle Ages.

Nevertheless, even at first glance, it is clear that the intimacy of Cortona's Madonna painting has more than just an aesthetic intention; it is meant to influence the mood of the spectator in a manner conducive to private prayer. The question of the devotional picture is somewhat complicated by Cortona's use of elements taken from the pagan vocabulary of early Roman Baroque – the idyllic, the pastoral, the antique bucolic landscape with its shady trees and wild wine – in keeping with the increasingly aesthetic interests of clients and buyers. Cortona's powers of synthesis are evident in the way he applies them successfully to create an ecclesiastical image of great atmosphere.

## MATTIA PRETI
1613–1699

Preti's biographer Dominici reports that this painting *The Tribute Money* was executed in Malta, where the painter had travelled in 1660 as a Knight of Malta in order to work on the decoration of the cathedral of San Giovanni. The painting is of particular interest in view of Preti's encounter with the works of Caravaggio who had executed some important paintings in Malta after 1607. The theme treated here is the biblical tale culminating in Christ's fateful words: "Render therefore unto Caesar the things which are Caesar's; and unto God the things that are God's." (St Matthew, 22:21) In the dark brown tones of the painting, we can barely make out the six figures half illuminated by a light from some indiscernible source. The tax collector pauses in his writing as Peter hands him the coin. Only this pause indicates the miracle that has just occurred: Peter found the coin in a fish he had caught at the command of Christ (St Matthew 17:24). The turban of a man, a hand holding a pen, another holding a coin, a face in profile with a deeply lined forehead, turned towards another face of which we can recognize only the temple and the nose, a bald head, a little red fabric and the heavy folds of a rough brown cloth are the scattered but not unconnected fragments from which our gaze wanders to and fro, reconstructing the narrative.

**Mattia Preti**
The Tribute Money, c. 1640
Oil on canvas, 193 x 143 cm
Milan, Pinacoteca di Brera

## SALVATOR ROSA
1615–1673

Democritus, the great pre-Socratic philosopher and founder of a strictly materialist concept of the world sought new explanations for birth and death, appearance and disappearance. According to his theory of "atomism", atoms are the smallest parts of all substancesl, uniting and dividing in eternal swirling movements. His ethical system called for a life of moderation and tranquillity foregoing most sensual joys.

Rosa depicts him in the traditional pose of melancholy, amidst a setting of decay, destruction and desolation. Animal skulls and bones, symbols of the past greatness of antiquity (vase, altar and herm) and symbols of fallen power (the dead eagle) are featured in this wasteland overcast with heavy grey clouds. An owl high in the tree is his only living companion, both a sign of night and of wisdom. Rosa's Democritus is not the philosopher who has reached the goal of his contemplation, nor does he represent serene tranquillity or the superior cognitive powers of the analytic mind. Instead, we see a forsaken thinker contemplating the things that have been the subject of his intellectual endeavours: death, the past, turbulent disquietude, fragmentation. The vanitas symbolism of the objects does not go unanswered: in the figure of the pensive philosopher lies the germ of a response, still caught in melancholy lethargy.

**Salvator Rosa**
Democritus in Meditation, c. 1650
Oil on canvas, 344 x 214 cm
Copenhagen, Statens Museum for Kunst

**Evaristo Baschenis**
Still Life with Musical Instruments, c. 1650
Oil on canvas, 115 x 160 cm
Bergamo, Galleria dell' Accademia Carrara

# EVARISTO BASCHENIS
## 1617–1677

Baschenis, an artist from Bergamo, was a highly specialized painter who worked almost exclusively on the portrayal of stringed instruments. The nearby town of Cremona, a famous centre of violin and lute making, provided him with his models. However, unlike the Netherlandish artists, who often used musical instruments as symbols of hearing, while the transience of the notes recalled the transience of life, Baschenis does not paint scenes of allegorical or moral significance. His emphasis lies on the aesthetic and decorative aspects, as reflected in his singular attention to painterly and ornamental detail in portraying these instruments.

A theorbo, a tenor lute and a descant lute, as well as a violin with bow can be seen together with a writing box, a quill and a book of music set on a table against which a cello is leaning. A mysterious life develops between these objects. The mild sheen on the surface of the woods and the changing hues on the body of the lute create a visual autonomy that almost makes us forget the actual purpose of these instruments. Their curves present unusual viewpoints as though by chance. These musical objects are an almost tangible feast of tranquillity for the eyes.

**Luca Giordano**
The Fall of the Rebel Angels, 1666
Oil on canvas, 419 x 283 cm
Vienna, Kunsthistorisches Museum

# LUCA GIORDANO
## 1634–1705

The fall of the rebel angels is the greatest single theme of the Counter-Reformation. It is a theme that allowed a church in conflict to present its propaganda in the form of its struggle against all forms of heresy. At the same time, the theme of the struggling angel also symbolized the triumph of light over the rebellion of the powers of darkness – giving the painter an opportunity to create a chiaroscuro charged with meaning, in which heaven and hell, the incense of the blessed and the brimstone of the damned are contrasted in an extremely confined space, creating an arc of tension within which the knight-like angel spreads his broad wings and wields his sword in a sweeping gesture of victory.

Giordano sets the scene with relatively few figures compared to, say, Rubens' *Great Last Judgement*. Against a background of deep golden light, the archangel balances with an almost balletic movement on the heavy breast of Lucifer, entangled amidst a group of his servants, his angular and batlike wings cutting through the hazy sfumato of the hellfire. What appears at first glance to be so dramatic is not in fact the depiction of a struggle as such. Michael is not attacking the figures from hell with his sword, but is holding it aloft like a sign, as though his mere appearance were enough to cast Satan and his followers into eternal damnation.

# BACICCIO
1639–1709

This small oil painting showing the *Apotheosis of St Ignatius*, the founder of the Jesuit order, is a bozzetto – a preparatory sketch for the fresco Baciccio executed for the vaulting of the left transept of the order's principal church of Il Gesù in Rome. The bozzetto differs from the fresco only in a few of the angel figures and in the use of stronger colours. Although the apotheosis of the saint has a firm place in the overall ecclesiastical programme of the church, from which it cannot be dissociated, this oil study is nevertheless an independent painting, executed with greater care than one might expect of a sketch.

The saint is carried heavenwards by a group of music-making, flower-strewing angels that are inebriated with joy. His arms spread wide, he soars towards a golden stream of light that is breaking through from the depths of the heavens. Baciccio does not treat this supernatural triumphal procession as a transcendental vision, but as a real occurrence. The body of the saint and the angels are not transcended by light, but are sculpturally tangible, and in its earthly corporeality, the painting mediates between the world of the spectator and the light whose source remains invisible to us, but which is perceptible in the figure of the saint.

**Baciccio**
The Apotheosis of St Ignatius, c. 1685
Oil on canvas, 48 x 63.5 cm
Rome, Galleria Nazionale

# GIUSEPPE MARIA CRESPI
1665–1747

Through the oiled paper in the window frame, a milky light falls into the humble servant's room. Clothing is scattered untidily on the floor and thrown over a roughly made bench. A few household objects and some washing on a bar hang against the bare brick wall, whose only remaining decoration consists of a few personal items. The pretty woman who lives in this room, a maid or servant girl, is sitting on the edge of the bed, dressed only in a shift. As she concentrates on her search for a flea that has probably hidden on her breast, she reveals her round knees, her plump arms and her well formed shoulder.

The complete intimacy of this scene and the still life of the utensils anticipates a theme that was to become typical of late 18th century taste: innocence glimpsed unawares. Although there are a number of allegorical reflections – the little dog at the end of the bed, the roses in the vase next to the cosmetic jar – they nevertheless do not seriously mean to identify this girl with Venus. The "keyhole perspective" also leaves it up to the spectator to choose his or her own interpretation of the scene.

**Giuseppe Maria Crespi**
The Flea, c. 1707–1709
Oil on copper, 46 x 34 cm
Florence, Galleria degli Uffizi

Quentin Varin
Presentation of Christ in
the Temple, c. 1618–1620
Grisaille, 46 x 36.5 cm
Beauvais, Musée
Départemental de l'Oise

## QUENTIN VARIN
### C. 1570–1634

The scene shows Mary, who has freed her son
from service in the temple by bringing a sacrifice, for Jewish custom requires that the first-
born belongs to Yaweh. In the gospel according to St Luke, this is linked to the purifica-
tion sacrifice of the mother, indicated here by
the doves in the basket of the servant girl. Old
Simeon is a seer who recognizes the divinity of
the child immediately.

Varin's painting, which is hardly a masterpiece of French art, gives some indication of
the high stylistic quality of even the minor
masters of the Baroque. This is a so-called grisaille picture, which means it is painted entirely in monochromatic grey tones. Similar
monochromatic paintings had existed since
the late Middle Ages in other forms, generally
derived from coloured earth. Varin's *Presentation of Christ in the Temple* explores the subtle
boundary between a palette reduced entirely
to black and white and the traces of a delicate
germ of colour. The grey is by no means colourless. Varin has mixed it using a dark greenish earth, brown and a slightly yellowish
white; what is more, he lets the dark red tone
of the canvas grounding shine through some
thinly painted areas, for example the altar
cloth, thereby achieving a texture of extreme
sensitivity.

Simon Vouet
Saturn, conquered by Amor,
Venus and Hope, c. 1645/46
Oil on canvas, 187 x 142 cm
Bourges, Musée du Berry

## SIMON VOUET
### 1590–1649

Vouet had spent 15 years in Italy when
Louis XIII and Cardinal Richelieu called him
back to France to make him the artistic representative of their ideas, ideals and ideology.
What made Vouet seem the right man for the
job was not only his virtuoso painterly skills,
but also his preference for large-scale yet beautifully balanced composition. In addition to
religious themes, he also favoured allegorical
depictions.

Saturn as an old man, with his attribute,
the scythe, in his hand, has fallen to the
ground – he embodies time. A young woman
is pulling hard at one of his wings and the anchor at her feet indicates that she represents
Hope. Beside her, a beautiful woman with a
bare breast is tugging at his grey hair – she
represents Truth. Above this group, in an
iridescent robe, floats Fama, the figure of
fame, who announces her presence with a
trumpet. She has placed her arm around a
figure whose hair is blowing forwards – the
traditional attribute of Occasio, the fortunate
occasion – with the insignia of power and
wealth in her hand, which are also the attributes of Fortuna, the allegory of luck or
good fortune. The luminous colours, the dramatic and yet masterly movement, are equivalents of the affirmative content of the allegory.

# LOUIS LE NAIN
c. 1593–1648

We cannot be entirely sure as to which of the three Le Nain brothers actually painted this picture. Right up to the present day, art historians have been unable to determine the individual contributions to their joint works. Their peasant paintings – which constitute only a part of their overall œuvre – brought them fame, particularly in the 19th century.

There is a considerable risk of judging them primarily on grounds of their humble rural genre scenes. They do not present poverty imbued with profound religious faith (as do the works of Murillo), but already show signs of interpreting the "simple life" in the sense of an idyll. The richly nuanced use of brown and grey tones, heightened by a few scarlet accents, takes on a sophisticated independence for which the subject matter serves merely as external legitimation. The delicacy of colour finds its counterpart in the composition. The children on the haycart, the mother with the infant on her lap, the little swineherd with two girls: each form distinctly separate groups which, at the same time, are like the verses of a song praising the beauties of rural life – a song sung by a city dweller of high society.

This is a picture of unforgettable gravity. Far removed from the so-called bambocciada with which Le Nain's peasant paintings are generally compared, there is not the slightest hint of caricature or humour here. The few figures grouped around an almost empty centre show nothing of the pleasant side of rural life so frequently depicted as serene and edifying. Le Nain's peasant family is not in Arcadia, and nobody familiar with the peasants and herds of this poetic realm in the 17th century is likely to have misconstrued it in this vein. Few paintings cast such an accusing shadow on the art of the Baroque with its exuberant celebration of sensual pleasures.

On the right, a man in rags stands beside a boy who is sitting on the ground, his legs stretched out before him with a cockerel on his lap; opposite him is a woman on a chair and, in the background, a young woman with a child in her arms stands on the steps of the dilapidated house from whose windows and doors the other inhabitants peer out shyly. The figures are quite motionless. Neither joy nor sadness, anticipation nor rejection can be detected in their faces. Only the great indifference of their earnest gaze calls upon the spectator to take a similar stance and underpins the realism of the composition in its portrayal of an unapproachable dignity that brooks neither the rhetoric of accusation nor transfiguration.

The art of Le Nain is direct. Neither allegory, nor symbol, nor history: everything is meant just as we see it.

Louis Le Nain
La Charette (The Cart), 1641
Oil on canvas, 56 x 72 cm
Paris, Musée National du Louvre

Louis Le Nain
Peasants at their Cottage Door, undated
Oil on canvas, 55 x 68 cm
San Francisco (CA), The Fine Arts Museums of San Francisco, California Palace of the Legion of Honor

## GEORGES DE LA TOUR
### 1593–1652

The brutal realism and brackish, earthy colours brightened by a single vibrant red immediately call to mind the Spanish painting to which the works of this artist from Lorraine have frequently been attributed. "Repulsive, cruel truth; a Spanish painting attributed to Bartolomé Esteban Murillo. It is not without charm. Fine colours, realistic expression..." Such was the ambivalence with which Stendhal, an experienced connoisseur of Italian and French painting, described his impressions in "Mémoires d'un touriste", astutely pinpointing the very core of this portrayal: its seemingly paradoxical attempt to apply the cultivated art of painting to a thoroughly miserable subject matter. We can almost hear the discordant voice of the blind man with his hurdy-gurdy. Yet this unflattering presentation does not represent a sympathetic attitude to the socially disadvantaged of the day. On the contrary. Subjects of this kind were intended to amuse high society, who enjoyed gracing the walls of their patrician homes with such melodramatic scenes.

The moralizing genre of painting made popular by Caravaggio includes the painting of the trickster. An inexperienced, wealthy and opulently dressed young man is being cheated at cards in the dubious company of a courtesan with her lover and a conspirative servant girl. Wine and the promise of erotic adventure have made the young dandy so light-headed that he does not notice the unsubtle trick of an ace being drawn from his opponent's belt. Such depictions may be regarded as brothel scenes – a woman drinking wine in the company of men could be nothing but a whore in the eyes of a 17th century spectator. The three accomplices are after the young man's money, and they communicate with each other through glances and subtle gestures. The spectator becomes a witness and the sideways glance of the servant girl seems to make the spectator an accomplice as well.

In the 17th century, St Sebastian was one of the most important of all patron saints. Prayers were offered to him seeking protection against disease, especially the plague, which had affected the region of Lorraine particularly severely. In reference to the medieval legend in which the widow Irene takes pity upon the martyr who has been left for dead, we clearly see the expectations of care and attendance demanded of this saint. La Tour has painted a night scene illuminated by the torch Irene is holding. Grief, empathy and a range of light that runs from dazzling brilliance to deepest darkness all add up to a moving and meditative comment on charitable kindness.

Georges de La Tour
Hurdy-Gurdy Player,
c. 1620–1630
Oil on canvas, 162 x 105 cm
Nantes, Musée des Beaux-Arts

Georges de La Tour
The Card-Sharp with the Ace of Spades, c. 1620–1640
Oil on canvas, 106 x 146 cm
Paris, Musée National du Louvre

Georges de La Tour
St Sebastian Attended by St Irene, c. 1634–1643
Oil on canvas, 160 x 129 cm
Berlin, Gemäldegalerie

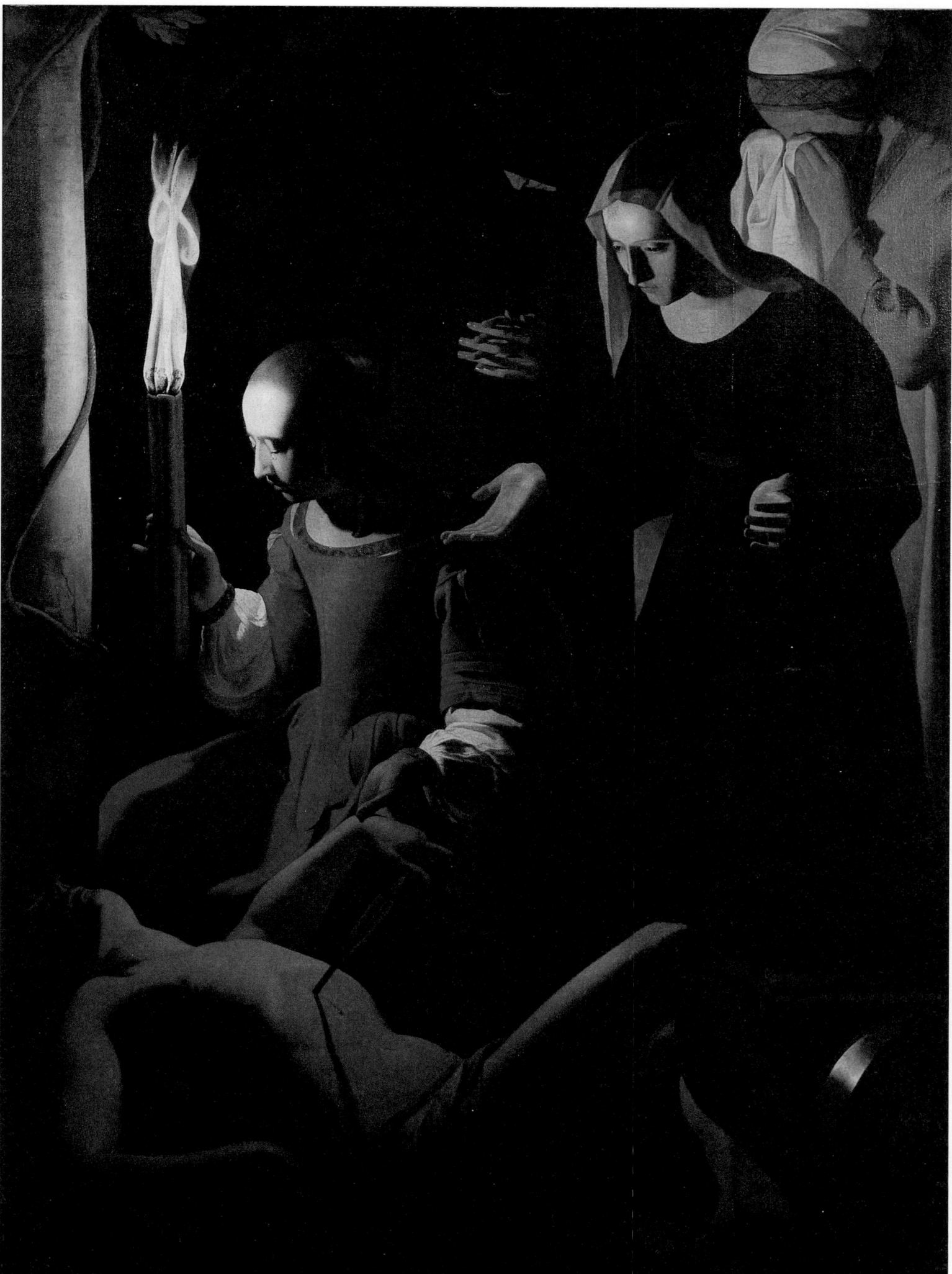

## VALENTIN DE BOULOGNE
### 1594–1632

He gave himself the epithet "Innamorato" –
the enamoured. In Rome, he led a life his bio-
graphers found despicable. He associated with
gamblers, whores, drunkards and, according to
Sandrart, favoured the company of Dutch and
Flemish artists. Valentin de Boulogne is of interest not only for his turbulent biography,
but also as one of the most remarkable of the
Caravaggisti. In a genre scene such as *The Concert* he proves his individuality as a follower of
Caravaggio, by interpreting the latter's pictorial approach in a completely new way. On the
other hand, Valentin is of only indirect significance for French painting.

A group of musicians with guitar, violin,
mandolin and music score is grouped around a
block of stone on which we can see an antique
relief. In their midst is a half-grown child,
while drinkers can be seen in front of and behind the stone. Formally, he employs the chiaroscuro technique "invented" by Caravaggio,
highlighting faces, a leg, feathers or a silken
sleeve. Yet here, the darkness takes on an ambivalent depth: its gloominess casts shadows on
the facial traits, filling them with a terrible
sadness (none of the figures is laughing or
even smiling). At the same time, it is the soil
or germ from which all colour, the source of
all life, springs.

Valentin de Boulogne
The Concert, c. 1622–1625
Oil on canvas, 173 x 214 cm
Paris, Musée National du Louvre

## LUBIN BAUGIN
### c. 1610/12–1663

The crisply structured still lifes signed "A.
Baudin" and attributed to Lubin Baugin rank
amongst the finest examples of French Baroque painting. What is typically French in
the artist's approach is the clear distribution of
the objects throughout the narrowly defined
space and the way they are spread out over the
picture plane. The absence of overcrowding
and the avoidance of all unclear overlapping results in a cool and almost mathematically ordered world whose tranquility brooks none of
the pathos so popular in the Netherlands at
the time. Each of the objects refers to one of
the five senses: the lute and the "rattling"
coins in the bag suggest hearing, while the
musical score, the chessboard and the cards indicate vision. The wine stands for taste, the
bread to be broken evokes the sense of touch
and the flowers the sense of smell. What appears at first glance to be a simple grouping of
otherwise meaningless objects is in fact the
figuration of an allegory in which earthly symbols stand for eternal values. Only superficially do the wine and bread represent an accompaniment to the joys of play, for they actually refer to the Last Supper, a fact further
underlined by the inclusion of carnations,
whose very name suggests the "incarnation" of
Christ. In this sense, the painting is an indication of God's presence in symbols of everyday
life.

Lubin Baugin
Still Life with Chessboard (The Five Senses), undated
Oil on panel, 55 x 73 cm
Paris, Musée National du Louvre

# NICOLAS POUSSIN

c. 1593/94–1665

French Baroque Classicism celebrates its greatest triumph in the work of Nicolas Poussin, who chose to live in Rome. The painting showing a rare portrayal of the Midas legend, is one of his most beautiful mythological compositions. His use of motifs taken from antique sculpture, on which most of the figures in the painting are based, also ensures the authenticity of the pictorial narrative whose material is taken from Ovid's Metamorphoses. Midas, King of Phrygia, dazzled by the thought of untold wealth, makes unwise use of a divine gift. Bacchus promises to fulfil one wish for him and Midas foolishly asks that everything he touches should turn to gold. Too late, he realizes his fateful error. Doomed to hunger and thirst because everything he puts to his lips turns to gold, he begs Bacchus to release him from his terrible gift and is finally allowed to wash away the spell in the river Pactolos, which has carried alluvial gold ever since.

Which scene is portrayed here in this Bacchalian realm? Is it the granting of Midas' foolish wish? Is it his plea for liberation from its spell? Or is it the king offering his thanks to Bacchus for saving him from certain death? It is probably the latter, for the figure kneeling in the background beside the river god seems to have discovered the gold in the sand of the river Pactolos, indicating that this scene depicts the situation after Midas has been liberated from the spell.

Poussin did not begin to treat landscape as an independent element until after 1648. One reason for this might lie in the fact that landscapes, unlike architecture and human figures, were not actually included in the artistic canon of classical antiquity. This meant that Poussin had to rely entirely on his own inspiration in evoking nature from the spirit of antiquity as he saw it. There is certainly a stroke of audacity in this painting, which hangs in the Prado, Madrid, in that Poussin does not portray any particular incident or activity. The three men are indeed merely figures in the landscape. Their gestures seem to describe distant routes, and their attitude suggests the repose of the wanderer who has walked great distances.

The artists of the 15th century perfected the construction and regulation of linear perspective. The artists of the early 16th century discovered the use of colour as a means of rendering spatial distance in aerial perspective, making it unthinkable for subsequent landscape paintings to ignore the way objects change their colour in the distance. In the 17th century, these techniques were adopted as a means of creating a spatial illusion of depth whose intangibility is generally described rather vaguely as "atmosphere". It is for this reason that the landscape paintings of the Baroque era never give the spectator the same sense of empty space as the works of earlier centuries. Atmosphere in the Baroque era is the very substance of a landscape that fills the whole painting, drawing it together to create a homogeneous whole.

**Nicolas Poussin**
Midas and Bacchus, c. 1630
Oil on canvas, 98 x 153 cm
Munich, Bayerische Staatsgemälde-
sammlungen, Alte Pinakothek

**Nicolas Poussin**
Landscape with Three Men, c. 1645–1650
Oil on canvas, 100 x 130 cm
Madrid, Museo del Prado

**Nicolas Poussin**
Echo and Narcissus, c. 1627/28
Oil on canvas, 74 x 100 cm
Paris, Musée National du Louvre

**Nicolas Poussin**
Moses Trampling on the Pharaoh's Crown, 1645
Oil on canvas, 99 x 142.2 cm
Woburn Abbey, Duke of Bedford collection

# NICOLAS POUSSIN
c. 1593/94–1665

According to Ovid's Metamorphoses, the nymph Echo fell in love with the beautiful young Narcissus. However, her love was unrequited and she wasted away in sorrow until only her voice – echo – remained. Later, Narcissus caught sight of his own reflection in a pool, and was so enamoured of the beautiful youth beyond his reach that his self-love destroyed him and he turned into the flower that bears his name.

Poussin has painted Narcissus reclining by the waterside with the pallor of death upon him, and narcissi already growing by his head. Behind him is Amor with the torch that ignited the love of Echo, whose incorporeally elegiac image can be seen amidst the rocks.

A text by Josephus Flavius, *Antiquitatis Judaicae*, tells how the daughter of the Pharaoh, finding the baby Moses amongst the rushes, decided to present the child to her father. Her father plays with the child and, in fun, places his crown on the baby's head. Moses casts the crown to the ground, so that it breaks. The high priest, recognizing the boy as the one who has been prophesied to overthrow the Pharaoh, makes to kill him. Only an appeal invoking the child's innocence and the future judgement of God save Moses.

Poussin uses a wide variety of rhetorical gestures in order to express the various reactions to the incident in a classical mode. The gestural drama reaches its climax in the "dialogue" between the high priest who has raised his dagger to strike the child and the raised left arm of the nurse-maid behind the Pharaoh's daughter.

The iconography of St Cecilia did not always depict the martyr as a musician. Raphael, for example, portrayed her listening enthralled to the sounds of celestial harmonies in such transports of delight that the instruments of earthly music fell from her hands. Poussin's interpretation, on the other hand, shows her playing music herself.

Against a background of landscape and classical architecture, a putto draws a red drape to the side above the saint, creating the backdrop for an intimate concert. St Cecilia is playing on a keyboard instrument, accompanied by two singing angels who are standing before a column. In this way, Poussin has created a synthesis between the earthly musicianship of the saint and the strains of celestial music. Through the involvement of the angels, the earthly sounds are transformed into celestial harmony, beyond the hearing of profane ears, but visualized in the full-toned chord created by the cardinal trio of red, yellow and blue, which is played in every possible modulation from brightly illuminated planes to areas of darkness.

**Nicolas Poussin**
St Cecilia, c. 1627/28
Oil on canvas, 118 x 88 cm
Madrid, Museo del Prado

**Claude Lorrain**
Landscape with Cephalus and Procris reunited by Diana, 1645
Oil on canvas, 102 x 132 cm
London, National Gallery

**Claude Lorrain**
Landscape with Apollo
and Mercury, c. 1645
Oil on canvas,
55 x 45 cm
Rome, Galleria
Doria-Pamphilj

## CLAUDE LORRAIN
### 1600–1682

Claude Lorrain is perhaps the first artist we may justly describe as a landscape painter in the modern sense. His specialization in this field was determined by his lifestyle and his working method, his intensively meditative observation of nature and his open-air sketches. His classification as a pure landscape painter seems at first to contradict the fact that, in spite of his obvious lack of talent in the portrayal of figures, he refused to forego their inclusion in his landscapes and frequently had them painted by his assistants or artist colleagues.

The people in his paintings, however small and seemingly irrelevant they may appear, are obviously more than mere staffage or props in the sense of a decorative element. They are part of the landscape itself, the embodiment of its respective character through mythological narrative, in which nature becomes the scene of an encounter between the mortal and the divine.

Nothing in this scene showing the reconciliation of Cephalus and Procris through Diana points towards the tragic end that begins to unfold here. The tale is told by Ovid in his Metamorphoses: Procris flees from her husband Cephalus, who has accused her of being unfaithful to him, and turns to Diana and her hunters. Diana gives her a hound and a magic javelin that never misses its mark. Procris gives both to Cephalus on their reconciliation, which Claude – unlike Ovid – describes as occurring in the presence of Diana. To the spectator at the time, the rest of the story, in which jealousy seals the fate of the couple, would have been evident. Tortured by fears of her husband's unfaithfulness, Procris hides in the bushes to spy on him. Cephalus, alarmed by a rustling sound, casts his spear into the bushes and unwittingly kills Procris. In view of this background, Claude's peaceful painting has to be interpreted as a warning against unfaithfulness and jealousy.

This pastoral scene with Apollo and Mercury suppresses all suggestion of enmity in this remarkable act of divine cattle-rustling related in the tale of the theft of Admetus' cattle. If ever the transposition of poetic concepts into works of painting were appropriate, then surely in a painting such as this one, in which a truly lyrical theme – Apollo playing, singing and so immersed in his music that he does not even notice Mercury surreptitiously leading away the peerless cattle of Admetus. The lyricism lies in the affinity between the rapt emotional state of Apollo, which seems to merge with the atmosphere of the landscape, and the light-drenched expanses of the plain through which the shimmering river flows. It was a widespread concept in Baroque art theory that poetry was verbal painting and painting was silent poetry, a concept fully expressed in this work.

The great "inner" theme of 17th century painting is light: illumination from some invisible
source contrasted with all-powerful darkness;
as in the work of Caravaggio, the living light
of a candle whose pale white flame permeates
every nuance of shadow; as in the work of
Georges de La Tour; or a view of the sun –
boldly attempted for the first time by Claude
Lorrain – shimmering through the fragile veil
of the morning haze and dissolving the wide
horizon of the sea with distant sails, landscapes with mountains, cities and towers.

This light seems to reach the spectator
from a world of the imagination rather than reality. The port with its Roman triumphal arch
and crumbling defence walls may well be the
setting for a scene from everday life in ancient
times. Yet what we see here is not a reconstruction of classical antiquity. The ancient buildings are overgrown by bushes and grass; antiquity is merely an image, a ruin recalling a
timeless world in which a transfiguring sun
casts a morning light without shadow. Just as
it is impossible to pinpoint the century in
which the people of a Claude Lorrain painting
live, so too is it impossible to name the countries where his landscapes might be found.

Like no other artist before him, Lorrain made
poetic reality the subject of his painting.

In the painting *Seaport at sunrise* Claude Lorrain shows bales of goods being transported between a cargo boat and the nearby shore using
small boats. We cannot even tell for sure
whether the goods are being transported towards the cargo boat or away from it. The labourers, the conversation on the shore and the
group by the triumphal arch are mere staffage,
little more than attributes of the landscape.
This is not a scene of contemporary or ancient
poetry, and the great classical ruins are not
peopled by figures from mythology. In his
own way, Claude Lorrain contributed towards
genre painting and the preference of his epoch
for portrayals of ordinary people. One might
describe this transposition of everyday life into
the past as "genre historié" – in much the
same way that we use the term "portrait historié" to describe the technique, so popular in
the Netherlands, of depicting living personalities as biblical or mythological figures.

**Claude Lorrain**
Seaport at Sunrise, 1674
Oil on canvas, 72 x 96cm
Munich, Bayerische Staatsgemälde-
sammlungen, Alte Pinakothek

**Philippe de Champaigne**
Ex Voto (Mother Superior Cathérine-Agnès Arnauld
und Sister Cathérine de Sainte-Suzanne, the daughter
of the artist), 1662
Oil on canvas, 165 x 229 cm
Paris, Musée National du Louvre

**Gaspard Dughet**
Landscape with St Augustine and the Mystery
of the Trinity, c. 1651–1653
Oil on canvas, 278.5 x 385.5 cm
Rome, Galleria Doria-Pamphilj

# PHILIPPE DE CHAMPAIGNE
## 1602–1674

The Flemish-born painter Philippe de Champaigne was the leading portraitist at the court of Marie de Médici and Louis XIII. His profound Catholic faith began to find increasingly clear expression in his art after a number of personal blows of fate; his wife died in 1638 and his son in 1642. Both his daughters entered the famous convent of Port-Royal. The youngest died in 1655 and one year later, the elder sister took her vows under the name Cathérine-Suzanne.

We have to be aware of these details in order to understand the *Ex Voto*, for this painting is closely linked with the personal sentiments of the artist. It shows two nuns dressed in the habit of their order. The elderly nun is kneeling and praying with an expression of contentment on her face, while the younger nun is seated on a chair, her legs stretched out to rest on a footstool, joining the elderly nun in prayer. A lengthy Latin inscript explains the story. Champaigne's daughter Cathérine, the younger of the two nuns in the painting, had been struck by paralysis and had regained her health after nine days of prayer. It is a mark of his faith that the artist does not portray the miraculous healing itself, but the prayer of his daughter and her Mother Superior.

# GASPARD DUGHET
## 1615–1675

A brother-in-law and student of Poussin, Dughet soon developed his own expressive syntax, particularly in landscape painting, which bears evidence of his familiarity with the works of Elsheimer, Rosa and Bril. Here, too, we sense his different temperament, for excitement and fantasy enliven the peaceful tranquillity of the landscape. The enigma of nature becomes the subject matter, creating new relationships between the pictorial space and the subject matter. According to legend, St Augustine was walking on the beach of Ostia, contemplating the problem of the Holy Trinity (which appears here as a vision in the clouds) when he noticed a child trying to spoon the sea into a hole in the sand. On pointing out the futility of the task, he received the response that it was equally futile to attempts to explain the mystery of the Holy Trinity.

In Dughet's painting, the legend is rendered plausible by the portrayal of the landscape. The intensive atmosphere – the brooding expanses of the sea, the looming storm, the gathering clouds – create a sense of anticipation as though the spectator, too, must seek to understand some mystery. At the same time, the spectator senses the triviality of human existence reflected in the small figures set in a universal landscape.

# SÉBASTIEN BOURDON
1616–1671

Because of his skilful mastery of a wide variety of styles, Sébastien Bourdon has never achieved a clear-cut position as an artist. One of the strongest influences on his painting was undoubtedly Nicolas Poussin. This is clearly reflected in *The Finding of Moses*, which is a particularly fine example of Bourdon's skill in handling the subjects of other artists with great originality.

An informal yet dignified procession of figures has approached the banks of the Nile where two men have recovered the basket with the infant and are handing it over to the servant women. However familiar the classical robes of Poussin may appear here, the treatment of landscape and the handling of colour are entirely different. A sense of distance is created, structured by light and shadow, silhouettes and laconic modelling, and dotted with dark masses of vegetation and grey architecture.

This imaginary landscape presented in sweeping planes contrasts sharply with the gentle modelling of the robes. Any association with Poussin or other artists tends to be dispelled by the strongly contrasting portrayal of the figures and the landscape.

**Sébastien Bourdon**
The Finding of Moses, c. 1650
Oil on canvas, 119.6 x 172.8 cm
Washington, National Gallery of Art

# PIERRE MIGNARD
1612–1695

Mignard's artistic career is condensed in this painting. He trained primarily in the Paris workshop of Vouet, the great master of finely balanced classicistic compositions, and elegantly allegorical formulation. This is reflected in the appealing pose of the girl and the dignified blue drapes of her robe, more appropriate to the Venus of Vouet than to the portrait of a child.

What is more, the allegory itself also refers to Mignard's teacher; the notion of the individual as a soap bubble – "homo bulla" – points to the transience of human existence, a concept that is further underlined by the watch Mignard has painted on the table. We might also muse on whether the shell containing the soap is intended to indicate Venus, whose attribute it is.

Mignard's close reading of Titian's works is also evidenced by the little dog and the landscape so frequently found in Titian's Madonna paintings. Just four years before his death, Mignard was appointed "peintre du roi" as successor to Le Brun, whose artistic bounds he surpasses in this portrait. The pathos of vanitas and the pomp of representation do not set a rigid pattern here, for the vitality of the child's personality clearly predominates over the Baroque pictorial traditions.

**Pierre Mignard**
Girl Blowing Soap Bubbles, 1674 (Marie-Anne de Bourbon)
Oil on canvas, 132 x 96 cm
Versailles, Châteaux de Versailles

**Charles Le Brun**
The Martyrdom of
St John the Evangelist
at the Porta Latina,
c. 1641/42
Oil on canvas,
282 x 224 cm
Paris, Saint-Nicolas
du Chardonnet

**Charles Le Brun**
Chancellor Séguier at the Entry of Louis XIV
into Paris in 1660, 1660
Oil on canvas, 295 x 351 cm
Paris, Musée National du Louvre

# CHARLES LE BRUN
## 1619–1690

Le Brun might well be described as the one figure who best symbolizes art policy under Louis XIV. In 1638, at the age of just nineteen, he became court painter and two years later Richelieu commissioned him to produce three major works. This painting, probably commissioned by the guild of painters, sculptors and gilders of the city of Paris, may well have constituted an important step in his meteoric career.

The martyrdom of John the Evangelist plays a special role amongst the reports and legends of the disciples of Christ. According to legend, John was arrested under Trajan in Rome at the Porta Latina and thrown into a vat of burning oil, but survived unhurt and was even rejuvenated. Although he later died a natural death, he was accorded the rank of martyr.

Le Brun has chosen to portray the dramatic moment at which he is lifted into the boiling, steaming vat. Menacing idols and horseback soldiers bearing the symbols of imperial power flank the scene. Yet just as his executors are making their final preparations and fanning the flames, the doomed man receives the divine message of martyrdom, with laurel wreaths and flowers. The visible triumph of faith at the moment of extreme physical danger is the subject of all portrayals of martyrdom, but only high Baroque painting found formulations capable of balancing the spiritual rapture of a saint against manifestations of physical brutality.

The equestrian portrait of the chancellor Séguier shows Le Brun's first great patron, for whom his own father, a minor sculptor, had already worked previously. Séguir helped the ambitious young painter to enter the studio of the famous Simon Vouet and financed his journey to Rome which not only allowed him to stay in the promised land of art study, but also gave him the opportunity of meeting Nicolas Poussin.

The chancellor, magnificently dressed and seated on a white horse draped in a sumptuous caparison is surrounded by six pages who are leading the horse at a suitable pace and shading their master with parasols as a sign of his high office. There is something almost exotic about the picture and we soon realize that this impression is due to a certain ambiguity in the subject matter.

On the one hand, the chancellor is presented in the highest ceremonial dignity, in an official portrait that says little about his individual personality; on the other hand, however, this equestrian portrait is only an imaginary aspect of the ceremonial entry of Louis XIV into Paris in the year 1660 and, as such, it is a history painting in the tradition of the "entrées solennelles" which were an important component in the ceremonial representation of monarchy and officialdom from the time of François I onwards.

## EUSTACHE LE SUEUR
### 1616–1655

Three girls, crowned with wreathes, are playing music in an Arcadian setting. One is
seated gracefully on the ground, with a musical score on her lap, singing to the accompaniment of the viola da gamba played by a second
girl, who has turned her gaze heavenwards for
inspiration. The third figure, slightly in the
background, is listening and casts an earnest
glance towards the spectator. There can be
little doubt as to their identity.

If they are not the Three Graces, they can
be none other than the three muses of poetry.
The first is probably Melpomene, the muse of
tragic poetry, the figure with the bare breast is
Erato, the muse of erotic poetry and mime,
while the singer is undoubtedly Polymnia, to
whom the writers of lyrical hymns turned for
inspiration.

Another trio is also indicated here: Le
Sueur has portrayed the close sisterly ties and
their various traits by a simple colouristic
means. He has used yellow, red and blue, the
primary colours from which all other colours
spring. In this way, just as the three muses
embody all of poetry, so too do their clothes
contain the entire colour spectrum of the
painter.

Eustache Le Sueur
Melpomene, Erato und Polymnia,
c. 1652–1655
Oil on canvas, 130 x 130 cm
Paris, Musée National du Louvre

## HYACINTHE RIGAUD
### 1659–1743

This famous portrait is regarded as the very
epitome of the absolutist ruler portrait. Yet it
represents more than just power, pomp and circumstance. The sumptuous red and gold
drapery is not only a motif of dignity, but also
creates a framework that echoes the drapes of
the ornate, ermine-lined robe. The blue velvet
brocade ornamented with the golden fleurs-de-
lis of the house of Bourbon is repeated in the
upholstery of the chair, the cushion and the
cloth draped over the table below it: the king
quite clearly "sets the tone".

A monumental marble column on a high
plinth is draped in such a way that it does not
detract from the height of the figure. Louis is
presented in an elegantly angled pose, situated
well above the standpoint of the spectator to
whom he seems to turn his attention gra-
ciously, but without reducing the stability of
his stance.

Rigaud's consummate mastery of portraiture is particularly evident in the way he depicts the king's facial expression: his distanced
unapproachability are not founded in Neoclassicist idealization, but in the candour of an
ageing, impenetrable physiognomy. The lips
are closed decisively and with a hint of irony,
the eyes have a harsh, dark sheen, while the
narrow nose suggests intolerance. This is a
ruler who is neither good nor evil, but beyond
all moral categories.

Hyacinthe Rigaud
Portrait of Louis XIV, 1701
Oil on canvas, 279 x 190 cm
Paris, Musée National du Louvre

**Nicholas Hilliard**
Portrait of George Clifford,
Earl of Cumberland, c. 1590
Mixed media on parchment,
25.7 x 17.8 cm
Greenwich, National Maritime
Museum

## NICHOLAS HILLIARD
### c. 1547–1619

Nicholas Hilliard, a goldsmith and miniaturist, is one of the lesser known yet highly important artists of early Baroque. His unique achievement lies in his creation of a type of courtly portraiture unparalleled in European painting at the time. By his own admission, he was influenced by Hans Holbein, that peerless master of the portrait miniature, for whom Hilliard expressed his unreserved admiration in his writings.

However, Hilliard's sophisticated and finely executed miniatures have little in common with the work of his German forerunner, apart from their mastery of fine technique and certain aesthetic principles such as the avoidance of chiaroscuro and strong modelling. These are features of an absolutely aristocratic stance in keeping with the attitudes displayed by the very people he painted.

Hilliard's portrait of George Clifford, Earl of Cumberland, from c. 1590, is a full-figure portrait, which is quite rare, and it is one of this artist's most complex works. This successful naval leader was a favourite of Elizabeth I and his feathered hat also bears the Queen's glove as a mark of distinction which adds the finishing touch to his courtly apparel in the guise of a knight.

**Peter Lely**
Henrietta Maria of
France, Queen of
England, 1660
Oil on canvas,
49 x 39 cm
Chantily, Musée Condé

## PETER LELY
### 1618–1680

Portraiture, which was to become the single most brilliant achievement of English painting in the 18th century, was a field dominated in the 17th century by foreign artists who received many commissions from the royal court. The leading exponents of this period were van Dyck and Lely. This portrait of Henrietta Maria, the daughter of King Henry IV of France and Marie de Médici is an idealized portrait.

In 1660, when her oldest son succeeded to the throne as Charles II of Great Britain and Ireland, Henrietta Maria returned to England where she died at the age of 51, marking the end of a turbulent life. She had married Charles I in 1625, but soon fell out of favour with Parliament and the people because of her support for English Catholics. Later, she tried in vain and with great personal commitment, to help her husband from the Netherlands. After his execution, she entered a French convent and later lived in bitter poverty in Paris.

Lely portrays her here as a beautiful and dignified woman in royal dress with an expression of suffering on her lips and a look of aloof mourning in her eyes. This is no longer a Baroque representative portrait, but tends far more in the direction of an individual interpretative portrayal. The nature of her life's journey is hidden by her reserved facial expression.

# ADAM ELSHEIMER
## 1578–1610

The cross as the focal point of the "gloria del paradiso" is revered by the saints and the elect of the heavenly realm who surround the cross on banks of clouds. On the right, we recognize the patriarchs, including Moses, Abraham and King David. We also see Jonas sitting on the fish, looking up towards the cross, and St Catherine and Mary Magdalene in a sisterly embrace. In the foreground, there is a disputation between St Sebastian and Pope Gregory, St Jerome, St Ambrose and St Augustine, with the first Christian martyrs St Stephen and St Laurence. The cross, clutched by a kneeling female figure who is probably an embodiment of Faith, is surrounded by angels bearing the instruments of the Passion, above which we can make out the Evangelists and Apostles. At the head of a procession of angels streaming into the dazzling light of the background, which is flooded with an overwhelming brightness, we can see the Coronation of the Virgin.

Elsheimer's unique art is evident in the astonishing illusion of remarkable breadth and depth achieved by this small panel painting. Here, space is no longer simply a problem of continuously reduced scale, but also one of simultaneous graduation of colour and the distribution of light and darkness. This creates interlocking areas of colour and light which, though perceived by the eye, nevertheless take on the quality of a vision. This painting, originally part of a triptych, is widely regarded as Elsheimer's greatest masterpiece.

**Adam Elsheimer**
The Glorification of the Cross, c. 1605
Oil on copper, 48.5 x 36cm
Frankfurt am Main,
Städelsches Kunstinstitut

This small painting is undoubtedly the most beautiful example of the night scenes that brought Elsheimer so much fame. Four sources of light illuminate the greenish-blue landscape with its starry sky: the full moon on the right above the trees fringing a lake, its reflection in the water, the campfire of the cowherds on the left, from which a column of sparks rises into the darkness of the tree tops, and finally the torch in the hand of Joseph, who is leading the ass with Mary and the child. Each of these sources of light models the objects in the immediate surroundings only fragmentarily, so that illuminated areas are directly juxtaposed with unlit areas. Our gaze is drawn across expanses of impenetrable darkness, settling upon islands of fine draughtsmanship, and following the vaulted silhouettes of the tree tops.

Here, night is portrayed as a miracle that can help the holy family on their flight to Egypt. Elsheimer has succeeded in evoking a sense of danger and comfort at the same time entirely by means of the atmospheric values of his use of light and shadow. It would therefore be wrong to place the emphasis entirely on the subject of landscape. This picture represents something entirely new in the field of religious imagery, with landscape opening up possibilities of exploring new narrative contents.

**Adam Elsheimer**
The Flight to Egypt, 1609
Oil auf Kupfer, 31 x 41cm
Munich, Bayerische Staatsgemälde-
sammlungen, Alte Pinakothek

**Georg Flegel**
Still Life, undated
Oil on copper, 78 x 67 cm
Munich, Bayerische Staatsgemälde-
sammlungen, Alte Pinakothek

## GEORG FLEGEL
### c. 1566–1638

Flegel, Germany's first purely still life painter, is believed to have worked in the studio of the Flemish artist Lukas van Valckenborch as a painter of flowers, metalware and fruit, a fact that would certainly appear to be borne out by this painting.

The very Netherlandish-looking bouquet of flowers with tulips, carnations, roses and narcissi, is as superbly painted as the silver vase ornamented with golden mascarons in which it has been placed. The different qualities of silver, gold and pewter, their various degrees of brilliance, hardness and finish have been rendered in painstaking detail. The heavy pewter plates are juxtaposed with an elegant, fine-rimmed silver dish and a golden-lidded chalice bearing a fine statuette of Mars. The blade of the knife at the edge of the table, the dish of hazelnuts, the lid and edge of the brown earthenware jug – all are variations on the artist's theme.

The display of foodstuffs seems less impressive at first glance, and arranged almost at random. Everything seems to be arranged by pure chance, so much so in fact that an allegorical interpretation seems unlikely. Though the composition may appear purely cumulative, it is nevertheless precisely calculated, especially in the masterly distribution of colour highlights.

**Johann Liss**
The Death of Cleopatra, c. 1622–1624
Oil on canvas, 97.5 x 85.5 cm
Munich, Bayerische Staatsgemälde-
sammlungen, Alte Pinakothek

## JOHANN LISS
### c. 1595–c. 1629/30

Cleopatra, Queen of Egypt, committed suicide to avoid being taken prisoner by Octavius, who had conquered Anthony, Cleopatra's lover and Octavius' rival for supremacy in Rome. Plutarch reports that the Queen wished to die by a serpent's bite, for the ancient Egyptians believed that this death ensured immortality.

The artist has not chosen to portray the dramatic climax, nor the decision to commit suicide, nor even the snake bite itself, but the moment in which the tension begins to subside. The serpent has done its deadly work, and the young black servant boy holding the basket of flowers is staring with terror-struck eyes at the snake in it, while a servant woman supports her swooning mistress. On the surface of things, very little seems to be happening in this picture, with everything concentrated on the transition between life and death. All the light falls on the young Queen, bathing her body in warm and sensuous colours. All of life itself seems to be concentrated in the colour of her flesh on the threshold of death, whose advent is suggested by her sinking arm and overcast gaze. The central moment in this painting is one of transition, and this is reflected in the move from light to darkness and in the strong graduation of colours from the background to the foreground.

## JOHANN HEINRICH SCHÖNFELD
1609–1682

We have little information about Schönfeld's life. One of the few reports available is a diary entry by the German architect and art collector, Joseph Furttenbach of Ulm, which tells us that "he spent eighteen years in Italy, twelve of them in Naples.". Living in Naples and experiencing its piety and its works of art had a profound effect on the work of this German artist from Biberach around 1643/44. During this period, the serenity and lightness of his mythological and Old Testament themes give way to dark renderings of predominantly Christian subjects, but also this picture of *Chronos*.

A thin, balding old man can be seen in a deeply melancholic pose in a gloomy setting, his arm resting on a plinth that bears the inscription "Il tempo" (time). On it stands an hourglass and an extinguished candle as symbols of transience and mortality, while in the foreground, a putto sits on a skull blowing soap bubbles – further metaphors of the triviality of human life. The predominant brown tones of the painting, broken only by the blue of the loincloth, make a similar statement: it is not a dark varnish, but an intrinsic quality of the painting itself. All colour as a sign of vitality and exitence have been purged from the pictorial realm. The Chronos we see before us is no longer the philosopher of decay and fragility, but part of it.

Johann Heinrich Schönfeld
Il Tempo (Chronos), c. 1645
Oil on canvas, 102 x 77 cm
Augsburg, Deutsche Barock-
galerie im Schaezlerpalais

## JOACHIM VON SANDRART
1609–1688

Sandrart, best known for his major art history published in 1675 under the title "Teutsche Academie" is one of the few artist-writers whose painterly œuvre was on a par with his literary ambitions.

For Prince Maximilian of Bavaria, Sandrart painted allegories of day and night as well as a cycle of twelve paintings of the months of the year for the dining room of the Old Palace in Schleissheim. The months, accompanied by verses, were widely distributed in the form of engravings. They are illustrated by life-size half figures set in landscapes or interiors and show characteristic activities associated with the respective seasons and surrounded by their natural attributes. November, under the zodiac sign of Sagittarius the hunter, shows a hunter's return. With his nervous dogs on a short leash and his catch slung over his shoulder, he is heading towards a castle in the middle distance. A keen wind tears the leaves from the trees and scatters them through the air.

Landscape and genre, still life and allegory are combined in a picture that epitomizes the month of November in concentrated form. Only briefly and in passing does the hunter glance to one side, and once more we find an allegorical personification of time passing.

Joachim von Sandrart
November, 1643
Oil on canvas,
149 x 123.5 cm
Munich, Bayerische
Staatsgemälde-
sammlungen

Johann Carl Loth
Mercury piping to Argus, before 1660
Oil on canvas, 117 x 100 cm
London, National Gallery

## JOHANN CARL LOTH
### 1632–1698

A certain form of half-figure painting had become modern through the influence of Caravaggio, who had painted a number of genre scenes, such as *The Fortune Teller* (ill. p. 229), and mythological paintings, such as *Bacchus* (ill. p. 230), in this manner and whose earliest works had conjured up an erotically mythological world full of half-figure portrayals of singularly feminine young boys. The tastes and preferences of certain patrons and collectors had also contributed to this trend, but the form as such continued to remain extremely popular, particularly in history paintings in which the intimacy of a moment called for the appeal of a heightened physical proximity.

In this painting, Loth tells how Argus of the many eyes was tricked by Mercury. Juno, the mistress of Jupiter, had set Argus to guard the nymph Io, who had been turned into a heifer. Mercury approached the herdsman and lulled him to sleep with the music of his pipe, then killed him. At first glance, one might think that Loth has transformed this cruel plan into an idyllic pastoral scene. Yet there is something menacing in the dark background and in the deep-set eyes of the two men. The fiery red drape covering Mercury's dagger and the flexing of his muscles herald the murder.

Johann Michael Rottmayr
St Benno, 1702
Oil on canvas, 118 x 100 cm
Munich, Bayerische Staatsgemäldesammlungen

## JOHANN MICHAEL ROTTMAYR
### 1654–1730

In 1688, the artist returned from a thirteen-year stay in Venice, where he had worked in Loth's studio. By the time this painting was executed, he had already developed the influence of the Venetian treatment of colour into a highly distinctive style, based on southern German traditions.

Benno, scion of a Thuringian noble family, was Bishop of Meissen from 1066–1106. According to legend, he is said to have thrown the keys of his cathedral into the river Elbe only to find them again in the belly of a fish on his return. From 1580 onwards, his relics were kept in the Frauenkirche in Munich, and he soon became the patron saint of Munich and Bavaria.

What is typically South German about Rottmayr's portrayal of the moment when the saint finds the key, is his handling of the human figures. Benno does not appear as an enraptured saint, but as an old man, pale with fright, incredulously pointing out the miraculous event to an angel. The angel, a figure of serene vitality, places a reassuring arm on the shoulder of the astonished man.

What is real in this painting is not the historic figure of Benno, but the fish with its belly slit open, the key and the young angel. The faith of the saint, and indeed that of the painter, is clearly reflected in the realism of the miracle.

258

# JUAN SÁNCHEZ COTÁN
## 1561–1627

Everyday objects: a melon, cut open to reveal its pale pink flesh, a knobbly cucumber, a yellow apple that is past its best, a cabbage with thick leaves. Parallel to the picture plane, a smooth frame delineates the opening for a window. From the direction of the spectator, light falls upon the parapet, on which the slice of melon and the cucumber are placed so that they jut over slightly and thereby they seem to be almost within reach – a *trompe l'œil* effect that was particularly popular in Netherlandish painting in the 17th century. The head of cabbage and the apple, suspended on threads that presumably have been attached to the upper frame, are dangling over the gaping darkness.

Even if the objects are arranged so that they seem close enough to touch, they are nevertheless distanced. For all the naturalism with which they are depicted, the isolation of each object, heightened further by the black background, makes each of them seem extremely artificial and lends them a monumental, almost sculptural gravity. The centre of the picture is empty and the arrangement seems coincidental; the dimension of the painted picture is denied. The disturbing evocation of the painted picture is the main theme.

Juan Sánchez Cotán
Still Life (Quince, Cabbage, Melon and Cucumber), c. 1602 (?)
Oil on canvas, 65 x 81 cm
San Diego (CA), The Fine Arts Gallery of San Diego

# JUSEPE DE RIBERA
## 1591–1652

Standing in a sweeping landscape, dressed in patched brown clothes, barefoot and shouldering a crutch, his disability is evident: his deformed foot is at the centre of the spectator's field of vision. In his left hand, this pitiable creature holds a note with the inscription: "DA MIHI ELIMO/SINAM PROPTER/ AMOREM DEI" ("Give me alms, for the love of God").

Described in this way, the painting would appear to be an image of misery, humiliation and begging. Yet what meets the eye, contradicts such an unequivocal statement. The boy whose face is aged beyond his years stands proud and upright against the landscape in the background. He looks directly downwards at the spectator with a relaxed gaze of experience and superiority. The boy's mouth is opened in a relatively unattractive gummy grin that permits no patronizing sympathy. Ribera has created a monument to the justice of God. He shows up our hierarchical thinking, our worldly expectations of the gratitude of the poor, to whom we give alms. The apparently miserable, valueless individual stands here like a monument admonishing us to remember that all creatures are equal before God. This boy is not begging for mercy. He is claiming his right to it.

Jusepe de Ribera
The Boy with the Clubfoot, 1642
Oil on canvas, 164 x 92 cm
Paris, Musée National du Louvre

## JUSEPE DE RIBERA
### 1591–1652

Jusepe de Ribera
Archimedes, 1630
Oil on canvas, 125 x 81 cm
Madrid, Museo del Prado

The image we have today of the ancient scholar owes much to the classicistic ideals of the 19th century. This concept of cool distance and noble gravity is contradicted sharply by such a painting as Ribera's *Archimedes*: the great physicist, mathematician and natural scientist is shown here as a toothless old Spaniard. His weathered, wrinkled face has none of the marbled pallor of scholarship. In one thin hand, he holds a pile of papers and in the other a compass. His nails are dirty, his dress unkempt, and an old cloak is thrown carelessly over his undershirt, open to reveal his chest. Archimedes looks at us with a broad grin, and seems as close to the everyday life of Ribera's contemporaries as the artist's paintings of the saints. We find no monumental dignity here, only the dignity of a strong personality.

Like Caravaggio in his *Crucifixion of St Peter* (ill. p. 231), Ribera contradicts the canonical concept of the heroic martyr who bears his torture with quiet patience and the serene assurance of salvation. Bartholomew, apostle and preacher, who was flayed and murdered by King Astyages in the Armenian town of Albanapolis, is portrayed by Ribera as a weak elderly man, whose fear of death and desperation are clearly written in his face. The louts dragging him up by a beam before the eyes of the curious onlookers are concentrating fully on their task. The question of guilt and innocence remains unanswered for the incident is still very much in the present.

*Bottom:*
Jusepe de Ribera
Martyrdom of
St Bartholomew, 1630
Oil on canvas, 234 x 234 cm
Madrid, Museo del Prado

According to legend, the giant Ophorus carried the infant Christ across a river at night, and was pressed down below the surface of the water by the weight of the child, thereby being baptized. Thereafter he received the name Christophorus ("bearer of Christ"). In this night scene, Ribera reiterates the legend, but he adds more: he brings life to the figure of the giant, lending him an expression of incredulity and astonishment at the sight of the infant Christ. His physical power is evident in the drawing of his muscles of arms and shoulders. Paradoxically yet fittingly, Ribera has given him the flickering shadow of all-devouring ecstasy that predominates in a heightened form in his depictions of monks. It is a scene of superficial poverty without the brilliance of colour and luminosity. The miraculous experience of Christophorus is neither majestic nor historic, but is a sacred occurrence repeated daily before our very eyes.

Jusepe de Ribera
St Christopher, 1637
Oil on canvas, 127 x 100 cm
Madrid, Museo del Prado

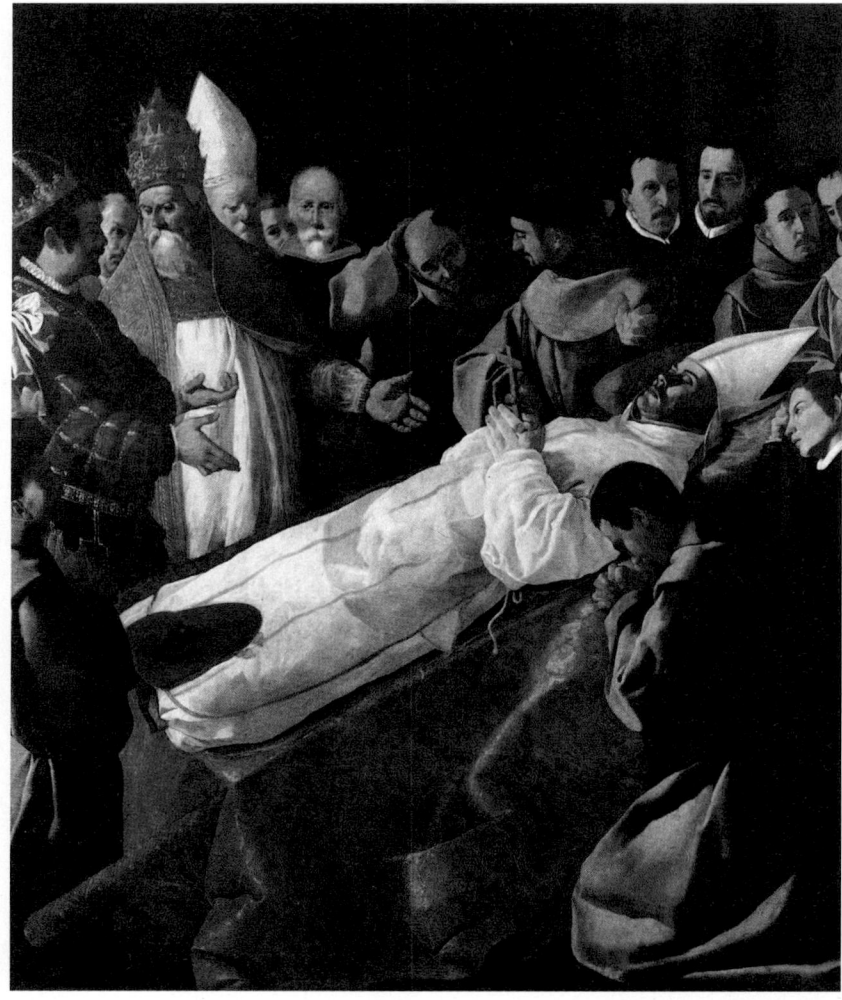

**Francisco de Zurbarán**
The Death of St Bonaventura, 1629
Oil on canvas, 245 x 220cm
Paris, Musée National du Louvre

**Francisco de Zurbarán** St Hugo of Grenoble
in the Carthusian Refectory, c. 1633
Oil on canvas, 102 x 168cm
Sevilla, Museo de Bellas Artes

# FRANCISCO DE ZURBARÁN
## 1598–1664

Dressed in the brilliant white robes of a bishop, grasping the cross in his folded hands, the body of the saint lies in state on a bier draped in sumptuous brocade, with the red biretta of the cardinal at his feet. Pope Gregory X, who had appointed him cardinal bishop of Albano in 1273 stands, a white bearded man, beside the king, to whom he appears to be explaining the merits of the dead man. Most of the mourners, however, are simple Franciscan monks in their greyish brown habits, pensively praying or meditatively contemplating the dead man. He is indeed one of them, and the wan complexion of his tranquil face appears to mirror the dull hue of the habits. The great scholar and administrator of his order is here placed between the representatives of ecclesiastical and worldly power and the world of simple Franciscan brotherhood. He was accorded the title of "doctor seraphicus", meaning the "brilliant teacher full of love". This is what Zurbarán paints: the teacher bound to practical life, his face filled with mystical desire even in death.

Zurbarán's painting of a Carthusian refectory intensely reflects the ideal of this order of hermit monks: simplicity, sobriety and quiet contemplation. The room is unadorned, but for a painting showing the Virgin and Child with John the Baptist in the wilderness – an inspiration to the monks. An arched doorway opens out towards a typically simple Carthusian church. The monks, dressed in white cassocks, are seated at the table on which there are only plates of bread. With the exception of one monk whose hands are folded in prayer, they are all completely immersed in introspective contemplation with their eyes cast down, apparently paying no attention to the guest to whom the elderly abbot, St Hugo, appears to be explaining the life of the monastery. This painting exudes an atmosphere of tranquillity unaffected by the event portrayed.

The apocryphal legend of the life and death of Margaret of Antioch was known in the western world as early as the 7th century. Cast out by her heathen father, she was martyred in the Diocletian persecution of Christians and decapitated. In the course of the centuries, more and more legends grew up around this popular martyr. Zurbarán has portrayed her with straw hat and staff, in the costume of a Spanish shepherdess. Behind her we see the dragon which she is said to have overcome with the sign of the cross. Completely inactive, with the Bible in her left hand and a woven shepherd's bag over her arm, she gazes at the spectator with a sweetly childish face. This painting does not tell the turbulent episodes of her life, but shows a saintly woman revered in the home country of the painter.

**Francisco de Zurbarán**
St Margaret, c. 1630–1635
Oil on canvas, 192 x 112cm
London, National Gallery

**Francisco de Zurbarán**
The Ecstacy of St Francis, c. 1660
Oil on canvas, 65 x 53 cm
Munich, Bayerische Staatsgemälde-
sammlungen, Alte Pinakothek

# FRANCISCO DE ZURBARÁN
## 1598–1664

Born in 1181 or 1182 in Assisi as the son of a
wealthy draper, he died in poverty in the same
town on 3 October 1226. Francis' life of poverty, humility, selflessness and serene neigh-
bourly love made the order of Friars Minor
which he founded one of the most widespread
religious orders in the entire western world.
Following the council of Trent in the mid
16th century, St Francis was invariably portrayed as an ascetic, penitent and ecstatic
monk, frequently dressed in the habit of the
Capuchin monks and with a skull as attribute.

Zurbarán's saint bears the entire complexity of this figure. This is Francis the ascetic,
dressed in a brown habit, without signs of office or adornment. This is the humble Francis
dressed in the colours of the earth. This is
Francis the ecstatic monk, who has received
the stigmata of the five wounds. His young
face is raised heavenwards in contemplation,
one hand placed upon his heart, the other on
the skull, the sign of meditation. He is shown
as a holy man of spiritual profundity and scholarly intellect, as reflected in his facial traits.
Yet he is not a monk who is alienated from
daily life and caught up entirely in his mystical passion, but a man close to life, as Zurbarán shows. His "portrait" is an allegory of faith
and simplicity.

**Francisco de Zurbarán**
Still Life with Lemons, Oranges and Rose, 1633
Oil on canvas, 60 x 107 cm
Pasadena (CA), Norton Simon Museum of Art

In the œuvre of Zurbarán, religious themes
predominate, with particular emphasis on asceticism. He also painted many still lifes, which,
however, reflect the same qualities of asceticism, quiet contemplation and introversion for
his choice of objects indicates the transience of
human life.

Zurbarán does not do so by presenting a
clock, a skull or an hourglass. Instead, on a
brilliantly polished table, he shows us a pewter plate with lemons, a basket of oranges complete with leaves and blossoms, and a fine
china cup on a silver saucer on which lies a
rose in full bloom. Though lemons signify
wealth in a Netherlandish still life, they have
a very different meaning here, in the country
where they actually grow. Even so, they are
not represented as the fruits of daily life, but
presented with all the solemn celebration of an
offering on an altar.

As in the paintings of his contemporary
Sánchez Cotán, Zurbarán isolates the individual objects from one another – even the composition appears to be a conscious though not
excessively artificial arrangement. Against the
dark background, the objects are completely
static, and appear to be torn out of the context
of everyday life. The human beings to whom
they apparently belong have no place here.

# ALONSO CANO
## 1601–1667

This painting, hailed by Cano's contemporaries as a masterpiece, was part of the main altar in the no longer extant church of Santa María in Madrid. Damaged and all but forgotten, the painting entered the Prado in 1941, where its qualities can now be appreciated as they fully deserve.

According to legend, the son of St Isidore fell into a well. Through the prayers of the saint and his wife, the water level rose miraculously so that the child was brought safely to the surface. Here, we see St Isidore standing in front of the well with his arms spread wide. The young woman is helping the child out of the well and looking towards her husband with an expression of astonishment on her face. Two servant girls in the background are commenting with eloquent gestures on the miracle. Two children and a dog, drawn towards the overflowing water, also discuss the event.

Cano links two themes in this painting: the miracle itself and the recognition of Isidore's saintliness by the women. For the artist, this means presenting him in the manner of history painting and religious portraiture at the same time. He has solved this problem of duality by presenting the saint as an almost incidental figure barely involved in the event, a fact which has frequently been misinterpreted as a weakness of this painting.

Alonso Cano
St Isidore and the Miracle of the Well, c. 1646–1648
Oil on canvas, 216 x 149cm
Madrid, Museo del Prado

# BARTOLOMÉ ESTEBAN MURILLO
## c. 1617/18–1682

She is not shown in the thralls of mystical rapture, nor in those of devotion. Murillo's Mary is a very young woman with an almost child-like face, who is kneeling at her prie-dieu, her eyes cast pensively downwards. She has set aside her basket of handiwork and seems to have been disturbed by an angel in the midst of her prayers. Were it not for the presence of his wings, even the angel would seem to be a very worldly creature. He is not floating in some uncertain sphere, nor is he a vision, but is kneeling on the floor tiles. Strong-limbed and barefoot, almost like a peasant, his pretty face is framed by dark locks. With one hand, he points towards the dove of the Holy Spirit, which floats above their heads in a truly unearthly and intangible celestial vision. With the other hand, he makes a gesture of persuasion: he seems to be explaining the purpose of his mission quite vigorously to Mary.

Although the event seems plausible in a distinctly earthly manner – even the putti in the clouds do not alter this impression – the miracle is clear. Mary's innocence, underlined by the lily as a symbol of purity, is of such intensity that the spectator senses her quiet reservation, the excited anticipation of the prophesied miracle and her astonishment at the experience.

Bartolomé Esteban Murillo
Annunciation,
c. 1660–1665
Oil on canvas,
125 x 103cm
Madrid, Museo del Prado

**Bartolomé Esteban Murillo**
La Immaculada, undated
Oil on canvas, 96 x 64 cm
Madrid, Museo del Prado

**Bartolomé Esteban Murillo**
The Toilette, c. 1670–1675
Oil on canvas, 147 x 113 cm
Munich, Bayerische Staats-
gemäldesammlungen,
Alte Pinakothek

# BARTOLOMÉ ESTEBAN MURILLO
## c. 1617/18–1682

Murillo's *Immaculada* has nothing of a Queen of Heavens. Standing on a crescent moon, as described in the Apocalypse, surrounded by angels holding the mirror as a sign of purity and the palm frond as a sign of suffering, she stands in a relatively unaffected poses. Her face is pale, her eyes gaze upwards in yearning. We can sense the pain she has experienced and her mourning for her son. Quiet and introverted, she epitomises the humble anticipation of the hereafter, transfigured only by a mild smile, that is a hallmark of Murillo's paintings of this period; the *Estilo vaporoso* – the vaporous style.

The room is so dark that we can hardly make out the objects in it: beneath the little window aperture stands a rough-hewn wooden table, on which there is an earthenware jug and a white cloth. Another earthenware jug stands on the floor. At the right-hand edge of the painting, we see a spindle and distaff on a stool. The old woman who has just set them aside is now crouching down to look for lice in the little boy's hair. He is sitting on the floor, leaning against her knee and petting a little dog that is begging for a piece of the bread the boy is stuffing into his mouth. Both figures are very poorly dressed, and the few details of the room further emphasize the impression of poverty.

Murillo is probably the only Baroque painter of rank to have portrayed poverty with such kind and conciliatory traits. There is no sign here of the wealthy man's notion of the picturesque simple life, so frequently found in this genre. Murillo chooses the colours of the earth. The earthenware dishes, the stones of the wall, the wood of the furniture, the faces and clothes of the two figures, all are united by this warm colouring which seems so natural that it does not even raise the question of poverty or wealth, happiness or unhappiness.

A little girl with the face of a Madonna, a contented little boy examining the earrings she holds in her hand and a basket full of grapes which is, in itself, a still life of the highest quality. Does this painting show us a life free from worry?

The apparent poverty of the two figures, their unchild-like but necessary employment suggest a sense of hopelessness and misery. And yet these children seem to exude an air of rapt serenity and contented enjoyment of life. Herein lies Murillo's Christian message: because these children do not see their poverty as a burden, and because they do not regard their existence as joyless, they are beautiful and "dignified". It is thus a painting that could adorn the walls of any ruler's palace.

**Bartolomé Esteban Murillo**
The Little Fruit Seller, c. 1670–1675
Oil on canvas, 149 x 113 cm
Munich, Bayerische Staatsgemälde-
sammlungen, Alte Pinakothek

**Juan de Valdés Leal**
Allegory of Death, 1672
Oil on canvas, 220 x 216cm
Sevilla, Hospital de la Caridad

## JUAN DE VALDÉS LEAL
### 1622–1690

Of all the great painters of the school of Seville – alongside Zurbarán, Velázquez and Murillo – the distinctive style of Valdés Leal is the most difficult to place. Only two major allegories on the transience of life and on death which he himself is said to have described as "hieroglyphs of our afterlife" have remained truly popular. His patron, Don Miguel de Mañara, was a Knight of the Order of Calatrava who became a benefactor of the brotherhood of the hospital and its church in penitence for his previous life of decadence. The epitaph on his grave succinctly describes the spirit that commissioned such a powerful vanitas still life: "Here lie the bones and ashes of the worst person who ever lived on earth". His last will and testament contains the most humble self-accusation not only as a great sinner, but also as an adulterer, robber and servant of the devil.

The *Allegory of Death* presents the triumph of the grim reaper, who sweeps into the picture as an imposing figure. One skeletal foot stands on the globe, while the other stands on armaments, the trappings of office and insignia of power. Under his arm, he carries a coffin and in his hand a scythe. As his right hand snuffs out the life-light represented by the candle, he stares at the spectator from the very depths of his empty eye-sockets.

**Claudio Coello**
King Charles II,
c. 1675–1680
Oil on canvas,
66 x 56cm
Madrid, Museo
del Prado

## CLAUDIO COELLO
### 1642–1693

One of the most important tasks of a court painter in the age of absolutism was portraiture, either in the form of an individual, family or group portrait. Most of these commissioned works were sent to other royal houses. Whatever the occasion in each respective case, a portrait of this kind invariably had the primary function of representing the court.

Coello's unfinished portrait of King Charles II gives us an opportunity of seeing how the artist worked. The three-quarter profile of the young king is set in a medallion. Coello has concentrated on depicting the brilliance of the shining armour and the rich folds of the bow, using free and spontaneous brush-strokes. Reproductions of a portrait of Charles II from the Städel in Frankfurt, lost in 1945, suggests that Coello toned down these lavish details somewhat in a later version. In comparison to paintings of Alsonso Sánchez Coello, who had worked for the Spanish court a hundred years earlier, Claudio Coello's view of the monarch has little of the stringency of courtly ceremony. He is the last major representative of the Spanish tradition of painting that reached its climax in the Mannerism of the 16th century.

# DIEGO VELÁZQUEZ
1599–1660

In this early work, Velázquez refers to the gospel according to St Luke, which tells of a visit by Christ to the house of Martha and Mary. While Mary sat at his feet to listen to his words, Martha busied herself with work in the kitchen; eventually, she came to him and said: "Lord, dost thou not care that my sister has left me to serve alone? Bid her therefore that she help me." To which Christ replied, "Martha, Martha, thou art careful and troubled about many things; but one thing is needful: and Mary has chosen that good part, which shall not be taken away from her." (St Luke 10:40–42).

The composition of the painting, with a kitchen scene in the tradition of the "bodegones" taking up the foreground, while the scene involving Christ is presented as a view or a mirror image, is clearly influenced by the art of the Netherlands. Even the plump, ruddy-cheeked figure of Martha and the still life arrangement of fish, garlic, eggs and paprika, recall examples of Northern European art. Moreover, this picture is charged with a strange sense of tension and restlessness. The events reflected in the mirror, bathed in a mild light and exuding an atmosphere peace and calm, are contrasted with the foreground image of loud and busy work. Through highlighting and formal diversity, the artist sets a scene that is clearly dissatisfactory to Martha. She is not concentrating on her work, but gazes full of yearning, on the verge of tears, and slightly angrily, as though she already realized that Mary had chosen the better part.

Velázquez painted this picture of Bacchus surrounded by eight drinkers for Philipp IV, who hung it in his summer bedroom. The painting is not only unique in his œuvre, but is very rare indeed in Spanish painting as a whole, which does not generally have the drinking scenes so familiar in Flemish and Netherlandish painting. Drunkenness was regarded in Spain as a contemptible vice and "borracho" (drunkard) was the most scathing of insults. At the royal court, it seems to have been considered highly entertaining to invite low-lifers from the comedy theatres and inebriate them for the amusement of the ladies. But what kind of a Wine God is this we see, crowning his followers with ivy, said to cool the heat of wine, and consorting with peasants who grin out of the painting and clearly find the spectator, that is to say the king, a very funny sight indeed? The authority of the god whose presence delights them lends them a sense of majesty as well. And in view of the delightful travesty of royal honours in which Bacchus is indulging, they too have turned the tables and are laughing in the faces of those who would laugh at them. Is this Bacchus merely a myth born of wine, an embodiment of those lowly joys which the nobleman snubs? Or is the god a courtier having precisely the kind of fun at which the ladies liked to laugh? As only Caravaggio before him, Velázquez has portrayed Bacchus (or rather Dionysos) as the God of the mask, the theatre and disguise.

Diego Velázquez
Christ in the House of Martha and Mary, 1618
Oil on canvas, 60 x 103.5 cm
London, National Gallery

Diego Velázquez
Los Borrachos (The Drinkers), 1628/29
Oil on canvas, 165.5 x 227.5 cm
Madrid, Museo del Prado

# DIEGO VELÁZQUEZ
## 1599–1660

The main problem of a history painting featuring a large number of figures is the question of how to handle the crowd scenes. Velázquez initially tackles this difficulty by dividing the picture plane into two levels – a higher area of action on which the main event is acted out as on a stage, and an area below it in which we see the city and harbour of Breda and the sea. The stage-like situation is further emphasized by various foreground elements. The two military leaders – the defeated commandant of Breda handing over the keys of the fortress to the Spanish commander Spinola – are immediately recognizable as the protagonists because the view opens up behind them towards the otherwise hidden background, whereas to the right and left the respective military entourage is grouped like stage extras. Yet Velázquez does not portray them as anonymous soldiers. Amongst the group of Spanish victors brandishing their lances, we can make out just as many individual expressions of exhaustion as we can amongst the resigned group of defeated Dutch soldiers.

In the field of royal portraiture, the portrait of the infant or child ruler poses a particular problem to the artist. A majestic pose, sumptuous clothing and the traditional outward trappings of dignity inevitably clash with the very nature of childhood. Velázquez solves this problem by placing the child on a sturdy horse so that the little figure is raised, as on a monumental plinth, to the "correct" position in the picture. This view is further vindicated by a sweeping landscape whose unspoilt nature creates an uncontrived link with the serious, yet still softly contoured and unspoilt mien of the child's face.

Although the dwarf Don Sebastián de Morra is portrayed in full figure, he is not standing in a self-confident pose or elegantly seated on a chair, but is sitting on the bare earth with his feet stretched out in front of him. This low position not only shows up the sumptuous clothing for the clownish apparel it is, but also heightens the intended effect: the court fool is at the mercy of the spectator. Such pictorial devices reveal the voyeurism with which the royal rulers made these people the objects of their shameless whimsy, caprice and power. At the same time, however, the artist is also making another statement: this court fool is giving nothing away, neither a smile, nor any buffoonery. Immobile, scrutinizing and impenetrable, his dark eyes are fixed on the spectator, who somehow feels caught out by such a gaze and turns away.

Diego Velázquez
The Surrender of Breda, 1634/35
Oil on canvas, 307.5 x 370.5 cm
Madrid, Museo del Prado

Diego Velázquez
Prince Baltasar Carlos,
Equestrian, c. 1634/35
Oil on canvas,
209.5 x 174 cm
Madrid, Museo del
Prado

Diego Velázquez
A Dwarf Sitting on the Floor
(Don Sebastián de Morra) c. 1645
Oil on canvas, 106.5 x 81.5 cm
Madrid, Museo del Prado

**Diego Velázquez**
Venus at her Mirror (The Rokeby Venus), c. 1644–1648
Oil on canvas, 122.5 x 177 cm
London, National Gallery

**Diego Velázquez**
Las Meninas (The Maids of Honour), 1656/57
Oil on canvas, 318 x 276 cm
Madrid, Museo del Prado

# DIEGO VELÁZQUEZ
1599–1660

The Rokeby Venus is widely regarded, along with Titian's *Venus of Urbino* (ill. p. 176), as one of the most beautiful and significant portrayals of Venus in the history of western painting. Yet it is virtually impossible to explain the magic of this painting. The consistent reduction of colour to lucid red, gentle blue, clear white and a warm reddish-brown allows the skin tone of Venus – blended, incidentally, only from the other colours in the painting – to emerge as an independent hue whose sumptuous sheen dominates everything else.

Venus is presented in a sensually erotic pose, and yet she seems chaste and is so completely merged with the overall image that she cannot be touched. Cupid, disarmed, without his bow and arrow, is holding a mirror, his hands bound by fragile pink fetters, condemned to do nothing and completely immersed in contemplation of the beautiful goddess. The mirror image – in defiance of all laws of optics – does not reveal the other side of Venus, but only permits a vague and blurred reflection of her facial traits. This may in fact indicate the underlying meaning of the picture: it is not intended as a specific female nude, nor even as a portrayal of Venus, but as an image of self-absorbed beauty. The goddess of love appears here as a mythical being with neither aim nor purpose, needing no scene of action, but blossoming before our very eyes as an image of beauty itself.

This is a composition of enormous representational impact. The Infanta Isabella stands proudly amongst her maids of honour, with a dwarf to the right. Although she is the smallest, she is clearly the central figure; one of her maids is kneeling before her, and the other leaning towards her, so that the standing Infanta, with her broad hooped skirt, becomes the fulcrum of the movement. The dwarf, about the same size as the Infanta, is so ugly that Isabella appears delicate, fragile and precious in comparison. On the left in the painting, dark and calm, the painter himself can be seen standing at his vast canvas. Above the head of the Infanta, we see the ruling couple reflected in the mirror.

The spatial structure and positioning of the figures is such that the group of Las Meninas around the Infanta appears to be standing on "our" side, opposite Philip and his wife. Not only is the "performance" for their benefit, but the attention of the painter is also concentrated on them, for he appears to be working on their portrait. Although they can only be seen in the mirror reflection, the king and queen are the actual focus of the painting towards which everything else is directed. As spectators, we realize that we are excluded from the scene, for in our place stands the ruling couple. What seems at first glance to be an "open" painting proves to be completely hermetic – a statement further intensified by the fact that the painting in front of Velázquez is completely hidden from our view.

Hermann Bauer

# BAROQUE IN THE NETHERLANDS

## Dutch and Flemish painting in the 17th century

In the 17th century, following the division of the country, painting in the Netherlands blossomed in what came to be known as its Golden Age. Rubens in the Catholic south of the country and Rembrandt in the Protestant north represent the contrasts and kinships of Baroque painting at its zenith.

Whereas Rubens, with his monumental creations for nobility and the Church, forged a link between the mortal, earthly world and the realms of Heaven or Olympus, Rembrandt's subtle chiaroscuro revealed the hidden depths of the human soul, creating a new dimension in portraiture.

Alongside these artists of genius, we also find the outstanding portraiture of Frans Hals and van Dyck, the landscapes of Ruisdael, van Goyen and Hobbema, the allegories of Jordaens, the still lifes of Heda and Kalf, the genre scenes of Brouwer, Steen, Terboch and de Hooch. The painting of the era culminates in Vermeer's interiors – masterpieces in the handling of light and harmony of colour.

## Rubens and Rembrandt:
## the Southern and Northern Netherlands

When Rembrandt was commissioned by Prince Frederick Henry of Orange (1584–1647) to paint five scenes from the Passion of Christ, most of which are now in the Alte Pinakothek in Munich (ill. p. 315), he corresponded between 1636 and 1639 with the Prince's governor-secretary Constantijn Huygens (1596–1687). In one of seven surviving letters, Rembrandt writes of the *Entombment*, stating that he had taken great care to render "die meeste ende natureelste beweechgelickheijt" ("the greatest and most natural movement") and explaining that this was why he had spent so much time on the painting. This "greatest and most natural movement" of which he speaks in his letter refers as much to the subtle and realistic portrayal of the figures as to the expression of their inner emotion.

A Mannerist artist of the 16th century would have couched a description of his work in very different terms. He would have emphasized the skill, artifice and inventiveness of the painting. Rembrandt's comment referred to something else. It evoked a quality that was to become a fundamental feature of Baroque painting, particularly in the Netherlands. Rembrandt was talking about realism and about a new and more intimate approach to the way the world looks. He was also talking about a new dimension of pathos and expression – "natureelste beweechgelikheijt".

Rembrandt's *Passion of Christ* cycle is the early work of a Dutch artist. It coincides with the late work of the Flemish painter Peter Paul Rubens. Between 1636 and 1638, Rubens was working on a series of designs for a major mythological cycle, part of which he executed personally, that had been commissioned by the King of Spain to decorate the royal hunting lodge of Torre de la Parada near Madrid. Irrelevant as the all too frequent attempts to compare Rembrandt and Rubens may often be, they can nevertheless provide some interesting insights: what Rembrandt regarded as a commission, Rubens regarded as the enriching culmination of his life's work. In Rubens' later work, we find an increase in pathos and dramatic expression.

"It is almost wondrous that the outstanding Rembrandt von Ryn, coming from the countryside, and from a milling family, should have been imbued by nature with such noble art that he has been able, through his own hard work, natural inclination and preference, to achieve such a high rank in art... and because of his natural talent, unstinting hard work and constant practice it was no disadvantage to him that he did not visit Italy and other places where one might study Antiquity and Art Theory, nor that he was unable to seek edification in books, for he could read only Netherlandish, and that but poorly. Nevertheless, he remained constant in his chosen custom and did not shy from defying our rules of art in anatomy and human proportion, defying perspective and the example of ancient statues, defying the draughtsmanship of Raphael and scholarly teachings, nor did he shy from railing against the academies that are so necessary to our profession, contradicting them, in vain, by proclaiming that we should look to nature alone and brook no other rules..." wrote Joachim von Sandrart in his *Teutsche Akademie*, an art history published in 1675, based on the Italian model and influenced by classical theory. His assessment is by no means incompetent. After all, Sandrart had spent several years in Holland and knew Rembrandt personally. His views are particularly interesting on two points: the fact that he feels obliged to add – alongside the academic values of the beautiful and the true – nature as Rembrandt's sole instance and, secondly, the fact that he acknowledges an independent Dutch, and indeed national, art.

National pride had already begun to emerge before Rembrandt arrived on the scene. Huygens, mentioned above, secretary to the Prince of Orange, wrote of Rembrandt's 1629 painting *Judas Returning the 30 Pieces of Silver*: "Let all of Italy come forth and all things magnificent and admirable since Antiquity..."

In Ruben's major paintings of the 1630s, from his altarpieces to his designs for civic stagings such as the *pompa introitus* designed to welcome the Infante Ferdinand as regent of Flanders, from his mythological scenes such as the decoration of the Torre de la Parada near Madrid, to his landscapes, we find an increasing density and centrality, with each painting gaining significance from the attribution of essential characteristic and objects to content – a density in which light and colour play an important role.

Certain criteria of Netherlandish painting were clearly established even before Rubens and Rembrandt: realism and the faithful rendering of objects. Their contribution, however, is the presentation of pathos and movement; increased pictorial expressiveness achieved by centering and by profound handling of colour and light.

There are limits to the usefulness of any comparison between the late Rubens and the early Rembrandt, and such comparisons invariably tend to be used to highlight certain polarities. On the one hand, we have an aristocratic painter and cosmpolitan sophisticate sought after by the ruling houses of Europe and the Church. On the other hand, we have a miller's son from Leiden whose attempts at running a patrician house in Amsterdam are doomed to failure, and who eventually withdraws to the margins of the ghetto, avoiding human contact and devoting himself entirely to his painting. Such clear-cut contrasts tend to overlook a number of factors that these men actually had in common. Rubens,

**Peter Paul Rubens**
Portrait of Susanne Fourment (Le chapeau de paille), c. 1625
Oil on panel, 79 x 54.5 cm
London, National Gallery

**Rembrandt Harmensz. van Rijn**
Self-portrait, 1658
Oil on canvas, 133.5 x 104cm
New York, The Frick Collection

had to look beyond the confines of Antwerp, to Italy, mother-land of the arts, in order to establish a name for himself. Under political pressure, Rubens' work became increasingly outward-looking, while the newly rich and proud city of Amsterdam boasted that Rembrandt had never been to Italy, and the latter's art became increasingly introverted and his radius of movement diminished in Amsterdam.

In 1566, the largely Calvinist Gueux who had revolted against Spanish rule sacked the Catholic churches and monasteries of Antwerp (at the time a city with a population of some 120,000) in a violent "breaking of the images". The Spanish rulers responded by calling in the Inquisition, Margaret of Austria, duchess of Parma (1522–1586) resigned from her post as governor-general, and troops headed by the Duke of Alba (1507–1582) marched in. Many Protestants fled the country, including the lawyer Jan Rubens, who went with the entourage of Prince William of Orange (1533–1584) to Cologne, where his intimate liaison with the wife of the governor-general resulted in his banishment to Siegen. It was in Siegen that his son Peter Paul was born and registered as "Lutheran".

After the death of Jan Rubens, his widow and children returned to Antwerp – she had evidently remained Catholic – where Peter Paul attended the Latin school, just as Rembrandt had briefly done in Leiden. However, he soon had to earn his own living, and became page to a widowed countess. Shortly afterwards, he was apprenticed to a painter of whom we know little more than the name: Tobias Verhaechts (1561–1631). Later, he was apprenticed to the renowned Adam van Noort (1562–1641) and finally studied for four years under Otto van Veen (1556–1629), a Mannerist of international stature.

Though Rubens went to Italy to learn his craft, his evident talent allowed him to launch his career at his very first port of call, Venice, where he came to the attention of the Duke of Mantua and was employed at his court. Rubens' tasks included producing copies of Italian masters and portraits of the ducal family. By the time he was sent on a diplomatic mission to Spain io 1603, he was creating his own paintings, producing copies and the works of old masters. He was back in Italy a year later, finally returning to settle in Antwerp in 1608.

In the Southern Netherlands, which had remained Spanish and Catholic, a certain degree of normality was beginning to return to everday life, with churches and monasteries being rebuilt and restored. Thanks to the patronage of the art-loving Infanta Isabel Clara Eugenia (1566–1633), a sister of King Philip III of Spain (1578–1621), Rubens had a more than adequate supply of work from court, municipality and church.

Rubens' great historical achievement was his synthesis of the traditions of classical painting in a previously unimaginable way that created dynamic perspectives rather than stati-

as the son of Protestant emigrants, did not embark upon the educational or professional path that had been charted for him and, like Rembrandt, he was largely self-taught, even though he later played the role of *uomo universale*. Both of them had an enormous impact on the world of art, becoming the masters of their century and forming schools of art – both literally and metaphorically – that shaped the development of painting. Moreover, they were the only artists in the Netherlands to practise every genre of painting, from history painting to portraiture; at the same time, they advocated a return to specialization in painting. Rubens trained and employed specialists for flowers, genre figures and even for "Rubens-style" painting. Virtually every Dutch specialist was indebted to Rembrandt, from "fine" painting to *trompe l'œil* illusionism and even portraiture.

The rise of painting in the Netherlands coincided with a period of political turbulence in which the country was divided once and for all both by religion and political rule. It was a period when Antwerp lost much of its wealth and power, just as Amsterdam's star was rising. The fact that Rubens was commissioned by the church and the nobility was due to some extent at least to the fact that he initially

cally retrospective structures. He was to become the painter of the new Baroque era, the exponent of an art that transcended the borders between reality and meta-reality, transforming the static props of the Renaissance into exuberantly theatrical scenes. He was to become the painter of a spiritual and worldly apotheosis, presenting by sensual means the deification of the great and the good, and their entry into the world of eternity and conceptuality. He adopted the *Assumption* or *Ascension* as his foremost theme, in all its variations, creating images of beings ascending to celestial heights and descending into the sphere of the sensually palpable, for his ecclesiastical patrons of the Counter-Reformation and "courtly society".

When Rembrandt was born in Leiden in 1606, the northern provinces of the Netherlands governed by stadholder Maurice of Nassau, Prince of Orange (1567–1625) had only been fully independent of Spanish rule since 1596, under the terms of a truce that was to last until 1621. The Peace of Westphalia in 1648, which also marked the end of the Thirty Years' War, recognized the Northern Netherlands and at the same time separated them for good from the southern provinces, which remained Spanish, coming under Austrian rule in 1714.

The province of Holland took the leading role within the union of Zeeland, Gelderland, Overijssel, Drenthe, Friesland and Groningen. By closing off the Scheldt, Antwerp's access to the sea, Holland crushed the city which, in the 16th century, had been the wealthiest trading centre of the north, while Amsterdam rose to unprecedented prosperity. Holland rivalled England as a seafaring power, gaining a virtual monopoly on cargo shipping, dominating the Baltic grain trade and establishing colonial bases in the East Indies, West Indies, North and South America. Above all, Amsterdam was a flourishing centre of finance, and the importance of its "exchange bank" was comparable to that of Wall Street today. In 1602, a number of trading companies joined forces to create the Dutch East Indian Trading Company, triggering a hitherto unimaginable flow of money into Amsterdam.

The political structure of the States-General was federal, with the Princes of the House of Orange acting as stadholders or chief executives of otherwise self-governing republics in which a monied nobility of wealthy burghers emerged to take over the administration, deriving their legitimation from the liberation struggle and their financial success.

The process of political independence in the Netherlands was largely a religious struggle in which various forms of Protestantism, most notably Calvinism, took firm hold. A national synod held at Dordrecht in 1618 prohibited Catholic religious services and permitted only Calvinists to hold office. Most of the members of the House of Orange were orthodox Calvinists, and only scattered pockets of the northern provinces remained Catholic.

The history of the new northern provinces began with the iconoclasts. In his "Decalogue", John Calvin had taken a stance on the question of imagery and had called for a ban on any representation of the divine. The almost sacramental dignity with which the Catholic faith had endowed the portrayal of saints had now become a sacrilege. This turn of events narrowed the field of artists' commissions by putting an end to church decoration and altarpieces.

## The creation of a new image

When Rembrandt created a series on the Passion of Christ for the Prince of Orange, these were intended as private devotional paintings. The landed nobility with their palaces provided few commissions for frescos or major decoration. The Orange palace of Huis ten Bosch was one of the few exceptions, albeit on a modest scale, and was decorated by Flemish painters. The extent to which the question of images was first and foremost a question of religious images is reflected in the fact that the production of paintings in the Netherlands grew enormously from the end of the 16th century and the balance between supply and demand became exceedingly complex. The now predominant genres showed

**Peter Paul Rubens**
Venus at a Mirror, c. 1615
Oil on panel, 124 x 98cm
Vaduz, Sammlung Fürst von Liechtenstein

that Christian iconography had not entirely disappeared from painting. As Calvin, in his doctrine of predestination, had accorded to each individual something akin to a personal priesthood, it was inevitable that the portrait, as the depiction of the individual, should take on a new significance. Accordingly, it became an outstanding instrument in Holland as well. The image of the individual, or of a group, also indicated the position of the individual between God and the world. Where the image of God was forbidden, the allegory was all the more important. Often, in Dutch painting, we find the so-called *portrait historié*, a specific likeness, generally of several people, but in a biblical or mythological role. For example, if two brothers were reconciled after a family dispute, they might commission a portrait depicting them in the roles of Jacob and Esau to celebrate their reconciliation.

What may appear at first glance in Netherlandish painting to be a genre scene – and was long regarded as such – is almost invariably an allegory or a pointer towards some accepted "truth". Scenes of gallantry and entertainment, originating in brothel scenes, have their roots in the parable of the prodigal son. Jan Steen (c. 1625/26–1679 painted humorous

**Jan Steen**
Rhetoricians at a Window, c. 1662–1666
Oil on canvas, 74 x 59 cm
Philadelphia, Philadelphia Museum of Art

scenes depicting folk wisdom, allegories or proverbs. The superficial humour could also be taken at face value. The Mannerist tendency to conceal the meaning of a picture by packaging it in a rebus or intricate puzzle, was adopted and presented, in the 17th century, in a less equivocal, simpler and more obvious form.

Probably the most striking example of the way in which the allegory took the place of the religious painting is the still life or, to be more precise, the vanitas still life. The very designation "vanitas" tells us that the beautiful and pleasingly painted objects are an indication of the transience of all earthly life. The figurative meaning of a skull or a dying candle is quite obvious, and we can easily deduce that a soap bubble is likely to symbolize the triviality of life. Over and above, there exists a vast repertoire of symbolic meanings, many of which are no longer familiar to us today, with which the objects in such paintings are endowed with specific significance in much the same way as the vanitas picture. The frequent depiction of bread and wine in Dutch still lifes is, for example, an indication of the increasing use of secular surrogates to evoke the liturgical rites of the Eucharist. With the decline of religious imagery, allegorical painting flourished. However, this particular development was not restricted to the Protestant Netherlands alone. It could be found in the southern provinces, too, albeit with a considerably stronger affinity to Italian art and the traditional subject matter of Catholic painting.

Just as, in the course of the 16th century, paintings had become less and less an integral part of the architectural whole, particularly in the Netherlands, so too did the painting itself become a commodity as well as a transportable object. One indication of this development is the emergence of an art trade and exhibitions. We know that, by this time, painted canvases had become objects of speculation and that they were regarded as capital assets, accepted as payment and taken as security. With the increasing emancipation of the middle classes, the circle of buyers of paintings grew to an extent that would have been unthinkable in the early years of the 16th century when the Church, nobility and a small circle of humanist thinkers had commissioned works. A frequently quoted report by an English traveller visiting Holland in 1641 describes how he arrived at Rotterdam late in the evening to find a fair in progress, where he was astonished at the number of pictures – especially landscapes and so-called drolleries – on offer. Surmising that the reason for this was the low price of the pictures and the lack of available land as a capital investment, the author goes on to explain that peasants had the habit of investing large sums in paintings, filling their homes with them and selling them at considerable profit during their fairs.

Whether or not the prices were indeed as high as this traveller claimed, the remarkable thing about this statement is his evident surprise at the very idea of paintings being such mobile goods. Sales exhibitions were first held in Antwerp, and in the course of the 17th century became commonplace throughout Holland. By 1640, the Guild of Painters in Utrecht had a permanent sales exhibition. In The Hague, the painters formed a corporation for sales purposes in 1656, and occasionally made attempts to standardize formats in order to rationalize sales and pricing. Even the Dutch picture frame became uniform and standardized. These ornate dark or black wooden frames were artistically formed, but also neutral and appropriate to the painting.

Whereas there had previously been agents who mediated between an aristocratic or ecclesiastical patron and the artist, the profession of art dealer now began to emerge, along with assessors and auctioneers, and Amsterdam became the centre of the art market. Painters frequently offered for sale not only their own works, but also paintings by other artists or antique works. We know, for example, that Rembrandt sold works by his students, and Arnold Houbraken (1660–1719); chronicler of 17th century art, reports that Frans Hals exploited his student Adriaen Brouwer (c.1605/06–1638).

Result and cause of the newfound mobility of paintings was the increasing specialization of individual painters on specific genres and subject matter. Delegation of work was the rule, rather than the exception. Rubens is known to have had specialists for certain aspects of painting; Jan Brueghel (1568–1625) collaborated with him, painting the flowers in some of his works. Nicolaes Berchem (1620–1683) painted incidental figures in the paintings of Jacob van Ruisdael (c.1628/29–1682). On the other hand, a landscape painting by Berchem includes a portrait of a man and woman by the portraitist Gerard Wons. In the church interiors by Pieter Saenredam (1597–1665) we frequently find incidental figures by Pieter Post (1608–1669).

As painting became increasingly equated with the production of a commodity, the status of the artist threatened to return to that of mere craftsman, the very status from which artists had emancipated themselves in the Renaissance. Rubens and Anthony van Dyck (1599–1641) succeeded in establishing themselves as a new form of artist-aristocrat, though Rubens was once sharply cut down to size by a real aristocrat. Rembrandt's attempt at this kind of upward mobility was a rather tragicomic expression of a prototype Bohemian lifestyle.

Painters who took on other kinds of work, or part-time painters, became fairly commonplace. Jan van Goyen (1596–1656) traded in tulips and real estate. Many artists of the day, including Jan Steen and Adriaen van de Velde (1636–1672) were publicans who could exhibit paintings in their taverns and who occasionally accepted them in payment. Jacob van Ruisdael was a surgeon, Philips Koninck (1619–1688) had a shipping line, Meindert Hobbema (1638–1709) was a tax collector. Few of them found painting a lucrative occupation.

**Jan Brueghel the Elder**
The Animals entering the Ark, 1615
Oil on copper, 25.7 x 37 cm
London, Wellington Museum

One of the many changes that swept the Netherlands in the turbulent years of the late 16th century, apart from the emancipation of the painting as such, was the fact that this "commodity" no longer needed to be a vehicle for a certain "content" in the traditional sense, but contained objects gathered together as genres. It became far less common for specific subjects to be commissioned. Instead, certain subjects tended to be preferred or rejected by purchasers. The concept of "subject matter" which became so important in the 19th century is best used here to describe what individual specialists now produced.

Understandably enough, orders were still frequently placed for individual and and group portraits, the latter being mainly for institutions and meeting halls such as the premises of the Civic Guards, where the painting had a permanent place. Only once was a building created on the scale of a royal palace with corresponding interior decor and iconography. It was the Amsterdam City Hall, often referred to as the Cathedral of Holland. It might in fact be better described as the Versailles of this republican city. The consistent iconographical programme throughout the building is a hymn to liberty and bourgeois republican virtues. The city fathers commissioned Ferdinand Bol (1616–1680), Govaert Flinck (1615–1660) and Rembrandt to contribute to the decor, while Artus Quellinus (1609–1668) was responsible for some outstanding sculptural work on the building. At any rate, the artists at work here were specialists in the field of history painting – the most highly esteemed genre of the time and the only one that was more or less independent of art market fluctuations.

The art market dealt primarily in specific themes and attracted an astute and critical audience who judged the works according to the conviction and skill with which a painter portrayed worldly objects and the subtlety with which he could convey an underlying message of "truth". Dutch Baroque painting emerged in this artistic climate of specialization in a wide variety of subjects. The more the artists specialized in individual sectors, the more intensive the impact of the individual paintings became.

**Jacob van Ruisdael**
The Windmill at Wijk bij Duurstede, c. 1670
Oil on canvas, 83 x 101 cm
Amsterdam, Rijksmuseum

A number of pictorial genres were developed to high standards of purity. Whereas, in Mannerist painting, the individual components had consituted a partial aspect of some wider context, a process of emancipation was now taking place which can best be illustrated by way of example of the still life. Initially, in the kitchen scenes, pantry scenes, marketplaces or households painted by such artists as Pieter Aertsen (1508–1575) or Joachim Beuckelaer (c.1530/35–c.1575/78), the objects and items of the kitchen or marketplace take up most of the painting, while a biblical scene tucked away somewhere in the background indicated the actual meaning of the work. One of the most important steps on the way towards Baroque painting lies in this rejection of the complex superimposition of different layers of meaning; by abandoning the overwrought breadth and scope of Mannerism, the picture could be broken down into individual and independently valid parts, liberating the close-up still life from such contextual strictures. Landscape painting evolved along similar lines. Pieter Brueghel the Elder (c.1525/30–1569) had already created landscapes of great intensity in their evocation of atmosphere, season and mood. Yet they are also invariably "universal landscapes" (like those

of Patinier) in which the range of the visible and the raised standpoint – potentially a bird's eye view – invariably add something increasingly conscious, considered, symbolic and significant, whereas the landscape painting of the 17th century no longer depicts "summer" or "winter" as such, but a landscape or a seascape on a summer's day or on a winter's day.

This should not be misconstrued. Baroque painters did not paint outdoors at their easels, as the artists of the School of Barbizon would later do in 19th century France. They might, at most, make some sketches outdoors, or they might take notes or even record a situation using the *camera obscura*, which aided accuracy in drawing details, before executing the painting in the studio. While bearing these facts in mind, we should nevertheless take care to avoid the pitfall of assuming that the Baroque artists of the Netherlands were simply "copying" reality. Even though their landscapes and vedutas may depict specific places, situations and cities, and even though their still lifes may seem almost "real" enough to touch, a number of factors provide overwhelming evidence that they are not intended to portray a detail of the visible world. We know that a number of painters, especially in Delft, used the camera obscura to make their initial studies of objects and city vedutas. Nevertheless, in the pictorial organization of a work such as the *View of Delft* (ill. p. 33) by Jan Vermeer (1632–1675) the cityscape has been altered in a barely perceptible yet highly energetic way to suit the scheme of the painting, as was common practice in such vedutas. In the still life, the process is more obvious. What appears to be a portrayal of found objects, of incidental and arbitrary items is actually specifically intended to indicate the transience and vanity of earthly existence. On another level, these objects are visually significant in terms of the way they have been arranged with the pictorial structure and aesthetic appearance of the painting in mind.

**Subject matter and content – specialists and masters**
One of the greatest achievements of Netherlandish Baroque painting was its creation of specific schemes within the various genres, in which a great diversity of individual objects gained their own distinctive and unprecedented dignity.

History painting ranked highest in the artistic hierarchies of the day. It referred to paintings which represented an "image of historic events" in which the actual portrayal of significant contemporary events played only a minor role. The painting by Gerard Terboch (1617–1681) depicting the Peace Treaty of Westphalia negotiated at Münster in 1648 (London, National Gallery) is in fact a group portrait showing the representatives of the signatory power. Battles and other warlike events were rather less popular subjects, with the possible exception of equestrian combat. At the same time, however, history paintings could also feature allegorical subjects from Antiquity, especially if they involved republican subjects.

Finally, history paintings might also be portrayals of biblical themes, particularly from the Old Testament.

Rembrandt addressed the Protestant variety of religious painting – the parable – in greater depth than any had done before, exploring the human factor as well as the divine. In the work of his students Flinck, Bol and Nicolaes Maes (1632–1693) this contemporaneity of the biblical and of man's relationship with God is more immediately evident, more direct and, in the "portrait historié", often dramatically presented. Nevertheless, in Dutch history painting, the ambitious aim of projecting contemporary life onto a backdrop of historical or biblical events and, on the other hand, updating ancient or biblical paradigms, are often naive, if invariably human, in its directness.

Flemish painters such as Rubens or Jacob Jordaens (1593–1678) were, in a similar sense, history painters: The difference between them and the Dutch painters lies in the distinct sensuality and corporeality of earthly appearances they achieved through their heightened colour and form, suggesting and at times revealing a sense of meta-reality.

Since the 15th century, the portrait had become an independent genre. So, too, since Dürer and the High Renaissance, had the self-portrait of the artist. In the Netherlands of the 17th century, the portrait became the primary vehicle not only for the representation of a person's social rank and standing, but also an excercise in exploring the psyche through the individual's expression. What is more, the portrait now came to represent the relationship between the individual and the community, either in the form of a family portrait (of which Rubens created some that showed bonds of deep affection), or in the group portraits of the Dutch artists in which Hals, Thomas de Keyser (c. 1596/97–1667) and Rembrandt sought successfully to depict individuality within a homogeneous group. The developments of the age are all the more evident in the light of a comparison with the group portraits created before the mid-16th century, for example by Jan van Scorel (1495–1562). Initially, they generally involved an accumulative juxtaposition of portraits (of pilgrims to Jerusalem, for instance). In the work of Hals, the occasion, the principle and the essence of a group are the determining factors in its composition. After all, Rembrandt's *Night Watch* (ill. p.313) is also a group portrait, albeit one in which the painter admittedly goes far beyond the conventions of this particular genre, creating a highly theatrical *mis en scène*.

With the increasing secularization of places of worship in Netherlands and the loss of votive and sacred images in the wake of the iconoclasts, the church interior, or rather architecture with churches as a prime motif, became popular subjects in painting. This "concretization" of the sacred might be regarded as a kind of compensation, in much the same way as elements of the Eucharist began appearing in still lifes. The paintings of church interiors, in particular, do tell

**Gerard Terborch**
A Concert, c. 1675
Oil on panel, 58.1 x 47.3 cm
Cincinnati (OH), Cincinnati Art Museum

us a great deal both about their development and the way they were regarded. In the works of Emanuel de Witte (c. 1617–1692) or Gerard Houckgeest (c.1600–1661), to name but two specialists in this genre, there are preachers and congregations to be seen, but it is far more common to find children playing in the outsized rooms, people strolling, or even dogs lifting a leg at a pillar – a motif that requires little interpretation. The actual subject matter of the picture is no longer the church interior itself, but the portrayal of light within a space that is perceived as space primarily because it is too large, unused and unaffected by the presence of people, its very existence as tranquil as an architectural still life.

Architectural painting developed along the following lines: Flemish artists, in particular, had a penchant for imagined spaces with surprise effects and unusual perspectives. This approach, which still bore many features of Mannerism, was later replaced by what Hans Jantzen (1881–1967) described as the "dream of reality" – views of interiors in which a portrait of architectural individuality was created, while the portrayal of the space itself remained largely dependent upon the actual detail and perspective of the picture itself. Peter Saenredam was the leading church portraitist of

Anthony van Dyck
Portrait of a Member of the Balbi Family, c. 1625
Oil on canvas, 132.7 x 120 cm
Cincinnati (OH), Cincinnati Art Museum

this period. In a final stage, of which de Witte was the fore-most representative, a considerably smaller detail of the inte-rior was portrayed and showed the play of light and shadow on individual parts, pillars (cut off at the top) or corner sites, rather than on architectural structures, thereby making the atmosphere the main focus of the image.

The objects in a room, especially objects bathed in light, and the room or space itself thus became a subject of Dutch painting. Each object – person, animal, room – is presented as though caught in a brief pause for thought. There are many variations in which elements of still life painting are combined with other objects. Vermeer's interiors are like an extended space surrounding a still life. In the work of Carel Fabritius (1622–1654) we can find a view of Delft seen through the shop of a merchant of musical instruments in which a lute and a cello lie in front of the townscape like a still life.

Together with portraiture, the still life is a key genre in Netherlandish painting. In this field, too, there was consider-able specialization and differences between individual schools. Haarlem concentrated on portraying banqueting tables laden with opulent dishes. Leiden focused more on vanitas still lifes full of books, jugs, tobacco pipes and writ-ing implements. In The Hague, seafood predominated. What is more, there were considerable differences between

Flemish and Dutch still lifes as well. In Antwerp, the work of Frans Snyders (1579–1657) presents sumptuous still lifes which are invariably a theatrical staging of extremely diverse objects and precious items. If Flemish still life can be de-scribed as "extensive", Dutch still life may be called "intens-ive" in the sense that it draws its appeal from its concentra-tion on only a few things. Even where the Haarlem "ban-quets" are based on the Flemish model, space and light are handled very differently indeed.

The landscape of the Low Countries and the sea, imagined memories of southern climes, Arcadian fields, landscape as a portrait of a certain place or an area and landscape as a projec-tion of imagination did not become an independent genre until the Baroque era and, when it did, the Netherlands led the field. Dürer's watercolour landscapes had already helped to emancipate the genre to some extent prior to 1500. With Pieter Bruegel, such elements as mood, atmosphere and indi-viduality took on greater independence. There is something celestial in his portrayal of the months and seasons. In the Baroque landscapes between van Goyen, Jacob van Ruisdael and Hobbema, a new element comes to the fore which had previously been a mode of illustration. Aerial views had been known since the days of Leonardo da Vinci, and artists were also well aware of the fact that objects in the distance change not only in terms of linear perspective but also in terms of light and colour. Netherlandish landscape painting took dis-tance, space and atmosphere – the interim zone between ob-jects in which light develops its effects – and made this the subject matter of their painting.

The French poet and playwright Paul Claudel (1868–1955) described it as follows: "I do indeed believe that we would better understand Dutch landscapes, these poems of tranquility, sources of silence, which owe their origins less to outward curiosity than to inward contemplation, if we would only learn to lend them an ear at the same time as we perceive them with our eyes. Compared to the overladen, overfilled paintings of the English and French, it is the enor-mous importance of emptiness over fullness that strikes us first of all. We are struck by the slowness with which a tone retained time and time again, through every shade and hue, finally alights upon an unequivocal line or form. Distance merges with the void, and the water on the wide, open spaces bears the cloud."

In other words, void and distance have become objects – a subject matter as calm as any part of a still life. The concreti-zation of space and light are the hallmarks of Netherlandish landscape painting. It is interesting to note that the horizon of land or sea is often very low, unlike that of the early land-scape paintings with their sweeping and almost universal dis-tances. From a bird's eye view, or at least from a raised view-point, a sense of distance is created by placing the centre of perspective and the horizon very low. "The moist haze of the sky with its atmospheric clouds plays the main role in the picture", according to Eduard Hüttinger. There are several versions of a view of Haarlem by Jacob van Ruisdael, in vertical format, seen from a raised point of view, but with the city so far in the distance that it actually forms the horizon, with the church spires soaring heavenwards and the clouds and haze forming a blurred boundary. It is situated in the lower third of the picture. The other two thirds are taken up by a cloudy sky. Between the spectator and the city there is a bleaching green on which lengths of locally manufactured fabric are stretched out, bathed in rays of light from the open skies. The spectator experiences the light through its effect on the objects, in the way the sun falls on the linen – as trivial as it is solemn. A similar phenomenon may be observed in the work of Vermeer, where a woman stands at a window, contemplating her pearl necklace in the light. Simple light is transformed into a ceremonious event, in its penetration of the room and in the way it falls on objects. Yet for all the mutability and transience of light, it is not brief moments that are portrayed in the interiors and landscapes, but "heightened" moments in which everday occurrences becomes celebratory moments.

Nowhere is the specialization of Netherlandish painting so evident as it is in landscape painting. There was an Italianate form which adopted elements of Italian painting as well as southern and ancient motifs. Many of these Italianate landscape painters had studied in Italy, including Herman van Swanevelt (c. 1600–1655), Berchem and Jan Asselijn (1610–1652), and they were profoundly influenced by Rosa and Lorrain. Then there were the Haarlem landscape painters who favoured low horizons and the sweeping expanses of the dykes and polders by the sea. Van Goyen initially painted in Haarlem, Jan Porcellis (c. 1584–1632), Hercules Seghers (1589/90 – c. 1633) and Salomon van Ruysdael (c. 1600/1603–1670) were members of the Haarlem Guild. Seascapes included the calm and tranquil scenes with a slight swell in the evening light (Jan van de Capelle, c. 1624/25–1679 as well as the stormy sea with endangered or capsized ships, favoured in Antwerp, and there were also paintings of shipping fleets (Willem van de Velde, 1633–1707), while the history painting of the fighting Dutch fleet barely played a role in the 17th century and lost its significance in much the same way as the battle painting.

In the Southern Netherlands, most notably under the influence of Rubens, a style of landscape painting developed which, for all their differences, bore many similarities with that of the Dutch school. This is evident, for example, in the work of Jan Siberechts (1627– c. 1700/1703) of Antwerp, who integrated Dutch elements into Flemish painting. Certain components which remained the preserve of individual specialists in Dutch painting can be found together in a single painting in the work of the Flemish artists: calm and sweeping plains together with bizarrely vibrant mountains or the idyll of of a river meandering through a shady forest

**Frans Hals**
Two Singing Boys, 1626
Oil on canvas, 62 x 54.5 cm
Cassel, Staatliche Kunstsammlungen

together with a sweeping view towards a distant horizon. Rubens' later work includes some of the finest landscape paintings in the history of European art. His *Landscape with Rainbow* (Munich, Alte Pinakothek, and London, National Gallery) and his *Landscape with Steen Castle* (London, National Gallery) executed around 1635 are more than mere views of the world around him. The wealth of nature is reflected in the colour spectrum, making Flemish rural life appear like some lost Arcadia, and the young men and women bringing in the harvest seem to hail from some strange metamorphosis of deities in disguise. In fact, the landscapes of Rubens are indeed frequently mythical scenes, often embodied by tiny figures. The difference between Dutch and Flemish painting might be described, albeit with some exaggeration, as follows: in Dutch painting, we find beauty rendered in a concentration of the representational, whereas in Flemish painting the representation of the world appears to be a vehicle for poetic metaphor.

Genre painting, as it has come to be known (for lack of a better description) encompasses the entire circle of social themes: portrayals of scenes from everyday life, music-making, love, rakish living, tooth-pulling, the doctor's visit or the self-portrait of the artist in his studio. Needless to say,

**Pieter de Hooch**
The Courtyard of a House in Delft, 1658
Oil on canvas, 73.5 x 60 cm
London, National Gallery

there were specialists for each individual type within the field of genre painting. Steen was regarded as a specialist of the wittily rendered "topsy-turvy world", involving moralizing or raucous scenes, while Gabriel Metsu (1629–1667) concentrated his efforts on minutely detailed portrayals of tranquil interiors. Brouwer and Adriaen van Ostade (1610–1685) made small-scale peasant genre paintings their speciality.

Though such a list could easily be extended ad infinitum, to do so would risk lending weight to a misunderstanding of Netherlandish genre painting that has been prevalent since the 19th century. This misunderstanding has tended to arise when the paintings are regarded as anecdotal, as portrayals of specific situations or as illustrations of certain activities. Such an interpretation should be treated with caution in view of the fact that, even though a work by Brouwer or Ostade may show a momentary situation or brief activity, certain elements of still life, a contemplatively introverted extension of time, may also frequently be found. This is particularly evident in the genre paintings by Vermeer, in which several people are gathered in a beautiful interior, perhaps drinking or making music, and the conversation piece with its elements of activity are continued in a traditional manner, but

where it is also clear that this is not a portrayal of activity between protagonists, but of concentration on the material world with its glasses of wine, musical intruments etc.

A scholarly debate has raged around the interpretation of one of the most important of these paintings, Vermeer's *Allegory of Painting,* also known as *The Fame of Painting* (ill. p. 334). On the one hand, it has been interpreted as an illustration, while on the other hand, successful attempts have been made to seek an iconographic interpretation at various levels, in which the artist at his easel with model is regarded not only as the theme of the painting, but also as a personification of the fame of painting. There are strong indications that such a painting is intended as a "truth" or iconographic rendering, especially as the entire range of Dutch painting has almost invariably been used as a vehicle for more or less obvious morals, proverbs or warnings. The question remains, however, as to whether, by deciphering such a painting, we can actually reveal its intended meaning or whether an anecdotal level is equally important. Much would seem to favour the latter possibility as well, given that the aesthetic value of the objects portrayed has always been of foremost importance in Dutch painting.

However, there is no need for us to choose between the extremes of iconographic coding and anecdotal genre. The very fact that such divergent interpretations of a Dutch genre painting are possible at all is in itself an indication of the ambivalence visible in the still life as well. These are pictures created by the sheer pleasure in substance, material and texture, in narrative, drama and wit, in the appearance of nature and everyday life, yet at the same time, they possess a moral and an edifying aspect. Behind the portrayal of a merry scene that an insider would immediately recognize as a brothel scene, lies the biblical parable of the prodigal son. When Steen or Gerard Dou (1613–1675) show a doctor visiting a sick patient and scrutinizing the contents of a glass phial against the light (ill. p.320), it is first and foremost an opportunity of painting a beautiful interior and of studying the effect of light in the room and on the glass. The moral of the story, however, is to be sought in its underlying jibe: the doctor sees in the urine the signs of a pregnancy that is causing the woman's distress.

Just as we can often find the symbols of vanitas behind a still life, so too can we find the iconography of the "five senses" behind the genre or moral painting. Initially, the five senses – touch, hearing, taste, sight and smell – were rendered in the form of personifications. A graphic series after Hendrick Goltzius (1558–1617) created around the end of the 16th or beginning of the 17th century, bears inscriptions warning against indulging in the senses. In a painting by Ludovicus Finson (c. 1580–1617) the personifications are united in a single picture. Around a table there are women with musical instruments, men fondling the women, tasting wine or smelling a rose.

If the Netherlandish genre painting can be traced back to such specific types, as it can in the early period and in the works of the Utrecht school with their adoption of such formulae from the Caravaggisti, we can no longer regard it as simply a portrayal of real life in the Netherlands. What we find here is not based on the depiction of a fleeting moment, but on rather more sophisticated visual formulae of enormous vitality, developed through longstanding tradition.

In the development of an independent Netherlandish painting, so-called "Caravaggism" was extremely important. Utrecht played a particularly important role in mediating between Italy and the north. The city, having remained largely Catholic, still commissioned religious works and, what is more, had retained its contacts with Rome. The later exponents of the Utrecht school, Hendrick Terbrugghen (c. 1588–1629), Gerrit van Honthorst (1590–1656) and Dirck van Baburen (c. 1590/95–1624) all spent several years in Italy, where they also received commissions. Honthorst was employed by the Grand Duke of Tuscany and became known as "Gherardo delle Notti" – Gerard, the painter of night scenes. This nickname indicates an extremely important characteristic of the Utrecht painters. They had adopted Caravaggio's chiaroscuro, which they tended to apply in a more representational manner. Whereas Caravaggio himself sought to create a contrast between his handling of light and the dark ground, Honthorst and Terbrugghe (who may well have known Caravaggio personally), use the technique to create a night scene in which artificial sources of light such as torches or candles illuminate part of the painting so that it stands out against the darkness. The possibilities of dramatic effects, the theatrical contrasts and surprises, as well as the pathos-laden modelling of the objects in chiaroscuro, came into fashion at the same time as Italian, Spanish and French painting. The Utrecht Caravaggisti and the Tenebrosi (from the Italian "tenebroso", meaning dark or shadowy) are thus an international phenomenon. Without them, the heightened chiaroscuro contrasts in the early works of Rembrandt would be unthinkable.

With the Caravaggisti, another specific type of genre painting entered Netherlandish painting: merry social gatherings full of music-making and drinking. Behind these scenes we can generally find the iconography of the "five senses". The history of Netherlandish chiaroscuro painting begins with the Utrecht Caravaggisti. In Rembrandt's early works of the 1630s, the tension between the darkened pictorial space and the spot-like areas of illumination correspond to the realism of expression and the portrayal of objects. The more "realistic" the objects became, the greater was the dramatic tension between unmotivated and sudden points of illumination in the dark pictorial space. This is true of more or less all Netherlandish painting: in the final phases of late Mannerism, it went through a phase of Caravaggesque chiaroscuro in which the concentrated intensity of Baroque painting emerged in response to the extensive elongations of Mannerism. Just as light emphasizes and delineates the key features of the painting by contrasting it with the darkness of the surrounding scene, so too does the painting seem to have shed the ballast of Mannerist improbability. In this context, some scholars have described Dutch painting as "concave", by which they mean that the essential objects are to be found together, as in the concave hollow of a dish.

One further phenomenon would also appear to be based on techniques of chiaroscuro in the manner of Caravaggio: light itself became the subject matter of the painting. Whereas earlier works featured artificial sources of light such as candles or lanterns, artists soon turned their attention to the portrayal of sunlight, in hazy atmospheres and in interiors lit by sunlight falling through a window. Even the works of Vermeer, who shows light lying on and even modelling objects, owe much to the influence of Caravaggesque genre painting.

The early phase of Caravaggesque painting gradually gave way to colority in Dutch painting. This is strikingly obvious if we compare, say, the landscapes of Pieter Brueghel with those of van Ruisdael or van Goyen. Whereas Brueghel's

Jan Vermeer
Street in Delft ("Het Straatje"), c. 1657/58
Oil on canvas, 54.3 x 44 cm
Amsterdam, Rijksmuseum

landscapes are made up of colours juxtaposed with more or less equal emphasis, the Dutch artists of the Baroque era use similar tones bound together by non-colours. They seem to be inherent in shades of grey and brown, with a potential for colour that can only be awakened through the light.

In the work of Rembrandt during the 1640s, the contrasts that lend shape and substance to objects begin to dissolve, the spot illuminations and their shadows recede, and colour becomes less of a determining factor. The space he portrays is no longer a dark space from which the objects stand out through the handling of light, but has become a colourless background in which light and colour are potentially immanent. In this way, brown takes on a new role as an underlying value. At first a non-colour, it nevertheless seems to contain colours – red and yellow, sometimes green – which can be called up at will.

What the 19th century admired so much in the work of the Dutch artists, particularly Rembrandt, as a "gallery tone", and regarded as a mysterious artistic sleight of hand, is not a brown coating applied over the original colority of the painting, but a tonal medium containing potentially vibrant colours. In landscape painting, the counterpart to Rembrandt's "gallery tone" can be found in the "tonal" period in which such artists as van Goyen, for example, reduced the range of colours in a coastal landscape to browns, olives and blues. Taken to an extreme, they can even be monochromatic brownish-green. These paintings may be described as "tonal" because their "tones" are subdued and reduced, yet nevertheless fully evident as tones. "We are struck by the slowness with which a tone retained time and time again, through every shade and hue, finally alights upon an unequivocal line or form. Distance merges with the void, and the water on the wide open spaces bears the cloud." With these words, Claudel speaks of the ability of Dutch paintings to portray proximity and distance, finity and infinity by means of this "tone retained".

The new Dutch painting also differs from its Mannerist forerunner in that it does not combine proximity and distance by forging some bold link, but by making the extremes of proximity and distance independent elements in their own right. Astonishing painterly methods are used to address not only distance and infinity, but also extreme proximity. For Dutch painting also tends to dissolve the visual boundaries of the painting towards the foreground, towards the spectator, in the kind of illusionistic paintings known as *trompe l'œil*. The imitation transcends the bounds of the pictorial plane towards the spectator. The curtain – a device frequently found in the works of Vermeer and Rembrandt – also has an illusionistic effect. It appears to lie within the picture plane and yet already seems to form part of the real space where the spectator is standing. In this way, the transition from real space to pictorial space is camouflaged.

## ABRAHAM BLOEMAERT
1564–1651

Bloemaert lived to the age of almost ninety. He was a contemporary of Rembrandt and yet he belonged to the generation of Rembrandt's teachers. He was the leading representative of the Utrecht Mannerists and the director and founder of the Utrecht Guild of St Luke, but he continued to work well into the Baroque 17th century when a third generation of landscape painters was already emerging.

His peasant landscape contains certain Mannerist elements such as the large distance between the foreground objects and the sweeping horizon, or in the way in which he has united contrasts. The aspects of Bloemaert's work adopted by Dutch landscape painters are the picturesque elements evident in his rendering of nature and architecture. The picturesque appeal of dilapidated cottages, damaged thatching, broken fences and rotten tree trunks were to become part and parcel of Netherlandish landscape painting.

Bloemaert's œuvre also forges a link between Flemish and Dutch painting. While his portrayals of mythological themes and biblical tales lean heavily on the syntax of the international Flemish Mannerists, the dramatic realism of his rural genre paintings influenced the Dutch artists.

**Abraham Bloemaert**
Landscape with Peasants Resting, 1650
Oil on canvas, 91 x 133 cm
Berlin, Gemäldegalerie, Staatliche Museen
zu Berlin – Preußischer Kulturbesitz

## JOOS DE MOMPER
1564– c. 1634/35

Momper is rightly regarded as the most important Flemish landscape painter between Pieter Brueghel and Rubens. Brueghel's influence is clearly evident in this winter landscape, and it is quite probable that his son Jan also painted a number of the figures in this picture.

Momper's personal achievement lies in his rendering of landscape as a picturesque subject matter in its own right. What we see here is no longer a great universal landscape full of symbolically charged allusions, but a scene whose aesthetic appeal is valued for its own sake. Momper's painting is divided into various planes by a kind of backdrop, against which silhouettes are highlighted by a pale light or dark, thundery clouds. People are making their way along tortuous paths on terrain that seems to be hazardous.

Rain-laden stormclouds, sunshine and snow set the atmosphere of the painting. In this respect, Momper has taken an important step towards emancipating the landscape painting as an autonomous genre in which the landscape is not merely a setting for some event, but is treated as a subject matter in its own right.

**Joos de Momper**
Winter Landscape, c. 1620
Oil on panel, 49.5 x 82.5 cm
Private collection

## JAN BRUEGHEL The Elder
### 1568–1625

**Jan Brueghel the Elder**
Great Fish-Market, 1603
Oil on panel, 58.5 x 91.5 cm
Munich, Bayerische Staatsgemälde-
sammlungen, Alte Pinakothek

Brueghel's *Great Fish-Market*, dating from the
year 1603, contains many elements of Mannerist landscape painting. Rendered in a perspective that is almost a bird's-eye-view, the scene
opens up across a downward-sloping foreground teeming with hundreds of figures
grouped around the stalls and booths of a fish-
market. The eye is drawn towards the harbour
in the background, out across the bay and
along the coastline, past entire towns with
ruins, piers and fortresses, into the depths of
the mountains, whose blue merges with the sea.

What we see here is a universal landscape,
but one broken down into individual themes
that are soon to establish themselves as genres
in their own right. Fish-market scenes of this
kind were to become an independent subject
in Flemish painting, for example in the works
of Snyder. Still life paintings of fish, such as
that displayed for sale here, would also begin
to emerge. Marine painting, ruins, and even
pure landscape are all to be found as elements
in this painting. We even seem to be able to
make out a family portrait: the group at the
centre of the foreground is thought to be a self-
portrait of the painter in the company of his
family.

In the second decade of the century, which
marks Brueghel's mature period, we find a
number of landscape paintings that differ considerably from his universal landscapes. They
show flat land broken by only a few motifs
such as windmills or isolated cottages bathed
in changing light. There is an increased sense
of portraiture and figure genre is used sparingly. As in the landscapes of Rubens, peasants' carts, cutting a diagonal path, give a
heightened impression of depth and distance.
One of the elements which indicates that this
is a Flemish landscape rather than a Dutch one
is the fact that the horizon is placed fairly
high in the painting.

*The Holy Family* leaves us in little doubt as to
why the second son of Pieter Brueghel was
given the nickname "Velvet" Brueghel. It is a
masterpiece of "fine" painting in which elements of floral still life, landscape painting
and devotional painting are combined into a
harmonious whole. A magnificent garland of
meticulously painted flowers and fruits reflecting the diversity of nature frames the idyllic
scene like a triumphal arch. It forms the letter
M for Mary, who is seated as in a "beszloz-
zenen garten" or hortus conclusus dominating
the middle ground with the Christ child on
her knee. Beside her are the angels and the
lamb, slightly behind her is Joseph and in the
background is a view of a landscape with grazing deer. The figures were painted by Pieter
van Avont – an excellent example of the way
specific painterly tasks were delegated according to artists' specializations within Netherlandish painting.

**Jan Brueghel the Elder**
Landscape with Windmills, c. 1607
Oil on panel, 34 x 50 cm
Madrid, Museo del Prado

**Jan Brueghel the Elder** The Holy Family, undated
Oil on panel, 93.5 x 72 cm. Munich, Bayerische
Staatsgemäldesammlungen, Alte Pinakothek

**Peter Paul Rubens**
The Four Philosophers (Self-portrait with the artist's brother Philipp,
Justus Lipsius und Johannes Wouverius), c. 1611
Oil on panel, 164 x 139 cm
Florence, Palazzo Pitti, Galleria Palatina

**Peter Paul Rubens**
Stormy Landscape with Philemon und Baucis, c. 1620
Oil on canvas, 147 x 209 cm
Vienna, Kunsthistorisches Museum

# PETER PAUL RUBENS
## 1577–1640

In 1611, the artist's brother Philip Rubens died suddenly. This group painting, probably executed shortly after his death, was intended to evoke the atmosphere of humanistic thinking in which the brothers grew up. On the left-hand edge of the painting stands the artist himself, next to him is his brother with a pen in his hand, then their teacher, the humanist Lipsius, and on the right Johannes van de Wouwere. The fifth in the group, watching over them all, is the bust of Seneca, set in a niche with a floral tribute of tulips. Lipsius published his writings. In the landscape in the background, we can see the Roman Palatine.

A stream has wreaked havoc after a storm, flooding fields and meadows, breaking trees and now rushing towards the foreground in a cascade. The stormy sky has begun to clear, and a small rainbow has formed beside the waterfall. The storm has destroyed the peaceful landscape.

The figures to the right of the painting indicate that this is an allegory of a greater cosmic event. When Jupiter and Mercury descended to earth in human form, only Philemon and Baucis gave them hospitality. The gods responded by flooding the entire land with a terrible storm which spared Philemon and Baucis and left their humble dwelling unscathed. Everything in this painting by Rubens is in the hands of divine powers and subject to metamorphis; there is no tree or river that cannot be transformed into a living being, no creature that cannot be turned back again into a river or a tree.

This double portrait was probably executed to celebrate the marriage of Rubens to Isabella Brant, the daughter of an Antwerp patrician. Rubens had returned from Italy the previous year, having achieved fame and renown at the court of Mantua. The marriage was in keeping with his social standing and this is also reflected in the painting. Rubens was familiar with such portrayals of happily married couples from Italian paintings of the 16th century. However, he heightens the significance through symbolic and emblematic references. The couple is seated in a bower of honeysuckle, a plant frequently associated with marital love and emotional constancy. Their hands are joined, indicating that the marriage ceremony has already taken place.

This portrait is remarkable for its painstakingly detailed treatment of each and every object and for the accuracy with which fabrics, lace and embroidery are rendered. Everything is worked like a piece of fine jewellery, as though Rubens sought to prove his skill as a painter.

**Peter Paul Rubens**
Rubens with his first wife Isabella Brant
in the Honeysuckle Bower, c. 1609/10
Oil on canvas-covered panel, 178 x 136.5 cm
Munich, Bayerische Staatsgemälde-
sammlungen, Alte Pinakothek

# PETER PAUL RUBENS
## 1577–1640

**Peter Paul Rubens**
The Landing of Marie de'
Médici at Marseilles,
c. 1622–1625
Oil on canvas,
394 x 295 cm
Paris, Musée National
du Louvre

*Below:*
**Peter Paul Rubens**
The Rape of the
Daughters of Leucippus,
c. 1618
Oil on canvas,
224 x 210.5 cm
Munich, Bayerische Staats-
gemäldesammlungen,
Alte Pinakothek

In 1621, Rubens received what was probably his most important commission: a cycle of paintings for Marie de' Médici, the widowed queen consort of Henry IV of France, to decorate the upper galleries of both wings of the newly built Palais du Luxembourg. The programme was worked out by the Abbé de Saint-Ambroise. The queen, Cardinal Richelieu and Rubens all put forward proposals for the paintings, documenting and glorifying the events and deeds in the life of King Henry IV and Marie de' Médici. The cycle of twenty-one paintings now hangs in the Louvre in Paris, while sixteen preparatory sketches are in the Alte Pinakothek in Munich.

This painting depicts Marie's arrival in Marseilles on 3 November 1600. She is greeted by allegories of France and the port city. Above her floats Fama; Neptune and the Nereids have accompanied the ship to ensure a safe passage.

The commission also had a distinctly political edge. Marie had been appointed regent by the King when he entered the Clèves-Jülich war of sucession, clearly with some foreboding of his death. On the day after the coronation, Henry IV was assassinated. The widowed queen was soon embroiled in conflict with her son, the future Louis XIII. The series of paintings was therefore intended as a highly visible sign of the legitimacy of Marie's rule.

No other artist could have executed this commission in such a way, transposing historical facts into images of timeless significance, blurring the boundaries between history, mortality and the realms of the eternal powers.

The subject matter of this painting was not recognized until 1777 when the German poet Wilhelm Heinse pinpointed a scene in the Idylls of Theocritus which corresponded precisely with the scene painted by Rubens: Leda's sons Castor and Pollux (Pollux, fathered by Zeus, was immortal) carried off the two daughters of Leucippos of Argos during a wedding ceremony, even though the Leucippides were already betrothed to the twins Lynceus and Idas.

However, this painting is clearly not simply an illustration of a mythological theme. The important point is what Rubens does not portray. For example, we do not see the fight that breaks out over the Leucippides, nor the wedding celebrations nor even the pursuit. The two horsemen do not even seem to be lifting the two naked maidens onto their horses, but simply lifting them from the ground, and both have turned their eyes heavenwards in rapture. Here, we find a typical device of Rubens.

What this painting actually portrays is an apotheosis: the Leucippides are lifted from the earthly realms into the Olympic heights of celestial Zeus. Although the scene appears at first glance to be full of movement and tension, Rubens has calmed the action by allowing the movements to flow gracefully into one another.

Around 1615, Maximilian I, Elector of Bavaria, commissioned Rubens to paint a series of four hunting scenes for the Old Palace in Schleissheim. In 1800, the paintings were seized by the French and removed to France, and only "a cruel hunt against monstrous crocodiles" (as Joachim von Sandrart described the painting in his *Teutsche Akademie* of 1675) was returned to Munich.

The wild hippopotamus is the focal point and centre of the composition. The action has already reached a dramatic climax; tha animal has been captured and is panting with rage, showing the hunters its teeth. The hippopotamus is rendered with such zoological precision that we must assume Rubens actually saw such an animal with his own eyes – perhaps in a royal menagerie – and drew it from nature, just as Dürer before him had drawn a rhinoceros.

Three Moorish riders are grouped around the wild animal on rearing horses, with their lances pointing towards the centre of the painting. The attack by the two dogs on the left and the hunter half-buried beneath the crocodile who is trying desperately to escape, also run in the same direction. The fight is already over for the figure lying lifeless on the ground, above whose body the view opens towards the horizon and an exotic landscape.

Far from being a realistic portrayal of a hunt, this painting is an allegory of the struggle between man and savage beast, and indeed between man and nature as a whole. Rubens uses a very similar approach in his battle scenes, underlining the fact that it is not so much the hunt as the struggle that is the theme – a struggle in which both man and beast have a chance.

The fiery horses, the snapping dogs, the clothed and unclothed bodies of the hunters – everything revolves around the body of the cumbersome yet dangerously enraged hippopotamus. Naked and clothed, smooth and scaly, black and white, mounted high and prostrate on the ground; the painting seems to be an exercise in every possible aspect of an exotic, mythical world that is both beautiful and disturbing at the same time.

**Peter Paul Rubens**
Hippopotamus and Crocodile Hunt, c. 1615/16
Oil on canvas, 248 x 321 cm
Munich, Bayerische Staatsgemälde-
sammlungen, Alte Pinakothek

Peter Paul Rubens
The Three Graces,
1639
Oil on canvas,
221 x 181 cm
Madrid, Museo del
Prado

## PETER PAUL RUBENS
### 1577–1640

*The Three Graces* is one of the artist's final works. He had portrayed this theme several times since about 1620, but only later adopted the form that prevailed in classical Antiquity, with the three figures forming a circle so that one of them has her back to the spectator. "They were the goddesses of pleasant charm, of charitable deeds and of gratitude… without them nothing would be graceful or pleasing. They gave people friendliness, uprightness of character, sweetness and conversation…They were presented as three beautiful virgins and were either completely naked or clothed in some fine, transparent fabric…They stood together all three so that two of their faces were turned towards the spectator and only one was turned away from him."

Rubens' late painting of three nude figures magnificently illustrates the artist's extraordinary handling of incarnate or human flesh tones. Rubens builds them up using the three primary colours yellow, red and blue. An unusually high proportion of blue is evident here. In this way, the human figure bears the same primary colours that make up the appearance of the world and the entire cosmos, and all that is gathered here in the landscape and flowers, the sky and the trees.

Pieter Lastman
Odysseus and Nausicaa, 1619
Oil on panel, 91.5 x 117.2 cm
Munich, Bayerische Staatsgemälde-
sammlungen, Alte Pinakothek

## PIETER LASTMAN
### 1583–1633

The fact that Lastman visited Italy and that, while he was there, he was profoundly influenced by Elsheimer, is evident in this painting of the shipwrecked Odysseus found naked by Nausicaa and her entourage. The pictorial structure, the individual gestures and formal pathos are theatrical, and the setting itself is charged with meaning. The artist has taken a highly original approach in placing the figures, with their gestures of surprise and fright and their outstretched arms, against a pale sky – a motif Rembrandt was soon to adopt. One thing, however, is particularly remarkable about this painting, and it foreshadows an element that is to emerge strongly in later Dutch painting: the element of the "portrait historié". We have the impression here that a historic event is being played by specific persons, as though in a theatrical role. History painting and the reality of the protagonists are widely divergent.

In this painting, the naked Odysseus not only looks like the great hero of the Trojan war, but he is also caricatured in his all too human role. Lastman increased the figurative detail of his staffage and with that the realism and narrative impact of his work. The young Rembrandt also adopted this sense of tension.

# FRANS HALS
## c. 1581/85–1666

The portrait of the *Officers of the St George Civic Guard* is the first major group portrait by Frans Hals, and the first monumental civic guard painting in the new era of Dutch painting. Together with the leaders of public, charitable and professional associations, the civic guard societies were the main patrons to commission group portraits. This patronage took on considerable proportions in the course of the century. These group portraits are also of value as historical documents, for which lists were drawn up giving the names of the figures portrayed. The paintings themselves were displayed prominently on the premises of the respective association.

These civic guard portraits were an expression of the Baroque will to representation, whose tradition is rooted in the medieval era. There had been civic guards in the Netherlands since the 13th century. They had played an important role in the emancipation of the cities and towns from feudal rule and had gained considerable political and military significance in the Netherlands' struggle for independence.

Cornelis van Haarlem had already painted the officers of the St George Civic Guard in 1599. Hals, however, revolutionizes this type of painting. Instead of merely painting a row of individual portraits, he places them within a specific context by creating a banquet scene. This is not simply a moment captured at a table, but an extremely witty and calculated composition in which a scenic context is created between all the figures involved, and, on the other hand, each of the figures poses and acts independently and individually. Hals has found a new and persuasive solution to the problem of portraying a large group without difference of rank.

Although the young man holding a skull in his hand has occasionally been identified as Hamlet, this interpretation is probably incorrect. It is much more likely to be a Dutch vanitas allegory. As in corresponding still lifes featuring the same attribute, it voices a warning, calling on the spectator to think of death, even in youth. Such an interpretation may describe the content of the painting, but it still does not touch upon the actual meaning of the image. This is to be found in the way Hals has created a variation on a theme of Utrecht Caravaggism by equipping the model, a young man, with certain props and portraying him as someone posing for a painting. It is this that is the actual event or action of the painting, and as such it is very similar to the work of the young Rembrandt, who painted himself in similar garb working at his easel.

In spite of the borrowings from the Utrecht school, there are nevertheless distinct differences. The figure does not develop from the darkness towards the light, but is lit from behind. The *trompe l'œil* effects, the foreshortened hand and the skull that almost seems to jut beyond the front of the pictorial plane, are all masterly devices in which illusion is less important than painterly wit.

**Frans Hals**
Banquet of the Officers of the St George
Civic Guard in Haarlem, 1616
Oil on canvas, 175 x 324 cm
Haarlem, Frans-Hals-Museum

**Frans Hals**
Young Man with a Skull (Vanitas), c. 1626
Oil on canvas, 92 x 81 cm
London, National Gallery

**Frans Hals**
The Merry Drinker,
1628
Oil on canvas,
81 x 66.5 cm
Amsterdam,
Rijksmuseum

# FRANS HALS
## c. 1581/85–1666

Dutch painting tends to break through the pictorial plane towards the foreground, creating *trompe-l'œil* effects. Not only does the *Merry Drinker* approach us by his gesture – offering his wine glass to us out of the painting – but the objects of the painting also seem so close that we might almost grasp them. This effect is achieved by the employment of painterly means which are almost diametrically opposed to those used in fine painting. The subject matter is not rendered imitatively but is brought to life by suggesting its appearance under the effect of light. This suggestion is evoked with such precision that the spectator gains a completely fresh impression of its appearance.

The painting known as *The Gipsy Girl* is situated somewhere between a portrait and a genre painting. Her insolent and provocative look are unequivocal, and this is also quite clearly the portrait of a specific person from the milieu of whores. As in other genre portraits of this kind, there is a certain coarseness and squalor that makes an interesting motif in itself, but these factors are offset by the brushwork.

What is important here is the sense of transience and spontaneity, the mutability of a fleeting impression that leaves no time for reflection on the moral content. Seen in this way, Hals' genre portraits are positively immoral. They glorify sensual perception and visual pleasure, making it seem ridiculous to reflect on the meaning behind them.

A wealthy merchant presents himself in noble guise. The bunch of roses, the vineleaf on the floor and the lovers in the background may well be intended as signs of mortality, recalling the labour of amassing earthly goods; perhaps the doorway draped with a curtain is the doorway of the temple of Mars, which was kept closed during times of peace in ancient Rome.

Dutch portraits tend to be full of such hidden codes which hint at the identity of the figure portrayed, and in this case they tell us that the man is a merchant who has responsibilities in times of peace and war. Neither the pose nor the symbolic attributes are meaningless signs; they are the lavish attributes of a man who presents himself as an important figure. The air of the *nouveau-riche* parvenu, to be found in so many Dutch portraits of this type, featuring showily dressed burghers, is offset by the duality of the composition in which all things of beauty are merely outward signs of dignity, full of vanity and masquerade, things of fragile and transient charm.

**Frans Hals**
The Gypsy Girl,
c. 1628–1630
Oil on panel,
58 x 52 cm
Paris, Musée
National du Louvre

**Frans Hals**
Portrait of Willem van Heythuysen, c. 1625–1630
Oil on canvas, 204.5 x 134.5 cm
Munich, Bayerische Staatsgemälde-
sammlungen, Alte Pinakothek

**Frans Hals**
Regentesses of the Old Men's Almshouse in Haarlem, 1664
Oil on canvas, 170.5 x 249.5 cm
Haarlem, Frans-Hals-Museum

## FRANS HALS
### C. 1581/85–1666

The two large format group portraits of the *Regents* and *Regentesses of the Old Men's Almshouse in Haarlem* are not only one of the last major work by this artist who ranks beside Rembrandt as the greatest of all portrait painters, they are also the last historically significant examples of this genre.

Whereas Hals previously presented individual gestures, attitudes and poses in a ceremonial and more than momentary context, here he isolates the individual parts and the individuals themselves. The faces above the white collars seem to float against the dark ground of a room that is difficult to distinguish. The "breakdown" of the figurative corresponds to the brushwork whose ductus is no longer fluid, but broken so that it seems to crumble into particles of colour. Here and there, a shimmer of red flares up through the black like the final glimmer of dying embers in the ashes.

Whereas the iconography of vanitas and the theme of transience were previously expressed through specific symbols in Dutch painting, we now find that the most vigorous genre of all – the group portrait – has also been imbued with the concept of mortality. Old age and death seem to menace, where once there was activity and sociability.

**Dirck Hals**
Merry Company, undated
Oil on panel, 45 x 67.5 cm
Private collection

## DIRCK HALS
### 1591–1656

Dirck Hals was apprenticed to his older brother Frans. Yet while Frans Hals specialized in portraiture, Dirck Hals concentrated primarily on genre paintings and conversation pieces in the manner of Esasias van de Velde and Willem Pietersz. Buytewech. From the 1620s onwards, he frequently had the figures in his paintings added by his own specialist, Dirck van Deelen. He preferred a courtly setting and noble society, whereas his *Merry Company* follows in the tradition of the brothel painting and the tale of the prodigal son.

The bed on the left in the background, and the body language of the couples leave us in little doubt as to the situation. At the same time, however, this is also a "five senses" scene: not only is the sense of touch satisfied, but there is also music and singing, smoking and drinking, while the eyes feast on an empty jug or a bodice.

The interior also gives us an idea of how paintings were displayed in Holland at the time. They have been hung on a shabby wall without any evident system: a landscape, a marine painting, a portrait. It is clear that paintings had by now become objects to be taken for granted. Some might be cheaper or more expensive, better or worse painted than others, but they were no longer laden with iconographic significance.

# ROELANT SAVERY
## 1576–1639

Savery's painting, outmoded both in type and composition, adheres to the style of late Mannerism. Landscape as an imaginary combination of heterogeneous, natural and invented components, had by now been replaced by details of familiar surroundings, and animal images that seem to be taken straight from the pages of a zoological almanac had given way to portraits of domestic pets.

Savery's painting calls for a close reading and an appreciative eye. His art lies in his scholarship and well-founded knowledge, reflecting the interest of the age in the natural sciences and exotic phenomena. The new Dutch painting, on the other hand, calls for a more sensually perceptive and contemplative approach. In its narrative, the landscape with birds is comparable to those Flemish floral still lifes which, for a period, presented botanic diversity in great detail. Savery's compositional form has its origins in the paradise portrayals of the 16th century, in which Adam and Eve are shown in harmony with the animal world around them. Picturesque ruins in the manner of Maerten van Heemskerck are also common features, soon to be adopted by the Italianate landscape painters. Savery's prolific drawings are spontaneous and precise, individual studies which he then transferred to his paintings.

Roelant Savery
Landscape with Birds, 1628
Oil on panel, 42 x 57 cm
Vienna, Kunsthistorisches
Museum

# FRANS SNYDERS
## 1579–1657

Just as a circle of specialists for individual genres gathered in Amsterdam around Rembrandt, the same was true in Antwerp around Rubens. Snyders frequently collaborated with him on arrangements of objects and staffage. On the other hand, Snyders also adopted Rubens' new Baroque principles into his own specialized area of still life. The result was a number of new pictorial types in this field.

He initially drew upon the great kitchen interiors and pantry paintings of the Flemish Mannerists such as Aertsen or Beuckelaer. However, whereas these artists created "epic" arrangements of enormous breadth, Snyders sought to produce more dynamic still lifes. He created the hunting still life which not only features game, but also includes certain elements of the hunt itself, and in which each animal, dead or alive, still has its own tale to tell. In his portrayal of animals, he was peerless in his time. Whereas Dutch still life presented coded "truths" and warned of the transience of earthly life, Snyders staged a theatrical drama portraying the riches of the world. Snyders' pantry scenes, a variation on the hunting still life, are equally dynamic.

Frans Snyders
Stil Life, 1614
Oil on canvas, 156 x 218 cm
Cologne, Wallraf-Richartz-Museum

**Frans Francken the Younger**
Supper at the House of Burgomaster Rockox,
c. 1630–1635
Oil on panel, 62.3 x 96.5 cm
Munich, Bayerische Staatsgemälde-
sammlungen, Alte Pinakothek

## FRANS FRANCKEN The Younger
### 1581–1642

The title of the painting tempts us to see it as the portrayal of a specific situation. Yet we are unable to recognize the master of the house and, on closer inspection, the gentlemen and ladies in the painting appear to represent a "five senses" scene (music = hearing; man contemplating painting = sight; lady smelling rose = smell; wine drinker = taste; warming at fire = touch). Above all, however, it is an allegory on the artistic taste of the client. The humanistically trained lawyer and burgomaster had purchased a large house in 1603 and had converted it into an art gallery. Francken's painting shows the main room with its finest pieces, including antiques. Above the fireplace hangs the Rubens painting of Samson and Delilah, now in London. In the background, through the doorway, we can just make out Rubens' *Incredulity of St Thomas* which was commissioned by Rockox for his burial chamber. Several other paintings, from Massys to Hemessen, can also be seen.

This glimpse of a wealthy art collection also gives us some idea of how difficult it must have been to use what is to all intents and purposes a medieval room as a place to display an art collection. A shelf has been installed on the walls for the antique busts, and some of the smaller paintings are hung above the moulding that holds the wall tapestry in place.

**Cornelis de Vos**
The Family of the Artist, c. 1630–1635
Oil on canvas, 144.5 x 203.5 cm
Ghent, Museum voor Schone Kunsten

## CORNELIS DE VOS
### c. 1584–1651

This portrait of the artist's family, created in the late 1620s, allows us to pinpoint some of the differences between Flemish and Dutch painting. De Vos was, for a while, a colleague of Rubens and, together with Jordaens, he executed designs by Rubens, including a triumphal arch for the entry of the Infante Ferdinand in Antwerp. He was the brother-in-law of Snyders, a skilled craftsman and a cog in the wheel of the great Baroque machinery of the Rubens studio.

When it came to painting in the domain dominated by the Dutch, namely the group portrait, he seems to have encountered some difficulties. Where the Dutch painters evoke nuanced psychological differences and individual traits, de Vos produces a rather dry inventory of persons. Flemish painting thrives on scenic movement. In an attempt to inventorize, it loses its character.

For the Dutch portrait painter, on the other hand, the group portrait is a welcome challenge. Solving the problem of breaking through the stereotype and presenting the characters individually gave them enough activity for any painting. De Vos was renowned for his ability to make the eyes of his subjects speak eloquently. Here, however, parents and children alike all seem to be looking at the spectator in the same way, with a slightly disturbing effect.

# HENDRIK AVERCAMP
## 1585–1635

The deaf and dumb artist Hendrik Avercamp, known as "De Stomme van Campen" was a pupil of Pieter Brueghel the Elder. As his work initially leaned heavily on his teacher's landscape paintings, it seems apt to compare the two. Whereas Brueghel imbued even the most apparently innocuous figures with some significance, some underlying moral "truth" or attribute, Avercamp made his scenes an independent genre in their own right. The rural setting of this winter scene is full of simple enjoyment.

Avercamp was particularly fond of portraying the mirror-smooth surfaces of frozen canals and lakes, on which villagers went skating or played golf, and where elegantly dressed burghers strolled.

Pieter Brueghel was the first to portray winter as an atmospheric landscape. Avercamp's winter scenes use atmosphere and the coolness of light and air as essential elements of the painting. Although his landscapes bear certain Mannerist traits, including the considerable divergence between the objects in the foreground and the depth of the painting, as well as his distribution of many figures across the scene as a whole, the tendency towards the tonality of the new Dutch landscape is already evident in his work.

Hendrik Avercamp
Winter Scene at Yselmuiden, c. 1613
Oil on panel, 47 x 73 cm
Geneva, Musée d'Art et d'Histoire

# HENDRICK TERBRUGGHEN
## c. 1588–1629

Terbrugghen's portrait of a lute player accompanied by a buxom singer who is clapping the rhythm was created a year before he died. Together with Baburen and van Honthorst, Terbrugghen was undoubtedly the most important of the Utrecht Caravaggisti, even though he gained little renown during his own lifetime.

His highly lit modelling draws the sensual and realistic appeal of his figures into the foreground of the painting. It is a "loud" painting in the sense that he makes a distinct attempt to reach the spectator with persuasively captivating painterly skills and sophisticated handling of light.

A popular and consistent iconographical structure sets the theme of such paintings, which can be broken down according to the "five senses": hearing (as in this example), smell, sight, touch and taste, often painted as a series, sometimes as personification and frequently found in Dutch genre paintings. Pictures of musicians, table rounds, banquets, raucous peasants – all are embodiments of the allegorical concepts of these "five senses". The compositional structures and formula of pathos were often adopted from existing paintings, particularly from the works of Italian artists, most notably Caravaggio.

Hendrick Terbrugghen
The Duo, 1628
Oil on canvas,
106 x 82 cm
Paris, Musée National
du Louvre

Jacob Jordaens
Allegory of Fertility, c. 1622
Oil on canvas, 180 x 241 cm
Brussels, Musées Royaux des Beaux-Arts

Jacob Jordaens
The Family of the Artist, c. 1621
Oil on canvas, 181 x 187 cm
Madrid, Museo del Prado

## JACOB JORDAENS
### 1593–1678

Amid a group of naked bodies stands a woman draped in a red robe which highlights her figure and frames the white and red grapes she is presenting to the admiring gaze of the other figures. The grapes, a divine gift, are the focal point of the painting. The female figure is probably Pomona, the goddess of fruits. At first it is the grapes that are admired by the nymphs and satyrs, who hold them contemplatively and wondering in their hands. On the left, however, we see another figure approaching, bearing a huge bundle of cherry branches, artichokes, fruit and melons. This, together with the way in which the fruits are distributed over the entire painting, recalls the sumptuous still lifes of fruit in the style of Snyders.

It is not unusual to find overlaps between two different pictorial genres in Netherlandish Baroque painting. Similarities can often be detected between a Rubens figure painting and a Brueghel flower still life, to name but one such example.

Further variations on this theme by Jordaens can be seen in Munich, Madrid and London. The liberal portrayal of human nudes is an astonishing feature of his œuvre. In this painting, which hangs in Brussels, the naked nymph with her back to us forms the symmetrical axis of the painting. To her left crouches a naked satyr, turned undaunted towards the spectator, mirrored on the right by the back of a semi-reclined female nude. Individual figures from these compositions by Jordaens can also be found in the works of Rubens.

The young woman sitting in a chair on the left can also be found in the Munich painting of *The Satyr and the Farmer's Family*. She is Catharina, the wife of the artist and daughter of Adam van Noort, to whom Jordaens was apprenticed and who also taught Rubens. She is well dressed, wearing a large ruff. She draws her cheekily smiling little daughter to her. Jordaens is standing by a chair with a lute in his hand, one foot placed slightly higher on the frame of the chair, reflecting the triumphal pose of the noble man (in the manner of placing a foot on the defeated enemy or the captured game). Slightly behind them stands a servant woman carrying a basket full of beautiful grapes.

Two further group portraits of highly original composition, *Jordaens and the Family of his Father-in-law* hang in Cassel (Gemäldegalerie) and St Petersburg (Hermitage).

The decor and the props in this family portrait clearly indicate the artist's claim to recognition as a nobleman in the sense of an artistic aristocracy. Rubens was the first to embody this status, by furnishing his home lavishly and by acquiring a palatial country house. Like Rubens, Jordaens also imbues the pathos formula and the props in his paintings with enormous vitality and humanity. Jordaens worked in Rubens' studio in 1618/19. After Rubens died in 1640, he took his place as the leading master of Flemish painting.

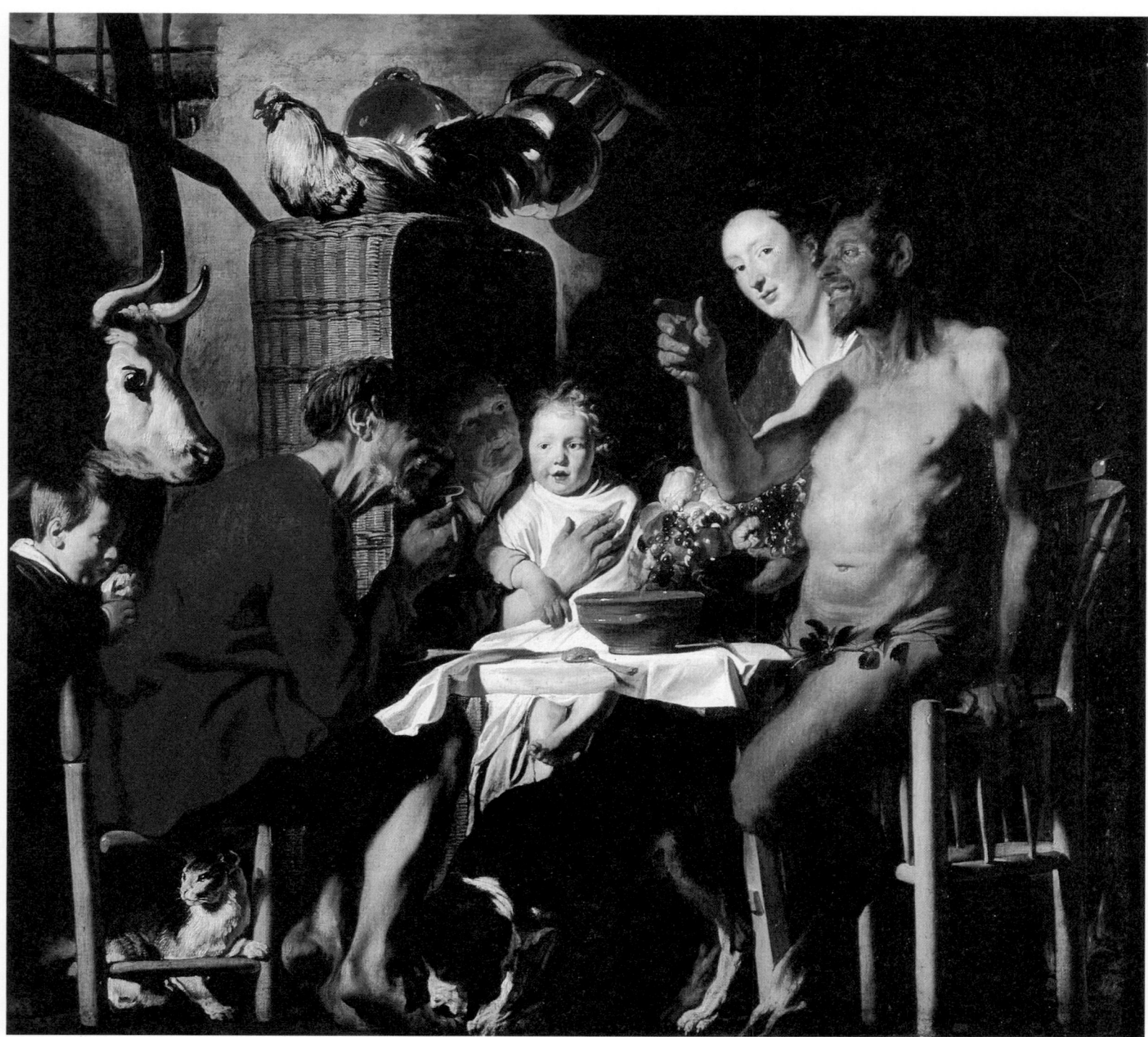

This painting is an early version of a theme Jordaens treated on numerous occasions. The strong contrasts of light and shade in the Munich version vividly recall Utrecht Caravaggism. Similarities with the works of Honthorst are also evident in the way the figures seem to be playing to the spectator, and in the modelling of the realistic corporeality against a dark ground. Contrasts are positively savoured, as in the juxtaposition of the ugly brown satyr and the pale-skinned young woman, the wrinkled old lady and the chubby-cheeked child.

This particular genre scene is based on a fable by Aesop in which a farmer invites a satyr into his home. First, he watches the farmer blowing on his hands to warm them and then blowing on his soup to cool it. The satyr, feeling he is being made a fool of, jumps up.

Jordaens does not simply illustrate the ancient fable, but links it with the genre and history painting that may be regarded as a Netherlandish invention. The naked satyr of Greek mythology has been integrated into a Flemish household. The young woman (Catherina Jordaens) and the children are almost certainly portraits. The rustic objects and the animals are typical of a Flemish household. This lively mixture of myth and genre, past and present, fable and moral was first introduced by Rubens. On another level – the finest example being the Medici cycle – Rubens also links historical reality and contemporary scenes with the world of mythology, in images that show how these intervene in human actions and deeds.

Jacob Jordaens
The Satyr and the Farmer's Family, after 1620
Oil on canvas-covered panel, 174 x 205 cm
Munich, Bayerische Staatsgemälde-sammlungen, Alte Pinakothek

## WILLEM CLAESZ. HEDA
c. 1593/94–1680

**Willem Claesz. Heda**
Still Life, 1631
Oil on panel, 54 x 82 cm
Dresden, Gemäldegalerie Alte Meister

This painting shows an "ontbijtje", or breakfast table. It is a term that hardly seems fitting as a description of the still life presented here. In fact, this particular designation was originally adopted in Holland where the term "still life" was unknown before about 1650. "Ontbijtjes" were a popular form of Haarlem vanitas painting. The leftovers of a meal are still standing on the table: the tablecloth has been pushed to one side, only part of the pie has been eaten, a goblet is overturned, a glass broken. The watch, in particular, reminds us of time passing. In these leftovers that remain after the joys of eating, we see the vanity of all earthly existence.

However, because this is such an artful arrangement, in which the individual things develop all the brilliance and appeal of their materials, a certain ambiguity arises. The things intended to recall transience, destruction and decay are a joy to the eye, and their iconographical function becomes an alibi.

The reduction of colour allows the reflections of the metal and glasses to appear all the more beautiful. Such works are known as monochrome "banketjes" in reference to the heightened appeal of surface finishes achieved by reducing tonal values.

## GERRIT VAN HONTHORST
1590–1656

**Gerrit van Honthorst**
The Incredulity of
St Thomas, c. 1620
Oil on canvas,
125 x 99 cm
Madrid, Museo del Prado

Honthorst stayed in Rome from 1610 onwards, where his preference for night scenes with special lighting effects earned him the name "Gherardo delle Notti". His *Incredulity of St Thomas* was probably painted towards the end of his stay in Italy, before his return to Utrecht in 1622. The influence of Caravaggio, whose works he had studied in Rome, cannot be overlooked. The contrast between the dark ground of the painting and the illumination of the key areas by some source of light that cannot be located enhances the realism of the scene rather than the miraculous nature of the event: Thomas has placed two fingers in the wound of Christ. Yet the superficial realism of the scene actually emphasizes its sacred character.

The source of illumination and the handling of light in the works of Caravaggio and his followers are independently determined, defying completely rational calculation. In the later works of Honthorst, light tends to be portrayed more figuratively by showing a candle or a lamp, frequently covered by a figure in the foreground.

On his return to Utrecht, Honthorst became the leading representative of a group of painters whose work was profoundly influenced by Caravaggio. It was here that he began translating the initially predominant religious themes of his chiaroscuro paintings into popular genre scenes.

# JAN VAN GOYEN
## 1596–1656

These two landscapes mark the beginning of a period in Goyen's œuvre that might be described as "monochrome" or "tonal". In other words, this was a period in which he reduced his colour palette in favour of achieving atmospheric effects, by presenting a space bathed in light and haze through which colour had to penetrate. The fact that the reduction of local colouring can actually increase a sense of colour, is described by the poet Paul Claudel as follows: "I felt drawn towards, or rather captivated by, a small painting almost hidden away in a corner… It was a landscape after the manner of van Goyen, painted in a single tone as though with gilded oil on luminous smoke. But what really made me tremble as I contemplated the painting from a distance, and what made this subdued work sound out like a trumpet clarion was, as I now realize, the tiny scarlet dot beside an atom of blue, like a crystal of salt and a peppercorn."

What is actually the subject matter of Goyen's landscapes? The sparse, barely vegetated dunes, the dilapidated wooden hovels, the marram grass, the scattered little figures busying themselves with who knows what? In order to find some indication of the answer, we must turn to other still lifes of the period in which reflections and the absorption of light on the surface of objects were gradually becoming the focal point of the picture, so that the sense of space and atmosphere created by the objects, rather than the objects themselves, had become the subject matter of the painting. This is also true of the landscapes of Jacob van Ruisdael. Dunes, water, hovels, trees, all gain their significance in their role as bearers of the pictorial subject matter: atmospheric light.

Though the word "atmosphere" may be used readily enough, it should first be defined. It is not so much a question of sentimentality as of melancholy. The things portrayed are mundane, decayed, ephemeral or they are the intangibly vast and sweeping spaces of sea and sky. As such, their importance lies less in the objects themselves than in their melancholy mutability. Trivial as they may be in themselves, their appearance is one of beauty.

We might even say, with some reservations, that certain elements of the vanitas still life can also be found in the landscape painting. There, as here, the objects are not only symbols of transience, but also things of beauty. The same may be said of the objects in a work by van Goyen or Ruisdael. The land and the marks of human labour may be ruined or decayed, but they radiate beauty. Such beauty is ephemeral, just as the lighting and atmosphere in this landscape are mutable.

Van Goyen left more than a thousand paintings and, along with Jacob van Ruisdael and Hobbema, ranks amongst the most important of Dutch landscape painters.

Jan van Goyen
Landscape with Dunes, c. 1630–1635
Oil on panel, 54 x 37.5 cm
Vienna, Kunsthistorisches Museum

Jan van Goyen
River Landscape, 1636
Oil on panel, 39.5 x 60 cm
Munich, Bayerische Staatsgemälde-
sammlungen, Alte Pinakothek

## PIETER CLAESZ.
### C. 1597/98–1661

**Pieter Claesz**
Still Life with Musical instruments, 1623
Oil on canvas, 69 x 122 cm
Paris, Musée National du Louvre

A certain dichotomy is often present in Dutch still lifes. On the one hand, we find a carefully composed arrangement of beautiful objects, yet on the other hand these things are "out of use", forgotten, almost coincidental, merely lying there. The picture itself is created through the brilliance and beauty of the surfaces and finishes, the reflections of light on glass and metal or, in this case, on the wooden body of the musical instruments. Certain Mannerist leanings can still be detected in the tense handling of space and perspectival depth, with a line of flight running from the large foreground objects to the tiny items in the background. Tradition would have it that the objects in such a still life have a specific statement to make: time passes in this vain and ephemeral earthly life. All is vanitas.

A great deal could be written about the individual metaphorical significance of the objects. Bread and wine are frequently intended as a worldly expression of the Eucharist. The flesh of a nut may be a sign of the divinity of Christ, its shell may stand for the cross, a pretzel may represent the fragility of human life, while a lemon may suggest the bitterness that lies within a thing of outward beauty; pleasure, it seems to say, may end bitterly.

Yet all the warnings that may be hidden in these things are undermined by the beauty of the same objects.

## THOMAS DE KEYSER
### C. 1596/97–1667

**Thomas de Keyser**
Equestrian Portrait of Pieter Schout, 1660
Oil on copper, 86 x 69.5 cm
Amsterdam, Rijksmuseum

The life-size equestrian portrait that found such widespread acceptance throughout the royal houses of Europe in the 17th century is rarely seen in Dutch art. The œuvre of Rembrandt and Potter includes only one example respectively. The republican attitudes prevailing in Holland seem to have been at odds with this feudal Baroque form of portrayal. On the other hand, we do find smaller equestrian portraits of wealthy burghers, especially in the work of Keyser.

In the summer of 1660, the ten-year-old Prince of Orange, later William III, visited Amsterdam with his mother Mary, daughter of Charles I of Great Britain, and entered the town in a magnificent parade of civic guards. Pieter Schout was also there and probably had this portrait painted to commemorate the event. He is mounted on his horse in noble garb with sparkling sword and yellow-brown doublet. The fine painting and tasteful colouring underline the noble attitude of this confident man. And yet his gaze seems to betray not so much the self-confidence of the ruler as the contemplative self-awareness of the citizen.

The amount of space taken up by landscape and sky is quite remarkable. The painting is not dominated by the central figure of the horseman and the space to which he is allocated. Indeed the horseman seems to have been set in the midst of a rural Dutch landscape.

# ANTHONY VAN DYCK
## 1599–1641

This painting of *Susanna and the Elders* was executed while van Dyck was in Italy, where he stayed until 1627. It clearly reflects the inspiration of Venetian painting. The deeply luminous colours, especially the strong red of Susanna's mantle, are reminiscent of Titian, while the dynamic contrasts of movement are influenced by Tintoretto. What is more, the portrayal as a whole owes much to Caravaggist trend that was at its height at the time. The way Susanna moves forward out of the dark background, in luminous flesh tones, and the way the heads of the two elderly men create the only light accent against the dark ground, are all reminiscent of the genre painting of Honthorst or Baburen during their Roman period.

Van Dyck deliberately calculated these effects. As Susanna recoils, chaste and anxious, from the lecherous old men, she turns towards the spectator who thus becomes her protector. Contacts of this kind in which the painting involves the spectator beyond the pictorial boundaries, are often found in the work of the Caravaggisti; another typical feature is the reduction of narrative to a detail involving only a few figures in a setting that is merely hinted at.

When the church of St Martin in Zaventem commissioned van Dyck to create an altarpiece in 1621, he sent them a painting that had probably been in his studio for some time and may well have been completed around 1618. The composition is based on a drawing by Rubens and is only one of many examples of the latter's seemingly inexhaustible reservoir of invention.

The legend of St Martin sharing his coat with a freezing beggar is portrayed here with great vigour and drama. The red cloth, one end of which the saint keeps for himself, giving the other end to the heroically naked beggar sitting in the straw, is almost cut through. The composition has been built up around this point in the action, and it is here that the lines of movement and action intersect. Even the horse adds to the pathos of the scene, lowering its head and raising its foreleg in a piaffe worthy of the *haute école* of dressage, so that the rider does not need to bend down. Although this early work does not display the full harmony of colour handling van Dyck was yet to achieve, the stark contrast of red and blue is successfully toned down by using a broad palette of greys for the body of the horse and the clothing of the two beggars.

For all his dependence on the painting of Rubens, certain differences are already quite clear. Whereas Rubens uses pathos formula to indicate some higher plane of significance, in this work by van Dyck they seem rather theatrical, as though performed by actors.

Anthony van Dyck
Susanna and the Elders,
c. 1621/22
Oil on canvas, 194 x 144 cm
Munich, Bayerische Staatsgemäldesammlungen, Alte
Pinakothek

*Below:*
**Anthony van Dyck**
St Martin Dividing his
Cloak , c. 1618
Oil on panel,
171.6 x 158 cm
Zaventem, St Martin

# ANTHONY VAN DYCK
## 1599–1641

Anthony van Dyck
Portrait of Maria Louisa de Tassis,
c. 1630
Oil on canvas, 130 x 93.5 cm
Vaduz, Fürst Liechtensteinische
Gemäldegalerie

The outward trappings of nobility are magnificent armour and sumptuous silks. Whereas, in the work of Rubens, colour is the expression of something deeply rooted in all things of the cosmos, colour is used in the work of van Dyck as a reflection of superficial beauty. The woman in this portrait was the daughter of a wealthy Antwerp patrician, and van Dyck painted her portrait before he left for London.

At the time of painting this portrait of the Duke of Arundel, van Dyck was already a favourite portraitist of the English nobility; it became *de rigueur* for anyone of rank and status to have their portrait painted by him. As court painter to the king, he developed compositional forms particularly suited to the requirements of his task, and in doing so he set a pattern that was to have a considerable influence until well into the 18th century.

Compositions featuring a landscape view on one side and a drapery or pillared architecture on the other originated in the religious painting of 16th century Venice. Van Dyck adopted these compositional forms and transferred them to courtly portraiture. Moreover, his backgrounds are imbued with a lyricism that clearly removes the subject matter from the banality of everyday life. Portraits of children were not only fashionable at the time, but also highly esteemed. The lyrical and even sentimental underlying atmosphere of this painting gave even the landed gentry and military men a touch of beauty and humanist intellect.

*Below:*
Anthony van Dyck
The Count of Arundel and his son
Thomas, 1636
Oil on canvas, 187 x 162 cm
Madrid, Museo del Prado

The Stuart monarch Charles I embodies Baroque absolutism as well as the traditional ideal of the cavalier. Firmly believing in the divine right of Kings, he regarded art as an excellent vehicle for presenting the monarch as the human embodiment of divine rule. CAROLUS/REX MAGNAE/BRITANIAE reads the inscription on the panel in the tree at the right.

Ever since Titian's equestrian portrait of the Emperor Charles V (1548; Madrid, Prado), landscape had established itself as a particular form for this kind of portrait. Rubens created one version and there is also a version by van Dyck dating from the early 1620s, showing Charles V on horseback. For his portrait of the British monarch, he returned to the same technique of placing the rider in a picturesque landscape with a distant view on one side and a shady tree on the other. In a previous equestrian portrait of the same king, the monarch is portrayed frontally under a triumphal arch. Here, the landscape itself becomes a triumphal motif.

Anthony van Dyck
Equestrian Portrait of Charles I,
c. 1635–1640
Oil on canvas, 367 x 292.1 cm
London, National Gallery

Salomon van Ruysdael
The Crossing at Nimwegen, 1647
Oil on canvas, 70 x 89 cm
Bonn, Rheinisches Landesmuseum

## SALOMON VAN RUYSDAEL
### c. 1600/03–1670

Although this painting portrays a flat river-scape with a city on its banks, the topographical situation of the Waal near Nimwegen is not entirely precise. Instead, Ruysdael combines individual elements also featured on some of his other paintings, such as the "Plompetoren" of Utrecht, whose tower was demolished in the 18th century. The artist is interested less in a faithful rendering of a certain geographic situation than in presenting the Netherlandish riverscape in the Rhine-Maas delta.

The river is broad and slow. Sailing boats and cargo tugs lie almost motionless on its mirror-smooth surface. In the muddy waters of a tongue of land, fishermen have cast out their nets and, slightly further into the distance, we see cattle standing in the shallow water near the riverbank. Right across the foreground of the painting, a ferry is crossing the river carrying a few passengers, two cows and two horses, with their riders still in the saddle. One of them is signalling his arrival with a trumpet blast.

This visible acoustic signal underlines the quiet calm of the landscape, emphasizing the fact that this tranquillity is in itself the actual subject matter of the painting. The colours of the painting are broken greys and blues, creating a tonality that makes everything appear as though seen through a veil of haze.

## PIETER JANSZ. SAENREDAM
### 1597–1665

This painting shows the interior of the Jakobikerk in Utrecht, built between the 14th and 15th centuries. Saenredam prepared the painting in a number of sketches and structural drawings.

Whereas earlier interiors tended to correspond more or less with the spectator's view into the painting, so that the picture frame acted as an introduction to the architecture portrayed, Saenredam has objectified the interior. Although Saenredam does not portray a diagonal detail of the room in which the movement of light is present, such as we find later in the work of de Witte, the painting nevertheless derives its sense of an interior through the handling of light and space rather than through perspective alone. The man walking alone with his dog seems almost lost in the church, further underlining the independence of the architecture as a motif. In contrast to the so-called "atmospheric interiors" of the following generation, Saenredam's interiors are described as "realistic spaces". What is meant by this, is that such rooms did not serve as a foil for something else, but were actually an independent, pictorial object. These were, to all intents and purposes, portraits, and were not adapted to fit in with any external compositional structure. In the work of Saenredam, the sparse colority and dry linearity of the architectural subject are fascinating.

Pieter Jansz.
Saenredam
Church Interior in
Utrecht, 1642
Oil on panel,
55.2 x 43.4 cm
Munich,
Bayerische
Staatsgemälde-
sammlungen,
Alte Pinakothek

# ADRIAEN BROUWER

c. 1605/06–1638

In the work of Brouwer, who was born in Flanders and lived in Amsterdam and Haarlem before returning to Antwerp, we find a blend of Flemish and Dutch traditions. His influence on both parts of the Netherlands was considerable. Whereas his rough peasant types recall the work of Pieter Brueghel, the sheer vitality with which he presents human emotions such as pain, rage or humour, are reminiscent of Frans Hals, in whose studio he worked for a time.

The elements Brouwer adopted from the peasant scenes and parables of Brueghel were still new to the Dutch art world. Yet his paintings did not possess the many-layered meanings of 16th century pictorial narratives, being reduced instead to drastic and edifying individual anecdotes whose very conciseness was echoed in their small format. They are cabinet pieces whose effect owes much to their ability to capture a sense of great vitality in sweeping painterly gestures on a tiny area.

Around the turn of the 17th century, allegories tended to take the form of personifications with appropriate attributes. Now, however, they began to take the form of realistic scenes apparently drawn from everyday life. The anecdotal "genre" style distracts from the original underlying message of a "truth" or proverb which is invariably present in Netherlandish paintings. Often, these tell the parable of the prodigal son, using it as a vehicle for the presentation of brothel scenes or taverns with singing and brawling peasants.

Bearing this in mind, paintings can occasionally be interpreted in ways that are not immediately obvious. The popular motif of the *Barber-Surgeon* in which we see someone having a painful corn cut out of his foot borrows the iconographic forms normally used in portrayals of Christian martyrdom, a fact which does not prevent Brouwer from taking his portrayal of the characters to the point of caricature. Such adaptations can frequently be found in the work of the Utrecht school around the turn of the 17th century, where there were contacts with Italian painting, especially with the realistic chiaroscuro painting of Caravaggio.

Though Brouwer's paintings are not always part of a series, they do generally belong to the category of "five senses" pictures. Just as the "foot surgery" we see here represents the sense of touch, so too do the brawling, drunken or smoking peasants represent embodiments of taste and smell rather than pure genre portrayals. In Antwerp, the dens where people went to savour the forbidden pleasures of tobacco were known as "tabagie". Through the short clay pipes, the smokers would inhale so much nicotine that they not only experienced an intoxicating rush, but sometimes even suffered serious poisoning.

**Adriaen Brouwer**
The Operation, undated
Oil on panel, 31.4 x 39.6cm
Munich, Bayerische Staatsgemälde-
sammlungen, Alte Pinakothek

**Adriaen Brouwer**
Peasants Smoking and
Drinking, c. 1635
Oil on panel, 35 x 26cm
Munich, Bayerische
Staatsgemäldesammlun-
gen, Alte Pinakothek

Rembrandt Harmensz. van Rijn
The Artist in his Studio, c. 1626–1628
Oil on canvas, 25.5 x 32 cm
Boston (MA), Museum of Fine Arts

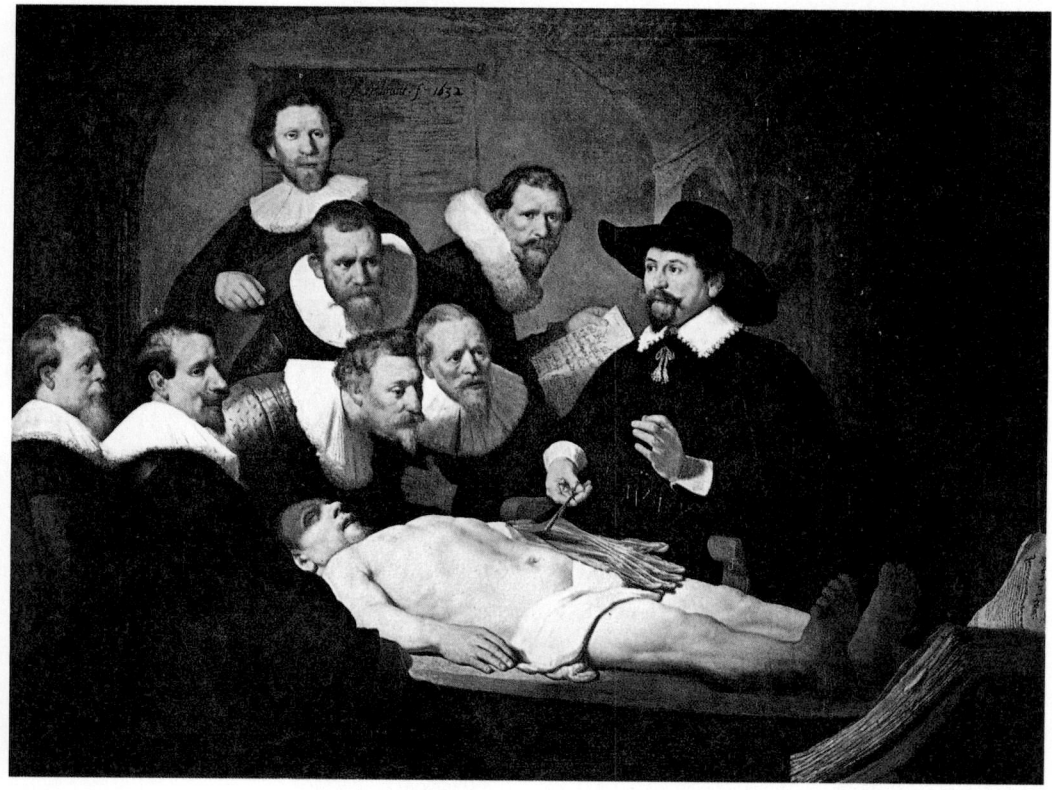

Rembrandt Harmensz. van Rijn
The Anatomy Lesson of Dr. Nicolaes Tulp, 1632
Oil on canvas, 162.5 x 216.5 cm
The Hague, Mauritshuis

# REMBRANDT
## 1606–1669

While he was still in Leiden, the young Rembrandt painted himself as an artist in front of his easel, in what was to be the first of many artist self-portraits in Holland. This form of portrait provided an opportunity of presenting the professional status and lifestyle of the artist. For this, Rembrandt chose a highly unusual form.

We see the painter standing before us in extravagant garb, wearing an oversized coat as though in a masquerade. Vermeer's later studio painting (ill. p. 334) also shows the artist dressed in finery that indicates his status as master of a noble art rather than that of a simple craftsman. When Rembrandt adopts the stance of the well-dressed artist – which has a tradition going back all the way to Leonardo da Vinci – he seems to call it into question at the same time by lending it the air of a masquerade. This interpretation would seem to be borne out by the fact that the studio itself is sparse and poorly furnished. The artist standing in these bare surroundings looks rather lost, confronted with his canvas on the easel. All we see of it is the back of the painting, submerged in shadow; the light bathing the front of the canvas reflects into the room.

The same light in otherwise dark rooms can also be found in the young Rembrandt's portrayals of biblical miracles which take on a sense of the supernatural; it is an artistic device adopted from the Caravaggisti. Here, the light makes the painting on the easel light up as though from within. Small and forlorn in his humble surroundings, the young artist faces the great challenge of art.

This group portrait shows a famous Amsterdam physician surrounded by colleagues, students and interested onlookers in the rare and spectacular act of giving an anatomy lesson. The first known treatment of this subject is a painting by Keyser dated 1619. Whereas earlier anatomy lessons tended to use a skeleton, here the subject is a corpse. The dead man has been laid out as in portrayals of the Lamentation over the Body of Christ.

Anatomical lectures involving the dissection of a corpse were rare occurrences for which entry fees were levied and they met with enormous interest. Only one such lecture is documented in Amsterdam in the year 1632, when this painting was executed. The corpse is the body of a hanged gunsmith. The composition of the painting in which the audience (their names are recorded on the sheet of paper one of them is holding in his hand) are grouped in a semicircle around the head of the corpse, while Tulp stands slightly to one side, is an innovative approach: Rembrandt does not simply document the momentary situation of an anatomy lesson in progress, but creates a symbolic image. This is evident from the fact that the arm muscles of the corpse are rendered in the manner of a drawing from a book of anatomy. Andreas Vesalius, the great 16th century physician and founder of modern anatomy had published just such a book. We find it here, propped up open at the feet of the corpse.

Probably Rembrandt's most famous and most controversial painting was given its errounious title *The Night Watch* in the early 19th century. The title referred to the subdued lighting and led art critics to seek all manner of hidden mysteries in the painting. The original title, recorded in the still extant family chronicle of Captain Banning Cocq, together with a sketch of the painting, sounds rather dry by comparison: "Sketch of the painting from the Great Hall of Cleveniers Doelen, in which the young Heer van Purmerlandt [Banning Cocq], as captain, orders his lieutenant, the Heer van Vlaerderdingen [Willem van Ruytenburch], to march the company out."

It is, therefore, a "Doelen" piece or group portrait in which the captain can be seen in the foreground wearing black and the lieutenant wearing yellow. What sets Rembrandt's group portrait apart from other comparable paintings is his use of chiaroscuro as a dramatic device. Interpretations seeking a plausible action fail to take into account that the scenery is made up more or less of individual "types". For example, the horseman with helmet and lance turns up again as *Alexander The Great* (Glasgow, Art Gallery) and we can also find the *Man with the Golden Helmet* (Berlin, Gemäldegalerie; recently no longer attributed to Rembrandt) in the *Night Watch*. Indeed, the painting includes the entire repertoire of portrait poses and gestures from Rembrandt's store of figures.

There is inevitably a sense of celebration in the portrayal of individuals in a Dutch group painting. Yet whereas Frans Hals, for example, draws together his individual participants around a banquet scene, Rembrandt breaks up the group, so that individual characters and participants become absorbed in their own actions, each standing alone.

**Rembrandt Harmensz. van Rijn**
The Night Watch (The Company of Captain Frans Banning Cocq and of Lieutnant Willem van Ruytenburgh), 1642
Oil on canvas, 363 x 437 cm
Amsterdam, Rijksmuseum

# REMBRANDT
## 1606–1669

This self-portrait painted by Rembrandt in the year of his death is an image of passiveness, resignation, scepticism and irony. The blustering show of props and artistic affectation has given way to a more humble and homely mode of dress. The portrait underlines all that is personal, withdrawn, lonely and even eccentric about this elderly man. The brushwork seems deliberately rough and cumbersome, as though details were unimportant. The paint is applied so thickly that it creates an almost relief-like surface and the image of the ageing artist seems to be disintegrating before our very eyes. The colour itself, on the other hand, has a stabilizing effect; a deep and brilliant red shimmers through the brown ground with profound luminosity. Whereas all that constitutes form seems to be caught in the grasp of mortality and decay, and while even the brushwork seems brittle and crumbling, the strength of the underlying colour tells of life and hope.

In his *Descent from the Cross* which is part of a cycle depicting the Passion of Christ commissioned by the stadholder of the Netherlands, Rembrandt cites the altarpiece painted by Rubens for Antwerp Cathedral. A comparison of these two works can give us some interesting insights into his specific painterly technique. The strong contrast between the dark ground and the use of light is not used to heighten the pathos and drama of the Passion, but to underline the very human aspect of suffering and pain in the face of death. Light is not used here to divide the darkness, for the artist does not seek to present the triumph of light over the forces of darkness, but to portray the wan pallor of the shroud and the waxen skin of the dead Christ. In the chiaroscuro of Rembrandt's early works, light is not so much a sign of the supernatural as an emphasis of worldly reality.

There is something deeply disturbing about this painting. The bloody, fatty mass of the *Slaughtered Ox* seems to fill the canvas in the manner of a still life with a certain aesthetic appeal. This is in fact an increasing feature of Rembrandt's later works. The subject matter, even in portraiture or history painting, is either treated with a brushwork of almost brutal vigour and subverted to the point of unleashing the brilliance of the underlying colour – especially red – or else, as here, he chooses to portray a subject matter that has inherently the same subversive effect, as luminous as the finest still life. This particular example also illustrates the role played by the brownish background colour in Rembrandt's work. There is nothing colourful about this background brown, and yet it seems to harbour within its depths an inherent luminosity and colority that can burst forth at any moment.

Rembrandt Harmensz. van Rijn
Self-portrait aged 63, 1669
Oil on canvas, 86 x 70.5 cm
London, National Gallery

Rembrandt Harmensz. van Rijn
The Descent from the Cross, 1633
Oil on panel,
89.4 x 65.2 cm
Munich, Bayerische Staatsgemäldesammlungen, Alte Pinakothek

Rembrandt Harmensz. van Rijn
The Slaughtered Ox, 1655
Oil on panel, 94 x 67 cm
Paris, Musée National du Louvre

**Rembrandt Harmensz. van Rijn**
The Syndics of the Amsterdam
Clothmakers' Guild (The Syndics), 1662
Oil on canvas, 191.5 x 279 cm
Amsterdam, Rijksmuseum

**Rembrandt Harmensz. van Rijn**
Aristotle Contemplating the Bust of Homer, 1653
Oil on canvas, 143.5 x 136.5 cm
New York, The Metropolitan Museum of Art

## REMBRANDT
### 1606–1669

Behind a table draped in a red tapestry, with a finely panelled wall in the background, sit the five "Staalmeesters". This is probably a committee of the clothmakers' guild, the "Waardijns van de Lakenen" who were in charge of inspecting the quality of the cloth samples. We know their names and the name of the servant standing in the background. On the back wall, we can just make out a small oil painting depicting a lighthouse as a metaphor for model behaviour and "lighting the right way".

As in the last two group portraits by Frans Hals dated 1664, Rembrandt also reduces drama and scenery (at its most lavish in his *Night Watch*) to a minimum. The pathos formula and showy stances have all but disappeared. For example, the "waardijn" second from the left is half standing and half sitting, and the gentleman next to him is quietly explaining something in the ledger. The lack of scenic interaction isolates the individuals.

For many years, this painting was wrongly interpreted. It was believed that the commission of cloth inspectors had to defend themselves against accusations, and that one of them was drawing up a bill, while another was greedily grasping the money bag. Such an interpretation of this painting could hardly be further from the truth. In fact, it is actually intended to show five men with a firm sense of responsibility, forming a group in which the individuality of each is more important than any pathos-laden dramatic scene. The main distinction between this group painting and the earlier *Night Watch*, however, is the reduction of vitality in the overall movement and the distance created between the group and the spectator.

*Aristotle Contemplating the Bust of Homer* was commissioned in 1653 by the Sicilian nobleman Don Antonio Ruffo, who paid Rembrandt five hundred guilders for it, about four times the price of a comparable Italian painting. Later, Don Ruffo also commissioned two further paintings, one of *Alexander the Great* and one of *Homer*. The plastercast of the antique Homer bust was in Rembrandt's home.

The pensive philosopher has placed his hand on the bald stone forehead of the poet. It is an encounter across the bounds of time, a meeting of minds, symbolized by the warm light that glows between the two figures. The bust seems to come alive, just as the objects in a Dutch vanitas still life speak to us.

At the same time, the living figure of Aristotle is drawn into the past; with an introverted and contemplative gaze. The blind eyes of Homer and the seeing eyes of Aristotle meet directly, as it were, and at the point where their gaze meets, the light of the painting is strongest.

## JAN DAVIDSZ. DE HEEM
1606–c. 1683/84

De Heem's still life paintings initially followed the style of the Haarlem school, but later drew closer to the more lavish Flemish style of large-scale still lifes. Nevertheless, certain Dutch elements cannot be overlooked. In this painting, they are particularly evident at the points where a "dialectical principle" determines the compositional structure.

A mass of fruit and flowers ranging from ripe chestnuts to blackberries, from columbine to roses, has been arranged on a stone slab. A wide variety of surfaces, each with a different effect in light, with pure or iridescent colours, is spread out before us. Yet snails are already crawling across the vine leaves, the foliage is discoloured and withering and, the ears of grain are curling, the peach has burst its skin, the citrus fruit is half peeled, the white carnation is dried and drooping over the table edge.

At the very point where the image bears an iconographic message of the transience of worldly life in the form of nature's riches, we see these things in their last bloom of beauty. Just as a ruin could represent the picturesque appeal of architecture, so too can a vine leaf riddled with snails seem picturesque in the full and final flowering of its beauty.

Jan Davidsz. de Heem
Still Life, undated
Oil on panel, 55.8 x 73.5 cm
Gent, Museum voor Schone Kunsten

## JUDITH LEYSTER
1609–1660

Judith Leyster is one of the very few women to have been accepted as a member of the Haarlem Guild of Painters. Although a contemporary historian described her as a leading light in art (punning on her name Leyster, which means "lodestar") she remained unknown for a long time and her works were either believed lost, or were attributed to Frans Hals. She probably worked in his studio around 1630 and was also a friend of his family, for one year later she became godmother to Hals' daughter Maria.

Like Hals at the same time, the young Leyster adopted the style of the Utrecht Caravaggisti, with their strong chiaroscuro modelling in the manner of Caravaggio. From the mid-1620s, she concentrated more on vividly illuminated genre scenes, generally featuring half figures of merry musicians, gamblers and whores, strongly influenced by the painting of Terbrugghen and Honthorst.

While the Utrecht school of painters still rounded the surfaces of their objects smoothly between light and shade, Hals and his school adopted a broad, vibrant and independent brushstroke. Leyster's work can be distinguished from that of Hals through her generally more discordant handling of colour, her sketchier treatment of hands, the wryly distorted smiles of her figures and her altogether flightier brushwork.

Judith Leyster
Carousing Couple, 1630
Oil on canvas,
68 x 54 cm
Paris, Musée National
du Louvre

**Jan Asselijn**
Italian Landscape with the Ruins of a Roman
Bridge and Aqueduct, undated
Oil on canvas, 67 x 82 cm
Amsterdam, Rijksmuseum

**Frans Post**
Hacienda, 1652
Oil on panel, 45 x 65 cm
Mainz, Mittelrheinisches Landesmuseum

## JAN ASSELIJN
### 1610–1652

Asselijn studied for some time in France and
Rome. On his return to Amsterdam, he specialized in painting animals and Italianate
landscapes, which occupied a firm place in
Dutch painting. Motifs of the Roman Campagna, ruins, rocks and castles generally dominate his settings peopled with riders and herdsmen. Yet his works owe less to real landscapes
than to painterly tradition. Some typical features of the work by this Italianate Dutch artist are the way he bathes his landscapes in atmospherically "romantic" golden hues influenced by Claude Lorrain's handling of light,
or adopts picturesque motifs in the manner of
Salvator Rosa.

Italianate as they may be, these paintings
are nevertheless easily identifiable as the work
of a Dutch artist, for the genre generally lacks
the pathos formula of the Baroque and the antique ruins tend to blend into the rest of the
landscape like elements in a still life. The
genre components can be found in the procession of mules, their riders and the figures
on the bridge.

Like a piece of broken bread or a cracked
earthenware jug, the ruins unfurl their melancholy beauty in the tranquil evening light, recalling the transience of earthly life in a
highly aesthetic way.

## FRANS POST
### 1612–1680

From 1637 to 1644, Post accompanied the
retinue of Prince Johan Maurits of Nassau
Siegen to Brazil, where he painted the landscape around Pernambuco and on a number of
oceanic islands, as well as genre scenes of local
life. This Dutch artist's sensitivity to specific
situations, landscape and people make Post's
Brazilian paintings an invaluable source of information regarding not only the flora and
fauna of the region, but also the dress and customs of the time.

On his return, Post settled in Haarlem and,
like all his Dutch colleagues, he specialized,
concentrating especially on tropical and exotic
views. In his paintings, we note that, although
he supplies details and specific information
about this far-off land, the paintings themselves are nevertheless organized along the
lines of conventional Dutch landscape paintings. The gaze of the spectator is drawn from
the foreground into the depths of the landscape. This distant view with atmospheric
changes and a large proportion of sky, are typical features of Dutch painting. Genre-type
figures are also included in the compositional
structure of these Brazilian scenes.

## ADRIAEN VAN OSTADE
### 1610–1685

Ostade's paintings of the 1630s bear eloquent witness to the influence of the early Rembrandt. Although Ostade studied in the Haarlem studio of Hals at the same time as Brouwer, the chiaroscuro of his paintings owes much to Rembrandt. Even his genre scenes of decayed and dilapidated inns and hovels, almost the sole motif in Ostade's œuvre, are to be found in the work of Rembrandt. For this reason, we should take any assertion that these paintings of brawling and drunken peasants represent everyday Dutch life with a considerable pinch of salt. A more likely explanation is that they represent a highly popular subject with a long tradition that had eventually developed into an independent genre.

In his early work, Ostade set his scenes in dark rooms using meticulously staged lighting. The handling of light and the humble architecture derive from the tradition of portraying the stable at Bethlehem. These peasant genre paintings were almost certainly aimed at an urban audience which saw its prejudices and clichéd notions of primitive and oafish peasant life confirmed by such caricatures and which could also appreciate the particular humour of such a painting. This perceived humour lay to some extent in the notion of "wasting" sophisticated artistic skills on such lowly motifs.

Adriaen van Ostade
Peasants Carousing in a Tavern, c. 1635
Oil on panel, 28.8 x 36.3 cm
Munich, Bayerische Staatsgemälde-
sammlungen, Alte Pinakothek

## DAVID TENIERS The Younger
### 1610–1690

Teniers was the most popular genre painter of the 17th century in Antwerp and the southern Netherlands – the Flemish counterpart to the Dutch artists Steen and Ostade. This painting of a *Twelfth Night* celebration is from his early period, the 1630s, in which we can still recognize the distinct influence of Adriaen Brouwer's genre paintings. Later, when Teniers became court painter and curator of the art collection of stadholder Archduke Leopold Wilhelm in Brussels, he painted vedutas and galleries full of people.

From the 16th century onwards, particularly in the Netherlands, but also elsewhere, Twelfth Night (January 6) was celebrated in the form of a so-called "bean feast". A bean was baked into a cake and the person who found it became the Bean King. This provided ample opportunity for raucous travesties of courtly ceremonies. Here, we see a Flemish household boisterously roaring the traditional toast "The King drinks!"

Teniers' painting differs from comparable Dutch presentations of the same theme in its obvious leanings towards the work of Pieter Brueghel the Elder, whose daughter he had married, as well as in the number of figures in the narrative. Similar Twelfth Night scenes in the work of Ostade or Metsus tend to concentrate more on the one particular aspect of the "bean feast" and are often more brightly illuminated.

David Teniers the Younger
Twelfth Night (The King Drinks), c. 1634–1640
Oil on canvas, 58 x 70 cm
Madrid, Museo del Prado

**Gerard Dou**
The Dropsical Lady
(The Doctor's Visit),
c. 1663 (?)
Oil on panel, 86 x 67 cm
Paris, Musée National
du Louvre

## GERARD DOU
### 1613–1675

Gerard Dou was the leading representative of
the Leiden "fine painters". In his work, the
longstanding Netherlandish tradition of the
meticulously detailed rendering of objects,
painted using a fine brush and a magnifying
glass, is blended with the Dutch love of *trompe-
l'œil*.

Dou, originally a stained glass artist, was renowned for his technique of illusion, created
by painting such objects as draperies or window openings in the foreground in such a way
that they appeared to belong to the spectator's
sphere. These objects – and in particular the
light falling on their surfaces – are painted
with the finest of brushes.

Dou has a preference for genre scenes and
interiors. As in the work of Steen, these generally involve some moral, parable or joke. This
particular painting, which hangs in the
Louvre, is entitled *The Dropsical Lady*. The
title is almost certainly a later fabrication, and
*The Doctor's Visit* is much more appropriate.
Here, we see a doctor holding a urine sample
up to the light. In most paintings of this kind,
the joke lies in the fact that the woman who
thinks she is sick is being given a pregnancy
test. The urine glass and its contents are illuminated as in a still life, and the doctor is
looking at it as though enraptured by a vision,
while the servant and daughter bewail the patient.

**Emanuel de Witte**
Church Interior,
c. 1660
Oil on canvas,
80 x 66 cm
St Petersburg,
Hermitage

## EMANUEL DE WITTE
### c. 1617–1692

Witte was evidently a representative of the
Delft school, even though he originally came
from Alkmaar and later settled in Amsterdam.
His church interiors bear comparison in many
respects with the work of Vermeer, in that the
light falling into the room is actually the subject matter of the painting.

The evolution of Witte's work sheds some
light on the practice of Dutch artists' specialization. Having initially tried his hand at genre
scenes and portraiture, he eventually settled for
church interiors, rendering the play of light and
wandering shadows on parts of the high, pillared architecture. The Haarlem painter Saenredam preceeded him in creating views that present not only the function and size of an architectural interior, but also its actual state. The work
of Witte has often been described as "atmospheric", indicating that, in his paintings, the
structure of the architecture is secondary to the
momentary appearance of the interior in the respective conditions of light.

This view of architecture no longer follows
the perspectives prescribed by the building,
but is determined as though by chance. Diagonals, corners and overlaps are the rule rather
than the exception. Light falling on certain
components is reflected as in a still life.

# GERARD TERBORCH
## 1617–1681

After mid-century, Dutch genre and social painting changed. There was a shift towards more noble and semi-courtly society. In purely formal terms, the subtle treatment of textures and portrayal of a diversity of materials and surfaces became increasingly important. Terborch, who was of Vermeer's generation, typically embodies this last significant phase of Dutch genre painting that spans the period from about 1650 to 1680.

In his painting *The Card-Players*, we still find echoes of the Caravaggisti and the Utrecht school, which influenced not only the theme, but also the handling of light. Otherwise, however, it differs distinctly from similar paintings by Terbrugghen or Hals.

The woman in the foreground has her back to us. Silent, pensive and concentrated, the man standing beside her reaches out to grasp her cards, the player opposite her looks on silently, but attentively. In the work of the Caravaggisti, the players would have played towards us, the spectators, and the card game would have prompted some action with consequences. In this painting by Terborch, there is neither drama nor pathos in the card game.

The same is true of *The Letter*. A young man, dressed in all the finery of a cavalier, has entered the living-room to delivery a letter to the elegantly dressed lady. She, however, recoils, concealing her hand beneath her cloak rather than reaching out to take the letter. Her servant looks astonished, and the lady's lapdog barks at the courier.

To insiders, the meaning is clear: the letter is a love letter. The bed in the background says it all. The lady, however, is virtuous and chaste, as the still life objects on the table indicate: washbasin, ewer and brush are all signs of her purity and cleanliness, though the mirror and pearls suggest vanity. A tale begins to unfold.

The pictorial narrative expresses a moment of tension and a turning point in the story. It is not clear what will happen next. What is the courier to do with the letter? The lady has hidden her hand. The servant is waiting. This is not the climax of the story, but the moment we might describe as the "still life point" when, in Dutch paintings, everything, objects and people alike, seems to stop for a moment.

Terborch was also a talented portraitist. His skill in portraying subtle surface textures also stood him in good stead in rendering carefully observed individual traits. "Attentiveness" was frequently cited as a key feature of Dutch group portraits and it can certainly be detected in the faces of Terborch's characters. The "five senses" are attentive and alert.

**Gerard Terborch**
The Card-Players,
c. 1650
Oil on panel,
25.5 x 20 cm
Winterthur,
Sammlung Reinhart

**Gerard Terborch**
The Letter, c. 1655
Oil on panel,
56 x 46.5 cm
Munich,
Bayerische
Staatsgemälde-
sammlungen,
Alte Pinakothek

**Philips Koninck**
Village on a Hill, 1651
Oil on canvas, 61 x 83 cm
Winterthur, Sammlung Reinhart

**Willem Kalf**
Still Life, c. 1653/54
Oil on canvas, 105 x 87.5 cm
St Petersburg, Hermitage

## PHILIPS KONINCK
### 1619–1688

Koninck is one of the last generation of Dutch landscape painters. In the 1660s, there was a general tendency to "upgrade" the various genres. During this period, the interiors of Vermeer and de Hooch became increasingly elegant, and even the still lifes were freighted with "noblesse". In the work of Koninck, this trend even affected the landscapes, in which he positioned courtly figures and palatial architecture.

In the 1650s, by contrast, when Koninck was at the height of his creative powers, he produced landscapes of exceptional purity, bringing the flat panoramic landscape to its greatest perfection. A soft and golden light is cast across the flat countryside, illuminating things that are, in themselves, uninteresting: sandy dunes, the occasional tree, some water, a village. There is nothing remarkable or jarring. The sensation is where the brown earth is bathed in sunlight to a golden hue.

Koninck was influenced by Rembrandt's landscape painting, which represents a chapter in its own right within his enormous œuvre. Rembrandt's influence is evident in the golden-brown tone of his paintings and in the way Koninck occasionally integrates unexpected and fantastic objects such as a glittering bridge spanning the water, a ruin or a fairy-tale castle.

## WILLEM KALF
### 1619–1693

Kalf's magnificent still lifes vary little in their structure, and most of them feature similar objects. A damask cloth or tapestry is draped upon a table on which there is sumptuous tableware, with gold and silver vessels, many of which have actually been identified as the work of specific goldsmiths such as Jan Lutmas. There is almost always a Chinese porcelain bowl, often tilted so that the beautiful fruits tumble out of it.

Nevertheless, it would be wrong to speak of "movement" in the still lifes of Kalf. The objects in his paintings possess a fragile equilibrium, and any suggestion of dynamic movement is reminiscent of a Flemish still lifes with its narrative component. However, in these still lifes, the painting is reduced to its contents alone and to the portrayal of the objects' beauty, captured at a single moment in time. They are brought to life by a seeming paradox. The objects are arranged almost coincidentally, in the manner of a vanitas painting: a half-peeled lemon, a loaf from which a piece has already been broken. At the same time, they are skilfully arranged, and it is this ordered coincidence that adds to their aesthetic appeal. The painterly technique recalls the work of Vermeer, another artist who portrays the appearance of light on the surfaces of objects in glittering points of luminosity and grainy precipitation.

## AELBERT CUYP
1620–1691

This portrayal of three brooding hens and a proudly prancing cockerel guarding them jealously might be described as a genre painting from the world of birds. Dutch art lovers saw in it something familiar and amusing. The hens are resting contentedly in the sand, having pecked at some leftover fish and shells. Only the cockerel is posing, otherwise all is calm, and we can almost hear the drowsy cackling of the hens.

The scene bears certain similarities with the kind of conversation piece in which a gentleman courts a lady. There seems to be a lengthy pause in the conversation, and the light falling on the objects, the sand and the feathers has taken over the action.

Cuyp was a specialist in animal and landscape painting. His landscapes are regarded as his masterpieces for the manner in which the objects in them are transfigured by a warm, golden light. It was this skill that earned him the nick-name "the Dutch Claude Lorrain". His animal paintings also show his talent for creating atmosphere through the handling of light on objects. Cuyp left a considerable œuvre, yet recognition of his artistic achievement came late in the Netherlands, even though his work was highly esteemed in England.

Aelbert Cuyp
Rooster and Hens,
undated
Oil on panel,
48 x 45 cm
Ghent, Museum
voor Schone
Kunsten

Abraham van Beyeren
Still Life with Lobster, 1653
Oil on canvas, 125.5 x 105 cm
Munich, Bayerische Staatsgemälde-
sammlungen, Alte Pinakothek

## ABRAHAM VAN BEYEREN
c. 1620/21–1690

Although still life paintings were a prominent feature of Flemish painting, as in the great decorative pieces by Snyders, they did not become widespread in the Dutch art world until after mid-century. Just as conversation pieces by such artists as Metsu or de Hooch became increasingly noble, so too did the still lifes. In the work of Beyeren, we find sumptuous goldsmithing and expensive fruits in magnificent arrangements, with the dignified forms of a column and a drape in the background.

The open pocket-watch placed almost coincidentally amidst the fruit is clearly allegorical. It recalls time passing. Yet the very character of this arrangement of diverse objects suggests that the trappings of Luxuria had already by this time become aesthetic objects in their own right.

In keeping with the trend towards "nobility" in Dutch painting at the time, the portrayal of objects becomes harsher, the contours sharper and the surface smoother. In the work of Beyeren, no great distinction is made between the various materials, the handling of light is brash and rather schematic. The atmospheric touch so important to Dutch painting is barely discernible here.

Carel Fabritius
The Goldfinch, 1654
Oil on panel, 33.5 x 22.8 cm
The Hague, Mauritshuis

*Below:*
**Paulus Potter**
Peasant Family with Animals, 1646
Oil on panel, 37.1 x 29.5 cm
Munich, Bayerische Staatsgemälde-
sammlungen, Alte Pinakothek

## CAREL FABRITIUS
### 1622–1654

Originally, this picture of a captured bird was probably painted on a cupboard door, as was often the case with *trompe-l'œil* paintings, including portrayals of letter-holders and writing implements. What was important was the effect of making the objects seem close enough to touch, and so realistic that they might be mistaken for real objects. Something of this imitation of reality can also be found in this painting of a goldfinch sitting on its perch. It is not portrayed in a room, but in front of a surface which would appear to be the front plane of the picture. This notion of painting as imitation is a distinctive feature of Dutch painting.

Another important element is the fact that not only objects, but also living creatures – animals and sometimes even people – could be portrayed with the calm immobility of still life. Here, the captive bird has become still and is merely present. If it were a person, we might use the words "introverted" or "contemplative".

By choosing a brightly lit background, against which the object stands out clearly, Fabritius distances himself from his teacher Rembrandt, who preferred dark-toned backgrounds. In doing so, he paved the way for the handling of light by his most famous student: Jan Vermeer.

## PAULUS POTTER
### 1625–1654

Potter, who died of consumption at the age of 29, loved the meadows, pastures and broad flatlands of his Dutch homeland, which he, like Jan van Goyen, portrayed bathed in warm sunlight. Perhaps his preference for bright and welcoming landscapes can be traced back to his Italianate contemporaries, such as Karel Dujardin, though he himself never actually visited Italy.

Potter specialized in animal painting, painstakingly detailed portraits of goats, sheep and, most notably, cows, which he presents in peasant surroundings. His most famous painting, the life-size *Young Steer* (The Hague, Mauritshuis) still astonishes spectators with its almost pedantic and obsessive detail.

The landscape, above which an atmospheric cloudy sky rises, is bathed in brownish-golden sunlight. In the foreground are the grazing animals, each one lovingly characterized and portrayed in typical pose, like people around a table in a group portrait. They are neither ornamentation nor mere staffage, but rather the main motif, taking precedence over space and landscape. Towards the end of the 19th century, Potter's art was renowned as "cabinet painting", particularly in England. Johan Heinrich Wilhelm Tischbein copied this painting in a watercolour study.

# JAN STEEN
## c. 1625/26–1679

Amongst the genre scenes that brought Steen popularity and fame, there are almost twenty showing a doctor's visit to a bourgeois home. As theatrical as any *Commedia dell'arte* play, they present scenes full of misunderstandings, secrets, assumptions and indiscretions. The "illnesses" of the patients are generally unforeseen pregnancy or lovesickness. The bed with the painting of lovers hanging over it, and the statue of Amor on the draughtscreen of the door immediately indicate to the spectator what is going on. The basin of coals in the foreground with the burning thread – quack doctors diagnosed pregnancy by "reading" the smoke – and the maid with her suitor at the door are further typical features of this genre. The patient, whose pulse the doctor is counting, has a note in her hand on which the following words are written: "Daar baat gen/medesyn/want het is/minepeyn" ("No medicine can cure the pain of love").

Though hardly a profound insight, these words constitute a moral of the kind that is almost invariably to be found behind these types of Dutch paintings. For all the autonomy of the subject matter, a painting without such a "deeper" meaning would have been inconceivable at the time, and indeed did not actually emerge until the 19th century.

Almost a century before Hogarth was to address a similar theme in England, Jan Steen created this painting of a fun-loving young couple letting their hair down. Drunk and sprawling in a most unmannerly way, but dressed in the very latest fashion, they are seated in the foreground. For the prim elderly couple lecturing him with their pious words from a book, the young man has only a mocking smile. Steen, although he worked for some time as a publican, was a pious Catholic. The house is extremely untidy. The servant has fallen asleep, the children are running free and the dog is stealing food from the table. A duck has alighted on the shoulder of the moral preacher and a pig is gobbling waste from the floor.

On the surface of it, this genre painting would appear to show a scene of utter chaos. On another level, however, it contains a number of morals. The panel on the steps at the right bears the inscription: "In weelde siet toe" (roughly equivalent to "better wit than wealth"). The basket hanging high and the precious things cast before swine are all references to morals and proverbs.

In this respect, the painting takes its place in a longstanding tradition that began even before Brueghel's proverb paintings. In the work of Steen, however, the painting can be regarded on different levels. The spectator can interpret the chaos as a collection of wise proverbs, but at the same time the drama and comedy of the situation can be seen as a source of pleasure and enjoyment in painting for its own sake.

Jan Steen
The Lovesick Woman, c. 1660
Oil on canvas, 61 x 52.1 cm
Munich, Bayerische Staatsgemälde-
sammlungen, Alte Pinakothek

Jan Steen
The World Upside Down, c. 1660
Oil on canvas, 105 x 145 cm
Vienna, Kunsthistorisches Museum

**Jan van de Capelle**
Shipping Scene with a Dutch Yacht Firing a Salute, 1650
Oil on panel, 85 x 115 cm
London, National Gallery

**Willem van de Velde the Younger**
The Cannon Shot, undated
Oil on canvas, 78.5 x 67 cm
Amsterdam, Rijksmuseum

## JAN VAN DE CAPELLE
### C. 1624/25–1679

There is little variation in Capelle's compositional structures. Around 1650, he painted
several similar versions of a calm sea in a shel-
tered haven, full of sloops, lighters, dinghies
and rowing boats, some of them carrying passengers, firing a salute, unrigged, almost motionless, lying at anchor.

A knowledgeable spectator may note the
details and structural features of the ships,
while at the same time being involved in a dramatic play of water, sky, clouds, haze, light
and atmosphere. The horizon of the sea is so
low that almost everything is dominated by a
hazy sky. At the same time, the sails and
clouds are reflected on the smooth surface of
the water in such a way that the entire scene
appears to be floating.

This painting shows more clearly than
most how Dutch painting often avoided stabilizing structural elements such as architecture;
here, the actual subject matter is the infinite
and the mutable. Dutch paintings are not
structured, but reflect characteristics of nature
and the elements. The appearance of the objects is determined by reflections. The light reflects on surfaces in such a way that colours appear. These, in turn, are subdued and broken.
The objects are often mirrored as well. Boats
are mirrored in the water, as is the cloudy sky.

## WILLEM VAN DE VELDE
### The Younger
### 1633–1707

Van de Velde was a specialist in marine pieces
or seascapes. More precisely, he was a portraitist of ships. Although he also executed history
paintings in the form of sea battles, his marine
pieces are differently structured. Ships of all
kinds are lying at anchor and, as such, are remarkable subject matter.

The painter certainly knew his subject, and
he would hardly have found any buyers for his
drawings if the details of his ships, from hull
to sails, had not been realistic. Yet the manner
in which he arranges his meticulously rendered vessels is reminiscent of a still life composition.

A ship is firing a salute. The acoustic effect
is rendered visibly as a cloud of smoke and
steam, as an atmospheric drama, ringing out
on a sea that looks like the resonating body of
a musical instrument.

The French poet Paul Claudel described
the painting as follows: "It is as though, at
this signal, at this sudden burst of sound in a
cloud of smoke, nature itself had paused for a
moment: fire! It is as though the sea were listening attentively, and the spectator too. This
is one of those paintings you can almost hear
rather than see."

# JACOB VAN RUISDAEL

C. 1628/29–1682

Jacob van Ruisdael's landscapes are poetic in a very special sense. They are first and foremost portraits of reality, in which each and every detail is drawn from daily experience and the Dutch landscape. In the context of the painting itself, however, these details are exaggerated and rearranged in such a way that they heighten the sense of atmosphere, sentiment and content.

In 1816 Goethe published an essay on "Ruisdael as poet" in the "Morgenblatt für gebildete Stände". In it, he wrote: "His works satisfy first and foremost all possible requirements in terms of appearance. Hand and brush, working with great freedom, achieve perfect precision. Light, shade, composition and overall effect leave nothing to be desired. Any art lover and connoisseur is aware of this at first glance. For the present, however, we wish to consider him as a thinking artist, indeed as a poet, and in this repect as well, we

must admit, that he deserves the highest accolade."

What caught Goethe's imagination was the fact that Ruisdael presented heightened versions of the familiar objects of local landscape that prompted contemplation and empathy: "The intention of the painting is to portray the present and the past, and this is achieved most admirably in a vivid combination of the living and the dead... opposite this building stands a nature copse of lime trees, planted long ago, yet still growing, indicating that the works of nature have a longer life than the works of man... this is an image successfully drawn from nature, successfully enhanced by cognition... an image that will always appeal to us..." Goethe wrote this essay at a time when landscape gardening was at its height as a means of appealing to the senses and arousing contemplation and sentiment with regard to landscape. The architects of this new 18th century gardening made the images of Ruisdael reality by copying them in their designs.

Jacob van Ruisdael
Two Watermills and an open Sluice
near Singraven, c. 1650–1652
Oil on canvas, 87.3 x 111.5 cm
London, National Gallery

**Jan Siberechts**
Landscape with Rainbow,
Henley-on-Thames, c. 1690
Oil on canvas, 82.5 x 103 cm
London, Tate Gallery

## JAN SIBERECHTS
1627– c. 1700/03

Even in its later period, Flemish landscape painting retains the main distinguishing characteristics that emerged as early as the 16th century in the works of such atrists as Pieter Brueghel and Momper.

This painting shows a sweeping view from a slightly elevated position, sloping down over the cattle pastures in the foreground towards a river plied by a cargo boat on the left and with a village on its banks to the right. Towards the background, the terrain slopes upwards again, with fields under changing sunlight and clouds, and a double rainbow in the sky. On the left, the view broadens out into the background towards the hills on the horizon.

A Dutch landscape painting, for example by Ruisdael, could hardly be described in this manner. Unlike Flemish landscape paintings. their Dutch counterparts rarely include so many different and contrasting elements. Here, we have proximity and distance, hill and plain, animals, people, boats and houses. While Flemish landscapes frequently have a universal theme, Dutch landscapes tend to concentrate on a single aspect. This painting is typical of the later work of Siberechts, who emigrated to England in 1672. Whereas his Flemish landscapes generally portray a small detail, his later work is topographically more precise; on the right we can recognize the village of Henley-on-Thames.

**Samuel van Hoogstraten**
Still Life, c. 1666–1668
Oil on canvas, 63 x 79 cm
Karlsruhe, Staatliche Kunsthalle

## SAMUEL VAN HOOGSTRATEN
1627–1678

In Dutch painting there is a tendency towards imitation and the dissolution of the boundary between real space and pictorial space. Even Rembrandt painted "window pictures" in which the person portrayed is standing in a door or window whose frame is identical with the frame of the painting. The generation of artists who followed him took a particularly keen interest in *trompe-l'œil* techniques. Hoogstraten was a specialist in this field and the work shown here is typical of the genre. Because such *trompe-l'œil* effects do not work well in depth, but are most effective on the surface, the artist chose to portray flat objects that could be placed on the picture plane, to which relatively flat items could be added. Here, for example, we see a variety of everyday objects held by two leather straps over a wooden frame. That old chestnut about the spectator who is actually fooled by such painted objects is quite easy to imagine in this case, but we should not forget that such *trompe-l'œil* paintings were actually intended as a joke and that they were meant to produce a sense of surprise on discovering that the objects were painted rather than real. Even so, this approach towards reproducing reality in painting does tell us something about Dutch painting in general: it is highly "figurative" in the sense that its content is conveyed entirely through the portrayal of objects.

# PIETER DE HOOCH
## 1629–AFTER 1684

Pieter de Hooch has gone down in art history as a painter who rendered Dutch domestic life with great precision. The private everyday life of the bourgeoisie in all its ordered tranquility, a world whose calm is never shattered by any sensational event, is the subject of his works. De Hooch opens a window on narrow alleyways, small gardens and courtyards, and gives us a glimpse into the antechambers and living-rooms of the Dutch citizens. Like Jan Vermeer, de Hooch specialized in the portrayal of interiors.

Yet, whereas the paintings of Vermeer tend to be dominated by a self-absorbed figure pausing momentarily in some activity, de Hooch's paintings are dominated by the room itself, by its perspectives and views through doors and windows, where people become an integral part of the interior. Light is an important factor, especially daylight, as in the work of Vermeer, with its refractions and reflections adding vitality to the rooms. Whereas people and animals interpose in their activities, light itself becomes the active element, permeating and moving over walls, floors and tiles, illuminating objects or casting them in shadow.

Like Vermeer, de Hooch also draws upon religious paintings, translating them into scenes of everyday life. His painting of the housewife and her maid cleaning fish in a neat backyard, for example, recalls the topos of the Virgin Mary in the hortus conclusus. Rooms flooded with light take on aspects of the Annunciation or recall Jan van Eyck's *Madonna in a Church* (ill. p. 124) in a church interior, lit by stained glass windows.

In the period between 1654 and 1665, when de Hooch was living in Delft, he created such works as *The Card-Players*, leaning heavily on the influence of Vermeer and the Rembrandt student Carel Fabritius. Although a certain tendency towards sumptuous interiors and elegant society is already evident here, the compositional organization is charming, and the architecture of the room with its checkerboard tiles heightening the sense of depth and perspective, is rendered with painstaking precision.

When de Hooch moved to Amsterdam in 1667, where he moved in high circles, his interiors became increasingly elegant, and his simple "households" were gradually replaced by palatial interiors. At the same time, the portrayal began to lose its precision and the vitality of the Dutch genre painting began to fade.

His paintings also began to lose the strong colour values so aptly described by Eugène Fromentin, a 19th century painter as follows: "The subtlety of Metsu and the enigma of Pieter de Hooch depend on there being much more air around the objects, shadow around the light, stability in volatile colours, blending of hues, pure invention in the portrayal of things, in a word: the most wonderful handling of light and shade there has ever been…"

**Pieter de Hooch**
A Woman and her Maid in a Courtyard, 1660
Oil on canvas, 73.7 x 62.6 cm
London, National Gallery

**Pieter de Hooch**  The Card-Players, c. 1663–1665
Oil on canvas, 67 x 77 cm
Paris, Musée National du Louvre

Frans van Mieris
Carousing Couple,
undated
Oil on panel
Private collection

## FRANS VAN MIERIS The Elder
### 1635–1681

The social or conversation piece was a particularly popular type of painting in Holland. Its origins reach back to late Mannerist painting, in which it was particularly the school of Utrecht that produced many portrayals of drinkers, musicians or lovers. There is undoubtedly a connection between the "privatization" of Netherlandish painting that went hand in hand with the decline in religious commissions and the increasing popularity of such "gallant" conversation pieces.

In this painting, the suitor is trying to fondle the woman of his choice, who is hesitantly drawing her clothes together. The payment for her services, however, is already lying in her lap. What is clearly a scene from the milieu of prostitution has been portrayed with beautiful objects from the world of still life and music in the tyle of the Leiden "fine" painters.

This particular theme originates in the biblical parable of the prodigal son who spent his money on whores and ended up in a pigsty. In spite of the underlying moral, the painting is a witty feast for the eyes.

There was also considerable specialization in the field of genre painting. In the work of Ostade or Brouwer, the peasant home and the inn were the most frequent setting, while the Leiden "fine" painters Dou, Metsu and Mieris included courtly elements.

Gabriel Metsu The King Drinks (The Beanfeast), c. 1650–1655
Oil on canvas, 80.9 x 97.9 cm
Munich, Bayerische Staatsgemäldesammlungen, Alte Pinakothek

## GABRIEL METSU
### 1629–1667

Metsu's *Twelfth Night* was painted under the influence of Steen. However, whereas most depictions of the toast to the person who has been arbitrarily elected "bean king" for a day show scenes of hilarious revelry (compare, for example, Teniers' *Twelfth Night*, ill. p. 319), Metsu has subdued the rough and raucous element. Even in the portrayal of such a dramatic and populistic scene, we can identify a trend that has been present in the genre painting since around the middle of the century. Even when a comic moment is illustrated, the portrayal pauses, becomes calm, takes on the traits of a still life.

The excesses of the "bean feast" celebrated on January 6 had become a thorn in the flesh of the Reformed church. The "king for a day" was granted a retinue of fools, and the joys of the table took on distinctly unmannerly forms in an otherwise strictly well-mannered country; what is more, this particular custom had its origins in Catholic countries. For these reasons, a number of cities banned such festivities for a time and portrayals of the revelries came to be regarded as something from the bizarre world of picturesque and raw peasant life.

Metsu's painting offers proof that Netherlandish painting never actually represented a direct report of reality, but that the art market incorporated certain fixed pictorial types in various forms.

## MEINDERT HOBBEMA
1638–1709

When Hobbema painted this view of the little town of Middelharnis and the avenue approaching it while he was staying there, Dutch landscape painting had already passed its zenith. Nevertheless, it continued to lean heavily upon that tradition, which provided a positively inexhaustible source of material.

Profoundly influenced by Jacob van Ruisdael, Hobbema initially painted gnarled old trees in picturesque contrast against smooth and luminous water, deep woodland shadows against brightly lit clearings in the sun, full of picturesque details of ruins, mills and peasant hovels. In his later works, however, such details became increasingly sparse, revealing the compositional structure of the painting.

The view of Middelharnis is a veduta, albeit of a typically Dutch kind, in which the town and its houses appear almost coincidentally at the end of the avenue, so that the path leading towards it seems to be the main subject matter of the painting. This path has made the painting famous. The upper two-thirds of the picture are taken up by the sky,

below which the flat land stretches out. Where the horizon line is drawn, we see the church and the houses of the town. The avenue runs from the spectator towards the exact centre of the horizon, and its vanishing point is exactly where the town covers the horizon. The perspective is of mathematical precision. Indeed, it is this very precision that underlines how strongly the land here has been shaped by the hand of man, by the people who dug ditches and built dykes.

Weather and time have made their mark upon this prosaic geometry. Gaps have been torn in the neat row of poplars lining the avenue and the wind has whipped their foliage into grotesque and spindly broomsticks. The straight path running between the two ditches is muddy, and the wheels of a cart have left their jolting tracks. A man, still small and distant, is coming towards us with his dog.

It is not easy to pinpoint just what it is that distinguishes Hobbema's late painting from his views of, say, the 1660s. The clearest distinguishing feature of his later work is the strong emphasis on linear structure and the scenes that intrude from either side, giving the impression of a stage setting viewed from a fixed standpoint.

Meindert Hobbema
Avenue at Middelharnis, 1689
Oil on canvas, 103.5 x 141 cm
London, National Gallery

√ **Jan Vermeer**
The Lacemaker,
c. 1665
Oil on canvas on
panel, 24 x 21 cm
Paris, Musée National
du Louvre

*Below:*
**Jan Vermeer**
Woman Holding a
Balance, c. 1665
Oil on canvas,
42 x 35.5 cm
Washington, National
Gallery of Art

# JAN VERMEER
## 1632–1675

Of the three great Dutch painters of the 17th
century –Vermeer, Rembrandt and Frans Hals
– Vermeer was the youngest. Very little is
known about his life. He left an œuvre of only
forty or so paintings, and his family suffered
constant poverty. For almost two hundred
years, his work was all but forgotten, only to
be rediscovered towards the end of the 19th
century at a time when the creation of pictorial light through colour had become a focal
concern of impressionist painting. For Renoir,
Vermeer's *Lacemaker*, along with Watteau's *Pilgrimage to Cythera*, were the most beautiful
paintings in the world.

The *Lacemaker* is crouched over her work
table, almost merging with it to create a
single plane, on which light sets the accents.
The light falls into this imaginary room from
the right – an exception in the work of Vermeer – and models the form of the head in an
interplay of shadow and light. Face, hair and
hands are modelled by the light itself. Simple
bright colours, the yellow of the blouse, the
blue of the cushion and the red of the threads
are not smoothly glazed, but grainy and interspersed with white, emphasizing the structure
of the canvas. We can almost see the light
lying on the body of the woman and the objects in the painting, creating the tranquility
of a still life. Moreover, the atmosphere of
light within the room itself seems almost
physically tangible.

A young woman – probably the pregnant Catharina Vermeer – is standing, lost in thought,
at a table in front of a curtained window. In
her right hand, she is holding a set of scales:
She is checking the weight of some gold coins;
in front of her lie coins and shimmering
threads of pearls, luminous against a deep blue
cloth. Her right hand, holding the scales,
forms the centre of the painting, where the
diagonals meet.

The process of weighing and the painting
on the wall depicting the Last Judgement suggest a possible interpretation: the trinkets of
this world are mere vanities, they weigh too
little in the scales, just as we ourselves shall be
found wanting if we bind our lives to earthly
things. Another interpretation is: life (including the life growing in a mother's womb) and
death are close together. Little time is granted
to us. The painting can be read like a vanitas
still life. Yet just as a Dutch still life is not
fully interpreted by determining its allegorical
meaning, the same is true of the paintings of
Vermeer. Here, interiors and even genre scenes
may take on aspects of still life painting, the
people in them are contemplative and pensive
–"out of time" .Thoughts of eternity arise
where everyday life comes to a standstill. Vermeer's great achievement lies in transposing
elements and principles of still life to interior
and genre paintings.

Even in the 17th century, it was already common practice to use optical aids in painting a veduta – a highly realistic view of a town or landscape. For his *View of Delft* Vermeer undoubtedly used a camera obscura. A few examples of such devices have survived. His hometown of Delft was in fact a centre of experimentation in the field of optics. Even the house from whose window Vermeer "drew" his view of Delft has been pinpointed. Yet the use of a technical aid by no means diminishes the artistic achievement of the painting, for the essential elements of the picture remain entirely the work of the artist.

Dutch views have a special place in the history of Baroque veduta painting. The artists were less concerned with an overall portrayal of the city than with finding certain "picturesque" aspects. In other words, the city is "characterized" rather than "represented" in the Dutch veduta.

A section of the port of Delft with its walls and gates, built mainly in red brick, forms the main view. The rooftops of the town sink behind it, and even the towers and spires are barely visible. The masonry is reflected in the water, and more than half the painting is taken up by the cloudy sky. The veduta shows the town of Delft in rapidly changing light and reflections on the water. There is no sense of action in this painting which portrays the town with all the remoteness and tranquility of a still life. Indeed, the actual subject matter of the painting would appear to be the atmospheric light, which shapes the appearance of Delft.

Here, as in his interiors, Vermeer has painted the effect of light on the brick walls of the houses and the hulls of the boats. A grainy white heightens the red and brown, conjuring up an impression of mutable and moving light on the old and immobile materials of wood and brick. A sense of quiet harmony is created in which the contrasts of tone and colour are finely balanced.

**Jan Vermeer**
View of Delft, c. 1658–1660
Oil on canvas, 98.5 x 117.5 cm
The Hague, Mauritshuis

**Jan Vermeer**
Allegory of Painting
(The Artist's Studio),
c. 1666
Oil on canvas,
120 x 100 cm
Vienna, Kunst-
historisches Museum

# JAN VERMEER
## 1632−1675

The studio painting is a frequent feature of
Dutch painting. Rembrandt painted himself
at his easel, as did Dou, Ostade and many
others after him. What is unusual about Vermeer's painting, however, is the fact that he
turns a self-portrait into a complex allegory.
Scholars and art historians have long debated
the "correct" interpretation of this allegory, a
fact which, in itself, merely underlines the
complexity of the painting. The interior is full
of artistic paraphernalia, and on the wall
hangs a map of the free Netherlandish provinces. The painter is elegantly dressed, and
working in an equally elegant room. He may
well have been citing Leonardo da Vinci's
treatise in which he says of painting: "…the
artist sits in great comfort before his work,
well dressed, and stirs the light paintbrush
with graceful colours. He is dressed in apparel
as he likes it." Could this be a reference to the
superiority of painting over architecture and
sculpture?

The artist is in the process of painting the
laurel wreath worn by the model; she also has
a trumpet and a book in her hands, identifying her as Fama, the allegorical embodiment
of fame. This studio scene, almost like a genre
painting, thus becomes an allegory of "the
fame of painting" in the Netherlands.

This corresponds to a generally widespread
Dutch possibility of incorporating "truths" or
general moral statements in what appears to
be a genre painting. An unusual feature in this
painting, however, is Vermeer's handling of
light, unparalleled in the art of the 17th century and rediscovered two hundred years later
by the Impressionists. The light falls through
an invisible window onto the model, whom
the painter has positioned in the most
brightly lit spot. In this way, natural light
becomes glorifying light − as befits an allegory.

In Vermeer's late work − this painting was
probably executed around 1675 − some weaknesses become evident. The system of distributing objects in the room − a painting on the
back wall, a drape to the left, the main figural
focus on the left − has become a stereotype formula. The objects have harsh contours and the
detail of surfaces and textures imitate the
work of the "fine" painters.
A comparison with Vermeer's greatest works
of the 1660s reveals the source of his later
weakness. In his later work, light itself is no
longer the main subject matter of the painting. Here, it is "merely" a means of illuminating the objects, whereas before − as in *The
Lacemaker* − light seeping onto the surfaces of
objects had been the actual theme of the painting. Also, we find an increasing use of deep
black in the portrayal of shadows, a technique
Vermeer had not used in his earlier works.

**Jan Vermeer**
Young Woman
Seated at a
Virginal, c. 1675
Oil on canvas,
51.5 x 45.5 cm
London, National
Gallery

Eva-Gesine Baur

# ROCOCO AND NEOCLASSICISM

## The painting in the 18th century

In Rococo, the sublimity of the Baroque gives way to a more relaxed style of almost whimsical ease. Sentiment and emotion prevail over reason. Yet the "fetes galantes" and pastoral idyll, the sophisticated elegance and amorous trysts are often little more than theatrical settings, serenely elegiac dreams behind which there lurks an awareness of paradise lost. The centres of Rococo painting were Paris, Venice and London. In the Parisian art world, "gallant" scenes by Watteau, Boucher and Fragonard predominated, along with the delicate still lifes and genre paintings of Chardin. In Venice, we find the magnificent cityscapes and veduta of Canaletto and Guardi, along with Tiepolo's brilliantly illuminated ceiling frescos. London society celebrated portraitists of stature such as Hogarth, Gainsborough and Reynolds, while in Southern Germany and Austria, pious images of celestial serenity spanned the church ceilings created by Asam and Zimmermann, Troger and Maulbertsch.

In stark contrast to Rococo stands the crisp, cool Neoclassicism of David, while in Spain, Goya's work plumbs the very depths of human existence, heralding the dawn of a new era.

In 1874, the brothers Edmond and Jules de Goncourt published the final volume of their joint œuvre *L'art du XVIIIe siècle*. In doing so, they took the first major step towards rehabilitating an era that has undergone a turbulent and constantly changing reception, right up to the present day, and which has so far defied virtually all attempts at elucidation and revival.

The misunderstandings began even before the era had come to an end: a still vibrant epoch was declared defunct, rejected by the very people who were themselves caught up in it and who now protested against a *Zeitgeist* of which they were still very much a part. Rococo was carried to its grave amidst the tumult of the French Revolution. Historians cite 1789 as the turning point that heralded its demise, and stress that the "outbreak" of the Revolution was the inevitable culmination of a process that had begun fermenting long before. The actual beginning of that process cannot be pinpointed; it can only be observed as a gradual change of consciousness.

The categorical distinction that tends to be made between Rococo and Neoclassicism has always been one of the major obstacles to understanding the 18th century as a whole. In the 1790s, Parisian artists coined the term "Rococo" from the word "rocaille", and even then it was applied disparagingly. The concept of florid superficiality and complacent serenity that continues to mar our view of Rococo art was already firmly established. In Germany, in particular, the widespread emergence of idyllic poetry, pastoral romance and convivial Anacreontic lyrics – often of mediocre quality – merely strengthened this view. The garlands of roses and bowers of love, the nightingales, whispering zephyrs and blushing Chloes represent only one rather narrow aspect of an era, but one which has tended to be mistaken for the whole story.

Small wonder, then, that the young Germans of the 1830s used the word "Rococo" pejoratively, as a term evoking stuffy courtesy, inflexible convention and an outmoded *ancien régime*. Even in 1859, when Wolfgang Menzel (1798–1873) introduced the term to literary history, it was synonymous with empty and meaningless ornamentation. The aesthetic theorist Friedrich Theodor Vischer (1807–1887) was probably the first to propose adopting it as a term in art history. Used in this context since the 1860s, it has gradually become a neutral term designating a historical epoch.

It is no coincidence that, towards the end of the 19th century, following the Neoclassicist trends of the previous century, the culture of Rococo should have been rediscovered by the exponents of Jugendstil (as Art Nouveau was known in

Germany), and echoed in the writings of Hugo von Hofmannsthal (1874–1929), Richard Dehmel (1863–1920) or Otto Julius Bierbaum (1865–1910); after all, they perceived an essential kinship in it, with which they could identify. However subjective this interpretation may have been, it nevertheless suceeded in liberating the Rococo era from the stigma of superficiality.

### Repression of fear

Apocalyptic fear and identity crises, visions of death and doubts about reality were the underlying factors in which this generation found its affinities with the "fall of the Baroque". Admittedly, there were certain similarities in the way these fears were repressed rather than overcome. Myth and fairytale, festivity and fantasy, theatre and music were called upon to create dream worlds and intermediate realms that would allow all this to be forgotten without losing an awareness of these mechanisms and without giving up reflection on appearance.

If we bear this in mind when we contemplate the "fetes venitiennes" and masquerades of Francesco Guardi (1712–1793), the concerts of Nicolas Lancrets (1690–1743), the love scenes of Watteau, the simple pleasures of the circus scenes and street scenes of Pietro Longhi (1702–1785), we can grasp an important aspect of their character. The avoidance of shadow is another major characteristic of the new techniques. The white grounding in the works of Jean-Honoré Fragonard (1732–1806), the light pastels of Rosalba Carriera (1675–1757), Maurice Quentin de La Tour (1704–1788) and Jean-Etiene Liotard (1702–1789), or the shallow sheen of porcelain figures in the work of Franz Anton Bustelli (1723–1763) are as symptomatic of this era as the fashion for powdered wigs. The "Ile enchantée" or enchanted island became a vehicle for the projection of a dream of carefree timelessness; it appears as *Cythera* in the work of Watteau or remains nameless in the work of Guardi, who painted a series of twenty-one islands. Venice attracted artists and travellers. The foreign and the exotic became the focus of a new view of life, "Russeries", "Chinoiseries" and "Japanoiseries" became treasure troves of disguise.

### Detachment as a pictorial device

At the same time, the ironic detachment and self-consciousness of the Rococo age became evident in the deliberate use, application and exploitation of all things foreign or different in terms of phenomena that are beyond understanding. A spirit of enlightened detachment underpins a wide variety of forms of expression. We find it in the synopsis of the "veduta ideata", the panoramic paintings of Canaletto (1697–1768) and Bernardo Bellotto (1721–1780) and it forms the basis for the art criticism of Denis Diderot (1713–1784) as well as providing fertile soil for the art of caricature which was to blossom in England especially.

François Boucher
The Toilette of Venus, 1751
Oil on canvas, 108 x 85 cm
New York, The Metropolitan Museum of Art

Canaletto
Venice: The Basin of San Marco on
Ascension Day, c. 1735–1741
Oil on canvas, 121.9 x 182.8cm
London, National Gallery

Detachment is also a fundamental aspect of the one field that has been most vehemently criticized as superficial and frivolous: eroticism. Giacomo Casanova (1725–1798), the figure who, more than any other, is popularly regarded as epitomizing the spirit of the era, reports in his memoirs of an experience that made him keenly aware of his own vanity. Having dismissed as prudish a girl who had resisted all his seductive wiles, he observed her one night with someone else, doing exactly what he had being trying to inspire her to do when he had shown her the engravings of Giulio Romano (c. 1499–1546).

Indirect or ironic deflection is another important factor that played a major role in shaping the portrait – surely the greatest achievement of 18th-century art. In the self-portrait of William Hogarth (1697–1764) the artist makes a merciless comparison with the dog whose physiognomy seems distinctly similar to his own (ill. p. 380). In the self-portait of La Tour, we find an arrogant and thin-lipped smile and a pose that denies all claims to beauty (ill. p. 362). Jean-Antoine Houdon's (1741–1828) sculpture of Voltaire (1694–1778) shows the great scholar as a man past his prime, cynical, balding and without a wig. Portraits depict their sitters in dressing gown or negligée, with a candour that is less than flattering. Such tongue-in-cheek revelation harbours a witty and critical balance of truth and untruth, semblance and reality.

Atttitudes to nature and landscape were similarly oblique. The landscaped gardens of Capability Brown (1715–1783) were designed to look natural, full of "chance" effects that had been precisely calculated and the "belt walk" was intended to guide the walker along a route revealing the gar-

den's precalculated surprises to greatest visual effect. Thomas Gainsborough's (1727–1788) landed gentry (ill. p. 384) are no more bound to the nature or landscape in which they are portrayed than Queen Marie Antoinette (1755–1793) was a milkmaid in her make-believe village of the Trianon at Versailles. While the role portrait or "portrait historié" by Joshua Reynold (1732–1792) emphasizes the boundary between play and identity, it does not do so brashly, but in the discreetly subdued tones of a secret, a slip, an unintentional betrayal of one's true self (ill. p. 383). The art of cultivating and addressing the question of superficial appearances achieves its greatest concentration and complexity in Rococo. The "rocaille" from which the era takes its name is both figurative and non-figurative. With its florid curves of coral, shell and plant, it forgoes all symmetry, axis and hierarchy, yet subjects itself at the same time to planarity and space. It is both artistically crafted and amorphous at one and the same time.

### The dissolution of contour

The dissolution of contour is a central concept in the formal rules and subject matter of painting. The German poet and man of letters Christoph Martin Wieland (1733–1813) once wrote, in a letter, of his epic fragment *Idris and Zenide*: "Imagine a fable after the manner of *Quatre Facardins* or the *Bélier* by Hamilton – but a fable unlike any other, one born of a healthy mind – the quintessence of all the adventures of Amadís and of all fairytales. And in this plan, under this frivolous exterior, metaphysics, morality, the most secret machinations of the human heart, criticism, satire, characters, paintings, passions, reflections, sentiments – in short, all you could wish for, with enchantments, ghosts, duels, centaurs, gorgons... beautifully penned and mixed together, and all in such variety of styles, so lightly painted, so lightly versified, so playfully rhymed – and in –ottava rime– at that." In the field of literary studies, Alfred Anger noted a phenomenon of considerable importance to art history when he spoke of the "dissolution of borders between genres": The blending and merging of forms, materials, different levels of reality, quotes and costumes (the classical Italian poetic form of *ottava rime* is to be regarded in this light).

The unhierarchical approach of Rococo merges the figure of the mistress with the figure of Venus, and combines characters from pagan mythology with utter disregard for rank or status. It brings together the tragic and the satirical in Hogarth's *Marriage à la Mode* or *The Harlot's Progress*, and presents a naively earnest child in Reynolds' painting of *The Infant Samuel* (ill. p. 383), while Watteau's harlequins, Gilles and Pulcinella combine elements of the comic and the tragic (ill. p. 350). Play and reality are as indistinguishable in Fragonard's *Blind Man's Buff* (ill. p. 360) as theatre and real life, mythology and eroticism, vision and episode are in the works of Watteau, Francois Boucher (1703–1770) or Alessandro Magnasco (1677–1749). In the paintings by Hubert Roberts (1733–1808) architectural ruins, street scenes, staffage and actual observations all become part of a vivaciously staged reality (ill. p. 367). Indeed, long before the French Revolution, we find categorical social boundaries disintegrating with the emergence of a new and self-confident bourgeoisie, evident in such paintings as Hogarth's *The Graham Children* (ill. p. 380).

What is more, we find an affinity for simplicity and rural life prevailing over sentimentality, especially in England. In Lawrence Sterne's (1713–1768) *A Sentimental Journey through France and Italy* (1768) sympathy for spiritual and material poverty is more than just a means of exploring one's own sentiments; it is also imbued with a sense of that utopian yearning which sought tranquility in intellectual or material deprivation. The very fact that Samuel Richardson (1689–1761) and his countless imitators presented servant girls as the heroines of their literature would also indicate a tendency to project their own concepts of happiness onto what they considered a "natural" and unspoilt environment, as in the "fancy pictures" of such artists as Gainsborough. Social hierarchies were being dissolved in an attempt to enter previously inaccessible lifestyles, where artists and writers imagined they would find some kind of Arcadian existence. The same approach also permitted a complex fragmentation of the Baroque system of order, opening up a wealth of possibilities by which to heighten the depiction of highly contrasting interests.

The rigours of ceremonious rules and regulations fuel the mordant satire of Hogarth's *Marriage à la Mode* (ill. p. 340), and indeed, the very existence of such rules and an awareness of them is fundamental to the sense of revelation in such paintings. Surveillance merely heightens the appeal of the clandestine: in Fragonard's *The Swing* (ill. p. 360) the presence of the foolish and elderly man stimulates the couple's erotic excitement. Occasionally, moral censorship was cloaked in pathos-laden sentimentality, a device so patently obvious in the paintings of Jean-Baptiste Greuze (1725–1805) that it simply adds further piquancy to the eroticism of his motifs (ill. p. 353). The social conventions of portraiture bring out the childlike qualities of the sitters in the portraits of children by Reynolds or Hogarth (ill. pp. 380, 383). Finally, the breakdown of inflexible systems also signifies the dissolution of Baroque typology, paving the ground for one of the greatest achievements of 18th century painting: the portrait.

### The images of life observed

The effects of a changing and enlightened consciousness are evident in the impartial observation and representation of the unique individual. A phenomenon such as the English animal portrait, odd as it may seem to us today, should certainly be considered in this context. In a painting by George Stubbs (1724–1806) a poodle is not simply a poodle, but an individual creature capable of specific and unique feelings. This cultivation of individuality is at the same time a cultivation of

**Giovanni Battista Tiepolo**
St Charles Borromeo, c. 1767–1769
Oil on canvas, 122.6 x 111.5 cm
Cincinnati (OH), Cincinnati Museum of Art

*339*

the very factors Jane Austen (1775–1817) addressed in the title of one of her novels: *Sense and Sensibility* (1811).

The astute and unprejudiced eye of Hogarth and, most notably, Francisco José de Goya (1746–1828), spawned very different forms of expression. Goya's unflattering group portrait of *The Family of Charles IV* (ill. p. 400) and his individual portraits of various members of Spanish royalty are fine examples of this neutral observation and a keen awareness of forms and conventions which have lost their significance. It was Goya's rigorous rejection of meaningless forms already devoid of all credibility that imbued his works with the pathos and monumentality of truth. This is undoubtedly

**William Hogarth**
Marriage à la Mode: Shortly after the Marriage, 1744
Oil on canvas, 70 x 91 cm
London, National Gallery

Goya's greatest pioneering achievement and the reason for his profound influence on the art of the 19th and even 20th centuries. In the privacy of his isolated and modestly furnished home, he dared to express the extreme consequences of his clarity of vision in his paintings; in the *Quinta del Sordo*, apocalyptic visions become reality, Saturn devours his children, an abandoned dog drowns in the sand dunes. Henry Fuseli's (1741–1825) *The Nightmare* undoubtedly stems from the same new concept of reality, in which dream, fantasy, foreboding and psychological phenomena are very real elements.

### Neoclassicist painting and the return of the moral message

While such pictures continue to strike a chord with us today, we find it considerably more difficult to identify with other contemporary works such as *The Oath of the Horatii* (ill. p. 365) by Jacques-Louis David (1748–1825). It is an

example of the kind of painting that seeks to reassert a system of moral, historical, social and artistic order of such uncompromising rigidity that it is very much bound within its own era. In contemplating these paintings, we must consider the question of a changing consciousness. Essential features of Neoclassicism are a sense of responsibility with regard to the pictorial message, the way its formulation is calculated, its systematic structure and the conscious evocation of a certain atmosphere or stylistic character.

This is particularly evident in France in the work of David, who lends the pictorial composition a new and didactic function through which he expresses and insinuates certain moral values. This didactic approach – a hallmark of Neoclassicist attitudes to art that can be traced all the way through to the annual competitions held by Goethe at Weimar for a design on some classical theme in the early 19th century – is evident, particularly in David's œuvre, in the fact that the iconological multiplicity, versatility or triviality of Rococo painting is abandoned in favour of an unequivocal and unambiguous, even ineluctable pictorial statement. The composition thus becomes an authority that censors the objects in the picture in advance, as it were – a phenomenon already evident in the work of Greuze when he shows his deliberately erotic images through a veil of morality and pathos (though this by no means reduces the erotic element). The fact that any kind of sensual eroticism is avoided in Neoclassicism – unless it is precisely calculated to underline some primary statement – is a logical consequence of Neoclassicism's aim of edification. The fickle intangibility of Eros is a contradiction of all it stands for.

In England, the transition to Neoclassicism is not so easy to pinpoint. The work of Thomas Lawrence (1769–1830), for example, still owes much to the portraiture of Reynolds, yet in the calculation of his effects, in the predominance of cool elegance over sensual appeal, in the stabilization and structuring of composition through the handling of colour, he may certainly be described as a Neoclassicist. The landscapes (ill. p. 387) of Richard Wilson (1714–782) and Philipp Hackert (1737–1807) in Germany, or those of Claude-Joseph Vernet (1714–1789) in France, are clear examples of the inversion of compositional technique: atmosphere is created by a mosaic-like juxtaposition of components. In other words, the reception of the painting is constructed. In the field of art reception, at least in the case of French art, we find motifs and impulses of a stylistic change formulated by the art critics.

### Art criticism as the product of a new spectatorship

It was not until the 18th century that art criticism as we know it emerged. When it did, it went hand in hand with the advent of the art exhibition and, with that, the rise of a new desire for publicity and a new understanding of art reception. Although there had already been a "salon" – an annual exhibition organized by the king – as early as 1667, this had taken place in the open air in the courtyard of the Palais Royal. In 1699 it was held in the Louvre, though not on a regular basis (ten times in all during the reign of Louis XIV). Eventually, in 1737, the Salon became a firmly established part of French artistic life and an important meeting place for artists and the public. The involvement of a wider public soon made its mark. Parisian society took every opportunity of voicing opinions, often vehemently, with regard to the exhibits, and of influencing the choice of exhibits in this way. Soon, a number of writers, journalists, philosophers and laypersons were publishing their opinions at every level in a wide variety of periodicals. The art critic had arrived on the scene.

Art criticism actually began with non-criticism. From the 1720s onwards, the "Mercure de France" occasionally published reports on exhibitions, consisting of little more than emphatic and uninformative eulogies of praise for the artists and their works. The desire for genuine criticism was voiced in a text published in 1747 by Lafont de Saint-Yenne entitled *Réflexions sur quelques causes de l'état présent de la peinture en France* in which he formulated the right to criticism as follows: "A painting exhibited is like a printed book, or a staged play – everyone has the right to judge it." Although Lafont claimed to regard common sense as the essential criterion of judgement, he nevertheless followed the dogma of academicism, as all the art publishers of the era were to do in his wake. Implacable in his criticism of Rococo painting, Lafont nevertheless couched his criticism in terms that reflected a profound change of attitude: he railed against what he saw as its inherent lack of force, its inauthenticity and its faddish triviality. Though the artists themselves, most notably Charles-Antoine Coypel (1694–1752) defended themselves vigorously against this kind of opinionformation, art criticism managed to esconce itself firmly in the role of arbitrator. Charles Montesquieu (1689–1755), Jean Baptiste d'Alembert (1717–1783), Voltaire, Jean-Francois Marmontel (1723–1799) and the Marquis d'Argens (1704–1771) and with them virtually all the leading literary figures and philosophers of the day penned their opinions on the subject of art, helping it to become a recognized and independently esteemed profession. Their writings were counterpointed by an equally prolific outpouring of popular and satirical brochures publishing criticism of a generally low standard.

It was also the art critics who drew up and evaluated the categories; Friedrich Melchior Baron von Grimm (1723–1807), who published his *Correspondances littéraire, philosophique et critique* from 1753 onwards, distinguished between the "poetic" and the "painterly", disparaging the former as art driven by the unfettered powers of the imagination and recommending the latter as art driven by the grand passions and emotions of the soul. Instead of the "happy

**Francisco de Goya**
Portrait of Doña Isabel de Porcel, 1805
Oil on canvas, 82 x 54.6cm
London, National Gallery

moment" that Fragonard, Boucher and Nicolas Lancret had sought to capture, artists were now called upon to portray the great and significant moment. The key concepts of the new style were "nature" and "truth" – terms which, in themselves, shed some light on the intellectual climate of the day.

### What is "nature"?

In the monumental 19th-century dictionary compiled by the German scholars J. and W. Grimm, nature is defined as "expression", meaning the expression of high civilization and sublimity of character. This is very much the same concept of nature that informed the extremely positive attitudes to sculpture reflected in the writings of Diderot and Voltaire; sculpture was regarded as an art with a "natural" affinity to classical antiquity. The stamp of Neoclassicism is evident in those aspects which the art critics of the day regarded as representative of the spirit of antiquity – in the works of Jean-

Jean-Antoine Watteau
Scale of Love (La gamme d'amour),
c. 1717–1719
Oil on canvas, 50.8 x 59.7 cm
London, National Gallery

Baptiste Pigalle (1724–1785), François Girardon (1628–1715), Etienne-Maurice Falconet (1716–1791) and Pierre Philippe Mignot (1715–1770). The statuesque quality of David's figures fitted well with this love of sculptural quality. Even though Diderot, who was probably the most important art critic of the 18th century, never abandoned the notion that art should imitate nature and the belief that the study of ancient Greek and Roman art taught us to see nature, this had little in common with the theory of imitation propagated by Johann Joachim Winckelmann (1717–1768). In 1755, Winckelmann published his *Gedanken über die Nachahmung der Griechischen Wercke in der Malerei und Bildhauerkunst* (Reflections on the imitation of Greek works in painting and sculpture) to considerable acclaim throughout Europe. In it, the portrayal of truth and the nature of things is already posited as the basis of artistic creativity, but interpreted in a rather different way. Winckelmann saw expression – especially "violent passion" or excitement – as a hindrance. "The soul is more evident and significant in a state of violent passion, but it is great and noble in the state of oneness and peace."

Anton Raphael Mengs (1728–1779) was closely acquainted with Winckelmann. Both men came from Saxony. They met in Rome and, though he would later repudiate them, Mengs initially adopted Winckelmann's theories as

the aim and content of his art. The extreme consequences of these programmatic theses are to be found, for example, in England. Though the author himself warned against unreflected imitation, believing that "ideal beauty" could only be found by "overcoming naturalism", he was frequently misconstrued. His emphasis on the primacy of drawing and the importance of contour was at the same time qualified by a warning: "Those who sought to avoid emaciated contour have succumbed to bombast; those who sought to avoid the bombastic have succumbed to leanness." The outline drawings of mythological scenes by John Flaxman (1755–1826) are a clear example of such "leanness".

The enhancement of the marginal is also a crucial stylistic change. This is evident in the fact that not only David, but also Ramon Bayeu y Subías (1746–1793) and, during a certain phase, Goya, presented harsh and clearly contoured figures against a monochromatic background. It is also evident in the ceiling paintings of southern Germany, where centred Baroque compositions were occasionally enriched and sometimes even ousted by a border area running parallel to the edges of the painting. The fact that this border area represents landscape is also an indication of a decisive change, heralding the end of the illusion of spatial extension created in the Baroque era by means of *trompe l'œil* architecture. The picture becomes a picture again. Seen in this way, the transcendental aspect of blurred borders and broken boundaries actually ends with Rococo, though in other areas it shapes the style of an epoch.

## What is truth?

The second central tenet of French art criticism is the concept of truth. Critics praised the truth of Greuze, referring to the intensity of feelings he evoked. Emotion as an experience of one's own capacity for empathy and sympathy was the most recent form of proving existence and was therefore regarded as "true". The same phenomenon could also be found in England, with the appearance of Sterne's *Sentimental Journey* or Richardson's servant maids in the world of literature, while the portraiture of George Romney (1734–1802), John Opie (1761–1807) and Henry Raeburn (1756–1832) was both sentimental and stiffly Neoclassical. Truth was also lauded in the works of Vernet, Jean-Baptiste Oudry (1686–1755) and Jean-Baptiste Siméon Chardin (1699–1779) – in those cases, in the sense of clarity and simplicity. In the work of Vernet, Diderot discerned an affinity with the much-admired Lorrain in terms of the similarity of pictorial composition – a misunderstanding that completely overlooks the compilatory technique used by Vernet in composing his landscapes out of cited individual motifs. If we consider the still lifes of Oudry and Chardin, it is easier to understand what prompted critics to describe them as "true": Their truth lies primarily in the reduction to a few generally simple pictorial objects, but also in the clarity of composition and the restraint of pictorial technique.

Chardin's *Still Life with Basket of Strawberries* (ill. p. 344) is a brilliant condensation of all these qualities. The pyramid of identical berries in a basket – presented to the spectator with neither ornament nor decoration – is monumental in its simplicity. The tranquility of the image thrives on its inherent significance; there are no allegorical references to that which is shown, beyond the confines of the painting itself. No stimulating light whose source must be sought, no enigmatic pictorial meaning puzzles the spectator. Neither the objects portrayed nor the picture as a whole seek to be anything more than they appear to be. It is this that makes the concept of truth appear justified in contemplating this work.

## English concepts of reality

If art criticism played a much less important role in 18th-century England, this is because the polarity of academicism versus non-academicism never reached such heights as it did in France. The change of style demanded by both the public and the critics did not come about suddenly in England, but in the form of a gradual development emanating from the work of individual artists. Nevertheless, the issue of truth was also discussed here – not in theory, nor in the aesthetics of reception, but in the work of many artists. It is not the critical form of a change of epoch, but the logical conse-

Jean-Honoré Fragonard
Progress of Love: The Lover Crowned, c. 1771–1773
Oil on canvas, 317.8 x 243.2 cm
New York, The Frick Collection

quence of the observation of social and spiritual or psychological processes.

At the very beginning of the "golden century" of English painting, we find, in Hogarth, an artist unfettered by academic rules, bound by no specific school, whose strong sense of individuality gave him the liberty of an impartial eye. The truth in the work of Hogarth resides primarily in the idiosyncracy of his style, in his unpretentious attitude that invariably puts all representational needs second to the faithful reproduction of what he has seen. In his series of prints *A Rake's Progress*, *A Harlot's Progress* and *Marriage à la Mode* he reveals the hypocrisy and insincerity of social mores and the cruelty of social obligations. In many of his paintings, he stresses the importance of the wig, satirically emphasizing its status as a ridiculous symbol of power used by ageing and disinterested judges, by dandies and complacent gentry, or showing a wig that has slipped from the balding head of some drunken gallant, set aside wearily, or deliberately removed, recalling the rake in his cycle *A Rake's Progress*, who appears in the end as a bald and repulsive madman. This is scathing criticism indeed. It has nothing whatsoever in common with the coquettish "déshabillé" of French society revealed in the paintings of Boucher or Jean-Marc Nattier (1685–1766). It is a mordant revelation tempered only by a distinctly English talent for bringing out the comic side of things. The rough and ready caricatures by Thomas Rowlandson (1756–1827), George Cruikshank (1792–1878) and James Gillray (1757–1815) may also be included in this category, as expressions of a quest for truth that is not moral and theoretical but observational. When Fuseli, for example, portrays scenes drawn from the depths of the unconscious, as in his *Nightmare* (Frankfurt am Main, Geothe Museum), he is working in the same tradition of art that shakes off the categories of aesthetic tradition and reproduction of reality in order to present the truth.

The greatest and most terrifying examples of an almost obsessive quest for truth can be found in the works of Goya. Not only in his portraits – including the Spanish royal family – but also, most notably, in his series of prints *Caprichos*, *Disparates*, the bull-fighting scenes of his *Tauromachia*, the *Proverbios* and the *Desastres de la guerra*. The brutality of the Inquisition, the horrors of the Napoleonic wars, the cruelty of ancient rites are not objective reports of injustice observed or experienced, but depictions that overstep the bounds of specific, cynical social criticism, lighting the path of a self-destructive obsession that drives him to look, see and understand. Truth no longer appears in the guise of allegory or mythology. It is neither noble nor fine, but merely inescapable.

Goya heightens this statement by foregoing the aesthetic escapism of beautiful colours in favour of black and white printing techniques such as etching, aquatint and even lithography – some of which were recent developments. The

18th century spawned an unprecedented pluralism of artistic techniques that were to shape the face of the era. The height of Rococo coincided with a rediscovery of camaieu and grisaille painting as techniques appropriate to the subject matter they conveyed. By constructing a monochromatic image – generally in grey or brown – there can be no pretence of reproducing reality. The picture can be regarded as a picture, emphasizing its artificiality as a medium and creating an artificial world governed by its own laws. What is more, the bounds of reality in the painting itself can be dissolved, and various levels of reality can merge with the irreality of monochromatic worlds.

## Rococo pastels

One of the most characteristic features of the era is its love of pastel. This is a technique that first emerged in 15th-century Italy. Yet although there are chalk drawings by Leonardo, Holbein, Philippe de Champaigne, Wallerant Vaillant (1623–1677) and many others, the technique first found real popularity with the artist often erroneously cited as its "inventor", Rosalba Carriera. Three aspects of her art and the genesis of her style are of importance to the development of pastel. First of all, there is her amateur approach: Rosalba, the daughter of an impoverished wood merchant, received second-rate training in her home town of Venice from Giovanni Antonio Lazzari (1639–1713), a student of Bassano, who recommended that she use coloured chalks for drawing. For the most part, however, she was self-taught. As her highly informative diaries tell us, she regarded herself as a successful amateur rather than a talented professional. Nevertheless. she soon became one of Europe's most sought-after portraitists, representing fashionable taste. Because the use of pastel does not require a high degree of technical skill, drawing with coloured chalks of bound pigment on vellum or coloured paper soon found favour amongst amateur artists. The blurring of contours with a pointed roll of paper known as a "tortillon" or "stump", the ease with which corrections and alterations could be made, the "clean" working technique that required no palette, not to mention the pleasing results of even the most unambitious works, made pastel a highly popular technique, particularly in England. What is more, it fitted in well with prevailing notions of what constituted a "suitable pastime for ladies".

A further typical feature of the paintings by Carriera indicates her grounding in miniature painting. The small detail and cumulative approach involved in this genre lend it a certain affinity to pastel techniques. The great pastellist Liotard, for example, also began as a miniaturist.

The rigidity of Carriera's pastels, so often a point of criticism, is also an essential feature of her work. In spite of the sfumato and the dissolution of sharp contours that appeal to Rococo taste, they possess a singular immobility that was perhaps first overcome by La Tour and which at the same

**Jean-Baptiste-Siméon Chardin**
Still Life with Basket of Strawberries, c. 1760/61
Oil on canvas, 37 x 45 cm
Paris, Private collection

time paves the way for the Neoclassicist pastel techniques in the works of Johann Heinrich Wilhelm Tischbein (1751–1829) and Angelica Kauffmann (1741–1807).

In 1720/21 Rosalba Carriera was in Paris, where she had a seminal influence on the great French pastellists. The cool discretion of pastels, reflecting the intimacy of the boudoir rather than any overweening pretensions, made the technique very appealing to French artists. Different talents were drawn to the possibilities offered by pastels. La Tour, the most important pastellist of all, favoured a bluish background which created a sense of distance right from the start and which, as in his self-portraits, harmonized with the irony inherent in his treatment of his subject matter. For characterization, he also used the rapid technique of superimposing layers of strokes without actually mixing the colours. A bold red stroke over a matt blue ground, a portrait such as that of La Tour's mistress, the singer *Mademoiselle Fel* (St-Quentin, Musée Dupouch) – these are the new and brilliant forms of portaiture that trace individual identity in the ephemeral.

Jean-Baptiste Perroneau (1715–1785), La Tour's rival for public favour, demonstrated in his works the heights that could be achieved with this technique. Using a pale ground, a matt luminosity dominates the colours. Perronau was a master of the art of creating an entire picture on the basis of only a few colours, sometimes no more than two. Foregoing all brash effects and directness in his quest for finesse, delicacy and restraint, his pastels are marked by a distanced artificiality. Liotard, on the other hand, emphasized colority. Apart from a number of pale, light-coloured works dominated by shades of white, we also find in his œuvre some "folkloric" Turkish scenes and portraits in which a strong and richly contrasted colority is created by adding extra pigmentation to the chalks. He, too, bans shadow from his works. Pastels are never gloomy, never non-commital. They brook neither the absolute nor the abrupt. It is for this reason that pastels blossomed in the Rococo age.

## Capriccio – Caprice – Capricho

In 1617, Callot published a series of prints entitled *Capricci* which already bore the hallmarks of what was to become an accepted genre known as the "Capriccio". The series had a cover sheet followed by relatively small-scale prints showing strongly improvised scenes with no programmatic link and moving from one subject matter to the next without any apparent system of order. The provenance of the term "capriccio" has never been satisfactorily explained, though it is generally accepted that it may be derived from "capra" (goat) in reference to that creature's moodiness and mind of its own. Vasari used the adjective "capriccioso" to mean idiosyncratic, witty, breaking the rules. Montana and Stefano della Bella (1610–1664) transposed the capriccio style into ornamental sequences in the 17th century and in the field of

**Alexander Roslin**
Woman with a Veil: Marie Suzanne Roslin, 1768
Oil on canvas, 65 x 54 cm
Stockholm, Nationalmuseum

copper engravings of ornamental patterns, it developed into the rocaille that was a hallmark of Rococo in the 18th century.

Around mid-century, François Cuvilliés the Elder (1695–1768) published his "morceaux de Caprices à divers usage" showing rocaille in all its versatility – as a frame, a decorative device, an ornament in furnishings, and even as the subject matter of a painting. At the beginning of this chapter, the dissolution of contours in the broadest sense was presented as a feature of Rococo art. This is clearly demonstrated in the case of rocaille, which unites such elements as corals, shells, sails, smoke or foliage without actually adopting any one of these definitively as its predominant motif. It transcends borders between image and frame, between architecture and image, spanning planes without filling them, yet at the same time acting as an ornamental subject matter or as the hidden principle of inherent movement within the picture.

In 1749, Giovanni Battista Tiepolo (1696–1770) created a series of etchings entitled *Varii Capricci* teeming with the characters which make the capriccio the very epitome of imaginative form: warriors, orientals, satyrs and shepherds, travelling people and all manner of animals, elements from antiquity and exotic objects; all become instruments by

**Joshua Reynolds**
Portrait of Susanna Beckford, 1756
Oil on canvas, 127 x 101 cm
London, Tate Gallery

If we interpret the concept of the capriccio a little more broadly, we may include the paintings of architectural ruins, a genre represented primarily by Giovanni Paolo Pannini (c. 1691/92–1765) and his student Hubert Robert, known as "Robert des ruines". In these works, ancient architectural fragments have yet to be incorporated with the same considered stylistic awareness that is evident in the landscaped gardens of the Romantic and Neoclassicist age. Nor do they act as individual vehicles for atmosphere and mood, as in the works of Wilson, Hackert or Vernet. Their appearance of decay is by no means intended as a symbol akin to the Baroque allegories on the transience of all earthly life. Instead, the ruins are perceived as objects whose imperfection permits the associative imagination of each individual observer a free rein. Their crumbling decay contradicts Baroque systems and represents a potential stage for vital events. In terms of this interpretation, Magnasco's night scenes may be regarded as having the character of a capriccio.

It is, however, the island series by Guardi which gives the clearest indication of the close thematic relationship between the capriccio and the "Ile enchantée". Its rejection of inner pictorial logic and programmatic concepts echoes the detachment of the island from the mainland; the private subjectivity of visual creation corresponds to the intimate bounds of an island. In the boundlessness of the subjective imagination, the individual discovers his or her own submerged golden isle or "vineta". It is here that the "fetes galantes" provide an alternative means of escape from apocalyptic fears. Perhaps we ought to regard a painting such as Goya's *Burial of the Sardine* (ill. p. 399) as the drastic culmination of these festive visions, transporting us away from reality: the celebration of love has disintegrated into an apocalyptic spectacle.

### Fragmentation and invention

In much the same way, Goya's *Caprichos* (1793–1798) marked the end of the capriccio as a field of serene enchantment, as an island removed from all bounds of reality, and as a field of subjective experience. Goya seems to use the capriccio to some extent as a thematic vehicle that allows him to ignore all prevailing rules of form and content. Yet the noncommital stance of the imagination is no longer in evidence. Visions of winged monsters, distorted physiognomies, surreal figures that are half human, half animal, sinister gnomes, masked falsehood, cruelty and destruction are likenesses, and the nightmares he portrays are reality. The beautiful witch bears a distinct resemblance to the Duchess of Alba, the bestial spirits are dressed in monks' habits, the hypocritical opportunists are wearing contemporary courtly dress; the adultress has the traits of a princess featured in his portrait of the royal family, the victims of horrific torture by the Inquisition are portrayed with all the lifelike precision of a "genre" painting; the woman sentenced to death, having taken a lover because she was so maltreated by her husband,

which to express a rich imagination. Another approach can be found in the work of his son Giovanni Domenicho (1727–1804) whose *Idee pittoresche sopra La Fuga in Egitto* created in 1753 blends the irreal magic of the capriccio with elements of the Flight into Eypt, resulting in wondrously tender fairy-tale scenes.

The *Carceri* by Giovanni Battista Piranesi (1720–1778), first published in 1745 under the title *Invenzioni Caprici di Carceri* are widely regarded as the artistic manifestation of an anti-Rococo movement within the Rococo age. Their capriccio-like character marks them as an art form of that era in much the same way as Piranesi's *Opere varie di Architettura* (1750), albeit of a rather different kind: specific architectural elements are condensed to create a labyrinth which no longer seeks to represent specific architecture, but which, in its figurative irreality, confirms the reality of the associations it triggers. Here, the capriccio is a means of uniting objects which have been removed from their original context. Unlike the Neoclassical approach, which unites such objects in a mosaic-like staffage, the capriccio merges them to create a new entity whose structural principles are based on the artist's own creative fantasy and imagination.

is based on an actual lawsuit. Goya makes it absolutely impossible for the observer to escape the reality of the seemingly unreal; he does not allow us to close our eyes to the fact that the supposedly imaginary is true in more than just an abstract sense. The captions function in the same way. They are generally literary quotations or proverbs, often in seeming contradiction to that which is portrayed: a witch appearing before two sorcerers bears the title *Pious Confession* – enigmatic as they may seem at first glance, they are invariably unequivocal if regarded within the social, political or literary context from which they are taken. No hermetic or mysterious knowledge bears the key to these works – the quotations and proverbs Goya cites were, after all, widely known. In his *Caprichos*, Goya proves his revolutionary discovery that the true underlying reality can be conveyed more strongly by abandoning a superficial portrayal of reality. He knows that imitating the appearance of things actually conceals their true essence. He knows that similarity breeds dissimilarity. Much of 20th century art, most notably the works of James Ensor (1860–1949) and Francis Bacon (1909–1992) cannot be fully understood without an awareness of this aspect of Goya's achievement.

The uncompromising radicality of Goya's approach still contains vestiges of the debate on "truth" and "reality" that dominated the 18th century. Truth and reality can take shape even in their opposites. Truth and reality are the content of the illusion. This is evident in that most illusionary of all illusions: the stage.

## Theatre and illusion

Around 1700, winds of change swept the world of stage design. The changes that took place are inextricably linked with the Galli Bibiena family, whose most famous representatives were Giovanni Maria (1625–1665), Ferdinando (1657–1743), Giuseppe (1696–1756) and Carlo (1728–1787). They worked in Venice, Berlin, Dresden, Munich, Prague, Vienna, Bayreuth and innumerable other cities. The single most lasting achievement was Ferdinando's invention of the diagonal axis sytem, first presented in 1703 at the Accademia del Porta in Bologna. This involved shifting the central axis to reveal additional rooms or spaces which were visible to the audience at an angle (*veder la scena per angolo*), so that the technique came to be known as *scena per angolo*. Ferdinando elaborated his theory of this technique in 1711, making it widely available. Yet there was more to this innovation than simply breaking the mould of traditional Baroque stage design. The very fact that it abandoned the hierarchy of axial systems is not only symptomatic of the very essence of Rococo, but also indicates a change in the interaction between the scene and the spectator. Having exhausted the illusory powers of the visible, the illusory powers of the labyrinthine now came into their own. The strict regulation of ceremony required by the Baroque stage set is not possible in a

Thomas Gainsborough
Miss Anne Ford (Mrs. Philip Thicknesse), 1760
Oil on canvas, 197.1 x 134.9 cm
Cincinnati (OH), Cincinnati Museum of Art

*scena per angolo*. The decentralization of the stage automatically results in a decentralization of movement on stage, leading to an interesting dissolution and simultaneous emphasis of the contradiction between "artifice" and "nature". If the events presented on such a stage are seen to occur "naturally", this is, of course, the result of artificially created conditions.

The stage designs of the Galli Bibiena herald the dawn of a new era in yet another important way. They are the visual expression of a new form of rhetoric whose persuasive powers lie in indirect statement rather than in clarity of structure and logic. Slanting walls provide concealment, corners harbour clandestine meetings, angles are sources of surprise. The spectator is entranced by the possibilities of the unexpected and the unforeseen, and illusion is catapulted out of invisibility. It thus becomes possible to transform an entrance into a portentous event – a development soon adopted in an area that seems diametrically opposed: religious art.

## Pious imagery of Rococo

The extension of real space into ceiling paintings by transposing architectural detail in the manner invented by Pozzo (who was himself a set designer) still owes much to Baroque rhetoric. In the ceiling frescoes created by Cosmas Damian Asam (1686–1739) for the monastic churches of Weingarten (1718/19) and Aldersbach (1720) celestial events unfold in hierarchical ranks. Even in Weltenburg (ill. p. 392) the boundaries between these individual planes of action are blurred. There, too, on another level, the "theatrum sacrum" or sacred theatre is staged. St George appears against a background of light. The stucco figure is freestanding in an illuminated, stage-like setting created specially for it. The *Assumption of the Virgin* in the monastic church of Rohr tells us that the miraculous event is a palpable occurrence close to human experience.

In this regard, it seems only logical that, for example, the ceiling painting in the pilgrimage church of Steinhausen by Johann Baptist Zimmermann (1680–1758), should show a landscape – the earthly zone, as it were – surrounding the celestial centre like a frame. In this way, the artist creates a stage for both sacred and mortal actors. The miracles are comprehensible, present and yet distant, at once tangible and inaccessible, for the human proximity and explanation of the appearance are countered by the hermeticism of the image that now makes no pretence to be anything but an image. This adaptation of theatrical and stage set devices is also evident when the stage remains empty. In Zimmermann's ceiling fresco for the church of Wies, the heavenly gates remain closed, the celestial throne unoccupied, and the Supreme Judge appears between them in the clouds on a rainbow of conciliation. The tension between the two unoccupied areas, facing each other at east and west like opposite poles, is further heightened in this way, and the focus is on the message announced by Christ in the centre. The spectator experiences the doctrine of salvation indirectly rather than directly, in anticipation of it, rather than in its fulfilment.

When Johann Evangelist Holzer (1709–1740), Franz Anton Maulbertsch (1724–1796), Zimmermann or Matthäus Günther (1705–1788) integrate folkloristic elements into the realms of religious art and when Tiepolo includes objects of everyday Italian life in biblical scenes, they are using a similar formal language. To interpret Rococo as an era of diminished piety is to misconstrue that language. It is a language that makes use of new vocabulary and new rhetorical means in order to convey its message.

## The significance of the individual and individuality

The only way to approach the art of the 18th century is by seeking to understand the forms, the techniques, the categories and the values of Baroque without actually accepting them as valid standards. Never before did individuality and subjectivity play such a major role in art. It is a focal theme in portraiture, which explores the unique and the individual, not only in human beings, but also in animals. Even the precision with which an urban landscape is rendered becomes a unique and individual portrait of a city. Moreover, individuality is also a mode of presentation that is included in the picture as an independent value, as in the capriccio. It is only by understanding the dominance of artistic personality over trends, stylistic characteristics and concepts of collusion in this era that we can understand the greatest artists of the period.

Tiepolo and Goya, Piranesi and Hogarth, William Blake (1757–1827) and Chardin cannot be classified as artists of a single stylistic epoch. Their works may be shaped by the visual experience and *Zeitgeist* of their generation, but they still transcend it and its terminological classifications. Perhaps it is precisely this blurring of boundaries in the Rococo era that made it possible for such unique talents to flourish in the first place.

# JEAN-ANTOINE WATTEAU
1684–1721

*L'Indifférent* has a counterpart – a woman playing the lute, whose pose and clothing correspond to the position and costume of the dancing man. But even without knowing the second painting, we can sense its presence here: the young man is listening and looking, so that we can almost see the young woman playing and can almost hear the sound of the strings.

Watteau has placed his figure on the central axis of the painting as though this might lend it the stability it seems to lack. The dancer's leg position seems very unstable, his left leg is turned outwards, the foot placed at a right angle, and with his right leg he balances on tiptoe in a rather unstable-looking step. Nevertheless, his gaze seems contemplative and his movement calm. It is a position of great grace and choreographic artistry, seeming to defy gravity, but precarious all the same.

We suspect that we already know how this moment will end; that he will place his foot back firmly on the ground to balance himself properly and gather strength. At the same time, however, the young man's pensiveness seems to radiate a tranquillity and timelessness that forbids such thoughts. Watteau also shows that such a step would be impossible in this painting: there is neither earth nor floorboards, no room we might step into, no contoured environment. The real physicality of movement, position and balance become unreal here. The moment the dancer abandons his pose of artificial grace, the picture disappears.

It is not clear whether this painting shows people leaving the island of Cytherian Venus or arriving. Art historians have put forward some well-founded evidence suggesting that this ambiguity is intended. It is precisely this sense of a temporal and physical no-man's-land that makes the "Ile enchantée" or enchanted isle what it is: the scene of living dreams and dreamed-of life, somewhere between reality and unreality. The statue of Venus, the Amor-like cherubs in the air and on the earth, the island of Cythera itself: these and other mythological references transfigure the sense of reality. Just as mythology itself draws its aura from its unclarity and scope for interpretation, so too does the haze cast over this Rubenesque universal landscape become a statement in itself. The motif of the pilgrimage, evident in the pilgrims' hats, pilgrims' staffs and cloaks, becomes a motif of profound yearning.

The aims of religious pilgrimages – the working of miracles, the satisfaction of hopes and the fulfilment of vows – are reinterpreted here on a non-religious level. In the timeless celebration of love lies immortality, in the declaration of love lies the sincerity of the vow and in love itself lies heavenly ecstasy. The pilgrims are not leaving, nor are they arriving; no journey is needed, for their yearning is to be found within themselves, to be satisfied by themselves.

Jean-Antoine Watteau
L'Indifférent, 1717
Oil on panel, 26 x 19cm
Paris, Musée National
du Louvre

Jean-Antoine Watteau
Pilgrimage to Cythera, c. 1718/19
Oil on canvas, 129 x 194cm
Berlin, Staatliche Museen zu Berlin,
Schloß Charlottenburg

Jean-Antoine Watteau
Gilles (Pierrot), 1721
Oil on canvas,
184 x 149 cm
Paris, Musée National
du Louvre

## JEAN-ANTOINE WATTEAU
1684–1721

Few people who have seen this painting are likely to forget it. Art historians have looked for explanatory texts, biographical references and indications of mellow old age in this painting executed the year that Watteau died. It has even been suggested that it was painted as the advertising sign of an Italian theatre troupe. None of this explains its fascination.

We see cedars, pines, bushes, the statue of a faun, actors of the *Commedia dell'arte*, and in front of them, above them, Gilles. There he stands, his arms hanging loose by his sides, wearing his baggy Pierrot costume. He is standing right at the front, but he is shy; he is meant to entertain us, but he gazes at us with dark, melancholy eyes; he is meant to be present and yet he seems withdrawn as in a dream; he is clumsy and awkward, although he is accustomed to the stage. His colleagues in the background belong to a different sphere, they are full of vitality and excitement, and are paying no attention to him. Gilles is lonely. Almost – for with just one eye, but with the same melancholy gaze, an ass is looking out across the stage. Is nature the backdrop, is the backdrop nature? Is Gilles simply playing the role of the wise fool and the shy dreamer, or is that really what he is? It is a quiet, unnoticed moment of tranquility amidst the hustle and bustle of the theatre, a moment of truth in the game of intrigue, nature pausing for breath in a world of artifice.

A young couple outdoors. Trees, bushes, flowers can only be imagined, for they are merely hinted at in the atmosphere of a bower laden with desire and an air of sweet clandestinity. The colours flow hazily into one another, as though all resistance had already been broken, with no foreboding darkness nor warning daylight. A bright red cloak lies in the grass; the act of undressing has already begun. The red becomes the centre of gravity of colour and seems to draw everything towards it. We see the strong hand of the man supporting and leading at the same time, his brownish face with its faun-like traits, and we see the white neck of the woman, her silvery-blue silk dress drawn across her firm shoulders. Her right hand is stretched out in resistance, but the lines of her neck and back are already moving in another direction. We have the pleasure of looking on unnoticed, but Watteau does not make us into voyeurs. He merely shows us the final moment of hesitation, the "not yet" that is so full of promise. In doing so, he makes us participants in the scene, calling on us to imagine what happens next, so that in the end, it is we who are seduced.

In this *fête galante* nothing and no one seems to be the centre of attention. The couple dancing a minuet seem completely absorbed, the bagpipe player gazes dreamily into space, a cavalier is busy in his conquest of a beautiful woman, a couple is strolling in front of the fountain, two women and an actor are engaged in deep conversation. All in all, the materials have a certain similarity, and all add to the sense of celebration.

Jean-Antoine Watteau
The Indiscretion, 1717
Oil on canvas,
50 x 41 cm
Paris, Musée National
du Louvre

FRANCE

**Jean-Antoine Watteau**
Fetes Vénetiennes, 1719
Oil on canvas, 56 x 46cm
Edinburgh, National Gallery of Scotland

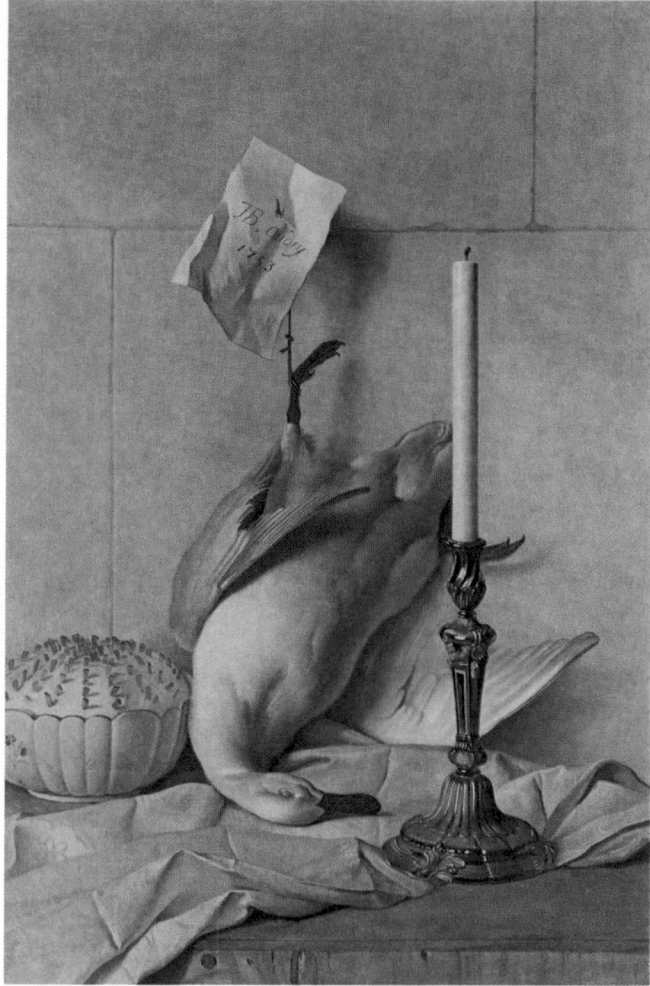

**Jean-Baptiste Oudry**
Still Life with White Duck, 1753
Oil on canvas, 95 x 63 cm
London, Marquise de Cholmondeley
collection (stolen)

*Below:*
**Nicolas de Largillière**
The Strasbourg Belle, 1703
Oil on canvas, 138 x 106 cm
Strasbourg, Musée des Beaux Arts

## JEAN-BAPTISTE OUDRY
### 1686–1755

Oudry was familiar with the Netherlandish still lifes of the 17th century. He had seen them and learned of them through his teachers Michel Serre and Nicolas de Largillière. Yet in a late work such as this one, he makes it radically clear that the French still life of the 18th century is of a completely different nature. Not only does the content of the painting forego any allegorical suggestion, it is virtually negated. The choice of objects – the white duck, the white dessert in a white china bowl, the white damask table cloth, the white candle in a silver candlestick, the white sheet of paper with signature and date, all set against a whitewashed wall – leaves us in no doubt whatsoever that this painting is not about the significance of the objects themselves, but about exploring a complex of white and silvery tones. It is a monochromatic painting with a difference: instead of portraying coloured objects drained of their colour, it portrays objects which are white in the first place. The artificiality of Rococo, so often cited as one of its main distinguishing features, is broken here with irony and skill. What we see here is not presented as something from the realms of fantasy, but as real objects in a real situation. The point, however, is that artificiality and finesse are thus presented as reality. In other words, reality is in the eye of the beholder.

## NICOLAS DE LARGILLIÈRE
### 1656–1746

We no longer know the name of this beautiful woman. Yet even though Nicolas de Largillière painted this as a portrait of a specific beauty, who sat as his model, her individuality seems to be secondary to her clothing and her origins. It is her traditional Strasbourg costume that is the real subject matter of the painting, rendered in meticulous detail with all the masterly skills that betray this artist's Flemish training. The lace trims of her shawl and jabot, the magnificent folds of the sleeves, the firmly laced corset with its sumptuous border and, by contrast, the simple skirt and unadorned wide-brimmed hat – these are certainly not just demonstrations of painterly skill. They indicate that this painting was intended to portray a specific costume, rather than a specific person.

The delicate beauty of the woman thus takes on a universal and non-committal quality, in contrast to which her clothing is special and characteristic. At the same time, the elegance of the pose and the fine facial traits suggest that this is not some rural beauty proudly presenting her finest clothes, but a sophisticated woman of the world, her lap-dog on her arm, who has chosen this peasant costume as a disguise in order to make the illusion of a naive sense of unbroken tradition the vehicle of a life of leisure.

## JEAN-MARC NATTIER
### The Younger
1685—1766

Towards the mid-18th century, the proportion of portraits shown at official art exhibitions increased considerably, prompting critics to demand that in future, only portraits presenting a specifically prescribed theme would be accepted. At the same time, this particular generation of artists produced a great many highly talented portraitists, including Roslin, La Tour and Nattier.

Nattier, more than any other artist, seized the opportunities offered by the Baroque form of "portrait historié", which presented contemporary persons as historical or mythological figures. He succeeded in linking thematic significance and universality with courtly elegance and decorative pose. When he was finally appointed "peintre du roi", most of his models were ladies of high society. Even the portraits the king commissioned for his bedroom in Choisy feature two of his daughters – Madame Adelaïde as Diana, Madame Henriette as Flora – with the costumes, according to contemporary documents, reflecting their different temperaments.

Nattier reports in his memoirs that, in accordance with the instructions of the queen, he painted the head first. Physiognomic similarity and mythological role, stylistic freedom and the instructions of the client had to be united in an elegant setting.

**Jean-Marc Nattier the Younger**
Madame Henriette as Flora, 1742
Oil on canvas, 94.5 x 128.5 cm
Florence, Galleria degli Uffizi

## NICOLAS LANCRET
1690—1743

Lancret is regarded alongside Jean-Baptiste Pater as the most important representative of the many artists influenced by Watteau, most of whom chose individual motifs or groups from his "fête galante" and made them independent themes. This process alone is indicative of a specific tendency in Rococo: the tendency towards small scale, intimate scenes. In Lancret's painting *The Swing* we find a highly popular motif of the time, treated not only by Fragonard, Boucher and Pater, but also by lesser painters of the era. Just what made the swing such a popular theme becomes clear here.

It is not only the erotic aura, whose "moment of happiness" is to be found in a glimpse under the petticoats, but also the fact that the swing is a metaphor of an interim realm belonging neither to the earth nor to the air. It remains intangible, allocated neither to an element nor to a physical place. Non-committal coquettishness, the freedom of intimacy, the bonds that do not tie: all these are evoked by the rope with which the desiring cavalier is moving the swing, not as a symbol, but certainly as an obvious suggestion.

**Nicolas Lancret**
The Swing, undated
Oil on canvas, 70 x 89 cm
London, Victoria and Albert Museum

**François Boucher**
The Education of Amor, 1742
Oil on canvas, 118 x 136cm
Berlin, Staatliche Museen zu Berlin,
Schloß Charlottenburg

**François Boucher**
Diana After the Hunt, 1745
Oil on canvas, 94 x 132 cm
Paris, Musée Cognacq-Jay

# FRANÇOIS BOUCHER
1703–1770

The strong and youthful figure of Mercury, messenger of the gods, reclines on clouds draped with a scarlet cloth. Beside him stands Venus, pressing a dove to her heart, knee-high in clouds, her shimmering mother-of-pearl back turned to us, glancing coquettishly towards Mercury, whose attention is concentrated on educating Amor. Amor, the coupler and mediator of love, seems uninvolved; he is studying a large folio that bears Boucher's name and the date of the painting. Yet his power conquers all, and his very presence is enough: already, Mercury is beginning to look over his shoulder towards Venus, who is tempting him with her looks and gestures. The fire of Amor's torch is not yet ablaze. But the sense of anticipation and the erotically charged atmosphere of expectation that dominates the situation already suggest his victory.

Diana, proud and triumphant, has returned from the hunt, laden with trophies, in the company of her entourage. For the Baroque artist, such a scene would have been presented as a great triumphal procession, for Boucher it becomes a vehicle for an intimate scene of undressing.
   He shows the chaste young goddess as a girl of seductive charm, a light shift slipping from her smooth shoulders. There is an air of slight tiredness, which merely heightens the erotic delicacy of the scene. The fruits of her hunt are incidental, and the three nymphs beside her, in the freshness of their beauty, add to the sense of this setting as an antechamber, while at the same time they emphasize the throbbing fatigue that weighs upon the goddess. The act of undressing has become the central, appealing theme and Diana has become a paraphrase of Louise O'Murphy, assisted by her servants, preparing for the visit of her royal lover.

This scene of a family breakfast does not radiate any sense of warmth, maternal happiness or security. The elegant young mother merely turns as though by chance towards the child who is busy with its toys. A nursemaid has a little girl on her lap, stiff as a china doll. Even the servant holding the jug seems uninvolved. The atmosphere in this painting is one of unqualified serenity and levity. The children are symbols of freedom from care, the women and the servant embody youth and beauty, the morning hour is free of shadow. The mirror, the gilding, the golden-yellow drapes, the pale porcelain and the high window are all bearers of lightness and brightness, with neither shadow, age nor poverty. Behind it all, the fears of transience are merely hinted at.

**François Boucher**
The Breakfast, 1739
Oil on canvas, 81.5 x 65.5cm
Paris, Musée National du Louvre

François Boucher
Blonde Odalisque
(Portrait of Louise O'Murphy), 1752
Oil on canvas, 59 x 73 cm
Munich, Bayerische Staatsgemälde-
sammlungen, Alte Pinakothek

# FRANÇOIS BOUCHER
1703–1770

In the salon reports of the *Nouvelles Littéraires* for the year 1750, Boucher is chided for painting "women's heads more pretty than beautiful, more vain than noble". Such criticism is vindicated in the portrait of Louise O'Murphy, a young Irish woman who worked as Boucher's model and who, in 1753, was briefly the mistress of Louis XV. The artist does not present her as a Venus of classical beauty, but portrays her instead in a provocative pose of unambiguously erotic persuasion as a sweet child-woman.

In spite of the high esteem in which Boucher was held by the public of the day, they frequently criticized the artificiality of his "porcelain heads" and his delicately coloured interiors. Here, too, his handling of colour is delicate in the extreme, creating a powdery surface without depth in which the hues are brought together by the use of white as a common ground. There are neither deep shadows nor sombre contrasts of light and shade. The white ground also takes the edge off the primary triad of red, yellow and blue, diluted here to discreet shades of pink, pale yellow and light blue. The unapproachable, aloof beauty is dethroned and a pretty little coquette is put in her place.

Everything seems to be in the foreground, like the pose of the mistress, and is nevertheless beyond reach of the spectator. The body that seems to be offered in such proximity, is not really present, but transported by the artificiality of the surface. The young girl's willing charms are paraded as attributes of naive beauty rather than as an appeal from within the painting. The artificiality of the colouring emphasizes the hermetic pictorial world governed by its own rules. Her pose of langorous waiting is not intended for the spectator. The pictorial space merely gives us an envious glimpse into a room whose door remains closed. Boucher does not destroy the sense of anticipation by allowing the figure she is waiting for to appear, but heightens it by the very fact that nothing happens. No person and no action stand in the way of indulging in these seductive charms – only the boundaries of the picture.

# JEAN-BAPTISTE SIMÉON CHARDIN
## 1699–1779

In 1885, Vincent van Gogh wrote to his brother Theo saying that he was "increasingly convinced that real painters do not complete their paintings in the sense so often associated with the word perfection, that perfection which has gone so far that things become tangible." This high art of distancing the objects in the painting from visual access was something van Gogh saw in the works of Chardin in particular. When we look at the painting *Boy with a Spinning Top* we realize what van Gogh meant and we sense the effect Chardin has created.

A young boy is standing near the foreground at a table drawn up to the very edge of the painting, on which he is watching the spinning top he has set in motion. The situation is a familiar scene of everyday life, and the action of the spinning top is rapid and ephemeral. The scene is "close" to the spectator in every sense. Nevertheless, nothing is "tangible", for the momentary and the proximate have been withdrawn, as much by painterly techniques (such as the blunt brushstroke) as by the possibilities of composition. By portraying the boy in profile rather than looking towards the spectator, Chardin emphasizes his concentration: he is completely immersed in the game and withdrawn from the spectator, whom he does not even notice. This painting radiates calm, tranquility and childhood happiness – a paradisical world we can only watch quietly, but cannot touch.

In the 18th century, allusions to play generally referred to adult games, erotic travesties, sensual theatre plays and flirtations with transformation. Chardin, on the other hand, takes the game seriously and returns it to the realms from which it originates: the world of the child that does not yet know the difference between fantasy and reality, between play and real life.

Like the great Netherlandish domestic genre scenes of the 17th century, Chardin's childhood scenes create a pictorial space full of calm and relaxation. The surface of the painting is matt and veiled, the pose of the girl with her toys in her hand is one of quiet and pensive relaxation. There is nothing sudden or loud in this scene; it shows a quiet life. Chardin was admitted to the academy as a still life painter and it was as a still life painter that he came to fame. When, as here, he renders his painting of a child like a still life, he juxtaposes the child with the fruits of nature, portraying a creature close to nature, unspoiled and pure. When he painted strawberries heaped up in a pyramid on a dish, or peaches, foregoing all sumptuous decor and ornamentation, Chardin was doing just what he does here: equating beauty with nature as it is. It is therefore only logical that this little girl is not looking out of the painting vainly in a bid to gain attention, but remains where no one will disturb her, in the world of childhood – paradise lost.

**Jean-Baptiste Siméon Chardin**
Boy with a Spinning Top, 1738
Oil on canvas, 67 x 76cm
Paris, Musée National du Louvre

**Jean-Baptiste Siméon Chardin**
Girl with a Racquet and Shuttlecock, c. 1740
Oil on canvas, 82 x 66cm
Florenz Galleria degli Uffizi

**Jean-Baptiste Siméon Chardin**
Pipe and Jug, c. 1755
Oil on canvas, 32.5 x 40 cm
Paris, Musée National du Louvre

**Jean-Baptiste Siméon Chardin**
The Grace, 1739
Oil on canvas, 49.5 x 38.5 cm
Paris, Musée National du Louvre

# JEAN-BAPTISTE SIMÉON CHARDIN
## 1699–1779

This painting clearly demonstrates why Chardin's fame is based primarily on his still life paintings. Yet his still lifes owe less to the Netherlandish painting of the 17th century than to a genuinely French tradition. There, we find the characteristics that distinguish the work of Chardin. The matt, "veiled" handling of colour, the even light that avoids all extremes of brilliance, the contentuality that is more or less identical with the objects portrayed. A simple jug, a dish with a lid, an open wooden box, the fragile clay pipe beside it – objects that do not seek to convey a symbolic meaning nor do they have any prestige or delicacy. The composition seems almost coincidental, with neither focal point nor climax in terms of colour and light. And yet it is a painting that gives the spectator a sense of harmonious perfection.

A contemporary art connoisseur described Chardin as "the French Teniers". Certainly, this interior is reminiscent of the interiors of Teniers' era. Light and colour are subdued, nothing is sudden or jarring. Even the movements seem slow, so that the picture appears to capture a moment of repose. The decor is simple; on the wall there is only a shelf with bottles and an earthenware dish, beneath which hangs a copper pot. The table is covered with a simple white cloth. The three figures in the painting are fully integrated into this system of reference. None of them glimpses beyond the windowless pictorial space – the unbroken calm of a hermetic microcosm is portrayed.

When we think of such painters as Fragonard or Boucher, this painting hardly seems to fit our concept of Rococo art. However, if we bear in mind that conscious repression and compensation of apocalyptic fears were fundamental characteristics of the Rococo age, then *The Kitchen Maid* is indeed a Rococo painting. The reference to Netherlandish kitchen scenes is soon found to be merely superficial, for the similarity is restricted only to the choice of props and the predominantly brown colouring. It would also be wrong to see any allegorical statement in this scene. It simply shows a kitchen maid in an indeterminate room, pausing for a moment in her work. Her expression is one of neither sadness nor joy, her gaze is aimless but not forlorn. The pictorial space, which initially appears to be firmly bounded, turns out to be a kind of nowhere, whose shelter is created entirely by an inner integrity. The moment of contentment and repose freezes into timelessness, into an eternity that harbours a refuge from fear and transience.

**Jean-Baptiste Siméon Chardin**
The Kitchen Maid, c. 1740
Oil on canvas, 46 x 37.5 cm
Washington, National Gallery of Art

**Jean-Honoré Fragonard**
Blind Man's Buff, c. 1760
Oil on canvas, 114 x 90 cm
Toledo (OH), Toledo
Museum of Art

**Jean-Honoré Fragonard**
The Swing, 1767
Oil on canvas, 81 x 65 cm
London, Wallace
Collection

## JEAN-HONORÉ FRAGONARD
### 1732–1806

The central figure in the painting is a young girl dressed as a shepherdess, trying to find someone with her eyes bound. But she is peeking out from beneath her white blindfold. And it is precisely this that is the fulcrum point of the picture. Just as the game turns out to be a mere cover for some coquettishly erotic play, the entire pictorial world itself is ambiguous. Is this a child or a woman who is cheating so subtly here? Is she a shepherdess and her playmate a shepherd, or are they perhaps a couple from high society, dressed in rural costumes and seeking to heighten the pleasures of flirtation by playing an "innocent" game of blind man's buff? Are these children or "amorettes" on the ground nearby, laughing at the players? Is it an outdoor scene or are they onstage?

The boundaries between various levels of reality seem blurred. Truth and falsehood, mythology and everyday play, bucolic life and theatre are merged in an artificial naturalness to create an evocative and beautiful unity. Yet this beauty also has something utterly evanescent, with neither aim nor purpose. The seeker is not seeking in order to catch or to find. In her gracefully outstretched arms, she holds nothing but the amorous atmosphere of an extended moment.

"Balance" is the French word for a swing. And balance is certainly the main theme of this painting, so typical of the era. After all, Rococo itself was one great balancing act, constantly teetering on the brink of a fall from its bold flights of grace. Here, too, the artist elegantly balances on the knife-edge of danger. The incident is unequivocal, but intention takes the guise of accident. The young suitor lies at the foot of a stone monument – incidentally crowned by Amor, the god of love – as though he had accidentally stumbled and fallen in the bushes, where, as though by chance, he catches a glimpse beneath the rustling petticoats of the pretty woman in the swing. Yet the scene shows more than a flirtatious play between voyeurism and exhibitionism. The face of the young man lying amidst the roses is illuminated as though by some invisible source of light – like a saint in the face of a celestial vision. However, it is not divine truth that reveals itself to him, but something much more human: what he glimpses is heaven on earth, and the joys it promises are of a very worldly nature.

The painting was originally commissioned by a wealthy baron in homage to his beloved. Yet Fragonard expresses more than a lover's devotion and the beauty of his beloved. The pretty woman's gaze is expressionless, and her eyes seem glazed in the charming blush of her face. What is happening here is already symbolized by the swing reaching the highest point in its arc. In a moment, it will fall again, drawn back by the elderly man in the dark background: a split second of erotic rapture, as blissfully lascivious and imperilled as Rococo itself.

FRANCE

Fragonard painted *The Stolen Shift* after his tour of Italy, when he was staying in Paris where he was very much a part of the city's social and artistic life. In this painting, the artist turns the spectator into a voyeur observing an intimate scene involving a young beauty who does not realize she is being watched. He shows her lying in her bed, which is draped towards the background by a red baldachin curtain. It is precisely this aspect of the painting, the background, that becomes the focal point, or foreground, of the spectator's curious gaze. It is as though Fragonard had hidden the spectator behind the bed, offering a "rear view" of the situation in a very literal sense indeed. However, having acted so indiscreetly, Fragonard plays down the erotic directness of the scene. Above the rosy-complexioned young girl with a blue ribbon in her hair, he paints a putto who is removing her shift. The putto is an attribute of Venus. Yet Venus does not generally wear a shift, nor does she tie her hair up so casually with a blue ribbon, nor is she a fresh rural beauty.

The double nature of the painting, the double view of the scene, the play on concealment and revelation all find their equivalents in the pictorial techniques. The beguiling sensuality of the shimmering, rosy flesh are permeated from within by a matt and powdery white, whose lack of sheen emphasizes our awareness that this is only a picture and that the entire incident is just a painting. The surface of the picture is placed like a barrier between the charms of the child-like Venus and the gaze of the spectator.

The tradition of the Baroque "five senses" allegory has come to an end. The artist does not grasp the opportunities offered by a motif of this kind. Instead of clearly defined statements, contoured and translatable pictorial language, we find a hint of unclarity that escapes all conceptual fixation. The dedication with which the young girl is immersed in her music does not differ in any way from the devotion in the gaze of her teacher as he muses on the charms of her décolleté. The power of such deep devotion to blur all boundaries is echoed in the fuzzy handling of colour and is more compelling than the objects themselves. The vagueness of Eros extends to all the senses. It negates the boundaries of age, time and space. The cat on the chair is not a symbol, but a pointer towards the meaning of the picture; it is sensual and fond of tenderness, but it cannot be controlled. It stalks its territory at all times of day and night. Like Eros, it is relentlessly on the prowl, in search of fulfilment.

Fragonard did not paint this picture as an allegory of the five senses, but as an allegory of sensuality. He makes eroticism the driving and creative force. The transience of sensual experience – hearing, seeing, feeling – is not used as a vehicle for any kind of vanitas allegory. In the depth of devotion, time itself is conquered. In the density of emotion, the hopes of a pagan lust for life seems to have reached its goal.

**Jean-Honoré Fragonard**
The Stolen Shift, c. 1767–1772
Oil on canvas, 36.5 x 43 cm
Paris, Musée National du Louvre

**Jean-Honoré Fragonard**
The Music Lesson, c. 1770–1772
Oil on canvas, 110 x 120 cm
Paris, Musée National du Louvre

Joseph-Siffred
Duplessis
Portrait of Christoph
Willibald Gluck, 1775
Oil on canvas,
99.5 x 80.5 cm
Vienna, Kunsthistori-
sches Museum

## JOSEPH-SIFFRED DUPLESSIS
### 1725—1802

His carrier began late in life and his rise to
fame as a portraitist was meteoric. In 1775, at
the height of his success, he created two
diametrically opposed works: a conservative
full-figure portrait of the young Louis XVI,
laden with pomp and circumstance in the Baroque tradition, and a half-figure portrait of
the composer Christoph Willibald Gluck that
was destined to become the epitome of a vibrant and individual artist portrait. At the
time, Gluck was a celebrity at the very centre
of the Parisian music scene and, together with
his librettist Calzabigi, he had triumphed over
an antiquated operatic genre with such innovative works as "Orpheus and Eurydice", "Al-
ceste" and "Iphigenia in Aulis", opening up
new dimensions of emotional expression in a
field that seemed to have reached the end of
the road.

In a sense, Duplessis takes much the same
approach. He imbues the traditional half-
figure portrait with a new content that revi-
talizes the classical canon. The emphasis on li-
bretto, so vital to Gluck's music, finds its
correlate in a literal interpretation of personality that brooks no idealization, but which
draws its authenticity from precise observation. The elderly, pockmarked face of the composer looks upwards, listening intently, enlightened only by the glow of a moment of inspiration.

Maurice Quentin
de La Tour
Self-Portrait, 1751
Pastel, 64.5 x 53 cm
Amiens, Musée de
Picardie

## MAURICE QUENTIN DE LA TOUR
### 1704—1788

When La Tour drew this self-portait (pastel,
being made of chalk, is not, strictly speaking,
a technique of painting) he was already one of
the most sought-after portraitists of his day.
Nevertheless, he foregoes all the trappings of
ostentation, dignity and solemnity. The intimacy of the pastel, hardly suited to large-scale
works or pathos-laden chiaroscuro, is further
heightened by the relaxed pose of the man
who smiles so courteously at the spectator.

On closer inspection, however, the look on
his face appears to turn almost imperceptibly
into supercilious sarcasm, and what seemed at
first to be candour becomes an impenetrable
expression. The cool blue tones of the painting
enclose the artist in a hermetic world of
precious artificiality that is neither vulnerable
nor accessible. Light as the colours may be, the
painting itself contains no light.

Strangely static, as though unaffected by
any change in light conditions, it denies the
fleeting aspect of fresh and spontaneous drawing. The pastel chalk does not simply portray
the powder of the wig – it is the powder, and
its dull, matt sheen is the sheen of velvet. Distance and intimacy alike are evident in La
Tour's pastels.

# JEAN-BAPTISTE GREUZE
## 1725–1805

"Let morality speak in painting" demanded the great critic Denis Diderot in 1763 and he saw this wish fulfilled in the works of Greuze. Today, especially in a painting such as *The Lamentation of Time Passing*, we see a delicately erotic image cloaked in a thin veil of moral piety.

The seeming contradiction is resolved if we interpret Diderot's concept of morality correctly. He was not calling for a total ban on the portrayal of sensual charms, but demanding a pictorial message or statement that was not restricted merely to a presentation of the erotic, in the manner so consummately mastered by Jean-Honoré Fragonard. His knowledge of Dutch and Flemish engravings gave Greuze the iconographic vocabulary with which to construct his pictorial narratives. The watch in the hand of the child-like young woman is a traditional symbol of transience and the fleeting ephemerality of a brief amorous adventure which is described here as false happiness.

Greuze's achievement lies in the way he has made the attractively half-bared breasts the "eyecatcher" around which he structures the narrative suggested by the title; we see the unmade bed, the loosened blouse, the abandoned handicraft, the scattered belts and bands, the discarded cap and, above all, the letter – the lover's letter of goodbye.

Jean-Baptiste Greuze
The Lamentation of
Time Passing, c. 1775
Oil on canvas,
79 x 61 cm
Munich, Bayerische
Staatsgemäldesamm-
lungen, Alte Pinakothek

When *L'Accordée du Village* (The Village Betrothal) was shown for the first time at the Paris Salon of 1761, it was greeted with great acclaim by critics and public alike. With his painting of the hesitant young bride with downcast eyes on the arm of her bridegroom, who is asking her elderly parents for her hand in marriage, Greuze satisfied the ethics of contemporary taste. The touching earnestness in the faces of the bridal couple, parents, notary, children, relatives and friends, the pure simplicity, the pious poverty and the unspoiled shyness of the situation as a whole gave expression to a new ideal. The elitist Arcadian idylls and erotic pastoral scenes were now countered by something new: the sentimental family genre. The images of simple contentment, homeliness and happy sentimentality, without which the 19th century could never have produced its "bower scenes", have their origins here.

And yet this painting is still very firmly rooted in the 18th century, charged with a pathos that can only be understood in terms of its direct contradiction with the pathos-free Rococo of Pater, Lancret, Drouais or Boucher. The narrative potential of this scene is the basis for the enormous popularity enjoyed by this painting and, at the same time, heralds a quest for new bourgeois ideals. Quiet tones of tender emotion are imbued with all the drama of the closing scene of a successful and moving play.

Jean-Baptiste Greuze
L'Accordée du Village
(The Village Betrothal), 1761
Oil on canvas, 90 x 118cm
Paris, Musée National du Louvre

# JACQUES-LOUIS DAVID
1748–1825

On 12 July 1793, David paid a visit to his Jacobin comrade Marat. "I found him", he reports, "in a situation that astonished me. Beside him was a wooden packing case, on it an inkwell and paper and, from his bath, he was noting his last thoughts for the welfare of the people." Next day, Marat was murdered by Charlotte Corday and David was commissioned by the Convention to paint him. David records his last impressions. The pen is slipping from Marat's hand, his head falling to one side. Marat's dying hand still holds Charlotte Corday's deceitful request for an audience; on the packing case lies a letter from an anonymous philanthropist; on the floor lies the murder weapon. At first glance, the scene appears too private for an official memorial painting. Yet on closer inspection, its compositional stringency makes it seem like a propagandistic memorial: the packing case with its inscription becomes a tombstone, the bath in which the murdered man lies, a coffin.

When David completed *The Oath of the Horatii* in Rome in 1784, his studio became a place of veritable pilgrimage. It is not the historic theme as such or the almost archaeological attention to detail that lie behind its triumphal success, but its highly effective compositional structure. Each of the rounded arches is allocated to a group of figures: on the right, the mourning women, on the left the three young Horatii raising their right hands to swear their oath, and in the centre the father holding the swords aloft at the moment before the battle. Effective choreography and handling of light concentrate all energies towards the oath, and everything culminates in the centre of the painting. Eagerness for action, determination and unity evoke a moral atmosphere of such intensity that suffering pales into insignificance beside it.

Madame Récamier's salon in Paris became a gathering place for royalists and opponents of Napoleon's government. When David painted her, she was 23 years old and her political sympathies were diametrically opposed to those of the artist, himself a former active Jacobin who had now become Napoleon's court painter. Nevertheless, he presents her as a heroine of the republic or protagonist of the Empire. Barefoot, wearing a simple white dress with neither adornment nor jewellery, she reclines in classical pose on a piece of furniture that has since become known as a "récamiere". The room itself contains only a footstool and a candelabrum. In spite of the lack of ostentation, she is clearly a woman of high society, who seems elegant, distanced and in no way populistic. The simple dress, the simple hairstyle, the bare feet – once attributes of a revolutionary attitude – are merely a fashion here.

**Jacques-Louis David**
The Oath of the Horatii, 1784
Oil on canvas, 330 x 425 cm
Paris, Musée National du Louvre

**Jacques-Louis David**
Madame Récamier, 1800
Oil on canvas, 173 x 243 cm
Paris, Musée National du Louvre

**Jacques-Louis David**
The Death of Marat, 1793
Oil on canvas, 165 x 128 cm
Brussels, Musées Royaux des Beaux-Arts

FRANCE

# JACQUES-LOUIS DAVID
1748–1825

Jacques-Louis David
Napoleon in his Study, 1812
Oil on canvas, 204 x 125 cm
Washington, National Gallery of Art

David's contemporaries admired the perfection of his technique just as later generations would. Yet he is not generally regarded as an artist of great psychological empathy. Nevertheless, if we examine this all too famous portrait of Napoleon with an impartial eye, we can detect the psychological depth behind its smooth surface. It was painted in 1812, a fateful year for Napoleon. In 1804, he had crowned himself Emperor in the presence of the Pope and David, who had been appointed painter to the imperial court that same year, recorded this official act of cold pomp and egomania.

In 1812, the life of the military man from Corsica reached a turning point. It was the year in which his triumph turned to defeat for the first time. On the retreat from Moscow, his army was crushed. In this painting, Napoleon does not look like a hero. His pale face is puffy, his body formless, his gaze melancholy rather than victorious. And the pose which is meant to appear confident seems uncertain instead. The emperor does not stand firm and dynamic, but slightly stooped amongst his lavish oriental-style furnishings.

We see a man who has already passed the zenith of his life and his success at the age of 43. There is almost nothing left of the bold hero, the storming conqueror painted by David in 1799/1800.

*Below:*
Jacques-Louis David
Napoleon Crossing the Alps, 1799
Oil on canvas, 259 x 221 cm
Rueil-Malmaison, Musée National du
Château de la Malmaison

This equestrian portrait of *Napoleon crossing the Alps* does not portray him as an intelligent strategist, nor as an unscrupulous and fearless general, but as a romantic hero elevated to a mythical figure crossing a mythical border – the Alps. David had met Napoleon for the first time some four years previously. In 1778, David's compatriot Etienne-Maurice Falconet (1716–1791) had created an equestrian statue of Tsar Peter the Great commissioned by Catherine II. David responds to this monument with his own equestrian portrait, which, though smaller, is no less imposing than Falconet's monument. And just as, in Falconet's sculpture, Tsar Peter rides up a steep slope, the rider in David's painting is charging up the rocky Alps. David glorifies Napoleon as a restless hero whose face unites the Neoclassicist ideals of beauty and determination. Napoleon did not sit as model for him for this painting any more than he did for the 1812 portrait. But in 1797, he had actually managed to spent two hours sitting for the esteemed court painter.

The oil sketch created at that sitting has less pathos and the expression of the general is less heroic, but even in this portrait, Napoleon can be seen as a handsome man with a strong jaw, a strong gaze and a strong will. The sketch actually served only as a preparatory sketch for a planned painting intended to show Napoleon contemplating the Alps which was never executed.

# HUBERT ROBERT
1733–1808

The paintings of ruins created by Pannini and Piranesi influenced the architectural paintings of Robert at a very early stage. The fact that he studied under Fragonard, with whom he travelled to Naples and Rome, and with whom he worked in Tivoli, is not evident in this late work exhibited at the 1789 Paris Salon any more than it is in his early work. Yet, even indirectly, something of Fragonard's spirit is tangible here.

The huge architectural ruins with their broken cornices, against which the human figures seem small and irrelevant, is not a gloomy warning or a symbol of the transience of earthly life, nor a monument of foreboding gloom. It is a place filled with life, used naturally, a place where fish are sold and food is cooked, a place for business, barter, play and work. High up on the once so majestic architecture, a railing has been installed to create a viewpoint and a trysting place for lovers or simply a convenient shortcut for hurried visitors. These witnesses of the past, portrayed in such detail, are part of life. It is precisely this dichotomy between the momentary and the permanent, the eventful and the immobile, between life and decay, chance and historicity, that shows Robert to be a true student of Fragonard.

Hubert Robert
The Porta Octavia in Rome
Oil on canvas, 161 x 117cm
Poughkeepsie (New York),
The Frances Lehman Loeb Art
Center at Vassar College

# ELISABETH VIGÉE-LEBRUN
1755–1842

Madame de Staël, daughter of the French minister of finance, Jacques Necker, achieved fame on the basis of her turbulent lifestyle and two literary works: *De l'Allemagne* (1810), a portrait of Germany, its customs, literature and philosophy, and her novel *Corinne ou l'Italie* (1807). In this work based on her travels in Italy in the company of August Wilhelm Schlegel, after Napoleon had exiled her from Paris, she records her impressions of Italy in glowing tones through the mouthpiece of the fictitious Italian poetess Corinne. Vigée-Lebrun portrays her in the role of Corinne wearing an antique robe, with a lyre on her lap, as a female Orpheus. Behind this figure there is a cliff crowned by a classical monopteros, and a sweeping landscape that fades into the distance with gentle, green hills and blue mountain peaks. The concept of the classical and the romantic which Madame de Staël was first to use in its present sense, are echoed in these two landscape types. The flawless idealization that marks so many of this artist's works is countered here by the powerful vitality of the face: a mature, confident and energetic woman of astute intellect who is by no means identical with the role of glowing and effusive rapture.

Elisabeth Vigée-Lebrun
Portrait of der Madame de Staël als Corinne, c. 1807/08
Oil on canvas, 140 x 118cm. Geneva, Musée d'Art et d'Histoire

**Alessandro Magnasco**
Seascape with Fishermen and Bathers, undated
Oil on canvas, 115 x 92 cm. Venice, Private collection

# ALESSANDRO MAGNASCO
1667–1749

Even if it was probably the work of the Impressionists that revived our interest in a painting such as this, there is nothing impressionistic about it. The "macchia" or daubed brushwork serves here as an expression of the imaginary and may well have its forerunner in the works of Salvator Rosa. The rapid, almost sketchy treatment of the foam, the rough and uncontoured trees and rocks along the jagged coast, the scudding clouds – all create a feverish and restless atmosphere as though a storm were about to break. The semi-naked fishermen endeavouring to bring their boat and their catch to safety are at the mercy of this atmosphere of tense anticipation. We do not see them as individuals, nor even as anonymous individual actors, but as an integral part of this stormy, drifting scene.

Magnasco does not delineate clearly, nor does he create boundaries. Sky, earth, water, people and vegetation all seem to merge. They seem to dissolve from within, without clear outlines, flowing and disintegrating. Because Magnasco does not let the eye of the spectator rest on any point, he succeeds in evoking this restlessness as something elementary, powerful and mysterious. This is not an episode whose end is in sight, but a state of excitement and uncertainty.

The composition forms no centres or focal points, rests nowhere and is fixed nowhere. The imaginary scene is not created out of individual components subjected to transformation and alienation, but finds its own completely independent form.

**Alessandro Magnasco**
The Wise Raven, c. 1703–1711
Oil on canvas, 47 x 61 cm. Florence, Galleria degli Uffizi

In the ruins of an ancient building, in a scene of unreal night, a strange rabble has gathered: in the foreground, with his back to us, is a mercenary who has fallen on hard times. On the rotting boards of the "stage" is an ageing mother with her ugly, gnome-like children and behind her is a figure in a strangely solemn scarlet toga. In front of them, sitting on part of a barrel, a semi-naked man with a note in his hand is reciting a text to the raven perched on the wine keg. Ragged, gnome-like children gather round the keg.

It is a genre scene. Yet just as all the props have been knocked over, broken, rotting, the scene itself shows the decay of the idyll. The raven on the barrel is the sovereign focal point, as though placed on a plinth, while his teacher is the shadow of the philosopher for whom the black bird is his last pupil. The solemnity of the red-robed figure is no more than a shabby and ridiculously theatrical display, the genre-like display of maternal happiness is merely a ragged crowd of urchins. This painting is an inversion of the familiar and the contemplative, the edifying and the moral. At the same time, however, the situation is charged with an exciting vitality and tension gleaned from the very fact that ideals void of credibility fail to find fulfilment.

## ROSALBA CARRIERA
1675-1757

In choosing pastel, Rosalba Carriera opted for a technique that allowed her to flatter her models without pretentiously idealizing them – which may explain the success she enjoyed despite her lack of artistic brilliance. Her best works were created when the gentle appeal and flattering softness of pastel complemented the personality of the sitter.

This is certainly true in this portrait of a young girl. The mother-of-pearl flesh tone has been rendered in classic pastel hues of blue, pink and pale grey, and the lack of depth in colority is perfectly suited to capturing this almost childlike face that has not yet experienced life. Pastel does not lend itself to the portrayal of shadow and is suited to depicting a life of carefree youth that knows no shadow either.

The softness of this charming face relates perfectly to the technique. Apart from the compatibility of subject matter and medium, Carriera's achievement consist in her ability to subordinate the facial expression to the mood of the picture without losing the individuality of the sitter's appearance. The girl looks at us with a mild and almost lustreless gaze, an almost imperceptible smile on her lips. All excitement, abruptness or suddenness that would contradict the pastel, is avoided. The quality of the painting lies in its delicate uniformity.

**Rosalba Carriera**
Portrait of a Young
Girl, after 1708
Pastel, 36.3 x 30.3 cm
Paris, Musée
National du Louvre

## GIOVANNI BATTISTA PIAZZETTA
1683-1754

The creation of an independent pictorial language capable of capturing the wealth and poverty, comedy and tragedy, serenity and gloom of Italian life is the achievement of such artists as Longhi, Magnasco and Piazzetta, who created a distinct counterpoint to the artificiality of French genre painting.

The young beggar boy here with his chubby cheeks, his strong neck and his childlike stature is not a pathos-laden appeal to the spectator, nor one that calls for sympathy. There is nothing servile in his bearing or his direct gaze and the rosary in his grubby hand is not a sign of hypocritical piety, but an object of his daily life.

Piazzetta allows the pictorial means to become bearers of expression in themselves. The background of the painting and the coat are brown as the naked earth: poverty is clearly something elementary, and not just picturesque decay. The red of the waistcoat is vigorous and strong. A vibrant southern light is reflected in the white of the sleeve, freshness and sunshine in the boy's brown complexion. There is no sentimentality in the harmony of technique and subject matter, but a certain candour that touches the spectator.

**Giovanni Battista
Piazzetta**
Beggar Boy,
c. 1740 (?)
Oil on canvas,
66 x 52 cm
Chicago (IL), The
Art Institute of
Chicago

**Canaletto**
The Courtyard of the Castle of Warwick, 1751
Oil on canvas, 75 x 122 cm
Warwick (Warwickshire), Duke of
Warwick Collection

**Canaletto**
Regatta on the Canale Grande, after 1735
Oil on canvas, 117 x 186 cm
London, National Gallery

# CANALETTO
## 1697–1768

The fact that, even in his own lifetime, Canaletto was not only imitated by such artists as Michele Marieschi, but was forged on a considerable scale, is proof indeed of the popularity of his paintings. His first buyers were predominantly English, commercial representatives, diplomats and travellers on the obligatory "grand tour". The Duke of Bedford commissioned a series of 24 veduta and John Smith, the English Consul in Venice, ordered 36. In 1746, Canaletto undertook his first journey to England, with understandable optimism, and returned after four years of intensive work.

The British nobility was by no means content simply to import a touch of southern warmth into their cool houses by purchasing the paintings of Canaletto, but also commissioned motifs of their homes. The detailed and objectively detached portraits of dogs or horses so popular at the time now extended to portraits of the patrons' property. For such a task, the Venetian guest seemed eminently suitable. The Duke of Warwick commissioned four views of his ducal residence, all painted from different angels. Even today, most of Canaletto's works are to be found in English collections.

In the example shown here, Canaletto does not simply aim to give a careful and true portrait of the property, but also demonstrates the versatility of his painterly technique: a cool northern light is cast across the symmetrically staged architecture, and colour, light and composition are perfectly balanced in their rigid stringency.

Processions and festivals, ceremonies and regattas – even Gentile Bellini's 15th century paintings bear witness to the brilliant pageantry of La Serenissima. Canaletto not only continues in this tradition, but actually revives it, adding to it his own views and temperament and clothing it in the garb of his own era. Whether he portrays the city's Ascension Day celebrations, the symbolic marriage of Venice with the sea, or the arrival of the Doge: it is no longer with the grand choreography and dignified regularity that dominates Bellini's paintings.

In this painting, Canaletto shows the Canale Grande teeming with boats, the gondolieri in their traditional costumes, the colourful decorations, the crowds lining the banks of the canal, the flags and pelmets on the windows and balconies. What is more, he conscientiously renders a specific location in Venice, seen from the Ca' Foscari, with its palatial facades, its simple houses, its stairways, rooftops, chimneys and terraces and between them all, the wide, azure expanse of the canal. He is fascinated by the contrast between the momentary pageantry with all its light and colour, its exhilarating presence, and the city itself, steeped in tradition, in which celebration after celebration passes through its ancient walls down the centuries.

Canaletto initially trained as a theatrical set painter in Venice before going to Rome in 1719, where he met Pannini, the painter of ruins. In this early work, we see some indication of this training. In the foreground, between blocks of marble, capitals, fragments and unworked blocks of hewn stone, we see the stonemasons at their work. On the right, a simple bothy has been hammered together with planks. In the middleground we see a canal, behind it the church and Scuola della Carità, painted with absolute precision as an easily identifiable Venetian building, set against a sky of silken blue. It is almost as though two paintings had been forced together on a single surface, with no reference to each other: one a genre scene heralding what would later become an independent theme, and the other a Venetian veduta.

Even if Canaletto does not make use of illusionistic effects here, he does profit from his theatre background. The veduta, clearly structured, remains in the distance of a background view, and the link between the two parts of the painting is created by tiny figures who seem like anonymous extras. A mother, children, stonemasons working outdoors, gondolieri and passers-by are scattered here and there, so that the entire painting merges into a single area of action.

What is happening in this space is not continuous. It is not a narrative episode with any moral or documentary character. The events serve to identify and delineate the space, and characterize it individually. The figures presented draw two very different areas together, blurring the border between them. Through these figures, Canaletto also creates a temporal unity: the temporality of each individual building, its respective age and its history are integrated in to the contemporary activity of communal life. The artist successfully avoids the pitfall of the sterility and academically sober detachment of a "veduta ideata". The architecture, monumentality and historicity of a city are not presented here as ideals, but are experienced as living elements in the painting. Fleeting and banal activity lends the built environment its identity.

**Canaletto**
Venice: Campo San Vitale and Santa Maria della Carità (The Stonemason's Yard), c. 1726/27
Oil on canvas, 123.8 x 162.9 cm
London, National Gallery

## FRANCESCO GUARDI

1712–1793

Grand Duke Pavel Petrovich, later Tsar Paul I, and his wife Maria Fyodorovna, arrived in Venice in January 1782, providing a welcome occasion for a city so fond of festivity to stage a number of brilliantly lavish celebrations and spectacles in their honour. The elderly Guardi was commissioned to chronicle their visit. He documented the ball at the Teatro di San Benedetto, the ceremonial procession on the Piazza San Marco, the regatta, bullfight and banquet. The artist, too, welcomed such an opportunity. Just as his distinctive drawings with their bold and vibrantly moving brushwork paid little heed to faithful detail in rendering palaces, towers, obelisks or figures, so too is his documentation of the royal visit hardly the work of a painstaking collector of data.

The gala concert in the philharmonic hall of the Procuratie Vecchie with a women's choir and a women's orchestra in the gallery, the shimmering silk robes in the warm candlelight, the glittering chandeliers, the gleaming mirrors and the vermilion floor all merge to a floating image of serene enchantment. The timelessness of the celebration and its carefree

*joie de vivre* are the legitimation for Guardi's painting. We cannot actually make out who exactly is the grand duke or his wife, for the artist did not create any individual physiognomic portraits. In the midst of celebration, the contours of all the individuals and the reality of time itself dissolve. In place of the strict regulated ceremony of the Baroque, what we see here is unceremonial; a choreography of coincidence has supplanted hierarchy. Whereas, in earlier times, the solemnity of the occasion would have been highlighted by contrast and difference, juxtaposing the wealthy with the less wealthy, the magnificent with the less magnificent, the highly esteemed with the less highly esteemed, these festivities gain their radiance from their sheer indissolubility; the celebration becomes a *Gesamtkunstwerk*.

In Guardi's painting, the light does not add brilliance to any individual person; it is diffuse. Nor are there any accents of colour that might serve to emphasize any individual. In dissolving the bounds of individuality and sensual perception we find a technique suited to escape from a sense of reality. Guardi's painting uses compositional techniques to express this illusion of an extended existence in which the participants taste immortality for a few hours.

Francesco Guardi
Venetian Gala Concert, c. 1782
Oil on canvas, 67.7 x 90.5 cm
Munich, Bayerische Staatsgemälde-
sammlungen, Alte Pinakothek

# FRANCESCO GUARDI

1712-1793

After his death, Guardi's name was quickly forgotten. Perhaps the rediscovery of his work is due in part to the new way of seeing that the Impressionists taught us. Nevertheless, it would not only be stylistically anachronistic to describe Guardi's work as "impressionistic", but would also be fundamentally incorrect. Whereas the Impressionists sought to present the unrepeatable individuality of an optical experience by portraying nature, rendering objects solely as a means of exploring the reflection of light and the perception of colour, Guardi takes exactly the opposite approach.

In this capriccio, he composes the subject matter of his painting on the basis of its individual components, building up the pictorial world from individual parts chosen according to their associative power: the melancholy of architectural ruins, the serenity of busy workers, the dignity of a domed building, the shadow creeping in from the side evoking a sense of the clandestine and the secret; the stone vase and the damaged bust evoking nostalgic memories of formerly blossoming gardens. The artist does not show us a subjective interpretation of what he actually saw, but chooses objects on the basis of their pictorial impact to express a subjective mood.

Francesco Guardi
Capriccio, c. 1745
Oil on canvas, 92 x 132 cm
Milan, Crespi Collection

# BERNARDO BELLOTTO

1721-1780

Bellotto, like his uncle, was also known by the name of Canaletto. Bellotto had studied under his uncle, Canaletto, and throughout his life he worked in the same field. Nevertheless, he quickly developed his own artistic profile and his works are easily distinguished from those of his uncle. In his younger years, Bellotto's distinctive style lay primarily in the way he enriched his vedutas with an intensity of atmosphere, either in the quiet melancholy of a cloudy sky, the magical illumination of a setting sun or the calm before an impending storm. Later, having worked in Vienna, Munich and Dresden, finally settling in Warsaw, his style began to lose its picturesque fluidity, gaining in clarity, becoming more sharply contoured, and tending increasingly towards draughtsmanship and line, whereby the emphasis on colour was reduced. In his painting of the *Piazza della Signoria in Florence* he portrays the Palazzo della Signoria, the Loggia dei Lanzi, the facades of churches and houses, rooftops and towers, with painstaking attention to detail. Yet he adds to these detailed documentations his observations of everyday life. The purely documentary is enlivened by the banal, the permanent by the transient. The piazza is bathed in afternoon light, making it unique in a double sense: as an urban architectural complex and as a contemporary urban scene personally experienced.

Bernardo Bellotto
Piazza della Signoria in Florence, c. 1740-1745
Oil on canvas, 61 x 90 cm
Budapest, Magyar Szépmüvészeti Múzeum

Pietro Longhi
The Rhinoceros, c. 1751
Oil on canvas, 62 x 50 cm
Venice, Ca' Rezzonico

Pietro Longhi
The Tooth-Puller, c. 1746–1752
Oil on canvas, 50 x 62 cm
Milan, Pinacoteca di Brera

## PIETRO LONGHI
### 1702–1785

In 1751, a rhinoceros was exhibited in Venice which had previously been put on show in Nuremberg, Stuttgart and Strasbourg. Longhi shows us some of the visitors who attended this spectacle standing on and before a wooden platform, in front of which the rhinoceros is eating its hay. Yet none of the guests is actually looking at the monstrous animal. The elegant lady in the lace shawl is looking straight at the spectator; her dark suitor, like the servant to her right, is staring ahead of him; the man at the edge of the picture with the clay pipe is deep in thought; the woman in the green shawl is looking towards the other side and her neighbour is gazing out of the picture through a black mask. Not even the little girl shows the slightest sign of astonishment. All of them seem to be caught in a rigid pose of supposed vitality, unreal behind their masks and physiognomies.

They seem like quotations of a Venetian life that is no longer within them, but only presented to them. And in front of this silent display of detachment stands the rhinoceros in its bulky and ponderous simplicity, painted with a certain naivity and described by the poster on the wall as "Vero Ritratto di un Rinoceronte". It is the "veritable portrait" of this animal which, in its strangeness, is the only reality. The familiar Venetian world behind it, has become the truly unfamiliar, because it is merely a shell, a costume, a mask or shadow of the reality to which it is no longer able to return a sense of wonder.

The relationship between Longhi's art and the plays written by his contemporary Carlo Goldoni has always been stressed. The relationship is particularly clear in this example. The *Commedia dell'arte* had become increasingly entrenched in the repetition of empty formula and had almost completely lost its original character of a popular theatre of improvization based on a number of specifically defined and easily identifiable characters. Goldoni revived them by bringing the small and great weaknesses of his contemporaries onto the stage. Longhi reiterates this form of expression in Venetian genre.

An everyday street scene becomes a stage. The tooth-puller on the platform is giving an improvised sales-talk to attract custom. At his feet crouches the patient, sympathetically observed by a passer-by whose companion is listening enthralled to the words of the miracle-working doctor. Three street urchins are eagerly involved in the performance, and the dwarf in the foreground profits from the attraction. Two masked couples, gloomy, rigid and ceremonial, represent a very different sphere. Just as Goldoni's comedy draws its wit, its depth and its vitality from the character sketches created by the heightened use of contrasts, so too does Longhi's painting gain its meaning from the juxtaposition of opposites. Ceremony and everyday situations, tradition and presence, wealth and poverty are combined in the aura of the theatre.

# GIOVANNI BATTISTA TIEPOLO
1696–1770

"Gerusalemme Liberata" ("Jerusalem Liberated"), the great heroic epos by Torquato Tasso (1544–1595), published in 1581, not only inspired Tiepolo to create his series of paintings in the Tasso Hall of the Villa Valmerana near Vicenza, but also to create individual portrayals such as this one. The episode involving Armida and the hero Rinaldo is set in the days of the crusades.

The enchantress Armida, resting after the rigours of battle, recognizes him as an enemy and is about to slay him. But at that moment, her hate turns to love and she bears him away to an enchanted island far from war, where Rinaldo is caught in the spell of her love. Two warriors sent to look for him make him aware of his error by holding up a shield as a mirror, reminding him of the battle, and take him back with them.

Tiepolo's Armida is a magnificent Venus figure carrying a mirror as the instrument of her magical powers and accompanied by Amor as the bringer of love. The young hero rests devoted at her breast, weating a garland of flowers as the sign of his entanglement. The theatricality of the foreground scene is heightened by the background scene in which, behind a "backdrop architecture" we can see the two warriors approaching. The wealth of colour, the sensual charms of Armida, the devotion of Rinaldo, the statue of a satyr and the parrot, the pale blue landscape behind the gate, the shimmering pink of the sky, the fantastic trees all conjure up the atmosphere of an "Ile enchantée".

A sense of duty, reality and order is embodied in the figures of the two soldiers who wish to draw Rinaldo back to their world. By investing all his painterly powers of conviction to mediate an episode of happiness, Tiepolo succeeds in drawing us, the spectators, into the spell: we, too, are beguiled by Armida; only in the distance do we perceive the warning of the vassals, the voices of everyday life. This scene of Tasso's lovers has been condensed to an exemplary form in which the victory of magic over reality becomes a quietly menacing actuality.

Giovanni Battista Tiepolo
Rinaldo and Armida, 1753
Oil on canvas, 104.8 x 143 cm
Munich, Bayerische Staatsgemäldesammlungen

**Giovanni Battista Tiepolo**
Rachel Hiding the Idols from her Father Laban, 1726–1728
Fresco (Detail), height c. 500 cm, width c. 400 cm
Udine, Palazzo Arcivescovile

**Giovanni Battista Tiepolo**
Sarah and the Archangel,
1726–1728
Fresco (Detail), height c. 400 cm,
width c. 200 cm
Udine, Palazzo Arcivescovile

# GIOVANNI BATTISTA TIEPOLO
## 1696–1770

After years of exploitation in the house of Laban, Jacob fled, taking with him his children, his livestock and his wives Rachel and Leah, the daughters of Laban. Rachel, cheated of her inheritance and property by Laban, had stolen her father's idols and had hidden them under the saddle of her camel. Three days later, the runaways were caught and accused of theft. Unaware of the truth, Jacob proclaims his innocence, while Laban searches the tent. In Tiepolo's fresco, the biblical narrative is presented as a skilfully structured scene of individual groups, positions and situations. The central group shows Jacob looking candidly out of the picture while the aged Laban talks irately to his daughter who is seated on the ground. On the left, a group of shepherd, maids, children and animals – almost an autonomous idyll – represents the aim of the runaways to lead a simple farming life. On the right, in front of a high drape which fringes the "stage", we see Leah carrying an amphora and watching the events. Behind the curtain, we see a couple resting, camel drivers and laden camels. The action is built up to a point of tension between "whence" and "whither" and is concentrated on the episode surrounding Rachel. Its compositional structure makes it a restless event of oppressive intensity.

In this fresco from Udine, Tiepolo once again explores an Old Testament theme: an angle brings the elderly Sarah the tidings that she will bear a son to her hundred-year-old husband, Abraham. Instead of creating an image of sublimity and solemnity, Tiepolo chooses to portray the presence and proximity of the event, lending it credibility by means of the candid humanity of the characters and the "Italian" reality of the surroundings.

Hagar, Isaac's maid, bore him a son, Ismael. When Isaac's wife Sarah drove Hagar and Ismael into the wilderness, an angel saved the child from thirst by showing Hagar the way to a well. Unlike Claude Lorrain, Tiepolo does not situate this Old Testament episode in an empty, sweeping landscape, but presses it into a dense composition. In the foreground lies the pale, exhausted and thirsting child, behind it the beautiful figure of Hagar, pleading with the angel and indicating Ismael's plight. The angel, a strong and very real figure, passing so close that he brushes against her shoulder, looks down with sympathy upon the suffering child and points the way to the well. The helplessness and urgency of the mother are not presented here by showing her as a forlorn figure in some vast expanse of space, but by portraying her in a gesture of mourning reminiscent of a pietà. The urgency with which Hagar pleads for help for her son is heightened by the density of this crowded composition.

**Giovanni Battista Tiepolo**
Hagar and Ismael in the Wilderness, c. 1732
Oil on canvas, 140 x 120 cm
Venice, Scuola di San Rocco

**Jean-Etienne Liotard**
Turkish Woman with a
Tambourine, c. 1738–1743
Oil on canvas, 63.5 x 48.5 cm
Geneva, Musée d'Art et
d'Histoire

# JEAN-ETIENNE LIOTARD
## 1702–1789

From 1738 to 1743, Liotard lived in Constantinople, where he learned the Turkish language and adopted the local clothing and lifestyle. The attention to detail in this painting indicates his astute powers of observation as well as his technical brilliance. Liotard's fame is founded primarily on his qualities as a pastellist and this painting is an oil replica of a smaller pastel. This allowed him to explore other aspects of the subject matter and set other accents. Whereas the powdery, velvety surface of the pastel and its predominantly whitish tones may be appropriate as a flattering medium for the portrait of an elegant woman of Parisian society, the strongly coloured charms of the Turkish costume can be rendered with considerably greater intensity in oil. The vibrant colours, the brilliance of the gold brocade, the silken sheen of the baggy trousers – everything in the picture is saturated with colour and light. Only the flesh tones are reminiscent of pastel techniques. The woman in this painting has the perfectly groomed face and pale complexion of a Frenchwoman whose picturesque pose seems to clash with the sumptuous richness of the costume and the setting. "Turquerie" was a popular exotic fashion imported during the Rococo period and this is not only the subject matter of the painting, but is also evident in the painterly techniques. The contrast between the "pastel style" and the "oil painting" indicates that this is a precious model in disguise who wishes to be recognized as such.

He had visited all the great cities of Europe, and had painted portraits of Pope Clemens XIII and Empress Maria Theresia by the time he returned to his home town of Geneva as portraitist to high society. There is no shortage of self-assurance in the way the artist writes of his talents, pointing out in particular his portraits of François Tronchin, scion of one of the oldest and wealthiest families of the city, and his wife. Here we see Tronchin, in half-figure and in three-quarter profile, dressed in the trappings of his office and seated at his desk. His gesture is reminiscent of the gesture of saints in a "Sacra Conversazione" pointing out the object of their devotion. Tronchin, however, is not pointing towards a Madonna with the Christ Child, but to a painting by Rembrandt which shows Rembrandt's second wife Hendrickje Stoffels in bed. Liotard informs the spectator in this way of Tronchin's art collection, and the esteem in which Rembrandt was held at the time, while at the same time establishing a connection between his own career as an artist and that of his famous colleague. We may be surprised to find a painting by Rembrandt on the easel, given that this artist of such finely detailed pasts would appear to have been influenced more by the smooth precision of Jan van Huysum. Yet in the deliberate contrast – the naked, almost peasant-like Hendrickje against a dark, deep space, with the smooth, elegant Tronchin in the foreground – Liotard displays his distinctive talent with great effect and little modesty.

**Jean-Etienne Liotard**
Portrait of François Tronchin, 1757
Pastel on parchment, 37.5 x 46 cm
Geneva, André Givaudon collection

# ANGELICA KAUFFMANN
1741–1807

Even at the age of eleven, she earned admiring praise for her portrait of Bishop Nevroni and although she would later concentrate on allegorical, antique, historical and religious themes in her paintings, the portrait was to remain the driving force behind her success throughout her life. She received so many commissions that her painting tended to become rather routine, taking on an increasing smoothness and superficial appeal at the expense of a more distinctive style. Goethe, whose portrait she painted in 1787 merely commented laconically: "A fine looking youth, but not a trace of me."

This self-portrait of the artist Angelica Kauffmann also has something routine about it, and is as pleasingly decorative as any interior decor that she might have created in her frequent collaboration with the English architect Robert Adam. Nevertheless, it does show her face as that of a highly sensitive personality. It is interesting to note that she illustrated Klopstock's "Messias" and that she frequented poets of literary sensitivity, such as Goethe, Herder, Winckelmann and Reynolds, which may explain this half natural, half artificial pose. On the other hand, there is something clear and decisive about her traits, which would certainly conform to Kauffmann's reputation as a draughtswoman. In her drawings, she presents a bold, free and "modern" technique that has all the distinctive individuality of real talent.

**Angelica Kauffmann**
Self-portrait, 1780
Oil on canvas,
130 x 102 cm
Frankfurt am Main,
Goethe-Museum

# HENRY FUSELI
1741–1825

Shakespeare's comedy *A Midsummer Night's Dream*, a bewildering romp through various planes of reality in which mythological and courtly elements are interwoven with tragedy, satire and fairytale, has prompted all manner of interpretations. Here, Fuseli depicts the revenge taken by Oberon, king of the fairies, on his wife Titania, with whom he has quarrelled. Oberon has the mischievous sprite Puck press the juice of a magic plant into Titania's eyes while she is sleeping, so that when she wakes, she will fall in love with the first creature she sees, "The next thing she waking looks upon, Be it on lion, bear, or wolf, or bull/ On meddling monkey or on busy ape, / She shall pursue it with the soul of love" (Act II, Sc. i). Puck heightens the mordant satire of the scene by choosing the talkative weaver Bottom as his victim and putting an ass's head on him. Fuseli turns this episode into a dream vision. He shows Titania as Venus triumphant, at whose feet the slow-witted and foolish Bottom seeks to demonstrate his power to a tiny elfin creature. The couple is flanked by two statuesque ladies-in-waiting, one dreaming and one waking, and surrounded by a group of beguiling, ugly and comic figures. Beauty and ugliness, pride and fear, youth and age, wit and foolishness are united here in a triumph of inventive power, condensed to the allegory of a dream.

**Henry Fuseli (Heinrich Füssli)**
Titania and Bottom, c. 1780–1790
Oil on canvas, 216 x 274 cm
London, Tate Gallery

# WILLIAM HOGARTH
## 1697–1764

Dr. Graham, apothecary at the Chelsea hospital, wished to show his wealth and success by commissioning this portrait of his four children in 1742. Hogarth certainly accommodated his desire to present a life of bourgeois comfort: the fine Sunday dresses of silk, the dignified drapery, the richness of the blossoms and fruit, a few items of fine and cultured furniture. Yet Hogarth offers more than simply a pleasing and decorative picture.

The children are posed in an almost ceremonial order reminiscent of Velázquez' *Las Meninas* (ill. p. 272) but at the same time they are full of life and merriment. With their fresh and rosy complexions, their pale dresses, their shadowless faces, they look at the world as a place of unqualified joy. And yet we sense that this innocent happiness is threatened. It is not simply the darkness of the room behind them, but also the way it is flanked by Baroque allegories: on the left we see time and transience in the figure of the childlike Chronos on the clock, on the right we see the cat preying on the birdcage as a metaphor of threatened sexual innocence. The perils of the adult world are already present in this room.

This is hardly a flattering portrait of the 48-year-old artist. There is nothing ornate about his clothing, and not the slightest trace of a smile to render his physiognomy more attractive. Indeed, it even seems to be caricatured in the face of the dog. The self-portrait is presented as an image within an image, as an oval canvas resting on a pile of books to indicate the craft of the painter. As the attribute of the artist, we also see a palette in the foreground bearing signature, date, and an S-curve with the inscription "line of beauty and grace". This "line of beauty and grace" was a concept central to Hogarth's aesthetic theory, which he outlined in his publication "The Analysis of Beauty", calling for its inclusion in all the visual arts. Theory is thus integrated into painting, and all pomp and idealization is banished in favour of carefully outlined character and unadulterated truth – just as Hogarth presents himself here. On the spines of the books, we can read the names of the authors – Shakespeare, Milton and Swift – respectively representing the English cultural tradition, moral criticism and hope of religious, ethical renewal, and mordant satire. Looked at from this angle, it is a self-confident portrait indeed.

In the improvised composition of this oil sketch of *The Shrimp Girl*, we see Hogarth's painterly talent at its very finest. Here, he succeeds in creating a spontaneous reiteration of his observations with all the impact of a first impression. The freshness of the moment is not transposed here into a smooth painterly technique, but is echoed in the vigorous and fleeting brushwork.

**William Hogarth**
The Graham Children, 1742
Oil on canvas, 160.5 x 181 cm
London, Tate Gallery

**William Hogarth**
Self-portrait, 1745
Oil on canvas,
90.2 x 69.8 cm
London, Tate Gallery

**William Hogarth**
The Shrimp Girl, c. 1740
Oil on canvas, 63.5 x 52.5 cm
London, National Gallery

**William Hogarth**
Heads of Six of Hogarth's Servants, c. 1750–1755
Oil on canvas, 62.2 x 74.9 cm
London, Tate Gallery

## WILLIAM HOGARTH
### 1697–1764

Hogarth originally wanted to become a history painter, but this ambition seems to have been thwarted by a singular lack of interest on the part of his contemporaries. Posterity, too, has chosen to remember a very different Hogarth. He characterized the individual personalities of his sitters, revealed the unique within the typical, and in his tongue-in-cheek portrayals of human nature he documented the social mores of the age in areas beyond the sphere of the "historic" event. Then, as now, he was regarded as the painter of the private, the forgotten and the overlooked.

Hogarth's later works include this painting of his servants. Although it is a portrait of a group, the artist has not arranged the figures in the conventional form we might normally expect. Instead, he has created a painting that looks for all the world like a study sheet. The brushwork is sketchy, yet each face has been painstakingly and lovingly given its own distinctive identity. The servants are dressed in their drab domestic uniforms, gathered together within a closed space, yet entirely free as individuals. Each is looking in a different direction, none refers to any of the others. No one betrays anything personal, even though each is depicted as a unique character. We know nothing about them, and their private lives remain a mystery.

**Joseph Wright of Derby**
Experiment with an Airpump, 1768
Oil on canvas, 183 x 244 cm
London, National Gallery

## JOSEPH WRIGHT
### 1734–1797

Most of Joseph Wright's paintings explore the effects of light and illumination. He counted amongst his close friends a number of factory owners and scientists, the very people who were the driving force behind the changes that came with the dawn of the industrial age, which was to bring so much profit and wreak such disaster. He was fascinated by mankind's encounter with technology, innovation and invention, and with the myth of a new era which he monumentalized in his paintings. The light that Caravaggio used to project his revelations and celestial visions seems to have fascinated Wright as well. But the spectator soon realizes that any similarity is misleading. In the work of Caravaggio, the source of light remains unknown so that it seems almost supernatural. Wright, on the other hand, uses light for dramatic effect. The experiment carried out by the elderly, long-haired scholar thus becomes an exciting theatrical scene.

The scholar is demonstrating the principle of the vacuum. Using a pump, he has emptied the glass sphere of air, creating a vacuum in which a bird seems to be struggling to gasp its last breath. Pained, the little girl turns her face away as though witnessing the martyrdom of a saint. Here, we find religious iconography being used to portray a worldly situation, elevating the scientific experiment to a para-religious event.

# JOSHUA REYNOLDS

1732–1792

Any educated Englishman who had been on his obligatory grand tour to the continent's centres of culture would have recognized this image immediately. The pose adopted by Mrs Siddons on a majestic throne cites Michelangelo's prophets in the Sixtine Chapel of the Vatican. The concept of the "portrait historié" which transposes contemporary portraits to a mythological or historical setting, was by no means new in 1784 when this painting was created. To choose the role of a tragic muse behind whom demons lurk as harbingers of doom, was fitting indeed; Sarah Siddons was the celebrated heroine of great tragic roles in Shakespearean drama.

Nevertheless, this painting, which the artist has so elegantly and confidently signed on the hem of the dress with the words "Joshua Reynolds pinxit 1784" is a brilliant pictorial invention. The scene in the clouds is not ethereally light, but rendered in earthy, Rembrandtesque hues of brown that lend it weight and dignity.

The pathos of the prophetic pose is alleviated by the relaxed elegance of the sitter. Moreover, the impersonal mythological role finds its counterpart in the brilliant character study of this actress who is not identical with the roles she played, but who remains an individual and sensitive woman of the 18th century. The traditional techniques Reynolds uses so confidently serve one sole purpose: that of heightening the portrait of Sarah Siddons as an inimitable personality.

**Joshua Reynolds**
Sarah Siddons as the Tragic Muse, 1784
Oil on canvas, 236 x 146cm
San Marino (CA), Huntington Library
and Art Gallery

Reynolds never tired of encouraging his students at the Royal Academy to bear in mind how important it was to study the contents and techniques of the old masters and, by copying them, to develop a style they could use. Though Reynolds himself was a highly distinctive painter, he mastered "à-la-mode" painting and could effortlessly slip into the guise of another style.

Here in his portrait of *The Infant Samuel*, the stylistic guise he dons is that of Rembrandt. In earthy shades of brown, he shows Samuel, the last judge and first prophet of Israel, as a child. The very choice of theme is unusual, considering the role of Samuel as the epitome of constant obedience, great wisdom and just but firm rule, a weighty role indeed for a child of such tender age, as Reynolds shows here. By using the light and colours of Rembrandt, he also cites the profound human piety of the Dutch artist's œuvre. In this way, the Rembrandtesque becomes a motif of dignity that not only enriches the painting and lends it profound significance, but also mediates between the religious Old Testament theme and the innocence of the child. The Rembrandtesque brown is also a gallery tone that makes the painting a collector's piece. In this context, the childishness also functions as mediating distance: the high religious theme becomes more adaptable and less pathosladen. It becomes a *Samuel* that can hang in any home.

**Joshua Reynolds**
The Infant Samuel, 1776
Oil on canvas, 89 x 70cm
Montpellier, Musée Fabre

## THOMAS GAINSBOROUGH
### 1727–1788

Thomas Gainsborough
Robert Andrews and his Wife Frances, c. 1750
Oil on canvas, 69.8 x 119.5 cm
London, National Gallery

When Gainsborough returned to live near his birthplace of Sudbury at the age of 21, the landed gentry of Suffolk became his main patrons. Landscapes were not in great demand in those circles at the time and they tended to be displayed for purely decorative purposes above the fireplace. Nevertheless, in what has come to be known as his Ipswich period, Gainsborough proves his skill as a portraitist and landscape artist whose cornfields, hills and trees are not fictional ideals, but images, even portraits, of specific properties. The young landowners are posed in front of their grounds in a relaxed attitude. Yet there is something artificial, staffage-like about them, which Gainsborough was to overcome in his more mature works. The 1740s fashion for full figures posed in front of a landscape background – introduced, incidentally, by his colleague Francis Hayman, is used quite charmingly here, but it still clearly betrays Gainsborough's practice of modelling and structuring cork, sand, fragments of mirrors, moss, asparagus shoots and dolls. At the same time, however, we find here the nucleus of a new technique, for this real Suffolk landscape had been recorded in sketches by the artist, working in the open air.

Gainsborough's individual portrait style found no followers. His landscape painting, influenced by the study of 17th century Netherlandish painting, particularly Ruisdael, was to shape the generation of artists who came after him, who saw in him a major pioneer of plein-air painting. In a painting such as *The Watering Place* his intensive observations of natural light conditions and illumination are evident. Gainsborough recorded these phenomena in sketches from nature and reworked them in his studio.

A comparison of this double portrait with the earlier double portrait of *Mr and Mrs Andrews* is tempting: once again, we see two full-figure portraits in an outdoor setting. Yet even in the attitude of the couple towards each other, we already sense that there is a marked difference from his earlier work. The disinterested and cool juxtaposition has been replaced by an attitude of natural intimacy, and in place of the rather stiff immobility we see a light and elegant step. Lightness also determines the atmosphere with its gentle morning light that no longer lies on the surface, but in all of the colours, creating a sense of weightlessness. Foliage, fabrics, hair, the feathers on Elizabeth's hat, the fur of the dog – everything seems to consist of the same airy and light material. The two figures are not standing against a landscape background, but, in spite of their elegant clothing, seem to be integrated into it.

Thomas Gainsborough
The Watering Place, 1777
Oil on canvas, 147.3 x 180.3 cm
London, National Gallery

Thomas Gainsborough
The Morning Walk, c. 1785/86
Oil on canvas, 263.3 x 179.1 cm
London, National Gallery

**Thomas Gainsborough**
Woman in Blue, before 1780
Oil on canvas, 76 x 64 cm
St Petersburg, Hermitage

**Thomas Gainsborough**
Lady and Gentleman in a Landscape, c. 1746/47
Oil on canvas, 73 x 86 cm
Paris, Musée National du Louvre

# THOMAS GAINSBOROUGH
## 1727–1788

What does English landscape gardening have
to do with an elegant portrait of a woman?
What do Gainsborough's famous portraits
have in common with the carefully calculated
yet subtly informal landscaping of the day?
Both demonstrate a decisive rejection of
pretentious artificiality. An acceptance of
forms that correspond to nature and are not
imposed on it. Even if the lightly powdered
hair of the woman in blue has been piled up
high, fixed with combs and decorated with a
ribbon in a blue to match her silken dress,
there is nevertheless something delightfully
natural about her portrait. Her slender face
with cheeks reddened by the country air seems
to need no make-up. There is no hint of coquettishness in her slightly shy smile and
gentle gaze. No corset pushes her breasts upwards, no deep décolleté distracts from her personal charm. John Locke, whose complete
works had been published in 1714, had popu-
larized the idea that beauty and grace are inextricably linked with nature and naturalness.
Gainsborough had had ample opportunity to
study and document the requirements of sophisticated dress and deportment between 1759
and 1774, when he lived in the elegant spa
town of Bath.

This painting is the culmination of a motif
Gainsborough had already been exploring for
some time as a young artist. In 1746, when he
painted his *Lady and Gentleman in a Landscape*,
he was just nineteen years old. Linguists have
traced the use of the word "sentimentality" for
the first time in English literature to that
same year, but language of that kind was already in the air long before the publication of
Laurence Sterne's famous novel *Sentimental Journey*. The painting is known to show Gainsborough with his young wife Margaret Burr,
whom he had recently married. There is more
than a hint of French Rococo spirit in this
painting, and much that reminds us of the
great Watteau. When Gainsborough, a child
prodigy, enrolled at art school at the age of
thirteen, he had already learned to place full
figures gracefully in an outdoor setting. His
models were landscapes he had built himself,
peopled with tiny dolls. In these pastoral
idylls he evoked and transfigured a sense of
"simplicity". His portraits, set in Netherland-
ish-style landscapes after the manner of Ruisdael and Wynants whose works he copied,
were meant to be anti-heroic and devoid of pathos. In spite of a certain stiffness in his early
work, there is something charming and
amiable about this marital conversation. The
young painter, a book in his hand, is talking
and gesturing enthusiastically; perhaps he is
discussing the literature with his young bride.
As in his intimate portrait of a couple in *Morning Walk*, the fragrant, light-filled landscape
seems to inspire conversation, allowing the
couple to become a part of nature.

## RICHARD WILSON

1714–1782

Paintings such as this were of seminal importance to the otherwise apparently unprecedented art of William Turner. Here, Wilson abandons the tradition of Poussin or Vernet and dispenses with the evocative power of pictorial objects.

He composes his landscape entirely in blues, greens and browns linked together in finely transparent shading. The atmosphere carries itself and no longer depends on individual pictorial components as its vehicle. The outlines of the mountains, trees, and shoreline, and the mirror image on the water, create their own system of movement and countermovement that requires no stabilizing compositional techniques.

The same applies to the density and restraint with which colour is handled; even in the colour composition, the artist does not use the tectonic structure of chiaroscuro. The gentle tones complement each other without blurring. The landscape itself has neither drama nor passion.

Richard Wilson
View of Snowdon from Llyn Nantlle, c. 1766
Oil on canvas, 100 x 127 cm
Nottingham, Castle Museum

## GEORGE STUBBS

1724–1806

Portraits of horses, such as this one, were not generally commissioned specifically unless the noble animal had won a thousand-guinea race, or had sired a generation of famous racing horses and gone down in the history of English sport. The portrait is a monument to individuality, and nowhere has there been a deeper and more natural understanding of the individuality of animals than in England.

When we think of monuments, we generally expect a gesture of pathos. In the work of Stubbs, there is little sign of pathos at first glance. The critical horse connoisseur will find more to feast his eyes on here than the lover of exuberant Baroque drama. Everything Molly Longlegs has in terms of characteristic traits is painstakingly and discreetly represented with the profound knowledge of anatomy possessed by Stubbs, who had given lectures on the subject. No perspectival foreshortening disturbs the objective portrayal; the saddle has been removed and is lying on the ground, the slender, nervous head of the animal is slightly turned to one side and its fiery eyes seek the admiration of the connoisseur, of which it can be certain.

George Stubbs
"Molly Longlegs" with Jockey, c. 1761/62
Oil on canvas, 102 x 127 cm
Liverpool, Walker Art Gallery

**George Romney**
The Leigh Family, c. 1767–1769
Oil on canvas, 180 x 197.5 cm
Melbourne, National Gallery of Victoria

## GEORGE ROMNEY
### 1734–1802

In England, which was spared the social upheaval of revolution, we find clear evidence that the transition from Rococo to Neoclassicism need not involve an abrupt break in style; nowhere is the continuity of this gradual evolution more obvious than in the field of portraiture. Romney's work combines the traits of a Reynolds-influenced style with a new brand of sentimentality – reflected in the numerous portraits of the divine Emma Hart, later Lady Hamilton – and a cool elegance that prefers elegiac detachment to lively expressiveness.

This group portrait also reflects Romney's admiration for the French artist Eustache Le Sueur, as indicated by the perfectly calculated composition and the clarity of the figures. Here, the conversation piece has lost the character of reality observed and no longer shows the hidden vitality behind the pose struck for the portraitist.

The painting foregoes all monumental theatrality and yet it is as immobile as a still, an effect that is further heightened by the total lack of contact between the closely grouped members of the family. None of them has eye-contact with any of the others, their gazes are melancholy and pensive. This lack of communication and the sense of calm disinterest adds to the relaxed elegance of the group.

**William Blake**
Beatrice addressing Dante from her Wagon,
c. 1824–1826
Aquarell, 36.5 x 52 cm
London, Tate Gallery

## WILLIAM BLAKE
### 1757–1827

Blake illustrated themes from the Old and New Testaments, Milton's *Paradise Regained*, Young's *Night Thoughts*, his own mythologies and poems such as the *Songs of Innocence* and William Blair's *The Grave*. From 1824 to 1826 he created a hundred watercolours on Dante's *Divina Commedia* commissioned by his great patron John Linnell, to be engraved in copper for a cycle of illustrations.

As in all his illustrations, Blake refers here to a specific place in the text, commenting on it individually in his pictures. In this case, in spite of his admiration for Dante, he formulates a vehement criticism of the writer's Catholic orthodoxy as a hindrance to his clarity and a barrier to his redemption through wisdom. Beatrice, Dante's ideal beloved, who was to remain a constantly repeated and idealized motif throughout his œuvre from *La Vita Nuova* onwards is, for Blake, the very epitome of seductive corruption to which the poet was enslaved.

Even in this illustration, in which (according to Purgatorio XXX, 31–81) she appears as a magnificent Venus-Madonna surrounded by Evangelist symbols in human form, the threat is clearly expressed in the innumerable eyes and the turbulence – it is the threat of the Babylonian harlot as harbinger of death, which Blake sees behind the mask of Beatrice's beauty.

# THOMAS LAWRENCE
1769–1830

He may be only four years old or thereabouts, but in his decorative pose he has the elegant attitude of a coveted society beauty. His traits are soft and childish, charming and unspoilt, with chubby arms and an innocent, direct gaze. Yet there is something almost coquettishly delicate in the way he grasps his ankle and holds the little posy of flowers. The foppish sash around his waist is artistically arranged, and a brilliant red drape rises behind him with pathos and dignity. It is as though the painter had little idea of what is appropriate to a child and childhood. Yet in this very inappropriateness, he succeeds in expressing the essence of the childlike.

All that is vain, pathos-laden and affected is cut short by the innocent clarity and purity of the face. At the same time, these decorative effects are used to express the fine flesh tones, the shimmer of ash-blonde hair and the delicate facial traits as skilfully as in any of Lawrence's portraits of women. To the sensitive mind, the child can thus appear as a fragile beauty without losing his credibility and without appearing doll-like.

In this painting, Lawrence shows how an individual portrait of little Master Ainslie can become a decorative *mise en scène* of the concept of perfect beauty.

**Thomas Lawrence**
Portrait of Master
Ainslie, 1794
Oil on canvas,
90 x 70 cm
Madrid, Museo
Lázaro Galdiano

In this portrait, Lawrence proves his mastery in the art of showing beauty in its best light. The contrast of brilliant dark hair and pale skin, further heightened by the transparency of the dress, the strong red of the lips echoed only in the red drapery around her hips: all these show the hand of a virtuoso portraitist. Yet Lawrence has more to offer than the mere technical virtuosity of an established portraitist. If we recall the portraits by Gainsborough set against a landscape background, we quickly realize what is new and different about this portrait. Not only does it not show the sitter at full length, but it does not interact in any way with nature or even seem part of it.

Nature is merely the backdrop for a carefully rehearsed performance. Although the lady is just putting the tuning key to her harp, the picture is almost static. The scattered accents of colour, such as red, seem to act as a counterpoint to her balanced pose. The harp and part of the stone socle may be intended as bearers of elegiac atmosphere, but first and foremost they are stabilizing compositional elements. "Sentimentality" and Neoclassicism are found hand in hand here. A clear and stringent compositional architecture is hidden behind an air of dreamy softness. The concept of the experienced portraitist is cloaked in the guise of chance inspiration.

**Thomas Lawrence**
Portrait of Lady
Elizabeth Conyngham,
c. 1821–1824
Oil on canvas,
91 x 71 cm
Lissabon, Museu
Calouste Gulbenkian

John Singleton Copley
Portrait of Rebecca Boylston, 1767
Oil on canvas, 127 x 101.6 cm
Boston (MA), Museum of Fine Arts

John Singleton Copley
The Death of Major Peirson, c. 1782–1784
Oil on canvas, 247 x 366 cm
London, Tate Gallery

## JOHN SINGLETON COPLEY
### 1738–1815

The woman who commissioned this portrait was already forty years old and, in her day, would have been considered an old maid – although, as a sister of the enormously wealthy Boston merchant Nicholas Boylston, she would undoubtedly have made a good match. Copley, an experienced portraitist, handled the task with panache. Without seeking to give this confident woman a look of youth that would have defied all credibility, he concentrates on her charming vitality. She sits for the artist, dressed in a silken negligée. This is intimate garb indeed.

In France, only the aristocracy had their portraits painted in such apparel. Yet it is the prerogative of the bourgeois Rebecca Boylston to adopt this dress as a sign of her confidence and imperturable dignity. The thin fabric also gives Copley a chance to emphasize Rebecca's slender figure, showing her firm and youthful breasts beneath the satin sheen. At the same time, in the intelligent and slightly mocking gaze of her dark eyes, Copley suggests that this is a woman of experience. Six years later, Rebecca married a wealthy landowner who commissioned Copley to paint a second portrait of his beautiful wife.

The fact that Copley did not portray his model in the stiffly prestigious setting of a salon, but in a park, further underlines the natural charm of this millionairess. There is nothing contrived or affected in the way she holds the little basket of rose blossoms in her hands; it is almost as though she had just picked the flowers in the famous gardens of the Boylston villa. The slightly cramped Rococo attitude of Copley's earlier paintings succumbs here to a new and distinctly American directness and spontaneity.

History painting on a grand scale is probably the one genre of painting that the Rococo neglected most of all. In France, the events of the revolution triggered a vigorous renaissance. But while such artists as David sought to express the significance of the events by heightening them with the rhetoric, style and pose of classical antiquity, Copley takes a different approach. He places the spectator in the very midst of the events, using the sense of turbulent chaos as a means of increasing the relevance of the scene.

At first glance, the dead Major Peirson lying in the arms of his soldiers, with flowing hair, is not immediately visible at the centre of the painting. The chaos of the situation with its various groups increases the sense of excitement in the scene. Nevertheless, the painting does possess a certain pathos-laden monumentality. The women at the right of the picture, fleeing with their children from the scene, act as a rhetorical means of guiding the spectator's attention to the focal point of the narrative. One of them has thrown her arms up in a grand gesture of lamentation, and the other has turned to look towards the body of the major; we follow her gaze. The significance of the event becomes all the more clear to us because we "discover" it ourselves.

# BENJAMIN WEST

1738—1820

It is no coincidence that Benjamin West should have enjoyed his greatest success in London. As this example demonstrates, he succeeded in uniting the great tradition of 18th century English portraiture with a reawakened interest in history painting. His particular appeal in the eyes of an English public lay in the fact that he did not use the historical situation to magnify the dignity of the sitter to the point of heroism, and did not stylize the figure of the colonel into a monumental bearer of history.

Colonel Johnson is shown in a relaxed pose, with an Indian cloak draped over his uniform and moccasins on his feet. Behind him, in the half shadow, stands an Indian chief who is smiling down on the seated man and pointing out, with a gesture of his left hand, the peaceful existence of his tribe, visible in the background. The fresh, clear face of the colonel, the Indian attributes and the chief himself all suggest a love of liberty without violence, and a sense of honest and egalitarian cooperation.

The portrait was to become the emblem of a new belief in liberty, expressed by the natural pose and friendly, relaxed attitude of the figures which indicate that liberty is no longer an unattainable and lifeless ideal, but something that comes to life in those who practise it.

Benjamin West
Colonel Guy Johnson, c. 1775/76
Oil on canvas, 203 x 138cm
Washington, National Gallery of Art

# GILBERT STUART

1755—1828

Gilbert Stuart once defined his rule of thumb for portraiture as follows: one third light, one third dark, one third half-tone. His American pragmatism permitted a prolific output. The English influence is obvious. As a young talent, Stuart had come to Edinburgh in 1772, but had returned only a year later to America as a penniless sailor.

The stars of portraiture at that time lived in Europe. So Stuart travelled there again, this time to London, where he sought to imitate Joshua Reynolds and Gainsborough and soon became the "gentlemen's portraitist", obliging Gainsborough to concentrate more on a female clientele.

In America, too, where this eccentric charmer had fled from his English creditors in 1792, he made a name for himself primarily with male portraits. Benjamin West praised him as the best portrait painter of his day. In 1794, he painted the Spanish businessman Don José de Jaudenes y Nebot.

If we consider the fine brushwork and the bravura in the style of van Dyck with which he portrays the richly embroidered jacket and the sumptuous waistcoat, it is not difficult to understand why Stuart was so popular. Here, however, we see little of the avant-garde boldness with which he was to create his legendary oil sketch of President George Washington two years later.

Gilbert Stuart
Portrait of Don José de
Jaudenes y Nebot, 1794
Oil on canvas,
128 x 100cm
New York, The Metropolitan Museum of Art

**Johann Baptist Zimmermann**
The Nymph as Symbol of Nymphenburg, 1757
Ceiling fresco (detail)
Munich, Schloß Nymphenburg, Steinerner Saal

## JOHANN BAPTIST ZIMMERMANN
### 1680–1758

In his last work, the ageing Zimmermann created an image of tremendous atmospheric power, finely balanced in terms of both composition and colour. This ceiling painting as a whole presents an allegory of flourishing welfare as a source of peaceful contentment, in harmony with the world of the gods. In the main view, the beautiful nymph appears in a charming Arcadian setting. She is enthroned on the steps of a garden architecture flanked on the right by an overgrown arched pergola and on the left by a fountain with a rocaille ornament.

Only a thin white veil cloaks the hips of the naked nymph and on her breast she wears a little blue cloth as an indication of the traditional colours of Bavaria: white and blue. A reed-crowned nymph brings her a shell heaped with pearls and corals, the fruits of the sea, while another female figure hands her a basket of blossoms. Just as these two figures embody the elements of water and earth, and just as the fountain suggests water and the foliage suggests earth, the nymph too belongs to both spheres. Nymphenburg Castle with its fountains is presented as a man-made idyll. The entire complex is interpreted as a vast nympheum in which the boundaries between the elements are dissolved.

**Cosmas Damian Asam**
St Georg worshipping Christ
and the Virgin, 1721
Ceiling fresco (detail)
Weltenburg, Monastery Church
of St Georg and St Martin

## COSMAS DAMIAN ASAM
### 1686–1739

Above the oval main room of the monastery church, a broad concave moulding marks the transition to a domed ceiling. The vaulting opens up into a diadem borne by angels, reiterating the oval groundplan. Illuminated by invisible windows, we see the saints of the Benedictine order in all the glory of the heavens.

It is quite impossible for the spectator to see that this domed setting is actually flat, and that the whole work is not, as is so often claimed, a domed ceiling fresco. By creating a transition from oval to circle, Asam is able to interweave the clouds amongst the pillars so that they help to conceal the base of the (painted) round temple on the oval ceiling aperture. A more intense metaphor for the heavens as a domed and pillared temple borne on clouds can hardly be imagined. On the main side of the fresco we see St George with his eyes raised towards Mary as she is carried upwards to Christ and God, who is holding a crown above the starry nimbus around her head. It is the triumph of the church that is displayed here against the golden background bathed in light, and its effect is all the more overwhelming because Asam has made the architecture his accomplice in illusion.

## PAUL TROGER
1698–1762

The cult of St Sebastian, who was probably a victim of Diocletian's persecution of the Christians, is documented in early Christian writings and has an unbroken tradition through to the 20th century. The scene Troger has chosen for his altarpiece refers to the legend that tells how Sebastian, Commander of the Praetorian Guard, was shot by archers on the orders of the emperor and later nursed back to health by the Christian Irene, widow of St Castulus the martyr. When he later continued to express his Christian faith, he was beaten to death.

Troger's Sebastian is not the youthful hero of Baroque paintings. There is no radiant certainty of salvation here. Instead, we see a wretched scene of suffering that does not even have the historic pathos of a key event. What is happening here is shown in a shabby, secluded setting, far from the public eye. With pragmatic energy, a young woman is untying him, while Irene gently draws an arrow from his body. The suffering of his martyrdom is as tangible as the suffering of any sick neighbour. The assistance is so pragmatic and utterly unheroic that the spectator perceives it as a natural action. In this way, Christianity is shown as a faith that can be applied to daily life.

Paul Troger
St Sebastian and the Women, c. 1746
Oil on canvas, 60 x 37 cm
Vienna, Österreichische Galerie,
Belvedere

## MATTHÄUS GÜNTHER
1705–1788

With his domed ceiling fresco in the monastic church of Münsterschwarzach, Johann Evangelist Holzer supplied the stylistic, compositional and contentual model for Günther. It was Holzer's pioneering achievement of finding an individual form of expression in a time of stylistic change that forged the link between Rococo and Neoclassicism. At Rott am Inn, Günther dispenses with Holzer's technique of architectural illusion. The real architecture is no longer continued into the painting, nor does it open up to a celestial illusion. The ceiling painting is like an easel painting projected onto the ceiling, avoiding exaggerated "sotto in sù" views from below.

As early as 1761, Mengs had already applied this Neoclassicist version of ceiling painting in the Roman Villa Albani. The detail from the overall painting which shows the Holy Trinity in the centre, presents the founders of the Benedictine order on concentrically aligned banks of clouds, with the angles bearing the symbols of his life – chastity, continence, survived assassination attempt (the poisoned chalice alludes to this) and the rules of the order. What is new here, and characteristic for Günther, is the predominantly grey colouring that replaces the bright colours of Asam and Zimmermann and heralds the advent of Neoclassicism.

Matthäus Günther
The Apotheosis of St
Benedict, c. 1761–1763
Ceiling fresco (detail)
Rott am Inn, Benediktinerklosterkirche

GERMANY/AUSTRIA

Franz Anton Maulbertsch
Adoration of the Virgin, 1757
Ceiling fresco (detail)
Heiligenkreuz-Guttenbrunn, Orgelchor

## FRANZ ANTON MAULBERTSCH
### 1724–1796

The main fresco of the Gnadenkirche portrays the legend of St Helen and the Miracle of the True Cross. From here, there is a transition to the theme of the fresco above the organ loft which shows the pilgrims of Heiligenkreuz-Guttenbrunn seeking to be cured by the miraculous waters. The cripple on his crutches, the mother with the sick child and many other ill and ailing persons have gathered around the spring. On the right, humble and friendly, the patron himself looks out of the painting; it is one of the earliest known portraits by Maulbertsch. The figures are grouped naturally in an earthly scene, set within a landscape reminiscent of Tiepolo's "capricci". In the clouds, we see the Virgin with a radiant aura, to whom some of the pilgrims have raised their eyes in prayer.

The light and serene colouring with its gentle hues of pink and pale blue, the gentle green shading of the trees and the bright white clothes all indicate the optimism of the sick people. There is no shadow here, nor any threat. The pilgrims constitute a community of ordinary people whose suffering seems sublimated through their faith in the promise of redemption. Everyday life and miracles, nature and the lyricism of an imaginary landscape have been convincingly united here.

Anton Raphael Mengs
Allegory of History, c. 1772/73
Fresco, 420 x 260 cm
Rome, Vatican, Biblioteca
Vaticana, Sala dei Papiri

## ANTON RAPHAEL MENGS
### 1728–1779

In a harmonious composition lacking any sense of tension or suspense, Mengs presents Clio, the muse of history, as the central figure in his allegory. She is looking up at a Janus-headed figure which represents history itself, as indicated in the opposites of time passing (youth and age). In its overall approach, this painting is still very much a part of the late Baroque. Chronos, crouched at the front, cradling his scythe, is an allegory of time. A youthful winged figure wreathed in ivy approaches from the left, carrying rolls of papyrus; on the one hand, he indicates the function of the room – a library – while on the other hand he evokes the art of poetry, whose attribute is ivy and which is one of the sources of history. Above the group, Fama announces their fame with her trumpet.

While Clio, Chronos and Fama all belong to the traditional canon of mythological figures, the figure of history is an allegorical neologism which sheds some interesting light on Mengs as a classicist and theoretician. History confidently strides past time without seeming to be touched by it or hindered in her progress. She points towards the antiquities exhibited in the museum and to the museum itself: history is shown here as being as timeless as historiography itself.

GERMANY/AUSTRIA

# JANUARIS ZICK

1730–1797

What seems at first to be a family scene turns out to be a rather strange blend of portrait, genre and mythology. The elderly factory owner in his Sunday best is sitting on a low stone wall instructing a small boy with an almost adult face who has bowed his head and is listening to the explanations. In his hand, the man holds a lump of the same stone with which the boy also seems to have filled his basket. Another little boy is sitting on the ground with an air of detached disinterest. Behind them, with disturbing realism, stands the figure of Mercury.

This strange scene is easily explained if we know that Mercury is the god of trade. He is the protector of those who manage their affairs well. The wealth of the successful merchant is evident, and his works and property are visible in the background. The basis of his professional success, over which Mercury holds his protective hand, lies in clear and carefully considered instruction and in obedience. Instruction in the broadest sense of the word is seen here as the basis of success – a didactic and therefore thoroughly Neoclassicist compositional programme. The specific quality of the painting lies in the ease with which it overcomes a seeming disparity: the figure of the god has been integrated into everyday reality.

Januarius Zick
Gottfried Peter de Requilé with his two sons
and Mercury, 1771
Oil on canvas, 96.7 x 83 cm
Bonn, Rheinisches Landesmuseum

# JOHANN HEINRICH WILHELM TISCHBEIN

1751–1829

In a letter to Lavater dated 9 December 1786, Tischbein writes of this portrait: "... on the ruins that have witnessed such great deeds, a mortal man also appears great, and it is as though we knew him better." He portrays Goethe in classical pose, reclining on the fragment of an obelisk behind which there is an antique relief, an Ionic capital and, in the distance of the sweeping Campagna, the ruins of ancient aqueducts and the tomb of Cecilia Metella. These monuments are components drawn from the repertoire of the educated individual, thereby documenting his awareness of style. Archaeological and historic objectivity are blended with a sensitivity that transforms the quotations from antiquity into bearers of atmosphere.

The background of fragments highlights the wholeness, or integrity, of the sitter's personality, and the atmosphere of transience reflects a sense of vitality which need not be emphasized by action, for it is mediated by presence and determination alone. The literalness with which the concept has been illustrated is both the strength and the weakness of this painting. It reduces the depth of significance and has something compilatory, yet at the same time these very features are a compelling expression of the *Zeitgeist* in an era that has begun to pay homage to a new cult of genius.

✔ Johann Heinrich Wilhelm Tischbein
Goethe in the Roman Campagna, 1787
Oil on canvas, 164 x 206 cm
Frankfurt am Main, Städelsches Kunstinstitut

Luis Eugenio Meléndez
Still Life with Melon and Pears, c. 1772
Oil on canvas, 64 x 85 cm
Boston (MA), Museum of Fine Arts

## LUIS EUGENIO MELÉNDEZ
### 1716–1780

The objects that furnish the still lifes of Meléndez are simple and almost impoverished.
Nevertheless, towards the end of the 18th century, forty-five of his paintings hung in the
royal palace of Aranjuez. In the first half of the
17th century, influenced by the kitchen scenes
of such artists as Aertsen and Beuckelaer,
Spain created its own style of still life which
differed distinctly from the great achievements of their Netherlandish colleagues.
Right from the start, this difference lay in the
specific choice of objects portrayed: peasant
tableware, plain foods, everyday items used in
the kitchen, and an extremely simple overall
arrangement.

What makes Meléndez stand out within
this tradition is not just his consummate painterly skill and his mastery of a wide variety of
surface finishes, but also the way he presents
the objects. The things themselves have no allegorical significance: not just one of the pears
is worm-eaten (indicating the transience of all
earthly existence) but all of them – as though
they had all been plucked from the same ailing tree. However, because he does not actually take this statement any further, Meléndez stresses something else. Against the dark,
abstract and even "non-spatial" background,
the things are presented in all the banality of
their everyday existence.

Ramon Bayeu y Subías
The Blind Singer, c. 1786
Oil on canvas, 93 x 145 cm
Madrid, Museo del Prado

## RAMON BAYEU Y SUBÍAS
### 1746–1793

The blind man is sitting on a grassy knoll in a
once smart but now ragged suit of brightest
blue with a yellowish-brown cloak draped over
his shoulders and the hurdy-gurdy on his lap.
A little further down the slope, dressed in rags
of grey, stands his young companion, playing
on the castanets; a dog, prancing on its hind
legs, is looking up at him. Bayeu shows a
scene of beggars in a genre of poverty that has
a long tradition in Spain. Yet this painting
shows poverty and humility only in its objects.

The composition itself is diametrically opposed to the content: the bright blue of the
clothing corresponds with the bright blue of
the sky. The face of the singer – the face of a
martyr and a poet – is solemnly illuminated
by a warm glow and the contours of his figure
are sharply and clearly outlined against the
background. The vibrant green of the grass,
the royal blue of the clothing, the flash of a
brilliant red waistcoat all combine to create a
magnificently elegant sense of harmony. Because the colour of the sky is linked with that
of the beggar's costume, it elevates his figure
to the level of great and memorable. The handling of colour, the clarity of composition turn
the figure of the blind singer into a monument. The Neoclassicist stylistic techniques
present their power to monumentalize a
"lowly" scene.

# FRANCISCO JOSÉ DE GOYA
1746–1828

In 1797, Goya travelled through Andalusia in the company of the beautiful and capricious Duchess of Alba. The two *Maja* paintings were executed around 1797. This fact, together with a certain superficial likeness, gave rise to considerable speculation. Yet even without projecting any such connection, these paintings would be no less provocative. Why?

"Maja" is the Spanish word used to de-scribe an ordinary girl of the lower classes when she dresses up in the latest fashion and finery. She is both simple and special, one of the people, and a feast for the eyes at the same time. Goya's *Maja* is no Venus; what we see here is not sublimated sensuality in the guise of antiquity, but sensuality itself. Her pose is unequivocal, her challenge bold. Goya shows her both clothed and naked: nudity is not a mythological attribute here, but simply a state of undress. By dispensing with tradi-tional patterns, the artist creates a scene of provocative reality.

Francisco José de Goya
The Clothed Maja, c. 1797
Oil on canvas, 95 x 190 cm
Madrid, Museo del Prado

Francisco José de Goya
The Naked Maja, c. 1797
Oil on canvas, 97 x 190 cm
Madrid, Museo del Prado

**Francisco José de Goya**
Don Manuel Osorio Manrique de Zúñiga, c. 1787
Oil on canvas, 110 x 80 cm
New York, The Metropolitan Museum of Art

**Francisco José de Goya**
Plucked Turkey, between 1810 and 1823
Oil on canvas, 44.8 x 62.5 cm
Munich, Bayerische Staatsgemäldesammlungen, Neue Pinakothek

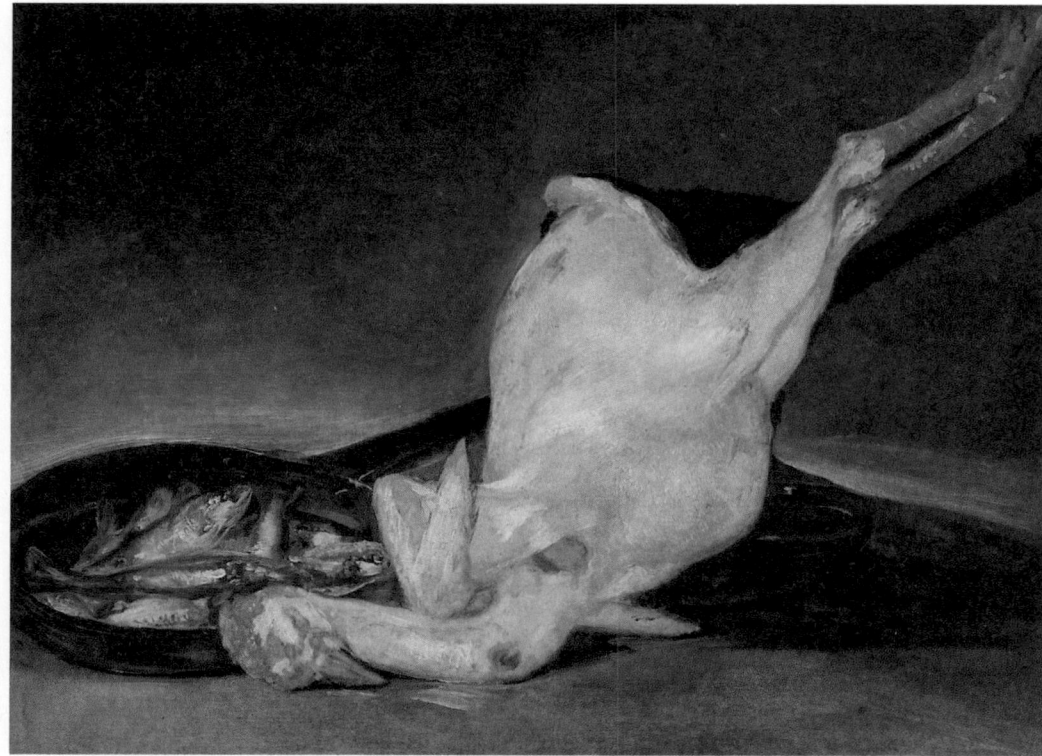

# FRANCISCO JOSÉ DE GOYA
## 1746–1828

Expressionless as a china doll, the youngest son of the Duke of Altamira gazes into the painting. He has a magpie on a string, and in its beak it holds a note bearing the name of the boy. Three cats are watching the bird with greedy eyes. On the other side, at Manuel's feet, is a birdcage. The painting is divided into two. On the one hand, there is the world of avaricious urges (the cats), curiosity (the magpie) and imprisonment (the birds), above which the boy rises with dispassionate sovereignty, representing a world of imperturbable freedom. This is no childish child. All the childlike characteristics have been transformed into their opposite: he is immobile rather than playful, introverted rather than merry, though we cannot quite define his mood.

In his cycle of engravings entitled *Caprichos* Goya portrays harlots fleecing their clients and chasing them away with empty pockets. The Spanish word for this is "desplumar" which means "to pluck feathers". He depicts them as ugly, plucked birds with the heads of men, as metaphors of exploitation and exposure, showing them up in all their mediocrity. In this still life, the plucked and naked bird represents the brutality of truth so violently revealed. Just as this painting does not allow the spectator to seek refuge in the comforts of moral edification, so too is it impossible to avoid the naked truth.

In a preliminary study for this painting, there are monks in the place of the women in their light coloured dresses, and the banner bears the inscription *mortus* ("dead"). An X-ray photograph has revealed this word beneath the grinning mask that Goya painted. It is clear that, in both cases, the message was the same, though the preliminary study actually indicates its origins. It is the medieval game of the world turned upside down in which the rights and customs of the church are perverted – with its permission – to utter anarchy, only to be followed all the more faithfully once order has been restored. In Spain at the time of the Inquisition, Goya's monks were eradicated from the composition, and the laconic clarity of the word *mortus* was replaced by a grotesquely grinning face. Its expression is now truly a banner, flying over a scene of uncanny happenings: an abyss of apocalyptic mania in which merriment is distorted to the point of menace. We are confronted with the image of a final, frenzied celebration in the face of death. Military men amongst the beggars, women and children are metaphors of order gone awry, order beyond all hope of restitution, subverted into the crazed desperation the anonymous masses hidden behind their masks.

**Francisco José de Goya**
The Burial of the Sardine (Carnival Scene),
c. 1808–1814
Oil on panel, 82.5 x 62 cm
Madrid, Academia de San Fernando

SPAIN

**Francisco José de Goya**
The Family of Charles IV, 1800
Oil on canvas, 280 x 336 cm
Madrid, Museo del Prado

# FRANCISCO JOSÉ DE GOYA
## 1746–1828

Goya was at the zenith of his carrier when he painted this portrait of the royal family in 1800. He paid meticulous attention to detail, preparing numerous sketches and ten individual studies, and he insisted on long sittings even though this displeased the royal family. The finished painting, however, was accepted and approved. This makes it all the more difficult to understand why both the studies and the completed painting are widely regarded today as caricatures. Such an interpretation would would not only be an arrogant underestimation of the well-documented intelligence of, for example, María Luisa, but would also misconstrue Goya's achievement in the field of portraiture.

By faithfully rendering the historically documented ugliness of the older Infanta María Josefa and Queen María Luisa or the dull physiognomy of the King, and further heightening this by contrasting them with the pretty

children, Goya actually developed a new form of dignity. The old technique of idealization had lost its credibility. In presenting the unadulterated truth, Goya discovered a new form of pathos. The latent malice in the face of the Queen, the fatigued expression of the King, the bitter, old-maidish stare of the Infanta do not trouble the sitters themselves. This is clear if we bear in mind the compositional similarity to Velázquez' *Las Meninas*. Goya, who had copied that painting as an etching and aquatinta, was well aware of its complex and fragmented structure. He even cites Velázquez here by presenting himself, like his forerunner, in front of the easel in the shadow at the left hand side of the painting.

The deliberate differences, however, are also extremely interesting. Goya's painting contains no mirror image, no picture within a picture, no spatial depth, no iconographic enigma or labyrinthine references. Vain and shameless, the figures are all pushing towards the front row, taking no interest in the others. It is a monument to royal self-esteem, for which moral and aesthetic values are of no significance.

PART II

# From the Romantic Age to the Present Day

PART II

# From the Romantic Age to the Present Day

by Barbara Eschenburg, Ingeborg Güssow,
Christa von Lengerke, Volkmar Essers

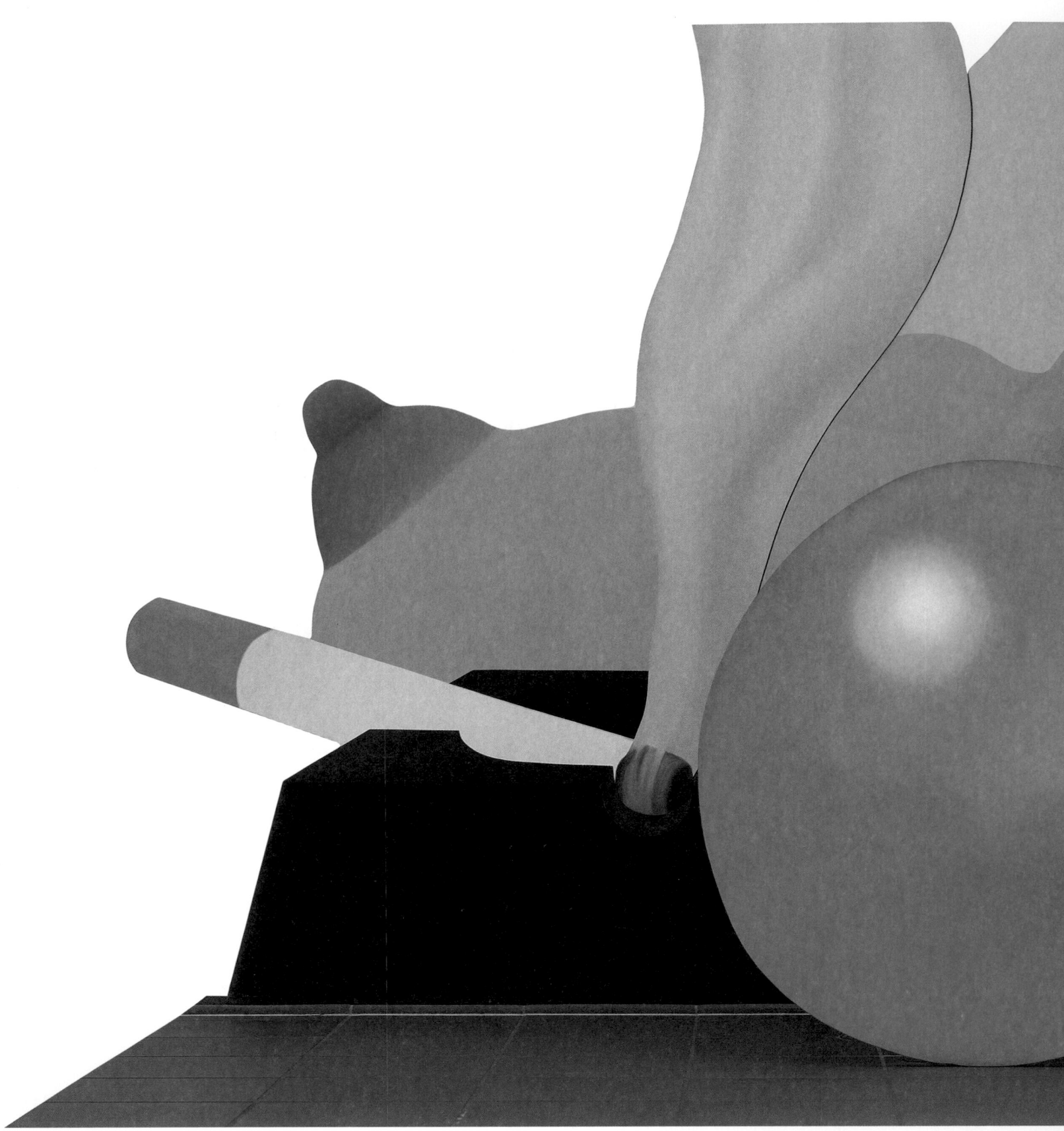

*Page 402:*
**Pablo Picasso**
The Kiss, 1925
Oil on canvas, 130 x 97 cm
Paris, Musée Picasso

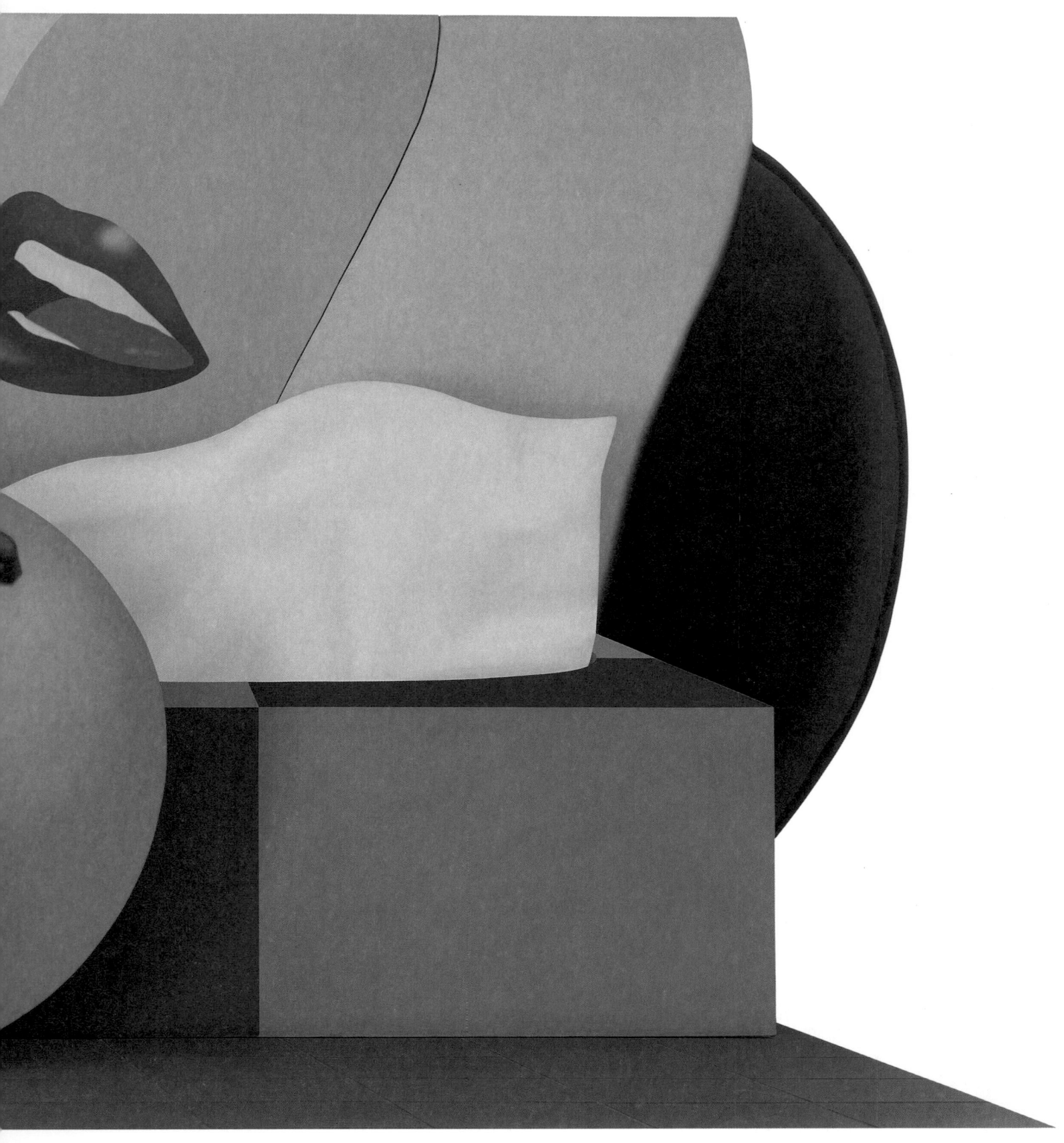

Tom Wesselmann
Great American Nude No. 98, 1967
Five canvases arranged behind
one another in three planes
250 x 380 x 130 cm
Cologne, Museum Ludwig
Photo: Rheinisches Bildarchiv, Cologne

Barbara Eschenburg/Ingeborg Güssow

# ROMANTICISM AND REALISM

## Painting in the 19th century

In the 19th century, for the first time, it was the bourgeoisie who determined the content and form of art throughout Europe. Major works by the French artists Géricault, Delacroix and Courbet were no longer dedicated to the glory of religious or secular power, but to heroic renderings of the nation and its people, workers, peasants or even artists.

The longstanding rivalry between idealism and realism was finally settled in favour of artistic subjectivity. Abandoning the stringent rules of the state academies, painters – whether they still regarded themselves as Neoclassicists, as Ingres did, or as romanticists and realists – now began claiming their own genius and nature as their sole sources of inspiration. Following the breakthrough of *plein-air* painting, such a claim could best be realized in landscape painting: in the work of Friedrich and Koch in Germany, Rousseau and Corot in France, Constable, Bonington and Turner in England, and Church and Cole in the USA.

The exploration of natural light, which was to culminate in the work of the Impressionists, completely changed the handling of colour in paintings and may be regarded as the single most important innovation in painting during this period.

**Eugène Delacroix**
Orphan Girl at the Cemetery, 1823
Oil on canvas, 66 x 54 cm
Paris, Musée National du Louvre

# I. IDEALISTS:

## Academicians in France

Since the absolutist state of the 17th and 18th centuries had begun bringing its influence to bear on art and taste through the founding of academies, the officially recognized art promoted by the academies had been locked in rivalry with those who, though they had to rely entirely on the art market, nevertheless endeavoured to find a place for their work in the official exhibitions monopolized by the academies. The first Académie Royale de Peinture et de Sculpture was founded in Paris in 1648 under Louis XIV. With the Salon exhibitions held at regular intervals, every two years, from the second half of the 18th century onwards, the Académie achieved an influence on artistic production and the art market that made it imperative for artists to deal with this institution and, if possible, to seek a good position in the Salon exhibitions.

Remarkably enough, the French Revolution of 1789 changed very little in this respect. Although the Académie Royale was disbanded in 1793, its successor, the Académie des Beaux-Arts, exerted just as strong an influence on the French art world right through to the second half of the 19th century. As a member of the art commission of the National Convention, the already famous painter Jacques-Louis David presided over the dissolution and re-establishment of the Académie. A keen partisan of the spirit of the Enlightenment, David was an ardent proponent of the French Revolution and later a great admirer of its heir, Napoleon I (1769–1821).

In his capacity as a teacher at the Académie, David propagated the ideas of the Enlightenment. He saw art as a discipline that could, in principle, be taught, and believed that an artist could and should learn considerably more than the mastery of technique alone.

In contrast to the approach that prevailed under the old Académie Royale, however, David placed considerable emphasis on the personal relationship between teacher and student. It was still widely believed that art should serve the edification and moral education of the citizen, for which the Roman republican virtues were still seen as a rich source of allegorical material. Before the revolution, such motifs had been used to hold up a mirror to the ruling classes. Now, in the name of the same virtues, it was possible to glorify the ideals of the French Revolution and the new state. The stringent Neoclassicism based on draughtsmanship which David had already developed under the *ancien régime* was regarded as a suitable means to this end. David's students François Gérard (1770–1837) and Antoine-Jean Gros (1771–1835) upheld the tradition of this style, albeit with a certain painterly modification in the case of Gros, who went on to become the leading war artist of the Napoleonic campaigns (ill. p. 424) which David had also glorified in his monumental canvases (ill. p. 366).

In the post-revolutionary and post-Napoleonic period of the Restoration, Jean Auguste Dominique Ingres (1780–1867), another student and faithful follower of David, continued to propagate his master's style. Though he, too, initially produced history paintings based on Roman themes, he later became the sought-after portraitist of the aristocracy and of those members of the bourgeoisie (ill. p. 430) who had risen to wealth and power with the July Monarchy. The emphasis on material and texture in Ingres' portraits sets them apart from David's paintings which feature predominantly light backgrounds and blocks of colour frequently juxtaposed without mellowing chiaroscuro. The rich colours of sumptuous, flowing garments are given added brilliance by the use of glazing. His works were to have a profound influence on portraiture throughout the first half of the 19th century, especially on the Biedermeier period between 1815 and 1848.

Apart from bourgeois portraiture, which was one of the main genres of painting in the 19th century, Ingres concentrated primarily on female nudes. In his famous *Valpinçon Bather* (ill. p. 429), the bold spirit of innovation that informed David's paintings of the revolutionary period is still manifest, reflected in the Neoclassical monumentality of an otherwise insignificant motif, with none of the mythological or oriental trappings for which Ingres would later develop a taste. Bearing in mind that, before the French Revolution, the portrayal of naked female bodies in Rococo painting had had a distinctly erotic flavour, the new morality of this artist is clear. The sensuality of his works lies in the pleasure of contemplating the quiet beauty of objects in a light-flooded room, whose vertical and horizontal structure they absorb. The painting is like a still life. It is the presence of the objects alone that is important. Even the human figure becomes an object too, for the face as a sign of individuality is turned away from the spectator, lending the body the same silent existence of the ambient materiality, transfigured by light.

## Opponents of the Academy in Germany: Neoclassicists in Rome

Just as the Académie in Paris was dependent on the French monarchy, so too were the academies founded by German territorial princes in the 18th century the instruments of their rulers. In Germany, as in France, the 1790s were marked by an increasing disaffection of artists with the stultifying strictures of academic regulations, which they saw as a restriction of their creativity. However, unlike France, where such resistance had resulted in the disbanding and reorganization of the Académie in the wake of the French Revolution, in Germany, where feudal rule continued, it remained a purely individual form of protest, the consequences of which were borne by the artists alone. It was not unusual towards the end of the 18th century for German artists to break with the academies in order to pursue their own aims in art. The Tyrolean artist Joseph Anton Koch (1768–1839) fled from the Karlsschule academy in Stuttgart, whose militaristic regimentation had also been reluctantly endured by Friedrich von Schiller (1759–1805). Asmus Jacob Carstens (1754–1798) was expelled from the Copenhagen academy for his oppositional views. Johann Friedrich Overbeck (1789–1869) and Franz Pforr (1788–1812) turned their backs on the Vienna academy out of protest. All these artists, to name but a few of the more famous, chose to live in Rome, which was then the leading international centre of art.

The French Académie was the first to hold regular competitions amongst its students on a topic of ancient history or mythology, awarding the winner an opportunity of studying art in Rome. England, Copenhagen and various German academies and art schools soon followed suit in sending their most accoladed artists to live and study in the Eternal City. The German artists mentioned above, however, all came to Rome as outsiders, without the support of the academies, and had to forgo the creature comforts such academic support could provide in Rome. Both Carstens and Koch actually went to Rome on foot and were obliged to undertake all manner of menial tasks to earn a living. They had to make considerable sacrifices in order to pursue their express aim of renewing German art by liberating it from courtly restrictions. Nor were they prepared, at the end of the normal study period, to return to the hated feudal society of their homeland, where outmoded conventions had survived well beyond the French Revolution. They had in common a deeply moral attitude to art and life, and an imperturbable faith in their own creative power and its ability to flourish without academic regulation. Carstens, who had already gone to Rome several years before, was joined there by his younger colleague Koch. Both were vehement anti-monarchists. Carstens even turned down an appointment as an academy professor in Berlin. On his journey to Rome, via Strasbourg and Switzerland, Koch joined the Jacobin Club in Strasbourg, opponents of the old order that still prevailed in Germany. It was an act of high treason.

Koch's paintings of the falls and mountains of Switzerland, such as his *Schmadribach* (ill. p. 450) or *Swiss Landscape* (ill. p. 450) reflect the spirit of the Enlightenment, which saw Switzerland as an exemplary country of free citizens. The sublime landscape was regarded as an appropriate symbol for the purported dignity of the people of this country. Koch's water-colours of his Swiss tour, executed in the 1790s, and on which these compositions are based, possess a painterly freedom no longer evident in his finished works. Their emphasis on the invention and construction of landscape leans heavily on the Neoclassical landscape painting of the 18th century, to which Koch added a remarkable degree of attention to detail, more akin to the art of the Renaissance and late Middle Ages than to that of the Baroque.

A stylistically freer approach would have been diametrically opposed to such a concept. Though a trend towards a more freely executed and sketchier style, even in the finished painting, had emerged in the 1830s and found increasing acceptance, Koch, who lived until 1839, did not adopt it himself. This goes some way towards explaining how an artist so bitterly opposed to the old-style academies and so openly disposed towards artistic and individual freedom eventually came to be held up as a shining example by the conservative academies in Germany against the emergence of *plein-air* painting, and how the radically oppositional art of Koch and his contemporaries finally came to be acknowledged by the prevailing authorities in Germany, from the second decade of the 19th century onwards, as the epitome of German art.

The artists who were the innovators of German art in the early years of the century had opposed the opinions of the academies in two ways. On the one hand, they acknowledged only the free invention of the creative individual, whereas academic tradition recognized invention in the skilled application of the acquired and the familiar. On the other hand, these artists valued an altogether unacademic concept of the dignity of craftsmanship, reminiscent of the late medieval and Renaissance tradition.

With their emphasis on free invention, they nevertheless embraced a tradition that owed its very existence to the academies. In the early modern age, artists had come to value intellectual creativity – that is to say, invention – more highly than skilled craftsmanship and had declared themselves the equal of poets and philosophers, who had been ranked as practitioners the liberal arts in the Middle Ages, when painting, sculpture and architecture were still regarded as merely mechanical crafts. The academies, which placed the main emphasis on the theoretical foundations of art, eventually became the guardians of fine art as an intellectual activity and therefore as a liberal art. The rebellious artists of the early 19th century wanted to uphold this basic concept, but in doing so, they looked back to the pre-academic or extra-academic tradition of the early modern period, in particular the Italian art of the 15th to 17th centuries.

## Catholic Romantics: The Nazarenes in Rome

Carstens and Koch had already turned their backs on mythological and historical motifs inspired by the Roman republic. They drew their motifs from contemporary life, from the Bible and the writings of Hesiod (c. 700 B.C.), Dante and Ossian (3rd century A.D.). One of the most popular themes was the portrayal of the Golden Age of human harmony at the dawn of history, in which many leading figures of the German Enlightenment, from Immanuel Kant (1724–1804) to Schiller, saw the promise of a future society of liberty and equality, free from feudal privilege, the seeds for which had already been sown in their lifetime.

The younger artists in Rome, grouped around Overbeck and Pforr, looked instead to medieval and Renaissance religious art for their models. For them, Christianity was the guarantee of a life untrammeled by courtly superficiality, in which the truth, humility and profundity of the German soul could find expression. Unlike the Neoclassicists Carstens and Koch, they did not seek a future society free of autocracy, but dreamt instead of the emergence of a powerful empire of German nations in which spiritual and secular rule would hold equal sway, as in the medieval Holy Roman Empire, with the former possibly even taking precedence. In order to set an example of humility, the former exiles of the Viennese academy – Overbeck and Pforr – followed by artists from Düsseldorf and Munich (Wilhelm von Schadow, 1788–1862; Peter von Cornelius, 1783–1867; Julius Schnorr von Carolsfeld, 1794–1872), set up their own brotherhood along monastic lines. The Protestants amongst them converted to Catholicism. Because of their manifest piety, the Italians sarcastically dubbed them *i nazareni* in reference to Jesus of Nazareth.

In a bid to emphasize the serious intent of their objectives, the Nazarenes were not content merely to adopt medieval and Renaissance themes superficially. Instead, they were also eager to revive medieval painting techniques. For example, instead of the more conventional large canvases, they revived the practice of painting on small wooden panels and they used an extremely fine glaze painting on a white ground, superimposing layers of transparent colour to achieve the depth and brilliance of late medieval painting. It would nevertheless be wrong to surmise that these artists were willing to place themselves on a par with medieval craftsmen, for their ideas and their lifestyle were entirely the product of their own free and creative will, their "invention", and were not imposed upon them by any craftsman's guild. In other words, for all the apparent humility of their religious craftsmanship, they were not lacking in self-esteem or sense of vocation, as the key works of Overbeck and Pforr confirm.

In Pforr's painting *Shulamith and Mary* (Euerbach, Schäfer Collection), together with Overbeck's *Italia and Germania* (ill. p. 454), begun in 1811, the iconography of the Renaissance and the late Middle Ages is used to portray the imagined brides, which both artists saw as the muses of their art, equating them with the Madonna. Pforr, who glorified medieval chivalry in his other works, whereas Overbeck dedicated himself almost exclusively to reviving religious painting, has gone furthest in his equation of creative, private and religious concepts. Shulamith, Overbeck's future bride, is presented on the left like the Madonna with Child, set in the landscape, while Pforr's Mary is placed in an old German chamber like the Madonna of the Annunciation. In the final version of his painting produced in 1828, however, Overbeck avoided direct references to the Madonna paintings of the period around 1500, and rendered his female figures as personifications of Italian and German art, to which the Nazarenes felt indebted.

The artists of the Nazarene Brotherhood also set about reviving medieval and Renaissance Italian fresco painting. This was, to all intents and purposes, a new start, as fresco painting had fallen out of favour in the age of the Enlightenment – even in Southern Germany, where it had been used to decorate innumerable Baroque churches – and the technique of painting on wet plaster had been all but forgotten. The Prussian Consul General in Rome, Jakob Salomon Bartholdy (1779–1825) offered a welcome opportunity of practising this technique by commissioning the Nazarenes to decorate his apartment in the Casa Zuccaro with scenes from the life of Joseph (ill. p. 454). The frescos they executed brought fame to Cornelius, in particular, who succeeded in creating figures of a monumentality that equalled their powerful gestural and physical expressiveness.

Such nationalistic fervour in the field of art did not go unrewarded. Three former Nazarenes received appointments as directors of academies, whose princely founders sought to employ the artistic ideals of these artists living in Rome for the purposes of reviving a monumental state art: Cornelius was appointed to Munich in 1825, Schadow to Düsseldorf in 1826 and Philipp Veit (1793–1877) to the Städel in Frankfurt am Main in 1828. Schnorr von Carolsfeld also received major public commissions in Munich. Their idealism in techniques of drawing prevailed in German monumental and history painting until well beyond mid-century. On the arrival of Karl Theodor Piloty (1826–1886) whose powerful realism was influenced by Belgian painting, this idealism began to fall into disfavour, and was no longer regarded as typically German, but simply as old-fashioned.

**Protestant Romantics: Runge and Friedrich**
Just as Rome was the centre of a southern Romanticism shaped by the spirit of Catholicism, Northern Germany was the home of another, northern, Romanticism imbued with the spirit of Protestantism. Its main exponents were Philipp Otto Runge (1777–1810) and Caspar David Friedrich (1774–1840). Both had trained at the Copenhagen academy, which had been founded in 1754 on the French model. During the period when Friedrich (from 1794) and Runge (from 1799) were students there, the training system of the 18th century still prevailed, with studies from plaster casts taking precedence over life studies. Runge had complained bitterly of this in his critique of the academy, entitled *Rembrandt-Traum* ("Dream of Rembrandt"), in December 1799. From the 1820s onwards, the situation in Copenhagen altered dramatically. Amongst the students of Christoffer Wilhelm Eckersberg (1783–1853), himself a student of David who had studied in Rome and taken up a professorship in Copenhagen in 1818, a light-toned realism emerged which was to influence the realism of the 1830s in Germany.

**Caspar David Friedrich**
The Stages of Life, c. 1835
Oil on canvas, 72.5 x 94 cm
Leipzig, Museum der bildenden Künste

Dresden was the next important station for Friedrich and Runge. Here, they were influenced less by the academy itself than by their studies in the municipal gallery. Friedrich remained in Dresden, becoming a member of the academy with a fixed salary in 1816, retaining his contacts with his home town of Greifswald on the Baltic coast and visiting the island of Rügen on numerous occasions. Runge, on the other hand, moved to Hamburg, where his family background afforded him considerable financial independence. It is interesting to note that Rome did not feature in the artistic development of either of these two artists, important as the city was for most artists at that time.

Both Runge and Friedrich were deeply religious men who sought a renewal of German art on the basis of the pious Protestant spirit which so influenced Germany's educated middle classes. If art was to be religious, or if it was to generate a sense of religious spirituality, then this was certainly not to be equated with the portrayal of biblical figures and legends such portrayals had been commonplace in Catholic churches until the 18th century and the Nazarenes had sought to revive this in the spirit of the Middle Ages and the Renaissance. The northern Romantics did not aim to present a specific content, but to convey a certain spirit or attitude. Such an undertaking called for new forms of presentation. Runge's observation of a general "convergence towards landscape" is a frequently cited description of the early Romantic movement that can also be applied to the 19th century, for it

invokes the late 18th century notion that the vision of a sublime landscape in art could guide the spectator directly towards an awareness of God's greatness.

In Runge's work, landscape came to symbolize man's close harmony with the divinity of the cosmos (ill. p. 453). In portraying this harmony, Runge transformed the colours of his objects into purely spectral colours, illustrating the natural cycle of life through light and darkness, or through symbolic figures merged with meticulously detailed plants and blossoms. Colours were thus used to lend a new and immaterial aspect to nature, while the symbolic figures added a psychological component that allowed the spectator to identify more closely with the cycle of nature. In this way, religion becomes a spiritual value whose content is inextricably linked with the subject itself. Indeed, it consists of an emotional perception of cosmic structures, for which art builds the psychological bridges.

Unlike Runge, Friedrich did not paint imagined, cosmic worlds of nature in which the earthly landscape is merely a part, but drew his inspiration instead from the real landscape, peopling it with figures from contemporary bourgeois reality. To this end, he undertook lengthy walks in the little-known and sparsely populated mountains of Saxony, Silesia and Bohemia, and on the island of Rügen. As neither tourism nor hiking trails existed, such travels were naturally fraught with difficulty. The works created on the basis of these journeys are quite evidently based on personal experience. Friedrich chose locations – a slope, a summit, the seashore – that had never before been presented in this form in landscape painting. He created, for the first time, images in which the viewer could identify directly with the standpoint of the painter or with the figures in the landscape. This standpoint is generally a perilous position from which the yearned-for expanses and the transfiguring light of distance are merely hinted at. In conventional landscape painting, the painter and the viewer generally remained at a safe distance from the image of nature. Now, in the work of Friedrich, the viewer became part of the scene, often teetering on the border between proximity and distance, darkness and light.

Friedrich's paintings convey a profoundly melancholic world view. Though they do express the hope that the divine light of the cosmos will reach the earthly existence of the individual, the fulfilment of that hope is almost invariably postponed to some future time. This individualistic piety, closely bound with nature, in which light is a symbol of divine power, was not only prevalent in Germany amongst painters. The poet Ludwig Theobul Kosegarten (1758–1818), a preacher on the island of Rügen, expressed similar views in his "sermons on the shore" which, as the name suggests, were not held in a church, but in the open air. Fried-

rich and Runge were amongst his followers. It is therefore no coincidence that two of the key works of romantic landscape painting, Runge's unfinished *Rest on the Flight into Egypt* (ill. p. 452) of 1805/06 and Friedrich's *Cross in the Mountains* for the the *Tetschen Altar* (Dresden, Gemäldegalerie) of 1807/08, were originally conceived as altarpieces – Runge's was meant for the Protestant church in the Baltic coastal town of Greifswald and Friedrich's for the private chapel of Tetschen Castle in Bohemia.

The landscape paintings of the Romantic age demanded a meticulously detailed study of nature and a religiously inspired interest in the fleeting atmosphere of changing light and weather conditions. In this respect at least, in spite of the smooth finish of glaze painting, it differed little from the sketchy *plein-air* painting already beginning to emerge, which, by the second half of the century, would become firmly established as "atmospheric" landscape painting. There was, however, a fundamental difference. In the controlled and sober paintings of the early years of the century, artists still sought to convey an objective content beyond the bounds of palpable reality – generally an awareness of cosmic divinity – through the vehicle of their own subjectivity. From the 1830s onwards, by contrast, artists began exploring the possibilities of capturing a spontaneous and natural

**Philipp Otto Runge**
The Hülsenbeck Children, 1805/06
Oil on canvas, 130.5 x 140.5 cm
Hamburg, Hamburger Kunsthalle

impression by using sketchy, impasto brushwork. The move towards this new surface finish did not originate in Germany, but in England and France, and was imparted to German artists in Rome. Moreover, artists from the north, such as the Norwegian painter Christian Claussen Dahl (1788–1857) also stimulated this new realism.

## II. COLORISTS AND REALISTS
### French Romantics
In the paintings of David and his followers, the finished picture was invariably worked through to the last detail. The Romantics, on the other hand, regarded a sketchy surface effect as a painterly principle in its own right, even in the finished work. The driving force and leading figure of this group was Eugène Delacroix (1798–1863). The contrast between his rough, painterly surfaces and the smooth linear style of David's student, Ingres, rekindled the age-old academy debate of the 17th and 18th centuries on the supremacy of line or colour as the theoretically appropriate vehicle for the portrayal of reality in painting. This does not mean that the idealists of the 19th century, who sought perfection in drawing could not be accomplished colorists, such as David and Ingres. The debate was more specifically about the ideal. Whereas the strict defendants of line over colour argued that only draughtsmanship could liberate portayals of nature from the impurities and debris of earthly imperfection, the proponents of colour over line took up the gauntlet for the transience of life in all its fleeting manifestations. They rallied to the defence of subjective sensual pleasure, which the moralists of draughtsmanship or line dismissed as an unintellectual pleasure. This did not mean, however, that the colorists were to be regarded as natural-

**Eugène Delacroix**
The Bark of Dante (Dante and Virgil in Hell), 1822
Oil on canvas, 189 x 242 cm
Paris, Musée National du Louvre

ists. For them, colour was actually a means of portraying a more lyrical view of the world. Their creed of subjectivity, propagated under the banner of "colorism", was a thorn in the side of the Neoclassicists, who sought perfection in the permanent continuity of life rather than in its arbitrary and temporal manifestations.

The first public contradiction levelled at such idealism was articulated in the names of romanticism and realism: the monumental *Raft of the Medusa* (Paris, Louvre, see ill. p. 426) exhibited at the Salon of 1819 by the young and audacious Théodore Géricault (1791–1824). His painting illustrates a contemporary event. It has nothing of the cool Neoclassicism and emotional control to be found in the paintings by David and his students. Profound empathy with the plight of the shipwrecked mariners is expressed in the very angle from which it is painted – from a slightly elevated stance and at close proximity. We almost have the feeling that the painter himself is poised on a plank that is being carried along on the crest of a wave, while the corner of the raft sinks into a trough. By placing the dominant object, the raft, on the diagonal, Géricault breaks every rule of classical painting, in which the spatial organization and the narrative are to be rendered parallel to the spectator. Géricault's studies of dead bodies add an element of harrowing realism: hope and despair, the quick and the dead, numbness and passion charge the painting with tension. The artist goes beyond the momentary situation to reveal just how precarious the human condition is; there are no heroes in the face of such vulnerability, but only individuals struggling for survival. The bleak mood is underpinned by the gloomy and brooding colours that have ousted the luminosity of David and his students. In this highly realistic image, the romantic aspect is the artist's empathy and identification with the suffering of human fate, expressed by the painterly composition and handling of colour.

In Géricault's *Raft of the Medusa*, a tale of ordinary people is elevated to the level of great history painting, hitherto reserved for the portrayal of heroic deeds for the state or important state events. Such people as those depicted here by Géricault are included, if at all, only as relatively minor "extras" in paintings of stormy seas. Géricault lends their fate (which he read of in contemporary newspaper reports) all the monumentality and sublimity of a state event.

The roots of Géricault's art lay in a different aspect of Baroque painting than that of David. Whereas David worked in the strictly moralistic tradition of 17th century French and Italian Neoclassicism, Géricault saw his artistic forebears in the romantic leanings of the Neapolitan and Roman painting of the 17th century and its successors. Both thematically – man forlorn at the mercy of fate embodied by nature – and in its dark-toned colority, his works recall this period. Yet he portrays such a scene with a new sense of drama and empathy, a new realism in the presentation of detail.

His first major work, a scene from Dante's *Divina Comme-dia* exhibited at the 1822 Paris Salon under the title *The Bark of Dante* (ill. p. 414; also known as *Dante and Virgil in Hell*), was based on the painting by his friend Géricault, for whom he held a deep admiration. Here, though the figures are not shipwrecked, they are at the mercy of the River Styx, and are desperately trying to reach the safety of the bark carrying Dante and Virgil (70–19 B.C.). Even in this early work, it is clearly evident that the younger artist, who was to go on to become the leading figure of the Romantic move-ment in France, has charted a new course. Whereas, in Géri-cault's painting, passionate excitement is expressed by a bleak, cold chiaroscuro, Delacroix employs extreme contrasts of colour: the garish red of Dante's cap against the green water and the white tones of the wan bodies in the river, ac-companied by the intensive greens, russets and blues of the other robes.

Delacroix's masterpiece, *Liberty Leading the People* (ill. p. 432) exhibited at the 1831 Salon following the July Revolu-tion, would have been inconceivable without Géricault's *Raft of the Medusa*. The pale bodies of those who have fallen at the barricades and the republican fighters led by the al-legory of Liberty storming away over them, their faces dis-torted by eagerness, passion and determination, addresses the same contrasts as Géricault's painting, albeit under differ-ent circumstances. Here, there is no sense of fatalism, for the dead and the fallen are shown as the necessary price of vic-tory. Accordingly, apart from the use of light and shade, it is the blue, white and red of the tricolore that strikes the dom-inant chord in the painting. This is certainly not a conven-tional blend of colours, but evidence of Delacroix's new method of lending each scene its own appropriate and unmis-takable colority. The artist's subjective empathy was in-tended to trigger the same emotion in the spectator, implied directly through the use of colour rather than indirectly through reflection on the content. The result is a remarkable reinterpretation of light and shade in stark contrast to the ap-proach employed in Baroque painting. In *Liberty Leading the People*, chiaroscuro is no longer a cosmic and moral principle of the material world, but the product of a juxtaposition of pale to white hues with dark to black or dark-blue objects complemented by pure red in reiteration of the tricolore.

By 1824, Delacroix' backgrounds, in particular, dispense with non-colour chiaroscuro and adopt a specific and intense colority. The first example of this approach in his œuvre is *The Massacre of Chios* (ill. p. 432) with its background of blue, ochre and green, while *Liberty Leading the People*, six years later, uses blue and white. From the 1830s onwards, in-spired by the sumptous oriental robes that had fascinated him on his Moroccan tour of 1831/32, Delacroix began breaking down bright colours in his figures into tiny par-ticles of pure colour, giving his paintings a sumptuous bril-liance, as in his famous *Women of Algiers* (ill. p. 433) of 1834.

**Théodore Géricault**
The Madwoman (Manomania of Envy), 1822/23
Oil on canvas, 72 x 58 cm
Lyon, Musée des Beaux-Arts

Delacroix's greatest contribution to the development of painting in the 19th century, the full impact of which was not to be felt until the late 1840s, was his handling of colour according to the principles of complementary con-trast. He noticed that colours situated close together in the colour circle tend to heighten each other's impact when jux-taposed, whereas opposites (red/green, yellow/violet, blue/orange) tend to detract from each other. From mid-cen-tury onwards, he applied this principle to the overall compo-sition of his paintings as well as to his handling of individ-ual zones. Whereas the composition as a whole is generally based on contrasting colours such as red and blue or red and green, the individual zones are heightened in their intensity by a dense application of short brushstrokes, in which a wide variety of greens or reds create a plane. This height-ened colority added lyricism to his pictorial world, trans-figuring it to sublime beauty and sensuality. Delacroix sought his motifs in literature and in literary descriptions of war or love.

William Shakespeare (1564–1616), Goethe, Torquato Tasso and Dante were his sources. Contemporary events were of interest to him if he felt that they could be rendered lyr-ically on the canvas: the Greek liberation struggle, for in-

**John Constable**
The White Horse, 1819
Oil on canvas, 131.4 x 188.3 cm
New York, The Frick Collection

stance, or other struggles such as a lion hunt, preferably featuring oriental horsemen – all topics which he saw as expressions of heightened sensuality.

### Plein-air Painting in England and France

The influential force behind this divisionistic handling of colour that was to pave the way towards Impressionism – in this case as an exploration of daylight and sunlight, rather than complementary contrasts – was the English landscape painter John Constable (1776–1837). His three paintings exhibited at the 1824 Paris Salon, including the famous *Hay Wain* (ill. p. 464) had a revolutionary impact on French painting and blazed a trail throughout the continent. Delacroix, who probably visited Constable in London following the Paris exhibition in May or June 1825, made a note in his diary on 25 September 1846 regarding Constable's principle of colour division: "Constable says that the superiority of the green of his meadows is due to the fact that it is made up of a great number of different greens. The lack of intensity of green in conventional landscape paintings results from its being portrayed by a single hue. What he says about the green of his meadows can be applied to all other colours." Delacroix proved as much in his own paintings.

Constable broke down his colours into tiny individual brushstrokes, juxtaposing various hues and shades. In these vibrant planes of colour, blackish and white brush-strokes create a sense of light and shade, surface and depth. The effect is one of density and vitality unparalleled in any previous landscape painting. The open spaces of Constable's paintings seem to be filled, from sky to earth, from far to near, with particles of matter bathed in light. The dominant impression is one of luxuriant growth, glistening, lush and moist. Constable succeeds in capturing by painterly means

alone the English woods and meadows that were the heritage of the 18th century. His handling of colour, light and shade is not based on observation, but constitutes an unprecedented painterly transcription of an overall impression.

Like Delacroix, Constable does not rely on convention to express his individual experience of nature, creating instead a colour system of his own in accordance with his subjective impression. The use of chiaroscuro is no longer a vehicle for projecting the theological or philosophical contrast between the darkness of the fallen and the light of the divine. Instead, it is part of a pure colour cosmos of enormous density and subtlety in which all things of colour possess a material quality imbued with properties of light and darkness. In this way, all matter – whether tree-trunk or cloud – is basically the same, differing only in terms of material density, which is distinguished in the painting by textural differences in the brushwork.

Constable was a pioneer of 19th century art, not only for his handling of colour, but also for the aspects of nature he chose to portray. He disdained to paint the cultivated park and garden landscapes of the wealthy landowners that were a source of such pride in England at the time and had been a favourite motif of 18th century artists. Instead, he chose to paint the unspoilt, wild and overgrown corners of English farmland.

The French landscape painters of the schools of Barbizon and Fontainebleau followed suit with what they termed *paysages intimes*. They withdrew to the unspoilt countryside of Fontainebleau near Paris, with its meadows, heaths and woodlands, in order to escape the hustle and bustle of the city and to avoid the landscaped gardens of the Park of Fontainebleau. They sought to paint an archetypal and hitherto neglected landscape with none of the heroic contrasts that had previously appealed to landscape painters. Like the works of Constable, the paintings of the Fontainebleau artists – most notably Théodore Rousseau (1812–1867), Jules Dupré (1811–1889) and Narcisse Diaz de la Peña (1808–1876) – possess a dense and patchy textural structure that seeks to do justice to the materiality of the subject matter. The slight shimmer of Constable's paintings that takes away the heaviness of the material, is absent here. Gustave Courbet (1819–1877) who was not directly associated with the Barbizon painters, went furthest in his landscapes, particularly in his younger years. He had a talent for echoing the ruggedness of stoney nature in the ruggedness of the way he handled colour.

### Plein-air Painting in Rome

In the development of *plein-air* painting, there was one road that travelled through England and France and another that travelled through Rome. Throughout the centuries, Rome had been the meeting point of painters from many countries. The French had been the first to arrive in the 17th century.

In the 18th century, the English followed, and after the Glorious Revolution of 1688, it was considered *de rigeur* for a nobleman to complete his education with a journey to Rome. English painters also took up this custom, for the increasing popularity of travel quite naturally brought with it an increased demand for interesting views of foreign countries. Finally, the Germans followed in the middle of the 18th century, and their great innovators in the field of art were also based in Rome: the art historian Winckelmann was there, as was the painter Mengs, who might justifiably be regarded as the German equivalent to France's David, for his monumental canvases sought to recapture the greatness and natural beauty of classical Antiquity, according to Winckelmann's views. All three had turned against the courtly art of Rococo in their call for morality and seriousness in art.

The French living in Rome, in particular, had been familiar with oil-paintings created directly from nature as early as the 17th century. In his *Teutsche Academie der edlen Bau-, Bild- und Malerey-Künste* (1675–1679), Sandrart wrote that the French artist Claude Lorrain had produced just such *plein-air* studies. In the late 18th and early 19th centuries, it was the French in particular who used this technique, whereas the Germans tended primarily to draw from nature and the English concentrated more on water-colours.

In his memoirs, published under the title *Lebenserinnerungen* in 1885, the German Romanticist Ludwig Richter (1803–1884) who lived in Rome in the 1820s describes the difference between German and French painters in Rome in their portrayal of nature: "The French painters, with their huge boxes, needed enormous quantities of paint for their studies, for they were wont to apply the paint with large brushes half a finger thick. They invariably painted from a certain distance, in order to achieve an overall effect or, as we would say, an impact. Of course, they also needed a great deal of canvas and paper, for they almost invariably painted and rarely drew; we, by contrast, tended to apply ourselves more to drawing than to painting. No pencil was hard enough nor sharp enough to capture the tiniest detail of each outline. Each and every artist would sit crouched over his work, no larger than a small sheet of paper, seeking to render painstakingly what he saw before him. We fell in love with every blade of grass, with every slender twig and did not want to miss a single appealing trait. The effects of air and light were avoided rather than sought; in short, each of us endeavoured to reiterate the object as objectively and truly as in a mirror."

When he writes of the German painters, he means those who were followers of the Nazarene or Neoclassicistic tradition, and with whom Richter, like the majority of German artists, identified. Yet in the 1820s such artists as Karl Blechen (1798–1840) from Berlin, were also living in Rome. As a colorist, Blechen certainly bears comparison with the French artist Jean-Baptiste Camille Corot (1796–1875) and the English painter J.M.W. Turner (1775–1851),

**Gustave Courbet**
The Cliff at Etretat after the Storm, 1870
Oil on canvas, 133 x 162 cm
Paris, Musée d'Orsay

**Camille Corot**
View of Genoa, 1834
Oil on canvas, 29.5 x 39 cm
Chicago (Il), The Art Institute
of Chicago

who were also staying in Rome around the same time in
1828. Turner and Corot are amongst the most important
painters of the early 19th century. On his return to Paris
from Rome, Corot became a founding member of the school
of Barbizon. In the studies he produced during his stay in
Rome, he developed a light-toned colorism similar to that
which was to become characteristic of landscape painting
towards the end of the 19th century. It was only with the
advent of Impressionism that the light-toned *plein-air*
painting became a generally adopted principle. However,
Corot's early sketches – in contrast to the impressionist
paintings – consist of sweeping and almost monochromatic
planes of vibrant colour, often contrasted with dark outlines
delimiting them from the next homogenous colour plane.
The chiaroscuro modelling that once dominated the entire
painting is now abandoned in favour of large areas of colour
in which there are no major differences in degrees of light
and shade.

A similar planarity can also be found in the Italian sketches
of Blechen. Unlike Corot, however, he preferred a pale
colority without warm reds: ochre and violet, white and blue
or white, blue and black are juxtaposed. Here we can recognise a principle similar to that applied by Delacroix: each
painting has its own colority in accordance with its specific
atmosphere or mood, whereby Blechen loved extreme opposites and was particularly interested in burnished or sparsely
vegetated areas where the rocks take on the character of
bleached bones. This alone was enough to attract the scorn of
German critics, who were used to seeing Italy portrayed as an
earthly paradise full of merry people and lush vegetation.

They expected to see a landscape based in the idyllic light
familiar to them from the paintings of Lorrain. The extreme
subjectivism in the choice of location and colority in Blechen's paintings annoyed the critics just as much as his
failure to deliver an overall tone.

Turner, the great English landscape painter who spent time
in Italy, particularly in Rome and Venice, in 1819 and
1828/29, had been influenced by Lorrain in his use of light,
but the results he produced were very different indeed. In Turner's paintings, light is not, as is it in the works of Claude Lorrain, an immaterial brilliance produced by the use of glazing
technique, but is directly linked with a certain colority or
lightness of individual brushstrokes. Like other painters of his
generation, Turner also structured each painting on the basis
of its own individual colour contrast; in this respect he may
well have influenced Blechen: for example black/brown/yel-
lowish white or yellow/red or black/ochre/white/blue. The pictorial theme is merely the vehicle for an exploration of colour
contrasts. By treating the colours more or less autonomously
and liberating them from all representational givens, they
become an expression of the struggle of elementary forces in
the universe, presented as light and dark or as climatic factors.
There are compositions whose swirling movement and title
refers directly to cosmic forces: *Shade and Darkness: The Evening of the Deluge* and *Light and Colour: The Morning after the Deluge*, both c.1843 (London, Tate Gallery).

Based on a scientific analysis of colour, a subjective view of
the cosmos was presented in a manner that was to remain unparalleled until the arrival of the Blaue Reiter group of artists
in the early 20th century, particularly Franz Marc (1880–

**J.M.W. Turner**
Rome from Mount Aventine, 1836
Oil on canvas, 91.6 x 124.6cm
Private collection

1916) and Wassily Kandinsky (1866–1944). In a calmer form and without the same claims to universal significance, Turner's autonomous colority influenced impressionism. This influence is distinctly evident in Claude Monet's (1840–1926) painting *Impression: Sunrise* (ill. p. 479) of 1873 that was to give the Impressionist movement its name.

The group of colorists dealt with in this chapter also included a number of idealists and realists – most of whom linked both these aspects. In the early 19th century, however, the word "realism" was rarely used. Instead, it was described as naturalism and generally meant that the artist had paid too much attention to the fleeting appearance of nature without idealistic refinement on the one hand, and on the other hand, colour – the most subjective of artistic means – had not been controlled enough by line. In this respect, Constable and the painters of the school of Barbizon were realists or naturalists. Blechen, on the other hand, was not content with a subjectivist portrayal of actual givens, but added a pessimistic view of the world that made him appear an antipode to the Romantics, who invariably used light as a sign of godly transfiguration. Blechen found that this aspect was missing from light. Yet even in this reversal, there is an indication of a Romantic view of the world.

Corot, in his early sketches, which are colorist gems, is primarily a realist. Yet in his great Salon pictures from the mid-19th century onwards, with their famous shimmering groups of grey-silver trees by riverbanks, he reintroduces light, inspired by the landscapes of Claude Lorrain, as an element that adds a paradisical brilliance to a charmingly

idyllic world (ill. p. 434). In these paintings – in spite of the fleeting brushwork indicative of Impressionism – he is an idealist, if not a Romantic. And this form of colorism was by far the most popular with the public.

Turner's colorism with its cosmic world view had nothing to do with realism, in spite of its impasto handling of colour. These are visions of a universal context – albeit without the religious touch of love and empathy – rendered in colour, similar in principle to the works of Runge, who also pursued scientific colour studies. However, whereas Runge's paintings are allegorical images of a Neo-Platonic light metaphysics, Turner's images are based on the far-sighted and purely objective views of the 18th century which he imbued with new meaning through his colorism based on colour theory and *plein-air* painting.

A closely related form of landscape painting was brought to America by the English artist John Crome (1768–1821). Frederic Edwin Church (1826–1900), the great American painter of panoramic landscapes who exhibited from the 1840s onwards, was his student. In his views, the wide expanses of such landscape compositions became symbols of the size and expanse of the American continent.

**Realist History Painting and Critical Realism in France**
The realism in landscape painting is characterised both by the choice of motif – undistinguished areas lying beyond land used for farming or gardens and off the beaten tourist track – as well as its form of presentation: colour material becomes a symbol for the materiality of the world. As this

genre of painting was dependent on the art market from a very early stage, it was here that the academic rules were first disregarded. After all, the highest task of art continued to be seen in the portrayal of human beings.

In this field, Delacroix and Ingres set the standards in France until 1848. Successors of Ingres such as Thomas Couture (1815–1879) pursued a staged Neoclassicism of erotic appeal. Théodore Chassériau (1819–1856), a former Ingres student, had joined Delacroix from the late 80s onwards and had continued his poetic colorism. He also shared Delacroix's preference for the portrayal of women and exotic subjects. These had developed into a genre of their own amongst such so-called orientalists as Alexandre Gabriel Decamps (1803–1860). The public's darlings, apart from that painter of modern wars, Emile Jean Horace Vernet (1789–1863), had been, since the 1830s, Jean Louis Ernest Meissonier (1815–1891) and Paul Hippolyte Delaroche (1797–1856), painters of historical genre scenes. They combined coloristic skill with an interest in detailed scenes from history.

This form of "historical genre painting" had originated in Belgium, where the break with the Kingdom of the United Netherlands (founded in 1815) had led in 1831 to a reflection on history and culture by the painters Louis Gallait (1810–1887) and Edouard de Bièfve (1808–1882), creators of a patriotic history painting in the grand style. The themes of these paintings – frequently public commissions or state purchases – were drawn from the struggle for liberation from Spanish rule in the 16th century. They caused a sensation throughout Europe. They were regarded as appropriate vehicles for the portrayal of bourgeois rule, appealing in their realism.

When the Belgian paintings were shown in Germany for the first time in 1845, this heralded the end of prevailing Neoclassicist historical painting. Leaders of the Neoclassicistic school in Germany, such as Cornelius and Moritz von Schwind (1804–1871) in Austria and their followers retaliated by declaring the strict morality of Neoclassicism to be synonymous with profundity and German art, and scorning the realism of the historical genre paintings as reprehensible and as "superficial Frenchness". Historical genre painting, involving colour accents that highlighted the presentation of materiality, was established in Germany by Piloty, whose works finally overcame Neoclassicism. All these portrayals of "accidents of history", as Schwind called them, appealed to the empathy of the viewer. The world is clearly divided into good and bad, noble and unnoble, and fate is merciless. The moralistic claims of Neoclassicism continued to survive at the level of a historical novel, relating patriotic legends even to the uneducated.

Although this particular genre of painting found favour with the public, critics questioned its dignity. They repeatedly asked, for example, whether such superficiality was

the necessary result of an art aimed at a broad sector of the bourgeoisie, or whether art should propagate an image of the individual suited to the democratic ideals of bourgeois rule. They also asked whether human dignity might be sought where historic greatness did not exist and where human greatness was an unembellished and unspectacular part of everyday life.

The painters who adopted such concepts after 1848 frequently chose to portray the peasant, for, from the point-of-view of the city dweller, the peasant embodied a life set apart from history. Even before 1848, rural life had been the subject of the so-called genre painting of the Biedermeier era. In this highly popular genre, the closeness and constraints of rural life, which had certainly not been alleviated by the onset of industrialisation, was presented as pious, humble and content. A distinction was made between those whose virtue and piety allowed them to enjoy "happiness in measure" (Jean Paul, 1763–1825) and those who did not belong. Koch's view of the community of Alpine peasants as the model for a future society of equality is no longer the theme of such portrayals. Instead, they present humble adaptation to the given circumstances as a prerequisite for happiness, as presented in the theories of the "Idyll" of such genre paintings.

The few socially critical peasant paintings by the Viennese artist Ferdinand Georg Waldmüller (1793–1865) created in the 1850s and 1860s, show the consequences of restriction and call such happiness into question. Nevertheless, a painting such as his *The Last Calf* (ill. p. 455) suggests that family bonds are strengthened in the face of misfortune, when the last calf has to be sold. The people leading the calf away are themselves only momentarily more fortunate members of the same social class and do not stand accused. The entire scene is primarily intended to present the different reactions of these people, who are confronted with bitter destiny. Scenes of misfortune were found to be particularly suitable vehicles for the kind of character studies that were a focus of 19th century genre painting. English artists of the late 18th and early 19th centuries, particularly David Wilkie (1785–1841), were driving forces in this respect. In the work of Waldmüller, the God-fearing fatalism of the rural population arouses the sympathy of the painter and the spectator. Such works are generally informed by the same principle that is to be found in the historical genre paintings of Delaroche or Piloty, but for the fact that pure genre painting does not portray outstanding historical personalities, but simple people, who have to bear their fate in much the same way as the famous and the great.

Even at first glance, Jean-François Millet's (1814–1875) *Gleaners* (ill. p. 442), executed at around the same time, clearly demonstrates a different attitude. Honoré Daumier's (1808–1879) *Washerwoman* (ill. p. 440), Millet's *Sower* (Boston, Museum of Fine Arts), Courbet's *Stonebreakers* (destroyed

1945; formerly Dresden, Gemäldegalerie) and his *Winnowers* (ill. p. 443) all have one thing in common: in all of these paintings, the faces of the characters portrayed are either ·turned away or their physiognomy is so reduced that there can be no question of an individual character (as in the work for example, of Wilkie or Waldmüller). Moreover, the figures are not presented at a dramatic moment of decision or fate, but busily going about the monotonously repetitive work that shapes their lives. These paintings convey the message that it is work and work alone that determines the movements and postures of these figures, most of them bowed, some of them seemingly weighed down under the horizon in a sign of their eternal subjection, as Courbet said of his *Stonebreakers*. If they appear to be moving freely in front of the sky, like Millet's *Sower*, which was exhibited in 1850/51 at the same Salon as Courbet's *Stonebreakers* and his *Burial at Ornans* (ill. pp. 444/445), then it is only the mastery of their work that produces this movement.

Nature is sparse and barren in these paintings; it is merely a working material. However great the personal variations between the artists may be, they retain one thing in common: in all these images, the members of the lowest classes are portrayed in monumental size, at their work, according to the rules of art hitherto reserved only for the ruling classes. The fact that the peasants were particularly disdained by the city-dwellers as uncultivated and uncouth made the sacrilege of such art works all the greater.

In an article published in 1855 on the separate exhibition of his friend Courbet, the writer Jules Champfleury (1821–1889) wrote: "One does not care to admit that a stonebreaker is worth as much as a prince. The aristocracy is appalled to find so many yards of canvas dedicated to such common people. Only rulers have the right to be portrayed in full figure…" Everything that flew in the face of good taste and good manners in such a way was dubbed with the negative epithet "realism", as Champfleury explained. Courbet took up the term as the slogan for his exhibition of 1855, declaring that he refused to be restricted in his choice of themes and that painting could and should give expression to the dignity of objects conventionally regarded as ugly. It was the first exhibition of an "independent" exhibition parallel to the official Salon exhibition during the Paris world fair of 1855. Many were to follow, and they would line the path of modern art.

In contrast to Millet, Courbet regarded himself as a revolutionary and a republican and he publicised his attitudes by actively participating in the Paris Commune of 1870. Millet, on the other hand, expressly rejected the honour of being appointed an artist of the Commune and announced on several occasions that his painting had nothing to do with politics, that it arose from human empathy alone. He saw the moral stature of the peasants in their humility and acceptance of their lot, in the necessity of their existence and

Jean Auguste Dominique Ingres
Madame Moitessier Seated, 1856
Oil on canvas, 120 x 92.1 cm
London, National Gallery

in the dignity of their close ties with the fertility of the soil. He wrote: "I try to show things in such a way that the necessity of their connections becomes clear, instead of making them seem as though fate had brought them together. I want to paint people so that the spectator can see which class they belong to and that it has nothing to do with the idea of wanting to be anything else."

His paintings thus had little to do with a struggle against the eviction of impoverished peasants from their land. The capitalist destruction of the peasant' livelihood since the 1840s was a fact lamented by many intellectuals. Yet one is unlikely to compare Millet's paintings with those of Pierre-Joseph Proudhon's (1809–1865) attack on property as the cause of poverty. Nor did Courbet have such ideas in mind with his *Stonebreakers* and, indeed, was only later persuaded by his friend Proudhon that he had created a painting that was revolutionary in more than just an artistic sense. Proudhon reported that the peasants of Courbet's hometown of Ornans wanted to purchase the painting and then display it on the main altar of their church, in an act of disrespect against the ruling order that was tantamount to an outright challenge.

The dignity of the impoverished peasant was invoked by others as well, including the historian Jules Michelet (1798–1874), who published a detailed work entitled *Le peuple (The People)* in 1846, prophesying the fall of France should the small farmers and crofters, the salt of its earth, be abandoned and left to ruin; for they had not only proved their heroism in their eternal struggle to cultivate the land, but as soldiers in Napoleon's armies. The peasants' love of their native soil and their French fatherland is held up as a shining example and the author calls for justice to be done, in the name of France's greatness, to these small farmers crushed by bourgeois creditors.

Whatever one's views may be on the question, the situation of the peasants had become an issue of national importance since the 1840s. As a result, the poverty of the farmers or rural workers also became the subject of art. At least art should do justice to a class that had won special dignity through its necessary and sacrificing service. The aim, however, was truth in art rather than the support of a political struggle through art, which Courbet, unlike Millet, did not reject.

In Courbet's view, for the modern artist it was necessary to make all social classes – regardless of questions of social prestige – subjects of his art. This view is reflected in his famous *Painter's Studio* (ill. p. 446) which he showed at a separate exhibition in 1855 together with his *Stonebreakers* and his *Burial at Ornans*. In the *Painter's Studio*, the artist is presented as the person who, through his work, invokes the equality of all, by dint of the fact that they possess the same value for him as individuals and as subjects of his painting.

(The descriptions on pp. 423 bottom, 425 bottom, 436 top, 437 bottom, 438 bottom, 439 bottom, 466 bottom, 468 bottom, 471 bottom and 474 top were written by Annemarie Menke-Schwinghammer, and those on pages 444f. by the editor)

## PIERRE-PAUL PRUD'HON
1758–1823

Napoleon commissioned this portrait of his wife a few months after her coronation. Although the Emperor had already considered a separation on grounds of her infertility, Joséphine persuaded him to marry her in church before the coronation. Nevertheless, her fears that Napoleon would abandon her in spite of coronation and marriage were confirmed in 1809.

Prud'hon shows the melancholy and loneliness of a woman confronted with this situation. Graceful and relaxed, she sits on a rocky outcrop in the park of Malmaison, far from the society she represents. The portrait employs the traditional visual syntax of 18th century English painting, in which the melancholy of the artistic intellectual is presented in a similar fashion. Prud'hon has exercised sensitivity in his depiction of Joséphine's inner turmoil, reflected in the gloomy autumnal atmosphere of her surroundings and has captured the special appeal radiated by this Creole woman born on the Island of Martinique. Her enigmatic gaze is reminiscent of Leonardo da Vinci, whose works influenced Prud'hon and from whom he has adopted the soft, silky sfumato of this painting.

**Pierre-Paul Prud'hon**
Empress Joséphine, 1805
Oil on canvas,
244 x 179 cm
Paris, Musée National du
Louvre

## FRANÇOIS GÉRARD
1770–1837

Juliette Bernard, who had married the considerably older Jacques Rose Récamier in 1793, invited artists and opponents of Napoleon to her Paris salon. Her beauty was famed. She was particularly delighted by the way in which Gérard emphasized her charms in this portrait. Five years earlier, she had commissioned Gérard's teacher Jacques-Louis David to paint her portrait, but was dissatisfied with the result and it remained unfinished (ill. p. 365). David had portrayed her reclining on the chaise longue that came to be known as a "récamiere" in the sparsely furnished surroundings of a Neoclassicist, cool room. Gérard, on the other hand, adds a glimpse of nature to the background and echoes the gently curving lines of her pose and the hue of her complexion in the forms and colours of her surroundings.

She is seated at a slight angle, allowing the painter to present her deep décolleté as effectively as her naked feet and thighs. This mode of dress and pose appeared perfectly natural at the time, in deliberate contrast to the mannered strictures of Rococo. In this respect, the great success of this portrait is also an indication of a new political attitude and a new, forward-looking image of humankind.

François Gérard
Madame Récamier, 1805
Oil on canvas, 225 x 145 cm
Paris, Musée Carnavalet

**Antoine-Jean Gros**
Napoleon at Arcola,
November 17, 1796, 1796
Oil on canvas, 73 x 59 cm
Paris, Musée National du Louvre

**Antoine-Jean Gros**
Napoleon on the Battlefield at Eylau, February 9, 1807, 1808
Oil on canvas, 533 x 800 cm
Paris, Musée National du Louvre

# ANTOINE-JEAN GROS
## 1771–1835

In his portrayal of a historic event – the storming of the bridge of Arcola, held by the Austrians – Gros has chosen to depict only the figure of Napoleon himself, showing him at the very moment when he rides towards victory at the head of his troops, hair flowing and flag flying. The compelling force he radiates is heightened by the swirling brushstrokes that surround him, making the actual scene unclear and the incident only emotionally discernable.

By presenting Napoleon in the full dynamic force of his military leadership – the role on which his fame is based – yet at the same time isolating him from the immediate context of the turbulent events around him, Gros has created a universal psychological portrait of the "great man" in which the triumph of victory is as vital as the solitude of the brilliant leader. Napoleon's face bears an expression of absolute determination, and his gestures have an almost magical effect, as he drives his soldiers on in battle.

The backward glance suggests a link with the past history of the *Grande nation* from which Napoleon drew his motivation, and the colours of the tricolore are subtly suggested in the painting.

25.000 were killed or wounded at the dreadful battle of Eylau in Prussia where Napoleon narrowly defeated the Russian army. In order to project a kindly and caring image, the Emperor called a competition for a memorial painting of the battle, specifying the content in considerable detail and calling for a portrayal of "Napoleon with consoling gaze".

On the day after the battle, the Emperor rides over the battle field. The procession slows when a group of wounded enemy soldiers catches Napoleon's attention. He turns towards a Lithuanian officer, who kisses the eagle emblem on Napoleon's boot in gratitude for the assistance the Emperor has ordered. Napoleon, with sorrowful gesture and heavenward gaze, expresses his horror. Whereas the medical staff actually took care of only the French wounded, the Emperor is seen here taking care of the enemy soldiers as well. His act of clemency is further glorified by depicting him showing kindness to an enemy characterized as barbaric. In his painting, Gros succeeds in presenting the instigator and victor of the war as a man who declaims war as an evil that has been thrust upon him against his will. Napoleon personally awarded the artist the cross of the Legion of Honour for his services.

Just how closely Gros' portrayal corresponds to Napoleon's own views is clear in a letter the Emperor wrote to Joséphine the day after the victory: "Yesterday there was a great battle. I gained a victory, but I have suffered heavy losses; the fact that the enemy's losses are even greater does not console me."

# THÉODORE GÉRICAULT
## 1791–1824

The inspiration for this painting, that brought Géricault instant fame at the Paris Salon of 1812, came from a fair at Saint-Cloud where a horse, frightened by the noise and commotion of the festivities, suddenly reared. That same evening, he executed innumerable sketches and studies of the motif. After that, a coachman let him borrow his horse as a model, and a friend stood model for the portrait of the officer. At the same time, Géricault studied the works of Peter Paul Rubens, the *Battle of Constantine* by the school of Raphael and David's equestrian portrait of Napoleon.

Exhaustive life studies and a profound awareness of artistic tradition resulted in this sumptuous portrayal of a fiery steed rearing up at the sound of cannon fire, carrying its rider, who has already drawn his sable, into the dusty haze of the distant battle.

Géricault has followed the Baroque tradition in having the horse leap at an angle into the pictorial space, with rider and horse moving dynamically in all directions in a blaze of sumptuous colour.

The earthy, monochromatic beige and brown tones of the scene show a break at work in the muddy courtyard of a chalk furnace. Three heavy, dappled work-horses in the left foreground, still bridled and laden, are eating their oats from nosebags, in front of the pale, high-wheeled work-cart. To the right in the centre foreground, in front of the ponderous horizontal mass of the factory building, another two dapple-greys are also eating their ration of oats, standing at an angle in front of the high entrance. Thick white smoke is pouring through an aperture on the left of the factory building and drifting upwards in a dense cloud. The only sign of work and activity in a scene void of human figures, it forms a clear visual contrast to the gloomy overcast sky that dominates the left hand side of the painting.

In the touching poverty and grim tranquility of the scene, the painting has little of the narrative character normally associated with genre painting. Géricault's balanced treatment of pictorial elements, all in the same light and hues lend it a quality akin to a landscape painting. The gloomy melancholy of the overall atmosphere has little to do with Romantic notions of landscape as the mirror of transcendental reality, but would appear to be based on the artist's own direct personal experience. Géricault had the misfortune to invest a considerable amount of capital in this rundown factory and on a visit there, he immediately made a sketch of his first impressions.

**Théodore Géricault**
Officer of the Imperial Guard (The Charging Chasseur), 1812
Oil on canvas, 292 x 194 cm
Paris, Musée National du Louvre

**Théodore Géricault**
The Quicklime Works, c. 1821/22
Oil on canvas, 50 x 60 cm
Paris, Musée National du Louvre

**Théodore Géricault**
The Raft of the Medusa (sketch), c. 1818/19
Oil on canvas, 65 x 83 cm
Paris, Musée National du Louvre

On 2 July 1816, the frigate Medusa, carrying French settlers bound for the colony of Senegal, ran aground off the West African coast. A raft carrying 149 passengers drifted on the high seas for twelve days before it was finally sighted. Only ten of them survived the terrible ordeal. The disaster was due primarily to the incompetence of the ship's captain who had gained his appointment solely as a favour from the regime. The report of two survivors caused a public outcry. Hardly surprisingly, the fact that Géricault should dare to rub salt in the wound by choosing this particular motif for the Salon of 1819 was seen as an affront to the new Bourbon rulers, and they accordingly prohibited the painting's title.

Nevertheless, Géricault's fascination with the subject matter was not necessarily politically motivated. Indeed, he was primarily interested in it as a vehicle for the portrayal of human existence under extreme conditions – a theme he explored soon afterwards in his paintings of the mentally ill. In his impassioned empathy with the victims of the Medusa shipwreck, he did everything in his power to

present the inconceivable suffering of real figures as drastically as possible. He contacted survivors, had a model raft built and made numerous studies of the dead and the dying in hospitals and morgues.

The viewer discerns the bodies and faces of the dead, the despairing and the hopeful in a diffuse twilight that bathes the scene in gloomy, heavy colours, seen from the slightly elevated position of the artist that brings the events frighteningly close. This painting is frequently compared with Michelangelo's portrayal of human suffering in the *Last Judgement*, which Géricault greatly admired and which he had studied closely when he was in Rome in 1816/17.

In the sketch shown here, Michelangelo's influence is particularly evident in the powerful chiaroscuro modelling of the bodies with their impressive gestures and distortions, portrayed at times in bold foreshortening.

# THÉODORE GÉRICAULT
1791–1824

There is a world of difference between the *Raft of the Medusa* and the *Epsom Derby*, painted only two years later during a visit to England. It was to have a strong influence on the later Impressionists. Instead of the monumental gravity with which he had previously presented human fate, he now depicts a moment of exciting tension in the Englishman's favourite sport, horse-racing, which captivated Géricault, himself a keen rider.

The artist seems to channel the viewer's gaze through a pair of binoculars focused sharply on the distant horses and jockeys, so that the surroundings remain unclear, disintegrating into blurred strips of colour. This technique heightens the illusion of the speed of the galloping horses, in a way unparalleled by the popular prints, lithographs and engravings of racehorses that were so widespread in England, and which undoubtedly inspired Géricault to treat the subject in the first place. The strong colority influenced by English painting – particularly the intense green of the meadows – and the strange luminosity of the stormy twilight heighten our sense of witnessing a specific moment that has been captured on canvas just as the artist himself experienced it at a race, when a thunderstorm suddenly broke

A few months before his death, the 32-year-old Géricault noted: "a barely describable yet undeniable inner disorder." It was during this time that he was commissioned by the leading psychiatrist of the day, Dr Georget, to execute portraits of ten inmates at the Parisian mental asylum of Salpêtrière. Georget is regarded as one of the founding fathers of social psychiatry. He regarded insanity as a specifically modern expression of bewildered confusion, caused for the most part by social progress in the enlightened industrialized countries. Accordingly, the mentally ill under his care were freed from their chains and treated as people requiring help.

Géricault did not portray these mental patients the way they had been depicted since the Middle Ages – as creatures possessed by the devil and punished by God, or as grotesque fools. Instead, his meticulous physiognomical studies and the objective sobriety of his unadorned portraiture explored the fate of individual human beings, underlining their proximity to the healthy individual and the threat of insanity in us all is suggested. In the image of the mad-man, the empty and fleeting gaze, permitting no contact with the observer, the tense, alert, but immobile facial expression, the unkempt hair and beard and the dishevelled collar indicate a deviation from normality and an individual living entirely in his own world.

Théodore Géricault
The Epsom Derby, 1821
Oil on canvas, 92 x 123 cm
Paris, Musée National du Louvre

Théodore Géricault
The Cleptomaniac, c. 1822/23
Oil on canvas, 61 x 51 cm
Ghent, Musée des Beaux-Arts

# JEAN AUGUSTE DOMINIQUE INGRES
## 1780–1867

**Jean Auguste Dominique Ingres**
Joan of Arc at the Coronation of Charles VII in Reims Cathedral, 1854
Oil on canvas, 240 x 178 cm
Paris, Musée National du Louvre

*Below:*
**Jean Auguste Dominique Ingres**
The Turkish Bath, 1862
Oil on canvas, diameter 108 cm
Paris, Musée National du Louvre

This painting was commissioned in 1852 by the director of the Academy of Fine Arts in Orléans for the memorial celebrations in honour of Joan of Arc. Ingres presented the victorious young woman who had liberated Orléans from the English siege in 1429 as a triumphant heroine whose heavenward gaze indicates the source of her fame. Three pages, the monk Paquerel and Ingres himself, in the guise of a royal servant, pay homage to Joan of Arc. The mood is one of great piety. A wealth of precious items and sumptuous materials painted with meticulous precision in superbly luminous colours, recall the origins of a nation in which church and state were once powerfully united.

In this painting, executed at the age of 82, Ingres reiterates the bathers and odalisques of his early years. The motifs for his idealized female forms, living for beauty and pleasure alone, are based on reports of the Orient describing the baths of the harem of Mahomet and the letters of Lady Montagu describing Turkish baths. He adhered in great detail to these reports, which describe the dignified grace of the women, their magnificent milk-white complexions, their beautifully formed bodies and their beautiful hair.

For all their sensuality, Ingres' bathers have an air of paradisical innocence, corresponding to the reports of Lady Montagu, who remarked with some astonishment that, in spite of their nakedness, there was never any indecorous gesture or behaviour amongst the women. The abstract and idealized beauty of these women, suspended in time and strangely intangible, is achieved through the economy of artistic means by which Ingres has portrayed them. The bodies are clearly defined, with particular emphasis on the surface, so that the subtle interplay of light creates a gentle modelling and the skin has a pellucid opalescence.

While the *Turkish Bath*, teeming with stretching and writhing nudes, is composed in a round format that creates a most unusual sense of unity, the aesthetic appeal of this famous nude study of 1808 lies in the monumentalization of the individual figure. Here, the artist already uses the approach that is the hallmark of his later work. "The more simple the lines and forms," says Ingres, "the greater the beauty and power."

**Jean Auguste Dominique Ingres**
Valpinçon Bather, 1808
Oil on canvas, 146 x 97.5 cm
Paris, Musée National du Louvre

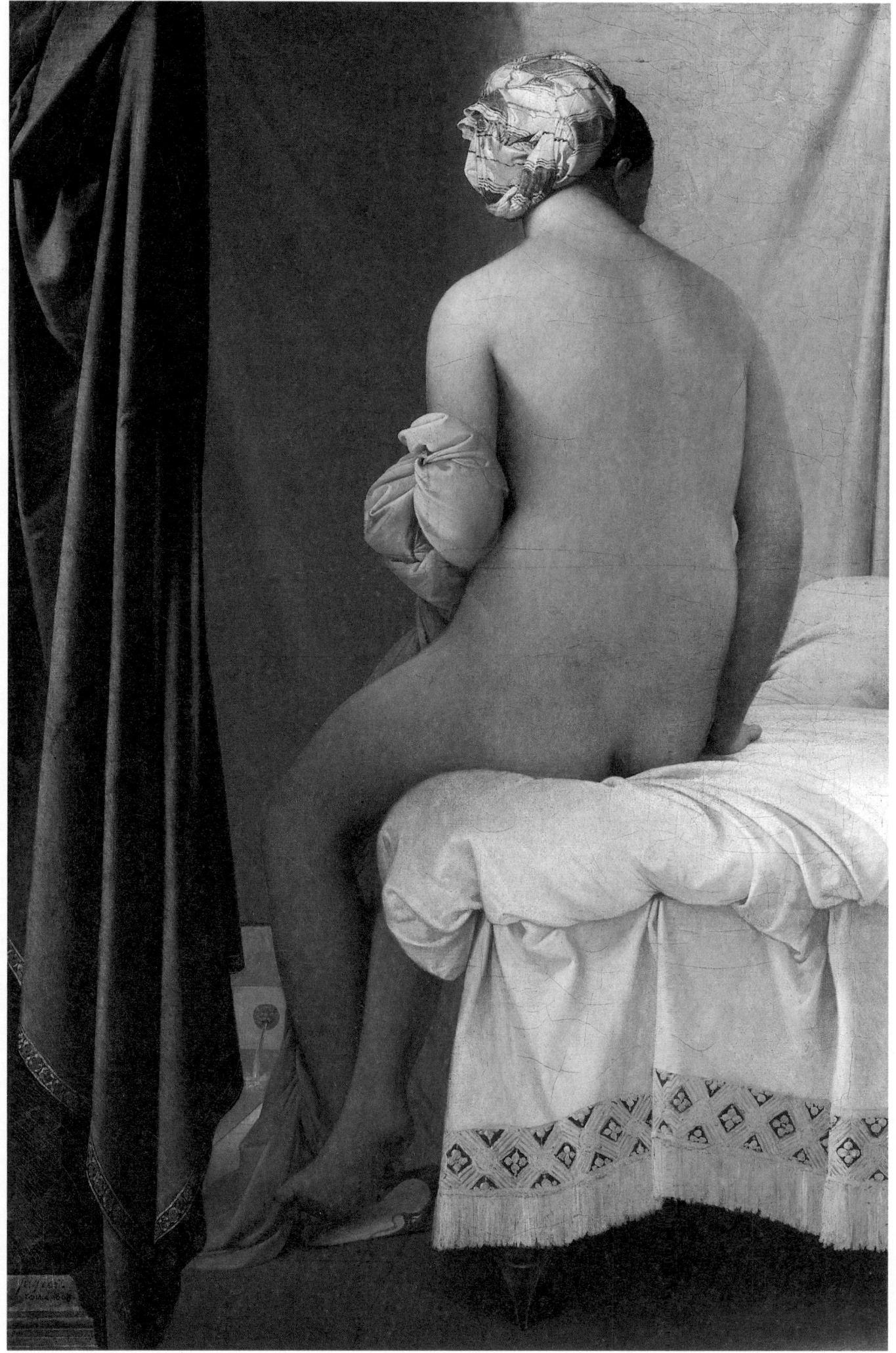

# JEAN AUGUSTE DOMINIQUE INGRES
## 1780–1867

Jean Auguste Dominique Ingres
Mademoiselle Rivière, 1806
Oil on canvas, 100 x 70 cm
Paris, Musée National du Louvre

This portrait of a young woman from an esteemed Parisian family was executed in the early years of Ingres' artistic career, when he painted portraits for his living. Even as an old man, Ingres still spoke affectionately of the "charming daughter" who died at the age of 15, only a few months after he had painted her.

Ingres demonstrated enormous sensitivity in his portrayal of this still child-like girl on the threshold of womanhood, already endowed with all the confidence of her social station. There is something charmingly stiff about her pose, even though she has already mastered the art of the gracious gesture in the way she holds the white boa draped around her body. Above all, in capturing her facial expression, Ingres has succeeded in capturing the indecisiveness of a girl who is not yet an adult. Though her large brown almond eyes seem to gaze dreamily and the suggestion of a smile plays around her slightly open lips, her gaze is alert and directed with earnest attentiveness towards the spectator.

Ingres has achieved this effect by using fragile yet contrasting colours, soft yet precise, and clear-cut precise forms and contours. Even the background is in perfect harmony with the mood of the model: the hazy riverscape of the Ile-de-France is offset against a pale blue sky reflected in the surface of the water, and the dark bushes with their little flowers are reiterated in the ochre of the gloves and in the fresh bunches of grass in the foreground.

*Below:*
Jean Auguste Dominique Ingres
Louis-François Bertin, 1832
Oil on canvas, 116 x 95 cm
Paris, Musée National du Louvre

Bertin, publisher of the *Journal des Débats*, was one of the most influential figures and spokesmen of public opinion under the constitutional monarchy of Louis Philippe I, and his newspaper was a force to be reckoned with in the state. His critics saw in him the very epitome of the complacent and self-righteous bourgeois who had been brought forth by the July Monarchy. Manet called him the Buddha of the well-heeled, world-weary, triumphant bourgeoisie. Ingres, who regarded him as one of "the best and most intelligent of men", was a close friend.

The portrait is astonishing for the directness and forceful presence with which Bertin confronts the viewer. All signs of prestige and ornamentation are lacking. The mighty silhouette of this colossal figure has been further emphasized by the fact that he is seen from a slightly lower position, as well as by the compact gesture of the pose and the curve of the chair that frames the body. The heavy head with its tousled hair is also impressive. The face exudes an air of utter imperturbability, the expression is one of sensitivity and energy, while the direct gaze indicates a vital intensity.

# EUGÈNE DELACROIX
1798–1863

The perilous struggle to the death between humans and wild animals held a particular fascination for Delacroix throughout his life, just as it had for Rubens, whose work he greatly admired. Following his journey to Morocco, Delacroix executed several studies and paintings exploring the theme of the forces of nature in terms of the confrontation between humans and animals. In *The Lion Hunt* the intensity of this struggle is expressed primarily through the creation of tempestuosly swirling movement. Set in a coastal landscape, the scene takes the form of a sweeping, circular movement, illuminated from above, with repetitions in individual body movements and in the details of clothing and clouds. At the same time, the scene is grouped around the point of intersection of two diagonals, along which the positions and movements of the individual figures are aligned.

Only on closer examination of this surging mass of animal and human bodies caught in the throes of a dramatic struggle, can we discern the balance of power and the imminent outcome. One Arab has been killed and two have been overwhelmed, but four others have already raised their lances and sables to attack the two wildly snarling beasts, while a rider is about to charge. This moment of tension when everything is still in the balance, is echoed by the indefinable weather conditions that bathe the entire event in a strangely shimmering light.

The presentation of nature is reduced to the elementary powers of heaven, water and earth, which merge in hues of bluish-green and in the structural formation radiating from the top right of the picture. In no other portrayal of a hunt by Delacroix are the primeval forces of nature so inextricably entwined with the struggle itself; even the human figures seem to share the suppleness and instinctive reactions of the animals.

**Eugène Delacroix**
The Lion Hunt, 1861
Oil on canvas, 76.5 x 98.5 cm
Chicago (IL), The Art Institute of Chicago

**Eugène Delacroix** The Massacre of Chios, 1824
Oil on canvas, 417 x 354cm
Paris, Musée National du Louvre

**Eugène Delacroix**
Liberty Leading the People (28th July 1830), 1830
Oil on canvas, 260 x 325cm
Paris, Musée National du Louvre

# EUGÈNE DELACROIX
## 1798–1863

The Greek struggle for liberation from Turkish rule fired the imagination of Europe's neo-Hellenistic liberal intellectuals. Delacroix chose the gruesome massacre of Chios in 1824 when 20.000 inhabitants of the Greek islands were murdered as an attention-catching subject. In 1821, he wrote to a friend: "For the next Salon, I want to make a painting based on the latest war between the Greeks and the Turks. I think that under the current circumstances, I shall be able to draw attention to myself in this way."

Delacroix skilfully structures the picture plane into three human pyramids of dead and dying Greeks, bathed in a harmonious light and colour. Although the painting had already been accepted by the exhibition committee of the Salon, he was no longer satisfied with it once he had seen some of the work Constable intended to submit to the Salon. Suddenly, his painting seemed to him "sad and void of light". Within four days, under the influence of Constable, he altered his painting, adding shimmering glazes and creating new effects with brief and forceful brushstrokes, densely juxtaposed.

The violation of the constitution by King Charles X, who sought the reinstatement of absolute monarchy, led to the bloody insurgency of 1830 which inspired Delacroix to create this painting of a modern subject, as he described it.

Delacroix portrays an extremely dramatic event within a strictly Neoclassical compositional structure based on an equilateral triangle. The people, fuelled by rage, are storming towards the viewer over a broad threshold of the dead and wounded and a barricade of stones and beams. The clouds of dust and gunpowder that envelope the central motif suggest the outlines of firearms in the background and, in spite of the relatively small number of figures in the painting, it gives the impression of a large crowd. The crowd is led on by the allegorical figure of Liberty, part goddess of antiquity and part Parisian marketwoman – wearing a Jacobin cap and brandishing a gun as she waves the tricolour. The crowd is fired by her enthusiasm, described as follows by Heinrich Heine: "These common people have one great thought, that gives them dignity and succour and re-awakens the dormant dignity within their souls."

The painter is the sole exception, portrayed in the guise of an intellectual – the student with the hat – as the counterpart of the goddess. Unlike the boy who is shooting around him indiscriminately, the artist holds his gun hesitantly. His gaze, sceptical and thoughtful, is directed into the distance, suggesting that he is seeking the deeper meaning and purpose of it all.

A highlight in Delacroix' tour of Africa which lasted of several months, was his opportunity to visit a harem. His companion, a French diplomat, reports that Delacroix was overwhelmed by the sight: "C'est beau! C'est comme au temps d'Homere!" ("It's beautiful! Just as in the days of Homer!") are said to have been his words. Here, in this enclave of women cut off from the world, he felt he had found the epitome of truth and beauty and the spirit of Antiquity.

These women exude the atmosphere that Charles Baudelaire described as "luxe, calme et volupté" and they seem to float somewhere between reality and dream. In the blend of oriental and Greek and the facial traits reminiscent of a sculpture by Phidias, these are embodiments of an ideal of womanhood which Delacroix describes as follows: "The magic that makes us love them is based on a thousand things… But what seduces the heart and fires its passion are beauties less defined and less delineated, unknown, unexplained, enigmatic and unspeakable."

In order to record his impressions reliably, Delacroix made water-colour sketches during his brief visit to the harem and noted the nuances of colour in pencil. The oil-painting, executed two years later, was to influence many artists, from Renoir to Matisse. This later generation of artists was particularly impressed by the heightened colority inspired by the overwhelming impressions of an oriental journey, and by the way in which Delacroix brightened the traditional brownish hues of the painting.

The handling of light, for example, is such that the light flooding into the room highlights the different materials of various objects, while the areas in the shadow have a deeper but nevertheless intensive colority which is graduated towards the points of transition between shadow and light. Given the sheer variety of magnificently opulent materials and the huge range of colours and reflections, the atmosphere is one of vibrant and vital commotion, woven into a bright and sumptuous tapestry of colour.

**Eugène Delacroix**
Women of Algiers, 1834
Oil on canvas, 180 x 229 cm
Paris, Musée National du Louvre

## JEAN-BAPTISTE CAMILLE COROT
### 1796–1875

**Jean-Baptiste Camille Corot**
View of the Colosseum from the Farnese Gardens, 1826
Oil on cardboard on canvas, 30 x 49 cm
Paris, Musée National du Louvre

Corot painted this picture while he was in Rome on his first tour of Italy, where he developed the style of his nature studies on the basis of the classical tradition. It is one of a series of three views – each seen from the Farnese gardens – which, together, create a triptych of different times of day; this one shows the evening. The painting portrays the city with its historic monuments from an idealized viewpoint. It possesses clarity and documentary authenticity without being overburdened with details.

Distance and ideal heightening of the view are achieved by the stage-like framing of trees and bushes of the garden. The contrast between the plants in the foreground, the tectonic forms of the central plane and the empty spaces of the almost cloudless and unusually low horizon in gently graded light and dark tones lend this painting its particular appeal. The handling of light adds a vibrant brilliance to the entire scene, suffused by the evening play of light and shadow, so that the abandoned remnants of the past appear to take on a fresh immediacy.

Although Corot is primarily a painter of serene and sun-drenched landscapes, he created about ten paintings after mid-century in which the scene is shaken by heavy gusts of wind. Most of the landscapes are situated in the north of France, as in this painting showing dunes in front of a low, light horizon, where the movement of the passing clouds seems almost palpable.

A group of windswept trees make the force of the gust particularly clear. The typically hazy air near the sea is depicted by the gently shimmering graduations of colour from light, greyish-green and brown tones and a silvery veil cast over the entire picture. The effect created is a strange blend of natural realism and Romantic, lyrical atmosphere, typical of Corot's mature style.

Monumental and strongly sculpted, the figure of the young Italian woman rises up in front of an atmospheric village background. Her classical face is framed by a warm autumnal light as though by a nimbus. The compact blue and black tones of her costume make her stand out even more distinctly from the background, which seems to dissolve in the luminosity and colority, particularly towards the right-hand side of the painting.

**Jean-Baptiste Camille Corot**
Le Coup de Vent (The Gust of Wind), c. 1865–1870
Oil on canvas, 47.4 x 58.9 cm
Reims, Musée Saint Denis

**Jean-Baptiste-Camille Corot**
Agostina, 1866
Oil on canvas, 130 x 95 cm
Washington, National Gallery of Art

Jean-Baptiste-Camille Corot
Woman in Blue, 1874
Oil on canvas, 80 x 51 cm
Paris, Musée National du Louvre

*Below:*
Jean-Baptiste Camille Corot
The Studio, 1866
(Young Woman with a Mandolin)
Oil on canvas, 64 x 48 cm
Paris, Musée National du Louvre

# JEAN-BAPTISTE CAMILLE COROT
## 1796—1875

Both the melancholy gesture of chin on hand, and the setting within the artist's own working area, places this portrayal of a young woman firmly amongst Corot's repertoire of figural and studio paintings. Most of his studio paintings belong to his mature phase and many show women in a mood of melancholic reverie. This particular painting is, however, unusual not only because it portrays a full figure standing, but also because the woman shown here is dressed in extremely elegant and fashionable garb, in stark contrast to Corot's more frequent renderings of nameless models dressed considerably more simply and representing "types" in their Italian, Greek or oriental-style costumes. For this reason, many art historians believe that this painting may well be a portrait of the young Madame G., with whom the artist had been friends since around 1870.

Although Corot had gained considerable acclaim for his landscape paintings, his figure studies, which he had also worked on for several decades, did not come to public attention until after his death. He plainly felt that they belonged to the private domain in which he could experiment with his art undisturbed. This painting is from the closing months of the artist's life, and may well be his last figure study. The sophisticated density of his handling of colour, restricted to only a few hues, is extremely progressive. It had an enormous influence on the much younger generation of Impressionists, most notably on several portraits by Renoir, painted in the same year.

In the last fifteen years of his life, Corot worked primarily in his Paris studio, where he produced a number of studio paintings featuring dreamily pensive young girls, to whom he allocated attributes from the world of music, painting or literature. The girl in this painting has clearly just stopped playing a mandolin and is now sitting meditatively, her head leaning on her right hand. In front of her is the artist's easel with a landscape painting, and further paintings are placed on a shelf in the background.

In the dark, brown-toned room, the light falls from above, touching the girl, the painting on the easel and the brightly upholstered chair. The focal point of the painting is the brilliant red of the girl's blouse, reiterated in her hairband. Its warm colority blends harmoniously with the silky sheen of her sand-coloured skirt, the pale complexion of her face, the reddish-brown of the mandolin, the luminous golden frames of the paintings and the ambient dark browns. The dreamy, melancholy mood surrounding the girl is emphasized by the harmonious colours. This, for Corot, is essential: "What I seek in painting is... an equilibrium of hues. Colour is only secondary to me."

# THÉODORE CHASSÉRIAU
1819–1856

Henri Lacordaire, who had abandoned his career as a lawyer in order to become a priest, was called to Rome in 1839 by Pope Gregor XVI to answer for his rebellious ideas. He submitted to the will of the papal chair and became an impassioned proponent of Catholicism, making a significant contribution to its renewal during the upheavals of the 1848 revolution.

Chassériau's portrait of Lacordaire, who had joined the Dominican order, was executed in Rome. The clergyman, dressed in a monk's habit, is standing in an attitude of meditation in front of the cloisters of Santa Sabina. Only the intelligent, sharply contoured face with the piercing eyes set firmly on the viewer indicate the passionate and courageous spirit of this man. Chassériau also expresses this in his painterly technique by having a ray of light fall upon the figure, creating strong *chiaroscuro* contrasts and contours in the face and robes, and at the same time separating the figure like a silhouette in relief against the softly painted architecture of the background. This is also in keeping with the reduced palette, consisting primarily of browns, that suffuses the background in a gentle reddish-brown, against which the dark brown and pale beige of the face and robes are distinctly set apart in their starkly contrasting hues of dark brown and light beige.

Théodore Chassériau
Pater Lacordaire, 1840
Oil on canvas,
146 x 107 cm
Paris, Musée National
du Louvre

In this painting of his two sisters, who often stood as models for him, Chassériau chose to portray a bond of harmony and tenderness. The double portrait, for which preparatory pencil studies exist, shows his older sister Adèle on the left and Aline, twelve years her junior, on the right.

The age difference between the two women is barely discernable in the painting. Both have the same fine, sleek, dark hair and delicate complexion, particularly evident in the portrayal of their intertwined hands and wrists. They also wear similar clothing and jewellery. The immobility of the scene and the emphasis of line embracing both figures and making them stand out clearly against the background, expresses the harmony of these two women. Only the magnificent blossoming rose on her belt sets Adèle apart from her much younger sister.

The bold use of colour is in stark contrast to the linearity which lends the painting its own decorative quality. The influence of Delacroix' modern and intensively coloured painting on this former student of Ingres is clearly evident not only in the fine, though by no means overweeningly elegant dresses, with their blend of light browns and pinks, but most notably in the long, brightly coloured red shawls.

Théodore Chassériau
The Sisters of the
Artist, 1843
Oil on canvas,
180 x 135 cm
Paris, Musée National
du Louvre

## PAUL HUET
### 1803–1869

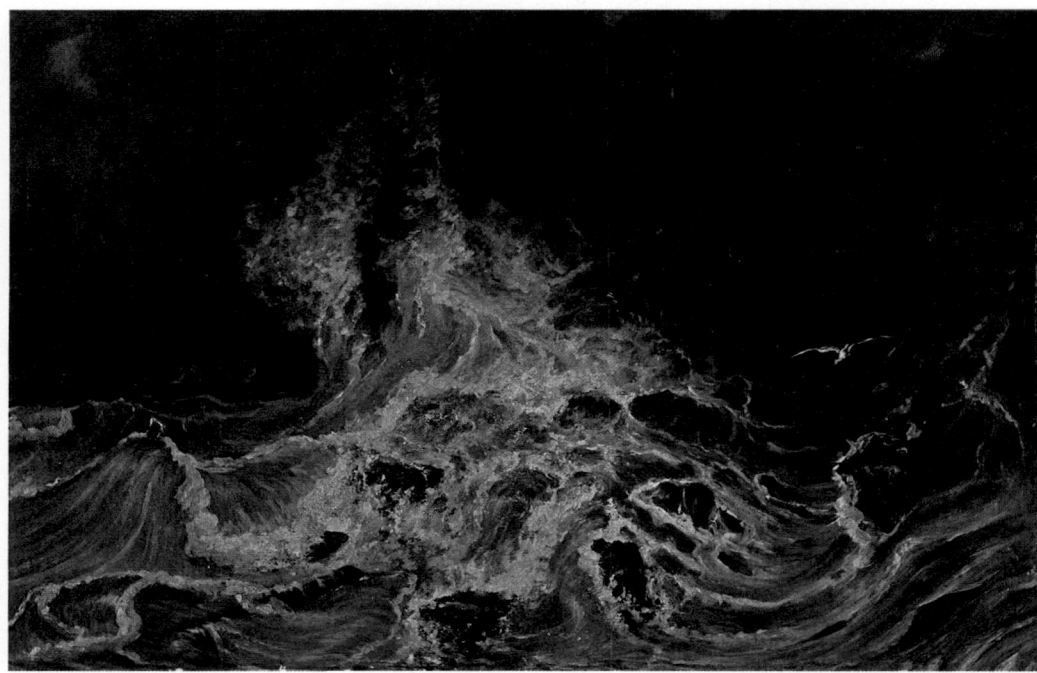

**Paul Huet**
Breakers at Granville, c. 1853
Oil on canvas, 68 x 103 cm
Paris, Musée National du Louvre

Unlike Daubigny, who portrayed the calm and meditative side of nature, most of Huet's landscapes are images of catastrophe, storm, and flood. The tempestuous seas lashing the peninsula at Granville, where the artist stayed in 1850, inspired numerous sketches, on which he based his famous wave paintings.

The sea dashing against the steep cliffs is painted at such proximity that it is almost as though Huet had set up his easel in the midst of the rising waves. The white crests of foam topping the breakers as they crash against the cliffs and the spray rising from them form the focal point of this dramatic display of the forces of nature. Broad brushstrokes create the brackishly green waves and the blurred and fleeting sketchiness of the dark brown rock formations. The menacing undertone of nature's powers unleashed is further heightened by the dark and thundery sky that makes the sea light up so strangely.

The famous critic Charles-Augustin Sainte-Beuve said of Huet's art: "In this way of observing and presenting location, the human being no longer plays any major role... nature comes first, nature alone."

**Charles-François Daubigny**
Landscape at Gylieu, 1853
Oil on canvas, 62.2 x 99.7 cm
Cincinnati (OH), Cincinnati Art Museum

## CHARLES-FRANÇOIS DAUBIGNY
### 1817–1878

One of Daubigny's favourite subjects is the changing character of landscapes with water. His aim was to capture the momentary mood created by a specific weather or light situation. The forms of the objects and their materiality are subordinate to this purpose. The paint is hastily applied so that forms appear to be dissolved by light. The traditional distinction between sketch and finished painting was thus abandoned by Daubigny.

From the late 1840s onwards, the artist also worked on his landscape paintings in the Rhone valley. The pond of Gyliau near Optévoz fascinated him for some time; he even created an oil-painting of it as late as 1869. This version of 1853 was painstakingly prepared with several preliminary studies.

Daubigny not only determined the composition in his small-scale pencil sketches, but also noted the colours in which he would execute the finished painting. The balanced composition and the finely gradated, sometimes shimmering greens render the calm atmosphere of this undisturbed place on a bright summer day seemingly effortlessly. In the realistic, atmospheric presentation of landscape without pathos, Daubigny paved the way for the Impressionists.

# THÉODORE ROUSSEAU
1812–1867

Rousseau painted the *Chestnut Avenue* in the park of Château Souliers in the Vendée, owned by the family of his friend, the painter Charles le Roux. The composition is reminiscent of a theatrical backdrop in which an illusion of great depth is created by means of architectonically structured and symmetrically graded trees on either side of the alley. The fact that the upper edges of the painting have been rounded heightens this stage-like effect. It is further emphasized by the position of the viewer, who perceives the alley at a distance, although he is actually standing in its midst.

A gloom-laden atmosphere is exuded by this painting, devoted for the most part to a dense and impenetrable vault of foliage with no sky above it. Only in the lower quarter of the painting is there some air and light to be seen through the short and stocky tree-trunks with their wizened branches, and even the horizon is merely a matt shimmer along the line where earth and sky meet.

Forest and trees are Rousseau's preferred subject matter. The atmosphere he expresses in his paintings is invariably based on a direct and unsentimental observation of nature. Nature never becomes a vehicle for the expression of human sentiment.

In his *Oak Trees near Apremont*, Rousseau brings to perfection an artistic endeavour that had previously been explored only by English painters, and one that was relatively new to the French art world. With objective precision, he portrays the burning mid-day light of high summer and its effect on the landscape. Like many of his artist colleagues from the school of Barbizon, Rousseau chose his local environment as the subject of his studies, painting it under different light and atmospheric conditions, then completing the painting in the studio.

A group of sturdy oaks takes up the central area, it is surrounded by grazing cows; a peasant can also be seen. The dark mass of the trees casts a short and compact shadow that is broken in only a few places by pools of light. To the right and left, the dark green outline dissolves into smaller, lighter foliage, shimmering in the sun. Behind the wide expanse of lush green meadow, dappled with patches of pale yellow, a small strip of yellowish vegetation stretches across the painting, cut by a sandy path.

The calm tranquillity of the scene and the compositional device of placing the horizon line at a low level, leaving considerable space for the sky, give us a clear indication of Rousseau's main influences, particularly amongst the Netherlandish landscape painters of the 17th century such as Meindert Hobbema or Jacob van Ruisdael.

**Théodore Rousseau**
The Chestnut Avenue, 1837
Oil on canvas, 79 x 144 cm
Paris, Musée National du Louvre

**Théodore Rousseau**
Oak Trees near Apremont, 1852
Oil on canvas, 63.5 x 99.5 cm
Paris, Musée National du Louvre

Honoré Daumier
The Emigrants, 1852/55
Oil on panel, 16.2 x 28.7 cm
Paris, Musée du Petit Palais

## HONORÉ DAUMIER
### 1808–1879

Through a barren dunescape beneath a low, overcast sky in shades of brown, a bowed and ragged group of stragglers makes its way – the scene is one of utter despair and destitution. The anonymity of the landscape and the people, their unknown destination and the unknown reason for their march that seems to stretch into infinity beyond the picture frame, do not even permit the viewer a direct sense of sympathy with the fate of these individuals. There is only an unsettling sense of anxiety.

Throwing all artistic convention to the wind, Daumier has reduced the means available to him as a painter to this single statement. In doing so, the figures have been reduced to gloomy, earthy lumps, like the clay of the landscape around them, and it is only the occasional thick, black outline and the contrast of light and shade that makes them recognisable as human beings at all.

The immediate circumstances that would give use to this deeply affecting picture, as well as a series of oil-paintings, lithographs and a relief bearing such titles as *The Emigrants*, *Refugees* and *The Lock-Up* was the with less cruelty with which the government of Louis Philippe had crushed the workers' uprising of June 1848, in which thousands were killed or imprisoned as a result and some four thousand were deported to the highlands of Algeria.

Honoré Daumier
The Washerwoman, c. 1860
Oil on panel, 49 x 34 cm
Paris, Musée National du Louvre

Against the sketchy backdrop of a row of houses bathed in evening light, the dark silhouette of the washerwoman at the end of her day's work, her child by the hand, ascending the steps at the banks of the Seine, appears monumental. This working mother is not starved and emaciated. She has the heavy, well-proportioned body of a strong woman: here we find the Romantic socialism which, in the age of new social ideas sees the working woman as a heroine, as a "monument of solid decency". The same notion can be found in the paintings of Millet, who felt that the people only had to be "saved" and new heroes would emerge, and who – like Daumier – heightened everyday situations to the point of monumentality.

This painting of the washerwoman is the most famous of a series of seven by Daumier on the same theme. In all of them, the empathy of the artist is clearly evident. Daumier's work is peopled by ideal figures such as the washerwoman in the form of a conventional woman fulfilling her role as mother and worker with dignity and a deep sense of duty. However, as soon as they rebelled against their appalling situation – politically engaged women at the time were struggling against their social status as citizens without rights – he would caricature them and portray them in his lithographs as ridiculous and ugly Xanthippes.

Although Daumier's fame is based primarily on his prints, he is also one of the most important painters of his century.

Daumier illustrated the tragi-comic epic of the Spanish author Miguel de Cervantes in some 25 oil-paintings, watercolours and a number of charcoal-drawings. Don Quixote, who sets out in quest of adventure, vowing that "he would right every manner of wrong, placing himself in situations of the greatest peril such as would redound to the eternal glory of his name" is an idealist who cannot come to terms with the world as it is and who therefore sets out to conquer it according to his own chivalrous ideals.

Daumier's Don Quixote is repeatedly interpreted as the creation of an artist who was also an outsider and who saw himself reflected in the figure of the travelling knight. In this painting, Daumier has expressed the loneliness of the knight by portraying him as a sad figure in an empty, barren wasteland, a thin body riding an emaciated horse, looking for all the world like a caricature.

The physiognomies of both man and horse are skeletally grotesque and have been stylized to the point of anatomical deformation. The light does not model the figures, but illuminates them in an eerie manner, robbing them of all palpable corporeality and making them appear to the viewer as mere illusion, almost like a spectre. The strangely unreal intensity of the background colority, which resembles a moonscape, further heightens this impression.

In this way, Daumier makes Don Quixote and his horse in their symbiotic portrayal, a tragicomic incarnation of the outsider in the world.

Honoré Daumier
Don Quixote, c. 1868
Oil on canvas, 52.2 x 32.8 cm
Munich, Bayerische Staatsgemälde-
sammlungen, Neue Pinakothek

"There are times when the audience becomes quite fanatical and the gallery is like a cage of wild beasts poised to leap into the fray and tear apart their victim, the conspirator, the traitor, the evil one, the faithless lover... Just imagine what they would be like if they were ever to break out seriously", writes Banville in his memoirs, describing a Paris theatre audience.

Daumier, who enjoyed visiting the theatre, has captured just such an audience in this painting. In fact, the audience tended to interest him more than the plays themselves. In front of the audience, on the stage, the pathetically triumphant murderer – it was clearly a good murder – shows a despairing and frantic woman the victim stretched out on the floor. The crowd is riveted in horror, unable to distinguish between fiction and reality. The highly effective one-sided lighting of the footlights, creating a contrast between the brightly lit stage and the dark auditorium, is used by Daumier to build up an atmosphere of high tension at the climax of the play. Daumier was the first major painter to portray the theatre stage, well before Toulouse-Lautrec and Degas.

Honoré Daumier  The Melodrama, c. 1860
Oil on canvas, 97.5 x 90.4 cm. Munich, Bayerische Staatsgemäldesammlungen, Neue Pinakothek

Jean-François Millet
The Gleaners, 1857
Oil on canvas, 83.5 x 111 cm
Paris, Musée National du Louvre

# JEAN-FRANÇOIS MILLET
## 1814–1875

Honoré de Balzac has described gleaning in some detail: "Gleaning was permitted only with a certificate of need issued by the mayor, and gleaning was permitted only to the poor in their own community." This background knowledge is needed in order to understand the impact this painting had on a contemporary audience. One critic, for example, suspected that *The Gleaners* bore "the thorn of revolution and the guillotine of 1793". Millet's themes alone, drawn primarily from peasant life, seemed revolutionary and therefore dangerous.

Taken at face value, the painting of the gleaners, the poorest of the poor, presents a picture of absolute harmony. Humans and nature in perfect harmony express a higher natural order. The evening sun bathes the people and the landscape in gently atmospheric hues. The ponderous figures of the women, whose monumental silhouettes fill the centre of the painting, have frequently prompted comparison with Michelangelo's sibyls. The uniformity of their bowed posture and their movements take the form of a harmonious working rhythm that betrays nothing of the sheer physical effort of this heavy work.

Jean-François Millet
The Evening Prayer, c. 1858/59
Oil on canvas, 55.5 x 66 cm
Paris, Musée National du Louvre

In this painting, two peasants are taking a break in their work at sunset in order to pray. A brief moment of peace is granted to them. They clearly have a hard day's work on the huge potato field behind them and the implements around them indicate that they will probably take up their work again once their prayer is over. They seem to be bound up in a natural order of things, within which they carry out their work "like priests in holy office" (according to a contemporary critic).

"It is quite impossible to imagine these people ever thinking of being anything but that which they are", Millet once said, "but we can see the oppression, even if they cannot. Perhaps it is revealed to us in the expectation that we shall respond to it." The socio-political intent behind Millet's paintings is not immediately evident. Clearly, however, he quite rightly anticipated a certain awareness on the part of his audience, who saw in him a republican revolutionary. Many of his contemporary critics, on the other hand, saw his paintings as sentimental. Cézanne even described Millet as a "tear-jerker", although Millet, as he himself once wrote, eschewed everything that might appear as pure sentimentality. Van Gogh, on the other hand, saw in Millet his spiritual father, and Dalí produced several variations on the theme of the *Evening Prayer* and devoted a book to it.

# GUSTAVE COURBET
## 1819–1877

Courbet himself described this painting as strange. Indeed, it is quite unlike any of his other paintings. Although the women are busy at their daily work and surrounded by the requisite objects, the scene nevertheless appears distinctly artificial. One need only regard the postures and gestures of the women. The woman leaning against the sacks seems to be working as though in a dream, with stiffly outstretched fingers. The other, kneeling, seems almost frozen in her exaggerated pose. What is more, all three figures are completely isolated from each other, each immersed in their own thoughts.

It may be assumed that, in creating this painting, Courbet was inspired by the fashion for Japanese art that had been all the rage since about 1855, most notably the Japanese wood cuts introduced during this period. The elements that suggest this are, for example, the handling of light, the monotone grey and ochre tones of the pictorial space delineated by vanishing lines, the empty background wall and the figures like cut-outs in strongly-coloured red and bluish-green robes, and the many round and oval forms, especially those of the vessels and containers, reminiscent of Japanese lanterns and vases. Even the pose of the woman sifting the grain is similar to a pose frequently adopted by players in traditional Japanese *kabuki* theatre. Such distinctive artifice is not to be found again until the works of Gaugin.

Today, we find it rather difficult to understand how Courbet's *Young Women on the Banks of the Seine*, exhibited at the Paris Salon of 1857, could possibly have caused such a scandal. Two pretty young women on a sunny summer's day are taking a rest in the shade of a tree and enjoying the calm tranquillity. Both are beautifully dressed in the fashion of the period. To contemporary critics, these women were shameless and vulgar, and described as "biches", the term generally used in French to describe "kept women", as featured in the pornographic works of the Second Empire. Pierre-Joseph Proudhon saw in them a moral accusation, with the brunette immersed in erotic dreams and the blonde coldly calculating shares, stocks and business. The shock-waves triggered by this painting can only be explained in the light of the completely new form of realism that Courbet introduced into painting, both with regard to his form of presentation – strong colours closely bound to the objects they portray, unchanged by the specific daylight or light and shadow – and the subject matter itself. Courbet portrayed neither the mythological nudes of the Salon painters, nor the oriental beauties of Delacroix, but simply the perfectly normal situation of a summer excursion. Nor has he transfigured the girls or created any distance between them and the viewer, placing them instead, as it were, at his feet.

**Gustave Courbet**
The Winnowers, 1853
Oil on canvas, 131 x 167 cm
Nantes, Musée des Beaux-Arts

**Gustave Courbet**
Young Women on the Banks of the Seine, 1857
Oil on canvas, 173.5 x 206.5 cm
Paris, Musée du Petit Palais

## GUSTAVE COURBET
1819–1877

Ornans, a little provincial town near Besançon, was Courbet's home town and the place of his birth. He painted his *Burial* here, in the little studio he kept in his grandfather's attic, itself barely wider than the finished canvas. Against the rugged landscape of the Roche du Mont, the mourners have gathered at the open grave: the citizens of Ornans, farmers and wine-growers, merchants and bourgeois, clergymen and officials. Courbet knew them all and they all wanted to be in the painting. In the end, 46 of them were included – life-size and just as the painter saw them, neither more beautiful nor more ugly.

Four pall-bearers in wide-brimmed hats are carrying the coffin, their heads turned slightly to one side to avoid the smell of the decaying corpse. Beside them, in his white robe, is the verger with the cross and two servers. Bonnet, the priest in the black robe, is reading the Prayer for the Dead; on the right, the two beadles in scarlet are the shoemaker Clemént with the long nose and the wine-grower Muselier. At their feet kneels the gravedigger in his shirt sleeves, and above him, next to the man in the top hat, is Courbet's father Régis.

On the right, with his hat in his hand, stands Proudhon, deputy Justice of the Peace. Next to him, is the plump mayor. Right beside the grave, two veterans of the revolution of 1793 attired in Jacobin garb, have come to pay their last respects. In front of them is a skull as the symbol of mortality. Perhaps it is also intended as a symbol of

Gustave Courbet
Burial at Ornans, c. 1849/50
Oil on canvas, 315 x 668cm
Paris, Musée d'Orsay

the failure of the revolution of 1793 and the dashed hopes of 1848?

Set apart from the men, as they would be if they were in church, are the mourning women who also complete the circle. Amongst them are the painter's sisters: Juliette crying, Zoé hiding her face, Zélie lost in thought. On the outside right, with a child holding her hand, is Courbet's mother.

But who are they mourning for? In 1848 Courbet's grandfather, Jean-Antoine Oudot, died. He was a keen republican and veteran of the 1793 revolution. He may be the dead person. Yet even as his Jacobin friends stand by his grave, he himself appears in the painting, at the left-hand edge, a witness to his own burial.

The composition is as simple as it is skilled. The horizontals of the background are reiterated in the parallels of the frieze-like group. The tonality is equally simple, with a distinct predominance of black and white, fractured by strong reds. The painting provoked an outrage.

The banality of a village burial, a genre scene, had been portrayed in the format of a history painting. The trivial had been treated as a state event. Courbet was accused of pursuing a "cult of ugliness" and of creating an "undignified, godless caricature". Above all, the "full-moon faces" of the beadles "smeared with scarlet, and their drunken posture" incensed the critics. Yet Courbet merely documented what he had seen.

**Gustave Courbet**
The Painter's Studio: A Real Allegory, 1855
Oil on canvas, 359 x 598 cm
Paris, Musée d'Orsay

# GUSTAVE COURBET
## 1819–1877

Courbet himself described the composition of this remarkable painting of enormous dimension as follows: "I'm in the centre, painting, on the right are all of the participants, that is to say my artistic and bohemian friends. On the left is the other world of daily life, the people, misery, wealth, poverty, the exploited and exploiters, people who live off of death." It was his expressed intention "to have the whole of human society pass through my painting".

Courbet showed this painting at a private exhibition, the Pavilion of Realism, organized in protest against the Salon of 1855. In the catalogue, he called it a "real allegory". For Courbet, being a realist meant "being an honest friend of full truth". As such, he divided human society into two groups, one impervious to the "world of art" and one participating in it. He presents himself as an artist working on a landscape painting of primal nature.

As ideal viewers, he shows the female nude model and the child; they represent the sensual and authentic perception of truth, untrammelled by reflection. The woman was immediately intepreted by contemporary critics as the "muse of truth". Both stand in contrast to that which Courbet presents as modern life. Jew, clergyman, old republican, hunter, reaper, fairground strongman, harlequin, peddler, working woman, labourer, gravedigger, Irishwoman, draper, specified by Courbet himself as personalities of the left side, are real allegories

in the sense that they represent specific spheres of life. Their reality comes from the fact that the painter has them appear on the stage of his studio, which means that the world becomes interesting through the significance with which the artist imbues it in his painting. Those accepted by him as spiritual participants in his "realistic" art (right) round off Courbet's world. We recognize his closest friends: Promayer, Bruyas, the socialist philosopher Pierre-Joseph Proudhon (in the centre of the standing group of five), Cuénot and Buchon; forefathers of literary realism, Jules Champfleury (seated) and Charles Baudelaire, the poet of the *Fleurs du Mal* (reading). In the window aperture in the background are two young lovers, while the elegant couple in the foreground represent lovers of art.

The focal point of the "reality" that he has created, is Courbet himself. Adopting the authoritarian and demonstrative posture of the demiurge, he is the only active person in the picture. The painter presents himself primarily as a protagonist and as the embodiment of the artist as such.

In contrast to previous studio paintings, which, since the Renaissance, had become a genre in its own right, Courbet is not interested in presenting his external surroundings and his social status, but in defining his special status on the basis of his creative powers. Courbet's studio is the stage on which the world evoked through his powers of imagination appears for the first time in all its authenticity.

# CASPAR DAVID FRIEDRICH
1774–1840

This painting was acquired by the Prussian king at the Berlin academy exhibition of 1810, together with Friedrich's famous *Monk by the Sea*. It is not known whether the artist intended these two paintings of identical format to be a pair. Certainly, it is not unusual in the œuvre of Friedrich for two or even four paintings to refer to each other or indicate seasons or times of day, symbolically evoking various periods of time or ages of human life, and such an aim is also conceivable in this case.

In the painting itself, the oaks and the Gothic ruins presumably indicate two historical epochs: the pre-Christian era of natural religions and the Christian era which has replaced the forest with the church – culminating in the medieval Gothic cathedral – as the place of worship. It is strange that the funeral procession of the monks should pass by the open grave towards the doorway of the church ruin and then through it. Friedrich based this painting on the ruined church of Eldena in Pomerania, adding the crucifix in the portal and the window tracery above it in order to make the religious aspect clearer still. The path the monks are treading evidently leads them towards a world of light that goes beyond death and history.

This painting was described by Friedrich's contemporary, the poet Theodor Körner, in his *Friedrichs Totenlandschaft* (Friedrich's Landscape of the Dead) as follows: "Der Quell der Gnade ist im Tod geflossen, / Und jene sind der Seligkeit Genossen. / Die durch das Grab zum ew'gen Lichte ziehen." ("The source of mercy has flowed in death / And they are comrades of beatitude / Who pass through the grave towards eternal light") The skies have cleared over the darkness that weighs down upon the bleak winter scene and we can just discern the faint outline of the moon.

The wanderer is resting at a place typical of Friedrich's landscapes: at a slope in the foreground, beyond which there is a yawning abyss from whose unknown depths the mountains rise up in the darkness. Friedrich loved this rugged transition between foreground and background, zones he tended to identify as two fundamentally different levels of existence. Whereas the foreground in this painting seems almost physically tangible in the dying light of day, further emphasized by the bright clothing of the wanderer, the background heralds a transformation of impenetrable darkness into enigmatic night.

Other Romantics, including the poet Novalis, saw night as the realm of the soul and spirit, indicative of a higher existence than daytime, which is the realm of real, earthly life, dominated by the demands of the material world. In Friedrich's painting, a rainbow divides these zones of day and night, itself an enigmatic sphere. At the time, the biblical concept of the rainbow as a symbol of reconciliation between God and man was widely prevalent.

**Caspar David Friedrich**
Abbey under Oak Trees, 1809
Oil on canvas, 110.4 x 171 cm
Berlin, Nationalgalerie, Staatliche Museen
zu Berlin – Preussischer Kulturbesitz

**Caspar David Friedrich**
Mountain Landscape with Rainbow, c. 1809/10
Oil on canvas, 70 x 102 cm
Essen, Museum Folkwang

GERMANY/AUSTRIA

**Caspar David Friedrich**
Wanderer watching a sea
of fog, c. 1817/18
Oil on canvas,
98.4 x 74.8 cm
Hamburg, Hamburger
Kunsthalle

# CASPAR DAVID FRIEDRICH
## 1774-1840

The figure portrayed may be an officer who
was killed in the Napoleonic wars of 1813-
1815, to which there is direct or indirect reference in many of Friedrich's works. With the
unification of the German states in these wars,
the bourgeoisie hoped not only to drive Napoleon from the territory of the former Empire,
but also to dismantle the feudal structures in
their own country. There have therefore been
many attempts to interpret the recurring dual-
ism in Friedrich's paintings – the restricted
foreground with figures (the present) and the
wide expanse of landscape in the background
(the future) as the political allegory of a better,
free Germany. The portrayal of the old-fashioned traditional German frock-coat, prohibited in 1818 and worn by the wanderer in
this painting, is taken as a validation for such
an interpretation. With this in mind, it is immediately evident that the wanderer has
reached the utmost point of the material
world and now, rising above its limitations, is
enjoying a new sense of liberty that goes beyond material considerations and is accessible
only to the spirit and the mind.

*The Lone Tree* is one of the works in which symbolism is actually secondary to the immediate
aesthetic effect. Nevertheless, here too, the
weathered oak is an entity with which the
viewer can identify as a metaphor of the
human being marked by the rigors and hardships of life.

In his *Chalk Cliffs* Friedrich has made a particularly unequivocal statement of his *Weltanschauung*. At the same time, this painting
indicates the extent of the artist's interest in
exploring hitherto unknown landscapes and
viewpoints in painting. The figures are situated on the very brink of an abyss bordering
two very different forms of existence. The inaccessible chalk cliffs elucidate the transition
from the physical world in which the wanderers are located and the great beyond which
is accessible only to the eyes and mind – a
boundary not everyone is willing to cross, and
one that divides opinions. We have little difficulty in determining which figure Friedrich
himself identified with: certainly not with the
bourgeois couple anxiously peering at some detail on the edge of the cliff, or searching for
some lost object and looking quite ridiculous
in doing so. The artist identifies with the man
in the old-style German frock-coat leaning
against the tree on the right and gazing pensively into the distance.
  The magnificent, endless expanses of the
sea were regarded in the 18th century as a
symbol of infinity. In Friedrich's paintings,
ships plying the wide ocean also indicate a certain yearning, for they suggest that the realm
bound by the limitations of earthly existence
has been overcome.

**Caspar David Friedrich**
The Lone Tree, 1822
(Village Landscape in Morning Light)
Oil on canvas, 55 x 71 cm
Berlin, Nationalgalerie, Staatliche Museen
zu Berlin – Preussischer Kulturbesitz

**Caspar David Friedrich**
Chalk Cliffs on Rügen, 1818
Oil on canvas, 90 x 70 cm
Winterthur, Stiftung Oskar Reinhart

**Joseph Anton Koch**
Swiss Landscape (Berner Oberland), 1817
Oil on canvas, 101 x 134 cm
Innsbruck, Tiroler Landesmuseum Ferdinandeum

**Joseph Anton Koch**
Schmadribach, c. 1821/22
Oil on canvas, 131.8 x 110 cm
Munich, Bayerische Staatsgemäldesammlungen,
Neue Pinakothek

# JOSEPH ANTON KOCH
## 1768–1839

This painting is composed in the grand format of the Neoclassical landscape of the 17th century. Accordingly, the picture planes are built up parallel behind one another, and the sides of the composition are framed by house and tree, while the mountains form a backdrop, creating a kind of interior space. Koch transfers Poussin's compositional structure, honed on Italian landscapes, to the world of the Alps, transforming the mythological and biblical figures that normally people such landscapes into figures of contemporary peasant life.

It is evening, and the people who have worked all day as hunters, herdsmen and gardeners are returning to the shelter of their village. The life of these people is clearly harsh, yet nature provides for them all. They are obviously happy and contented.

Here, Koch recalls concepts of 18th century Enlightenment, with its criticism of prevailing feudal structures and its evocation of a natural human existence, free of such structure and which they saw embodied in the free peasant communities of the Swiss Alps. In his famous poem *Die Alpen* ("The Alps") of 1729, the Swiss poet Albrecht von Haller praises the simple yet free life of the Alpine peasants and holds it up as a shining example against the envy, selfishness and evil of urban and court life.

In this view of the *Berner Oberland*, based on the impressions he gained during his tour of Switzerland in the 1890s, Koch projects an image of a holistic, natural world. The mountains have been recorded without distortion, from an angle that invites the observer to "read" the picture.

Our gaze is guided by the central axis, delineated by the waterfall, through various zones of vegetation and waste land. From top to bottom, these zones recall the sequence of natural history or creation, whose path also follows through from anorganic forms to various forms of vegetation and finally to animals and human beings, all of which are dependent on the life-sustaining and life-destroying element of water.

Water is also accorded its own individual features, being portrayed in every state from the haze of clouds to ice and snow, until, fed at first by a mere trickle, it becomes a rushing waterfall that carries away everything in its path. In Koch's lifetime, the path taken by water was frequently seen as a symbol of the path of human life.

Koch had already used the motif of the *Schmadribach* waterfall in a water-colour of 1794 (Basle, Kunstmuseum) and in an earlier version executed around 1811 (Leipzig, Museum der bildenden Künste).

# GEORG FRIEDRICH KERSTING
## 1785–1847

The Enlightenment sought to change society through knowledge. Accordingly, the reading-circles that had sprung up throughout Germany towards the end of the 18th century were placed under strict supervision of censorship, for it was feared that they were potential hotbeds of free-thinking intellectuals. Education was wielded, if not as the weapon, then at least as the intellectual property of the bourgeoisie, against the superficial luxury of the ancient feudal order.

Kersting, who belonged to the circle of Romantics around Friedrich, liked to portray people working, especially reading, in an interior. His readers are invariably people of middle or upper social standing, as is evident from their surroundings. Yet nowhere in these paintings does the main emphasis fall on the useful or useless comforts of life, as is so often the case in the later Biedermeier period. Instead, the material world, as in Friedrich's landscapes, is merely the starting-point for the presentation of a spiritual world created within the reader and symbolized here by the immaterial play of light on the wall. The fact that this world of spiritual concentration stands in contrast to the real world is also made evident by the cumbersome bookshelves delineating a certain area of their own that has no outward appearance of beauty, in a splendidly proportioned room.

**Georg Friedrich Kersting**
Reader by Lamplight, 1814
Oil on canvas, 47.5 x 37 cm
Winterthur, Stiftung
Oskar Reinhart

# GOTTLIEB SCHICK
## 1776–1812

In 1794, Wilhelmine von Cotta married the famous Tübingen-based publisher Johann Friedrich von Cotta, who had made a name for himself with his editions of classics. The artist painted this young woman at the age of 31. The painting bears obvious traces of Schick's training in the Paris studio of David, especially in his adaptation of the type and posture in David's portrait of Madame Récamier. Nevertheless, Schick does not adopt the elegance of the French painting. Instead, his model has an air of freshness and relaxation in spite of her highly fashionable Empire-style clothing. The broad face, the laughing eyes, the curls and rounded arms all contribute to this impression. Moreover, Schick has replaced David' Neoclassicistic furnishings with a cubic stone bench that by no means follows the lines of the body. We also notice Schick's training as a sculptor in the fact that he is evidently interested in sculptural forms. More importance is placed on individuality of form than on its harmonization within an overall movement.

Full figure portraits set against a landscape background emerged in England in the 18th century and were adopted by the French. Schick's painting is reminiscent of Goethe's *Wahlverwandtschaften* (Kindred by Choice) in which the emerging landscape garden is closely linked with the fate of the heroine Ottilie.

**Gottlieb Schick** Wilhelmine von Cotta, 1802
Oil on canvas, 133 x 140.5 cm
Stuttgart, Staatsgalerie Stuttgart

**Philipp Otto Runge**
Rest on the Flight into Egypt, c. 1805/06
Oil on canvas, 98 x 132 cm
Hamburg, Hamburger Kunsthalle

## PHILIPP OTTO RUNGE
1777—1810

The *Rest on the Flight into Egypt* is a recurrent theme in Christian art. Runge has interpreted it as the "dawning of western civilization", adding the Nile riverscape and the blossoming tree with symbolic figures. As in his painting *Morning*, he explores the various stages in which the light of divinity reaches the earth. Joseph is more brightly lit by the glow of the fire he is putting out than by the morning light of the landscape behind him. The brilliance that lights up Mary's face, however, seems to come both from the morning sun and from the child who is let by the sun, but nevertheless seems to be the point of radiance of all light in the painting.

Runge executed a portrait of his parents at the age of 69, together with their grandchildren. Old age and youth are contrasted here as the extremes of the life-cycle: the children, illuminated by the light of the landscape and with floral attributes, are still within the boundaries of the garden, whereas the elderly couple have already withdrawn into the shadow of the house. The strict expression on their faces expresses "the spirit of undemanding piety devoted to the holy writings and the catechism" (Runge's brother Daniel on his parents).

*Morning* was originally intended as part of a cycle of paintings portraying the different times of day, but only drawings and etchings of the four stages exist. The "times" or "ages" that interested Runge from 1802 onwards are the visual form of his Neoplatonic-Christian view of the world and art. According to Runge, colours and the appearance of light contain "the entire symbol of the trinity:... we cannot grasp light and we should not grasp darkness, man has been given the Revelation and colours have come into the world, that is to say: blue and red and yellow."

In *Morning*, an intangible white light – in the cupola, the morning star and the lily – radiates down to earth through the red of the roses and the fiery hair of Aurora/Venus/Mary and the yellow aura, finally reaching the place where the Eros/Christ child lies as its incarnation. What is seen as light falling in the centre of the picture appears around the edges as light rising from the darkness of an eclipse of the sun, through the yellow light of the sun and the red of the amaryllis to the blue and white of the cupola. Here, landscape is by no means the view of an area, but rather the presentation of the soul's progress along the path of the metamorphosis of lightless material into immaterial light.

**Philipp Otto Runge**
The Artist's Parents, 1806
Oil on canvas, 196 x 131 cm
Hamburg, Hamburger Kunsthalle

**Philipp Otto Runge**
Morning (first version), 1808
Oil on canvas, 109 x 85.5 cm
Hamburg, Hamburger Kunsthalle

**Peter von Cornelius**
Joseph makes himself known to his brothers, c. 1816/17
(from the Casa Zuccaro, Rome). Fresco, 236 x 290 cm
Berlin, Nationalgalerie, Staatliche Museen
zu Berlin – Preussischer Kulturbesitz

## PETER VON CORNELIUS
### 1783–1867

When the Prussian consul general in Rome had his flat decorated with a cycle of pictures from the life of Joseph, the Nazarenes were provided with an opportunity for the first time of putting into practice their aim of a revival of Renaissance fresco painting.

Cornelius' work achieves its monumentality from the exaggerated scale of the figures in relationship to their surroundings. This is further heightened by the narrow "stage" with its classical architecture and the allocation of only one specific, brilliant colour combination to each figure. By arranging the figures in two closely knit groups, the movement of the main figures is emphasized without making the others seem secondary in importance. The group on the right-hand side recoils on recognizing their brother, who, in his office as a high Egyptian dignitary, now holds in his hands the lives of the same brothers who sold him into slavery in his youth. The group on the left is dominated by the show of affection between Joseph and Benjamin, the favourite brother. The main technique used by Cornelius to express the inner emotion of the figures was, in keeping with the aims of the Nazarenes, concentration on the eyes and various ways of looking. Here we can see how intensively the artist had studied the frescos of Raphael and Michelangelo, as well as Dürer's *Four Apostles*.

**Johann Friedrich Overbeck**
Italia and Germania (Shulamith and Mary), 1828
Oil on canvas, 94.4 x 104.7 cm. Munich, Neue Pinakothek

## JOHANN FRIEDRICH OVERBECK
### 1789–1869

This painting was begun in 1811 as a gesture of friendship to Franz Pforr and as a counterpart to his painting *Shulamith and Mary*. After the death of his friend in 1812, it remained unfinished. When Overbeck took up the idea again in 1828, the personal aspect of the wish to find a partner who shared the same goals in life, was no longer as important as it had previously been. As in Pforr's small picture, the future, ideal brides of these two friends were portrayed as Shulamith, the bride of the Song of Solomon and Mary, the mother of Jesus. Overbeck, who was by this time an acclaimed artist, gave the painting a new content and a new name. Now it was entitled *Italia and Germania*, a title indicating that the artistic ideals of the friends now took precedence. On the left sits Shulamith, Overbeck's ideal bride, as a dark-haired Italian woman crowned with laurels. On the right is Pforr's ideal bride Mary, a German Gretel with blonde braids and a wreath of myrtle in her hair. The background is also divided in two and pertains to the figures: behind Shulamith/Italia we see an Italian landscape, behind Mary/Germania a German landscape.

In the strong figures reminiscent of Raphael's female studies, we find two models for German Romantic art: Italian and German painting of the late Middle Ages and the Renaissance, the revival of which was Overbeck's aim.

# FERDINAND GEORG WALDMÜLLER

1793–1865

*The Last Calf* is one of this artist's later works in which he tends to show the darker side of modern rural life, conventionally glorified in images of festive merrymaking. For him, the impoverishment of the small farmer is not, however, a reason to point an accusing finger at those who have caused the misery, for the true wrong-doers are unlikely to be the same people who finally purchase the calf cheaply. The sale of the last calf by a poor crofting family is seen as a blow of fate in which the reactions of loser and winner are portrayed. In this, Waldmüller adheres entirely to the principle of genre painting as a means of presenting the character of the people. The fact that this character is generally shown as one of patient fatalism is also in keeping with this genre, which tends to take as its theme the subject of "happiness in measure" (Jean Paul). The artist concentrates on the effect of the sunlight. Even the facial expressions of the figures are determined not only by the event, but also by the bright light that meets them as they leave their dark house.

In Waldmüller's work, light tends to overemphasize all things; later, it would serve the Impressionists as a means of dissolving outlines and blending the objects with their surroundings.

**Ferdinand Georg Waldmüller**
The Last Calf, 1857
Oil on panel, 44 x 56.3 cm
Stuttgart, Staatsgalerie Stuttgart

# CARL ROTTMANN

1797–1850

This painting is a variation on the painting of the same name from the so-called *Greek Cycle* featuring twenty-three views of Greece which can now be seen in the Niedersächsische Landesgalerie in Hanover. The liberation struggle of the Greeks against the Turks with the backing of the major European powers provided considerable new material for landscape painting. In Bavaria, the subject was particularly topical, as a Bavarian prince had become King Otto I of Greece in 1832. Whereas Italian views tended to be idyllic landscapes, Rottmann's Greek paintings show a war-torn country, impoverished, infertile and hostile to life. Nevertheless it also lends an impression of sublime greatness, as the geological formations are shown here starkly and without any covering of vegetation.

The great days of ancient Greece, evident only in a few fragments that are barely distinguishable from the rocks, gives the landscape a melancholy atmosphere. Like the monk, gazing pensively into the depths and reflecting on the transience of human civilization in the face of nature's destructive power, the viewer, too, is called upon to consider the primal forces of nature and time, reflected in the geological lines as the true driving force behind history.

**Carl Rottmann**
Sicyon and Corinth, c. 1836–1838
Oil on canvas, 85.2 x 102 cm. Munich, Bayerische
Staatsgemäldesammlungen, Neue Pinakothek

**Karl Blechen**
Monks at the Gulf of Naples,
c. 1829
Oil on panel, 37.5 x 29 cm
Cologne, Wallraf-Richartz-
Museum

## KARL BLECHEN
### 1798–1840

The motif of this painting is comparable to that of Caspar David Friedrich's *Chalk Cliffs on Rügen* (ill. p. 449). Here, too, there is an abrupt break between foreground and background, with steep white cliffs contrasted against the blue of the sea. The subject matter, however, could hardly be more different. The monks in their black habits have turned away from the distance and are sheltering in the shadow of the cave. The distance holds no appeal, but seems impenetrable and neutral. The lack of vegetation heightens the impression of lifelessness, echoed in the appearance of the rocks, which look like bleached bones. The painter is interested in the effect of indirect light reflected brightly on objects which, like the rocks, place no bounds upon his creative imagination.

Whereas, for Friedrich, the distant sea evoked the longed-for infinity of future spiritual freedom, in Blechen's painting it is the point of departure for a reclusive existence in areas increasingly withdrawn from life and light.

Here, it is the future that is the foreground. There is an atmosphere of the spectral and the extinct, and of the victory of the life of privation to which the monks have subjected themselves. In this painting, Blechen has created an image of Italy that contradicts all coventional idyllic notions.

**Karl Blechen**
The Gardens of the Villa
d'Este, c. 1830
Oil on canvas, 126 x 93 cm
Berlin, Nationalgalerie,
Staatliche Museen zu Berlin –
Preussischer Kulturbesitz

The Villa d'Este and its park were created in the mid 16th century by Cardinal Ippolito d'Este. Anyone visiting an Italian Renaissance park is astonished by the extreme contrast of light and dark created by the huge cypress alleys. Blechen has taken this phenomenon as the basis for his painting. Eerie figures from some past era move like ghosts through the fiery, multicoloured light that falls through the mature trees lining the path and sweeping over the edge of the long, vertical painting. Yet Blechen does not observe the past with the sober eye of the historian. Instead, these figures of the late 16th century have sprung from the imagination of an artist inebriated by contrasts of light. He lets history come to life in his mind's eye and in his mind it becomes inextricably linked with reality.

As this is a Romantic, imaginary world rather than a reconstruction of reality, the colours in the area where the figures are located have been heightened in a dream-like manner, with a most unusual predominance of violet hues. The subject matter alone determines the appearance of the world in this painting, lending it a magical aura that verges at times on the uncanny. The painting has nothing to do with any objectively documentary historicism, but draws its charm entirely from the feverish sensitivity of an artist in thrall to visions of the past, who seeks to lend expression to these visions through colour.

# LUDWIG RICHTER
## 1803–1884

Richter stayed in Rome between 1823 and 1826, where he painted Italian landscapes in the manner of Joseph Anton Koch. Later, in Dresden, he initially continued to work in the same vein. It was not until the 1830s, inspired by walking tours through Saxony and Bohemia, that he turned to the landscapes of his homeland. Although he continued to portray the same idyllic subjects he had treated in Rome – monks and herdsmen's families, simple people living in harmony with nature – he now sought his motifs in Germany rather than Italy. Neolassicists like Koch had presented the life of the people as a primal form of society for which nature was the only non-human point of reference. Romantics like Richter felt that the purest expression of the essence of nature required some reference to the Christian God as its creator. It was for this reason that they so frequently portrayed churches, in whose shadow people could be seen leading a life of harmony and piety guided by the rules of the church and thus according to God's will. The abrupt contrast between proximity and distance was interpreted by the early Romanticist Friedrich as a symbol of the contrast between material and spiritual existence. Richter eliminates this distinction by placing his church on the borderline, so that nature is now portrayed as an all-embracing unity.

Ludwig Richter
Church at Graupen in Bohemia, 1836
Oil on panel, 56.7 x 70.2 cm
Hanover, Niedersächsische Landesgalerie

# MORITZ VON SCHWIND
## 1804–1871

Elves and fairies are creatures of nature in the Nordic sagas. Handed down through the generations, they can be found in the works of Shakespeare and entered the German literature of the day through translations of the eras of the Enlightenment and Romanticism and through the collections of folk-tales and fairy-tales that were made around that time. From then on, they came to be regarded as independent nordic creatures and as counterparts to the classical nymphs of Antiquity. For writers and artists who, like Schwind, had set themselves the task of placing German art firmly on an equal footing with French art, these creatures of fable were a favoured subject. The artists grouped around Schwind defended Neoclassical linearity as a fundamentally German approach to art and claimed that it possessed greater profundity than the painterly realism of the French artists.

In Schwind's group of dancing elves, an intimate community of children and women is presented. In this respect, the painting is very much in keeping with the glorification of the family as the haven of intimacy and the nucleus of the state, so prevalent in the constitutional theories of the Restoration and in the art of the Biedermeier era. As these are "human" circumstances, the life of these "natural creatures" differs in no way from the ideal image of the "better part" of the German bourgeoisie presented by Schwind in his society paintings.

Moritz von Schwind
Fairy Dance in the Alder Grove, c. 1844
Oil on panel, 62.8 x 84 cm
Frankfurt am Main, Städelsches Kunstinstitut

Adolph von Menzel
The Berlin-Potsdam Railway, 1847
Oil on canvas, 43 x 52 cm
Berlin, Nationalgalerie, Staatliche Museen
zu Berlin – Preussischer Kulturbesitz

Adolph von Menzel
A Paris Day, 1869
Oil on canvas, 50 x 71 cm
Düsseldorf, Kunstmuseum Düsseldorf

## ADOLPH VON MENZEL
### 1815–1905

The subject of this painting is speed, a dimension that had become part and parcel of everyday life with the advent of railway travel in the 1830s. Movement is presented here in two ways. On the one hand, the landscape appears blurred at the edges, as though seen flashing past through the window of a train compartment. On the other hand, the movement of the train is seen from outside, whereby the contours of the locomotive merge with the surroundings. Menzel has chosen a subject that was soon to become a central theme in the work of the Impressionists. However, the Impressionists, for whom the railway was no longer a novelty, were even more fascinated by the movement of horses on the racetrack. The sunny racecourses with their clouds of dust gave them ample opportunity to explore light and atmosphere. Menzel, however, still preferred a sombre brown tonality of a more traditional kind, which, further heightened here by the use of black, is actually a perfectly appropriate means of portraying the dirt of an industrialized suburban landscape, where even the air and the atmosphere see bleak and gloomy.

In 1867, Menzel painted scenes of everyday Parisian life for the first time. He prepared them *in situ* in the form of pencil sketches and later executed them in his studio in Berlin. Unlike the street scenes of the French Impressionists only a few years later, Menzel still uses the traditional brown tones in the foreground to bind the colours together, while light pastels are used for the background.

Menzel's sister, who was very close to him, is standing on the doorstep of the room in which she spent her childhood, gazing dreamily outwards into a new world that has yet to reveal itself entirely to her as a young girl. The past, embodied by the room where her mother is sitting working, can be clearly discerned. The doorstep is certainly intended here in the metaphorical sense of a threshold between two stages of her life, with background and foreground related to each other as past and future. For all its sketchiness, and the fleeting transience of the light, this composition points to a permanent state of human community. In the three figures, the young girl, the old woman and the *putto* suspended from the ceiling, we see the three ages of life, whose sequence is presented as a cycle. The life of the young girl will end like that of her mother. In this presentation of life as a series of pre-ordained natural stages, the painting is a typical example of the Biedermeier style.

Adolph von Menzel
The Artist's Sisters, 1847
Oil on canvas, 46.1 x 31.6 cm
Munich, Neue Pinakothek

Ferdinand von
Rayski
Portrait of a Young
Girl, c. 1840
Oil on canvas,
68.5 x 57 cm
Altenburg, Linde-
nau-Museum

## FERDINAND VON RAYSKI
### 1806–1890

Artists from the late 18th century onwards sought the essence of unspoiled nature in all things. It was therefore only logical that they should turn to the portrayal of children. For the first time, children are portrayed as independent individuals whose innocence has not yet been tainted, rather than simply as a smaller version of adults.

The care with which the girl is holding the basket shows how tentatively she seeks to conquer her world. The basket does not contain a magnificently arranged bouquet, but a bunch of fragile wildflowers and grasses that have not yet been cultivated. In this respect, they may be compared with the child who still regards and treats the world with an earnestness that lends weight to the smallest thing – an earnestness the educated adult lacks. The dog adds emphasis to the theme, as a creature that may express its temperament naturally.

Unlike the portraits of the 18th century, nature is not perceived here as a generalized or universal landscape, but as a precisely definable place: the child's actual home. The ideal of the natural is found by patient and loving observation of reality, rather than reality being shaped to fit the notion of the natural ideal. In contrast, all the outer trappings of materiality, so prevalent in the portraits of the Biedermeier era, are avoided.

**Carl Spitzweg** The Poor Poet, 1839
Oil on canvas, 36.3 x 44.7 cm. Berlin, Nationalgalerie

## CARL SPITZWEG
### 1808–1885

*The Poor Poet* is one of Spitzweg's earliest works and the painting that made him famous. The image of the poet or philosopher living in poverty in a garret originated in 18th-century France. Yet Spitzweg is not interested here in pointing an accusing finger at some wicked landlord for charging extortionate rents, but in attacking idealist art on behalf of the realism that had begun to take hold in Germany as well. Spitzweg's poet, who is clearly in thrall to the muses, is scanning a hexameter (the metre can just be discerned, written on the wall above the bed.) The hexameter was the metre of the epic poem and, with that, the measure of what was still regarded in those days as the highest form of art. There is something equally pompous about the stack of papers lying by the stove to be used as fuel, entitled in Latin: *Gradus ad Parnassum* (The Road to Parnassus). The pursuit of high art is made to seem all the more ridiculous in view of the impoverished setting which it is clearly incapable of improving. At the same time, the fine tonality and meticulous attention to realistic detail seems to be Spitzweg's admonishment to idealist artists: "like this poet, you may be able to portray high but fundamentally impracticable ideals, but you can't paint."

# CHRISTOFFER WILHELM ECKERSBERG

1783–1853

Like the Baroque Italian architect, Giovanni Battista Piranesi, who created copperplate engravings depicting monuments of Antiquity, Eckersberg has filled his canvas with a classical architectural motif. Eckersberg, however, uses this motif as a vehicle to draw our attention to the transience of human greatness. Just as the bright light of day has ousted the *chiaroscuro* of the Baroque, so too has our view of history become more sober and objective. Yet the notion still persists that a view of ancient Rome must necessarily involve a statement on its history.

The three arches of the Colosseum, part of the curved inner wall of the ancient area, span the picture with such perfect regularity that the three background views seen through them with no intermediate transition seem to be of equal importance: to the left is the Capitol, the seat of power in ancient Rome, in the centre is the Torre delle Milizie, part of a 13th century fortress, alluding here to the power of the medieval princes, and on the right is the early Christian church of San Pietro in Vincoli, which underwent major alterations and extension in the Renaissance and which may be regarded here as an indication of the power held by the Christian church in Rome since the early modern period. The frontal view of the Colosseum arches is reminiscent of the compositional approach of Ingres, another student of David.

Christoffer Wilhelm Eckersberg
View through three northwest arches of the Colosseum in Rome. Storm gathering over the city, 1815
Oil on canvas, 32 x 49.5 cm
Copenhagen, Statens Museum for Kunst

The sculptural plasticity and balanced contraposto of this nude – a girl with her back to us wearing a cloth draped in deep folds around her hips – is reminiscent of a classical statue. The motion of pinning up her hair and the items of her toilette are merely hinted at. The girl's face appears in the mirror as though in a picture.

The mirror image itself, the downward glance and the chin hidden from view, seems to transport her facial features to a much less tangible sphere than the nude in the foreground. The two views seem like a meeting of sculpture and painting, two forms of imagery that can illuminate very different aspects of one and the same object.

The age-old rivalry between painting and sculpture – a source of heated debate since the Renaissance – is alluded to here once more. In doing so, Eckersberg may also have been paying homage to his friend, the sculptor Bertel Thorvaldsen, whose work had impressed him greatly in Rome. At the same time, the discretion and tranquility of the action, and the handling of light that falls from an unknown source, give this painting something of the vibrant intensity of a 17th century Netherlandish interior.

Eckersberg, who taught at the Copenhagen academy and profoundly influenced Romantic painting, is justifiably described as the father of Danish painting.

Christoffer Wilhelm Eckersberg
Nude (Morning Toilette), c. 1837
Oil on canvas, 32 x 25 cm
Copenhagen, Den Hirschsprungske Samling

**Johann Christian Claussen Dahl**
View through a Window to the
Chateau of Pillnitz, c. 1824
Oil on canvas, 70 x 45.5 cm
Essen, Museum Folkwang

## JOHANN CHRISTIAN CLAUSSEN DAHL
### 1788–1857

This painting was executed in Dresden in the 1820s. It documents the friendship that bound the Norwegian artist, who had been living and teaching in Dresden since 1818, with Friedrich and his circle of friends. The view is through the window towards the chateau of Pillnitz on the River Elbe, built in the early 18th century by Pöppelmann. Such window views were a favourite motif amongst the German Romantics. There are comparable paintings by Friedrich and Carus and even by Menzel as late as the 1860s. The contrast between the expanse of the landscape and the dark confines of the interior was regarded by the Romantics as a symbol of human existence between the temporal presence and eternity. Dahl's paintings, like Menzel's, do not lend themselves to such interpretation. Both artists were realists right from the start. Dahl is interested in light solely as a natural phenomenon and not as an expression of divine powers. In spite of the intensive colour of the sky, the landscape retains a certain sobriety, particularly because the colour is presented in its own right rather than as a sublimation of coloured matter. The transformation of the landscape into the realms of the irreal through its reflection in the window panes has only physical rather than metaphysical reasons. It sewes to present a different colouristic level and to stimulate the imagination.

**Christen Schjellerup Købke**
The Shore at Dosseringen, 1838
Oil on canvas, 53 x 71.5 cm
Copenhagen, Statens Museum for Kunst

## CHRISTEN SCHJELLERUP KØBKE
### 1810–1848

Købke was one of the younger generation of Danish naturalists who consciously sought to create an independent Danish painting. Whereas his teacher Eckersberg was devoted to the international Neoclassicism of the school of David and had gained important experience in Rome, the younger painters turned increasingly to the landscape of their homeland, whose unprepossessing views they perceived as equalling any sun-drenched Italian landscape or dramatic nordic vista, both themes with a strong tradition. The tranquillity of nature in the environs of villages and towns, the clarity of colour and light and the unspectacular life of the people who live there, are Købke's subjects.

The fact that this is Denmark is emphasized by the red and white flag, whose colours further heighten the other hues in this painting. The fact that the women have their backs to us as they gaze out over the lake is not imbued with the same significance as such a gesture in the works of Friedrich. Here, they do not embody the consciousness of the viewer, but seem instead like quiet objects in a quiet landscape in which life always goes on in the same way. A charming finesse, dedicated to subtle detail, prevails in this work, which seeks to reflect something of the clear order of this life.

# JOHN CONSTABLE
1776–1837

In the late summer of 1816, Constable spent his honeymoon with his wife Maria at Osmington, a village near Weymouth Bay. Only his honeymoon could have prompted him to paint such a wild and naked landscape, claimed one of his critics, for he was an artist who did not otherwise explore such solitary regions.

This quiet bay ringed by rocks and cliffs is painted in reddish-brown, muddy tones with fleeting brushstrokes and dabs of paint. The heavy sea, neither calm nor stormy, seems to push into the landscape. It is a rather unspectacular landscape, neither particularly beautiful, nor particularly ugly, neither sublime nor Romantic. Its charm derives from the singular atmosphere, with the expanse of overcast sky suffusing the entire landscape in an indefinable twilight.

The specific atmosphere is familiar enough to the viewer from personal experience and Constable presents it entirely unsentimentally. He initially documented it in a sketch prepared at the bay before producing two larger versions. It is precisely this unpretentious way of seeing that appeals so directly to the viewer and makes it clear what Constable meant when he said that, for him, feeling and painting are one and the same thing.

**John Constable**
Weymouth Bay, c. 1816
Oil on canvas, 53 x 75 cm
London, National Gallery

This painting was commissioned by Constable's friend, the Bishop of Salisbury, who also specified that the cathedral should be portrayed as seen from the garden of the bishop's palace. The bishop himself is present in the painting taking a walk with his wife and pointing towards the cathedral. "My cathedral looks very good," wrote Constable, who felt that it was the most difficult landscape painting he had ever had on his easel. Whereas he normally painted seemingly coincidental details of the English countryside, he now had to keep to precise specifications in his painting of the cathedral.

The view of the cathedral through the framing arch of trees is nevertheless most skilfully arranged, giving an impression of harmony between nature and human endeavour. Man has formed nature according to his needs, both for agricultural purposes, as indicated by the grazing cattle, and for his own edification, as a park. The further spiritual achievements of humankind are evident in the central motif – the cathedral bathed in sunlight.

The only disturbing factor in this altogether harmonious painting seemed to be, in the opinion of the bishop, the dark clouds forming in the sky. "If only Constable had left out the black clouds! Clouds are black when it begins to rain. When the weather is fine, the sky is blue," he wrote, and sent the painting back to the artist to be reworked.

**John Constable**
Salisbury Cathedral from the Bishop's Grounds, 1828
Oil on canvas, 34 x 44 cm
Berlin, Nationalgalerie, Staatliche Museen
zu Berlin – Preussischer Kulturbesitz

# JOHN CONSTABLE
## 1776–1837

Unlike the primarily idyllic images of rural life in the 18th century, with shepherds and shepherdesses frolicking in the fields, Constable presents objective, unadorned depictions of peasant life during the changing seasons. *The Hay Wain* shows a scene in the Stour Valley where Constable grew up. A horse drawing a hay cart is wading through the clear water of the river, a dog is watching the cart draw past; on the right a figure in the bushes is mooring a boat, while to the left an old farmhouse is almost completely hidden by trees and bushes. In this painting, Constable has drawn together many familiar details of rural life which, as a whole, evoke a concept of a natural universe in which man, animals and landscape are still bound together in primal harmony. The weather conditions, which Constable invariably based on direct study, show an overcast sky that promises a rapid succession of rain and sunshine.

In his painterly technique, Constable liberates himself from conventional principles of composition and colour handling. His bright colourity and often sketchy brushstrokes create a new and direct experience of the English countryside that goes some way towards explaining the enormous attention attracted by his paintings, particularly by *The Hay Wain* at the Paris Salon of 1824.

**John Constable**
The Hay Wain, 1821
Oil on canvas, 130.5 x 185.5 cm
London, National Gallery

Constable preferred to paint in areas he had known since his childhood. This painting, one of three such atmospheric views created between 1818 and 1820, shows the mill at Dedham Vale owned by his father, the miller Golding Constable, where Constable himself had worked as a child.

Farmer Willy Lott's house in Flatford is a recurrent motif in Constable's œuvre, and it also appears in his famous painting, *The Hay Wain*. This Romantic view shows the house, set slightly in the background, nestled in the lush greenery of the Stour Valley. Only a few golden highlights cast by the last rays of a late sun illuminate the sombre brown tones of the gloomy autumn atmosphere. Constable himself was not satisfied with the painting and worked on it for several months after it had been returned from the Royal Academy exhibition. Even once he felt he had got rid of the "hailstones" and "snow" that covered the painting, attracting so much criticism, the surface nevertheless remained rough and grainy and did not achieve the brilliance of colour to be found in his masterpieces. Remarkably, however, Constable actually received the sum of 300 pounds for this particular painting, the largest sum he ever received for any of his works. Long before its completion, it was purchased by Robert Vernon.

**John Constable**
Dedham Lock and Mill, 1820
Oil on canvas, 53.7 x 76.2 cm
London, Victoria and Albert Museum

**John Constable**
The Valley Farm, 1835
Oil on canvas, 147.3 x 125 cm
London, Tate Gallery

**Richard Parkes Bonington**
Beach in Normandy, c. 1826/27
Oil on canvas, 33 x 44 cm
London, Tate Gallery

**Richard Parkes Bonington**
The Column of St Mark in Venice, c. 1826–1828
Oil on canvas, 45.7 x 37.5 cm
London, Tate Gallery

# RICHARD PARKES BONINGTON
1802–1828

In 1824, Bonington was working on a series of lithographs to illustrate a volume on Normandy for Baron Taylor's *Voyage Pittoresque dans l'Ancienne France*. In this connection, he also created a number of oil-paintings showing the Normandy coast. These were highly acclaimed for their fresh and natural approach.

The tradition of English watercolour-painting, devoted to the exploration of atmosphere, light and colour, is as evident here as the influence of Flemish and Venetian painting. It is a charming genre scene portrayed with a delicately nuanced tonality that alternates between warm browns and cool blues, the predominantly brown tones of the foreground contrasting with the pale hues of the hazy distance in the light of the midday sun. In the foreground is a picturesque group of seated women with a child and fishbaskets. Behind them is the sea at low tide with ships, a distant strip of coastline and a broad expanse of sky.

The colourful dresses of the women with their high hats indicates that these are the wives of fishermen from Pollet, a suburb of Dieppe, whose inhabitants still wore the same traditional costumes they had worn in the 16th century.

The immediate visual appeal of this painting lies in the use of luminous colours more reminiscent of a watercolour than an oil-painting. The radiant blue sky is a dominant feature which, as in many works by Bonington, takes up more than half the picture and is contrasted with shades of white and – in the two pillars – a honeyed brown. In this painting too, the artist applies the stylistic device of an upward view, in which the dark lion of Saint Mark on the towering pillar at the left stands out sharply against the bright Italian sky.

The scene, captured during a one-month tour Bonington made to Venice in 1826, is an architecturally correct and detailed rendering of the actual topography, in the tradition of the veduta. Nevertheless, it is more than simply a superficial documentation: it is a deliberately structured composition, as is evident not only in the chosen angle, but also in the avoidance of symmetrical pictorial organization. Bonington was heavily attacked by French art critics for orienting his work towards a specific location rather than the ideal landscape painting of the 17th century.

However, his views of Venice proved so popular with the public that he executed innumerable variations in oils and watercolours. It was precisely this merging of realistic, topographically precise description with painterly elements that constituted the progressive trait of his art and was, at the same time, the target of criticism. In this respect, his work already anticipates the "pure" *plein-air* painting that was not to become established for another twenty years.

# DAVID WILKIE

1785–1841

Wilkie was the most popular English genre painter of his day. His famous painting *Reading the Will* was commissioned by the Bavarian king Maximilian Joseph, who hung it in his bedroom. The subject had been proposed to Wilkie by the English actor and comic Charles Bannister, and he had undoubtedly also been inspired by similar scenes from contemporary plays, such as Armand Charlemagne's *My Uncle's Will* or by *Guy Mannering* written by his friend Walter Scott.

The stage-like lighting and spatial organization which Wilkie designed beforehand using model figures, create the effect of a theatre scene capturing the exciting climax of the plot. A motley crowd of relatives has gathered in the dead man's study, where his portrait is hanging on the wall, to hear the lawyer read the last will and testament. Only a child and the dog crouching below the empty armchair seem to be affected by the death. Already, a suitor is leaning attentively over the young widow who looks towards the viewer in an affected pose. The others are all listening to the words of the lawyer with a mixture of emotions, from curiosity and greed to undisguised irritation. Wilkie leaves us in no doubt whatsoever as to their characters.

David Wilkie
Reading the Will, 1820
Oil on panel, 76 x 115 cm
Munich, Bayerische Staatsgemälde-
sammlungen, Neue Pinakothek

# WILLIAM DYCE

1806–1864

The painting shows a scene during a holiday the artist spent with his family in Kent. In the foreground is his wife, her two sisters gathering shells and one of his sons. The title indicates that the artist was eager to regard the painting as a souvenir. As such, it prompts ambivalent feelings which he clearly linked with the event. On the one hand, presumably assisted by preliminary sketches, he reproduces each and every detail with almost photographic precision, lovingly capturing an image of the people he knows so well at some chance moment of repose and contemplation. With the same precision, he meticulously documents the bay with its chalk cliffs and the sea at low tide, evoking the specific atmosphere of a cool October day in the late afternoon light. On the other hand, in spite of this faithfully exact reproduction and in spite of the proximity of the figures in the foreground, the entire scene seems strangely distant and dreamlike. Dyce has used realism here as a means of portraying a sense of timelessness at a specific moment. One indication of this may be the fact that, on the very same date, the Donati comet appeared in the sky, an astronomical event that occurs only once every 2,100 years.

William Dyce
Pegwell Bay in Kent. A Recollection
of October 5th 1858, c. 1859/60
Oil on canvas, 63 x 89 cm
London, Tate Gallery

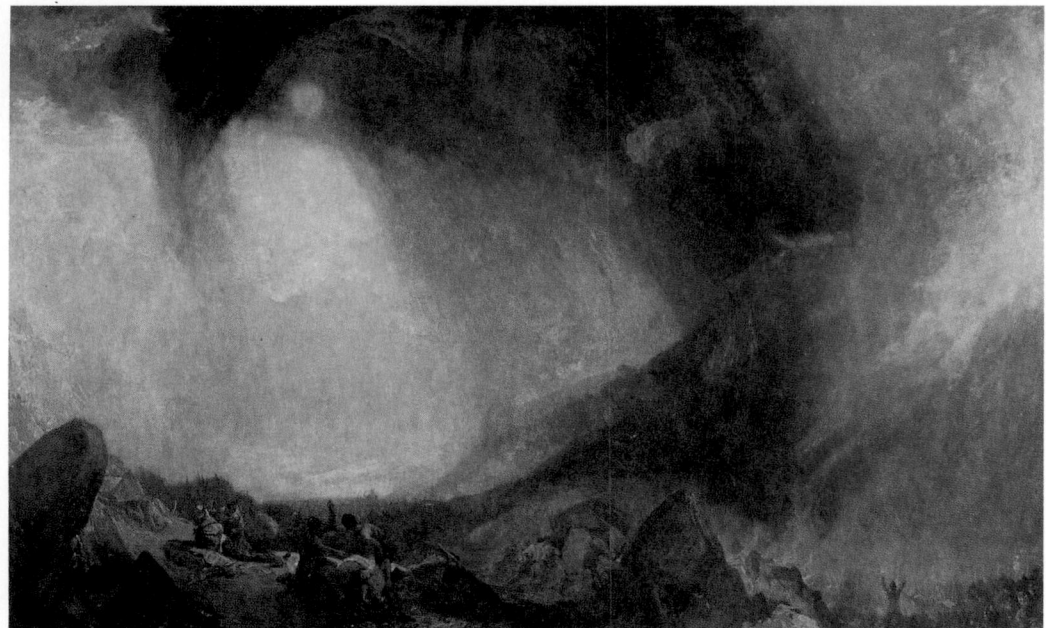

**J. M. W. Turner**
Snow Storm. Hannibal and his Army
crossing the Alps, c. 1810–1812
Oil on canvas, 144.7 x 236cm
London, Tate Gallery

**J. M. W. Turner**
Peace – Burial at Sea, 1842
Oil on canvas, 87 x 86.5 cm
London, Tate Gallery

# J. M. W. TURNER
## 1775–1851

A terrible snowstorm lashes the Alps. The dark, menacing sky unloads its masses of snow. A milky orange disc of sun lights up the blackish-grey sky and eerily illuminates the mountains. At the very lower edge of the painting, there are scenes of robbery, murder and plunder between the rocks. In the middle ground, we see the vague outline of Hannibal's army. The Carthaginian military leader himself can just be discerned as a tiny speck in the middle distance, seated on an elephant and looking out onto the far-off, sun-drenched plains of Italy. Turner regarded the painting as a warning to England. With this example from history, he sought to point out that England could be subject to a fate that Rome was spared.

The main content of Turner's painting is not, however, the historic event in its metaphorical significance – this is merely indicated anecdotally at the edge of the painting. It is, instead, the whirling chaos of the forces of nature, enigmatic and magical, creating strange metamorphoses of colour and luminosity as the sunlight filters through the dark cloud. This painting is the first example of Turner's innovative compositional approach which disregards conventional structures of horizontal, vertical and diagonal, employing instead irregularly bisected arcs and cones that do not offer the viewer any point of reference, but draw him into the fray instead.

In his painting *Peace – Burial at Sea*, Turner pays homage to the Scottish painter David Wilkie who died on board a steamer on his return from a study tour of Palestine on 1 June 1841. As the port authorities at nearby Gibraltar had closed the harbour for fear of the plaque that had infested the Middle East, Wilkie had to be buried at sea that same evening.

The scene is dominated by a pale haziness that suffuses the water and the sky in the same cold light. The only warm and luminous point of the painting is at the scene of the burial itself, where Wilkie's corpse is lowered into the water by the light of flaming torches. The black of the dark ship's keel is dominant, and its compact mass seems to be rent in two by the searing shaft of light. The two black sails stand out starkly against the milky white of the sky. Their sharp outlines contrast with the blurring of borders, as for example, the reflection of the black ship in the water running menacingly into the foreground in a way that underlines the universal inevitability of transience and death.

Turner exhibited this painting in 1842 together with *War. The Exile and the Rock Limpet* (London, Tate Gallery), an allegorical picture of Napoleon that suggests a further political dimension to this pair of paintings.

During Turner's lifetime, England rose to become Europe's leading maritime power. Turner depicted many of the great sea battles of the time. His early paintings, in particular, painted with realistic precision, brought him considerable success. In this painting of the *Fighting Téméraire*, objective presentation – a certain attention to detail is still evident in the portrayal of the ship – is combined with the predominant organization of light and atmosphere in a sweeping sky with a deep horizon, and its reflection on the surface of the water.

Turner, who was in fact a witness to the event, renders the tugging of Nelson's warship, Téméraire, in the summer of 1838 from the fleet base at Sheerness on the mouth of the Thames to a wrecker's shipyard, as a melodramatic event.

"Seen against and almost absorbed by a molten sunset, the fighting Téméraire, once a glory of British navel prowess in the Napoleonic wars, becomes a spectre on its way to a maritime grave. The poignancy of this symbolic burial is further underlined by the sooty little tugboat in the foreground, which offers a realistic foil of the mundane here and now to the visionary spectacle of the passing of man's achievements beyond some distant horizon," writes Robert Rosenblum.

The pathos-laden depiction of the wrecked ship in the evening light becomes an enigmatic metaphor suggestive of the path of history and human life. The rise and fall of worldly power are thus closely tied with the progress of natural history. The art critic John Ruskin was to come to similar conclusions in his melancholy observations on the end of the Téméraire, in which he lamented that the sunset would never again dress her in golden robes, nor the light of stars shiver on the waves that ripple forth as she glides across the sea, and that even the child of the seaman would neither reply nor know that the dew of night lay deep in the war-torn timbers of the old Téméraire.

This painting, which Turner called his favourite, is also regarded as a reflection by the artist on his own age and on death.

J. M. W. Turner
The "Fighting Téméraire" Tugged to her Last Berth to be Broken Up, 1838
Oil on canvas, 90.8 x 121.9 cm
London, National Gallery

J. M. W. Turner
Rain, Steam and Speed –
The Great Western Railway, 1844
Oil on canvas, 91 x 122 cm
London, National Gallery

# J. M. W. TURNER
## 1775–1851

Turner admired modern technology. His painting shows a locomotive, the most modern of its kind, crossing the Maidenhead Bridge, which itself was a masterpiece of progressive engineering by Isambard Brunel. This railway painting was intended to show the beauty inherent in the merging of nature and technology. In this respect, Turner stood apart from most of his artist colleagues, who regarded industrial progress with suspicion and certainly did not consider it a worthy subject for art.

Although the painting is based on his own observations, it is not a realistic portrayal of an event, but, typically for Turner, its mythical exaggeration; in the words of Werner Hofmann, it is "the merging of natural forces and technically guided energies".

It is said that Turner frequently sought to create atmospheric tonality in his paintings by smearing the paint in short, broad brushstrokes from a dirty palette onto the canvas and then gradually drawing objective codes out of this colour ground. As in a dream, the haze rising from the water blurs with the veil of rain in the sky, and the steam of the locomotive, creating an atmospheric unity of colour.

Turner got sailors to lash him to the mast on board the Ariel Harwich for four hours so that he could observe a storm at sea. In the resulting painting, ships are swept between the whipped-up sea and the swirling clouds of snow. Sky and sea blend into a foaming mass of black/brown/grey/green and white whirling around the ships and only a tiny blue patch of sky gives any hope of an end to this situation. The viewer is drawn into the events in which his eye can find no fixed point. Atmosphere and the elemental forces of nature are the subject matter of the painting, even more so than in the painting that depicts Hannibal.

Turner's means of presenting the forces of nature lies primarily in his handling of colour freed from all precise representation. The magically abstracted colouring also makes the actual subject matter of the painting an enigmatic metaphor for underlying reflections, for example, on the creation of the world. The snowstorm conjures up the chaos at the beginning of the world, in which water was separated from earth and light from darkness. In his free handling of colour, Turner influenced not only the Impressionists, but also paved the way for abstract painting. In his later years, Turner's quest was to create a tapestry of light and colour independent of objects.

J. M. W. Turner
Snow Storm – Steam Boat off a Harbour's Mouth making Signals
in Shallow Water, and going by the Lead. The Author was in this
Storm on the Night the Ariel Left Harwich, 1842
Oil on canvas, 91.5 x 122 cm. London, Tate Gallery

# GEORGE CALEB BINGHAM
1811–1879

Even at the time when Bingham painted this picture, it appeared as a nostalgic memory of a lost world. The fur trade had long since been taken over by the great trading companies of the Mid-West who shipped their goods on large steamers and freighters. In Bingham's painting, father and son are bringing the furs they have trapped themselves to the nearest trading-post. The father, at the rudder, is an amiable grey-haired elderly man of French origins; his son, the child of an Indian mother, leans dreamily against the cargo and the gun with which he has shot a duck. Both men look directly at the viewer, drawing us into their peaceful existence.

The riverscape, with scattered bushes fading into the horizon is quite enchanting. Branches jut out of the water, whose surface is smooth as a mirror, unruffled by any breath of wind. It reflects the boat in pale colours. Everything is bathed in the pale pinkish-silvery mist of twilight, against which the half-savage, half-civilized clothing of the boatmen, with their black cat, stand out sharply.

George Caleb Bingham
Fur Traders Descending the Missouri, c. 1845
Oil on canvas, 73.5 x 93 cm
New York, The Metropolitan Museum of Art

# WILLIAM SIDNEY MOUNT
1807–1868

Mount makes us eye-witnesses to a village incident in which two men are striking a deal on the brown horse, saddled and quietly standing on the left. In accordance with local custom, the two men are whittling twigs until they have agreed on a price for the horse.

The anecdotal narrative of this scene is the focal point of the painting. Mount has taken great care to portray the rural atmosphere which, like the topic, has been drawn from his immediate surroundings and related with painstaking attention to detail. In the background is his own farm in Stony Brook, a small settlement on Long Island. The summer sun lights the scene as on a stage.

Mount was the leading representative of rural genre painting of the period in America. With evident self-confidence, he rejected a patron's suggestion to enhance his painterly skills by continuing his studies in Europe. Nevertheless, his paintings do possess certain similarities with European art, especially with German Biedermeier painting which emerged around the same time and which he may have known from reproductions.

William Sidney Mount
The Horse Dealers, 1835
Oil on canvas, 61 x 76 cm
New York, The New York Historical Society

## FREDERIC EDWIN CHURCH

1826–1900

The magnificent Niagara Falls, a wonder of nature famed throughout the world, are commemorated by the American artist Church in this painting. The predominant impression is the sense of nature's boundless powers and the sweeping expanses of the open landscape. This is achieved on the one hand by the unusual pictorial format (almost twice as wide as it is high) and on the other hand by the bold compositional device of presenting the horseshoe-shaped waterfall in the full force of its roaring masses of tumbling masses directly frontal to the viewer, while at the same time underlining the sheer enormity of its vast dimensions by means of the narrow horizontal strip of land in the background that runs right across the painting.

The realism of the portrayal heightens the immediacy with which the forces of nature are perceived by the viewer. Numerous studies on location and a profound interest in natural sciences (optics, surveying techniques, geometry) equipped Church admirably for the task.

In contrast to the powerful motif, the painter employs a palette of remarkably pale and delicate hues, particularly the violet sky that merges with the rainbow and the haze of the spray and is even reflected in the darkly rippling water of the foreground. An air of

mystery elevates the motif to the realms of the symbolic. The powerful and irresistible (in both positive and negative sense) spirit of a huge, new nation is presented to without offering the viewer a firm position from which to view its gigantic force. The painting, exhibited for the first time in 1857 in New York, was a huge success for Church, not only in America. It was particularly important in enhancing the reputation of young American art in Europe, where it attracted considerable attention.

In London, where the painting was exhibited in the same year, *The Times* noted the arrival of this major work by an American

landscape artist on an American theme, underlining the achievement of sober authenticity. The painting was also highly acclaimed in France, where it was awarded a medal ten years later at the Paris World Fair of 1867.

**Frederic Edwin Church**
Niagara Falls, 1857
Oil on canvas, 108 x 229.9 cm
Washington, The Corcoran Gallery of Art

**Thomas Cole**
The Voyage of Life. Youth, 1842
Oil on canvas, 134.3 x 194.9 cm
Washington, National Gallery of Art

## THOMAS COLE
### 1801–1848

Cole's portrayal of *Youth* is bathed in the pale midday blue of summer. In a boat accompanied by angels, the young man holds the rudder himself and guides the boat, his right arm held aloft emphatically, along the path of life, which is frequently expressed by the metaphor of a river. In the distance, a "castle in the air" alludes to the optimistic ideals this young person still nurtures for his future. Even the lush and fertile landscape in all its tranquillity and mild luminosity clearly underlines the positive characteristics Cole attributes to this stage of life.

The three other scenes in the cycle, *Childhood*, *Maturity* and *Old Age*, are by no means entirely positive. In them, the figures are also accompanied by guardian angels, but the path of life is often shadowed and surrounded by high mountains, or lashed by storms.

The entire series, executed twice by Cole and originally commissioned by a profoundly religious banker for his private villa, combines various metaphors of age, time and season with literary concepts in a way that would be unthinkable without the European Romantic movement. It is no coincidence, that *Youth* was the most popular motif in the series, and the one most widely distributed in numerous reproductions. It is a fitting reflection of the prevailing mood in 19th century America following the economic crisis of the 1840s.

In a panoramic landscape of mountains, plains and oceans, in which enclaves of human life are indicated by a small town on the seashore and some tiny ships, rises a gigantic chalice of stone. It is clearly a remnant of the long lost era of the Titans who, according to Greek myth, lived on earth before the days of men and gods. Now the chalice has lost its original function, its rim is overgrown, ancient settlements can be seen around it and ships sail on its surface. Only the painter and the viewer, in their all-seeing position, can recognize the contexts in which human life goes on.

Cole's known interest in the creation myth prompted him to code many of his landscape paintings with religious and allegorical allusions. *The Giant's Chalice* is intended to show that civilizations have no awareness of the powers of their development and renewal nor any sense of the vast dimensions of other worlds beyond their own. This painting, highly original for its time, was not fully appreciated until the advent of the surrealists.

**Thomas Cole**
The Giant's Chalice, 1833
Oil on canvas, 49.3 x 41 cm
New York, The Metropolitan Museum of Art

Christa von Lengerke

# IMPRESSIONISM, ART NOUVEAU AND JUGENDSTIL

## Painting from 1860 to 1910

The second half of the 19th century spawned a wide diversity of stylistic trends in painting and brought forth a number of highly distinctive personalities. The very fact that so many different terms are associated with this period – Salon painting, Impressionism, Pointillism, Historicism, Pre-Raphaelites, Jugendstil, Art Nouveau and Belle Epoque – bears witness to the sheer variety of artistic movements.

In France, inspired by the revolutionary painting of Manet, the Impressionists shook off the fetters of a rigid and outmoded artistic canon and determined the subject-matter and compositional organization of their paintings, themselves; Monet and Renoir, Pissarro and Sisley painted what they wanted as they wanted. Others soon followed suit, including Liebermann and Corinth in Germany and Cassatt and Chase in the USA.

The Pre-Raphaelites in England, Millais and Rossetti among them, called for a more profound and reflective intellectual approach to art and paved the way for the decoratively ornamental style known as Art Nouveau and its German-Austrian equivalent, Jugendstil, which was embodied in its purest form by the work of Klimt, while Symbolists like Moreau conjured up visions from the world of dreams and the realms of the imagination.

Dynamic brushwork and a highly expressive handling of colour are the predominant features of Van Gogh's paintings. Gauguin's images of the South Seas represent a journey of discovery to a more primeval life, while Cézanne's autonomy of form and colour brought him widespread recognition as the father of modern art.

Impressionism and Art Nouveau, or Jugendstil as it was known in Germany and Austria, are terms used to stake out the boundaries of a development in painting that took place within a period of about five decades, from the mid-19th century to the early years of the 20th century. On the one hand, there was so-called Salon painting, art cloaked in traditional means, whose meticulously crafted and often brilliantly executed works reflected a conservative attitude that did not question the prevailing order. On the other hand, a new painting was beginning to emerge whose creative freedom and forceful impact undermined conventional structures and pointed towards the dawn of a new era.

Although we have become accustomed to talking of stylistic pluralism as a 20th century phenomenon, it can already be observed in the 19th century, when a number of stylistic directions developed in rapid succession and at times even simultaneously. The origins of these styles are often difficult to trace. Some of them were full of innovative vitality and paved the way for subsequent developments, while others were merely the emasculated remnants of a movement whose energies were already spent. A few key words suffice to indicate just how heterogeneous the situation was in the field of painting during the period under discussion: Salon painting – Impressionism – Historicism – Pre-Raphaelites – Post-Impressionism – Japonisme – Symbolism – Fin de Siècle – Jugendstil – Art Nouveau – Belle Epoque.

## Paris as the centre of art

Around the mid-19th century, the world was highly Eurocentric. Europe was seen as the model of progress, and its colonies, friendly states and even countries subjugated by force recognized European civilization and culture, whereas Europe continued, as it had done ever since the discovery of distant lands, to plunder the treasures of foreign lands for things of value, exotic rarities and fashionable articles. Since the reign of Louis XIV, France had embodied the very epitome of elegant life in the eyes of the European courts, aristocracy and *haute bourgeoisie* – a reputation it continued to savour in spite of a change of ruler, a revolution, a new empire and even a republic. Finally, in the second half of the 19th century, Paris was the exciting and scintillating centre of the art world, and justly so.

A number of favourable circumstances had secured France and thereby Paris, a foremost position in the world of art, which it was to maintain for many years, well into the 20th century. Rome's hegemony as a seat of learning and a coveted base for artists had declined almost unnoticed and Paris had stepped in to fill the breach. Artists still went on study tours of Rome and Italy, visiting museums and classical monuments, but the major events in the world of art were now taking place in Paris. It was the powerful *Institut de France* which directed and regulated cultural life under the auspices of monarch or parliament. This institution was in charge of the Ecole des Beaux-Arts in Paris and the Académie de France in Rome, constituting the only official training facility for painters and sculptors, who hoped that their training there would be a passport to status, recognition and wealth. Prizes, awards, public purchases and commissions, election to the Académie des Beaux-Arts from which the professors were appointed to the art schools in Paris and Rome and from which the jury members were chosen for the Salon exhibitions, constituted coveted career goals accessible only by this path.

The Salon was a high-profile exhibition and sales forum that drew many visitors and stimulated the kind of lively debate and public attention so important for artists in a period when art-dealing and commercial galleries were only beginning to develop. Salons were public and had enjoyed enormous popularity since Louis XIV had begun holding them in the court of the Palais Royal and later in the Louvre – events attended by *le tout Paris*. Each Salon prompted a flood of art criticism from amateurs and professionals alike. The tradition of art theory as the basis for the development of art goes back to the 17th century when it was first established by Académie members like Le Brun and other active painters, later by connoisseurs and collectors who described themselves as "amateurs" and who had a distinct sense of responsibility towards the world of art. The proponents of the individual stylistic directions fiercely defended their controversial views and did not shy from even the most vehement debate. Just as the Rubenistes and Poussinistes had been implacable rivals in the 17th century, in the mid-19th century it was the disciples of Eugène Delacroix who pinned the banner of "colour" to their mast and railed against the predominance of line and drawing propagated by Ingres and the other academists. Out of these rivalries and controversies there grew a phenomenon that has come to be taken for granted in our day and age: publicity.

The Salon reports published in the form of newspaper articles, custom printed brochures or in letter form, as plays, satires or essays, were equally popular. Often renowned intellectuals – Denis Diderot, Charles Baudelaire (1821–1867), Emile Zola (1840–1902), Théophile Thoré-Bürger (1807–1869), Joris-Karl Huysmans (1848–1907) wrote the Salon reviews, defending the work of one painter and his art or tearing others to pieces, and fuelling the already raging fire of debate. In an era not yet inundated with information overflow, they were received with eager interest, and pro-

**Pierre-Auguste Renoir**
The Swing, 1876
Oil on canvas, 92 x 73 cm
Paris, Musée d'Orsay

vided welcome material for discussion in the salons of high society.

The situation in the rest of Europe was similar. In almost all the capital cities there were subsidized academies which awarded grants and prizes and organized exhibitions; there was no shortage of theoreticians and critics, nor of buyers, and yet it was Paris alone that was the main focus of attention. Elsewhere, there were capable artists, many of them outstanding individuals, whose talent remained in the wings, generally enjoying modest local patronage, but burdened with the disadvantage or even the stigma of not having achieved fame in France or in Paris.

Of course, in other countries – in England and Scandinavia, in Belgium, Holland, Germany, the Alpine countries, Eastern Europe, Russia and the USA – old and new trends, coloured by a regional and local vernacular or by the strong signature of an individual artist also existed. Yet it often took longer for these to emerge from the shadow of dominant French painting and find the attention and acclaim their significance deserved.

## Official art and countermovements

The Paris World Fair of 1855, which included a separate section for the presentation of international art, was a major event. Twenty-eight nations exhibited, and it was the showcase for the first continental exhibition of the English Pre-Raphaelites. The section for French painting was not only accorded the most space, but was also the main focus of attention and admiration. The selection of French artists chosen to appear in the exhibition sheds some light on the situation of the Paris art scene at the time.

Ingres, represented by over forty works, was the radiant and highly accoladed star, and all the prizes and honours were awarded to artists who adopted his approach and painted in accordance with the doctrines of the Académie. As so often, Delacroix had to forego academic and state merits, although Baudelaire dedicated a brilliant eulogy to his work, and the painters of the school of Barbizon, referred to somewhat pejoratively as realists and naturalists, were allowed to display only a few poorly-placed paintings.

Only those painters conventional enough to follow the official artistic career-path by producing Salon art were well received. A hierarchy of motifs was applied as a scale of values that seems quite ridiculous from today's point of view. Historical, religious and allegorically idealizing themes met with the highest praise, followed by swagger portraits. Landscapes, genre painting and still lifes were even less highly thought of. Moreover, a certain technical skill was demanded in the execution of ceremonial postures, dignified reminiscences and academically correct classicism. The paintings that complied with these outward criteria often had little more than fashionable appeal and empty rhetorical brilliance and they were purchased and accoladed by a public that saw

itself mirrored in them. Unchanged for decades, and determined by civil servants, the requirements of academic perfection and the academic structures were a hindrance to vitality and an innovative spirit. Creative freedom and personal artistic development were quite unthinkable.

A tentative protest against the rules of the academy had already been voiced in the first half of the 19th century by groups of artists, such as the St Lukas Bruderschaft (Brotherhood of St Luke) in Vienna in 1809, while in France the rebel artists were those who had settled in rural Barbizon to paint outdoors and in the studio. Corot, Courbet, Millet, Rousseau, Charles-François Daubigny (1817–1878), Constant Troyon (1810–1865) and Diaz de la Peña had joined forces to step out in a new direction in painting and lend each other support when they could expect none from any official authority. In England, the Pre-Raphaelite Brotherhood was founded in 1848, adopting as their model the painting of 15th century Italy, the age of Raphael, and seeking a complete renewal in art. In Paris, the gradually awakening self-confidence of non-academic painters or those rejected by the academy led in 1863 to the creation of a Salon des Refusés which, though it did not achieve the hoped-for success, caused a major scandal and unleashed storms of uncomprehending protest.

The eight group-exhibitions mounted by the Impressionists in Paris out of necessity and protest between 1874 and 1886 were initially doomed to failure, but they nevertheless contributed towards making the artists concerned better known. In their wake came the Neo-Impressionists and the Symbolists. Throughout Europe, groups of artists began to form, culminating in the Secessions that sprang up everywhere, with their firmly anti-academic programme and regular exhibitions. It was not only the *avant-garde* painters who were in search of new contents and forms for their art. Similar trends could be found in literature and music, and it is therefore hardly surprising that interdisciplinary groups were also founded.

Cafés and restaurants played an important role in cultural life, and were often places of debate and lively discussion rather than mere watering-places. At that time, the Brasserie des Martyrs in Montmartre and the Andler-Keller were frequented by the realists grouped around Corot and Courbet, by the critics and writers Jules Castagnary (1830–1888), Champfleury and Baudelaire. Henri Fantin-Latour (1836–1904) and Gustave Flaubert (1821–1880) preferred the Café Taranne. Café Fleurus, decorated with murals by Corot, was a favourite meeting place amongst the students of Charles Gleyre (1806–1874).

Until 1866, Edouard Manet (1832–1883) was a regular at Café Bade, before he switched to Café Guerbois on the Boulevard de Batignolles, which was soon to become a popular haunt of the Impressionists and their friends. Later, they would also meet in the Café Nouvelle-Athènes, where Edgar

**Claude Monet**
Impression: Sunrise, 1873
Oil on canvas, 48 x 63 cm
Paris, Musée Marmottan

Degas (1834–1917), Pierre-Auguste Renoir (1841–1919), Monet and Alfred Sisley (1839–1899) were frequent guests, as were the critics and writers Armand Silvestre (1837–1901), Ernest Renan (1823–1892), Auguste Villiers de L'Isle-Adam (1838–1889), Paul Cézanne (1839–1906), the musician Cabaner (1832–1881) and George Moore (1852–1933), who initially wished to become a painter and then ended up as a writer. Café Volpini was later to become the meeting place and exhibition venue of the Nabis and the Post-Impressionists.

## Impressionism and the Impressionists

At the Ecole des Beaux-Arts, the studio of Charles Gleyre was regarded as the most liberal. Though Gleyre himself painted very much in line with contemporary taste, he did not seek to impose this style on his students in any way, preferring to allow them to develop their own skills. His classes were understandably the most popular, particularly amongst young artists eager to explore new avenues in painting. At the Atelier Suisse on the Quai des Orfèvres, painters would gather to work for a small fee, without a teacher telling them what to do.

In the 1860s, these places attracted the young painters Monet, Frédéric Bazille (1841–1870), Sisley, Renoir and Camille Pissarro (1830–1903). These were the artists who were to develop the purest form of Impressionism, which reached its zenith in the 1870s and 1880s and, for several decades, constituted the "new painting" that swelled to become a

broad international movement and paved the way for the art of the future. They initially joined forces on a friendly basis with the intention of taking their training as painters into their own hands, in order to avoid the impasse of academic teaching.

Monet had come from Le Havre where he had been introduced to *plein-air* painting by the aimiably helpful, slightly older Eugène Boudin (1824–1898) and had learned to observe various different light situations from the same standpoint under different conditions. He passed on what he had learned to his friends and persuaded them to take up the experiment of *plein-air* painting so disdained by the traditionalists. In Paris, they studied the old masters in the Louvre and practised with dedication in the studio, executing innumerable studies and sketches before creating their compositions in oil. They never tired of studying the works of the painters of previous generations who had also gone against the academic direction. They revered Delacroix, who had died in 1863, and they sought the friendship and advice of the painters of Barbizon; Corot and Courbet earned their highest esteem.

Brought together by their common quest for a new spirit in painting and by their mutual admiration and friendship, an increasing number of painters, writers, musicians and other artists and critics as well as a few collectors, art dealers and patrons soon joined their circle. The two slightly older *plein-air* painters Boudin and Johan Barthold Jongkind (1819–1891) were invariably willing to undertake work

479

together, to spend time in the country and to hold discussions. With their light-flooded landscapes, they built a bridge between the school of Barbizon and purely Impressionist painting.

It was Monet, with his ideas and paintings, who made the most decisive contribution to the development of Impressionism. The fascination of capturing a fleeting moment, the observation and reproduction of colours and surface appearances changing under the influence of natural light became an increasingly important aim in his works. He chose to leave out the narrative, the sublime and the historic from his paintings, preferring from the start to portray simple motifs: landscapes, still lifes, tranquil scenes of his family and friends, urban and rural life, portraits of his mistress. All of his models and motifs were portrayed in close-up or at a distance in a manner that allowed an intimacy to be retained.

His new way of seeing – the outward appearance as the harmony of colour and light – could be expressed only by a new approach. The possibilities of Neoclassicist painting were exhausted and so he sought other models, gradually banning linearity and stark planarity from his paintings, and relaxing his brushwork until it came to resemble scumbled daubs.

Pissarro and Sisley were closest in style to Monet, both in their choice of motif and overall organization, and to Bazille, who died in the Franco-Prussian war in 1870. Renoir, with whom they frequently explored the same motifs, worked entirely according to the increasingly clearly defined principles of Impressionism.

Time and time again, with varying degrees of success, the young artists would submit their paintings to the Salon jury in the hope that they might be accepted, for these exhibitions were virtually their only opportunity of presenting their works to the public and of selling them. The further they strayed from the paths of academic tradition towards their own style, the more futile their chances became until the constant rejections finally drove them to take their own initiative.

They were also joined by painters like Edouard Manet, who was not entirely outside of the Neoclassicist camp. He had trained in the studio of Couture at the Ecole des Beaux-Arts and had enjoyed some initial success at the Salon. Manet's work is as much a milestone on the road to Modernism as that of the pure Impressionists, but it is based entirely on classical predecessors. Manet was a close friend of Monet and even adopted certain Impressionistic aspects of the latter's works, but he was never prepared to sever all ties with the Salon and the society that supported it, even though he suffered rejection because of the risqué liberality of his *Déjeuner sur l'herbe* (ill. p. 491) and his *Olympia* (both Paris, Musée d'Orsay) both of which caused a scandal. Degas also belonged to their circle and in his early work his clas-

sical training is still plainly evident. His gradual development towards a painterly technique in which structured fields of colour dominate in the portrayal of seemingly banal motifs positions him near the Impressionists.

The maverick Cézanne would meet up with the Impressionists whenever he came to Paris and he also exhibited with them from time to time. He adopted their *plein-air* techniques and explored Impressionist influences, but his struggle to find a pure new art eventually led him to adopt a highly analytic approach to the exploration of compositional structure.

Fantin-Latour was one of the group around Jean-Baptiste Armand Guillaumin (1841–1927) and Armand Gautier (1825–1895), Mary Cassatt (1845–1926) and Berthe Morisot (1841–1895). James Abbott McNeill Whistler (1834–1903) visited his Impressionist friends whenever he came to Paris, and their influence and inspiration are undeniable in his work.

Long before there was any precise term to describe it, a certain way of seeing and portraying had been developed which was pejoratively dubbed *Impressionnisme* and which soon came into common usage as an accepted term without negative connotations. The artists themselves often referred to the concept of "impression" in explaining the focus of their art. They forswore a precisely delineated reproduction of photographic precision in favour of atmosphere in their paintings – using painterly techniques to transfigure portrayals of distance and close-up objects, breaking down homogenous colour planes and lines, and using brushwork and texture as creative media in themselves

In their enthusiasm for *plein-air* painting, Monet, Sisley, Pissarro and Renoir had gone furthest in their experimentation with light, colours and shadows. They had instinctively recognized the psychological effects and characteristics of colour. Monet was the first to ban gloomy black from his palette, replacing it with a vital, vibrant blue. Today, in retrospect, it is often said that these artists were not particularly revolutionary. In the eyes of their contemporaries, however, they were revolutionary indeed, for the storms of indignation, outrage and ridicule triggered by their works were acutely and genuinely felt. Like their forerunners, the painters of Barbizon, they were referred to as realists and naturalists. This, however, applied to only one aspect of their painting: they sought their motifs in their actual surroundings and in nature, and they did not seek to imbue them with any sublime significance. The gentle anarchy of these painters aroused protest for many reasons. Even their lifestyle indicated that they were not artists in search of social approval and integration; they were interested first and foremost in true art and in the joys of their family life and their circle of friends. They turned their backs on the ideals of high society and broke the taboos of its superficial morality. Whereas the painters of Barbizon had been sober reporters of what they saw, the Impressionists glorified everything that had no place in the Salons: unspoilt nature, the simple life, people without airs and graces, nudity, Paris by day and by night.

Although the French Revolution had aimed to create a classless society, class differences had once again become firmly entrenched and were alien to a social dogma. The artists had dared to cross the borders of class difference. That alone was enough to provoke anyone who adhered to this divine order. After all, the higher echelons of society and academic art needed the artists as a mirror for themselves, and the bourgeoisie needed them too, for upward mobility was their heart's desire, and their bid to achieve it also meant adopting high society's taste in art.

The Impressionists, however, ignored the sublime motifs of Salon art, calling instead for the viewer to look at the artist's life, to see the snow in Normandy with them, to catch Madame Monet unawares sitting beneath the lilac tree, to look at the bar girl in the Moulin de la Galette – a bar that no gentlemen of fine society would actually admit to frequenting – to join them on a pleasure-steamer with ordinary citizens or to watch shirt-sleeved rowers in their boats. They asked the viewer to see as art things that had hitherto been arrogantly dismissed out of hand. That was quite simply going too far.

Even such painters as Manet, himself a wealthy man with social connections, were not immune from rejection if they took too many artistic liberties. One might be forgiven for asking whether they did so innocently or with some ulterior motive. Manet's *Nana* (Hamburg, Kunsthalle), a cocotte in her underwear, applying her make-up in the presence of a suitor, was viewed with considerable disapproval.

Their painterly technique was also seen as sacrilegious. It was not the first time since the Middle Ages that colours had been allocated a symbolic significance or that painters had discovered the power of colour as a stylistic device. According to the maxim *ars superante materiam* (art over matter) colour had long been subjugated and placed in the service of an exact fulfilment of the lines and planes of the motif. Whenever painters had liberated colour or brushwork and impasto from the strictures of line – Titian, Rubens, Frans Hals and Rembrandt, and in the 19th century Delacroix – it had been held against them. It was an act of artistic freedom that went against the grain of theory. The Impressionists and many of their contemporaries broke the mould of classical pictorial structure with its painstaking compositional approach, replacing it with a dynamic juxtaposition and contrast of bold and seemingly arbitrary colour planes which became an image when viewed at a distance.

Monet's famous painting *Impression: Sunrise* (ill. p. 479), from which Impressionist painting takes its name, shows a veil of mist enveloping water, sky, outlines of ships and

**Edgar Degas**
Ballet (The Star), 1876/77
Pastel on monotype, 58 x 42 cm
Paris, Musée d'Orsay

boats, a red sunrise and its reflection on the water. It has atmosphere and a touch of the unfinished, lightly daubed, that leaves room for the imagination. It does not tell the whole story. Looking at it, the viewer perceives the beauty with which light imbues matter.

Impressionist paintings do not express high ideals, but then again, that is not their intention. They pay homage to an attitude to life that is firmly rooted in the private sphere. They do not narrate, nor do they give us food for thought, but they invite us to take a brief break from the flow of time and delight in the beauty of a fleeting moment. They do not appeal to reason, but to the senses.

The phenomenon we describe as Impressionism is no longer associated solely with the painting of the 19th century. Today, we may speak of the Impressionistic painting of antiquity, Impressionist phases in the work of Titian, or the Impressionism of late 17th century Netherlandish landscape painting. Claude Debussy's (1862–1918) music is described as impressionist, as are the writings of Marcel Proust (1871–

Camille Pissarro
Landscape at Chaponval, 1880
Oil on canvas, 54.5 x 65 cm
Paris, Musée d'Orsay

1922). The term is rarely applied to sculpture – though Auguste Rodin (1840–1917) and Medardo Rosso (1858–1928) are often referred to as impressionist sculptors – and it is not used for architecture at all.

The history of Impressionism is, at the same time, a history of the great bonds of friendship between artists, as is true of most of the non-academic art movements in the 19th century. The support offered by a circle of friends, including the often necessary financial assistance, gave the painters who had turned their backs on tradition and society the power and peace of mind to pursue their painterly aims unerringly. Even before the painters, worn out over the years by the constant rejection of their work by the Salon, joined forces and formed the Société des Artistes Independants in 1874, they had already found buyers for their paintings amongst a few aficionados and patrons.

### Art dealers, patrons, critics
Most of the art dealers in Paris in those days were conservative and the few who supported the new painting at first paid dearly for it. Louis Martinet (1810–1894), a courageous art dealer with a gallery on the Boulevard des Italiens, had shown many artists from the Salon des Refusés at his gallery. Nevertheless, his programme was still fairly conservative and he was more supportive of the school of Barbizon and Manet than he was of such extremists as Monet, Renoir, Sisley or Pissarro.

The art dealer Paul Durand-Ruel (1831–1922), whose rival was Georges Petit (1835–1900), insisted, even in the face of bankruptcy, on representing the Impressionists and he made an immense contribution to their recognition. Ambroise Vollard (1865–1939) AND "PÈRE" MARTIN (C. 1810-c. 1880) had faith in their talent and supported them with purchases and small exhibitions.

The Romanian doctor Georges de Bellio (1828–1894) began collecting Impressionist works and the French doctor Paul-Ferdinand Gachet (1828–1909) not only provided medical care and advice for two generations of painters, but also came to their rescue in moments of need by purchasing their works. The customs officer Victor Choquet (1821–1891) invested his entire savings in his collection of paintings. He possessed many works by Delacroix, Cézanne, Monet, Renoir, Manet, Pissarro and Sisley. The singer and composer Jean-Baptiste Faure (1830–1914) was a customer of Durand-Ruel and he also purchased from the artists themselves. Eugène Murer (1846–1906), restaurant owner and patissier, expressed his approval and support by holding the famous Wednesday dinners so greatly appreciated by the painters.

Ernest Hoschedé (1838–1890), owner of the Au Gagne-Petit department store on the Avenue de l'Opéra, was enthusiastic about the work of the Impressionists, collected their paintings and organized two auctions. When he went bankrupt, Monet was able to return the favour by taking him and his large family in. After the death of both Monet's wife and Hoschedé, the latter's widow Alice (1844–1911) became Monet's second wife.

Politicians such as Georges Benjamin Clemenceau (1841–1929), who would later become Prime Minister, and Antonin Proust (1832–1905) admired the Impressionists, bought their paintings, and even dedicated their writings to them. Critics and writers like Baudelaire, Zola, Thoré-Bürger and Champfleury, who praised the new painting in several articles, have already been mentioned in this connection. In 1878, the art critic Théodore Duret (1838–1927) published his ground-breaking study *Les Peintres impressionnistes* which brought them recognition, and his views were soon echoed by other critics, including Philippe Burty (1830–1890), Castagnary, Ernest Chesneau (1833–1890) and Edmond Duranty (1833–1880).

## Japonisme

When Japan opened up to trade with the United States and Europe, Japanese art and Japanese crafts were imported in quantity, particularly to Paris. At the Paris World Fair of 1867, there was a highly acclaimed section dedicated to objects from Japan. On the European art market, particularly in Holland, England and France, Japanese art was available and large, exclusive department stores also stocked these coveted articles.

The rage for beautiful fans, kimonos, china, enamel, lacquer work and metal work, parasols and coloured woodcuts triggered a veritable passion for all things Japanese. People began collecting Japanese art for their homes and so-called "Japonisme" was to have a lasting impact on the artists, that was particularly evident in the period from Impressionism to Art Nouveau.

On the face of it, this Japanese fashion was similar to the craze for Chinese fashions in the 17th and 18th centuries. At that time, exotic, beautiful and precious items had been imported from China, and then Europeanized by modifying or copying them. China cabinets and lacquer cabinets were used to display collections, gilded decorations were applied to vases, wall-screens were dismantled and integrated into Rococo wall decorations as picture panels, Chinese painting was imitated as Chinoiserie. China responded to this fashion by producing export goods specifically for European taste. This simple mechanism also took effect in the case of Japanese works. At first, the fact that a painting included a Japanese object was merely an indication of the widespread popularity of Japanese crafts in Europe at the time – a phenomenon no more noteworthy than any other fashion or fad.

Yet it was the artists, in particular, who were inspired by Japanese art and who integrated it into their work, modifying it to sent their purposes. They were particularly impressed by the woodcuts, but also by the painted paravents, textiles, fans, lacquerwork and porcelain. The boldly fore-

shortened perspectives, figures cut off at the edge of the picture, elongated vertical picture formats, the quiet intimacy of the genre scenes, the fragile beauty of landscapes and plants, stylized almost to the point of ornament, and the partial abstraction were all sources of inspiration for the artists.

Whistler's tall, narrow formats have their origins here, and they will also occur later in the work of Edouard Vuillard (1868–1940) and Pierre Bonnard (1867–1947), going on to dominate the field of poster design from the 1880s onwards. The cut-out simplification of planar figure schemes in the work of Paul Gauguin (1848–1903), Synthesists and Nabis as well as in the work of Henri de Toulouse-Lautrec (1864–1901) is Japanese-inspired, as are the figures clipped at the edge in the works of Manet.

Monet's great cycles of paintings – the cathedral of Rouen, the Gare Saint-Lazare, poplars and grainstacks – showing the same objects again and again in changing light conditions, are inspired by the serial paintings of Katsushika Hokusai (1760–1849) and Utagawa Hiroshige (1797–1858). Vincent van Gogh (1853–1890) loved Japanese woodcuts so much that he translated them into oils, seeking inspiration in their rhythmic linearity and planarity as he did so. Symbolism, Art Nouveau and Jugendstil are unthinkable without the influence of Japanese art.

The recognition of Japanese art as such indicates the changing consciousness of the 19th century in comparison to earlier times. It is conceivable only with an understanding of the Historicism that re-evaluates the art of earlier epochs and prepares the ground for an appreciation of primitive and naive art.

**Paul Signac**
Riverbank, Petit-Andely, 1886
Oil on canvas, 65 x 81 cm
Paris, Private collection

## Impressionism in Germany

The term German Impressionism is generally used with certain reservations. Although there was no widespread and uniform movement as there was in France, certain Impressionistic traits can be found in the works of individual artists such as Wilhelm Leibl (1844–1900), Max Liebermann (1847–1935), Max Slevogt (1868–1932), Lovis Corinth (1858–1925), Wilhelm Trübner (1851–1917) or Fritz von Uhde (1848–1911).

In the second half of the century, official painting in Germany was the preserve of society painters. Swagger portraits, history paintings in which size and pathos were equated with quality, cloying allegory, idealization and sentimentality predominated and were celebrated and purchased by a public whose taste reflected the wealth and pomp of the economic boom years known in Germany as the *Gründerzeit*. Many painters saw this as a dead end, turned their backs on tradition and academic painting and sought a fundamental renewal of art. The realism of the *plein-air* painters of Barbizon and the French Impressionists was welcomed as a stimulating source of inspiration.

**Pierre-Auguste Renoir**
Two Girls, c. 1881
Oil on canvas, 80 x 65 cm
Moscow, Pushkin Museum

Leibl, who achieved considerable early success with his highly acclaimed portraits, left his chosen home in Munich for the solitude of Bavarian village life, creating an œuvre that went against prevailing concepts of art. Influenced by Courbet and the Impressionists, he did not seek to pander to prevailing taste either in his choice of motif nor in his presentation. His portraits and the peasant paintings he created from 1873 onwards show him to be a master of acute observation (ill. p. 532).

With meticulous finesse and the calm of a still life study, he shaped his motifs and models with coloristic inventiveness from the distance of a neutral observer. He developed a subtle realism whose mordant edge is invariably softened by the brilliance of his colours. Occasionally, especially in his later works, we find Leibl moving closer to his Impressionistic sources of inspiration. His friends and colleagues included the painter Johann Sperl (1840–1914), Carl Schuch (1846–1903) and Wilhelm Trübner. Like the French Impressionists, they painted together in the open air and, like them also preferred subjects drawn from their personal surroundings and explored the outward appearance of things and their relationship to light. Schuch's still lifes and Trübner's landscape paintings may best be described as Impressionist.

Liebermann's work evolved from an almost raw realism to *plein-air* painting and an Impressionistic approach. The clear linearity of his early works dissolves increasingly as he models with light. Liebermann had a considerable influence on Uhde. Uhde's painting, which was realistic for some time, began to move towards Impressionism both thematically and technically once he gave up religious motifs around 1900.

Slevogt is frequently mentioned in connection with German Impressionism, and many of his paintings, especially his landscapes, do owe much to the Impessionist movement. His art nevertheless also contains certain naturalistic traits of the old masters that bear witness to the broad range of his artistic imagination and talent, making him difficult to classify under a single stylistic scheme.

Apart from Liebermann and Slevogt, Corinth should also be mentioned in this context. Whereas his early works are still dominated by a dark-toned palette, his colours become lighter and brighter, especially under the influence of Manet and the *plein-air* artist Jongkind, taking on distinctly Impressionistic hues. His later work, however, the rhythmic Alpine landscapes of the Walchensee region with their strongly expressive colority, and his portraits and self-portraits, have rather more in common with Expressionism.

## England – from the Pre-Raphaelites to Modern Style

The Pre-Raphaelite Brotherhood of artists was founded in England in 1848 and their aims of achieving a renewal in art were to hold sway until the advent of Symbolism and Art

**Edouard Manet**
A Bar at the Folies-Bergère,
c. 1881/82
Oil on canvas, 96 x 130 cm
London, Courtauld Institute
Galleries

Nouveau. The founding members of the Pre-Raphaelite
Brotherhood included the painter and poet Dante Gabriel
Rossetti (1828–1882), the painters William Holman Hunt
(1827–1910) and John Everett Millais (1829–1896), the
writer William Michael Rossetti (1829–1919) and the sculptor Thomas Woolner (1825–1892). Their close circle also included the painters Ford Madox Brown (1821–1893) and
Edward Coley Burne-Jones (1833–1898), William Morris
(1834–1896) and John Ruskin (1819–1900), who, as art
critic and writer, provided the literary and ideological background.

They adopted a primarily anti-academic line directed
against the official canon of Victorian art. Right from the
start, their concept of renewal included not only the field of
painting but also that of poetry. Over time the applied arts
and crafts came to be included as well – innovations in interior decoration, and even the revival of the printer's craft towards the end of the century would owe much to their endeavours. Although the aims of the group were never actually formulated in writing, they were clearly expressed in
the works of the individual artists.

New forms of presentation based on the works of the old
masters were to be used to generate authentic sentiments.
They drew their motifs from literary and religious sources,
undertook studies from nature and practised *plein-air* painting. In their treatment of fairy-tales and sagas, they became
the first to explore such thoroughly English themes as Ar-
thurian legend or tales from Shakespeare. Religious motifs
were frequently transposed to a contemporary setting – a

modern step indeed – and occasionally portrayed in a fairy-
tale or historicizing setting.

The Pre-Raphaelite faible for medieval themes and meticulously detailed landscapes also betrayed a certain affinity
with the Romantic artists. Though it is rather difficult for
us today to appreciate what appeal they could possibly have
found in the cloying sentimentality of the loving couples
that people a small proportion of their pictorial themes,
some of the Pre-Raphaelite artists, most notably Brown and
Millais, did address socially critical subjects as well. They
also dealt with allegorical and mythological material, in
which the pathos and sublime gravity of the beautiful
woman was often a dominant feature. In many of their
works, it is not difficult to trace the sources of inspiration
from art history.

From the 1870s onwards, the Pre-Raphaelites drew
closer to Symbolism, as some of their titles, such as Burne-
Jones' *The Heart of the Rose* (London, Tate Gallery), or Rossetti's *The Daydream* (Karlsruhe, Badisches Landesmuseum)
indicate. With their aims of renewing craftsmanship and interior decoration, they instigated the Modern Style that was
equivalent to Art Nouveau in France or Jugendstil in Germany.

Philip Speakman Webb (1831–1915), Rossetti and Burne-
Jones were all involved in the firm of Morris, Marshall,
Faulkner and Co., which was founded in 1861. They designed large friezes and panel cycles as well as fabrics, wall-
papers, tapestries and stained glass. Morris was particularly
inventive in creating variations on organic and floral forms,

whose sweeping, ornamental curves already anticipate the emergence of Modern Style. Later, they also turned their attention to furnishings, tiles, picture-frames and bookbindings. The idea behind the firm – unity in the arts and harmony in decorative form and function – was to emerge later in the Art Nouveau and Jugendstil movements of the continent. In Scotland, this development was represented by the work of Charles Rennie Mackintosh (1868–1942) and the artists grouped around him, and in England by the Arts and Crafts movement.

The collaboration between Burne-Jones and Morris at Kelmscott Press resulted in a series of magnificently designed book editions which were truly works of art for biblio-

**Paul Cézanne**
Boy with a Red Waistcoat, c. 1888–1890
Oil on canvas, 80 x 64.5 cm
Zurich, Stiftung Sammlung E. G. Bührle

philes. Walter Crane (1845–1915), a friend of Morris, was also a designer, a political caricaturist, and designer of posters and prints. Aubrey Vincent Beardsley (1872–1898) created numerous illustrations based on the work of the Pre-Raphaelites and inspired by Japanese woodcuts, in an œuvre with a distinct hint of decadence that embodied the *fin de siècle* spirit in a formal syntax that bore distinct affinities to Jugendstil and Art Nouveau.

## Symbolism – Fin de Siècle

As a counter-movement to the realistic and naturalistic trends in art, and diametrically opposed to the Impressionistic glorification of superficial beauty, the Symbolists brooded on an aspect of human existence that cannot be grasped by reason and rational observation: the realm of the soul, the sentiments and the imagination, which they articulated by drawing upon the ability of the individual to symbolize such immaterial phenomena and lend them form.

There have always been individual artists who condensed the unemotional allegorical language of allegory into the language of Symbolism in order to appeal to the emotions or express them. Now, towards the end of the 19th century, a distinct approach to art was emerging which had evidently been nurtured by these roots and which, without necessarily following in the footsteps of French art, spread throughout Europe and even as far as Russia. Symbolism in painting would have been unthinkable without the literary connection and the *fin de siècle* mood.

The 19th century, so enthusiastically hailed as the century of discovery, invention, science and progress, was drawing to a close and with the growing realization that these high aspirations had not been fulfilled and had failed to bring the hoped-for paradise, the disappointed hopes of a generation were channeled into a melancholy sense of the end of an era. On the one hand, it triggered an egocentric avoidance of reality and quest for oblivion and an exaggerated interest in individual personality, together with reveries on the hidden forces of life and feverishly angst-ridden lust, while on the other hand it prompted escapism in the apocalyptic pursuit of pleasure, aestheticism or mysticism.

Few artists can actually be classed as pure Symbolists. Most of them combine Symbolism with certain other stylistic features, such as Historicism, Jugendstil or Art Nouveau – and later, Expressionism – or display a strongly idiosyncratic creativity, as in the case of Van Gogh. Sigmund Freud (1856–1939), who posited the importance of the subconscious as an element of the individual's psychological make-up and explored the coded Symbolism of mood and emotion in dreams, was working at around the same time as the Symbolist movement.

The symbiotic coexistence of literature and painting is a distinctive feature of Symbolism: many artists were not only painters, but also writers. The Symbolist ideal or the narrative material was frequently articulated in words before being translated into a visual language, while the work of painters often inspired poets as well. Certain topics, frequently contradictory, were preferred by the Symbolist painters and expressed by them in ways specifically aimed at triggering emotions. Romantic motifs from fairy-tales and sagas, pathos-laden references to the world of mythology, feverish visions, lyrical relationships between man and woman, overweening sexuality and the sophisticated pleasure of eroticism, woman as demonic *femme fatale*, evil seductress, good or bad mother, elfin innocent or beguiling nymph. Sickness, death, fear, solitude as threats to the individual stood in contrast to the expectation of redemption through religion and virtue.

The means of evoking emotion and a mood charged with significance are more limited in painting than they are in literature and were handled in very different ways. Apart from using familiar allegorical symbols such as a skull, fantastic imaginary creatures were invented, the psychological effect of colours was exploited, facial expressions, gestures and poses were exaggerated and underlined by breaking down realistic proportions and dissolving the unity of time and space.

In England, the Pre-Raphaelites, following in the footsteps of Fuseli and Blake, had reintroduced symbolist elements into their painting, interwoven with historical ideas and underlined by literature. In France, the circle of painters and writers grouped around the poet Stéphane Mallarmé (1842–1898) presented their ideas in the magazine *Le Symboliste* published by Gustave Kahn (1859–1936). Pierre Puvis de Chavannes (1824–1898) placed his symbolist ideals (hope, dove) in coolly inaccessible landscapes and settings. Gustave Moreau (1826–1898) was fond of highly-charged imaginary landscapes, pompous architecture, fantastic creatures and baroquely bejewelled beautiful women as harbingers of death. Odilon Redon (1840–1916) whose graphic works were described as "strange, enigmatic, sick visions, hallucinations", developed a fragile and subtle symbolism in his later works.

In Belgium, Fernand Khnopff (1858–1921) remains the most famous representative of Symbolism. His preferred topics, inspired by Symbolist poetry, are tranquility, solitude, the deserted city, mystery and woman as Sphinx. Jan Toorop (1858–1928) and Jan Thorn-Prikker (1868–1932) represent Symbolism and Jugendstil in the Netherlands, while the Norwegian artist Edvard Munch (1863–1944) created visions of fear and menace, not unlike the works of the Symbolists, but which integrated the sweeping curves and distorted forms of Art Nouveau or Jugendstil with a highly dramatic psychological force that anticipates Expressionism. In Rome, the German expatriates Hans von Marées (1837–1887) and Anselm Feuerbach (1829–1880) and the Swiss artist Arnold Böcklin (1827–1901) looked to the classical art of Italy and ancient Rome and blended the emergent Neoclassicism with Symbolistic traits.

## Gauguin, the School of Pont-Aven and the Nabis

Gauguin belonged to the generation of painters who had already begun to regard Impressionism with scepticism. Although, for some time, he had painted Impressionistic landscapes of captivating fragility and tonal transparency, around the age of forty, he had begun to seek other forms of expression and statements for his painting. By this time, he re-

**Henri de Toulouse-Lautrec**
Jane Avril Dancing, 1892
Oil on cardboard, 85.5 x 45 cm
Paris, Musée d'Orsay

garded Impressionism as empty and meaningless, and sought an antithesis to it as a basis for his work. It was this quest that finally resulted in the compelling and forceful visual language that put him firmly on the path to modern art without ever entirely abandoning all aspects of Impressionism. Throughout his life, he loved to paint outdoors, and in his handling of large colour planes he would fragment them into a tapestry of nuances and a patchwork of varying intensity.

✔ **Vincent van Gogh**
Garden in Bloom, 1888
Oil on canvas, 92 x 73 cm
Private collection, on loan to Metropolitan
Museum of Art, New York

On his return from a journey to Martinique in 1888, he took up work again in the Breton village of Pont-Aven. Together with his younger colleague Emile Bernard (1868–1941), who admired him greatly, Gauguin developed Synthesism and Cloisonnism, a style of painting in boldly contoured, flat colour areas, derived from stained glass and *cloisonné* enamel techniques. In Gauguin's painting *The Vision after the Sermon* (Edinburgh, National Gallery of Scotland) Symbolist elements occur for the first time: from now on, his paintings are frequently charged with a religious symbolism that imbues them with higher meaning. Later, on his return to the South Pacific islands, he would transpose biblical scenes into the local setting, in an early step towards acknowledging their equality.

Together with Bernard, whose Synthesist paintings are laden with Symbolistic content, he gathered other painters around him, and this circle, which came to be known as the school of Pont-Aven, explored new concepts in painting. Gauguin himself, regarded by the members of the movement as the leader of the Symbolists, did not always adhere to the criteria of symbolic reference in his paintings. He worked on strong simplification of linearity and forms, creating images of enormous intensity, whose greatest strength lies in the impact of their colours.

Influenced by Gauguin and the Pont-Aven group, Paul Sérusier (1864–1927) gave the the Hebrew name "nabis", meaning prophets, to the association of painters he had founded in 1889. They, too, sought to counter Impressionism with a religiously mystical painting of intensive colority and decorative planarity. They saw the principles of Bernard and Gauguin as their artistic message of redemption. This group included Bonnard and Vuillard as well as Maurice Denis (1870–1943) and later Félix Vallotton (1865–1925); they were joined still later by Aristide Maillol (1861–1944) who was then a painter, and Henry van de Velde (1863–1957), who was to achieve fame primarily as an Art Nouveau architect and designer. The forum for their ideas was the *Revue Blanche*.

Symbolism had never been a predominant aspect of the group's work, which turned increasingly towards the decorative arts in the early stages of Art Nouveau. In keeping with contemporary trends, they soon began exploring the possibilities of book illustrations and posters, theatre décor and interiors. Denis concentrated strongly on religious Symbolism and in 1919 he founded the Ateliers d'art sacré (Studios of religious art). Bonnard and Vuillard left the group.

### Post-Impressionism and Pointillism

Following the achievements of Impressionism, which took pure, free painting as its aim and content, calls for a consolidation of content and form began to take hold again in art. The Impressionists had experimented with colour and with the effects of light on colour. Their findings had been gained intuitively and through observation, and were not bound by rules or regulations.

The colour theories of Charles Blanc (1813–1882) and Eugène Chevreul (1786–1889), based on chemical research, attracted considerable attention and were also adopted by artists. Pissarro had begun drawing up a theory as foundation for his painting, an experiment that never got beyond its early stages. Before recording it in writing, he abandoned the experiment, feeling that it restricted his spontaneous creativity. Georges Seurat (1859–1891) and Paul Signac (1863–1935), the main protagonists of Pointillism, also known as Divisionism, sought to make a systematic science of the Impressionist painting process. Carefully calculated dots of pure colour juxtaposed so that they would add up to an image in the eye of the observer were intended to create a precalculated impact. The motif became the vehicle for technical experimentation. Purely divisionistic paintings, however, remained considerably less effective than those of the Impressionists, for they lacked the magic of the fleeting moment.

Vuillard and Bonnard, a generation younger than the first Impressionists, followed on from the initial experiments of Impressionism, which they developed further and brought to a worthy conclusion in the early years of the 20th century. These two artists remained friends for life and even shared a studio at times. Their œuvre, not surprisingly, has many similarities. After a brief association with the Nabis, which had no major impact on their style, they took up the ideas of the Impressionists and remained faithful to them. The influence of Japanese art is undeniable, especially in their prints. Their interiors, still lifes and cityscapes bear the hallmarks of a subtle, but intoxicating enthusiasm for the miracle of colour and light, its beauty and harmony, as the quintessence of life's quiet joys.

## Van Gogh, Toulouse-Lautrec, Cézanne

Apart from Gauguin, there are three other artists, in particular, whose work paves the way towards modern painting on the basis of Impressionist achievement. They are Van Gogh, Toulouse-Lautrec and Cézanne.

Van Gogh, who said of himself that he painted everything with true passion, saw his task as an artist to strive for the good of mankind. His paintings were intended to be of significance in this endeavour. The stark simplicity of his forms and the absoluteness of his colours had an enormous impact on the generations of artists who followed him. The dynamic expressiveness of his brushwork and his planar distortion of perspective to the point of negation constitute major steps towards 20th century painting. The Symbolism of his colours and motifs arose from his individual mood and situation, but nevertheless make a universal statement to the viewer that goes far beyond the mediation of aesthetic values, opening a window on a psychological view.

Toulouse-Lautrec elevated the sketchy, the unfinished and the fragmentary to the level of a stylistic principle in his paintings at around the same time as Rodin's sculptures were establishing the torso as an independent motif. In many of his paintings, Toulouse-Lautrec comes very close indeed to dissolving form and space to the point of abstraction. He ignored class differences and hierarchies, seeking his motifs in the aristocratic circles into which he had been born as well as in the *demi-monde* he chose to frequent. He saw the beautiful, the ugly and the vulgar and he interpreted it in a way that went far deeper than a mere social or character study; his form of presentation was capable of arousing an understanding far removed from aesthetic exaggeration, sympathy or social criticism. With subtle psychological empathy, he stylized typical features, creating an astonishingly modern image of individuals and their daily lives by means of laconic reduction and strong, expressive colours.

Cézanne is frequently referred to as the father of modern art. From the very beginning of his artistic career, he sought to achieve more than his contemporaries, the realists and Impressionists. Though he strictly rejected Neoclassicism, he saw himself as a classical artist; he sought to express a universal and timeless truth, based on his exploration of the fun-

**Paul Gauguin**
When will you marry? ("Nafea faa ipoipo?"), 1892
Oil on canvas, 101.5 x 77.5 cm
Basle, Öffentliche Kunstsammlung Basel, Kunstmuseum,
Rudolf Staechlin'sche Familienstiftung

damental principles of painting. He regarded narrative, idealist and symbolist factors as detrimental. He invariably worked from nature, seeking to capture the essence without creating a mere reproduction of what he saw. In his analysis of the relationship between colour, form, light and space, he gradually achieved a unity of drawing, colour and forms of presentation that paved the way for Cubism and abstraction. He modelled and modulated with colours and colour values. Gradually, the classical perspective disappeared from his compositions and he constructed objects, volumes and space on the basis of painterly interpretations of basic geometric patterns and forms.

## Jugendstil – Art Nouveau – Modern Style – Secessionism

These various terms, current in Germany, France, England and Austria respectively, have not been applied to painting for quite as long as they have actually existed. Originally, they belonged to the field of applied arts and crafts. In the last two decades of the 19th century, applied arts, crafts and interior decoration achieved artistic heights that made them the main bearers of creative design. A kind of prototypical Art Nouveau initially emerged amongst the Pre-Raphaelites in England, and went on to influence the paintings as well as in the boldly structured posters and illustrations of Crane. Beardsley worked as a draughtsman and illustrator. His works may be regarded as important documents of a refined Art Nouveau, in which object and ornament are playfully interwoven to the point of illusion.

The continental art of the poster is superbly represented in the work of Bonnard, Toulouse-Lautrec and Alfons Maria Mucha (1860–1939). The most characteristic features of Art Nouveau are the unsymmetrical curve which lends vitality to the ornament (occasionally with a leaning towards abstraction), floral forms and geometric variations. Frequently, the assimilation of Japanese elements is also evident. In the painting of the turn of the century, which can be regarded according to this stylistic aspect, symbolistic content is coupled with the fluid ornamental forms of Art Nouveau.

Ferdinand Hodler (1853–1918) and Giovanni Segantini (1858–1899) in Switzerland, van de Velde in Belgium, Toorop and Thorn-Prikker in Holland, Max Klinger (1857–1920) and Franz von Stuck (1863–1928) in Germany were the leading proponents of an art in which Symbolist content merged with the formal syntax of Art Nouveau.

In the last two decades of the 19th century, in Paris, Berlin, Munich and Vienna, Secessions were founded. The Secessions were organizations based on anti-academic principles uniting all artists who had no truck with conventional artistic tradition and the accepted canons of art. Having no fixed programme, they were in favour of the realization of new, unconventional and free artistic ideas. After the turn of the century, it was the artists of the Secession who paved the way for Expressionism and related stylistic directions.

In Vienna, the Secession is closely linked with Jugendstil. Indeed, it is used to refer to everything associated with the Viennese Art Nouveau, which reached its scintillating zenith in the work of Gustav Klimt (1862–1918). His figures, mostly women, are presented against an abstract background, swathed in mystery and ornament. His colours range from subtle nuance to sumptuous oriental magnificence, on radiant gold backgrounds. Egon Schiele (1890–1918) overcame the dominant aestheticism of his paintings to achieve a tensely expressive illumination of his motifs. In doing so, he broke away from Jugendstil and forged a link to Expressionism.

(The descriptions on pp. 496 bottom, 497 bottom, 507f., 518 bottom, 519 bottom, 539 bottom and 541 top were written by the editor)

# EDOUARD MANET
## 1832–1883

Manet's *Déjeuner sur l'herbe* or *Luncheon on the Grass,* as it is sometimes known, caused a scandal in 1863. Rejected by the official Paris Salon, together with almost 3,000 other paintings submitted, it was then exhibited at the instigation of Napoleon III in the Salon des Refusés. *Déjeuner sur l'herbe* was the most controversial painting in an exhibition of works rejected by the Salon jury and therefore unlikely to meet with public praise. Several of the works shown at that exhibition are today the pride of many a major museum. Though Manet was acknowledged as a talented artist on the basis of his skilled draughtsmanship and his mastery of perspective, his choice of motif – two fully clothed men in the company of a female nude outdoors – met with utter incomprehension and earned him accusations of decadence and bad taste. The public was outraged not only by the provocative way in which his naked model looks directly at the viewer, but also by the fact that the artist did not trouble to cloak the scene in the guise of some allegorical title.

Manet struck upon the idea for this painting on a Sunday outing to Argenteuil, on the banks of the Seine. When he decided to capture the peaceful artistic idyll in a painting, he was already aware that he would be torn to pieces on grounds of the subject matter. Nevertheless, the idea obviously appealed to him so strongly that he set about conscientiously working out his design. Having taken the Spanish masters as his source of inspiration for a long time, he now turned to Italian art, and sought to create a modern version of Giorgione's *Concert Champêtre* (ill. p. 164). Because the motif is drawn directly from the immediate personal environment of the artist, critics refer to Manet's work as Pre-Impressionist, while the technical execution of the painting is Neoclassical in style.

Emile Zola, a friend of Cézanne since his youth, had always taken a keen interest in painting. He was particularly enthusiastic about the work of the artists rejected by the official art critics, and in 1866 he wrote an article about Manet, who had been rejected by the Salon jury yet again, claiming him to be a master of the future, whose path would lead straight to the Louvre. In order to express his thanks for the article, Manet proposed making a portrait of the critic. Zola was 27 years old at the time. His writings document that he sat for Manet in the artist's studio in February 1868. Manet presented Zola in an environment that characterizes his personality, his life and his profession. He is seated at a desk, on which Manet has arranged a busy still life of books, inkwell and other utensils – including the brochure Zola had written in Manet's defence. The book Zola is holding in his hand is very probably *L'Histoire des Peintres* by Charles Blanc. To the left behind the writer we can see part of a Japanese screen, and above him, in a frame, a sketch of Manet's *Olympia* – another painting Zola had defended in his writings – and a Japanese woodcut.

Edouard Manet  *Déjeuner sur l'herbe,* 1863
Oil on canvas, 208 x 264.5 cm
Paris, Musée d'Orsay

Edouard Manet  *Portrait of Emile Zola,* 1868
Oil on canvas, 146.3 x 114 cm
Paris, Musée d'Orsay

**Edouard Manet**
Luncheon in the Studio, 1868
Oil on canvas, 118 x 154 cm
Munich, Bayerische Staatsgemälde-
sammlungen, Neue Pinakothek

**Edouard Manet**
Argenteuil (The Boating
Party), 1874
Oil on canvas,
149 x 115 cm
Tournai, Musée des
Beaux-Arts

# EDOUARD MANET
1832–1883

This breakfast scene – the subject of widely
varying interpretations over the years – was
in fact originally conceived as a representation
of a studio, as an X-ray of the painting has
shown. In its original state, the grey back wall
had a typical studio window with metal spars.
The figures, who seem to have no relation to
each other, have also been clearly identified.
The young man in the foreground is Léon
Koëlla-Leenhoff, who is thought to be Manet's
son. For some time, Monet was the model for
the cigar-smoking man at the table, but in the
final version it is Auguste Rosselin, a student
friend of Manet from the Gleyre and Couture
studios. The woman with the silver coffee pot
is a housemaid and not, as was previously believed, Madame Manet.

 This painting also includes a number of
still life features reminiscent of Netherlandish
compositions of the 17th century: the arrangement on the checkered table cloth and the
weapons on the left are typical studio props.
The black cat, often a feature of Manet's work,
adds a certain intimacy to the painting.

Monet lived in Argenteuil, Manet spent his
summers in nearby Genevilliers, Caillebotte
lived in Petite Genevilliers and Renoir also
joined them frequently. It was here, under the
influence of Monet, that Manet began to explore the possibilities of *plein-air* painting. *Argenteuil* or *The Boating Party* may well be one of
the paintings created in this way. It is certainly one of the most Impressionistic of
Manet's paintings in terms of the handling of
light, colour and atmosphere. Rudolph Leen-
hoff was his model here. The identity of the
female figure is unknown.

Manet found his inspiration for the painting
*The Balcony* in 1868 during a visit to Boulogne-sur-Mer. The arrangement is a transposition of Goya's *Manolas on the Balcony*. For this
painting, whose chief appeal is the superb use
of only a few colours, three friends of the family stood model, sometimes finding it quite tir-
ing. The figures of the three young people
emerge against a dark background, in which
the outline of a servant with a water-jug can
just be discerned. The man standing with a
cigar in his hand is the landscape painter Antoine Guillemet. He is wearing a deep purple
tie that seems almost luminous against the
white of his shirt. The woman beside him in a
white dress with an emerald-green silk parasol
and a white, green-edged hat is the violinist
Fanny Clauss. In the foreground, dreamily
leaning against the balcony railing is the
painter Berthe Morisot, seated on a black stool
wearing a white voile dress. Next to her is a
white plant pot with purple rhododendrons.

**Edouard Manet**
The Balcony, c. 1868/69
Oil on canvas, 170 x 124.5 cm
Paris, Musée d'Orsay

# EDGAR DEGAS
## 1834–1917

**Edgar Degas**
The Gentlemen's Race: Before the Start, 1862
Oil on canvas, 49 x 62 cm
Paris, Musée d'Orsay

**Edgar Degas**
Dance Class at the Opéra, 1872
Oil on canvas, 32 x 46 cm
Paris, Musée d'Orsay

Degas was fascinated by the atmosphere of the racecourse, which was very much a part of "la vie parisienne" and the meeting-point of elegant society, the *demi-monde* and ordinary citizens in search of entertainment. The racecourse paintings that constitute such a significant part of Degas' œuvre were created on the basis of many *in situ* studies.

Here, the painter has chosen the position of an observer at the start, just before the race. The gentlemen riders (as opposed to professional jockeys) form the dominant group in the foreground. The impression of spontaneous immediacy is created by a portrayal in the manner of a snapshot in which the riders are shown in relaxed pose, further heightened by the apparently arbitrary way in which the front right edge of the painting is cut off. The riders in their garishly coloured tricots and the well-groomed horses have an almost sculptural presence, whereas the background is matt, diffuse and extremely reduced: the row of viewers, the green and rolling meadow and an industrial area which, in spite of its smoke stacks and slagheaps, is by now means bleak or gloomy, under a hazy sky.

In the world of the theatre, it was the young ballet girls in their little tutus, their satin shoes and bows that Degas observed at rehearsals and performances. He created innumerable variations on this motif in oils, pastels and as sculptures. In this painting, he gives us a glimpse of the rehearsal room at the Paris Opéra. The ballet master has just interrupted a young dancer. He is leaning on the stick he uses to tap out the beat and explain corrections, and is giving instructions to the gracefully posed girl in front of him with a gesture that calls for discretion and subtlety in the passage they are rehearsing at the moment. A violinist, who provides the melody and tempo, is sitting waiting by his music stand. The other girls of the *corps de ballet* are taking note attentively or are practising at the barre.

Degas himself often frequented cafés. In his younger years, he preferred the Café Guerbois, later the Café la Nouvelle-Athènes at Place Pigalle. It was here that he was inspired to paint his portrait of Desboutins and the actress Ellen Andrée known variously as *In a Café, The Absinthe Drinker* or, quite simply, *Absinthe*. This painting of two people sitting side by side yet in total isolation is a virtuoso psychological portrait that conveys the different moods of the figures with great precision but without pathos. Desboutin, in bohemian dress, drawing on his pipe, gazes sceptically into the interior of the café which the viewer cannot see. The woman, resigned and lost in thought, is lost in solitary thought, contemplating the glass with the drink that will bring oblivion.

**Edgar Degas** Absinthe, 1876
Oil on canvas, 92 x 68 cm
Paris, Musée d'Orsay

# CAMILLE PISSARRO
## 1830–1903

**Camille Pissarro**
Red Roofs (Village Corner, Impression of Winter), 1877
Oil on canvas, 54.5 x 65.6 cm
Paris, Musée d'Orsay

The Louvre acquired this small-scale work as part of the bequest of Caillebotte, a friend and patron of the Impressionists. The painting is one of the earliest Impressionist motifs by Pissarro. It shows a few houses in a humble little village at the foot of a hill, surrounded by fields, orchards and bushes, under a strip of blue sky.

Only the leafless trees give us some indication of the time of year. It is a winter day without snow.

The landscape is bathed in sunshine and the red roofs of the houses are echoed in the red of the earth, the distant trees and bushes. The individual parts of the painting are merged in small, rapid brushstrokes, and the texture of the paint and the brushwork are easily recognizable.

The intertwined branches, the uneven ground, the roofs and the chimneys are consolidated by the play of light on the colours in a charmingly natural way. The artist thus captures only the momentary impression of a a brief and specific instant, while the precise location of the village is of lesser importance. Like Cézanne, with whom he had a long friendship that benefited both, Pissarro loved simple and unaffected rural motifs.

**Camille Pissarro**
The Old Marketplace in Rouen and the Rue de l'Epicerie, 1898
Oil on canvas, 81 x 65 cm
New York, The Metropolitan Museum of Art

In 1894, Monet painted his famous series of twenty views of the cathedral of Rouen, capturing its appearance at various times of the day and in various light conditions. Sisley had attempted a similar series for the Gothic church of his home town of Moret. Pissarro, on the other hand, studied the effect of different times of day on the thronged boulevards of Paris. In Paris, modern life as he sought to chronicle it was easier to portray than elsewhere. Nevertheless, he made several journeys to Normandy, to Dieppe and Rouen, in order to paint street life from his hotel windows. Here, too, he produced cycles of paintings and sought to sublimate the harmony of a cityscape entirely in its colourity, creating a new, interactive tonality.

In this painting of Rouen, the bustling old marketplace seems to channel the crowd into the Rue de l'Epicerie which leads into the maze of streets in the historic heart of the town. The carefully considered composition draws the viewer's gaze far into the pictorial space. Numerous breaks and tiny details arrest the gaze, making it sweep anew over the façades. The towers of the cathedral seem to float above the picturesque roofs of the houses.

Nevertheless, for all the medieval romanticism of the scene, Pissarro makes it quite clear in a few laconic details, such as the advertising posters on a house wall, that modern life has taken firm hold in the town. The writer Octave Mirbeau had nothing but the very highest praise for this painting: "Here, life is invoked, the dream ascends, floating, and what seems so simple and so familiar to our eyes is transformed into an ideal image."

## ALFRED SISLEY
### 1839–1899

This painting was executed at a time when the hard core of the Impressionist group – Monet, Sisley, Pissarro and Renoir – frequently painted together outdoors. It was a time when the main principles of their painting had already been determined by constant observation, experimentation and discussion. These artists often chose to portray the same motif, preferring to work outdoors in order to capture aspects of nature and landscape or characteristic features of particular seasons which had aroused their visual curiosity. It is a period when the works of Monet, Pissarro and Sisley bear a close stylistic resemblance, as they were produced according to the same principles. Cityscapes and landscapes were frequent themes during this period.

*The Flood* was a particularly fascinating natural phenomenon for Sisley; in his painting, he does not portray the tragic effects of the flood, nor the inconvenience it caused to those affected by it, as Emile Zola, his contemporary and close friend of the Impressionists was to do, so realistically and dramatically in his novel *L'inondation* ("The Flood"). Sisley has chosen to portray the moment when the clouds have begun to clear from a pale sky which casts its light onto the flooded banks and streets of Marly, shimmering bright and golden with the reflections of sunlight on the water.

**Alfred Sisley**
The Bark during the Flood, Port Marly, 1876
Oil on canvas, 50.5 x 61 cm
Paris, Musée d'Orsay

A lapse of twenty years lies between these two paintings. We can see that Sisley's love of simple, rural motifs has not altered during this time. In his depiction of this view of a small town near Paris, his brushwork seems to have changed little, though it has perhaps become a little finer. Throughout his life, Sisley preferred to live in the country, where he could lead a simple and modest life. The famous and often lyrically evoked light of the Ile-de-France, the light of changing days and seasons, the experience of natural elements, sky, clouds, water, snow – it was this that he sought to capture in his paintings. The landscapes themselves, the villages, bridges, streets and rivers, meant more to him than a mere occasion to set up his easel. Yet in his limited choice of motifs – Sisley seldom painted interiors, portraits or still lifes – he created an œuvre that faithfully documents France's rural charms. There are no factories here, no city sounds, but no labouring peasants either. What comes across most strongly is the tranquility of the landscape.

A skilfully structured composition draws the gaze along the bridge and into the picture. The scattered figures and the horse and cart are mere staffage. Our gaze is drawn directly into the centre of the picture, where the white walls of the mill break the line of flight of the bridge. Sisley intended to convey an impression of calm tranquillity in his balanced distribution of the groups of houses, the river and the trees, spanned by a mild, blue sky.

**Alfred Sisley**
The Bridge of Moret, 1893
Oil on canvas, 73.5 x 92.5 cm
Paris, Musée d'Orsay

**Claude Monet**
The Red Boats, Argenteuil, 1875
Oil on canvas, 60 x 81 cm
Cambridge (MA), Fogg Art Museum, Harvard University

**Claude Monet**
Le Pont de l'Europe, Gare Saint-Lazare, 1877
Oil on canvas, 64 x 81 cm
Paris, Musée Marmottan

# CLAUDE MONET
## 1840—1926

Monet's painting of *The Red Boats, Argenteuil* indicates that he has already, by this time, reached the point of concentrating entirely on the principles of free Impressionistic painting. He explores the luminosity, radiance and shimmering light in its interaction with matter. He is not interested in the structure of matter or its characteristics, but in surface appearances and the way they change under the effect of light. Monet's light is gentle and mild. He explores the finest nuances of shimmering objects. Water, sky, smoke, clouds, boats, houses and trees merge here to evoke a summer idyll that exudes an air of calm and invigorating freshness. Monet dedicated his œuvre to capturing fleeting moments of appearance, which he himself described as "impressions".

Monet never ceased to be fascinated by the way in which one and the same object, one and the same place, could change under differing light conditions, and he never tired of observing and portraying his motifs in different conditions. Haystacks, poplars, his beloved waterlilies, the façade of the cathedral of Rouen and the Gare Saint-Lazare in Paris are just a few such motifs. Monet may well have adopted the idea of creating cycles of paintings from the world of Japanese art, which he collected, and which was a rich source of inspiration to him. The steam of a locomotive, otherwise regarded as a nuisance, is transformed here by Monet's brush into a beautiful bearer of light. It blends with the pale light of the sky and lies like a shimmering silken veil over the railway tracks and the façades of the houses. At the Impressionist exhibition of 1877, Monet showed seven variations on this theme.

Monet's *Women in the Garden* was created at a time when he had already turned his back entirely on academic painting and was well on the way towards Impressionistic painting. Light, which was to become the focus of his œuvre, already plays an important role in this painting. The group of women in summerdresses, enjoying the delights of a flower garden, is portrayed by the artist as though glimpsed by some chance observer of whom they are unaware. Light, shadow and half-shadow create magical reflexes on their hair, their skin, their sumptuous, light dresses, on the blossoms and leaves, and on the path. None of the women is shown here as in a portrait; instead, Monet has captured the atmosphere of a happy summer day. This large canvas was painted in the studio, and apparently posed a considerable challenge to the artist. One of his models was his wife. The relatively dark palette, so typical of his early works, still bears some of the hallmarks of classical inspiration and the masters of the school of Barbizon.

**Claude Monet**
Women in the Garden, 1867
Oil on canvas, 256 x 208 cm
Paris, Musée d'Orsay

**Claude Monet**
The Waterlily Pond, 1900
Oil on canvas, 90 x 92 cm
Boston (MA), Museum of Fine Arts

**Claude Monet**
Waterlilies (Green Reflections), c. 1916–1921
Hall I, detail of the east wall
Oil on canvas, 200 x 850 cm
Paris, Musée de l'Orangerie des Tuileries

# CLAUDE MONET
## 1840–1926

Monet had lived with his large family in Giverny since 1883. There, he dedicated himself daily to creating the fairy-tale garden which Marcel Proust once said was as dear to him as a favourite wife to a king. He had plants sent to him from all over the world, and liked to spend his time by the waterlily ponds. The waterlilies themselves, which he affectionately called *Nénuphars* were a constant source of pleasure to him.

He chose his motifs with an inner tranquillity reminiscent of oriental contemplation, from which he drew his visual sensitivity and acute awareness of the finest nuances of almost imperceptible changes. Nature, for him, was not red in tooth and claw, but a quiet, shimmering beauty, manifested in the landscape, flowers, trees, water, sky, clouds and snow.

Monet loved all that was plant-like, slow and languorous; he was captivated by the phenomena of the changing seasons and weather conditions, and he had the peace of mind to spend hours watching blossoms open and close, observing hoarfrost come and go, or the changing appearances and reflections of snow, rain and ice.

His meditative observation of objects and his meditative contemplation of colour blending with light, is fundamental to his art. This explains why all of Monet's paintings have an air of harmony, and why most of them are imbued with calm serenity.

Monet painted the Japanese bridge in his garden many times, with the waterlilies below it, the reed-covered banks, the exotic bushes and trees, all in the shade of magnificent weeping willows. The bright summer light bathes the scene in dancing reflections.

*Nymphéas*, shimmering waterlilies on shimmering water: this is the key theme of his later work. Monet's attitude towards his waterlilies became almost religious in the last years of his life. In 1916, he had a particularly large and airy studio built for him and began work on nineteen monumental canvases of waterlilies, to which he dedicated several years, finally bequeathing them to the French state in 1922 through the mediation of his friend Clemenceau. Since 1927, they have been on permanent display in the Musée de l'Orangerie, where they are a deeply moving source of pleasure to visitors. They completely fill the walls of two large halls, giving the visitor the impression of standing on an island surrounded by waterlily ponds.

Monet's waterlily paintings in the monumental *Nymphéas* cycle culminate in a virtual dissolution of naturalistic form. They are a hymn to colour and light. Nevertheless, for Monet, they do not represent a step towards total abstraction, for they are not intended as something abstract, but as something spiritual, requiring neither firm contour nor strictly delineated form.

# HENRI FANTIN-LATOUR
## 1836–1904

Fantin-Latour, whose superb still lifes are a highlight in many museums and collections, is frequently mentioned in the same breath as his contemporaries and friends, the Impressionists. At the Musée d'Orsay, the museum of Impressionism in Paris, he is represented by a number of group portraits showing the French *avant-garde* intellegentia of the day and a few still lifes. Nevertheless, he never was a true Impressionist. He spent many hours in the Louvre, where he studied and copied the old masters, and his work bears eloquent witness to this training, without forgoing its distinctiveness.

Fantin-Latour's still lifes echo the classical sublimity and dignity of the great French, Italian and Spanish artists who influenced him. The structure of his *Nature morte dite aux fiançailles* could well have been inspired by Zurbarán. A few objects are arranged on a table against a pale background of a single colour. A white china dish of ripe strawberries, with pale red cherries and a single strawberry in the foreground, next to it a blue and white china vase with a magnificent bouquet, to the right of that a white camelia with shining green leaves and behind it a glass of red wine. The painting has an air of cool dignity and sublime aesthetic elegance.

Henri Fantin-Latour
Still Life ("Aux Fiançailles"), 1869
Oil on canvas, 32 x 29.5 cm
Grenoble, Musée de Peinture et de Sculpture

# BERTHE MORISOT
## 1841–1895

Like Mary Cassatt, Berthe Morisot was one of the few women artists who were active members of the Impressionist circle. She had undergone a long and comprehensive training and her works subtly indicate the influence of Corot, Jongkind, later of Manet and Renoir. Although she often exhibited with the Impressionists, she did not play as important a role within the group as Monet, Renoir or Pissarro, for she was not actually instrumental in furthering the movement. Nevertheless, her works were highly esteemed and, in spite of her assimilation of Impressionistic principles, they have their own highly distinctive style. She sat as a model for Manet on several occasions, and is one of the figures in his painting *The Balcony* (ill. p. 493). In 1874, she married Manet's brother Eugène.

This intimate interior showing a young woman in *déshabillé*, sitting at a table and powdering her face at a tilted mirror, unites all the typical features of Morisot's painting. Her own outward appearance is said to have been distinctly feminine, graceful and gentle, and her works also have something of these qualities. Delicate, contrasting tones are used to depict this young woman in her boudoir, and light is used to model the scene gently. Morisot's strength lay in her ability to present her models as contemplative without falling into the trap of banality or sentimentality.

Berthe Morisot
Young Woman Powdering
Herself, 1877
Oil on canvas, 46 x 38 cm
Paris, Musée d'Orsay

**Pierre-Auguste Renoir**
The Painter Sisley and his Wife,
1868
Oil on canvas, 105 x 70 cm
Cologne, Wallraf-Richartz-
Museum

# PIERRE-AUGUSTE RENOIR
## 1841–1919

There is a the continuity in Renoir's œuvre in which we can recognize not only his strongly distinctive personal style, but also his eagerly experimental exploration of a wide variety of compositional approaches. In fact, he actually started out as a painter of porcelain and the brilliant radiance and luminosity of his colours certainly reflect that early training.

*The Painter Sisley and his Wife* is an early work dating from a period when he and his friends were beginning to move towards an impressionistic style. The overall structure of the composition with its large-scale figures is still very much in the traditional mode, with the devoted couple expressing their bond in a rather awkward gesture of affection, portrayed in considerable detail and faithful portraiture. The background, however – a garden or park bathed in light – is already distinctly Impressionistic. The choice of motif – scenes and figures from his own immediate environment – also indicates that, even at this early stage, he was already on the way towards pure Impressionism.

Renoir himself liked to frequent the taverns and nightclubs of Montmartre, and he was a frequent guest at the Moulin de la Galette, which had a large garden for dining, drinking and dancing in summer. It was an unpretentious and popular place, rarely visited by society ladies.

Renoir observed the predominantly young clientele of the Moulin de la Galette as they enjoyed their Sunday leisure, dancing, drinking, seeing and being seen, chatting and relaxing. In the foreground, seated at a table, is the writer and critic George Rivière, a friend of the artist and a major supporter of the Impressionists.

*La Première Sortie* gives what appears to be a chance glimpse into a box at the opera, where two pretty young women are sitting, looking down onto another theatre-box below them.

The main figure is seen in profile, with her face turned slightly away from the painter, who has captured the charming contrast of her youthful fresh pale complexion, her reddish hair, her dark dress and the light blue and mauve of her hat and lace at a moment when she is looking down into the lively audience in the other theatre-boxes. Large colour planes and contours dissolve in a vibrant shimmer of light and colour. The atmosphere of intimacy in the foreground theatre-box and the teeming vitality of the opera audience who are not there simply for the pleasure of culture alone, has been wonderfully captured in this painting.

**Pierre-Auguste Renoir**
Bal au Moulin de la Galette, 1876
Oil on canvas, 131 x 175 cm
Paris, Musée d'Orsay

**Pierre-Auguste Renoir**
La Première Sortie (The First
Outing), c. 1876/77
Oil on canvas, 65 x 49.5 cm
London, Tate Gallery

# PIERRE-AUGUSTE RENOIR
## 1841–1919

Pierre-Auguste Renoir
On the Terrace, 1881
Oil on canvas,
100 x 80 cm
Chicago (IL), The Art
Institute of Chicago

Although Renoir's œuvre went through a
number of different stylistic phases, it always
remained true to the modern direction, as an
art based on visual experience in which the artist himself selected the motifs and their pictorial organization on the basis of his own aesthetic criteria. Renoir never wanted anything
ugly in his paintings, nor any dramatic action.
He found his inspiration in his immediate environment, in nature and landscape. Landscape
interested him only when it was enlivened by
the vitality of spring and summer, perhaps by
the colours of autumn. Unlike his Impressionist friends, he never painted snow, hoarfrost or
ice, all of which he considered ugly. This lends
all his paintings an atmosphere of peace, tranquility, relaxed serenity and charming beauty
echoed in the combination of colours, nuances
and dissonances.

Renoir's entire œuvre is dominated by the
depiction of people. He found his models in
the studios of the artists, amongst his friends,
in the environs of Montmartre where he lived
for many years and in the high society he studied and scrutinized and which inspired him
to his aesthetic compositions.

In the painting, *On the Terrace*, in front of a
wrought iron railing, we see a young woman
in a dark blue dress, with her little daughter
dressed in white beside her. The woman is
wearing a red hat with a bouquet of poppies
and a posy on her chest, while the little girl's
straw hat is garnished liberally with blossoms.
The woman's hands are calmly folded on her
lap, and she is smiling amiably, apparently enjoying the calm of a fine day in the country.
The intensive colours of this peaceful group in
the foreground are echoed in the basket of
brightly coloured skeins of wool and in the
green pot of plants. Looking into the background, we see an overgrown area of bushes
and trees in blossom, and a riverbank bounding the bright band of glittering water. Sky,
houses, water and trees are all painted in delicate colours which lend the scene a radiant
aura.

*Bathers* gave Renoir an opportunity of exploring variations on the theme of the female
nude, a motif to which he returned time and
time again. This *Bather with Long Blonde Hair*
is seated on a light-coloured cloth, her legs
crossed, displaying the charms of her ample
young body, the freshness of her pale complexion and the healthy blush of her lips and
cheeks, and the beguiling mane of reddish-
blond hair that flows down to her hips. This
unapologetic homage to beauty underlines
once again one of Renoir's primary working
principles: only to paint what seemed to him
serene, beautiful and appealing.

Pierre-Auguste Renoir
Bather with Long Blonde
Hair, 1895
Oil on canvas,
92.7 x 74.3 cm
Vienna, Kunsthistori-
sches Museum

# FRÉDÉRIC BAZILLE
1841–1870

It is a hot summer day. Some young men are taking a refreshing dip in the cool blue water of a pond, others are relaxing in the shade of a tree. Some are undressed or in the process of undressing, most of them are wearing bathing trunks. Two young men are wrestling on the meadow. The lush green grass with a few shady trees, a gently rolling landscape in the background and the hint of a village, under a radiant blue sky in which white summer clouds drift along, provides the setting for this calm and carefree scene.

Bazille has drawn the motif from his own environment in his own day, and what he has recorded in his painting is very probably based on personal experience. The handling of light and shadow already indicates the move towards Impressionist techniques, while the figures of the young men, their various actions and postures suggest a precise study of motion and the intention of incorporating this into the composition, are features more reminiscent of realism. The handling of colour is also early Impressionist. The organization of the theme – a comparatively trivial motif for the prevailing taste of the time – is a far cry from the ideals of Salon painting.

**Frédéric Bazille**
Bathers, 1869
Oil on canvas, 158 x 159 cm
Cambridge (MA), Fogg Art Museum,
Harvard University

# GUSTAVE CAILLEBOTTE
1848–1894

Although the Impressionists were his friends and although he exhibited with their group, Caillebotte did not adopt their principles and techniques lock, stock and barrel, preferring instead to retain his own distinctive style. In this large canvas of a Paris street scene, Caillebotte's intentions are quite evident.

The artist has captured a chance moment, an everyday motif, with neither pose nor artificial sublimity. In this respect, his painting is very much in the spirit of Impressionism. He draws the viewer into a typical street scene, showing the spacious and – at the time this painting was executed – extremely modern architecture and urban planning of Baron Haussmann. At the time, the cobbled streets were still the preserve of horse-drawn carriages and pedestrians. Nevertheless, the painting is strictly organized in a carefully conceived structure of horizontal and vertical zones. The foreground has extraordinary clarity and smoothness, with painstaking attention to detail. The figures walking with umbrellas are painted with the precision of portraiture and every object in the foreground is meticulously rendered with sharply delineated contours. Towards the background, however, the painter has adopted more impressionistic means, introducing slight unclarities.

**Gustave Caillebotte**
Paris Street: A Rainy Day, 1877
Oil on canvas, 209 x 300 cm
Chicago (IL), The Art Institute of Chicago

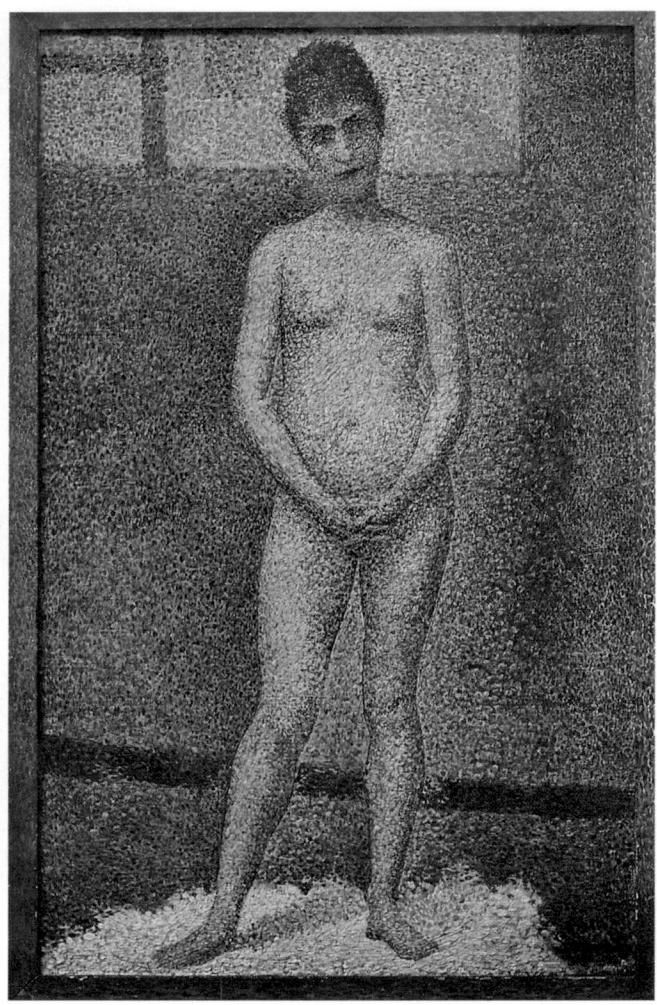

**Georges Seurat**
Model, Front View, 1887
(study for "The Models")
Oil on panel, 26 x 17 cm
Paris, Musée d'Orsay

**Georges Seurat**
Bathers at Asnières, c. 1883/84
Oil on canvas, 201 x 301.5 cm
London, National Gallery

# GEORGES SEURAT
## 1859–1891

Seurat based his painting firmly on theory, believing that Impressionism had exhausted its possibilities and required a complete renewal. He studied not only the writings of painters and art philosophers, but also the theories of chemists and physicists: Charles Blanc, Eugène Delacroix, Eugène Chevreul, Ogden Rood, David Sutter. For his own theoretical treatises, he adopted entire passages from the books that had influenced him.

Seurat was the main protagonist of Post-Impressionism, also known as Neo-Impressionism, as his works followed on from the paintings of the Impressionists. He gathered a group of artists around him who adopted his theories and worked in the manner he had developed.

The main foundations of his pictorial conception were the chemical and physical findings of colour studies and colour theories, which he sought to transpose to the field of painting without any regard for the fact that these were very different media indeed. Seurat's painterly ideal was to break down the colour plane and lines into dots of contrasting colours or complementary colours in close juxtaposition. This stylistic direction, which was also adopted by his friend Signac, was known as Divisionism, and the painterly technique of dots or points was known as Pointillism.

At a distance from the painting, the myriad dots are intended to add up in the eye of the observer. This theory does not quite work in practice, as Seurat's paintings invariably have a shimmering, dancing effect of oscillating dots of colour. On the basis of the theories posited by Humbert de Supervilles, he integrated his own guidelines of positive and negative effects of specific colours, of horizontal and vertical dominance, and of rising and falling lines. This manner of painting, in which technique clearly dominates the handling of colour, permits only specific results. Nothing is left to chance, to the spontaneous artistic idea, to experimentation or imperfection.

In terms of colour handling, the possibilities are also restricted; there are no gentle transitions and no sharp contrasts, no drastic emphasis or de-emphasis, no voids, and no precisely detailed portrayals.

It is for this reason that *Bathers at Asnières* does not have the light-hearted atmosphere of a hot summer day that has drawn people to the riverside. The divisionistic method has robbed the figures of their individuality, just as it has in the nude female study for *The Models*.

The atmosphere and appeal that gives the Impressionist paintings their charm are incalculable, for they have their roots in creativity itself, and Seurat has failed to take into account the profound significance of this. Occasionally, Seurat actually broke his own rules and painted in an unorthodox manner.

Seurat worked on this painting for more than two years. When he presented it to the public for the first time at the eighth and last Impressionist exhibition in May 1886, he was immediately hailed as the most important painter in a new generation of artists. The painting was like the statement of a manifesto and this, together with its huge format, made it the hotly debated centrepiece of the exhibition.

The painstaking preparation involving no less than sixty-two sketches in oils which he then put together in his studio in a precisely calculated composition, corresponds to the extremely precise and detailed application of the tiny dots of paint. Depending on the object to be portrayed, the paint is applied in a variety of ways: the dabs of paint are superimposed crosswise to achieve the green of the grass, while they are applied in horizontal layers for the water. The colours are reduced more or less to the basic tones. Nuances are created by varying the distance between the dabs of colour: lilac, for example, is created by juxtaposing red and blue. The lines in the painting are also created by delineating colour areas or by creating contrasts.

All the forms have been reduced to simple, stereometric bodies distinctly separated from their respective surroundings. In his schematic handling of form, Seurat may be regarded as a forerunner of cubism.

In painting a summer day in a park full of people, Seurat chose a topic that had also been popular amongst the first generation of Impressionists. He showed the bourgeoisie of Paris on a weekend excursion to an island in the Seine between Neuilly and Courbevoie, to the west of the Bois de Boulogne, where there were restaurants, cafés and dance-halls and meadows, and where it was possible to hire boats or go fishing. At first glance, it appears as though Seurat has captured a fleeting moment of an ordinary day, in the manner or Renoir. Yet the careful positioning of the forty or so figures, void of all individuality and strangely rigid in their distribution throughout the pictorial structure, indicates the highly structured and theoretical character of this painting. The everyday world has been integrated into an almost classical framework of verticals and horizontals, which give the picture its stability. The Pointillist technique has been extended through to the frame, so that even the painting itself is distinctly separated from its surroundings.

Seurat lived only five more years after exhibiting the *Grande Jatte*. An attack of diphtheria forced him to give up *plein-air* painting. He withdrew to his studio and painted exclusively interior scenes, such as *The Models*, which he used as a vehicle for portraying the work of the artist with his models. Other motifs included music-halls and circus scenes.

**Georges Seurat**
Sunday Afternoon on the Island of La Grande Jatte, 1884–1886
Oil on canvas, 206.4 x 305.4 cm
Chicago (IL), The Art Institute of Chicago

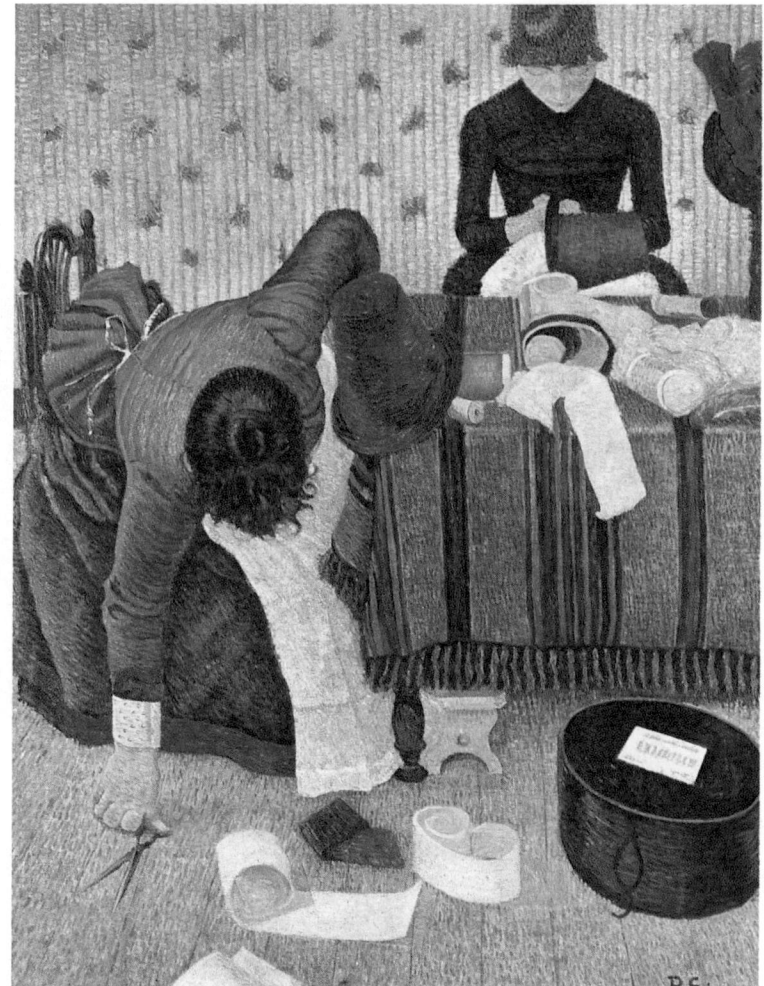

**Paul Signac**
Two Milliners, Rue du
Caire, c. 1885/86
Oil on canvas,
111.8 x 89 cm
Zurich, Stiftung Sammlung
E.G. Bührle

**Paul Signac**
The Port of Saint-Tropez, 1907
Oil on canvas, 131 x 161.5 cm
Essen, Museum Folkwang

## PAUL SIGNAC
### 1863–1935

The early work of Paul Signac was strongly influenced by Monet and Sisley, and it was his
friendship with both these painters that led
him to develop his first Impressionistic phase.
A wealthy man with no financial cares, he
painted incessantly and was personally committed to the advancement of contemporary
*avant-garde* art. Through his friendship with
Caillebotte, he became an enthusiastic yachts-
man. In June 1884, he met Seurat and, under
the influence of this new artistic friendship, he
increasingly integrated structural compositions into his paintings. From around 1885,
he identified so strongly with the ideas propagated by Seurat that he also began painting
in a strictly Divisionistic style and creating
purely Pointillist paintings.

*The Milliners* shows how well Divisionist
theories can be applied to the portrayal of interior scenes. Here, Signac has endeavoured to
overcome a number of compositional problems
at the same time. The milliner who is bending
down to pick up the fallen scissors is presented
in extreme foreshortening – a device intended
to add depth to the pictorial space. This is contrasted by the flatness of the still life featuring
a hatbox, rolls of felt and fabric in the lower
right-hand corner. The even application of
short brushstrokes for the tablecloth and wallpaper is interrupted in the portrayal of the
rounded forms, such as the back of the woman
bending down and the hatbox. This device fa-
cilitates the portrayal of corporeal volumes.
The scene itself is familiar from a number of
Impressionist paintings. However, in contrast
to, say, one of Degas' women ironing, the atmosphere of a fleeting moment captured on
the canvas is secondary to the controlled handling of colours and forms. In spite of the technical similarities, Signac's palette has always
been more generous and fresh than the increasingly gloomy and rigid colorism of Seurat.

Signac's book *D'Eugène Delacroix aux néo-im-
pressionnistes* published in 1889, in which he
presents the history of the Pointillist movement and the scientific foundations of his theories, is an important document of Pointillist
theory. Signac shared libertarian and even anarchist convictions with his friends Félix Fé-
néon and Maximilien Luce, which placed him
in constant opposition to bourgeois conventions. After Seurat's death, Signac decided to
continue his school and keep alive his artistic
memory.

In 1892, he discovered the picturesque port
of Saint-Tropez, which he portrays here, as in
many other paintings, using the Pointillist
technique so characteristic of his work. From
this point in time onwards, he stopped composing his paintings directly from the motif,
but merely took notes instead and thus liberated himself gradually from the self-imposed
doctrines of strict theory. His style became
more relaxed and free, and his compositions
more picturesque.

# PIERRE PUVIS DE CHAVANNES
## 1824–1898

Apart from his major mural cycles and the mordant caricatures published after his death, Puvis de Chavannes also created a large number of panel paintings with religious and allegorical themes. Together with Moreau and Redon, he belongs to the Symbolist movement, whose aim it was to lend expression to the realms of the imagination, fantasy and magic. The motif of *The Poor Fisherman* is one he treated several times, the best known version being this one, which hangs in the Musée d'Orsay.

On the banks of a quietly meandering stream, we see a humble little boat, in colours as grey and earthy as the stoney tongue of land bordering the brackish water. Only a few scattered shrubs grow on the land. A woman, presumably the fisherman's wife, is kneeling to pick flowers, and near her lies a small child asleep. The boat is reflected in the still waters of the river that stretches to the horizon, bounded by dark, flat land, and the sky in the background has the same melancholic, dull colours as the river. At the front of the boat, a net has been attached to a tilted mast and dipped into the river. Behind it, in humble attitude, his hands folded as if to pray, stands the bearded fisherman with his eyes closed.

**Pierre Puvis de Chavannes**
The Poor Fisherman, 1881
Oil on canvas, 155 x 192.5 cm
Paris, Musée d'Orsay

# GUSTAVE MOREAU
## 1826–1898

André Breton said of the beguiling charms and corrupting decadence of Moreau's female figures that "This type of woman has probably concealed all others from me; it was complete enchantment. The myths rekindled here as nowhere else have had their effect. She is the woman, who almost without any external changes becomes, in turn, Salome, Helen, Delilah, Chimere or Semele, shaping herself into these different embodiments." In his motifs and in his painterly technique, Moreau consciously turned away from reality, lending form to dreams of morbid eroticism, mystically fascinating death and pathos-laden suffering.

*The Apparition* is placed in an architectural setting which might equally be a church, a temple or a palace. The background remains unclear, like a relief carved in sonorous, russet tones with a paucity of light reflexes, almost swallowing up the outlines of the sketchy figures in their rigid poses.

Only the apparition itself has a sculptural presence: the bloody, decapitated head of John the Baptist, eyes wide open and staring at Salome, surrounded by gleaming rays of light, and Salome herself, her nudity veiled in a diaphanous robe, dripping with gold and jewels. Her arm and her gaze are directed imperiously towards the victim whose death she has caused.

**Gustave Moreau**
The Apparition (Salome),
c. 1875
Oil on canvas, 142 x 102 cm
Paris, Musée Gustave Moreau

**Paul Cézanne**
The Card-Players, c. 1885–1890
Oil on canvas, 47.5 x 57 cm
Paris, Musée d'Orsay

# PAUL CÉZANNE
### 1839-1906

Cézanne defied the wishes of his father, a banker, in order to become an artist. The role of misunderstood outsider, however, was to remain with him all his life, even as an artist. His difficult, uncompromising character and his self-doubts, nurtured by the high standards he set for himself and the quality of his art, frequently drove him into isolation and spawned works which, from today's point-of-view, make him the father of modern art.

His interest focused, often for years at a time, on a few key themes which he frequently repeated. It was not unusual for him to rework his paintings over lengthy periods. Cézanne regarded the work on each new version as an attempt to gain new and progressive aspects from his painting. *The Card-Players* presents a topic he was to treat no less than five times in the course of the 1890s.

Throughout his long friendship with Pissarro, he had explored the possibilities of *plein-air* painting and Impressionism. Pissarro proved a sympathetic mentor and sought only to encourage Cézanne, whose artistic prowess he had fully recognizad. Cézanne benefited from their collaboration. He adopted a new, lighter approach to colour and a stronger brushstroke and developed a lasting love of *plein-air* painting and landscape.

Two simple peasants, slightly awkward, are seated opposite each other, completely immersed in their game of cards. A bottle of wine on which the light is reflected forms the central axis. This structure gives the composition an almost geometric stringency and order, as well as a timeless atmosphere. Although the subject matter itself is Impressionistic, the painting has a density, strength and gravity that goes well beyond the Impressionist aesthetic.

Cézanne had abandoned conventional ways of seeing and the spatial organization of central perspective in his paintings. Instead, he created a non-illusionistic pictorial space in which a new planar dimension is won by means of colour and its modulation.

He liked to work on still lifes, arranging the objects at will in positions permitting detailed studies. It was on this basis that he developed his distinctive means of expression. He preferred using apples and oranges in his still lifes for the very simple reason that they did not perish quickly, as he often spent a considerable time working on each painting.

In his *Still Life with Apples and Oranges* specific objects (in this case dishes, fruit and a jug) are juxtaposed in a picture plane with hardly any depth. The vibrant colour contrasts and graduations give the painting a deceptive hint of a naturalistic portrayal. Almost ironically, this impression is offset by the considerable abstraction of the pictorial space achieved by deliberately displacing the planes and fields of colour in a way that densifies the composition, creating a sense of reality all its own.

Cézanne's creative endeavours invariably involved certain self-imposed tasks and creative challenges that dominated his motifs. He produced a series of portraits, including self-portraits and figural compositions of models. For each of these paintings, a great number of sittings were required. The physiognomical similarity, however, played only a secondary role.

In his own invariably highly critical self-reflections, the painter noted that he had not achieved as much in portraiture as he had in other genres. Today, we might be tempted to regard this as an unjustified sense of inferiority or insecurity. In fact, the identity of the people he painted at close quarters is not the main problem. Cézanne's portraits are not character studies. In fact, he uses them, as he uses all his objects, to explore the rules of painting he has established for himself.

*Woman with Coffee Pot* is an example of Cézanne's pictorial reality and the new concept of space gained in the previous years. He admired Courbet as a realist and also considered himself a realist. Nevertheless, he did not seek to give a photographic rendering of the essential features and characteristics of his models or motifs (he saw each of his motifs as something imbued with a constantly changing vitality) but sought instead to construct truth creatively by his own means. The quiet strength of this woman and her simple, stylized physiognomy characterize the kind of person for whom time is a static dimension — as in *The Card-Players*. In her motionless pose, the woman is as much a part of a still life as the cup and the coffee pot on the table beside her.

Paul Cézanne
Still Life with Apples and Oranges, c. 1895–1900
Oil on canvas, 74 x 93 cm
Paris, Musée d'Orsay

Paul Cézanne
Woman with Coffee
Pot, c. 1890–1895
Oil on canvas,
130.5 x 96.5 cm
Paris, Musée d'Orsay

## PAUL CÉZANNE
### 1839–1906

Paul Cézanne
Les grandes baigneuses (Large Bathers), c. 1895–1904
Oil on canvas, 127.2 x 196.1 cm
London, National Gallery

The motif of *Bathers*, in which figural compositions are merged with landscape was a concept
that fascinated Cézanne right from the start of
his artistic career. Many versions, some of
them in large formats, were created over a
lengthy period. One critic, having seen the *Reclining Bathers* (1875/76), dubbed the painter a
radical. Although this was intended as an insult, it nevertheless contained an element of
truth. With each new version of his bathers,
Cézanne forged on in a direction that involved
not only a radical break with the traditional
possibilities of painterly presentation, but also
meant turning his back on the prevailing ultra-
modern trends of the day, seeking to overcome
them and create paintings of timeless value. In
doing so, he paved the way for subsequent
generations of painters. He deliberately structured his paintings so that they would not
appeal superficially to the fleeting viewer,
radically banning all decorative, anecdotal
elements which might detract from the true
essence.

The nude female bodies of the *Large Bathers*
have not been included in the picture because
of their female charms, as some almost sarcastic details would indicate. The group is reduced, both in body and posture, to elements
too true to life to appear stylizad. This is already a step on the way towards abstraction.
Cézanne handles space in much the same way,
with depth playing no major role in the spatial organization. Abstractive and already abstract formations take over the function of specific landscape details, giving the painting
enormous tension and density.

The Mont Sainte-Victoire is a central motif in
Cézanne's œuvre and one that he painted repeatedly from a number of diffferent angles,
analysing it artistically. The mountain, which
dominates the Provencial landscape, was to be
a recurrent motif in the œuvre of this artist,
particularly in his later years, and one which
allowed him to test and explore his own laws
of painting.

Cézanne subjected each and every brushstroke to the merciless scrutiny of his analytical mind, seeking a unity of colour, composition, planarity and tectonics. He sought to
underpin his experience and experiments theoretically. Although he painted only by observation, using models, and often in the open
air, he sought neither to achieve a static rendering of what he had seen nor to capture a fleeting glimpse.

"Everything we see disperses, disappears.
Nature is always the same, yet nothing of its
visible appearance remains. Our art must lend
nature the sublimity of duration, with the elements and the appearance of all its changes.
Art must make nature eternal in our imagination. What is behind nature? Nothing, perhaps. Or perhaps everything."

Paul Cézanne
Mont Sainte-Victoire Seen from the Quarry at Bibémus, c. 1898–1906
Oil on canvas, 65 x 81 cm
Baltimore (MD), The Baltimore Museum of Art

## ODILON REDON
1840–1916

Redon was, in his day, a completely isolated figure who stood like a stranger in his era, distantly linked at most to writers like Edgar Allan Poe or Charles Baudelaire. Born at the same time as the first generation of Impressionists, he did not share their artistic style. His art has no impressionistic approach. There is no dominance of colour or line, but a synthesis of both, for they exist side by side in his compositions.

After he had exhausted the possibilities of his lengthy Symbolistic phase, he began to devote his attention to floral paintings, watercolours and pastels. The change coincided with the advent of a new century, and followed a trip to Venice which deeply impressed Redon. The demons of his Symbolistic visions now began to make way for an air of serene tranquillity, as evidenced most clearly in the many variations of his floral still lifes.

In this flat composition, the spatial organization may only be understood in terms of visual experience. The decorative alignment of the vases and their contents, bouquets of flowers which cannot necessarily be identified, alongside easily recognizable types, dominate the composition. The three vases and their contents seem to emerge without location out of an incandescent surrounding to unfurl their many-coloured charms.

Odilon Redon
Still Life (Flowers), c. 1910
Oil on canvas, 73 x 54 cm
Wuppertal, Von der Heydt-Museum

## HENRI ROUSSEAU
1844–1910

With no artistic training, and without respect for traditions or the painters who had gone before him, driven solely by his wish to paint only the works he imagined, Rousseau represents the type of artist who draws his inspiration entirely from the powers of his own lively imagination and individuality. He serenely ignores classical compositional structures. His lack of technical skill is offset by his disarming improvisation, creating images of elementary force that are nurtured by the unspoiled originality of his ideas. Rousseau's fascinating appeal lies in the immediacy with which he organizes his frequently heavy and cumbersome forms, his carefree symbolic language and the unspoiled freshness and luminosity of his colours.

His painting *War* was preceded by a lithograph already containing the main elements of the composition, which took on a colossal force of expression and density in the oil-painting. The galloping, black horse takes up almost the entire width of the painting, leaving the fallen beneath it. Black birds of death have lighted upon the dead and dying, drawing on their blood, as they lie on the charred black earth. The horse is the bearer of war with its flaming torch and sword, symbol of the ineluctable madness of war.

Henri Rousseau
War, 1894
Oil on canvas, 114 x 195 cm
Paris, Musée d'Orsay

**Paul Gauguin**
Tahitian Women (On the Beach), 1891
Oil on canvas, 69 x 91.5 cm
Paris, Musée d'Orsay

**Paul Gauguin**
Breton Peasants, 1894
Oil on canvas, 66 x 92 cm
Paris, Musée d'Orsay

## PAUL GAUGUIN
### 1848–1903

Gauguin arrived in Tahiti in June 1891 and, after a brief stay in Papeete, withdrew to a secluded part of the island as yet unspoiled by civilization and colonialism. There, he lived amongst the natives, "far from those prisons of European houses," in a Maori hut which "never banishes people nor severs them from life, from space, from infinity." He painted daily, and worked on carved sculptures and reliefs, taking his motifs from the everyday life and spiritual world of the islanders to whom he now felt a closer bond than to his own origins.

In the strong Maori women, Gauguin discovered a beauty nurtured by other sources than that of European women. He admired their unspoiled naturalness, their strength, their pride, their dignity and the nonchalance with which they took it upon themselves to work hard or enjoy relaxing and doing nothing. He found the lifestyle of the islanders, their religion, their morality and their inextricable involvement in their rich, natural surroundings considerably more attractive and purer than life in Paris and he completely submerged himself in their world.

On his return from the South Seas in 1894, Gauguin visited Brittany once again to paint there. An exhibition of the paintings he had created on Tahiti was mounted at the Galerie Durand-Ruel. It was a total failure. Throughout his life, Gauguin would always be plagued by financial cares. Nevertheless, he worked on relentlessly, and his new paintings – like the *Breton Peasants* in their traditional costumes with the starched white caps – also reflect his Tahitian experience. The painting still bears certain elements of Cloisonnism – stark contours, bold, flat planes of colour – but it is dominated by the delicate magic of Gauguin's colours. The figures of the women are simplified and stylized in their postures, gestures and facial traits. The right half of the painting is bordered by large grey rocks flanking the pale path and by a copse in strangely delicate colours, while the left side of the painting shows a view onto green fields and a group of buildings.

The title of this painting is a symbolic translation of a situation in which reality merges with the realms of the imagination. Two native women, dressed only in loincloths, with blossoms in their hair, are sitting side by side – one of them in lotus position – surrounded by grey clouds, exotic flowers and sumptuous vegetation. Behind them, like a magician, or perhaps like someone spellbound, sits a man in a lilac robe, with fiery red hair, whose physiognomy is similar to that of the painter Meyer de Haan.

**Paul Gauguin**
Contes barbares (Barbarian Tales), 1902
Oil on canvas, 131.5 x 90.5 cm
Essen, Museum Folkwang

**Henri de Toulouse-Lautrec**
Two Women Dancing at the Moulin Rouge, 1892
Oil on cardboard, 95 x 80 cm
Prague, Národni Galeri

# HENRI DE TOULOUSE-LAUTREC
## 1864–1901

Toulouse-Lautrec spent much of his time exploring the haunts of Paris night-life with its
twilight pleasures and it was here that he
sought the inspiration and motifs for his work.
He did not see this *demi-monde* through the
eyes of his own social class, but through the
eyes of a man for whom all barriers of class difference had long since fallen. He reports without the complacent superciliousness of one of
higher social standing, but he also avoids the
pitfall of sympathy and false sentimentality.
With subtle empathy, he translates his observations into realistic images charged with atmosphere and creates character studies that give a
lively insight into their respective situations.
Colour in all its nuances and graduations is
the main vehicle of expression for Toulouse-
Lautrec.

The painting of two women dancing
together shows a detail of the lively night-life
at the famous Moulin Rouge in Montmartre,
where Toulouse-Lautrec was a frequent guest
and for which he created a series of magnificent posters. In the foreground we see the
dancing women. Behind them is a railing that
sections off a larger, crowded room where
guests are seated at tables. The dancing
women are dressed simply in plain dark
dresses and hats. The woman on the right
with the rather masculine traits often stood
model for the artist for his Moulin Rouge
paintings. The women are preoccupied with
each other and their dance. They are part of
the Moulin Rouge scene where bourgeois morality holds no sway, where high society and
the proletariat merge, where simplicity and
vice exist side by side.

Toulouse-Lautrec had a keen eye for such
detail and a talent for portraying life as it was
lived. For him, all are equal – the top-hatted
dandy, the intellectual, the worker, the elegant
cocotte and the servant girl. On the right in
the painting, he has shown the painter Charles
Conder, and on the left, François Ganzi. The
woman in the red jacket is Jane Avril, the
singer and dancer who became world-famous
as a figure on Toulouse-Lautrec's paintings and
posters.

The actor Henry Samary belonged to the ensemble of the Comédie-Française. Here, he is
portrayed in full figure on the stage in the role
of Raoul Vaubert in a popular comedy. He is
in fashionable dress, with French jacket, lace
cravat and collar and black patent leather
shoes, his top hat in his hand, the very epitome of the Parisian dandy.

The clowness, Cha-V-Kao, an onomatopoeic
name meaning something like "noise and
chaos" (which was exactly what her performances at the circus and music-hall caused)
frequently stood as model for the artist. Here
she can be seen as a blowsy, ample figure, sitting on the sofa of her dressing room, wearing
a funny white wig. The contrast of dominant
colours, brilliant yellow, quiet lilac, red and
turquoise, lends the scene a spontaneous vi-
vacity.

Henri de Toulouse-Lautrec
Henry Samary, 1889
Oil on cardboard, 74.9 x 51.9 cm
Paris, Musée d'Orsay

Henri de Toulouse-Lautrec
The Clowness Cha-U-Kao,
1895
Oil on cardboard, 64 x 49 cm
Paris, Musée d'Orsay

# HENRI DE TOULOUSE-LAUTREC
## 1864–1901

Henri de Tou-
louse-Lautrec
The Toilette, 1896
Oil on cardboard,
67 x 54 cm
Paris, Musée d'Orsay

The painting *The Toilette* is one of a number of female nudes by this artist. It shows a young woman sitting on the floor with her back to the viewer. Ignoring the rules of classical perspective, the artist conveys the room and setting from an elevated standpoint, with objects overlapping and juxtaposed to create the atmosphere.

The young woman with her red hair caught at the nape of her neck is sitting in a relaxed pose on a rug with a light garment wrapped around her hips, her right leg still stockinged. On the two wicker chairs in front of her are her crumpled clothes, and between them stands a bluish bathtub. The painter portrays his model as though looking over her shoulder just as she is taking a rest, without striking any pose.

Irrespective of whether Toulouse-Lautrec used oil-paints, pastels or the lithographic technique in which he was so consummately skilled, he invariably preferred a matt surface, which heightened the cool luminosity of his colours, his bold and unusual tonality and his forceful brushwork. Like so many of his pictures, this too has a touch of unfinished sketchiness.

This glimpse into the salon of a brothel in the Rue des Moulins is less sketchy. In the translucence of the clothing in which the lightly dressed women ply their wares, Toulouse-Lautrec had nevertheless used the possibilities of the incomplete to reveal their wan flesh. The tired faces of the women are portrayed with unflattering candour, but nevertheless with kindness and sympathy. The dusty pomp of the velvet furnishings exudes a tired and hackneyed charm. The wide sofa keeps the spectator at a distance, under the scrutinizing and almost pitying gaze of the elderly lady with the chignon, who is the madam of the establishment.

Toulouse-Lautrec would sometimes spend weeks in this brothel, sketching and painting the life of the prostitutes there. Because of his physical disability, he felt rejected by aristocratic and bourgeois society; sickness and disgust with life made him seek refuge amongst the exploited and the disdained. With his paintings of the *demi-monde*, he documented the hidden side of bourgeois civilization, which sought to indulge in vice only in specially secluded places and denigated physical love to the level of a business transaction. His paintings stand in stark contrast to the works of the academic and Symbolist painters who were his contemporaries, or to the illustrations of, for example, the novels of Huysmas, which barely conceal their voyeuristic attitude. Toulouse-Lautrec counters the hypocritical allegories of the day by casting an almost clinical eye on the life of the social outcasts with whom he identified.

Henri de Toulouse-Lautrec
Interior in the Rue des Moulins, c. 1894
Oil on canvas, 111.5 x 132.5 cm. Albi, Musée Toulouse-Lautrec

# EDOUARD VUILLARD
1868–1940

Vuillard has been described as an "intimist". This applies not so much to the way he portrays his figures, for he never actually violates the intimacy of his models in his paintings, but to his choice of motifs and models, which he invariably sought in the immediate surroundings of his own life. In this respect, at least, he has much in common with the Impressionist choice of motifs.

Vuillard's life and work were always inextricably linked, and he constantly portrays the same subjects and models, his environs, his close circle of friends, impressions of the few journeys he made. Although, like Bonnard, he belonged to the nabis group of artists, his works do not necessarily bear the hallmarks of their style, nor can any links with Symbolism be detected. He was an independent and rather reclusive artist.

This portrait of his friend and colleague Toulouse-Lautrec shows the artist dressed in bright yellow, baggy trousers and a red shirt with a red-and-white kerchief, and a jaunty little hat on his head, standing at a table and glancing over in the direction of his portraitist. Vuillard, who invariably portrayed his surroundings with great empathy, has conveyed an image of Toulouse-Lautrec as a stocky and affable character and has played down his disability.

**Edouard Vuillard**
Portrait of Toulouse-Lautrec,
1898
Oil on cardboard, 39 x 30 cm
Albi, Musée Toulouse-Lautrec

# MAURICE DENIS
1870–1943

Maurice Denis is regarded as the theoretician of the group of young artists who called themselves the nabis. His most famous statement is also regarded as one of the fundamental tenets of modern art: "A picture – before being a warhorse, a female nude, or some anecdote – is essentially a flat surface covered with colours assembled in a particular order."

The radicalism of this statement is not fully realized in his early work. Admittedly, the colours, like the lines, are painstakingly selected in accordance with ornamental considerations, and the painterly means already anticipate the decorative curves of Art Nouveau. This gives the painting a rhythmically structured planarity, but the artist has not yet taken the step of dissociating colours and forms from the object portrayed.

The theme of this painting is influenced by the *Sacred Grove* motif adopted from antiquity by Puvis de Chavannes. Denis, however, has transposed the motif of *The Muses* entirely into contemporary life: here, the muses have become mortal. Under the strictly stylized trees, a young girl is sharpening her crayon; she is the goddess of painting. Another looks up from her book; she is the goddess of poetry. This contemporary treatment of ancient mythology and the stringent stylization make this painting appear both ambivalent and enigmatic.

**Maurice Denis**
The Muses, 1893
Oil on canvas,
171.5 x 137.5 cm
Paris, Musée
d'Orsay

Pierre Bonnard
At the Circus, c. 1879
Oil on canvas, 54 x 65 cm
Paris, Private collection

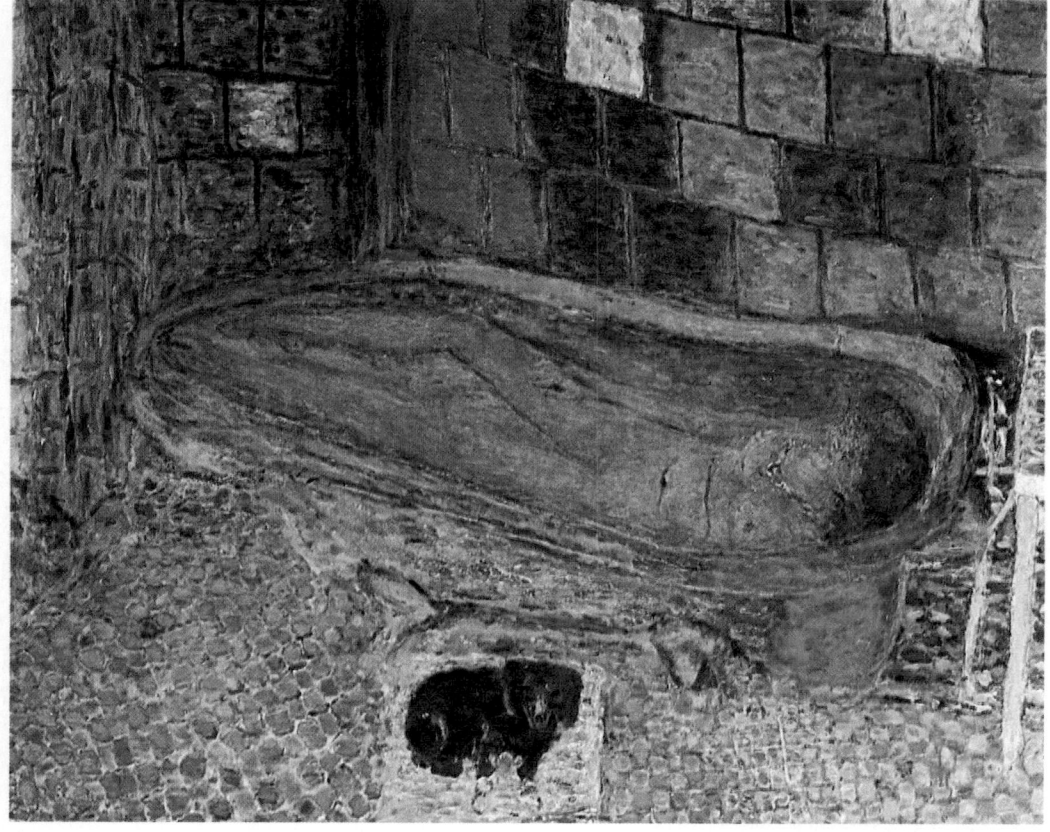

Pierre Bonnard
Female Nude in the Bathtub, c. 1938
Oil on canvas, 122 x 151 cm
New York, The Museum of Modern Art

# PIERRE BONNARD
*1867–1947*

All of Bonnard's paintings express a certain *joie de vivre*, and seem to be full of sheer enjoyment at the events and occurrences life brings. His profound admiration for Monet and Renoir prompted him to continue along the path paved by the older generation of Impressionists. Like many of his contemporaries, Bonnard also encountered the strong influences of Japanese art which was imported in large quantity to Paris at the time, and he also closely studied the works of his contemporaries Gauguin and Cézanne.

Having painted continuously for some sixty years of his long life, Bonnard left us a rich œuvre that reflects a number of different stylistic trends – Post-Impressionist works as well as those influenced by Art Nouveau and by East Asian art. Nevertheless, his own distinctive style predominates throughout and his rendition of sensual perception remains very much in the foreground. He does not narrate, analyse or moralize. He merely conveys what he has selected from the wealth of his surroundings, coloured by his own personal way of seeing. A peaceful serenity permeates his motifs, and a sense of joy is conveyed in his sumptuous mosaics and tapestries of delicate colour and form.

The circus was a welcome event in an era before the age of entertainment overkill and one people could look back on with pleasure. Circus motifs are frequent in painting. Bonnard, Toulouse-Lautrec, Picasso and other artists treated themes from the famous Médrano circus and the Cirque d'Hiver.

Here, we see a detail of the circus ring with the anonymous grey mass of viewers and an artiste in a pink tricot with a tutu riding on a dappled horse, painted in a strangely alienating shade of green. A red-coated rider in black trousers and a black top hat is galloping across the foreground on a white horse, and next to him we see part of a figure in black with red headgear. The forms and details have been deliberately executed in bold brushstrokes to give even greater vibrancy to the individual colour areas.

In this much later female nude which could, however, just as easily be mistaken for an early work, Bonnard creates a kaleidoscope of shimmering and luminescent colour areas. A young woman lies naked in a bathtub filled with water which is standing on a blue and gold mosaic-tiled floor. The reflections of light on the water and on her skin vie with those to be seen on the wall. Light, gold, blue, orange, lilac, pink, and a few daubs of bright red shimmer side by side in a visual symphony that is a delight to the eye. The young nude body seems to merge completely with the dominant colours and light.

# VINCENT VAN GOGH
## 1853–1890

In 1888, van Gogh moved to the south of France, where the landscape, the light and the people of the Provence brought him a sense of happiness that triggered an almost feverish burst of activity on his part. He saw in everything around him a vibrant beauty that moved him deeply, it was a beauty he had not encountered in the previous places that he had painted – whether at be his Netherlandish home, Paris, the Île-de-France, as northern France.

The Langlois bridge near Arles was a motif van Gogh painted several times (Otterlo, Rijksmuseum Kröller-Müller; Cologne, Wallraf-Richartz-Museum; Paris, private collection). In this version, he has chosen a position close to the bridge, on a grassy and reedgrown strip of the left bank. A bark, tiled on its side and filled with water, is moored at a little jetty built into the river, where a group of women is busy at their washing.

The entire painting is filled with the bright, crystalline light of the Mediterranean. The hazy blue of the sunny sky is reflected in the water of the river, its surface rippled by the washerwomen's work. The solid masonry of the bridge creates a horizontal framework. The draw-bridge construction is light and pale against the sky, as are the smouldering red trunks and branches of the leafless poplars. A two-wheeled covered wagon is crossing the bridge. Reeds grow on the river bank, and on the left we see a strip of the fertile red soil of the Provence. It is a painting that conveys all the hope and strength of a spring day.

Van Gogh's love of Mediterranean light and colour constantly drew him outdoors and many open air works were created by him during this period. The plain of La Crau with Mont Majour in the background is another motif he treated frequently. He found it invigorating to paint a landscape that Cézanne, whom he deeply revered, had also known. Unfortunately, the admiration was not mutual and Cézanne was quite unmoved by van Gogh's work.

In this painting, van Gogh guides the viewer's eye with masterly skill in handling of perspective, across the ripe harvest fields to the distant mountains and the vibrantly blue summer sky. In shimmering reflections, the light dances on the waving fields of grain, the fences and hedgerows, the carts and houses.

Van Gogh was fascinated by the art of Japanese woodcuts and this is clearly reflected in his work. He believed that the contrasts of Japanese prints could be heightened in their intensity by the use of oil-paints. A delicate touch of East Asian charm certainly comes across in both paintings. Van Gogh himself called his beloved landscape "my provençale Japan".

Vincent van Gogh
The Langlois Bridge at Arles, 1888
Oil on canvas, 54 x 65 cm
Otterlo, Rijksmuseum Kröller-Müller

Vincent van Gogh
Harvest at La Crau, with Montmajour in the Background (Blue Cart), 1888
Oil on canvas, 73 x 92 cm
Amsterdam, Rijksmuseum Vincent van Gogh, Vincent van Gogh Foundation

Vincent van Gogh
The Artist's Bedroom in Arles, 1889
Oil on canvas, 73 x 92 cm
Chicago (IL), The Art Institute of Chicago

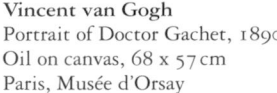

Vincent van Gogh
Portrait of Doctor Gachet, 1890
Oil on canvas, 68 x 57 cm
Paris, Musée d'Orsay

# VINCENT VAN GOGH
## 1853–1890

Van Gogh's bedroom in the Yellow House he rented at Arles gives us a precise document of his simple abode. Only the bare necessities were there: a bed, with some hooks for his clothes behind it, two chairs, a small wooden table, some paintings on the wall. For the artist, however, it was a place of promise and the first place he could call a home of his own. Although the shutters are closed, the room is flooded with a bright light that lets each object appear with all the force and clarity of its colours. In the crowded perspective with its characteristic slight distortions, the painting also reiterates van Gogh's belief, expressed in a letter to his brother Theo, that "colour expresses something in itself, one cannot do without this, one must use it;…the result is more beautiful than the exact imitation of the things themselves."

The Parisian homeopathic doctor and psychiatrist Paul Gachet was a close friend of the artist. He had a small practice in Paris that brought him little pleasure and in his free time he painted and etched, and was not without talent. Gachet was a patron and friend to many artists, including Pissarro and Cézanne, and was one of the first to purchase their paintings. In 1952 Dr Gachet's son bequeathed this major collection to the French nation. Dr Gachet had agreed to look after van Gogh in Auvers-sur-Oise after his discharge from the asylum at Saint-Rémy. Vincent lived there in an attic room above a café and spent much of his time at the doctor's house.

Soon after his arrival, Vincent expressed a wish to paint the doctor's portrait. Pensive, almost careworn, with a slight hint of scepticism, his pale face, framed by blonde hair and topped by a white cap, stands out against the blue of the jacket and background. The artist felt a distinct affinity between the doctor and himself, of whom he said that he was "at least as nervous as I am".

Van Gogh spent some time painting the flowers in the doctor's garden before he began to explore the little village and its surroundings. The late Gothic village church sits like a plump and brooding hen on a small rise spanned by a blue summer sky. It is surrounded by green grass and sunlit paths, and the blue of the sky is reflected in the broad windows with their fine tracery. At the edge of the painting, we see the houses and trees of the village. A peasant woman is making her way towards them. Although this is one of his last works, it betrays nothing of the deep despair that finally drove van Gogh to take his life. A calm tranquillity lies in this painting. The force of the colours and the decisive brushstroke seem to be anchored in the redeeming principle of hope.

Vincent van Gogh
The Church at Auvers-sur-Oise, 1890
Oil on canvas, 94 x 74 cm
Paris, Musée d'Orsay

**Johan Barthold Jongkind**
The Maas at Maassluis, 1866
Oil on canvas, 33 x 47 cm
Le Havre, Musée des Beaux-Arts

# JOHAN BARTHOLD JONGKIND
## 1819–1891

This Dutch, artist whose work is rooted in the great artistic tradition of his home country, and who dedicated himself primarily to landscape painting, was to become a key figure in French painting rather than in Dutch painting. He lived in France from 1846 onwards and it was here that he found the inspiration that liberated his painting from the technical and coloristic heritage of the 17th century masters. Light tonality and a deliberate dissolution of line and contour appear initially in his watercolours, later in his oil-paintings as well. He is rarely accorded the recognition he deserves as a forerunner of Impressionism, which he anticipated with his *plein-air* painting.

His choice of motif and his structuring of the horizontal plane – a low horizon, broad stretches of water with boats, and a narrow strip of land – certainly place this painting firmly within the Netherlandish landscape tradition. In formal terms, however, it already uses the new structural elements that Jongkind was to pass on to the young Monet and his friends: expressing the motif through the qualities of light, reiterating a brief and fleeting moment, strong brushstrokes without firm delineation, capturing reflections on surfaces. His invariably small-format paintings were the first impressionistic landscapes.

**Fernand Khnopff**
I Lock my Door upon Myself, 1891
Oil on canvas, 72 x 140 cm
Munich, Bayerische Staatsgemälde-
sammlungen, Neue Pinakothek

# FERNAND KHNOPFF
## 1858–1921

Towards the end of the 19th century, Belgium, and most notably Brussels, was an important centre of the artistic *avant-garde*. Symbolist art, in particular, was well represented in this period. Khnopff is one of the great masters of Belgian Symbolism. He was a member of the groups L'Essor, Les XX and Libre Esthétique and enjoyed an international reputation. He frequently adopted motifs from Symbolist literature, for example from the works of Maurice Maeterlinck and Emile Verhaeren, as the themes of his paintings. *I Lock the Door upon Myself* is the seventh line of a poem by Christina Georgina Rossetti, sister of the English painter Dante Gabriel Rossetti.

This narrow, horizontal painting is executed in delicate, translucent colours, in which a pearly and by no means gloomy grey is predominant. A red-haired woman with grey eyes is leaning dreamily in front of a stage-like background: it is a "picture within a picture" that gives a glimpse into a monastery garden on the right, and a view of a locked grey door in the middle. The atmosphere is vaguely melancholic, reminiscent of Khnopff's enigmatic cityscapes at night, and contains such Symbolistic signs as the withered red lilies, the poppy, and the blue-winged head of Hypnos.

# JAN TOOROP
1858–1928

This painting, whose tonality is restricted to only a few hues – white, black and various degrees of russet brown – combines various typical elements of Symbolism and Art Nouveau. The young girl – the woman as bride – was a popular theme at the turn of the century. The scene is organized with the symmetry of a ballet choreography and filled with symbolic props and a large cast of main characters, a background choir and right and left in the foreground two groups of semi-naked women, whose flowing hair – a symbol of female charms – is woven into curving ornaments.

This initiation scene focuses on three very different brides, all dressed in white robes and bathed in a bright light. On the left, pious and primly clad, is the bride of anxious innocence. In the centre is the crowned and willing bride who offers herself naked beneath her veils. On the right is the enigmatic and demonic bride with Egyptian headwear, her breasts shimmering through her magnificent robe.

White blossoms, bells from which tresses flow, sacrificial bowls and jugs, curls of rising smoke, crucified hands, nuns shielding their gaze – the picture is teeming with Symbolistic motifs, yet it is executed in the fluid planarity of ornamental Art Nouveau.

Jan Toorop
The Three Brides, c. 1892/93
Pencil, black and coloured chalk on paper, 78 x 98cm
Otterloo, Rijksmuseum Kröller-Müller

# JAN THORN-PRIKKER
1868–1932

In Thorn-Prikker's painting *Madonna among the Tulips* we find a number of elements showing the transition from Impressionism to Art Nouveau. The background is almost conventional: a sky with clouds, beneath it a village, a rural house to the right and endless tulip fields whose coloured rows lead towards the foreground, lending spatial depth and dimension as well as a certain atmosphere.

This vertical-format painting is divided by the beam of what may be assumed to be a cross, on which only the feet of Christ can be seen, as in a stylized wooden sculpture. The head and body of Mary are completely dematerialized, merging with the beam of the cross like a planar ornament. The sweeping curves of the sumptuous robe divided into magnificent ornamental zones seems almost anachronistic in view of the theme. Mary has become an Art Nouveau ornament.

The division of planes into individual decorative zones is a technique borrowed from French Cloisonnism. The draughtsmanship anticipates Thorn-Prikker's later stained glass and mosaic works. The colours themselves also have a symbolic significance. The *Madonna among the Tulips* creates a patron saint for Holland.

Jan Thorn Prikker
Madonna among the Tulips (Before the Cross), 1893
Oil on canvas, 146 x 86cm
Otterloo, Rijksmuseum Kröller-Müller

**William Holman Hunt**
The Hireling Shepherd, 1851
Oil on canvas, 76.4 x 109.5 cm
Manchester, City of Manchester Art Gallery

## WILLIAM HOLMAN HUNT
### 1827–1910

Apart from glorifying medieval themes, the Pre-Raphaelites also concentrated on landscape painting. Landscape was seen from a romantic point of view and gave them the opportunity of presenting each detail with loving care, meticulously portraying blades of grass, flowers, leaves, light and shadow. Nevertheless, for Hunt, being true to nature was not an end in itself.

Instead, he sought to give art a firm moral foundation and to make it a "servant of justice and truth". He was the only one of the Pre-Raphaelite artists who sought to portray nature and the events within it in all their colority as something to be grasped emotionally – in accordance with the principles propounded by John Ruskin.

The purity and naivety with which he portrays the shepherd leaning over the pretty young girl's shoulder in order to catch a glimpse of the little lamb sitting on her lap is quite disarming. It is a fine summer day, the corn is ripe, the sheep are grazing and resting, and the couple is linked in perfect harmony. The flowers, the grasses and the marshy stream are portrayed with almost microscopic precision, as are the figures and robes of the shepherd and the girl. The colours are as brilliant as enamel.

**Edward Coley Burne-Jones**
King Cophetua and the
Beggar Maid, 1884
Oil on canvas, 290 x 136 cm
London, Tate Gallery

## EDWARD COLEY BURNE-JONES
### 1833–1898

The wide range of Pre-Raphaelite pictorial themes includes religious, allegorical and historical material as well as motifs from the world of saga and fairy-tale. Most of the paintings portray a literary scene that can be precisely pinpointed. The theme of this painting, for example, is taken from an old Elizabethan ballad that also made a considerable impression on Shakespeare. It tells of King Cophetua's love for a poor beggar-girl whom he marries and enthrones as his queen.

Burne-Jones' paintings, like those of his Pre-Raphaelite friends, were executed on the basis of detailed preliminary studies and preparatory sketches. He began work on this painting in 1880 and did not complete it until four years later. In 1883, he executed a large watercolour on the same theme for a Mr Graham. When the oil painting was completed in 1884, it was hailed as a masterpiece. On the basis of this work, the artist was offered membership in the Academy one year later and in 1889 he was awarded the first class medal and the Order of the Legion of Honour in Paris for this painting.

Within a framework of historicizing ornament, the king, in full armour with the crown in his hands, sits at the feet of the young beggar-girl dressed in grey as specified in the ballad, gazing up at his beloved, who shyly sits on one half of the throne, while two pageboys look down on the scene from above.

# JOHN EVERETT MILLAIS
## 1829–1896

The tragi-romantic character of Ophelia was frequently portrayed by 19th century artists. A fascinating figure dangerously linked with water, she belongs in the same category of motifs as Undine and Nymphe, who were adopted in Symbolist painting. In an attitude of transfigured pathos, with her scattered garland, she drifts on the water, bouyed only by her robes. Millais depicts with almost literal precision the scene in Shakespeare's tragedy *Hamlet* that describes Ophelia's death.

The narrow stream is framed by reeds, bushes and trees and Ophelia's long dress has the same earthy colour as the soil of the river bank and the mysteriously dark marshy riverside. The water on which she floats is like a still moorland pool, adding a touch of demonic melancholy. In her euphoric, hallucinatory madness, she has no awareness of the danger of drowning. According to Shakespeare, "Her clothes spread wide / And mermaid-like awhile they bore her up, / Which time she chanted snatches of old lauds / As one incapable of her own distress / Or like a creature native and in-dued / Unto that element."

In this painting, Millais has created a framework within which he draws the viewer into a close-up view of Ophelia's perilous situation. In spite of the painstaking precision with which he portrays the details, he succeeds in giving the scene an air of credible tragedy.

**John Everett Millais**
Ophelia, 1851
Oil on canvas, 76 x 112 cm
London, Tate Gallery

# DANTE GABRIEL ROSSETTI
## 1828–1882

We know from the letters of Rossetti that this painting already existed in his mind's eye as early as 1863 and that he had even made a start on it then. It was originally intended as a *Beatrice* commissioned by Ellen Heaton. Force of circumstances, however, dictated a change of motif and the painting was given an entirely new meaning.

Rossetti invariably worked with models and his working method was strictly aimed at depicting exactly what he saw. In 1863, for example, he wrote to Ellen Heaton telling her that he had already painted the entire face and that he felt the painting would be one of his best works, but that the model Mary Ford was simply not the perfect Beatrice, though he did not dare to paint over the figure and give her the facial traits of another model. He went on to explain that he now had the idea of presenting the young woman as a bride inspired by the biblical Song of Solomon.

The artist prepared several sketches of other models and then merged the group of young women into a static arrangement in which the adorned young woman forms the centre, framed by her companions bearing flowers.

**Dante Gabriel Rossetti**  The Bride, 1865
Oil on canvas, 80 x 76 cm
London, Tate Gallery

**Arnold Böcklin**
The Waves, 1883
Oil on canvas, 180.3 x 237.5 cm
Munich, Bayerische Staatsgemälde-
sammlungen, Neue Pinakothek

## ARNOLD BÖCKLIN
### 1827–1901

With this painting, Böcklin draws us into the fabulous world of sea creatures, nymphs Nereids, nixens and Tritons. It is one of a large cycle of works featuring imaginary creatures whom he brings to life in his paintings. These creatures do not have an ideal human form; they are plump, course, often arrogant and clumsy.

In *The Waves* we see a group of such creatures at play in the sea. Crowned with water plants and flowers, seaweed and coral, their pale, bronzed or coppery-red bodies shimmer in a bluish-green sea with white foam, and the waves merge with the greyish-pink horizon. Böcklin has captured their movements and gestures, which are drastically heightened to the point of being grotesque. This impression is further underlined by their coarse and almost exaggerated facial expressions. Such are the expressive qualities and characteristic traits that the painter allocates to this world. Portrayals of this kind prompted his critics to claim that he had no artistic talent whatsoever. Yet the powerful colours, their luminosity and contrast, are carefully calculated and deliberately used as a forceful means of expression. This, in fact, is the key to understanding how this particular painting is related to Böcklin's other mystic and Symbolistic themes.

**Félix Vallotton**
Sandbanks on the Loire, 1923
Oil on canvas, 73 x 100 cm
Zurich, Kunsthaus Zürich

## FELIX VALLOTTON
### 1865–1925

This landscape by Vallotton was created in the final years of his life. In his œuvre, he covered a wide range of stylistic influences; Pointillism, Naturalism, a late Impressionism that was inspired by Hodler and he also benefited from the influence of Japanese woodcuts. After the turn of the century, his works move clearly in the direction of modern art with neo-realistic and Expressionist features, and the Surrealists see in him a forerunner. In all of his works, Vallotton sought simplicity, regarding his subject matter soberly and critically in an unsentimental light, purifying his forms of all ornamentation and reducing them to essentials.

The *Sandbanks on the Loire* is one of a group of paintings widely acknowledged as anticipating *pittura metafisica*. At first glance, the gentle slopes and curves of the sand, the arms of the river, the riverbanks and the groups of trees standing in the bright light under a limpid blue sky, the lone fisherman on the bank, all seem to present a peaceful situation with no deeper significance. The reduction of colours to blue, green, the yellow of the sand and the deep shadows nevertheless create an atmosphere that makes us pensive.

# FERDINAND HODLER

## 1853–1918

"It is the mission of the artist to lend form to the eternal in nature and to reveal its inner beauty. The artist tells of nature by rendering things visible; he pays homage to the forms of the human body..." Hodler's maxims were certainly not evident to all viewers of his works. During his lifetime, the response to his work was extremely ambivalent and often negative. Just as he had begun to gain some recognition in his own country, and just as people were beginning to understand and appreciate his works, he introduced a change of style around 1890, heralding the creative period in which he was to produce the paintings we regard today as typical of Hodler's style.

In the early phase of his work, spanning almost seventeen years, he created paintings closely modelled on the example of the old masters both in subject matter and in tonality. With the beginning of this new period, his palette became distinctly lighter, achieving that intensity of colour so typical of his work, and introducing the element of expression and movement.

For the painting *Autumn Evening* Hodler was awarded second prize at the Concours Calame in 1893. It is a composition created in the studio along the lines of earlier landscape paintings. Nevertheless, this painting is more than just the portrayal of a large-format landscape. The path strewn with fallen russet leaves and flanked by chestnut trees that have lost most of their foliage, leads into nothingness. The upper half of the painting is taken up by a sky in which the evocative colours of sunset flare up briefly before darkness falls. The sky is tinged with yellow, the clouds are radiantly lilac, and just above the end of the path we see a red strip – the last rays of the dying sun.

This painting already gives a strong indication of Hodler's new approach and his intention of imbuing his paintings with a more profound significance than that of simply illustrating nature. In doing so, he makes use of the strongly expressive powers of colour as a bearer of atmosphere and the universally comprehensible symbolism inherent in the theme "autumn evening".

Another of Hodler's newfound aims was to evolve new ways of addressing new topics. The success of his Symbolistic painting *The Night* (Bern, Kunstmuseum) in several European cities confirmed that he had been right to choose this new, monumental approach. In *Communication with the Infinite* he created a single figure composition in which a sense of space is secondary to planarity. A nude woman (for which Augustine Dupin, the mother of Hodler's son Hector, was the model) standing on a grey cloth lifts her eyes and hands in a gesture of prayer towards the pale strip of sky above the green hill before which she stands. This zone of light may be regarded as the universe or the infinite.

Ferdinand Hodler
Autumn Evening, 1892
Oil on canvas, 100 x 130 cm
Neuchâtel, Musée des Beaux-Arts

Ferdinand Hodler
Communication with the Infinite,
1892
Oil on canvas, 159 x 97 cm
Basle, Öffentliche Kunstsammlung
Basel, Kunstmuseum

## GIOVANNI FATTORI
1825–1908

**Giovanni Fattori**
Roman Carts, 1873
Oil on canvas, 21 x 32 cm
Florence, Galleria d'Arte Moderna, Palazzo Pitti

Fattori, the most productive and most expressive painter in the Macchiaioli group of artists, preferred to paint on small wooden panels. His *Roman Carts* is one of the first works he painted in macchia technique, which involves a rapid juxtaposition of individual daubs of colour. This type of brushwork, closely related to that of Impressionism, also broke with traditional classical techniques. The motif, in its simplicity, also broke with academic doctrines. Apart from landscapes and rural scenes, Fattori's preferred motifs were battle paintings.

The laden, two-wheeled carts to which the horses are harnessed are standing in the bright sunlight on cracked dry earth in front of a high wall. A man is lying on the ground, in the foreground a horse is resting on straw, and behind it stands a saddled horse. The motif cannot be interpreted as romantic, for the atmosphere is too sober and realistic.

Here, the light has more than a coloristic function: it is a bearer of atmosphere. The midday sun has broken the blue of the sky and the trees behind the wall into a light and shimmering haze, bathing the scene in a paralyzing brightness that even robs the colours of their strength.

## GIOVANNI SEGANTINI
1858–1899

*The Hay Harvest* was completed in the last year of Segantini's life, ten years after he had begun to paint. It belongs to a part of his œuvre that earned him the rather inapt epithet "the Italian Millet".

Apart from his major Symbolist themes and cycles, Segantini also studied the life of the mountain peasants, the quiet mysteries of the mountain world, and the majestic sublimity of nature. Like most of his contemporaries, Segantini undertook studies of nature and painted in the open air. In the quiet solitude of the mountains, he explored the changing light conditions in the course of the day, and the changing seasons. He developed a kind of Divisionism, involving a technique of dividing the picture plane into individually juxtaposed brushstrokes that was closely related to Impressionistic techniques.

This painting shows peasants gathering in their hay on a plateau fringed by mountains, with a young woman in a white apron and white cap in the foreground bending down to gather a bundle. A brilliant blue sky with stylized grey and pink clouds spans this peaceful scene. The people and animals are integrated into the landscape, transfigured by the radiance of the light and the gentle lyricism of the scene.

**Giovanni Segantini**  The Hay Harvest, 1899
Oil on canvas, 135 x 149 cm. St. Moritz, Museum Segantini

ITALY

# ANSELM FEUERBACH
1829–1880

Feuerbach saw his ideals reflected in the classical sovereignty and beauty associated with Antiquity and the Renaissance. These ideals, together with his romantically transfigured notion of the past, permeate his entire œuvre. As the son of an archaeologist, he was not only familiar with the literary themes he treated in his paintings, but he also had an eye trained from an early age on the monuments of classical Antiquity and the Renaissance.

According to the artist himself, this painting, originally entitled *Ariosto at the Court of Ferrara*, caught the attention of Count von Schack, who purchased it and thereupon commissioned further works. It was the literary reference in the painting that appealed particularly to von Schack, and because of this, critics accused him of failing to recognize Feuerbach's true genius and of forcing him to repeat his treatment of literary material.

Ariosto, one of the great poets of the Renaissance, is portrayed here wearing a laurel wreath in the manner of Dante. Ercole d'Este, the theatre-loving Prince of Ferrara, was one of the first to put Ariosto's plays on the stage. Ariosto is seen strolling here amongst a group of intellectuals and beautiful women, in a magnificent garden-setting before an architectural backdrop that reiterates the majestic forms of classical Antiquity. In this painting, Feuerbach also takes up an earlier Dante theme.

Anselm Feuerbach
The Garden of Ariosto, 1863
Oil on canvas, 102 x 153 cm
Munich, Bayerische Staatsgemälde-
sammlungen, Schack-Galerie

# FRANZ VON LENBACH
1836–1904

Lenbach was regarded by his contemporaries, as he is today, primarily as a brilliant portraitist of high society. Using a predominantly brown and golden tonality in the manner of the old masters, he painted Bismarck, the Prince Regent Luitpold, Emperor Wilhelm I, Pope Leo XIII, Richard Wagner and many other famous personalities and figures in politics and high society. All these portraits are objective depictions of the respective persons in the dignity of their office and their position. However, when younger women with less famous names are his models or when he paints his wife and children, a distinct tendency towards cloying sentimentality is undeniable.

Lenbach also created a cycle of paintings depicting peasants and shepherds, standing, sitting or reclining, which clearly appealed to his visual interest. He showed them in all their simplicity, in their rural surroundings. The *Young Boy in the Sun* sitting on a grassy, sandy knoll looks sweet and simple. He is blonde, with a ruddy complexion, a little dirty, simply dressed and portrayed against the limpid blue of a summer sky. This harmless idyll undoubtedly appealed to the emotions of Lenbach's late 19th century spectators. His skill in the portrayal of plants is as virtuoso as any old master.

Franz von Lenbach
Young Boy in the Sun,
c. 1860
Oil on canvas,
33.5 x 26 cm
Darmstadt, Hessisches
Landesmuseum

**Wilhelm Leibl**
Three Women in Church, 1881
Oil on panel, 113 x 77 cm
Hamburg, Hamburger Kunsthalle

## WILHELM LEIBL
### 1844–1900

The painting of *Three Women in Church* shows Leibl at the height of his creative powers. A slow worker, who considered and composed even the tiniest areas of his paintings with painstaking care, he has succeeded here in creating a perfect example of his realist phase with all the consummate skill of the fine artists of the old school.

The painting shows two old women and one young woman in rural dress, seated side by side on a church pew, deep in prayer. The Baroque carving of the church pews is rendered with the same photographic precision as the figures of the women themselves.

Leibl achieved a superb mastery of colour, allowing its luminosity to speak for itself. In front of the light-coloured background, the peasant woman in her dark dress and dark headwear stands out strongly, her gaze turned away from the viewer towards an altar that is situated somewhere beyond the picture frame. Beside her, in the centre of the painting, an old peasant woman bends over the prayer book she holds in her large, rough hands. Her striped dress acts as a compositional transition to the young woman with her light shoulder-covering and apron, her fresh complexion and the golden bands of her hat. The dispassionate precision of this portrayal draws the viewer into the quiet contemplation of the scene.

**Wilhelm Trübner**
Landscape with Flagpole, 1891
Oil on canvas, 48 x 65 cm
Winterthur, Stiftung Oskar Reinhart

## WILHELM TRÜBNER
### 1851–1917

Like the work of his friends in the circle of artists grouped around Leibl, Trübner's approach is anti-academic, invariably seeking the new and the lively, even though he was trained in the tradition of the old Netherlandish, German, Spanish and Italian masters. His talent lies in his unerring sense of colority, authenticity of form, and in the simplicity and reduction of his structures. He countered the widespread contemporary rejection of his works by taking up the pen and anonymously publishing, in 1892 and 1898 respectively, two polemical tracts entitled *Das Kunstverständnis von heute* (Attitudes to art today) and *Die Verwirrung der Kunstbegriffe* (The confusion of artistic concepts). From 1890 onwards, he dedicated himself increasingly to *plein-air* painting and travelled widely during the summer months.

His *Landscape with Flagpole* at Chiemsee documents one such journey, and it is quite evident that he has now reduced his early principle – "stringency of draughtsmanship and supreme handling of colour" – to the principle of coloristic painting in the Impressionist mode. The short, angular brushstrokes of his earlier works are increasingly replaced by freer, broader and longer strokes. Clear and bright, the sky and the blue lake contrast sharply with the village and the lakeside. In addition to landscapes, Trübner's œuvre also includes portraits, still lifes and interiors.

# MAX KLINGER
1857–1920

Klinger invariably created his works with the inner calm of an artist who had withdrawn from society and who was nevertheless open to all contemporary influences. In his complex and prolifid œuvre, we find elements reflecting all the prevailing stylistic tendencies of contemporary art.

In addition to realist paintings, he also created works of imaginary and fantastic motifs, history paintings and mythological themes. In Paris, he became closely involved with Impressionism, and in his later years he came to be regarded as one of the leading masters of German Jugendstil.

The *Landscape at the Unstrut* is a relatively unusual work in Klinger's œuvre. Whereas he generally tended to prefer scenic portrayals with an allegorical, imaginary, religious or historical content, he turns here to a purely landscape motif. The hilly landscape divided horizontally in the centre by a narrow river, is completely uninhabited and the tranquillity of nature is disturbed neither by narrative nor by any human figure.

The foreground is dominated by reeds, and the water flows down a series of steps, with a steep riverbank on one side, upon which there are three trees, with bushes of glowing russet, bluish mountains and an almost violet sky in the background. This is a typical Jugendstil landscape.

**Max Klinger**
Landscape at the Unstrut, 1912
Oil on canvas, 192 x 126cm
Altenburg, Lindenau-Museum

# FRANZ VON STUCK
1863–1928

*The Dinner Party* documents an authentic event: the great gala dinner held to celebrate Stuck's fiftieth birthday on 23 February 1913 in the studio of the Villa Stuck in Munich. The artist is not interested in creating portraits of the guests, but in capturing the festive atmosphere and the majestic effect of the room he had designed and decorated himself.

Ladies and gentlemen in formal dress are seated at a long table lit by magnificent candelabra. That is almost all we can recognize. They are dark figures in the shadow or pale outlines in the light. The dignified surroundings of this gathering, the high ceiling of the aristocratic artist's studio, is designed in the Neoclassicist style inspired by the architecture of ancient Rome. On the walls, between pilasters, hang magnificent tapestries, and the room is spanned by a richly ornamented coffered ceiling.

The guests are celebrating Stuck's birthday; he accepts their attention and even celebrates himself by documenting the event, thereby merging life and art. Imagination, pomp and circumstance are the main motifs here. At the time this painting was created, Cubism was already in its second phase. War was to break out in 1914.

**Franz von Stuck**
The Dinner Party, 1913
Oil on canvas, 57.5 x 68.5cm
Munich, Bayerische Staatsgemälde-
sammlungen, Neue Pinakothek

**Max Liebermann**
The Parrot Walk
at Amsterdam Zoo,
1902
Oil on canvas,
88.1 x 72.5 cm
Bremen, Kunsthalle
Bremen

## MAX LIEBERMANN
### 1847–1935

This painting was created at a time when Liebermann had already found his own personal style. After some initial work in which the realist influence of the Hungarian artist Mihály Munkácsy and the school of Barbizon were undeniable, he began a close study of the old Dutch masters, the French Impressionists and contemporary German painters. In the end, he chose to break with tradition and became the most important representative of German Impressionism.

In this *Parrot Walk* he has captured the atmosphere of a warm summer day. A pale, broad sandy path is flanked by high trees with dense foliage, between which magnificent parrots are perched, rustling their feathers, to the delight of the women and children in their light summer dresses and straw hats. On the benches by the side of the path, some of the walkers are taking a rest.

The viewer remains an outsider, for the events captured in the painting are not directed towards his perspective and all the people in the picture are busy strolling about, looking at or feeding the exotic birds. The pools of light on the path and on the grass indicate the sunlight falling through the dense foliage. Everything in this painting is modelled with light.

**Fritz von Uhde**
In the Garden (The Artist's Daughters), 1906
Oil on canvas, 70 x 100 cm
Mannheim, Städtische Kunsthalle Mannheim

## FRITZ VON UHDE
### 1848–1911

Uhde created the modern religious painting as a vehicle for his quest to endow his work with deeper meaning. He also devoted his attention to themes inspired by an observation of his immediate surroundings. Invariably, people are at the centre of his work.

Although traditional motifs abound in his œuvre – history paintings, allegorical or mythological motifs, narrative genre scenes – and although many of his early works show the influence of classical painting, he eventually developed his own unacademic style. Both the subject matter and the technique are closely related to French naturalism and Impressionism which he adapted in his own way. His close family life, the figures of his wife and his three daughters, provided a motif Uhde frequently painted.

In a garden with trees, through which the sunlight falls, casting pools of light on the ground, his three adult daughters are clearly engaged in conversation. A parasol is leaning against the fence, there is a chair to rest on and the white and brown dog stands faithfully waiting. The calm contentedness of this summer idyll is an example of Uhde's tendency towards the picturesque.

# LOVIS CORINTH

1858–1925

Corinth's *Self-Portrait with Straw Hat* executed in 1923, two years before his death, unites two of this artist's main motifs: self-portraiture and the landscape of Walchensee in the Bavarian Alps. Like Rembrandt and Beckmann, Corinth was an artist who frequently subjected his own physiognomy to critical and considered study, making it the subject matter of his painting.

We know that Corinth had undertaken to create a self-portrait each year to mark his birthday. He suffered a stroke in 1911, which severely affected his life and forced him to withdraw from many of his Berlin activities as president of the Secession and director of a school of painting for women. From then on, he spent most of his time in the south of Germany and, from 1919 onwards, at his house by the lake, Walchensee.

Most of the picture area is taken up by the head and shoulders of the straw-hatted artist in the middle of this small horizontal painting, viewed from an elevated position above the lake, which is fringed by mountains on the opposite shore. This is not a psychologically detailed portrait. The sun-tanned artist, wearing a moustache, is gazing almost absent-mindedly into the distance. He appears introverted and pensive. Stylistically, this painting is closely related to the works of the Impressionists.

**Lovis Corinth**
Self-Portrait with Straw Hat, 1923
Oil on cardboard, 70 x 85 cm
Bern, Kunstmuseum Bern

# MAX SLEVOGT

1868–1932

Slevogt is frequently described as the master of German Impressionism, a description which is justified in many ways if we do not make too close a comparison with French Impressionism. After all, Slevogt developed his own highly distinctive and modern forms of expression. Apart from his considerable graphic output, he dedicated his time intensively to painting. Portraits, figural compositions and still lifes were, for a long time, his preferred subjects. He turned to landscape painting at a fairly late stage, after he had begun to paint all his motifs in natural light.

When Slevogt travelled to Hamburg on the invitation of the art historian Alfred Lichtwark in order to paint the portrait of senator William Henry Oswald, he took the opportunity of painting some scenes of Hamburg as well. None of these is, strictly speaking, a veduta. Nevertheless, this painting with a view of the river Alster does show a detail of a real scene which can be precisely pinpointed. Slevogt's main aim is to clarify the spatial situation. He shows an clearly defined area with a distinct background formed by the opposite lakeshore and gives an authentic rendering of the atmosphere between daytime and twilight.

**Max Slevogt**
The Alster at Hamburg, 1905
Oil on canvas, 59 x 76 cm
Berlin, Nationalgalerie, Staatliche Museen
zu Berlin – Preussischer Kulturbesitz

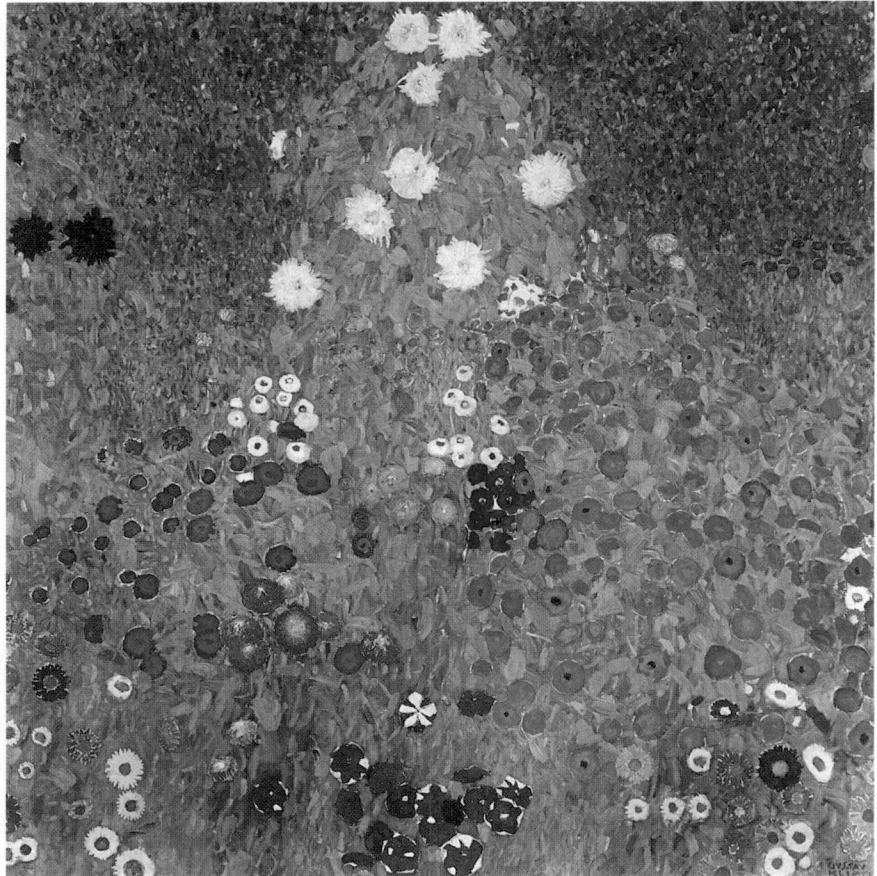

**Gustav Klimt**
Flower Garden, c. 1905/06
Oil on canvas, 110 x 110 cm
Prague, Národni Galeri

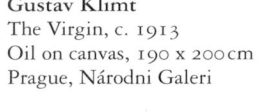

**Gustav Klimt**
The Virgin, c. 1913
Oil on canvas, 190 x 200 cm
Prague, Národni Galeri

# GUSTAV KLIMT
## 1862–1918

Many of Klimt's paintings are created in a kind of millefiori technique, in which colours, patterns, figurative areas, ornaments are juxtaposed and merged into a plane in which the boundaries between seemingly arbitrary pattern and real materiality are often blurred. He invariably uses colours of sumptuously oriental luminosity or with a precious, enigmatic shimmer, heightening the intensity with gold backgrounds or gold ornaments. For his landscapes, he chooses a different handling of colour, in subtly impressionistic tones.

His *Flower Garden* is a tiny landscape detail portrayed in close-up. Klimt does not indicate spatiality, showing instead a rich cornucopia of summer flowers, a dense tapestry of blossoms through which no soil shows, over which no sky is spanned, crossed by no path, flanked by neither tree nor bush.

The flatness and planarity of the picture make it seem as though it is suspended in some indefinable place. The blossoms are like a pattern that could be repeated *ad infinitum*, a chance glimpse of a vast sea of flowers. In a technique verging on Pointillism, the colours have been juxtaposed in tiny, rapid brushstrokes in which the blue and green of the little leaves merge together and the bright splashes of the flowers seem to have been dabbed on the canvas at random. The painting thrives on the contrast of vibrant colours in an oscillating tonality that creates a dynamically rhythmic effect.

In this large and almost perfectly square painting, which Klimt entitled *The Virgin*, an interwoven group of bodies, ornaments, flowers and bands seems to float like an island within a dark, diffuse area. We see the faces, arms and naked bodies of young women nestled there, drowsily interlaced in symbolic unison with the blossoms, bands and ornaments on which they lie. Some of the girls are still fast asleep, others have opened their eyes slightly and, still gazing dreamily, are looking out of the picture. They are in various stages of the unconscious, before awakening as women. A lascivious tranquility prevails; the colours have a magical and potent radiance, and the entire ensemble is orientally sumptuous.

The painter plays a confusing game with the appeal and sensation of materials, colours and ornaments, with the contrast of concrete materiality and abstraction and with the wealth of what he portrays. Corporeality and décor merge completely.

The subject of "woman" is a key motif in Klimt's work and he invariably shows woman in all her corporeality as an essentially attractive creature – enigmatic, mysteriously beautiful and sublime.

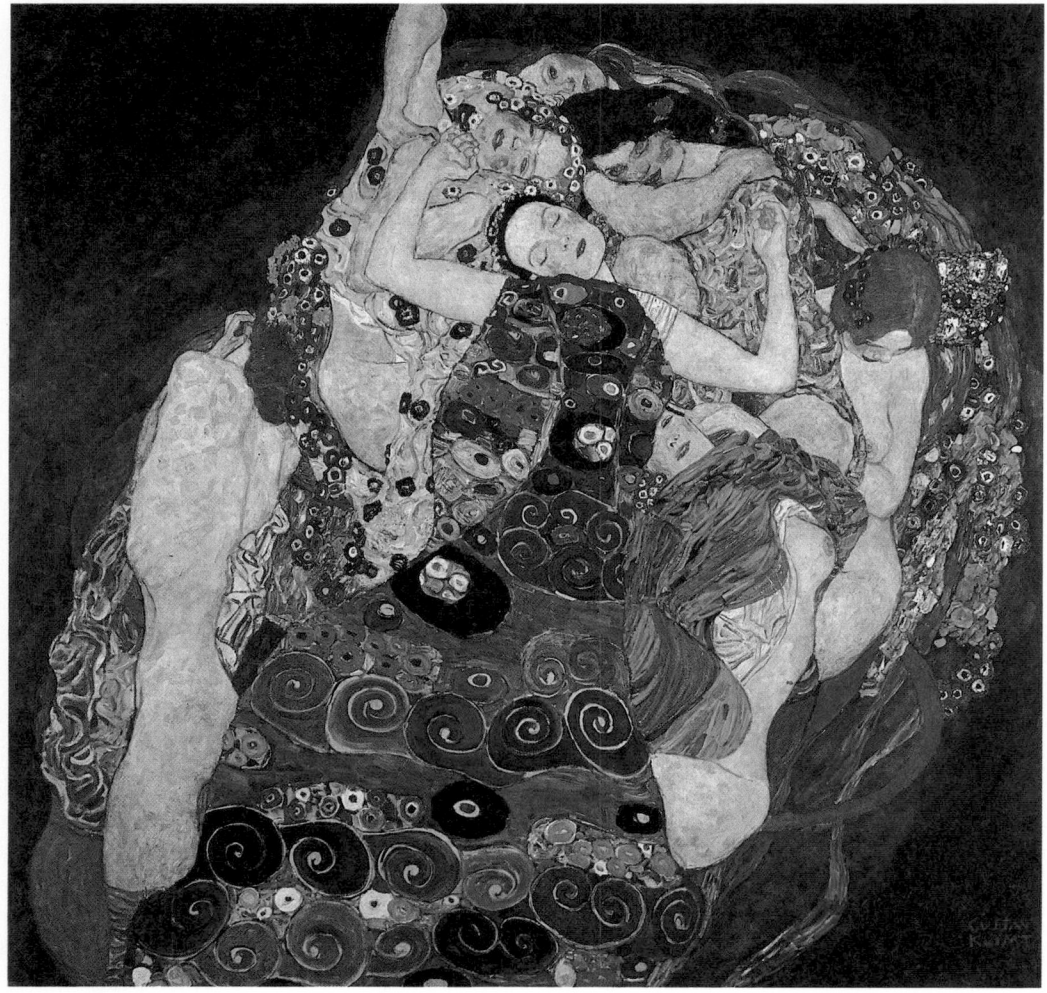

# EGON SCHIELE

1890–1918

Like van Gogh, Schiele's creative career as an artist spanned barely a decade and yet, even in this brief period, he succeeded in producing works of such arresting power and outstanding quality that he is regarded today as one of the most important of Austrian painters.

Though his art would have been inconceivable without the work of his mentor, friend and Secession colleague Klimt, the work in which Schiele follows on from Klimt's groundbreaking œuvre nevertheless possesses its own highly distinctive style.

"In the case of Schiele, as with anyone who died so young, one cannot avoid seeing the traces of what Trakl calls the November destruction – what the hopelessly healthy calls morbid and the smart nascal calls decadent." With these words, the Viennese academy professor Albert Paris Gütersloh, painter, writer and a contemporary of Schiele ironically characterized his work. Yet he touches upon only one aspect of Schiele's œuvre, whose body of artistic work also lays bare the underlying structural forces of life, expressively symbolized in glowing colours.

Schiele's overriding interest was the human figure, the body and the face. With sceptical curiosity and an anatomically coloristic attention to detail, he analyzed himself and his models time and time again. Another aspect of his work is his landscape painting. With flighty, almost nervous brushwork he applies colours whose vibrant luminosity is morethe-less often translucent. He elongates his objects and fragments them into many parts. Light, empty areas contrast with sonorous, dark colours in tonal passages of alternating intensity and density.

*Female Model in Red* shows the importance of movement in his work, portrayed by means of a distortion akin to that of the Expressionists: movement as a strong and colourful independent entity, merging to a singular and almost unsettling tonal conglomerate. The fiery red of the robe is picked out again here and there on the skin of the model – on her cheeks, arms and legs – while the brown of the undefinable garment into which the model is trying to slip her foot is reiterated in the hair and on the skin. No sense of space is indicated; in spite of the heavy physicality of the woman, her body remains flat. The vertical angle, the planarity, the way the head is deliberately clipped at the upper edge, the expressive movement – all these features suggest the influence of Japanese woodcuts. Many of Schiele's nudes have a similar structure and frequently radiate a powerful eroticism, while, as in this work, they are also overlaid with quite different sensations: the reciprocal tension of form and colour.

Schiele spent a lot of time in the picturesque little southern Bohemian town of Krumau, which he immortalized in many of his paintings. Here, the individual elements – houses, gardens, river, sky and fields – are broken down into myriad mutable patches of colour.

**Egon Schiele**
Female Model in Bright Red Jacket and
Pants, 1914
Gouache and Pencil,
46.5 x 29.7 cm
Vienna, Graphische Sammlung
Albertina

**Egon Schiele**
Krumau Landscape (Town and River), 1915/16
Oil on canvas, 110 x 140.5 cm
Linz, Wolfgang-Gurlitt-Sammlung in der
Neuen Galerie der Stadt Linz

**James Abbott McNeill Whistler**
Rose and Silver: La Princesse du
Pays de la Porcelaine, 1864
Oil on canvas, 216 x 109.2 cm
Washington, Freer Gallery of Art

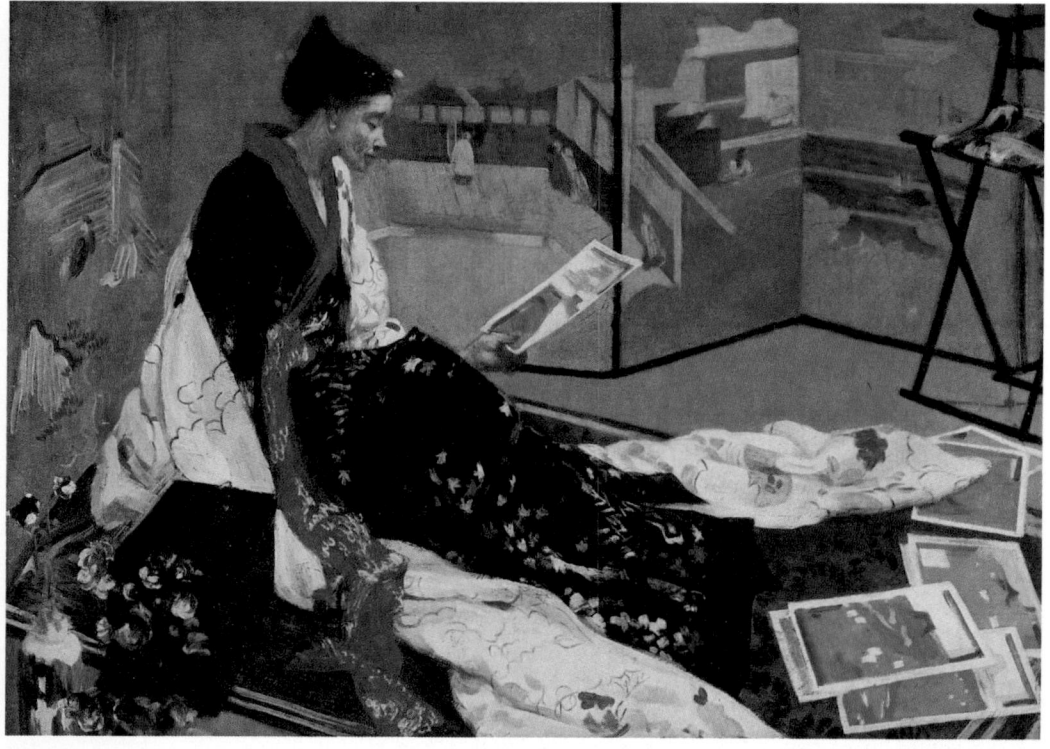

**James Abbott McNeill Whistler**
Caprice in Purple and Gold, No. 2:
The Golden Screen, 1864
Oil on panel, 51 x 68.5 cm
Washington, Freer Gallery of Art

# JAMES ABBOTT McNEILL WHISTLER
## 1834–1903

Whistler loved to title his paintings according
to the gentle colour harmonies that dominated
their respective tonality. His work is informed
by the subtle and compelling charm of finely
nuanced hues in a shimmering luminosity that
conjures up a sense of materiality. A profound
love of East Asian art influenced Whistler's
life as much as it did his art. This affinity is
clearly based on a certain inner harmony that
prepared him for the influences from a world
in which a heightened aesthetic sensibility
played a predominant role. He collected East
Asian porcelain, textiles, paintings and *objets
d'art* of all kinds and lived surrounded by
them.

A profound identification with Far Eastern
principles of design, motifs and aestheticism is
evident in all his work and he loved to portray
objects from his collection in his paintings.
Like Japanese and Chinese artists, Whistler
created for himself a stamp-like seal with a
stylized design. Far from leading to superficial
imitation, Whistler's close study of Eastern art
produced independent interpretations which
nevertheless bear clear witness to their sources
of inspiration.

In *Rose and Silver: La Princesse du Pays de la
Porcelaine* we see a European woman of lyrical
beauty dressed in a magnificent silver bro-
caded kimono and a pink, silk robe standing
on a Chinese rug in front of a screen. Painted
fans, a tall vase, part of a pink, silk tablecloth,
a glimpse of flooring and the background all
reiterate the tonal variations on pink and silver. These are extremely delicate colours juxtaposed without contrast, drawing their vibrancy from the charm of their delicate gradations.

In the painting *Caprice in Purple and Gold,
No. 2: The Golden Screen* the colours and contrasts that determine the composition are
stronger. The upper half of the painting is
dominated by a Japanese folding screen with a
warm golden ground on which, in character-
istically sharp perspectival depth, we can discern buildings and landscape elements.

In front of it, a European lady with a pale
complexion, her hair piled high, is seated on a
red rug. She is dressed in a dark, embroidered
silk kimono with a scarlet shawl collar, a scarlet embroidered obi (a long broad sash) tied
around her waist, with a cream-coloured silk
shawl embroidered in gold and red thrown
loosely over her shoulder. Beside her are a
small lacquer cabinet and a porcelain vase
with pink flowers. Here, Whistler explores the
delightful contrasts between light and shade
and between the shimmering of nuances of
similar colours. He felt that his work bore a
profound relationship to music, which explains why he so often gave his paintings such
titles as *Caprice* or *Harmony*.

# MARY CASSATT
1845–1926

It was through her friendship with Degas, who was extremely critical when it came to accepting his friends as artists, that Mary Cassatt came into contact with the Impressionists. An invitation to take part in their exhibitions liberated her from the pressure of presenting her works to the jury of the Salon and allowed her to concentrate on painting quite independently the subjects of her choice as she saw fit. Yet the direct influence of the Impressionists on her art remained limited. Though she brightened her palette and worked with broader and bolder brushstrokes, her forms remained self-contained and were not broken down into colours and light.

*The Boating Party* is a typical composition in the œuvre of Mary Cassatt and one that involves one of her favourite motifs: mother and child. The choice of detail, the silhouette of the rowing man in black, whose back is turned to the viewer and who fills much of the foreground, the deep blue surface of the water and the corner of the greyish sail all indicate that Mary Cassatt was thoroughly familiar with the Japanese masters of the woodcut. The woman holding her child on her arm is turned towards the man, looking at the him, so that the viewer is excluded from the painting. The cool, discreet handling of the scene is typical of her work, while the strong colour contrasts add a sense of tension.

Mary Cassatt generally found her models within her close circle of friends; in fact, these two little girls, fully immersed in their game on the beach, were the children of a friend. The artist concentrates mainly on the little children whom she has placed in a narrow and almost photographically structured detail, as can be seen by the way the edge of the picture clips the legs of the girl with the hat. Cassatt painstakingly captured the charming facial traits of the little girl with the shovel. The textile structures of their aprons are brilliantly mastered. The surrounding area, on the other hand, is fleeting and sketchy: sand and sea, cliffs and sailing boats are reduced to colour impressions. In this way, the observer is led through the composition and through the various brushstrokes into the centre of the picture.

Contemporary critics applauded the way Cassatt had succeeded in presenting this scene naturally and authentically, praising her rendering of the children's cheeks, their chubby arms and their little legs, and comparing their wonderful, sun-tanned skin to the firm, dense texture of nectarines. The artist was certainly not interested merely in the picturesque effects she could achieve in this picture. She approaches the children at their own level rather than looking down on them from above. In this way she regards their game seriously as a means of exploring the world. The very fact that Cassatt's children could be regarded as independent personalities is a sign of the changing perception of humanity towards the end of the 19th century, in the wake of Darwin's theories.

Mary Cassatt
The Boating Party, c. 1893/94
Oil on canvas, 90 x 117 cm
Washington, National Gallery of Art

Mary Cassatt
Two Children on the Beach, 1884
Oil on canvas, 97.6 x 74.2 cm
Washington, National Gallery of Art

## WINSLOW HOMER
### 1836–1910

**Winslow Homer**
Breezing up, 1876
Oil on canvas, 61 x 96.5 cm
Washington, National Gallery of Art

Before Homer had the opportunity of seeing the paintings of French artists on a European tour, he had independently arrived at an almost Impressionistic handling of light. He painted outdoors, painstakingly observed the times of day and weather conditions and reproduced them authentically. Yet in doing so, he never went so far as to break down the entire surface of the painting, adopting a realistic approach to reproduce certain elements instead. His colours invariably remained subdued and almost cool. The atmosphere he does achieve verges on tension. Homer loved to spending time by the sea and to portray man's struggle with the elements – wind, waves and weather.

*Breezing Up (A Fair Wind)* is one of his more mature works. It shows a bearded man with three young boys enjoying a sailing trip just as the wind begins to come up and their sport may be expected to become rather more strenuous. The breeze is beginning to ruffle the tops of the waves, and dark clouds are drawing across the sky, on the right side of the horizon we can see the dark outline of a large sailing-boat.

The vast presence of the sea was to remain one of Homer's key motifs to the end of his life. Henry James wrote of him: "He is almost barbarously simple, and, to our eye, he is horribly ugly; but there is nevertheless something one likes about him."

## JOHN SINGER SARGENT
### 1856–1925

**John Singer Sargent** The Daughters of Edward Darley Boit, 1882
Oil on canvas, 222.5 x 222.5 cm
Boston (MA), Museum of Fine Arts

In the second half of the 19th century, American artists began once again to look to Europe, just as they had done a century before. This time, however, they did not do so only in order to learn from the European artists, but also in order to follow the stylistic developments that were emerging there. Sargent, a cosmopolitan man of the world, had trained in Europe, and had spent his formative years there amongst Americans who had chosen to live in the Old World. Sargent's teacher for many years was Carolus-Duran, a friend of Manet, who also was a great admirer of Velázquez. In his day, Carolus-Duran was a celebrated and sought-after portraitist. It was from him that Sargent learned to study his models and motifs with precision and to pay attention to balancing the tonal values. Portraiture was his preferred genre and the field in which he achieved his most skilfully structured works.

Although we can undoubtedly detect the influence of Whistler, a friend of Sargent, as well as that of Velázquez and other Spanish masters, the artist nevertheless retained his own distinctive artistic style. *The Daughters of Edward Darley Boit*, showing four little girls in delightfully relaxed pose in their bourgeois surroundings.reflects the influence of the old masters, blended with Impressionist brushwork.

## WILLIAM MERRIT CHASE
1849–1916

In his country home near Shinnecock, Chase held a summer school of *plein-air* painting for twelve successive summers. Before beginning with this school, he had tended to paint in the darker, earthier tones used by his teachers at the Munich academy. Now, with an increasing interest in a more relaxed depiction of landscape, he turned in the 1890s to the stylistic techniques of the French Impressionists and, in doing so, influenced an entire generation of American painters. The brighter palette and the more relaxed brushwork of the new style perfectly suited his concept of an atmospheric portrayal of landscape.

The sweeping beaches and dunes of Long Island were ideal motifs to use as a vehicle for portraying the carefree mood of a summer day. The two women and the children are splashes of white on the grassy dunes: figures in a landscape. The atmosphere of the landscape is transferred to the figures themselves. Yet unlike his French colleagues, Chase did not explore the impact of modern industrialized life on people. His landscapes tend to be pictures of escape from hectic city life to the unspoiled freedom of the countryside.

**William Merrit Chase**
Leisure, 1894
Oil on canvas, 64.8 x 90.2 cm
Fort Worth (TX), Amon Carter Museum

## MAURICE PRENDERGAST
1859–1924

Prendergast, who was born in the same year as Seurat, went one important step further than the French Impressionists who influenced him. He, too, structured his picture plane with rough brushstrokes of pure colour; yet the reduction of his forms already indicates the direction that art was to take in the 20th century. He ignored the fashionable colour theories of the day and allowed himself to be guided by his own painterly intuition in the composition of his pictures, juxtaposing daubs of colour in a bid to capture the glittering and shimmering light of fleeting movement. Prendergast's painting never demonstrated any political commitment or critical social commentary and he chose peaceful scenes as his motifs, transposing them to the canvas like a prism of ever-changing colour.

Around the turn of the century, the path from Piazza San Marco to the Riva degli Schiavoni was thronged with crowds, their hats, parasols and dresses creating a refreshing and colourful contrast to the expanses of water and sky and the huddled houses. Stylistically, Prendergast represents the end of American Impressionism and the beginning of a truly modern style of painting in the United States.

**Maurice Prendergast**
Ponte della Paglia in Venice, 1899
Oil on canvas,
71 x 58.5 cm
Washington,
Philipps Collection

**Ilya Yefimovich Repin**
Zaporozhian Cossacks (sketch), c. 1878
Oil on canvas, 67 x 87 cm
Moscow, State Tretyakov Gallery

# ILYA YEFIMOVICH REPIN
## 1844–1930

Repin was very much an artist of his time and of his country, and in his art he naturally united the influences he had drawn from seemingly contradictory sources. On the one hand, the painting associated with the royal court and high society would have been quite inconceivable without the constant contacts with Central Europe and, of course, Paris. On the other hand, enormously expressive popular and religious art of high quality had always existed in Russia. The liberal intelligentsia of the day was full of unrest, and many new directions were beginning to evolve, heralding a reorientation of lifestyles and social structures.

For Russian art, this brought with it a nascent self-confidence in its own achievements, emancipation from the European model and recognition of the country's own specific characteristics and requirements. This found expression in distinctly Russian forms of realism, Impressionism and symbolism.

Repin's oil sketch of *Zaporozhian Cossacks* exists in two further monumental versions in Kharkov and St Petersburg. The motif has an authentic historical background: in 1675, the Cossacks had crushed the Turkish sultan, but the sultan nevertheless sought a capitulation agreement with the victors. In strong, bright colours, Repin gives a realistic portrayal of the Cossacks and their exuberant delight at penning a reply to the sultan. The wording of the letter still exists; it is a flood of florid oriental metaphor and ridicule.

**Ilya Yefimovich Repin**
Portrait of Vera Alekseevna Repina, 1882
Oil on canvas, 140 x 91.5 cm
Moscow, State Tretyakov Gallery

Repin was also a talented and sought-after portraitist. In his *Portrait of Vera Alekseevna Repina* he combines the subtle skills of his portraiture with his ability to capture the mood of a fleeting moment. In doing so, he has created a symphony of dark reds and browns that bears comparison with Titian's handling of colour. Every tone and nuance has been explored, blended and contrasted with the paler hues of skin and fabric. The actual subject has been rendered with the meticulous precision of fine painting, bringing out each detail of the materials, their surface textures and the effect of light, while the ambient surroundings are more diffuse and impressionistic – in itself a delightful contrast. A young woman is resting in a large armchair upholstered in wine red. Her eyes are closed, her posture graceful, with one hand at her head, and with her legs crossed. Though Repin has portrayed the young woman at a moment of rest, he is a quiet observer and not an intruder, for she presents herself in an attitude of perfection that brooks no indiscretion.

Volkmar Essers

# CLASSICAL MODERNISM

## Painting in the first half of the 20th century

Classical Modernism evolved within the atmosphere of tension generated by the dichotomy between figurative and non-figurative art, realistic portrayal and abstraction. Changing perceptions of society brought in their wake new perceptions of form, space, light, time and movement.
In France, Matisse created images of peerless harmony born of his enthusiasm for colour, while Braque and Picasso broke the mould of conventional concepts of form. Delaunay combined form and colour in a way that influenced the painters of the Blauer Reiter group. Whereas such new movements as Fauvism, Cubism and Futurism still retained certain figurative elements, Kandinsky was the first to take the radical step to pure abstraction. For Klee, on the other hand, abstract forms were a source of inspiration for his highly imaginative creative approach.
Painting as a vehicle of personal expression was taken to new heights by Chagall, Modigliani, Kirchner and Beckmann. The surrealists Dalí, Magritte, Max Ernst and Miró plumbed the depths of the subconscious in their works. In Russia and the Netherlands, Malevich and Mondrian sought to ban all that was personal from the new visual world they created, using strictly geometric forms of abstraction.

The painting of the 20th century, from the earliest works of classical Modernism onwards, simply cannot be understood as long as we expect artistic freedom to remain within certain bounds or demand that a painting should have some recognizable subject matter. Not only the abstract painters, but also those who still retained some signs of a mimetic relationship between art and visible reality, took art to extremes in the context of their day and age, permanently rolling back the boundaries of traditional ways of seeing.

When El Lissitzky (1890–1941) and Hans Arp (1887–1966) published *Die Kunstismen* (The Artisms) in 1925, they were able to list as many as fifteen different movements, with illustrations by way of example, even though their treatise was restricted to the ten years between 1914 and 1924. "Cubism, Futurism, Expressionism, abstract art, metaphysics, Suprematism, simultanism, Dadaism, purism, neoplasticity, merz, proun, verism, constructivism, abstract film." The sheer diversity they presented seems all the more confusing given the fact that, in the 20th century, so many different visual approaches were explored in rapid succession and sometimes even antithetical movements occurred simultaneously. Nevertheless, it is possible to identify certain correlations and basic undercurrents which permit us to link individual movements or understand how they influenced each other.

In terms of form and content, the many and varied changes that took place in the painting of classical Modernism can be pinnned down to a few fundamental transformations in visual concepts. These were: the liberation of colour and form from the reproduction of the object, culminating in abstraction; an emphasis on emotion and heightened personal expression on the one hand and a depersonalisation of the image in favour of structure and a new collective order on the other hand; the exploration of the subconscious in dreamlike and fantastic images.

## The Liberation of Colour

The use of pure, unbroken colours irrespective of the natural colour of the objects portrayed is the single most obvious characteristic of a group of artists that included Henri Matisse (1869–1954), Maurice de Vlaminck (1876–1958), André Derain (1880–1954), Albert Marquet (1875–1947), Georges Rouault (1871–1958), Raoul Dufy (1877–1953) and Georges Braque (1882–1963). When they exhibited together at the Salon d'Automne in Paris in 1905, their strident colours prompted the critic Louis Vauxcelles (*1870) to ridicule them as "fauves", meaning "wild beasts". The exhilarating abandon with which they handled colour liberated one of the most fundamental elements of painting.

**Pablo Picasso**
Portrait of Dora Maar, 1937
Oil on canvas, 92 x 65 cm
Paris, Musée Picasso

The explosive tonality of the Fauves was not without precursors. Other painters before them had sought to use colour in new ways, either by making it the foremost structuring element in the composition, as Seurat had done, or by using it to express emotions, as in the work of van Gogh, whose memorial exhibition in Paris in 1901 was the single most important event leading up to the formation of the Fauves. Apart from the influence of van Gogh, a keen interest in divisionism had also been aroused by the 1904 exhibition of paintings by Signac.

The Fauves rejected the gentle nuances of the Impressionist palette and sought a new expressive force in colour. They were not interested in a realistic rendering of nature. Instead, they created visions of green skies, yellow trees, blue roads and emerald green faces, by using the paints just as they were, straight from the tubes – or "dynamite cartridges", as Derain called them. A sense of space was created with neither perspectival depth nor shading, simply by superimposing, juxtaposing and interweaving areas of colour. The subject matter was no longer an independent entity, but merely a function of colour, and it was only through the distribution of colour in varying proportions on the canvas that the context and equilibrium of the picture was created. As a vindication of their aims rather than an explanation of its sources, the Fauves invoked an astonishing panoply of influences: the primitives, Gothic art, Rubens, El Greco, folk art, African sculpture.

Within five years, the shock of the Fauves had lost its sting. Some of the original members of the group began to turn once again to more traditional artistic values. Others, like Braque, moved on to explore new terrain. Matisse alone developed his life's work continuously on the basis of his enthusiasm for colour. Though he used garish and discordant tones, he was capable of profoundly subtle gradations of hues and, by limiting his palette to only a few colours and distributing them to create a delicately balanced structure, he produced images of incomparable harmony, as in his early masterpiece *Le luxe* (Paris, Musée d'Art Moderne) executed in 1907.

In Germany, Ernst Ludwig Kirchner (1880–1938), Karl Schmidt-Rottluff (1884–1976), Erich Heckel (1883–1970) and Fritz Bleyl (1880–1966) adopted an approach similar to that of the Fauves, and very possibly influenced by them. In 1905, they founded the Die Brücke group in Dresden. In 1906, when they held their first group exhibition, they were joined by Max Pechstein (1881–1995) and Emil Nolde (1867–1956) who remained with them for only two years.

The name Die Brücke, which means "the bridge", was intended to symbolize their aim of linking all the revolutionary tendencies of the day in Germany. Their sense of innovation and of moving forward into a new era is expressed in their programme, formulated by Kirchner in 1906: "With faith in progress and in a new generation of creators and spectators we call together all youth. As youth, we carry the future and want to create for ourselves freedom of life and of movement against the long established older forces. Everyone who reproduces that which drives him to creation with directness and authenticity belongs to us." Clearly, for the artists of Die Brücke, their innovative approach was not a question of exploring colour for its own sake, but one that addressed existential issues right from the start.

Like the Fauves, van Gogh, whose paintings were shown in Dresden in 1905 and 1908, was an important influence on the artists of Die Brücke, as were Gauguin and Seurat. Munch was also exhibited, and his ecstatic imagery, in which colour reflects inner emotion and turmoil, did not miss its mark. In fact, the work of this German group is often charged with an emotional and psychological tension quite alien to the paintings of Matisse, and it is this, in particular, that sets them apart from the pure colorism of the Fauves. The clear distinction between their respective styles was not diluted by the increasingly direct contact between the two groups; Pechstein met the Fauve artists in Paris in 1907, and in 1908 they exhibited in Dresden. In 1909, Kirchner visited the Matisse exhibition in Berlin. Another important factor in their development was the fact that an interest in folk art and visits to ethnological museums were gradually becoming a must for any progressive artist.

The artists of Die Brücke heightened colority to the point of dissonance. Kirchner and Heckel outlined their ornamental

**Alexei von Jawlensky**
The Red Shawl, 1909
Oil on canvas, 54 x 49 cm
Private collection

colour fields with bold, angular contours, while Schmidt-Rottluff openly juxtaposed them. They also explored the possibilities of the woodcut, a technique ill-suited to the more light-hearted approach of the Fauves, and adopted some of its formal severity and angularity in their paintings. Their motifs were drawn from their immediate surroundings: the studio, a holiday landscape, their artist friends, nudes and still lifes. The period in which Die Brücke produced paintings of unbroken, radiant colour was as brief as it had been for the Fauves. When the group moved to Berlin in 1911, the explosion of colour calmed to a more subdued tonality and a renewed emphasis was placed on content.

## The Renewal of Form

Shortly after the liberation of colour from the representation of objects, form and structure underwent a similar process. Influenced by a close study of Iberian and African sculpture, Pablo Picasso (1881–1973) began preparing preliminary sketches in 1906 for his 1907 painting, *Les Demoiselles d'Avignon* (ill. p. 569). The influence of the "primitives" was further consolidated by the impact of the 1907 Cézanne exhibition in Paris. According to Cézanne, "Everything in nature is modelled on the sphere, the cone and the cylinder." When Braque began to apply these ideas in his landscapes of L'Estaque, the critic Vauxcellles referred to the results disdainfully as "little cubes". So it was that the selfsame person whose scorn had given the Fauves their name was also instrumental in coining the term "Cubism". During the brief period between 1908 and 1914, Picasso and Braque developed the key aspects of this style that was to revolutionize our way of seeing.

In the first phase of Cubism in 1908/09, a few pictorial themes such as landscape, still life and figure (usually a half-figure with a musical instrument) were built up of basic geometric forms, resulting in angular entities whose self-contained corporeality underlines the sculptural quality of the objects. The palette, reduced to ochre, brown and green, has no independent value, but serves solely to lend clarity to the form. The illusionistic depth of central perspective is replaced by the simultaneous projection of different views and angles. Instead of a uniform pictorial space, we find an independent network of interconnected volumetric forms.

During the second Cubist phase, from 1910 to 1912, the term analytic Cubism gained currency, referring to the increasing deconstruction and dissection of volumes, lines and planes and the breakdown of clear delineation into a fluid interpenetration of planes that created an alternating interaction of positive and negative forms. Volume and space became inextricably linked. The break with a realistic representation of objects was pushed to its limits until the subject matter or theme of the painting became barely recognizable and pictorial structures verged on abstraction. Colour alternated in fragments of ochre and grey, and short, abrupt lines created a rhythmic formal texture.

**Henri Matisse**
Dance (La Danse), 1910
Oil on canvas, 260 x 391 cm
St Petersburg, Hermitage

Between 1912 and 1914, the third phase, known as synthetic Cubism, began with a technical innovation: a wide variety of everyday materials such as newspaper cuttings, cigarette packs, matchboxes and scraps of wallpaper were pasted into the pictures. The introduction of collage exerted an influence on 20th century art that was destined to go far beyond the bounds of Cubism. Picasso and Braque increasingly integrated aspects of daily reality into their work, while at the same time drawing attention to the materiality of the picture itself as an object. The carefully constructed layering of paper fragments influenced their overall style. Large-scale structuring created a more self-contained imagery, while the abbreviated portrayal of objects in distinctly contoured planar fragments took on a new representational clarity. Everything seemed to be pressed together in a single, flat layer. A return to a broader and brighter palette structured the planarity of the paintings and heightened the tension inherent in its forms. At the same time, however, the renewed colority began to regain an independent significance that verges on the garishly bright in Picasso's case.

Although Picasso and Braque eschewed exhibitions while they were systematically developing Cubism, their innovations fired the imagination of young artists in Paris right from the start. As early as 1910, Robert Delaunay (1885–1941), Albert Gleizes (1881–1953), Jean Metzinger (1883–1956) and Henri Le Fauconnier (1881–1946) joined the ranks of the Cubists, followed a year later, by Juan Gris (1887–1927). In 1911, the Cubists, with the exception of Picasso and Braque, exhibited their works as a group for the first time. Gleizes and Metzinger undertook the first attempt at a comprehensive definition and vindication of the new painting in *Du Cubism* (On Cubism), published in 1912. Amongst the circle of writers who supported the new movement, Guillaume Apollinaire published his book *Les peintres cubistes* (The Cubist Painters) in 1913.

Whereas Picasso and Braque explored the possibilities of Cubism in the domain of landscape, still life and figure, Fernand Léger (1881–1955) addressed the visual world of the machine age. Explaining his choice of motifs, he wrote: "Each artist possesses a weapon that allows him to attack tradition. In

**Georges Braque**
Fruit Bowl and Glass, 1912
Charcoal and papier collé, 62 x 44.5 cm
Private collection

tionships form the basis of a painting that is no longer imitative, but inherently creative on grounds of technique alone." Delaunay's paintings and theoretical statements had an enormous impact on the German artists of his day, most notably Marc, August Macke (1887–1914) and Paul Klee (1879–1940). Delaunay's treatise *Sur la lumière* (On Light) was translated into German by Klee and published in his Berlin magazine *Der Sturm* in 1913 under the title *Über das Licht*.

## Movement and Time

By breaking down the object and structuring images of simultaneity, Cubism prepared the ground for the portrayal of movement. Movement defies direct, realistic representation in painting. Whereas in film, it can be captured in temporal sequences, in painting it is represented by the simultaneous reiteration of a series of different stages of movement.

The aim of visualizing movement and time, dynamics and energy was taken up by a group of Italian artists who called themselves futurists in reference to their forward-looking orientation. Their *Manifesto of Futurism*, penned by the Italian poet Filippo Tommaso Marinetti (1876–1944) was published on the front page of the renowned Parisian daily *Le Figaro*, marking the birth of a movement that went on to produce some 180 manifestos addressing every domain of life and art. The very fact that it was published in Paris ensured that the manifesto gained international attention. Marinetti announced provocatively: "We affirm that the world's magnificence has been enriched by a new beauty: the beauty of speed. A racing-car whose hood is adorned with great pipes, like serpents of explosive breath – a roaring car that seems to ride on grapeshot is more beautiful than the *Victory of Samothrace*."

Umberto Boccioni (1882–1916), Carlo Carrà (1881–1966), Luigi Russolo (1885–1947), Giacomo Balla (1871–1958) and Gino Severini (1883–1966) followed suit on 11 February 1910 by drawing up and signing their *Futurist Painting: Technical Manifesto*. They were enthusiastic supporters of modern technology, the exhilaration of velocity and a new beauty that is not born of harmony, but of aggression and struggle. They had little interest in the past or in tradition, which they felt merely hindered their own powers. They saw war as a means of destroying the past and starting anew out of chaos. Their artistic ideas did not stand the test that came with the outbreak of the First World War, in which several of them were killed.

For the Futurist painters, the late Impressionist division of colours and, above all, the influence of Cubism since 1911, paved the way for them to put their new creed into practice. On this basis, Boccioni succeeded in heightening the dynamics of simultaneous permeation into a vivid impression of the spiralling movement of a maelstrom in his 1911 painting *The Noise of the Street Enters the House* (ill. p. 576). Boccioni even portrays time in his painting. The futurists did at least draw the viewer's gaze towards simultaneous perception and succeeded in raising the question of visualizing movement, time and space.

search of the explosive and the intense, I looked to the machine, just as others look to the nude or the still life. I try, with mechanical elements, to create a beautiful image." Léger developed a special form of Cubism whose leitmotif is the tube or cylinder. In 1913, Léger began work on a series of paintings entitled *Contrastes et formes* (Contrasts of Form) in which various constellations of cylindrical forms are presented in shades of blue-evoking metal, machinery and technology without any specific functional correlation. Though Léger was fascinated by the machine age, he did not seek to reproduce it in his paintings, preferring instead to adopt individual machine forms for his imagery.

Colour, which the Cubists had neglected for several years, giving precedence to form, became Delaunay's focal theme. In 1912, in his series of *Window* paintings, he explored the dissolution of form in colour. The lyricism of his work prompted Apollinaire to speak of a cubism of light and colour, for which he coined the term "orphism". Delaunay proclaimed the independence of the image: "Not a copy of nature – but the first abstract painting in colour. Colour, colours with their own laws, their contrasts, their slow vibrations, their intervals – all these rela-

**Pablo Picasso**
Guernica, 1937
Oil on canvas, 349.3 x 776.6cm
Madrid, Centro de Arte Reina Sofía

## The Advent of Abstract Art

Although every new movement since 1900 – Fauvism, Die Brücke, Cubism and Futurism – had radically questioned the mimetic function of the image and focused instead on the inherent laws of painting, all of them had retained signs of visual reality. The total break with figurative painting that was to revolutionize traditional attitudes to art was achieved by a small circle of progressive artists who had grouped together in Munich under the name Neue Künstlervereinigung (New Artists' Association).They included Adolf Erbslöh (1881–1947), Alexander Kanoldt (1881–1939), Marianne von Werefkin (1860–1938) and Gabriele Münter (1877–1962). Marc, Karl Hofer (1878–1955) and the brothers David (1882–1967) and Vladimir Burliuk (1886–1917) soon joined them. The spokesmen of the Neue Künstlervereinigung were Kandinsky and Alexei von Jawlensky (1864–1941). Their work was closely related to Fauvism and folk art traditions.

In his autobiography *Rückblicke* (Reminiscences) Kandinsky reports on an incident he experienced in his Munich studio in 1909: "I was returning, immersed in thought, from my sketching, when on opening the studio door, I was suddenly confronted by a picture of indescribable and incandescent loveliness. Bewildered, I stopped, staring at it. The painting lacked all subject, depicted no identifiable object and was entirely composed on bright colour patches. Finally I approached closer and only then saw it for what it really was – my own painting, standing on its side against the wall. Next day I tried to recapture the same impression in daylight, but I did not succeed fully: even lying on its side, I could still recognize the ob-

jects and the fine sheen of twilight was missing. One thing became clear to me: that objectiveness, the depiction of objects, needed no place in my paintings, and was indeed harmful to them."

In 1913, Kandinsky painted his first abstract watercolour, later backdating it to 1910. Between 1910 and 1914 he painted figurative, abstract and mixed figurative-abstract works. Although a number of painters since 1900, including Fancis Picabia (1879–1953), František Kupka (1871–1957), Robert Delaunay, Franz Marc, Hans Arp, Mikhail Larionov (1881–1957), Kasimir Malevich (1878–1935) and Piet Mondrian (1872–1944), had independently abandoned the figurative in their work, Kandinsky is generally acknowledged as the founder of abstract art. This is because he is the one artist who consistently pursued the path of abstract painting and systematically underpinned his innovations and discoveries in theoretic writings.

Kandinsky's conversion to abstraction led, in 1911, to the break-up of the Neue Künstlervereinigung. That same year, Kandinsky and Marc founded the Blauer Reiter as an association of like-minded artists with a committee for exhibitions and publications. Apart from Kandinsky and Marc, the first exhibition of the Blauer Reiter group included Heinrich Campendonk (1889–1957), Macke, Münter and, as a guest from Paris, Delaunay. Klee was represented in the second exhibition in 1912. 1912 was also the year in which Kandinsky and Marc issued the *Blaue Reiter Almanach* addressing painting, music and folk art, and the year in which Kandinsky published his major programmatic treatise *Über das Geistige in der Kunst* (On the Spiritual in

**Wassily Kandinsky**
Untitled, 1910 (1913)
Pencil, watercolour and ink on paper,
49.6 x 64.8 cm
Paris, Musée National d'Art Moderne,
Centre Georges Pompidou

Art). Inaccessibly complex as the fundamental principles of his book may be, it has remained a key text on abstract art right up to the present day.

Kandinsky rejected materialism and embraced spirituality. He made a clear distinction between nature and art, regarding art as separate from the practicalitites of life. For him, art did not mirror nature, but arose from an inner emotional urge capable of expressing itself independently of the external forms of nature. He saw "the principle of internal necessity" as the yardstick of all art, meaning that art renders perceptible something otherwise imperceptible, namely the universal law of a *harmonia mundi*. He considered two painters as the pioneers of abstract art: "Matisse - colour. Picasso - form. Two indicators of a great aim."

Music, which requires neither words nor tangible content, was a central point of reference for Kandinsky, who also linked various emotions and synaesthetic relationships in a simultaneous perception of colours and sounds. According to Kandinsky: "Colour is the keyboard. The eye is the hammer. The soul is the piano, with its many strings. The artist is the hand that purposefully sets the soul vibrating by means of this or that key." Kandinsky's theory of art had its roots in turn of the century Symbolism and bore affinities with the pre-war Expressionist movement. His orientation towards the cosmic was in keeping with the spirit of the times. Only in their choice of words do we discern a difference between Kandinsky and Klee: "The making of a work of art is inherently cosmic. The originator of the work is the spirit. That is the cosmic tragedy in which hu-

mankind is only a sound, just one single voice among many and in which the centre is pushed into a sphere that approaches divinity."

For Kandinsky, colour had a musical, symbolic and cosmic significance. Yellow sounds to him like a trumpet, an aggressive and typically earthly colour. Blue, depending on how dark or pale it is, sounds like a flute, a cello, a double bass, or an organ; it is the colour of tranquility, the typical celestial colour. Red, depending on the shade, sounds like a tuba or a violin; it is passion and channeled force. White means the nothingness before the beginning, before the birth, symbol of a world high above us. Black, on the other hand, is a silence with neither future nor hope. Marc, who went furthest of all the Blauer Reiter artists along Kandinsky's road towards abstraction, also attributes symbolic meanings to colours. For him, blue is the male principle, yellow the female principle, while red signifies matter in general.

Music, so frequently invoked in legitimizing the abandonment of subject matter, was represented in the exhibition and the *Blauer Reiter Almanach* by the composer Arnold Schönberg (1874–1951). At the same time as Kandinsky was developing abstract paintings, Schönberg took the decisive step towards atonal music. Driven by them same urge to underpin his works theoretically, Schönberg published his *Harmonielehre* (Theory of Harmony) in 1911. Schönberg's influential publication bears some remarkable correspondences to Kandinsky's *On the Spiritual in Art*. Both are interested in the hidden inner sound of the world; both posit and document the spiritual principle of art.

After visiting a Schönberg concert in Munich in January 1911, Marc wrote to Macke: "Can you imagine a music from which tonality (that is to say, the adherence to a certain key) is entirely absent? I couldn't help thinking of Kandinsky's great compositions and of Kandinsky's 'leaping colours' when I heard this music, which lets each note stand for itself (a kind of white canvas between the patches of colour!) Arnold Schönberg seems to be convinved of the ineluctable dissolution of the European laws of art and harmony in the same way as the Munich Artists'Association." Marc regarded this dissolution as a positive and liberating gain, as the revelation of a new creative beginning, whereas the critics saw in it only a decline into utter chaos. On the outbreak of the First World War, in which both Marc and Macke fell, Kandinsky left Munich and returned to Russia.

## Unsettling Reality

An important motivation for the Brücke artists – Kirchner, Heckel, Pechstein and Schmidt-Rottluff – to move to Berlin in the autumn of 1911 was their hope of reaching a broader and more enlightened public in the capital city. In Berlin, Herwarth Walden (1878–1941) had been publishing his art magazine *Der Sturm* since 1910. It was to become the most important forum for introducing the German public to contemporary French and German art. At the same time, Walden was also a talented organizer of exhibitions, which he held at the Sturm gallery or sent on tour. In 1912 he showed the work of the Blauer Reiter artists.

In 1911, the art historian Wilhelm Worringer (1881–1965) published an article in *Der Sturm* in which the word Expressionism was used for the first time to describe the visual arts. Worringer actually applied the term to Cézanne, van Gogh and Matisse, for whom it is no longer used today. Nevertheless, this would certainly seem to indicate that the work of these artists was regarded at the time as a heightened form of expression and that their work was felt to be in some way related. With respect to the Blauer Reiter exhibition at the Sturm gallery the term was also used in connection with the modern trend in German art; that is to say, with artists whose new formal language sought to express both emotional and social perceptions. Expressionism is not a uniform movement in terms of either form or content. The spectrum ranges from Marc's endeavour to "pantheistically sense the trembling and flowing of blood in nature" to Max Beckmann's (1884–1950) fascination for the "great human orchestra" of the city.

The bewildering diversity of impressions and perceptions and the hustle and bustle of the city was what captured the imagination of the Expressionists, providing them with a complex subject, that would be taken up by them in their art, literature and film. The city was a mirror of existential struggle and sensual pleasure, teeming masses and solitude, affluence and poverty, exhilaration and danger. For the Expressionists, the people were more important than the backdrop, and they often portrayed figures on the margins of bourgeois society as typical representatives of urban life.

Amongst the artists of the Brücke, the most vehement reaction was that of Kirchner. His Berlin street scenes of 1913/14 are images of urban alienaticn. His protagonists are prostitutes and their clients. Their encounters are rituals of soliciting and selling. Sharp, incisive lines and stark contrasts of light and shadow give the figures something threatening and aggressive. Their faces are as anonymous as masks. His works describe the lonely, the forlorn and the loveless. Apart from these images of alienation, Kirchner also portrayed a life of freedom in nature, executed during the summer months he spent on the Baltic island of Fehmarn or at Lake Moritzburg near Dresden.

**Marc Chagall**
Double Portrait with Wineglass (Bella and Marc), 1917
Oil on canvas, 235 x 137cm
Paris, Musée National d'Art Moderne, Centre Georges Pompidou

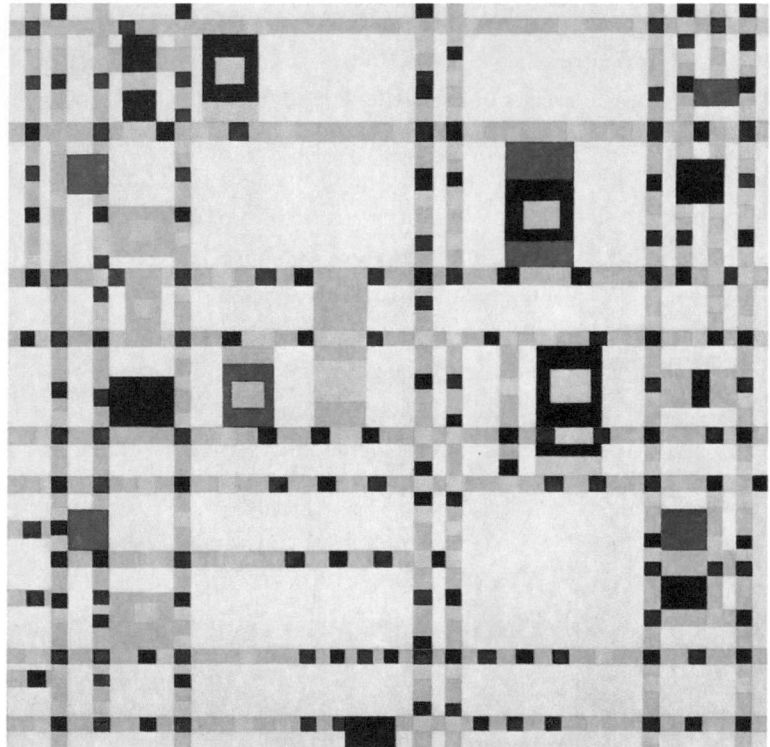

**Piet Mondrian**
Broadway Boogie-Woogie, 1942/43
Oil on canvas, 127 x 127 cm
New York, The Museum of Modern Art

In Ludwig Meidner's (1884–1966) *Anleitung zum Malen von Großstadtbildern* (Guidelines for Painting Urban Scenes) published in 1914, he writes: "We have to start painting our home at last, the city, which we love infinitely. On countless canvases the size of frescos, our trembling hands should scribble all that is magnificent and strange, monstrous and dramatic, in the avenues, railway stations, factories and towers." Meidner's street scenes and cityscapes of 1913 have an unsettling futuristic dynamism full of plunging perspectives. Meidner's apocalyptic visions are bursting with an angst-ridden sense of being cast at the mercy of civilization's destructive potential. One year before the outbreak of the First World War, the cities in his canvases were harbingers of impending doom.

The war unleashed a deep moral crisis amongst the German artists Beckmann, Otto Dix (1891–1969), George Grosz (1893–1959), Kirchner and many others. In 1915 Kirchner painted himself as a drinker and as a soldier with his hand shot away, even though he had not even been to the front during his brief military service. Nevertheless, his fear was barely under control. Kirchner wrote in a letter in 1916: "The pressure of war and the increasing superficiality weighs heaviest of all. I constantly have the impression of a bloody carnival. It is as though the decision is hanging in the air and everything is topsy-turvy. Bloated, staggering to work, though all work is futile and mediocrity is storming everything in its path. Becoming like the whores I used to paint. Washed out, gone next time. All the same, I still try to order my thoughts and create an image of our time out of the confusion, which is, after all, my task."

Grosz, who was invalided out of the armed forces, described the motivation behind his artistic production: "I drew and painted out of contradiction and tried, through my work, to portray the world in all its ugliness, sickness and mendacity." For Grosz, the street was a place of violence, terror and brutality; he castigated the bourgeoisie by revealing its perverse and even criminal side.

Beckmann took a rather different stance in his *Schöpferische Konfession* (Creative Credo), published in Berlin in 1920: "The war has now dragged to its miserable end. But it hasn't changed my ideas about life in the least, it has only confirmed them. We are on our way to very difficult times. But right now, perhaps more than before the war, I need to be with people. In the city. That is just where we belong these days. We must be a part of all the misery which is coming. We have to surrender our heart and our nerves, we must abandon ourselves to the horrible cries of pain of a poor, deluded people. Right now we have to get as close to the people as possible. It's the only course of action which might give some purpose to our superfluous and selfish existence – that we give people a picture of their fate. And we can only do that if we love humanity." In his paintings, Beckmann shows people in harrowingly claustrophobic situations, deformed by brutality and passions.

In contrast to the dismay and suffering expressed by some at the circumstances of the time, there were other artists who vociferously proclaimed their sarcastic criticism of outmoded values, monotony and empty functionalism. From Zurich, where the members of the Cabaret Voltaire had adopted the meaningless name Dada, the anti-art movement spread through the art centres of New York, Paris, Berlin, and even took hold in Hanover and Cologne.

Max Ernst (1891–1979) who was a member of the Cologne Dada group from 1918 to 1922, wrote: "A war as terrible as it is was senseless robbed us of five years of our lives. We were there when everything we had been taught was right, beautiful and true was plunged into an abyss of ridicule and shame. My works of that period were not meant to please, they were meant to make you howl."

### Designs for a New World
Even during the First World War, artists in Russia and the Netherlands were joining forces with the aim of creating designs for a new world, and breaking down the barriers between art and technology. Every field of modern life was to be included: fine arts, architecture and urban planning, typography and advertising, photography and film. Geometric forms began to predominate in the visual arts.

In Russia, Kasimir Malevich presented his *Black Square* (St Petersburg, Russian Museum). In an accompanying text, he described his new style: "The midnight hour of art has tolled. The fine arts have been banned and ostracized. The artist as idol is a prejudice of the past. Suprematism compresses all painting into a black square on a white canvas. I have invented nothing. All I sensed within me was night and in night I glimpsed that which is new, that which I called suprematism. It is expressed in the black area that forms a square."

After the October Revolution of 1917, Suprematism became the predominant style in Moscow. Apart from painting, Malevich also turned his attention to architecture, and his suprematist theory was aimed at a universe with neither aims nor boundaries. According to Malevich, the world in which we live is an illusion born of our habit of separating individual entities from the universe by giving them names and allocating certain functions to them. He sought to present the true universe pictorially in coloured planarity, but even this, he felt, was not going far enough, and so he exhorted his readers to "swim in the white, free abyss; infinity is before you." In the west, his ideas had reached a wider public by 1927 at the latest, when Malevich had an exhibition in Berlin and his book *The Non-Objective World* was published by the Bauhaus under the German title *Die gegenstandslose Welt*.

El Lissitzky was also working on the realization of new ideas. Between 1919 and 1924, he created the abstract paintings he called *Prouns*. The word "proun" is actually an acronym made up of the first letters of the Russian phrase meaning "foundation of new forms in art". As Lissitzky said of his "prouns": "the canvas has become too small for me, and I have created the proun as a transition between painting and architecture. I treated the canvas and wooden panels as a plot of ground where my structural concepts are subject to a minimum of inhibitions. I used the range of black and white (with a blaze of red) as matter and material. In this way, a reality is created that is clear to all." Like Malevich, Lissitzky was fascinated by movement in space: "New inventions enable us to move in space in a new way with new rapidity will create a new reality. The static architecture of the Egyptian pyramids is overcome: our architecture rolls, swims, flies. Floating oscillation emerges. I want to be involved in inventing and designing this reality." In accordance with his concepts, Lissitzky turned his back on autonomous creative work after 1924 and worked as an inventor, constructor, photographer and typographer.

After 1921, the terms "Suprematism" and "proun" were superseded by the more all-embracing term "Constructivism" – a term derived from the relief constructions of Vladimir Tatlin (1885–1952), who concentrated on formal and material qualities and on the relationship between matter and space. Tatlin's 1919/20 design for the *Monument to the 3rd International* has come to be regarded as the very epitome of revolutionary art in Russia. A gradual reaction against Constructivism began to set in, culminating in the dismissal of their work as "degenerate" by 1931; Socialist Realism was gaining the upper hand.

In the Netherlands in 1917, a group of painters, sculptors and architects were associated with the magazine *De Stijl* which was published until 1928 by Theo van Doesburg (1883–1931).

**Kasimir Malevich**
Suprematist Painting, 1916
Oil on canvas, 88 x 70.5 cm
Amsterdam, Stedelijk Museum

Their aim was to present a universal harmony in which individualism was overcome. Like the Russian artists, geometrism and constructivism are their artistic means of creating a better world.

The artist who transposed their ideas into painting most persuasively was Mondrian, who also introduced the term "new plasticity". His images show full-blown abstraction in the sense that they completely dismiss sensual perception of visual reality. The pictorial elements are reduced to their basic elements: straight line, right angle – horizontals and verticals – and the primary colours red, yellow and blue with the non-colours black and white. It is a highly disciplined and reduced painting. Mondrian, however, is not interested primarily in designing elementary forms, but in elementary correlations. The balanced interrelationship of various proportions is the expression of his *Weltbild* based on the antagonism between microcosm and macrocosm, or, as Mondrian himself said: "Through the horizontal-vertical division of the rectangle, the neoplasticist gains the tranquility and equilibrium of duality: of the universe and of the individual."

In Germany, the design for a new world did not begin until after the end of the First World War. Following on from van de

Velde's Kunstgewerbeschule (school of applied arts), the Staat- liches Bauhaus was founded in Weimar in 1919. Its aims were less utopian than those of Malevich's Suprematism or Mon- drian's neoplasticity. As a training facility, it was also rather more down-to-earth. The students were to be taught to apply artistic experience to the design of architecture and everyday ob- jects. The programme issued by Walter Gropius stated: "Archi- tects, painters, sculptors, we must all return to the crafts! For there is no such thing as 'professional art'. There is no essential difference between the artist and the craftsman. The artist is an exalted craftsman. By the grace of heaven and in rare moments of inspiration which transcend his will, art may unconsciously blossom from the labour of his hand, but a foundation in handi- craft is essential for every artist. It is there that the primary source of creativity lies."

Lyonel Feininger (1871–1956), who illustrated Gropius' Bauhaus programme with a woodcut of a cathedral in his own distinctive style of crystalline cubism, was a painter at the Bau- haus since its foundation. He was followed by Paul Klee, Oskar Schlemmer (1888–1943), László Moholy-Nagy (1895– 1946) and Kandinsky, who had returned from Russia. Teach- ing at the Bauhaus encouraged painters to become more aware of their attitudes in order to enable them to pass on their knowledge of the effects of colour, form and materials to their students.

Klee published his *Wege des Naturstudiums* (Towards a Study of Nature) in 1923 and his *Pädagogisches Skizzenbuch* (Pedago- gical Sketchbook) in 1925 as Bauhaus Book 2. At the art associ- ation in Jena, Klee held his famous lecture "On Modern Art". Kandinsky's teaching at the Bauhaus produced his *Punkt und Linie zu Fläche* (Point and Line to Plane), which was published in 1926 as Bauhaus Book 9. He drew up a grammar of element- ary forms and explored planimetric figures to determine their fundamental properties and their expressive value, by combin- ing the objective with the subjective. He defined composition as "an exact, regulated organization of vital forces contained within the elements in the form of tension."

The *avant-garde* music of the day also underwent a similar transformation. Schönberg systematized free atonality to create the twelve-tone method. The strictly atonal compositional ap- proach based on this row or sequence of twelve notes was ex- tremely strict. It arose from the composer's urge to "create the greatest possible interrelationship between the various parts" and it also meant a reduction in individuality.

The rational atmosphere of the Bauhaus encouraged the use of geometric elements by painters. Between 1914 and 1921, while he was in Russia, Kandinsky used geoemtric forms along- side irregular, organic forms for the first time, possibly under the influence of Suprematism and Constructivism.

At the Bauhaus, he completely abandoned the free structure of his early abstract pictures. Geometric forms are superimposed and seem to move as though within an endless space. Whereas

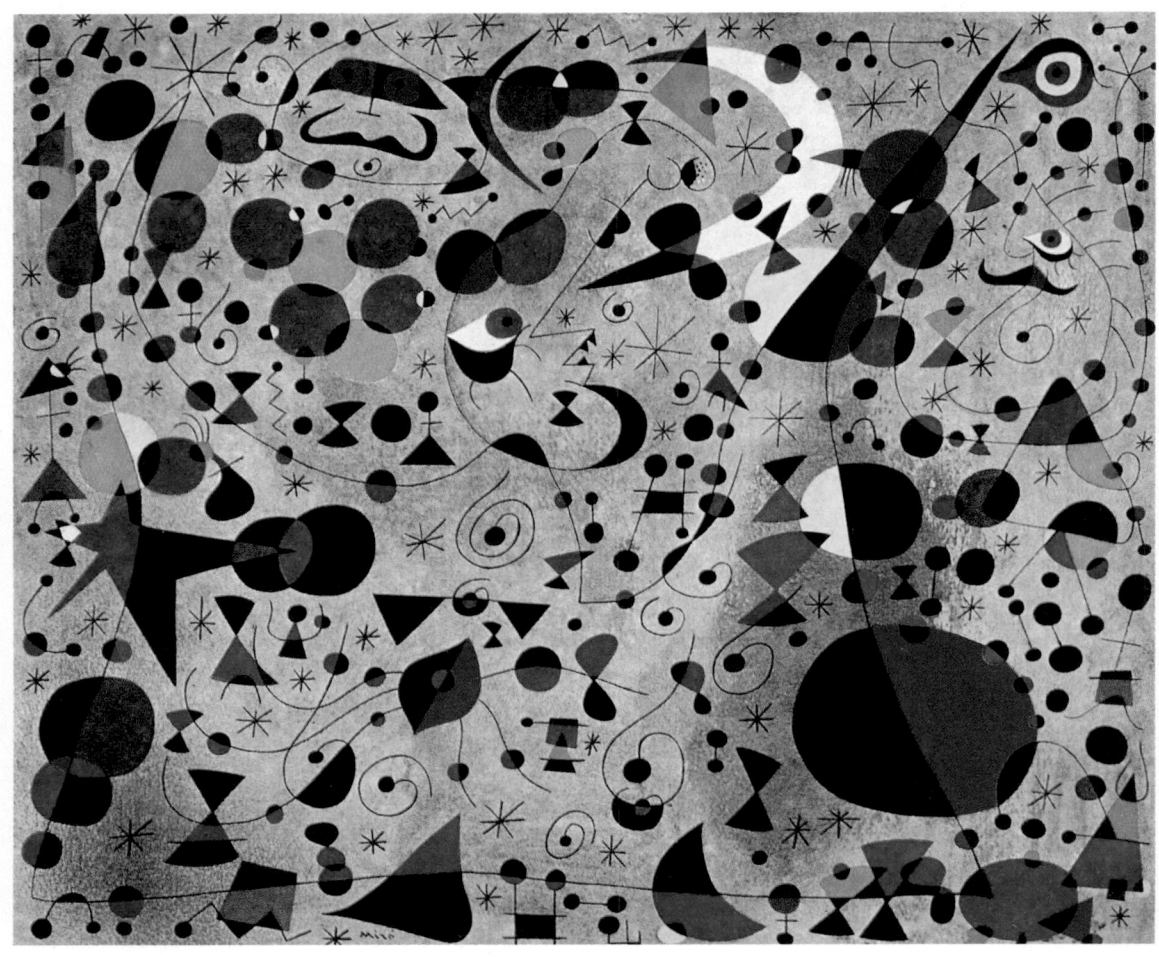

Joan Miró
The Poetess, 1940
Gouache and turpentine paints on paper, 38.1 x 45.7 cm
New York, Collection Colin

**Edward Hopper** Nighthawks, 1942
Oil on canvas, 76.2 x 152.4 cm. Chicago (IL), The Art Institute of Chicago

Kandinsky avoided figurative associations, Klee positively sought them. Unlike Kandinsky, Klee sought to combine the laws of nature and art. Both these artists, however, retained the fundamental principles of the Blaue Reiter period, seeing a network of interactive forces in geometric forms as well, and maintaining the cosmic dimension of their art. In the work of Moholy-Nagy, on the other hand, the constructivist images are linked with a new order of concrete reality.

The tension between fine art and applied art was not entirely swept aside at the Bauhaus. Schlemmer, in his many activities as painter, sculptor, set designer, ballet choreographer and art teacher, acted as a mediator between various disciplines, but rather than seeing a bond between them, he retained their individual independence. On 18 March 1924, he noted in his diary: "I see the way towards the future like this: the paths diverge. The architectural, constructive tendencies of recent movements in art lead to direct application, constituting a solution for so many recent problems. Application: designing the everyday objects around us or, even better – house construction and everything that entails. On the other hand, the death of art proclaimed by the proponents of application (the true, non-painting Constructivists, incidentally) is found to be untrue; I mean the picture, painting, the metaphysical, are saved and demonstrated by the same constructivist tendencies that some apply pragmatically and others apply ideally in design."

As the political situation in Germany became increasingly tense, the Bauhaus was forced to move from Weimar to Dessau in 1924/25 and then to Berlin in 1932. Ludwig Mies van der Rohe (1886–1969), the last director of the Bauhaus, endeavoured to keep the school going, but had to give up in 1933. The National Socialists equated abstract art with Bolshevism and proclaimed the entire modern movement to be *entartet* ("degenerate"). A touring exhibition entitled *Entartete Kunst* (Degenerate Art) was organized to pillory modern art.

## Beyond Reality

Giorgio de Chirico (1888–1978) sought to go beyond the bounds of mere physical reality with an art he called *pittura metafisica*. Impressed by the city of Turin, we wrote: "On the city squares, shadows cast their geometric riddles. Above the walls stand senseless towers, heightened by bright little flags," and, continuing in this vein, he added, "it is the frosty twilight hour of a clear day towards the end of spring. The depths of the celestial dome, green as the ocean, makes anyone who gazes at it dizzy."

For de Chirico, it was clear that "madness is an inherent element of any profound artistic statement." In his view, madness meant the loss of memory: "The logic of our normal actions and daily lives is a continuous band of memory of the relationships between the environment and ourselves." In de Chirico's metaphysical paintings of the period between 1909 and 1919, this

**Salvador Dalí**
The Temptation of St Anthony, 1946
Oil on canvas, 89.7 x 119.5 cm
Brussels, Musée Royaux des Beaux-Arts
de Belgique

memory is erased. He could already look back on a considerable œuvre of metaphysical paintings when he was joined in 1917 by Ferrara Carrà, who had left the Futurists, Alberto Savinio (1891–1952) and Filippo de Pisis (1896–1956). Together, they founded the *arte metafisica* group. Giorgio Morandi (1890–1964) joined them a year later. *Pittura metafisica* became a direct precursor of surrealist art, which recognizes de Chirico as its main influence.

Surrealism emerged in the mid 1920s in response to increasing rationalization and perfectionism on the one hand, and as a counterpart to the rediscovered realities of the unconscious on the other hand. André Breton (1896–1966), the spokesman of the Surrealists, claimed in 1924, provocatively referring to the Christian credo: "I believe in the future dissolution of these apparently contradictory states of dream and reality into a kind of absolute reality, as one might say: *sur-réalité*." Each of the Surrealist painters had their own personal language, their individual mythology, their personal pictorial themes. The enigma lay in the spiritual approach rather than in the artistic form. The poet and *avant-garde* spokesman Apollinaire used the word "surrealist" for the first time in 1917.

As the description of an art movement, however, the term only began to take hold gradually once the writers Breton, Louis Aragon (1879–1982) and Philippe Soupault (1897–1990) had founded the magazine *Littérature* in Paris in 1919. Under the influence of Tristan Tzara (1896–1963), *Littérature* was initially concerned with Dadaism, before turning increasingly towards Surrealism. In 1922, with the arrival of Ernst and Man

Ray (1890–1976) in Paris, the circle of writers extended to include the visual arts a year before the actual founding of Surrealism. In 1924, Breton published the first *Manifeste du surréalisme* (Surrealist Manifesto). At the same time, the magazine *La Révolution Surréaliste* was launched and the Bureau de Recherches Surréalistes was opened in Paris.

Surrealism rendered the realms of the subconscious visible in paintings. It was an artistic revolution which, unlike Fauvism and Cubism, was not interested primarily in questions of colour and form, but in seeking new artistic possibilities and processes as a vehicle for expressing new subjects. By combining scientific research into the subconscious with findings on painful and pleasurable experiences, the Surrealists drew upon many contemporary and historical sources: psychoanalysis and the Fredian interpretation of dreams, fairytales and myths, spiritualism and alchemy, German romanticism and fantastic elements of art from the earliest days to the 20th century, naive painting and the art of the mentally ill, children and "primitive" peoples. In the world of literature, they acknowledged the influence of the Marquis de Sade (1740–1814), Edgar Allan Poe (1809–1849), Count Lautréamont (1846–1870), Arthur Rimbaud (1854–1891) and Alfred Jarry (1873–1907).

In their quest for appropriate means of expression, the Surrealists developed a number of processes which include chance as a source of artistic inspiration: *frottage*, in which a paper is placed over a relief and the design is transferred to the paper by rubbing with charcoal or crayon; "decalcomania" in which ink or paint is applied to paper, then folded or blotted onto another paper and the chance image obtained in this way is then elaborated by the artist; the scratch technique known as "grattage", the smoke technique known as "fumage" and the "sand painting" technique of scattering sand onto a canvas primed with paste. By alternating between different forms but also by combining them – automatic handwriting, chance and deliberate processes – multi-layered possibilities of expression emerged and the fantastic was also given a new dimension.

The first Surrealist exhibition at the Galerie Pierre in Paris included works by Arp, de Chirico, Ernst, André Masson (1896–1987), Joan Miró (1893–1983), Picasso, Man Ray, Pierre Roy (1880–1950) and Klee. Yves Tanguy (1900–1955), René Magritte (1898–1967), Salvador Dalí (1904–1989) and Alberto Giacometti (1901–1966) joined them and widened the spectrum that ranged from traces of subconscious painting to the principle of "automatic writing", including coded and symbolic portrayals and even representational renderings of dreams or enigmatic reality. The Surrealists explored literary, artistic and above all political questions with an intensity that led to changes in the magazine, which eventually adopted the name *Le Surréalisme au Service de la Révolution* and also prompted Breton to publish the second *Surrealist Manifesto* in 1930. During the Second World War, many of the surrealists emigrated to New York, where they were to have a profound influence on American art.

## Abstract or Concrete Art?

Around 1930, Paris once again became the centre of an international artistic *avant-garde*. Devotees of abstract art formed groups such as the Cercle et Carré and Art Concret. These two groups were the precursors of Abstraction-Création, which was founded as an association to organize exhibitions of non-figurative art and publish statements on it in their *Cahiers* or yearbooks. "Abstraction, because certain artists have come to the concept of non-figuration by the progressive abstraction of forms from nature. Creation, because other artists have attained non-figuration direct, purely via geometry, or by the exclusive use of elements commonly called abstract such as circles, planes, bars, lines, etc..." What is referred to here as "creation" was to become established under the term "concrete art" from 1930 onwards – a term also adopted by Kandinsky, who emigrated to Paris in 1933. It refers to an art with no relation to the visual reality of purely geometric forms and correspondences, and whose painterly technique is precise, immaterial and impersonal.

Alongside the cool geometry of abstract art, however, more and more lyrical and coded aspects were developed. The geometry of Kandinsky's Bauhaus paintings was combined wih organic, semiotic and even musical forms and movements. The Symbolists also adopted semiotic aspects of form. In the 1930s, the work of Miró and Masson moved closer towards abstraction. The work of Arp, with its mutable organic forms, bears distinct

affinities to that of the Surrealists. The semiotic aspect became a key factor in art after 1945, influenced more by Kandinsky, Klee, the Surrealists and, in Germany, Willi Baumeister (1889–1955) than by the geometrists. This influence spread to the USA in the early 1940s, where Kandinsky's early *Improvisations* together with the surrealism of such painters as Arshile Gorky (1905–1948), Willem de Kooning (* 1904) and Jackson Pollock (1912–1956) led to the painting that came to be known as abstract Expressionism.

Never before in the history of art had the appearance of things – their colour, form and spatiality – changed so much, and never before had the range of concepts involved been so broad. The *avant-garde* movements added new dimensions of perception to what was already familiar, but also narrowed the view of their specificity and fragmented the holism of experience. Many important artists adopted aspects of the *avant-garde* movements, but nevertheless continued to develop their œuvre in concert with both their own inner motivation and with past tradition.

Such artists as Amedeo Modigliani (1884–1920), Marc Chagall (1887–1985), Chaïm Soutine (1893–1943) and Georges Rouault (1871–1958) spring to mind in this context. Others

**Yves Tanguy**
The Five Strangers, 1941
Oil on canvas, 98 x 81.3 cm
Hartford (CT), The Wadsworth Atheneum,
The Ella Gallup Sumner and Mary Catlin Sumner Collection

flirted briefly with the revolutionary movement in art before returning to a more traditional approach; they include Derain, Carrà, de Chirico, to name but a few. Severini, who had distanced himself from Futurism and was one of the first to try to merge *avant-garde* portrayals with tradition, published his book *From Cubism to Classicism* in 1921. In 1915, Picasso produced drawings in the Neoclassicist style of Ingres and even applied this approach to other themes in drawings and paintings in 1917. For Léger, the cubist and mechanical period in which he broke down the planes to create a distinct dynamism, was followed in 1920 by his monumental period which reintegrated the human form.

The history of painting during the period of classical Modernism is rather more complex than a mere sequence of fresh starts. Indeed, these many and varied innovations and changes of direction may be regarded as its constitutive framework, rather than as a means of evaluation. In 1912, Kandinsky wrote in *Über die Formfrage* (On the Question of Form): "The embodiments torn by the mind out of the storehouse of painting can be ordered quite easily between two extremes: 1. great abstraction, 2. great realism. These two extremes open up two paths which lead eventually to one destination." In other words, both figurative and non-figurative art are based on a creative force and not just on a representative force.

(The descriptions of pages 562 bottom, 610 top, 612 and 614 were written by the editor.)

# JAMES ENSOR
## 1860–1949

Because of the ambiguity of this painting, with its blurring of boundaries between masquerade and fantasy, it has come to be known variously as *Skeletons Fighting over the Body of a Hanged Man* or *Masks Fighting over the Body of a Hanged Man*.

One of the three female figures who have been fighting with each other is lying on the ground, but continues to keep up the fight by attempting to pull the others down, clutching at the hems of their skirts. The figure on the left in a richly embroidered cloak over a long dress is a lady. Her opponent with a feathered hat, pseudo-military jacket and patent leather boots is a girl of easy virtue. The defeated figure lying prostrate on the ground in a cotton jacket and striped skirt is a domestic servant.

The three figures could be the wife, the mistress and the housemaid of the dead man. A number of threads linking the hanged man with the stick his wife is wielding as a weapon indicate that, in his lifetime, the man was the puppet of his wife. The sign saying CIVET (a stew of hare and other game) suggests that he is to be devoured. Greedy masks are pushing into the room from both sides in an embodiment of raw passion. This painting is an expression of Ensor's hatred of women, his repulsion of marriage and his view of humankind as a barbarous hoard.

**James Ensor**
Skeletons Fighting for the Body of a Hanged Man, 1891
Oil on canvas, 59 x 74 cm
Antwerp, Koninklijk Museum voor Schone Kunsten

Ensor's desire to flee daily existence and seek refuge in the world of make-believe prompted him to turn to masks as a central means of expression. Ensor's self-portrait of 1899 shows him gazing sadly out at the spectator wearing a rather eccentric hat and surrounded, indeed stormed, by a mob of masks. Behind his back, the masks are in the company of skulls. They have a threatening and menacing air. Those in front of him, with their bizarre faces and long noses, seem more friendly.

In Ensor's œuvre, the self-portrait turns to role-play. Here, Ensor plays the part of Peter Paul Rubens, whose self-portrait (Vienna, Kunsthistorisches Museum) he assimilates fully. Only the hat is a parody. As early as 1883, Ensor had taken Rubens' self-portrait as his inspiration for a self-portrait with a floral hat (Ostende, Museum voor Schone Kunsten). The various levels of role play, self-scrutiny and parody are difficult to distinguish. Ensor said of the meaning the mask had for him: "I have happily abandoned myself to the realms of solitude in which the mask is enthroned in all its violence, light and magnificence. To me, the mask means freshness of tone, exaggerated expression, sumptuous decor, grand and unexpected gesture, uninhibited movement, selected turbulence."

The intense and highly expressive colority of Ensor's paintings influenced the Expressionists, while his bizarre and often macabre fantasy inventions influenced the Surrealists.

**James Ensor**
Portrait of the Artist Surrounded by Masks, 1899
Oil on canvas, 120 x 80 cm
Antwerp, Collection Jussiant

# EDVARD MUNCH
## 1863–1944

Edvard Munch
Puberty, 1895
Oil on canvas,
151.4 x 109.9 cm
Oslo, Nasjonalgalleriet

In this painting, *Puberty*, Munch explores the anxieties of being on the threshold of adult life. He dares to enter the borderland between the physical and the psychological. Sitting rather awkwardly on the edge of the bed, a naked adolescent girl stares wide-eyed out of the picture. Her pale body cuts across the white sheet. Her lanky arms are crossed over her lap, as though seeking to conceal the source of her anxiety. The deeply disturbing new experience has created a stage of great excitement. In the unornamented surroundings, the shadow of the girl does not appear as a natural accompaniment, but has something mysteriously threatening, dark and fluid. The girl is helplessly confronted with her own sexuality.

Munch's simultaneous evocation of attraction and repulsion lies in the subtly expressive presentation of the same themes explored by Sigmund Freud. It is evident that Munch was not interested in revealing the girl's vulnerability, but in showing understanding and empathy, for in spite of the inner turmoil, the portrait possesses a formal austerity and solemnity reminiscent of portrayals of Christ in suffering.

*Below:*
Edvard Munch
Girls on a Bridge, 1901
Oil on canvas,
135.9 x 125.4 cm
Oslo, Nasjonalgalleriet

The three *Girls on a Bridge* which Munch painted during a summer sojourn in Aasgaardstrand possesses a quiet lyricism. Munch did not invent this situation, but actually portrayed a specific point on the Oslofjord: the long bridge that continues into a sloping street, the sandy shoreline with its green patches of grass, the old house with its shady trees, framed by a white wooden fence. Yet he has drawn all these elements together into large, melancholic forms that are mirrored in even darker tones on the surface of the water. Only the yellow star, whose silvery light makes it unclear whether it is sun or moon, does not appear in the reflection.

Three girls are standing at the railing of the bridge. Sketchily portrayed in white, red and green, they appear more as a triad of colour than as human figures. They have turned away from the viewer so that they cannot be grasped as individuals. Apart from their compositional function in the painting, they also pose a challenge to the viewer, calling us to observe the landscape and its atmosphere in the same way as they do. It is the mood of the painter that is reflected in the viscous forms of what is an almost melancholy gravity.

This interpretation is confirmed by Edvard Munch's own words: "In a strong emotional mood, a landscape has a specific effect on people – by portraying such a landscape one can arrive at an image of one's own mood – it is this mood that is the main thing – nature is merely the medium."

As in so many themes that were important to him, Edvard Munch painted several versions of this oil-painting and also portrayed the scene in various different printing techniques.

# GEORGES ROUAULT
## 1871–1958

Throughout his life, Rouault endeavoured to find the meaning of life through the Christian faith. The theme of *The Holy Face* is one he treated repeatedly. According to legend, Veronica approached Christ on the road to Calvary and wiped his face, and the imprint of his face was left on the cloth. Rouault's painting is based on this apocryphal text.

The face of Christ is presented frontally, with solemn ceremony, on the white cloth. In order to underline the precious value of this honoured relic, Rouault has painted a frame of roses and fine ornaments around the cloth. The expression of the face is heightened by strong black contours, the proportions painfully elongated. Repeated overpainting of individual parts has created an encrusted surface structure, lending the painting the character of something ancient, venerable and timeless. The artist has combined his painterly means with his faith in the permanent validity of the pictorial theme.

Time and time again, Rouault's pictorial themes expressed his faith. Even *The Old King* is not a spontaneous pictorial creation, but one based on designs from the year 1916. As in *The Holy Face* we are reminded of a much more distant past. The biblical Book of Kings and the tale of King David spring to mind. This king, however, is not dressed in the garb of a specific era, even if the portrayal tempts us to think of Gothic stained glass windows.

Rouault's distinctive ability to emphasize contours so that each plane of colour is bounded by a broad line like a fragment of stained glass in its lead setting, has frequently been cited as evidence of the continuing influence of his apprenticeship as a stained glass maker. The contoured weave of black lines and figural stylization create clarity in various respects: it divides the various zones of the painting and at the same time heightens the iconographic and compositional clarity, the completely planar approach without perspectival depth, is frontal to the viewer and, finally, the detail is restricted to only the most essential aspects of expression.

Rouault retained this technique of linear compositional structuring to the end of his life. But it has to be complemented by colour. It is colour that determines the overall atmospheric character of his work and it is applied in a technique that occasionally appears "scarred": in the red of the robe, the yellow of the crown and chain, in the white of the flowers. Because they are applied in several layers, the colours develop an enormous luminosity that is almost phosphorescent. All these artistic techniques serve to heighten the impression of stringency, earnestness and solemnity. As Rouault himself said: "I do not seek beauty, but expression."

Georges Rouault
The Holy Face, 1933
Oil on canvas, 91 x 65 cm
Paris, Musée National d'Art
Moderne, Centre Georges
Pompidou

Georges Rouault
The Old King, 1937
Oil on cardboard,
77 x 54 cm
Pittsburgh (PA), The Carnegie
Museum of Art

**Albert Marquet**
The Beach at Fécamp, 1906
Oil on canvas, 51 x 61 cm
Paris, Musée National d'Art Moderne,
Centre Georges Pompidou

## ALBERT MARQUET
### 1875–1947

Marquet met Matisse at the Ecole des Arts Décoratifs in Paris in 1890 and remained a friend all his life. In 1905, his paintings were shown alongside those of Matisse, Derain and Vlaminck in the exhibition that brought them the name Fauves. It is important to recall this connection in the case of Marquet.

The motif of the Mediterranean beach so beloved by the other Fauves, seems singularly subdued in Marquet's work. There is no brilliant sunshine, no explosion of brilliant colourity, no brio of frenzied brushwork. His painting is sweeping and tranquil, and does not break the boundaries of convention; it seems to posses a subdued harmony. The beach running diagonally into the painting is cut off in the background by a hill sloping downwards and protruding into the sea like a wall. People walking on the beach and sailing boats at sea are portrayed in laconic, dark brushstrokes. The only colourful figures are the two sailors in the foreground on the wall. Their blue collars are as bright as the red flag in front of the green hill behind them. This build-up of colour on the left hand side of the painting creates a contrast to the quiet planes of colour of the beach, sea and sky, in their self-contained forms. The proximity to Matisse is evident.

**Maurice Utrillo**
Impasse Cottin, 1911
Oil on cardboard,
62 x 46 cm
Paris, Musée National d'Art
Moderne, Centre Georges
Pompidou

## MAURICE UTRILLO
### 1883–1955

A distinction is made between various different phases in Utrillo's œuvre. *Impasse Cottin* dates from his "white period" between 1910 and 1914 when he explored the sensual qualities of the pale facades of Parisian houses by experimenting with the use of zinc white, plaster, cement and adhesive. This gives his paintings a highly distinctive, material aesthetic. Ridges and streaks create a shallow surface relief that gives the impression of a slightly dilapidated street, and the peeling paintwork of the houses is hinted at with plasticity. His paintings of this period thus become signs of his search for tangible reality, symbols of his quest to breathe some real life into the canvas.

This "impasse" in Montmartre, a district far from the grand boulevards, and one whose quiet streets and picturesque buildings Utrillo recorded in innumerable paintings, ends with a steep stairway towards which the lines of perspective run. The alleyway is virtually empty. Only in the background, in front of the entrance to a house, do we see a silhouette. A few women making their way up the steep stairway add rhythm and movement to the painting, drawing the viewer's gaze upwards along the flight of steps. Yet before our gaze actually reaches the sky, it meets with a burst of blossoming life, in the form of the quivering foliage of a group of trees.

## ANDRÉ DERAIN
### 1880–1954

In the company of Matisse, Derain spent the summer of 1903 in Collioure on the Mediterranean coast, where he painted. From Collioure, he wrote to his friend Vlaminck: "I have been seduced by colour as colour."

The harbour of Collioure is shown here from a strongly elevated vantage point. A few people are moving around on the shore of the bay, where three boats are lying at anchor. Everything is compiled of luminous daubs of colour which are elongated to lines only in the boats and masonry or in figures. The individual colours are not broken down into their basic hues in the manner of the pointillist Paul Signac, but in larger daubs that allow the colour to stand for itself. In retrospect, Derain once said: "The colours become dynamite. They detonate in light." Derain does not use Divisionism in the sense of breaking down colours, but as a means of structuring space. Paintings using this technique can be found in the œuvre of Derain only in the period between 1905 and 1906. After that, his brushstrokes become longer again and he uses colour planes, frequently framed by contrasting lines of colour.

André Derain
Boats at Collioure, 1905
Oil on canvas, 60 x 73 cm
Düsseldorf, Kunstsammlung
Nordrhein-Westfalen

## RAOUL DUFY
### 1877–1953

Like Braque, Raoul Dufy also started out with a dark-toned palette and was influenced by the Fauvist handling of colour at the Salon of 1905. However, it was not until the period when he painted his *Sailing Boat at Sainte-Adresse* that he developed his distinctive personal style which is essentially based on techniques of line drawing and watercolour. An abbreviated description of the objective repertoire is projected onto coloured backgrounds whose colours are to all intents and purposes independent of the objects themselves, and generally based on variations of one colour hue.

In this view of the bay of Sainte-Adresse, the decorative form of the detailed drawing and the almost calligraphic contours project a consciously intended naiveté that integrates the predominant rhythm of colours. The crests of waves, houses, rooftops and the boat seem like written signs or codes featuring deliberate rhythmic repetitions. From the pier with its fencing and flagpole in the foreground, a diagonal cascade of colours rushes towards the shore with its broad, horizontal structure, while the white of the boat and the houses creates a second diagonal.

Dufy's approach gives the impression of a playful levity that may well owe much to Impressionism and folk art, both of which he studied closely in his early period.

Raoul Dufy
Sailing Boat at Sainte-Adresse, 1912
Oil on canvas, 86.4 x 114.3 cm
New York, The Museum of Modern Art

**Kees van Dongen**
Portrait of Fernande,
1905
Oil on canvas,
100 x 81 cm
Private collection

# KEES VAN DONGEN
## 1877–1968

It was through Picasso, who lived in the famous Bateau-Lavoir studio complex in Paris,
that the Dutch artist Kees van Dongen heard
in 1905 of an available apartment. In December, he moved in with his wife and daughter,
and he stayed there until February 1907. Occasionally, Fernande Olivier, then Picasso's
mistress, would act as his model. Whereas Picasso was in his "rose period" in 1905, van
Dongen was exploring the richly contrasted
and garish colority of the Fauvists grouped
around Matisse. Van Dongen toned down the
brashness of the Fauvists in his own paintigs,
creating modulated planes, but at the same
time choosing strong colours and harmonies
which influenced and enhanced each other
mutually.

In his *Portrait of Fernande* van Dongen
brackets the foreground and the background
in a cool shade of blue. Fernande is holding a
blue cloth in front of her naked body, and it
casts a greenish shadow on part of her un-
covered skin. A fiery red in the lower background zone emphasizes the green highlight.
The figure is bounded by strong contouring
lines, which also increase the intensity of the
colours without creating an effect of plasticity.
This large painting, in which the palette is reduced to only a few colours, coolly distances
the woman from the spectator in spite of the
frontal view.

**Maurice de Vlaminck**
Les Bateaux-Lavoirs, 1906
Oil on canvas, 50 x 73 cm
Paris, Musée National d'Art Moderne, Centre Georges Pompidou

# MAURICE DE VLAMINCK
## 1876–1958

Of all the Fauves, Maurice de Vlaminck was
the most impetuous. His contempt for all conventions applied not only to art, but also to
life in general: "My passion pushed me to all
kinds of bold risks against convention in
painting. I wanted a revolution of social
mores... I gave myself no other goal but this:
to use new media to express the profound relationships that link me with the old earth... I
suffered at not being able to hammer more
strongly, at having arrived at the maximum of
intensity, limited by the blue and red of the
paint-seller."

1906 is regarded as the zenith of Vlaminck's vital and instinctive painting, an artist who did not hesitate to use his fingers instead of the paintbrush in order to apply his
paint to the canvas. Yet he never ignored the
question of compositional balance. At the foreground riverbank where the *Bateaux-Lavoirs*
are anchored, the triad of primary colours –
red, blue and yellow, is strongest. It is echoed
in a milder form on the other shore. The
painting gains its compositional stability
from the bridge with its horizontals, intersected and touched by the verticals of the
boats' masts.

# HENRI MATISSE

1869–1954

*Dance* is one piece of a two-part decoration commissioned by the Russian collector Shchukin on the basis that the design shown here had struck him for its *noblesse*. Its counterpart is *Music*. The main difference between the two versions – the final version is now hanging in the Hermitage in St Petersburg – is the intensity of their colours (cf. ill. p. 547).

Hands join to create a whirling circle that appears as an oval in the spatial perspective. The confined space drives the dance on the hill to the point of frenzy. Between the figure on the left and her neighbour on her right there is a considerable distance. In order to fill up the empty space and close ranks again, she is leaning forward to stretch her hand out to the other, who is leaning backward and endeavouring with all her might to stem the movement that is pulling her towards the background, but they do not quite connect. The effort of the dance changes the figures to the point of distortion, which at the same time adds to the expressiveness of the image. In *Dance* the "religion of happiness" takes shape. Lust for life is conveyed by the subconsciously contagious effect. The "decorative" style merges with the sacred content. According to Matisse, "What I am most interested in is neither still-life nor landscape, but the human figure. In it, my religious attitude to life is best expressed."

The "character of elevated dignity" that these figures possess can be explained on formal grounds. Their majestic monumentality is the result of increasingly simplified painterly means: a few colours applied in large homogenous planes, a drawing that tends towards pure line and the outlining of forms.

*The Piano Lesson* is an elegiac, earnest image in transparent and geometric forms. Its predominant form is the triangle, the form of the metronome, the sign of music that may also be regarded as the emblem of Matisse's art. The triangle is also the distinctive feature in the face of the young boy Pierre, the artist's son, at the piano. The multiple significance of the triangle is highly informative: Matisse had decided, against the boy's wishes, that Pierre should study music. The rather earnest-looking child is subjugated completely to his father's will, and this is expressed in the painting's unmitigated formal severity. The boy is confined between quotations of the painter's own work: to the lower left, the *Decorative Figure* (1908) and behind him the *Woman on a Stool* (1914). In the stringent and static structure of geometric forms, there is a calm and clarity strengthened by the cool grey of the background. As in a mosaic, the colour planes of complementary contrasts – green to red and blue to orange – are integrated into the background.

**Henri Matisse**
Dance (La Danse, first version), 1909
Oil on canvas, 259.7 x 390 cm
New York, The Museum of Modern Art

**Henri Matisse** The Piano Lesson, 1916
Oil on canvas, 245.1 x 212.7 cm
New York, The Museum of Modern Art

**Henri Matisse**
The Green Stripe (Madame Matisse), 1905
Oil on canvas, 40.5 x 32.8 cm
Copenhagen, Statens Museum for Kunst

**Henri Matisse**
Odalisque with Red Trousers, 1921
Oil on canvas, 65 x 90 cm
Paris, Musée National d'Art Moderne, Centre Georges Pompidou

# HENRI MATISSE
## 1869–1954

In the summer of 1905, Matisse created a painting of great tranquility in spite of its strident colours. It is a portrait of Madame Matisse. Here, Matisse has simplified the forms of his model to the essentials. In its sovereign frontal attitude, the portrait has the air of an icon. The green stripe which seems so unnatural at first glance is by no means arbitrary. In fact, it designates the border between the zones of light and shadow on the face. At the same time, it emphasizes the beautiful and regular facial structure of the model. Yet it is also symptomatic of a painting structured into colour fields which are reciprocally enhancing without actually imposing on each other, because they are clearly divided.

Complete concentration on colour gave way in the 1920s to a combination of great reality, spatial depth and rich detail, as in the *Odalisque*. Of the apparent conventionality of his odalisques, who recall the work of Delacroix, Matisse said: "The oriental decoration of the interiors,… the sumptuous costumes, the sensuality of the heavy, slumbering bodies… all the magnificence of the siesta, in which arabesque and colour are heightened to a maximum, should not deceive us: I have always rejected the merely anecdotal. Under this atmosphere of voluptuous languor and sun-drenched lassitude in which people and object are bathed, smoulders an enormous tension that is purely painterly and based on the relationships between the elements."

While the *Odalisque* in her plasticity and diagonal position in the room effortlessly stands apart from the decorative elements of her surroundings, the *Decorative Figure on an Ornamental Background* is almost drowned out by the loud colours and florid details. The kitschy French baroque wallpaper has been exaggerated to the very limit. The tastelessly eclectic mix of objects in this corner of the room has been arranged to create an unbroken wall of garish motifs. The seated woman stands out against the surroundings that seem liable to overwhelm her completely. Her body parts seem cylindrical, as though she were merely a "life-machine". The position of the figure makes it possible to distinguish between the verticals of the back wall and the horizontals of the floor. The position of her legs reiterates the two directions in which the floor stretches. A shadow borders the figure in the upper area against the background. In the contrast between the angularity of the figure and the arabesque background, Matisse attempts to maintain dimensional depth within a decorative space.

**Henri Matisse**
Decorative Figure on an Ornamental Background, 1925
Oil on canvas, 131 x 98 cm
Paris, Musée National d'Art Moderne, Centre Geoges Pompidou

**Juan Gris**
The Teacups, 1914
Papier collé, oil and charcoal on canvas, 65 x 92 cm
Düsseldorf, Kunstsammlung Nordrhein-Westfalen

**Juan Gris** Le Déjeuner, 1915
Oil and charcoal on canvas, 92 x 73 cm
Paris, Musée National d'Art Moderne,
Centre Georges Pompidou

# JUAN GRIS
## 1887–1927

In 1912, Picasso and Braque introduced a new artistic process of integrating pieces of paper in their pictures. The technique came to be known as collage. It was an innovation that was to have far-reaching consequences for the art of the 20th century, for it broke the hegemony of oil-painting and went on to be adopted by many art movements. In his collage *The Washstand* of 1912, he even incorporates a fragment of mirror.

In the work illustrated here, the surface of the table with its teacups, glasses, a bottle and a pipe, is not painted by hand, but represented by a piece of imitation wood-grain wallpaper which has been pasted into the picture. Further pieces of wallpaper, snippets of paper and newspaper also add to the structural contrasts. The pieces of paper pasted into the picture do not seem like foreign bodies, but are fully assimilated into the architectonic pictorial structure.

Spatiality is not unequivocally determined in terms of foreground and background, but seems ambivalent and puzzling. The planarity of the objects makes them seem alternately positive and negative, tangible and intangible. The reduction of colours to only black and white in addition to the wooden tone gives the work a delicate equilibrium that creates an overall sense of pictorial harmony in spite of the enormous contrasts.

Just like *The Teacups* his picture *Le Déjeuner* is also representative of the phase known as synthetic Cubism. Even though all the parts of this picture are actually painted, it nevertheless looks like a collage in which various differently contoured planes have been superimposed; above all, the way it imitates wood-grain is reminiscent of collage technique.

The individual planes with their different colours and structures form the architectonics of the painting. The result is an almost abstract planar structure with very little depth. Figurative elements have been drawn onto the abstract composition: newspaper, bottle, glass, coffee-pot and bowl. The very fact that they have been drawn in this way clearly underlines the fact that the painting is a surface onto which the objects have been projected. In the centre of the picture, the portrayal of the coffee-pot on three different coloured planes demonstrates various degrees of pictorial presentation: as a negative form in a pale outline on a black ground, as a sculpturally tangible object in the midfield and as a contour on the right, green field. The degree of reality becomes a pictorial problem.

The first art dealer to represent the Cubist artists, and one of their most important chroniclers, Daniel Henry Kahnweiler, praised Gris particularly for his pictorial structure: "If we consider regaining the integrity of the artwork to be one of the most important aims of Cubism, the will to create perfect organisms rather than sketches, then none of the Cubists has pursued that aim more consistently and successfully than Juan Gris."

# PABLO PICASSO
1881–1973

This painting represents a revolutionary breakthrough in the history of modern art. Whereas the central figures are still indicative of that stage in which the painting was begun, the nudes that frame the composition already demonstrate the decisive change of direction in Picasso's art that was to be of such seminal importance to Cubism. The motif of five female nudes grouped around a still life, remains indebted to classical convention. The structure itself can be traced back to Cézanne's *Bathers*. The large figures are angular, with the influence of ancient Iberian sculpture evident in the heads of the central figures, whereas the corner figures with their large, firmly contoured planes herald an entirely new approach. The faces themselves possess a compelling force that owes much to African sculpture. The figures and the background seem to form a relief that forgoes all pursuit of spatial depth and retains the close relationship to the pictorial surface.

Pablo Picasso
Les Demoiselles d'Avignon, 1907
Oil on canvas, 244 x 234 cm
New York, The Museum of Modern Art

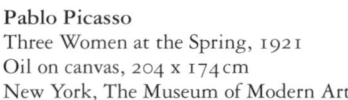

**Pablo Picasso**
Ma Jolie, 1914
Oil on canvas, 45 x 40 cm
Collection Berggruen

**Pablo Picasso**
Three Women at the Spring, 1921
Oil on canvas, 204 x 174 cm
New York, The Museum of Modern Art

## PABLO PICASSO
### 1881–1973

The still life *Ma Jolie* belongs to a group of
works created in 1914 whose light-hearted
mood and elegant articulation have earned
them the epithet rococo Cubism. The objects
are recognizable, the formal syntax more relaxed, and the attitude more playful than before. The objects are arranged on a small table
portrayed in a contour drawing of straight
lines on the pictorial ground. In their planar
graduation they seem to be stuck together
rather than painted. Stippled brushwork is
used to indicate areas where light and shadow
permeate. The words "Ma Jolie" on the musical score leaning on the back wall are taken
from a popular song of the time. It was also
the name by which Picasso called his new mistress Marcelle Humbert in 1912.

The painting *Three Women at the Spring* may be
regarded as a model example of Picasso's Neoclassicism. His new found interest in the sculptural volumes of the human figure, suppressed
during his phase of formal cubist analysis, may
have been reawakened in 1917 on a journey to
Italy, where he encountered the art of classical
Antiquity. One standing, one sitting and one
leaning on the rocks, three women have gathered at the well around which their hands
seem to circle. Their corporeality has been
heightened to the point of the colossal. The
folds of their robes are vaguely reminiscent of
Roman sculptures and Pompeian frescos and,
even more so, they recall the fluting of classical columns. The subdued, fresco-like colours
add to the sculptural effect of volume that creates the overall effect of a relief rather than
that of a free-standing sculpture. The painting
expresses an awareness of just how near and
yet how far the influence of classical Antiquity
remains.

Picasso may well have been inspired to paint
this *Girl before a Mirror* by his love for the
sensual Marie-Thérèse Walter. Of all his
paintings of the early 1930s, this is the most
painstakingly executed in its lavish luminosity, its decorative pattern and its expressive
yet coolly analytical traits. In the world of
art, women with mirrors traditionally represent vanitas images, suggesting the vanity or
transience of earthly life. In the case of Picasso, we are tempted to think of the mirror
as representing the idea of the painter's superiority in terms of his ability to create an
image more lasting than that of a mirror. The
girl does not hold the mirror like an attribute, but embraces it like a second self. She is
both clothed and naked and seems to be radiated by x-rays. The rounded form of the
womb is the formal *leitmotif* of this distinctly
erotic painting.

**Pablo Picasso**
Girl before a Mirror, 1932
Oil on canvas, 162 x 130 cm
New York, The Museum of Modern Art

**Georges Braque**
The Portuguese, 1911
Oil on canvas, 117 x 81.5 cm
Basle, Öffentliche Kunstsammlung
Basel, Kunstmuseum

# GEORGES BRAQUE
1882–1963

Towards the end of 1910, a new phase of Cubism began, in which the deconstruction of the object was taken further than ever before. The central figure in *The Portuguese* is broken down into its individual formal components to such an extent that they can be recognized only with difficulty: eye, nose, shoulders, upper and lower arms. *The Portuguese* is holding a guitar. The surface is rhythmically divided into the many facets of objective forms. The convex cubes and concave spatial fragments have been flattened to create a self-contained effect. Colour has been reduced to two tones: grey and brown.

The stencilling that appears for the first time in *The Portuguese* is not contexturally associative, but formally rhythmic. Braque explained, "In my constant search for reality, I introduced letters into my paintings in 1911. These were forms that were not to be changed; because they are flat, letters are situated outside space, and their presence in the picture made it possible to distinguish the objects within the space from those outside it."

After the still lifes of the 1920s and 1930s with their wealth of objects, Braque devoted his energies between 1936 and 1939 to a group of key works in which there is a return to classical figure compositions. His painting *The Duo* belongs to this phase. The scene is framed theatrically by curtains at the side. An ornamental wallpaper pattern forms the background, with one light and one dark half contrasting. The figure of the singer holding a score by Debussy, whom Braque admired, is divided into a black zone and a pink zone. The piano in the middle has been cubistically compacted. Its brown colour unites it with the pianist. The interaction of light and shade determines the enigmatic dialogue between the two musicians.

At a later state of Cubism, Braque began presenting objects in the form of differently contoured planes whose distinctive, earthy tonality creates a harmonious whole, as in the *Still Life with Bowl of Fruit, Bottle and Mandolin* dating from 1930. The still-life is architectonically structured, but in spite of the handling of space, it avoids any perspectival illusionism. The individual zones are layered and superimposed in the manner of a collage and, as in earlier collages, the marbling of the table top is emphasized as a reiteration of material surface finishes.

**Georges Braque**
The Duo, 1937
Oil on canvas, 131 x 162.5 cm
Paris, Musée National d'Art Moderne,
Centre Georges Pompidou

**Georges Braque**
Still Life with Bowl of Fruit, Bottle and
Mandolin, 1930
Oil on canvas, 116 x 90 cm
Düsseldorf, Kunstsammlung Nordrhein-Westfalen

Fernand Léger
The Stairway, 1914
Oil on canvas, 130 x 100 cm
New York, The Museum of
Modern Art

Fernand Léger
Three Women (Le Grand Déjeuner), 1921
Oil on canvas, 182 x 251 cm
New York, The Museum of Modern Art

# FERNAND LÉGER
1881–1955

In 1913/14, Léger painted several pictures featuring a stairway as an important motif. Everything is geared towards the contrast of cylindrical components and angular steps, and towards the contrast between the primary colours red, blue and yellow, outlined in black on a pale grey ground. The sculptural volume has been emphasized effectively, without allowing us to forget that it is the surface of the painting that forms the plane of projection. In this way, "the simultaneous coordination of the three basic elements, line, form and colour," are embodied for Léger.

However, unlike his *Contrastes et formes* (Contrasts of Form), the cylindrical components in this work remind us not only of the machine world that fascinated Léger, but of the human world as well. These are creatures who seem to consist only of a coat of armour, and who move like mechanized robots. The face, in which all human expression is concentrated, becomes a black and white visor. All sentimentality has been exorcized. Léger was perfectly aware of the break with tradition when he noted: "Since abstract art has liberated us entirely from the fetters of tradition, it has become possible for us to consider the human figure as a purely pictorial component rather than as a sentimental component."

After 1920, a phase began which Fernand Léger himself described as his "monumental era," and of which he said: "I have increased the sense of planarity by applying the same formal approach to my figures and objects as in the machine era, but without the same dynamism. I had smashed the human body, so I began putting it together again, finding the face again."

When Léger put the human figure back together again after 1920, he nevertheless portrayed the collective rather than the individual. He is not interested in emotion. Nor in psychology. In his painting *The Three Women (Le Grand Déjeuner)* the compositional arrangement of the three nude women is determined by horizontals and verticals. The two reclining women are intersected by the seated woman. Their bodies are mainly made up of basic geometric forms. The colour is modelled at the edges to give them some corporeality. The faces show no emotion.

The detachment of his portrayal does not, however, have the effect of separating the figures from their surroundings. The interior has merged with the persons to a geometrically patterned surface. The tonality of the painting is as clear and harsh as its forms. The grey tones used for the bodies seem to break the colourful geometry of the entire room. Léger said of the use of these techniques: "I contrast curved lines with straight lines, flat surfaces with modelled surfaces, purely local colours with finely nuanced tones."

# ROBERT DELAUNAY

1885–1941

At the centre of the prismatic cubic forms of houses and rooftops stands the Eiffel Tower. The transparent colour planes seem to radiate from it like facets. They are not restricted to the pictorial field alone, but are continued onto the frame. The colour becomes the sole carrier of pictorial structure. It is used in planes as light, form and movement in space, with individual colours receding or protruding on grounds of various intensities. Guillaum Apollinaire described these paintings by Delaunay as "orphism", in reference to their lyrical character. This painting inspired him to one of his finest poems, *Les Fenêtres* (The Windows).

In 1933, Delaunay wrote about the design principle behind his *Window* paintings: "No nature – more like initial abstract painting in colours. The paint, the colours with their inherent laws, their contrasts, their slow vibrations, their intervals – all these relationships form the basis of the painting that is no longer imitative, but creative in itself through its inherent technique."

Whereas Delaunay was rejected as Impressionistic by the Cubists, whose handling of colour he had described as "web-like", his *Window* paintings were enthusiastically received immediately by the German artists Marc, Macke and Klee.

**Robert Delaunay**
Simultaneous Windows on the City, 1912
Oil on canvas and wood (painted frame),
46 x 40 cm
Hamburg, Hamburger Kunsthalle

In his *Sun and Moon* series, Delaunay sought to capture the different light effects of sun and moon. The painting does not aim to give a descriptive portrayal of the celestial bodies themselves. What the artist is interested in is in reiterating the specific light through colour forms.

On the right in the painting, the disk of the sun spreads out, with a circle and axial cross at its centre, around which contrasting fields radiate and interweave, heightening the atmosphere. On the left, we see the floating sphere of the moon, based on a simple formal motif of two dark ovals on a tilted axis holding an oval light form between them, enveloped in circular colour zones of iridescent blue, green, pink and violet.

The light gains substance from the colours perceived simultaneously by the viewer. The more intense the light, the more the colours have to activate. Each colour is an amorphous entity in itself; only the juxtaposition with a contrasting or related colour gives it expression, intensity and movement, and certain dimensions have to be sustained to determine the form. In this way, form is born of colour and becomes one with it. In his portrayal of both worlds of light, Delaunay was interested in exploring the concept of "pure" painting.

**Robert Delaunay**
Simulaneous Contrasts: Sun and Moon, c. 1912/13
Oil on canvas, diameter 134.5 cm
New York, The Museum of Modern Art

**Umberto Boccioni**
State of Mind II: The Farewells, 1911
Oil on canvas, 71.2 x 94.2 cm
New York, The Museum of Modern Art

**Umberto Boccioni**
The Noise of the Street Enters the House, 1911
Oil on canvas, 100 x 106.5 cm
Hanover, Sprengel Museum Hannover

# UMBERTO BOCCIONI
## 1882–1916

In May 1911, Boccioni was working on his first series of paintings entitled *States of Mind*. Each of the three paintings in this series was given a subtitle: *The Farewells, Those Who Stay,* and *Those Who Go.* In the melting swirl of his first version, Boccioni presents the concept of separation. Farewells at railway stations are his metaphor of the pain of breaking a sense of community. At the end of 1911, following a visit to Paris where he had been particularly impressed by the work of Picasso, Boccioni began a second version: *States of Mind II*.

In his painting *The Farewells* the influence of Cubism in the fragmentation of forms and compositional structure is evident. The numbers integrated by the Cubists as flat, non-spatial elements and indications of reality, have been adopted by Boccioni in the centre of the picture.

Guillaume Apollinaire, who was familiar with the artists of his day, immediately recognized the significance of the numbers: "Boccioni's best painting is the one that is most directly inspired by Picasso's latest works. They even have those stencilled numbers that give Picasso's recent works such simplicity and magnificent reality." Boccioni's number is the number of the locomotive that drives apart the embracing couples to the right and left. A red, diagonal snaking line of velocity accompanies the machine. The red highlights and dramatizes the clouds of smoke, the evening sun, the stop signals and the tail lights. The excitement of the moment is captured.

"Let us praise the hubbub of voices, the mathematical division of work in the laboratories, the whistling of the railway trains, the confusion on the station platforms and the restlessness! And the speed! And the precision! Let us praise the screech of the sirens as a substitute for the boring, bronze peal of the church bells, the sound of engines and the ear-clipping rattle of the drive-belts!" wrote Boccioni in 1912.

A square flanked by houses has become a building site. A woman looks down from the balcony of her room into the hustle and bustle that swirls around her like a maelstrom. All structure seems to have been abandoned. Everything seems to be collapsing towards the centre – and the centre is the woman leaning out. Her head, in which all these impressions are gathering, is positioned precisely at the point where the diagonals of the painting cross. Just as the square and the houses seem to vibrate with the distortions, displacements and fragmentations, so too do the colours vibrate in order to heighten this impression. The paint has been applied in every possible variation from smooth and flat to daubed and striped, but it is always radiant and, above all, juxtaposed in colours so stridently clashing that they almost scream aloud.

# GIACOMO BALLA
## 1871–1958

Of all the Futurists, it was Balla, more than any other, whose dissolution of the pictorial motif into fields of movement came closest to the abstract compositions of Kandinsky. Yet in the superimposition and permeation of the forms, we find the "plastic dynamism" and simultaneity so characteristic of Futurism. The artist aimed to present various phases of movement and aspects of a sculptural body at the same time. The radiating rhythm of the "window" colour facets fractured by the light in the work of Robert Delaunay are very different indeed from Balla's emphatic dynamism.

Balla expanded the cognition of movement to cosmic dimensions. His painting *Mercury Passing before the Sun* is based on an eclipse of the sun that he observed on 7 November 1914 with a telescope and dark glass filter. It is a worldly enthusiasm for cosmic expanses and movements, informed by an awareness that not only the visual medium of painting, but also the forces of life have cosmic origins. The *Futurist Technical Manifesto* of 1910 claims: "We Futurists shall climb the most sublime and radiant summit and proclaim ourselves lords of light, for we drink from the source of the sun!"

**Giacomo Balla**
Mercury Passing before the Sun, 1914
Oil on canvas,
120 x 100 cm
Milan, Private collection

# GINO SEVERINI
## 1883–1966

Severini's 1913 manifesto begins with the words "We want to capture the universe in the art work. Objects no longer exist." For Severini, there is only the reality of consciousness with its mechanisms of memory and analogy: "The sensation reality invokes in us, of which we know that it is square in shape and blue in colour, can also be expressed in its complementary forms and colours, which means in round forms and yellow colours."

The rhythm of the picture is determined by the radiation and refraction of light. There is nothing figurative at all. Only triangles and circles structure the plane. The paint is applied in tiny rather than flat dots, in order to render the process of dissolution even more clearly. From the pale yellow in the centre, it darkens towards the edges on all sides, right through to black. Its radiant force spreads out. Whereas Divisionism created the basis for breaking objects down into light and colour, it was Cubism that provided the fragmentation by which the handling of space could be determined. In this painting, the density of colour creates a rhythmic ebb and flow.

**Gino Severini**
Spherical Expansion of Light (Centrifugal), 1914
Oil on canvas,
61 x 50 cm
Milan, Private collection

**Amedeo Modigliani**
Bride and Groom, c. 1915/16
Oil on canvas, 55.2 x 46.4 cm
New York, The Museum of Modern Art

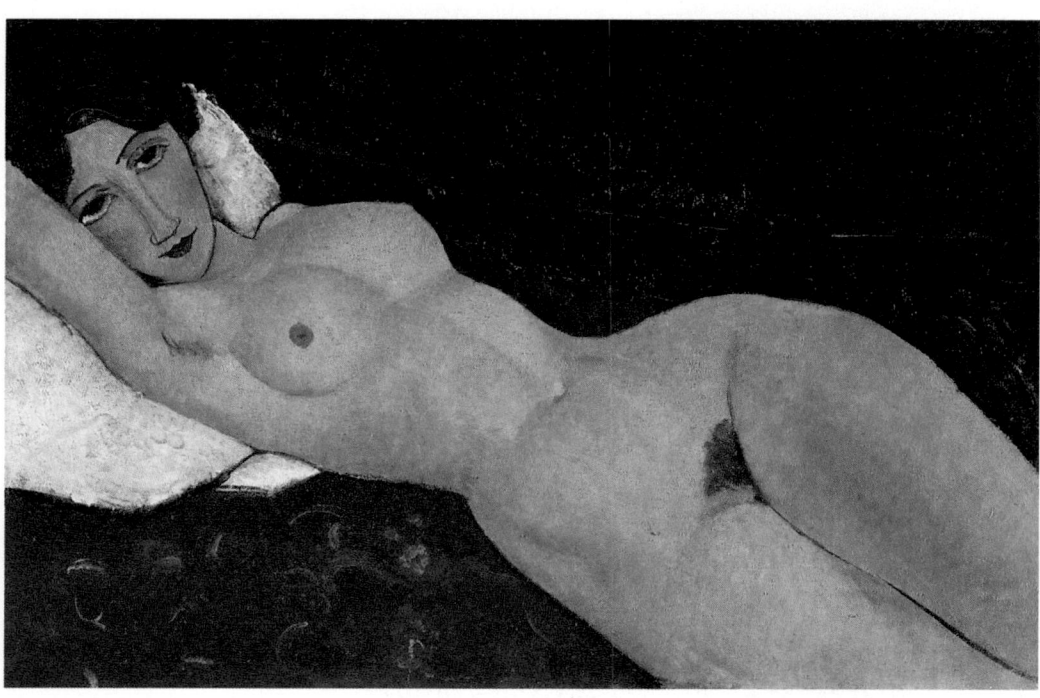

**Amedeo Modigliani**
Reclining Nude on White Pillow, 1917
Oil on canvas, 60 x 92 cm
Stuttgart, Staatsgalerie Stuttgart

# AMEDEO MODIGLIANI
## 1884–1920

Modigliani concentrated primarily on individual portraits. This painting is one of the few exceptions. The poet Jean Cocteau pointed out that this painting was probably inspired by some *nouveau riche* couple the painter had seen on the boulevard.

Both are elegantly dressed. The man is wearing an evening suit with a stiff white collar and bow-tie. The rim of his top-hat is discernible just below the upper edge of the picture. The woman's earrings are somewhat larger than discreetly elegant understatement might allow. They are too showy to seem entirely serious. The age difference also indicates that the title of the painting is ironic. This constellation of elderly playboy and young mistress is a common motif in painting.

What is unusual about the composition is the way the figures are arranged in the pictorial space. The woman can only be seen just above the lower edge of the painting to her shoulders, whereas the man is shown from the chest upwards, so that his head reaches the upper edge of the painting. There is a clear interaction between sweeping space and detailed areas.

In their facets and geometric simplification, the faces reflect the influence of Cubism, but also have something of the austerity of African masks. In large capital letters of the kind the Cubists also used as non-spatial pictorial elements, Modigliani has included his name in the composition like a company logo.

Modigliani's first and only solo exhibition was in 1917 at the Berthe Weill gallery in Paris. Most of the paintings exhibited there were nudes. The police of a city accustomed to considerably more erotic images declared the nudes a public nuisance and closed the exhibition.

While this reclining nude is certainly not unerotic, nor is it in any way obscene; it is far too consciously unreal as an art product for that. Whereas other artists surrounded their nudes with furniture, draperies and flowers, sometimes adding a clothed male figure as a dramatic accent, Modigliani avoids all such effects. The woman lies like a Venus on the red divan, her gaze transfigured. While the upper half of the body is portrayed in three-quarter view, the lower half has been turned to an almost frontal view. In comparison to the rest of the body, her lap takes on the dimensions of a fertility goddess. The interior forms have been modelled sparsely with light and shadow. The main focus is on the outline of the body with its flat, pale red. The stringency of the contour underlines the planarity of the body, while the volume is subdued. The few strong colour contrasts have no spatial effect.

## ALEXEI VON JAWLENSKY
### 1864–1941

From around 1907, it was the influence of
the Fauves, most notably Matisse, that helped
Jawlensky to develop his pictorial concept on
the basis of colour. He adopted Matisse's concept that: "It is not possible for me to copy
nature slavishly; I am obliged to interpret it
and subjugate myself to the spirit of the
painting. From all my relationships of found
tones, a vital chord of colour must result; a
harmony similar to that of a musical composition."

Jawlensky's *Woman with a Fan* is painted as
a purely planar composition, just as the French
artists required. Yet, unlike paintings of the
same period by Matisse, the handling of colour
is more strongly modulated and the black outlines and bands of colour seem to vibrate.
Areas of different shades of blue in the blouse
and hat of the woman contrast with the red of
the background and the flowers on her hat.
The structure of the painting draws together
all the details, ornamentally arranging them
in the picture plane. Jawlensky has retained
something of the tonality of his Russian
origins: exaggeration and eastern folk art. His
painting deliberately lacks the lightness of Matisse. The colour is not an end in itself, but is
combined with an emotional mood dominated
by the slightly melancholy expression of the
woman.

Alexei von Jawlensky
Woman with a Fan, 1909
Oil on cardboard, 92 x 68 cm
Wiesbaden, Museum Wiesbaden

## WASSILY KANDINSKY
### 1866–1944

In his 1912 treatise *On the Spiritual in Art* Kandinsky distinguishes between three types of
paintings in his œuvre – impressions, improvisations, compositions – according to their
various sources of origin. He describes his "improvisations" as mainly unconscious, sudden
expressions of inner processes or impressions of
inner nature. This wish to explore inner nature
led Kandinsky to choose religious themes occasionally in his works of the period 1909–
1912, which form a transition from figurative
to abstract art. They show how profoundly
rooted he was in the Christian concept of redemption and how he translated it into imagery.

*Improvisation 8* and the preliminary study
for it which, like most preliminary studies, is
very different from the finished version, both
date from 1910. On the left stands an archangel holding the sword in the centre of the
picture. On the right, crouching or standing
figures await judgement. Above them, as
though floating in a yellow valley, we see a
Russian town with its churches and domes,
the Kremlin or Heavenly Jerusalem. Then
again, it could just as easily be the upper Bavarian town of Murnau where Kandinsky lived
and worked at the time.

Wassily Kandinsky
Study for "Improvisation 8", 1910
Oil on cardboard on canvas,
98 x 70 cm
Winterthur, Kunstmuseum

RUSSIA

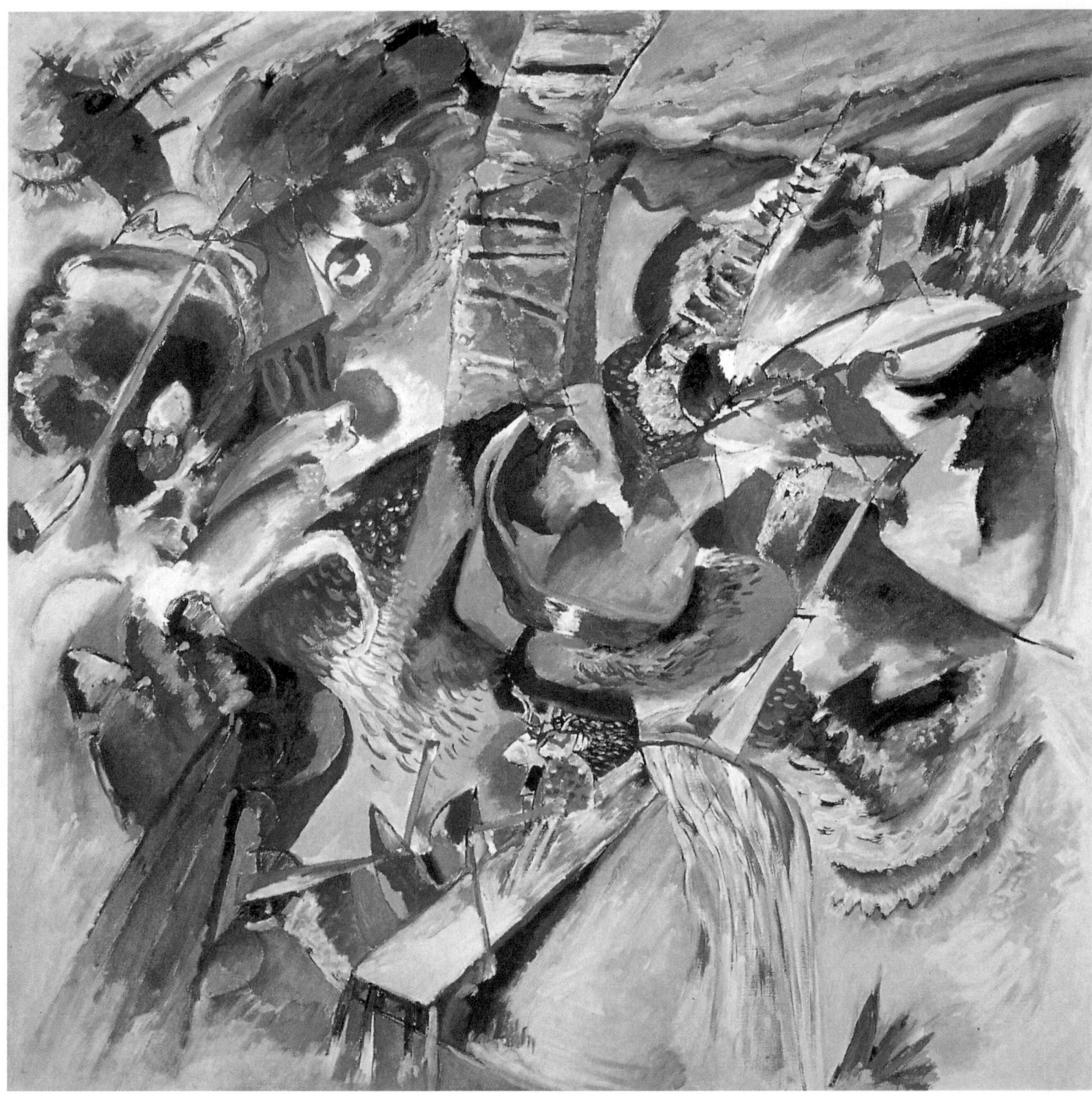

**Wassily Kandinsky**
Improvisation Gorge, 1914
Oil on canvas, 110 x 110cm
Munich, Städtische Galerie im Lenbachhaus

## WASSILY KANDINSKY
### 1866–1944

Around 1910, Kandinsky began dismantling the function of black outlines as definers of figures and boundaries, replacing them with bold curves, angles and zigzag lines as direct expressions of inner movement without actually portraying any external reality. Opposites play a subordinate role in this whirl of colours and forms in *Improvisation Gorge*. Like a landing-jetty, we see a pathway penetrating diagonally into the picture in the lower half.

On it stands a couple in Bavarian costume. Beside them, a colourful cascade rushes like a waterfall. The other forms cannot be figuratively interpreted with quite the same clarity. They are in the field of the visionary. The mountain landscape with the evening sky and red sun is only the starting point. In the open pictorial structure, there seems to be no top or bottom. Some of the lines are taut, others seem distorted by the force of energy. The handling of colour alternates between clear delineation and fluidity. The forms float freely in space.

From 1914 to 1921 – the period of the First World War and the Russian revolution – Kandinsky was living in Russia. During this time, possibly influenced by Suprematism and Constructivism, we find geometric forms occurring alongside the irregular, organic forms in his paintings for the first time. During the period 1921 to 1932 – when he was teaching at the Bauhaus in Weimar and Dessau – Kandinsky used almost exclusively geometric forms, cool colours, dynamic lines and frequently chose the circle as his central motif. In 1933, he moved to Paris. Freed from the obligations of teaching, his art now turned in a new direction, in which we find a synthesis between natural forms and the geometric forms of his Bauhaus period. Unaffected by the events in Germany, he created a serene and light-hearted œuvre in Paris in his later years.

Strange creatures inhabit the world of his *Sky-Blue* painting, whose title is derived from the background colour. The colour blurs at the edges, suggesting infinity rather than firm delineation. Against this lucid background, clearly delineated forms of luminous colority stand out. Geometric basic forms swell into irregular shapes, becoming organic, resembling fantastic animals. They are reminiscent of the little animals which Kandinsky created in 1926 to illustrate his Bauhaus book *Point and Line to Plane*. Cold and cloying colours are harmoniously balanced. The predominant basic tone scatters the figures, creating the impression that they are hovering in space. Kandinsky gives us no hint as to the interpretation of this painting. He merely speaks vaguely of a "hitherto unknown world" he has discovered.

**Wassily Kandinsky**
Sky-Blue, 1940
Oil on canvas,
100 x 73 cm
Paris, Musée National d'Art
Moderne, Centre
Georges Pompidou

In his painting *The Arrow* Kandinsky once again presents a highly charged figuration in a seemingly playful manner. In the interaction of rest and movement, geometric forms can be transformed into organic forms. The arrow at the centre of a midnight-blue field of action symbolically emphasizes the direction of attack launched by two amorphous forms on a geometric entity that recoils under the onslaught. To the right and left, unstably stacked geometric forms manage to hold their balance. As in Kandinsky's early paintings, there is a sense of cosmos with the forces that affect it.

The formal syntax of Kandinsky's paintings may have changed in the course of time, but the basis for his imaginary world remained constant. For him, art was a spiritual world alongside the natural world. Both are subject to the laws of the cosmic world, the laws of an overall harmony. In 1938, Kandinsky stated "The abstract world constitutes a new world alongside the 'real world', and one which, on the surface of it, has nothing to do with 'reality'. In this way, a new 'art world' is placed alongside the 'natural world' – a world just as real and concrete. Which is why I personally prefer to refer to so-called 'abstract' art as concrete art."

**Wassily Kandinsky**  The Arrow (La Flèche), 1943
Oil on cardboard, 42 x 58 cm
Basle, Öffentliche Kunstsammlung
Basel, Kunstmuseum

**Emil Nolde**
Christ among the Children, 1910
Oil on canvas, 86.8 x 106.4 cm
New York, The Museum of Modern Art

## EMIL NOLDE
### 1867–1956

In the summer of 1910, Nolde painted several religious pictures at Ruttebüll in northern Silesia. In these paintings, he expresses the religious sentiments of his youth: "The biblical images are intensive memories of youth, to which I have given form as an adult."

Christ's words "Suffer the little children to come on to me, and forbid them not: for of such is the kingdom of God" is the basis for Nolde's painting in which a division into dark and light graphically expresses the biblical story, which continues "whosoever shall not receive the kingdom of God as a little child, he shall not enter therein."

In the darker part of the painting, we see the astonished apostles, who believe themselves to be the chosen ones, in discussion. Their robes are dark blue and violet. Christ is bending forwards away from them in his bluish-green robe, towards the children with their candid expressions. They are of light-hearted innocence. Shades of yellow and red flare up like a bright light in their area. Everything radiates serenity. The yellow of the bodies and faces is also reflected in the faces of the apostles, bracketing the antithetically structured picture. The expressiveness of the colours red-yellow and blue-violet is evident. Nolde developed his expressive approach to painting entirely on the basis of colour.

**Emil Nolde**
Nordermühle, 1932
Oil on canvas, 73 x 88 cm
Munich, Bayerische Staatsgemälde-
sammlungen, Staatsgalerie moderner Kunst

Just as the mature painter turns to his youth in *Christ among the children* so too does he return to his youth in *Nordermühle*. The sight of windmills standing majestically on the sweeping flat land left a deep impression on Nolde. He recalled "the great thatched grainmill soaring high above everything. As a young boy, when we were driving our livestock in the spring or autumn, I would look up to those powerful sails cutting through the air and my impressionable child-like self was deeply moved. It seemed to me as though the great mills, confident and proud, were calling to the humans: See my beauty! And as though their sails were reflected in the surrounding canals."

In this painting, the mill seems huge and inaccessible, as though surrounded by something enigmatic. There is not a breath of wind to move its heavy sails. They seem to be a firm and unmovable part of the building. In black and white, the mill stands out against the dark, streaming colours of the landscape. Dark clouds loom over the flat horizon. In a brilliant yellowish-red, the reflection of the setting sun breaks through, lighting up the sky and fading on the surface of the water. It evokes the first day of creation, before the elements had been separated from each other, one flowing into the other, while only the mill seems to stand fast. It is a theme to which Nolde returned time and time again. The landscape, as in the work of Munch, expresses the sentiments of the painter and the way he experiences colour.

## ERICH HECKEL

1883–1970

For four years, from 1907 to 1910, the fishing village of Dangast am Jadebusen became Heckel's summer workplace, apart from his Dresden studio. It was here that he created the first of the works that were to distinguish him as a unique creative force.

*Windmill at Dangast* clearly indicates his contribution to the expansion of colour. The few, but extremely intensive, colours of northern Germany's coastal landscape – the green of the meadows and trees, the yellow of the sand, the red of the path and the houses, the radiant blue of the sky – are heightened to the greatest possible luminosity. The two sets of colour opposites – green and red, orange/yellow and blue – underlines the effect. The spontaneity of the painterly act is legible in the fluidity of the brushstrokes. The traces of movement turn the entire picture into a field charged with energy. Black lines swirl and spiral above the fence, the meadow and the mill, breaking off at its sails. The spiral movement is not a spatial element, but a structural and compositional one. The flat effect of the dry pigments the artist ground himself stands in stark contrast to the more impasto brushwork of the Fauves, but it is also unlike Heckel's own earlier works as it has been diluted like watercolour, leaving parts of the background free. In this way, the paint unfurls all its vital, energetic powers.

**Erich Heckel**
Windmill at Dangast, 1909
Oil on canvas, 70.7 x 80.5 cm
Duisburg, Wilhelm-Lehmbruck-Museum

## KARL SCHMIDT-ROTTLUFF

1884–1976

Like Heckel, which whom he spent the summer of 1910 in Dangast, Schmidt-Rottluff abandoned the thickly applied paint of previous years, influenced by the Neo-Impressionists and van Gogh, in favour of a flatter application of broad bands of colour in his *Gap in the Dyke*. Heckel's *Windmill* and Schmidt-Rottluff's *Gap in the Dyke* bear witness to the common ground they share from the early period of the Die Brücke group.

All the vitality of this painting lies in the way the painter has handled colour. The dominant, unbroken red of the earth in the foreground finds its basis and its hold in the black fence that curves like the rim of a plate. In the paths running up the banks of the dyke, the red is carried on up over the roof of the house at the level of the strip of evening clouds. Its effect is heightened by the contrast with the deep blue of the sky that penetrates from the upper edge of the picture into the red zone that sweeps across the dyke and the figures on the path. The tension is further increased by the few yellowish-greenish tones that seem to echo the sparse, sandy coastal landscape, which has been circumscribed only sketchily with broad brushstrokes. The process of composition is here at one with emotion. Schmidt-Rottluff had "only the inexplicable yearning to capture what I see and feel and to find the purest expression for that."

**Karl Schmidt-Rottluff** Gap in the Dyke, 1910
Oil on canvas, 76 x 84 cm. Berlin, Brücke-Museum

GERMANY

**Ernst Ludwig Kirchner**
Negro Dance, c. 1911
Oil on canvas,
151.5 x 120 cm.
Düsseldorf, Kunstsamm-
lung Nordrhein-Westfalen

**Ernst Ludwig Kirchner**
The Red Tower in Halle,
1915
Oil on canvas, 120 x 90.5 cm
Essen, Museum Folkwang

# ERNST LUDWIG KIRCHNER
## 1880–1938

In October 1911, Kirchner moved with
Heckel, Pechstein and Schmidt-Rottluff from
Dresden to Berlin. Like no other painter of
the Brücke group, Kirchner explored the
theme of the city in his paintings with a mixture of fascination and unease. He painted
street scenes or music-hall performances such
as *Negro Dance*. He was interested in music-
hall performances for their movement and dynamism, their hustle and bustle, the erotic
*frisson*, the tension created between the girls
on stage and the uninvolved musicians. In
the foreground, we see the orchestra pit with
the conductor and musicians. On the stage,
two black girls are dancing in flouncing
skirts. Their pose forms an x-shape. The angular movements correspond to the angular
hand movements of the conductor. This
highly dynamic presentation is clearly structured and composed. Amidst the fragmented
colority, only the flash of red stands out
sharply, and for the first time, Kirchner uses
white in his scale of colours – as though exoticism had paled in the eyes of the civilized
world.

With the outbreak of the First World War
and military conscription, Kirchner's psychological crisis was exacerbated. Already emotionally unstable, the artist broke down completely. The conflicts of the era and the conflicts of his life could not be solved by art
alone. Nevertheless, in 1915, he entered one
further brief and feverish creative period in
which his urban landscape *The Red Tower in
Halle* was produced.

This painting shows the so-called "red
tower" a freestanding late Gothic belltower
with a neo-Gothic brick base, one of the land-
marks of the city of Halle. It stands on same
square as the Marktkirche (the church to the
left in the background) which Feininger chose
as a motif in his work. The square is portrayed at such a strongly distorted angle that
it seems to have been folded into the picture
plane. It is surrounded on all sides by high
buildings. Within this setting, the tower combines stability and aggression. In order to
underline its monumentality, Kirchner chose
a larger scale for the tower than for its surroundings.

The square base, distorted to a rhombus by
the perspectival angle, points towards the
lower edge of the picture. In this position, the
tower exudes an air of aggression as well as
stability. The point of the base seems to stand
like a breakwater against the tide of the approaching tram. The red streets emphasize the
rhomboid form of the square and the tower
base. The aggressive red of the lower floor, the
streets and the tram cut through the cold blue
that dominates the surrounding area. Violet
cumulus clouds are gathering behind the
tower. Yet the cold tonality predominates, expressing Kirchner's sense of forlorn solitude.
No passers-by add life to the square.

*The Street* was one of the first high points of Kirchner's early artistic career. The street scenes he painted in Dresden and Berlin between 1908 and 1909 record his views of city life more intensely than the other artists of Die Brücke. Kirchner himself always regarded his first Dresden street scene as a milestone on his artistic path. In his diary he called it "the first great painting".

The painting shows a lively street with passers-by. The background is a closed wall of people, broken in the middle by a tram. On the right, women in lavish hats and a man are moving frontally towards the viewer, while the passers-by on the left are moving away with their backs to us. Between these two directions of movement on either side of the road, a little girl is standing in the middle of the road. Her huge hat seems like a nimbus or even a target against the red street.

The rhythm of curved lines within the composition, set in motion by the hats of the women with their various rims, builds up to a vortex in the centre of the painting. It is the surging movement of curved lines, spiralling out from this vortex, and the contours of the figures in all parts of the composition that creates a restless dynamism on which the exuberant vitality of this painting thrives.

**Ernst Ludwig Kirchner**
The Street, 1908/19
Oil on canvas 150.5 x 200.4 cm
New York, The Museum of Modern Art

## OTTO MUELLER

1874–1930

The focus of Mueller's art is the human condition and paradise lost. He saw his ideal of primordial existence embodied in the life of the gypsies, which explains why they are his preferred models. They are often presented as lovers in a landscape or natural setting. Even when the situation is by no means as explicit as it is in this portrayal of *Lovers*, the erotic aspect is nevertheless muted.

The theme is approached with considerable simplicity. A young couple is gently leaning on each other. The elongation of the figures and their slender, angular features make them appear almost Gothic. Their angular movements subdue the erotic appeal of the clothed young boy embracing his lover in her unbuttoned blouse. The predominant mood is one of an indefinably passive love that closes out the external world.

The composition is dominated by vertical lines, further heightened by the fence and the tree trunks. This makes the interaction of diagonals – the line of the arms and hips – all the more effective. The muted palette is limited to only a few shades of green, yellow and brown. The cool blue creates a contrast and adds the necessary touch of tension.

**Otto Mueller**
Lovers, 1919
Distemper on burlap,
106 x 80 cm
Ravensburg, Private
collection

**Max Beckmann**
The Night, 1918/19
Oil on canvas, 133 x 154 cm
Düsseldorf, Kunstsammlung Nordrhein-Westfalen

## MAX BECKMANN
### 1884–1950

In 1920, Max Beckmann admitted "It is really pointless to love humankind, that egotistical heap (of which one is also a part). But I do, all the same. I love them in all their pettiness and banality." In Beckmann's paintings, his pessimistic world view is expressed in disturbing images of distress, especially in *Night*.

The scene is a crowded attic with seven people and various props. A family is being attacked in their home by a gang. A semi-clothed man on a table is being strangled and tortured by two men with bandaged heads. In the background stands a woman, and under the table a dog is howling. An almost naked woman is sinking to the floor with her legs spread wide. Her hands are tied to the window frame.

A man whose face is shaded by the peak of his cap is dragging another woman into the room. He is pulling down the curtain. The bodies of the figures, with their angular movements, seem deformed. Their faces are distorted by pain or brutality. Victims and perpetrators alike have lost their humanity. The scene appears to be lit by pale moonlight. Only a few colours flare up amidst the structure of pale tones and black lines, as though Beckmann had coloured a woodcut.

**Max Beckmann**
Dance in Baden-Baden, 1923
Oil on canvas, 100.5 x 65.5 cm
Munich, Bayerische Staatsgemälde-
sammlungen, Staatsgalerie moderner
Kunst, Stiftung Günther Franke

As in *Night*, Beckmann's *Dance at Baden-Baden* is also crowded with figures. Fashionably dressed couples are jostling past each other in an elegant dance-bar. The figures fill out every available space in the picture so that the floor and the back wall of the bar are barely visible. The close physical contact and angular movements suggest that the couples are moving to the rhythms of a tango.

The dance does not seem to have any particularly enjoyable or relaxing effect. Slender and cool, the figures stand stiffly, arms jutting out and hands pointing downwards. While the blonde gentleman scrutinizes his dark-haired companion, she turns her face away with a calculated look of world-weary disdain. The other couple, in similar pose, are both looking in the same direction, but not at each other. All the figures seem to be watching the others.

Beckmann has condensed his impressions of the spa resort of Baden-Baden into an image of society but he has done so without the accusing directness and aggression of Dix or Grosz. The painter appreciated the expensive elegance of low cut, sequined dresses and the masquerade of the black tuxedo. Nevertheless, the magnificence of this society game does not make him blind to human weakness disguised at great expense. The coolly shimmering tonality of the painting is merely an accompaniment. The large faces with their expressions of grim determination tell us all too clearly that the game is, in reality, a struggle.

# GEORGE GROSZ

1893–1959

Grosz painted this picture during the First World War, when his feelings of disgust and repulsion for bourgeois society were at their strongest. In a letter dated 15 December 1917, he wrote: "At the moment I am working on a large hell painting – schnapps alley of grotesque dead men and madmen, there is lots going on – the man himself is riding on a coffin through the painting, on the right a boy is vomiting, vomiting all those beautiful illusions of youth onto the canvas – I have dedicated this picture to Oskar Panizza. Teeming with obsessive human animals – I am convinced that this era is sailing into destruction – our soiled paradise…"

Panizza, to whom the painting is dedicated, was a writer and psychiatrist. He had appeared in court twice for his satirical statements, accused of blasphemy and *lèse majesté*. From 1904, he was in a mental asylum near Munich. Grosz himself had spent three months in a psychiatric hospital in 1917.

As in an apocalyptic vision, the funeral procession pushes through the abyss of a city street. The human with the animal traits is painted in the tradition of Hieronymus Bosch, while the dynamic movement of the painting with its fragmented faces and falling perspective owes much to Futurism.

**George Grosz**
The Funeral –
Dedicated to Oskar
Panizza, 1917/18
Oil on canvas,
140 x 110 cm
Stuttgart, Staats-
galerie Stuttgart

# OTTO DIX

1891–1969

The importance *Portrait of the Artist's Parents* in the œuvre of Dix was recognized as early as 1925 by contemporary critics: "In the life of each young artist, there is a great work. As far as we know this artist, he achieved that great work in July 1921. He painted his parents. Apron and blouse, rough hands and the signs of age are portrayed mercilessly and without tenderness, but with deep understanding. Cold hate gleams in the clear eyes of the old worker: I'll do it if I have to."

Otto and Louise Dix are portrayed with enormous objectivity and painstaking care, not only as familiar figures, but also as representatives of the working-class. The parents are not looking at each other, and they are looking past the viewer. They are seated in a pose of dull and almost menacing inactivity, their oversized hands resting on the arm of the sofa, or on a thigh or knee. The angle at which father and mother are seated close to each other captures them in this narrow room as a mirror image of the cramped conditions of their life. The light falling in from the side creates a sculptural quality, but also emphasizes the harshness of the modelling. Dix once said of the art of portraiture: "Each artistic statement is, to some extent, self-projection." His emotional involvement has been transformed here to a revealing accusation.

**Otto Dix** Portrait of the Artist's Parents, 1921, Oil on canvas,
101 x 115 cm. Basle, Öffentliche Kunstsammlung Basel, Kunstmuseum

**Marc Chagall**
I and the Village, 1911
Oil on canvas, 192 x
151.5 cm. New York,
The Museum of Modern
Art

## MARC CHAGALL
### 1887–1985

Marc Chagall moved from St Petersburg to
Paris in 1910, where he met Fernand Léger,
Robert Delaunay and Amedeo Modigliani. He
adopted the formal possibilities of Cubism and
orphism, constructing a mirror of his memories in his painting *I and the Village*. The stringent form of circle and diagonal cross forms
the structure of order for the dream of his
Russian home village of Vitebsk, in which individual facets are reiterated like transparent
fragments. The stylized profile of the artist,
holding a glittering posy in his hand, crowds
into the painting opposite a cow whose mouth
is pushed forward to meet the point of intersection of the diagonals. In the head of the
cow, we see a milking scene.

For Chagall, the cow is the epitome of village
security and, for him, it is almost human. Between the two heads, we see a farmer with a
scythe going to the fields, while a woman points
the way. The fact that she is upside-down is
quite unimportant in this dream-like scene, but
on the other hand it emphasizes counter-movement in space. The synagogue and the houses
are on the horizon. It is as though the cosmos of
memory circles round a hub.

In 1913, Chagall returned to Russia, where he
met his beloved Bella once again. The emotional enthusiasm that inspired Bella and Chagall was expressed in the flying motif of lovers
– almost a *leitmotif* in the work of Chagall –
first presented in *The Birthday*.

Bella visited the artist in his room overlooking the Ilych church and brought with her a
bouquet of flowers. We see her hurrying
weightlessly towards her lover, who floats
around her with a malleable body, expressing
his inner emotion in outward movement. In
the sparse colours of the painting, the red floor
over which Bella glides and the green jacket of
the floating artist create complementary contrasts.

Against a blue background, the bride appears
as in a dream. She has raised one hand to her
head, as though to check whether she is awake
or dreaming. Although Chagall and his wife
were in Paris at the time this picture was
painted, we see a small Russian-style wooden
cottage beside Bella, indicating the village life
of her origins and, as though to indicate joy
and happiness, a huge bunch of flowers is
growing over the hut. Yet nothing really takes
on firm contours – neither the daubed bunch
of flowers, nor the lightly contoured hut. Even
the bride is partly swallowed up by the dark
blue. Everything in this picture is drawn
together, as though there were no firm place
on earth, but only in the imagination of the
painter.

**Marc Chagall**
The Birthday, 1915
Oil on canvas, 80.7 x 99.7 cm
New York, The Museum of Modern Art

**Marc Chagall**
Bride with Bouquet, c. 1924/25
Oil on canvas, 69 x 55 cm
Mannheim, Städtische Kunsthalle Mannheim

**Lázló Moholy-Nagy**
Composition Z VIII, 1924
Distemper on canvas, 114 x 132 cm
Berlin, Nationalgalerie, Staatliche Museen
zu Berlin – Preußischer Kulturbesitz

## LÁZLÓ MOHOLY-NAGY
### 1895–1946

Vigorously dynamic movement energizes the
Constructivist paintings of Moholy-Nagy, for
all their compositional stringency. His *Composition Z VIII* is made up of an alignment of segments and bars against an unprimed canvas.
Between the black and pale blue segments,
placed on a diagonal, there are two closely
linked constellations: a central one that dominates the picture and a secondary one that appears as a distant projection of the first. The
large configuration is spanned by a yellow
stripe between the two segments. One black
and one grey parallel component are placed
vertically, as though they were meant to meet
the ground. Further stability is offered by two
red bars of colour that cut through the dominant black segment. The intersections create
a colourful blend of superimpositions. Subordinated configurations are shown as lighter
colours. Some form sections, however, do not
consistently follow this system and have been
treated in retrospect according to compositional criteria.

The lightness of colours and the way the
formations are integrated in the picture space
suggest a fragile constellation.

**František Kupka**
The Language of
Verticals, 1911
Oil on canvas,
78 x 63 cm
Madrid, Museo
Thyssen-Bornemisza

## FRANTIŠEK KUPKA
### 1871–1957

Bohemian-born Kupka exhibited abstract
paintings in Paris in 1912. Yet three years earlier, he had already come very close to abstraction. The floral and ornamental forms of Jugendstil and symbolism had prepared the
ground for him to break away from figurative
painting. Like Kandinsky, who moved towards
abstraction at the same time, Kupka was also
inspired by music. *The Language of the Vertical*
may well have been inspired by the artist's experience of the interior of a Gothic cathedral.
The slender vertical stripes could well be the
pillars of a church aisle, through which the
purple light of the stained glass windows
flows. They could just as easily be a set of
organ pipes. The visual relationship with the
original object, triggered by the picture, can
no longer be reconstructed.

For Kupka, observation of the real world is
merely the starting point for an abstract composition structured according to strict rules.
Although there is an obvious displacement in
space between the surface strips and others
that seem to recede into the background, the
overall impression is one of a picture plane
evenly divided by stripes. The pattern created
by the change of colours follows the basic compositional alignment.

# KASIMIR MALEVICH
## 1878–1935

Although Malevich drew international acclaim as a Cubo-Futurist, from 1915 onwards, he continued to guide his art away from figurative painting in the direction he had begun to take with his *Black Square* (St Petersburg, Russian Museum). According to the artist, the concept of the *Square* can be traced back to a stage design he created in 1913 for the premiere of A. Kruchenych's opera *Victory over the Sun* in St Petersburg. Lissitzky reports that the stage curtain featured a black square. This is the most radical contrast imaginable to the sunlight apotheosis of Delaunay.

While the motif of the black square may still have been vaguely compatible with conventional concepts of art in the context of a stage set, it was bound to provoke a challenge to viewers as the sole subject matter of a panel painting, especially as it was hung over a corner in an elevated position, in the tradition of Russian icons, at its first showing in St Petersburg in 1915. The intended religious allusion was confirmed by Malevich himself in a letter he wrote in 1920: "In the square, I see what people first saw in the face of God."

*Suprematist Composition* shows a black square and a red square on a white ground, with the red square tilted until it is almost standing on one corner. The variation of colours, proportions, and position of the squares in relation to each other and their alignment on the picture plane creates a subtle dynamics whose source of impetus remains invisible. The painting gives an impression of both movement and stability, as though some eternal power were meant to be rendered visible.

*The Knife-Grinder* is generally regarded as the most important Futurist-style painting by a Russian artist. Malevich explores the repeated movements of the knife-grinder by gradating the individual phases of movement in front of each other: the foot driving the wheel of the grindstone, the arms and hands holding the knife to be ground. These are movements that oscillate according to the principle of shimmering around a centre, without destabilizing the picture. Malevich not only presents the movement of the knife-grinder, but also shows his surroundings shimmering from the knife-grinder's own point of view: On the left we see the table with the knives and on the right we see the steps. The Futurists intended to transpose the vibration of the figure and surroundings to the viewer.

In 1912, the Futurists wrote: "In their lines, even inanimate objects reveal languor or wildness, sadness or happiness. By its lines, each object shows how it would deconstruct if it could follow the tendencies of its inner forces."

Kasimir Malevich
Suprematist Composition, c. 1914–1916
Oil on canvas, 71 x 44.4 cm
New York, The Museum of Modern Art

*Below:*
**Kasimir Malevich**
Knife-Grinder, 1912
Oil on canvas, 79.5 x 79.5 cm
New Haven, Yale University Art Gallery

**Marcel Duchamp**
Nude Descending a Staircase No. 2, 1912
Oil on canvas, 146 x 89cm
Philadelphia (PA), Philadelphia Museum of Art,
Collection Louise and Walter Arensberg

**Marcel Duchamp**
The Bride Stripped Bare by Her
Bachelors, Even or The Large Glass,
c. 1915–1923
Oil, lead, wire, foil, dust and quick-
silver on plate glass, 278 x 176cm
Philadelphia (PA), Philadelphia Museum
of Art

# MARCEL DUCHAMP
## 1887–1968

1911 was an important year in the painterly
œuvre of Duchamp. Elements of Cubist and
Futurist painting, evoking processes of movement, herald the development that was to culminate in his most famous painting *Nude Descending a Staircase* in 1912. Immediately before that, in December 1911, he had painted
his *Sad Youth in a Train* in which the torso,
legs and head of a male figure are recognizable in spite of their cubistically deconstructed form. The repeated forms, like parallel strips, withdraw increasingly from the
centre so that a spatial effect is created.
Through the repetition of forms, Duchamp
rendered visible a movement based on the
method of serial photography that had also inspired the Futurists. Duchamp, however, does
not show the inherent movement of the man,
but the effects of the shuddering railway carriage.

In his *Nude Descending a Staircase* the inherent movements of the figure are presented and
the individual phases of movement are clearly
separated. With the aid of Cubist formal vocabulary, Duchamp has radically mechanized the
*Nude* which is barely recognizable as a naked
woman. The monochrome colouring distinctly
emphasizes the mechanical movement, contributing to a further alienation. Contemporaries
ridiculed the painting as "an explosion in a
shingle factory".

In a later work, *The Bride Stripped Bare by Her
Bachelors, Even*, which is also known as *The
Large Glass*, there are no longer any indication-
s of a human figure. The mechanical aspect is
entirely dominant. With perspectival precision, Duchamp portrays a series of cones, a
waterwheel, a kind of metal rack, piston-like
components of wire, a grinder and geometric
figures from the eye-test panels of an optician
projected onto glass. This picture remained
very much an enigma until Duchamp himself,
a decade later, published an accompanying
text.

The picture consists of two glass panels of
equal size. The upper panel is the domain of
the "bride", and the lower panel is the domain of the "bachelor machine". Both are separated by the three "insulation slabs" also
known as the "bride's dress" or horizon. In the
centre of the "bachelor apparatus" is a "chocolate grinder" which Duchamp defined as a
symbol of masturbation: "The bachelor grinds
his chocolate himself." The bachelors are
presented as "nine manly moulded forms", piston-like components framed in wire. Duchamp has created the "bride" from an analogy with a combustion engine. The bride is
stripped bare not by her contact with the bachelors in the male sphere, but by the bachelors inherent within her, the pistons of the
motor. This picture is a pseudo-scientific dia-
gram of the psychology of a wedding night.
Duchamp was interested in exploring an anti-
painterly, anti-traditional principle. He
wanted his pictures to have something of the
precision, rationality and emotional indifference of technical articles.

# MAN RAY
1890–1976

Man Ray's intention was to present the movement of the shadows cast by a dancer in space. The dancer has dissolved in movement. Lines mark the movement and colour planes mark the shadows. Man Ray himself described the creative process of this picture, the motif for which was a rope dancer he had seen in a music-hall performance. First of all, he sketched various positions of acrobats, each on a different piece of coloured paper, intending to indicate movement not only through drawing, but also through the transition from one colour to another. He cut out these forms and arranged them in various sequences. Having changed the composition several times, he became increasingly dissatisfied. Then he noticed the coloured paper cuttings that had fallen on the floor. He threw away the original forms of the dancer and went to work on the canvas, producing large planes of unbroken colour, whose forms corresponded to the pieces that had been thrown away when he created the first drafts of the dancer. He explained that he had made no attempt to achieve harmony of colour, using red against blue, purple against yellow, green against orange, with the greatest possible contrast, and applying the paint so generously that he used up all his supplies.

**Man Ray**
The Rope Dancer Accompanies Herself
with her Shadows, 1916
Oil on canvas, 132.1 x 186.4 cm
New York, The Museum of Modern Art

**Francis Picabia**
Catch as catch can, 1913
Oil on canvas, 101 x 82 cm
Philadelphia (PA), Philadelphia Museum of Art

# FRANCIS PICABIA
1879–1953

Picabia arrived at orphism – whose driving force was Delaunay – in 1910. Orphism sought a pictorial solution to the problem of simultaneity of space and movement, taking as its starting-point proportions borne by colour alone, through which figurative elements may occasionally appear. The first exhibition of Futurist paintings in Paris in 1912 confirmed Picabia's own intentions.

Not unlike the *Contrastes et formes* (Contrasts of Form) by Léger, with whom Picabia had exhibited his work at the Salon de la Section d'Or in Paris in 1912, the forms take on a machine-like character. The moment of movement in space, illustrated by the reciprocal emphasis and overlapping and at times portrayed by the permeation of forms has taken on a harsher edge than orphism. The individual form gains independence. The smooth surfaces of the sharply contoured forms evoke associations with machine elements. The structural parts are arranged freely, consistently foregoing conventional rules and laws of composition. Picabia is not interested in the design of functioning machinery, but in its absolutely free variations. In 1914, Marc had entitled one of his paintings *Fighting Forms*. Picabia's title is *Catch as catch can*.

El Lissitzky
Proun 19D, c. 1922 (?)
Gesso, oil and collage on plywood, 97.5 x 97.2 cm
New York, The Museum of Modern Art

## EL LISSITZKY
1890–1941

The pale background of the picture is not seen as a two-dimensional surface, but as a three-dimensional space with different axes of projection. This explains why there is no immutable orientation from above or below, right or left. That, at least, is Lissitzky's intention. In *Proun 19* D he achieves this effect by means of a black triangle pushing up from the lower edge of the picture, thereby creating the visual field of reference for the two structural relationships with their different directions of movement.

The influence of his Russian compatriot Malevich is evident not only in the white ground and the use of grey, yellow and black, but above all in the system of planes crossing the pictorial plane diagonally with eccentrically aligned circular areas. The picture becomes a *proun* in the sense Lissitzky intended by the fact that the diagonal planar system appears to be overlapped by a horizontal component and a spatial system running at right angles to it.

What Lissitzky was preparing in his pictures was the completely new design of the environment. He enthused: "the new elements we have brought forth in painting we shall pour over the entire world to be constructed by us and we shall make the rawness of concrete, the smoothness of metal and the mirror of glass the skin of a new life."

Theo van Doesburg
Simultaneous Counter-Composition, c. 1929/30
Oil on canvas, 50.1 x 49.8 cm. New York, The Museum of Modern Art

## THEO VAN DOESBURG
1883–1931

In his article entitled *Painting – from Composition to Counter-Composition* published in the *De Stijl* magazine, Doesburg wrote in 1923: "On the one hand, the term counter-composition contrasts with the classical and even the abstract concept of composition and design. On the other hand, it contrasts with the fundamental, predominant structural elements of nature and architecture." Van Doesburg sought to break free from all regulations that had structured composition in a traditional sense: "Elementary (antistatic) counter-composition: it adds a new, angular dimension to the orthogonal, peripheral composition. In this way, it dispels the horizontal-vertical tension in a very real way. Introducing angular planes, areas of dissonance in opposition to gravity and architecturally static structure... introduction of colour as independent energy."

Van Doesburg has veered away from the strict concept of the right angle in this counter-composition by tilting and cropping the yellow, blue and red colour planes. Compositionally, however, he has created a balance through the position and size and repetition of certain angles. The black of the right angle repeats itself in the bars that frame the colour fields.

# PIET MONDRIAN

1872–1944

When Piet Mondrian moved from Amsterdam to Paris in 1911, he came into contact with the Cubists. He adopted their preference for an oval frame and their compositional principles.

In his *Oval Composition*, he elaborates on the phase of analytical Cubism in which the greatest possible degree of abstraction is achieved. In Mondrian's work, too, the figurative starting-point – in this case, trees – has been dissolved to the point of unrecognizability. The colour changes between grey and ochre tones, applied in brief brushstrokes in the Cubist manner, and the use of short black lines that add a distinctive rhythm to the picture is also Cubist. The basic directions of horizontal, vertical, diagonal and round, however, create a network of greater density than we might normally find in Cubist painting. The picture is more tense and more stable.

For Mondrian, Cubism was only a preliminary stage in the quest for more absolute solutions: "Gradually, I began to realize that Cubism did not take on the logical consequences of its own discoveries. It did not develop abstraction through to its ultimate goal of expressing pure reality. I felt that it could only be achieved through pure compositional design and that this should not be determined essentially by subjective feelings and imaginings. For a long time, I endeavoured to discover the special qualities of form and natural colour that arouse subjective emotional states and obscure pure reality. Natural forms thus have to be traced back to pure and immutable conditions."

Mondrian made the contrast of vertical and diagonal principle the basis of what he called the "nieuwe beelding", or "new plastic" as it has come to be known in English. His aim was to create a universal harmony and overcome individualism. He saw total abstraction as the only possible means of doing so, by completely eradicating any element of the sensual perception of visual reality. This meant limiting the pictorial means to their basic elements: straight line, right angle, primary colours red, yellow and blue, non-colours black and white. The radical application of these principles in a large scale structuring of his paintings and their reduced colourity began in 1921.

The degree of reduction is most advanced in those paintings which are not based on the three primary colours, but on the dominant tone of one basic colour. The larger red field is both enhanced and subdued by the smaller blue field. Most of the areas delineated by the black lines of varying thicknesses are taken up by the non-colour white, in accordance with Mondrian's view that "Equilibrium generally requires a large expanse of non-colour or empty space and a small expanse of colour or matter."

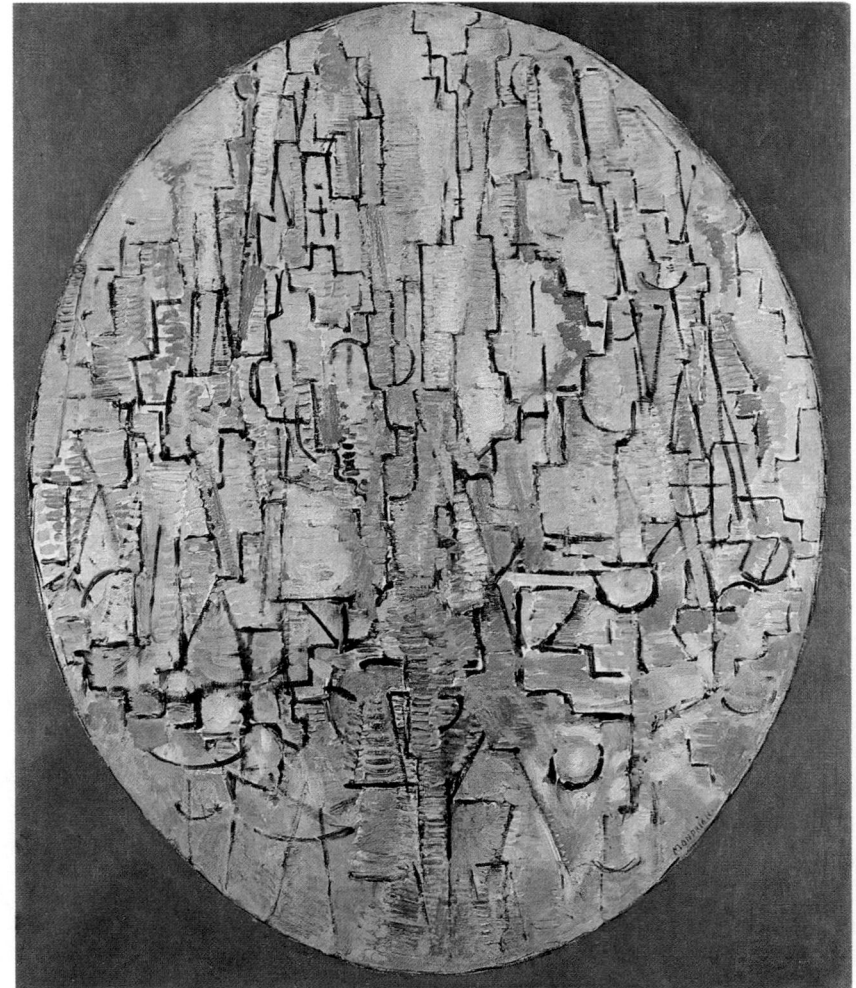

*Above:*
**Piet Mondrian**
Oval Composition
(Tree Study), 1913
Oil on canvas,
94 x 78cm
Amsterdam,
Stedelijk Museum

**Piet Mondrian**
Composition No. II;
Composition With
Blue and Red, 1929
Oil on canvas,
40.5 x 32cm
New York,
The Museum of
Modern Art

**Paul Klee**
Villa R, 1919
Oil on cardboard, 26.5 x 22 cm
Basle, Öffentliche Kunstsammlung
Basel, Kunstmuseum, Imv. Nr. 1744

# PAUL KLEE
## 1879–1940

The foreground of the painting *Villa R* consists of a grassy knoll with graphically suggested trees. Behind them, like a monument, stands a large green R. A red path winds diagonally across the landscape past an architectural structure that looks like a house made of building bricks. It looks more like a backdrop than a real and inhabitable house. It is flat and unreal, and even the mountains in the background seem ornamental, without any structural volume. They are framed by a large green crescent moon on the left and a yellow sun on the right. The brighter corner areas at the upper edge draw the picture together. Klee has given this picture the magical depth of a glass window through his contrast of dark and luminous colours.

When Klee described the *Wege eines Naturstudiums* (Ways towards a study of nature) in 1923 to students at the Bauhaus, he explained the aim of studying as follows: "The development of the student in the observation of nature enables him, the closer he comes to a world view, to achieve a new naturalness, the naturalness of the work".

In *Senecio* Klee takes the circle as his basic form, dividing it into geometric colour fields, drawing a flat figure of eight and placing round red discs in the almond-shaped eyes. The figurative association becomes all the more clear and is further developed. The forms become eyes, the vertical line becomes a nose, the squares become a mouth, the circle a head. It seems like the head of a child with the wisdom of an adult. Klee has created his "little old person" *Senecio* on the basis of geometric components.

**Paul Klee** Senecio, 1922
Oil on gauze on cardboard, 40.5 x 38 cm
Basle, Öffentliche Kunstsammlung
Basel, Kunstmuseum

**Paul Klee** Around the Fish, 1926
Tempera and oil on cotton, 46.7 x 63.8 cm
New York, The Museum of Modern Art, Abby
Aldrich Rockefeller Fund, Inv. Nr. 271.39

The blue dish with the fish and bunches of dill seems to float in the middle of the picture against the dark background, surrounded by various figures and objects that have been symbolically reduced: above the table, a full and a crescent moon; on the left, emphasized by the arrow and the exclamation mark, the head of a person growing on a stem that protrudes from a cylinder; on the right, a cross under a trefoil that seems to grow like a flower out of another cylinder; at the lower edge of the picture, another flower and a cut lemon.

The fish, symbol of Christianity, forms the centre, around which the cycle of death and resurrection moves. It appears in two forms: as a living creature superimposed over its own shadowy shape. The two cylinders are channels of transformation; the one on the right is recognizable as the channel of death, signified by the cross, and the one on the left as the channel of resurrection, symbolized by the branch, the head and the banner. The double moon underlines the concept of the cycle. This painting is one of the first Klee produced in Dessau after the Bauhaus moved there from Weimar in 1925.

Oskar Schlemmer
Bauhaus Stairway, 1932
Oil on canvas, 162.3 x 114.3 cm
New York, The Museum of
Modern Art

## OSKAR SCHLEMMER
### 1888–1943

In spite of the wide range of his creative work, Schlemmer concentrated almost exclusively on a single theme: people and space. In 1923, he noted in his diary: "The birth pangs of the new – controversial – unacknowledged. Yet a major theme remains, ancient forever new, object and creator of all time: man, the human figure, of which it is said that it is the measure of all things."

After nine years at the Bauhaus, where it proved impossible to resolve the conflict between fine and applied arts, Oskar Schlemmer moved to the academy in Wroclaw in 1929. There, he painted from memory the stairway of the Bauhaus in Dessau, designed by Walter Gropius, which undoubtedly embodied an ideal architecture for him. The stairway allows him to gradate a number of male and female figures in the space. They are aligned at various angles; back, frontal and profile. Bodies, heads and faces are all made up of standardized basic forms that avoid any sign of individuality. The result is a distinctive vertical, horizontal and diagonal linearity in the painting.

The square panes of the window form the background. Plane and volume, architecture and figure interact. Here, Schlemmer has used the colours that tend to predominate in his œuvre as a whole: shades of grey, blue and reddish brown.

Lyonel Feininger
Marktkirche in Halle,
1930
Oil on canvas,
100.7 x 85 cm
Munich, Bayerische
Staatsgemäldesamm-
lungen, Staatsgalerie
moderner Kunst

## LYONEL FEININGER
### 1871–1956

The Cubists had a decisive influence on Feininger's stylistic development. In Paris, he met Delaunay, with whom he shared an interest in the refraction of light and questions of colour. However, he was not interested in exploring the problem of form detached from sensual perception of the environment. In 1913, he began working on architectonic compositions, whose themes were primarily the villages and towns of Thuringia. Feininger once said of his preference for these motifs: "The church, the mill, the house – and the cemetery – have filled me with a profound sense of reverence since my childhood."

The *Marktkirche in Halle* was painted in 1930, when he had a studio in a tower at the invitation of the museum director of Halle. The west façade of the church, with its double spires, is positioned frontally at the centre of the picture, and the nave is portrayed in foreshortening. There are some houses around the church. On the square in front of it, we see tiny little figures, and their small scale underlines the monumentality of the building. The church and the sky are prismatically divided in the same manner. The forms are transparent and flooded with light. Although Feininger adopted the Cubist method of deconstructing down objects, he developed his own set of rules, which he called "prismaism".

# GRANT WOOD
1892–1942

When Grant Wood exhibited his painting *American Gothic* at the Art Institute of Chicago, he was accused of caricaturing American rural life. On the other hand, he was also accused of idealizing Mid-Western antipathy to civilization and the rural rejection of progressive urban attitudes. Wood was not interested in taking sides, but chose the themes he felt he could portray best because he knew them best.

A farming couple, described by Wood as father and daughter, are standing in front of a wooden house with the kind of pointed window arch that earned this form of architecture the epithet "carpenter's Gothic". Wood's sister Nan and his dentist Doctor McKeeby were the models for this couple with their old-fashioned clothes and direct gaze. The prongs of the hay-fork, a metaphor for rural America, reiterate the Gothic window. Like the hay-fork the man is holding, the flower-pots behind the woman, the house, the barn and the church tower are all indications of the property, profession and attitudes of the two figures. The puritanical sobriety of the couple corresponds to the dry realism of the portrayal which corresponds in many ways to the Neue Sachlichkeit (New Objectivity) movement in Europe.

**Grant Wood**
✔ American Gothic, 1930
Oil on beaverboard, 75.9 x 63.2 cm
Chicago (IL), The Art Institute of Chicago

**Edward Hopper**
Night Windows, 1928
Oil on canvas, 73.7 x 86.4 cm
New York, The Museum of Modern Art

# EDWARD HOPPER
1882–1967

A key motif in the work of Edward Hopper, who was always interested in the question of lighting, is the portrayal of various times of day and, in particular, night. The special atmosphere of night is portrayed here in the simple motif of a corner building with three illuminated windows.

In the confrontation between the dark outside world and the brightly lit room, he places the viewer in the situation of a voyeur. In order to allow the spectator to participate in what is going on in the room, he chooses an elevated point of view. The cornice of the building and the floor of the room are seen from above. Through the central window, we can recognize the figure of a woman in a petticoat with her back to us. The intimacy of the situation makes the spectator's gaze seem intrusive.

Unlike other artists, Hopper uses the window as a motif that intensely clarifies feelings of separation, uninvolvement and alienation. On the one hand, the artist and the spectator are shut out from the scene they are observing, but on the other hand, those observed are also shut out from the outside world. In order to add tension to the contrast between the contemplative mood of the self-contained interior and the frequently more vibrant outer world, Hopper often uses motifs such as fluttering curtains, as he does here.

UNITED STATES

**Giorgio de Chirico**
The Silent Statue (Ariadne), 1913
Oil on canvas, 99.5 x 125.5 cm
Düsseldorf, Kunstsammlung Nordrhein-Westfalen

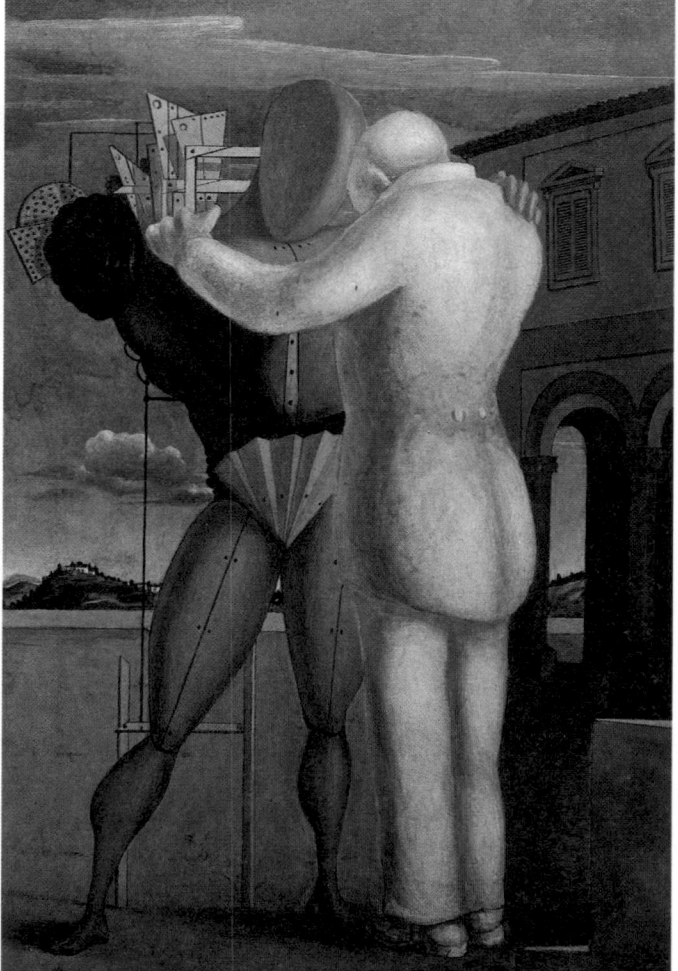

**Giorgio de Chirico**
The Prodigal Son, 1922
Tempera on canvas, 87 x 58 cm
Milan, Civico Museo d'Arte
Contemporanea

# GIORGIO DE CHIRICO
## 1888–1978

De Chirico painted six important pictures in 1913 featuring the statue of Ariadne as a motif. This ancient Greek work was familiar to him in the form of Roman copies in the Vatican and Florence. The statue shows the restless sleep of Minos' daughter, plagued by nightmares, on Naxos. Ariadne was abandoned by her husband Theseus as she slept.

De Chirico has placed the statue diagonally in the picture and has moved so close to it, closer than in his other paintings, that the motif appears in detail. The face, worn by sleep and dream, is the main motif. In his essay *The Desire of the Statue* De Chirico states: "She loves her strange soul. She conquers. The sun is high in the centre of the sky. And in constant contentment the statue bathes her soul in the contemplation of her shadow."

The statue stands on a square in front of a building with deeply shadowed arcades and in front of a tower with fluttering flags. De Chirico explains: "The Roman arcade is fate. Its voice speaks in riddles filled with singular Roman lyricism." In the background, the sea appears as a black plane. The volumes of the objects have been projected into the plane so that everything appears incorporeal and intangible.

In the early 1920s, De Chirico began to take an interest in the techniques of Renaissance artists. The Russian painter Nicola Lochoff introduced him to the secrets of *tempera grassa vernicata*. *The Prodigal Son* is painted in this revived technique, but nevertheless retains the ambiguity of *pittura metafisica*.

In De Chirico's painting, we find none of the stirring pathos that normally imbues portrayals of this encounter between father and son. De Chirico's painting shows their meeting as the meeting of two representatives of different ages, an encounter between fossilized tradition and helpless modernity. The father stands as a stoney monumental figure in front of the son, on whose shoulder he has placed his hand. The son stands there, large and powerful, but as a puppet without facial traits and incomplete limbs, requiring the support of a complex structural frame. For De Chirico, the puppet is a metaphor of the modern anti-hero in a universe in which the heroism of classical Antiquity – the heroism of Achilles, Hector or Roger – is no longer possible. The place at which the monumental figure and the puppet meet has all the stability and dignity of Renaissance architecture. In the background, we see a cultivated, hilly landscape. The yearning for refuge in tradition is not fulfilled.

# CARLO CARRÀ
## 1881–1966

In the early 1920s, Carrà began painting sea-scapes in the manner of Giotto. Carrà, who had distanced himself from the principles of *pittura metafisica*, published a book on Giotto in 1924, in which he pointed out: "In the magical tranquillity of Giotto's forms our gaze comes to rest; our ecstasy grows and gradually dissolves in a sense of transfiguration."

Carrà's *Summer* also exudes an air of tranquillity. It is an everyday scene on the beach. The woman on the left in profile is drying her hair, her face covered by the towel, while the woman on the right with her back to us is drying her knees with the towel wrapped around her waist. Between them sits a dog, and the right-hand side of the picture is bounded by a bathing cabin. Behind it, we see the bay, with a boat and some hills.

The appeal of this painting does not lie in the subject matter, but in the almost monumental simplicity of the composition. In their strength, simplicity and unornamented stringency, the large figures herald the emergence of a new Classicism after the formal experiments of the early decades of the 20th century. Time seems to stand still. Both of the figures have turned away from the viewer. Not even the dog reacts. In this way, Carrà closes the picture, and at the same time arouses our curiosity which is satisfied only by the form.

**Carlo Carrà**
Summer, 1930
Oil on canvas, 166 x 121.5 cm
Milan, Civico Museo d'Arte
Contemporanea

# GIORGIO MORANDI
## 1890–1964

The work of Morandi has only one brief close link to the movements of classical Modernism: the metaphysical still lifes of the period 1918/19. Just one year later, Morandi was to go his own way – entirely independent of the trends of his time.

In his still lifes, Morandi explored an artistic problem which he explains quite simply: "The only interest that the visible world arouses in me has to do with space, light, colour and form." Morandi severely restricts the traditional handling of space based on the use of central perspective. The depth of the table surface foreshortened in a flat curve is reduced by the wall immediately behind it parallel to the picture plane.

The components of the still life are arranged on the table: bottle, vases, round fruit, a box with a fruit dish on it. Light models the objects only to the point of creating an impression of tangible volume, but the self-contained form remains. The result is a balancing act, combining planar elements with volume and space. The colours, limited to ochre, brown and white, creating a soft *chiaroscuro*, underline the ambivalence of positive and negative forms.

**Giorgio Morandi** Still Life, 1920
Oil on canvas, 60.5 x 66.5 cm
Milan, Private collection

**Diego Rivera**
The History of Mexico: Huastec
Civilization, 1930–1932
Fresco (detail)
Mexico City, Palacio Nacionale

## DIEGO RIVERA
### 1886–1957

Rivera, who had closely studied contemporary art in Europe, particularly in Paris, returned to Mexico in 1921, where he joined the Communist Party. Drawing on the traditions of Mexican folk art, he began painting murals intended to present the country's history to its uneducated people. For the National Palace of Mexico City, he created a narrative sequence of pictures on the theme of Mexican culture in the period before the arrival of the Spanish conquistador Hernán Cortés. With the painstaking thoroughness of a historical researcher, he gathered all the available sources and translated them into realistic paintings of compelling clarity and monumental impact.

*Huastec Civilization* shows grain and corn being milled and made into tortillas. In the foreground, a woman is kneeling on the ground, grinding grain to flour on a stone. Behind her, four women are seated on the ground. A young woman is shaping tortillas by hand, while the older woman beside her is stirring. A mother is removing the grains of maize from the cobs and her neighbour is making tamales. On the right beside the five women, a man is planting corn.

The scene is watched over by protective gods, of whom all we can see in this particular detail is the feet. In the background there are cornfields. Rivera's didactic intention is reflected in the clarity of the composition.

**Frida Kahlo**
Self Portrait with Monkey,
1938
Oil on hardboard,
40.6 x 30.5 cm
Buffalo (NY), Albright-
Knox Art Gallery, A. Conger
Goodyear Bequest, 1966

## FRIDA KAHLO
### 1907–1954

With a proud and almost imperious gaze, the artist looks directly at the viewer in this self portrait. Her deep brown eyes are fixed on us and her pink lips demand our attention. Frida Kahlo stylizes herself as a confident artist and woman.

The simple, apparently naive pictorial language, in which elements of Mexican devotional painting are blended with classical portraiture, emphasize the symbolic meaning of the attributes. The necklace of bones around her neck may be read as a metaphor of death. The foliage in the background indicates the jungle as the origin of nature and all life.

The little monkey is one of the many animals that lived in the Blue House of Diego Rivera and Frida Kahlo. He has placed his arm around the artist, and behind his large eyes, we seem to perceive a vulnerable soul. In Western and Mexican iconography, the monkey is a symbol of lust, though Mexican mythology also treats the monkey as a patron god of dance.

Here, Kahlo is making a reference to her complex relationship with her husband Rivera who had an affair with her sister Christina a few years earlier. In 1938, as an expression of her new found independence, she travelled alone to New York for the opening of her solo exhibition.

# CHAÏM SOUTINE

1893–1943

Between 1927 and 1929, Soutine painted many pictures of choirboys, restaurant staff and hotel porters. The *Page Boy at Maxim's* is shown as a frontal three-quarter figure. He is wearing a red uniform with gold buttons. He stands, arms akimbo, as though seeking to demonstrate the sleekness of his slender, wiry figure. The instability of his stance is underlined by the little hat balancing on his head. The cap also makes the face of the boy seem caught between it and the uniform. The rather audacious, tongue-in-cheek expression also has something tortured about it. The background is formed by the instable movement of a heavy blue velvet drape.

Soutine was probably fascinated by the single colour and identical structures of uniforms, which have fewer variations than civilian clothing. What is more, uniforms tend to subdue individuality, depersonalizing the unique and emphasizing anonymity. Painted in thick, heavy brushstrokes, it becomes a vibrant material, an artificial skin. In his work, Soutine explored one colour after another: the white of the chef, the red, dark green and blue of the page and valet, the white and purple of the choirboy. He was constantly seeking the right form for his motif.

Chaïm Soutine
Page Boy at Maxim's, c. 1925
Oil on canvas, 81.9 x 74.9 cm
USA, Private collection

André Masson
Meditation on an Oak Leaf, 1942
Tempera, pastel and sand on canvas, 101.6 x 83.8 cm
New York, The Museum of Modern Art

# ANDRÉ MASSON

1896–1987

Masson, who fled to America from France during the Second World War, wrote that he still imagined the country in which he was exiled in terms of a virgin forest, and that this had a psychological influence on his painting in America. The cities, he claimed, did not affect him in any way; it was the proximity to nature that became a typical characteristic of his American work.

Concentrating on an oak leaf triggered associations for Masson. The picture is positively teeming with biological symbols of germination and growth of individual cells or larvae to the point of totemic configurations of floral, faunal and human nature. The link in this chain of associations is the oak leaf which can be seen as a silhouette and blue shadow at the top left. Within this silhouette, its outline is reiterated in a smaller form like a cell division. The result is a labyrinthine constellation reminiscent of the cycles of nature, and the trauma and fantasy of the soul. The forms as a whole create a totem, crowned by a cat's head symbolizing the animal kingdom.

## JOAN MIRÓ
### 1893–1983

**Joan Miró**
Harlequin's Carnival, c. 1924/25
Oil on canvas, 66 x 95 cm
Buffalo (NY), Albright-Knox Art Gallery

*Harlequin's Carnival* shows Miró's break-through to the portrayal of the imaginary and the miraculous in an atmosphere of levity and serenity. Many figures, objects and signs appear, overlap and take part in the magical game that is a mixture of carnival, theatre and fairytale. A harlequin with a moustache and a mechanical guitarist with a wind-up key take the leading roles. Around them we see cats playing with a ball of wool, birds of paradise laying eggs from which strange butterflies emerge, flying fish encountering comets. An insect is crawling out of a cube. On a ladder hangs a huge human ear, and between its rungs there lurks an eye. Eyes open on cubes, cylinders and cones between the living fairy-tale toys scattered on the floor. A window gives a view of a black triangle, a red flame and a star against a blue sky. The luminous colours are subordinated to the precise drawing of the forms. Through repetition and distribution of colours, reference and pictorial rhythm are created.

Miró did not distinguish between painting and poetry. Time and time again, he painted pictures in which he includes words or poetic phrases. The freely associative inscript "hirondelle amour" that inserts the two words without any syntactic connection, corresponds to the Surrealist refusal to insist on certain qualities or intrinsic properties of objects. Yet the signs bear such an unequivocal significance that a sexual element is clearly evident in their playful levity.

From 1926 onwards, Miró developed his own highly distinctive alphabet of pictorial signs, which he continued to use increasingly freely over the years and, in the course of which, his pictorial world became more serene and humorous. The material and grain of the canvas play an important role in a number of paintings towards the end of the 1940s. The priming is irregular and emphasizes the coarse texture. On the other hand, the forms appear more planar. The result is an attractive interaction between the background, the colour planes on it and the black lines. Two figures are interwoven. The form of the red sun corresponds to the large head of the figure directly on the lower edge. The body of the figure soars vertically into the air. Only if we turn the picture around does the figure stand on its feet. As on a playing card, the concepts of "above" and "below" are no longer valid.

**Joan Miró** Hirondelle Amour, 1934
Oil on canvas, 199.3 x 247.6 cm
New York, Collection, The Museum of Modern Art,
Gift of Nelson A. Rockefeller

**Joan Miró**
People and Dogs before the Sun, 1949
Tempera on canvas, 81 x 54.5 cm
Basle, Öffentliche Kunstsammlung Basel,
Kunstmuseum, Stiftung Emanuel Hoffmann

# MAX ERNST
## 1891–1979

The basic concept of this painting is based on the work of de Chirico. Behind a square, stage-like floor we see a brief indication of a landscape with a low-lying horizon spanned by the high arch of the sky. A two-legged, drum-like monster stands firmly on the ground, crowned by a figure based on one of de Chirico's geometric elements. In the foreground, a headless female figure raises her arm, and we see fish swimming in the sky. The objects are unreal, yet the precision of the painterly technique lends them the appearance of reality.

Max Ernst did not actually invent the name *Celebes*. In fact, Celebes is one of the Greater Sunda Islands of Indonesia. The island has a singular four-armed shape consisting of an almost square central part with large peninsulas. The form of the elephant is derived from a picture of an African grain silo.

Found objects have been combined in this picture as in a collage, of which Max Ernst explained: "Collage technique is the systematic exploitation of the coincidental or artificially provoked encounter of two or more unrelated realities on an apparently inappropriate plane and the spark of poetry created by the proximity of these realities." For the Surrealists, collage served to find new contents, rather than new forms, as in the work of the Cubists.

*Above:*
**Max Ernst**
Elephant of the
Celebes, 1921
Oil on canvas,
125 x 106 cm
London, Tate Gallery

**Max Ernst**
Après nous la
maternité, 1927
Oil on canvas,
146.5 x 114.5 cm
Düsseldorf,
Kunstsammlung
Nordrhein-Westfalen

Birds play an important role in the work of Max Ernst. The repertoire of birds is ambivalent in its significance. It is both evil and tender, coy and demonic, a metaphor of liberty and of menace.

In the painting *Après nous la maternité*, creatures that are part bird and part human are grouped in a triangular hierarchy. The character of the painting itself is as ambivalent as the creatures. The central figure embraces a smaller bird-like creature in an attitude of matriarchal security, while the soaring bird-like creature above it embodies independence from that security and, therefore, liberty. The central group is an ironic reference to Raphael's Madonna paintings.

As in many other pictorial motifs, Max Ernst traces the blend of bird and human to an experience in his youth: "A friend by the name of Hornebom, a clever, colourful, loyal bird, dies in the night: a child, the sixth, comes to life that same night. Confusion in the brain of the otherwise healthy boy. A kind of interpretative madness as through the innocence just born, sister Loni, had taken the dear bird's vital juices. The crisis is soon overcome. Yet in the boy's imagination, there is a voluntary, irrational imaginative blurring of people and birds and other creatures; and this is mirrored in the emblems of his art."

In 1945, Max Ernst won a painting competition held by an American film company on the theme of *The Temptation of St Antony* for Albert Lewin's film *The Private Life of Bel-Ami*. One of the eleven artists who entered the competition was Dalí, Max Ernst gave the following statement on his painting: "Over the brackish water of his dark, sick soul, St Anthony receives the echo of his fear as a reply: the laughter of the monsters born of his imagination."

St Antony in the red monk's habit is suffering terrible tortures in the hallucinations embodied by the fantastic creatures surrounding him. They are creatures made up of parts of mammals, birds, reptiles and humans. Though the concept and artistic technique in this painting are closely linked with surrealism, this work also owes much to the tradition of medieval German painting, especially the same theme treated by Grünewald.

Max Ernst has used the technique of decalcomania for a considerable proportion of the image, in which paint is applied to a sheet of paper or glass and a second sheet is then superimposed on this background and raised, creating characteristic structures on the painted surface. The painter can then use the imprints or blots created in this way to identify forms and find in them the structure of the monsters. The figure of St Antony himself was created by conventional painterly techniques.

Max Ernst
The Temptation of St Anthony, 1945
Oil on canvas, 108 x 128cm
Duisburg, Wilhelm-Lehmbruck-Museum

## KURT SCHWITTERS

1887–1948

Schwitters began creating pictures made of waste materials in 1919, one year after the end of the First World War. He called them *Merz* pictures. They correspond to his mood at the end of the war: "I felt free and I had to cry out my joy to the world... You can also cry out with waste products, and that was what I did by gluing them and nailing them together."

The *Merz* pictures blur the boundaries between painting and relief. Different materials are mounted on the cardboard background: snippets of paper, can lids, pieces of cardboard, wooden batons, wire, string, tickets and newspaper cuttings. The objects have not been left in their found state, but most of them have been painted over. Against the earthy brown background, lighter colours stand out in faceted fragmentation: ochre, red, blue and green.

Only fragments of the newspaper clippings are legible: *Offener Brief* [open letter], *(R)eichsk(anzler)* [chancellor of the Reich], *Die Korrupt(ion)* [corruption], *Mathias (Erzberger)*. The mention of Mathias Erzberger, who signed the ceasefire at Compiègne in 1918 and who was Minister of Finance in 1919/20 gives the picture a specific time-frame. The found items are used in terms of their formal quality, while the disks reiterate the late Expressionist concept of the cosmic.

Kurt Schwitters
Merz 25 A. The Constellation, 1920
Montage, collage and mixed media on cardboard,
104.5 x 79cm
Düsseldorf, Kunstsammlung Nordrhein-Westfalen

**Paul Delvaux**
The Encounter, 1938
Oil on canvas, 90.5 x 120.7 cm
Private collection

**Yves Tanguy**
The Palace of the Window Cliffs, 1942
Oil on canvas, 163 x 132 cm
Paris, Musée National d'Art Moderne, Centre Georges Pompidou

## PAUL DELVAUX
### 1897–1994

The frozen stillness and stage-like scenery of *The Encounter* is derived from the metaphysical urban imagery of de Chirico, which profoundly influenced Delvaux and Magritte from 1936 onwards. From this treasure-trove of motifs, Delvaux created a distinctive pictorial cosmos that explores the impossibility of communication between the sexes. Like Magritte, Delvaux used a meticulously detailed technique to present improbable, dream-like encounters.

Delvaux also adopted from René Magritte the motif of the well-dressed man in the bowler hat with the traits of the artist. He greets his model and ideal human: an academic female nude barely clothed in a magnificent drape. In the windows of the stage-like facades of Renaissance buildings running towards the background, we see further classically dressed women. Disturbed by the arrival of a streetcar, another woman flees into the forest in the background. Here, the Surrealist love of expectations confused by combinations of improbability is evident. Encounters between civilization and nature, modern man and antique Venus are possible in a moment of frozen time in which reality is interrupted and undermined.

## YVES TANGUY
### 1900–1955

Around 1926, Tanguy found the theme that he was to vary continuously until his death: the Surrealist landscape. In *The Palace of the Window Cliffs* no horizon line divides the sky from the earth. They merge in a mutual, pale, greyish-blue tone. In the foreground are indefinable objects – some like stone, some like coloured plastic. Some stone-like elements have the regular form of architectural components. Apertures are placed like noses. The individual components are linked with each other by lines and points of connotation, as though to present them dissolving into the infinite space.

André Breton, who, like Tanguy, had emigrated to the USA during the Second World War, wrote of Tanguy in the year this painting was created: "Until Tanguy, the object, even though it was subject to a number of external attacks, remained unmistakable and a prisoner of its identiy. With him we enter the world of complete indeterminability for the first time: 'at any rate no actual appearances' promised Rimbaud. The elixir of life seeks to set itself apart from all the upheavals of our transient individual existence."

# RENÉ MAGRITTE

### 1898–1967

The combination of eroticism and sadism finds its extreme expression in the theme of the crime of passion that played such an important role in German art in the 1920s. In French and Belgian art of the same period, Magritte's painting is a thematic anomaly.

The room is structured like a stage. A red *chaise-longue*, on which the pale corpse of a naked woman is lying, juts into the room. Her throat has been cut. Blood is streaming from her mouth.

At the front of the room, a man is standing beside a small table on which there is a gramophone. The distinctly well-dressed man is listening to music. His face shows no sign of emotion. It is as though a doctor had made his visit in this bright, sparsely furnished room and was listening to a little music to help him relax after his strenuous work. But the room is surrounded. Three men, a rugged mountain landscape behind them, are looking into the room over the balcony railing. In the foreground, a man with a club is standing to the left of the entrance to the room, while a man on the other side is waiting with a net. In their neat clothing, the gentlemen look distinctly bourgeois. They are all quite immobile, and everything has frozen to a state of uneventfulness.

Magritte has coupled the horror of the situation with bourgeois harmlessness. The picture shows the dichotomy between social adaptation and the overstepping of social norms. The Surrealists took the provocative stance of seeing the positive aspect of the criminal as an individual who does not comply with social strictures.

In August 1927, Magritte moved from Brussels to the Parisian suburb of Perreux-sur-Marne, where he became involved with the Parisian surrealists. In his new circle of friends, he gained fresh inspiration and it was here that he produced his first paintings involving words.

Interpretations of these paintings frequently refer to the philosopher Ludwig Wittgenstein and his critique of the inadequacy of language. This approach tends to underestimate the influence of Magritte's direct contact with André Breton in Paris. In 1927, Breton criticised the fact that poets were incorrigible word fetishists, and that words took the place of things and even of living creatures and that for a poet to move from language to reality merely signified a tautology. For Magritte, a picture or a word can never be identical with reality.

The designation alone says nothing. Magritte points out this problem of "naming" in his *Palace of Curtains III* by juxtaposing image and word. Two irregularly-shaped framed panels are leaned against the panelling of an interior room. One frame contains a painterly portrayal of the sky, while the other contains the word "ciel" (sky). Language and image mean the same and, for Magritte, are both equally detached from reality.

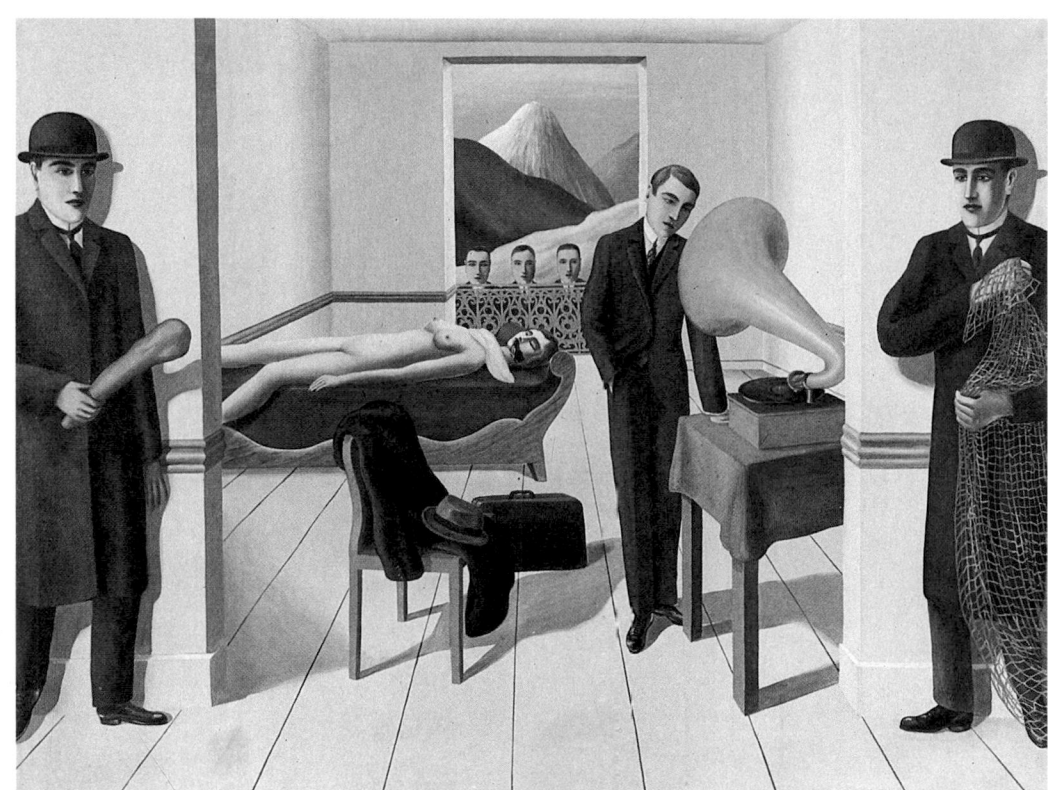

René Magritte
The Menaced Assassin, 1927
Oil on canvas, 150.4 x 195.2 cm
New York, The Museum of Modern Art

René Magritte
Palace of Curtains III, c. 1928/29
Oil on canvas, 81 x 116.5 cm
New York, The Museum of Modern Art

**Victor Brauner**
Miroir de l'incréé (Mirror of the uncreated), 1945
Oil on canvas, 77 x 56.2 cm
Private collection

# VICTOR BRAUNER
1903–1966

Victor Brauner painted in wax on canvas from the early 1940s onwards. In his place of exile in the Alps, he initially used this technique quite simply due to a lack of other materials. The warm wax, thinly applied with a trowel, covers a drawing on the canvas, whose contours and colouring are added by scratching the wax.

Brauner was obliged to simplify his enigmatically emblematic imagery with enormous stringency. For him, the layer of wax possessed alchemistic qualities, and transformed a banal canvas into an esoteric image.

A chimera-like female creature with a double head is seated at a small table. One of the heads gazes at the viewer with large, visionary eyes, opened wide. The other head, resting in the crook of her arm, is contemplating its reflection in a mirror on the table with closed eyes.

Brauner would appear to be referring to the séances frequently held by the Surrealists, in which mediums in a trance delighted the participants with their prophecies and enigmatic utterances. Above the creature floats a male torso, heated by two candles. This may be a reference to the actual production process of the picture itself.

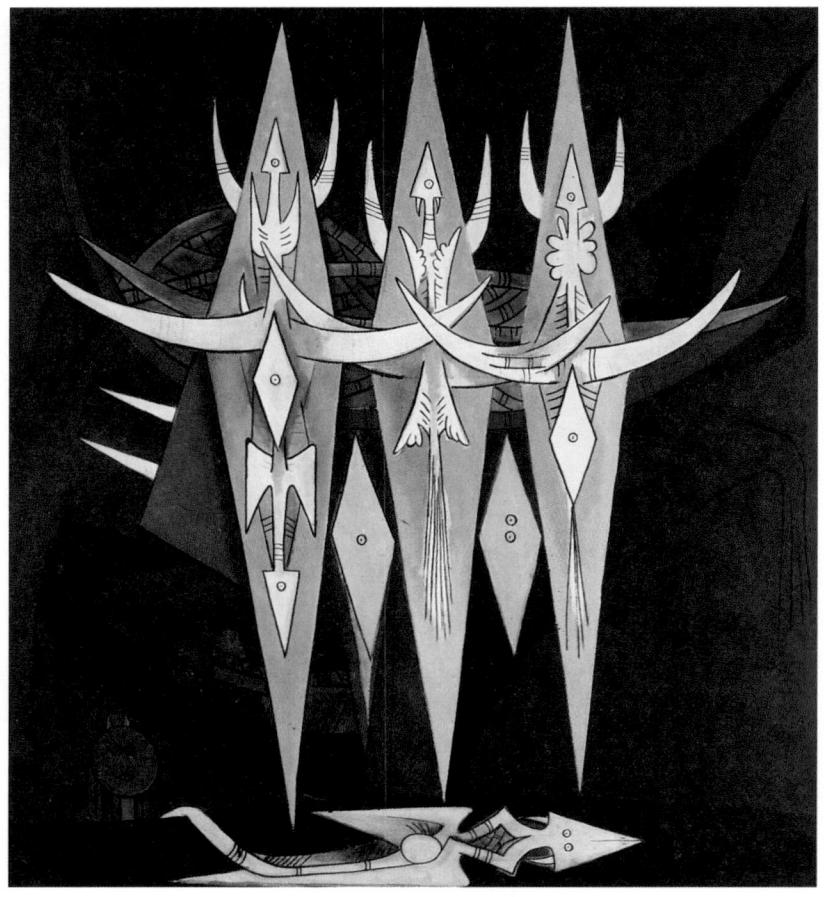

**Wifredo Lam**
Umbral (Senil), 1950/51
Oil on canvas, 188 x 173 cm
Paris, Musée National d'Art, Centre Georges Pompidou

# WIFREDO LAM
1902–1982

Wifredo Lam's pictorial motifs and his distinctive surrealist style are rooted in the exotic imagery of his homeland, where Caribbean, European and African cultures blend. His mythical figures are inspired by the voodoo spirits of Cuba and by African jungle motifs. Since the 1940s, Lam's formal syntax, previously influenced by his imitation of the entangled organic forms of the jungle, becomes firmer and clearer. *Leitmotifs* such as the vertical rhomboid figure are developed and their obsessive repetition gives them a fetish character.

*Umbral* is a work from this phase of clarification and emblematic condensation. Three-horned rhomboids, enigmatically enlivened totemic figures, seem to float and dance against a dark, night-like background in some obscure ritual. The structure of their bodies is reduced to a sign by the geometric figure. The object of this sacrificial act lies before them. Another creature with a moon-like face and plaited hair is watching the scene from the background. Beyond such figurative interpretation, the strict composition of the picture with its harshly delineated forms accentuated by the two smaller yellow rhomboid figures, is particularly striking.

# SALVADOR DALÍ

1904–1989

It was around 1930 that Dalí developed his theory of the "paranoid-critical" method. Paranoia is expressed in chronic hallucination, megalomania, persecution complex.

In a sparse landscape with a high horizon lies an amorphous form and, on the left, a platform with a tree stump, on which a deformed clock is draped, following the forms of the object on which it has been placed. The amorphous form on the ground has human traits, not unlike those of the artist himself. But the mouth is missing. The Surrealists adopted the psychoanalytical correlation of the mouth as a symbol for the female genitals. The lack of a mouth maybe interpreted as a fear of impotence with regard to the partner. The soft clocks have the form of relaxed tongues. Tongue-like entities are frequently featured in Dalí's paintings, supported by crutches, again expressing a fear of impotence. The clock that has been turned over so that we cannot see its face maybe regarded as a symbol of fear of revelation.

Dalí himself derives the *Persistence of Memory* from an everyday situation without exploring the reasons for his association: "We had finished our dinner with an excellent camembert and, as I was alone, I remained for a moment with my elbows on the table, thinking about the problems of this super-soft runny cheese… The picture I was working on at the time showed a landscape near Port Lligat, whose cliffs seemed to be illuminated by the transparent light of the dying day. This landscape was to serve as the backdrop for an idea, but for which idea? I needed a surprising image and I could not find it. I switched the light off and was about to go out when I literally "saw" the solution: two soft clocks, one of which would be hanging miserably on the branch of an olive tree."

In a similar landscape with a low horizon and distant blue mountains where the evening light throws long shadows, we see the *Burning Giraffe* standing calmly. Stranger still is the female figure in the foreground. Tongue-like entities supported by crutches jut out of the back of her body, while a number of opened drawers jut from the front. Dalí, who had intensively studied psycho-analysis, may have been familiar with Freud's essay *The Theme of the Three Caskets* when he created paintings and sculptures in 1936 featuring many caskets built into the human body. In view of these works, Dalí spoke of the "narcissistic pleasure", perceived in the "observation of each of our caskets". The burning giraffe is an elementary object of desire yearned for by the female who is devitalized by the strictures of moral caskets and by the painter with his fear of impotence.

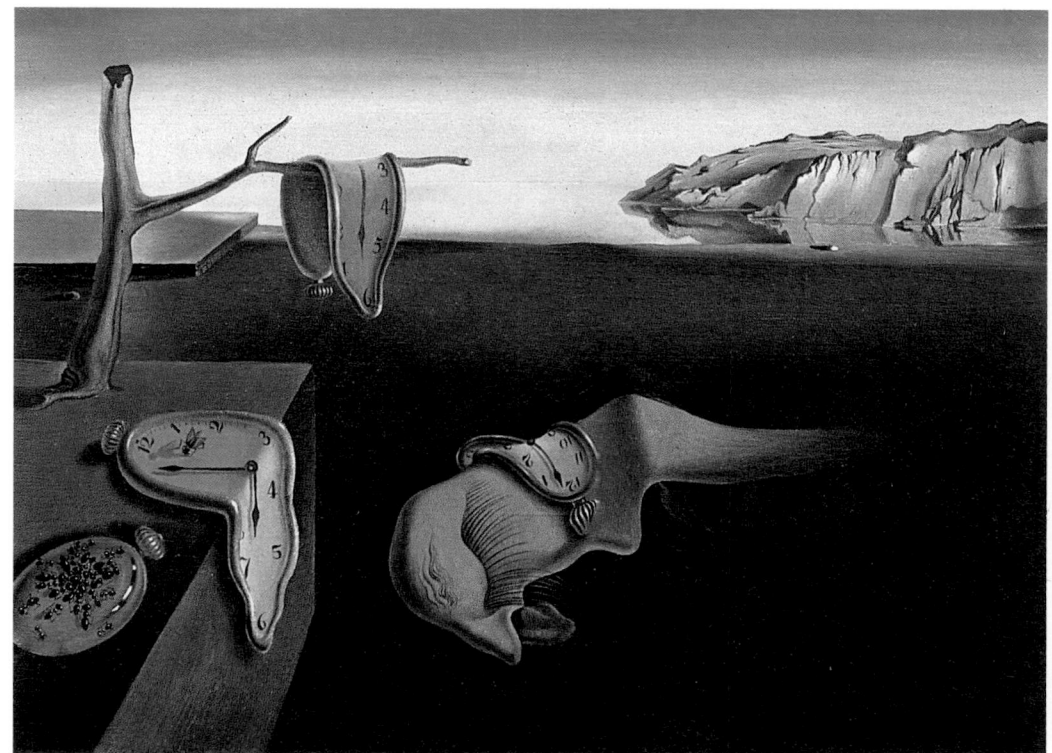

Salvador Dalí
The Persistence of Memory, 1931
Oil on cancas, 24 x 33 cm
New York, The Museum of Modern Art

Salvador Dalí
The Burning Giraffe,
1936–1937
Oil on panel, 35 x 27 cm
Basle, Öffentliche
Kunstsammlung Basel,
Kunstmuseum

Ben Nicholson
Still Life, 1947
Oil and pencil
on canvas,
61 x 50.8 cm
Private collection

Graham
Sutherland
The Bridle Path,
1939
Oil on canvas,
60 x 50 cm
London, Tate
Gallery

# BEN NICHOLSON
## 1894–1982

For Nicholson, the late 1940s were a period
of recollection and collection. He attempted
to consolidate the pictorial forms he had already developed in his major series, and collect them within a secure canon. Whereas,
until the outbreak of war, he had explored
questions of organic connections between
image and canvas by way of abstract reliefs,
he now began to return to more traditional
motifs.

In his still life, Nicholson draws upon the
pictorial syntax of synthetic Cubism. The
classical motifs such as a jug and a glass are reduced to flat forms and interconnected groups.
Although they are still recognizable as objects,
they can now be used as material with which
to create a balanced, planar composition. Soft
and hard colour tones are contrasted, allocated
associatively to the pictorial objects, and juxtaposed.

Nicholson said of his paintings of this
period: "In painting a still life one takes the
simple everyday forms of a bottle – mug – jug
– plate-on-table as the basis for the expression
of an idea: the forms are not entirely free,
though they are free to the extent that each object can be seen from as many viewpoints as
you wish at one and the same time, but the
colours are free."

# GRAHAM SUTHERLAND
## 1903–1980

To Sutherland, the landscape of western
Wales, and especially of Pembrokeshire, was a
revelation. He had learned from the Surrealists
to awaken the unobserved, and to breathe life
into arbitrary forms of nature in a visionary
moment. It is this that creates the magic of his
paintings. The point of departure for his *Bridle
Path,* which is regarded as exemplary for this
process of vitalization, was the precise observation of nature. In a number of preparatory
sketches, he worked out the dramatic and
mysterious aspect of the landscape.

Sutherland once described his approach as a
process of starting to learn again, stressing
that he found himself incapable of simply sitting down and painting from nature what he
saw: "I did not feel that my imagination was
in conflict with the real, but that reality was
a dispersal and disintegrated form of imagination."

In the painting, the forms used in the drawings were further simplified and accentuated.
Sutherland was interested primarily in the
curving line of the village road. Brilliant
white and yellow give the impression of
strongly reflecting sunlight with branches reduced to coded signs and surrounded by fields
of colour that can barely be interpreted as landscape motifs.

Christa von Lengerke

# CONTEMPORARY PAINTING

## New movements in painting since 1945

Contemporary painting reveals new techniques, new materials, new pictorial forms – emerging in parallel or in sequence. It spans a range from abstraction to realism, from purist stylization to the monumentalization of trivia, from tongue-in-cheek revelations of subculture to sober and even visionary presentations of political or personal trauma.

In the USA, Pollock and de Kooning developed free abstraction to its zenith. Their abstract Expressionism has its lyrical counterpart in European informel or Tachisme. The pictorial statements of Reinhardt, Newman and Noland are determined by the quality of colour. The world of the object and the metaphysical qualities of material are united in the work of Dubuffet and Tàpies to symbolistic assemblages.

Vasarély, with his decorative, rhythmic grids, is the founder of Op Art. Warhol and Lichtenstein follow on from Jasper Johns and Rauschenberg in elevating the clichés of the consumer world to the realms of Pop Art, scrutinizing them with an ironical eye. In the portraits by Bacon or in the works of Baselitz, Kiefer and Richter, the classical painting, once declared dead, seems to find its continuation.

## The artistic environment after 1945

The end of the Second World War marked a break with the past, whose impact went far beyond the political dimension alone. It heralded the end of European hegemony, dividing the world into a system of eastern and western power blocs that was to last for more than forty years. Against this background, artistic life in America ranked for the first time on an equal footing with art in Europe.

In the post-war years, the western world built up and perfected interactive institutions and instrumentaria that facilitated the dissemination and popularization of art: museums and exhibitions, art trade and art criticism. Until the 1970s, the art of the socialist world was barely acknowledged in the west. The eastern bloc produced commissioned art that was strongly influenced by politics; until the end of the 1980s, creative freedom in that part of the world was possible only in underground movements.

Ever since the discovery and settlement of America by the Old World, everything considered to be of a higher standard – and that included art – had to be imported from Europe. Invariably, it was measured by a European yardstick, and all things European were copied and imitated: America's consciousness was defined by the Old World. Paris, the capital city of the 19th century, had to share its previously unchallenged position as cultural leader with other centres after the turn of the century: initially, within Europe, with Berlin, Milan, Vienna and Zurich, and even with such provincial towns as Weimar, where the *avant-garde* created its forum at the Bauhaus.

Now, after the end of the Second World War, the situation was entirely different. Although strong artistic personalities and groups continued to emerge in Europe, new stylistic directions also began to evolve that were acknowledged everywhere; just as the eyes of the art world had focused for centuries on Europe, they turned now increasingly towards North America. For a good two decades, it was North America that produced the most exciting innovations and vibrant impulses for art. As a world power, the USA developed its own cultural consciousness. Confidence in the power of industrial society was as boundless as the faith in the blessings of the American way of life. Those beliefs were to be shattered politically in the 1970s, first by Vietnam and Watergate, then artistically in the 1980s by the advent of Neo-Expressionist "wild" painting.

New York has been able to maintain its position as an international centre of art up to the present day. The relationship between art and commerce that emerged there has been taken up elsewhere. This liaison between media and management has made art as consumable as any mass-produced wares, though the enormous profits involved in art and its surrogates and in art ownership, connoisseurship and understanding remain the preserve of an elite.

Since 1929, the Museum of Modern Art and since 1939 the Solomon R. Guggenheim Museum in New York have held exhibitions. Both go beyond their primary function of presenting art works. With their wide-ranging activities, they have become highly influential cultural institutions. They heralded a new era of museumship and still have a lasting influence on artistic activity. A small group of exhibition organizers, museum curators, critics, academics, patrons and collectors, together with the powerful lobby of the art dealers, thus ensure that the latest art is not only accessible to the public, but is also made attractive through interpretation. The art of the past decades is not neglected, for it is meant to retain its ideal and material value. Finally, the artists themselves have also turned their eyes towards New York. The hustle and bustle of the world's capital city seems to create a fertile working atmosphere, for not only do many artists exhibit here, but they also have their studios in New York.

## Painting today – traditions and trends

Once the long days of war were finally over, there was a general sense of starting out in a new direction. Art, too, called for a new start instead of merely upholding old traditions. As in the first half of the century, it was art that sought new ways and new solutions in keeping with the spirit of the times. Much had already been achieved by the artists of Expressionism and Cubism, by the Dadaists, Futurists, Surrealists, Constructivists and the painters of the Neue Sachlichkeit. Even the most revolutionary innovators of our day continue to draw upon ideas that were developed in the first decades of the 20th century.

The most lasting influences on contemporary art come from Dada and Surrealism. "Dada invited misunderstanding, challenged it, supported every kind of confusion: on principle, on whim, out of fundamental opposition" (Hans Richter, 1888–1976). The combination of a wide variety of materials and techniques became the means of expressing this will to provocation: Marcel Janco (1895–1984) was the first to integrate *objets trouvés* (found objects) into his work. Johannes Baader (1876–1955), a founding member of the Dada movement, called for the use of new materials in painting as early as 1918. The ideas of Marcel Duchamp (1887–1968) proved the strongest basis for new approaches. By declaring everyday objects to be art simply by adding his signature, Duchamp demonstrated the artist's demiurgic powers. The object is no longer portrayed or represented, but represents itself, so that everyday reality and artistic reality become one.

The "psychic automatism" of the Surrealists liberated painting from pre-formulated, intellectually guided concepts. Psy-

**Willem de Kooning**
Untitled, 1970
Oil on parchment on canvas, 182.8 x 107.9 cm
Zurich, Thomas Ammann Fine Art

chic occurrences and stirrings, the unconscious and the spontaneous, trauma, dreams and visions found a place in painting and expanded the realm of motifs to previously unexplored limits. Carl Gustav Jung (1875–1961) described chance as an order outside causality. Arp and Tzara then discovered chance as an artistic principle.

After 1945, painting adopted this approach in its search for a pictorial language that can not only be discovered through education and intellect, but which is also capable of triggering complex psychological processes in the viewer. Irrespective of whether it is figurative or abstract, this is art that is intended to be regarded and understood as a bearer of meaning, as an exploration of the materials and realities of the socio-political environs, and the dreams and nightmares of our time and culture. It represents a quest for truth free of values, far from social conventions and aesthetic structures. It is a question of new pictorial forms, approaches and functions in the integration of external reality. This involves the need for a redefinition of such concepts as "painting" and "picture".

The painterly process is no longer an exclusively manual application of paint onto a ground. It can also take the form of a physical action with its own forceful dynamics (Action painting, Tachisme). It can be complemented or substituted by collecting, selecting and arranging found objects (Combine painting). The manual act of painting can be aided or substituted by the use of reproductive processes such as photography or silk-screen printing (Pop Art, Photo-Realism). This de-individualization culminates in the concept art of the 1970s. With his maxim "concept over reality" Raymond Roussel (1877–1933) anticipated the artistic approach of the 1920s. The intellectual concept, rather than the material realization, constitutes the art work.

The idea of image as representation is no longer crucial to contemporary art. The path towards abstraction opened up new expressive possibilities for the artists and new dimensions of experience for the spectator. It is no longer nature alone that creates the store of pictorial motifs; the individual's psyche, the forms and colours used by foreign or "primitive" cultures, the elementary power of children and the mentally ill are all discovered as creative sources.

Pictures also take on a more political function. They are rarely intended merely to confuse, provoke or shock. They are invariably used with the intention of tearing away a veil that cloaks something sacred or perilous. A picture can be its own protest against its consumption as a purely aesthetic object. Pictures can also express philosophical and religious concepts, or can be brought back to their original function as a call to meditation.

The viewer's encounter with the art work is a vital, dynamic and constantly changing process in which personal mood and leanings, *Zeitgeist* and the passing of time constantly determine and influence the reception of the work and its impact. These components are variable. The constant givens are the contents intended by the artist, the statements intended by him, frequently supported by a written instruction or explanatory title. For the active viewer, however, it can take on its own dynamics. Through his or her own ideas and associations, the viewer can construct a personal pictorial truth and an individual pictorial expression. Through distance in time or changing awareness, the original statement can be dissolved or guided in completely different directions.

## The New York School

It was the painters of the Ash Can School who turned their backs on European ideals and ideas. As early as 1908, they portrayed monotonous rural existence and the hard life of America's streets and slums with a critical and realistic eye. In doing so, they created an approach that was entirely independent of the European art tradition. At the same time, they elevated themselves above the provincial and naive level of American folk art. The leading representatives of this socially committed realism were Edward Hopper (1881–1967), Grant Wood (1892–1942) and Ben Shahn (1898–1969). Arshile Gorky (1904–1948), whose development away from the objective figurative towards expressive abstraction was the link between this "American scene" painting and post-war art.

Alongside this national development in the world of art, the names of certain European emigrants are closely linked with the emergence of the New York School. Duchamp, the most popular and by then the most influential visitor, brought Dadaistic ideas to New York in 1915, together with Francis Picabia. Hans Hofmann (1880–1966) and Josef Albers (1888–1976) followed, and both went on to become highly influential teachers of art in the USA. Ernst, Robert Matta (* 1912), Tanguy and Breton also brought their Surrealist ideas with them.

In response to the Ecole de Paris, which had become ossified in its virtuoso aestheticism, the New York School emerged full of self-confidence in the 1940s. For a full two decades, it would shape the world of art on an international scale, breaking new ground with abstract Expressionism, Drip Painting and Action Painting.

At her progressive Art of this Century gallery in New York, Peggy Guggenheim (1898–1979) offered the emigrants and the entirely unknown painters of the American *avant-garde* the chance to exhibit their works. As a patron and collector, she was able to build up relationships with such artists as Pollock, Franz Kline (1910–1962), de Kooning, Robert Motherwell (1915–1991), Clyfford Still (1904–1980), Barnett Newman (1905–1970), Mark Rothko (1903–1970) and Ad Reinhardt (1913–1967). In the independent processing of Dadaist and Surrealist elements, these painters forged an individual path towards abstraction.

Gorky is the main pioneer of abstract Expressionism. Initially, his work leaned heavily on Cézanne and Picasso, but later, under the influence of Matta, he arrived at a new and inde-

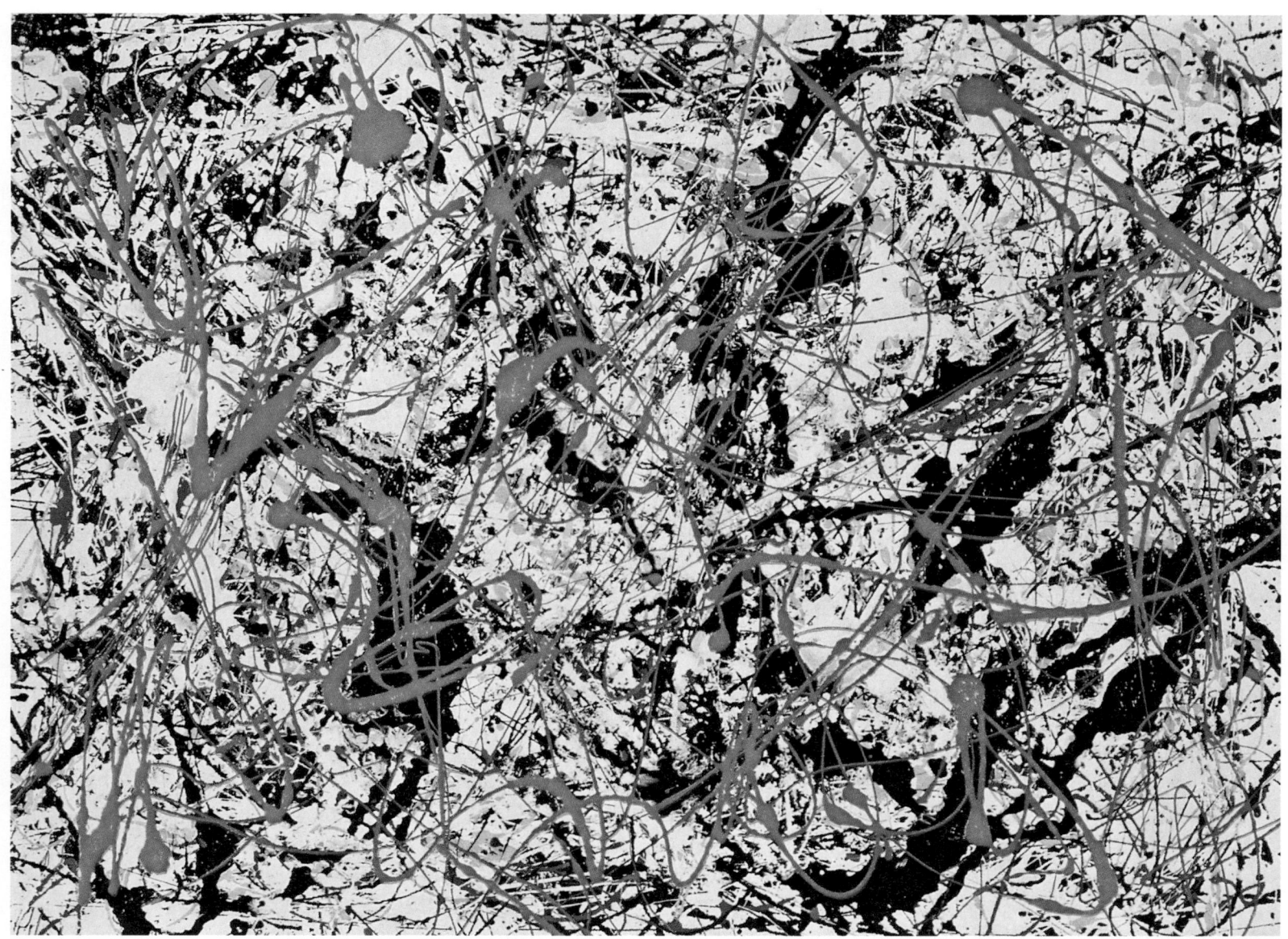

**Jackson Pollock**  Painting, 1948
Oil on paper, 57.3 x 78.1 cm
Private collection

pendent pictorial language. Gorky's later work already contains the nucleus of every characteristic of the later movement. He took his life just as their ideas were beginning to develop more widely.

Pollock was the first to adopt Gorky's pictorial formulations. In his tendency towards folk art, Pollock was inspired by the Indian culture with its symbolic forms, brilliant colours and interlaced patterns, which led him directly to abstract painting. The partially figurative motifs of his early work cover the canvas with density and regularity. The combination of these painterly forms with psycholgical processes indicates an affinity with certain principles of Surrealism. On the basis of their psychic automatism, Pollock eventually developed an automatism that involved the entire person. In a rapid action, while his senses and his body were entirely concentrated on the energy-charged act of painting, he worked on the canvas spread out on the floor. Conventional instruments such as brush, easel or pallet were a hindrance and would have inhibited the spontaneous process.

He let the paint drip out of cans and tubes, mixed it with all manner of materials such as sand or ground fragments and distributed the dripping colours with sticks and rags. This technique of drip painting soon earned him the epithet Jack the Dripper. For all the vehemence of his gestures, his works indicate a strong inner control over the creative process in these expressive pictorial patterns. In this way, Pollock created a new aesthetics – an aesthetics of action.

The fully abstract paintings created after 1946 indicate a radical break with classical painting. They demand an entirely new way of seeing, in order to acknowledge this iconography of energy as a physical reality. Harold Rosenberg (1906–1978), who gave this painting the name Action Painting, wrote: "At a certain moment the canvas began to appear to one Amercian painter after another as an arena in which to act – rather than as a space in which to reproduce, redesign, analyze or 'express' an object, actual or imagined. What was to go on the canvas was not a picture but an event." This trend determined artistic creativity until well into the 1950s.

Motherwell, who had worked with Pollock and exhibited with him at Guggenheim's gallery, developed more tranquil forms of expression in his paintings, in keeping with his calmer personality. They are the result of careful consideration and, because of Motherwell's love of history and literature, they often have a profound ideal significance, as in his *Elegy to the Spanish Republic* (ill. p. 634) series. In his large-format paintings, the subdued, expressive brushwork is often dominated by a lyrical atmosphere. Motherwell's activities went beyond the field of painting, and he was influential as an author, publisher and lecturer.

In the 1950s, de Kooning was the leading exponent of abstract Expressionism. For de Kooning, who came from Europe, a link with western tradition was a matter of course, though he upheld that heritage with a progressive and vitalizing approach. Against this background, he developed an unparalleled convergence of abstract and figurative painting. In 1928, he met Gorky in New York.

As in the work of Pollock, the painterly process took on a life of its own in de Kooning's works, with a vehement brushstroke and brilliant colours documenting unleashed aggression. The vulgarity of his motifs correspond to this exalted formal syntax. His series of male and female figures project a brutally distorted image of the human condition.

Kline was relatively late in joining the abstract Expressionist movement. At first, he painted small-format Cubist impressions of city life and realistic portraits and landscapes. Under the influence of de Kooning, his characteristic black and white paintings emerged from the early 1950s onwards: broad, beam-like brushstrokes on large white canvases. These works have a distinct similarity with East Asian calligraphy. More important still in Kline's pictorial language, however, is its distinction from calligraphy: his paintings are not to be regarded as black traces of paint on a white ground, but as an equal interaction of both. The manual preparation of priming and the creative act of applying the paint thus contribute essentially to the creation of pictorial tension. It was not until the late 1950s that Kline also began including colour in his work.

Attempts to categorize various artists according to a single stylistic concept on the basis that they worked around the same time are not always entirely convincing. The term abstract Expressionism linked with the artistic production of the New York scene between the end of the Second World War and the end of the 1950s applies, strictly speaking, only to the work of Jackson Pollock, Robert Motherwell, Willem de Kooning and Franz Kline.

## Abstract Symbolism

For some artists, the path towards abstraction meant developing a symbolically coded pictorial language. Individual abstract, non-figurative forms, can be indicative of appearances in reality.

The work of Mark Tobey (1890–1976) is largely influenced by philosophical reflections. His attempt to exclude definable forms and structures from his art is influenced by his close reading of Cubism and his conversion to the Bahai faith, which emphasizes the spiritual unity of human kind. From 1935 onwards, Tobey developed his mature style with his *White Writings*: a network of thin white lines against a dark background. He regards these abstract compositions as symbols of the unity of form and movement in the universe.

Mark Rothko, Clifford Still, Barnett Newman and Ad Reinhardt tended to work primarily in monumental formats on monolithically abstract pictorial blocks. By deliberately going beyond the familiar dimensions of a classical easel painting, the artist gives the viewer a sense of the sublation of the pictorial boundary. The aim is the experience of space as such.

Around 1950, Rothko reduced his forms to large, rectangular, converging "colorfields" which shimmer out of the monochromatic background. The simple presentation of colours takes on a sophisticated artistry. The colours themselves are neutralized in a sonorous tonal harmony, and their effect materializes purely in the shimmering substance of the paint itself. Instead of many colours, the potential wealth of monochromatic gradations and carefully chosen colours create solemn and celebratory accents. In his paintings, Rothko associates archetypes, metaphors of possible responses to fundamen-

**Mark Rothko**
Red, Green, Blue, 1955
Oil on canvas, 207 x 197.5 cm
Milwaukee (WI), Milwaukee Art Museum

tal questions of human existence and life, mystic formula that cannot be named, but repose within the magical twilight of their appearance.

Still also addresses metaphysical themes in his paintings. In 1947, through his interest in the presentation of universal ideas, he arrived at his distinctive style: a characteristic hallmark of his huge canvases is the large monochromatic ground that covers almost the entire surface of the painting, framed at the edges by flaming forms.

Newman concentrated on colour, which he sought to "create". In his huge horizontal or vertical canvases, we note a tendency towards ever larger and ever simpler forms. The rudimentary composition develops on a calm surface that tends to negate the personal brushwork. Newman's distinctive formal reductions created the basis for the purist formal syntax of minimal art. The philosophical implications of his work, however, were not adapted by his followers.

As a critic, art historian and painter, Reinhardt sought to create a purely abstract art. From 1950 onwards, he divided the canvas into sharply contoured rectangles which he filled with slightly varying hues of a single colour. Whereas the colority of his early paintings was still light and vibrant, his later works are painted in darker tones, culminating in his characteristic *Black Paintings* which are probably the most subtle of all color-field paintings. For Reinhardt, art was a clearly defined object, independent and separated from all other objects and circumstances, whose significance is not explicable or translatable. For him, artistic progress meant increasing negation of its formal means.

Jasper Johns
False Start, 1959
Oil on canvas, 171.5 x 134.7 cm
New York, Private collection

## Tachisme and Informel in Europe

In Europe, at almost exactly the same time as American abstract Expressionism, a new direction in painting was developing which had many essential similarities: *informel*. This new expressive painting initially developed under the influence of the École de Paris, but from the 1950s onwards there were artists all over Europe seeking new means and concretizations. All of them followed a similar path.

It was Antoni Tàpies (* 1923) who coined the term *informel* and who first spoke in 1950 of the "significance of formlessness" in new painting. *Informel* as a style can only be outlined in its fundamental traits. The emergence of *informel* paintings has its roots in the Surrealist concept of psychic automatism. *Informel* has no traces of the figurative, and its formal syntax emerges from the spontaneity of movement. Colour is predominant as a coloristic and mutable element as well as in terms of its materiality.

New techniques involving the use of unconventional media or mixing colours with materials not previously employed in painting, such as sand, resulted in new visual impressions, requiring also that the viewer to adopt new ways of seeing. Working from the spontaneous inspiration of the subcon-

scious, the rapidity of the act of painting and the inclusion of the principle of chance determine the process of creation of *informel* paintings.

In France, it was Jean Fautrier (1898–1964), the German immigrant Wols (1913–1951) and Hans Hartung (1904–1989) together with Georges Mathieu (* 1921) who represented the new painting emancipated from traditional rules of composition. As a synonym for *informel*, the term *tachisme* took hold in French, derived from the French *la tache* meaning a "daub" or "stain". The work of Wols, in particular, is often described as lyrical abstraction.

The pictorial worlds of Pierre Soulages (* 1919) bear certain similarities to the structures of Kline's work. His œuvre and that of Mathieu are often subsumed under the term calligraphic abstraction. Two painters who emigrated to France in the wake of the Russian Revolution, Serge Poliakoff (1906–1969) and Nicolas de Staël (1914–1955) complete this broad spectrum of French *informel* painting.

In Germany, Ernst Wilhelm Nay (1902–1968) Emil Schumacher (* 1912), Baumeister and Bernhard Schultze (* 1915) worked out new artistic aims entirely in accordance with their individual painterly temperament.

## Jean Dubuffet – The CoBrA Group

Jean Dubuffet (1901–1985) paved the way for an extended concept of art that included formulations by children and the mentally ill. The expressive potential of primitive art had already been recognized and put to use by the Expressionists in the first half of the century. Inspired by them, he initially began collecting what he described as "art brut". It became the point of departure and orientation for his own pictorial inventions, through which he sought to emancipate himself from conventional principles of design and aesthetic guidelines. This allowed him to declare as superfluous the stylistic, contentual and thematic values of the western culture he disdained. He found a correlation to this anti-traditional view of art in the visual worlds of the mentally ill. He created backgrounds of plaster, sand, paste, putty and other materials, working them over with a palette knife, scratching and scoring them, in flights of lyrical imagination. Dubuffet's preference for cycles of works culminated in his *Hourloupes*, puzzle-like juxtapositions of amorphous forms which overgrow the background.

The members of the CoBrA group pursued similar aims. Their programmatic rejection of the aesthetic dictates of the Ecole de Paris was accompanied and legitimized by their vociferous condemnation of a civilization that was responsible for unleashing two world wars. The CoBrA artists came from Denmark, Belgium and the Netherlands, and the first letters of the capital cities of these countries were used to form the group's name. The main representative of the artists association that lasted for only three years, from 1948 to 1951, were Pierre Alechinsky (* 1927), Karel Appel (* 1921), Constant (* 1920) and Asger Jorn (1914–1973). Like Dubuffet, they, too, saw more originality and vitality in the pictures by children and the mentally ill than in the classical canon of art history and, accordingly, they called for a break with all aesthetic norms in a total liberation of thought. The group's ideas were expressed in joint exhibitions, publications and a magazine of the same name.

## Geometric Abstraction, Op Art

Geometric abstraction developed out of the Bauhaus tradition, as a sober art bearing no personal signature and no trace of craftsmanship. Based on the ideas of the Constructivists and the De Stijl group, they followed in the footsteps of the *abstraction-création* movement which had united the leading representatives of modern abstract art in the 1930s.

Van Doesburg, one of the spokesmen of geometric abstraction, described it as "concrete art", feeling that it was not bound to a process of abstraction, but based entirely on concrete geometric elements. This fundamental concept was also adopted by Max Bill (1908–1994), who substituted geometric abstraction for a naturalist art, distinguishing it clearly from Cubism and from the intuitive and naturalist movements. Like the work of Bill, the œuvre of Albers is accompanied by art theoretical reflections and academic teaching. "When I paint, the first thing I see and think is – colour." Albers used the form of the square to exemplify the changing effects of colour in a multitude of variations.

Op Art once again addressed a number of the questions Albers had already raised in his work. For example, a row of geometric forms was aligned in an area in such a way that colour variations or gradations of light and shade optically confused the viewer. Victor de Vasarély (* 1908) is the most inventive and varied designer of Op Art objects. He regards himself as the creator of a harmonious order that does not exist in this form in the real world. Vasarely aims to transform the "monotony of modern life into a determination of beauty with manifold forms". Op Art seeks to unsettle the viewer by involving him in the visual confusion that it has deliberately created and which in fact serves as its structural concept.

## Post-Painterly Abstraction: Colorfield and Hard Edge

Like Op Art, so-called post-painterly abstraction also originated in the *Gestalt* psychology colour studies of the Bauhaus system. Disseminated by Albers in America, it provided fertile ground for the painting of the 1960s which superseded abstract Expressionism. Following on from the tranquil, intensively coloured paintings of Rothko and Newman, it sought to achieve an absolute application of colour while avoiding spatial illusion by emphasizing planarity in large and even huge formats. It was painting for its own sake, unfettered by any thematic strictures. No longer the bearer of a message or a *Weltanschauung*, it is not at the service of literature, religion or philosophy, does not narrate and does not imitate. Anyone can understand the language of this painting without initiation, for it transports no coded messages or personal experience of the artist. Its variations are called colorfield and hard edge, terms that tend to overlap.

With new paints, thinners and unorthodox methods of application, Kenneth Noland (* 1924) and Morris Louis (1912–1962) explored the dimension of colour. Paint with all its inherent characteristics – opacity, transparency, impasto and sheen – is merely the bearer of coloristic qualities and visual sensations. The colorfields consist of elementary geometric forms. These paintings can be regarded as a purist emancipation in which a deliberately simple form is linked to the chromatic.

Frank Stella (* 1936) took the reduction of colorfields one step further in his *Shaped Canvas*. The elementary basic form was no longer the prescribed rectangular canvas; instead, the colorfield determined the pictorial format, resulting in paintings with a triangular, V-shaped, or polygonal outline. Colour is treated as an object bounded by external form. In this way, it becomes part of the third dimension, developing sideways and parallel to the wall into the room itself.

Ellsworth Kelly (* 1923) also regards the picture plane as a neutral container of colour. He was the first to use ready coloured canvases which merely had to be sewn together as standardized pictorial forms. Colour thus took on its own, "concrete" reality, inherent in the original carrier and no longer perceptible as material.

## Combine Painting, Material Painting

The Dadaists had already discovered the lyrical appeal and painterly quality of *objets trouvés*. In the same way, Cubist collages contain fragments of everyday objects, and a fascination with the fragmentary is evident, which exerted an influence on Surrealist montage.

Following abstract Expressionism, artists returned again to this integration of everyday objects in their work. In classical Modernism, this stood for an extension of pictorial language, an emphasis of the lyrical and chromatic qualities of things, ensuring the homogeneity of the art work, whereas the artists from the late 1950s onwards clearly sought to use them – in a combination and convergence of art with daily reality – as a means of questioning the effectiveness of an art language. Their exploration of everyday subjects is to be seen as a response to introverted and intellectualized abstract Expressionism. It ensures an element of recognition and familiarity. The painting now becomes the bearer of relief-like arrangements that combine a variety of materials, techniques and objects. By fixing them on a ground, it is their identification that creates the image.

In the spirit of *informel* and lyrical abstraction, Tàpies created his early material paintings. Paint mixed with sand and binder takes on a relievo structure. Code-like scratching and splitting are reminiscent of old masonry. Representational elements – the canvas that becomes a relief through the combination with sand – and the object they represent – the wall – become virtually synonymous.

Joseph Beuys (1921–1986) also integrated found objects and materials in his drawings and his painterly, sculptural works. For Beuys, each material and each object was the bearer of symbolic meaning, because it was linked to some universal tradition or personal experience. In his life and in his work, Beuys sought a reconstruction of the lost unity of nature and spirit, countering rationalism with a way of thinking that included the archetypal, the mythical and the magical religious. For example, fat, in accordance with its functions in nature, also functions as an energy store in the œuvre of Beuys.

Alberto Burri (1915–1995) composed his material paintings using burnt, torn sack-cloth and colour areas. Eventually, many painters turned to a free application of diverse materials and techniques, when painting alone no longer seemed capable of making a forceful statement. Appel and Jorn applied paint like thick plaster, thereby dissolving the purely painterly impression of their works.

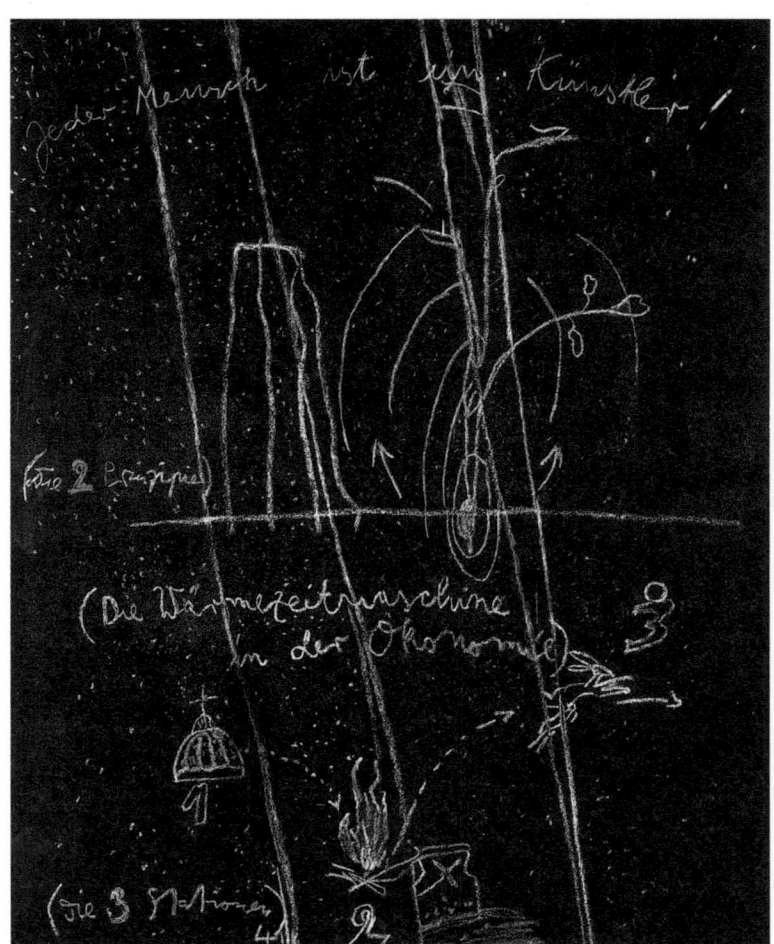

**Joseph Beuys**
Is it about a bicycle? IV, 1982
Coloured chalk on panel, 150 x 122 cm
Private collection

In the USA, it was Robert Rauschenberg (* 1925) who invented combine paintings after some earlier experimentation with Action Painting. He began to integrate individual elements in collage technique into his expressive painting. These were objects that he had found and that belonged to the waste thrown up by civilization. They certainly possessed no lyrical flair, merely the misery of a short existence as cheap mass-produced articles.

This Junk Art blossomed in the 60s, and found an increasing number of exponents, including the sculptors John Angus Chamberlain (* 1927), Robert Mallary (* 1917) and Richard Peter Stankiewicz (* 1922). The movement culminated in the creation of *Watts Towers*, towers built of garbage and decorated with garbage, in the slums of Los Angeles.

If we look at Junk Art from today's viewpoint, with our awareness of certain social and environmental problems, we are tempted to perceive it as an eloquent incrimination. However, these works were not created with the intention of making a socially critical statement. At the time they were produced, the problems implied by them were not part of the public consciousness. Nevertheless, creative design is no longer an act of creation, that produces aesthetic objects alien to reality. This uninhibited foray into the treasure-trove of shabby symbols of mass culture may be regarded as a breaking-down of social barriers.

Jasper Johns (* 1930) created monumentalized everyday clichés such as the American flag, targets and maps. In presenting these deliberately simple things, he forged a correspondence between the object of the painting and the painted surface for the first time, thereby raising the question of the identity of thing and its portrayal: "Is it a flag or is it a painting?" asked one critic when his first flags emerged. The simplicity of the motifs and their relationship to large format images with advertising panels and advertising hoardings anticipate certain characteristics of Pop Art.

In his early work, Jim Dine (* 1935) was strongly influenced by Johns and for both these artists abstract Expressionism had been the starting-point. The repertoire of Dine's motifs, like that of Johns, is fairly limited: household objects, furniture, tools, items of clothing. In his paintings, he often integrates real objects with painted shadows, reiterating them in paint on the canvas or underpinning their existence in the painting by an accompanying text.

## Pop Art

Pop Art is a term coined by the critic Lawrence Alloway (1926–1990). In the 60s, the American variant of Pop Art achieved a degree of popularity unparalleled by any previous art movement. Pop Art derived its inspirations and motifs from the world of mass consumer society, industrial mass production, the consumer – oriented and taste – defining influences of advertising and the media. The resulting phenomena such as sensationalism, star cult, loss of individuality and glorification of the banal and the trivial, in short, the eminent significance and effectiveness of clichés, were the foundations on which Pop Art was built and the soil that nurtured its success.

The motifs of American Pop Art were generally adopted from other media: magazine cut-outs, film stills, advertising images. Special printing techniques and printing processes were used to transfer the image to its ground, whereby it was coloured and alienated. Everyday themes from politics to gossip were adopted. The motifs, which already reduced the complexity of the statement, were transformed into an effective trivial *cliché* by enlarging the format, simplifying the colours and repeating the motif. Although the Pop artists drew their motifs from a generally accessible store, their works are distinctly different. Their respective styles are constituted by their personal selection of pictorial patterns, technical processes and specific colours.

Andy Warhol (1928–1987), who was the most famous representative of Pop Art, staged spectacular public appearances along the lines of advertising campaigns, thereby creating a true symbiosis of personality and work. He himself was a superstar, and in his view it was through his work that other persons, events and products became superstars themselves: Elvis Presley, Marilyn Monroe, Albert Einstein and Mao Tse-tung all share the same entertainment quality as the stars of short-lived daily news-spots: accidents, catastrophes, executions. The stars of American life can also be dollar bills, cola bottles, soup cans, packs of washing powder. Warhol's creed was: "Everybody is plastic, but I love plastic, I'd like to be plastic."

Roy Lichtenstein (* 1923) cited the trivial fantasy world of the comic strip in his large-scale canvases. The screening of the print is reiterated in the painting as a pattern of painted dots. Individual images are torn out of their narrative context and the selected image reveals the triviality of the story as a whole, while at the same time, this isolation emphasizes the formal properties of the original medium.

Tom Wesselmann (* 1931) is famous first and foremost for his artistically stylized presentations of the naked female body. Sex as a consumer article has developed its own clichés in the course of its marketing. By reducing the body to flat, simple forms, in which mouth, breasts, thighs are emphasized, Wesselmann varies uniform gender traits in his *Great American Nudes*. James Rosenquist (* 1933) started out as a painter of billboards. For his monumental paintings, he had no need to change his theme or his technique.

Trivial pictorial forms – comics, advertisements, reports – in magazines or on television have a broader impact than art. In Pop Art, ennobled by the selection by an artist, they return as art. Removed from their normal context, monumentalized, in an exhibition, gallery, a museum, a private collection or a prestigious apartment, they serve as an affirmation of consumption.

Before the emergence of American Pop Art, English Pop Art arose in the 1950s, and was echoed in other European countries. The themes explored by the English artists were much the same as those chosen by their American counterparts, but apart from printing processes, they also used collage and other methods of integrating everyday objects. In doing so, they developed principles similar to those used by their contemporaries Rauschenberg and Johns in their combine paintings. On the whole, European Pop Art had a more socially critical approach.

Richard Hamilton (* 1922) caricatured the double-edged blessings of the consumer world and fashion in his collages. Peter Blake's (* 1932) painted collages contain mordant comments on familiar emblems, clichés and trademarks from the world of media. Reducing woman to an object of sex and lust was an approach pursued by Allen Jones (* 1937) in his paintings and objects to the point of affrontary. Such artists as David Hockney (* 1937) and Ronald B. Kitaj (* 1932) adopted elements of Pop Art without committing themselves completely to this direction.

**Roy Lichtenstein**  Razzmatazz, 1978
Oil and magna on canvas, 243.9 x 304.8 cm
Boston (MA), Collection Graham Grund

## Concept Art

The dematerialization of art was taken to the limit in Concept Art. The ground was broken by the art forms of the 1960s and early 1970s, such as colorfield painting and minimal art. They appeared to reject any emotional involvement on the part of the artist and avoided creating a reference to any reality beyond the world of art. Concept Art sought to provide objective information as the documentation and fixing of thought processes. The traditional art form in its material existence is abandoned and presented purely as thought, as concept in the form of texts, photos, diagrams.

Two artists anticipated the development towards Concept Art in the 1950s: Lucio Fontana (1899–1968) whose *Concetti Spaziali* (Spatial Concepts, see ill. p. 654) sought to interpret and present the void as a positive principle, and Yves Klein (1928–1962) whose characteristic blue does not reiterate a fragment of reality, but seeks to master all of reality through the medium of colour.

## Photo-Realism

Photographs form the basis for all the paintings in this hyper-realistic style. They are clearly not art photos, as they seem like snapshots, polaroids or passport photos with trivial motifs, as though they had been captured at some arbitrary moment. Projected as a slide onto the canvas, they provide the motif for a painting executed with a spray gun or a brush. Not only the choice of subject, but also the way in which colour and form are intensified, transfigured and alienated, the nuances added by the painter, indicate the personal signature of the artist. Reality is represented here illusionistically. An apparent lack of professionality – the photos seem to be underdeveloped, unsharp, amateurish – is compensated by the precision with which they are transformed into a highly artificial form of painting.

Richard Estes (* 1936) prefers to take urban life as the motif for his paintings, with its neon sterility and sober anonymity. Chuck Close (* 1940) is interested more in questions of percep-

625

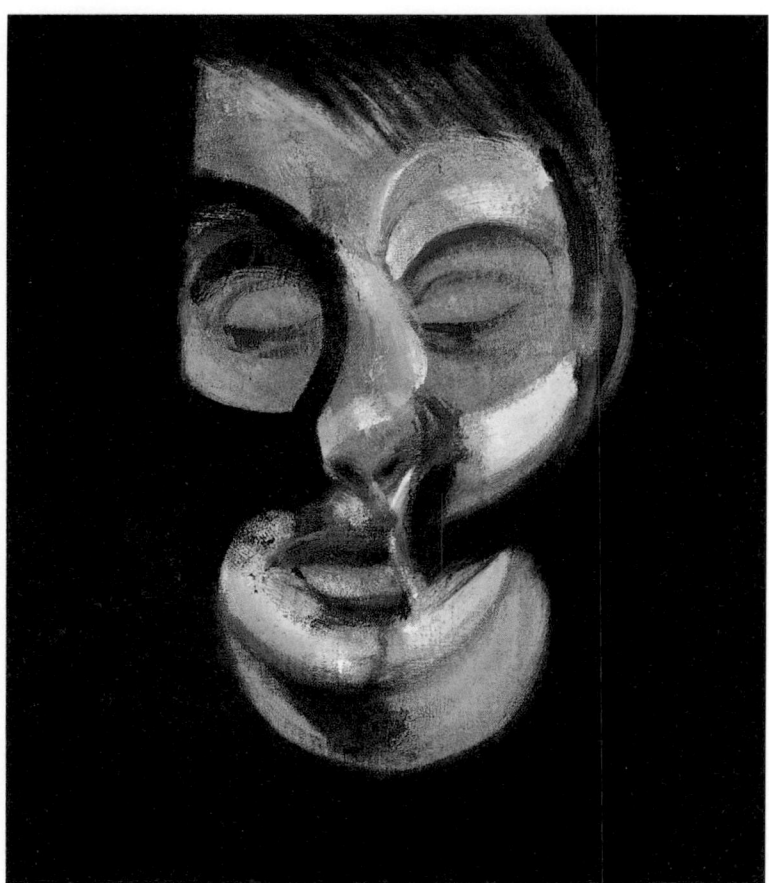

**Francis Bacon**
Self-Portrait, 1973
Oil on canvas, 35.5 x 31.8 cm
Private collection

label "socialist realism". Following on in the tradition of Expressionism and Neue Sachlichkeit, this art permitted, to some extent, an exploration of certain problems of classical painting, but in the choice of themes it remained subject to the dictates of a state-run cultural bureaucracy. The main premise was universal comprehensibility. Werner Tübke (* 1929) clothes his themes in the rich colours and forms of the Italian Renaissance. Werner Heisig (* 1925) creates gloomy visions of human impulses comparable to the works of Goya and Beckmann.

Defying all classification, Giacometti pursued a concept of figure and space in his sculptures and paintings that was profoundly influenced by existentialism. Francis Bacon (1909–1992), whose overall world view was similar to that of Giacometti, also explored the ideas of Jean-Paul Sartre (1905–1980) and Albert Camus (1913–1960), especially in his early work. Bacon's later work adopts some of the characteristics of Pop Art in the planarity of presentation and in the ornamentalization of colority. Lucian Freud (* 1922) has continued to concentrate for decades on the portrayal of the human body, apparently uninfluenced by all trends in art.

tion: he applies the three primary colours in separate layers, so that the fragmented colour scheme of the painting is put back together again by the spectator. Europe's leading photo-realist is the Swiss artist Franz Gertsch (* 1930) who fills monumental canvases with portraits of his friends.

## Figurative Painting in Europe

In an event in Düsseldorf in 1963, the ironic expression "capitalist realism" was coined, which is associated with the names Sigmar Polke (* 1942) and Gerhard Richter (* 1932). Polke is the more sarcastic of the two; independent of all group involvement, he developed a distinctive and ironic pictorial language that presents humorous pictorial puzzles full of visual puns, contradictions and clichés.

Richter endeavours in his large-scale series, to transpose newspaper articles, colour sample charts and amateur photographs into painting. He is interested in painting as painting. Konrad Klapheck (* 1935), who, like Richter, teaches at the Düsseldorf academy, interweaves the magical materiality and associative aspects of technical apparatus such as telephones and typewriters with distinctly human qualities in an approach that bears certain affinities with magic realism.

Until the fall of the Iron Curtain, all official art that was permitted and encouraged in eastern Europe went under the

**Georg Baselitz**
Motivschimmel Zerbrochene Brücke
(Dappled motif broken bridge), 1986
Oil on canvas, 173 x 139 cm. Private collection

## Painting in the 1980s

In reaction to past movements in art in which painting gradually lost its creative inspiration and individual message, a number of personalities emerged, especially in Germany and Italy, to revive a new and distinctly subjective form of expression.

In Germany, Georg Baselitz (* 1938) has been exploring the possibilities of expressive painting for many years. He became famous particularly for his paintings in which the subjects are turned upside down. The demonic expressiveness of his style and, most notably, its visionary distortion of the human figure, clearly reflects the influence of German Expressionism and the later work of Corinth.

All the representatives of new painting in Germany such as A. R. Penck (* 1939), Anselm Kiefer (* 1945) or Markus Lüpertz (* 1941), and in the group of Italian artists (Sandro Chia, * 1946; Francesco Clemente, * 1952; Enzo Cucchi, * 1950; Mimmo Paladino, * 1948) aim to liberate themselves from the fetters of ideology in expressing their dismay and unease, visualizing their individual and intuitive experiences, or clothing their impressions, experiences and nightmares in explosive or meditative forms. Theirs is a deliberate and conscious return to painting, albeit without the stringent framework of regulations posited by academic dictates.

The quest for liberty, and the wish to elevate themselves above all stylistic, iconographic and aesthetic strictures is already evident in their respective choice of unconventional motifs. The new painting draws upon Expressionism, Futurism and Surrealism; yet at the same time it does not constitute a complete break with the tradition of art.

In the 1980s, initially in New York and later in Europe, those on the margins of society, the underprivileged, the ethnic minorities began to establish themselves on the art scene, as did women, to an extent previously unparalleled. It was no longer imperative to have studied at an academy in order to exhibit at the leading galleries and museums of the capital cities. The first wave of these new artists emerged from the North American graffiti scene.

The heroes of this subculture such as Keith Haring (1958–1990) and Jean-Michel Basquiat (1960–1988) were able to introduce their semiotically imbued art in the New York subway as well as in the highest circles of the art world. Gallerists hoped that by showing their work, they could revitalize an art form increasingly perceived as jaded and spiritless. Other ethnic minority painters soon followed, some of them vehemently representing the rights of their respective ethnic groups in images that abandoned the traditions of European painting and returned to the stylistic means and pictorial forms of their own cultural roots, albeit occasionally falling into the trap of a rather anodyne political correctness.

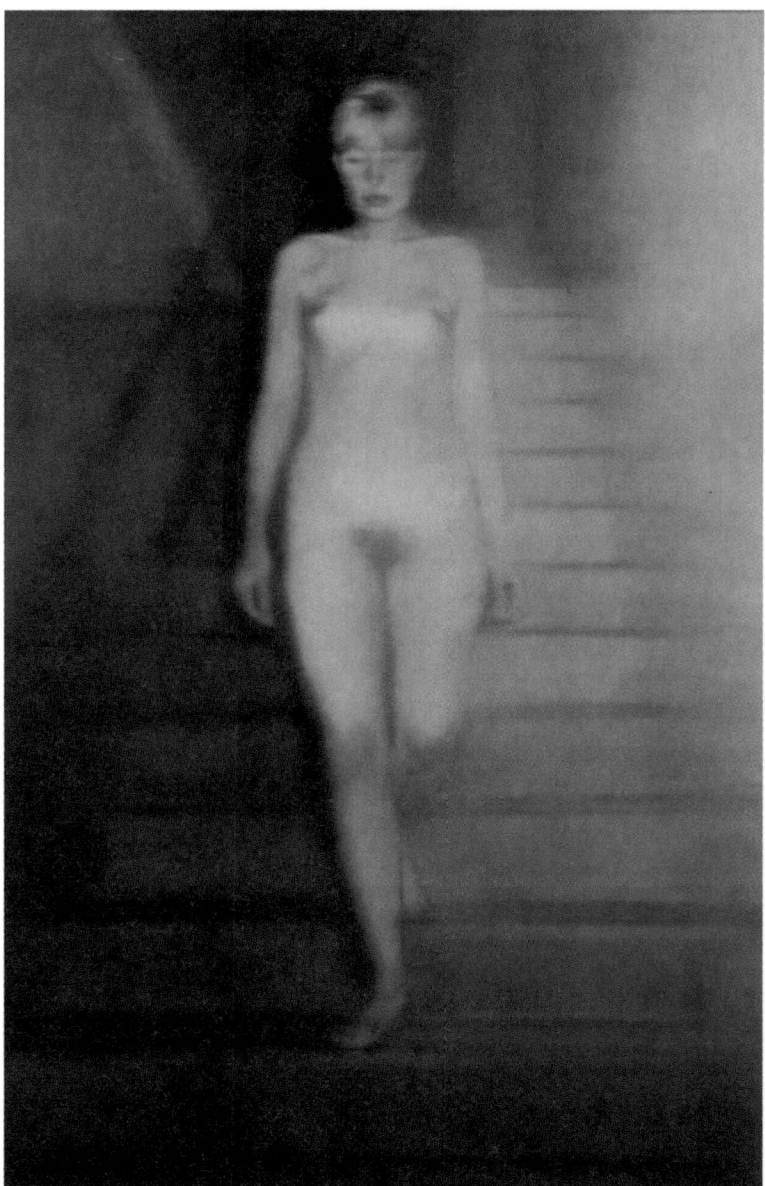

**Gerhard Richter**
Ema – Akt auf einer Treppe (Ema – Nude descending a staircase), 1966
Oil on canvas, 200 x 130 cm
Cologne, Museum Ludwig

## Painting and Post-Modernism

A typical feature of painting around 1990 is its utterly confusing stylistic pluralism. With the death of Beuys and Warhol in 1986 and 1987 respectively, two of the last great heroes of art died, and the history of 20th century art as a continuous project of constantly developing sequences of mutually enriching *avant-garde* movements seemed to have come to an end. It was therefore only logical that the painting of the 1990s came to be known as post-*avant-garde*. This term also refers to the term Post-Modernism which was initially coined for architecture and similarly indicated the end of an era without having a fitting description for the coming period.

Admittedly, in recent years, there have still been such classic artistic careers as that of the New York stars Julian Schnabel (* 1951) and David Salle (* 1952) whose meteoric rise to fame seemed to follow the pattern set by Warhol. Both these artists achieved success with large-format paintings for which they plundered the treasure-trove of art history and the consumer world.

In the meantime, however, there was no longer any style or artistic direction that could clearly make its mark on the period. The painting of the 1990s is shaped by a detached attitude and a clear awareness of what has been achieved. There are painters such as the Dutch artist Rob Scholte (* 1958) who have followed on from pop art, while others, such as the German artist Martin Kippenberger (* 1953) and the brothers Albert (* 1954) and Markus Oehlen (* 1956) cultivate a Dadaistic attitude. There are Neo-Constructivist tendencies as rep-

resented by the Swiss artists John Armleder (* 1958) and Helmut Federle (* 1944) and by the German artist Günther Förg (* 1952). In the USA, on the other hand, minimal art is undergoing a revival in the work of Brice Marden (* 1938) and Agnes Martin (* 1912). The same is true of Concept Art; with such forebears as Duchamp and Malevich in the background, artists like Sherrie Levine (* 1947), Philip Taaffe (* 1955) and Jeff Koons (* 1955) reprocess citations of acknowledged *avant-garde* positions, questioning their effectiveness. Though much of their work may appear calculated and superficial, it nevertheless makes one thing clear: a canon of painting vindicated by an exemplary ethical attitude no longer exists.

(The text on the last page of the introductory essay and the descriptions of works on pages 630, 643 bottom, 645 bottom, 648, 651 bottom, 653 top, 659, 663 bottom, 673, 674 top, 675 bottom, 677, 678 top, 679 and 680 were written by the editor)

# ARSHILE GORKY

1904–1948

This painting is one of Gorky's most important works. It was created at a time when he succeeded in breaking away from the influence of his early role models Paul Cézanne, Pablo Picasso and Joan Miró and had already begun constructively integrating the Surrealist elements which were to shape his work decisively from then on. From the early 1940s onwards, Gorky began moving away from figurative painting, developing fluid, organic forms and a subtle colourity full of luminosity, calligraphic lines and symbolic codes.

The painting is extraordinarily bright, and includes almost every possible permutation of the palette. The title indicates its origins in Surrealist language. Even the colour fields and "hybrid" forms are juxtaposed in a distinctly Surrealistic manner creating a partly painterly, partly sketch-like effect. The image on the whole is full of vibrant motion, almost to the point of aggression, even when it foregoes figuratively realistic elements. The spontaneity of colour and the direct gestures of the brushstrokes already contain elements of action painting and abstract Expressionism. In this work, warmth of colour alternates with cool zones, giving the painting a distinctive rhythm through the repetition of individual forms and colour areas. In this respect, it may be regarded as a summary of all his creative ideas.

**Arshile Gorky**
The Liver is the Cock's Comb, 1944
Oil on canvas, 183 x 249 cm
Buffalo (NY), Albright-Knox Art Gallery

# ROBERTO MATTA

*1912

Matta, who joined the Surrealists towards the end of the 1930s, based his painting on the psychic automatism propounded by André Breton and practised by André Masson. *Le Vertige d'Eros* is one of his many large-scale paintings with a title that gives some indication of its interpretation and the painter's intent. Important as the aspect of automatism may have been, Matta nevertheless felt obliged to make a statement in his work. He unites messages received through the psyche from the subconscious, with reflected perceptions, considerations and findings. In this way, he formulates questions.

With his paintings, he reacts to certain political situations (he was a volunteer in the Spanish Civil War) and at the same time, seeks to express states of mind. He is interested more in collective, timeless issues than personal or momentary issues. The overall mood of his insights is one of scepticism and even pessimism. He regards the human individual as a creature open to threat, illusion and surprise. His pictorial syntax is made up of symbolic signs, some of which possess an archaic magic, others a modern abstraction, with remnants of the figurative. In this respect, his paintings have a strongly dynamic and expressive aspect.

**Roberto Matta**
Le Vertige d'Eros, 1944
Oil on canvas, 195.6 x 251.5 cm
New York, The Museum of Modern Art

**Hans Hofmann**
Blue in Blue, 1954
Oil on canvas,
127 x 101.5 cm
Private collection

## HANS HOFMANN
### 1880–1966

Hans Hofmann was one of the great mediators, who brought European abstract art to America. Although his work in New York as a teacher of generations of abstract painters was widely acknowledged at an early stage, his own paintings were long neglected. They do, however, take a special place within abstract Expressionism through their specific personal touch. Hofmann was often inspired by particularly moving events, to which he reacted with dynamic streams of colour reminiscent of calligraphy. Abrupt brushstrokes charged with energy form the colour planes in *Blue in Blue* which are generally derived from rectangular forms. These forms collide, blend and dissolve. It is a pure painting, but one charged with significance through its sheer force and physical presence. It is not a question of aesthetic pleasure, but the expression of a profound inner sentiment.

Hofmann himself, in writing of his artistic career, pointed out that he had devoted his entire life to the quest for the real in painting: "The only values which make a work of art great are emotional and sensory. Life-content. Expressed experience." He claimed he had never believed in academic training, which he had not undergone himself. His maxim was instinct alone, and he believed that he had to find everything within himself if he was to achieve anything meaningful in the course of his artistic development.

**Clyfford Still**  Untitled, 1954
Oil on canvas, 297.2 x 256.3 cm
Private collection

## CLYFFORD STILL
### 1904–1980

Still banned all reference to the visual world from his paintings. He sought to liberate colours from the significance allocated to them and keep his painting free from all characteristics of an individual signature. He was one of the most vociferous proponents of artistic autonomy: "We are now committed to an unqualified art, not illustrating outworn myths or contemporary alibis. The artist must accept total responsibility for what he executes. And the measure of his greatness will be lie in his inner depth and in his courage in realizing his own vision." After a few years, he gave up giving his paintings significant titles.

The irregular colour planes, which seem to have been torn apart, are generally vertical. The colours are interlocked as though in battle, and reciprocally heighten their effect and intensity. Until well into the early 1940s, Still preferred to inundate his canvases with menacing, and at times meditative, black tones. The painting shown here was created during a phase when Still was increasingly interested in coloristic confrontation, in which black invariably played the most important role.

# WILLEM DE KOONING

## 1904–1997

*Woman, I* was created when de Kooning was at the height of his artistic vitality. Abstract compositions from the same period indicate the purely painterly intentions of the artist: art as an action linked with energy and physical movement. He works in a state of outer emptiness and inner concentration, oriented solely towards the act of creativity. The result is not pre-programmed, but completely open and is constituted by the end of the painterly act.

In the violent, tension-charged composition of this painting with its aggressive colours, the image of a woman is integrated. The figure is monstrously ugly, a distorted image of woman. She is not Venus, an idol of ideal figure, a fertility Goddess – attempts at interpretations that have been tried but have proofed unconvincing. She is the fading, decadent woman. Robbed by society of her inner self, her better characteristics and abilities, she remains reduced to exaggerated physical features – large eyes, flashing teeth, huge breasts, heavy thighs.

The subject of "woman" captivated him for more than ten years and each interpretation he attempted resulted in a new version of a caricature, a travesty of the stylized media clichés of femininity. De Kooning's paintings not only show what is missing, they scream it out: soul and humanity. He uses a shocking anti-aesthetics to reveal the alarming background of this appearance – a stylistic medium that was to be adopted once again decades later by Germany's *Neue Wilde* artists.

In this later work by de Kooning, we can see his stylistic development from the abstract expressionism of the 1950s to his mature work in the 1980s. The figurative elements have completely disappeared from his paintings, and even his abstract compositions are structured differently. They are still strongly rhythmic in their structure, but there is less movement than before. The colours are almost all mixed with white, some only through their application on the canvas. The large area is tectonically structured by multi-faceted colour fields and zones.

Art of this kind can be interpreted only through the artist. Traditional canons of aesthetic standards are of little help to us here, for they do not apply to this kind of painting. The way in which the artist integrates his emotional and intellectual energy into the act of painting, as though he were in an existential situation, gives the canvas its statement. Painting as a physical process is invariably dependent on the constitution of the artist at the moment of painting. De Kooning works in an attitude of open possibilities in which nothing is pre-programmed, and only the result of the spontaneous painterly act is evaluated.

**Willem de Kooning**
Woman, I, 1950–1952
Oil on canvas,
192.7 x 147.3 cm
New York, The Museum
of Modern Art

**Willem de Kooning**  Untitled, III, 1980
Oil on canvas, 178 x 203 cm
New York, Collection Xavier Fourcade Inc.

## JACKSON POLLOCK
1912–1956

Jackson Pollock is the pioneer of the American post-war *avant-garde*. Today, he is recognized as the artist who fundamentally renewed abstract painting. *Blue Pole* a painting dating from 1953, was created using the painterly technique he himself described as drip painting. His early figurative works possess an almost coarse and even ungainly formal syntax full of raw vitality. Later, he adopted elements of Surrealism, and the works of the early 1940s are marked by an impetuous brushstroke.

The decisive break with his earlier ideas came in 1947. Pollock no longer wanted to create carefully considered and constructed compositions. The brush as instrument seemed to him too restrictive, as was the easel. He cleansed his art of all previously existing forms and motifs. He placed his canvases on the floor. In this way, he could work

on them from all four sides, a method he had seen used by Indian sand painters in the American West. In this type of process, he felt he was literally "in the painting". As the substratum of his Surrealistic endeavours, he retained psychic automatism, the spontaneity of the painterly act, that led him to the creation of his drip painting method. He no longer took a brush in his hand, but dripped and sprayed the colour onto the canvas instead. In doing so, he followed an inner willingness and tension geared entirely to the action with his materials. He himself described this state as follows: "When I am in the painting I'm not aware of what I'm doing... the painting has a life of its own. I try to let it come through." In a painting like this one, however, we can also see the control with which Pollock pursued the direction, thick-

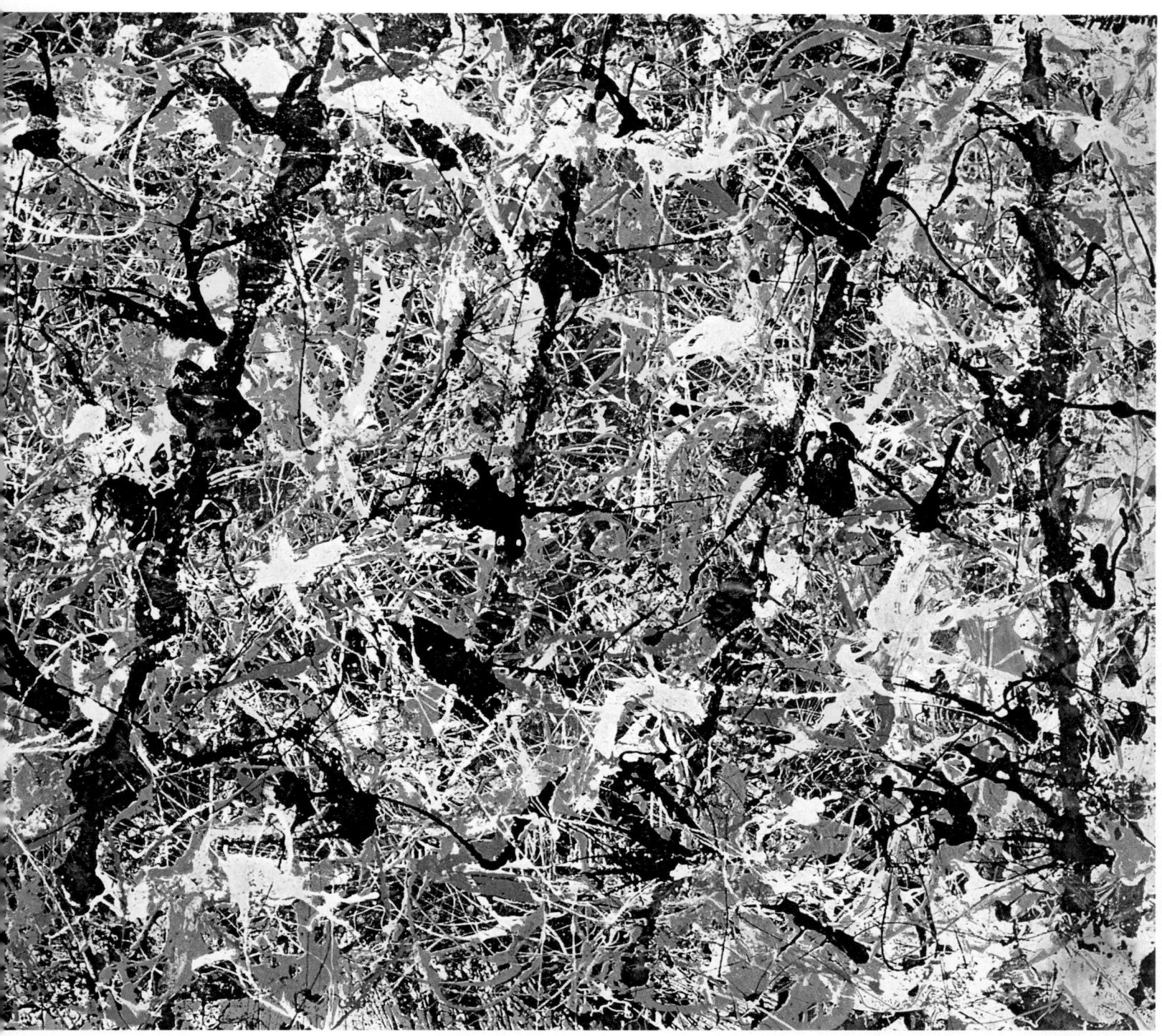

ness and continuity of the drops and rhythmic lines.

*Blue Pole* is well-organized and balanced in colours and forms. In 1951, the critic Harold Rosenberg coined the term "action painting" for Pollock's work. The paintings were created out of fluid drops of paint, heavy pastes, mixed with sand, glass splinters and other additives.

Pollock used sticks, cloths, knives to apply and distribute the paint. When the action and the material harmonized, the rhythmically abstract pictorial patterns were created. Strongly charged with expression, they reflect the dynamics of their creative process. *Blue Pole* was created a good four years after the first drip paintings. It is situated at a lower level of reflection than the first paintings in the new technique, in which the joy of experimenta-

tion and automatism are more clearly evident in the painterly technique. By 1953, Pollock had gained more confidence in his painterly technique and was able to control the application of paint more precisely without losing his spontaneity. The colours no longer refer to some natural impression. The dark blue, luminous orange, yellow, black, white and silver, are all artificial colours – the painter used a rapidly drying, brilliant car paint and aluminium. These were blended to a garish tonal chord, in keeping with the strong and confident application of paint. The colours are distinctly American and a sign of the radical break with the European painterly traditions. Finally, with his large-scale pictorial format, Pollock virtually forces the viewer to confront his new visual world. The overwhelming dimensions permit no escape.

**Jackson Pollock**
Blue Pole, 1953
Oil, car lacquer and aluminium
paint on canvas, 210.8 x 488.9 cm
Canberra, Australian National Gallery

**Franz Kline**
New York, 1953
Oil on canvas, 201 x 128.5 cm
Buffalo (NY), Albright-Knox Art
Gallery

## FRANZ KLINE
### 1910–1962

Kline's *New York*, a canvas of monumental
dimensions and boldly abstract forms created
in strong, broad brushstrokes, is a highlight of
action painting and abstract Expressionism.
Although the painting looks spontaneous, it is
painstakingly prepared, for Kline invariably
worked on the basis of carefully considered
and organized draft sketches. Only the final execution was then created with concentrated
speed and intensity in a motoric action, in
which the physical movements were intended
to be integrated into the colour fields as "signs
of power". He used large decorators' paint-
brushes and preferred industrial paints to oil-
paints because of their effects and their quick-
drying properties.
  Although this painting bears the specific
title *New York,* the painter denied any reference to bridges or scaffolding in his tectonic
black and white structures. Nor did he ap-
prove of comparisons with calligraphy. He saw
only the painterly aspect of his works and he
wanted them to be understood as the end results of a painterly act, as the confrontation of
the artist with the vital "act of painting". The
colours black and white are intended to be
equally valid and mutually permeable.

**Robert Motherwell**
Elegy to the Spanish Republic No. 34, 1953/54
Oil on canvas, 203 x 254 cm
Buffalo (NY), Albright-Knox Art Gallery

## ROBERT MOTHERWELL
### 1915–1991

Although Robert Motherwell is an action
painter, and a key figure of abstract Expressionism in New York, the elements of this
spontaneous, gestural painting are relatively
subdued in his work. His paintings are invariably intellectual. In 1948, when he founded
the short-lived cooperative The Subjects of
the Artist together with Rothko, Newman
and other artists, he discovered the theme
that he would continue to work with over the
next three decades in more than a hundred
versions: his *Elegy to the Spanish Republic.* The
civil war in Spain triggered a moral crisis in
the late 1930s comparable to that of the Vietnam war.
  With his *Elegies to the Spanish Republic*,
Motherwell did not intend to give a coded report, nor to describe a local situation, nor even
to refer to a special event. According to
Motherwell, "I take an elegy to be a funeral
lamentation or funeral song for something one
cared about. The Spanish elegies are not "political" but my private insistence that a terrible
death happened that should not be forgotten.
They are as eloquent as I could make them.
But the pictures are also general metaphors of
the contrast between life and death and their
interrelation." Whereas black and white dominate in the *Elegies*, his palette later becomes
more colourful.

## SAM FRANCIS

1923–1994

Sam Francis' painting is closely linked to the work of the American abstract Expressionists. Even before he began to study art at the University of Berkeley, he had already developed his own style in abstract painting. Two elements are typical of his approach: irregular, cell-like structures or daub-like colour areas and a preference for undiluted acrylic and oil-paints.

Though he was born and brought up in California, Francis is not exactly a typical representative of American painting. His travels to Eastern Asia and lengthy stays in his chosen home of France, where he lived in Paris, make him a cosmopolitan artist whose work integrates a wide variety of influences. The large-scale *Basle Mural* thrives on the tension between a rhythmically structured network of interconnected colour zones and a uniformly pale ground. The few colours – red, blue and yellow – are applied, partly with a palette knife, in overlapping, cell-like zones that create a pictorial pattern. The works of Sam Francis from this period have a scintillating colour force. The intellectual concepts behind his work are frequently influenced by Asiatic philosophies.

**Sam Francis**
Basel Mural II, 1956–1958
Oil on canvas, 400 x 608 cm
Amsterdam, Stedelijk Museum

## MARK TOBEY

1890–1976

Tobey developed his painterly style relatively independently of prevailing artistic trends. His pictorial patterns are vaguely reminiscent of Pollock's drip paintings, but they are derived from very different roots. Although, as in Pollock's paintings, a kind of calligraphic pattern covers the entire canvas, Tobey's paintings, like Newman's work, have their origins in the religious sphere.

Until the discovery of his own pictorial pattern, Tobey's involvement with the Bahai sect and his study of oriental brushwork were decisive influences on his artistic development. In his calligraphic paintings, Tobey found a possibility of uniting Eastern and Western cultures.

Tobey's paintings invariably involve similar conceptual structures. Colours, signs and patterns are varied respectively. Their limitation at the edge of the painting seems arbitrary, as though they could continue *ad infinitum* to all sides. Tobey's transition from figurative art to abstract art is not founded in his formal development, but in his wish to create an art that is an internationally comprehensible pictorial language. He sees humane ideals and aims in the harmony of his intimate picture patterns, as well as the restlessness of human endeavour and the interweaving of human fates.

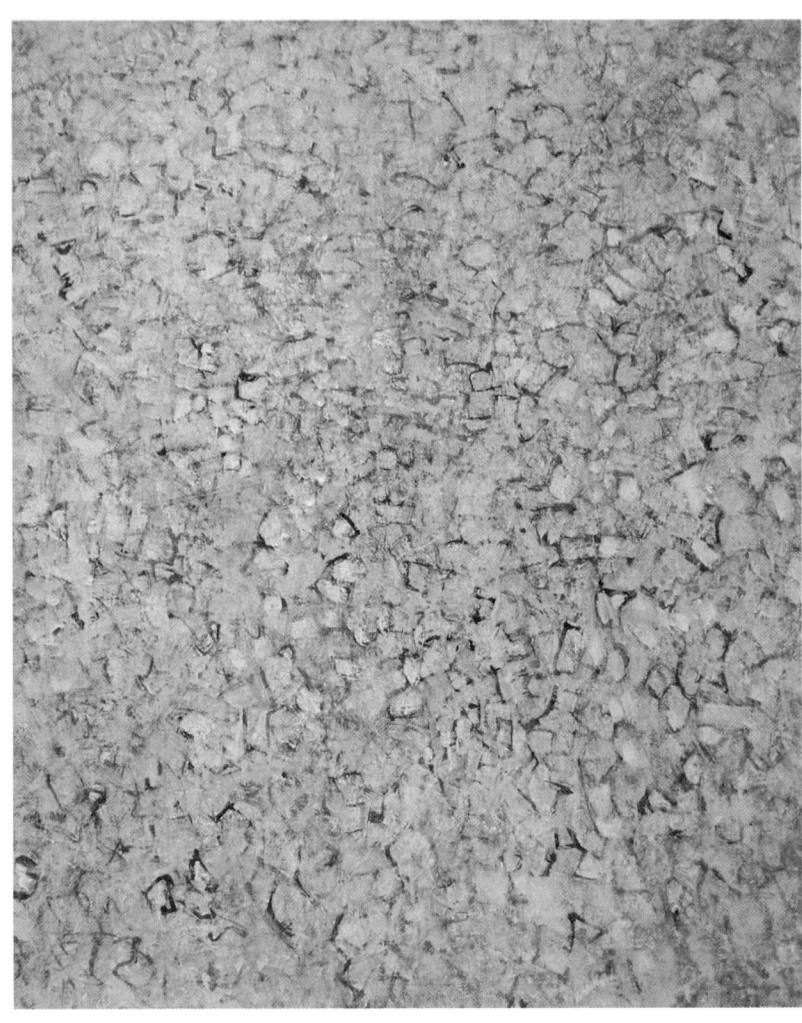

**Mark Tobey**
North-west current,
1958
Oil on cardboard,
117 x 100 cm
London, Tate Gallery

**Hans Hartung**
T 1956–9, 1956
Oil on canvas,
180 x 137 cm
Private collection

## HANS HARTUNG
1904–1989

In the 30s, the work of Hans Hartung was understood neither by the representatives of abstraction, nor by the equally influential Surrealist movement. It took a good ten years for his simple harmonic, graphically structured compositions to gain recognition as significant works. At a very early stage, Hartung developed the idea that no form can be created without movement and the idea of the large line of one colour that breaks into rays.

This painting, created in 1956, is typical of the forms developed and frequently varied by Hartung: the colour palette is restricted to a few yellow/brown/black tones that create a vibrant, but harmonious pattern on a pale ground. The large, lens-like signs are superimposed and interconnected. Out of a meditative painterly movement, a vital organism seems to have grown. The structures of the bundles of lines take on a balanced tectonic structure through the various intensities of pale and dark, yellow and brown. The alternating thickness of the brushstroke, the complexity of the superimpositions and the gentleness and vehemence with which the brushstrokes are executed are reminiscent of Oriental ink drawings. It seems only logical to compare Hartung's work with Japanese Zen calligraphy.

**Pierre Soulages**
Painting 21. 6. 53, 1953
Oil on canvas, 195 x 130 cm
Private collection

## PIERRE SOULAGES
*1919

After 1945, Soulages, who had visited the academy only briefly, presented his paintings to the public. He is one of the best known representatives of the École de Paris and French *tachisme*. His abstract compositions do not generally have explanatory titles. The paintings are coloristically and formally reduced, restricted to a relatively narrow canon of forms. The luminosity of the colours is rarely in the foreground, and is generally mixed with black. The connection of black with brown, grey, green or blue, determines the mood of each painting. The strength of the colour layer, alternating between the strongly impasto and the gently transparent, creates the subtle gradations and effects.

Soulages' pictorial codes are mutable. The contrast of dark and light, reflection and opaqueness, add vitality to his compositions. The plasticity of his pictorial structure suggests density in the dark areas, while the paler semi-transparent parts create a vague impression of space. Soulages' formal syntax, although abstract, is inspired by the impressions he gained during his childhood in the Massif Central where he was familiar with prehistoric menhirs and the sculptures of Romanesque churches. Later, the influence of calligraphy was added.

# GEORGES MATHIEU

\*1921

In the post-war years, Mathieu was one of the most famous representatives of the Ecole de Paris. After a brief realistic early phase, inspired by his reading of Joseph Conrad's texts, he began exploring questions of the essence of art and decided to work abstractly. His first non-realistic paintings already include the elements that were to become the hallmark of his painting from then on. *The Decapitation of Olivier III* is one of this group of works.

There is no unequivocal relationship between the title and the painting. Mathieu's preference for historic-sounding titles can be explained by his philosophy and his readings in history; he studied the Capetian dynasty of French rulers particularly intensively. Against a calm, black ground, two white geometric forms appear in balanced alignment to the right and left: a rectangle and a rectangle from which a circular shape has been cut out. In the centre, we see Mathieu's "hallmark", an impulsively drawn emblem in brown-beige impasto. It is clear that Mathieu regarded the painting of a picture as an action, and that he enjoyed celebrating a painting in a kind of performance before an audience. Various attempts have been made to classify his works as "lyrical abstraction", "tachisme", "informel" and "calligraphic abstraction".

**Georges Mathieu**
The Decapitation of Olivier III, 1958
Oil on canvas, 60 x 92 cm
Paris, Private collection

# SERGE POLIAKOFF

1906–1969

Although Poliakoff left his Russian homeland at the age of twelve and spent his artistically formative years in Paris, his works nevertheless betray certain subtle Russian elements. The icon painting of his homeland and the decor of the orthodox churches undoubtedly influenced Poliakoff's work. His paintings are abstract and cannot actually be described as religious, yet their overall mood is one that invites meditation. The mystical colour chords, the gentle shimmer of light that seems to be inherent within the colours, the tension that emanates from his formally similar compositions, are all unthinkable without the influence of Russian art. The generally angular forms interact, rarely overlapping, thereby creating a spatial illusion.

The diversity of Poliakoff's oeuvre is based on his virtuoso handling of colour. It varies in tonality and luminosity within a single field, and even the material character of the colour changes from area to area, becoming more gentle or appearing more grainy. Unlike his contemporaries Kasimir Malevich, Wassily Kandinsky and Robert Delaunay, Poliakoff did not place his painting at the service of political agitation or functionality. He remained a painter of decorative easel works, concentrating on a few colours.

**Serge Poliakoff**
Composition, 1959
Oil on canvas,
130 x 96.5 cm
Vienna, Museum
moderner Kunst,
Sammlung Ludwig

**Maria-Elena Vieira da Silva**
The Library, 1949
Oil on canvas, 114.5 x 147.5 cm
Paris, Musée d'Art Moderne,
Centre Georges Pompidou

## MARIA-ELENA VIEIRA DA SILVA

### 1908–1992

Though its overall format is large, the painting *The Library*, executed in 1949, is structured in small detail. At first glance, it appears abstract, with many small areas interacting to create a pictorial surface. Vieira da Silva's paintings guide the spectator's gaze across the canvas, inviting us to ponder some detail or go on a journey of discovery with fantastic associations. The way she plays with various pattern zones, anchored in a sweeping and bold network of lines, turns out to be a virtuoso interaction of frontal, angular views from above and below. The painting is a dream-like, visionary illusion of space, independent of real dimensions.

An atmosphere of timelessness informs the architecture, structured on several levels. In the same way, the painting has the possibility of a connection with reality even though it seems to have no real boundary at top or bottom. In the mosaic-like facets, we recognize endless walls of books, stairways, corridors, ceilings, floors and galleries. The wide-spanned arches and angles and the irreal spatial layering create a realistic situation and distort it to the point of absurdity. After all, this is not the image of a specific library; instead, it draws our imagination into spheres that can be reached through the treasures of a library.

**Nicolas de Staël**
Figure on the Beach,
1952
Oil on canvas,
161.5 x 129.5 cm
Düsseldorf, Kunst-
sammlung Nordrhein-
Westfalen

## NICOLAS DE STAËL

### 1914–1955

Hans Arp, Sonia and Robert Delaunay and Alberto Magnelli were the first artist friends to recognize de Staël's talent and encourage him to paint. Abstraction had entered the world of art four decades earlier, and already seemed to have exhausted its possibilities when it experienced a revival in the 1940s in the USA and Europe. De Staël initially joined the European abstract movement and created *tachiste-informel* works. Today, they appear fashionably faddish, unexperimental and void of personal characteristics. Only the paintings that bear the inimitable hallmark of his own highly distinctive style are truly convincing.

The *Figure on the Beach* is one of the great classic paintings by de Staël. Although it is actually non-figurative and has no reference to the external visual world, its proximity to reality is determined by the title. The various large colour fields that define the tectonic structure of the painting have a direct relationship to the spectator. The colour is recognizable in its materiality and the traces of the palette knife at work suggest the moment of creation. The juxtaposition and interconnection of the many zones with their shimmering layers is captivating in the appeal of its sublime choice of colour whose luminosity is reminiscent of the Impressionists.

# WILLI BAUMEISTER
1889–1955

Around the same time that a number of major upheavals affected his life – the loss of his professorship in Frankfurt am Main and the Nazi threat – Baumeister turned his back on an art that was still geared towards reality and reflective of it. After a phase in the late 1930s and early 1940s, when he experimented with interpretations of prehistoric patterns and concepts of collective subconsciousness, he turned increasingly towards abstraction.

*Montaru*, *Aru*, *Monturi* and *Han-i* are series of abstract compositions on which he worked for many years. For Baumeister, abstract forms were not void of content. Instead, he saw in them the bearers of metaphysical powers and perceived abstraction as a contemporary form of expression with intellectual parallels to science. "The paintings show forms, colours with their contasts and intersections, lines and rhythms so that, through these, they arrive at an order or so-called harmony. Order can help us to gain a standpoint in the confusion and multiplicity of the world... the modern painter does not create his work after nature, but in the manner of nature." In other words, the artist no longer studies creation, but is himself the creator of a world in the picture.

**Willi Baumeister**
Montaru-G VI, 1954
Oil auf Hartfaserplatte,
185 x 130 cm
Düsseldorf, Kunstsammlung
Nordrhein-Westfalen

# ERNST WILHELM NAY
1902–1968

Ernst Wilhelm Nay was one of the most important and renowned representatives of abstract painting in post-war Germany. In a process that lasted more than three decades, he moved his earlier figurative topics – still lives, landscapes and mythological themes – further and further from the real world and the world of imagination. During his final period of figurative painting, a distinct tendency towards expressive portrayal was evident. In the mid-1950s, he broke entirely with all figurative motifs and devoted himself entirely to purely abstract painting, and it was at this time that painting took on a new meaning for him. His own aims best describe his intentions: "Painting means forming a picture with colour."

Nay's abstractions contain no coded message. They are painting for its own sake. The most important formal statement is the coloristic and material quality of the paint. The title *Yellow Chromatic* indicates that the impulsively applied colour fields, daubs and circle segments are a question of harmony. Colour and form stand in a tense relationship to one another, in contrasts and harmonies. An expressive motion creates a sense of space.

**Ernst Wilhelm Nay**
Yellow Chromatic, 1960
Oil on canvas, 125 x 200 cm
Essen, Museum Folkwang

# JEAN DUBUFFET
## 1901–1985

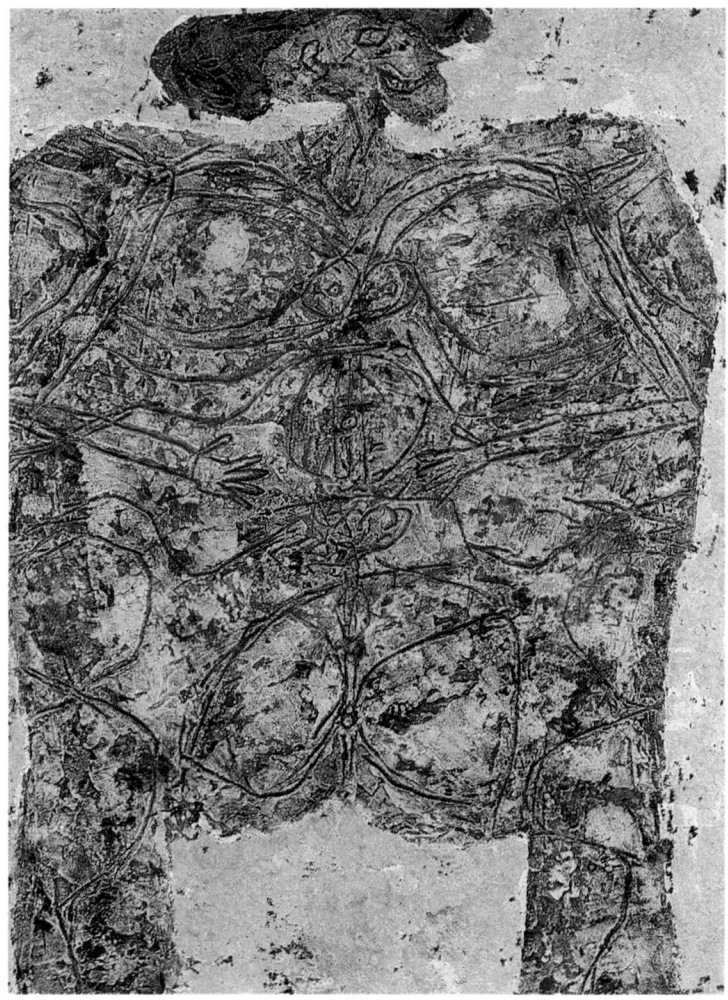

**Jean Dubuffet**
Le Métafisyx, 1950
Oil on canvas, 116 x 89.5 cm
Paris, Musée National d'Art
Moderne, Centre Georges
Pompidou

Dubuffet did not seek his inspiration or role models in academic painterly tradition or in the generally acknowledged and binding aesthetic canons. For him, true art, expressed in creativity, spontaneity, vitality, freshness and originality, came from other realms. In the drawings and scribbles of children, in the painterly endeavours of the mentally ill, mavericks, prisoners or in the art of primitive peoples, he saw an unspoiled approach that he himself sought to achieve.

In the forms of expression used by people beyond the bounds of academic art training, he recognized a magical and spontaneous force that he described as "art brut". The bizarre lyricism of his paintings, drawings and sculptures stand apart from the various movements of art to which he never wanted to belong. They are a response to the appealingly beautiful, academic and intellectual art, whose formal syntax and colour rules Dubuffet deliberately ignored.

*Le Métafisyx* is a wild, raw figure, bluntly scratched into the pictorial ground, not carefully painted, and with an archaically brutal expressive force, full of terrifying, simple and symbolic coding. Dubuffet himself was attracted to the ugly and the chaotic, because it is an integral part of the world. He did not intend his world to contain anything ordered and adapted. Nothing that subjugated itself to any other rule than that of total freedom: "Seek spiritual worlds that have nothing to do with culture… it should always be badly made like a clumsy dance."

*Business Prospers* is a broad, horizontal-format painting. Individual, divided forms seem to blend with each other in the manner of millefiori (a technique involving polychromatic floral patterning). On closer inspection, we see that it is indeed an ordered and interactive tapestry of individual forms: blocks of houses, streets, squares, cars, a bus and many people. The individual buildings are schematized into colour fields so strongly that they are designated as "bank", "butcher" etc. The vehicles look as though they had been flattened, but on the inside we can see the passengers. People have been simplified to matchstick figures with total disregard for proportion and perspective.

Dubuffet's painterly approach, which he himself described as "art brut" goes beyond traditional and *avant-garde* modes of presentation, and pits itself against all conventional aesthetics. It denies all the achievements of centuries of pictorial technique. The result is a painting that looks more like a living organism with all its growing forms and multiple layers.

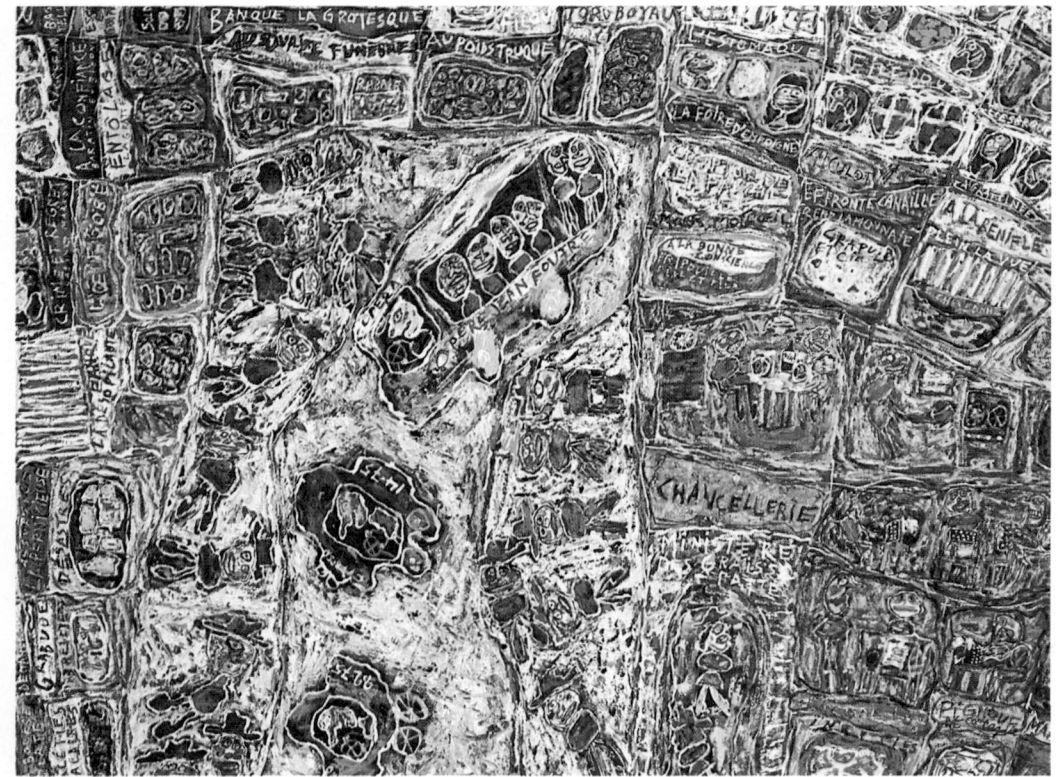

**Jean Dubuffet**
Business Prospers, 1961
Oil on canvas, 165 x 221 cm
New York, The Museum of Modern Art

## WOLS

1913–1951

*Le Bateau ivre* is the title of a poem by Arthur Rimbaud describing the journey of life. Wols adopted it as a poetic metaphor for his own brief, painful and often aimless life. The title of the painting is therefore more metaphoric than literal. From around 1941/42, Wols' paintings, which had previously been figurative, began to become increasingly abstract. *Ecriture automatique* became his pictorial language. The abstract forms and the fine and delicately selected colours still maintain a fragile relationship to real concepts. Wols did not regard himself as a professional artist, and he hated the official art trade, the cultural circus, and the self-projection of all those involved in it.

His works distinctly reflect the influence of Paul Klee, Max Ernst, Joan Miró, but also that of George Grosz and Otto Dix; yet Wols used all these sources of inspiration only in order to create his own highly individual oeuvre. With his work, he belongs to an artistic movement that influenced the painting of artists in many countries and came to be known from country to country under different names: *informel*, abstract Expressionism, *tachisme*, abstraction *lyrique*.

**Wols**
Le Bateau ivre, 1945
Oil on canvas,
92 x 73 cm
Zurich,
Kunsthaus Zürich

## JEAN FAUTRIER

1898–1964

Fautrier worked for well over twenty years without his work attracting widespread attention. He started out as a painter of nudes and animals and, from 1932 onwards, he developed his new technique. It was only after the Second World War that he achieved recognition as the creator of an *art autre*, an other art, through which he distinguished himself particularly from the American painters. The term "art autre" could also be used to describe his own development, for his early works appear to be preparatory to his path towards non-figurative post-war works. He called these paintings *Otages (Hostages)*. They are not pure painting, but an interaction of many technical processes and reworkings that constitute an interim stage on the path towards material and object art.

The canvas is generally prepared by creating a ground. For example, paper may be pasted onto it. On the still damp ground, a drawing is sketched with the brush, onto which pastel powder and pigment substances are then distributed.

Finally, Fautrier adds a thick layer of paint over the outline of the first drawing. With coloured powders, brush and palette knife, he works in various layers in which different areas are more or less intensively processed, repeating the procedure and then adding grooves and scratches.

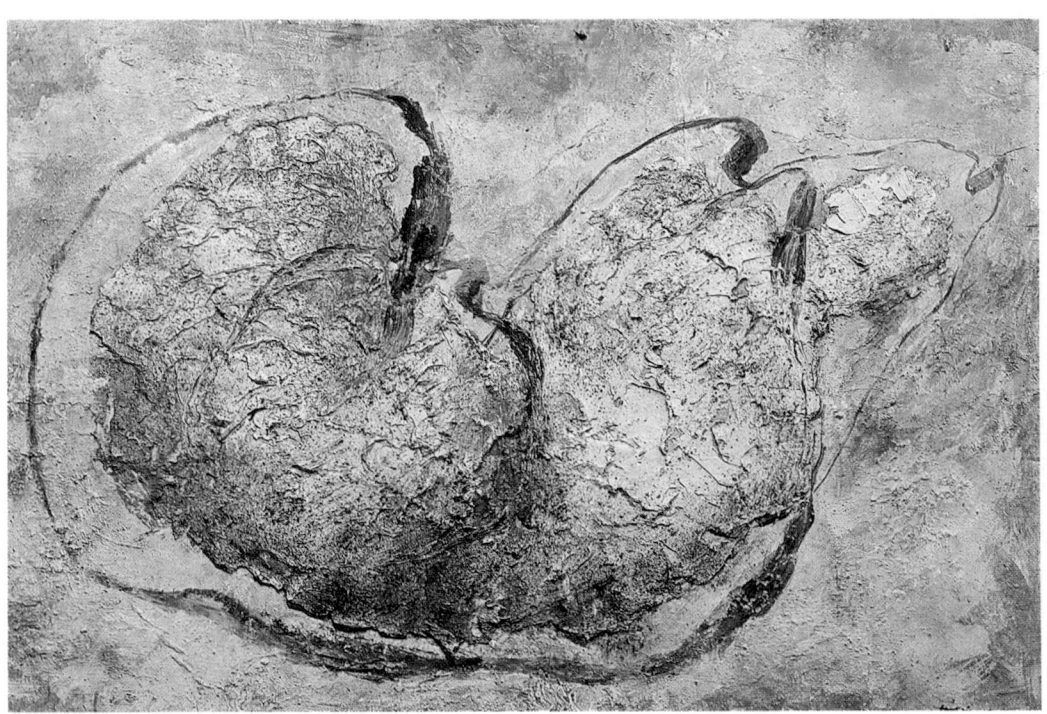

**Jean Fautrier**
Nude, 1946
Oil on canvas, 114 x 146 cm
Private collection

**Antoni Tàpies**
Relief in Brick Red,
1963
Mixed media with
sand on canvas,
260 x 195 cm
Düsseldorf,
Kunstsammlung
Nordrhein-Westfalen

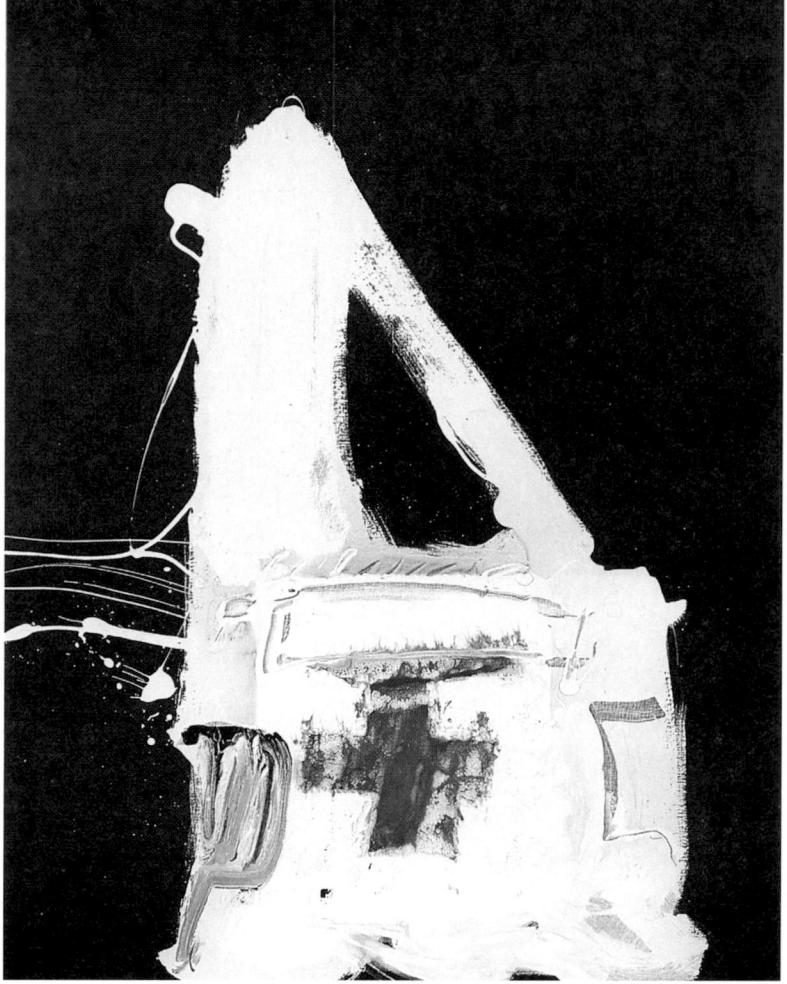

**Antoni Tàpies**
Armchair,
1982/83
Oil on canvas,
146 x 114 cm
Private collection

# ANTONI TÀPIES
## *1923

Tàpies is regarded as the most important master of *informel* and *tachisme* in Europe. In this material painting, he not only uses painterly means. The heavily applied binder is mixed with sand. This gives the painting the character of a relief, with signs and scoring applied to the still soft surface. The range of colours used here is reduced to reddish-brown hues, black, white and grey. Painterly and sculptural forms interact in this abstract painting in which not everything is actually meant in an abstract sense. Both the colours and the signs scratched into or painted onto the surface have a meaning. However, Tàpies has no intention of telling the spectator what to think. He does not even want his work to be analysed intellectually. "It is more important that the spectator should follow the intuition that sets his spirit moving. Art affects our general sensibilities, and not just our intellect."

Tàpies sees himself as someone who has retained his universal connection with nature and a certain mysticism. For him, art should have depth and should contain a design for a new positive awareness that also includes philosophy and ethics, and gives everything a new meaning. In addition to the laws of pure pictorial design, he expects the artist to possess an inner dynamic force or emotional power that enables him to undertake his own development, with the aim of finding new formula that will make his work more efficient.

Tàpies' paintings are created through intuition, following lengthy meditation. In their finished form, they are often beyond the control of his feelings and his intellect. After a Surrealistic early phase influenced by his reverence for the two great Spanish painters Miró and Dalí, Tàpies turned to abstract painting. For many years, he created the stringent panels known as his *Wall Paintings*. The composition of *Arm Chair* is also stringent. We see a white outline on a black background, which, on closer inspection, might come to be recognized as the shell of a chair or arm chair. Yet the painting is so planar, so strongly abstracted, that we might just as well consider it to have no figurative meaning.

Black, white, grey and earthy brown, occasionally mixed with white, are the few colours used in this picture. The sign of the cross, which Tàpies so often uses, grooves scored into the thickly applied paint, splashes of paint and scraped areas all give this work a strongly dynamic feeling. Tàpies believes that all those who are as strongly bound to a tradition as he is can "read" or interpret his paintings: "I am not in favour of making it easier for people to understand by lowering our language to their level; the people have to come up to our level. The struggle to find the necessary materials for this process is everyone's responsibility."

# ALBERTO BURRI

## 1915–1995

The prosaic title *Sack No. 5* that Burri gave this painting clearly indicates that this material collage is not a question of content rooted in narrative, and that Burri did not actually intend to portray any particular object. Instead, he was turning his back on the traditional media of painting. The sack is not a substitute for the canvas as the carrier of the picture, but, together with the painterly elements used, is a component part of the work with its own significance. Objects and materials are no longer taken as a motif and painted illusionistically. In the sense of a new realism, they are self-referential.

Here, the act of painting is translated into an action whose result is no longer an unreal painting. In this respect, he adopts the concepts of early Cubist collages and Surrealist montages. The materials combined in a pictorial format on a single plane with all their injuries, repairs, knots and painted areas, have their own poetic pictorial language that allows the spectator to develop his or her own associations. As Burri frequently used burnt and shabby materials, the spectator's feelings are guided in a specific direction. Often, his works are regarded as a challenge. From the 1950s onwards, other artists also used similar materials, as did Tàpies and Beuys.

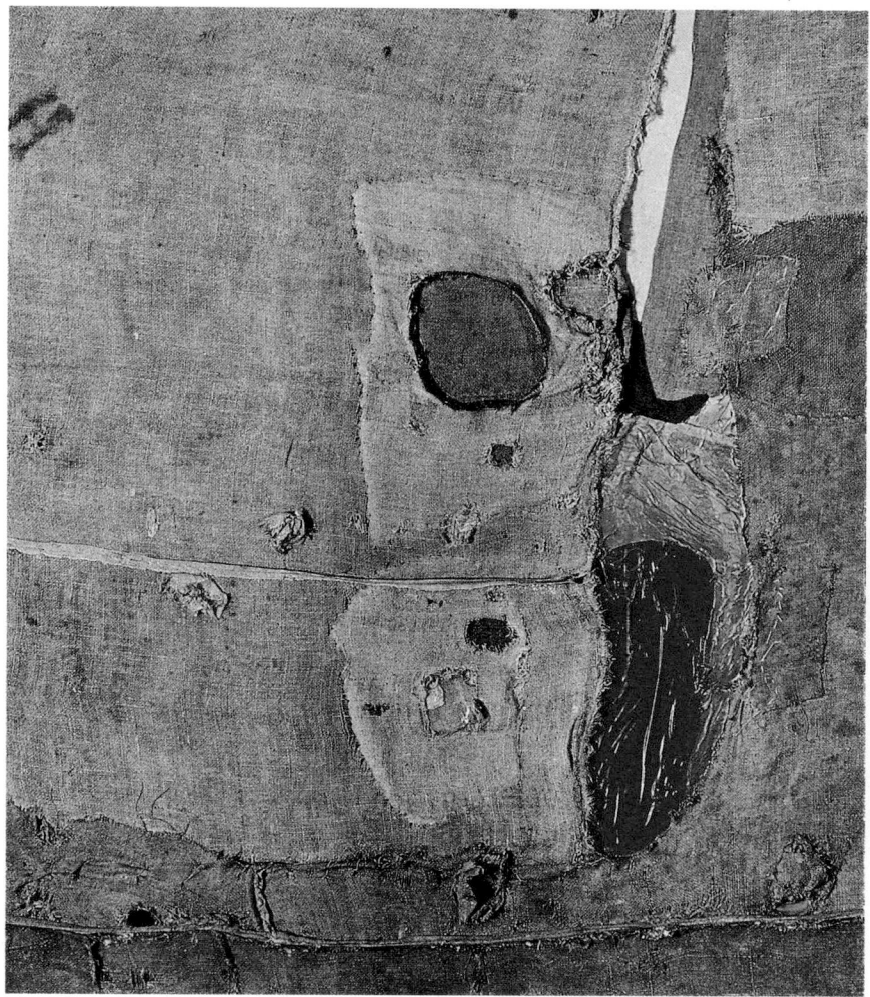

*Above:*
**Alberto Burri**
Sack No. 5, 1953
Mixed media and collage,
150 x 130 cm
Città di Castello,
Fondazione Palazzo
Albizzini, Collezione Burri

# EMIL SCHUMACHER

## *1912

In this painting, Schumacher achieves a new quality. Although the composition of large geometric components is still vaguely reminiscent of the Cubist landscapes he painted directly after the Second World War, the paint is already used here as material. It is no longer a question of using paint or colour to portray something, either figurative or abstract. The paint or colour is no longer the medium, but the subject matter of the design. The constructive framework of the forms will disappear completely in the years to follow. The two deep blue, luminous pictorial zones contrast effectively with the areas of earthy brown and beige. At some points, Schumacher has scratched the heavily applied paint with a knife or the handle of the brush, and in other places black trails of colour lie across the canvas like threads, drawn together at some point – such as the centre – to create relief-like structures. With his ability to lend the colours a sense of palpability, Schumacher goes beyond the bounds of the *informel*. The emphasis on material that was soon to lead him to integrate lead, asphalt, straw and paper into his paintings, was to influence a new generation of painters who, like Anselm Kiefer, sought to charge such materials with mythical meaning.

Emil Schumacher
Spatial Division, 1955
Oil on canvas, 90.6 x 74.3 cm. Private collection

**Asger Jorn**
Without Boundaries, c. 1959/60
Oil on canvas, 46 x 55 cm
Private collection

# ASGER JORN
## 1914–1973

Jorn was an active member of the CoBrA group and his painting was oriented towards the group's aims. Even after the group was disbanded in 1951, he continued to uphold their basic intentions as the foundation of his work. For his painting, that meant turning away from Surrealist influences and ideas, but also from lyrical and aesthetic *informel* approaches, but without radically breaking with abstraction.

*Without Boundaries* is a painting in strong, highly contrasted colours with three formless, but strongly modelled, restless zones set within colour fields. The brushwork is strong and spontaneous, the oil-paint emphasized in its materiality, and in the intensity of the individual colour zones. The colours are simple, but charged with tension and contrast, even slightly aggressive, as is the brushwork itself, legible on the surface of the painting.

Given the concepts of the CoBrA group, associations with the figurative are legitimate. The original, "uneducated" art of children is regarded as a source of inspiration, as is the work of the mentally ill, indigenous peoples, and the truth and magic of ancient mythology, or the forces of nature. Art and artists are meant to be socially effective in this respect.

**Karel Appel**
Reclining Nude, 1966
Oil on canvas, 190 x 230 cm
Private collection

# KAREL APPEL
## *1921

In the history of painting, the theme of the "reclining female nude" is to be found throughout the centuries. The unclothed reclining woman is invariably seductive, as Venus, Odalisque or some anonymous model whose name the painter does not tell us, even if, as in Francisco de Goya's *Naked Maja* (ill. p. 397) the viewer has some sense of recognizing a specific person. Only rarely do we find portraits of audacious and frivolous women in such intimate poses.

Appel's *Reclining Nude* follows on in this tradition. Somewhere between figuration and abstraction, the vaguely discernible body forms dissolve into planes of colour. The physical characteristics are reduced, and yet the female attributes are discernible. However, they do not exude any aesthetic or even erotic appeal, nor do they recall any specific figure. Space and body are blended in the plane. Masses of colour seem to be juxtaposed with neither rule nor order, applied with brush and palette knife, superimposed. The strong, bright colours, in their impasto materiality, give the painting a unique quality to which the subject matter itself seems secondary. Together with Constant Nieuwenhuis, Corneille and Jorn, Appel was a member of the CoBrA group. Though only seven years his senior, Jorn was Appel's teacher.

# ALBERTO GIACOMETTI
1901–1966

On his death, Giacometti left a painterly oeuvre to equal the quality of his sculptures. This portrait of the writer Jean Genet is situated within an intangible space of light and shadow, bounded by a painted frame. The face and figure are rendered in a manner that is not portrait-like.

Genet said of himself that he had a rather rounder face, but Giacometti has made it longer. The tonality, as in all Giacometti's paintings, is strongly reduced and limited to only a few shades of white, graphite grey and brown.

In his sculptures and paintings, the artist sought to understand "how the world is really made, even if it is only a small part of it, such as a human figure." The needs, visions and experiences of the writer Genet and those of his figure are what Giacometti seeks to capture. For this reason, he places Genet's portrait within its own impenetrable spatiality, thereby creating a sense of place as a setting for *angst* and trauma. Throughout his life, Giacometti's main concern was to master the world of space that seemed to him so boundless and terrifying, and to master the sense of misery in the face of silent existence around him and the oppressiveness of human alienation.

**Alberto Giacometti**
Portrait of Jean
Genet, 1955
Oil on canvas,
73 x 60 cm
Paris, Musée National d'Art Moderne,
Centre Georges
Pompidou

# LUCIAN FREUD
*1922

Lucian Freud paints what he knows: his family, his lovers, his friends, still lifes, and the area around his home. He might spent years working on a painting, and some of his friends sit as models for entire series. *The Big Man* is a typical painting for Freud, created in his studio, in which he has portrayed a friend from an unusual angle. The man, placed in front of a mirror, is painted from above, adding a certain distance and objectivity. The heaviness of the body, sunk into the shabby armchair, is emphasized by this choice of perspective. Freud renders visible different textures and finishes through his painterly technique. He has paid considerable attention to detail in his rendering of the flesh tones of the hands and head of the man.

The uncompromising directness of this artist is reminiscent of the paintings of the Neue Sachlichkeit movement and some of his statements echo their programme. According to Freud, "I want paint to *work* as *flesh,* which is something different. I have always had a scorn for *la belle peinture* and *la delicatesse des touches.* I know my idea of portraiture came from dissatisfaction with portraits that resembled people. I would wish my portraits to be *of* the people, not *like* them. Not having a look of the sitter, *being* them. I didn't want to get a likeness like a mimic, but to *portray* them, like an actor… As far as I am concerned the paint *is* the person. I want it to work for me just as flesh does."

**Lucian Freud**  The Big Man, c. 1976/77
Oil on canvas, 91.5 x 91.5 cm
Private collection

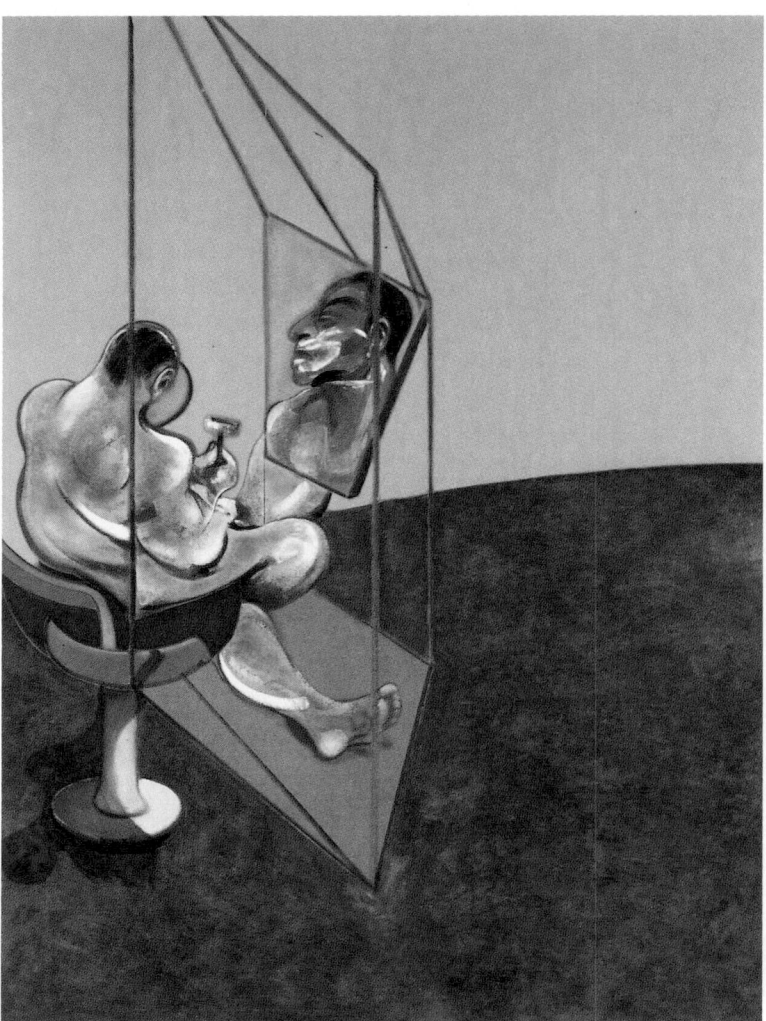

**Francis Bacon**
Three Studies of the Male Back, 1970
Triptych. Oil on canvas, each 198 x 147.5 cm
Zurich, Kunsthaus Zürich

# FRANCIS BACON

## 1909–1992

A triptych was originally a three-part altar-piece whose central panel was the focus, both formally and in terms of content. Bacon used this format for the first time in his work *Three Studies at the Foot of a Crucifixion* (1944). From then on, he frequently adopted the theme of the crucifixion and used three-part canvases even for profane portrayals. He saw the triptych as an opportunity for multiplying his motif. It is presented in several paintings from different angles which are to be regarded simultaneously. In his portrayals of people and his portraits, Bacon often used only one model for large series. His subject matter would sometimes occupy him for years. The finished versions were then frequently titled "studies" in order to rob them of the absoluteness of perfection and completion.

The three panels in this triptych show a naked man sitting in an armchair with a magnifying mirror in front of him. On both the outer panels, the man is shaving, and his face can be seen in the mirror. In the central panel, we see the man reading a newspaper; the mirror is dark, without a reflection. The man is fleshy, muscular, corporeal. His face, like his heavy body, is distorted in curves that seem to follow the strands of his muscles. He is seated within a framelike structure that Bacon often

used as an artistic device. It is certainly not to be understood in real terms, but, like the large colour planes of the floor and wall, is intended to emphasize and intensify the figure. It is a kind of cage in which the figure has only a limited sphere of action. The observer is standing outside the space, but can watch the man unhindered. Private rooms and actions are rendered visible and therefore public.

Bacon was a figurative painter, in many ways related to Giacometti, but more expressive and radical. He was not the chronicler of a "world in order". Of all the possibilities of human existence and sentiment, he chose to portray despairing extremes. In his paintings, Bacon created "mythical translations of our inner structures". He rendered subconscious perception visible. His pictorial language thrives on the elementary force of his forms and colours. In his work, colour became a physical substance with which he recreated the brutality of daily life in his paintings. His exploration of painting was a constant act of looking chaos in the face, a constant awareness of transience and death, resigned to the meaninglessness of human existence.

**Ad Reinhardt**
Red Abstract, 1952
Oil on canvas, 152.4 x 101.3 cm
New Haven (CT), Yale University
Art Gallery

## AD REINHARDT
### 1913–1967

Reinhardt, who was also a consistent art critic and art historian, sought to present the absolute in his paintings. Following on from the tradition of the Constructivists, primarily Piet Mondrian, he increasingly reduced his painterly means, colours and forms in order to ban all that was irrational and arbitrary from his pictures. For Reinhardt, the first rule and absolute measure of beautiful art and painting, which he regards as the highest and freest of the arts, was its purity. He believed that the more references and additions a painting had, the wose it was. Reinhardt called for the revival of art as art, rejecting the expressive gestures of his American colleagues as vehemently as those of the Surrealist automatisms. At the end of his development, we find monochrome black panels that he painted from 1960 onwards in the same format until his death.

Red Abstract illustrates the process by which his monochrome paintings emerged. Reinhardt superimposed rectangles of almost identical colours over one another, so that a cruciform could be seen in their structure. This cruciform was the last still portrayable step before his works turned to purely spiritual appearances that could only be grasped mentally.

**Josef Albers**
Study for "Homage to the Square": Star Blue, 1958
Oil on Masonit, 121.8 x 121.8 cm. Private collection

## JOSEF ALBERS
### 1888–1976

From 1950 onwards, Josef Albers worked on a series that he called Homage to the Square. He determned two formats at an early stage (60 x 60 cm and 120 x 120 cm) and also settled on the alignment of squares within a vertical symmetrical axis. On the basis of this strictly regulated form, he spent more than 25 years of concentrated work creating a large series of oilpaintings on hardwood panels, offset-prints and serigraphies. Albers varied only the number of squares and the colours. For many of these square paintings, the colours were determined after a series of studies. There are paintings with contrasting colours and variations on single colours, in which the transition from square to square is minimal. Albers himself described the process in a prose poem: "When I paint and construct / I seek visual articulation / ... / In my work it is enough for me / To compete with myself / To attempt multiple instrumentation / With a simple palette and simple colours / And to dare to make further variations" Albers gave his paintings freely associative poetic titles that would give the spectator scope for individual interpretation. On the other hand, the simple pictorial structure makes us consider the actual process of painting.

## MARK ROTHKO

1903–1970

Following a realistic phase in the 1930s, Rothko began experimenting with the automatic painting propagated by the Surrealists. His own personal and artistic development did not profit much from it, for he went in an entirely different direction. Rothko was particularly interested in Greek and Roman mythology and in the theories of Freud and Jung, particularly in their theory of symbols. For Rothko himself, symbols were tragic, timeless expressions of primitive fears and impulses, in every country and in all situations. On the basis of this notion, Rothko began treating forms and colours like an adventure into an unknown world: "Ideas and plans that existed in the mind at the start were simply the doorway through which one left the world in which they occur."

In the 1940s, he often painted with watercolours or gouache, to achieve a transparent effect. Soon he turned to abstraction, believing that reminders of the world of the figurative and nature would disturb his exploration of ideas. He wanted to avoid any object-oriented association in his portrayal of objects, in order to be able to create entirely value-free statements. For this reason, he simplified his work methods and motifs increasingly, reducing his formal repertoire drastically to the rectangle.

By the end of the 1940s, he had developed the typical pictorial form with its two or three rectangles, which he continued to vary from then on. Rothko was one of the most important figures in the New York School of abstract Expressionism, but he was not an action painter. His abstract compositions were not created in a process of frenzied action, but in a contemplative attitude. His paintings are the result of an inner calm, and they mirror meditative processes. The theme in Rothko's large paintings, including *Number 10* is the theme of the infinite, of the universe. He sought transcendence through the constant equilibrium of only a few forms in his paintings and through the powerful statement of his colours. Applied thinly, not delineated at the edges, linked with the structure of the canvas, with a matt, almost dull surface, the colour fields give an illusion of atmosphere and the impression of an aura. The dynamics of the painting lies in the tension between the floating colour fields.

As in the work of Albers and Poliakoff, Rothko explores painting through colour: a form once found is subjected to minimal variations, while colour is constantly re-explored and, thereby leading to new atmospheres and moods. His paintings possess an atmospheric quality of spiritual, contemplative nature, in contrast to the dynamic mood of Pollock, Kline or de Kooning.

**Mark Rothko**
Number 10, 1950
Oil on canvas, 228.6 x 114.6cm
New York, The Museum of Modern Art

**Morris Louis**
The Third Element, 1965
Acryl on canvas, 217.8 x 129.5cm
New York, The Museum of Modern Art

## MORRIS LOUIS
### 1912–1962

Morris Louis founded the Washington Color School together with Kenneth Noland. They wanted to devote themselves entirely to the painterly process, exploring the interaction between artist, colour and canvas, the properties of colour and the resulting possibilities for painting.

*The Third Element* is a typical result of these experiments in a new pictorial structure invented by Louis. Technically, it is based on the method he developed on the basis of an approach differing from that of classical painting, which has much in common with the approach of the abstract Expressionists and action painters.

Paint is poured onto an unprimed canvas and the colour is guided into stripes. Diluted colours, which would shine through at certain points, gave his early paintings their typically veiled effect. What is more, he often allowed several layers of colour to permeate each other. All his colours were combined on the canvas. In this way, the subtle gradations of colour on the surface of the painting give a sense of depth and warmth. His experiments with the new water soluble latex paints also give his work an impression of sublime levity and spontaneity. In his last paintings, he abandoned symmetry altogether.

**Barnett Newman**
Vir Heroicus Sublimus, 1950/51
Oil on canvas, 242.2 x 513.6cm
New York, The Museum of Modern Art

## BARNETT NEWMAN
### 1905–1970

Newman, together with Rothko, was one of the main exponents of colorfield painting. Colorfield painting emerged in the 1950s in reaction to abstract Expressionism. Newman painted very large-format works. Taking as his starting point the rectangular canvas, he divided the painting horizontally or vertically. Just as Motherwell was the intellectual amongst the abstract Expressionists, Newman was the scholar amongst the colorfield painters.

Schooled in the Jewish tradition of the Bible, the rabbinic teachings of the Talmud and the mystical teachings of the Kabbalah, he had painted works in the 1940s featuring magical signs inspired by the symbols of primitive cultures.

From 1948 onwards, however, he limited his expression to line and plane. For him, the line was the first creative act, the gesture with which God intervened in the great void and parted light and darkness. For Newman, the creative act was a repetition of the Creation. By limiting his form of expression to a few structuring lines on a large colour plane, he sought to banish the chaos of possible forms. For him, this pictorial structure was ordered truth, reflecting his attitude to the mysteries of life and death.

# KENNETH NOLAND
\*1924

Kenneth Noland was a member of the Washington Color School. Together with Morris Louis, he put Washington firmly on the map of the art world. Like Louis and Helen Frankenthaler, Noland colours the canvas. He uses colour to create an illusion of changing spatial impressions. He returns time and time again to a few basic forms, which he reiterates in different colours. In the past, these forms were mainly targets and V-motifs, later horizontal stripes. The square canvas of *Ember* is unprimed, so that the motif and its colours appears to float in a diffuse space. The simple form of concentric colour rings is the only subject matter of the painting. There is no philosophical metaphor behind it that might permit a subjective interpretation. Correspondingly, the title bears no relationship to the world beyond the painting itself.

In his art, Noland represents a new kind of abstraction that breaks away from the concept of the active artistic personality and the notion of an interaction between body, spirit and painting, so that it becomes more objectified. The restriction to a few emblematic forms and the rejection of all traces of the pictorial process create a cool sense of distance. The emergence of a new spirit of objectivity is evident.

Kenneth Noland
Ember, 1960
Acrylic on canvas, 179 x 178 cm
Private collection

# ELLSWORTH KELLY
\*1923

Intensifying perception through drastically reduced means has been Ellsworth Kelly's aim since his return to the USA in 1954, having studied the stringent compositions of the European Constructivists. Kelly uses pure colours, and tries to avoid all traces of the painter's hand on the surface of his paintings in order to create perfect pictorial objects. Whereas Kelly initially chose traditional rectangular frames at first, like Frank Stella, he began developing irregularly shaped canvases, and a large range of different carriers. The forms of his canvases were increasingly determined by the intensity of the colours, and the painting thus took on the characteristics of an object.

In *Red Blue* the combination of two triangles creates a fragile equilibrium. The new pictorial structure is an open parallelogram created by the juxtaposition of two coloured triangles. The different qualities of the two colours, their "temperatures" as it were, are linked with the alignment of the triangles. The quiet blue stands on its broad base like a pyramid; the aggressive red, by contrast, is a triangle standing on its point. Where the two colours meet without transition, there is a flickering that grants no respite to the eye of the spectator.

Ellsworth Kelly
Red Blue, 1968
Oil on canvas, 228 x 244 cm
Düsseldorf, Kunstsammlung Nordrhein-Westfalen

Jasper Johns
Flag, 1954/55
Oil and collage on plywood, 107.3 x 153.8 cm
New York, The Museum of Modern Art

# JASPER JOHNS
*1930

The American flag is one of the most frequently painted motifs in Johns' oeuvre. Using various techniques and materials, he seeks to retain a certain relationship to reality, but at the same time appeals to the viewer, catching his attention, perhaps disturbing him, and making him think. This is not a photographic portrayal, nor does it have the texture of real cloth.

Johns works entirely with the painterly means of abstract Expressionism, with paint applied in free gestures, leaving obvious traces of his work. Yet his subjects are as trivial as those of the Pop artists: in addition to the national flag, he has repeatedly painted numbers, targets and maps.

Johns chose to portray objects that seemed typical of everyday life, "things which are seen and not looked at" because they are so familiar and their aesthetic qualities so inconspicuous. "Using the design of the American flag took care of a great deal for me because I didn't have to design it." Johns believes that seeing familiar objects can prompt the viewer to explore their poetic qualities. There are a number of versions of the American flag, executed in a variety of formats and techniques. This re-

peated treatment of a simple pictorial pattern is not something Johns regards as monotonous. Instead, there is an aspect of Dadaistic irony behind it. Johns' use of encaustic wax technique is very rare today.

Johns' paintings in the early 1950s made him famous almost overnight; they were an important source of inspiration for the Pop artists. A motif from a prefigured repertoire of forms, a kind of symbol or emblem, calm instead of chaos – these were the things that fascinated him. His first alphabet paintings were created in 1956, and in 1959 he began painting numbers. In 1958, he created his first painted sculpture in bronze, and in 1960 he turned his attention to the serial production of lithographs. Johns himself finds everything he makes "pre-formed, de-personalized, conventional". His works remain impersonal, irrespective of what we might interpret into them. This stands in deliberate contrast to the process of creation and the end-products of the abstract Expressionists, who include the emotions and physical movements of the artists in their work. Many of Johns' newer paintings do not lack realism, but depth, and the traditional belief in the necessity of meaningful motifs is firmly negated. These paintings are an important preliminary step on the path towards minimal art.

From the mid 1970s on, Johns created works that might be described as purely abstract. This painting is created entirely from a single pattern of "cross-hatching" which Johns also used later in the background of two figurative paintings. According to the artist, "I was riding in a car... when a car came in the opposite direction. It was covered with these marks, but I only saw it for a moment – then it was gone – just a brief glimpse. But I immediately thought that I would use it for my next painting." Even if the patterns are based on a real source, this is no longer evident in the pattern repetition of the finished work. Johns refers to the *Drip Paintings* by Pollock. He tried to reiterate the overall compositions of the action painters in a less improvised and more controlled pattern on a similarly proportioned canvas.

The painting is divided into three, citing the traditional altarpiece form of European painting. The dividing lines have been subtly emphasized by Johns. At the point of transition from the left panel to the central panel, the direction of the cross-hatching changes, while the colours are retained. At the point of transition from the right panel, the direction of the lines is maintained, but the colours are changed. If we imagine the two outer edges of the left and right panels joining up, the cross-hatching continues unbroken. The choice of colours is as carefully considered as the composition itself. Johns has painted on a black background in the three primary colours and their complementary colours.

Jasper Johns
Untitled, 1980
Acrylic on plastic on canvas,
77.5 x 138.2 cm
Private collection

# FRANK STELLA
*1936

Whereas other artists pared down their paintings, increasingly freeing them from optical additions of all kinds, Stella's oeuvre developed in precisely the opposite direction. He invented the "shaped canvas" in which the outline of the canvas is adapted according to the composition of the painting and not, as traditionally, the painting composed into the limitations of the given canvas.

With his shaped canvas in the form of a V, an X or a circle, he fundamentally changed conventional concepts of composition and their relationship to the form of the canvas. Until the early 1970s, not only was the repertoire of his forms deliberately limited to a few repeated forms, but his colour scale was also purist.

In his painting *Guadalupe Island* he has made the move from sparse reductionism to lavish opulence. The painting is made up of a number of material components, all painted in the same way as the background. The brushstrokes and patterns are wholly abstract, comparable with the paintings of the abstract Expressionists. The colours are garish and loud, but the brushwork is gentle and there is no concentration in a single centre. Some of the component parts are cut out and superimposed over the background. As Stella himself said: "You can see the whole idea without confusion."

Frank Stella
Guadalupe Island, Caracara, 1979
Mixed media and aluminium,
238 x 307.5 cm
London, Tate Gallery

UNITED STATES

**Yves Klein**
Monochrome Blue, Un-
titled (IKB 3), 1960
Sponges, pigment and
resin on panel on canvas,
199 x 153 x 2.5 cm
Paris, Musée National
d'Art Moderne, Centre
Georges Pompidou

## YVES KLEIN
### 1928–1962

In 1946, Yves Klein symbolically divided
the world with his friends Arman and
Claude Pascal: lying on the beach at Nice,
looking up at the sky, he chose for himself
the sky and its colour blue. From then on,
blue was of central significance in his œuvre.
The focus of his later painterly experiments
was on the monochrome, and even though he
later worked with other colours, including
gold, blue continued to remain his preferred
colour. In order to achieve the greatest possible intensity for his blue canvases, he applied
pure, dry pigment onto the canvas which
had been moistened with petroleum. He explored all the possibilities of blue tones until
he finally found the luminous ultramarine
that became his trademark IKB (international
Klein Blue).

In 1957, in Milan, Klein announced the advent of the Blue Epoch. From then on, he created further monochromatic canvases, in IKB,
some of which included dyed objects, such as
sponges, which he regarded as relics of the real
world. His blue canvases were intended to sen-
sitize the viewer, giving a sense of the infinity
of space and wide expanses, stimulating an experience of his own reality. Klein was an important pioneer of Concept Art.

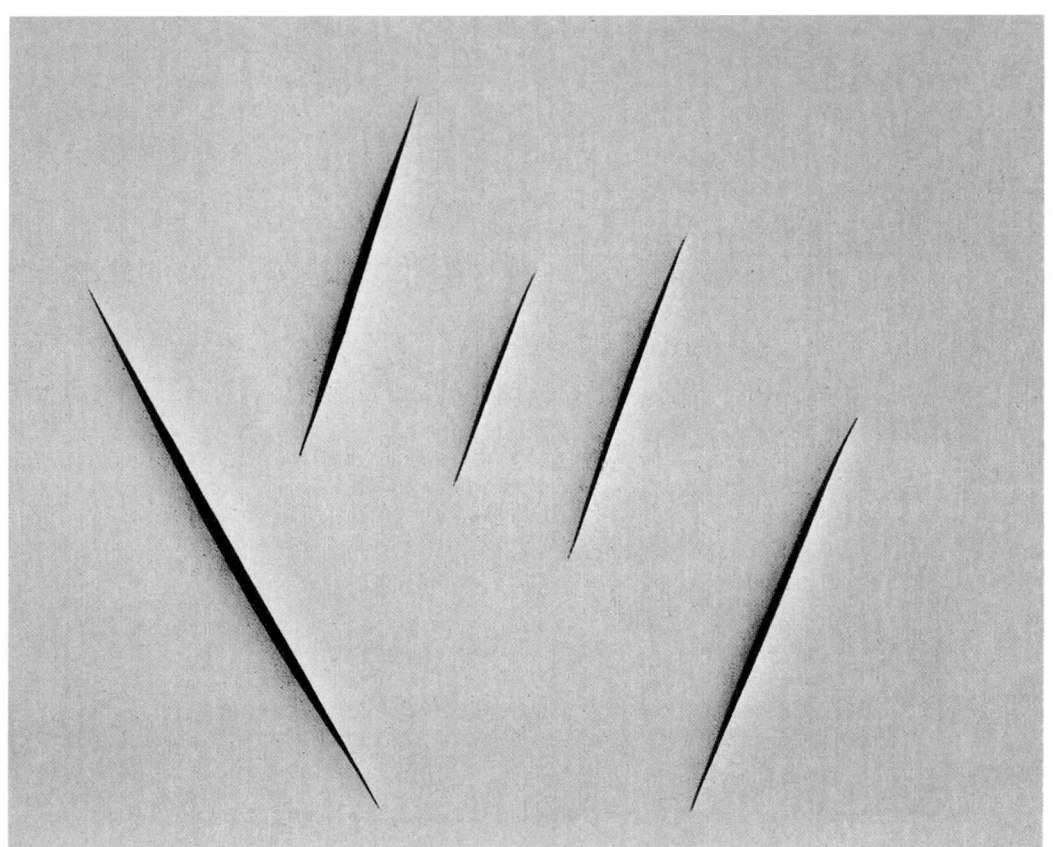

**Lucio Fontana**
Concetto spaziale, Attese (Spatial Concept), 1959
Water-based paint on canvas, 100 x 125 cm
Milan, Fondazione Lucio Fontana

## LUCIO FONTANA
### 1899–1968

Lucio Fontana's paintings, which he himself described as "concetto spaziale" demonstrate just
how far the boundaries of painting were rolled
back after 1945. The classical concept of the
painting had to be extended, for the canvas
had by now become the bearer of a painterly
message in only a restricted sense. We can
hardly even use the word "painting" in its
original sense. With the advent of abstraction,
the canvas, which, for centuries, had been the
material fundament for the painted illusion of
reality, took on a new function as the background for signs both with and without meaning, for colours signifying only themselves,
their coloristic qualities or their materiality.

Here, the canvas is so uniformly and evenly covered in luminous yellow that we cannot
discern any brushstrokes, nor any signs of
the act of painting, though we do recognize
the rough structure of the canvas itself. A
few bold, long slashes with a sharp knife
have cut the surface; the traditionally hermetic picture plane has been given apertures.
The edges of these abrupt incisions curve
inwards, creating a spatial impression – not as
a window on the world, but as a sparse and
abstract spatiality.

# VICTOR DE VASARÉLY

1908–1997

Vasarély's art is intended to have a positive impact on society. He is not interested in creating intellectually complex content, nor in producing entirely dysfunctional decoration. Gradually, he removed all anecdotal narrative from his work, replacing it with formal structures intended to appeal to the eye of the viewer through their impression alone. He developed a kind of modular system involving a repertoire of geometric forms and colours. With these fundamental prototypes, he experimented until he had worked out the "score" or basic pattern for a model. It can then be executed as a painting, as a panel, as a silk-screen print or as a multiple. The mass distribution of his works are intended to have a profound and far-reaching influence on our lives, and on urban planning, for Vasarély is particularly interested in having his optical creations included in the design of buildings and urban facilities, whose bleak monotony he attacks. According to Vasarély, people without a more profound knowledge perceive the rhythm of sound in exactly the same way as they perceive the rhythm of form and colour. With regard to his Op Art works, the artist believes it is extremely important for contemporary productions to be presented to a broad public so that they can train their eyes and their sensibilities. *Arcturus II* with its architectonic, square grids, is a typical example of Vasarély's Op Art.

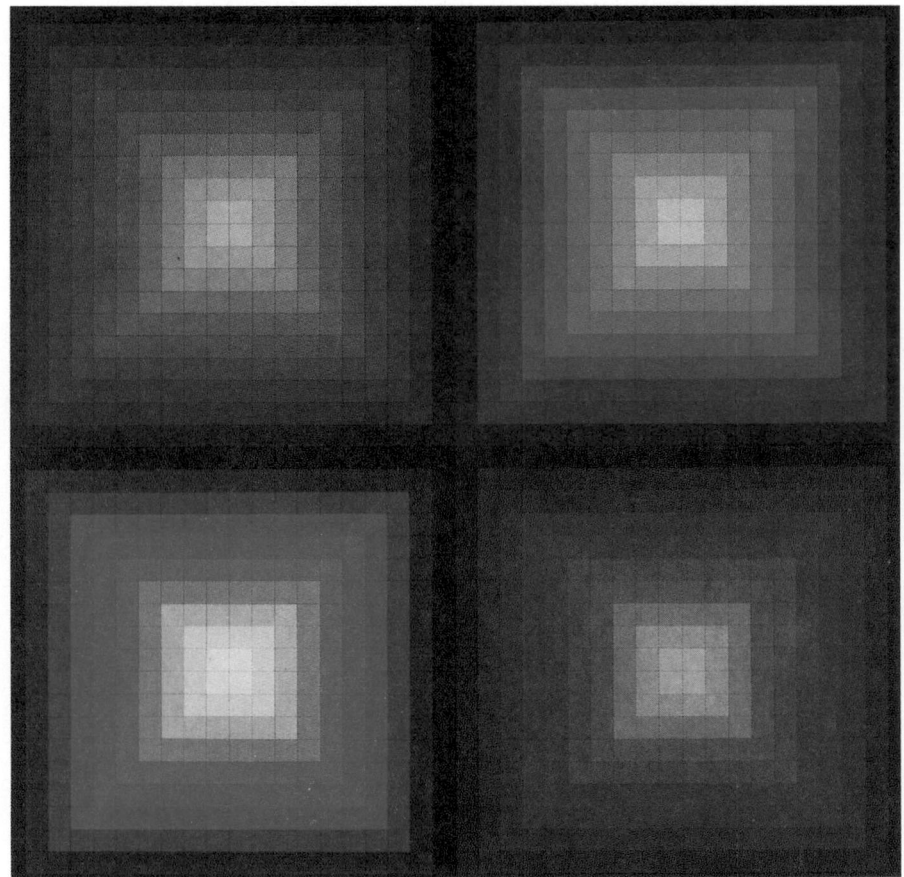

Victor de Vasarély
Arcturus II, 1966
Oil on canvas, 160 x 159.7 cm
Washington, Hirshhorn Museum and
Sculpture Garden, Smithsonian Institution

# FRIEDENSREICH HUNDERTWASSER

*1928

The spiral, in ever new variations, is one of the key motifs in the work of Hundertwasser (born Friedrich Stowasser). Here, it is set like a labyrinth against an almost square background with a blue core, transverse links and inserts on the left-hand side. Hundertwasser's art is based on Viennese Jugendstil, and would be unthinkable without such forerunners as Egon Schiele or Gustav Klimt. Although Hundertwasser takes abstraction a step further, he uses the same luminous and vibrant colours. Spiral and labyrinth are closely related in terms of symbolic content. In the work of Hundertwasser, universal and traditional symbolism are still closely linked with specific personal issues.

*The Great Way* is a self-contained image, in which the lines of the spiral can lead inwards to the centre, or outwards from the centre, on a path that does not lead to infinity, but to an outward point of rest. This creates a double possibility of exclusion or inclusion. In the spiral, there is at the same time the motif of a constant dynamic, an action that is always in motion and never static. Comparisons with plant forms spring to mind, or with the rings of a tree or with the skin and core of a fruit.

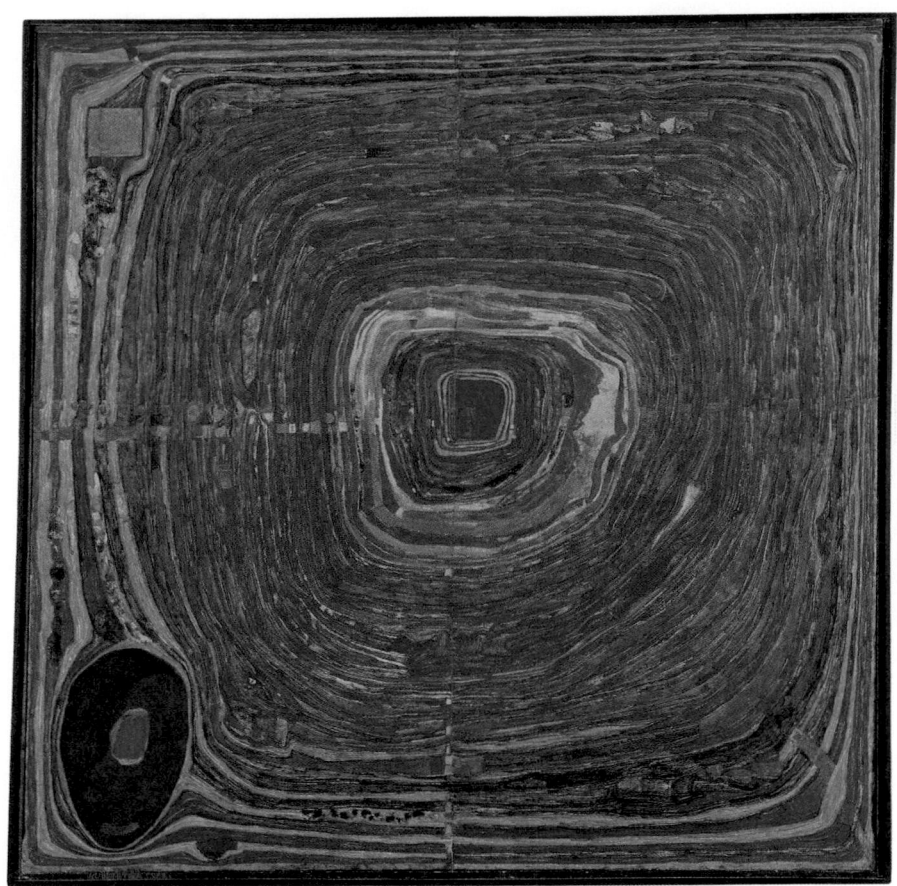

**Friedensreich Hundertwasser**  The Great Way, 1955
Polyvinyl on two joined strips of canvas primed with chalk
and zinc white, 162 x 160 cm. Vienna, Österreichische Galerie

**Richard Lindner**
The Meeting, 1953
Oil on canvas, 152.4 x 182.9 cm
New York, The Museum of Modern Art

## RICHARD LINDNER

### 1901–1978

Lindner's painting *The Meeting* is one of his most important works. All the typical elements of his art can be found here. His creative oeuvre was invariably closely linked with his personal experience, his memories and his current situation. Throughout his life, Lindner's topics remained the same, though after his emigration they took on increasingly American features with some reminiscences of Europe. Lindner's figures and scenes are always set in a very flat space, whose volume is expressed in planes. He uses strong and often garish colours.

The figures in the painting are arranged in a strictly pyramidal structure and portayed in frontal, rear and profile views. In terms of content, they have no relationship to one another: the Bavarian fairy-tale king Ludwig II, the lady in the prim grey coat, the frivolous

red-head showing her leg, the old-fashioned couple in the sailor suit and *belle-époque* costume, the lady in the red evening dress, the casually dressed gentleman, the huge ginger cat and the woman in the tightly laced corset with suspenders, a cabinet of motley marionettes, full of ambiguous references, a meeting of past and present, dream and reality. It is this inner quality that sets Lindner's paintings apart from Pop Art. Here, we find cold scepticism clothed in the garb of the burlesque. Style and subject matter are congruent.

Lindner's planar pictorial zones are filled with bright and sometimes garish colours, the individual parts are clearly separated by sharp edges, with passages of blurred perspective. He models with the poster-like forms of clothing, shells, bodies, external appearances. His figures often possess erotic qualities expressed by such props as corsets, suspenders, high-heeled shoes and boots. His figures are standard types, strangers, spectators.

# ROBERT RAUSCHENBERG
## *1925

Having started out by painting in the manner of the abstract Expressionists, Rauschenberg arrived at his own new pictorial concept in the early 1950s. *Charlene* is typical of the so-called Junk Art he produced for two decades. Pure painting is no longer the foremost consideration. Instead, objects and fragments have been included in the pictorial surface, some of them left as they were found, some of them re-worked with paint. Purely painterly passages in the forceful, spontaneous style of action painting fill the interim spaces.

The technique of these works is similar to the collages of the Cubists and Surrealists, but the lyrical aesthetic appeal and the distinct element of surprise inherent in the collages and paintings of Georges Braque, Pablo Picasso and Kurt Schwitters take on a different aspect in Junk Art. After all, these are objects drawn from the garbage heap of the affluent society and, instead of lyricism or poetry, they exude a raw, banale realism that is further heightened by the rough brushstrokes over or between them. The discarded and the worthless is thus elevated to a higher plane by its integration into a work of art. At the same time, this act calls into question the aesthetic standards of today's mass culture and consumer society.

Like Jasper Johns, who is a close friend of his, Rauschenberg adopted the large-scale canvases and brushwork of the abstract Expressionists. By addressing banal everyday subjects, they guided art in a new direction. Both these artists are regarded as mediators on the way to Pop Art.

Robert Rauschenberg
Charlene, 1954
Collage, 225 x 320 cm
Amsterdam, Stedelijk Museum

The title *Trophy I* may be regarded both ironically and as a laconic narrative. The trophy in question consists of the waste of our consumer society. The found objects of mass production, having reached the end of their brief life-cycle and having ended up on the garbage heap, are collected by Rauschenberg. Integrated into what he describes as his combine painting, they are transformed into artistic objects. *Trophy I* may be the house-altar, the collecting cabinet of a naive and unthinking consumer who has not had the fortune to live in more noble spheres; for him, the found items are valued as reminiscences. At the same time, the painting can also call into question contemporary lifestyles and the medium of contemporary art.

Rauschenberg's fellow artist Allan Kaprow called for artists to deliberately dispense with craftsmanship and permanence and to turn instead to distinctly perishable media such as newspaper, string, adhesive tape, grass and real foodstuffs so that there could be no doubt whatsoever, right from the start, that the work would soon become garbage or dust. The ideas of Junk Art were adopted by many other artists.

Robert Rauschenberg
Trophy I, 1959
Combine Painting, 168 x 104 cm
Zurich, Kunsthaus Zürich

UNITED STATES

Andy Warhol
200 Campbell's Soup Cans, 1962
Oil on canvas, 183 x 254 cm
Private collection

## ANDY WARHOL
### 1928–1987

When Warhol began putting Jacqueline Kennedy and Marilyn Monroe onto the canvas in silk-screen prints, creating entire series of these pictures, painting entered realms that had certainly never before been associated with painting. Warhol's pictures have nothing whatsoever to do with painting in the classical sense. He deliberately depersonalized the art work, and in all his portrait series the origins of the image in a commercial print and the technical process of production are clearly evident.

Warhol has portrayed the famous face of Marilyn Monroe against a blue background. This picture is based on a photograph which has been enlarged and silk-screened onto the canvas. Warhol often left the actual printing and colouring of his pictures to his assistants, thereby negating the identity of the person portrayed as well as the individuality of the artist who designed and executed the art work. Long before Warhol adopted her image as a motif, Marilyn Monroe was already an idol. Warhol's presentation of the isolated, enlarged individual image underlines this status. In a sequence of several different work processes, the photo was reproduced by superimposing monochrome silk-screens in different colours. This has in no way detracted from Monroe's appeal: the blonde hair, the sensually painted lips, the eye-shadowed lids veiling an enigmatic gaze, and the arch of the eyebrows.

In other motifs, such as the soup cans, the same picture is repeated in series, with variations only in the lettering of the label. Here, advertising becomes Pop Art and the image is at the same time an indication of the mechanization and dehumanization of modern society with its alienation and boredom.

While gourmets may turn up their noses at the very idea of opening a can of soup, here we find two hundred of them stacked up. They are the stars of the supermarkets. In the iconography of Pop Art, they take up the same position that was once held by Chinese vases, Venetian glasses, oysters or lemons in early still lifes. The two hundred soup cans create a contemporary still life. Here, Warhol has taken a do-it-yourself, painting-by-numbers picture as his motif.

The very idea of do-it-yourself hardly sounds like high culture; after all, the pattern, the material and the instructions are all supplied so that all you have to do is apply the right colour to the area labelled accordingly. It is a more or less foolproof method. The finished painting then exists in countless copies, decorating the walls of countless homes. This prefabricated art prompted Warhol to make an ironic comment on the fundamental principles of his own production process. Warhol intended to use industrially produced pictorial series to call into question the classical notion of originality.

Andy Warhol
Do it yourself – Landscape,
1962
Acrylic on canvas,
178 x 137 cm
Cologne, Museum Ludwig

UNITED STATES

It was only logical that Warhol should have named the loft where he produced his images of the consumer society and the glamour world, The Factory. In a bid to compete with Picasso's legendary prolific output, Warhol employed a number of assistants who helped him to create his silk-screen prints. Within six months, from August to the end of 1962, some 2,000 pictures were produced.

Warhol also produced underground films at The Factory with the many friends and fans who lived with him there. The topics of these films were generally trivial, showing people going about their daily life, sleeping or smoking a cigar. His eight-hour film *Empire* shows the Empire State Building in the course of the day from a static camera viewpoint. True to the maxim that every individual could be famous, Warhol described his actors as superstars, caricaturing the myth-machine of Hollywood. When the films approached the conventional narrative structures they had some commercial success. Warhol, the self-styled universal genius, geared his life entirely to the principles of pop stardom.

**Andy Warhol**
Marilyn, 1964
Silk-screen, ink and acrylic on canvas,
101.5 x 101.5 cm
Private collection

Jim Dine
Cardinal, 1976
Mixed media on canvas,
274.3 x 182.8cm
New York, Pace Gallery

## JIM DINE
*1935

Jim Dine has explored the motif of the coat in
various versions, techniques and materials,
ranging from silk-screen print to combine
painting (a painting involving the montage of
materials). The item is invariably some kind
of bathrobe in the posture of the person who
would be wearing it.

    *Cardinal* is a brilliant red bathrobe with a
shawl collar and belt, painted in an extremely
sculptural, corporeal way on a dark background through which lighter patches shimmer. The arms akimbo recalling the bathrobe's
wearer, hands comfortably in the pockets, give
the picture a direct vitality that is surprisingly
cancelled by the lack of a head. The impression of immediacy is heightened by the
painterly approach: many layers, some superimposed, add light and fluctuating motion to
the picture.

    In a variety of techniques which he ex-
plored in his motifs, Dine also saw an opportunity for self-exploration. Constantly reiterated motifs in his art, such as tools, hearts,
palettes and coats, have a personal significance
for him. For Dine, these headless bathrobes
embody the person who is meant to be wearing them. Sometimes it is a self-portrait, but
here it is a cardinal, symbolically expressed by
the colour red.

Robert Indiana
The American
Dream, I, 1961
Oil on canvas,
183 x 152.7cm
New York, The
Museum of
Modern Art

## ROBERT INDIANA
*1928

*The American Dream* is the dream of fairy-tale
wealth and freedom: everybody can take their
chance. Yet the American dream has come
true only for a few. Like many Pop artists, Indiana gleans his motifs from the immediate
daily environment of those consumers and
citizens for whom the American dream has
not brought the splendid isolation of a world
full of unique luxury goods. His planar codes
and emblems are taken from the daily iconography of a trivial sphere. These four discs
are taken from the world of the gambling
casino, inspired by one-armed-bandits and
targets.

    Indiana chooses large formats to lend his
colour panels, full of signs, numbers and slogans, the impact of posters. In this lettered
painting, he deliberately chooses pre-existing
signs, and his own creative contribution is restricted to the arrangement, the combination
and the choice of colour.

    In contrast to early Dadaist play with typo-
graphy, Robert Indiana's *American Dream* has
a significance, a deeper meaning, almost an
ambiguity. The slogans TAKE ALL and TILT,
the many stars and the promise of The American Dream may be taken literally as goals
that can be achieved only in a game.

# TOM WESSELMANN

*1931

A bathroom setting undoubtedly lends itself to the portrayal of a female nude. Painted panels and real objects have been juxtaposed here in a huge assemblage. This is not an environment the spectator can enter, but a pictorial object to be viewed frontally.

In *Bathtub III* we see a naked, pale-skinned woman in a bathtub. She is drying her back with a red and white striped towel. Her femininity is underlined by the emphasis on her lips, blonde hair, red fingernails, navel, nipples and pubic hair. Her slender figure is painted in a flat, poster-like way. The image of the woman is degraded to a faceless cliché. The blue bathtub in which she is standing, the dark-blue tiled wall of the niche and the yolk-yellow wall

bordered by a blue stripe are all painted. These painted panels are given an unexpected element of reality by the juxtaposition of objects that turn the painting into an assemblage. In the perspectively painted niche, a shower rail has been fitted above the bathtub, from which a red shower curtain is hanging. In front of the bathtub, a blue synthetic bath mat has been placed, next to which stands a blue laundry basket. A real white door concludes the right-hand side of the object, with a door handle and a towel rail on which a bath towel is hanging. The curtain is in the tradition of European painterly motifs. Yet the intimacy of the nude is completely offset by the functionality of the ambient surroundings and trivialized by the act of drying.

**Tom Wesselmann**
Bathtub 3, 1963
Oil on canvas, plastic and various objects (Bathroom door, towel and laundry basket), 213 x 270 x 45 cm
Cologne, Museum Ludwig

**Roy Lichtenstein**
M-Maybe (A Girl's Picture), 1965
Magna on canvas, 152 x 152 cm
Cologne, Museum Ludwig

### ROY LICHTENSTEIN

### 1923–1997

Lichtenstein is one of the key figures of American Pop Art. He took the motif for this picture from a comic, magnifying one frame enormously onto the canvas. In doing so, he creates an outline drawing of his chosen motif, projects it through an episcope onto the canvas and fixes it there with the brush. Using stencils, he then grids individual areas or the entire painting using what is known as the benday process.

Finally, he applies the colour, concluding with the black outlines. He uses only primary colours. Because they are easily soluble in turpentine, he uses magna-acrylic paints. Because these paints leave no traces on the background when they are removed, they permit corrections to be made easily. Like other Pop artists, he uses motifs with which everyone is familiar, and also cites the old masters or Japanese woodcuts. In this respect, Lichtenstein aims at an audience that will recognize his quotes and understand the irony in his work. He has reached the threshold at which Pop Art becomes intellectual.

# JAMES ROSENQUIST
*1933

Marilyn Monroe is the prototype of the famous film star. During the Vietnam war, she was the pin-up in every GI's locker, but with the advent of Pop Art, her image graced the walls of museums. Rosenquist created a simultaneous collage with the face of Marilyn Monroe; her smiling mouth and her eye are blended over and alienated by lettering from the advertisement. The individual parts of the picture are placed at different angles and are interconnected.

Before Rosenquist turned to art, he had been a painter of billboards. While he was working on a huge advertising image, he suddenly realized how much the effect of an image changes when seen close up. Deeply impressed by the constant impact of advertising on the citizens of the consumer society, he sought to use the persuasive powers of these billboards and their visual language for his art. A preference for oversized formats and poster-like painting became his hallmark. He used all the available reproduction procedures and every possible technical aid. Rosenquist considered other kinds of painting to be outmoded and lacking in impact. Behind these apparently superficial aspects lies a distinctly critical approach.

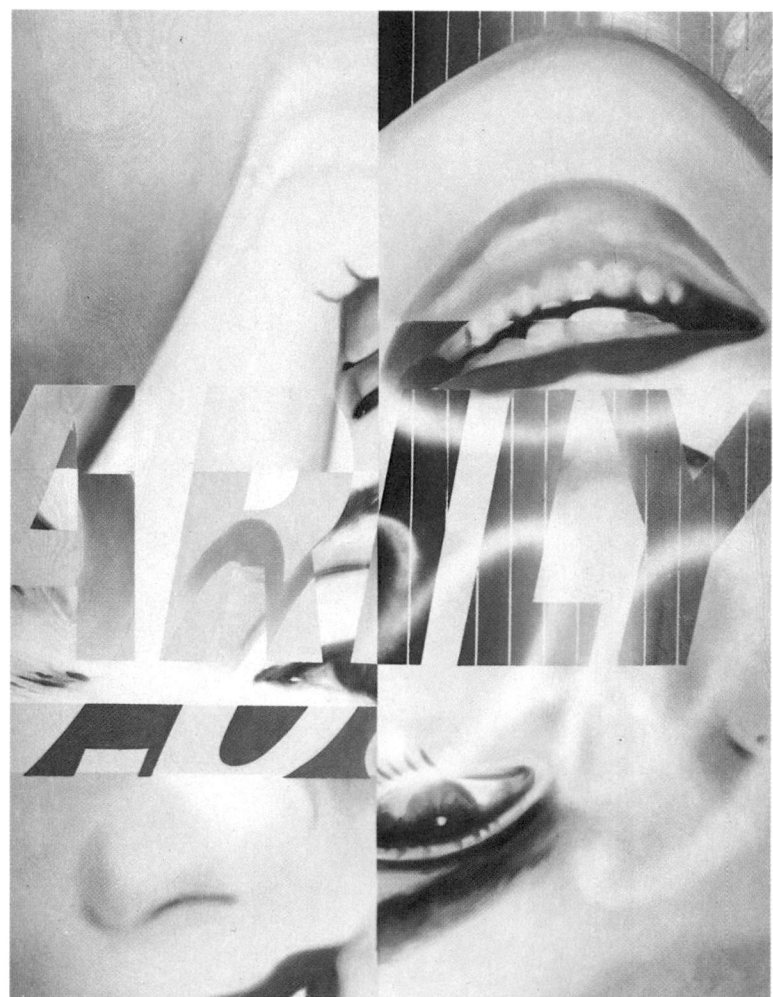

**James Rosenquist**
Marilyn Monroe, I, 1962
Oil and spray enamel on
canvas, 236.2 x 183.5 cm
New York, The Museum
of Modern Art, Collection
Sidney and Harriet Janis

# RONALD B. KITAJ
*1932

Kitaj is regarded as one of the mediators between American and English Pop Art, since arriving in London on a scholarship in 1958 and staying there. He soon joined the group of artists gathered around the Institute for Contemporary Art and familiarized them with developments in America. However, as he himself tended to draw his motifs primarily from philosophy and cultural history rather than from the trivial myths of everyday life, he soon began to distance himself increasingly from Pop Art during the early 60s.

Kitaj presents his critical social stance in *Value, Price and Profit*. The three mainstays of capitalism are transposed as in a collage onto the golden-yellow surface of the picture, true to the maxim that a painting can only be the surface for the projection of events in the world. The three figures have been made up of fragments taken from different contexts; we recognize parts of photographs and drawings, monochrome colour areas and ornaments that may be part of a wallpaper pattern. The foolish facial expression on each of the three figures also suggests that Kitaj does not hold any of the concepts mentioned in his title in particularly high esteem. For him, they are mere formula, which cannot mediate any actual content.

**Ronald B. Kitaj**  Value, Price and Profit, 1963
Oil on canvas, 153 x 153 cm
Private collection

UNITED STATES

Peter Blake
Bo Diddley, 1963/64
Acrylic, adhesive-tape on hard-
board panel, 122.4 x 78.3 cm
Cologne, Museum Ludwig

*Below:*
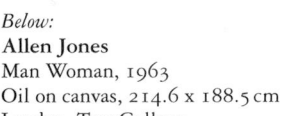
Allen Jones
Man Woman, 1963
Oil on canvas, 214.6 x 188.5 cm
London, Tate Gallery

## PETER BLAKE
*1932

Together with Hamilton, Blake was one of the
first to use the motifs and techniques that
were to shape English Pop Art. The style,
reminiscent of advertising graphics, and the
choice of daily mythologies as a pictorial motif
are the hallmarks of Pop Art. In spite of all
the innovation, however, Blake also retained
certain painterly elements.

The 1950s and 1960s were the heyday of
rock 'n' roll bands and stars. *Bo Diddley* was a
hit for Elias McDaniel, who adopted the title
of his smash hit as his stage name.

The painting is composed in the manner of
a poster, with a bright red edge and garish yellow lettering. The contours of the guitar and
the blue outline of the legs light up like thin
neon striplights, the instrument and the legs
are flat, as though they had been cut out. The
shimmering Havanna brown of the background has a subtle, painterly quality. The
body language of the singer is vivaciously
lively. His facial expression reflects his total
devotion to music, and might even be described as a physiognomic study. *Bo Diddley* is
more than just a poster: it is the individual
portrait of the singer at his work. In other
paintings, Blake projects a critical, detached
attitude and an almost ironic approach to the
material.

## ALLEN JONES
*1937

Jones' motifs almost invariably address erotic
themes. Within this genre, he always remains
on a very direct and even drastic level, although he varies his motifs and works in different techniques. Jones is one of the most significant representatives of English Pop Art of
the 1960s. This explains certain basic elements in his choice, composition and statement of motifs. Eroticism is not seen here as
the sophisticated fulfilment of an individual
life, but is degraded to mere sex – just another
consumer article amongst many. Like everything that can be consumed, even sex has
taken on its own symbols and clichés in the
simplified yet highly effective visual language
of advertising and mass media.

In *Man Woman* Jones echoes this *cliché*. A
long, female leg, stockinged and high-heeled,
the hint of a skirt that has ridden up, a tie,
part of a man's suit, headless and so flat that
it seems bodiless; all these features conjure up
an unequivocal situation. There is something
banale and vulgar about the entire scene, but
it is not without humour. Although Jones
uses simple visual means, the painterly execution of the picture prevents a sense of embarrassment in the face of such an intimate
presence.

## RICHARD HAMILTON

*1922

From the beginning of his artistic career in the 1950s, Richard Hamilton used technical achievements in the field of visual arts. Photographs are a fundamental and important element in many of his works. Hamilton ranks amongst the leading representatives of English Pop Art. The special visual language of the media and advertising is attacked in his work, and he rails against the banal and trivial existence of the masses. His artistic statements on the spirit of the times are aimed at an audience beyond the already interested group of specialists.

On some universal beach, seen from a distant standpoint, bathers swarm like ants. The picture has been created on the basis of a postcard, sprayed over and transposed to the canvas in a complicated reproduction process. In doing so, the documentary aspect of the picture is called into question. The garish bathing accessories, a bathing-cap and a piece of flowered fabric that seem all the more garish set against the dreary colours of the actual bathing-scene, remind us of the business of pleasure and leisure that has taken on ever increasing dimensions in the world of mass tourism. Everyday images and objects, combined anew, add an absurd accent to the apparently normal.

**Richard Hamilton**
Bathers I, 1966/67
Photo on canvas, bathing-cap and textile,
84 x 117 cm. Cologne, Museum Ludwig

## DAVID HOCKNEY

*1937

The English painter David Hockney is fascinated by California. Time and time again he draws his motifs from this American coastal state. Where California is densely populated, landscape and nature become little more than a backdrop of secondary importance, destroyed by far-reaching interventions. Streets, architectural complexes and leisure areas predominate, imposed on the environment by man's unceasing need to make his mark. The epitome of Californian lifestyle and comfort is the bungalow with swimming-pool.

A flat-roofed bungalow with a glass wall, in which the buildings and palm trees opposite are mirrored, a long strip of patio, in front of which is a large swimming-pool, all set against the lucid background of a cloudless blue sky. Someone has just dived into the pool from the springboard in the foreground right; all we see is the spray of water. The chair in front of the house in empty: splendid isolation. An atmosphere of traumatic calm and unreality is briefly interrupted by the splash. The sense of cool artificiality is heightened by the static, planar, horizontal and vertical composition and by the powdery pale, subtle colours. The small strip of grass and the palm trees have remained as codes for nature.

**David Hockney**  A Bigger Splash, 1967
Acrylic on canvas, 243.8 x 243.8 cm
London, Tate Gallery

**Richard Estes**
Candy Store, 1969
Oil on canvas, 121.3 x 174 cm
New York, Whitney Museum of American Art

## RICHARD ESTES
*1936

Estes adopts spontaneous situations in modern cities which, completely devoid of human presence, take on an aura of chill isolation. The glass window-front of a coffee-shop, with a view through the entrance door into the interior and the huge display window, is the trivial subject of this painting. Nuts and candies, presented on several layers, have been displayed in the window as a "picture within a picture" set behind glass in a metal frame, illuminated by neon strip-lighting. It is a confusing play of mirroring and reflections from the interior and from the opposite side of the street that ironically adds a touch of life to this huge, unpeopled still life.

The painting presents the spectral presence of a highly civilized subculture that pays homage to the fetish of consumption, viewed from a safe distance as though through a glass darkly. This kind of painting plays on the perceptions and observations of the viewer. It heightens the motifs, charging them with tension, filling them with light and shadow, reflections, mirroring, prismatic refraction and lending them an intensity that would never actually be found in such concentrated form in the real world. Throughout the painting, we find visual tension and overlapping levels of reality that arrest the viewer's gaze and provoke reflection on the situation.

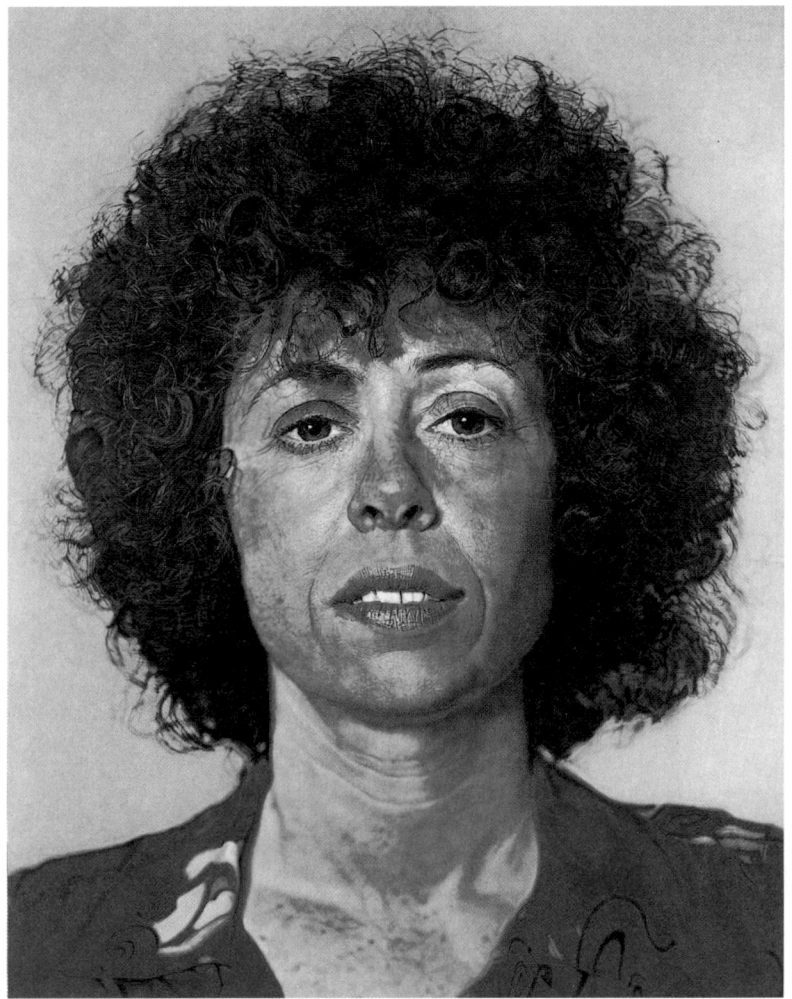

**Chuck Close**
Linda, 1975/76
Acrylic on canvas,
274.3 x 213.4 cm
Akron (OH), Akron
Art Museum

## CHUCK CLOSE
*1940

Chuck Close drew the attention of the critics for the first time in 1967 with his large, realistic black and white paintings: frontal portrayals of heads, like a kind of oversized passport photo, in the form of a painting on canvas. Though he remained true to his subject, he soon went on to paint in colour. *Linda* is staring directly at the viewer, as though into the lens of a photo booth, which coldly reproduces the facial traits, curly hair, lines and freckles, and the collar and shoulders of the dress. Although the painting is in colour, it does not seem realistic. Its photographic realism lies in the reiteration of the reddish-brown tone so frequently found in photos that are developed by automatic processes.

Close's paintings are created according to a grid system by which he divides a photo into zones of light and shade and then transposes the grid onto the canvas. He applies the paints by hand, but adds blue, yellow and red layers over his backgrounds as in a technical printing process. Close's paintings are related both to Pop Art and to Photo-Realism. His interest lies, as he claims himself, in not painting in a certain style. The technical process of painting and the photographic motif also place his work close to the field of minimal art.

# FRANZ GERTSCH

\*1930

The art created by Gertsch is often described as Hyper-Realism or Photo-Realism; in Europe. He is one of the best-known and most consistent representatives of this style. The monumental painting *Medici* shows a group of casually dressed young people standing behind a red and white wooden barrier. The title, reminiscent of the former, powerful Tuscan dynasty, merely refers to the word that can be read on the white stripe of the painted barrier.

Although Gertsch works with slides, his paintings are not simply photographs transposed to the canvas. Even at the moment of photographing, he consciously chooses the motif, the detail and the lighting. When he transposes his hugely enlarged projections onto the canvas, he remains true to the original in terms of pictorial composition, but he also undertakes some major changes. The viewer is likely to notice these changes only after lengthy observation, and the painting thus takes on the signum of an original and an almost shocking proximity: emphasis or transfiguration of colority and brushwork can vary the intensity of the painting, and in its extreme close-up view it seems to penetrate into the real space beyond the frame.

**Franz Gertsch**
Medici, 1971
Dispersionsfarbe on canvas, 400 x 600 cm
Aachen, Ludwig Forum

# ARNULF RAINER

\*1929

As early as 1951, Rainer turned his back on the fantastic realism of his early years. He was more interested in the painterly process of the composition of paintings and the potential for formal destruction. From 1952 onwards, he explored so-called "centralizations" and "central compositions"; in these compositions, the line is the point of departure. The paintings are an expressive accumulation of arbitrary strokes. One year later, he began photographing himself and then painting over these photos. Overpainting is a focal point in Rainer's works.

From 1969 onwards, Rainer began exploring the question of body language. During this period, his first "grimacing" photos were created, and accentuated by overpainting. *Zünglein ohne Waage* is one of a series of heavily reworked grimacing photos, and its strangely punning title (paraphrasing the German saying "Zünglein an der Waage" which means "the little tongue that tips the scales" in the sense of "holding the balance of power") places it close to the world of Surrealist art. All that is left of the photo is the face in soft focus. All the other parts have been aggressively overpainted, and the paint is dripping down the canvas. Rainer also seeks inspiration in hallucinatory mind-altering substances, and in art created by the mentally ill.

**Arnulf Rainer**
Zünglein ohne Waage (Tongue that tips no scales), 1975
Oil on photo on panel, 44.5 x 60.5 cm
Private collection

**Balthus**
The Artist and his Model, 1980/81
Oil on canvas, 227 x 235 cm
Paris, Musée d'Art Moderne, Centre Georges Pompidou

## BALTHUS
*1908

This painting by Balthus, whose full name is Balthasar Klossowski de Rola, is a late work of great maturity and serenity. Even in his twenties, the artist had created images of enormous intensity which he continued to use and perfect. In some of his landscapes and portraits, this purely artistic mastery appears to be predominant in the subtle handling of colour and light and in the reduction of forms heightened by colour structuring. Most of his paintings, however, especially those featuring his key motif – the young girl approaching womanhood – but also some of his street scenes, still lifes and portraits, have a distinctly erotic tension. In the paintings of Caravaggio, for example, Balthus saw the arousal of desire and latent violence as a metamorphosis of Eros.

This mood is now sublimated in an atmosphere whose tension is transposed to the realms of the enigmatic and allegorical. The model no longer beguiles with her maturing charms, and does not arouse any corrupting impulses. With the countenance of a Renaissance madonna, the girl is completely immersed in her reading. The painter, with his back to her, is contemplative and moderate.

**Fernando Botero**  The Family of the President, 1967
Oil on canvas, 203.2 x 195.5 cm
New York, The Museum of Modern Art

## FERNANDO BOTERO
*1932

In a freely paraphrased version of Francisco de Goya's painting *The Family of Charles IV* of 1800 (ill. p.400) showing all the members of the ruling house of Bourbon on a large, broad canvas, Botero has created his *Family of the President*. Goya's painting is far more than just a group portrait. It is a shocking indictment of the social mores of the day, critical and ironic to the point of mordant sarcasm, due to the sheer technical brilliance of his realism. Like the incorruptible eye of the camera, which neither flatters nor omits, Goya uses a fine brush to present all the figures as they really are.

Unlike Goya, Botero's *Family of the President* is not intended as a portrait. It could be the presidential family of any country. Yet criticism, irony and sarcasm are evidently directed at these powerful representatives who have taken the place of former monarchs with similar powers and aims. Botero uses his own methods to portray this. His stylistic means of alienation of blowing up all the figures and objects gives them a doll-like stiffness, and an exaggerated presence. The bishop and the saluting dictator or general are revealed as parasites like the others in the painting. They have their tasks and pursue them entirely for their own ends.

# WERNER TÜBKE

*1929

One of the ideals that Tübke sought to express in his art is the dignity of humankind. This theme was addressed by the Renaissance philosopher Pico della Mirandola in a text that remains valid today. Tübke is not only interested in the spiritual approach of this great era; his painting is also oriented towards the masters of the past: Mantegna, Titian, Veronese, Caravaggio, van Eyck, Bruegel, Bosch, Dürer, Cranach and Grünewald. He has painted the *Livestock Brigadier Bodlenkov* – a man who has earned his laurels for a socialist planned economy and is therefore deserving of a portrait, even of a museum place, just as an Old Master would have painted him.

This hero of the people sits in the saddle like a *condottiere*, on a horse that might have been painted by the brush of Verrocchio, surrounded by dogs that could be taken from the ceremonial procession of some Burgundian duke, and set against a meticulously painted background landscape filled with details, stretching into the far distance, reminiscent of a universal landscape of the 16th century. Tübke has said of himself that he has no sense of historical distance and that he means to "bring periods of art history to life productively and realitically". An important aspect of his art is therefore the exemplary presentation of active persons faced with a difficult fate.

Werner Tübke
Portrait of the Libvestock
Brigadier Bodlenkov, 1962
Mixed media on canvas on
panel, 145.5 x 97 cm
Leipzig, Museum der bildenden
Künste

# BERNHARD HEISIG

*1925

Heisig's major influences are Beckmann, Dix, Corinth, Kokoschka and Picasso, who, in parts of their oeuvre, accusingly present the horrors of this world. Heisig's figures are deformed, disfigured, injured, like all the objects in his paintings. His imagery is provocative, strident, brash.

Even paintings with a non-political content – portraits, nudes, landscapes – betray his awareness of a fragmented world. Heisig's painterly technique, like his colours and his symbolism, is accordingly expressive. He paints the same scenes over and over again, lending them a new form according to the insights gained from new angles. He often returns to work on paintings he had already considered finished.

The motif from Goethe's poem *Der Zauberlehrling* (The Sorcerer's Apprentice) was already familiar as a parable in the days of classical Antiquity and was handed down by Lucian. Heisig's *Zauberlehrling,* however, unlike the figure in Goethe's poem, cannot expect his antics to end well. Here, we see the tragic point of the poem: "The spirits I invoked . . ." They are the evil spirits of war, of terror, fascism and violence. Even the most powerful master cannot undo what has been done.

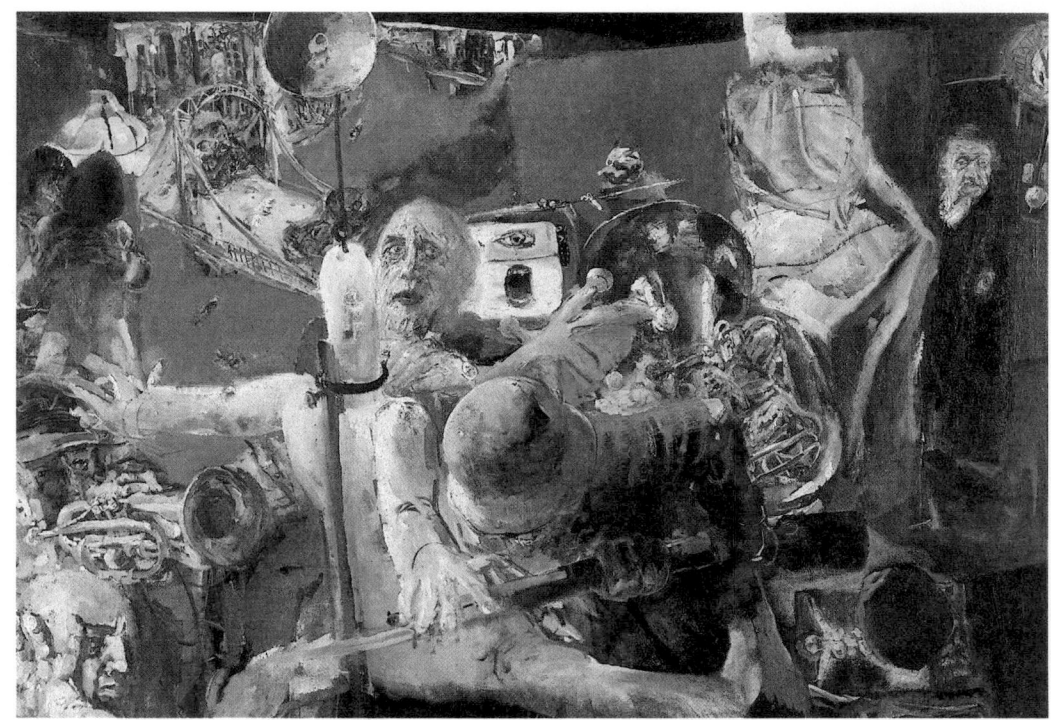

Bernhard Heisig
The Sorcerer's Apprentice (second version),
1978–1981
Oil on canvas, 150 x 200 cm
Private collection

**Renato Guttuso**
Wall of News – May 1968, 1968
Oil on cardboard on canvas, 280 x 480 cm
Aachen, Ludwig Forum

# RENATO GUTTUSO
## 1912–1987

Long before he began to paint (1931) Guttuso
was a convinced socialist. In his painting, he
returned time and time again to such bold
themes as fascism, war and the power of the
church. Trained by the Futuristic artist Pippo
Rizzo, he has adopted several stylistic ways of
expressing his ideas. His early work leans heavily on Futurism and Cubism, later turning to
a more expressive imagery.

For his *Wall of News – May 1968* he has
chosen as his basis a collection of realistic
motifs, that are reduced to poster-like symbols and arranged in a dynamically charged
composition. The signs of inexorable power
are glass skyscrapers, wrecked cars, furniture
and machine parts scattered across the painting. It is the flotsam and jetsam of Western
civilization. At the bottom of the picture, we
see a group of armed police moving in closed
ranks, brandishing their riot shields against a
group of demonstrators. Below them is the
caricature of a status symbol, a white sports-
car, next to which we see a procession bearing red flags.

In the upper part of the picture, we see the
horrors of Vietnam and the violence of whites
against blacks. These are the events of 1968
evoked by Guttuso in this socially committed
painting.

**Mimmo Paladino**
Ronda Notturna (Nightwatch), 1982
Oil on canvas, 300 x 400 cm
Munich, Städtische Galerie im Lenbachhaus

# MIMMO PALADINO
## *1948

Paladino's oeuvre contains a wide range of expressive possibilities, uniting apparently contradictory elements. His paintings are abstract
and figurative at the same time, pure paintings as well as assemblages with relievo character and three-dimensionality, what should
really be described as sculptures.

The title of his monumental painting
*Nightwatch* is a more or less coincidental reference to Rembrandt's famous painting in
the Rijksmuseum, Amsterdam (ill. p. 313).
Paladino's *Ronda notturna* is not quite as easily legible as the Dutch painting of three centuries before, for its iconography is not subject to any convention. He invents codes,
figures and action according to his own subjective concept.

Paladino applies a number of different spatial interpretations in this painting. The
stylized couple in the pale, tent-like structure is keeping watch to ensure that the
perils and spirits of the night do not gain
the upper hand. The larger part of the painting is filled with flat, dislocated, weightlessly hovering bodies and fantastic creatures,
patterns and symbols. These are stylized references to the real world in which we can detect certain parallels with Ottonian and Romanesque art.

# ENZO CUCCHI
*1949

The hero has no face. The blood-red head with the red, swollen lips, has slipped down between his legs. He has raised his hands towards the black and flaming sky in a gesture of impotence, despair and accusation, like the praying gesture of classical Antiquity. Like Moses parting the waters of the Red Sea, he is himself caught between two threateningly close, high walls, one fiery yellow and red, the other gloomy black. He seems to have no influence or power over these forces, and is at the mercy of their inherent threat.

Cucchi, like Paladino and Clemente, has returned to the traditional medium of painting. Colour is used in an expressive, gestural painting as a material and colouristic element of strongly symbolic power. Layers of colour of enormous force, rough forms and emotionally charged simplicity give this picture its highly expressive syntax.

Cucchi's paintings are a reaction to the art forms of the 1960s and early 1970s which formed the basis on which a young generation of painters was able to build their work, albeit using their own forms of subjective and forcefully expressive visual language. His motifs explore personal feelings of threat, *angst* and aggression directed against the impotence of the individual.

**Enzo Cucchi**
Headless Hero, 1981/82
Oil on canvas, 203 x 255 cm
Private collection

# FRANCESCO CLEMENTE
*1952

Together with Mimmo Paladino, Enzo Cucchi and Sandro Chia, Clemente is one of the main representatives of new Italian painting. It is new in the sense that it has broken away from familiar directions such as politically committed painting or *arte povera*, and places more emphasis on the personality of the painter. The images speak eloquently for themselves.

The huge head in Clemente's painting conceals something mysterious. In the orifices – eyes, nose, ears and gaping mouth – we see chalk-white heads with fiery red lips. Heads within a head: the interpretation of this symbolism is left entirely to the spectator. The physical act of painting is not negated in the image; the rough and heavy brushwork is clearly evident, lending the composition its dramatic vitality. The view through the train window towards a green strip of landscape with a blue sky and the yellow interior with pillar, is reminiscent of Surrealist associations.

This painting does not attempt to create any connection with reality, but mirrors the inner realities of the painter, his states of mind, visions and imaginings. In formal terms, it tends towards expressive painting. The artist has deliberately eschewed carefully ordered brushwork and draughtsmanship.

**Francesco Clemente**
Untitled, 1983
Oil and wax on canvas, 200 x 236 cm
Private collection

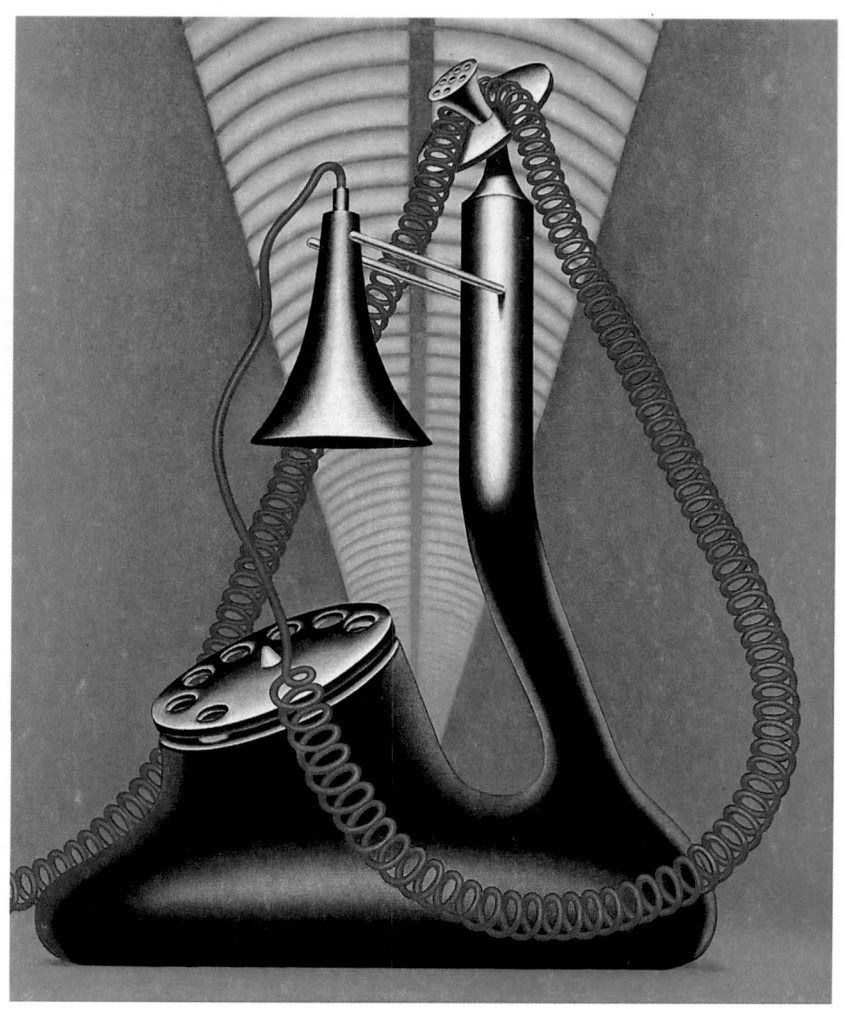

## KONRAD KLAPHECK
\*1935

Even as a student at the Düsseldorf art academy, Klapheck arrived at the themes and form of presentation so typical of his work and to which he has remained true until today. At the time, he saw his painting as an antithesis to the prevailing *informel*. Time and time again, he chooses to paint machinery and technical objects, smoothly schematized, and stylized into monuments. A relatively limited repertoire of everyday objects takes on an independent and almost symbolic statement in Klapheck's visual world. Liberated from their functionality and the cycle of use, in brilliantly sober portraiture, generally filling the entire picture space, and presented in close-up to the viewer, they take on a challenging and at times almost threatening presence.

Klapheck sees certain human aspects embodied in this material world: standardized types, male and female, typical situations and behaviour patterns. His titles trigger distinct associations and their subtly ironic references are also reminiscent of Marcel Duchamp and the Surrealists. Klapheck's lovingly lyrical view of these products from the lower spheres of technical banality links him with the magic realism of the 1920s.

**Konrad Klapheck**
The Mother's Prayers, 1984
Oil on canvas, 120 x 100 cm
Private collection

## SIGMAR POLKE
\*1941

The title sounds like an advertising slogan. In German, it not only rhymes ("Traum" = "dream" with "Schaum" = "foam") but also presents a pun on the word "Schaum" which can means either "foam" in the literal sense or "hot air" in the sense of meaningless hype. The sharp wit of the title indicates how it is to be interpreted. We see the outlines of two male heads, taken from a shaving cream advertisement, transposed as stencils onto a background of pink synthetic fur. Yellow, red, green and white patches of colour, drips and daubs, have been integrated energetically and irreverently into this strange ensemble.

In 1963, together with Gerhard Richter and Konrad Fischer, Polke founded the group Capitalist Realism, whose exhibition Leben mit Pop (Living with Pop) in a Düsseldorf furniture store called into question the mechanisms with which consumer society manipulates the individual. Polke continued to explore these themes in his later works. All his paintings and assemblages address the effects of the pseudo-comforts provided by mass production. With mordant irony, he confronts the viewer with the worst products of mass design kitsch, adopting synthetic fur, printed plastic film and patterned fabrics as his backgrounds. The contrast between these trivial materials and the motifs, gestures and slogans he presents on them, are invariably intended to create a shock effect.

**Sigmar Polke**
Remingtons Museums-Traum ist des Besuchers Schaum, 1979
Oil and spray technique, stencils, on pink synthetic fur, 212 x 135.5 cm
Bonn, Städtisches Kunstmuseum

GERMANY

# GERHARD RICHTER
*1932

In the early 1960s, around the same time as the American Pop artists, Gerhard Richter was painting images from illustrated magazines: grey in grey, slightly blurred, he transposed these images to the canvas. He was interested in gaining the pictorial worlds of the mass media for art. However, unlike his American contemporaries, he was interested less in such phenomena as star cult or sensationalism as in the banality to which the media reduce images of all kinds. He wanted to transfer the neutrality and indifference reflected in the media onto his oil-paintings. Often, he would also adopt the captions from the illustrated magazines in order to make the original context clear.

Later, Richter also sought to apply this principle of transposal to paintings created according to other models. In this way, he also created paintings based on private family snapshots or the sample charts of the paint industry. His *Mountains (Himalaya)* raises the question of the character of images and their relation to reality with direct reference to the medium of oil-painting. The image of nature is transformed in painting, for on closer inspection of this large canvas, the areas of rock and snow dissolve into fields of black, white or grey that might just as well be abstract.

Richter works in series, returning time and time again to the same motifs, which he often repeats. In addition to a series of monochromatic grey paintings, he has also created a large cycle of generally large-scale paintings with some resemblance to the expressive gestural painting of the post-war years. These neo-abstract paintings are executed in garish acrylic paints. The abstract imagery regarded in the 1950s as the expression of artistic personality is now used by Richter to create coldly calculated effects, as he explains himself: "The overall effect then looks very spontaneous. However, there are generally lengthy periods in-between that destroy an atmosphere. It is a very carefully planned spontaneity." Richter exploits all the potential and possibilities of paint – from fine brushstroke to sprayed-on colour or paint smeared with a cloth and even raked – in order to create highlights of enormous subtlety that defy reproduction.

It took a relatively long time for Gerhard Richter to achieve international recognition. In the USA, especially, his work met with incomprehension. The constant change of motif and working techniques created a climate of insecurity that has been allayed by the major retrospective exhibitions of recent years. Today, the question of image and reproduction, reality and portrayal, addressed in all his series, is more clearly evident.

**Gerhard Richter**
Mountains (Himalaya), 1968
Oil on canvas,
199.5 x 159.5 cm
Private collection

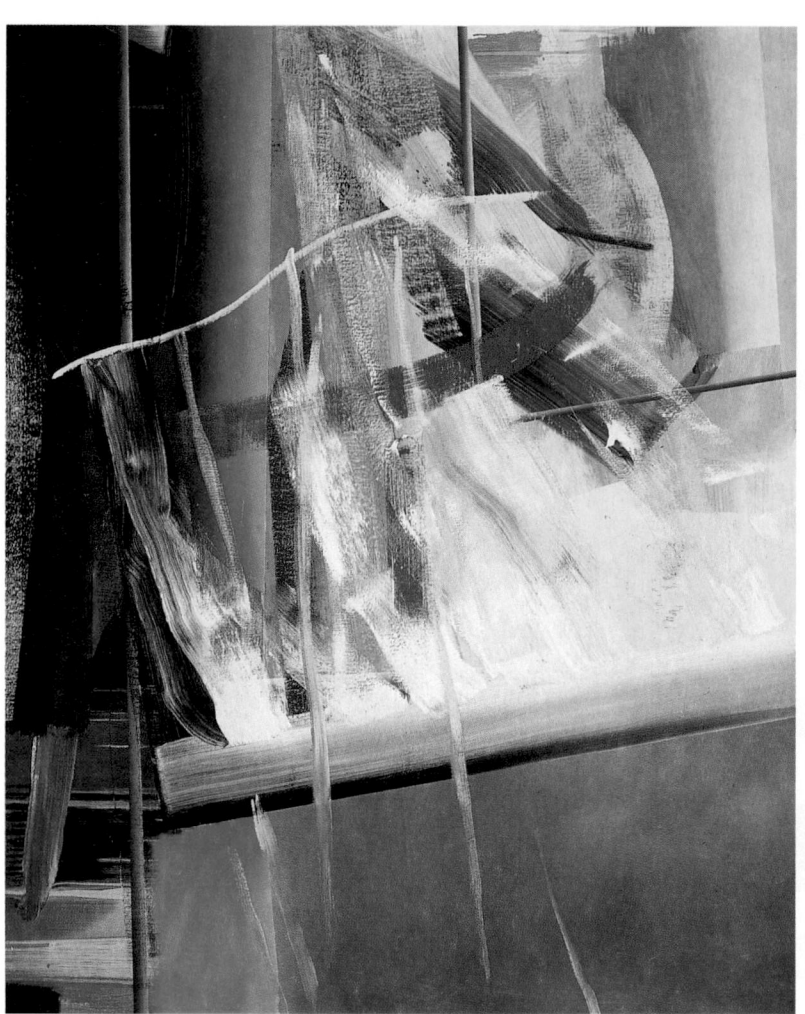

**Gerhard Richter**
Untitled, 1984
Oil on canvas,
200.7 x 160.3 cm
Private collection

**Markus Lüpertz**
Babylon-dithyrambic VI, 1975
Distemper on canvas, 162 x 130 cm
Galerie Michael Werner, Cologne and New York

# MARKUS LÜPERTZ
*1941

Together with Georg Baselitz and Jörg Immendorf, Markus Lüpertz ranks as one of the "new masters" of German painting, who studiously copies the approach of such 19th century artists as Makart and Lenbach. Apart from an almost imperial and thoroughly choreographed public projection, this involves the creation of large-scale paintings in which highly significant gestures indicate momentous phenomena. *Babylon-dithyrambic VI* is one of a series of works all bearing the same title, with which Lüpertz concluded his phase of dithyrambic paintings between 1963 and 1976. The choice of title indicates his painterly approach, evoking a Nietzschean reference and thematizing the sacrifical ode to the god Dionysos.

All the paintings of this period feature voluminous, sculptural objects with simple structures. Lüpertz related these pictorial symbols to the archaic ode. Towering entities formed of letters of the alphabet soar monumentally into a blue sky. The motif of the ornamental skyscraper with its abstract brushwork, decorative ornaments and stripes is linked to alphabetic signs that form the roof of the tower. These motifs belong to different linguistic levels or registers. Lüpertz attempts to combine writing and object by painterly means.

**A. R. Penck**  The Birth of Mike Hammer, 1974
Acrylic on canvas, 285 x 285 cm. Basle, Öffentliche
Kunstsammlung Basel, Museum für Gegenwartskunst

# A. R. PENCK
*1939

Mike Hammer is one of the pseudonyms adopted by Penck. The painting of the same name illustrates the birth of the figure of a painter who uses a pseudonym. Penck has always been in search of an anti-style that runs against the grain of fashionable prevailing tastes or intellectual standards. In order to paint realistically, he wanted to break illusionism as a painterly style. Penck is a critical thinker, constantly in opposition to the dominant system. In his painting, he invariably endeavours to achieve the pure realisation of his idea.

He does not see the ground of his painting as a smooth surface, but as a field centred with lines of energy. The simple signs with which he constructs his paintings are often aligned around a central axis according to an evaluation of the individual elements in the picture. The individual codes are selected in such a way that they appear as pairs of opposites in the painting, subjected to an inherent axiality that determines the horizontal format of the image.

The signs and codes are reduced and condensed so that they create a general concept of objects and figure, which Penck calls "standard". This "standard" provides the possibility of repetition. Accordingly, signs from this painting can also be found in his other paintings.

# GEORG BASELITZ
## *1938

The *Family Portrait* is upside-down. Looking at it in the way it is intended to be seen abruptly breaks the mould of habitual ways of seeing. The second shock comes when the spectator realises the discrepancy between the title, evoking traditional concepts of portraiture, and content: a naked couple representing the family. Since around 1969, Baselitz has been painting landscapes and figures upside-down. In doing so, he consciously seeks to change traditional ways of seeing, and does not attempt to make things easy for himself or the viewers of his paintings. At the same time, he creates a distinctive hallmark that has established his reputation on the international art market: Baselitz has become synonymous with upside-down painting. He does not draw his themes from the field of easy entertainment, nor does he simplify his objects or aestheticise them in order to ensure "easy viewing".

Georg Baselitz works with purely painterly means. His influences are the Mannerist painters and the school of Fontainebleau. Through his close study of 1950s *tachisme*, he arrived at a subjective figurative painting. He draws upon dynamically gestural form of expressions and employs a frequently brutal rawness and distortion in order to present his themes and motifs in a way that is highly unsettling.

The starting point of *Ciao America I* was a woodcut Baselitz had made for the fortieth anniversary of the Springer gallery in Berlin. For each of the forty years, as he reports, he carved one more bird in the panel: "There are forty or more birds, but because they are upside-down and consist only of lines, patches and fragments of bright colour flashing through the black surface, it is difficult to tell that these are birds and how many of them there are." In transposing this motif to the canvas, he retained the black background, but heavily reduced the number of birds, capturing them within a grid-like network of colour. The choice of motif is relatively arbitrary; Baselitz' work is geared towards traditional themes of European painting, but he radically denies any interest in his pictorial motifs: "The problem is not the object in the picture, the problem is the picture as object. And the question of what is being dealt with here, whether it is a chair or a cube or a portrait, is simply not an issue." In recent years, he has thus been able to create works that lean heavily on the forms of the abstract painting of the 1950s. In this way, Baselitz not only indicates that these paintings are already an acknowledged part of the history of painting, but also attempts to take his "painting about painting" into new dimensions. Whereas the figurative motifs of his paintings had previously been intended as a means of ensuring that his work did not fall into the trap of arbitrary subjectivism, he now sought to protect his work from purely decorative effects through his brushwork and his handling of colour.

**Georg Baselitz**
Family Portrait,
1975
Oil on canvas,
250 x 200 cm
Cassel, Staatliche
Kunstsammlungen, Neue Galerie

Georg Baselitz  Ciao America I, 1988
Oil on canvas, 250 x 200 cm
Washington, Hirshhorn Museum and Sculpture Garden

**Anselm Kiefer**
Bilderstreit (Iconoclastic Controversy), 1979
Oil on canvas, 220 x 300 cm
Eindhoven, Stedelijk van Abbemuseum

## ANSELM KIEFER

*1945

*Bilderstreit* (Iconoclastic Controversy) is a theme of enormous cultural and historical importance. Is it possible to create an image of divinity and to worship the imaged god in this way? This question serves Kiefer merely as a foil for his own interpretation of the Iconoclastic Controversy. He is interested primarily in the harrowing consequences of this theological and philosophical dispute which did not stop at rhetorical argument; he addresses the madness of war, which is a central and ever present theme in his work. His paintings are not designed as large-scale narratives, nor does he seek to present the position of the iconoclasts or image worshippers.

His *Bilderstreit* is an "image of burnt earth", an image of devastation, of brutal destruction – the invariable consequences of war, irrespective of whether it was a holy war or one conducted on baser grounds. Against the torn and scorched earth, the outlines of modern tanks are painted in white, the colour of peace, as are the names of those who were involved in the Iconoclastic Controversy that raged in the By-

zantine Empire in the 8th and 9th centuries: Theophilos, Photius, John of Damascus, Theodos Studites, Leo III, Artavasdos, Theoctistos, Theodora, Staurakios, Theodoros Melissenos. Added to the list are the names Doris and Charles Saatchi, collectors of ultra-modern art in London. In the centre is the outline of a palette, the embodiment of "art" as a field of energy.

Kiefer's paintings are a blend of landscape and history paintings. Landscape and earth signify unspoiled nature for Kiefer, remodelled by humankind into a landscape of culture and imbued with historical implications. Here, it is the earth destroyed by the horrors of war.

Kiefer does not seek to portray outward appearances, even in his images of interiors. What he shows is invariably intended as a metaphor or codification, triggering some impulse. The colours, too, have a symbolic significance in the work of Kiefer, capable of triggering atmosphere and emotion. His images invariably focus on the past that has already been experienced and suffered. It has left its traces – the traces of death, violence and destruction. His images are not direct accusations. Nevertheless, they set thought processes in motion that must necessarily bring some insight.

# MARTIN KIPPENBERGER
1953–1997

Kippenberger is one of the representatives of a generation of artists whose initial success came in the early 1980s in the wake of the *Neue Wilden* painting. His concept of art differs fundamentally from that of his colleagues, however, for his oeuvre is not limited to a single medium. Painting, drawing, sculpture and photography make reciprocal comments, with the artist invariably taking up central themes of his work in various techniques. In this context, painting is only one of several forms of expression, whose potential and possibilities the artist calls into question conceptually. Kippenberger avoids a personal painterly style; he sees art history as a storehouse of forms, universally available and compatible.

Heute denken – morgen fertig (Think today – finished tomorrow) painted in 1983 is typical of Kippenberger's oeuvre. A modern artist in this sense is concerned less with questions of detail than with central statements translated into painting. A marionette of the kind that painters use for anatomic studies is subjected to this pragmatic approach that grasps painting as a means to an end. Kippenberger, a self-styled "non-painter" once claimed: "I am more like a salesman. Sell and negotiate ideas. I am far more to people than someone who paints pictures."

# ALBERT OEHLEN
*1954

Albert Oehlen belongs to a generation of artists who rediscovered painting at the end of the 1970s in a kind of counter-reaction to conceptual art. Together with Werner Büttner (*1954) he founded the Liga zur Bekämpfung des widersprüchlichen Verhaltens (League to Combat Contradictory Behaviour) in 1978. His early paintings are thematically provocative, his brushwork rapid, but highly virtuoso. He seems to feel that everything and anything can be painted, from a garden fence (*Fence*, 1982) to *Four Suitcases* (1991). In 1984, he created his first *Mirror Images* in which the artist applies fragments of mirror onto the canvas and works them in to the surface structure of his painting. By mirroring the ambient space in his painting, Oehlen takes an ironic attitude to the maxims of abstract Expressionism which allow the viewer to enter the painting. Over the years, Oehlen has increasingly turned away from reality and has developed the abstract paintings so typical of his oeuvre. *Untitled* is characteristic of this development. The painting consists of three canvases which the artist has joined together. As a basis, he has chosen to use printed fabrics that remain visible in the background. In garish colours, he paints against the stridency of the fabric patterns. The illusory space of the picture is systematically deconstructed by asserting the presence of the fabric patterns in places and completely covering them with forms and colours in other places.

**Martin Kippenberger**
Heute denken – morgen fertig, 1983
Oil on canvas, 160 x 133 cm
Private collection

**Albert Oehlen**
Untitled, 1983
Oil on canvas, 240 x 240 cm
Private collection

## ROBERT RYMAN
*1930

Starting anew time after time, Robert Ryman explores the elements that are indispensable for the creation of a painting and essential to it. His work is generally classified as minimal art, and his paintings can certainly be described as minimalist.

Ryman reduced his field of exploration gradually to square, white paintings. Because he regards the painting as an autonomous object, he has also devoted considerable energy to exploring the possibilities of affixing it to the wall. He has designed holders that become a constitutive part of the work itself and keep the painting at a distance from the wall, thereby emphasising the independence and autonomy of his paintings. In barely varied series, he underlines the significance of each pictorial component.

The application of paint is of key importance. Ryman's brushwork is geared entirely to the width of the brush and its capacity to absorb paint. He generally avoids completely covering the canvas with paint. The canvas often shimmers through as a contrast to the colour. The almost meditative act of painting can be experienced by the viewer who views the original, as there are no additional elements or content to distract from it.

**Robert Ryman** Summit, 1978
Oil on canvas with metal holders, 191.7 x 183 cm
Private collection

## CY TWOMBLY
*1929

The time Twombly spent at the Black Mountain College was of enormous importance to his artistic development. His teachers there included Motherwell and Kline, and his fellow-students included Rauschenberg. All of his later works, including the series *Pan,* consisting of seven paintings of equal size, mirror the elements that he chose to include in his art at that time.

Like his teachers, who were abstract Expressionists, Twombly does not portray figurative motifs. On a monochrome background, he scratches or paints in swift and energetic brushstrokes or crayon strokes in what might be described as a "scribble". In spite of this completely abstract visual language, Twombly's titles have a reference to reality, albeit a reality that is to be grasped intellectually, as embodied by Pan, the Greek god of the fields and woods.

Twombly's paintings invariably follow a previously thought-out concept and are subject to the strict rules of an inherent law. In his work, line has a significant function. Like Paul Klee, he regards this element as a persuasive means of presenting movement and, therefore, time. His main aim has always been to express time and movement in an imaginary space. He uses colour very sparingly.

Cy Twombly
Pan (part four), 1980
Mixed media on paper in seven parts, 132.5 x 150 cm
Private collection

UNITED STATES

# JEAN-MICHEL BASQUIAT
1960–1988

Basquiat had already achieved some local fame as a graffiti artist in New York before he began to transpose his abbreviated pictorial codes to canvas. His cryptograms, or tags, were scattered throughout the city under the pseudonym Samo, particularly in the subway. Basquiat came from a socially under-privileged background.

He was one of a generation of artists of the black and Hispanic ethnic minorities who began to break down the social barriers in the early 1980s and established themselves on the art scene. Unlike many other graffiti stars, Basquiat never gave up his social critique or his artistic protest.

*ISBN* contains a rich repertoire of paint traces, figural fragments, written fragments and collage elements. The black skull with the rasta hair that Basquiat has placed in a prominent position, is evidently a self-portrait. Other pictorial fragments are borrowed from the language of comics, and the small pictorial narratives in the painting tell of the popular myths of American culture. However, Basquiat also includes the art history of the 20th century. His paintings bear a remarkable affinity to the images of Cy Twombly and the *art brut* of Jean Dubuffet.

Jean Michel
Basquiat
ISBN, 1985
Acrylic and collage
on canvas,
218.5 x 172.7 cm
Private collection

# KEITH HARING
1958–1990

Of all the graffiti artists, Haring was the most consistent in seeking to link "low" popular street culture with the "high" art of galleries and museums. His more or less traditional training at several art schools gave him a solid grounding in his craft, and he combined these techniques in his images with the new stylistic characteristics he was obliged to adopt in order to spray as rapidly as possible on walls and subway trains. Haring preferred to use large, codified pictorial elements, ensuring easy legibility and rapid recognition of motifs. Like the Pop artists of the 1960s, he frequently drew his motifs from the trivial myths of American urban life. Unlike the Pop artists, however, he did not merely quote. Comic figures such as Mickey Mouse are modified by Haring and adopted into a highly personal symbolic system in which the artist critically questions political and social problems in the USA. Haring commented on such phenomena as idol worship, mass protest and mass phenomena. His decorative talent was never limited to conventional canvases alone, and his symbols were soon to be found on all manner of everyday objects. Haring himself had become a star, and, glorified by his early death, achieved a cult-following for several years.

Keith Haring
Untitled (M. Mouse), 1985
Acrylic on canvas, 296 x 364 cm
Private collection

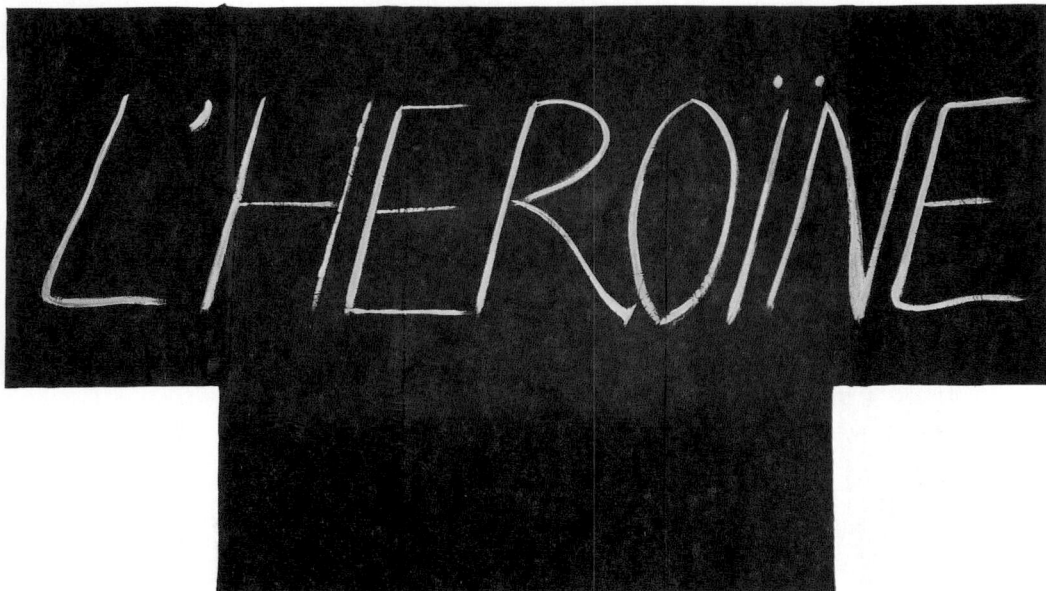

**Julian Schnabel**
L'Heroïne, 1987
Gesso on tarpaulin, 259 x 457 cm
Private collection

## JULIAN SCHNABEL
*1951

Schnabel's paintings often possess the sculptural quality of a relief. Unusual materials and found objects, from broken plates and straw to antlers, are applied to painterly backgrounds which themselves are frequently beyond the pale of the conventional artistic canon. Schnabel paints and creates collages on velvet, animal skins, Oriental rugs and sackcloth. The paintings are often of enormous dimensions, in garish colours, with calculated, hard-hitting effects. He draws his pictorial themes from American popular culture and from the European world of mythology, drawing them together with elements of expressive abstract art.

L'Heroïne is one of a series of fourteen *Cognition* paintings which introduced a new phase in his oeuvre. He named them after a novel by the American writer William Gaddis and exhibited them for the first time in 1987/88 in a ruined Carmelite monastery in Sevilla. The form of the cross is a reference to the stations of the cross which Schnabel "spells" as in a monumental piece of graffiti, with the names of saints, mysics and monks. The background is made of found tarpaulins from military trucks, whose rough structure, stains, rips and seams are painted with large codified forms like the war banners of the early modern era.

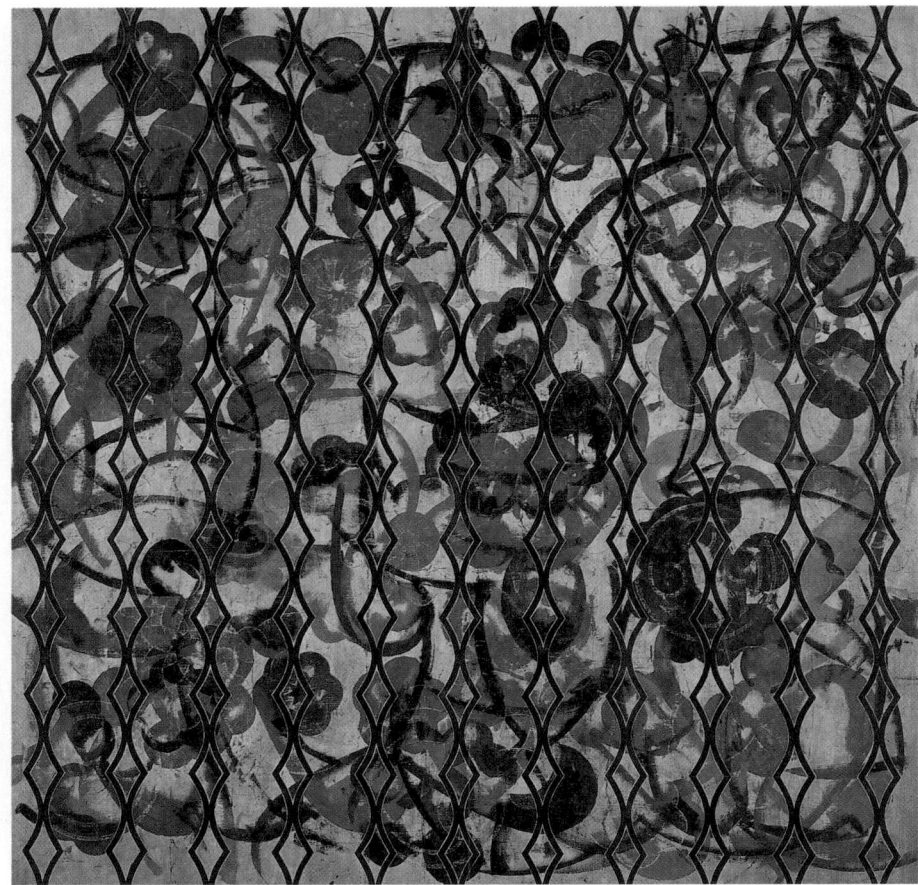

**Philipp Taaffe**  Conflagration, 1991
Mixed media on canvas, 290 x 293 cm
Private collection

## PHILIP TAAFFE
*1955

Taaffe lives in New York and sometimes on the Gulf of Naples. This clash of cultural influences has had an enormous impact on his more recent works. Whereas his American paintings can be seen as a direct exploration of abstract Expressionism, the work he created in Italy is a symbiosis of western painting and Arabic ornament. The source of inspiration is the specific atmosphere of Naples, which, in the course of history, has provided fertile soil for many different cultures. In Taaffe's paintings, we constantly find borrowings from a variety of eras, including Renaissance coats of arms, 19th century tile patterns and Saracen arabesques, collaged to created ornamental friezes. These historic fragments are still an important feature of the Neapolitan urban scene.

Generally taking the form of monotypes, these ornaments are printed on a canvas primed with various shades. The background fading and spatial logic of these patterns create a productive contrast that defines the tension in Taaffe's work. In *Conflagration* the indifference of the patinated canvas takes on an almost architectural order through the vertical garlands, calming the hectic interaction between foreground and background.

# APPENDIX

## ALBANI Francesco
1578 Bologna – 1660 Bologna

Although soon falling into oblivion after his death, Albani achieved considerable fame and prosperity during his lifetime. With Reni and Domenichino, he studied c. 1600 under Annibale Carracci in Rome. He assisted in decorating the Aldobrandi lynettes, designed the apse of Santa Maria della Pace in Rome and worked at the court of Mantua in 1621/22. In 1625 he settled in Bologna for good. He owed his reputation as the "Anacreon of painting" to his landscapes with staffage figures. They were mostly mythological, gently balanced, set in an arcadian landscape. He was rediscovered in the 20th century because his manner of representing nature is reminiscent of Poussin and Claude Lorrain.
*Illustration:*
233    Sacra Famiglia (The Holy Family),
       c. 1630–1635

## ALBERS Josef
1888 Bottrop – 1976 New Haven, Connecticut

After studying at the Berlin Academy 1913–1915, then at the College of Decorative Arts at Essen under Thorn-Prikker 1916–1920 and at Munich Academy under Franz von Stuck 1919/20, Albers continued his studies for another two years at the Weimar Bauhaus. In 1922 he took his final examinations, taught preparatory courses, supervised first the workshop for painted glass and then for furniture. In 1925 he became a Bauhaus master and married the artist Anneliese Fleischmann. In 1933 he was invited to the newly founded Black Mountain College in North Carolina where he taught until 1949, having giving an entire generation of American artists an insight into the ideals of the Bauhaus. His students included Motherwell, de Kooning and Rauschenberg.

From 1950 to 1960 he lectured in the Department of Design at Yale University School of Art, New Haven. He worked as visiting lecturer at many universities and institutes in America as well as at the College of Design in Ulm, Germany. As an influential art theoretician and teacher he wrote the book *Interaction of Colour* (1963), a School of Seeing. Albers, who had already turned to abstract art in 1920, became primarily known for his severe square-pictures, analysing problems of depth and colour in two-dimensional art which he called "Homage to the Square" from 1950 onwards. He is considered a precursor of Op Art and Minimal Art.
*Illustration:*
648    Study for "Homage to the Square": Star Blue, 1958

## ALLORI Cristofano
1577 Florence – 1621 Florence

Allori received his initial training from his father Alessandro, through whom he had contact with his uncle Bronzino. But it was through his teacher Gregorio Pagani that he found his direction, initially as a painter of religious subjects. Soon he also established himself as a painter of portraits and mythological scenes. While his output was somewhat sparse on account of the painstaking care he took in preparing and executing a painting, the result was always of an unvaryingly high quality. In "Judith with the Head of Holofernes" (ill., p.233), presumably a picture of his mistress and her mother, the rich materials vie with the deep, glowing colours and sensuous naturalness. Allori was a painter who overcame the cold stiffness in Florentine painting.
*Illustration:*
233    Judith with the Head of Holofernes, 1613

## ALTDORFER Albrecht
c. 1480 Regensburg (?) – 1538 Regensburg

Altdorfer is one of the most talented painters in the whole of German art. Although also a draughtsman and engraver, his importance lies in the field of coloured representation. Here, only Grünewald can be compared to him because all other contemporary painters were committed to the conventions of outline and drawing qualities. Altdorfer achieved, through his colour modulation, completely new ways of expression directed at the emotions. His tendency towards the "romantic" is particularly noticeable in his landscapes. Thus it was he who painted the first picture in European art that is purely a landscape ("Danube Landscape near Regensburg", Munich, Alte Pinakothek, c. 1530), and in many of his other paintings figure and landscape merge in such a way that the scenic becomes background ("St George in the Forest", Munich, Alte Pinakothek, 1510). Altdorfer, who travelled in the Alpine countries in 1510, became the leading light of the so-called "Danube School".

There is no actual proof that he went to Italy. This seems highly probable, however, when looking at his virtuoso handling of spatial construction in the St Florian passion altar panels (after 1510). In his later work Altdorfer moves towards Mannerism in his complex depiction of moving elements, the daring approach to depth and new handling of colour.

Nothing is known about the painter's formative years and early beginnings. There is evidence that in 1505 he lived in Regensburg, where he bought property in 1513. His election to the town council in 1519 and to the inner council in 1526 shows his good standing. At the same time he served as civic architect. There is no information about his architectural work, but it is possible that he was involved in the design of the pilgrim church "Zur Schönen Madonna" (now the new Neupfarrkirche) at Regensburg.
*Illustrations:*
192    The Agony in the Garden, c. 1515
192    Susanna at her Bath and The Stoning of the Old Men, 1526
193    Alexander's Victory (The Battle on the Issus), 1529

## ALTICHIERO DA ZEVIO
c. 1320/30 Zevio (near Verona) – c. 1385/90

Only a single work by Altichiero's own hand remains in Verona, but there are two series of large fresco paintings in Padua, both commissioned by the aristocratic family of Lupi during the years 1379 to 1384. Otherwise there is little known about this outstanding artist, who deserves to be better treated by posterity. Records show that he lived at Verona and Padua between 1379 and 1384.

Altichiero worked almost exclusively for the despotic rulers of northern Italy. His fame was established after working for the Scaliger family in Verona, who for half a century had been great patrons of the arts, taking in Dante and employing Giotto. Altichiero, although following the example of Giotto, differs from him in that he portrays groups more distinctly, even giving them individual features, while making single figures, including holy images, appear less heroic and monumental. He looks with cool detachment at human life and emotions. He found a new way of relating religious stories, not by changing the principal figures, but by close observation of the minor characters' reactions, which he renders almost dispassionately. This is a new kind of social realism; therefore the inclusion of portraits does not seem intrusive.
*Illustration:*
47     The Beheading of St George, c. 1382

## ANGELICO Fra
(Beato Angelico, Guido di Piero da Mugello, Fra Giovanni da Fiesole)
c. 1395–1400 Vicchio di Mugello (near Florence) – 1455 Rome

Angelico came from a well-to-do family and learned his craft from obscure painters and miniaturists. On completing his training he entered the Dominican monastery at Fiesole, between 1418 and 1421, where a strict rule was observed. This reformed branch of the Dominican order enhanced the prestige and intellectual importance of the order in the Tuscan region. Angelico held various offices as a friar, such as that of prior between 1450 and 1452. During his beatification process at the beginning of the 16th century it was claimed on various occasions that Fra Angelico was to have been appointed Archbishop of Florence in 1446 but that, at his own suggestion, the friar Antoninus (who was later canonised) was given the office. This suggests that the painter was by no means just a naive, contemplative monk, detached from reality. In 1436 Cosimo de'Medici left the San Marco monastery in Florence to the reformed Dominicans, using it as a private family chapel, and both the church and the monastery were restored at his expense. The architect Michelozzo added some new parts, including the famous library. Fra Angelico carried out the paintwork with the help of assistants between 1436 and 1445 and also after 1449. Angelico did not only undertake work for churches and monasteries of his own order, but was also some years in the service of the popes in Rome (the chapel of St Nicolas in the Vatican still remains) and in Orvieto where, according to records, he worked in 1447 with four assistants, amongst them Gozzoli.

Fra Angelico was a contemporary of Masaccio. Artistically, however, he tended towards the masters of the 14th century, such as Orcagna, and the somewhat older painters like Lorenzo Monaco and Gentile da Fabriano. With his advancing age the new discoveries of Masaccio and other young Florentines became detectable in his handling of light and the architectural severity of composition. With regard to figures and surroundings he upheld his deeply spiritualised ideal. This religious ideal of "sweetness", as it was called in contemporary tracts, had been a dominant feature of monastic piety in the 12th century.
*Illustrations:*
23     St Lawrence Receiving the Church Treasures, c. 1447–1450
57     Annalena Panel, c. 1445
58     The Lamentation of Christ, 1436
59     Entombment, 1438–1443
59     The Annunciation, c. 1450
59     The Coronation of the Virgin, c. 1430–1435

## ANTONELLO DA MESSINA
c. 1430 Messina – 1479 Messina

Antonello was born c. 1430 in Messina where he studied under local artists. His creative talent developed and found direction during his years of travel which took him as far as northern Italy. He probably worked in Naples around 1450. Here, the young painter was able to study major works of the Netherlandish school of painting, as King Alfonso I possessed a good collection of paintings by Jan van Eyck and Rogier van der Weyden. It is also thought that the painter Colantonio, who had studied the art of the Netherlands, taught Antonello in Naples. It was in this environment that Antonello discovered his talent for fine detail, whose textual reality is achieved by adding oil as binder, thus allowing the application of several transparent coats of colour. Learning about artistic devices employed in the Netherlands was so important that Vasari later, in the mid-16th century, assumed that Antonello must have visited Flanders, studying under Jan van Eyck (which in terms of time alone could not have been the case).

On his northern travels Antonello met Piero della Francesca in Urbino, whose works taught him the art of perspective and clear geometric disposition of space. With this combination of talents unique in 15th century Italian painting, he reached Venice in 1475 where he stayed until 1476. His arrival must have been a revelation to the Venetian painters. He acted as catalyst, helping Venetian art to come into its own: colour modulation instead of the hitherto predominant outline. Because of this function, and the equally important one of mediator between north and south, Antonello is regarded as one of the most important figures in early Renaissance painting.

*Illustrations:*
116   St Jerome in His Study, c. 1456
116   Virgin Annunciate, c. 1475
117   St Sebastian, c. 1476
117   Sacra Conversazione, 1475/76

## ANTWERP POLYPTYCHON → Master

## APPEL Karel
born 1921 Amsterdam
Appel studied art at the Amsterdam Rijksakademie from 1940 to 1943. In 1948 he was cofounder of the Experimental Group, later called "CoBrA". To this avant-garde group belonged, besides Appel, Pierre Alechinsky, Jorn, Benjamin Constant and Corneille, and others. Together they edited a magazine and organised exhibitions. Appel's pictures express spontaneity, and are painted in powerful, gestural strokes in strong, thickly applied colours. In 1948 he received a commission for a large relief in wood for the Amsterdam town hall which provoked an outcry when unveiled. In 1950 Appel settled in Paris, and a year later the CoBrA group was dissolved. Besides oil-paintings, he produced works in ceramics, church windows, reliefs and sculptures made of wood and polyester, murals for the Stedelijk Museum in Amsterdam (1955) and for UNESCO in Paris (1959) as well as the 100 metre long Energy Wall in Rotterdam. Since 1977 Appel has lived in Monaco and New York.

*Illustration:*
644   Reclining Nude, 1966

## ARCIMBOLDO Giuseppe (also: Arcimboldi)
c. 1527 Milan – 1593 Milan
His father Biagio Arcimboldo was descended from a noble Milan family and worked as a painter on the Milan Cathedral. From 1549 to 1558 Arcimboldo was assistant to his father at the Milan Cathedral workshops and engaged in designing stained glass windows. In 1562 he was called to the court of Ferdinand I in Prague as a portrait and copy painter. In 1563 Arcimboldo painted his first set of "Seasons". The unique artistic conception of these pictures established his fame even then as master of the fantastic art of composing portraits, still lifes, landscapes and allegories consisting of plants, animals and everyday objects. In 1566 he painted the four "Elements", and there is evidence that he went to Italy in the same year. In 1569, on New Year's day, the "Seasons" and the "Elements" were presented to Ferdinand's successor, Emperor Maximilian. At the court Arcimboldo worked as architect, stage designer, engineer, art expert and organiser of festivities and tournaments. In the early seventies he produced several replicas of his "Seasons" pictures. In 1587 he left the court of Rudolf II, the successor to Maximilian, to return to Milan. As a mark of recognition he received 1550 florins from the Em-

peror. In 1591 he sent to Prague a portrait of Rudolf II depicted as *Vertumnus*. In the following year the Emperor bestowed on him the non-hereditary title of count palatine. The Surrealists regarded him as one of their precursors.

*Illustration:*
157   Spring, 1563

## ASAM Cosmas Damian
1686 Benediktbeuren – 1739 Munich
Cosmas Damian, together with his brother Egid Quirin, with whom he worked later, was trained by his father Hans Georg Asam, who is considered to be the founder of Baroque ceiling painting in Bavaria. In the years 1712 to 1714 the brothers travelled to Rome, where Cosmas Damian took up his studies under Pierleone Ghezzi and won an academy prize. He concentrated mainly on wall and ceiling painting of the High Baroque, in particular in the style of Cortona and Pozzo, who in 1702 had published a book of rules on quadratura, a form of ceiling decoration with architectural elements, which give the illusion of perspective and imaginary space. The work which he carried out on his return in south Germany, Bohemia, Silesia and the Tyrol betrays his Roman schooling. However, he gradually abandoned the Italian quadratura technique in which the illusionism is solely directed at the viewer (Weingarten, Aldersbach). Finally, as in the principal fresco at Osterhofen, each side commands its own viewpoint. His work, both sacred and secular, such as at Weltenburg on the Danube 1716–1721, in which his brother was also engaged as sculptor and ornamental plasterer, contains examples of late Baroque art which was to become important for the Rococo in southern Germany.

*Illustration:*
392   The Patron of Churches St George in Adoration of Christ and Mary, 1721

## ASSELIJN Jan
(also: Asselyn; "Crabbetje")
1610 Diemen or Dieppe – 1652 Amsterdam
He received his fundamental training from Esasias van de Velde, who influenced Asselijn's early work, as his equestrian scenes reveal. He then went through France to Italy, where he worked in Rome for a long time. Because of his crippled left hand he was given the nickname "Crabbetje", meaning little crab, by the Dutch "Bent" school of painters in Rome. Here he received encouragement from Jan Both, Pieter van Laer and most of all Claude Lorrain, whose lucid manner he transferred to the Dutch landscape. Around 1645 he returned to Holland and settled in 1647 in Amsterdam, specialising in two categories: the animal portrait, of which "The Threatened Swan" (Rijksmuseum, Amsterdam) is the most famous example, and the landscape. His landscapes with motifs of the Roman Campagna, ruins and pastoral elements in chiaroscuro with well-observed light reflexes are representative of the Italianised direction of Dutch painting.

*Illustration:*
318   Italian Landscape with the Ruins of a Roman Bridge and Aqueduct, undated

## AVERCAMP Hendrick
(Hendrick van Avercamp)
1585 Amsterdam – 1635 Kampen
Although born two generations after Pieter Brueghel the Elder, Avercamp showed himself a receptive student of the famous Flemish painter. He learned his art under Pieter Isaacsz in Amsterdam and subsequently in the studio of Gillis van Coninxloo. After 1610 he went to Kampen, where his father had settled as an apothecary. Avercamp was

deaf and dumb which earned him the nickname "De Stomme van Campen". Besides landscapes depicting the sea and herds of cattle, Avercamp is known mainly for his atmospheric winter scenes in which he shows, with great skill in the art of perspective combined with a strong colour sense, the frolickings of peasants and burghers on the ice of the lakes and canals of his homeland. Although not without an undertone of the comical, his pictures seem to belong to the pure genre, as opposed to those of his exemplar Brueghel who operated on various levels.

*Illustration:*
301   Winter Scene at Yselmuiden, c. 1613

## BACICCIO
(Giovanni Battista Gaulli; also: Baciccia)
1639 Genoa – 1709 Rome
Baciccio's success and prosperity can be ascribed to his chosen fields: portraiture and the painting of ceilings. The style of his portraits shows the influence of van Dyck's pictures executed at Genoa. His portraits of Pope Clement IX (Rome, Galleria dell' Accademia Nazionale di San Luca) and Cardinal Leopoldo de' Medici (Florence, Uffizi) bear, however, the stamp of Baciccio's own lively perception and handling of light. When painting ceilings, he follows Cortona's decorative style to which he was introduced when in Rome, developing it further by extreme perspectival foreshortening. His principal works are the cupola of San Agnese and the nave vaulting and apse of Il Gesù. The sculptor and architect Bernini was Bacaccio's protector: he took the young man in when he had to flee from the plague to Rome. In 1662 he became a member of the painters' academy of San Luca, in 1674 its director. His influence as fresco painter continued into the 18th century.

*Illustration:*
239   The Apotheosis of St Ignatius, c. 1685

## BACON Francis
1909 Dublin – 1992 Madrid
Bacon was just 16 years old when he went to London. Two years later, while working as a decorator in Berlin and Paris, his first drawings and water-colours appeared, showing the influence of Picasso. He destroyed his early oil-paintings, painted under the influence of French Surrealism in 1944, after he had found his own form of expression. He depicted almost without exception distorted human bodies and faces against diffuse-oppressive backgrounds. His paintings, often consisting of several parts, are reflections of some inner reality, a foreboding and feeling of dissolution. As early as 1955 Bacon had his first retrospective at the London Institute for Contemporary Arts. Along with his compatriot Sutherland, Bacon is one of the most important representatives of visionary painting of the post-war era.

*Illustrations:*
626   Self-Portrait, 1973
646   Three Studies of the Male Back, 1970

## BALDUNG Hans
(called: Grien)
c. 1484/85 Schwäbisch Gmünd – 1545 Strasbourg
Baldung probably completed his apprenticeship in Strasbourg at the early age of 15, when he was given the byname "Grien" (Green) because of his youth. In 1503 he entered the workshop of Dürer in Nuremberg to become one of his most prominent pupils. As one of the most eminent German artists of the 16th century, both as painter and as master of the graphic arts, his works are remarkable for their unusual combination of unveiled sensuality and dispassionate intellect which often pro-

duces a "cold fire". Besides religious commission work, Baldung preferred secular themes in which the female body, worked up into a demonic frenzy in his witch scenes, is given a major role. He was also highly regarded as a portraitist, and from about 1530 he was considered to be one of the best artists on the Upper Rhine. His development leads from the latest Gothic forms via the Italian Renaissance, whose harmony he never strove to achieve, into Mannerism. In his treatment of colour he rejected the conventional norm of clear, harmonious tones in favour of dissonance alien to nature. In this respect he represents a parallel to the masters of early Florentine Mannerism (Pontormo, Rosso Fiorentino).
*Illustration:*
189   The Nativity, 1520


## BALLA Giacomo
1871 Turin – 1958 Rome
Except for attending some courses at the Accademia Albertina di Belle Arti in Turin, Balla was self-taught. In 1895 he moved to Rome, where he worked as an illustrator, caricaturist and portraitist. In 1900 he spent seven months in Paris on the occasion of the World Exhibition, where he was particularly impressed by the Neo-Impressionists. On his return, he was joined by Boccioni, Severini and Sironi whom he taught the new Parisian method of painting.
    In 1910 he signed, together with his friends, *Marinetti's Manifesto of Futuristic Painters*, but did not take part in the activities of the group until 1913. From then on Balla attempted, often in co-operation with his Futuristic friends, to find by experiment newer forms not only for painting and sculpture, but also for theatrical scenery, the applied arts and the film. Balla's pictures stand out on account of their unusual, almost photographic qualities and the dissolution of objects into lines of movement, expressing dynamism and speed. In 1935 he became a member of the Accademia di San Luca in Rome.
*Illustration:*
577   Mercury Passing before the Sun, 1914


## BALTHUS
(Balthasar Klossovski de Rola)
born 1908 Paris
Balthus is a descendent of an old Polish family which moved to Paris in the mid-19th century. He spent his youth in Paris, Berlin and Switzerland, and Rainer Maria Rilke discovered and promoted Balthus' talent in his early years. In 1921 Rilke published a collection of forty of the boy's panels in a folder under the title *Mitsou* and wrote the introduction. After his military service in 1933 Balthus became friendly with some of the Surrealists, including Giacometti and Artaud. Artistically, however, Balthus held a special postion: his extensive knowledge of the history of art explains the quotations from Giotto to Caravaggio in his paintings. Balthus painted still lifes, portraits and landscapes. Most fascinating, however, are his representations of young, still immature girls, whom he surrounds with an almost demonic atmosphere. In the thirties Balthus began to explore his second subject area: Paris street scenes. In 1961 Malraux appointed him director of the Villa Medici, the French academy in Rome. In 1977 he moved to Switzerland. Balthus' work has been shown at major exhibitions, including the New York Museum of Modern Art in 1956, the Tate Gallery London in 1968 and the Pompidou Centre in Paris in 1983. He has been an honorary member of the Royal Academy, London, since 1981.
*Illustration:*
668   The Artist and his Model, 1980/81


## BARNABA DA MODENA
active 1361 – 1383 Genoa
The Emilia region within Modena borders on Tuscany and Lombardy as well as Veneto. But the Roman papal states, which at some periods also ruled Bologna, had some influence here too. It is significant that in the mid-14th century when Tuscan art declined and Lombardian and Venetian art were at their zenith, the painters of Emilia continued to be successful beyond their home ground (Tommaso da Modena). Barnaba da Modena comes to us through his signed works and some source material, yet we know nothing of his artistic origins. No doubt he followed the example of Sienese art and would also have been conversant with the Byzantine works of Venice. Most of the time he worked in Genoa; his panels were exported from there as far as Spain. Written commissions from Piemont and Pisa have also survived.
*Illustration:*
47   Madonna and Child, 1370


## BARTOLOMMEO Fra
(Bartolommeo di Pagola del Fattorino, known as: Baccio della Porta)
1472 Soffignano (near Florence) – 1517 Florence
The twelve-year-old Bartolommeo, called "della Porta" because his family home was at the Porta di San Pier Gattolino, was sent to the workshop of Cosimo Rosselli, where he was given an education in the full spirit of the late 15th century. In 1490 he founded his own workshop, together with Mariotto Albertinelli. Evidently equipped with a social sense and filled with religious fervour, he became a follower of Savonarola and entered the Dominican order in the late nineties. His creative work, briefly disrupted, led him to abandon tradition in the early years of the 16th century, and to come under Flemish influences. He explores Perugino in his representations of landscape and his drawings; he becomes fascinated with Giovanni Bellini while in Venice in 1508; and on his return studies Leonardo's new colour theories. The combined effect of these influences resulted after 1512 in works which stand out in the art of the Florentine High Renaissance. Bartolommeo not only made a lasting impression on Raphael, but as a teacher also gave direction to Rosso Fiorentino, Pontormo and the Sienese painter Domenico Beccafumi.
*Illustration:*
166   Annunciation, c. 1500


## BASCHENIS Evaristo
1617 Bergamo (?) – 1677 Bergamo
Today his name no longer conjures up the battle scenes of his early years, but rather the still lifes with musical instruments from the legendary Cremona workshops of Amati, Girolama and Nicola. By employing artistic devices imported from the Netherlands, in particular the *trompe l'œil* effect, Baschenis represents his lutes and violins as strongly expressive special objects. He puts these rotund sound chambers in juxtaposition to clear, flat surfaces and uses the warm tones of their wood to produce the overall colour effect. About his life we only know that he comes from a painting family and was a priest before devoting himself entirely to painting.
*Illustration:*
238   Still Life with Musical Instruments, c. 1650


## BASELITZ Georg
(Hans-Georg Kern)
born 1938 Deutschbaselitz (Saxony)
From 1956 Baselitz studied at the School of Fine and Applied Arts in East Berlin under Walter Womacks, where he met Peter Graf and Ralf Winkler (A.R. Penck). A year later he changed over to the Academy in West Berlin where he studied painting under Hann Trier until 1962. He adopted the pseudonym Baselitz in 1961. Stimulated by the Surrealist manifestos of Breton, he, too, wrote manifestos to accompany his action pictures "The Night of Pandemonium" (1962), and "Why the Picture 'Great Friends' is a Good Picture" (1966). His first strictly representational pictures are directed against Tachisme and abstract art. Since 1969 he has been painting upside-down portraits and landscapes. The first woodcuts were produced in 1966; roughly-hewn wooden sculptures since 1979. A scholarship took him in 1965 to the Villa Romana at Florence. Since then he has been visiting Italy most years, taking a studio in Imperia in 1987. In 1978 he was given a professorship at the Academy of Arts at Karlsruhe. From 1983 to 1988 and then again in 1992 he lectured at the Berlin Academy. In 1995 a large retrospective was arranged for him at the Guggenheim Museum, New York. Baselitz lives at Derneburg near Hildesheim.
*Illustrations:*
626   Motivschimmel Zerbrochene Brücke (Dappled motif broken bridge), 1986
675   Familienbild (Family Portrait), 1975
675   Ciao America I, 1988


## BASQUIAT Jean Michel
1960 New York – 1988 New York
Basquiat was born in New York as the son of a Haitian book-keeper and a Puerto-Rican mother. After a difficult childhood he began at the age of 17, together with Al Diaz, to paint graffiti in underground stations and on house-fronts under the assumed name of Samo. He did casual work and played the guitar and synthethiser in a band. The art market soon discovered Basquiat; by taking part in the documenta at Kassel in 1982 and the Whitney Biennale in New York in 1983, he became a media star. He made friends with Warhol. They painted portraits of each other and designed a number of works together. Basquiat introduced the graffiti art form to the art world without disowning his Brooklyn ghetto origins. He constructed assemblages from waste objects; materials used as surface could range from a torn bit of paper to a fridge door. He died from a drug overdose.
*Illustration:*
679   ISBN, 1985


## BASSANO Jacopo
(Giacomo da Ponte)
c. 1517/18 Bassano – 1592 Bassano
Bassano stems from a family of painters and received his training from his father, Francesco. In 1530 he was apprenticed for 5 years to the Venetian painter Bonifazio de' Pitatis. In 1549 he was appointed a councillor and consul of his home town, whose name he adopted and where he lived all his life, untroubled by great events. Bassano had a large workshop, where later four of his seven children worked. Here he produced about 180 paintings which would not have been feasible without assistance. His works show the influence of Titian and Lorenzo Lotto and late Venetian Renaissance art (Tintoretto and Veronese), whose insights he developed further. The strength of his work lies in the concentration on objects and in telling a story simply but effectively. In his realistic representation of

landscape Bassano developed a style of his own; genre painting outweighs work with religious content.

*Illustration:*

179   The Procession to Calvary, c. 1540

## BAUGIN Lubin

c. 1610–1612 Pithiviers (Loiret) – 1663 Paris
Several religious paintings of Baugin survive, including "Virgin with Child and St John" (London, Nancy, Rennes), "Birth of Mary" (Aix-en-Provence, Musée Granet). Because of his large-figured, mellow style and clear, extensive planes of colour, he was rightly called "Le petit Guide", the little Guido Reni, for he was strongly influenced by the work of this Italian painter. In contrast, his still lifes, signed "A. Baugin", are in the late style of the "School of Fontainebleau" with late Mannerist elements. Before 1789 the Cathedral of Notre Dame possessed eleven of his religious paintings. Baugin studied in Rome under Vouet, was accepted by the Académie de Saint Luc in Paris in 1645, was appointed "Peintre du Roi" in 1651, was expelled from the Academy on the grounds of founding a private school, and on closing it was re-elected. Baugin's long disputed identity is now established as these details tally exactly with those of the still life master.

*Illustration:*

244   Still Life with Chessboard (The Five Senses), undated

## BAUMEISTER Willi

1889 Stuttgart – 1955 Stuttgart
Baumeister began his artistic career as a decorative painter. From 1908 he attended the Stuttgart Academy and from 1909 studied composition with Schlemmer under Adolf Hölzel. Repeated visits to France aroused his interest in French art, and he made friends with Léger and others. In 1919 he was one of the founders of Üecht, a group of Stuttgart artists. Baumeister was initially under the influence of the Cubists and produced figurative work which was superseded by the "wall pictures". After becoming a member of the "Circle of New Promotional Designers" in 1927, he worked a year later as teacher of typography at the Städelsche Kunstschule in Frankfurt/Main. In 1933 he was dismissed and professionally banned as a "degenerate" artist, but he continued to paint secretly at Stuttgart. His works became increasingly removed from the representational. From 1939 to 1944 he worked alongside Schlemmer at the paint manufacturer Kurt Herberts in Wuppertal. Baumeister's theoretical work *The Unknown in Art* was written between 1943 and 1947. From 1946 to 1955 he held a chair at the Stuttgart Academy. He is still regarded the master of abstract art in Germany.

*Illustration:*

639   Montaru-G VI, 1954

## BAYEU Y SUBIAS Ramón

1746 Saragossa – 1793 Aranjuez
Like his brother Manuel, Ramón was eclipsed by his brother Francisco who, not least because he was Goya's brother-in-law, found a place in the history of art. Ramón accompanied his brother Francisco to Madrid in 1763, where he worked in an artistic climate dictated both by the late Baroque and by Classicism, embodied by the old Tiepolo and the increasingly influential arbiter of taste, Mengs. Ramón seems to have been less clearly associated with a particular school than his brother. For example, the prevailing influence of Classicism shows in the jointly executed frescos in the Zaragoza cathedral, while in his portraits, but especially in his etchings which he carried out to his

own design or after those of his brother or of older masters, the technique and picturesque gracefulness of Tiepolo are still detectable.

*Illustration:*

396   The Blind Singer, c. 1786

## BAZILLE Frédéric

1841 Montpellier – 1870 Beaune-la-Rolande (near Orléans)
Bazille, who came from a well-to-do, cultured background, began to study medicine in his home town in 1859. His general interest in art induced him to study painting at the Gleyre studio when he went to Paris in 1862 for further medical studies. Here he met Monet, Renoir and Sisley. At Easter 1863 he painted with Monet at Fontainebleau, and again in June 1864 at Honfleur, where he met Boudin and Jongkind. He abandoned his medical studies. In 1865 he put up Monet at his studio in the Rue de Furstenberg, and in 1866 he exhibited at the Salon. He then shared a studio with Renoir in the Rue de la Visconti. He supported both Monet and Renoir, partly by buying their work. As Bazille was only 29 years old when he was killed in the war, his œuvre is relatively small, including portraits of members of his family and friends in various studios. His still, clear landscapes and harmonious family scenes in muted colours make him one of the most important forerunners of Impressionism.

*Illustration:*

505   Bathers, 1869

## BEAUNEVEU André

1335 Valencienne – before 1413 Bourges
Beauneveu, whose life is documented between 1360 and 1403, stemmed from Valencienne which only became French under King Louis XIV. As Bondol served King Charles V as court painter, so his fellow Fleming Beauneveu became his court sculptor. In 1371 he was ennobled by Charles V. He also worked for the Flemish Count Louis de Mâle who in addition engaged Broederlam. However, Beauneveu's most important patron was the Duc de Berry who put him in charge of all his artistic projects, including the building of the palace of Méhun-sur-Yèvre. All designs and plans were worked out jointly by the duke and Beauneveu, and the latter also undertook miniature and glass painting. Beauneveu was regarded as an outstanding artist by his contemporaries. Thus, in 1393, the Duke of Burgundy sent his court sculptor Sluter and painter Jean de Beaumetz to Méhun to study the work in progress. The authenticated works of Beauneveu show that he took the academic rules of French art in the first half of the 14th century as a starting point, but handled them with great virtuosity and delicacy. Among his early work his portraits quite rightly receive most praise, such as the tomb statue of Charles V at St Denis. In his later work he explored Italian innovations, leading to richly vibrant forms.

*Illustrations:*

65   The Duc de Berry between his Patron Saints Andrew and John the Baptist, c. 1390

## BECKMANN Max

1884 Leipzig – 1950 New York
After spending his youth in Brunswick and Pommerania, Beckmann studied from 1900 at the Weimar Academy of Art before moving to Berlin in 1904. With the "Scene from the Sinking of the Messina" (St Louis, Saint Louis Art Museum) he formulated in 1909 the theme which was to preoccupy him all his life: the threat of catastrophe to the individual and all humanity. When war broke out in 1914 he volunteered as medical orderly,

but a nervous breakdown only a year later brought his discharge. He moved to Frankfurt am Main where he lived until 1933. Having experienced mass killing in the trenches, he abandoned biblical, historical and allegorical subjects and turned to man in his physical and spiritual anguish, as depicted in his work "The Night" (ill. p. 588) of 1918/19. In this, forms are simplified and reduced so that harsh contours and direct transition become dominant. In the following years the severity and harshness of his style seem to mellow. The contour becomes less angular and colours more brilliant, while the monumentality remains. The theatre, circus, fun fair and night-club, music-hall and cabaret, are seen as analogies of human existence. In 1925 Beckmann accepted a chair at the Städelsche Art School, Frankfurt/M. In 1933 he was compelled to leave, moving to Berlin. In the triptych "Departure" (New York, Museum of Modern Art) of 1932/33, a title full of associations, he foresaw his emigration. This work started a series of nine similar, monumental compositions, all having as their theme the futility of human endeavour and our subjection to a higher power. When the "Degenerate Art" exhibition was opened in 1937, he left Germany for ever, spending the war years in Amsterdam before departing for New York in 1947.

*Illustrations:*

588   The Night, 1918/19
588   Dancing in Baden-Baden, 1923

## BELLECHOSE Henri

c. 1380 Breda (Brabant) – c. 1440/44 Dijon
In 1415 Bellechose took over from Malouel as court painter and *valet de chambre* to the Dukes of Burgundy in Dijon. He worked at the ducal residences at Talant and Saulx and the monastery Champmol near Dijon, for which he painted an altarpiece of the life of St Dionysius and a scene from the life of Mary. At court he was responsible for the decorations at festivities and also the painting of coats of arms and standards. For a time he received a good income from the duke, but when the court was removed from Dijon he had to carry out private commissions. Bellechose is regarded as the major representative of the French-Flemish version of International Gothic.

*Illustration:*

66   The Last Communion and Martyrdom of St Denis, c. 1416

## BELLINI Gentile

1429 Venice – 1507 Venice
Gentile, who was somewhat older than Giovanni, was trained at the workshop of his father Jacopo. The keenness of observation with which he rendered perspective, scenery or antique fragments in his sketches became a decisive factor in his artistic development. It predestined him to be the most important portraitist of Venetian art in the 15th century. From 1450 until his death Gentile acted as official painter to the Republic. He was sent to Constantinople in 1479/80, as the Signoria of Venice had been requested by Sultan Mehmed II to send him the best portraitist. The famous portrait of this oriental potentate is now in the National Gallery, London. Next to portraiture, Gentile also excelled at large-scale historical scenes painted in the style of the early Venetian Renaissance. There is nothing in Venice to equal his panels with scenes from the Legend of the True Cross, painted c. 1500. The faithful and precise rendering of St Mark's Square and the medieval Rialto bridge make him the forerunner of Canaletto. It is true that in terms of coloration he remains well within the boundaries of 15th century traditions, whereas his younger brother was even then opening up new fields in colour modulation.

Gentile's most significant pupil and successor was Carpaccio.
*Illustration:*
118    Procession in St Mark's Square, 1496

## BELLINI Giovanni
(also: Giambellino)
c. 1430 Venice – 1516 Venice
Giovanni was initially taught by his father Jacopo whose drawings of almost icon-like precision in the traditional 14th century method and manner influenced his early work. When Giovanni's sister Nicosia married Mantegna in 1453, close relations between Venice and Padua were established, and Giovanni began to explore the physical and spatial representation of the Early Renaissance. Under Mantegna's influence his style assumes temporarily a certain calligraphic precision ("The Transfiguration of Christ", Venice, Museo Correr, c. 1460; "The Mount of Olives", London, National Gallery, c. 1470.)

The visit of Antonello da Messina to Venice in 1475/76 seems to have liberated Giovanni's innermost talents. Without abandoning the rational structure and interaction of form and space, his colours gain in luminosity and depth; modulation of tone increasingly replaces the dividing outline, light floods the canvas. The landscape, as can be seen in many of his representations of the Virgin and Child and the Pietà, achieves a quality that marks Bellini as the most important Italian landscape painter of the Early Renaissance. His ability to endow his figures with an expression of quiet contemplation while fully conveying movement and human anatomy, remains a secret that raises him above all his contemporaries. The great works of his late art, in particular his portrayals of the Sacra Conversazione, already cross the border from Early to High Renaissance in the way artistic freedom and convention merge. As teacher of Giorgione and Titian, Giovanni, whom Dürer on his second visit to Venice from 1505 to 1507 still called the greatest painter of his time, was of immeasurable significance for Venetian art in the 16th century.
*Illustrations:*
84     St Francis in the Wilderness, c. 1480
120    Sacra Conversazione (Pala di San Giobbe), c. 1487/88
120    Transfiguration of Christ, c. 1460
121    Portrait of Doge Leonardo Loredan, c. 1501–1505
121    Christian Allegory, c. 1490

## BELLOTTO Bernardo
(known as: Canaletto; also: Beloto)
1721 Venice – 1780 Warsaw
Bellotto began his artistic career at the age of fifteen in the workshop of his uncle Antonio Canal and took over not only his speciality of veduta painting, but also largely his style and finally even his name Canaletto. Like his uncle, he also visited Rome and probably Tuscany. He worked in several regions of Italy, including Lombardy and Turin, before travelling to England in 1746. A year later he was welcomed in Dresden by Augustus the Strong. He carried out work for Maria Theresa and the Austrian nobility in Vienna, returning 1762 via Munich to Dresden where, after losing his position as court painter, he took a post as teacher of perspective painting at the Academy founded in 1764. Bellotto finally settled in Warsaw where he became court painter to Stanislas II. The close connection between uncle and nephew makes it difficult to draw a clear line between Bellotto's early work and the late work of his teacher. A cooler palette and the even greater precision of his topographical views distinguish his independent work from that of Canal. His principal works, such as the 14 Dresden vedutas, or the view of Warsaw, make him the

equal of his uncle. His topographical representations of the European royal capitals are also an important historical record on account of their exactitude and faithfulness.
*Illustration:*
373    Piazza della Signoria in Florence, c. 1740–1745

## BERLIN NATIVITY → Master

## BERLINGHIERI Bonaventura
c. 1205–1210 – after 1274
Berlinghieri was the son of the Milan painter Berlinghiero Berlinghieri, of whom some works survive. Records show that he lived in Lucca from 1228 to 1274. The sources mention his brother Barone, also a painter, and a further brother, Marco, the miniaturist. The only authenticated work of Berlinghieri is the St Francis panel in Pescia, bearing the inscription: "Anno Domini MCCXXXV Bonaventura Berlinghieri de Luc…". Thanks to the Berlinghieri family, the painting school of Lucca gained prestige far beyond the city boundaries. The Byzantine element in the father's art became even more pronounced in the works of the son, resulting in a peculiar flatness and stiffness.
*Illustration:*
28     St Francis and Scenes from his Life, 1235

## BERRUGUETE Pedro
c. 1450–1455 Parades de Nava – c. 1504 Avila (?)
The combination of a great variety of traditions makes Berruguete one of the most versatile and important Spanish painters of the 15th century. Having been raised in the cultural ambience of the court of the Castilian "Catholic Kings", who collected pictures in Granada from the Netherlands as well as employing painters from the North, he became, after a lengthy stay in Italy, one of the most important mediators between Spanish art and the Italian Early Renaissance. In 1477 he worked with Justus of Ghent at the court of Urbino. Here Berruguete painted his portraits of famous figures, using with great sensitivity the innovations of the Italian Early Renaissance regarding form and space. Clearly he was highly thought of in Italy, not only receiving stimulation but also giving it to others, such as at the court of Ferrara. In 1483 he returned to Toledo. Unfortunately his frescos in the sacristy and cloister of Toledo Cathedral did not survive, but his mature works, including the altarpieces for the monastery of Santo Tomás and for Avila Cathedral show to this day his symbiosis of Spanish medieval tradition, Dutch faithfulness in detail, and Italian clarity of composition. Pedro was the father of the sculptor Alonso Berruguete.
*Illustration:*
138    Court of Inquisition chaired by St Dominic, c. 1500

## BEUYS Joseph
1921 Kleve – 1986 Düsseldorf
Beuys grew up in Kleve near the Dutch border. In the war he flew a fighter plane from 1941 to 1945, crashing over the Crimea. He was found by Tartars who wrapped him in fat and felt. These two materials took on great significance in his later work. From 1947 to 1951 he studied at the Academy of Art in Düsseldorf, where he was the principal pupil of Ewald Mataré, and where Beuys himself taught from 1961 to 1972. By combining several artistic media and merging them with his life story, he attempted to achieve a unity of art and life in his work. In doing so, he also drew on anthroposophy, mythology and religion. In 1962 he became ac-

quainted with the Fluxus movement through the Korean Nam June Paik and through George Maciunas, and began to exhibit his own actions from 1963. He also produced sketches and plastic works and designed objects and environments. The symbolism of his work is drawn from magical-religious, mythical and archetypal contexts, or from personal experience. Thus the idea of felt as an insulator against the cold and fat as a source of energy and warmth stems from his own experience, representing a closeness to nature lost in our culture. Beuys advocated creativy in all walks of life – hence his attempt to gain political influence.
*Illustration:*
623    Is it about a bicycle? IV, 1982

## BEYEREN Abraham van
(also: Beijeren)
c. 1620/21 The Hague – 1690 Alkmaar or Overschie (Rotterdam)
Beyeren found scant recognition in his lifetime, yet today he is among the most important still life painters of his country. He was taught by his brother-in-law, the painter of fish, Pieter de Putter, which may be the reason why Beyeren began his career with the same subject matter. In 1640 he joined the Painters' Guild in The Hague, where he became a co-founder of the *Confrerie Pictura* in 1656. In 1657 he went to Delft, in 1663 he returned to The Hague, in 1672 he lived in Amsterdam and in 1674 in Alkmaar. He was always in financial straits; fleeing from creditors may have been the reason for his many moves and restless life. His true métier were sumptuous, tastefully arranged still lifes, breakfast tables with magnificent cloths, flowers, glasses, fruit and animals, showing the influence of de Heem. There are also fragrant flower pieces in the style of Jan Brueghel, seascapes, and his fish still lifes.
*Illustration:*
323    Still Life with Lobster, 1653

## BINGHAM George Caleb
1811 Augusta County (Virginia) – 1879 Kansas City
Bingham grew up at Franklin on the Missouri river, on his father's tobacco farm. After an apprenticeship as cabinet-maker, and then briefly studying theology and law, he went to Philadelphia, where he attended the Academy of Arts in 1837/38. In 1844 he returned to Missouri and painted scenes from the everyday lives of farmers, trappers, traders and raftsmen, as well as genre pictures, which made him famous as the narrator of the domestic customs and traditions of the Western States. In particular, the mass distribution of copper engravings made from his own drawings brought him great popularity. On a visit to Europe from 1856 to 1859 Bingham spent most of his time in Paris and in Düsseldorf where he had contacts with the German-American painter Emanuel Leutze and the Düsseldorf School. On his return to the USA he held political posts which severely restricted his artistic activities. As expressed in his own words, his aim was to depict "social and political characteristics". His poetical, delicately coloured renderings of the Missouri river area seem, however, to be reminiscent of the early days of settlement as celebrated in Mark Twain's books.
*Illustration:*
471    Fur Traders Descending the Missouri, c. 1845

## BLAKE Peter
born 1932 Dartford, Kent
Blake studied graphic art at the Gravesend School of Art, and from 1953 to 1956 he attended the Royal College of Art, London. In 1956/57 he

toured Europe for study purposes, then from 1964 taught at the St Martin School of Art. After an initial realistic period he became, together with Hamilton and Richard Smith, one of the key figures of English Pop Art. Compared with other pop artists, though, he does not employ trivial pictorial clichés, but nostalgically approaches the aesthetics of the thirties. The painted collages produced since 1959 express a disarming wit and cheerful colourfulness. In 1967 he designed the record sleeve of the Beatles' LP "Sergeant Pepper". From 1969 to 1979 he lived with the "Brotherhood of Ruralists" near Bath, and then returned to London.
*Illustration:*
664    Bo Diddley, 1963/64

## BLAKE William
1757 London – 1827 London
Blake, the son of a stocking weaver, already had visionary experiences as a child, and this was to influence the "prophetic" character of his singular artistic combination of visual art and poetry. At the age of 10 he was given drawing lessons by Henry Pars; then was taught engraving by James Basire for whom he painted medieval pictures. His own works showed very early the influence of Michelangelo in particular, whose vast human figures later became central to his work. While studying at the Royal Academy (from 1778), he became embroiled in an argument with Reynolds about the relative importance of colour and drawing. Blake took the classical view, and his entire work shows his disinclination to use colour for effect. In his illustrations of the Bible, Dante, or his own writings, the traditional relationship between picture and text was abandoned, achieving a symbolic unity of word and picture which would not be accepted until decades after his death.
*Illustration:*
388    Beatrice addressing Dante from her Wagon,
       c. 1824–1826

## BLECHEN Karl Eduard Ferdinand
1798 Cottbus – 1840 Berlin
Blechen was born in Cottbus as the son of a tax official, and first worked in a bank in Berlin. In 1822 he began his art studies at the Berlin Academy. His acquaintance with the painters Friedrich and Dahl at Dresden was an important stimulus. These two artists represent the two poles covered by Blechen's work: Romanticism and Realism. His visit to Italy in 1828/29 was decisive in his development. The innumerable oil-studies carried out in Italy show him to be an open-air painter with an affinity to Turner, who was then also working there, as well as to the French painter Corot who had settled there. These studies make Blechen the most important representative of early Realism in Germany. In subsequent years his romantic strain again comes to the fore. The mood is often sombre; the figures on the brink of catastrophe or just overtaken by it. Although he was given a professorship in 1831 at the Berlin Academy, the desired public recognition was withheld. The extreme subjectivity of his work was too much out of tune with contemporary German painting. In 1835 he fell into deep depression and finally mental derangement in 1839.
*Illustrations:*
456    Monks on the Gulf of Naples, c. 1829
456    The Gardens of the Villa d'Este, c. 1830

## BLOEMAERT Abraham
1564 Dordrecht or Gorinchem – 1651 Utrecht
Bloemaert was trained in the workshop of his father Cornelis, a sculptor and later city architect in Amsterdam. At the age of 16 he went to Paris, where he worked under Jean Bassot and Hieronymus Francken, but was most influenced by Frans Floris, an important representative of Dutch Mannerism. He returned in 1583 to his father in Amsterdam, but then lived most of his life at Utrecht where he became superintendent of the painters' guild in 1611 and was given permission to keep a studio in the St Clare nunnery. His pupils included Cuyp, Terbrugghen, Honthorst, Weenix and Both. Bloemaert's work includes historical paintings, dramatic, multi-figured mythological scenes, and bucolic landscapes with "picturesque" huts. He never went to Italy, but through his pupils became familiar with Caravaggist chiaroscuro which had first been taken up in Utrecht and was to influence the entire country. Bloemaert's life spanned both the Mannerist 16th century at one end and the period of Rembrandt at the other.
*Illustration:*
287    Landscape with Peasants Resting , 1650

## BOCCIONI Umberto
1882 Reggio di Calabria – 1916 near Verona
Boccioni studied painting in Rome from 1898 to 1902. While there, he met Severini and Balla, who introduced him to French Neo-Impressionist ideas. In Paris he explored Divisionism and in particular Seurat's work, but its contemplative air and atmospheric stillness did not satisfy him for long. On his return to Italy he settled in Milan in 1907, the place where the greatest technical advances had been made. In 1910 he signed the Manifesto of Futuristic Painters, together with Carrà, Luigi Russolo, Balla and Severini. When with Severini in Paris in 1911, he met Apollinaire, Picasso, Braque and Dufy. Via Cubism he arrived at pictures which represent the Futuristic ideal of speed and movement. In 1914 his book *Pittura, scultura futurista, dinamismo plastico* was published, the definitive work on the theory and practice of Futurism.
*Illustrations:*
576    State of Mind II: Farewells, 1911
576    The Noise of the Street Enters the House,
       1911

## BÖCKLIN Arnold
1827 Basle – 1901 San Domenico (near Fiesole)
Böcklin went in 1845 from Basle to Düsseldorf to study at the Academy for three years under J. W. Schirmer who painted heroic landscapes in the style of Claude Lorrain. Via Geneva, Brussels and Paris he arrived at Rome in 1850. He was full of enthusiam for the Italian landscape and the culture of Antiquity. His friendship with Reinhold Begas, Feuerbach, H. Franz-Dreber and Hans von Marées, the "German Romans", was decisive for his work. Seven years later he went via Basle to Germany, achieving his first success in Munich. Adolf Friedrich, Count of Schack, became his patron, and in 1859 King Ludwig I of Bavaria bought his picture "Pan in the Reeds" for the Neue Pinakothek. At this period his friendship with Lenbach began; a year later he became a professor at Weimar. Böcklin loved and painted Symbolist themes full of pathos, mythological scenes set in fantastic landscapes, and allegories. Towards the end of his life his work became darkly visionary, almost apocalyptic. His emotionalism, at times bordering on the humorous, brought him much criticism, but his supporters admired him fervently. He experimented with colour, explored old and new techniques and materials, including underpainting. He used a wide range of colours, and the intensity of value deepened the mood of his themes. His yearning for independence soon induced him to resign his Weimar post. He moved to Basle, in 1871 back to Munich, then to Florence. In 1887 he went to Zurich for seven years before finally settling at San Domenico, where he died in 1901.
*Illustration:*
528    The Waves, 1883

## BONDOL Jean
(also: Bandol, Bandolf)
born in Bruges, active 1368–1381 in Paris
Bondol is first mentioned in 1368 as court painter to Charles V (the Wise) of France. He was well rewarded, and was later granted a life pension, a mark of high esteem. The inscription on the title page of the bible of Jean de Vaudetar, his only surviving work, reads as follows in translation: "In the year of our Lord 1371 this work was painted at the behest and to the glory of our illustrious lord Charles, King of France, in the 35th year of his life and the 8th year of his reign, and John of Bruges, painter to the afore-mentioned King, created this painting with his own hand." Today this picture stands alone in the history of early panel painting of the Netherlands; all other examples have been lost. The esteem accorded to this painter's person and art suggests that the affected style which was the tradition in art at the regal court did not always meet the patron's expectations. The need was met by engaging realistic panel painters and sculptors from the Netherlands. Bondol also did work for other members of the royal household, such as the cartoons produced between 1376 and 1379 for Charles' brother Louis I of Anjou for the famous tapestry series of the Apocalypse of Angers, drawing on an English apocalyptic manuscript from the 13th century in royal possession.
*Illustration:*
60    Title page of the Bible of Jean de Vaudetar,
      1371

## BONINGTON Richard Parkes
1802 Arnold (Nottingham) – 1828 London
Bonington came from a Nottingham family who left England in 1817 to settle in Calais. There the 15-year-old was taught the aquarelle technique by Louis Francia. In 1818 Bonington went to Paris, where he met Delacroix and made aquarelle copies in the Louvre of Dutch and Flemish landscapes. In 1821–22 he studied under Gros at the École des Beaux-Arts. In 1824 he won a gold medal at the Paris Salon. He travelled all over France and especially Normandy, painting a number of atmospheric coastal and seaport scenes, and also went to England and Scotland, occasionally accompanied by his friend Delacroix in whose studio he later worked. His journey to Italy in 1826 brought him to Venice where he was much impressed by Veronese and Canaletto. Bonington, like Constable, was one of the English artists whose landscape paintings were highly regarded in France on account of their fresh and spontaneous composition. He was one of the first in France to use watercolour paints in the open. His approach to nature as well as his technique stimulated the Barbizon painters and – with E. Isabey, Boudin and Jongkind as mediators – paved the way to Impressionism.
*Illustrations:*
466    Beach in Normandy, c. 1826/27
466    The Column of St Mark in Venice,
       c. 1826–1828

## BONNARD Pierre

1867 Fontenay-aux-Roses (near Paris) – 1947 Le Cannet (near Cannes)

From 1886 to 1889 Bonnard studied law in Paris. However, he rejected a possible career in this field as he had already been studying art in 1888/89 at the Académie des Beaux-Arts and the Académie Julian. There he met Denis, Vuillard and Sérusier, who introduced him to Gauguin's art. In 1889 he sold a stylistically innovative poster design ("France-Champagne"). After a brief period of military service he shared a studio in 1890 with Denis and Vuillard and became co-founder of Nabis, a group of painters favouring symbolist and anti-naturalist ideas. From 1891 to 1905 he exhibited at the Independents. His first poster was published, and he met Toulouse-Lautrec. From 1893 his lithographs appeared in *La Revue Blanche*; from 1895 Vollard published his lithographs and book illustrations which show some influence by Redon. In 1903 he exhibited for the first time at the new Autumn Salon. In 1906 he taught at the Académie Ranson. In 1905 he travelled with Vuillard to Spain; in subsequent years to Belgium, Holland, England, Italy, Algeria and Tunisia. In 1909 he visited southern France for the first time, where he bought a house in Le Cannet in 1925 and settled there for good. Best known and most popular are Bonnard's paintings in the late Impressionist manner with delicate colours of porcelain-like translucence, including interiors, portraits and female nudes as well as landscapes and street scenes. Many of his works appear intimate but are executed with a fine sense of propriety. Although a member of Nabis, Bonnard cannot be classed as belonging to a specific school or group. As with many of his contemporaries, he was fascinated by Japanese art, and this interest comes out in his work.

*Illustrations:*
520   At the Circus, c. 1897
520   Female Nude in the Bathtub, c. 1938

## BOSCH Hieronymus

(Iheronymus van Aken)

c. 1450 s'Hertogenbosch – 1516 s'Hertogenbosch

Bosch, a contemporary of Leonardo da Vinci, is one of the great European painters of his time. The need to decodify his symbolic language, which is no longer generally accessible, although it is essential to an understanding of the spirit of the time, often deflects from the great artistic worth of his works. Bosch's training and early work remain largely in the dark. His attention to minute detail, which also characterises his large triptychs, has led to the assumption that he was trained as miniaturist ("Garden of Delights", ill., p. 135; the "Haywain" triptych, several versions, of which one at the Prado, Madrid; "Last Judgement", Vienna, Gallery of the Akademie der Bildenden Künste). There is no proof of this, however. The disturbing world of his paintings, which often scourges the moral decadence and folly of the world, may have been induced by religious unrest before the Reformation. In the course of his development, Bosch increasingly refined his devices until he achieved a distinctive way of handling colour, combined with an equally distinctive clear outline. This marks him as a contemporary of Leonardo, whose works he may or may not have known. Bosch was, besides Geertgen tot Sint Jans, the great landscape painter in the Netherlands in the 15th and early 16th centuries. He gave the impetus to the development of the "world landscape" – such as by Patinir – and also of the autonomous landscape, such as Pieter Brueghel's Seasons. It is significant that Bosch, already highly regarded in his lifetime, should have found particular favour with his "morality" pictures in the very place where the 16th century Inquisition had its worst excesses: in Spain.

*Illustrations:*
135   The Garden of Delights, c. 1510
136   The Ship of Fools, after 1490
137   St Jerome, c. 1500

## BOTERO Fernando

born 1932 Medellín, Columbia

Botero grew up in Medellín, an industrial region of Columbia, and then went to Bogotá where he had his first exhibition. Only then did he take up his art studies at the Academía San Fernando in Madrid. In Florence he studied art history. The distinctive feature of his work is the sumptuous shape. He succeeds in combining simple narrative delight with cleverly applied traditional methods and respect for the old masters to achieve a new sensualism and grotesque drollery. In the early 1990s he caused a sensation with his monumental bronze figures of overly stout human beings, which were displayed in public places, including the Champs-Elysées in Paris. Since 1960 Botero has been living in New York.

*Illustration:*
668   The Family of the President, 1967

## BOTTICELLI Sandro

(Alessandro di Mariano Filipepi)

1445 Florence – 1510 Florence

After an apprenticeship as a goldsmith, which was to influence his entire work, he became the pupil of Filippo Lippi from whom he took over the madonna and angel figures, but giving them more expression. There is no proof that he worked under Verrocchio, though this is probable for stylistic reasons. There he would have perfected his talent as master of the sensitively drawn line. His early work takes up the plastic realism of the past generation: the "Adoration of the Magi" (Florence, Uffizi, c. 1475) is characteristic with its clear composition, three-dimensional figures, strong, bright colours and individual treatment of the faces (Medici portraits). Later, the interest in space and physical form diminishes in favour of the richly moving line of slender figures and fine detail of jewels and richly embroidered dress ("Birth of Venus", "Primavera", ill., p. 107). But as his three frescos begun in 1481 on the lower wall of the Sistine Chapel show, Botticelli was well able to achieve monumental effects. He soon became a master of the large format: in his "Cleansing Sacrifice of the Lepers" the centre emerges naturally, the multi-figured groups connect, giving unity to the scene, and foreground, middle ground and background merge into each other.

In his late work the line gains in sensitivity (92 silver point drawings for Dante's *Divine Comedy*) and in emotional expressiveness ("Annunciation", Florence, Uffizi, 1490–1495). The religious fervour depicted in these later works may have been the result of Savonarola's sermons calling for repentance, but this tendency was already noticeable in his mature work. With his death in 1510 the 15th-century period of Italian painting came to a close.

*Illustrations:*
90    Camilla and the Centaur, c. 1482
104   Venus and Mars, c. 1480
106   Madonna del Magnificat, c. 1481/82
106   Pietà, after 1490
107   La Primavera (Spring), c. 1477/78
107   The Birth of Venus, c. 1485

## BOUCHER François

1703 Paris – 1770 Paris

His father, a designer of embroidery patterns and ornaments, apprenticed the 17-year-old to François Lemoine. Apparently he stayed there for only three months, and then went to work under the engraver Jean François Cars. Already in 1723 he won the Grand Prix de Rome, but did not visit Italy until four years later. On his return in 1731 he was admitted to the Academy as historical painter and in 1734 became a member. Rising from professor to rector and director of the Academy, his brilliant career culminated in his appointment as head of the Royal Gobelin factory (1755) and finally as "Premier Peintre du Roi" (1765). The young Boucher developed his style by drawing primarily on Bloemaert, Rubens and Watteau. His early work celebrates the pastoral and idyllic, sometimes in childlike diminutive. He depicts nature with ingenious artifice, also creating pure landscape. The eroticism of his shepherds and shepherdesses is given a very thin veneer of innocence. Mythological scenes with Venus as the focal point are treated on the level of mere amorousness and sensuality; there is no heroism: Mount Olympus has been replaced by the boudoir seen from the perspective of the keyhole. In his portraits, too, Boucher's work realises the Rococo in its purest form. In his final creative years he became the butt of the critics of the new morality and pathos as advocated by Diderot.

*Illustrations:*
336   The Toilette of Venus, 1751
354   The Education of Eros, 1742
354   Diana returning from the Hunt, 1745
355   The Breakfast, 1739
356   Blonde Odalisque (Portrait of Louise O'Murphy), 1752

## BOURDON Sébastien

1616 Montpellier – 1671 Paris

Bourdon led a restless life. At the age of seven he became apprenticed, and he was already painting the ceiling in a château near Bordeaux when fourteen. Lacking commissions, he became a soldier, but was, however, discharged and went to Rome in 1634, where he painted pictures for an art dealer in the styles of Claude Lorrain, Sacchi, Poussin, Castiglione and L. Carracci. His brilliant technique and skill in copying were obstacles to the development of a personal style. He returned to Paris in 1637, feeling that as a Huguenot he was not welcome in Rome, and again produced "Italian" hunting and battle scenes for a dealer. Bourdon was highly regarded by his contemporaries. In 1648 he was a co-founder of the Académie Royale, where he held a chair and was appointed rector in 1655. In 1652 he acted briefly as court painter to Queen Christina of Sweden, where he painted her seated on a horse (Madrid, Prado). In Paris he decorated the Galerie des Hôtel de Bretonvilliers, later destroyed, which, according to records, seems to have been his best and most individual piece of work.

*Illustration:*
251   The Finding of Moses, c. 1650

## BOUTS Dieric

(also: Dierick, Dirk)

c. 1410–1420 Haarlem – 1475 Leuven

Bouts can, besides Memling, be considered the most significant successor to van der Weyden. Little is known about his training and early work. It is not clear whether he was Rogier's pupil or not, but this painter's work certainly became a lasting influence. Bouts developed Rogier's style almost to a radical degree in his verticalization of architecture and figures, the minute rendering of costly garments behind which the body recedes, and the reduction of the individualistic in favour of typification. It is difficult to decide whether Bouts was the representative of a specific, Protestant art of the northern part of the Netherlands, or whether he was caught up by the wave of "re-go-thicisation" sweeping over Europe after the mid-century. In any case, the characteristics already described, intensified, from the Lord's Supper altar in Leuven (1464–1467) to the justice pictures in Brussels (begun 1468). In 1475 Bouts' name first appears in the records of Leuven, where he married Katharina van der Brugghen. He worked in Leuven and became a highly respected painter. His last mention in the records dates from 17 April 1475. As to his work, a clear line still cannot be drawn between his own work and that of others, including his son Dieric Bouts the Younger. It is therefore impossible to make a fair assessment of his art. If the winged altar at Munich known as "the pearl of Brabant" is indeed by his hand, then he must have been one of the greatest landscape painters of his generation.

*Illustrations:*
130   The Empress' Ordeal by Fire in front of Emperor Otto III, c. 1470–1475
130   Last Supper, 1464–1467

## BRAQUE Georges
1882 Argenteuil-sur-Seine – 1963 Paris
Braque was apprenticed to a decorative painter in Le Havre, before studying in Paris from 1900. He attended the Académie Humbert and in 1903 the École des Beaux-Arts. The exhibition of the Fauves in 1905 impressed him so profoundly that he joined the group. In contrast to the other Fauves, Braque preferred broken colours: violet and pink. The Cézanne commemorative exhibition in 1907 and his acquaintance with Picasso, in whose studio he had seen the "Demoiselles d'Avignon" (ill. p. 569), altered his direction. He now painted surfaces penetrating each other and arched planes, a system of volumes which in 1908 the critic Louis Vauxcelles called cubes. He also reduced colour to a few tones in favour of form. During the period of analytical Cubism from 1909 to 1912 objects were broken down to become unrecognisable multi-faceted planes. The resolution came after 1912 with the large-scale representation which re-united synthetic Cubism in a compositional whole. Until World War I, when Braque was called up, he worked closely with Picasso. When Braque returned after being wounded in 1917 and took up painting again, he developed his own style based on his Fauvist and Cubist experiences. Form was again combined with colour. Braque painted monumental figures and a series of mantel and table pictures. He also re-discovered landscape. After World War II he produced studio interiors and bird pictures in which objects and space, and severity and poetry, are united. The studio interiors are considered the crowning achievement of Braque's œuvre.

*Illustrations:*
548   Fruit bowl and glass, 1912
572   The Portuguese, 1911
572   The Duo, 1937
573   Still Life with Bowl of Fruit , Bottle and Mandolin, 1930

## BRAUNER Victor
1903 Piatra Neamt (Rumania) – 1966 Paris
After studying at the Academy of Fine Arts in Bucharest from 1921 to 1924 and an initial visit to Paris in 1925, Brauner settled in the French capital in 1930. He met Brancusi, Giacometti and Tanguy and in 1933 joined the Surrealists whose ideas he tried to pass on when back in Bucharest. In August 1938 he lost an eye while trying to settle an argument, having portrayed himself as one-eyed seven years earlier. His flight in 1940 took him first into the Pyrenees and then the Alps where, for lack of utensils, he discovered wax

painting. In his years of solitude he developed a comprehensive private mythology which he sought to express both visually and in verse. He returned to Paris in 1945 and broke with the Surrealists in 1948. Recurring severe illness induced him to spend three years on the Côte d'Azur where he began work with the potters at Vallauris. In the 1950s, stimulated by Heidegger's existentialism, he produced pictures which dealt prophetically with death.

*Illustration:*
612   Miroir de l'incréé, 1945

## BRUEGEL, BREUGHEL → Brueghel

## BROEDERLAM Melchior
active 1381 – 1409 Ypern (West Flanders)
There are earlier references to people of this name in Ypern, yet nothing is known about his upbringing and what affected him artistically. As in so many cases, iconoclasm and wars in the Flemish/French border lands are probably responsible for this. If it were not for the surviving altar in the Carthusian monastery at Dijon, we would not have known of his existence, except for written sources. They tell us that he was highly esteemed by Duke Philipp the Bold of Burgundy whose court painter and *valet de chambre* he was. He participated in the decoration of Château Hesdin, one of the richest and most finely furnished of its kind. As court artist he also painted portraits and designed costumes. It is recorded that he accompanied the altar to Dijon and visited Paris. The two surviving pictures at Dijon, which adorn a carved altar by Jacques de Baerze, show him to be a painter whose handling of the effect of light and gradation of tone was so masterly that, when in front of these pictures, one actually feels how necessary the refinement of the old technique was to oil-painting.

*Illustration:*
61   The Presentation in the Temple and The Flight to Egypt, 1394–1399

## BRONZINO Agnolo
(Agnolo Tori, Agnoli di Cosimo)
1503 Monticelli (near Florence) – 1572 Florence
After an apprenticeship with Raffaelino del Garbo, the young Bronzino assisted Pontormo in 1522 with the frescos in the Certosa di Galuzzo near Florence, where he received decisive artistic impulses for his future. But he moved increasingly away from Pontormo's spiritual tendencies, favouring a highly refined, detached aestheticism. In 1539 he participated in the decorations for the wedding of Cosimo I de' Medici with Eleonora of Toledo and won such favour that he became their court painter and portraitist. His portraits, usually painted in cool colours and in which the figures are placed silhouette-like before the background, are the most refined of their kind in the 16th century. During his visit to Rome from 1546 to 1548 Bronzino studied in particular the works of Raphael and Michelangelo, from whose novel ways of portraying the figure he benefited, as is apparent in such works as the fresco "Martyrdom of St Lawrence" (Florence, 1565–1569). In his later work he developed under the influence of what were then the latest theories seeking to unlock the code of allegorical representation. In these works he manages to balance cool sensuality with an elaborate composition. The colour surface often attains an enamelled smoothness.

*Illustrations:*
159   Eleonora of Toledo and her Son Giovanni, c. 1545
180   An Allegory (Venus, Cupid, Time and Folly), before 1545

## BROUWER Adriaen
c. 1605/06 Oudenaarde (Flanders) – 1638 Antwerp
By birth Brouwer was Flemish, by training Dutch. After the death of his father he probably went at the age of sixteen to Antwerp, a year later to Haarlem. Presumably he had contacts with Frans Hals at this time. In 1631 he returned to Antwerp, became a member of the Lukas Guild and ran a small workshop. Brouwer was always in debt, spending some months in prison. Rubens, who owned 17 of his pictures, probably obtained his release. On his early death during the Plague seven creditors fought over his estate. Brouwer's work always calls to mind scenes of card-playing, smoking, quaffing and brawling peasants – his favourite subjects along with "operations" by the village barber. While early paintings are of strong colour, the more mature work, under Hals' influence, is in deep brown tones, and carried out with great artistic skill and precise psychological observation. After Brueghel, Brouwer is considered the foremost painter of bucolic themes, the greatest collection of 16 of his works being in the possession of the Alte Pinakothek at Munich.

*Illustrations:*
311   The Operation, undated
311   Peasants Smoking and Drinking, c. 1635

## BRUEGHEL Jan the Elder
(also: Bruegel, Breughel, Breugel)
1568 Brussels – 1625 Antwerp
Because of his penchant for certain themes and glowing enamel paint, Jan, the second son of Pieter Brueghel the Elder, was given the nickname "Velvet" or "Flower" Brueghel. His work, which distinguishes itself from his father's by a refined technique and miniature-like delicateness, was given direction by his grandmother, a miniaturist painter, and his teachers, including Pieter Goetkint and Gillis van Coninxloo. Brueghel spent the years 1589–1596 in Italy; he worked in Rome in 1593/94 and then in Milan in 1596 for Cardinal Federigo Borromeo, who became his patron. In 1597 he returned to Amsterdam and became a member of the Lukas Guild. In 1610 the Archduke of Austria, governor of the Netherlands, appointed him court painter. Brueghel was well-to-do and respected, owning several houses in Antwerp as well as a considerable art collection. He was a friend of Rubens with whom he collaborated, including the magnificent flower garland in Rubens' "Madonna in the Flower Wreath" (Munich, Alte Pinakothek) while Rubens painted Adam and Eve in Brueghel's "Paradise" (The Hague, Mauritshuis). Besides historical scenes, paradisiacal images of animals, and genre scenes, he was above all a painter of landscape, often with staffage figures and animals in the foreground, and of flower pieces. As a specialist of "accessories" he collaborated with Frans Francken, Hans Rottenhammer and Momper.

*Illustrations:*
279   The Animals entering the Ark, 1615
288   Great Fishmarket, 1603
288   Landscape with Windmills, c. 1607
289   The Holy Family, undated

## BRUEGHEL Pieter the Elder
(also: Bruegel, Breughel, Breugel)
c. 1525–1530 Breda (?) – 1569 Brussels
His nickname "Peasant Brueghel" harks back to his depiction of peasant life, proverb and genre scenes, unduly diminishing the importance of this great Netherlandish painter of the 16th century. In his representations of the life of peasants and the underprivileged, Brueghel penetrated the outer shell, converting them to images applicable to human life in general, such as in the folly of the World

("Country of the Blind", Naples, Museo Nazionale di Capodimonte), the transience of material values ("The Land of Cockaigne", ill. p. 205), or the fate awaiting the power-greedy (various versions of the "Tower of Babel", ill. p. 205).
In some respects Brueghel takes up the concerns of Bosch. He undoubtedly belongs to the phase of European Mannerism in breaking up the composition into small parts ("Proverb" pictures), or the suggestion of movement ("Country of the Blind"). On the other hand, with his later works which show a new overall unity of structure and also greater use of large figures, he paves the way for the Baroque north of the Alps. His visit to Italy in the 1550s, which took him to the far South, might have contributed to this change. His significant place as a landscape painter in the whole of European art in the 16th century is undisputed. In the "Months" pictures created around 1565, colour developed into an elemental force, pointing far into the 17th century.
*Illustrations:*
204   Netherlandish Proverbs, 1559
205   The Tower of Babel, 1563
205   The Land of Cockaigne, 1567
206   The Corn Harvest, 1565
206   Hunters in the Snow, 1565

BRUGGHEN → Terbrugghen

## BURGKMAIR Hans the Elder
1473 Augsburg – 1531 Augsburg
After an initial training by his father, Burgkmair was apprenticed to Schongauer at Colmar, whose style influenced his early work. After 1490 he probably travelled in Northern Italy, spending time in Venice. In 1498 he finally settled in Augsburg and took over his father's workshop. His reputation grew rapidly judging by the commissions he received (e.g. "Basilica Pictures" for the Catharine Foundation, today at Augsburg, Altdeutsche Galerie, 1501–1504). These are still in the tradition of the late 15th century, as fine detail still dominates the overall structure and composition. With the knowledge gained in Italy, Burgkmair later explored the monumental form of the High Renaissance, combining it with a brilliant, warm coloration. (St John's Altar, ill. p. 189). He also made drawings for woodcuts, especially from 1512 to 1518 with his contributions to the large commissions for Emperor Maximilian (Weißkunig, Theuerdank, Triumphal Procession of the Emperor Maximilian). Burgkmair was a key figure in opening the Augsburg art world to the Renaissance.
*Illustration:*
189   John the Evangelist on Patmos, 1518

## BURNE-JONES Edward Coley
1833 Birmingham – 1898 London
After studying theology, Burne-Jones turned to art, and with his friends William Morris and Rossetti formed the nucleus of the Pre-Raphaelite Brotherhood. His work was extensive and varied, including paintings, drawings, designs and illustrations. Like the other members of the group, he endeavoured to revive craftsmanship, paving the way for the Art Noveau movement. He produced designs for interior decoration, furniture, stained glass, tiles, tapestries and wall paintings for the company Morris, Marshal, Faulkner & Co, of which he was also a partner. His admiration for the Italian Renaissance found expression in his paintings. His themes are of a mythological-allegorical nature and drawn from legends and history, often including heroines with a slightly menacing air. John Ruskin was one of his friends and admirers. In 1890 he was elected to the Royal Academy, an honour from which he resigned three years later.
*Illustration:*
526   King Cophetua and the Beggar Maid, 1884

## BURRI Alberto
1915 Città di Castello (Umbria) – 1995 Nice
From 1934 to 1939 Burri studied medicine in Perugia, and then served four years as a doctor in the Italian Army in North Africa. During this period he began to paint. When he returned from an American prisoner-of-war camp in 1945, he devoted himself almost wholly to painting. His first abstract paintings appeared in 1949. Together with Giuseppe Capogrossi, Ettore Colla and others he founded the Gruppo Origine in Rome in 1951. Burri then went to America where he earned his living by giving art lessons. From 1960 he worked again in Rome. His work consists of abstract pictures of closely-assembled materials, lacking any formula, in part collage, in part material montage. Colour and the origin and type of materials express strong statements. Since the early 1960s he had been experimenting with burned plastics, working with another group of artists.
*Illustration:*
643   Sack No. 5, 1953

## CAILLEBOTTE Gustave
1848 Paris – 1894 Gennevilliers (near Paris)
The son of a middle-class family, Caillebotte was left a large legacy by his father, giving him lifelong independence. In 1870 he completed his law studies and entered the École des Beaux Arts in Paris in 1873. Here he came into contact with the Impressionists and met Monet. He found his motifs in his immediate surroundings: family, street scenes, working life, and scenes from his summer visits to Yerres, especially boat parties. In 1876 he contributed for the first time to the second Impressionist exhibition; then he financed and organised subsequent events. Caillebotte was generous to his needy painter friends, including Monet, Renoir, Sisley and Pissarro, buying many of their pictures and staging exhibitions of their work. In his will, made in 1883, he left his large collection of Impressionist paintings to the French nation on condition that all 67 works were to remain together in the Louvre. He died of a stroke in 1894, and the Institute de France scandalously refused to accept the collection on the grounds that it included works by Cézanne. It was not housed in the Louvre until 1928; today it is at the Musée d'Orsay.
*Illustration:*
505   Paris Street: A Rainy Day, 1877

## CAMPIN Robert
c. 1380 Tournai (?) – 1444 Tournai
Recent research is agreed on the identification of Robert Campin as the painter who was long called "Master of Flémalle" (named after a triptych said to have been in the Abbey Flémalle near Liège, now kept at the Städelsche Kunstinstitut at Frankfurt/Main). Some of the problem remains unsolved, however: although he is referred to in documentary records, none of his signed works survives. Sometimes he has been placed alongside the young van der Weyden, but stylistic differences speak against this. Rather, a teacher-pupil relationship should be assumed. Campin was born in about 1380 in Tournai, where he was made master in 1406/07 and presumably taught van der Weyden from 1427 to 1432. Together with the brothers van Eyck he can be considered the founder of the Early Renaissance in Netherlandish painting. Evidently outgrowing the Burgundian art of the brothers Limburg, whose influence could still be felt in Campin's early work ("Betrothal and Annunciation of Mary", Madrid, Prado, c. 1410), he soon turned to three-dimensional figure representation and the exploration of depth ("Adoration of the Shepherds", Dijon, c. 1420). These are late works, when the painter was almost obsessed with all aspects of perspective (e.g. the Mérode altar, so called after its original location; now in New York, Metropolitan Museum, c. 1430; Werl altar, ill. p. 126). Terborch
*Illustrations:*
86    Annunciation, undated
126   St Barbara, 1438
126   Portrait of a Man, c. 1435

## CANALETTO
(Giovanni Antonio Canal)
1697 Venice – 1768 Venice
As the son of a painter of stage sets, Canaletto was trained in the craft of perspective painting for the theatre, and this was to be a decisive influence on his later work. When in Rome in 1719 he became acquainted with veduta painters. His friendship with Pannini, Vanvitelli and Carlevari resulted in his emphasis on chiaroscuro in his early work. Besides topographical views, his early work also included architectural fantasies and ruin capricci. His pictures were particularly sought after by English collectors, and Canaletto used agents who sold his pictures. The demand was so great that he went to England to paint views of London and of country houses. These pictures are already in the lighter, clearer coloration which he had adopted in the 1730s – a quality he transferred to a certain degree to his graphic work. His avoidance of strong chiaroscuro contrasts in his middle and late work led to the erroneous assumption that Canaletto had abandoned the Baroque. His treatment of light does, indeed, belong to the Baroque, while his discoveries in the coloured rendition of views were to prepare the way to the open-air painting of the 19th century.
*Illustrations:*
338   Venice: The Basin of San Marco on Ascension Day c. 1735–1741
370   The Courtyard of the Warwick Castle, 1751
370   Regatta on the Canale Grande, after 1735
371   Venice: Campo San Vitale and Santa Maria della Carità (The Stonemasons' Yard), c. 1726/27

CANALETTO → Bellotto

## CANO Alonso
1601 Granada – 1667 Granada
Cano, one of the most versatile talents in 17th century Spain, learned architectural drawing from his father, carpenter and altar builder Miguel Cano, the art of sculpting under Juan Martinez Montañés in Seville, finally studying painting from 1616 to 1621 under Francisco Pacheco, the teacher of Velásquez. His best known architectural work is the facade of Granada Cathedral with its theatrically-baroque triumphal arch motif. On Velásquez' recommendation the king appointed Cano court painter and drawing teacher to prince Balthasar Carlos. In 1643 he painted idealised images of Gothic kings for the Alcázar, which show him to be a painter with an individual style. He has been unfairly accused of eclecticism: his large-scale colour planes may be reminiscent of Reni, but the general approach is genuinely Spanish in its realistic observation and combines an independent manner with an imaginative historicism. Cano's life was eventful. In 1637 he had to flee from Seville to Madrid after injuring a duelling partner. In 1644 he was accused of the murder of his wife and threatened with torture

and imprisonment, so he escaped to his estates in Valencia. In 1650, with the king's help, he was given a sinecure by the cathedral of Granada, fell out with the clerics, was dismissed, took legal action, was ordained as priest in Madrid, and reinstated at Granada as sub-deacon, where he died impoverished.
*Illustration:*
265   St Isidore and the Miracle of the Well, c. 1646–1648

## CAPELLE Jan van de
(also: Cappelle)
c. 1624/25 Amsterdam – 1679 Amsterdam
Although quite untrained, this son of a prosperous cloth merchant belongs among the most important marine painters of the Netherlands. Painting was a pastime to him, sparked off through the study of Simon de Vlieger's drawings. It was within his means to have his portrait painted by Frans Hals and Rembrandt, and on his death he left not only a large legacy but also a collection of 197 paintings, including some by Rembrandt, Hals, van Goyen, Brouwer, and van de Velde. Capelle's seascapes, mostly in early morning or evening mood, depict ships on a calm sea or wide river estuaries, with the sunlight reflected on water, sky and ship silhouettes. Less important are his winter scenes, rustic idylls in the style of Aert van der Neer, of which some 40 remain.
*Illustration:*
326   Ship Scene with a Dutch Yacht Firing A Salute, 1650

## CARAVAGGIO
(Michelangelo Merisi, Amerighi da Caravaggio)
1573 Caravaggio (near Milan) – 1610 Porto Ercole
Michelangelo Merisi was born in Caravaggio as the son of a ducal architect. His early training was under a little-known pupil of Titian. In 1592 he went to Rome, where he earned his livelihood by painting run-of-the-mill pictures. His contact with Cesare d'Arpino, the most popular painter and art dealer in Rome at the turn of the century, brought recognition but no material independence. However, it is through the art business that Caravaggio met his first patron, Cardinal del Monte, who not only held out the possibility of working independently, but also secured for him his first public commission, from the Contarelli Chapel in San Luigi dei Francesi. Here, Caravaggio developed his characteristic treatment of light, which shoots dramatically into the dark world of his pictures, creating an intensely sharp yet alien reality.
From then on he was inundated by public commissions. Yet because of his violent temper he was constantly in trouble with the authorities. In 1606 he became embroiled in murder and had to flee, finding refuge on the estates of Prince Marzio Colonna, where he painted the Vienna "Rosary Madonna". On his wanderings he paused at Naples, painting exclusively religious themes. In Malta he was put up by the Knights of St John and painted several portraits of the grand master, Alof de Wignacourt. In 1608 he was granted the title "Cavaliere d'Obbedienza". The artistically fertile Maltese period was again interrupted by imprisonment and renewed flight. Going through Syracuse and Messina, where some major late works came into being, Caravaggio went on to Palermo and from there again to Naples. Here the news of the Pope's pardon reached him and, on arriving at Porto Ercole by ship, he was again arrested but later released. By then the ship had sailed, including all he possessed. Struck down by a fever, he died without setting foot in Rome again.
The main stages of this story of a restless and finally hounded man are reflected in his work, albeit in an unexpected way. Just before 1600 the light, clear coloration of the early work is replaced, almost without transition, by his famous chiaroscuro, combining dynamism with dramatic expression. Then, from the Maltese period onwards, the intensity of this combination is steadily reduced. Perhaps because of his need to paint more rapidly, he began to paint more thinly, and the dark background becomes increasingly part of the overall composition, while the strong contrasting chiaroscuro effect is lessened to such a degree that it can no longer be understood merely as light and shade but as an indication of an increasing spiritualisation.
*Illustrations:*
214   The young Bacchus, c. 1591–1593
228   Basket of Fruit , c. 1596
229   The Fortune Teller (La Zingara), c. 1594/95
229   The Supper at Emmaus, c. 1596–1602
230   Bacchus, c. 1598
231   The Crucifixion of St Peter, 1601
231   The Entombment, c. 1602–1604

## CARPACCIO Vittore
c. 1455 (1465 ?) Venice (?) – 1526 Venice
Carpaccio was the principal pupil of Gentile Bellini. In his workshop he learned the precise observation of detail, the "staging" of multi-figured historical scenes and the composition of large-scale paintings. Artistically, however, teacher and pupil differed widely. While Bellini can be considered the "chronicler" of Venice in the late 15th century, Carpaccio was the born "novelist", intermingling freely what was actually before his eyes with his own inventions or with the material of legends. At a higher level he could be called the Benozzo Gozzoli of Venetian art. If Bellini's panels of the "Legend of the True Cross" can only be imagined in their large format, it is possible to see Carpaccio's efforts as book illustrations. This impression is reinforced by his choice of colours, sometimes bordering on pastel shades, as opposed to his teacher's adherence to those colours which are typically associated with the subject matter. Carpaccio created all his major works for Venice: one of the earliest consisted of nine large panels depicting scenes from the legend of St Ursula (ill. p. 122); from 1502 to 1507 followed the scenes from the Lives of Saints George and Jerome for the Scuola di San Giorgio degli Schiavoni. A great number of panel pictures, mostly of religious content, are to be found in collections all over Europe. His mode of telling a story still belongs to the Early Renaissance, but in his brilliant rendering of the light and atmosphere of landscape and interiors, as well as in his handling of perspective, Carpaccio is already abreast of the innovations of the late work of Giovanni Bellini.
*Illustration:*
122   Scenes from the Life of St Ursula, c. 1491

## CARRÀ Carlo
1881 Quargnento (Piedmont) – 1966 Milan
After attending classes at the Milan Brera School and working as an independent painter, Carrà joined the Futurists in 1909 and signed their manifesto. When in Paris in 1911, he met Modigliani, Picasso and Apollinaire. His work from this period shows the influence of Cubism, but in a manner that is more dynamic and not restricted to studio subjects. As early as 1915 he terminated his Futurist membership. During his military service he became acquainted with de Chirico and his ideas on "metaphysical" art when at Ferrara in 1917. The vehemence of his Futuristic period was now replaced by stillness, toned coloration and structural objectivity. His former relationship with tradition was renewed: he again occcupied himself with Masaccio, Uccello and Giotto. The result was a new Italian realism of melancholy solemnity – Carrà's third contribution to his chosen art.
*Illustration:*
603   Summer, 1930

## CARRACCI Agostino
1557 Bologna – 1602 Parma
## CARRACCI Annibale
1560 Bologna – 1609 Rome
## CARRACCI Lodovico
1555 Bologna – 1619 Bologna
Amongst the trio of Carraccis, Agostino, Annibale's elder brother, was probably less endowed artistically and rather more important in the role of scholarly theoretician, as emerged in the task of decorating the Palazzo Farnese for which he supplied the programme and iconography. As teacher, he advocated the often disputed "academic Carraccisms". Annibale took as his starting point the Mannerist style in his early work ("Butcher's Shop", Oxford, Christ Church Library Collections), developing it through his study of Correggio at Parma (1584/85) and the works of Titian and Veronese, to a sensual classicism enlivened by an inner unrest and true-to-life naturalness, as exemplified by his "Triumph of Bacchus and Ariadne" (ill. p. 227) in the frescos at the Palazzo Farnese. He had already left the "Accademia del Naturale", later called the "eclectic" school, in 1595, which he had founded in Bologna together with his cousin Lodovico and brother Agostino. In the 49 years of his life Annibale gained importance not only for his frescos, but also as a painter of Baroque altar pieces. Lodovico was the head of the school known for its rejection of Mannerism. He also trained both his cousins in his workshop at Bologna. In 1584 they collaborated in the decoration of the Palazzo Fava, in their native city, with mythological friezes which were attacked by the Mannerists and led to the founding of the school, enabling them to uphold their views artistically and theoretically. Lodovico's religious work, in particular, radiates a new, natural and genuine devoutness.
*Illustrations:*
225   The Beaneater, c. 1580–1590
225   "Domine, quo vadis?" (Christ's appearing to St Peter on the Appian Way), c. 1601/02
226   The Martyrdom of St Stephen, c. 1603/04
226   The Lamentation of Christ, 1606
227   Triumph of Bacchus and Ariadne, c. 1595–1605

## CARRIERA Rosalba Giovanna
1675 Venice – 1757 Venice
As a pupil of Giuseppe Diamantini and Antonio Balestra, Rosalba Carriera initially gained her reputation as a painter of miniaturist portraits. August the Strong, King of Poland, was portrayed by her on several occasions. Her brother-in-law Giovanni Antonio Pellegrini seems to have encouraged her to take up pastel painting. By using this technique in portraiture and perfecting its artistic possibilities, which lie between drawing and painting, Carriera was, if not the inventor of pastel painting, at least the creator of a new influential form of portraiture – the face of the age. At the age of thirty she became a member of the Accademia di San Luca in Rome. Her visit to Paris in 1720, where she painted Louis XV as dauphin (Dresden, Gemäldegalerie) and exchanged pictures with Watteau, was of great significance to French pastel painting.
*Illustration:*
369   Portrait of a Young Girl, after 1708

## CASSATT Mary Stevenson
1845 Allegheny City (Pennsylvania) – 1926 Le Mesnil-Théribus (Oise)

The daughter of a banker, she moved with her family to Paris in 1851. From 1853 to 1855 she lived at Heidelberg and Darmstadt. From 1861–1865 she studied at the Pennsylvania Academy of Fine Arts in Philadelphia, then in the studio of Charles Chaplin in Paris. In 1868 she exhibited for the first time at the Salon. While studying at the Academy Raimondi in Parma in 1871, she copied Correggio and Parmigianino and became an admirer of Velázquez and Rembrandt. In 1873 she travelled to Madrid, Seville, Belgium and the Netherlands, and made copies especially of Velázquez and Rubens, before finally settling in Paris. There she met Degas in 1877, who suggested her joining the Impressionists. Her work was greatly influenced by Degas and Renoir, taking as principal subject portraits of women and children. Cassatt took part in the IV to VI and again in the VIII Impressionist exhibition. Her own work was shown by Durand-Ruel in 1891. In 1898 she visited the United States, went to Italy and Spain in 1901, and for the last time to the United States in 1908. In 1910 she became a member of the National Academy of Design in New York. In 1914 she was awarded the gold medal of the Pennsylvanian Academy of Art. Cassatt gradually lost her sight and was compelled to give up painting. It was due to her efforts that French Impressionism became known and understood in America, and also thanks to her initiative that the Havemeyer collection, now at the New York Metropolitan Museum, came into being.

*Illustrations:*
539   The Boating Party, c. 1893/94
539   Two Children on the Beach, 1884

## CASTAGNO Andrea del
c. 1421–1423 Castagno near Florence (?) – 1457 Florence

Castagno's work must be seen in close connection with the older painter Uccello. In their major work, both take as starting point Masaccio and the great sculptors of the Early Renaissance. If Uccello's greatest concern was the art of perspective, Castagno strove to make his figures appear solid and real, although, of course, these two aspects often overlap. We know nothing of Castagno's training. When painting the prophets in the vault the of Capella di San Tarasio on the Santa Zaccaria in Venice in 1442 – the first influx of the Florentine Renaissance into Venetian art – his style was already established. Castagno's art was closest to Donatello. It was probably between 1445 and 1450 that he received a commission for frescos from the monastery Santa Apollonia in Florence. His Last Supper in the refectory represents an important step towards Leonardo's work in Milan. The "naturalness" of the frescos is due to the virtuosity of construction in which perspectival elements and real space merge, giving the illusion of great depth, as well as the lively movement and gestures of the life-sized, ample figures. Probably shortly after 1450 he painted the "Uomini famosi" fresco series in the Villa Pandolfini at Legnaia near Florence (ill. p.98) for which the sculptural style had been prescribed. Castagno's interest in sculpture and its effect on painting were central to his work.

*Illustration:*
98   Farinata degli Uberti. From the series "Uomini famosi", c. 1450

## CÉZANNE Paul
1839 Aix-en-Provence – 1906 Aix-en-Provence

Born during the first generation of Impressionists and spasmodically also belonging to the group, Cézanne nevertheless always went his own way. He was to become a great influence on subsequent generations of painters and can be regarded as the forerunner of modern painting. Introverted, never satisfied with himself, he worked steadily, partly in Aix, partly in Paris, Auvers-sur-Oise, Pontoise, or L'Estaque, and finally only at Aix where he settled. He quarrelled with his boyhood friend Zola, believing that he had been portrayed as an unsuccessful painter in one of Zola's novels. He smarted under the rejection of his contemporaries, feeling that only a few understood him, and worked untiringly, always in doubt whether he would reach his goal of transmitting artistically his perceptions rather than merely rendering them. Financially, he was always dependent on his father, but in his advanced years he at least received recognition of his art. At first destined for a banking career in his father's business house, he gave up his law studies in 1859/60, against his father's wishes, in order to study art. He went to the Académie Suisse from 1862–1865, studied the old masters, and was rejected by the École des Beaux-Arts. Until about 1870 he used thick, dense colours, later called his "baroque" style, painting narrative themes, still lifes, portraits, and studio-painted landscapes based on sketches. Although an admirer of other painters' works, he often used them as the basis of uncomplimentary versions, such as Manet's "Olympia" (Paris, Musée d'Orsay). Pissaro introduced him to the Impressionist circle with whom he exhibited unsuccessfully in 1874 and 1877. Pissaro became his mentor and persuaded him to paint in the open. Despite his close contact with the Impressionists, he did not adopt their methods, preferring to produce something "solid and lasting". He abandoned his early style and used light tone values to define the structures of forms in space, reducing them to their essential features, and so using ideas and structures in order to convey a representation of deeper meaning.

*Illustrations:*
486   Boy with a Red Waistcoat, c. 1890–1895
510   The Card Players, c. 1890–1892
511   Still Life with Apples and Oranges, c. 1895–1900
511   Woman with Coffee-Pot, c. 1890–1895
512   Les grandes baigneuses (Bathers), c. 1900–1905
512   Mont Sainte-Victoire Seen from the Quarry at Bibémus, c. 1898–1900

## CHAGALL Marc
1887 Liosno (near Vitebsk) – 1985 Saint-Paul-de-Vence (near Nice)

His Jewish origins and rural upbringing in Russia had a lasting effect on Chagall's life. In 1907 he began to study painting at St Petersburg. In 1910 he visited Paris, where he came under the influence of van Gogh and the Fauves, also meeting Modigliani and especially the Cubists, whose ideas of form he explored. Through Apollinaire he came into contact with Herwarth Walden, in whose Berlin gallery Der Sturm his works were exhibited in 1914. From Berlin he returned to Russia, where he was detained by the outbreak of World War I. During this period Chagall succeeded in connecting his own ideas with those of the western *avant-garde*. His themes centre on his home ground at Vitebsk. On returning to France in 1922, he added to his repertoire scenes of the Mediterranean coast, the Eiffel Tower, Notre-Dame and Pont-Neuf. With Vollard's commission in 1923 to illustrate Gogol's *Dead Souls*, his extensive and brilliant career as an illustrator began. In 1925 he discovered the circus world which fired his imagination. His darkly glowing pictures give way to brilliant coloration. More than ever his figures and creatures seem to float in the air. With political tension and the threat of war, his subject matter changed temporarily, such as the symbolic composition "The White Crucifixion" (Chicago, Art Institute) of 1938. Chagall spent the war and immediate postwar period in New York. After a big exhibition at the Museum of Modern Art in 1946, he returned the following year to France where, in 1950, he settled in Vence.

*Illustrations:*
551   Double Portrait with Wineglass (Bella and Marc), 1917
590   I and the Village, 1911
590   The Birthday, 1915
591   Bride with Bouquet, c. 1924/25

## CHAMPAIGNE Philippe de
(also: Philippe de Champagne)
1602 Brussels – 1674 Paris

First in the studio of Jean Bouillon, then at the workshop of the miniature painter Michel de Bourdeaux, Champaigne acquired in his native city the technical knowledge on which he drew in his later work, particularly his treatment of the surface of materials. In 1620 he entered the workshop of Fouquière, a landscapist and friend of Rubens, where he came into indirect contact with Rubens. He then went to Paris, met Poussin and worked under Georges Lallemand.

In 1628 he had to abandon plans for a visit to Italy as he was appointed court painter to the Catholic Dowager Queen Maria de' Medici, succeeding Duchesnes, whose daughter he married. He worked for the Palais du Luxembourg and decorated churches with frescos. The patronage of Louis XIII and Richelieu soon opened opportunities for portrait painting which he carried out with a new classical refinement and precision, a style that was taken over by the next generation. The loss of his wife in 1638 and of his son in 1642 deepened his religious devotion and he sought closer links to a Jansenist monastery, Port-Royale de Champs, where he sent his two daughters in 1648. During this period his fine portraits of Mother Angélique Arnauld and the Paris Councillors (all in Paris, Louvre) were produced, and the recovery of his last remaining daughter Cathérine inspired him to his famous "Ex-Voto" painting (ill. p.250).

*Illustration:*
250   Ex Voto (Mother Superior Cathérine-Agnès Arnauld and Sister Cathérine de Sainte-Suzanne, the daughter of the artist), 1662

## CHARDIN Jean-Baptiste Siméon
1699 Paris – 1779 Paris

His father, a decorative cabinet-maker and legal adviser to his guild, first sent his son to an insignificant teacher, then in 1720 to Nicolas Coypel, who taught him painting until 1728. Since 1724 he had also been enrolled at the Academy of St Luc. He gained further experience by restoring the frescos of Rosso and Primaticcio at Fontainebleau under van Loo. He first came to public notice in 1728 when he exhibited some works at the "Exposition de la Jeunesse", including the famous still life "The Ray" (Paris, Louvre), and at the recommendation of Largillière, became a member of the Academy as an "animal and fruit painter". Chardin, who had shown his work at the Salon since 1737, now also painted genre pictures as well as still lifes, but the academic hierarchy considered both these categories not worthy of much attention. In 1740 he showed the King his pictures "The Diligent Mother" (Paris, Louvre) and "Saying Grace" (ill. p.358), and under his patronage was appointed adviser to the Academy in 1743. Public recognition of his still lifes came in the 1750s and 1760s. By now he was also trying his hand at portraiture, though with little success.

Chardin had to resign his various Academy posts in 1774 because of an eye disease. Soon afterwards his friend, the influential engraver Cochin, who had secured many commissions for him, fell out of favour. As for Chardin, his period had come to an end. The new classicism left no room for his style and choice of subjects, but he was rediscovered in the 19th century by the brothers Goncourt and especially the Impressionist painters with their new treatment of light, who saw Chardin as the last outstanding master of the *ancien régime*.
*Illustrations:*
344   Still Life with Basket of Strawberries, c. 1760/61
357   Child with Teetotum, 1738
357   Girl with a Racquet and Shuttlecock, c. 1740
358   Pipe and Jug, c. 1755
358   The Grace, 1739
359   The Kitchen Maid, c. 1740

## CHARONTON → Quarton

## CHASE William Merrit
1849 Williamsburg (Indiana) – 1916 New York
After his initial training by a local portrait painter from 1867 to 1869 and in New York at the National Academy of Design during the years 1869–1871, Chase went in 1872 to the Munich Academy where he was a pupil of Karl von Piloty until 1876. Together with his American friends Frank Duveneck and John H. Twachtman he spent nine months of the year 1877 in Venice, where he was particularly impressed by Tintoretto's work. After his return to New York in 1878 he taught painting at the newly-founded Art Students League. He was an influential teacher, and his studio became the meeting place of young American artists. His contributions to many of the great American Exhibitions established his reputation. After a visit to Paris in 1881 he abandoned his brown-toned Munich style and turned to open-air painting, showing the influence of Impressionism in his lighter colours and more fluid brushwork. Further visits to Europe followed. In 1885 he became acquainted with Whistler. In 1891 he founded at his summer house on Long Island the Shinnecock Summer Art School where he taught primarily landscape painting. In 1896 the Chase Art School in New York followed, which was renamed New York Art School two years later. In 1903 he became a member of the group The Ten American Painters, and in 1908 a member of the Academy of Arts and Letters. Chase, like Whistler, can be seen as one of the great mediators of modern European painting in the USA.
*Illustration:*
541   Leisure, 1894

## CHASSÉRIAU Théodore
1819 Sainte-Barbe-de-Samana (Santo Domingo) – 1856 Paris
At the early age of twelve years Chassériau became a pupil of Ingres who was to influence him all his life. The clarity and severity of his compositions, as well as his emphasis on outline, can be traced back to Ingres' classicism, particularly in his portraits. However, he gradually developed more independence from this dominant model and included elements of Romantic painting. He combined the classical style of Ingres with a lively and contrasting coloration reminiscent of Delacroix, under whose influence he had been since 1838. Chassériau was the only painter who succeeded in combining two such antithetical modes of painting, and so finding a style of his own. This was especially apparent in his representations of the female nude. His picture "Esther before meeting Ahasuerus" (Paris, Louvre, 1841), shows restrained sensuousness and a refined approach to colour, and Degas regarded "The Sisters of the Artist" (ill. p. 437) as the best painting of the century. After a visit to Algeria in 1846 he concentrated on oriental scenes. Towards the end of his life he devoted himself to mural painting, his principal work being scenes of war and peace at the Court des Comptes of the Palais d'Orsay.
*Illustrations:*
437   Pater Lacordaire, 1840
437   The Sisters of the Artist, 1843

## CHIRICO Giorgio de
1888 Volos (Thessalia) – 1978 Rome
The son of a Sicilian railway engineer, Chirico attended drawing classes at the Polytechnic Institute in Athens, then went on to serious artistic education at the Munich Academy from 1906 to 1908, where he became fascinated by Max Klinger's phantastical work and Böcklin's mythological scenes. He returned to Italy in 1909 and began to paint pictures which combine object and scene in a unique way. From 1911 to 1915 he lived in Paris, almost completely untouched by Cubism. The most significant work of this Paris period is the series of "Italian Squares", combining his memories of Turin and Florence squares with antique architecture. The squares are filled with melancholy and enigmatic stillness; shadowy figures, sometimes turning into marble smoothness, hover in front of rows of arcades and windows like dead eyes. They are altogether a vision of alienation and desolation. As a soldier in World War I he met Carrà when in Ferrara in 1917, and both began to paint in this manner. Chirico also produced marionette-like display dummies besides still lifes and interiors.
*Illustrations:*
602   The Silent Statue (Ariadne), 1913
602   The Prodigal Son, 1922

## CHRISTUS Petrus
(also: Cristus)
between 1415 and 1420 Baerle (Brabant) – 1472 or 1473 Bruges
After a long period in oblivion, Christus is today regarded as Jan van Eyck's successor. He was probably van Eyck's pupil, and on his death took over the workshop and completed van Eyck's unfinished work. His significance today lies in his further development of the art of perspective. He was the first painter in the North who arrived empirically at the law of linear perspective and who applied it. His significant portraits are marked by their concentration on just a few characteristic details. He was also the first Dutch master to place the sitter not before a neutral background but in front of a recognisable interior. After he was made master and burgher of Bruges in 1444, van Eyck's influence waned and was replaced by his interest in van der Weyden and Campin. His representation of background, often in the form of landscapes in a mood of quiet harmony, influenced later Netherlandish painters, in particular Bouts, Ouwater and Geertgen. There was no further development in his later work, of which only six signed and dated pictures survive.
*Illustration:*
134   Portrait of a Lady, c. 1470

## CHURCH Frederic Edwin
1826 Hartford (Connecticut) – 1900 New York
After receiving instruction from two local artists at Hartford, Church studied under Cole at Catskill from 1844 to 1848 and was soon seen as Cole's successor in the American school of landscape painting. His large-scope, large-format landscapes differ from Cole's in their more objective and detailed representation of nature, indicating a profound knowledge of the natural sciences. In 1853 and 1857 Church visited the unexplored parts of South America. A European visit in 1868 took him by way of Greece to the Middle East; in 1869 he travelled through Labrador. The pictures he produced in the various countries show a special interest in botany, geology and metereological phenomena, but rendered in a poetic, even romantic manner in the pale-coloured light of dawn or dusk. Like Fitz Hugh Lane, Church belonged to that generation of artists after Cole who did not think it essential to go to Paris or London for inspiration. Their aim was to paint nature in the state in which God has created it before He created man. To Church, the "paradise" America in its "virginal" charm represented the elemental powers of nature. His portrayal of natural forces in America was also an expression of his belief in the powers of the New World, in the "holy fate of America", as he put it.
*Illustration:*
472   Niagara Falls, 1857

## CIMABUE
(Cenni di Pepo, called Cimabue)
c. 1240 Florence (?) – after 1302
The most famous painter of his generation (documented 1272–1302), and one of the first great painters of Tuscany, Cimabue also undertook commissions outside his home ground, such as work for ecclesiastical clients in Rome, the series of large frescos in the Upper and Lower Church of St Francis at Assisi, painted glass for Siena Cathedral and mosaics for Pisa Cathedral. He obviously had a large, well-organised workshop, one of the first of its kind in 14th century Tuscany. This is probably where Giotto was trained. The kind of work produced can best be judged by the panel paintings (Madonnas, painted crucifixes): generosity of form; restriction of colour to few, usually schematically distributed tones and clear outline, but in summarily executed detail. As a panel painter the young Sienese Duccio soon became Cimabue's rival. His Santa Trinità picture may have been an attempt at accepting Duccio's challenge, but his alignment to the clever new manner of Duccio merely serves to reinforce the latter's influence, as can be seen from the panels at the Louvre from St Francis in Pisa.
*Illustrations:*
16   Maestà (Madonna Enthroned), c. 1270 (?)
28   Madonna and Child Enthroned with Angels and Prophets (Maestà), after 1285

## CLAESZ. Pieter
c. 1597/98 Burgsteinfurt (Westphalia) – 1661 Haarlem
Born in Westphalia, Claesz settled in Haarlem in 1617. Through him and the painter Willem Claesz Heda, with whom he was often confused, Haarlem became the centre of Dutch still life painting. While in his early work he usually depicted a collection and arrangement of various striking objects, he later developed his so-called "monochrome Banketje", or "breakfast pieces", which show objects on a white cloth, such as filled glasses, a bowl of bread, a plate of fruit, or a cut cake, all arranged as if by chance. He worked in tones of brown, ochre, white and grey, and with only a few sharp accents. The attraction of his still lifes lies in the beautifully executed reflection of light on glass, pewter and copper. Claesz was the father of the landscape painter Nicolaes Berchem.
*Illustration:*
306   Still Life with Musical Instruments, 1623

**CLAUDE LORRAIN** → Lorrain

**CLEMENTE Francesco**
born 1952 Naples
Clemente attended the Humanist Gymnasium in his home town where his passion for Latin, Greek, philosophy and Italian literature was awakened. When in Rome in 1968, he me Twombly, whose work made a great impression on him. In 1970 he began to study architecture in Rome, and a year later he showed his first collages. He spent some time travelling, and visited India and Afghanistan in 1973, later revisiting these countries for a longer period and absorbing some elements of their foreign cultures into his work. In 1980 he went for the first time to New York, where he set up a studio two years later. Besides New York, he lives and works also in Rome and Madras. Clemente's pictures combine abstract forms with figurative elements.
*Illustration:*
671    Untitled, 1983

**CLOSE Chuck**
(Charles Close)
born 1940 Monroe (Washington, D.C.)
Since 1958 Close has studied at several American universities, including the Yale University School of Art, and since 1964/65 at the Academy of Fine Arts in Vienna. He subsequently taught at the University of Massachusetts in Amherst, and in New York, where he has been living since 1967. Close is one of the most important representatives of American Hyper-Realism and Photo-Realism. He paints portraits almost exclusively. Since 1965 he has been using photographs in the passport style which he produces himself, as the basis of his work. The model's head covers the entire surface, and because of the extremely close view, even the pores of the skin and single hairs show up with great clarity in some pictures. His early work is in monochrome; since 1970 he has been experimenting with colour, using layers of primary colours to imitate printing techniques. Since 1979 he has been using Polaroid photographs as models. Since the 1980s he has been trying to lay a separate screen over the pictures, sometimes by means of papier-mâché collages.
*Illustration:*
666    Linda, 1975/76

**CLOUET François**
(also: François Janet)
c. 1505–1510 Tours (?) – 1572 Paris
Clouet was trained by his father Jean Clouet, but little is known of the life of either of them. François went to the French court at an early age, and on the death of his father about 1540 was granted a salary by Francis I. His successor Henry II appointed Clouet *valet de chambre* and painter-in-ordinary. Contemporary documents give evidence of his high reputation. Only two pictures of importance remain: the "Portrait of Apothecary Pierre Quthe" (Paris, Louvre, 1562) and the "Lady in her Bath" (ill. p.207). Both works prove Clouet's involvement with the Italian Renaissance, in particular with Leonardo's Lombardic successors. The painter may also have had contacts with the School of Fontainebleau.
*Illustration:*
207    Lady in her Bath (Diane de Poitiers ?),
        c. 1570

**CLOUET Jean**
(also: Jean Janet)
c. 1475 Brussels – c. 1540/41 Paris
The origins, training, life and work of the elder Clouet lie largely in the dark. He was probably born in Flanders and perhaps trained by Quentin Massy or one of his circle. On moving to France, he rose to become court painter to King Francis I. The works attributed to him show an undeniably Netherlandish influence, particularly in the rendering of detail. While not a single signed or reliably authenticated work exists, a great number of drawings survive – probably from the period 1515–1540 – which give an insight into his artistic temperament and stylistic development. These drawings formed the basis of the attribution of paintings; no documentary records survive. It is a fact that Clouet was an accomplished, sought-after portraitist. His works appeal on account of their elegance and a quality of portrayal which is personal and yet presented with a cool detachment.
*Illustration:*
207    Portrait of Francis I, King of France,
        c. 1535

**COELLO Claudio**
1642 Madrid – 1693 Madrid
His father, a bronze caster from Portugal, apprenticed him to the painter Francesco Rizi in order to equip him for taking over his workshop. Rizi, however, recognised the boy's talent for painting. Coello's further training included a visit to Italy and the study of the works of Titian, Rubens and Jan van Eyck, which were kept at the Spanish royal palaces. The court painter Juan Carreño de Miranda obtained access for him, and Coello became his successor in 1685. In 1691 the Chapter of Toledo Cathedral appointed him "titular painter" to the cathedral, where he had already painted the vestry in 1671 in collaboration with José Jiminez Donoso. Coello was predominantly a decorator of sacred buildings, including several frescos in the churches of Madrid, in the monastery of Paular and in the church of the Augustinian monastery La Manteria in Zaragoza – all painted by 1683. His masterpiece is the altar panel for the sacristy in the Escorial: "King Charles II and his Entourage Adoring the Host". Coello was pushed into the background when Giordano arrived in Madrid in 1692.
*Illustration:*
268    King Charles II, c. 1675–1680

**COLE Thomas**
1801 Bolton-le-Moor (Lancashire) – 1848 Catskill (New York)
Cole came from an Anglo-American family which left England in 1818 to return to America. In England, Thomas had already been trained in drawing and woodcut. From 1823 he studied at the Academy of Art in Philadelphia and later settled in Catskill on the Hudson where he became a co-founder and an important representative of the Hudson River School which established Romantic landscape painting in America. His direct, spontaneous landscapes which he painted in the wilderness of the Catskill mountains soon found recognition and attracted New York buyers. In 1829 and 1841/42 he visited Europe, including England, Switzerland and Italy, studying in particluar the landscapes of Poussin, Claude Lorrain, Salvator Rosa and Jacob van Ruisdael. Having also absorbed philosophical and literary ideas, he introduced a new type of painting in America on his return: the symbolic-moral landscape, such as the thematic series "The Course of the Empire" (New York, Historical Society 1832) and "The Voyage of Life" (Utica, Mun-

son-William-Proctor Institute, 1839/40). These have fantastic, symbolic settings and are full of didactic, allegorical references. In their somewhat kitschy colourfulness, accentuated by theatrical lighting, they do not attain the fine quality of his earlier atmospheric landscapes.
*Illustrations:*
474    The Voyage of Life. Youth, 1842
474    The Giant's Chalice, 1833

**CONSTABLE John**
1776 East Bergholt (Suffolk) – 1837 London
Constable was the son of a prosperous mill-owner in Suffolk a landscape whose scenery became central to his work. He took painting lessons in Suffolk but was largely self-taught. In 1795 he went to London and took courses at the Royal Academy in 1799. As a student he copied the works of the old landscape painters, in particular Jacob van Ruisdael. He was especially impressed by the work of Claude Lorrain and the water-colour paintings of Thomas Girtin; but to him, the actual study of nature was still more important than any artistic model. He refused to "learn the truth second-hand". Unlike any other painter before him, he based his work on precisely drawn sketches made directly from nature. His early work also included portraits and some religious pictures, but from 1820 onwards he devoted himself almost exclusively to landscape painting. His themes were taken from the parts of England that he knew best, mainly Suffolk and Essex, and also Brighton.
   In his pictures, Constable succeeded in capturing the light-and-shade effects of clouds and the various moods of landscape. After 1820/21, a period in which he produced a series of cloud studies, the "wind and weather" and their varying light conditions determined his landscapes as never before. His oil sketches were mostly of the same size as the finished picture, if not larger. This leads to the conclusion that to him the study was the original, containing all that mattered. And although public recognition was slowly growing, the critics never tired of pointing out that his works often resembled sketches rather than finished pictures. In 1824 his paintings were shown in Paris and were an instant success, crowned by a gold medal from the Salon. Constable's art became an enduring influence on French painting. In 1829 he became a Member of the Royal Academy.
*Illustrations:*
416    The White Horse, 1819
463    Weymouth Bay, c. 1816
463    Salisbury Cathedral from the Bishop's
        Grounds, 1828
464    The Hay-Wain, 1821
464    Dedham Lock and Mill, 1820
465    The Valley Farm, 1835

**COPLEY John Singleton**
1738 in or near Boston (Massachusetts) – 1815 London
After the death of his father, a tobacco merchant of Irish descent, Copley first received instruction from his stepfather, the etcher Peter Pelham. As a painter Copley was largely self-taught, studying copies of old masters and also printing techniques and using all available sources of contemporary European painting. In his early twenties he was already a popular portraitist, receiving commissions from New York, Philadelphia and Canada. From 1765 onwards he exhibited in London, where his work was well received by his fellow painters. Following West's invitation, he at last visited England himself in 1774 to perfect his technique. His travels on the Continent were short but intensive. When in London he painted several striking historical pictures, including "Brook Watson being attacked by a

Shark" (Boston, Museum of Fine Arts, 1778), whose topicality had a revolutionary effect. He was made an associate (1775) and then a full member of the Royal Academy (1783). Around this time he began to align himself more with European conventions, a tendency which became more pronounced with advancing years.

*Illustrations:*
390 Portrait of Rebecca Boylston, 1767
390 The Death of Major Peirson, c. 1782–1784

## CORINTH Lovis

1858 Tapiau (East Prussia) – 1925 Zandvoort
Corinth studied from 1876 to 1880 at the Königsberg Academy and from 1880 to 1884 under Defregger in Munich. After a visit to Antwerp, where he admired Rubens, he took up further studies at the Paris Académie Julian under Bouguereau and Robert-Fleury from 1884 to 1886. While there, he was particularly impressed by the works of Courbet. From 1887 to 1891 he lived in Berlin; in 1891 he moved to Munich, where he had his first success with his landscapes, religious paintings and portraits. In Berlin, where he went in 1901, he became a member of the Secessionists and then president when Liebermann left. In collaboration with his friend Walter Leistikow he founded a painting school for women. Through his contacts with Slevogt and Liebermann he developed his Impressionist style. In 1911 he became chairman of the Berlin Secession, and in the same year suffered a stroke. From 1918 onwards he lived mostly in his country house at Urfeld on the Walchensee. Corinth's artistic development can be traced throughout his work. From the Impressionists and their forerunners he adopted the technique of broken colour planes and realistic representation. In his narrative themes this realism often borders on the grotesque. Violent brush-strokes, strong colour and compact representation, sometimes in a sombre mood, mark his later work, moving it closer to Expressionism.

*Illustration:*
535 Self-Portrait with Straw Hat, 1923

## CORNEILLE DE LYON

(Corneille de La Haye)
c. 1500/10 The Hague – after 1574 Lyon (?)
The life and work of this master, who was not rediscovered until the end of the 19th century, even now remain obscure. A number of stylistically related, miniature-like portraits painted against a usually light, neutral background, are attributed to him. Corneille is first mentioned in 1534 in Lyon, where in 1541 he became painter to the dauphin, later King Henry II. In a document dated 1547, The Hague is given as his birthplace. In 1564 Katharina de'Medici is said to have visited Lyon in order to see the painter and his work. The last record dated 30th March 1574 confirms his privileges as painter and *valet de chambre* to the King.

*Illustration:*
208 Portrait of Gabrielle de Rochechouart, c. 1574

## CORNELIUS Peter von

1783 Düsseldorf – 1867 Berlin
Cornelius belonged to the instigators of idealistic fresco painting in 19th century Germany. In 1811 he had joined the Nazarenes in Rome, having already made "old German art" his model, at the encouragement of the brothers Boisserée and Canon Wallraf. In 1816 he painted two frescos of the Old Testament story of the life of Joseph for the Prussian consul-general Bartholdy at the Palace Zuccari. These brought him such fame that he was called both to the Düsseldorf and Munich

Academies simultaneously in 1819. He accepted both appointments, commuting between these cities, but finally deciding on Munich. Here he was appointed director of the Academy in 1824 and, unlike in Düsseldorf, he had the opportunity to paint large frescos. However, he fell out with King Ludwig I of Bavaria over his wall paintings in the Ludwigskirche in Munich, and went to Berlin in 1840 where he made the designs for the planned Camposanto. With their exhibition in 1859 in Berlin and Düsseldorf, Idealism celebrated a late triumph.

*Illustration:*
454 Joseph makes himself known to his brothers, c. 1816/17

## COROT Jean-Baptiste Camille

1796 Paris – 1875 Paris
After an apprenticeship of five years in a drapery business, Corot studied painting from 1822 to 1825, first under the painter Michallon, then under the Classical landscape painter Victor Bertin, and copying works by Joseph Vernet and others, including the 17th century Dutch masters. Convinced that "man can only be an artist when he has recognised in himself a strong passion for nature", he painted, or mostly sketched, outdoors, working in the forest of Fontainebleau, at Dieppe, Le Havre, Rouen and at Ville d'Avray where his father owned a house. His first visit to Rome from 1825 to 1828, which was to become decisive in his artistic development, produced a number of oil-studies painted from nature, views of historical Roman monuments and the scenery surrounding Rome. They are of an unusual freshness, catching the light and atmosphere of different times of the day with delightfully subtle variations in tonal values. The actual paintings based on these studies, for example, the "View of Narni" (Ottawa, National Gallery of Canada, 1826), painted for the 1827 Paris Salon, are in comparison rather formal, in the manner of the New Classicism.

On his return from Italy Corot worked in various parts of France. He also visited Italy again (in 1834 and 1843), and went to Holland (1854) and England (1862). His friendship in the late 1840s with the Barbizon painters Rosseau, Millet, Troyon and Dupré greatly influenced his art. Around this time he changed his style; his romantic-lyrical landscapes ("Paysages intimes") interpret nature in her various moods, and in the most delicate dull silver tones. His landscapes had an inspiring influence on the Impressionists, who wished to include him in their first Exhibition.

*Illustrations:*
418 View of Genoa, 1834
434 View of the Colosseum from the Farnese Gardens, 1826
434 Le Coup de Vent (The Gust of Wind), c. 1865–1870
435 Agostina, 1866
436 Woman in Blue, 1874
436 The Studio (Young woman with a mandolin), 1866

## CORREGGIO

(Antonio Allegri)
c. 1489 Correggio (near Modena) – 1534 Correggio
After his training, probably in Bologna and Ferrara, Correggio developed his own style based on Leonardo and 16th century Venetian painting. His innovations were of the utmost importance to European art. He developed new ways of handling light and colour, creating the illusion of open walls and ceilings. Stimulated by the treatment of light by Mantegna (Camera degli Sposi in Mantua, Palazzo Ducale) and Leonardo (Sala delle Asse, Milan, Cas-

tello Sforcesco), Correggio opened up the refectory ceiling in the Convento di San Paolo in Parma (1518/19) purely by using his new painterly devices. The cupola frescos in San Giovanni Evangelista (Christ ascending to heaven, 1521–1523) and in Parma Cathedral ("Ascension of Christ in Glory", 1526–1530), show that he did away completely with the upper margin so that his frescos cover the entire cupola.

In his altar pieces and mythological scenes Correggio increasingly abandoned outline, using colour and light to balance forms and in this way achieving an overwhelming radiance. The High Renaissance structure, whose principle was founded on the antithesis of statics and dynamics, was transformed by Correggio to asymmetry and movement, as shown by his foreshortened figures whose posture is often complicated.("Madonna and St Sebastian", Dresden, Gemäldegallerie, c. 1525; "Madonna and St Jerome", Parma, Galleria Nazionale, c. 1527). Correggio's treatment of light and shade ("The Nativity", Dresden, Gemäldegallerie, c. 1530; "Zeus and Io", ill. p. 175) was to point far into the future.

*Illustrations:*
174 Leda and the Swan, c. 1531/32
174 Zeus and Antiope, c. 1524/25
175 Zeus and Io, c. 1531/32
175 The Abduction of Ganymede, c. 1531/32

## CORTONA Pietro da

(Pietro Berrettini)
1596 Cortona – 1669 Rome
As an architect and painter of easel pictures and interior decorations, this versatile and talented artist already achieved fame in his lifetime. He received his initial training under the Florentine Andrea Commodi with whom he went to Rome in 1613 to complete his studies under Baccio Ciarpi. Early works, such as the "Triumph of Bacchus" (Rome, Pinacoteca Capitolina, c. 1625), still show the marked influence of Carracci. From 1623 he worked under the patronage of the Sacchetti, decorating their villas in Ostia and Castelfusano with frescos. His greatest patrons were, however, the Barberini. He not only painted for them the frescos for the Santa Bibiana church (1624–1626), including various altar pieces, but also the ceiling of the salon in the Palazzo Barberini (Rome, 1633–1639) which contained the greatest number of frescos in contemporary Rome. Here, Cortona proved himself as a great innovator of interior decoration. From 1640 to 1647 he worked in Florence where, under Ferdinand II, he painted the entire upper floor rooms facing the street in the Palazzo Pitti. Cortona also had great talent as a panel painter, as can be seen in such works as "The Sacrifice of Polyxena" or the "Rape of the Sabines" (both Rome, Pinacoteca Capitolina).

*Illustration:*
236 Holy Family Resting on the Flight to Egypt, c. 1643

## COSSA Francesco del

1436 Ferrara – 1477/78 Bologna
With Cosmè Tura and Ercole de' Roberti, Cossa was one of the great trio of the Ferrara school of painting. Although less fantastic in temperament than Tura, it is sometimes difficult to distinguish the one from the other. For example, the "Allegory of Autumn" has been variously ascribed to either, but the powerful, statuary representation, the purity of outline reminiscent of Piero della Francesca, the brilliance of colour and the abundance of light flooding the landscape – which can also be traced back to Piero – point to Cossa rather than Tura (Berlin, Gemäldegalerie). Very possibly Donatello's work in Padua also played an important role in formulating the young painter's style. In his early work he en-

deavoured to create solid figures despite the dominance of dress, using the devices of perspective in his construction of space. In the 1460s he collaborated with Tura on the most important project of the Early Renaissance in Ferrara: the decoration of the Sala dei Mesi in the Palazzo Schifanoia. Although only fragments of it survive, Cossa's contribution depicting the months of March, April (ill. p. 113) and May fortunately remain in good condition. It appears that Cossa, though a master of the fresco, received less recognition and financial reward than Tura. He moved to Bologna where he died in 1477/78.

*Illustration:*

113   Allegory of the Month of April, 1470

## COTÁN Juan Sánchez
1561 Orgaz (near Toledo) – 1627 Granada
Cotán's life was uneventful. He was trained by the Mannerist painter Blas del Prado from Toledo. In 1604 he joined the Carthusian order and entered El Paular monastery near Segovia. Eight years later he moved to the order's monastery in Granada which he decorated with frescos. He died there aged 66. Although the influence of his realism continued into the later part of the 17th century in various respects, during his lifetime Cotán's style seems to have been uniquely personal. In particular in his "Bodegones", the kitchen pictures, and in his still lifes, he developed an unmistakable language of his own in its umcompromising clarity and downright expression. The ascetic, so often emphasised in the scenes of monastic life and images of saints in baroque Spanish painting, does not enter into the world of inanimate objects in Cotán's work.

*Illustration:*

259   Still Life (Quince, Cabbage, Melon and Cucumber), c. 1602 (?)

## COURBET Gustave
(Jean-Désiré Gustave Courbet)
1819 Ornans (near Besançon) – 1877 La Tour-de-Peilz (near Vevey)
After attending the grammar school at Besançon, Courbet began to study law in Paris in 1840. In painting he was largely self-taught, learning his art by copying the old masters (Velázquez, Hals, Rembrandt and the Venetians) in the Louvre, and in Holland where he stayed in 1846. In 1844 he exhibited for the first time at the Salon. In 1848 he met Corot, Daumier and Baudelaire. The themes of his early works, taken from Goethe's Faust and the books of Victor Hugo and George Sand, still bear the strong mark of Romanticism which he was soon to reject. These early works include landscapes, painted at Fontainebleau, and portraits of members of his family ("Juliette Courbet", Paris, Musée du Petit Palais, 1844) as well as self- portraits. He was first accepted at the Salon in 1843 with his picture "Courbet with Black Dog" (Paris, Musée du Petit Palais, 1842).

In 1849/50 his first "realistic" pictures are produced at his home town of Ornans: "Peasants from Flagey returning from Market", "The Stone Masons" (destroyed in 1945, kept at Dresden, Gemäldegalerie), and "Burial at Ornans" (ill. p. 444) which were considered revolutionary. Revolutionary they certainly were in their choice of subject, depicting the life of simple people (Courbet rejected all traditional subject matter) with an unsentimental, down-to-earth manner of representation. Courbet aimed at a realistic art with a social function. "I maintain that painting is clearly a concrete art whose existence lies only in the representation of real and existing objects..." Courbet's work is characteristic in its strong brush strokes, sometimes applying paint directly with the spatula,

mostly in dark tones. Maupassant observed the painter at work at Etretat in 1869, giving a pointed account of his method: "In a large, empty room a gigantic, grimy and untidy man applied blobs of white paint to a large, empty canvas with a kitchen knife. From time to time he went to the window, pressed his face against the pane and looked out at the storm. The sea came so close as if to smash the house, covering it with spume and noise... The work became "The Wave" and brought disquiet to the world."

When, in 1855, Courbet was rejected by the jury of the World Exhibition, he set up his own "Pavillon du Réalisme" next door to the exhibition building in protest and as an example of his perception of art, demonstrating it by displaying forty of his pictures. One of them was the "Painter's Studio" (ill. p. 446), which included a picture of his friend, the Socialist philosopher Proudhon, whose political convictions had a great influence on Courbet. Courbet was very successful with his work in Germany where he stayed in Frankfurt am Main in 1858/59 and in Munich in 1869. He joined the Paris Commune in 1871 and was given the task of protecting the museums from war damage. When the Commune was defeated, he was sentenced to six months' imprisonment. He took refuge in Switzerland in 1873. Courbet, who influenced and advised the budding Impressionists, has become a major representative world-wide of a naturalistic realism which shows up inconsistencies in reality by means of artistic devices.

*Illustrations:*

417   The Cliffs at Etretat after the Storm, 1870
443   The Winnowers, 1853
443   Young Woman on the Banks of the Seine, 1857
444   Burial at Ornans, c. 1849/50
446   The Painter's Studio: A Real Allegory, 1855

## COUSIN Jean the Elder
c. 1490/1500 Soucy (near Sens) – c. 1560 Paris
Cousin achieved high recognition during his lifetime. Registered as master in his Paris guild in 1538, he received all kinds of commissions from representative bodies, including some for panel pictures, decorations for festivities, tapestry cartoons and clerical dress designs. There was no need for him to serve at the court and so he was able to live the independent life of a prosperous burgher. His book on perspective, *Livre de perspective*, was for a long time a kind of textbook used in French workshops. The extent of his œuvre is as yet unclear. His best-known panel painting, "Eva prima Pandora" (Paris, Louvre, c. 1550), encourages the assumption that he was connected with the School of Fontainebleau. In any case, the plastic rendering of figures as well as the coloured modulation of outline indicate his interest in the art of the Italian High Renaissance.

*Illustration:*

208   St Mammès and Duke Alexander, 1541

## CRANACH Lucas the Elder
1472 Kronach – 1553 Weimar
Lucas Sunder or Müller, who named himself after his Upper Franconian home town Kronach, probably spent his first years of training in his father's workshop. Nothing is known about his further training and his years of travelling. There is evidence that he worked c. 1500–1504 in Vienna, making drawings for woodcuts and also painting. He had evidently studied Dürer's graphic art intensively. In his paintings, however, he showed at this time an imagination tending towards "romanticism", combined with an emotionalism heightened by colour – characteristics which formed the basis

of his genius ("Crucifixion", Vienna, Kunsthistorisches Museum, c. 1500; "Crucifixion", Munich, Alte Pinakothek, 1503; "Resting on the Flight to Egypt", ill. p. 196). In the works of this period, today regarded as the "true" Cranach, landscape and theme are brought to an atmospheric unity which must have impressed the young Altdorfer deeply. Cranach can be regarded as one of the founders of the Danube school.

In 1504 he moved to Thuringia, following an invitation to become court painter to Frederick the Wise, and in 1505 settled permanently at Wittenberg. This concluded his first creative phase in which he produced his most important work belonging to the Dürer era. This gave place to a completely new style for which the courtly climate must at least in part have been responsible. A visit to the Netherlands in 1508 brought him into contact with Dutch art and indirectly with the conventions of the Italian Renaissance. Cranach's love of fine detail increased at the same rate as his intellectual perception of construction ("Torgau Altar", Frankfurt am Main, Städelsches Kunstinstitut, 1509), proportionally losing the rapt spontaneity of his early work. There is a faint echo of it in some works, such as his picture of "Cardinal Albrecht of Brandenburg before the Crucified One" (ill. p. 196). Cranach soon gained great esteem in Wittenberg. As a friend of Luther, he became the great portraitist during the Reformation without, however, committing himself to any particular confession. In the second quarter of the 16th century, while his workshop was flourishing, Cranach increasingly favoured a style tending towards the over-refined and Mannerist. This is especially noticeable in his depiction of the female nude, such as the panels of the Fall of Man and of Venus and Lucretia. This, too, may have been partly induced by courtly life with its predilection for erotic representation.

*Illustrations:*

196   Rest on the Flight to Egypt, 1504
196   Cardinal Albrecht of Brandenburg before the Crucified One, c. 1520–1530
197   Hercules and Omphale, 1537

## CRANACH Lucas the Younger
1515 Wittenberg – 1586 Weimar
Cranach the Younger was a pupil of his father. In the mid-1530s he began to play an increasingly important role in his father's workshop, finally taking it over at his death. Although generally just as successful as his father, he never achieved his artistic greatness. Because he adopted his father's late style, there have been problems with attributing some of the works ("The Fountain of Youth", ill. p. 197; "Portrait of Lucas Cranach the Elder, Florence, Uffizi, 1550). His work, however, lacked the breadth of emotion and imaginative spontaneity which mark his father's art. His best works include portraits and simple versions of allegorical and mythical scenes.

*Illustration:*

197   The Fountain of Youth, 1546

## CRESPI Giuseppe Maria
(called: Lo Spagnuolo)
1665 Bologna – 1747 Bologna
Despite the fact that Crespi never left his home town, he has nothing in common with what marked the academic school of painting at Bologna two generations earlier. Crespi abandoned the heavy corporeality in favour of mobile, strong figures of a new naturalness. Luigi Crespi, his son, a mediocre painter and his father's biographer, stated that his father had studied the effect of light in nature. In his set of paintings "The Seven Sacraments" (Dresden, Gemäldegalerie) Crespi not only proves to be a

close observer of gesture, movement and facial expression, but that he also found new ways regarding chiaroscuro. It is this irregularity and unpredictability of light and shade which animates his genre scenes ("Peasant Family", Budapest, National Museum; the "Fair of Poggio a Caiano", Florence, Uffizi). In pictures, such as "The Flea" (ill. p. 239) or "Kitchen Maid" (Florence, Uffizi), his persuasive power lies in the total abstention from excessive allegorical elevation and the humorous lightness of the narrative style.

*Illustration:*
239   The Flea, c. 1707–1709

## CRIVELLI Carlo
c. 1430–1435 Venice – before 5 August 1500 Ascoli Piceno (?)
Although an outstanding talent within Venetian art of the Early Renaissance, Crivelli never succeeded in achieving a synthesis of his artistic abilities. He received his decisive impressions by working within the circle surrounding the workshop of Francesco Squarciones at Padua and studying the early works of Mantegna. The school of Ferrara, in particular Cosmè Tura, also became important in his later work, not only in developing his "goldsmith's style", but also in his combined depiction of several unrelated scenes set in unreal spatial surroundings ("Madonna della Passione", Verona, Museo di Castelvecchio). He lived in Venice until 1457 and then went into exile after being threatened with imprisonment, working first at Zara (today Zadar, Dalmatia), then in the late 1460s at Ascoli Piceno where he painted his major works. The large polyptych in the cathedral of Ascoli Piceno (1473) is characteristic of his style: sharply-angled, modelled figures clad in stiff-textured garments, often as if made of metal, which in this way create a unity with the splendour of the painted jewels and carved frame.

*Illustration:*
112   Annunciation with St Emidius, 1486

## CUCCHI Enzo
born 1949 Morro d'Alba (near Ancona)
Cucchi lives and works in Ancona and Rome. After his training by a restorer, he worked from 1966 to 1968 as a surveyor before devoting himself entirely to art. Together with Sandro Chia, Francesco Clemente and Mimmo Paladino, he is a member of the Arte cifra group. This movement does not advocate concentration, but rather openness; not clarity of expression, but, as its name suggests, "chiffre". With his drawings and pictures, Cucchi enters an enigmatic world that is sometimes demonic, sometimes slightly comical. His with drawal to an entirely self-contained artistic subject may, however, not be as absolute as it appears.

*Illustration:*
671   Headless Hero, 1981/82

## CUYP Aelbert
(also: Cuijp)
1620 Dordrecht – 1691 Dordrecht
Cuyp, whose repertoire embraces portraits, landscapes, animals and still lifes, could best be compared to Rembrandt in terms of versatility, although his reputation was based on landscape painting. He was a pupil of his father Jacob Gerritsz, and also a pupil of Bloemaert, but his study of the works of van Goyen with his harmonious golden-yellow coloration became the decisive factor in his art. His favourite subject matter was Dordrecht and its surroundings with the canals, the peaceful river flats and plains where the cattle graze under a radiant sky imparting a warm glow to the scene. Because of his fine handling of light in all its nuances

he was called the "Dutch Claude Lorrain". In his later work, after 1660, the influence of the Italianised landscape and classical pastoral, as depicted by Jan Both, became even more pronounced. The range of colours is extended, and mountains and rocks, antique ruins and idyllic shepherds enter his pictures.

*Illustration:*
323   Rooster and Hens, undated

## DAHL Johann Christian Claussen
1788 Bergen – 1857 Dresden
After working as a decorative painter in his Norwegian home town of Bergen, Dahl studied landscape painting at the Copenhagen Academy from 1811 to 1818. Here he was impressed with Jens Juel and Eckersberg, but his decisive influence was the study of the Dutch masters of landscape of the 17th century. One of them, Allaert Everdingen, had visited Norway and subsequently developed a type of "northern landscape" based on his impressions. This style was later taken up by the Norwegian national movement in the 19th century. Alongside the "Italian landscape", the "northern landscape" also became established on the Continent in the early 19th century. Stimulated by his first extensive travels through Norway in 1826, Dahl added to his existing range of motifs – waterfalls, moving clouds and windswept trees – by exploring the bare plains of the high mountain regions and their cloud formations. Dahl was an innovator in the art of German as well as Norwegian landscape painting. In 1818 he settled at Dresden, joining the circle of Friedrich and Carus. In 1824 he was, like Friedrich, appointed professor at the Dresden Academy. Dresden and its surroundings feature frequently in his work, in which the sky often occupies the largest part of the canvas. During his visit to Italy in 1820/21 he found subject matter for a third range of themes.

*Illustration:*
462   View through a Window to the Chateau of Pillnitz, c. 1824

## DALÍ Salvador
(Salvador Felipe Jacinto Dalí y Domenech)
1904 Figueras (Catalonia) – 1989 Figueras
Dalí was a trouble-maker even in his student days. After three years at Madrid Academy he was expelled in 1924. In 1925 he became interested in Sigmund Freud's psychoanalysis, but his dreams and visions did not take centre stage until the height of Surrealism in Paris, where Dalí settled in 1929. He interpreted "The Evening Prayer" or "Angelus" by Jean-François Millet (ill. p. 442) as a symbol of sexual repression, and the story of William Tell as a legend of incestuous mutilation ("The Enigma of William Tell", Stockholm, Moderna Museet).

Dalí described his way of not portraying the visible object but rather its associations, as a "paranoid-critical method". After a stay at Cadaqués with René Magritte, Luis Buñuel and Paul Eluard and his wife Gala, the Muse of the Surrealists, Gala remained with Dalí. He took part in all the activities of the Surrealists until 1937, when Breton announced his official expulsion. He travelled in Italy from 1937 to 1939, studying Andrea Palladio's architecture and Renaissance and Baroque painting. In 1940 he went to America where he proclaimed his return to classical art. In 1949 he returned to Port Lligat in Spain and converted to Catholicism. In 1951 his *Mystical Manifesto* appeared. In 1971 a Dalí Museum was opened, and it was transferred to St. Petersburg in Florida in 1982. In 1979 the Pompidou Centre in Paris put on the largest-ever Dalí retrospective, afterwards moving on to London.

*Illustrations:*
556   The Temptation of St Anthony, 1946
613   The Persistence of Memory, 1931
613   Burning Giraffe, 1936–1937

## DAUBIGNY Charles-François
1817 Paris – 1878 Auvers-sur-Oise
Daubigny was given instruction by his father, a landscape painter. After visiting Italy, he worked at the Louvre in Paris as a restorer and also as an illustrator in 1836. In 1840 he studied briefly under Delaroche. He had his first success at the Salon in 1840 with a picture painted in the heroic landscape style, but his graphic work became more important in the 1840s. He met Corot in 1852, who encouraged him to paint directly from nature, and this friendship became decisive. Daubigny, the youngest of the Barbizon school of painters, took as his motif the river scenery of the Seine, Oise and Marne. The strong coloration, the light and fluid brushwork, as well as the light-flooded atmosphere of his work make him a direct precursor of the Impressionists. In order to capture the changing character of river life, he had a studio boat fitted out in 1857. In it he cruised the Seine and Oise all summer, enabling him to paint larger pictures from nature. Monet later adopted the same method. From Auvers-sur-Oise, where he settled in 1860, he undertook various journeys: in 1866 and again in 1870/71 to England, in 1868 to Spain, and in 1870 and subsequent years to the coast in Holland. In 1872 he acted as adviser to Cézanne. In 1874 he was invited to show his work at the first Impressionist exhibition. Although the pictures he produced in the 1850s won the admiration of buyers and also official public recognition – he received the first-place medal of the Salon three times – his later works, which, under the influence of Courbet, were of a larger format with less careful brushwork, aroused strong criticism, with his pictures described as "unfinished" and sketchy.

*Illustration:*
438   Landscape at Gylieu, 1853

## DAUMIER Honoré
1808 Marseille – 1879 Valmondois (near Paris)
Daumier was first sent as trainee and errand-boy to a legal official, then worked in a bookshop, and in 1822 finally entered the studio of Alexandre Lenoir, a former pupil of David. At the same time he studied antique sculpture in the Louvre as well as copying Titian and Rubens. In about 1828 he learned the new technique of lithography. As an enthusiastic Republican he began to draw political caricatures, one of which led to six months' imprisonment. From 1832–1835 he was a member of the staff of the paper *La Caricature* which published his "masks" – caricatures of politicians and scathing satires. When the law against the freedom of the press put an end to this work in 1835, he changed over to the *Charivari*, a paper committed to social criticism. His caricatures of the Parisian petty-bourgeoisie soon attracted attention. He was also ruthless in exposing the upper classes and directed his scathing wit against legal restrictions and against the monarchy and parliament, against the Church and the Establishment as well as the Academy and Classicism. To him, only the lowest class deserved his sympathy.

In 1845 Daumier began to paint pictures, primarily using literary subjects taken from the writings of Cervantes and Molière, and also from the lives of ordinary people. With paintings such as "Washerwoman" (ill. p. 440) and "Third Class Carriage" (New York, Metropolitan Museum of Art, c. 1862) he became a major representative of social realism in painting. There is no other painter in the 19th century to equal the succinctness with which he presented his figures like monumental silhouettes with wide brushstrokes in pasto on the canvas. Balzac quite rightly compared him to Michelangelo. Daumier strove for a career as painter and sculptor but was constantly compelled to resort to lithography for journalistic purposes as a means of earning a livelihood. In 1865 he retired to Valmondois near Auvers-sur-Oise where, in 1879, he died impoverished and almost blind in a house which Corot had given him.

*Illustrations:*

| | | |
|---|---|---|
| 440 | The Emigrants, 1852/55 |
| 440 | The Washerwoman, c. 1860 |
| 441 | Don Quixote, c. 1868 |
| 441 | The Melodrama, c. 1860 |

## DAVID Gerard

c. 1460 Oudewater (near Gouda) – 1523 Bruges
David is the only Dutch painter who, without direct knowledge of Italy, achieved an overall unity of structure comparable to that of the Italian High Renaissance. For his starting point he went back over two generations to the brothers van Eyck, combining their concept of reality with current ideas on the representation of space and figure in 15th century Netherlandish painting. It is not known where David received instruction, but the influence of Rogier van der Weyden and Hugo van der Goes in his early work is undeniable. In 1484 he was registered as a member of the Bruges guild. His commissioned work was predominantly for ecclesiastical clients and reached its highest perfection when the subject matter portrayed a certain fixed state (triptych "The Baptism of Christ", ill. p. 199). Scenic elevation did not always suit his temperament ("The Wedding at Canaan", Paris, Louvre, c. 1503). David's great skill in unifying figure and landscape was of great importance for future development. Many followed his example in Bruges, particularly in book illumination.

*Illustrations:*

| | | |
|---|---|---|
| 199 | The Mystic Marriage of St Catherine, c. 1505–1510 |
| 199 | The Baptism of Christ, c. 1505 |

## DAVID Jacques-Louis

1748 Paris – 1825 Brussels
David's beginnings still had their roots in Rococo painting. After the early death of his father, a haberdasher, he was brought up by two uncles, an architect and a builder, who fostered his artistic talent. Boucher became his friend and adviser. At his recommendation David began studying under Vien in 1766. Several attempts to win the first Academy Prize failed, plunging him into despair. Finally, in 1774, he gained the prize which opened his way to Rome, where his teacher Vien had just been appointed director of the French Academy. Here David copied antiquities with great dedication; Rome became his most important experience, effecting the change from a painter of the Rococo to Neoclassicism.

On his return from Rome in 1781 he was accepted by the Academy, becoming a full member two years later. Besides portraits, he painted almost exclusively historical works with classical themes. His basic attitude found expression in the "Oath of the Horatii" (ill. p. 365). For its completion David went to Rome with his family where the picture was a triumphant success, just as at the Paris Salon in 1785. Politically, David ranged himself with the extreme left-wing of the Revolution, voting for the death of the King. In 1794 he headed the Convention and abolished the Academy. French art history owes much to his defence of artists and works of art as well as medieval monuments. After periods of imprisonment, he became a follower of Napoleon who appointed him

first painter to the Emperor in 1804. After the fall of Napoleon David was banished, and he went to live in Brussels where he spent his remaining creative years. Today, David's reputation owes more to the portraits than to his large historical pictures. As teacher of the most important painters of 19th century France he is the true artistic founder of the new epoch.

*Illustrations:*

| | | |
|---|---|---|
| 364 | The Death of Marat, 1793 |
| 365 | The Oath of the Horatii, 1784 |
| 365 | Madame Récamier, 1800 |
| 366 | Napoleon in his Study, 1812 |
| 366 | Napoleon Crossing the Alps, 1799 |

## DEGAS Edgar

(Hilaire Germain Edgar de Gas)
1834 Paris – 1917 Paris
Degas came from a cosmopolitan, well-to-do family. Soon after taking up legal studies, he discovered his interest in painting, in particular in Ingres and the masters of the Italian Renaissance. Between 1853 and 1859 he studied at the Ecole des Beaux-Arts in Paris, worked at the studio of Louis Lamothe and travelled widely for study purposes. His early work showed his concern with classical painting in terms of subject matter as well as composition. But he was open to other influences, such as Japanese art, and also Symbolist tendencies to which he was introduced by his friends Moreau and Puvis de Chavannes. He joined the Impressionist group and exhibited with them between 1876 and 1881, and again in 1886, though he loathed the label and never painted in a purely Impressionist style. His work was suffused by a very personal kind of psychological observation and a profound interest in modern life. His themes always deal with people and city life; raw nature did not inspire him.

Degas painted a great number of portraits. From 1862 onwards he liked to present a subject repeatedly, looking at it from various angles and aspects, such as the scenes of horse-racing, later washer-women and ironing-women, the world of the theatre – he was particularly fond of dancers – street and city scenes, and the female nude. From 1880 he began to work in pastel, developing his technique and finding new applications. Detail and narrative elements were abandoned in favour of a more generous disposition of space and the exploration of colour in all its tints and tones, aiming deliberately at sketchiness, the "unfinished". Degas also produced a great number of lithographs, drawings, engravings and monotypes. From 1909 failing eyesight caused him to turn to sculpture, leaving many wax models of dancers, horses and female nudes to be cast in bronze after his death.

*Illustrations:*

| | | |
|---|---|---|
| 481 | Ballet (The Star), 1876/77 |
| 494 | The Gentlemen's Race: Before the Start, 1862 |
| 494 | Dance Class at the Opéra, 1872 |
| 495 | Absinthe, 1876 |

## DELACROIX Eugène

(Ferdinand Victor Eugène Delacroix)
1798 Saint-Maurice-Charenton (near Paris) – 1863 Paris
After studying music, Delacroix first received instruction in painting at the studio of P. Guérin in Paris. In 1816 he entered the Ecole des Beaux-Arts, where he met Géricault, his junior by seven years, whom he much admired. He was also impressed by Goya's drawings and the work of Veronese and Rubens. His first great work "Dante and Virgil in Hell" (ill. p. 414), shown at the Salon in 1822, excited great attention. Two years later his "Massacre of Chios" (ill. p. 432) led to still greater

recognition. Having seen Constable's pictures at the Salon, he overpainted this painting and added highlights a few days before the opening of the Salon. The discovery of Constable and his friendship with Bonington caused Delacroix to visit London in 1825. Through the study of Constable's work he adopted a fresher and livelier coloration.

Back in Paris, Delacroix was now the leader of Romantic painting in France. This brought him much criticism from the Classicists, most of all from Ingres. He drew his subject matter from literary sources, such as Dante, Shakespeare and Goethe; also from the works of the Romantics, the novels of Walter Scott and Byron's poetry. In 1832 he visited Morocco, being a member of an ambassadorial mission sent to the Sultan of Morocco, also taking in Algiers, Oran, Tangiers and southern Spain. His enthusiasm for this exotic world with its brilliant light knew no bounds, inspiring him to produce hundreds of drawings and water-colours. From these, he painted later in Paris his most beautiful and colourful pictures, including the famous harem scenes (ill. p. 433) and the series of lion hunts (ill. p. 431). From 1834 he was engaged in large-scale decorative works, including those in the Salon du Roi in the Palais Bourbon (1833–37), the library in the Palais du Luxembourg (1845–47) and the church St. Sulpice (1861). In 1857 he finally became a member of the Academy, after seven years of candidature. Mounting criticism caused him to withdraw from the world in his final years, and he died in complete isolation in 1863. The passion, subjectivity and sensualism of his subject matter, as well as his methods of composition and coloration, made him a Romantic of a kind all his own and one of the greatest painters of the century. His conception of the intrinsic value of the overall colour effect was to be an emboldening influence on the Impressionists.

*Illustrations:*

| | | |
|---|---|---|
| 408 | Orphan Girl at the Cemetery, 1823 |
| 414 | The Bark of Dante (Dante and Virgin in Hell), 1822 |
| 431 | The Lion Hunt, 1861 |
| 432 | The Massacre of Chios, 1824 |
| 432 | Liberty Leading the People (28th July 1830), 1830 |
| 433 | Women of Algiers, 1834 |

## DELAUNAY Robert

1885 Paris – 1941 Montpellier
After an apprenticeship with a decorative painter, Delaunay became acquainted with the ideas of the Pont-Aven group while visiting Brittany in 1904. He began to study in depth the Neo-Impressionistic colour principles as well as philosophical works. His Eiffel Tower series, 1910, proclaimed his Cubist tendencies. With his "Windows" (ill. p. 575) and "Contrasts" (ill. p. 575), 1912/13, he established his artistic independence and significance. Apollinaire coined the term "Orphism" to describe Delaunay's colour Cubism, transforming the idea of colour into sound and musical resonances. His pictures were based on the principle that all colour tones develop from the circling rhythm inherent in the colour. This idea determined Delaunay's work until 1921, moving steadily closer to abstract art. In 1937 he designed the decorations for the pavilions of aviation and railways at the Paris World Exhibition.

*Illustrations:*

| | | |
|---|---|---|
| 575 | Simultaneous Windows on the City, 1912 |
| 575 | Simultaneous Contrasts: Sun and Moon, c. 1912/13 |

## DELVAUX Paul

1897 Antheit (near Liège) – 1994 Furnes
Delvaux first studied architecture from 1917 to

1924, and then painting at the Académie des Beaux-Arts in Brussels. His early work was marked by the influence of Belgian Expressionism and his admiration for Ensor. In 1932, at a Brussels fairground, he saw the waxwork figures of the Musée Spitzner. The impression of these figures was so strong that they repeatedly became the subject of his pictures. His acquaintance with the work of Chirico, Magritte and Max Ernst, whose pictures were shown at the "Minotaure" exhibition, 1934, caused him to produce pictures in the style of veristic Surrealism and to contribute to several international Surrealist exhibitions. After his visits to Italy in 1938 and 1939 his palette lightened, and, influenced by the Italian Renaissance, he began to include classical landscapes in his pictures. In the late 1940s and in the 1950s he produced stage sets and wall paintings. In 1950 he was called to the École Nationale d'Art et d'Architecture as professor of monumental painting, where he taught until 1962. He was president of the Académie des Beaux-Arts in 1965/66. Delvaux, who was the most important representative of Belgian Surrealism after Magritte, was in his old age honoured by many retrospectives and decorations.
*Illustration:*
610   The Encounter, 1938

**DENIS Maurice**
1870 Grandville (Manche) – 1943 Saint-Germain-en-Laye
From 1888 Denis studied at the Paris Académie Julian where he made the acquaintance of Bernard, Bonnard and Sérusier. He also knew Vuillard from his schooldays. Sérusier introduced him to the ideas of the school of Pont-Aven, and Gauguin in particular made a profound impression on Denis. In 1890 Denis founded with his friends from the Académie Julian the Nabis group. He shared a studio with Bonnard and Vuillard. In 1892/93 he designed the scenery for the Théâtre de l'Œuvre. His group portrait of the Nabis painters, entitled "Hommage à Cézanne", was painted in 1901. He visited Germany in 1903. In 1906 he visited Cézanne at Aix with Bernard and Roussel. Besides his impressionistic portrait studies and garden scenes he painted Symbolist pictures of an increasingly religious character, using a predominantly two-dimensional Art-Nouveau style. While visiting Italy he had become inspired by the masters of religious art in the Early Renaissance, in particular Piero della Francesca and Fra Angelico, and this he now expressed in his series of large-scale paintings for churches. He was also a book illustrator and lithographer, and his theoretical publications explored the ideas of Symbolism. He taught, at the Académie Ranson from 1908. In 1919 he founded, together with Rouault, workshops for religious art. He is considered one of the great restorers of French religious art.
*Illustration:*
519   The Muses, 1893

**DERAIN André**
1880 Chatou (near Paris) – 1954 Garches
Derain was self-taught before attending the Académie Carrière in Paris from 1898 to 1900. Matisse and Vlaminck, whom he met in 1901, were to become important for his art. Military service disrupted his studies from 1901 to 1904, though he resumed them briefly at the Académie Julian. In the summer of 1905 he worked with Matisse in Collioure on the Mediterranean, and showed his work at the Paris autumn Salon which led to his being classed as one of Les Fauves (wild beasts). Shortly afterwards he came under the influence of Cubism, after having spent several months with Picasso in Avignon in 1908. His study of Antiquity

led him back to a traditional manner of painting in 1921.
*Illustration:*
563   Boats at Collioure, 1905

**DINE Jim**
(James Dine)
born 1935 Cincinnati
Dine studied from 1935 to 1957 at the University of Cincinnati, the Boston Museum School and finally at Ohio University. Since 1958 he has been living in New York. As a challenge to Abstract Expressionism, he began by setting up "environments" and staging "happenings". As he felt artistically close to English Pop Art, he went to London in 1967. In his paintings, too, he remained true to the third dimension, working with collages and assemblages, and creating several levels of reality by overlapping canvases in one picture. His work usually shows everyday objects in unusual surroundings. In this way the objects take on a significance of their own, such as a dressing gown which Dine calls a self-portrait. Subsequently, heart shapes and classical sculpture, such as the Venus of Milo, became his subject matter. In the 1980s he produced large wall pictures for outdoor display in Boston and San Francisco. Dine has been a member of the American Academy of Art and Letters since 1980.
*Illustration:*
660   Cardinal, 1976

**DIX Otto**
1891 Untermhaus (near Gera) – 1969 Hemmenhofen (Lake Constance)
Dix was the son of a railwayman. After an apprenticeship with a decorative painter he studied at the Arts and Crafts School in Dresden. After World War I he continued his studies at the Academy in 1919. In 1920 Dix adopted a relentless, committed verism concerned with contemporary issues. In 1922 he began to work in Düsseldorf, where his etching "The War" was produced in 1924. During this time he also painted a large number of pictures with a technical skill little short of that of the old masters but with exaggerated facial expressions and physical features. He continued painting portraits when in Berlin from 1925 to 1927, including those of children. After his call to the Dresden Academy in 1927 he produced the triptychs "The City" (Stuttgart, Galerie der Stadt) and "The War" (Dresden, Gemäldegalerie Neue Meister) – visions of experienced and impending dread. After his dismissal from the Academy in 1933 he retired to Hemmenhofen on Lake Constance where he continued to devote himself to apocalyptic themes.
*Illustration:*
589   Portrait of the Artist's Parents, 1921

**DOESBURG Theo van**
(Christian Emil Marie Küpper)
1883 Utrecht – 1931 Davos
When Doesburg had a first exhibition of his work in The Hague in 1908, he still painted in an Impressionistic style. It was not until 1916 that he adopted geometric painting. Together with the architects Oud and Wils he worked on architectural projects. In 1917 he changed to Neo-Plasticism and founded with Mondrian the group De Stijl and became the publisher of, and contributor to the magazine bearing the same name. He sympathised briefly with the Dada movement, introducing it to Holland in 1922 and founding the magazine *Mecano*. He moved to Paris in 1923. He published his theoretical work *Principles of the New Art* in 1924 as one of the series of Bauhaus textbooks.

From this period also date his first contra-compositions which announced a new development of his art, describing it as "elementarism". The dynamic diagonal became the most important structural element.
*Illustration:*
596   Simultaneous Counter-Composition,
       c. 1929/30

**DOMENICHINO**
(Domenico Zampieri)
1581 Bologna – 1641 Naples
Domenichino was, with Reni, one of the most important successors of the Carraccis. He was trained by Lodovico Carracci in his home town, then assisted Annibale Carracci in Rome from 1602 onwards. His early work, such as the "Maiden and the Unicorn" (ill. p. 234) shows that besides the influence of both Carraccis there was already an individual, classically clear style which found expression in his characteristic monumental work, including the fresco in the oratorio of San Gregori Magno (Rome), his depiction of the martyrdom of Andrew, and also his frescos of the Nilus Legend in the Abbey of Grotta Ferrato (1609/10). On Annibale's death (1609) Domenichino became the foremost Bolognese landscape painter. In his landscapes of a typically greenish-grey coloration he explored during the years 1610–1615 new principles of composition which were later taken over by Claude Lorrain. In the field of interior decoration he demonstrated alternatives to the formulations of Cortona, as can be seen in the choir and cupola pendentives of Sant' Andrea della Valle, Rome. His panel paintings were masterly in their complex yet clearly structured composition and dramatic effect. Dominichino later worked in Naples, but there he met with hostility. He died there without having completed his work in the cathedral, leaving a great number of drawings which tell us how meticulous his preparatory work was.
*Illustrations:*
218   The Assumption of Mary Magdalene into
       Heaven, c. 1617–1621
234   The Maiden and the Unicorn, c. 1602

**DOMENICO VENEZIANO**
(Domenico di Bartolomea da Venezia)
c. 1410 Venice or Florence – 1461 Florence
Although Domenico was a highly important painter, few of his works survive. He called himself a Venetian yet we do not know whether he was born in Venice or whether his father moved from Venice to Florence before his birth. But it is not unreasonable to assume that his background was such as to promote an artistic talent which made him a unique figure in the development of colour in early 15th century Florentine painting. Little is known about his life. In the 1430s he worked in Perugia. In 1438 he wrote to Piero de'Medici, asking for help in obtaining commissions in Florence and expressing his intention of producing work comparable to that of the greatest living masters – Fra Angelico and Filippo Lippi. The choice of names was significant. Domenico was not primarily interested in problems of space and figure treatment, but in those of colour. His letter of application was evidently successful. In about 1440 he painted the frescos in San Egidio (now Santa Maria Nuova) with the assistance of his greatest pupil, Piero della Francesca. Not a trace of them has survived. Its loss may have left what is possibly the greatest gap in our knowledge of the development of Florentine Early Renaissance painting. With his signed "Sacra Conversazione" (ill. p. 98) he proves himself as a painter of the highest order. Although he had studied Masaccio, Uccello and Castagno with regard to the representation of space and figure, his first

concern was to find new ways of colour treatment. The intensity of colour can be increased by adding more oil as binder, and this technique was used in modern times to create "atmospheric" light effects.

*Illustrations:*
91 Portrait of a Young Woman, c. 1465
98 Madonna and Child with Saints (St Lucy Altarpiece), c. 1442–1448

## DONGEN Kees van
(Cornelis Theodorus Maria van Dongen)
1877 Delfshaven (near Rotterdam) – 1968 Paris
Dongen was first sent by his family to a decorative art school to be trained as a technical draughtsman. He felt drawn to painting, however, and at the age of twenty broke with his family and settled in Montmartre in Paris. At first he had to take on casual work, such as porter in the market halls, but once he had joined the Fauves in 1906 and somewhat later had become a guest member of the Dresden Brücke group, he could live from his painting. Around 1907 he lived at Bateau-Lavoir in the Rue Ravignan, where he met Picasso. His financial security was assured after signing a contract with the Galerie Bernheim-Jeune in 1908. Van Dongen was a masterly colourist; his paintings stand out for their intensive, voluptuous colour effects and emotive contrasts. After World War I he became a sought-after portraitist of high-society personalities, probably because he did not prettify his sitters.

*Illustration:*
564 Portrait of Fernande, 1905

## DOU Gerard
(also: Gerrit Dou)
1613 Leyden – 1675 Leyden
Dou was, during his lifetime and throughout the 19th century, one of the most respected genre painters in Holland. He was taught by his father, a stained glass artist, and went on to be trained by Bartholomeus Dolendo, a copper engraver, where he painted on small copper plates. After a further spell of training with another stained glass artist and also in his father's workshop, Dou studied from 1628 to 1631 under Rembrandt, who was then just 22 years old. When Rembrandt moved to Amsterdam, Dou remained in Leyden, set up his own workshop in 1632 and became a founding member of the Leyden Lukas Guild in 1648. Dou was one of the most talented and independent pupils of Rembrandt, from whom he took over the chiaroscuro effects and structuring of interiors, sometimes rendered in the light of candles or lamps ("Evening Class", Amsterdam, Rijksmuseum), and also the scenes of ordinary life. He is considered the most important representative of the so-called "fine painting", a very detailed style of painting, requiring the finest brushes and often a magnifying-glass to give a realistic rendering of the smallest detail. His work ranged from small genre scenes, with old women and men at work, interiors of small general stores, medical consultations ("The Dropsical Lady", ill. p. 320), to biblical subjects, portraits ("Young Mother", The Hague, Maritshuis) and still lifes. Dou remained all his life in Leyden, even declining an invitation to work at the English court of King Charles II. His best known pupils were Frans van Mieris the Elder and Gabriel Metsu.

*Illustration:*
320 The Dropsical Lady (The Doctor's Visit), c. 1663 (?)

## DUBUFFET Jean
1901 Le Havre – 1985 Paris
After obtaining his higher school-leaving certificate and doing two-years' training in painting at the Academy in Le Havre, Dubuffet went to Paris in 1918 to complete his studies at the Académie Julian. A year later he met Suzanne Valadon, Max Jacob, Léger and Dufy. In 1924 he went to Buenos Aires as a technical draughtsman, and a year later entered his father's wine business. He did not paint again until 1942, showing his work in Paris two years later. From 1945 he began to collect *art brut*, pictures of children and mental patients, which fascinated him because of their elemental powerfulness, and which he admired for their originality and independence from traditional, conventional subjects. In 1947 he founded the *art brut* movement and opened a gallery in order to disseminate and gain recognition for this art form. In July 1962 he began to produce two- and three-dimensional work under the title "L'Hourloupe", and in the 1960s he added musical experiments. In 1976 he presented his *art brut* collection to the city of Lausanne. He then returned to the simple forms of his early years, producing pictures, panels and sculptures.

*Illustrations:*
640 Le Métafisyx, 1950
640 Business Prospers, 1961

## DUCCIO DI BUONINSEGNA
c. 1255 Siena (?) – c. 1318 Siena
Duccio is first mentioned in 1278 in connection with small commissions for book-cover paintings. His first great unquestioned work was the Madonna in the Uffizi in Florence, executed for the Chapel of the Brotherhood of the Laudesi in the Dominican church Santa Maria Novella in Florence (ill. p. 17), probably to rival Cimabue. With this work Duccio's artistic standing was established before that of Giotto, despite the enmity between Duccio's home town of Siena and Florence. Besides smaller pictures destined to enhance private devotion, Duccio painted the famous altarpiece for Siena cathedral, the Maestà (the Virgin in Majesty). This huge work, painted on both sides, represents on the front the enthroned Madonna with angels and saints ranged by her side and, kneeling at her feet, the patrons of Siena. The predella depicts episodes from the Life of Christ; the retable those of Mary's death. The back shows the Passion and Resurrection of Christ. The work is no longer complete, having been dismantled in the 18th century. Some of the smaller panels are in various museums, others were lost.

Duccio's work is known for its profound closeness to Byzantine art. He used it, however, as a starting point for finding his own individual style which became independent of Byzantine origins. He was very open to contemporary art, represented by the sculptors to the Siena cathedral, Niccolò and Giovanni Pisano, whose adherence to antique and Gothic sculpture coupled with passion of expression led to the modification of Byzantine rules (most apparent in the Crucifixion depicted on the back of the Maestà altarpiece). Also noticeable is the influence of French art and of Duccio's older Florentine contemporary Cimabue – perhaps also the innovations of Giotto. Duccio exercised great influence in his time; he left behind him a prosperous workshop with painters who carried on in his style. He was remarkable for his stimulating effect on others – unlike that of Giotto and the Florentine painters – who had a stultifying influence on the younger generation of Sienese painters such as Simone Martini and the brothers Lorenzetti. These, however, were to overshadow their teacher's fame with their own great artistic contribution.

*Illustrations:*
15 The Temptation of Christ on the Mountain, c. 1308–1311
17 Ruccellai Madonna (Maestà), c. 1285
21 Christ Entering Jerusalem, 1308–1311

33 Madonna of the Franciscans, c. 1300
33 Adoration of the Magi, 1308–1311
34 Peter's First Denial of Christ and Christ Before the High Priest Annas, 1308–1311

## DUCHAMP Marcel
1887 Blainville-Crevon (near Rouen) – 1968 Neuilly-sur-Seine
As the son of a Normandy lawyer, whose other three children – Jacques Villon, Raymond Duchamp-Villon and Suzanne Crotti – also devoted themselves to art, Duchamp studied first at the Académie Julian in Paris, where he was initially influenced by Cézanne, then by the Fauves, the Cubists and the Futurists. His picture "Nude Descending a Staircase" (ill. p. 594), which was shown for the first time in New York in 1913, made him famous overnight in the USA, while he remained a marginal Cubist in France. Duchamp introduced the phrase "ready-made". He maintained the view that the creation of a work of art is already implied in the choice of subject matter, as exemplified in 1913 by his "Bicycle-Wheel on a Kitchen Stool". In 1915 Duchamp went to the USA, but returned via Buenos Aires to Paris, where he established contact with the Dadaists gathering around Tristan Tzara. Shortly afterwards he went again to New York, where he collaborated with Man Ray in publishing *New York Dada* in 1921. With his principal work "The Bride Stripped Bare By Her Bachelors", also called "Large Glass" (ill. p. 594), on which he worked from 1915 to 1923, he broke finally with traditional painting. He experimented with a great variety of techniques.

*Illustrations:*
594 Nude Descending a Staircase, No. 2, 1912
594 The Bride Stripped Bare By Her Bachelors (The Large Glass), c. 1915–1923

## DUFY Raoul
1877 Le Havre – 1953 Forcalquier (Basses-Alpes)
Dufy already worked in a coffee import business at the age of 14, attending evening classes at art school. In 1900 he was granted a scholarship at the Ecole des Beaux-Arts in Paris. From 1904 he had contact with the Fauves and was greatly influenced by Matisse. When staying with Braque in L'Estaque, he briefly moved closer to Cubism, and his palette became almost monochrome. From 1912 his coloration began to brighten and his style to become freer. He travelled widely, transmitting his impressions to his landscapes which combined intensive light effects with brilliant colour. In 1920 he settled at Vence, and his preferred subjects became horse-racing, beach scenes and concert scenes. For the World Exhibition in Paris in 1937 he produced his most important work, the huge mural "Fée Electricité" in which figures and objects are inserted with deliberate naivety into the overlapping colour planes.

*Illustration:*
563 Sailing Boat at Sainte-Adresse, 1912

## DUGHET Gaspard
(called: Gaspard Poussin)
1615 Rome – 1675 Rome
His brother-in-law Nicolas Poussin was his teacher, but Dughet soon became independent both financially and artistically, devoting himself almost entirely to landscape painting, including series of large frescos (Palazzo Dora, Palazzo Colonna and San Martino ai Monti, all of them in Rome). Although he never left Italy, he absorbed into his work a great variety of influences including foreign ones. Bril, Elsheimer, Domenichino, Rosa and Claude Lorrain were all just as important as Poussin

in developing Dughet's style. His work was particularly popular in England and Germany in the 18th and 19th centuries. Goethe said that in these pictures there "seemed to live a human race of few necessities and noble thoughts".

*Illustration:*

250    Landscape with St Augustine and the Mystery of the Trinity, c. 1651–1653

## DUPLESSIS Joseph-Siffred
(also: Silfrède Duplessis)
1725 Carpentras – 1802 Versailles
Duplessis' father was a surgeon who abandoned his profession in order to devote himself to painting, so Duplessis obtained his earliest instruction from him. When in Rome he made the acquaintance of Vernet and Subleyras, whose pupil he became. In 1749 he returned to his home town and painted landscapes for the local hospital. In 1752 he went to Paris and introduced himself to the Academy with his portrait of the Abbé Arnaud (Carpentras, Musée Duplessis). In 1774 he became a member of the Academy and court painter to Louis XV. Perhaps his best-known work is the magnificent picture of the composer "Portrait of Christoph Willibald Gluck" (ill. p. 362). Failing eyesight and hearing caused him to leave his apartment in the Louvre in 1792. He retired to the monastery of Villeneuve-lès-Avignon where he had already spent four years in his childhood. However, he returned to Paris in 1796 in order to take up the post of curator at the Versailles museum.

*Illustration:*

362    Portrait of Christoph Willibald Gluck, 1775

## DÜRER Albrecht
1471 Nuremberg – 1528 Nuremberg
Dürer's work is often, and quite rightly, regarded as the quintessence of the spirit of German art. A master of the graphic arts as well as painting, Dürer, through his extraordinarily dynamic development, laid the foundations of the German High Renaissance. He was the most important mediator between Italian and German art, and it could be said that there was an interactive effect. While Italian art opened up for him new vistas of artistic conception and painterly representation, Dürer's graphic art acted as a stimulus on Italian painting of the 16th century. In his late period he began to assess in his theoretical writings his new insights on realistic representation as well as the problems posed by it, a process whose intellectual penetration had already been set in motion in Italy three generations earlier.

As the son of a Hungarian goldsmith who settled in Germany, he may well have learned his father's craft before entering the workshop of Nuremberg's leading painter, Michael Wolgemut, in 1486. In 1490 he went on tour through the southwestern parts of the country, also visiting Basle and Colmar where he discovered that Schongauer, whom he admired and who had given him direction in his early work, was no longer alive. In 1494 he went to Venice for the first time. A year later he opened his own workshop in Nuremberg and became acquainted with a circle of humanists, one of whom, Willibald Pirckheimer, was to become a life-long friend. Graphic works featured largely in his early period. The linear design of his fifteen woodcuts of the "Apocalypse" achieved a height of expression never reached before. This was followed by sets of woodcuts entitled "The Great Passion" (1498–1500) and the "Life of Mary" (1501–1511).

His second visit to Italy from 1505 to 1507, which again centred on Venice and where he studied in particular Giovanni Bellini, brought his

development to maturity, making him one of the great European painters of the High Renaissance. His "Feast of the Rosary" (Prague, Národni Galeri), which he painted for the German merchant group in Venice, is the first proof of his new conception. Apart from a visit to the Netherlands (1520/21), Dürer remained in Nuremberg, highly esteemed and becoming a great supporter of the Reformation in the last decade of his life. There he produced his major works ("The Adoration of the Trinity", ill. p. 188; "Four Apostles", ill. p. 187), also painting many portraits, including "Hieronymus Holzschuher" (ill. p. 149). His famous, so-called master engravings date from the period 1513/14 ("The Knight, Death and the Devil", "Melancholia", "Jerome in his Cell"). Dürer's aquarelles depicting topographically accurate views represented a first step in the development of pure landscape painting. The extent of his surviving work is astounding: about 70 paintings, 350 woodcuts, 100 copper engravings, 900 drawings plus the water-colours. Dürer's influence on subsequent generations was immense. In the 19th century, when German "medieval" art was rediscovered, a veritable Dürer renaissance occured which often led to a falsified image of the artist.

*Illustrations:*

149    Portrait of Hieronymus Holzschuher, 1526
186    Self-Portrait, 1498
187    Portrait of a Young Venetian Woman, 1505
187    Four Apostles (John, Peter, Paul and Mark), 1526
188    The Nativity (Paumgartner Altar), c. 1502–1504
188    The Adoration of the Trinity, 1511

## DYCE William
1806 Aberdeen – 1864 Streatham (Surrey)
Dyce studied at the Scottish Academy, Edinburgh, and the Schools of the Royal Academy, London, becoming a member in 1848. In 1825 and again from 1827 to 1830 he stayed in Italy, mainly Rome, where he studied the works of Raphael and the earlier masters, and had close contacts with the German Nazarenes, Overbeck, Cornelius and Schnorr von Carolsfeld who greatly influenced his art. From 1830 to 1837 he worked as a portraitist in Edinburgh. His interest in art education and industrial design brought him an appointment by the newly founded Government School of Design in London to visit and report on the methods of the state-run art colleges in France, Prussia and Bavaria. In 1840 he became Director of the School of Design in London. Through his connections with the Nazarenes, Dyce was considered in England to be an expert on fresco painting, resulting in various commissions for murals, including in 1844 the frescos in the robing-room of the House of Lords and later for Lambeth Palace, Buckingham Palace and others. He also produced stained glass designs, usually on religious themes. Himself devout, he was an ardent supporter of the High Church. He maintained that society's aim should be to create a government which combined powers temporal and spiritual. This corresponded with the views of the German Nazarenes, whose often dry and hard method of painting he adopted in his early work, later becoming influenced by the Pre-Raphaelites, such as Millais and Hunt.

*Illustration:*

467    Pegwell Bay in Kent. A Recollection of October 5th, 1858), c. 1859/60

## DYCK Anthony van
1599 Antwerp – 1641 London
Van Dyck, next to Rubens the most important Flemish painter, was the seventh child of a well-to-

do silk merchant in Antwerp. After the early death of his mother he was sent at the young age of eleven to be trained by the Romanist Hendrik van Balen. In 1615 he already had his own workshop and an apprentice. In 1618 he was accepted as a full member of the Lukas Guild. From 1617 to 1620 he was the pupil and assistant of Rubens, who considered him his best pupil. They became friends, van Dyck living at Rubens' house and painting many pictures on his own after Rubens' design. Van Dyck's great talent, his untiring diligence and perhaps also Rubens' friendship combined to bring him commissions of his own very soon. Besides religious and mythological scenes he also painted some important life-like portraits, which were to become his main work. His pride and ambition made it hard for him to stand in Rubens' shadow in Antwerp. He therefore followed an invitation from the Earl of Arundel to London, where he stayed several months. From 1621 to 1627 he lived in Italy, studying the works of Giorgione and Titian. He entered Genoa on a white horse, a present from Rubens, also visiting Rome, Venice, Turin and Palermo. Titian's influence shows clearly in his paintings of Madonnas and Holy Families; works such as the "The Tribute Money" or "The Four Ages of Man" could almost have been by the great Venetian painter himself.

In 1627 he returned to Antwerp, where he was given a triumphal welcome. He received many commissions for churches, and became court painter to the Archduchess Isabella in 1630. In March 1632 King Charles I called him to England as court painter where he remained, apart from short visits abroad, until his end. Van Dyck became the celebrated portraitist of the English court and aristocracy, and created in this field a style typically his own. In under ten years he painted over 350 pictures, of which 37 were of the King and 35 of the Queen. His extravagant way of life – he had five servants – required a constant flow of commissions and a large studio. Often he merely made a portrait sketch, painting face and hands and leaving the rest to be completed by his assistants. He worked feverishly, weakened by thirty years' hard work and perhaps already feeling signs of his impending illness, rushing in his last years between England, Antwerp, Paris and back to England. But his great plans – frescos in the Banqueting Hall in Whitehall for the English kings, the decoration of the hunting castle of Philip IV in Madrid and a series of paintings in the Louvre for the French monarch – did not materialise, perhaps partly because his fees were exorbitant. Although van Dyck lacked the necessary vitality that Rubens possessed in addition to his genius, he created with his representative portraits, which are marked by their dignity, elegance and detachment as well as close psychological observation and fine use of colours, a type of painting that influenced many generations. He was in particular a stimulus to English painters, such as Gainsborough, Reynolds and Lawrence.

*Illustrations:*

282    Portrait of a Member of the Balbi Family, c. 1625
307    Susanna and the Elders, c. 1621/22
307    St Martin Dividing his Cloak, c. 1618
308    Portrait of Maria Louisa de Tassis, c. 1630
308    The Count of Arundel and his son Thomas, 1636
309    Equestrian Portrait of Charles I, c. 1635–1640

## ECKERSBERG Christoffer Wilhelm
1783 Sundeved – 1853 Copenhagen
Eckersberg's artistic standing in Danish painting is comparable to that of Ingres' in France. As the pupil of the classicist Abraham Abildgaard at the

Copenhagen Academy, Eckersberg established his style while working at David's studio in Paris from 1811 to 1813. He favoured a classicism mellowed by a natural surface treatment. A visit to Rome, 1813–1816, extended his repertoire to include light-toned, strictly perspectival veduta painting. On his return he settled in Copenhagen and became a professor at the Academy in 1818 and one of the most sought-after Danish portraitists. He also painted seascapes. Although upholding the old traditions, which are given expression through his objectivity in representation using a strong line, his unambiguity of colour and his perspectival construction, as a teacher he was always open to new ideas. Many of his pupils became the Danish realists of the second generation in the 19th century, preferring sketchiness, unusual perspective and subjective colour and light treatment.

*Illustrations:*
461 View through three northwest arches of the Colosseum in Rome. Storm gathering over the city, 1815
461 Nude (Morning Toilette), c. 1837

## ELSHEIMER Adam
1578 Frankfurt am Main – 1610 Rome
If coping with mass was a central problem of Baroque painting, it seems surprising that one of its most prominent founders worked only in small, even tiny, formats. Nevertheless the work of Elsheimer, who died at the age of 32, was largely taken up with this question. His earliest known work "Sermon of John the Baptist" (Munich, Alte Pinakothek, c. 1598) showed some new impressions in addition to the influence of the painters of the Danube School to whom his teacher Philipp Uffenbach had introduced him. In 1598 Elsheimer had come by way of Munich to Venice, where he was much impressed by the work of Bassano and Tintoretto. These new influences already find expression in his "Conflagration of Troja" (Munich, Alte Pinakothek), probably produced while still in Venice. On the small copper plate (Elsheimer painted exclusively on copper) he created a night-time drama of great fascination, achieved through his handling of light and with a bold combination of foreground scene and background.

In 1600 he moved to Rome where Bril and Rubens as well as Caravaggio and Annibale Carracci became of great importance to the gregarious and popular Elsheimer. The figures of Caravaggio and the landscapes of Carracci enabled Elsheimer to find his own direction, which was to make him famous: a new relationship between figure and space which is absolutely natural and convincing. This becomes apparent in works, such as "Myrrha" (Frankfurt am Main, Städelsches Kunstinstitut) and "Flight to Egypt" (ill. p. 255). The end of his not always very easy life was tragic. Goudt, the Dutch patron, imitator, copyist and posthumous forger of Elsheimer, who had supported him financially and found customers for his engravings, had Elsheimer thrown into the debtors' prison, presumably because not enough work was forthcoming. Shortly after his release Elsheimer died.

*Illustrations:*
255 The Glorification of the Cross, c. 1605
255 The Flight to Egypt, 1609

## ENSOR James
1860 Ostend – 1949 Ostend
Ensor received his earliest instruction in Ostend before attending the Academies of Ostend and Brussels from 1877 to 1880. His darkly dramatic interiors, landscapes and portraits were a renunciation of traditional conventions as taught by the academies. His landscapes owe something to both realism and Impressionism. From 1885 he sent

work regularly to be exhibited by the Les XX group, of which he was a founder member in 1883, his work having been rejected by the Salons. On a visit to England in 1886 he discovered the light and airy world of Turner. This experience induced him to move closer to the Impressionists. In his principal work, "Christ Entering Brussels in 1888" (Antwerp, Koninklijk Museum voor Schone Kunsten), religious ideas mingle with the realities of life. The analogy to Christ entering Jerusalem is depicted as a ghostly and uncanny identification of the artist's rejection by the world. After 1900 Ensor's creativity diminished. The themes of his pictures painted in sublime, rich colours, and also of his bizarre etchings, were the expressions of nightmares and a fantastic imagination: ghosts, masks, skeletons tussling over a herring, and scenes ridiculing the legal and medical professions.

*Illustrations:*
559 Skeletons Fighting for the Body of a Hanged Man, 1891
559 Portrait of the Artist Surrounded by Masks, 1899

## ERNST Max
1891 Brühl (near Cologne) – 1979 Paris
Ernst studied philosophy at Bonn University from 1909 to 1914, painting only in his spare time. After military service he returned to Cologne in 1918 where he founded a Dada group, with Arp. In 1921 he showed his collages in Paris at the invitation of Breton. He settled in Paris in 1922 and became one of the founders of the Surrealist group, which gathered around Breton. His initial interest in hollow pipe forms was partly due to de Chirico's influence and partly based on the Surrealist idea of tension between interior and exterior, the conscious and unconscious. His subject matter in the late 1920s included forest scenes, crowds, whirlwinds and bird monuments. He introduced several new painting techniques, such as frottage, grattage and decalcomany, which were to bring the stimulus of the coincidental into the creative process. Many collage sets were produced from engravings extracted from old illustrated papers. In 1938 Ernst left the Surrealists; in 1939 he was interned, leaving France and emigrating to the USA in 1941. Despite the recognition he received in America he returned to Paris in 1953, where he settled.

*Illustrations:*
608 Elephant of the Celebes, 1921
608 Après nous la maternité, 1927
609 The Temptation of St Anthony, 1945

## ESTES Richard
born 1936 Kewanee (Illinois)
Estes studied at the Art Institute of Chicago from 1952 to 1956, moving to New York in 1959 where he has since been living and working. At first he worked as illustrator and layouter to support himself, but from 1966 he has devoted himself entirely to painting. Only a year later he had his first one-man exhibition at a New York gallery. His works belong to the category of American Hyper-Realism and Photo-Realism. Like the painters of Pop Art, Estes chooses his subjects from everyday surroundings. Photographs and picture postcards are his raw material. He sometimes uses phosphorescent colours to highlight a scene and give it glamour. The streets, house facades, shopwindows and drugstores in his pictures are void of life. Although he uses real situations as a starting point, his pictures are more than a silent, minute reportage of his chosen detail of reality. He imbues them with an atmosphere of glassy stillness, an aura of abandonment and loneliness, giving them an almost magical light. They are hypermodern mystifications, fic-

tions of a mood, aroused by the magic of an otherwise ordinary material world heightened by neon lights and reflections.
*Illustration:*
666 Candy Store, 1969

## EYCK Jan van
c. 1390 Maaseyck (near Maastricht) – 1441 Bruges
Jan van Eyck can claim as much importance for northern painting as must be conceded to Masaccio in Italian art. His mastery in rendering the human figure, his modern understanding of portraiture, his minutely observed landscapes and brilliant perspectival construction of interiors combine to give a suggestion of reality which can only be called "Renaissance" to distinguish it from medieval art. In addition, van Eyck was the principal representative of a new epoch in colour technique. Though not the inventor of oil-painting, as Vasari assumed, van Eyck was the first master of this medium and developed a process called glazing, in which successive transparent layers of paint are applied to the canvas, thus achieving a high colour depth. He used this method with very great success, particularly in imparting an amazing degree of realism when painting jewels and richly adorned fabrics. He was highly respected and esteemed. Until 1422 he served at the court of Duke Johann of Bavaria in The Hague, painting and restoring pictures. He was also highly regarded at the court of Philip the Good of Burgundy who entrusted him with various diplomatic missions. From about 1430 he lived and worked in Bruges as painter to the court and city. His overall contribution to Flemish painting in the first half of the 15th century remains unclear as long as there is no authenticated work by his brother Hubert, with whom he collaborated on the famous altarpiece in the cathedral of Ghent (ill. p. 125) which was completed in 1432 and bears his brother's inscription. As Hubert died in 1426, Jan van Eyck continued to work alone on the altar for another six years on his own to complete it.
*Illustrations:*
87 Portrait of Cardinal Nicola Albergati, c. 1432
123 Giovanni Arnolfini and His Wife Giovanna Cenami (The Arnolfini Marriage), 1434
123 The Virgin of Chancellor Rolin, 1434–1436
124 Madonna in a Church, c. 1437–1439
124 The Virgin and Child in a Church, 1437
125 Ghent Altar (central section), 1432

## FABRITIUS Carel
1622 Midden-Beemster – 1654 Delft
His name is the Latinised form of "carpenter", a trade which Fabritius, the son of a schoolmaster, had at first taken up. Between 1641 and 1643 he worked in Rembrandt's workshop in Amsterdam, whose most individual and important pupil he was to become. In 1650 he moved to Delft, entering the Lukas Guild two years later. His short life ended tragically. He died in the explosion of a powder magazine, which devastated almost a quarter of Delft, and with him perished the greater part of his work. Those that survive – only just under a dozen – are, however, quite unlike what would be expected of a Rembrandt pupil. Fabritius did not take up a speciality as so many others did, but covered the wide range of portraiture, genre pictures and still life. In particular, he opened up new ways in handling space and perspective, sometimes using *trompe l'œil* effects. He also differed from Rembrandt in the treatment of light, placing dark figures against a light background. During the few years he worked in Delft he had a great influence on the local school of painters, especially on de Hooch and Vermeer. The latter was his pupil and continued to develop his particular conception of how light should be used.

*Illustration:*
324   The Goldfinch, 1654

## FANTIN-LATOUR Henri
(Henri Ignace Jean Théodore Fantin-Latour)
1836 Grenoble – 1904 Buré (Orne)
Fantin-Latour was the son of an Italian painter and drawing master and a Russian mother who moved to Paris in 1841. He received his earliest instruction from his father, attended the drawing school of Lecocq de Boisbaudran from 1850 to 1854, studied briefly at the Ecole des Beaux-Arts and worked spasmodically in the studio of Courbet. He copied the drawings of Flaxman and the paintings of Titian and Veronese at the Louvre, admired Delacroix, Corot and Courbet and became friendly with Manet and Whistler. He was rejected by the Salon in 1859. He visited England three times between 1859 and 1864 where he worked and sold some of his pictures. In 1861 he exhibited for the first time at the Salon, then regularly, and also at the controversial Salon des Refusés from 1863. Fantin-Latour painted a great number of landscapes, genre scenes and most of all still lifes of flowers, which established his fame in France, as well as portraits of artists. In 1870 he painted the famous picture "Un Atelier aux Batignolles" (Paris, Musée d'Orsay) with portraits of his friends. Despite his contact with the Impressionists he rejected their principles and did not take part in their exhibitions.
*Illustration:*
501   Still Life ("Aux Fiancailles"), 1869

## FATTORI Giovanni
1825 Livorno – 1908 Florence
Fattori studied under Antonio Baldini in Livorno and from 1846 to 1848 under Giuseppe Bezzuoli at the Accademia di Belle Arte in Florence. In 1850 he continued his studies in Florence. He moved in the circles of the Caffè Michelangelo where discussions ranged from politics to new forms of art. He painted his first open-air studies. In 1861 he won first prize at the "Concorso Ricasoli" with his painting "The Italian Field after the Battle of Magenta". From 1861 to 1867 he lived mostly at Livorno, painting realistic scenes of the country population. He spent the summer of 1867 at Castiglioncello with Martelli, the supporter and theoretician of the Macchiaioli. In 1869 he taught at the Florentine Instituto di Belle Arti. In 1872 he went to Rome and in 1875 to Paris where he became very interested in Corot. In 1891 he published a scathing polemic against the Pointillists. In 1900 he became a member of the Accademia Albertina in Turin. Fattori is regarded as one of the major representatives of the Macchiaioli although he disapproved of the Impressionists all his life.
*Illustration:*
530   Roman Carts, 1873

## FAUTRIER Jean
1898 Paris – 1964 Châtenay-Malabry (near Paris)
In 1908 Fautrier went to live in London and later to study at the Royal Academy and the Slade School of Art. In 1917 he returned to France. At first his work met with little success although he had the strong support of André Malraux and Jean Paulhan. He therefore gave up painting between 1934 and 1939 and worked as hotelier and ski-instructor in the French Alps. It was not until after the war, when he showed the picture series "Otages" on which he had been working since 1941, that he received recognition as an innovator. In 1960 he received the Grand Prix of the Venice Biennale.
*Illustration:*
641   Nude, 1946

## FEININGER Lyonel
1871 New York – 1956 New York
Feininger's parents were both musicians of German origin. He left New York at the age of sixteen to continue his music studies at Hamburg but changed his mind and turned to painting. From 1887 to 1891 he studied at the School of Decorative Arts in Hamburg, moving on to the Academy of Arts in Berlin and finally, for six months in 1892, to the Académie Colarossi in Paris. The following year he returned to Berlin, producing caricatures for magazines to support himself. In 1906 he went to Paris for a further two years where he met the circle of German painters around Matisse and also made contact with the Cubists, becoming particularly drawn towards Delaunay. From 1908 to 1919 Feininger lived again in Berlin. The Blauer Reiter group of painters invited him to exhibit at their first German Autumn Salon in 1913. His first architectural compositions were produced in 1912. In subsequent years he painted again his Thuringia village and town scenes in the style he had developed and named "Prismaism", a type of crystalline cubism. Walter Gropius called him in 1919 to the newly-founded Bauhaus at Weimar, where he taught painting and graphic art until 1933.
*Illustration:*
600   Marktkirche in Halle, 1930

## FETTI Domenico
(also: Feti)
c. 1589 Rome – 1623 Venice
In his early years in Rome Fetti had discovered the landscape style of Elsheimer which was clearly discernible in his work, such as "The Flight to Egypt" (Vienna, Kunsthistorisches Museum). At that period he also became influenced by Saraceni and the Caravaggists in his handling of light although in his work it became looser, more diffuse, hinting already at Guardi. In 1614 he was appointed court painter to Duke Ferdinand II of Gonzaga in Mantua whose collection of paintings Fetti was able to admire. He was particularly enthusiastic about the brilliance of colour in Rubens' works.

Fetti is primarily known for his small parable pictures which in this form had not been painted before. The "Parable of the Labourers in the Vineyard" (Dresden, Gemäldegalerie) and the "Parable of the Pearl of Great Price" (Kansas City, Nelson Gallery and Atkins Museum), in particular, demonstrate in their genre-like conception and flowing brushwork Fetti's artistic individuality. In Mantua Fetti also painted frescos, including some monumental work carried out in the cathedral and the Palazzo Ducale. On returning to Rome, at the age of only 34, he died. He can be considered as one of the founders of northern Italian painting of the 17th century.
*Illustration:*
235   Melancholy, c. 1620

## FEUERBACH Anselm
1829 Speyer – 1880 Venice
Like so many artists who settled in Rome, Feuerbach belonged to the German Romans. He came from a family of intellectuals and also received a thorough education, studying at Düsseldorf Academy (under Wilhelm von Schadow), and at Munich, Antwerp and Paris. In 1855 he briefly kept a studio in Karlsruhe before starting on a visit to Italy. In 1857 he settled in Rome, making friends with Arnold Böcklin and Reinhold Begas. His greatest influences were Andrea del Sarto and Raphael and, having had a classical education, he painted primarily sublime allegorical, mythological and religious subjects. In 1872 he received a call to the Academy in Vienna, but did not feel happy there. Feuerbach died in 1880 on a visit to Venice.
*Illustration:*
531   The Garden of Ariosto, 1863

## FLEGEL Georg
c. 1566 Olmütz (Moravia) – 1638 Frankfurt am Main
Nothing is known of Flegel's beginnings, but presumably he received his training in the Netherlands. There is evidence that he worked at least from 1594 in Frankfurt am Main, at first as an assistant to Martin van Valckenborch, whose paintings he adorned with fruit and flowers. On his way to becoming the first, pure still life painter in Germany, his work as a miniaturist was of particular importance; for example, in about 1607 he illuminated the breviary of Duke Maximilian I of Bavaria. Flegel's early still lifes therefore bear strong marks of this finely detailed art, including small decorative additions ("Fruit Still Life", Kassel, Staatliche Kunstsammlungen, 1589; "Still Life", ill. p. 256). Flegel subsequently (since 1611) arrived at a much more unified, considered composition. With one of his last pictures, the "Still Life with Candle" (Cologne, Wallraf-Richartz-Museum, 1636), he succeeded in creating a work of tremendous atmospheric power and artistic simplicity.
*Illustration:*
256   Still Life, undated

## FONTAINEBLEAU → School of Fontainebleau

## FONTANA Lucio
1899 Rosario di Santa Fé (Argentina) – 1968 Comabbio (near Varese)
In 1914/15 Fontana studied in Milan at the Instituto Tecnico Carlo Cattaneo, then at the Accademia di Brera from 1920 to 1922. In 1922 he returned to Buenos Aires, where he worked at sculpting in his father's studio. In 1930 he went back to the Brera in Milan for further advanced studies. Until 1934, in this middle period of his artistic development, his work centred on the human body, but he then founded an association of Italian abstract artists and a year later became a member of the group Abstraction-Création in Paris. Despite this he also produced representational work until 1947. In 1936 his manifesto on Italian abstract art was published in Milan. From 1940 to 1947 he again lived in Buenos Aires where the *Manifesto Blanco* was published, to which he had contributed. The first "Concetti Spaziali" were not produced until 1949. Fontana became known for these spatial concepts and also for his monochrome, slit or torn canvases.
*Illustration:*
654   Spatial Concept, 1959

## FOUQUET Jean
c. 1415–1420 Tours (?) – c. 1480 Tours
Historical records give us almost no direct information about the life and work of the most famous French painter of his day. The only authenticated works are the miniatures in the "Antiquités judaïques" (Paris, Bibliothèque National). Documentary sources of the 15th and 16th centuries show that he was a painter of international repute, and these allow a reconstruction of his artistic development. Fouquet probably received instruction in the illumination of manuscripts under Flemish-Burgundian masters, possibly the brothers von Limburg. In any case, the decoration of precious manuscripts took a prominent place throughout his life. In the 1440s Fouquet went to Italy where

he painted a portrait (now lost) of Pope Eugene IV, who died in 1447, which provides a clue to when Fouquet must have stayed there. A commission from this high quarter allows us to assume that the painter must have been of an age to justify his reputation. Fouquet's contact with Italian art – in particular with Uccello's and Castagno's advanced treatment of figures – were decisive in developing his style further. As court painter to the French monarch from 1475, he succeeded in combining these diverse influences to achieve a courtly classicism, marked by a certain detachment and severe construction, which is unique in the art of the 15th century.

*Illustrations:*

140   Madonna and Child, c. 1450
140   Portrait of Guillaume Juvenal des Ursins, c. 1460

## FRAGONARD Jean-Honoré
### 1732 Grasse (Provence) – 1806 Paris

Fragonard was the son of a glove-maker and tanner. He came to Paris in his childhood. At first he worked as assistant to a lawyer who noticed his artistic talent. In 1747 he was given instruction by Chardin, and a year later was accepted by Boucher who had insisted on prior grounding. Boucher entered him for the Rome 1752 competition, which he won. Fragonard then studied three years at the Ecole des élèves privilégés under van Loo, concentrating in particular on the Dutch masters, before being accepted by the Académie de France in Rome. He travelled through Italy and on his return to Paris became a member of the Academy. He soon resigned, however, as the membership – he had entered the Academy as an historical painter – evidently did not suit his artistic interests and social tastes. Between 1765 and 1770 his subject matter was frequently of an amorous-erotic nature. He also painted landscapes and portraits. "The Swing" (ill. p. 360), 1767, dates from that period. Fragonard was not very successful with prominent givers of commissions, such as Madame Dubarry.

Fragonard remained a brilliant colourist to the end. Works such as the "Love Vow" (Orléans, Musée de Peinture et de Sculpture) or "Sacrifice of Roses" (Buenos Aires, Museo Nacional de Arte Decorativo) show the pathos of a monumentalised passion in the Classicist manner. Under David's protection he survived the turmoil of the French Revolution, but the new generation, in particular the Empire period, had no use for his aesthetics which were still rooted in the Rococo. He had to leave his residence in the Louvre in 1806 and died in the same year, almost forgotten.

*Illustrations:*

343   Progress of Love: The Lover Crowned , c. 1771–1773
360   Blind Man's Bluff, c. 1760
360   The Swing, 1767
361   The Stolen Shift, c. 1767–1772
361   The Music Lesson, c. 1770–1772

## FRANCIS Sam
### 1923 San Mateo (California) – 1994 Santa Monica

Francis studied botany and medicine at Berkeley from 1941 to 1943, then, after military service in the air force, studied painting and art history from 1948 to 1950. In a crash during a test flight he sustained injuries to his spine, and he began to paint while in hospital and sanatorium in 1944. On his recovery he visited France, Italy, Mexico, India, Japan and Thailand. His work is related to Abstract Expressionism. Until 1949 Francis painted primarily irregular, cell-like colour forms with thinned-down oil or acrylic paints. From 1950, during a stay in Paris, these characteristic

designs began to resemble monochrome planes. Soon, however, he returned to brilliant colour designs. In 1959 Francis settled in Santa Monica, California. His vast murals excited particular attention.

*Illustration:*

635   Basel Mural II, 1956–1958

## FRANCKE → Master

## FRANCKEN Frans the Younger
### 1581 Antwerp – 1642 Antwerp

Francken was the most successful and productive member of an Antwerp family of artists. He received instruction from his father Frans the Elder, became master in 1605 and deacon of the Lukas Guild in Antwerp in 1614. He painted works for churches ("Altar of the Four Crowned", Antwerp, Koninklijk Museum voor Schone Kunsten), biblical and historical scenes as well as genre pictures. However, his special domain was the so-called "Kunstkammer" – the depiction of a picture gallery. His meticulous rendering of rooms with hung paintings or antiquities are a cultural and historical source of the first order. These works give us an insight into art, not only at court, but also in private hands.

*Illustration:*

300   Supper at the Burgomaster Rockox, c. 1630–1635

## FREUD Lucian
### born 1922 Berlin

The grandson of Sigmund Freud and son of the architect Ernst Freud, Lucian Freud spent his early childhood in Germany. The family emigrated to England in 1932. After a brief spell in the merchant navy he began to study art at the Dedham School of Arts and Crafts in 1942 and then at Goldsmiths' College in London. Despite the war and lack of opportunity to follow the development of modern art, Freud had already established his style by 1947. From the start he found his subject matter in his immediate surroundings. With psychological exactitude and an analytical eye he dissects on the canvas familiar objects, acquaintances and friends. The result is that Freud succeeds in conveying in his work an unusual closeness between the painter and his model. Most of his sitters, to whom he repeatedly returns, remain anonymous, an exception being the portrait of Francis Bacon from 1952, recording the close friendship between the two painters. Towards the late 1950s his precise, realistic style became a little looser and the compositions lost some of their severity, without any reduction in care and precision.

*Illustration:*

645   The Big Man, c. 1976/77

## FRIEDRICH Caspar David
### 1774 Greifswald – 1840 Dresden

Friedrich was the son of a soap-maker and chandler, and studied under Jens Juel at Copenhagen Academy from 1794 to 1798. From 1798 he lived in Dresden until his death, interrupted only by his travels to Greifswald, Rügen, Neubrandenburg, the Harz mountains and northern Bohemia. In 1816 he became a member of the Dresden Academy, in 1824 professor extraordinary. Friedrich was the founder of German Romantic landscape painting. He combined in his work a hitherto unknown closeness to reality, the impressions of his travels and wanderings, with the metaphysics of light aroused by Christian and Neo-Platonic ideas. The origins of his landscape art lie in 18th century veduta painting.

This already comprised a foreground with viewing level against a background of an interesting landscape, and there was already an interest in the grandeur of nature; in the idiom of the time, the "sublime" natural phenomena, such as lonely mountain ranges and seas which served the enlightened as a trigger for religious feeling and insight. But Friedrich's pictures have no longer any of the touristic interest of the 18th century landscape. His nature scenes embody the externalised mood of the figures in the foreground; they are "atmospheric landscapes", to use 19th century terminology. They are always determined by two components: the objective conditions of nature and the mood of the observer, the back of whose figure is often magnified in the picture. The limitless distance, as opposed to the limited position of the onlooker in the foreground in Friedrich's pictures, points at the two sides of human existence – body and soul, the earthbound and the divine – which from early times have comprised the fundamental dichotomy of Christian and Neo-Platonic thinking. Friedrich was a philosophical painter. His friends included not only painters such as Runge, Dahl, Kersting and Gerhard van Kügelgen, but also poets like Ludwig Tieck as well as scientists and philosophers. He was a fervent patriot, which explains the symbolism hinting at the wars of independence in many of his pictures.

*Illustrations:*

412   The Stages of Life, c. 1835
447   Abbey under Oak Trees, 1809
447   Mountain Landscape with Rainbow, c. 1809/10
448   Wanderer looking over a sea of mist, c. 1817/18
448   The Lone Tree (Village Landscape in Morning Light), 1822
449   Chalk Cliffs on Rügen, 1818

## FROMENT Nicolas
### c. 1430 Uzès (Gard) – c. 1485 Avignon

Together with the Master of the Annunciation of Aix and Enguerrand Quarton, Froment explored the artistic possibilities of 15th century Provençal painting. Thanks to its geographical location, Provençe was open to the most diverse influences. As Froment painted the Lazarus triptych (Florence, Uffizi) for the Minorite monastery in Mugello near Florence in 1461, his first authenticated work, his date of birth may be assumed to have been around 1430 at the latest. Although this work must have been produced in Italy, it shows no Italian influence whatsoever, but rather points to his training in the Netherlands in the neighbourhood of Bouts. Records show Uzès as his place of birth. The possession of several houses in Uzès about 1470 indicates prosperity obtained through substantial commissions. Since 1475/76 he worked for King René, who commissioned the surviving major work, the Moses triptych in Aix-en-Provence (ill. p. 141). He then decorated the King's palace in Avignon, and his name appears repeatedly in account books until 1479. Unfortunately none of these works, nor his designs for tapestries and festive decorations, have survived. Froment, whose work consists mainly of unauthorised attributions, remained all his life a follower of the Dutch school. However, his few authenticated works show a dynamic development towards a more liberal treatment of space and landscape and a more realistic approach to detail.

*Illustration:*

141   Moses and the Burning Bush, 1476

## FUSELI Henry

(also: Füssli, Füßli, Fuessli, Fueslin, Füßlin, Johann Heinrich)

1741 Zurich – 1825 Putney Hill (near London)

Füssli was the second son of the Zurich portraitist and author Johann Caspar Füssli. His early contact with the teachings of Johann Jakob Bodmer familiarised him with the figures of world literature, and these were to remain a major source for his artistic inspiration. Ordained in 1761 as a pastor in the Zwinglian Reformed church, he left Zurich two years later for political reasons, travelling via Berlin to London where he made his new home. Initially he made his living from literary work. Artistically he was engaged in illustrating the works of his favourite authors, particularly Shakespeare. It was Reynolds who persuaded him to concentrate entirely on the fine arts. He travelled through Italy, visiting Florence, Venice and Naples and lived for eight years in Rome. This period, during which Michelangelo's monumental style left deep impressions on his artistic feeling, became a lasting influence. After a short stay in Zurich on his return from Italy, he began to paint extensively in London. "The Nightmare" (Detroit, Institute of Arts, and Frankfurt am Main, Goethe-Museum), probably his most popular work, excited great attention when it was exhibited at the Royal Academy, to which he was elected in 1790. In the history of style, Füssli's significance lies in his early romantic Classicism which allowed him to develop a strange monumentalisation of the dreamlike and macabre. His often misunderstood importance as colourist probably lies in his novel, draughtsman-like treatment of colour.

*Illustration:*

379   Titania and Bottom, c. 1780–1790

## GAINSBOROUGH Thomas

1727 Sudbury (Suffolk) – 1788 London

Gainsborough was the fifth son of a well-to-do cloth manufacturer. Because of his early talent for drawing he was sent to London at the age of thirteen. There he studied etching under the Frenchman Gravelot, a pupil of Boucher. Apart from being influenced by the French Rococo, to which he was introduced by Hayman at St Martin's Academy, Gainsborough's landscapes were particularly affected by 17th century Dutch landscape pictures which he had copied and restored in his early years. Between 1747 and 1759, in Sudbury and Ipswich, he produced this type of landscape as well as working in the style of the French pastoral idyll. In 1746 he secretly married Margaret Burr, the illegitimate daughter of the Duke of Beaufort, which ensured him financial independence.

While the pure landscape was not highly appreciated in England, Gainsborough succeeded in combining full-length figure portraits with landscape, mostly depicting a location on the estate of the nobility he portrayed, and thereby becoming the founder of a new version of arcadia in the dispassionate English style. In 1759 he moved to the fashionable resort of Bath, where, inundated with portrait commissions, he developed his style further by studying van Dyck, whose work could be seen in many country houses around Bath. In 1774 he removed to London where as portrait-painter he had to vie with Reynolds and his pupils. He became increasingly interested in lighting effects, as popularised by experiments carried out by the theatrical decorator Loutherbourgh. Gainsborough succeeded in becoming the favoured portraitist of the royal family. In 1782 he painted in Windsor a series of oval portraits of the royal couple and their thirteen children.

After some dispute he retired from the Royal Academy, of which he had been a founder member in 1768, and in the 1780s he began to arrange summer exhibitions at his private house. His final creative years are marked by a sensitive, poetic style and ethereal coloration. His free compositions, or fancy pictures as he called them, date from this time. In these Gainsborough surpassed his exemplar Murillo, sensitively exploring the theme of this childlike and rustic genre in an old-masterly brown-toned tenebrism. Gainsborough was a pioneer in landscape painting. Apart from his extremely personal style of portraiture and a short-lived fashion of imitating his "fancy pictures", he had an important influence on 19th century landscape painting.

*Illustrations:*

347   Miss Anne Ford (Mrs. Philip Thicknesse), 1760

384   Robert Andrews and his Wife Frances, c. 1750

384   The Watering Place, 1777

385   The Morning Walk, c. 1785/86

386   Woman in Blue, before 1780

386   Lady and Gentlemen in a Landscape, c. 1746/47

## GAUGUIN Paul

1848 Paris – 1903 Atuona Hiva-Oa (Marquesa Islands)

The son of an émigré Republican journalist, Gauguin spent his earliest years 1849–1855 in Lima (Peru); then he went back to Orléans and Paris. He went to sea from 1865 to 1871, then worked in banking from 1871 to 1883 in Paris. In 1873 he married the Danish woman Mette Gad with whom he had five children. In 1874 he met Pissarro and other Impressionists, began to study at the Académie Colarossi and exhibited at the Salon for the first time in 1876. In 1879 he painted with Pissarro in Pontoise and exhibited with the Impressionists at their exhibitions IV to VIII from 1879 to 1886. In 1881 he painted with Pissarro and Cézanne. In 1882 he moved to Rouen, then to Copenhagen, and got into financial distress. He returned to Paris in 1885, leaving his family behind in Denmark. In 1886 he painted for the first time at Pont-Aven where he met Bernard. In Paris he became acquainted with the brothers van Gogh and travelled with the painter Laval to Panama and Martinique in 1887. While with Bernard and others at Pont-Aven in 1888, he changed to a "synthetic symbolism" in his Brittany paintings. He exhibited at Theo van Gogh's gallery. His stay with Vincent van Gogh at Arles ended the friendship. In 1889 he contributed to the Les XX exhibition at Brussels and at the Café Volpini during the Paris World Exhibition. He painted at Pont-Aven and Le Pouldu, influenced by Sérusier, Denis and Bonnard.

In 1891, after auctioning his works and quarrelling with Bernard, Gauguin travelled to Tahiti in order to escape from European urban civilisation. While there he contracted syphilis. From 1893 to 1895 he stayed in Paris, Copenhagen and Brittany. He was not successful with his large, colourful South Seas pictures symbolising life, the incunabula of "exoticism" and "primitivism". From 1895 to 1901 he was again in Tahiti, also producing sculptural work. His physical condition worsened, aggravated by alcohol. In 1897 he published his autobiographical writings Noa Noa, which are still read. In 1898 he tried to commit suicide. In 1900 the art dealer Vollard offered him a contract. In 1901 Gauguin removed to the Marquesa island of Dominique, where he fought against the colonial administration and was sentenced in 1903. He died utterly exhausted and impoverished at the age of 54.

*Illustrations:*

489   When will you marry? ("Nafea faa ipiopo?"), 1892

514   Tahitian Women (On the Beach), 1891

514   Breton Peasants, 1894

515   Contes barbares (Barbarian Tales), 1902

## GEERTGEN TOT SINT JANS

(Gerrit van Haarlem)

c. 1460–1465 Leyden (?) – before 1495 Haarlem

Geertgen's great importance for late 15th century Dutch painting is in inverse proportion to the small number of authenticated works. Probably born in Leyden, he may have been trained in the southern parts of the Netherlands, perhaps under Aelbert van Ouwater. But more important to his art were van der Weyden and van der Goes. Geertgen's reputation rests equally on the expressive gravity of his figures and on his masterly skill in landscape painting. In his early works, such as the "Three Kings" triptych (Prague, Národni Galeri), Geertgen drew on van der Weyden, but interpreting his style to suit his generation's courtly, refined, more elaborate taste. The "Crucifixion" altar painted for Haarlem's St John's church, probably after 1484, of which only the right wing of the Lamentation survives (Vienna, Kunsthistorisches Museum), shows a freer arrangement and treatment of figures with regard to size as well as expression, and also his characteristic depiction of landscape which was to culminate in the small panel of "St John the Baptist" (ill. p. 134). With these tendencies Geertgen seems to have represented an opposing current to that of contemporaries who, like him, worked for the order of the Knights of St John at Haarlem, and from which his name derived. His "Nativity" (London, National Gallery), with its amazing chiaroscuro, also shows how difficult it is to put Geertgen into a general category.

*Illustration:*

134   St John the Baptist in the Wilderness, c. 1485–1490

## GENTILE DA FABRIANO

(Gentile di Niccolò di Giovanni Massi)

c. 1370 Fabriano – 1427 Rome

Gentile, born in Fabriano, was the son of a cloth merchant. He probably received a thorough introduction to Sienese art at an early age, but there are signs which speak for his training at the great cultural centres of Milan and Verona. The clear evidence is that he visited Venice between 1408 and 1414. There he became famous with his paintings, particularly those in the Doge's Palace. One of his Venetian pupils was Jacopo Bellini who became a famous painter in his own right although later overshadowed by his sons Giovanni and Gentile. Nothing of Gentile da Fabriano's Venetian work survives, nor of the commissions carried out for the Malatesta in Breseia, or for the Pope in the Lateran Basilica in Rome or his Sienese works. In 1427 he died while working on the frescos in the Lateran Basilica; his assistant and pupil Pisanello carried on this work, taking over the workshop and also taking up the artistic legacy of his mentor.

Gentile can be regarded as fulfilling that for which Sienese art was striving in the first half of the 15th century. With his methods of gilding and wealth of colour effects and surface structures, he created an art of great charm both to the eye and to the touch. His style was eminently suitable for expressing the ruling classes' love for splendour and magnificence, and this may have contributed to his extraordinary success. Amongst his contemporaries he ranked as the master of the masters, and perhaps rightly so. Art history singles him out for other reasons, and particularly for his innovative treatment of light which was far ahead of his time: the gilded background is seen as a source of light irradiating the scene or casting shadows. He was also one of the first to use the medium of freehand drawing as a basis of further studies and sketches.

*Illustrations:*

53   A Miracle of St Nicholas, 1425

53   St Nicholas and the Three Gold Balls,
     1425
54   The Adoration of the Magi, 1423

## GENTILESCHI Orazio
(Orazio Gentileschi Lomi)
1563 Pisa – c. 1639/40 London
During his apprenticeship with Aurelio Lomi, his
brother or half-brother, and Bacci Lomi, his uncle,
Gentileschi familiarised himself with the Florentine
Mannerist tradition of Agnolo Bronzino and Jacopo
Carrucci da Pontormo. In Rome, where he stayed in
1580, he studied the art of Caravaggio. Gentileschi
was successful in uniting both these strands to a
style of his own, such as in the "Baptism of Christ"
for Santa Maria della Pace in Rome or the "Stigmata
of St Francis" for San Silvestro in Capite (Rome).
After a two years' stay each at Genoa and Paris,
where he was in the service of Maria de' Medici, he
followed the call of the Duke of Buckingham to the
English court in 1625 where he executed interior
decorations on a monumental scale though on
canvas. Late works, such as the "Lute Player" (ill.
p.228), are captivating because of their balanced coloration and composition as well as their brilliant
painterly technique. Orazio's daughter Artemisia,
stylistically close to her father, also achieved fame
among her contemporaries.
*Illustration:*
228   The Lute Player, c. 1626

## GÉRARD François Pascal Simon
1770 Rome – 1837 Paris
Gérard's family lived in Rome until 1780, where
his father served as steward at various courts. After
the family's return to Paris, Gérard entered the studio of Jacques Louis David at the age of 16 and soon
became his favourite pupil. In 1790 he travelled to
Rome to sort out some family affairs after his father's death. He married a younger sister of his
mother. Soon Gérard had to return to Paris to avoid
being registered as an emigrant. As the Revolution
deprived him of the ability to earn his living as a
portraitist, he worked as an illustrator of the works
of Racine and Virgil. He became successful as a
painter of historical scenes, winning the competition to commemorate the meeting of the National
Assembly of 10 August 1792. However, he soon
turned again to the painting of portraits which enjoyed popularity on account of their careful preparation and classical detachment. He remained successful through the period of the Restoration. In 1817
he became court painter to Louis XVIII, and was
ennobled in 1819.
*Illustration:*
423   Madame Récamier, 1805

## GÉRICAULT Théodore
(Jean Louis André Théodore Géricault)
1791 Rouen – 1824 Paris
Géricault's large œuvre came into being during a
creative period lasting only twelve years. He loved
horses and was a passionate rider, and therefore left
numerous sketches and pictures dealing with this
subject which are unsurpassed in their vividness
and realism. He became famous with one of these
equestrian pictures, "The Charging Chasseur" (ill.
p.425), which in 1812 was his first work to be exhibited at the Salon. The passionate, impetuous
manner of his depiction was a renunciation of Classicism, heralding the Romantic period. With his
"Epsom Derby" (ill. p.427), produced just a few
years before his death, he paved the way for the Impressionists. Géricault entered the studio of the
equestrian artist and battlefield painter Carle Vernet in 1808, changing in 1810 to Guérin, whose
Classicism did not appeal to him. His intensive ex-

ploration of the Antiquity and the masters of the
16th and 17th centuries became decisive for his art.
He made innumerable copies in the Louvre of the
works of Rubens, Caravaggio, Velázquez, Rembrandt, van Dyck and Raphael. When in Italy in
1816/17, he was particularly impressed by Michelangelo. In England, where he stayed from 1820 to
1822, Constable became important, and also Wilkie
and Hogarth. It is possible to trace the influence of
most of these painters in his work.
   The unequalled realism of Géricault's portraits
and pictures of animals, however, is founded on the
intensive study of nature – in the countryside, at
race courses, in stables and at public festivals. His
determination to capture human nature under the
most extreme conditions meant that he never
avoided working in hospitals, institutions for the
insane, and morgues. These pictures give an account
of Géricault's own eventful life – his spasmodic political enthusiasms, his joining the Musketeers of
the King's army, and also his passionate, unrequited
love for many years for the wife of a friend. He died
painfully at the age of 33 as the result of a riding
accident.
*Illustration:*
415   The Madwoman (Manomania of Envy),
      1822/23
425   Officer of the Imperial Guard (The Charging
      Chasseur), 1812
425   The Quicklime Works, c. 1821/22
426   The Raft of the Medusa (sketch),
      c. 1818/19
427   The Epsom Derby, 1821
427   The Kleptomaniac, c. 1822/23

## GERTSCH Franz
born 1930 Möhringen (near Bern)
Gertsch studied from 1947 tof 1950 at the paint-
ing-school of Max von Mühlenen in Bern. He is one
of the European exponents of Photo-Realism. In his
monumental canvases, produced since 1969, the
motifs appear in extreme magnification. As an
image to start from, he uses slides produced by himself. By intensifying and accentuating the projected
image on the canvas, Gertsch not only achieves a
hyperrealistic effect, but also attempts to demateri-
alise his subject. In the 1970s he produced family
and group scenes. After painting his last picture in
oil in 1986, the portrait "Johanna II", he began to
produce numerous large-scale woodcuts in the
hyperrealistic manner.
*Illustration:*
667   Medici, 1971

## GHIRLANDAIO Domenico
(Domenico di Tommaso Bigordi)
1449 Florence – 1494 Florence
Ghirlandaio was the antithesis to Botticelli in Florentine painting of the second half of the 15th century.
Botticelli's refined, courtly art stands in juxtaposition to Ghirlandaio's depiction of the prosperous
middle-class, where love of detail is dominated by
brilliantly marshalled mass scenes. In his lavishly
decorated "contemporary" architecture and distant
landscapes, Ghirlandaio owed more to the traditions
of the first half of the century. Above all, he is the one
painter of his generation in Florence to have been
destined for large-scale work, and therefore a born
fresco painter. Already in 1481 he was one of the
circle of selected artists to paint the lower half of the
Sistine Chapel. His second major work was the decoration of the private chapel of the Sassetti family at
Santa Trinità in Florence from 1483 to 1485. Scenes
from the Life of St Francis were given the setting of
15th century Florence, and even now some of his
views of the city are of particular value as an historical source. Ghirlandaio told his stories in a lively
manner, easily grasped by the imagination. Some de-

tails, such as figure arrangement, point to a Dutch
influence, as demonstrated by his altar picture in the
Sassetti chapel. The Last Supper fresco in the refectory of Ognissanti (ill. p.108) painted in 1480, a subject he used again in San Marco, was important in
the way Ghirlandaio succeeded in bringing actual
architecture into the scene. His creativity reached its
culmination with his work in the main choir of Santa
Maria Novella (1485–1490).
*Illustrations:*
108   Last Supper, 1480
108   Old Man and Young Boy, 1488

## GIACOMETTI Alberto
1901 Stampa (Graubünden) – 1966 Chur
Giacometti studied sculpture at the Ecole des Arts
et Metiers in Geneva. In 1920/21 he went to Italy
and remained in Rome for some time. In 1922 he
went to Paris and became a pupil of the sculptor
Émile Bourdelle at the Académie de la Grande
Chaumiére. In 1929 he met Aragon, Dalí and Breton and joined the Surrealists in 1932. Sartre and Simone de Beauvoir introduced him to Existentialism. Both his sculptural art and his painting deal almost exclusively with the human figure. Giacometti spent the years 1942 to 1945 in Geneva. He
then returned again to Paris, devoting himself intensively to painting. In protracted and frequently
repeated attempts he produced portraits principally
of his wife Annette and close friends. His concern
was to apply the principles of his late sculpture to
painting, with particular emphasis on the development of the human head.
*Illustration:*
645   Portrait of Jean Genet, 1955

## GIORDANO Luca
1634 Naples – 1705 Naples
Giordano, who obtained instruction from his father
Antonio and from Ribera, ranks as the first Baroque
"virtuoso" in the sense of the 18th century. The
number of his oil-paintings is estimated to be over
5000, which brought him the nickname "fa presto"
(do it quickly). He also had the ability to copy any
style. While he was greatly influenced by Ribera in
his early years, he later developed a style which
showed his familiarity with Rubens, van Dyck, Cortona, and most of all the great Venetian painters
such as Titian and Veronese whom he had discovered on a visit to the northern parts of Italy in
the early 1650s.
   In 1654, having returned to his home town, he
received a commission for two paintings for the
choir of San Pietro ad Aram, and he produced the
"Madonna of the Rosary" (Naples, Galleria Nazionale), the "Ecstasy of St Alexius" (Arco, Chiesa del
Purgatorio) and "Tarquinius and Lucretia" (Naples,
Galleria Nazionale). On a second visit to Venice in
1667 he painted there the "Ascension of Mary" for
Santa Maria della Salute, which in its generous conception is reminiscent of Cortona. Giordano's fame
was established with his two large St Benedict
cycles for Monte Cassino (destroyed 1943) and San
Gregorio Armeno (Naples). From 1679–1682 he
worked spasmodically on the ceiling of the gallery
in the Palazzo Medici-Riccardi in Florence. Charles
II called him to the Spanish court in 1692, and in
the following ten years Giordano produced major
works, such as the frescos in the San Lorenzo church
at Escorial and the bible scenes in the Buen Retiro
palace near Madrid. He returned via Genoa,
Florence and Rome to Naples in 1702. One of his
last important works was the fresco in the cupola of
Tesoro Certosa di San Martino.
*Illustration:*
238   The Fall of the Rebel Angels, 1666

## GIORGIONE
(Giorgio Barbarelli, Giorgio da Castelfranco)
c. 1477/78 Castelfranco Veneto – 1510 Venice
In the development of Venetian painting Giorgione's work provides the link between Giovanni Bellini and Titian. Giorgione was trained by Bellini, who also provided a decisive stimulus. Giorgione's "Madonna di Castelfranco" (ill. p. 164) shows the influence of both Bellini and Antonello da Messina in its clarity of composition and richness of colour scale, while already revealing greater dynamism in the articulation of surface and less dependence on the drawing. In subsequent works, landscape gains in importance, by far exceeding Bellini's possibilities. The aim was not, however, to create "pure" landscape, as was the case north of the Alps with Dürer, Altdorfer and Wolf Huber. Giorgione's starting point was always the representation of the human being, whose moods and dreams are reflected in the landscape. But this was not the only way in which he achieved the fusion of figure and landscape; rather, it was done through acute sensitivity of colour aimed at producing the right atmospheric effect ("La Tempesta", ill. p. 165; "Concert Champêtre", ill. p. 164, perhaps completed by Titian; "Venus", Dresden, Gemäldegalerie, c. 1505–1510). Giorgione's works are often mysterious in subject matter. He certainly exercised a lasting influence on the younger Titian with his soft modelling of forms in which line is replaced by colour. Giorgio Vasari stated with great admiration that Giorgione would put brush straight to canvas without preliminary sketch.

Only a few of his paintings survive, although it is difficult to identify those works that can be attributed to him with certainty. The versatility of his talent can be assessed only from the remaining frescos for the façade of the Fondaco dei Tedeschi (Hall of the German Merchants in Venice, 1508). His most significant contribution was the representation of the figure in space, freely moving and from all sides visible, and this idea was further developed by the great Venetian painters of the 16th century.
*Illustrations:*
164  Virgin and Child with SS Francis and
     Liberalis (Madonna di Castelfranco),
     c. 1504/05
164  Concert Champêtre, c. 1510/11
165  La Tempesta, c. 1510

## GIOTTO DI BONDONE
1266 (?) Colle di Vespignano (near Florence) –
1337 Florence
According to legend – Giotto was one of the first artists to become a legend – he was discovered by Cimabue as a boy, making drawings of his father's sheep. He certainly was a pupil of Cimabue. But he was able to work independently, as the frescos in the Upper Church in Assisi show and which can be attributed to him with complete certainty. Impressed by ancient Roman art, French sculpture (in particular Rheims and eastern France) and the Tuscan sculptors Giovanni Pisano and Arnolfo di Cambio, he developed his own conception which showed no particular influence. It is not certain whether he was involved in the painting of the famous cycle of the Life of St Francis in the Upper Church of Assisi. Considering that several masters and any number of assistants were engaged in carrying out this work, and also that Giotto had at that time not yet fully developed his own characteristic style, the main works of the cycle could well have been painted by him. However, his masterpiece was undoubtedly the decoration of the private chapel built by the financier Enrico Scrovegni for his family in the Arena of Padua, 1303 to 1305. Documentary sources tell us that he was the most famous painter of his generation in Italy. He received innumerable offers of

work from leading lords and princes, including from the Pope and his cardinals in Rome (copy surviving) and Bologna, from King Robert of Anjou for the large cycles in Naples, the Scaligers in Verona and Visconti in Milan. He probably also worked in other Italian cities. All these works, and also some cycles dealing with profane subjects, have been lost. Of his late work only some badly preserved frescos in the side chapels of Santa Croce in Florence survive in outline.

Giotto was an excellent organiser. He had a large workshop with a great number of well-trained assistants so that he was in a position to undertake even the largest of commissions. In this he is comparable to Rubens. And it is safe to assume that he was also a good businessman which, at the time, meant that as a leading painter he was able to charge exorbitant fees. This was customary up to the times of Dürer and Titian. Towards the end of his life he was appointed chief architect of the city of Florence. This was often no more than a title, but Giotto seems to have worked at it. He is generally considered to be the pioneer of modern painting, but his effect on his professional contemporaries in Florence was so overwhelming that they were reduced to mere followers, albeit capable ones. His influence was more fruitful in Siena and the northern parts of Italy; in Florence not until a century later with the generation of Masaccio.
*Illustrations:*
 8   The Devils Cast out of Arezzo,
     c. 1296–1297
13   The Crucifixion, 1303–1305
14   The Marriage Procession of the Virgin,
     1303–1305
29   Enthroned Madonna with Saints (Ognissanti
     Madonna), c. 1305–1310
30   Joachim Takes Refuge in the Wilderness,
     c. 1303–1305
31   Anna and Joachim Meet at the Golden Gate,
     1303–1305
32   The Lamentation of Christ, 1303–1305
32   St Francis Giving his Cloak to a Poor Man,
     between 1296 and 1299

## GIOVANNI DA MILANO
(Giovanni di Jacopo di Guido da Caversago)
born in Caversaccio (near Milan), active between 1346 and 1369, mostly in Florence
Giovanni was probably trained in Lombardy which had its own painting school of good reputation. Like Giotto, he was brought to Milan by the Viscontis (though in the last year of Giotto's life). From the start Giovanni was thus in touch with Florentine innovations. There is evidence that he himself lived in Florence from 1346 but continued to carry out commissions in Lombardy. It was not until 1366 that he became a Florentine citizen. His major work are the frescos of the Capella Rinuccini in the sacristy chancel of Santa Croce in Florence. Giovanni proved himself to be one of the few painters who went beyond Giotto in Florence. He owed his fine colour modulation and his evenness of application to Sienese panel painting, but without becoming an imitator. From his background in northern Italy he brought a close study of nature, especially of animals. His figures appear solemn, their faces idealised. The ambivalence between ideal beauty and actual nature – so typical in the International Gothic style – is already evident in Giovanni's work.
*Illustration:*
64   Pietà, 1365

## GIRARD D'ORLÉANS
active 1344–1361 in Paris
Probably coming from the family of the painter Evrard d'Orléans, Girard worked as a furniture decorator at the French court from 1344. In 1352 he was

appointed court painter and *valet de chambre* to John II, at whose direction he added to the collection of oil-paintings by Jean Coste at the Vaudreuil palace in Normandy. Only a few of his authenticated works survive: apart from the portrait of John II, taken from a square triptych and produced during his incarceration in England, there is information about a much admired Madonna, which he painted for the small Carthusian monastery in Paris and at whose feet he was buried.
*Illustration:*
67   Portrait of John II "the Good", King of
     France, c. 1349

## GOES Hugo van der
c. 1440–1445 Ghent – 1482 near Brussels
Van der Goes is, apart from the somewhat younger Bosch, the most important Dutch painter in the second half of the 15th century. Little is known about his life, and his artistic origins are also unclear. A certificate of 1480 confirms that his home town was Ghent, and as he was granted the master title in Ghent in 1467, he must have been born about 1440–1445. As early as 1477 he abandoned his workshop, entering the Red Monastery near Brussels where he died in 1482 after a severe mental illness. His masterpiece, known as the Portinari Altarpiece (ill. p. 133) is the only surviving work that can be attributed to him with absolute certainty, although there are others that can be assigned to him with some safety (Monforte Altarpiece, ill. p. 132; diptych depicting the "Fall of Adam, the Lamentation of Christ and St Genoveva", Vienna, Kunsthistorisches Museum, ill. p. 132). Hugo van der Goes had at his disposal all the techniques of the earlier Dutch masters, in particular Rogier van der Weyden, as regards spatial disposition, the true-to-life construction of the human body and the representation of luxurious detail to look like the real thing. Yet he handled these devices in a completely different sense, putting to service the heightened expressiveness of gestures and faces, and not excluding the "uncomely". With his Portinari Altarpiece he brought about a revolution in Florentine painting, as the works of Ghirlandaio and Filippino Lippi demonstrate, but which becomes most evident in Leonardo da Vinci's work.
*Illustrations:*
132  The Fall of Adam, before 1470
132  Adoration of the Magi (Monforte Altar),
     c. 1470
133  Adoration of the Shepherds (Portinari Altar),
     1476–1478

## GOGH Vincent van
1853 Groot-Zundert (Northern Brabant) – 1890
Auvers-sur-Oise (near Paris)
This Dutch painter, son of a clergyman, only had a short creative period of about ten years. All his life he remained very close to his younger brother Theo, who provided for him, as Vincent only sold one single picture during his painting career. Van Gogh worked first for art dealers in The Hague, London and Paris; then as a private teacher. Later he became a Methodist preacher among the Belgian miners of the Borinage, to bring them help and salvation. After his dismissal there, he decided to become an artist. Initially he painted sombre scenes from the life of the poor which show his personal engagement with his subject, using dark-toned colours and a rough, sharp-edged technique ("Potato Eaters", various versions). Although he sought friendship, all his relationships failed because of his tragic and melancholic temperament and his emotional outbursts. All his life he suffered from loneliness, his only consolation being painting. He often went back to his parents' home at

Nuenen, where the most important of his Dutch pictures were painted between 1883 and 1885. Until 1886 he was at Antwerp, where he entered the Academy for a few months, but he preferred to paint in the open. After discovering the charms of Japanese woodcuts he tried to transfer some of the motifs into oil. These woodcuts had a revolutionary effect on his style. He began to use lighter colours, and his two years in Paris from 1886 to 1888 became the most important period in his artistic career. He was introduced to the Impressionists, Symbolists and Pointillists, and also met Gauguin. In 1888, in search of the southern light, he went to Arles, where Gauguin visited him. In 1889 he went at his own request into an asylum at St Rémy, where he continued to paint, and in 1890 moved to Auvers-sur-Oise, where his friend and patron Doctor Paul Gachet lived. Unfortunately this medical attention could not help him, and, in despair of his condition, he shot himself. Between 1888 and his death van Gogh produced, in just thirty months of feverish creativity, those 463 paintings which established his worldwide fame and made him one of the founders of modern 20th century painting, in particular in the fields of Expressionism and Fauvism.

*Illustrations:*
488   Flower-Garden, 1888
521   The Langlois Bridge at Arles, 1888
521   Harvest at La Crau, with Montmajour in the
        Background (Blue Cart), 1888
522   The Artist's Bedroom in Arles, 1889
522   Portrait of Doctor Gachet, 1890
523   The Church at Auvers-sur-Oise, 1890

## GORKY Arshile

(Vosdanik Adoian)
1904 Khorkom Vari (Armenia) – 1948 Sherman (Connecticut)
Gorky was one of the key figures of abstract Expressionism in the USA. He was born in the cultural centre of Armenia, famous for its fresco painting, book illumination, architecture and sculpture. In 1908 his father emigrated to America, and the family followed in 1920, as they lived in fear of the Turks. Gorky taught himself to paint, guided by Cézanne's work. From 1922 to 1924 he studied at the Boston New School of Design. Exhibitions of Surrealist art in New York introduced him in the 1930s to the works of Picasso, Miró and Masson. While under their influence he painted some murals which had been commissioned by the American government. Gorky developed an idiom which became less and less objective until it arrived at the purely abstract. His pictures and drawings are divided into colour fields and "hybrid forms". Around 1947 he turned away from Surrealism and also spoke against abstract Expressionism, in spite of having himself exercised great influence on the painters of that tendency. When, after a serious road accident, his right-hand became paralysed, Gorky committed suicide.

*Illustration:*
629   The Liver is the Cock's Comb, 1944

## GOSSAERT Jan

(called: Mabuse)
about 1478/88 Maubeuge (Hennegau) – about 1533–1536 Breda (?)
It is not known where Gossaert was trained, and the stylistic assessment has not yet offered many clues about this. From 1503 to 1507 he lived and worked in Antwerp. Decisive in his development was a visit to Rome in 1508/09 in company with Philip of Burgundy for whom he had to draw ancient architecture and sculpture. On his return he nevertheless adhered at first to the traditions of the Dutch masters, copying the works of Jan van

Eyck, for example. However, after 1515 his Italian experience gradually took effect as can be seen particularly in his depiction of architecture as well as his interest in three-dimensional figure painting. His "Neptune and Amphitrite" (Berlin, Gemäldegalerie, 1516) reflects, in the Herculean representation of the nude figures, the impressions Gossaert had received from Michelangelo's ceiling in the Sistine Chapel. When called in 1515 by Philip of Burgundy to decorate the Soubourg palace near Middelburg, Gossaert was able to carry out court commissions without being bound by Guild regulations. He concentrated on mythological scenes and portraiture, favouring large-scale, "statuary" figures which, although modelled on the ideal body of Italian antiquity, nevertheless bear traces of ordinary characters of the day. Gossaert played an important role in introducing a northern Renaissance style with an Italian flavour.

*Illustration:*
201   Danaë, 1527

## GOYA Francisco José de

(Francisco José de Goya y Lucientes)
1746 Fuendetodos (near Saragossa) – 1828 Bordeaux
Goya was trained in Saragossa by José Luzan, a pupil of Giordano and Solimena, before going to Madrid. There he entered the studio of Francisco Bayeu, his future brother-in-law, who worked under Mengs at the court of Charles III. After visiting Italy in 1770/71, Goya was asked to provide designs for the royal tapestry works. In 1780 he became a member of the Real Academia de San Fernando, later to become its deputy principal and then principal. Having carried out court commissions since 1781, he was appointed as a court painter in 1786, painter to the royal chamber in 1789, and principal court painter in 1799.

Goya started painting in the Spanish version of the Rococo manner, intermingled with French and Italian elements, but from 1792 his style changed drastically. During that year he became deaf as a result of a severe illness. In a series of uncommissioned paintings he created, under the mask of ordinary genre scenes, a world of terror and nightmare ("The Burial of the Sardine", ill. p. 399; "Procession of the Flagellants"; the "Mad-House"; the "Session of the Inquisition" – all Madrid, Academia de San Fernando). During the same period he produced "Los Caprichos", consisting of 80 etchings (published 1799) to "scourge human vices and errors", as he wrote. With his "black paintings" of the Quinta del Sordo (Madrid, Prado) he reached the pitch of his portrayal of the negative and unaccountable in human existence. Under the pressure of the Restoration Goya left Spain and emigrated to Bordeaux. The deeply questionable in human nature, which is also expressed in Goya's portraits, did not find full recognition until the 20th century.

*Illustrations:*
341   Portrait of Doña Isabel de Porcel, 1805
397   The Clothed Maja, c. 1797
397   The Naked Maja, c. 1797
398   Don Manuel Osorio Manrique de Zúñiga,
        c. 1787
398   Plucked Turkey, between 1810 and 1823
399   The Burial of the Sardine (Carnival scene),
        c. 1808–1814
400   The Family of Charles IV, 1800

## GOYEN Jan van

1596 Leiden – 1656 The Hague
Van Goyen was born ten years before Rembrandt in Leiden. His father sent him as a child to learn drawing, then to several unimportant painters to

be trained, but van Goyen does not seem to have much profited by it. He travelled for a year in France, then in 1616 took up studies under the skilled landscape painter Esaias van de Velde in Haarlem. He then returned to Leiden, became a member of the Lukas Guild in 1618 and moved to the Hague in 1631. He won and lost money in property speculations and became the victim of a large tulip-bulb swindle. This compelled him to produce a large output, which in turn had a negative effect on the price of his pictures, although all his work was of a high standard. Van Goyen specialised in landscape painting and was one of the most important painters in this field at the time, although his true worth was not recognised until he was rediscovered by the Impressionists. He depicted quiet, peaceful scenery with dunes, the sea and rivers, also seascapes and winter scenes in a style quite of his own. His early work showed the influence of van de Velde with strong colouring, a great many figures, coral-like trees and heavy clouds. From about 1630 his style changed, becoming more simplified with almost monochrome colouring in green-greys or yellow-browns. After 1640, in his "toned period", he used almost exclusively a warm brown. Uncluttered river scenes with low horizons and vast areas of sky predominate. His most important pupil was his son-in-law Jan Steen.

*Illustrations:*
305   Landscape with Dunes, c. 1630–1635
305   River Landscape, 1636

## GOZZOLI Benozzo

(Benozzo di Lese di Sandro)
1420 Florence – 1497 Pistoia
Like many other painters of the early Renaissance, Gozzoli initially trained as a goldsmith, which enabled him to work in Ghiberti's workshop, 1444–1447, and assist him on the Paradise Gates. At the age of 27 he began to work with Fra Angelico in Orvieto and Rome. Both these masters were to influence his entire work. From Ghiberti he learned precision in depicting the finest detail and how to tell a story vividly, and Fra Angelico's legacy was his bright coloration, which Gozzoli succeeded in transmitting to the art of fresco painting. It is an astounding phenomenon that Gozzoli, the greatest "fanatic of detail" amongst all the Florentine masters of the early Renaissance, should have been primarily involved in the field of monumental painting. His first major independent commission was the fresco work in the choir of San Francesco in Montefalco with scenes from the Life of St Francis (1450–1452). This cycle could have helped him to secure another commission in 1458, the decoration of the chapel of the Medici Palace (ill. pp. 80, 102). Stimulated by the prestige attached to this commission and the abundance of materials at his disposal (including gold), Gozzoli created the most fascinating "story" of a 15th century Florentine. His subsequent cycles were of an equally high standard. Sienese and Umbrian art of later generations derived a great stimulus from Gozzoli's work.

*Illustrations:*
  80   Procession of the Magi (detail),
         1459–1461
102   Procession of the Magi (detail),
         1459–1461

## GRASSI Giovannino de'

documented from 1389, died 1398
Giovannino was court artist to the Visconti in Milan. He is first mentioned in connection with work on the building of Milan cathedral by the Visconti. His versatility was amazing. He produced several sculptures (a medium which, according to

records, did not suit him), decorated church banners, painted altarpieces, made designs for church windows, probably also made a wooden model of the cathedral, and acted as adviser on the building of the Pavia monastery. Of all this work, almost nothing has survived. As with Michelino da Besozzo we have to resort to his book illuminations in order to get an idea of his work. There remains in the Bergamo library a book of signed sketches which is of the greatest artistic value with its astonishing animal studies and other scenes. But there is the problem that some of the drawings seem to have been done direct from nature, some copied from paintings, and also that the sketches are not all by the same hand. So it was probably a workshop production, especially as it is known that Grassi was assisted in his work by his brother Porrino and his son Salomone as well as others. His artistic origins are not clear – much of the older Lombardian art has been lost. But he had many followers, his most important pupil and successor being Michelino da Besozzo.

*Illustration:*

49   Onions. From the herbal "Tacuinum Sanitatis", c. 1380–1390

## GRECO El

(Domenikos Theotokópoulos, called: "El Greco", The Greek)

c. 1541 Phodele (Crete) – 1614 Toledo

As a most unusual phenomenon in 16th century European painting, El Greco combined the strict Byzantine style of his homeland with influences received during his studies in Venice and the medieval tradition of his country of adoption, Spain. El Greco obtained his training as icon-maker in a monastery. He then went to Venice where Titian became his greatest mentor. In Titian's workshop he developed the brilliance of colour which became a lasting element in his entire work. But he was also moulded by Tintoretto's Mannerist style, as is shown in his delight in bold perspectival foreshortening, the complicated movements of figures and groups of figures, the elongation of proportions and his strong chiaroscuro.

In 1570 El Greco went by way of Parma to Rome, where he met Michelangelo. He criticised his "Last Judgment" severely, offering to produce a better composition. This attitude is a particularly telling example of historical irony. The only painter of the very highest order to come from the land where the art of classical Antiquity was born, failed to understand the High Renaissance ideal of bodily beauty. El Greco's acquaintance with Spanish humanists in Rome and the expectation of commissions in connection with the rebuilding of the monastery of El Escorial might have been what led him to migrate to Spain in 1577. At first he was in the service of Philip II ("Dream of Philip II", El Escorial, 1580), then settled in Toledo in 1580 where he received a great number of church commissions and also became a popular portraitist. Historical records tell us of many disputes with commissioners about inappropriate interpretation of religious themes, unusual coloration, elongation of figures, but also old-fashioned representation.

In the course of his development El Greco became gradually detached from the reality of representation. He distorted the human figure, abandoned logical space construction and also used colour no longer objectively. It is possible that his Byzantine legacy may have been responsible for his growing asceticism. For a long time almost forgotten, interest in him revived in the early 20th century on account of his tendency towards the abstract and his depiction of dream-like scenes. He is now considered as one of the most important representatives of European Mannerism.

*Illustrations:*

210   The Dispoiling of Christ (El Espolio), c. 1590–1600
210   The Agony in the Garden, c. 1595
211   The Burial of Count Orgaz, c. 1586
212   The Holy Family with St Anne and the young St John Baptist, c. 1594–1604
212   View of Toledo, c. 1604–1614

## GREUZE Jean-Baptiste

1725 Tournus (Sâone-et-Loire) – 1805 Paris

Greuze was the sixth of nine children. His father was a slater and wanted to have his son trained as an architect. But the son's talent won, and in 1749 he was sent to Lyon to study under the painter Charles Grandon. In 1750 Greuze went to Paris, and from 1755 studied at the Academy under Natoire. He spent two years in Italy, but this visit left no deep impressions. With his moralising genre pictures Greuze satisfied public taste, which had undergone a change and had grown tired of the Rococo manner. Subjects such as "The Cheated Blind Man", "The Paralytic Served by his Children", "The Much-Loved Mother", "The Ungrateful Son" and "The Chastened Son" found favour with the influential critic Diderot, who called this kind of painting "peinture morale", and so greatly contributed to Greuze's success. A parallel in the literary world could be found in the works of Jean-Jacques Rousseau. Although received by the Academy on the strength of an historical painting, he was categorised as a genre painter which disappointed him. His genre paintings gradually assumed heroic elements normally found in historical painting. Today he is held in high esteem as a portraitist.

*Illustrations:*

363   The Lamentation of Time Passing, c. 1775
363   L'Accordée du Village (The Village Betrothal), 1761

## GRIS Juan

(José Victoriano Gonzáles)

1887 Madrid – 1927 Boulogne-sur-Seine

Gonzáles changed his name to Gris when studying at the Arts and Crafts School at Madrid from 1902 to 1904. At the same time he worked as an illustrator for satirical papers. In 1906 he went to Paris and rented a studio in the Bateau-Lavoir where Picasso lived at the same time. The art dealer Kahnweiler encouraged him to follow the example of the Cubists, Picasso and Braque. Gris' first oil-paintings were produced in 1911. His Cubist pictures showed from the start a richer colour scale, as did his collages. It was his intention to bring together in a synthesis the various phases of Cubism. He used strong colours and lively forms, like a chequer-board pattern, and triangles. This was followed by his architecturally arranged pictures, a period which lasted three years. These works, in which composition governs form and colour, have an air of great calm. It was not until 1919, when the art dealer Léonce Rosenberg exhibited his works, that Gris received public attention, which enabled him to live from his painting.

*Illustrations:*

568   The Teacups, 1914
568   Le Déjeuner, 1915

## GROS Antoine-Jean

1771 Paris – 1835 Bas-Meudon (near Paris)

Already at the age of 14 Gros became a pupil of David after having received instruction from his father, a miniature painter. He was accused of Royalist tendencies and had to flee to Italy in

1793. There he lived mainly in Florence and Genoa, producing miniatures and portraits for his livelihood. A meeting with Napoleon in Milan in 1796 established his career. His first commission was "Napoleon at Arcola" (ill. p. 424). The dynamism displayed in this work already set it apart from David's cool severity of style. On his return to France in 1799 he painted with great success colossal battle scenes to celebrate Napoleon's martial prowess, including "Bonaparte Visiting the Plague-Stricken at Jaffa" (Paris, Louvre, 1804) and "Napoleon on the Battlefield at Eylau" (ill. p. 424). Under Rubens' influence his compositions became more lively and his handling of colour more intensive. The Romantics, in particular Delacroix, were impressed by the freshness and vigour of his work. As under Napoleon, Gros was also during the Restoration the official portrait painter of society. In 1824 he was made a baron. When David went into exile to Brussels in 1816, he handed over his studio to Gros and urged him as head of the Classicist school to strive against the Romantics. Gros' lifeless compositions of mythological subjects which then followed were rejected by the Romantics and also by his own pupils, who turned to the great Classicist Ingres. At the age of 65, depressed by his failures, he committed suicide.

*Illustrations:*

424   Napoleon at Arcole, November 17, 1796, 1796
424   Napoleon on the Battlefield at Eylau, February 9, 1807, 1808

## GROSZ George

1893 Berlin – 1959 Berlin

Grosz, who was expelled from school because of unruliness, studied at the Dresden Academy from 1909, then at the Arts and Crafts School in Berlin from 1911. He found his direction by studying the satirical draughtsmen of the *Simplicissimus*. In 1913 he spent six months in Paris and began painting in oils. After two years' military service, Grosz returned wounded to Berlin in 1916. His pictures dating from that period were futuristically structured visions, dominated by caricature-like, distorted figures who are embroiled in a hopeless muddle of things. In 1917 Grosz was again called up, but was soon transferred to a mental institution. On his recovery in 1918 he became connected with the politically active Berlin Dadaist group around Johannes Baader, Raoul Hausmann, Richard Huelsenbeck and John Heartfield. In about 1920 Grosz developed a decidedly naturalistic style with a dissecting perspicacity and biting sarcasm. He was several times summoned to appear in court about his graphic work. A visit to New York led to a decision to settle there in 1932, before the suppression of his art under the Hitler regime began.

*Illustration:*

589   The Funeral – Dedication to Oskar Panizza, 1917/18

## GRÜNEWALD Matthias

(Mathis Gothart Nithart)

c. 1470–1480 Würzburg (?) – 1528 Halle

Joachim von Sandrart entered this painter's name erroneously as Grünewald in his *Teutsche Akademie* (1675). His real name was Mathis Neithart or Nithart, and he later called himself Gothart. Grünewald is, beside Dürer, the most important representative of Northern painting at the turn of the 15th to the 16th century, and he is also Dürer's complete opposite. As Dürer's foremost artistic device was the line, so was Grünewald's colour, which he used to achieve new heights of expressiveness. And while Dürer turned to the new discoveries of the Renaissance in the course of his development, Grünewald generally continued to adhere to the Middle Ages. Tradition and "progress" cross each other in unexpected ways in the works of these two masters. And yet Grünewald was a man of the Renaissance in the way he lived and applied his many talents. In 1509 he became court painter to archbishop Uriel von Gemmingen at Aschaffenburg, and in this capacity he had to supervise the rebuilding of the palace there. In 1516 he started on a fixed income at the court of the elector Albrecht von Brandenburg where he worked as a painter and architect and also as a designer of fountains. He had to leave this post in 1520 because of his Lutheran convictions.

His major works include the "Isenheim Altar" (ill. p. 190), "The Mocking of Christ" (ill. p. 190) and the "Erasmus-Mauritius" panel (ill. p. 191); two pictures of the Crucifixion (Basle, Kunstmuseum, 1505; Washington, National Gallery, c. 1520); four figures of saints in grisaille for the wings of Dürer's Heller Altar (Donaueschingen, Fürstliche Gemäldegalerie, and Frankfurt am Main, Städelsches Kunstinstitut, 1501–1512); the "Stuppach Madonna" (Stuppach, Pfarrkirche) which formed part of the Maria-Schnee-Altar in Aschaffenburg (1517–1519), as did the "Founding of Santa Maria Maggiore" (Freiburg, Augustinermuseum); and the "Crucifixion" and "Christ Carrying the Cross" of the Tauberbischofsheim Altar (Karlsruhe, Kunsthalle, c. 1525).
*Illustrations:*
190    The Mocking of Christ, c. 1503
190    Crucifixion (Isenheim Altar), 1512–1516
191    The Meeting of St Erasmus and St Maurice, c. 1520–1524

## GUARDI Francesco
1712 Venice – 1793 Venice
Guardi obtained his initial training at the workshop of his older brother, together with whom he also seems to have worked later. As a veduta painter he took as starting point the work of Michele Marieschi and Canaletto, while his figure painting owed something to Magnasco and Tiepolo, the Guardis' brother-in-law. Like Canaletto and Bellotto, Guardi took his veduta production abroad, where the demand was, primarily the English art market. But he increasingly moved away from mere topographical rendition and towards a poetical view, in which Venetian effects of light are used to convey mood. His sensitive brushwork sets off the shimmering air and reflections of light on water, making the objects in the picture tremble and vibrate. Besides this, Guardi was also engaged in figurative painting, but it was not until mid-century that he carried out independent commissions. Around 1770 he painted the twelve-part series "Feste dogali", in which he depicted Venetian state ceremonies. Francesco, whose work is sometimes not easy to distinguish from his brother's, was also a graphic artist. His work in this field has a captivating spontaneity, and belongs among the best produced in the 18th century.
*Illustrations:*
372    Venetian Gala Concert, c. 1782
373    Capriccio, c. 1745

## GUERCINO
(Giovanni Francesco Barbieri)
1591 Cento (near Bologna) – 1666 Bologna
"Il Guercino" (the squint-eyed) was a nickname given because of the squint in his right eye. He was the leading painter of the Bolognese school alongside Reni. He was taught by Paolo Zagnoni in Bologna and was influenced by the work of Lodovico Carracci. Between 1615 and 1617 he painted interior decorations in Cento and produced religious works ("The Four Evangelists", Dresden, Gemäldegalerie) and landscapes ("Landscape in Moonlight", Stockholm, National Museum). At the commission of Cardinal Alessandro Ludovisi, later Pope Gregory XV, he painted the frescos in the oratorio of San Rocco, Bologna. His visit to Venice in 1618, where he met Palma il Vecchio, served to develop his style further ("Et in Arcadia ego", Rome, Galleria Nazionale d'Arte Antica; "Martyrdom of St Paul", Modena, Galleria Estense). In subsequent years his pictures became increasingly lively and dramatic, primarily achieved by the contrast of light and shade. In 1621 he followed a call to Rome by Pope Gregory XV, for whom he worked until his death. Here he painted his best-known work, the "Aurora", on a ceiling of the Villa Ludovisi. He explored his Roman experience when he returned to his home town, drawing in particular on Domenichino and Reni ("The Virgin with St Bruno", Ferrara, Pinacoteca Nazionale; "Ecstasy of St Francis", Dresden, Gemäldegalerie). There was now more pathos, and his freshness was replaced by an idealised Classicism; light and colour became cooler. On Reni's death in 1642 Guercino became the head of the Bolognese school. His attempts at regaining his former lively style were, however, not always successful.
*Illustration:*
236    The Return of the Prodigal Son, 1619

## GUILLAUME DE MACHAUT → Master

## GÜNTHER Matthäus
1705 Tritschengreith (Upper Bavaria) – 1788 Haid (near Wessobrunn)
After basic instruction in Murnau, Günther became the pupil and assistant of Cosmas Damian Asam. He had no direct contact with Johann Evangelist Holzer, who was his junior, but he acquired out of his estate various drawings and can be considered his legitimate artistic successor. He was made master in Augsburg in 1731 and subsequently worked as an independent fresco painter. In 55 years he decorated over sixty rooms. His main works were produced in the Benedictine churches at Amorbach and Rott am Inn, the Augustinian Canonical churches at Indersdorf and Rottenbuch, the parish churches at Sterzing, Mittenwald and Oberammergau, and the Great Hall at Sünching castle. Günther worked in Bavaria, Swabia, Franconia and the Tyrol and can be considered as one of the most important representatives of south German fresco painting.
*Illustration:*
393    The Apotheosis of St Benedict, c. 1761–1763

## GUTTUSO Renato
1912 Bagheria (near Palermo) – 1987 Rome
After studying law for a year in Rome, Guttuso, who was self-taught, began to paint. His political attitude was unmistakably anti-Fascist. In 1940 he joined the Communist Party and three years later a partisan group. In 1947 he was co-founder of the Fronte Nuovo delle Arti in Rome. Guttuso is the leading personality of Italian Social Realism. His socio-critical themes are given emphasis by his dramatic, expressive style. His art had its roots in the folk art of his Sicilian birthplace. He regarded himself as working in the tradition of Dürer, Courbet and Picasso. Between 1948 and 1960 he participated regularly in the Biennale in Venice. In 1952 and 1972 he received the Soviet Lenin Prize. In 1968 he accepted a chair at the Hamburg Kunsthochschule. From 1975 his political activities became more and more demanding, culminating in his election as a senator of the Italian Republic.
*Illustration:*
670    Wall of News – May 1968, 1968

## HALS Dirck
1591 Haarlem – 1656 Haarlem
Dirck was the younger brother of Frans Hals who was probably also his teacher, but the painters who influenced Dirck were Esaias van de Velde and Willem Buytewech. Apart from a few small portraits, he devoted himself exclusively to the painting of conversation pieces – the cheerful domestic life of prosperous burghers in their houses or gardens. He was not interested in the serious side of life; in his work he depicted people in conversation or while flirting, making music and dancing, eating and drinking. His interiors are hardly worked out, all the emphasis is put on fashionable dress and colourful representation. He succeeded in putting across people's high spirits through facial expression, costly dress, posture and loose grouping.
*Illustration:*
298    Merry Company, undated

## HALS Frans
c. 1581–1585 Antwerp (?) – 1666 Haarlem
Frans Hals was the son of a cloth-maker from Mecheln. He was Flemish by birth and was born in Antwerp or Mechelen. His parents moved to Haarlem, where his younger brother Dirck was born in 1591. Apart from one or two short visits to Antwerp and Amsterdam, Hals never left Haarlem. About 1600–1603 he was trained in the workshop of Karel van Mander who is most remembered for his writings on the history of art. In 1610 he became a member of the Lukas Guild, and in 1644 its head. He was highly esteemed in Haarlem, as is shown by the fact that he received altogether eight commissions for the large civic guard pictures. But Hals was often in debt as his portraits were not "elegant" enough for contemporary taste, so that he never became a fashionable painter. Also, he had to provide for ten children from his two marriages. In 1652 he had to auction his furniture and his paintings to pay the baker, and shortly before his death he received poor relief in the form of money and peat. It is often maintained that his poverty was the result of his extravagant life-style, but there is no evidence for this.

Hals is the most important Dutch portrait painter. His surviving work comprises about 300 paintings, and the majority of these are portraits and group portraits. Although also a genre painter after 1626 when he had become familiar with the Utrecht Caravaggists, these still remained portraits except that they also contained symbolic accessories or were painted in a narrative manner. Hals certainly was the foremost painter of the Dutch group portrayal. Already with his first commission, 1616, the "Banquet of the Officers of the St George Civic Guard" (ill. p. 295), he revolutionised this branch of painting which had so far been restricted to lining up several single portraits. But he never presented the scene in a theatrical fashion, as Rembrandt did with his "Night Watch", and each of his sitters is given individual and equal attention. His last two group portraits were the "Regents" (Haarlem, Frans-Hals-Museum, 1664) and "Regentesses of the Old Men's Almshouse in Haarlem" (ill. p. 298). These represent the end of the great era of this type of painting – there are just a few examples of it in the 18th century, and with its waning, the vitality and Baroque theatricality are replaced by a pessimistic, melancholic resignation about the human condition.

In his large single or double portraits, as in the life-size "Portrait of Willem van Heythuysen" (ill. p. 297), Flemish elements and the influence of Rubens become evident, with the background showing views and scenic staffage. His special devices used for livening up the picture are most evident in his genre portraits ("The Gypsy Girl", ill. p. 296; "The Merry Drinker", ill. p. 296; "Malle

Babbe", Berlin, Gemäldegalerie, c. 1629). With a spontaneous and seemingly improvised brushstroke, he produces light reflections on the faces, objects, cloth and lace, thus creating an effect of immediacy as well as vitality. Apart from his son Dirck and the imitator of his style, Judith Leyster, his pupils included the Ostade brothers; he also greatly influenced Steen and Terborch.

*Illustrations:*

283 Two Singing Boys, 1626
295 Banquet of the Officers of the St George Civic Guard in Haarlem, 1616
295 Young Man with a Skull (Vanitas), c. 1626
296 The Merry Drinker, 1628
296 The Gypsy Girl, c. 1628–1630
297 Portrait of Willem van Heythuysen, c. 1625–1630
298 Regentesses of the Old Men's Almshouse in Haarlem, 1664

## HAMILTON Richard
born 1922 London

Hamilton, an important representative of critical English Pop Art, was trained as a draughtsman, then attended the Royal Academy Schools and Slade School of Art from 1948 to 1951. He taught at the Central School of Arts and Crafts in London, at King's College of the University of Durham and at the Royal College of Art in London. Since 1953 he has collaborated closely with other artists in organising exhibitions at the London Institute of Contemporary Arts and the Hatton Gallery of Newcastle University. Hamilton is a great admirer of Duchamp; he reconstructed his "Large Glass" and organised in 1966 the comprehensive Duchamp retrospective at the Tate Gallery in London. Hamilton's work, which deals critically with the world of consumerism, is always ironic and sometimes full of biting sarcasm. After having experimented with polaroid self-portraits in the 1970s, he turned to computer art in the 1980s.

*Illustration:*

665 Bathers I, 1966/67

## HARING Keith
1958 Kutztown (Pennsylvania) – 1990 New York

Haring began early, drawing comic characters, using as models figures from television cartoon films. After high school he went to the Ivy School of Art in Pittsburgh, changing over in 1978 to the New York School of Visual Arts, where he studied under Keith Sonnier and Joseph Kosuth. Already in 1982 he had his first one-man exhibition at the Tony Shafrazi Gallery, and in the same year took part in the Kassel documenta.

Haring developed a simple, symbolic sign language in which thick black lines surround schematic figures in fluorescent colours. In the New York underground he used empty spaces on walls between advertising posters, and he painted T-shirts, buttons and also plaster casts of sculptures. In 1986 he opened the "Pop Shop" which sold multiples and everyday objects painted by Haring. In this way he set out to remove the division between high and trivial cultures. In 1989 he founded the Keith Haring Foundation for the support of social projects, and a year later he died of AIDS.

*Illustration:*

679 Untitled (M. Mouse), 1985

## HARTUNG Hans
1904 Leipzig – 1989 Antibes

Hartung already made drawings and painted watercolours in his schooldays. In 1924/25 he studied philosophy and history of art at Leipzig University and then attended the Academies at Leipzig and Dresden. After spending a year on Menorca in

1932, he settled in Paris. In 1939 he joined the Foreign Legion. After the war he became a French citizen and returned to painting, for which he found wide recognition from 1949. Hartung's abstract pictures are compositions of bundles of brushstrokes, whose effect is based on extreme reduction. Besides graphic art he also produced an extensive photographic work, mostly in the 1960s and 1970s.

*Illustration:*

636 T 1956–9, 1956

## HAY Jean → Master of Moulins

## HECKEL Erich
1883 Döbeln (Saxony) – 1970 Hemmenhofen (Lake Constance)

Heckel, the son of a railway engineer, began to study architecture in Dresden in 1904, but then gave up after three terms. In 1905 he became the organiser of the Brücke, a group of Expressionist artists. In 1910 Heckel turned away from his former Brücke style, replacing flowing lines, rounded contours and his light decorative rhythm, with sharper edges which in their extreme simplification resembled woodcuts. When he moved to Berlin in 1911, he took over the studio of Otto Mueller.

In 1913 the Brücke was dissolved, and Heckel developed his own individual style which achieved a crystalline density. Out of this he developed his many-layered meditative lyricism. From 1915 he served as a medical orderly in Flanders, where he met Beckmann. He explored social problems, depicting poverty and despair, the old and hungry, the blind, wounded and mentally deficient. But nature had always had a special attraction for him, and later he painted mountain scenes and views with dunes and hills, forests and lakes.

*Illustration:*

583 Windmill at Dangast, 1909

## HEDA Willem Claesz.
c. 1593/94 Haarlem – 1680 Haarlem

Along with Pieter Claesz., with whom he is often confused, Heda was the most important representative of the Haarlem school of still life painting. Little is known about his life. In 1631 he was a member of the Lukas Guild, and in 1637 he is mentioned several times as its chairman. After painting a small number of portraits and religious pictures, he began to specialise in the "breakfast" still lifes with their tasteful arrangements. These are not depictions of heavily-laden, magnificently appointed festive boards, but ordinary tables with just a few items, such as the remains of a cake, a half-empty wineglass, a pewter jug, cracked nuts or a burnt-out clay pipe, giving the impression that a simple meal has just been finished. The description "still life" did not exist until mid-century. There was the distinction between "Ontbijtje", the breakfast arrangement, and the "Banketje", the light meal. Heda's still lifes are conservative in their coloration, moving between a golden yellow, brown, grey and a silvery white. Therefore Heda's and also Claesz.'s works are referred to as "monochrome banketjes".

*Illustration:*

304 Still Life, 1631

## HEEM Jan Davidsz. de
1606 Utrecht – c. 1683/84 Antwerp

De Heem came from a family of Dutch-Flemish still life painters. He probably received his early training from his father, then from Balthasar van der Ast in Utrecht. The years between 1628 and

1631 he spent in Leiden, then settled at Antwerp where he became a member of the Lukas Guild in 1636. In 1669 he returned to Utrecht, and records show that he was again in Antwerp in 1672. This shows that he was active in both the northern and southern parts of the Netherlands, and this is reflected in his work. His first still lifes are in tone still reminiscent of Heda and Claesz., while later flower pieces and fruit baskets suggest the influence of the Flemish painters Daniel Seghers and Snyders in their Baroque-like magnificence of coloration. De Heem's speciality were large, elaborate pictures of opulently appointed dining tables laid with silverware, fine glass and fruit baskets, often accompanied by a large lobster to provide a brilliantly coloured accent. He also painted beautifully arranged and minutely detailed flower and fruit pieces, combining subtly painted botanical details with elements of the vanitas type of still life (caterpillars attacking the fruit, beetles in the flower buds). These pictures, in all their richness and glory, are almost without comparison in Dutch painting.

*Illustration:*

317 Still Life, undated

## HEEMSKERCK Maerten van
1498 Heemskerk (near Haarlem) – 1574 Haarlem

Heemskerck is one of the main representatives of the so-called Netherlandish Romanists. After training in Haarlem and Delft he entered the workshop of Jan van Scorel, only by a few years his senior, in 1527, probably working as his assistant rather than pupil. He visited Rome in 1532 and remained there probably until 1537. The exact archaeological precision of his drawings of ancient structures makes them highly valuable source documents on Roman monuments at the time. He was certainly back in Haarlem in 1538 as he received a commission for a winged altar with scenes of the Passion of Christ and the Legend of St Lawrence in that year. He soon acquired a high reputation as a painter of altarpieces and portraits. His contact with Haarlem humanist circles was reflected in his allegorically encoded representations. In 1540 he was appointed deacon of the Lukas Guild in Haarlem and was granted tax exemption in 1572 on account of his artistic achievements. After his period in Rome, Michelangelo's influence made itself felt in Heemskerck's three-dimensional modelling of figures. His coloration was often cool and his painting technique smooth, to suit the wooden panel rather than the canvas.

*Illustration:*

203 Family Portrait, c. 1530

## HEISIG Bernhard
born 1925 Breslau

Heisig, who now lives in Leipzig, is probably the most important painter of the former GDR. In 1941/42 he went to the College of Decorative Arts in Breslau, but his studies were interrupted by military service. In 1946/47 he worked as a graphic artist in Breslau and recommended his studies in 1948 at the College of Applied Art in Leipzig, continuing at the College of Graphic Art and Book Production until 1951. In 1961 he became principal of the Leipzig Art College, but was dismissed in 1964 for his criticism of the state of the arts and for demanding more artistic freedom. From 1968 to 1976 he worked freelance as a painter and graphic artist. In 1976 he again became principal of the Leipzig Art College, remaining in this post until his retirement in 1987. In 1989, in protest against the "misuse of power and corruption", he returned his two national prizes (1972 and 1978) awarded under the former regime.

*Illustration:*
669 Der Zauberlehrling (The Sorcerer's Apprentice), 1978–1981

## HILLIARD Nicholas
(also: Heliard, Hildyard, Helier)
c. 1547 Exeter – 1619 London
The great English art of portraiture of the 18th century had its beginnings in the works of Hilliard more than a hundred years earlier. Having no examples in this field to draw on, he used as a starting point for his painting the highly developed traditions of book illumination and the goldsmith's art. Himself the son of a goldsmith, he went to London to be trained by the goldsmith and jeweller to Queen Elizabeth I from 1562 to 1569. With great technical precision, he painted a portrait of the Queen as early as 1570 (Welbeck Abbey). In the next decade Hilliard's style gained in elegance of both form and conception (Self-Portrait, London, Victoria and Albert Museum, 1577). Already in the late 1560s, and after a visit to France, Hilliard was the leading miniature portraitist of royalty, as confirmed by his picture of James I, and going on to include the entire royal court. After 1580 he introduced the oval form of his, now often full-length, miniatures of which the "Young Man among the Roses" (London, Victoria and Albert Museum, c. 1588) is one of the finest examples. During this period he also succeeded in conveying individual expression in his pictures, and it is in this that he was of particularly valuable service to the next generation.
*Illustration:*
254 Portrait of George Clifford, Earl of Cumberland, c. 1590

## HOBBEMA Meindert
1638 Amsterdam – 1709 Amsterdam
Hobbema was the son of a bargee. He lost his mother early and grew up in an orphanage. Between 1657 and 1660 he was a pupil of Jacob van Ruisdael, on whose style his work was largely based, to the extent that it is easy to confuse their works. He always lived in his home town, except for brief visits to Deventer, Haarlem and Middelharnis. In 1668 he married a servant of the mayor, who procured him the position of weights and measures inspector, which involved calculating wine and oil casks according to Amsterdam measures. During this time he seems to have given up painting, especially as it had not provided him with an income. One of the few authenticated works dating from this late period is "Avenue of Middelharnis", 1689 (ill. p.331). Hobbema was a landscape painter, but not of the typically flat Dutch coastal scenery. He rendered overgrown dunes and wooded tracts with powerful trees and dark, dense foliage, enlivened by rivulets and mills, cottages and small figures. His colours were a strong green, yellow and brown, later interspersed with light, silvery tones. His landscapes provide a bridge to 18th century landscape painting.
*Illustration:*
331 Avenue of Middelharnis, 1689

## HOCKNEY David
born 1937 Bradford (Yorkshire)
Hockney studied from 1953 to 1957 at the Bradford College of Art, then from 1959 to 1962 at the Royal College of Art in London. Even before he left the Royal College, he had been awarded his first prize for his art; he found recognition and success from the start. In 1961/62 he went to New York and Berlin; later he paid another, prolonged visit to the USA and also to Egypt, and went to other European countries and East Asia.

His first theatre designs date from 1966. He taught at Iowa University, the Universities of Colorado, Berkeley and others. In 1969 Hockney worked as visiting professor at the Hamburg Kunsthochschule. He lives in London and California. Hockney developed a stylised realism combined with two-dimensional ornamentations. He has a penchant for cool to shrill acrylic colours and often works with his own photographs as models. Since 1982 he has been producing polaroid collages. In the late 1980s his first computer and fax drawings appeared.
*Illustration:*
665 A Bigger Splash, 1967

## HODLER Ferdinand
1853 Gürzelen (near Berne) – 1918 Geneva
Hodler was one of the few Swiss painters to achieve international fame. He had a difficult childhood, lost his parents early, and had a hard life as a young man. From 1871 to 1876 he studied at Geneva Art School under B. Menn who promoted him and introduced him to the works of his friends Ingres, Delacroix, Corot, Courbet and Manet. Hodler took a special interest in Corot and the French Impressionists, and his painting technique became moulded by Impressionism and realism. In 1878/79 he spent nine months in Madrid. He then developed his monumental style, which contained Symbolist and Art Noveau elements, with flat coloration, definite outline, symmetrical composition and parallel forms. He produced portraits and historical pictures, mostly of a symbolic nature. In 1891 he travelled to Paris and joined the Rose-Croix group, exhibiting at the Salon de la Rose-Croix in Paris in 1892. His tendency towards monumental representation resulted in many mural commissions, receiving first prize in 1897 for his design for the armory in the Zurich national museum. Critical opinion was divided on his achievements.

From 1901 to 1905 he took part in the Vienna Secession, and also showed his work at the Secessions in Munich and Berlin. He visited Italy in 1905 and 1911. In 1907 he decorated walls in Jena University. In 1913 Hodler was made an Officer of the French Legion of Honour. During this time he produced the decorations in the town hall of Hanover. A great retrospective of his work was held in 1917 in Zurich. His detractors thought him an exponent of the unattractive; his followers praised his honest, energetic exploration of his subject matter.
*Illustrations:*
529 Autumn Evening, 1892
529 Communication with the Infinite, 1892

## HOFMANN Hans
1880 Weißenburg (Bavaria) – 1966 New York
Hofmann spent his childhood and youth in Munich. In 1904 he went to Paris, where he studied at the Académie de la Grande Chaumière and became acquainted with Matisse, Delaunay, Braque, Pascin, Gris and Picasso. On his return to Munich he opened a school of modern art. In 1930–1931 he held summer seminars at Berkeley University in California and taught the following year at the Arts Student League in New York, where he settled. At his own school in New York, which he ran from 1934 to 1958, he greatly influenced that generation of American abstract painters through his teachings and theories. Until the early 1940s Hofmann adhered to Expressionist traditions; then he developed an abstract Expressionism which achieved its powerfulness through strong form, unbroken colours and free manner of painting.

*Illustration:*
630 Blue in Blue, 1954

## HOGARTH William
1697 London – 1764 London
Hogarth, the son of a schoolmaster, was apprenticed to a silversmith and engraver in 1712, where his interest in copperplate engraving was aroused. He studied at Vanderbank's Academy in St Martin's Lane and at the art school of the court painter Thornhill, whose daughter he married in 1729, and whose work left him with a life-long ambition to become an historical painter. While he was never to be successful in this field ("Sigismunda", London, Tate Gallery, 1759), he soon became well-known as an engraver and painter of pictures, such as the series " A Harlot's Progress" (1732), "A Rake's Progress" (1735) and "Marriage à la Mode" (1742–1744). These became so popular that he had to to take precautions against plagiarism. Hogarth was unfairly accused of uncouth dilettantism in his religious work ("Ascension" triptych, St Mary Redcliffe, Bristol, 1756). His versatility also extended to art theory, such as his treatise directed against academic rigidity, "The Analysis of Beauty", published in 1753. In portraiture, one of his best works was "Captain Thomas Coram" (London, Foundling Hospital, 1740). Although Hogarth, who on Sir James Thornhill's death became the principal of his art school, had no direct followers, he is regarded as the founder of the English school of painting, and especially of portraiture.
*Illustrations:*
340 Marriage à la Mode: Shortly after the Marriage, 1744
380 The Graham Children, 1742
380 Self-Portrait, 1745
381 The Shrimp Girl, c. 1740
382 Heads of Six of Hogarth's Servants, c. 1750–1755

## HOHENFURTH → Master

## HOLBEIN Hans the Younger
c. 1497/98 Augsburg – 1543 London
Amongst the great German masters of the 16th century Holbein may be singled out without reservation as the only Renaissance artist. Unlike any other he was, both in education and career, a cosmopolitan. At the early age of sixteen, after instruction by his father, he went off as a journeyman with his brother Ambrosius. He is first mentioned in 1515 in Basle, where he entered the workshop of Hans Herbster. His first public commissions were carried out in Lucerne in 1517. From there he probably visited Lombardy and Emilia in northern Italy. This is not supported by documentary evidence, but it is reflected in his work of the early 1520s. In 1519 Holbein became a member of the painters' guild in Basle, and in 1524 he stayed in France. The watershed of his career was his journey to England in 1526, where he went by way of the Netherlands, equipped with a letter of recommendation from Erasmus of Rotterdam. There he lived from 1532, despite tempting offers from the city of Basle.

Between 1515 and 1528 he carried out a number of outstanding religious commissions ("Madonna of Solothurn", Solothurn, Städtisches Museum, 1522; "The Dead Christ in the Tomb", Basle, Kunstmuseum, 1521). In the Basle painting one can see in his powerfully expressive depiction of Christ a parallel to Grünewald, which Holbein succeeded in combining with razor-sharp observation, which showed his genius for portraiture.

From 1528 he indeed concentrated solely on

portrait painting. In London he executed portraits of the German merchants of the Steelyard, then soon came to the notice of Henry VIII and members of his court. His observation of detail, psychological penetration of his sitters and superb handling of colour made him the greatest portrait painter of German art. He also produced excellent graphic work (e.g. the series of woodcuts "Dance of Death", completed about 1526; 91 woodcut designs on the *Old Testament*, completed 1538).
*Illustrations:*
194   The Ambassadors (Jean de Dinteville and Georges de Selve), 1533
195   Madonna of Mercy and the Family of Jakob Meyer zum Hansen (Darmstadt Madonna), c. 1528/29
195   Portrait of the Merchant Georg Gisze, 1532

## HOMER Winslow

1836 Boston – 1910 Prout's Neck (Maine)
Together with Thomas Eakins, Homer is one of the most important American painters of the second half of the 19th century. He began his career as a lithographer in Boston, but soon decided to work as an independent artist. He studied the woodcut technique which had not yet become popular in America. His chroniclers speak of Impressionistic influences and those of the Japanese woodcut in his work. In 1859 he moved to New York, where he worked as an illustrator on *Harper's Weekly*. From the time of the Civil War, his drawings for this magazine depict war scenes and daily life in time of war without sentimentality or false heroism. When he began painting in oil, he transferred to it the principles of woodcut design, developing a fine sense of colour in his composition. Homer preferred open-air subjects and excelled in pictures of popular life. In later life he lost interest in figurative representation and turned to marine painting.
*Illustration:*
540   Breezing Up, 1876

## HONTHORST Gerrit van

(also: Gerard van Honthorst; called: Gherardo della Notte)
1590 Utrecht – 1656 Utrecht
Honthorst was one of the most versatile Dutch artists. His work included biblical scenes, allegories, genre pictures, portraits and wall and ceiling decorations. He was also one of the few to achieve great prosperity. At first he studied under Bloemaert in Utrecht. In 1610 he went to Rome for ten years, where he was greatly influenced by Caravaggio and, although he did not meet this great artist himself, he systematically explored his chiaroscuro effects in his work. Dark rooms lit by candles, torchlight, hidden or channelled sources of light in dark spaces – these became typical subjects of his work. Because of his taste for artificially lit night scenes he was called "Gherardo della Notte" while in Italy. On his return to Utrecht in 1622 he became a member of the Lukas Guild. In Rome he had painted mostly religious subjects ("The Nativity", "Adoration of the Shepherds", both Florence, Uffizi), but now he turned to mythological subjects and genre scenes of soldiers, card-players and carousers ("Cheerful Company", Munich, Alte Pinakothek). Most of his many commissions were for portraits. In 1628 he went to England to paint portraits of King Charles I and the Queen. In 1637 he became court painter to Prince William of Orange and settled in The Hague. He painted many illustrious persons, including King Christian VI of Denmark and the Elector of Brandenburg, and he gave painting lessons to the Bohemian Queen Elizabeth and her

daughter. His financial position was such that he could lend her the large sum of 35,000 guilders in 1651. Honthorst spent his final six years in his home town of Utrecht.
*Illustration:*
304   The Incredulity of St Thomas, c. 1620

## HOOCH Pieter de

(also: Hoogh, Hooghe)
1629 Rotterdam – after 1684 Amsterdam (?)
His career as a painter developed very slowly. The son of a bricklayer, he received his early training under Nicolaes Berchem in Haarlem. Around 1650 he worked for a cloth merchant and art collecter in Rotterdam as painter and *valet de chambre*, whom he had to accompany on his travels to Leiden, The Hague and Delft. After his marriage in Delft he was accepted as a member of the Lukas Guild in 1655 although not actually a citizen of the town. In about 1667 he moved to Amsterdam, where he remained to the end of his life. De Hooch's most important creative period was his years at Delft. Under the influence of Vermeer and the Rembrandt-pupil Fabritius he painted genre scenes which depict the idyll of Dutch domestic life, including interiors, courtyards and garden scenes. A gentle light radiates the scenes, and the figures and objects seem to pause as if in a still life. Typical for de Hooch, whose colours are warmer and softer than Vermeer's, are perspectival rooms and vistas through open doors. In his Amsterdam period, where he liked to move in elegant society, his often plain and simple interiors were replaced by grand rooms with marble mantelpieces and pilasters. His rendering became hard and over-meticulous, his coloration cold and dry.
*Illustrations:*
284   The Courtyard of a House in Delft, 1658
329   A Woman and her Maid in a Courtyard, 1660
329   The Card-Players, c. 1663–1665

## HOOGSTRATEN Samuel van

(also: Hoogstraaten, Hoogstraeten)
1627 Dordrecht – 1678 Dordrecht
Hoogstraten received his earliest training from his father Dirck at Dordrecht, then in 1642 entered the workshop of Rembrandt and returned in 1648 to his home town. In the 1650s he stayed in Vienna to carry out work for the Emperor Ferdinand III and also visited Rome, which was exceptional in the tradition of Dutch painting. He married in 1656 in Dordrecht and went with his wife to London from 1662 to 1666. On his return to The Hague he joined the painters' guild "Pictura". In 1670 he finally settled in Dordrecht, where he was appointed provost of the mint. Hoogstraten was less known as a painter than as an experimenter and art theorist. In 1678 he wrote his *Inleyding tot de Hooghe Schoole der Schilderkonst*. He worked with optical instruments and constructed perspectival "peepshow" boxes (London, National Gallery), specialising in *trompe l'œil* illusionism. In his painting he initially followed Rembrandt, but then developed his own manner and subject matter.
*Illustration:*
328   Still Life, c. 1666–1678

## HOPPER Edward

1882 Nyack (New York) – 1967 New York
Hopper studied at the New York School of Art from 1900 to 1906. Between 1906 and 1910 he travelled widely in Europe, spending a great deal of time in Paris, where he painted street scenes in the Impressionist manner. He settled permanently in New York in 1908. From 1924 onwards, after the exhibition of his work at the Frank K.M. Rehn

Gallery, his subject matter moved away from the world of French painting and he concentrated entirely on American life. Modern civilisation became his subject, and he was particularly fascinated by urbanization, the expansion of industry and the excesses of American architecture. Many of his pictures are realistic depictions of street scenes, views over roofs and abandoned houses. He intensifies the sinister atmosphere by showing them at different times of the day and in different weathers. Hopper, who kept aloof from the *avant-garde* stream in Europe and America, created as no other a realistic picture of American urban life and landscape. In 1968 his widow gave all the works he left to the Whitney Museum of American Art in New York.
*Illustrations:*
555   Nighthawks, 1942
601   Nightwindows, 1928

## HUET Paul

1803 Paris – 1869 Paris
As a student of the Ecole de Beaux-Arts, Huet worked in the studios of Guérin and Gros, where he made life-long friends of Delacroix and Bonington. His greatest influence was Bonington, with whom he often worked and he spent some time studying in Normandy in 1827. More important still for his further development, as for that of Delacroix, was his encounter with Constable's work at the Paris Salon in 1824.
This is how he described it: "The young school's admiration was boundless... It was perhaps for the first time that one felt such warmth, such luxuriant nature, such greens, no blacks, no rawness, no mannerism." Stimulated by Constable, whom he often copied, Huet painted his landscapes mostly in Normandy and the forest of Compiègne, where he moved to in the early 1820s. Unlike the other painters of the Barbizon school to which he belonged, Huet was primarily interested in the dynamism of nature. His wildly romantic pictures of primeval forests, the excited play of the sea and billowing clouds in wind and weather, made him one of the founders of French "Paysage intime" landscape painting.
*Illustration:*
438   Breakers at Granville, c. 1853

## HUGUET Jaume

(Jaime)
before 1414 Valls (near Tarragona) – 1492 Barcelona
Huguet is the principal representative of 15th century Catalan art, which remained almost untouched by the innovations of the early Renaissance and so continued in the medieval tradition. There are no records documenting his work before the year 1448, when he received a commission for the James altar at Arbeca. Until 1486 he produced a great number of multi-sectioned altar retables, including those of St Abdon and Sennen (today in Santa María at Tarasa, 1458–1460) the the Three Kings altar (Barcelona, Museo de Historia de la Ciudad, 1464). Huguet's style was not remarkable; he kept to a background of gold, with a minimum of spatial features and little indication of depth. The growing abundance of commissions led over time to an ever-increasing share of work being done by assistants in his workshop. This in turn led to the use of stereotyped characters and a loss of painterly quality.
*Illustration:*
138   Last Supper, after 1450

**HUNDERTWASSER Friedensreich**
(Friedrich Stowasser)
born 1928 Vienna
Hundertwasser attended the Montessori school in Vienna and studied briefly at the Vienna Kunstakademie in 1948. In 1949 he adopted his pseudonym. His colourful work is influenced by Viennese Art Noveau and also by Klee. He has become a well-known figure for his spectacular appearances in public, his commitment to environmental issues and his general way of life. In 1959 he arranged with Bazon Brock the happening "Endless Line" in Hamburg. Hundertwasser travelled widely; since the 1970s he has been spending much time in the South Sea islands. After producing ceramic mural pictures for the decoration of buildings (such as for the Rosenthal company in Selb), he has become involved since 1982 in ecological architecture and has designed several buildings. Hundertwasser lives in New Zealand.
*Illustration:*
655   The Great Way, 1955

**HUNT William Holman**
1827 London – 1910 London
Hunt already began to paint during his training for commerce, copying works of the old masters, including those of the 15th century Flemish and Italian schools, which were to remain influential throughout his life. Much of his work is marked by an intense, fine colouring, a meticulous sense of detail, a preference for painting from nature, and a tendency to symbolism in presenting his subjects. In 1845 he joined the Royal Academy schools and met Rossetti and Millais. This acquaintance was significant in that it eventually led to the foundation of the Pre-Raphaelite Brotherhood, a group of idealistic young men whose aim it was to return English painting to former heights. John Ruskin felt close to this group and supplied the theoretical foundations for their aims. Hunt believed that if art was to be reformed it had to go back to the old religious, moral ideas, and these became central to his work, which was executed in a solid, craftsman-like manner. Besides Biblical subjects, he often returned to old English myths and sagas. Hunt's works are intensely symbolic, every small detail contributing to the intended message. By today's standards, this often meant crossing the border into sentimentality. However, he based his work on realistic observation and natural rendition and showed great skill in his treatment of colour and light. Hunt visited Palestine several times to paint the scenery and spent the years 1866–1868 in Florence. His work was greatly respected in his time and he received the Order of Merit in 1905.
*Illustration:*
526   The Hireling Shepherd, 1851

**INDIANA Robert**
(Robert Clark)
born 1928 New Castle (Indiana)
Indiana studied Pop Art at the John Herron School of Art at Indianapolis, the Art Institute of Chicago and, when staying in Scotland in 1953/54, at the Edinburgh College of Art. He has been living in New York since 1954. He produces Pop Art works based on letters, words and symbols of a poster-like character in a large, planar hard edged manner. Since 1966 the word "Love" has been his favourite motif, of which he designed a stamp for the American postal service in 1973. In New York he became acquainted with Kelly whose concepts made an impression on his work. Besides his pictures he has also produced a great number of silkscreen prints. Since 1969 Indiana has lived in Vinalhaven (Maine).
*Illustration:*
660   The American Dream, I, 1961

**INGEBORG-PSALTER** → Workshop

**INGRES Jean Auguste Dominique**
1780 Montauban – 1867 Paris
Ingres' father, a sculptor and decorative plasterer, instructed his son in drawing and sent him to Toulouse Academy in 1791. In 1797 he became a pupil of David and in 1799 was accepted by the Ecole des Beaux-Arts. In 1801 he won the Grand Prix de Rome with "The Envoys of Agamemnon" (Paris, Musée de l'Ecole Nationale Supérieure des Beaux-Arts). In 1806 he introduced himself as a portraitist at the Salon but received much criticism for his works, among them his great portraits of the Rivière family. During the same year he went on an Academy scholarship to Rome, where he stayed until 1819, producing his much admired portrait drawings of French society. Here he studied Antiquity and the works of Raphael, Holbein and Titian and became greatly influenced by Masaccio's work when he came to Florence in 1819. He developed his own style, independent of his master David, as his early work, the "Valpinçon Bather" (ill. p.429) from 1808, shows.
He returned to Paris in 1824 and began to teach. In 1825 he received the Order of the Legion of Honour from King Charles X and was elected a member of the Academy. His "Apotheosis of Homer" (Paris, Louvre, 1827), which seems to embody Ingres' own artistic and literary beliefs, is characteristic of his classicism based on the study of Raphael. His precisely drawn and painted portraits show more freedom than his other works in their life-like perception. He was also a master draughtsman, perhaps the most important of the 19th century, leaving 4000 sketches and drawings to his home town of Montauban. The Salon's disapproving attitude to his "Martyrdom of St Symphorian", 1834, (Autun Cathedral), caused him to accept the directorship of the French Academy in Rome from 1835 to 1841. On his return to Paris he met at last with enormous success and received the Order of Merit in 1845. As president of the Ecole des Beaux-Arts (from 1850) he became the leader of the Classical school. At the World Exhibition 1855 he was represented by 48 of his works. In opposition to Delacroix and other Romantics and the Realism of Courbet, Ingres upheld the Classic idealism with its clarity of line and sensuality of colouring based on a close study of nature.
*Illustrations:*
421   Madame Inès Moitessier Seated, 1856
428   Joan of Arc at the Coronation of Charles VII in Reims Cathedral, 1854, 1854
428   The Turkish Bath, 1862
429   Valpinçon Bather, 1808
430   Mademoiselle Rivière, 1806
430   Louis-François Bertin, 1832

**IVERNY Jacques**
active 1411–1435 in Avignon
The attribution of the fresco cycle of La Manta to Iverny has been disputed, but no acceptable alternative has instead been put forward. Doubters have been reluctant to accept that in early 15th century representation there was a wide gap between profane and sacred subjects, and that there is also a great similarity between Iverny's signed altarpieces and the religious scenes contained in this cycle. There is no doubt, however, that these frescos are the work of a French artist, which is not surprising as both the older and the younger Marchese of Saluzzo, whose palace was about forty miles south of Turin, lived most of their time at the French court. The frescos are also remarkable in that they comprise a large picture of the fountain of youth, which makes those who bathe in it young again and amorous. This is unaccountably placed in the same room with a picture of an altarpiece showing the Crucifixion. Very little is known about Iverny, except that he spent his longest period at Avignon. It appears that he travelled widely and was familiar with the art as practised at the courts of northern France.
*Illustration:*
61   Five Heroines; c. 1420

**JAWLENSKY Alexei von**
(Alexei Georgevich von Jawlensky)
1864 Torschok (Russia) – 1941 Wiesbaden
Jawlensky began to paint when still a young lieutenant in Moscow. As an officer he was transferred to St Petersburg in 1889, where he attended the academy of arts. He asked for his discharge in 1896 and went with Marianne von Werefkin to Munich, where he studied at the Ažbè school and met Kandinsky. In 1903 and 1905 he went to France to show his work at the Salon d'Automne and became acquainted with Matisse, whom he met again in Paris in 1907 and 1911. Together with Kandinsky he founded the New Artists' Association Munich in 1909. During this time his work reached a culmination with its large figure paintings, such as the "Woman with the Fan" (ill. p.579). At the outbreak of the First World War he had to leave Germany and settled in Switzerland. In the following years expression was gradually replaced by contemplation, piety and self-examination, becoming most apparent in his "meditations" in which his icon-like portraits became pictures of devotion.
*Illustrations:*
546   The Red Shawl, 1909
579   Woman with a Fan, 1909

**JOHNS Jasper**
born 1930 Augusta (Georgia)
Johns studied at the University of South Carolina in 1947/48. Military service took him to Japan in 1949. On his return in 1952 he worked as a bookseller and in New York with Rauschenberg as a window-dresser at Tiffany's. In 1966 he designed scenery and costumes for the Merce Cunningham Dance Company and worked with the composer John Cage. With Rauschenberg, Johns belongs to those artists who introduced decisive new elements into the art which followed Abstract Expressionism. His one-man exhibition in 1958 is seen as the beginning of Pop Art, yet his art also goes in other directions. Initially John's works concentrated on a relatively small repertoire of subjects, such as the American flag, letters, numbers and shooting targets produced in the early 1950s. He also produced assemblages of actual objects and everyday artefacts in cast metal. Johns lives at Stony Point (New York).
*Illustrations:*
621   False Start, 1959
652   Flag, 1954/55
653   Untitled, 1980

**JONES Allen**
born 1937 Southampton
From 1955 to 1959 Jones studied at the Hornsey School of Art in London and then for a further year at the Royal College of Art with Kitaj and Hockney. He is one of the best-known English Pop artists. From the early 1970s he taught at art colleges in the United States, Canada and Germany. He presents his motifs extracted from sex magazines in a cool yet provoking manner. His female bodies made of fibreglass – clad in corsets and high-heeled shoes, and intended as furniture – are disarming in their cheekiness. For these he finds his motifs in the sadomasochistic literature of the subculture.
*Illustration:*
664   Man Woman, 1963

**JONGKIND Johan Barthold**
1819 Lattrop (near Rotterdam) – 1891 La Côte
Saint-André (near Grenoble)
Jongkind grew up in Vlaardingen near Rotterdam, where he worked as a solicitor's clerk. After
his father's death he studied at the drawing
academy in The Hague in 1836/37. From 1846 to
1853 he lived in Paris, working in the studio of
Isabey and studying at the Picot studio. He met
Israëls and Chassériau and became friends with
Stevens, Courbet and Troyon. In 1848 he exhibited for the first time at the Salon. In 1850 he
went to Etretat in Normandy and again in 1851
with Isabey to Le Havre. Under the influence of
French landscape painting his style became
sketchy and his colours more brilliant, taking on
Impressionist elements. In 1855 he returned to
Holland and lived until 1860 in Rotterdam. His
work seems beset by psychological problems. He
met Courbet when in Paris in 1857. From 1860
to 1870 he again lived in poverty as a bohemian
in Paris. He met Boudin, Monet and Mme Fesser,
a compatriot, with whose support he conquered
his personal problems. In 1862 he worked with
Monet and Boudin at Le Havre and from then on
was more successful in selling his brilliantly coloured pictures. He settled at La Côte-Saint-André
near Grenoble in 1874 where, apart from short
visits to the Provence and Paris, he lived until his
death. Here his colours became visibly airier and
his style more simplified. Be set by mental illness,
paranoia and the misuse of alcohol, Jongkind died
at the mental institution of Saint-Rambert near
Grenoble.
*Illustration:*
524 The Maas at Maasluis, 1866

**JORDAENS Jacob**
1593 Antwerp – 1678 Antwerp
The son of a linen merchant, Jordaens was the
pupil of Adam van Noort, under whom Rubens
had studied briefly. He was classed as a "water
painter" when joining the Lukas Guild in 1615,
probably because he painted water-colours on linen
which served as wall-hangings and which his father
sold. In 1621 he was appointed deacon of the
Guild. His reputation as designer of decorations
brought in 1634 a commission from the Antwerp
magistrate to collaborate on the decorations for
Prince Ferdinand's visit under the supervision of
Rubens, in whose workshop Jordaens had been employed previously. Within the orbit of Rubens he
not only carried out the latter's designs, such as the
large canvases for the Torre de la Parada near Madrid, but adopted his style, making it his own.
After Rubens' death, he became the leader of the
Antwerp school, carrying out innumerable commissions for Church and Court between 1640 and
1650, including 22 pictures for the salon of Queen
Henrietta Maria at Greenwich, work for the Scandinavian and French courts, as well as the "Triumphs
of Prince Friedrich Heinrich of Nassau" at the Huis
den Bosch near The Hague, one of the few decorations of this kind to be found in Dutch palaces. Jordaens painted historical, allegorical and mythological scenes and was also a painter of religious themes
and genre pictures. He was one of the great Flemish Baroque painters along with Rubens and van
Dyck.
*Illustrations:*
302 Allegory of Fertility, c. 1622
302 The Family of the Artist, c. 1621
303 The Satyr and the Farmer's Family, after
1620

**JORN Asger**
(Asger Oluf Jorgensen)
1914 Vejrum (Jutland) – 1973 Århus
In 1929 Jorn moved to Silkeborg, where he began
to paint a year later. In 1936/37 he worked in the
studio of Léger while in Paris. In 1941 he was a cofounder of the magazine *Helhesten*, and while under
German occupation he published the paper *Long og
Folk*. He was one of the founders of the CoBrA
group and published monographs about its members. His first book *Salvation and Chance* was produced while recovering from tuberculosis at a sanatorium in Silkeborg. Jorn often explored a subject
in a series of works, such as the "Wheel of Life",
1952/53, "From a Silent Myth", and the "Swiss
Suite", a series of 32 etchings produced on a prolonged visit to Switzerland. Jorn also wrote on art
and its relationship to society. From 1956 he lived
in Albisola (Italy) and Paris. He was a member of
the group of International Situationists from 1956
to 1961. He founded the Institute for Comparative
Vandalism in 1962.
*Illustration:*
644 Without Boundaries, c. 1959/60

**KAHLO Frida**
(Magdalena Carmen Frieda Kahlo Calderón)
1907 Coyoacán (Mexico City) – 1954 Coyoacán
In a motoring accident in 1925 the 17-year-old
Frida Kahlo suffered severe spinal injuries which
led to a number of operations and hence her preoccupation with the subject in her work. Her very
personal pictures express her mental state and view
of the world in a direct, popular idiom. In 1928
Kahlo joined the Mexican Communist Party and
met the painter Rivera whom she married a year
later. In 1932 they both went to the USA for two
years, where Rivera painted several murals. In
1938 Kahlo had her first one-woman exhibition in
New York. In the same year Breton, who had
come to Mexico to meet Leon Trotski, stayed at
her house. In 1939 she went to Paris to exhibit
her work, and met Surrealist painters and writers.
In 1943 she began to teach at the art school La Esmeralda, but because of her former injury was soon
forced to hold her classes at home. Her condition
deteriorated rapidly in the late 1940s; she had to
wear a steel corset and could only get about in a
wheelchair. She had her first one-woman exhibition in Mexico in 1953 and died of pneumonia a
year later.
*Illustration:*
604 Self-Portrait with Monkey, 1938

**KALF Willem** (also: Kalff)
1619 Rotterdam – 1693 Amsterdam
Kalf was considered by his contemporaries as having exceptional intellectual gifts and being wellversed in the arts. He probably received his training
from Frans Ryckhals and Hendrick Pot. In 1640 he
went to Paris for six years, where he was a success
with his pictures of kitchens and interiors of peasant dwellings. With these pictures of untidy storage
rooms and passages cluttered with tools and female
servants, he created a genre that Chardin was to revive in the 18th century. But he was first and foremost a still life painter, initially depicting simply
laid breakfast tables with the remains of the repast,
glasses and pewter or silver vessels, which were
reminiscent of the "monochrome banketjes" of the
Haarlem painters Claesz. and Heda. In compliance
with the demands of the well-to-do Dutch merchant class, Kalf later produced luxurious still lifes
with rich table covers, Venetian glass, Chinese
porcelain and silver bowls containing tempting
fruit. These are never gaudy, as can be the case with
Flemish pieces, and they captivate by their suggestion of texture. Brilliant colours and the sensitive

use of light effects suggest Rembrandt's influence.
Most of these pictures date from the Amsterdam
period between 1646 and 1663. From then on Kalf
seems to have given up painting in favour of art
dealing.
*Illustration:*
322 Still Life, c. 1653/54

**KANDINSKY Wassily**
1866 Moscow – 1944 Neuilly-sur-Seine
Kandinsky abandoned his legal career by turning
down a lectureship at the university in 1896 in favour of studying painting at the Ažbè school in Munich. There he met his compatriot Jawlensky. In
1900 he changed over to the Academy, studying
under Franz von Stuck, and where he met Klee. In
1901 he was a co-founder of the Phalanx group of
artists. His pictures from 1901 to 1905 evoke a
Russian fairy-tale world with Art Nouveau and
Neo-Impressionist elements. He travelled all over
Europe between 1904 and 1908. When he moved
with Gabriele Münter from Munich to Murnau in
1908, his painting became influenced by the Fauves
and Bavarian glass painting. In 1909 he was one
of the founders of the New Artists' Association
Munich. In 1913 he painted his first abstract
water-colour which he later dated as from 1910
(ill. p. 550), soon to be followed by his first abstract
painting in oils. This step he had already discussed
in his book *Concerning the Spiritual in Art*, 1912. He
also expounded his ideas in the Almanac *Der Blaue
Reiter* which he published in collaboration with
Marc. At the outbreak of the First World War he
returned to Moscow, and now the dramatic in his
Munich work was replaced by a stricter order. He
returned to Germany in 1921, and Walter Gropius
called him to the Weimar Bauhaus in 1922 where
he met Klee again. While there he developed a disciplined geometrical style, which he again substantiated theoretically in 1926. In 1926 he published his book
*Punkt und Linie zu Fläche* (Point and Line to Plane).
The political opposition to the Bauhaus caused Kandinsky to leave Germany again in 1933. He moved
to Neuilly-sur-Seine near Paris, where he met many
leading painters, including Chagall, Léger, Miró,
Mondrian and Hans Arp, the last named becoming
his close friend. Through the influence of Arp and
Miró he returned to the organic form combined
with the geometric structure already in his pictures,
and his coloration became brighter.
*Illustrations:*
550 Untitled, 1910 (1913)
579 Study for "Improvisation 8", 1910
580 Improvisation George, 1914
581 Sky Blue, 1940
581 The Arrow (La Flèche), 1943

**KAUFFMANN Angelica**
1741 Chur (Switzerland) – 1807 Rome
Taught by her father, a Vorarlberg painter,
Angelica Kauffmann already painted remarkable
pastel portraits at the early age of 15. On extensive
Italian travels she developed a thorough knowledge
by copying the old masters. She became a member
of the Academies of Florence and Rome, and her
meeting with Johann Joachim Winckelmann was
decisive in pointing her in the Classical direction.
From 1766 she lived in London for 15 years, becoming a Royal Academician and working with
the architect Robert Adam, amongst others. On
her return to Rome she became the centre of a
salon which Goethe and Herder attended. Her portraits owe much to Reynolds and Mengs, while
her Classical religious and mythological pictures
were based on the study of Antiquity seen with the
eyes of Winckelmann.
*Illustration:*
379 Self-Portrait, 1780

**KELLY Ellsworth**
born 1923 Newburgh (New York)
After studying at the Pratt Institute, then doing military service from 1943 to 1945, and then further studies at the School of the Museum of Fine Arts, Kelly went to Paris in 1948 to attend the Ecole des Beaux-Arts. Under the influence of Constructivist painters, such as Hans Arp and Georges Vantangerloo, as well as the geometric abstractions of Vasarely, Kelly soon developed an abstract style in which geometric planes in different colour tones were slotted into each other. On his return to the USA in 1954 he worked on a further reduction of his visual language, returning to single, precisely structured, objectified pictures. Through his mathematically calculated sculptures, Kelly achieved a new type of representation in the 1970s, the so-called "shaped canvas", in which neutrally applied colours are coordinated with clearly defined planar forms.
*Illustration:*
651   Red Blue, 1968

**KERSTING Georg Friedrich**
1785 Güstrow – 1847 Meißen
Like many German artists of his time, Kersting came from a narrow middle-class background. After the death of his father, a glazier and glass painter, a well-to-do relative sent Kersting to the Copenhagen Academy from 1805 to 1808. He then settled in Dresden, where a friendship developed with Gerhard von Kügelgen and with Friedrich. With the latter he went on a walking tour through Silesia and Bohemia. Kersting painted exclusively interiors, a branch of painting which had become established in the Netherlands in the 17th century. His pictures often show sparse working and living quarters as an image of the concentrated intellectual life led by their inmates. These are often occupied with reading, his favourite subject apart from painting his friend Friedrich, and quite in tune with his unemphatic but delicately coloured work.
*Illustration:*
451   Reader by Lamplight, 1814

**KEYSER Thomas de**
c. 1596/97 Amsterdam – 1667 Amsterdam
De Keyser was the son of a sculptor and architect and, until Rembrandt's arrival in Amsterdam in 1632 the town's leading portraitist. He specialised in large-scale group portraits and also painted smaller, crowded pictures of families and groups ("The Anatomy of Dr Sebastiaen Egbertsz. de Vry", Amsterdam, Rijksmuseum). He abandoned painting altogether between 1640 to 1654 and became a dealer in basalt stone. Later he produced pictures of the rich Amsterdam middle classes mounted on their steeds – a way of depiction formerly reserved for the aristocracy. From 1662 until his death he supervised the building of the new Amsterdam town hall.
*Illustration:*
306   Equestrian Portrait of Pieter Schout, 1660

**KHNOPFF Fernand**
1858 Grembergen (East Flanders) – 1921 Brussels
Khnopff's work included oil-paintings, water-colours, coloured drawings and etchings. Like Klinger he also produced polychrome sculpture and designed interiors and theatre scenery. He abandoned his legal studies to attend art school in Brussels under Xavier Mellery, who gave him an understanding of painting as the bearer of a profound, hidden meaning, and so introduced him to the rudiments of Symbolism. In 1877 Khnopff visited Paris, where he was much impressed by the work of Moreau and

Delacroix. He was also an admirer of the Pre-Raphaelite painters. In 1883 he was a founder member of "Les XX", to which both painters and writers belonged. Many of his friends were writers, and he illustrated some books for Georges Rodenbach and Gregoire Le Roy. His work is characterised by delicate coloration and an aesthetic, reticent manner of painting, wrapping his subjects in idealised and generalised allegories. His female figures are inscrutable sphinxes and chimaeras, strangely beautiful creatures of an icy eroticism. Khnopff himself embodied the dandified type of artist, who lived in a fantasy house with blind windows, decorated to his own design.
*Illustration:*
524   I Lock My Door upon Myself, 1891

**KIEFER Anselm**
born 1945 Donaueschingen
Kiefer studied law and Romance languages at Freiburg (Breisgau) and took drawing lessons from Peter Dreher. He decided to concentrate on art and attended the Karlsruhe Academy in 1969, where he was taught by Horst Antes. The following year he went to study under Beuys at the Academy in Düsseldorf, where he produced his first paintings in a poetic, expressive style. His themes were always heroic or mythological allegories. Since 1980 he has been interested in "Margarete" and "Sulamit" from the Death Fugue by Paul Celan. In the 1990s he has produced large plastic works, such as his fighter planes constructed of lead sheets, carrying a mythical freight. A travelling exhibition has also shown the great number of *Künstlerbücher* (artists' books) produced over several decades.
*Illustration:*
676   Bilderstreit (Iconoclastic Controversy), 1979

**KIPPENBERGER Martin**
1953 Dortmund – 1997 Viena
In 1972 Kippenberger studied briefly at the Art College in Hamburg. He moved to Berlin in 1978, where he opened the Kippenberger Office and organised exhibitions with Walter Dahn, Werner Büttner, Albert Oehlen and others. The exhibition "Arbeit ist Wahrheit" with Büttner, Kippenberger and Oehlen was at the Folkwang Museum, Essen in 1984. In 1986 he went to study in Brazil, and in 1988 moved to Los Angeles. In 1990 he was visiting professor at the Städelschule, Frankfurt am Main. He had a one-man exhibition at the Museum of Modern Art, San Francisco in 1991. In 1993 he founded the Museum of Modern Art on Syros and had a one-man exhibition at the Pompidou Centre, Paris. His 1994 exhibition "The Happy End of Franz Kafka's America" was at the Boymans van Beuningen Museum, Rotterdam. His sculpture "Exit of the Underground Station Dawson City West" was unveiled in 1995 for an open-air public display in Dawson City, Canada. Kippenberger lives and works in Cologne and on Syros, Greece.
*Illustration:*
677   Heute denken – morgen fertig, 1983

**KIRCHNER Ernst Ludwig**
1880 Aschaffenburg – 1938 Frauenkirch (Switzerland)
Kirchner went to Dresden in 1901 to study architecture. He interrupted these studies briefly in 1903 to go to art school in Munich. After his examinations he devoted himself to painting, although largely self-taught. In 1905 he founded the Brücke group with Heckel, Schmidt-Rottluff and Fritz Bleyl. Initially he and his friends were influenced

by Neo-Impressionism and van Gogh's work, developing a style based on flat, pure colours which represented a parallel to the Fauvism in Paris. Ideas of "primitive" art, seen in the Museum of Ethnology, were added later. Faces became masks, bodies were depicted in grotesque positions, and limbs distorted. Kirchner left Dresden in 1911 and moved to Berlin. There he found the subject matter suited to his lively, restless temperament: the large city, to whose hectic and unnaturalness he could give expression as no other. His street scenes seem to hum with the city's hustle and bustle. In 1914, after having just been called up for military service, he suffered a severe nervous breakdown. He never quite recovered, convalescing at first in Germany and then moving to Switzerland in 1917, where he remained until taking his own life. Here, in depicting the peaceful landscape of mountains and valleys, he found a new, spiritualised form of expression.
*Illustrations:*
584   Negro Dance, c. 1911
584   The Red Tower in Halle, 1915
585   The Street, 1908/19

**KITAJ Ronald B.**
born 1932 Chagrin Falls (Ohio)
Kitaj studied at the Cooper Union in New York in 1950, at the Vienna Academy in 1951, at the Ruskin School of Drawing, Oxford, in 1958, and finally from 1959 to 1961 at the Royal College of Art in London. Between his studies in Vienna and Oxford he went to sea and taught himself painting. In London he influenced his fellow students Jones and Hockney, who were to become Pop Artists. Kitaj himself, however, never belonged to this movement as he did not take his subjects from mass culture but from philosophy and the works of poets, such as T.S. Eliot and Ezra Pound, as well as from the world of politics. By applying Surrealist collage methods he succeeded in combining a variety of subjects into a startling arrangement full of allusions. In 1970 he taught as visiting professor at the University of California in Berkeley, then at several art institutions in Britain. In 1995 he was awarded the prize for painting at the Venice Biennale.
*Illustration:*
663   Value, Price and Profit, 1963

**KLAPHECK Konrad**
born 1935 Düsseldorf
Klapheck studied from 1954 to 1958 under Bruno Goller at the Düsseldorf Academy. While still a student he found his subject matter, which he has used since then in a variety of new ways: figurative machine pictures in "prosaic super-representationalism". His first picture with typewriter dates from 1955. While in Paris for six months, he came to know the work of Duchamp. In the early 1960s he became friendly with the Surrealists around Breton. Klapheck had his first one-man exhibition at the Galerie Schmela in Dusseldorf in 1959. In 1979 he was given a professorship at the Dusseldorf Academy.
*Illustration:*
672   The mother's prayers, 1984

**KLEE Paul**
1879 Münchenbuchsee (near Berne) – 1940 Muralto (near Locarno)
Klee's father, a music teacher, was German, his mother Swiss. He himself played the violin and stayed close to music all his life. The decision whether to devote himself to music or painting fell in 1898 when he went to study painting in Munich. After attending the private art school of

Heinrich Knirr, he studied from 1900 at the Academy under Franz von Stuck. In 1901 he went to Italy, in 1905 to Paris. During the years 1902–1906, which he spent in Bern, he produced etchings inspired by Francisco de Goya, Ensor and Aubrey Beardsley. He then returned to Munich where he met Macke and in 1911 Kandinsky and took part in the second exhibition of the Blauer Reiter. During a further visit to Paris in 1912 he became acquainted with Delaunay whose essay *About the Light* he translated. He also saw the works of Braque and Picasso. His particular concern with both the potential and the demands of colour caused him to travel to Tunis with Louis Moilliet and Macke in April 1914. His impressions were fused with the predetermined order of colour fields. The water-colours of this period were masterful.

In 1916 Klee was called up for military service. On his discharge in 1919 he began painting in oil. In his pictures he developed the representational out of abstract forms. His essay *Creative Confessions*, started in 1918, appeared in 1920, and in the same year he was given an appointment at the Bauhaus. His geometric grid now was often accompanied by drawings of a subtle humour. In 1931 Klee became professor at the Academy in Düsseldorf. From this period date his divisionist pictures in which colour is applied in small dots similar to the method of pointillism. To evade the pressures of rising fascism, he returned to Bern in 1933, where he began to produce large-scale pictures. His work is often ambiguous or somewhat ironic, but it never loses touch with the real world.
*Illustrations:*
598    Villa R, 1919
599    Senecio, 1922
599    Around the Fish, 1926

**KLEIN Yves**
1928 Nice – 1962 Paris
Klein, who had studied Oriental languages amongst other subjects, had the idea in 1947 to explore the monochrome in music. He composed the *Monotone Symphony* based on a single tone, of which further versions appeared until 1961. He travelled to various countries and stayed in Japan for two years, where he became a black belt in judo in 1953. On returning to Paris he ran a judo school. From 1949 onwards he produced monochrome pictures; the "International Klein Blue" (IKB) dates from 1956, an ultramarine he developed by himself. To him, the monochrome canvases were the embodiment of his mystical ideas about the cosmic power of colour. At the Avant-Garde Festival in Paris in November 1960 a photograph was shown of Klein flying, in the only edition of the magazine *Dimanche*. He experimented with unorthodox subject matter, such as presenting empty rooms, creating "Anthropometrias" (impressions of female bodies dipped into "Klein"-blue) and "Cosmogonias" (traces of the effects of nature) and from 1961 fire pictures.
*Illustration:*
654    Monochrome Blue, Untitled (IKB 3), 1960

**KLIMT Gustav**
1862 Baumgarten (near Vienna) – 1918 Vienna
From 1876 to 1882 Klimt studied at the Vienna Arts and Crafts School and, together with nineteen other artists, joined the Jugendstil (Art Noveau) movement in 1897. He became a co-founder of the Vienna Secession and was its president until his resignation in 1905. To this day his work still has both its admirers and its detractors. He is criticised for his massed repetitive decorative elements, and his gold backgrounds and jewelled co-

loration are considered to be outside the bounds of "great art". Stylisation carried to the point of ornamental dissolution is typical of his style, as is the craftsmanlike execution. Like many of his contemporaries he favoured Symbolist representations, such as "Hope" (Turin, Galleria Galatea), "Music" (Munich, Neue Pinakothek) and "Fulfilment" (Strasbourg, Musée des Beaux-Arts). His portraits are both delicate and magnificent, his less numerous landscapes mosaic-like, with their dotted brushwork. Klimt's work, which is now highly esteemed, greatly influenced the development of the Vienna Jugendstil and also the arts and crafts movement, as represented by the Wiener Werkstätte founded in 1903.
*Illustrations:*
536    Flower Garden, c. 1905/06
536    The Virgin, c. 1913

**KLINE Franz**
1910 Wilkes-Barre (Pennsylvania) – 1962 New York
From 1931 to 1935 Kline studied in Boston, and from 1936 at the Heatherley School of Fine Art in London. He moved to New York in 1938, where he met de Kooning who aroused his interest in abstraction. He began to paint portraits, seated figures in rocking chairs, pictures of trains and the Pennsylvania landscape. He often gave his abstract paintings titles associated with his Pennsylvanian childhood memories. Towards the late 1940s he established his personal attention-grabbing style, painting increasingly large canvases and restricting himself almost totally to black and white. Around 1950 he produced powerful tectonic constructions which, by his own admission, had been influenced by Mondrian. From the mid-fifties he returned to brilliant reds, yellow, orange and purple, also browns and greys, but remaining true to his former idiom.
*Illustration:*
634    New York, 1953

**KLINGER Max**
1857 Leipzig – 1920 Großjena (near Naumburg)
Together with Slevogt and Hodler, Klinger studied under Karl Gussow in Karlsruhe and Berlin. He was much impressed by Goya, Menzel and Rembrandt, studying in particular their graphic work. He began his career with a series of etchings which successfully appeared in 1878. Subsequently he also produced paintings, but later devoted himself almost entirely to sculpture, using variously coloured materials. His works tended towards the dreamlike and imaginative, and contain Symbolist as well as Jugendstil (Art Noveau) elements.
*Illustration:*
533    Landscape by Unstrut, 1912

**KØBKE Christen Schjellerup**
1810 Copenhagen – 1848 Copenhagen
Købke became Eckersberg's pupil in 1828, after having studied at the Copenhagen Academy since 1822. Like his teacher, he concentrated on portrait and landscape painting. His pictures of Danish life are usually small in format, carried out in fine, broken or dotted brushwork capable of putting life into the smallest detail. Contrary to Eckersberg he did not choose the all-inclusive panoramic view, but discovered small, secret corners in the country or near the towns, which he rendered from an unexpected perspective and in limpid daylight. Købke was one of the most important representatives of light-toned, open-air painting and early realism in Copenhagen. Following his Italian sojourn from 1838 to 1840 he painted primarily from his

Italian travel sketches, abandoning the small format. His work lost the fresh directness of the earlier period.
*Illustration:*
462    The Shore at Dosseringen, 1838

**KOCH Joseph Anton**
1768 Obergiblen (Tyrol) – 1839 Rome
Coming from a poor background, Koch started work as a shepherd. He gained the support of the Bishop of Augsburg and was sent for his education to the Dilling Seminary and finally to the Karlsschule in Stuttgart for artistic training. As Schiller before him, Koch escaped from the intolerable constraints imposed at this school, making his way first to Strasbourg and then Switzerland. He had joined the Jacobin Club at Strasbourg, but the Swiss countryside, removed from all political strife, allowed him to express his ideals of freedom artistically. The mountain studies, which Koch made on his extensive walking tours, formed the basis for his large compositions, including "Schmadribachfall" (ill. p.450), "Swiss Landscape" (ill. p.450) and "The Hospice on the Grimselwald Glacier" (destroyed, formerly Leipzig, Museum der bildenden Künste). These works were not produced, however, until Koch had studied contemporary classic landscape painting in Rome, which enabled him to create a new monumental type of Alpine painting. Apart from a brief period in Vienna from 1812 to 1815, Koch lived in Rome from 1795 until his death. Here he found his subject matter for his landscapes in the Alban mountains and especially the area around Olevano. In these he combined Poussin's classic approach to landscape with direct observation of nature, which he captured in his sketches and water-colours.
*Illustrations:*
450    Swiss Landscape (Berner Oberland), 1817
450    Schmadribachfall, c. 1821/22

**KOKOSCHKA Oskar**
1886 Pöchlarn (Danube) – 1980 Villeneuve (Lake Geneva)
Kokoschka studied from 1905 to 1909 at the Vienna School of Applied Arts, simultaneously working at the Wiener Werkstätte from 1907, and received from 1908 the active support of the architect Adolf Loos and writer Karl Kraus. The Wiener Werkstätte edited his colour lithographs for his work of poetic writing *The Dreaming Boys*, which represent a high point in the art of illustration in the Jugendstil (Art Noveau style). In 1909/10, his period of the psychological portrait, the model is not so much depicted, but rather dissected. In 1910 he went to Berlin to work on Herwarth Walden's Sturm, but returned a year later to become an assistant at the Vienna School of Applied Arts. The male – female conflict, already dealt with in the drama *Mörder, Hoffnung der Frauen* (Murder, Women's Hope), was transformed in 1914 into an allegory of unrestrained love relationships in his pictures "Whirlwind" (Basel, Kunstmuseum). In 1915 Kokoschka returned seriously wounded from the front, having volunteered for service. In 1917 he settled in Dresden, becoming a teacher at the Academy in 1919. In addition to his portraits, he discovered the cityscape as a new subject. From 1924 he travelled all over Europe, painting large-scale pictures of famous cities in strong colours. He left for Prague in 1934 and emigrated from there to London in 1938, but finally settled in Switzerland in 1953.
*Illustration:*
586    Venice, Boats at the Dogana, 1924

## KONINCK Philips
(also: Coning, Coningh, Goningh, Koning)
1619 Amsterdam – 1688 Amsterdam
Konincks' father was a goldsmith, his older brother
Jacob a painter, who taught him from 1639 to 1641
in Rotterdam. He returned to Amsterdam in 1641,
possibly becoming a pupil of Rembrandt who became a friend to whom he owed much. Characteristic of his work are large-scale panoramic landscapes,
mostly seen from a slight elevation allowing a view
over wide stretches of flat or slightly hilly land
under a great expanse of sky. Waterways and paths
intersect the landscape, houses are dotted in the
foreground. These landscapes were most mostly carried out in warm, brown-yellow tones. As a sideline, Koninck operated a ferry service between Amsterdam and Rotterdam.
*Illustration:*
322   Village on a Hill, 1651

## KONRAD OF SOEST
c. 1370 Dortmund – after 1422 Dortmund
Konrad came from a family of painters who had settled in Dortmund two generations before his birth,
while still retaining connections to Soest. A record
of his marriage in 1394 survives; the witnesses,
came from some of the town's more respected
families. He was possibly trained in Westphalia, as
the structure and thematic perception of his work
follow older local traditions. However, other elements point at his extensive knowledge of French
and Netherlandish art, so much so that one could
be tempted to draw inferences from his painting
about much that has been lost in those countries.
During the period that produced the Wildung altar
retables (1403) he must have had a large workshop
with distinct areas of allocated responsibility, as it is
inconceivable that all the scenes could come from
one hand (ill. p.75). A major work from his later
work is the retable in the Marienkirche in Dortmund, of which only fragments remain. During
1413 to 1422 he is mentioned in connection with
his membership in the Brotherhood in St Nicolai in
Dortmund. He probably died soon afterwards. Konrad's fame went far beyond his home boundaries,
making his influence felt as far as the coast and central Germany.
*Illustration:*
75   The Nativity, 1403

## KOONING Willem de
1904 Rotterdam – 1997 New York
From 1916 de Kooning worked for four years for
an art dealer in Rotterdam, attending evening
courses at the Academy. In 1926 he entered the
USA illegally. In 1930 he met Gorky, with whom
he then shared a studio and who was to be an important influence. He taught summer courses at
the Black Mountain College and at Yale, and
travelled to Rome and San Francisco. In the 1930s
he painted several murals as part of an official arts
support programme. De Kooning is, with Pollock,
one of the most important painters of abstract Expressionism. His first one-man exhibition was not
held until 1948, and he became one of the leading
*avant-garde* personalities and influential artists of
the 1950s. During the 1930s and 1940s de Kooning specialised in the depiction of three main
themes: men, women and abstractions; towards the
end of this period his manner of painting grew in
intensity. After 1950 he returned to his subject
"Woman", while continuing with his abstract compositions. During this period his work was marked
by a heightened colour intensity and density which
in turn was replaced by lighter tones and larger,
more reduced forms. He painted abstract landscapes after 1955 and, encouraged by Henry
Moore, started producing large-scale sculpture in

1970. In 1963 he built himself a studio at Springs
on Long Island. In spite of a serious illness in 1989
he continues to paint incessantly while cared for by
his daughter.
*Illustrations:*
616   Untitled, 1970
631   Woman, I, 1950–1952
631   Untitled, III, 1980

## KUPKA František
1871 Opocno (Bohemia) – 1957 Puteaux (near
Paris)
After an apprenticeship as a saddler and attendance
at the Prague Academy from 1888 to 1891, Kupka
studied at the Vienna Academy for two years. In
1895 he moved to Paris, then to Puteaux in 1904,
where he associated with Jacques Villon, Léger,
Gris, Duchamp, Metzinger and Archipenko. He
regularly exhibited his Neo-Impressionist pictures
at the autumn Salon, supplementing his income by
producing illustrations. He became deeply interested in theosophy, Eastern philosophy and spiritualism. Around 1910 he turned to abstract painting. His knowledge of colour theory and the discoveries of modern physics inspired this work in
which he attempted to express both movement and
light in terms of colour. At the Paris autumn Salon
in 1912 he showed his first entirely non-representational paintings whose titles already give an indication of their closeness to music ("Amorpha: Fugue à
deux couleurs" and "Chromatique chaude"). In
1914 he volunteered for military service. From
1918 to 1920 he was a visiting professor in Prague,
when his work began to show the influence of the
world of machines and of jazz music. During the
years 1931–1934 he was a member of the group Abstraction-Création. It was not until the 1940s and
1950s that through exhibitions and acquisition of
his work by the world's great galleries Kupka received due recognition as one of the pioneers of abstract art.
*Illustration:*
592   The Language of Verticals, 1911

## LAM Wifredo
1902 Sagua la Grande (Cuba) – 1982 Paris
Lam came from a cosmopolitan family – a Chinese
father and a European-African mother, and was
trained at the San Alejandro Academy in Havana,
continuing his studies in Madrid and Barcelona in
1924. In 1928 he saw for the first time African
sculptures from Guinea and the Congo. These were
to influence his art as much as the work of Picasso,
whom he met in Paris in 1937. While in Paris he
met artists of the Surrealist group with whom he
took flight to Marseilles in 1940. In 1941 he took
ship with Breton, Masson and Lévi-Strauss to Martinique, going on to Cuba. On his return to Paris
in 1945 he began to lead a restless life between continents. He moved to Albisola Mare in Italy in
1964. Lam can be regarded as an outstanding exponent of the Surrealist endeavour to incorporate African and Caribbean mythology into art. His subject
matter centred around Cuban gods and myths,
voodoo culture and the dangers and wildness of the
jungel.
*Illustration:*
612   Umbral (Senil), 1950/51

## LANCRET Nicolas
1690 Paris – 1743 Paris
Lancret received early instruction in engraving and
drawing, then at the age of 17 became the assistant
of the history painter Pierre Dulin in Paris. He was
not very successful in this field and the hoped for
Rome prize of the Academy was not forthcoming,
so on entering the studio of Gillot, who had also

been the master of Watteau, Lancret gave up history painting. Two landscapes secured him membership of the Academy in 1718. His pictures show
from the very beginning the influence of Watteau,
with whom he soon quarrelled. A renewed attempt
at history painting failed in 1723/24. He now
devoted himself to the pastoral idyll and "fêtes galantes". Pictures such as "The Swing" (ill. p.353)
made him something of a mediator between Watteau and Fragonard, although he never achieved
their subtle poetic qualities. On Pater's death, Lancret completed the series of illustrations for La Fon-
taine's fables. With the exception of the "Tiger
Hunt' (Amiens, Musée de Picardie) and his portraits, Lancret remained faithful to his so-called
"Watteau genre".
*Illustration:*
353   The Swing, undated

## LANFRANCO Giovanni
(also: Giovanni di Stefano)
1582 Terenzo (near Parma) – 1647 Rome
As the pupil of Agostino Carracci he worked from
1600 to 1602 on the decoration of the Palazzo del
Giardino in Parma. A short time after his master's
death he was mentioned in Rome in the circle surrounding Annibale Carracci. In 1605, while in
Rome. he decorated the Camerino degli Eremiti in
the Palazzo Farnese (destroyed). Around 1610 he returned briefly to his home town, painting altarpieces for churches in Parma and Piacenza. Again in
Rome. he carried out the two works which were to
make him famous: the ceiling in the Loggia des Casino Borghese with its extreme foreshortenings
("Olympian Meeting") and the fresco in the cupola
with the "Assumption of the Virgin" for Sant'Andrea della Valle. These were to serve as an example
to Pozzo and Baciccio with their characteristic
powerfulness and monumental grandeur. In
1633/34 Giovanni Lanfranco made his way to
Naples, where he carried out a number of large commissions, including the cupola of Gesù Nuovo and
the frescos in Santi Apostoli, where he concentrated
on achieving dramatic vividness rather than careful
execution.
*Illustration:*
235   Hagar in the Wilderness, undated

## LARGILLIÈRE Nicolas de
1656 Paris – 1746 Paris
Largillière first studied art in Antwerp, qualifying
as a master artist in 1672. Two years later he went
to London, working with the Flemish-born Peter
Lely and also for the court. To avoid persecution as a
Catholic he had to return to Paris in 1682. With a
portrait of Charles Le Brun he was accepted as a
member of the Academy. He was again in London
in 1685/86 in order to paint the royal couple at the
coronation. Alongside Hyacinthe Rigaud, Largillière was the most sought-after portraitist among
royalty, nobility and the middle classes. As a teacher
– he became professor at the Academy in 1705 –
he upheld the Flemish tradition which had long
played an important part in French painting.
He was also a master of the group portrait and the
still life.
*Illustration:*
352   The Strasbourg Belle, 1703

## LASTMAN Pieter
1583 Amsterdam – 1633 Amsterdam
Rembrandt was briefly a pupil of Lastman around
1622/23 and copied his master's work in his early
career, and yet Lastman has almost been forgotten.
The son of a messenger, Lastman was apprenticed to
Gerrit Sweelinck, a pupil of Cornelis van Haarlem,
which explains the influence of the old Haarlem

school on his work. However, more important was his visit to Italy in about 1603–1607 which took him to Venice and Rome. His meeting with Caravaggio and the Carraccis, and most of all his close contact with Elsheimer, whose landscape composition and figure painting impressed him deeply, gave him a new direction. On his return to Amsterdam he dedicated himself to history painting centering on biblical scenes and ancient mythology. He tells his stories in a manner that is both realistic and original. His landscapes of Antiquity are often arranged with groups of figures in splendid dress and rich colours ("Odysseus and Nausicaa", various versions are at Brunswik, Augsburg, Munich; ill. p. 294).
*Illustration:*
294   Odysseus and Nausicaa, 1619

## LA TOUR Georges de
1593 Vic-sur-Seille (near Nancy) – 1652 Lunéville
Even in his lifetime La Tour must have been one of the most admired painters. He was ennobled, appointed "peintre du Roi", lived a luxurious life, had powerful patrons and so was able to charge enormous fees (such as for his "Peter Denying Christ", Nantes, Musée des Beaux-Arts, 1650). This is especially surprising as he never left his home ground, except for a brief visit to Paris and a still disputed journey to Rome, and yet he produced up-to-date work without subordinating himself to modish tendencies. He soon fell into oblivion after his death, until the revival of his work in the 1920s when artists of the New Objectivity (Neue Sachlichkeit) mistakenly thought they discovered in him an artistic predecessor of their own concepts. Only about twenty of his works survive, and these can be divided into his early stylised "day pieces" and the later "night pieces". But both attribution (he only rarely signed his work) and chronological order must remain questionable. Unlike the Utrecht Caravaggisti, La Tour, who was probably introduced to Saraceni, Caravaggio or Gentileschi by his colleague Leclerc, gave less and less attention to accurate detail. His strange lighting effects, particularly in his late work, do not create blurred forms but instead sharp contours. His figures, even when only barely and in part illuminated, have an extraordinary plasticity. In a work like the "The Card-Sharp with the Ace of Spades" (ill. p. 242) the figures seem to embody an inscrutability which is further enhanced by the enamel-like, opaque painting technique.
*Illustrations:*
242   Hurdy-Gurdy Player, c. 1620–1630
242   The Card-Sharp with the Ace of Spades, c. 1620–1640
243   St Sebastian Attended by St Irene, c. 1634–1643

## LA TOUR Maurice Quentin de
1704 St-Quentin (Aisne) – 1788 St-Quentin
Leaving his poverty-stricken home at the age of 15, La Tour first entered the workshop of an etcher in Paris, then worked in the studio of the painter Jacques-Jean Spoëde. With a letter of recommendation from an English ambassador he went to England where he was much impressed by van Dyck's art of portrayal. On his return to Paris he took up pastel painting, possibly inspired by Rosalba Carriera's success in Paris in 1720/21. After some experiments he soon came to excel at pastel portraits, surpassing all his rivals, even Perronneau, and gaining great favour at court. La Tour was most demanding in his art so that the execution of a work was often slow, and it was nine years before he produced a work which would admit him to the Academy. His portrait of Mme de Pompadour of

1755 (Paris, Louvre) and of the "President de Rieux in his Study" (Paris, Louvre) represent two of the few full-length pastel portraits in existence. His portraits show a vigorous handling and a perceptive grasp of character.
*Illustration:*
362   Self-Portrait, 1751

## LAWRENCE Thomas
1769 Bristol – 1830 London
Thomas Lawrence was the 14th of sixteen children of a customs officer and later publican. An early fondness of acting and drawing drew attention to the child prodigy. When only ten he drew portraits of fifty prominent Oxford personalities. He was given some instruction sin pastel and oil-painting, but was largely self-taught, studying private art collections. In 1789 he introduced himself with the full-length portrait of Lady Cremorne (Bristol, City Art Gallery) at the Royal Academy. He was a great admirer of Reynolds, and in effect became his successor on his death. Lawrence's acting talent showed itself in the way he posed and presented his sitters. In 1792 he became principal painter to the king, two years later a member and in 1820 president of the Royal Academy. He received his peerage in 1815, the same year he was asked to paint the leading personalities at the Congress of Vienna. His influence on Victorian portrait painting was fundamental.
*Illustrations:*
389   Portrait of Master Ainslie, 1794
389   Portrait of Lady Elizabeth Conyngham, c. 1821–1824

## LE BRUN Charles
1619 Paris – 1690 Paris
Having been the pupil of Perrier and Vouet, Le Brun was appointed "peintre du Roi" at the age of eighteen and received his first commissions from Cardinal Richelieu in 1640. Two years later he went with Poussin to Rome, where he studied and copied the works of Reni, the Carraccis, Raphael and Cortona. After returning to Paris in 1646 he soon developed his own style and was commissioned to decorate various great houses (Hôtel Lambert, Hôtel Nouveau), became co-founder of the Académie Royale in 1648 and there held the first of his famous "leçons" in the same year. His contact in 1657 with the government minister Fouquet resulted in the commission for the design of decorations in the Vaux palace (ceiling and wall frescos, 1658) and his appointment as director of the Gobelins manufactory. His introduction at court by Mazarin in 1660 brought him many commissions and the appointment as "first court painter" (1662). As the virtual dictator of the arts, Le Brun also designed furniture of massive silver, triumphal arches, fireworks and catafalques. Twenty years later he worked with his assistants on the decorations of the Petit Galérie des Louvre, designed decorations for Versailles, where he also decorated the Grand Escalier (1674–1678, destroyed) and decorated Colbert's Sceaux palace (destroyed) and Marly (destroyed). Le Brun, who in his lifetime was the most comprehensive, famous and influential artist of his epoch, is almost forgotten today.
*Illustrations:*
252   Martyrdom of St John the Evangelist at the Porta Latina, c. 1641/42
252   Chancellor Séguir at the Entrance of Louis XIV into Paris in 1660, 1660

## LÉGER Fernand
1881 Argentan (Normandy) – 1955 Gif-sur-Yvette
Léger worked as an architect's draughtsman in Paris until 1903. Like so many other painters, he was

deeply impressed by the 1907 Cézanne exhibition at the Salon d'Automne. From 1908 he lived in the artists' colony Zone with Delaunay, Archipenko, Laurens, Lipchitz and others. From 1910 he exhibited at Kahnweiler's gallery, who also represented Picasso and Braque, and began to move towards Cubism. However, the analytic dissection of surface did not appeal to him; he was much more interested in an art evolving from pure colours and rhythms as realised in his "form contrasts".

Léger's war experience 1914–1916 helped him find his true subject matter: the mechanisation of our world. His forms since 1917 took on such a tubular appearance that a critic remarked mockingly that Léger's art should not be called Cubism, but "tubism". In these works, figures enliven the inanimate mechanised world. His friendship with Le Corbusier inspired him to produce designs for wall decorations, mosaic and stained glass from 1920. The beginning of his "monumental" period was marked by his depiction of figures with stencil-like outlines. From 1927 they again began to take on forms that became increasingly organic and realistic.
*Illustrations:*
574   The Stairway, 1914
574   Three Women (Le Grand Déjeuner), 1921

## LEIBL Wilhelm
1844 Cologne – 1900 Würzburg
Today regarded as one of the great German painters, Leibl found little recognition and success in his lifetime. From 1864 to 1869 he studied in Munich under Karl Theodor von Piloty and Wilhelm von Kaulbach. At first he adhered to the old-masterly manner, painting portraits and genre scenes in muted tones. Already in his student days he had formed the "Leibl circle", gathering like-minded painters, such as Trübner, around him. However, this group did not organise itself formally or put forward any specific ideas. At the first International Art Exhibition at the Munich Glaspalast in 1869 Leibl had his first success with his "Portrait of Frau Gedon" (Munich, Neue Pinakothek). Here he met Courbet, whose work, and in particular the "Stonemasons" (formerly Dresden, Gemäldegalerie), impressed him so strongly that he spent 1869/70 in Paris. Here he saw the work of the early Impressionists, but it was Manet who inspired him most. In opposition to the "city art trade" he left Munich in 1873, retiring to remote Bavarian villages. From this period date his genre-like scenes of gloomily-lit interiors of peasant dwellings and rural life ("Three Women in Church", ill. p. 532). His fine detail and technical skill are reminiscent of the old Dutch masters, while his late work is marked by Impressionist influences.
*Illustration:*
532   Three Women in Church, 1881

## LELY Peter
(Pieter van der Faes)
1618 Soest (near Utrecht) – 1680 London
After studying in Haarlem, Lely travelled to England in 1641 when William of Orange married Mary of England; he obtained access to the court by painting the bridal couple. He also was in the service of the Earl of Northumberland, copying paintings by van Dyck for him. This work was to have a key influence on his style. Lely also admired the work of Dobson and Fuller, as can be seen from his portraits of the "Duke of York" (London, Syon House) and the "Children of Charles II" (Petworth). In 1656 he was given leave to visit Holland; the effect was the replacement of the van Dyck elegance of his painting with Flemish elements, such as landscape backgrounds in his por-

BIOGRAPHIES OF THE ARTISTS

traits. Charles II appointed him principal painter in 1661 at a considerable salary, and at the time of the Restoration Lely dominated Stuart portrait painting. During this period he painted his best work, including portraits of ten ladies of the court known a the "Windsor Beauties", 1662–1665 (Hampton Court). His late work is characterised by a velvety chiaroscuro – again close to van Dyck's work – and looser brushwork. His success was crowned by the bestowal of a knighthood in 1680.
*Illustration:*
254  Henrietta Maria of France, Queen of
     England, 1660

## LE NAIN Antoine
c. 1588 Laon – 1648 Paris
## LE NAIN Louis
c. 1593 Laon – 1648 Paris
## LE NAIN Mathieu
1607 Laon – 1677 Paris
The three brothers, who all used the same signature on their work and therefore represent an attribution problem to this day, probably trained under an unknown Dutch master in Laon and then settled in Paris.

Antoine, master painter to the Abbey St Germain-des-Près from 1629, showed the Dutch influence most. He preferred the small format, painting single and group portraits in a strong, dramatic manner ("Family Meeting", Paris, Louvre, 1642). In 1629 he became a citizen of Paris, where the three unmarried brothers amassed a considerable fortune, appointing each other heirs to their estates. He and his brother Louis were founding members of the Academy (1648).

Louis, also called "Le Romain" because of the Italian influence in his style, was probably artistically the most important of the three. Starting with the narrative genre of the so-called "Bambocciades", he developed an individual manner of portraying rural life ("Peasants at their Cottage Door", ill. p. 241). His work is marked by sparse but cleverly used coloration in tones of brown and grey and an atmosphere of solemnity and peace.

Mathieu seems to have concentrated on religious subjects, such as "The Nativity" (Paris, Louvre). Van Dyck's influence is apparent in such works as the "Tric-Trac Player" (Paris, Louvre), whose elegance stands out against the rustic pictures of Antoine and Louis. On the death of his two brothers Mathieu completed their unfinished works, adding to the already existing difficulty of distinguishing between them.
*Illustration:*
241  La Charette (The Cart), 1641
241  Peasants at their Cottage Door, undated

## LENBACH Franz von
1836 Schrobenhausen (near Munich) – 1904 Munich
Lenbach came to painting by a circuitous route. He studied it briefly in the Munich studio of Karl Theodor von Piloty, then travelled to Italy and Spain and went with Hans Makart and L. C. Müller to Egypt. Lenbach was a portrait painter, and in his work he clearly showed his admiration for the old masters, whom he had copied and whose sonorous tonal values came out in his own work. Like his friend Makart he was a society painter and liked to present himself as a painter-prince. He lived in a splendid Italian-style villa in Munich, now a museum, where he received his friends, including Otto von Bismarck. He had other well-appointed residences in Berlin and Vienna, and from 1882 he spent his winters at the Palazzo Borghese in Rome.
*Illustration:*
531  Young Boy in the Sun, c. 1860

## LEONARDO DA VINCI
1452 Vinci (near Empoli, Tuscany) – 1519 Cloux (near Amboise, Loire)
Leonardo was the embodiment of the Renaissance ideal of the universal man, the first artist to attain complete mastery of all branches of art. He was a painter, sculptor, architect and engineer besides being a scholar in the natural sciences, medicine and philosophy. He received his artistic training under Verocchio in Florence, with whose workshop he retained contacts even after having become an independent master. He left Florence for Milan in 1482, working at the court of Duke Lodovico Sforza in the capacities of painter, sculptor and engineer until 1499. When the French invasion of the city caused the Duke to leave, Leonardo returned to his home ground, but worked again in Milan from 1506 to 1513. In 1513 he went to Rome, and in 1516, at the invitation of King Francis I, to France as court painter.

With his "Last Supper" in Milan (ill. p. 161) Leonardo created the first work of the High Renaissance. His representation of the theme has become the epitome of all Last Supper compositions. Even Rembrandt, generally standing aloof from Italian art, was unable to resist its impact. Leonardo's work revolutionised both pictorial and painterly possibilities. While drawing had dominated over colour in the Early Renaissance, with Leonardo the outline was increasingly replaced by the use of mellowed colours which allowed one form to merge with another.

Leonardo was never quite understood in Florence, but this was more than made up for by his influence on 16th century Venetian art. His theories on art too were influential. He also supported his new ideas about painting with a sound theoretical basis. A number of projects remained uncompleted, such as the wall painting of the Battle of Anghiari in the Palazzo Vecchio in Florence, the numerous designs for the two equestrian monuments of Lodovico Sforza and Marshal Trivulzio in Milan, and also some architectural designs (Pavia cathedral).
*Illustrations:*
146  Virgin and Child with St Anne and St John
     the Baptist, c. 1495
148  Mona Lisa, c. 1503–1505
161  Last Supper, 1495–1498
161  Adoration of the Magi, c. 1481
162  Virgin of the Rocks, c. 1483
162  Virgin of the Rocks, completed c. 1506
163  The Virgin and St Anne, c. 1508

## LE SUEUR Eustache
1616 Paris – 1655 Paris
The decoration of the Hôtel Lambert in Paris announced a new style which was established by Le Sueur in the 1640s. While his early mythological paintings from 1644 still owed much to his master and friend Vouet, whose workshop he entered at the age of fifteen and with whom he had painted the ceilings in the Cour des Aides and the Hôtel Bouillon, his later work, such as "Melpomene, Erato and Polymnia" (ill. p. 253) or "Phaëthon in the Chariot" (1647–1649) were strongly influenced by Poussin. The academic classicism of Le Sueur, who also made Gobelin designs after Raphael's loggia frescos, is shown clearly in his 22 panels on the life of St Bruno for the Chartreuse de Vauvert (1645–1648). He often collaborated with his brothers Pierre, Antoine and Philippe, and at times was also assisted by his brother-in-law, Thomas Goussé. Le Sueur, who was one of the founders of the Academy in 1648 and was appointed court painter in the same year, combined cool clarity with an almost sentimental sensitivity, detached dignity and skill at conveying the idea of movement.

*Illustration:*
253  Melpomene, Erato and Polymnia,
     c. 1652–1655

## LEYDEN Lucas van
1494 Leiden – 1533 Leiden
Besides being taught painting in his father's workshop, the young Lucas also learned the goldsmith's and armouror's craft which must have brought his outstanding talent in the art of engraving to its full development. He certainly was exceedingly precocious in that art, as Carel van Mander confirmed. After 1508 Lucas worked in the workshop of Cornelis Engelbrechtsz. His passion for the realistic depiction of figure, landscape and architecture became merged with the coloration and characteristic outline of Italian Mannerism after his meeting with Gossaert around 1527. Problems still exist with the attribution of his painted works and their stylistic development. But he left a great number of engravings which were greatly influenced by Dürer, whom he had met on his visit to Antwerp in 1521.
*Illustration:*
202  Lot and his Daughters, c. 1520

## LEYSTER Judith
(also: Leijster)
1609 Haarlem – 1660 Heemstede
With her father, a Haarlem brewer, Judith came to Utrecht in the 1620s. There she was introduced to the characteristic handling of light by the Utrecht Caravaggisti, such as Honthorst and Terbrugghen. In about 1630 she was probably a pupil of Frans Hals in Haarlem, whose style she followed in her portraits and genre scenes, but giving the impression of some superficiality compared with her mentor. In 1636 she married the genre painter Jan Miense Molenaer and achieved for a brief period a personal note with her small multi-figured genre scenes and her preference for light blue and light grey tonality.
*Illustration:*
317  Carousing Couple, 1630

## LICHTENSTEIN Roy
1923 New York – 1997 New York
Lichtenstein studied art at the Ohio State University in Columbus from 1940 to 1943. From 1946 to 1950 followed a period of further study, concluding this at the Art Students League in New York. He at first followed in terms of both motif and style Frederic Remington, the major representative of the glorification of the "wild West", but came under the influence of abstract Expressionism in 1957. This period ended in 1961 when he found his personal idiom which made him an exponent of American Pop Art. For models he used comic strips and cartoons which he applied to the canvas greatly enlarged, sometimes with dotted grids after the Beday system. He produced Pop versions of famous paintings by Picasso, Mondrian and others. His colours are brilliant, clear and limited to a few primary tones, and his outlines are always boldly drawn in black.

Between 1964 and 1966 he produced sunsets, landscapes, ancient ruins and a series with brush strokes. In 1966 he discovered an interest in Art Deco of which he became a collector and which provides the inspiration for his paintings and sculptures. Lichtenstein is primarily a painter, but he has also produced designs for works in ceramic, steel and glass which have been produced industrially.
*Illustrations:*
625  Razzmatazz, 1978
662  M-Maybe (A Girl's Picture), 1965

## LIEBERMANN Max
1847 Berlin – 1935 Berlin
Liebermann was taught drawing before attending the Weimar Academy from 1868 to 1872. In 1871 he met in Düsseldorf the Hungarian painter Mihály von Munkácsy who inspired him to work on his successful painting "The Goose-Pluckers" (Berlin, Nationalgalerie). In the same year he visited Holland for the first time, and from 1913 he travelled there every year. From 1873 to 1878 he lived in Paris, where he followed the work of Courbet, Millet and Ribot, spending the summer months in Barbizon. He visited Venice in 1878 and settled in Munich for six years. In 1884 he returned to Berlin. Liebermann went three times to Italy, was co-founder of the Berlin Sezession in 1899, was elected to the board of the German Artists' Association in 1904 and became the president of the Academy of Fine Arts in 1920. Initially he adhered to realism, but towards 1890 came under the influence of Impressionism. Besides paintings, he produced drawings, watercolours and etchings, and also wrote theoretical works.
*Illustration:*
534   The Parrot Walk at Amsterdam Zoo, 1902

## LIMBURG Paul, Jean, Herman
after 1385 Nimwegen (?) – c. 1416 Bourges (?)
The three brothers came from the Aachen area. Their father was a picture-carver, their uncle the celebrated Burgundy court painter Jean Malouel (Malwael). According to records the two younger brothers Jean and Herman were apprenticed to a Paris goldsmith in 1399. In 1402 the three received a commission from Duke Philip the Bold of Burgundy to illuminate a so-called *Bible Moralisée* (which still survives). The fee was considerable, which leads to the assumption that they must already have had a good reputation. On Philip's death all three went into the service of the Duke of Berry. On the Duke's moving the workshop to Bourges in 1411, Paul, the eldest and most prominent of the brothers, was presented with a grand house previously inhabited by the Duke's treasurer. A close relationship existed between the Duke and the artists, and, according to records, Paul in particular often received presents and was appointed "valet de chambre" in 1413, while another brother was made a canon of the cathedral chapter at Bourges. The death of all three brothers is documented in 1416, probably caused by an epidemic. They had not yet reached their thirtieth year, leaving *Très Riches Heures* uncompleted. The Duke died in the same year at the age of 76. The brothers seem to have based their work on the art of Malouel. The Duke of Berry admired the art of Lombardy, and it is probable that the three miniature-painters visited that part of Italy with commissions from the Duke. Their work can be seen as the climax of painting around the turn of the century, being the culmination of one period and a transition to the next.
*Illustrations:*
62   Miniature on the Prayer "On preparing for a journey", after 1410
62   Expulsion from Paradise, 1414–1416
63   Calendar of the months: January, 1414–1416
63   The Temptation of Christ and The Castle Méhun-sur-Yèvre, 1414–1416
64   Calendar of the month: June, 1414–1416

## LINDNER Richard
1901 Hamburg – 1978 New York
Lindner studied at the school of applied arts in Nuremberg from 1922 to 1924, then at the Munich school and academy, and finally in 1927/28 at the Berlin academy. From 1929 to 1933 he was artistic director of the publisher Knorr & Hirth in Munich. Nazism forced him to leave for Paris in 1933, where he worked as a graphic designer. He then emigrated to the USA in 1941. There he supported himself as an illustrator of books and magazines, including *Vogue* and *Harper's Bazaar*. He was naturalised in 1948, and from 1950 he devoted himself again to painting. In his early years Lindner had been involved with German Expressionism, then with the Neue Sachlichkeit. He now developed a style combining his early impressions with his experiences as an illustrator and his encounter with American Pop Art. Lindner taught at the Pratt Institute in Brooklyn from 1952 to 1965. From 1971 he had made his home in New York and Paris.
*Illustration:*
656   The Meeting, 1953

## LIOTARD Jean-Étienne
1702 Geneva – 1789 Geneva
Liotard, whose family was French, was trained as a miniature-painter and engraver in Geneva. In 1723 Jean-Baptiste Masse became his teacher in Paris. His friendship with Lemoine inspired him to take up pastel and portrait painting. A visit to Rome, where he copied old masters, in particular Correggio, was followed by eastern travels in 1738, accompanied by Sir William Ponsby. During his five-year stay in Constantinople he adopted Turkish customs and traditions. In Vienna he painted the Empress Maria Theresia's family and the famous "Chocolate Girl" (Dresden, Gemäldegalerie). As portrait painter he worked in Venice, Lyon, Paris and London before settling finally in his home town in 1757. His work is characterised by light coloration and detailed rendering of a world almost without shadows. Liotard's perfectly even surfaces give away the fact that he had trained as an enamel painter.
*Illustrations:*
378   Turkish Woman with Tambourine, c. 1738–1743
378   Portrait of François Tronchin, 1757

## LIPPI Filippino
c. 1457 Prato – 1504 Florence
The son of Fra Filippo Lippi studied under his father, assisting on his last work, the apse decoration in Spoleto cathedral. In 1472 he is mentioned in connection with Botticelli, who influenced him greatly. His earliest panels are hardly distinguishable from those of his great master. Around 1481 Filippino must already have had a reputation in Florence as he was commissioned to complete the fresco cycle in Brancacci chapel which Masaccio and Masolino had left unfinished. By incorporating Flemish elements which determined the brilliance of his colours, the young painter reached the pinnacle of his career over the next few years ("The Vision of St Bernard", ill. p. 109). In the 1490s Filippino intensified Botticelli's melodious lines to convey a feverish unrest ("Adoration of the Magi", 1496). While in Rome, where he studied ancient monuments with great passion, he painted the frescos in the Caraffa Chapel of Santa Maria sopra Minerva. In these, he explored Antiquity, but appointed it a place restricted to detail, and in the overall conception and exuberant ornamentation brother all principles of this era's art. He again adopted this manner in the Strozzi Chapel of Santa Maria Novella in Florence, completed in 1502. In these works the vitality of the figures, the freedom of line and the complexity of architecture often seem to approach a complete lack of restraint. Here, the gates were thrown open for the "anti-classical" stance of 16th century art, where Mannerism would find its stimulus; even Michelangelo must have acquainted himself with Filippino's repertoire of figures before embarking on the Sistine Chapel in 1506.
*Illustration:*
109   The Vision of St Bernard, c. 1486

## LIPPI Fra Filippo
c. 1406 Florence – 1469 Spoleto
Lippi is one of the most important successors to Masaccio. In 1421 he entered the monastery of Santa Maria del Carmine in Florence and was able to observe the decorative work in progress in the Brancacci Chapel. He used this experience in his first work, the frescos in the cloisters of the monastery (1432), now only surviving in fragments, with their plastic figures and individual facial expressions. His Madonna of Tarquinia, 1437 (Rome, Galleria Nazionale), is in her clear articulation reminiscent of Masaccio's altarpiece in Pisa. In the 1440s, complex movements and a restless treatment of drapery are discernible ("Annunciation", Florence, San Lorenzo). These were the elements on which his great pupil Botticelli informed himself. With the decoration of the cathedral choir in Prato between 1452 and 1465, his artistic development reached its culmination, ranking him with Fra Angelico among the most outstanding fresco painters of his time.

Lippi was chaplain to Santa Margherita in Prato from 1456, but he had to leave the order as he had formed a relationship with the nun Lucretia Buti, who bore him a son, Filippino (born about 1457), who as a pupil and assistant of Botticelli was to give the latter's late style certain Mannerist features. In his own late period Lippi painted various versions of the "Adoration of the Child", the most famous being the one produced for the house chapel of the Palazzo Medici (now in Berlin, Gemäldegalerie). With its fairy-tale atmosphere created by light and shade, the rich use of gold and the magnificent flower carpet, this panel represents one of the finest achievements of the period.
*Illustration:*
102   The Feast of Herod. Salome's Dance, c. 1460–1464

## LISS Johann
(also: Jan Lys)
c. 1595 Oldenburg – c. 1629/30 Venice
His surviving works are few, the facts about his life sparse. After an early training by his father, he went by way of Amsterdam, Haarlem, Antwerp and Paris to Venice where he remained, except for a stay in Rome of unknown duration, until his death during the Plague. The significance of his time in Haarlem can be seen clearly in his many genre scenes which show his familiarity with late Haarlem Mannerism, specifically the works of Goltzius and Buytewech. His later work in high Baroque owed more to the young Jordaens in Antwerp. When in Rome, Liss became influenced by Fetti, the Carracci and Bril, as well as by the Caravaggists, whose ideas were already known to him through the Flemish branch. Poelenburg in Rome provided a contact with mythological painting which in Liss's work, however, always remained bound up in landscape. While the "Outdoor Morra-Game" (Kassel, Staatliche Kunstsammlungen, c. 1622) still showed the Dutch genre painter, his late religious work, such as the altarpiece with the "Inspiration of St Jerome" (Venice, San Niccolò da Tolentini), characterised by its flaky-loose brushwork and light coloration, was to become significant for 18th century Venetian painting.
*Illustration:*
256   The Death of Cleopatra, c. 1622–1624

## LISSITZKY El
(Eliezer Markovic Lissitzky)
1890 Polschinok (near Smolensk) – 1941 Moscow
After studying architecture, which he began in Darmstadt in 1909, Lissitzky returned to Moscow in 1914. Chagall called him to the art school at Witebsk in 1919. He joined the Unovis (new art) group led by Malevich and started painting his "Proun" series aimed at complete spatial reorganisation. "Proun" (= pro unovis), in combining Suprematist and Constructivist ideas, aimed to burst open closed space by means of asymmetry, disharmony and arythm, and so offering the human being a non-Euclidian, dynamic, spatial consciousness, open on all sides. In 1921 he became the head of the architectural faculty "Wchutemas". In the 1920s Lissitzky was the most important artistic mediator between eastern and western Europe. In 1923 he was able to realise a "proun" room in Berlin, and he arranged exhibition rooms in Dresden and Hanover for non-representational art.
*Illustration:*
596   Proun 19D, c. 1922 (?)

## LOCHNER Stefan
c. 1400 Meersburg (?) – 1451 Cologne
According to records, Lochner (documented 1442–1451) was born in Meersburg, Lake Constance, but came from Constance to Cologne. It is not known where he was trained and when he came to Cologne. The dating of his work points to the fifth decade of the 15th century. Lochner must have been familiar with contemporary Dutch art (Campin and van Eyck), but direct thematic adoptions are rare. Undoubted is the fact that he orientated himself towards the older masters when in Cologne. The personal always comes first in his art; any connections with schools or contemporary painting stand back. Lochner always used his artistic devices to correspond closely with subject matter, purpose and requirements. With his freshness of colour and charm of style he had no equal in central Germany until Schongauer. Lochner was elected to the city council of Cologne in 1447 and 1450 which proves that he was highly respected. He also had a flourishing workshop, where his book illuminations were produced, and where the work was carried on after his death during the Plague in 1451.
*Illustrations:*
76   Adoration of the Child, 1445
76   The Presentation in the Temple, 1447
77   The Virgin of the Rose Garden, c. 1448

## LONDON THRONE OF GRACE → Master

## LONGHI Pietro (Pietro Falca)
1702 Venice – 1785 Venice
Like other Venetian painters of the Rococo, Longhi studied in Bologna, first under Antonio Balestra, then under Crespi. In about 1730 he was back in Venice. He was not successful, either with his early historical paintings nor with his religious works, so, from the 1740s, under Crespi's influence, he began to paint mainly genre pictures recording Venetian life. In the manner of Watteau and his successors he created a personal form of conversation piece, depicting fashionable Venetian society with a fine, wry irony. In 1756 he became a member of the Academy, where he taught from 1758 to 1780. The affinity between Longhi's genre pictures and Goldoni's comedies (Longhi had contacts with him) is often pointed out, and rightly so. Longhi was also a considerable portrait painter.
*Illustrations:*
374   The Rhinoceros, c. 1751
374   The Tooth-Puller, c. 1746–1752

## LORENZETTI Ambrogio
c. 1290 Siena (?) – c. 1348 (?) Siena (?)
Ambrogio was probably the younger brother of Pietro Lorenzetti and so came from the same artistic background. Ambrogio, who is recorded as active in Siena from 1319 to 1347, paid at least two lengthy visits to Florence. This might explain his profound knowledge of Giotto's art and of his successors, and also the interaction in his work between Sienese and Florentine art, particularly with respect to the small-scale devotional picture. His treatment of space was the most advanced of his time, and his observation of nature was as remarkable as his brother's. His manner of painting was light and assured, using movement to express rhythm and emotion. Unlike Pietro's sombre air, Ambrogio created a bright, relaxed atmosphere.
*Illustrations:*
39   Madonna and Child Enthroned, with Angels and Saints, c. 1340
40   Allegory of Good Government, c. 1337–1340
41   Life in the City. From: The Effects of Good Government, c. 1337–1340
41   Life in the Country. From: The Effects of Good Government", c. 1337–1340
42   Nursing Madonna, c. 1320–1330

## LORENZETTI Pietro
c. 1280–1290 Siena (?) – 1348 (?) Siena (?)
Lorenzetti is recorded as active from 1306 (?) until 1345, but as is the case with other great Sienese masters we know little about his life, and the chronology of his work presents problems, although some signed and dated paintings survive. If the work carried out in 1306 for the city of Siena was by his hand, then he must have been born no later than around 1290. The first dated work is the altarpiece (1320) in the Pieve di Arezzo. The frescos in the Lower Church of Assisi (ill. p. 38) are possibly somewhat earlier. These show that Pietro attempted a synthesis of Duccio and Giotto, whose work he must have studied. Even elements of Cimabue can be recognised, as can the innovations of Simone Martini and the expressive powerfulness of Giovanni Pisano. And yet an individual style emerges, showing an astounding feeling for time and season, light and shade, and an acute awareness of the realities surrounding human life. In his frescos Pietro aimed at massed effects, sometimes at the cost of thematic clarity, while using a completely different approach in his panel works. The contrast demonstrates the scope and adaptability of his art. He preferred cool colours, particulary green and grey tones. Pietro, who was probably the elder brother of Ambrogio, sometimes collaborated with his brother, and it is probable that both died during the great Plague of 1348 which wiped out half the population of Siena.
*Illustrations:*
37   Birth of the Virgin, 1342
38   Sobach's Dream, 1329
38   The Deposition, c. 1320–1330

## LORENZO MONACO
(Piero di Giovanni)
c. 1370 Siena (?) – c. 1425
Records show that Lorenzo Monaco was active in Florence between 1388 and 1422, and he was probably born in Siena. Of the Sienese painters, the most influential for his work was Simone Martini, but his tonal sequence also suggests the influence of Pietro Lorenzetti. His early Florentine work showed his involvement with the Giotto successors, such as Agnolo Gaddi. Although these influences again became subordinate, Lorenzo Monaco never returned to the planar strictness of the older Sienese school. In 1390 he became a Camaldolese monk in Florence, entering the monastery of Santa Maria

degli Angeli. In 1402 he was accepted by the Florentine Guild. It seems that he left the closed monastic community at this time, but without giving up his orders. In 1414 he rented a house belonging to the monastery. He produced a number of miniatures in the service of the monastery. No other painter in Florence around 1400 went as far as Lorenzo in terms of stylisation of form and colour: sometimes he departed entirely from plausibility. But it would be unjust to call him a mere decorative artist; he opened up possibilities in the representation of the spiritual and visionary.
*Illustrations:*
56   The Annunciation, c. 1410–1415
56   Adoration of the Magi, 1421/22

## LORRAIN Claude
(Claude Gellée, called: Le Lorrain)
1600 Chamage (Lorraine) – 1682 Rome
At the age of fourteen Lorrain came to Rome and, while working in artists' studios, came to the notice of Agostino Tassi, the landscape painter, who gave him lessons. Except for a period in Naples (1619–1624) and in his home country (1625–1627), he always remained in Rome. There he painted frescos of landscapes in the Palazzo Crescenzi and Palazzo Muti. He became a member of the Accademia di San Luca in 1634, and three years later was regarded as the leading landscape painter in Rome. He attracted the attention of the leading nobility and church dignitaries. Amongst others, the King of Spain commissioned seven religious paintings for his palace Buen Retiro. However, all his life his speciality remained the landscape in various forms, presenting it as veduta, as mythological scene and as a stage for stories from the Old Testament. His figure representation, influenced by the so-called multi-figured "bambocciades", was not very adept and often not carried out by himself. His landscapes, unlike those of Poussin, are characteristic in their relaxed, peaceful air, and painted in a large range of muted tones. With their bright atmosphere and their use of pieces of architecture of Antiquity as items of stage scenery they set an example for classical landscape painting in the 18th and 19th centuries.
*Illustrations:*
248   Landscape with Cephalus and Procris reunited by Diana, 1645
248   Landscape with Apollo and Mercury, c. 1645
249   Seascape in Sunrise, 1674

## LOTH Johann Carl
(also: Lotto, Carlotto)
1632 Munich – 1698 Venice
After receiving instruction from his mother and father Johann Ulrich, who himself had been inspired by Caravaggio and Saraceni in Rome, Loth went to Italy in 1653, stopping first in Rome. There he studied the works of Caravaggio and his successors, and proceeded to Venice where, in 1663 he was given the title "gran miniatore" by his fellow artists. His lively manner of depiction was to set an example for southern German Baroque painting, introduced by his pupils Rottmayr, Strudel and Saiter. This style already marked his work in the churches of Venice and the Terra Ferma. Loth's contact with the Venetian Tenebrosi (so-called because of their contrasting use of light and shade and sombre coloration) is apparent in his "Death of St Andrew Avellino" (Munich, Theatinerkirche, 1677). This work also shows his own, closely human approach to the subject. For his mythological and religious scenes he favoured large-figured compositions, defined and dominated by the figures in the foreground. Late works, such as "St Joseph and the Child Jesus, God in his Glory, and Mary" (Venice,

San Silvestro, 1681), show his great talent in fusing earthly and heavenly elements to achieve a realistic whole. Loth, who was greatly esteemed in his lifetime, is now largely, though unfairly, forgotten.
*Illustration:*
258    Mercury piping to Argus, before 1660

## LOTTO Lorenzo
c. 1480 Venice – 1556 Loreto (Marches)
Lotto, one of the most important 16th century Venetian painters, lived an unsettled life far away from his home town. He grew up in Venice under the influence of Giovanni Bellini and the works of Antonello da Messina before travelling in the Marches and being introduced to the works of Melozzo da Forlì and Signorelli. These sharpened his understanding of perspectival construction and precise presentation of human movement. His work in the Vatican (1509–1511), of which no traces remain, indicates early success which, however, did not endure. Although recognised while working in Bergamo from 1513 to 1525, his lack of success in Venice caused him to retire to the Marches in 1549. In his religious works Lotto abandoned traditional patterns of composition. He was also an outstanding portraitist.
*Illustrations:*
158    Portrait of a Young Man, c. 1506–1508
179    Portrait of a Lady as Lucretia, c. 1530

## LOUIS Morris
(Morris Louis Bernstein)
1912 Baltimore – 1962 Washington
Louis studied from 1927 to 1932 at the Maryland Institute of Fine and Applied Arts. Between 1936 and 1943 he lived in New York, then in Baltimore until settling in Washington in 1952. Initially, he was totally under the influence of abstract Expressionism, and it was not until 1957, liberated by the destruction of over 300 pictures, that he developed his purely colouristic style and became an important personality in American painting. He worked on four large series: Veils (1954–1959), Blossoms (1959/60), Unfurleds (1960) and Stripes (1961/62). He saturated unprimed canvases with thinned-down acrylic paint, occasionally using a stick to direct the stream of paint. As the colours were absorbed into the canvas, a soft fusion was created. His friendship with Noland from 1952 had a reciprocal influence on their work. They both taught at the Washington Workshop Center of the Arts.
*Illustration:*
650    The Third Element, 1965

## LUDWIG PSALTER → Workshop

## LÜPERTZ Markus
born 1941 Liberec (Reichenberg, Bohemia)
From 1956 to 1961 Lüpertz studied at the Krefeld College of Applied Arts and at the Düsseldorf Academy. In 1963 he moved to Berlin. In opposition to all contemporary abstract trends, he began to paint simple, representational pictures in the Expressionist manner. From 1966 he called his style "dithyrambic", after the ancient Greek choral hymn in honour of Dionysus, the god of fertility. His pictures, intended to express the beauty of even ordinary everyday objects, were to be comparable to poetry. From 1969 to 1977 he produced a series of "motif" pictures, aking to still lifes compositions which consist of combinations of objects symbolising the past, such as steel helmets, shovels and flags. His "style" pictures from 1977, in which he used abstract ideas of the 1950s, were again replaced by more objective subjects in the

late 1980s and 1990s. He also produces monumental polychrome bronze figures. In 1976 Lüpitz was appointed professor at the Karlsruhe Academy of Fine Arts, and since 1986 he has been teaching at the Düsseldorf Academy, becoming its rector in 1988.
*Illustration:*
674    Babylon-dithyrambic VI, 1975

## MABUSE → Gossaert

## MACKE August
1887 Meschede (Sauerland) – 1914 Perthes-les-Hurlus (Champagne)
While studying at the Düsseldorf Academy, Macke designed stage sets for Louise Dumont, the director of the city's theatre. In 1907 he went to Paris for the first time where he was introduced to French Impressionism and Gauguin. In 1907/08 he studied under Corinth in Berlin. He met Marc in 1909, and contact was established with the New Artists' Association Munich. Macke worked on the Almanac, and on the Blauer Reiter exhibition at the Galerie Thannhauser in Munich, and in 1912 was one of the organisers of the Sonderbund exhibition in Cologne. He went once more to Paris, accompanied by Marc, to visit Apollinaire and Delaunay. He became the German Orphist, with his carefree, brightly coloured paintings in prismaic structure. In the spring of 1914 he travelled to Tunis with Moilliet and Klee for a brief but most fruitful time: his brilliant, clearly arranged water-colours executed there became the highlight of his work. A few weeks after the outbreak of war he was killed in action.
*Illustration:*
587    Girls among Trees, 1914

## MADONNA OF EICHHORN → Master

## MADONNA OF NEUHAUS → Master

## MADONNA OF ST VEIT → Master

## MAGNASCO Alessandro
(called: Il Lissandrino)
1677 Genoa – 1749 Genoa
Magnasco was trained in Milan in the workshop of the Venetian painter F. Abbiati. Starting off as a portrait painter, he soon discovered his true, lifelong theme: landscapes peopled with mysterious, often sinister figures. In 1703 he returned to Genoa, travelled in Emilia and became a court painter at Florence. He worked again in Florence from 1711 to 1735, then finally settled in Genoa. Various strands affected his development. Apart from the Genoan tradition, there are Lombardian traces of Morazzone and Crespi, which he owed to his training. The 17th century Neapolitan "macchia" manner – a spontaneous, patchy method of painting with a penchant for small, genre-like figures – also seems to have influenced his work. His monastic scenes, rendered in browns applied in impasto, were his favourite subject, together with religious and mythological themes. This points to a close affinity to Jacques Callot.
*Illustrations:*
368    Seascape with Fishermen and Bathers, undated
368    The Wise Raven, c. 1703–1711

## MAGRITTE René
1898 Lessines (Hennegau) – 1967 Brussels
After the family had moved to Brussels, Magritte at-

tended there the Académie des Beaux-Arts from 1916 to 1919. He met the Constructivist Victor Servranckx and began to paint abstract geometric pictures, supporting himself by designing posters and advertisements. In 1924 he saw a reproduction of Giorgio de Chirico's "Le chant d'amour" which made a deep impression and caused him to change direction. He founded a group whose aims resembled those of the Paris Surrealists. In 1927 he moved to Perreux-sur-Marne near Paris, living in close contact with Paul Eluard and André Breton. Magritte occupies a special place within the Surrealist movement. He did not experiment, nor did he adopt new techniques. His style was conventional in that he attempted to express comprehensible ideas and perceptions. In 1930 he returned to Brussels, and from then onwards was represented at all Surrealist exhibitions.
*Illustrations:*
611    The Menaced Assassin, 1927
611    Palace of Curtains III, c. 1928/29

## MALEVICH Kasimir
1878 Kiev – 1935 Leningrad
In 1895 Malevich began to study at the Kiev academy. From 1900 he lived in Moscow, where he met Larionov and Gontscharova. In 1910 he took part in the first exhibition of the Jack of Diamonds group of artists. In the following years he passed through phases of Symbolism, Fauvism, Cubism and Futurism, while developing his own style. He reached an important point in his career with the design of scenery in 1913 for the Futuristic opera "The Triumph over the Sun", using abstract, geometrical shapes. At the last Futurist exhibition in Petrograd in 1915 he showed his Suprematist compositions, including the famous picture "Black Square on White Ground" (St Petersburg, Russian Museum).
In 1916 in his paper *From Cubism and Futurism to Suprematism* he made a plea for the necessity of abstract art. After the October Revolution in 1917 he taught at the Moscow State Art School. From 1919 he was involved in the establishment of modern art schools in Witebsk and from 1922 in Petrograd, where he worked with his pupils on the plastic transposition of his ideas. With the "new economic policy" in 1921 began the attacks on the "new art". At the exhibition "15 Years of Soviet Art" in 1932 the works of the "revolutionary artists", including those of Malevich, hung in a separate room – as a warning.
*Illustrations:*
553    Suprematist Painting, 1916
593    Suprematist Composition, c. 1914–1916
593    Knife-Grinder, 1912

## MALOUEL Jean
(Jan Maelwael)
documented 1397 in Paris, died 1415 Dijon
Malouel came from the Dutch province of Geldern. In 1397 he was recorded as a painter to the French Queen. A year later he became court painter to the Dukes of Burgundy in Dijon. He supervised the decoration of the Carthusian monastery of Champmol and was commissioned to paint five altarpieces. He also designed the decorations for court festivities. Malouel, alongside Bellechose, is regarded as one of the outstanding exponents of the International Gothic style in Burgundy. The two paintings attributed to him, "Madonna with Angels and Butterflies" (Berlin, Gemäldegalerie, c. 1410) and "Pietà" (ill. p.66) stand out for their skilled composition, plasticity of figures and sensitive handling of colour.
*Illustration:*
66    Pietà (La grande Pietà ronde), c. 1400

## MANET Édouard

1832 Paris – 1883 Paris

Manet came from a well-to-do background. He came to painting by an indirect route. First he studied law, and then went to naval college, before taking up an artist's career. In 1855 he began six years of study under Couture at the Paris Académie des Beaux-Arts. He devoted much time to copying the old masters in the Louvre, and completed his training by making a number of study tours of Italy, Holland, Germany and Spain. The works of Velázquez and particularly Goya helped form his outlook. Therefore in his early work he often chose Spanish subjects and those of other old masters, giving them his own stamp, however. Initially he gained acceptance at Salon exhibitions with his almost conventional choice of colours and themes, but his famous "Déjeuner sur l'herbe" (ill. p.491) was rejected and caused a scandal because of the presence of a completely naked female model sitting among clothed men.

Although a contemporary and friend of the Impressionists, whose work he admired, he did not follow the aims of pure Impressionism in his own painting. However, when painting in the open, elements of this style can be detected in his work. To him, colours were the supreme device, and in his art he explored their tonal values, limiting himself to a small range of colours, and sometimes contrasting them. As with Degas, his themes were contemporary Paris life, but Manet also portrayed political events, such as the "Execution of Maximilian" (Mannheim, Kunsthalle). Serene interior scenes and the depiction of familiar surroundings and friends occur frequently. He painted portraits of his friend Morisot, of his wife, and of the writers Zola and Mallarmé, and also of politicians and art patrons, including Georges Clemenceau and Antonin Proust. With great skill he captured the peaceful atmosphere in country scenes or by the sea, or cheerful moments in Paris cafés or at the races, making no emotional statements, but using colour tones for expression. His delicate handling of tones is most apparent in his still lifes. Zola, Mallarmé and Baudelaire admired him and paid tribute to his art. In 1881 he was made a member of the Legion of Honour.
*Illustrations:*
485 A Bar at the Folies-Bergère, 1881/82
491 Déjeuner sur l'herbe, 1863
491 Portrait of Émile Zola, 1868
492 Luncheon in the Studio, 1868
492 Argenteuil (The Boating Party), 1874
493 The Balcony, c. 1868/69

## MAN RAY → Ray

## MANTEGNA Andrea

1431 Isola di Carturo (near Padua) – 1506 Mantua
Together with Giovanni Bellini, albeit with different artistic aims, Mantegna was largely responsible for spreading the ideas of Early Renaissance painting in northern Italy. He studied in Padua under Francesco Squarcione, who also collected and sold antiquities and coins, thus introducing his pupil to this field. But most important for Mantegna's artistic development was the sculptor Donatello, who from 1443 created the high altar for San Antonio in Padua. From him he learned how to paint anatomically correct figures, how to achieve precision when tracing details, and not least how to compose a picture with accurate perspective. By 1448 the young painter showed himself almost independent in style when decorating the Ovetary Chapel of the Eremitani Church in Padua (most of it destroyed in World War II). In 1460 Mantegna became court painter to the Gonzaga family in Mantua. There he painted the frescos of the Ca-

mera degli Sposi in the Castello, whose illusionistic ceiling painting and other elements point forward to the structural problems of Mannerism and the Baroque (ill. p.115). In about 1490 he began to produce engravings of great artistic and technical perfection which contributed greatly to the dissemination of Early Renaissance innovations north of the Alps.
*Illustrations:*
85 Portrait of Cardinal Ludovico Trevisano, c. 1459/60
114 Agony in the Garden, c. 1460
114 Dead Christ, c. 1480
115 The Gonzaga Family and Retinue, finished 1474

## MANUEL Niklaus

(called: Deutsch)
c. 1484 Berne – 1530 Berne
Equally talented as painter, draughtsman and woodcarver, Manuel was also a statesman, reformer and poet. He was probably trained as a glass painter. His early works, documented from about 1515, point to the tradition of late Gothic, Swiss painting. Manuel later developed in the direction of the Danube School, with strong, atmospheric emphasis on landscape and lively movement of figures ("Death as Mercenary Soldier Embracing a Girl", "Bathsheba in the Bath", Berne, Kunstmuseum, both 1517). Sudden foreshortenings also show the Mannerist influence. His later works deal mainly with secular subjects. Like all artists of his generation, Manuel was deeply interested in political and religious affairs of the day. In 1516 he joined the French army during the Lombardic war. From 1518 he travelled on political missions and became one of the principal representatives of the Swiss Reformation.
*Illustration:*
198 The Judgment of Paris, c. 1517/18

## MARC Franz

1880 Munich – 1916 Verdun
After studying theology and philology, Marc turned to painting in 1900 and studied art at the Munich Academy. After a lengthy visit to Brittany and Paris and to the Athos monasteries in Greece, he returned to the mountains of Upper Bavaria and also to his studio in Munich in 1905. In the same year Marc found a theme of his own: the animal. In 1909 he moved to Sindelsdorf in Upper Bavaria. A year later he met Kandinsky, Jawlensky and Marianne von Werefkin, became friends with Macke, and soon his first "blue horses" appeared. The colour was meant to depict basic essence, not actual appearance. Together with Kandinsky he organised the two Blauer Reiter exhibitions in 1911/12 and published the Almanac of the same name. With Macke he visited Delaunay in Paris in 1912. From then on, his classical animal pictures took the form of crystalline divisions. Colour, form and movement became a unity, serving at the same time as a symbol of his view of the world: the unison of all creatures with Creation.
*Illustration:*
587 Tyrol, c. 1913/14

## MARQUET Albert

1875 Bordeaux – 1947 Paris
In 1890 Marquet began his studies at the Ecole des Beaux-Arts in Paris, where he met Matisse who became his life-long friend. In 1897 he studied under Gustave Moreau. In order to support himself, he worked with Matisse on the decorations of the Grand Palais of the World Exhibition of 1900. At the 1905 exhibition of the Salon d'Automne his pic-

tures were shown alongside those of Matisse, Derain and Vlaminck, and these caused the critic Louis Vauxcelles to coin the description Fauves. Marquet's name became known, and he travelled widely, visiting Saint-Tropez and Normandy, Hamburg, Naples, Munich, Morocco, Holland and Algeria. He also went to Egypt, Rumania, Russia and Scandinavia. He always came back to Paris, and finally settled there in 1945. His works reflect his many experiences. His technique was to apply colour sparingly, in muted tones of grey and green, setting few accents.
*Illustration:*
562 The Beach at Fécamp, 1906

## MARTINI → Simone Martini

## MARTYROLOGY OF GERONA → Workshop

## MASACCIO

(Tommaso di Ser Giovanni di Simone Guidi Cassai)
1401 San Giovanni Valdarno (Arezzo) – 1428 Rome
Masaccio is considered the greatest master of Italian Early Renaissance painting. Within a time span of about five years he practically formulated the programme for future generations. Little is known about his training. Decisive for his development were the great Florentine sculptors Donatello and Nanni di Banco, and he also explored the early works of Brunelleschi. In the field of painting the only adequate comparison possible is with Giotto: over a period of about a century, Masaccio was the only painter whose work ranked with that of Giotto, in that Masaccio used all painterly devices at his disposal to convey genuine human feeling. In 1422 he was appointed master of the Florentine guild. From 1424 he worked with Masolino on the decoration of the Brancacci Chapel in the Carmine in Florence (ill. p.93 ff.), creating a little later the great fresco of the Holy Trinity in Santa Maria Novella (ill. p.93). With these works he achieved the high point of his artistic creativity, showing absolute assurance in the use of the perspective system together with the ability to suggest the mass and volume of objects in the round. Architecture and landscape appear natural but do not serve as ends in themselves. As in the works of Giotto, they are used to heighten the central scene, further emphasised by a completely novel handling of light and shade.
*Illustrations:*
82 Adoration of the Magi, 1426
93 The Trinity, 1425/26
93 St Peter distributes the Goods of the Community and The Death of Ananias, c. 1426/27
94 The Tribute-Money, 1426/27

## MASO DI BANCO

active in Florence 1320 – 1350
As a master painter Maso worked under Giotto on the great frescos in the Castel Nuovo at Naples, commissioned by King Robert d'Anjou. With Taddeo Gaddi, Maso is one of the most important pupils of Giotto known to us. He is noted for his strict spatial compositions. Between 1340 and 1350, Florence went through a crisis, suffering under a famine and economic and political upheaval. According to records, Maso di Banco was adversely affected by all this.
*Illustration:*
42 St Sylvester Sealing the Dragon's Mouth, between 1340 and 1350

## MASSON André
1896 Balagny-sur-Thérain (Oise) – 1987 Paris
After studies at the Brussels academy, Masson went on the advice of Émile Verhaeren to Paris in 1912. He was called up in 1914 and, severely wounded, and had to spend some time in a sanatorium. In 1922 he returned to Paris, joining the Surrealists gathered around Breton in 1924. He belonged to the group until 1929 and then again from 1937. Masson developed a method of automatic drawing which came close to the Surrealist concept of uncontrolled thought processes and which he later applied to his linear paintings. From 1934 to 1936 he lived in Catalonia, returning to Paris in 1937. From 1941 to 1945 he lived in New York and Connecticut. After the war he lived again in Paris and Aix-en-Provence. Masson illustrated a number of books and developed new graphic printing techniques.
*Illustration:*
605   Meditation on an Oak Leaf, 1942

## MASSYS Quentin
(also: Matsys, Metsys)
c. 1465/66 Leuven – 1530 Antwerp
Massys probably received his training in Leuven under the influence of Bouts. His work remained rooted in Netherlandish art, but he adopted elements of the Italian Renaissance to which he must have been introduced indirectly. Little is know about his early work. His "Anna Altar" (Brussels, Musées Royaux, 1507–1509) shows his fully developed style. Elements of van der Weyden and the use of new insights into figure and space representation are combined in his "St John Altar" (Antwerp, Koninklijk Museum voor Schone Kunsten, 1508–1511). For Massys, the figure, often monumentalised, formed the central point of his work. Hence his talent for portraiture, which he sometimes used as the starting point in his genre paintings (ill. p.200).
*Illustrations:*
200   The Money-Changer and his Wife, 1514
200   Portrait of a Canon, c. 1510–1520 (?)

## MASTER OF THE ANTWERP POLYPTYCH
active about 1400 in southern Holland and on the Lower Rhine
Stylistic and iconographic details suggest that the painter of these six small panels lived in the region of Aachen around 1400. Some of them are now in the Walters Art Gallery in Baltimore and the rest are in the Museum Meyer van den Bergh in Antwerp. The work probably comes from the Champmol monastery near Dijon; its construction is very much like the Orsini polyptych by Simone Martini (ill. p.36). The centre piece consists of two pictures, the Nativity and the Crucifixion; on the left we see the Annunciation, and on the right the Resurrection. The backs of the outer pieces show (without a gold background) the Baptism of Christ and a picture of St Christopher.
*Illustration:*
60   Nativity, c. 1400

## MASTER OF THE BERLIN NATIVITY
active c. 1330–1340 in southern Germany
Because of its resemblance to the manuscript clm 17005 dating from the years 1330–1340 in the Bavarian Staatsbibliothek (state library), Munich, it is possible to date and place the Berlin picture fairly accurately. The manuscript was given by the Emperor Ludwig the Bavarian to the Schäftlarn monastery, south of Munich. The painter probably worked in Munich, possibly also in Nuremberg, as the Heilsbronn altarpiece from c. 1346 is in the same tradition. Other works from his circle can be seen at the Bavarian Nationalmuseum, Munich. The

painter had direct knowledge of Italian art. In form and coloration, but also in the way of embossing and applying the gold ground, he came particularly close to Florentine art. He also seems to have been familiar with Sienese painting.
*Illustration:*
44   Nativity, c. 1330–1340

## MASTER OF THE EICHHORN MADONNA
active c. 1350 in Prague
Named after the Madonna panel which came from Eichhorn castle in Moravia, but probably originating in Prague. No other work of this master survives. In terms of motifs, there is an affinity with the Master of Hohenfurth, but he surpasses the latter's work. If there had been a connection at all, it could only have been a master-pupil relationship between Eichhorn and Hohenfurth. The picture seems to be an early work, taking into account the desire of Emperor Charles IV for greater dignity and monumentality in works of art.
*Illustration:*
45   Eichhorn Madonna (from Eichhorn, Moravia), c. 1350

## MASTER FRANCKE
c. 1380 Hamburg (?) – c. 1436 Hamburg
Francke (documented 1424–1436) seems to have come from a family of shoemakers who had moved to Hamburg from Zutphen in Geldern. His probable date of birth was about 1380, as he was several years younger than Konrad von Soest, who was one of his masters. Francke entered the Dominican monastery of St John in Hamburg, where he worked as a painter. He probably did not have a large workshop, but even as a monk his freedom of movement was barely restricted, and he probably gained extensive knowledge of Western art through travelling. He was highly regarded by the Hamburg merchants who supplied him liberally with commissions, and he even produced work for Reval and for the See of Münster. His influence was great and continued well into the 1460s. Unfortunately, the major part of his work was destroyed in the iconoclasm of the Reformation.
*Illustration:*
75   The Miracle of the Wall, 1414

## MASTER OF GUILLAUME DE MACHAUT
active c. 1350–1355 in Paris
This illuminator's work, which was discovered and dated by François Avril, comprises several manuscripts mainly produced for the court. He is called after the most important of these, the collected works of Guillaume de Machaut who, although a theologian, wrote courtly literature. His main subject was courtly love, allegorically veiled with many adorning and erotic elements, and presented in the over-refined manner of courtly life of about 1340. This style of writing ran parallel to contemporary tastes in art. It also reflected that fashion in dress, which was designed to emphasise the rounded contours of the body, using rich materials with a wealth of adornments, such as flounces, frills and ribbons. In painting, nature was beginning to find a place, but in a most artificial manner. The Master of Guillaume de Machaut succeeded in producing in his large workshop a fantasy world that met the demands of contemporary taste.
*Illustration:*
43   The Tale of the Lion: The Secret Garden, c. 1350–1355

## MASTER OF HOHENFURTH
active c. 1350 in Bohemia
The master is named after a series of nine panels

from the Cistercian monastery of Hohenfurth in southern Bohemia, now at the Národni Galeri in Prague. As G. Schmidt rightly stated, this not very significant artist combined elements of varying origins and traditions and used a variety of motifs without much originality. This may explain the heterogeneity of the works.
*Illustration:*
44   The Agony in the Garden, c. 1350

## MASTER OF THE KAUFMANN CRUCIFIXION
active c. 1340 in Prague
Of this important master only this one panel from the Kaufmann collection survives (now Berlin, Gemäldegalerie). This painting is doubly precious as it proves the excellence of Bohemian panel painting in central Europe around 1330–1340, and that already several significant painters were active in Prague at the beginning of the reign of Charles IV, including the masters of the Glatzer Madonna and the Boston Death of Mary. Although the work still cannot be placed with full authority, it contains two motifs used by the Master of Hohenfurth (ill. p.44), and also its underpainting and flesh colour as well as choice of colours and method of application, all are similar to that only found in contemporary Bohemian painting. The Master of the Kaufmann Crucifixion was familiar with the new insights of Italian art, but he showed no preference for a particular painter or school, and he certainly was no imitator. He seems to have delighted in strange head-dress, some of which are clearly the product of his own imagination. His artistic achievement lies in his creation of stark contrasts, so unlike the homogeneous opposites in Italian concepts. Expressiveness and ideality, the beautiful and the ugly, are placed side by side.
*Illustration:*
45   The Crucifixion, c. 1340

## MASTER OF THE LONDON THRONE OF GRACE
active c. 1420–1440 in Austria
Named after a painting of the Throne of Grace at the National Gallery, London, probably originating in Styria. This master belonged to the same group of painters as the Master of the Offerings. Whether they worked wholly in Vienna and surroundings or in Styria is not yet clear. Nor could be established satisfactorily whether the little panel from St Lambrecht was, in fact, the work of the Master of the London Throne of Grace. This panel shows in terms of coloration the influence both of Bohemian and Franco-Flemish art. The dating of it of "around 1420" is the result of a hypothetical identification by the Benedictine monks of St Lambrecht.
*Illustration:*
73   Madonna, c. 1420

## MASTER OF MOULINS
(Jean Hay or Hey)
active c. 1480– after 1504
A French painter and miniaturist of Dutch origin, he was named after a triptych in the cathedral of Moulins. The portraits on the altarpiece of the patrons Duke Peter II of Bourbon and his wife Anna would indicate that the painter worked in court circles, and from about 1483 in the province of Bourbonnais. In contrast to the somewhat older Fouquet, the Master of Moulins rejected a worldly approach. To the number of late 15th century panel paintings grouped around the triptych also belong, amongst others, "Charles II of Bourbon, Cardinal Archbishop of Lyon" (Munich, Alte Pinakothek), "Joachim and Anna Meeting at the Golden Gate" (London, National Gallery, 1500) and "St Mauritius

with Patron" (Glasgow, Art Gallery and Museum, c. 1500). It cannot be accepted that the Master of Moulins was identical with Jean Perréal, who worked for the Bourbons about 1500 and subsequently for the French royal court until his death in 1529. Instead, it now seems certain that he was the Dutch painter Jean Hay (or Hey). His oil tempera technique shows Dutch influences, as does his emphasis on sumptuous detail, while the clarity of composition indicates a knowledge of Italian art. The reticence of expression and discipline of construction anticipate "classicist" tendencies, which were to determine French painting in the 16th and particularly in the 17th centuries.

*Illustrations:*

89   The Virgin in Glory, surrounded by Angels, c. 1489–1499
141  The Nativity of Cardinal Jean Rolin, c. 1480

### MASTER OF THE NEUHAUS MADONNA
active c. 1400 in Prague

It is not certain whether the painting was destined for Neuhaus. This was probably one of those pictures which were painted in Prague studios and stored in readiness to be acquired by visitors to the city. There is, however, a fresco of a Madonna of the same type in the Minorite church at Neuhaus, albeit from a later date, which might be significant in terms of provenance. The work itself is in bad condition, the upper part having been restored. There is a stylistic similarity with the book illuminations of the missal dated 1409 of the Prague Archbishop Sbinko von Hasenburg (in Vienna).

*Illustration:*

71   Madonna, c. 1400

### MASTER OF THE OFFERINGS
active c. 1420–1435 in Austria

This is the tentative name for a number of pictures which, according to G. Schmidt, should be subdivided. This convinces on close scrutiny. The artists were certainly Austrian, and were active in and around Vienna, probably also in Styria, around the time 1420–1440. They were partly influenced by the paintings of the Bohemian Master of Wittingau, but also by Italian painting of the 14th century, as well as Western tendencies, such as the Limburg brothers (note the execution of dress). The workshop produced a great number of drawings, not so much in the sense of the Italian sketch but rather in the manner of a pattern book. Very possibly a group of painters worked here under a master around 1420. They followed and varied his style, but always repeated the same type of picture and individual motifs. Their influence was noticeable as far as Regensburg and central Franconia. The panel shown here probably belongs to one of the earliest and best works.

*Illustration:*

73   Christ at the Foot of the Cross with Mary and John, c. 1420

### MASTER OF THE PARADISE GARDEN
active c. 1410–1430 on the Upper Rhine

Because of iconoclasm and periods of war in the Upper Rhine region much of the work was destroyed, but remaining examples show that the art of this region exercised a great influence during the 14th and 15th centuries. During the first part of the 15th century the Councils of Constance and Basle would have had a stimulating effect on art production. Because of its affinity to other local works, such as the Strawberry Madonna at Solothurn, the Frankfurt Paradise Garden is undoubtedly a work of Upper Rhenish art, but it cannot be stated with authority whether it was

painted at Strasbourg, Basle, Constance or elsewhere. The Crucifixion panel at the Colmar Museum gives some indication as to its style. This panel dates from 1410 and was painted by a painter trained at the Bruges school, as the study of illuminations carried out there demonstrates. This explains the closeness of some of the motifs used in the Paradise Garden to the early works of the van Eyck brothers.

*Illustration:*

74   Garden of Paradise (Virgin in Hortus conclusus with Saints), c. 1410

### MASTER OF THE PÄHL ALTAR
active c. 1400 in Prague

The provenance of the altar retable from Pähl castle on the Ammersee, which belonged to the Augsburg bishops, is still posing problems because it seems very unlikely that it was painted for this chapel, dedicated to St George. All attempts to trace its origins to Salzburg or Augsburg have failed. In terms of motif and composition it is undoubtedly Bohemian; there are elements which point back to Master Theoderich or the Master of Wittingau. This allows it to be placed in Prague around 1400. This master's art aimed less at invention than at the modification of old motifs. Dress, gestures and heads are typified but at the same time refined, a process analogous to French art of about 1300. Great importance is attached to subtle colour toning and clever surface effects. These were works which appealed to a circle of buyers less interested in thematic innovation than in aesthetic refinement.

*Illustration:*

70   The Crucifixion of Christ between John the Baptist and St Barbara, c. 1400

### MASTER OF THE RAIGERN ROAD TO CALVARY
active c. 1415–1430 in southern Moravia

The master is named after a group of picture panels which came from the Benedictine monastery at Raigern. There is no certainty, however, that they were specifically created for the monastery. Most of his surviving works come from Moravia, the eastern part of what is now the Czech Republic. This, in turn, does not mean that they were painted there: other, similar works were produced in Prague. Besides, it is certain that in terms of motif the Prague school, perhaps that of the Master of Wittingau, served as their example. There is also some affinity to the early works of the illumination workshops and the Martyrdom of Gerona (ill. p. 72), which is another argument in favour of Prague. The painter seems to have sympathised with Hussite reform without breaking entirely with the old church; at least he painted subjects, such as the legends of saints, which do not correspond with Hussite ideas.

*Illustration:*

72   The Road to Calvary, c. 1415–1420

### MASTER OF THE ROHAN BOOK OF HOURS
documented c. 1420–1430 in Paris

The master was named after a book of hours in the Bibliothèque Nationale in Paris, formerly in the possession of the Rohan family. But it was produced for Jolanthe of Aragon, of the French house of Anjou. She also owned the *Belles Heures* and the *Très Riches Heures* of the Duc de Berry, on whose death in 1416 they had come down to her. The master was therefore able to study them there, as well as the many illuminated manuscripts produced for the family in Italy, mostly in Naples. In this book of hours only very few pictures are by the master's own hand, either in the preliminary drawing or comple-

tion. This was generally the case with manuscripts created for the nobility. He was probably a panel painter (at the Laon museum are kept some from his workshop) who carried out book illumination as a sideline. He was not a model court painter, belonging to the generation of the Bohemian Hussite painters, producing unlovely, inelegant work, with a dislike of all decoration. Not without reason did he become the first painter to specialise in the theme of death.

*Illustration:*

65   Lamentation, c. 1420–1427

### MASTER THEODERICH
active from 1359, died c. 1381

In 1359 there was mention of a property owned by Theoderich, court painter to the emperor. He was later entitled "familiaris" in the court records, suggesting that he was a court painter in only a limited sense. In 1367 he received tax exemption for an estate at Morin, at the foot of Karlstein castle, which formerly probably belonged to his predecessor at the court, the Strasbourg painter Nikolaus Wurmser. The exemption was granted for Theoderich's "artistic and solemn paintings" for the chapel which were "innovative" (also in the technical sense). These words from the emperor's own lips were praise indeed. Yet nothing is known about the master's origins and artistic training. His starting point was Bohemian and Italian art, with some elements of north German art. This can be seen especially in the sculpture of the Parler-Hütte, which incorporates the style of 13th century heftiness with a monumental heaviness. It appears that Theoderich met his patron's taste absolutely with his backward-looking monumentality and the integration of various tendencies, including Italian, western and Byzantine elements. Between 1355 and 1375 Bohemian art was entirely under his domination.

*Illustrations:*

25   St Gregory, c. 1360–1365
68   The Crucifixion, c. 1370
68   St Jerome, c. 1360–1365

### MASTER OF TREBON
active c. 1380–1390 in Bohemia

Nothing is known about this master. He was named after his principal work, the altarpiece in the Augustinian canonical church at Wittingau in southern Bohemia. The high altar was consecrated in 1378, so the work was then already completed or perhaps very soon afterwards. The Jérén epitaph, modelled on Wittingau's art, was completed in 1395, setting the upper limit on the date of the altarpiece. The work carried out at Wittingau coincided with the monastic reforms instituted by the emperor. It is therefore presumed that the master's workshop was in the capital city rather than in southern Bohemia. A Madonna panel from his workshop discovered in Raudnitz north of Prague seems to confirm this. The reconstruction of the altarpiece still presents problems. It can be assumed that the two panels shown are from the so-called "working-day side" of the retable as the painter used as reddish ground instead of gold.

In this work the master made use of assistants. It is certain that he had a large workshop and was very influential. We can only speculate about his artistic origins; Italian elements are entirely lacking in his work, while the influence of early Bohemian art is detectable. For example, the motif for the soldier on the left in the Resurrection is taken from the Master of the Madonna of Eichhorn (ill., p. 45), and his handling of light can be traced to Master Theoderich. It is possible that the Wittingau master received inspiration from Franco-Flemish panel painting, but of this nothing survives except for the works of Broederlam which belong to a somewhat later period. The Master of Wittingau was an innovator with regard to contextual and formal representation, and his excellence as a colorist made him the outstanding artist in central Europe between 1350 and 1400.

*Illustrations:*
69    The Agony in the Garden, c. 1380–1390
69    The Resurrection, c. 1380–1390

## MASTER OF ST VERONICA
active c. 1400–1420 in Cologne
This master, whose work was typical of Cologne art of about 1400–1420, is named after the Munich painting. Due to the fact that his style was typical of many Cologne artists of the time and also because Cologne had its own traditional school of painting, and this master greatly influenced other contemporary painters, it is difficult to attribute and date individual panels with any authority. In the course of secularisation all historical sources were lost, none of his works is dated, nor can patrons be established with accuracy.

*Illustration:*
74    St Veronica with the Sudarium, c. 1420

## MASTER OF THE ST VITUS MADONNA
active c. 1390–1400 in Prague
The only surviving work of this painter of the late 14th century is the panel in St Vitus cathedral, Prague. It is not known whether it was destined for the cathedral or whether it actually depicts one of the bishops. The mitre could signify a canon of Prague cathedral or even one of the Benedictine or Cistercian abbots of Bohemia. The saints shown around the frame, namely Wenceslaus, Vitus, Sigismund, Adalbert and Procopius, are all patron saints of Prague cathedral, but at the same time also major saints of Bohemia. Of the stylistic factors which might suggest a date of origin, the small frame reliefs would date the panel clearly before 1400.

*Illustration:*
71    Madonna, c. 1390–1400

## MASTER OF THE WILTON DIPTYCH
active c. 1390–1395
The unknown master of the Wilton diptych was probably English and worked at the English court from about 1380 to 1395. He painted in the International Style and was given this name because his diptych was formerly housed at Wilton, the seat of the Earl of Pembroke. This is his only surviving work. It is outstanding in its delicate coloration, fine handling of line and precisely developed ornamentation.

*Illustration:*
67    The Wilton Diptych, c. 1395 (or later)

## MATHIEU Georges
born 1921 Boulogne-sur-Mer (Pas-de-Calais)
After going to school in Boulogne, Versailles and Rouen, Mathieu studied law and English. For a year he taught English at the Lycée de Douai, then French at the American University in Biarritz. A book by Edward Crankshaw about Joseph Conrad inspired him to paint. His first attempts in 1947 were abstract works. In turn he was influenced by Wols, Pollock and de Kooning, finding his own style in about 1948 and becoming one of the most important representatives of French Tachism. He became noted for his public appearances, at which he produced instant, improvised pictures, often applying the colour to the canvas straight from the tube – a method used in Action Painting. Since 1962 he also produced large sculptures and murals as well as designs for furniture and tapestries. In

1967 he designed a series of posters for Air France. He also produced theoretical works and organised group exhibitions.

*Illustration:*
637    The Decapitation of Olivier III, 1958

## MATISSE Henri
1869 Le Cateau-Cambrésis – 1954 Nice
Matisse studied law and worked in a solicitor's office in his home town. While recovering from an appendicectomy in 1890 he began to paint, moving to Paris in order to study art. Rejecting an academic training, he became a pupil of Moreau, like Rouault and Marquet. In the Louvre he copied the works of Poussin and Chardin, painting in their chiaroscuro manner. While staying in Brittany in 1896 he returned to Impressionist painting. In about 1900 he recognised the independent value of colour and the effect of its luminosity. He began to analyse the works of Cézanne, van Gogh and Gauguin in order to find a new synthesis. While with Signac at Saint-Tropez in 1904 he adopted this painter's pointillist manner. This he gradually abandoned, using longer brushstrokes which finally became areas of colour divided by darker outlines. His work "Luxe, calme et volupté" (Luxury, Peace and Voluptuousness), 1907, became a landmark of the Fauvist style inspired by him. In 1909 he painted the large pictures "Dance" (ill. p.547) and "Music" (St Petersburg, Hermitage) for the Russian collector, Shtshukin.

Towards 1910 he adopted intensy brilliant coloration and simplified forms, lines and colour contrasts to a high degree, creating images of pure joy, unhampered by decorative and ornamental effects. In 1913 he visited Morocco. In the following years, up to 1917, his work temporarily tended towards Cubism. In 1918 he moved to Nice, and his style became looser and softer. From 1943 he lived at Vence near Nice. During this period he produced *papiers découpés*, stuck-together arrangements of cut-out shapes from painted-over paper. His late work lacked the serenity and ease which marked his former concern with perfection and harmony.

*Illustrations:*
547    Dance (La Danse), 1910
565    Dance (La Danse, first version), 1909
565    The Piano Lesson, 1916
566    The Green Stripe (Madame Matisse), 1905
566    Odalisque with Red Trousers, 1921
567    Decorative Figure on an Ornamental Background, c. 1925/26

## MATTA Roberto
(Roberto Sebastián Antonio Matta Echaurren)
born 1911 Santiago de Chile
Matta studied architecture until 1932, then went to work with Le Corbusier in Paris from 1934 to 1935. He met Picasso and observed the progress of his work on "Guernica", and travelled around Europe and the Soviet Union. His first pictures in the Surrealist manner date from about 1937. Two years later he went to New York, joining the Surrealists and becoming greatly influential in the New York art scene, with his abstract works comprising all the elements of psychic automatism. His contribution to abstract Expressionism was significant, and he greatly influenced Gorky and Motherwell. With the latter he worked and visited Mexico. In 1948 he returned to Europe, living in Rome from 1949 to 1954, then in Paris and Tarquinia (Italy). During the 1960s and 1970s he was involved in the peace movement and travelled several times to Cuba. He painted a number of large murals, including those at the University of Santiago de Chile and the UNESCO building in Paris.

*Illustration:*
629    Le Vertige d'Eros, 1944

## MAULBERTSCH Franz Anton
(also: Maulpertsch)
1724 Langenargen (Lake Constance) – 1796 Vienna
After an unremarkable apprenticeship Maulbertsch studied at the Vienna Academy. He was particularly impressed by the frescos of Paul Troger. This influence can be seen in, for example, his work in the Piarist Church in Vienna (completed 1753). There are also Venetian influences (Piazzetta) in his work, and these he used to arrive at his very specific and personal style. Troger's chiaroscuro reappears in mysteriously glowing colours, conveying a hazy atmosphere. In addition to his large and varied productions on walls and ceilings, Maulbertsch also made sketches in oil, and these became works of art in their own right. In the second half of his life Maulbertsch showed an amazing adaptibility to the Classicist movement without abandoning his Rococo origins entirely. His 1794 ceiling fresco in the Strahov monastery library could be called a counterpart of Mengs' Parnassus in the Villa Albani.

*Illustration:*
394    Adoration of the Virgin, 1757

## MELÉNDEZ Luis Eugenio
(also: Menéndez)
1716 Naples – 1780 Madrid
Meléndez received early instruction from his father, a well-known painter of miniatures who worked for the Spanish court. His self-portrait of 1746 (Paris, Louvre) shows his outstanding ability as a portrait painter. After visiting Rome and Naples he worked for King Charles III of Spain. Apart from religious works, he was particularly noted for his still lifes. He painted 44 still life panels for the palace at Aranjuez, of which 39 are now kept at various European and American museums. Meléndez continued the Spanish still life tradition in terms of motif and in coloration, as represented by Sanchez Cotán and Zurbarán: simple pottery, fruits of the fields and gardens, and wooden kitchen utensils in unpretentious arrangements and in colours which stand back from the glow of muted accents.

*Illustration:*
396    Still Life with Melon and Pears, c. 1772

## MELOZZO DA FORLÌ
1438 Forlì – 1494 Forlì
Melozzo came from an artistic family: his uncle was an architect, his brother a goldsmith and his brother-in-law a painter. He was trained in his home town by the painter Ansuino da Forlì, who introduced him to perspectival principles as developed by Mantegna and Piero della Francesca. He first worked in Forlì, then in the 1470s and early 1480s mostly in Rome, where he painted several frescos of which only fragments survive. Around 1475 and then again after 1480 he collaborated with Justus van Gent on the portraits of scholars and allegories of the "Liberal Arts" for the Palazzo Ducale in Urbino. In 1484 Melozzo returned to Forlì where he worked on frescos in the churches of Loreto and Forlì. His work is noted for its precise representation of character and mastery of perspective laws, which make him the precursor of illusionistic ceiling painting.

*Illustration:*
103    Sixtus IV; his Nephews, and his Librarian Platina, c. 1480

## MEMLING Hans
(also: Memlinc or Hemling)
c. 1430–1440 Seligenstadt (Main) – 1494 Bruges
After having long been regarded as the greatest Dutch painter of the late 15th century, Memling is now less admired. Little is known about his train-

ing and early work. Perhaps he was trained in Cologne or one of the workshops in the Rhine region, before moving to the Netherlands. In 1465 he is mentioned in Brussels; from 1466 he worked in Bruges. He was possibly a pupil of Rogier van der Weyden; in any case, Memling's earliest authenticated works were greatly influenced by him. He also drew on Bouts, as shown in his altarpiece of the Life of Mary, 1468 (London, National Gallery). However, he soon developed his own style which is characterised by the great charm of the figures in movement and expression, beautiful colours and narrative richness. Memling could be called the Dutch Gozzoli except that he did not achieve the latter's depth of expression and great skill in figure arrangement. His paintings form the sum of accurately observed and life-like details ("Scenes from the Life of Mary", Munich, Alte Pinakothek, 1480), but there is generally little personal development. His late work shows elements of the Early Italian Renaissance ("Madonna and Child", Florence, Uffizi).
*Illustrations:*
131 The Martyrdom of St Ursula's Companions and The Martyrdom of St Ursula, consecrated 1489
131 Portrait of a Praying Man, c. 1480–1485

## MENGS Anton Raphael
1728 Aussig (Bohemia) – 1779 Rome
By giving him the Christian names of Corregio and Raphael, Mengs' father, a painter of miniature and director of the Dresden Academy, destined his son for a painting career. At the early age of 12 he copied Raphael's frescos in the Vatican. Mengs began his career in Dresden, where he became noted for his fine pastel portraits, and was appointed court painter in 1746. While in Rome he converted to Catholicism and received a professorship at the Capitolinist Academy. A turning point was his meeting with Winckelmann, with whom he developed the theoretical principles of Classicism. In 1762 his book *Thoughts on Beauty and Taste in Painting* appeared. He broke away from the Baroque manner of ceiling painting, using realistic perspectival principles in his ceiling painting at the Villa Albani, 1761. He accompanied Charles III of Spain via Sicily to Madrid, where he executed various paintings for the king and reorganised the royal academy, becoming an authority on matters of art. His classicist-eclectic doctrine ushered out the Rococo, as represented by Tiepolo, in Madrid.
*Illustration:*
394 Allegory of History, c. 1772/73

## MENZEL Adolph Friedrich Erdmann von
1815 Breslau – 1905 Berlin
The son of a teacher and lithographer, Menzel taught himself the art of engraving and painting. After the early death of his father in 1832, he had to support his family, which had moved to Berlin in 1830. His first success came with his illustrations for Kugler's *Geschichte Friedrichs des Großen* (The Life of Frederick the Great), 1838–1842. This gave Menzel his subject-matter. Subsequently he made a name for himself with his scenes depicting the life of Frederick the Great, such as the "Flute Concert at Sanssouci" of 1852 (Berlin, Nationalgalerie), becoming established as the painter of Prussian history. From then on he retained his connections with the house of Hohenzollern in Berlin, later also painting contemporary royal scenes, including the "Coronation of King William I at Königsberg on 18 October 1861" (Hanover, Niedersächsische Landesgalerie). In 1853 he became a member of the Prussian Academy of Arts, in 1856 he received a professorship, in 1883 he was made vice-chancellor of the Order "Pour le mérite"; and in 1898 he was ennobled.

Menzel was not only a masterly and tireless draughtsman, but also a brilliant painter of oil-studies made straight from nature. In this field he had no equal in Germany at the time. Beginning with members of his family and friends, he later added views from windows and country scenery. In his late period he often chose multi-figured scenes which are somewhat reminiscent of the works of the Impressionists in their directness of capturing a moment in time, but nevertheless distinct in their great range of colours, handling of light and careful preparation. His most important realistic work dating from this period was the "Iron Rolling Mill" (Berlin, Nationalgalerie) of 1875 showing industrial workers during production. Before painting it he made innumerable studies at the Königshütte works in Silesia. He was highly esteemed, and decorated by the court at Berlin.
*Illustrations:*
458 The Berlin-Potsdam Railway, 1847
458 A Paris Day, 1869
459 The Artist's Sister, 1847

## METSU Gabriel
(also: Metzu)
1629 Leiden – 1667 Amsterdam
Metsu received early instruction from his parents who were both painters. Later he probably studied under Nicolaus Knüpfer in Utrecht, as did Steen. Initially he worked in Leiden, where he became a founding member of the Lukas Guild in 1648, but moved to Amsterdam in 1657. His early work comprised historical, biblical, mythological and allegorical works influenced by the Rembrandt school. After 1650 he concentrated on interiors and genre scenes, depicting refined middle-class life in warm colours and soft outline. Under the influence of the Leiden fine manner he later paid great attention to detail, particularly rich fabrics, without becoming over-polished.
*Illustration:*
330 The King Drinks (Beanfeast), c. 1650–1655

## MICHELANGELO BUONARROTI
(Michelagniolo di Ludovico di Lionardo di Buonarroti Simoni)
1475 Caprese (Tuscany) – 1564 Rome
As western art's giant of sculpture, no equal can be found for Michelangelo except in classical art. His painting as well as his architectural design was always based on plastic concepts. Though intended by his father to be a scientist, the boy's passionately felt vocation for art soon put an end to any such plans. When aged thirteen, he was allowed to become an apprentice in the workshop of the painter Ghirlandaio, where he probably only learned basic skills. Michelangelo greatly admired Giotto and Masaccio, as his early drawings after their works testify. He might also have known the famous goldsmith and bronze caster Bertoldo di Giovanni. His first works, the bas-relief "Battle of Centaurs and Lapiths" and the "Madonna on the Staircase" (Florence, Casa Buonarroti) reveal the true sources of his plastic art: on the one hand Antiquity, and on the other the highly expressive works of Donatello. Lorenzo de' Medici, showing uncanny intuition for spotting artistic talent, accepted the promising youth to work in the school in the Medici garden which contained a collection of classical sculptures.

Michelangelo reinforced these early impressions while in Rome from 1496 to 1501. Here he created the "Pietà" for St Peter's, his only signed work. Returning to Florence, aged 25, he was next engaged on the colossal "David". In this work he fully realised his perception of the human figure born in the spirit of Antiquity, which filled his contempo-

raries with an uneasy reverence. Between 1501 and 1505 he also received his first painting commissions, including the only authenticated panel of the "Holy Family" (so-called "Doni-Tondo", ill. p. 167). The fresco "Battle of Cascina", of which detail drawings for the cartoon survive, was never executed. In 1505 Michelangelo was summoned to Rome by Pope Julius II to design his sepulchral monument – a gigantic venture which was thwarted by lack of finance and eventually by the Pope's death. Meanwhile the Pope had a new project in mind. In 1508 Julius asked Michelangelo to paint the ceiling of the Sistine Chapel (ill. p. 167 ff). Michelangelo had completed this monumental task by 1512, after having done the work in two stages and under great pressure. As a painter he had produced his masterpiece with its great interpretation of Genesis, the whole concept being conveyed by the human figure and gesture alone.

Michelangelo's subsequent works were also dominated by the human figure. In 1534 he finally settled in Rome. Required to paint the altar wall of the Sistine Chapel, he produced a second masterpiece, the "Last Judgement" (ill. p. 153), 1536–1541. He also painted the frescos for the Vatican's Capella Paolina of the "Martyrdom of St Peter" and the "Conversion of St Paul" (1542–1550). As distinct from all Last Judgement representations that had gone before, Michelangelo's rendering of the subject, which covers the entire altar wall (14.83 x 13.30), is a vision of the end of the human race in which the light of redemption cannot overcome the powers of darkness. With this work he overstepped the limits of contemporary religious understanding; his naked figures in particular were thought offensive. In 1559 the first alterations were made to it by Daniele da Volterra at the behest of Pope Paul IV; after that, the work was four more times over-painted. It remains in this state to this day.

In his later life Michelangelo devoted himself increasingly to architectural projects. In 1546 he directed the building of the Palazzo Farnese and began the new design of Capitol Square. A year later he was made chief architect of St Peter's. With his design for the dome he gave the Eternal City its distinctive landmark. But just as the painter in Michelangelo could never forget the born sculptor, neither could the architect: he did not create "rooms" in the ordinary sense, but "modelled" walls and surfaces.

As no artist before him, Michelangelo threw off the shackles of tradition, opening up entirely new worlds of artistic expressiveness. His work bears witness to his own lived-through experiences and sufferings, and no-one knew better from bitter experience what abandoning the rules meant. There were immense dangers in shaking off restrictions in order to broaden the scale of expression, even when upholding artistic tradition at the same time. With Michelangelo a new kind of artist was born, and he has had an enormous influence on artists ever since. Rubens, who during his 8 years in Italy studied Michelangelo with an intensity and devotion as no other, carried over many of his innovations into the Baroque.
*Illustrations:*
153 Damned soul descending into Hell (detail from the Last Judgement), 1536–1541
167 The Holy Family (Doni-Tondo), c. 1504/05
167 Delphic Sibyl, c. 1506–1509
168 The Creation of Adam, c. 1510

## MICHELINO DA BESOZZO
(Michelino Molinari)
active 1388–1442
Michelino came from Pavia and is mentioned as a fresco painter in 1388, according to which he must have been born around 1370 at the latest. A contemporary source states that he could paint animals

excellently before learning to speak. His contemporary Alcherius, who in his capacity as artistic agent to the Duc de Berry met Michelino in 1410 in Venice, called him "the most outstanding of all painters in the world". Documents in connection with the building of Milan cathedral praise him as "pictor supremus", the greatest painter, and master of stained glass art. None of these works carried out for the cathedral, which was founded by Gian Galeazzo Visconti, survives, nor does any of his architectural work. His talent for animal painting would indicate a training under Giovannino de' Grassi; Stefano di Giovanni (or da Verona) was probably his pupil. His remaining work comprises mostly miniatures in the French manner, which he surrounded with backgrounds of flowers and other ornamentation invented by himself. He was a fine colourist and accomplished portrait painter.
*Illustrations:*
48  The Christ Child Crowns the Duke. Illustration to P. da Castelletto's obituary of Giangaleazzo Visconti, c. 1402/03
48  The Mystic Marriage of St Catherine, c. 1410–1420

## MIERIS Frans van the Elder
1635 Leiden – 1681 Leiden
Mieris, whose father was a goldsmith and diamond cutter, was first apprenticed to a glass painter. He then studied under Dou, the grand master of the very detailed style of painting developed in Leiden, who called him "a prince amongst his pupils". In 1655 he became a member of the Lukas Guild, in 1658 its deacon. He never left Leiden, even refusing an invitation from Archduke Leopold William, governor of Holland, to work at the court in Vienna. He specialised in portraiture and small-sized domestic scenes as well as conversation pieces with an erotic overtone. His cabinet pictures are considered his best work with their delicate handling of light and colour and precise rendering of detail ("House Concert", Schwerin, Gemäldegalerie; "Oyster Feast", St Petersburg, Hermitage).
*Illustration:*
330  Carousing Couple, undated

## MIGNARD Pierre
1612 Troyes – 1695 Paris
At the age of twelve Mignard entered the workshop of Bouchers in Bourges, then continued his studies at Fontainebleau, decorating the chapel of the palace Coubert en Brie when aged fifteen. After studying several years under Vouet in Paris, he went to Rome in 1636, where he worked first as a copyist but soon received commissions for portraits, altarpieces and room decorations. His Madonna pictures, known as "Mignardes", met popular taste in their soft, light manner. The portrait of Pope Alexander VII, painted in 1655 after visits to Mantua, Parma, Bologna, Modena and Venice, showed his great skill in characterisation. On his return to Paris in 1660, his artistic and stylistic approach brought him the enmity of Le Brun but also a great number of commissions, including portraits of the Queen Mother, Mazarin and King Louis XIV. In collaboration with his friend Dufresnoy, he painted the much admired decorations in the cupola of Val-de-Grâce in 1663. In 1664 he was appointed director of the Académie de St Luc, and he was ennobled in 1687. On the death of Le Brun in 1690 he became "principal court painter" and director of the Royal Academy.
*Illustration:*
251  Girl blowing soap bubbles (Marie-Anne de Bourbon), 1674

## MILLAIS John Everett
1829 Southampton – 1896 London
Millais was one of the few artists whose life and career were not marred by difficulties and enmities, and who was rewarded and honoured in his lifetime. When studying at the Royal Academy in London, he met William Holman Hunt and Dante Gabriel Rossetti and, contemptuous of contemporary English art and its academic rules, they founded the Pre-Raphaelite Brotherhood. Lofty moral ideals and ideas were to be made the subject of painting. The painters of this group chose intense imaginative scenes with close imitation of the smallest details of nature. Millais later abandoned the Pre-Raphaelite manner – he broke with John Ruskin, the group's great supporter – and adapted his style to popular taste as he cared about his standing in society. He was eventually ennobled and became president of the Royal Academy.
*Illustration:*
527  Ophelia, 1851

## MILLET Jean-François
1814 Gruchy (near Gréville) – 1875 Barbizon
The son of a Normandy peasant, he received his first art training in Cherbourg. A civic scholarship enabled him to go to Paris and work in the studio of the history painter P. Delaroche from 1837 to 1839. Subsequently he scraped a living together by selling portraits and pictures of gallant scenes in the Rococo manner. Between 1841 and 1845 he lived in Cherbourg, a town he often returned to later in life. Here, and also in Le Havre, he produced his few seascapes. In 1849 he joined the Barbizon school and lived in relative poverty at Barbizon, where he had the companionship of Troyon, Diaz, Dupré and Rousseau. In the early 1850s he found his true métier, the depiction of peasant life.

His best-known pictures date from this period, including "The Sower" (Boston, Museum of Fine Arts, 1850), which brought him success at the Salon in 1851; "The Binders" (Paris, Louvre, 1850), "The Gleaners" (ill. p.442) and "The Angelus" or "Evening Prayer" (ill. p.442). In these works he depicted the hardships of peasant life, but not in the rational and unemotional manner of Courbet. Rather, he endows the frugal existence of these people with an almost religious solemnity created by a twilight atmosphere cast over their large figures. "True humanity full of great poetry" is revealed in the plight of the peasants. In 1867 Millet received a prize at the Paris World Exhibition, but generally he found little recognition. His social conscience made him suspect, and also his works were often considered sentimental. But nevertheless they exercised great influence worldwide in the development of Realism, and in particular on the works of Pissarro and van Gogh. At an auction in 1889 his "The Angelus" (ill. p.442) fetched the sensational sum of 553000 francs.
*Illustrations:*
442  The Gleaners, 1857
442  The Evening Prayer, c. 1858/59

## MIRÓ Joan
1893 Montroig (near Barcelona) – 1983 Palma de Mallorca
While attending a business school, Miró was already going to art classes at the Academy La Lonja in Barcelona. He then worked briefly in a chemist's shop before taking up his studies at the Francisco Gali art academy, 1912–1915, where he was introduced to Impressionist and Fauvist painting. In 1917 he met Picabia in Barcelona, and when visiting Paris in 1919 he made the acquaintance of Picasso and his circle. He began to explore Cubism, was briefly interested in the Dada movement, and moved to Paris in 1920.

Here his art achieved its first height with the poetic realism of his paradisiacal landscapes. Gradually his pictures lost depth, giving way to purely flat painting when Miró joined the Surrealists in 1924 and signed their Manifesto. A strong element of fantasy entered his work, and he also made more abstract paintings.

In 1925 he first showed his works at the Surrealist exhibition. In collaboration with Max Ernst he designed in 1926 the costumes and scenery for Sergei Diaghilev's Ballets Russes. In 1928 he went to Holland to paint his "imaginary portraits" after old masters, at the same time producing his first collages. New forms appeared, and Miró's work turned into a fantastic play of realistic attributes and imagery. In the 1930s, with looming political events, the wittily playful element in his works, of airy figures and floating phantoms with spindly limbs, disappeared. In 1937 he designed the wall decorations for the Spanish pavilion at the Paris World Exhibition, and posters proclaiming the Spanish Republic. Returning to Barcelona in 1942, he began to produce his first ceramics in 1944. In 1956 he finally settled in Palma de Mallorca. His late works again combined lithe figurations of human and animal elements with an artful, naive cosmology.
*Illustrations:*
554  The Poetess, 1940
606  Harlequin's Carnival, c. 1924/25
606  Hirondelle/Amour, 1934
607  People and Dogs before the Sun, 1949

## MODIGLIANI Amedeo
1884 Leghorn – 1920 Paris
After studying briefly at the academies of Florence and Venice, Modigliani came to Paris in 1906 where he led a life dominated by illness, alcohol and drugs. He met Picasso and became friends with Maurice Utrillo and Soutine and was for a time the neighbour of the sculptor Constantin Brancusi who encouraged him to take up sculpture. As a result, he produced caryatids and female heads – influenced in part by the African sulpture he so admired. After experimenting with new media of expression, his own style became fully established around 1915/16. He preferred rust colours, and his subjects were elongated figures with curiously shaped eyes and noses, and oval heads sitting on tube-like necks. In his nudes, a permissive sensuality is encased within severe outlines. All his life he portrayed the people who surrounded him: artists, writers, friends, servants and children, and only when staying with the painter Survage at Cannes and Nice did he paint some landscapes influenced by Cubism.
*Illustrations:*
578  Bride and Groom, c. 1915/16
578  Reclining Nude on White Pillow, 1917

## MOHOLY-NAGY Lázló
1895 Bácsborsod (Hungary) – 1946 Chicago
After studying law in Budapest, Moholy-Nagy did military service from 1914 to 1917; he was badly wounded and began to draw while recovering. He completed his studies in 1918, but decided to turn to painting. He went via Vienna to Berlin in 1919/20, where he produced his first "photogrammes" in collaboration with his wife, the photographer Lucia Schulz. His early work was influenced by the Constructivists Malevich and El Lissitsky, but all his life he constantly experimented with materials and techniques. In 1923 he became a teacher at the Weimar Bauhaus, where he worked with metals and in 1926 published his book *Painting, Photography, Film*. After 1928 he worked in Berlin in various capacities, including scenery builder, exhibition organiser and

art theoretician. In 1934/35 he went to live in London, where he made films and published several documentary works. He also produced sculptural artefacts of plexiglass. In 1937 he was appointed principal of the New Bauhaus at Chicago which, however, soon closed down due to lack of funds. He founded his own School of Design, which he ran until his death.
*Illustration:*
592   Composition Z VIII, 1924

## MOMPER Joos de
(also: Joost, Joes, Josse, Jodocus de Momper)
1564 Antwerp – c. 1634/35 Antwerp
As Bloemaert's influence in Utrecht reached far into 17th century Baroque, so did Momper's in Antwerp. He was a member of an artistic family and was trained by his father Bartholomew. In 1581 he joined the Lukas Guild and became its principal in 1611. It can be assumed that Momper went to Italy and that this journey also took him to Treviso, where the Flemish landscape painter Lodewijk Toeput (Pozzoserrato) worked. In 1594 he was engaged for the decorations for Archduke Ernst's reception in Antwerp. Momper's landscapes, whose subject is frequently mountain scenery, were reminiscent of Pieter Brueghel and followed the usual colour scheme: brown foreground, grey-green middle ground and blue background. But he avoided all Mannerist artificiality, letting nature speak for itself, as also did his successor Seghers. Momper also painted summer and winter scenes of his home country.
*Illustration:*
287   Winter Landscape, c. 1620

## MONDRIAN Piet
(Pieter Cornelius Mondriaan)
1872 Amersfoort (near Utrecht) – 1944 New York
Mondrian came from an artistic family. He studied at the Rijksakademie in Amsterdam under A. Allebé from 1892 to 1897, where he was particularly impressed by Breitner and the landscapes of The Hague and Amsterdam schools. In 1904/05, while on a painting tour in Brabant and Overijssel, he was already painting in a manner detached from what one sees. He continued painting landscapes in the Impressionist style of The Hague and Amsterdam schools until 1906. In 1909 he incurred severe criticism with his fauvist-like landscapes at the exhibition at the Stedelijk Museum in Amsterdam. His years in Paris from 1911 to 1914 were greatly influenced by Cubism. The following years in Amsterdam were decisive in his development. In 1915 he met van Doesburg, with whom he formed the group De Stijl in 1917. In the journal bearing the same title he published a series of articles on new directions in painting. His journey into abstraction started in 1917 with his first paintings of rhythmical horizontals and verticals (plus-minus compositions), followed by those with geometrical grid patterns. Returning to Paris in 1919, he published *Le Neo Plasticisme* in 1920. From this period date his pictures of coloured rectangles with black outlines, the colours being soon reduced to the primaries plus black, grey and white. This trend continued over the next few years, developing an increasing purity of style. In 1930 Mondrian joined the Cercle et carré group and a year later the Abstraction-Création. In 1938 he went to London, then emigrated to New York in 1940. There his style changed once more, replacing the black grid with coloured lines dividing small, colour rectangles.
*Illustrations:*
552   Broadway Boogie-Woogie, 1942/43
597   Oval Composition (Tree Study), 1913
597   Composition No. II; Composition with Blue and Red, 1929

## MORANDI Giorgio
1890 Bologna – 1964 Bologna
Morandi grew up in an old patrician villa, where he lived until his death. He worked briefly in his father's trading business, then studied art at the Accademia di Belli Arti in Bologna from 1907 until

## MONET Claude
1840 Paris – 1925 Giverny (near Paris)
Monet's family moved from Paris to Le Havre in 1843, where the young Claude met the painter Boudin in 1855 in the latter's long-established framing shop, where artists could also display and sell their works. Boudin recognised the boy's talent and began to work with him, converting him to painting in the open. Boudin was soon urging his protégé to go to Paris for a proper training, so Monet took up his studies at the Académie Suisse in 1859, where he met Pissarro. Monet was at this time a great admirer of Delacroix, Corot, Millet and Courbet, and he visited Daubigny and Constant Troyon to get their advice. He also met the open-air painter Jongkind, who impressed him greatly. He was called up for military service in Algeria in 1861, but for health reasons was allowed to return to Paris the following year. He was not on good terms with his family, who refused to support him financially. He found more congenial company amongst intellectuals and artists at the Brasserie des Martyrs – a meeting-point of the Realists and their followers. From 1862 he also frequented the studio of Gleyre, where he met Bazille, Sisley and Renoir, and together with Pissarro these painters formed a friendly group.
   Monet had his first public success at the Salon in 1865, receiving a good review from the critic Paul Mantz in the *Gazette des Beaux-Arts*. But Monet was to pursue aims which led away from the accepted taste of the art establishment. The siege of Paris caused him to go to London with his family in 1870/71 where he met the art dealer Durand-Ruel through the mediation of Daubigny. He then spent some time in Holland. Although he had rented a house in Argenteuil from 1872 to 1877, he often returned to Paris to meet his friends and try to sell his pictures. Only Durand-Ruel, his painting friends and a few collectors appreciated his work, for which he charged little. By the 1870s he had fully developed his style and had banned black from his palette altogether, replacing it with blue. As a means of mutual support several artists formed the Société des Artistes Indépendants, which one critic derided by calling them the "Impressionists" after the title of one of Monet's works. The centre of the group consisted of Monet, Sisley, Pissarro and Renoir, but others joined although they did not conform stylistically, including Cézanne, Degas, Morisot and Cassatt. Manet, like Fantin-Latour, remained aloof although sympathetic to their aims. Between 1874 and 1886 the group held eight exhibitions and several auctions of their pictures, and gradually small successes and some recognition followed.
   In 1878 Monet lived at Vétheuil near his beloved Seine; in 1879 his wife died. In 1881 he moved to Poissy, and from 1883 he finally settled at Giverny, where he created his famous garden with water-lily ponds, finding at last some measure of peace and also inspiration. Here he spent his final years, often receiving friends and never losing interest in what went on in the world.
*Illustrations:*
479   Impression: Sunrise, 1873
498   The Red Boat, Argenteuil, 1875
498   Le Pont de l'Europe, Gare Saint-Lazare, 1877
499   Women in the Garden, 1867
500   The Waterlily Pond, 1900
500   Waterlilies (Green Reflections), c. 1916–1921

1913. Early influences on his work were Cézanne, Renoir and Monet. His first still lifes and landscapes date from 1911. He supported himself by working as a drawing-master at various schools in Bologna. In 1918 his first, strangely constructed, "metaphysical" still lifes were produced, but by 1920, again under the influence of Cézanne, Morandi had returned to a more traditional manner of representation, albeit in a style completely his own. His still lifes show everyday objects, such as cups, salad bowls, bottles and vases. Colour, form and light melt into each other, whereby the distinction between objects and space becomes ever less defined.
*Illustration:*
603   Still Life, 1920

## MOREAU Gustave
1826 Paris – 1898 Paris
Moreau's talent for painting showed itself early and, after studying briefly at the Ecole des Beaux-Arts, he continued his studies with Picot whose studio had a high reputation academically. Moreau admired Delacroix and classical art, and was greatly influenced by Chassériau, a fellow painter who died early. In 1857 he went to Italy for four years, returning with a number of landscape sketches in watercolour and pastel. From then on his direction was clear: themes with allegorical, symbolist content presented in a rich, glowing manner. In 1892 he was appointed professor at the Ecole des Beaux-Arts, his pupils including Matisse, Rouault and Marquet. Some time before his death, he gave his house to the nation for conversion to a museum; it can still be visited.
*Illustration:*
509   The Apparition (Salome), c. 1875

## MORISOT Berthe
1841 Bourges – 1895 Paris
Morisot was the daughter of a senior civil servant of the Département Cher and a great-niece of the Rococo painter Fragonard. She received her first drawing lessons in 1857. In 1859 she made the acquaintance of Fantin-Latour in the Louvre. From 1860 to 1862 she studied with her sister Edma (later Mme Pontillon) under Corot. He encouraged her to paint in the open at Auvers-sur-Oise. There she met Daubigny. Her first landscapes were shown at the Salon in 1864. Her friendship with Manet began in 1868. He painted her and became her mentor. Between 1874 and 1886 she took part in all the Impressionist exhibitions except the fourth, which she missed because of illness. In 1874 she married Manet's brother Eugène. From 1881 to 1883 she had a house built in Paris, opening it as a meeting-place for painters and writers every Thursday. Her visitors included Degas, Caillebotte, Monet, Pissarro, Whistler; also Puvis de Chavannes, Duret, Renoir and Mallarmé, the last becoming her best friend and greatest admirer. In 1882 she showed her work at the G. Petit gallery, and in 1887 at Les XX in Brussels. In 1894, for the first time, the nation acquired one of her paintings. A commemorative exhibition in 1895 at Durand-Ruel's showed 300 of her works and was introduced by Mallarmé. Her daughter Julie married a son of the collector and painter Henri Rouart, her niece Nini Gobillard became the wife of Valéry. Morisot contributed greatly to Impressionism with her fresh and sensitive studies of women and children.
*Illustration:*
501   Young Woman Powdering Herself, 1877

## MOSER Lukas
c. 1390 Weil der Stadt – after 1434
Lukas Moser (documented 1419–1434) was born in Weil der Stadt near Stuttgart, but probably

worked mostly in Ulm, where he also produced designs for glass paintings. Moser is noted for his retable of the Magdalen altar in Tiefenbronn (ill. p. 78), this being his only signed and authenticated work. This is remarkable for its inscription on the frame which sounds like the plaintive cry of an ageing artist: "Schri kunst schri und klag dich ser, din begert iecz niemen mer so o we 1432 lucas moser, maler von wil maister dez werx bit got vir in." But in terms of style Moser was one of the most modern of painters in his time, which might have been the reason why he felt rejected and not understood. Or perhaps his cry can be traced back to the hostile Hussite attitude to art, or to the reforms of the Council of Constance. No doubt Moser had knowledge of the art of northern Italy, perhaps even of the older Tuscan painters. He probably visited the Provence and southern France and had direct knowledge of Franco-Flemish innovations.
*Illustration:*
78    Magdalene Altar, 1432

## MOTHERWELL Robert
1915 Aberdeen (Washington) – 1991 Provincetown (Massachusetts)
From 1935 Motherwell studied at Stanford University in California, the California School of Fine Arts, Valencia, at Harvard, and at New York's Columbia University. He studied philosophy, art history and archaeology. He was a painter, writer, editor of art journals, and teacher. Apart from his paintings, he was also noted for his collages and prints. In 1941 experimented with printing techniques with Kurt Seligman, and consolidated these in 1945 in Stanley William Hayter's "Studio 17". He made a name for himself with his Surrealist theories and automatism in 1941, and soon became one of the most important exponents of abstract Expressionism and Action Painting, along with Pollock and de Kooning. His works are intellectually thought through, and without the spontaneous ferocity and sensualism of those of Pollock and de Kooning, as well as less aggressive. Motherwell also designed wall paintings, including those for the Kennedy Building in Boston. He also was an influential writer and publisher on art. In 1944 he began to publish modern art documents in book form. Together with William Baziotes, Newman and Rothko he founded the *avant-garde* art school "Subjects of the Artists", teaching there for a year. He also taught at Hunter College as well as Black Mountain College, 1950–1959. From 1970 until his death he lived in Greenwich (Connecticut).
*Illustration:*
634    Elegy to the Spanish Republic No. 34, 1953/54

## MOUNT William Sidney
1807 Setauket (New York) – 1868 Setauket
William Mount was apprenticed to his brother Henry, a sign painter, in 1824. After further studies at the National Academy of Design he returned in 1827 for two years to his home in Long Island. Until 1836 he earned his living in New York by portrait painting, but he made a name for himself with his scenes of contemporary life, today seen as typically American folk scenes. With these, he became one of the first American open-air painters. He soon became popular, with his fresh, almost Impressionist manner of painting and uncomplicated compositions, which were to become available in mass-produced reproductions. He kept open house for a circle of writers and painters at his farm Stony Brook. In the 1850s, when his creativity declined, he became engaged in spiritualist studies.

*Illustration:*
471    The Horse Dealers, 1835

## MUELLER Otto
1874 Liebau (Silesia) – 1930 Breslau
After leaving school, Mueller was trained as a lithographer until 1894. On the advice of Gerhart Hauptmann he studied at Dresden Academy until 1896. In 1898 he studied briefly with Franz von Stuck in Munich and began to paint under the influence of Böcklin, Hans von Marées and Ludwig von Hofmann. After working quietly in his home town, he moved to Berlin in 1908, where his friendship with the sculptor Wilhelm Lehmbruck became important for his development. Here he became co-founder of the Neue Sezession and a member of Die Brücke. As his style developed, he used a limited range of colours, painting in a dull, fresco-like, distemper technique. He painted variations on his lyrical theme of people in harmony with nature. During military service, 1916–1918, he made sketches of scenes untouched by war, which he later used for his paintings. In 1919 he received an invitation to teach at Breslau Academy. The summers of 1920 and 1923 he spent with Heckel, to whom he was greatly attached, at the Flensburg Förde, where he produced his few landscapes. In subsequent years he visited Dalmatia, Hungary and Rumania, often travelling with gipsies.
*Illustration:*
585    Lovers, 1919

## MULTSCHER Hans
c. 1390 Reichenhofen – c. 1467 Ulm
Together with Witz, Multscher is regarded as the most important German painter and sculptor of the first half of the 15th century. During the iconoclastic disruptions his first signed work, the sculpted Karg altarpiece in Ulm Cathedral, was badly damaged in 1531. All that remains is the spatial structure divided into several levels, with the window opening backwards, and some figures of angels. The Man of Sorrows on the central pillar of the Western portal of the Cathedral probably dates from the same period. The sandstone model for the sepulchral monument of Duke Ludwig the Bearded (Munich, Bayerisches Nationalmuseum) can be dated around 1434. While the master endowed this work with painterly qualities which hint at his sculptural interests, his painted panels of 1447 of the Wurzach altarpiece are full of sculptural vitality. (It is presumed that this altarpiece came from the parish church in Landsberg on the Lech, ill. p. 143). In the 1450s Multscher added woodcarving to his repertoire. The figures of St Barbara and St Magdalen (Rottweil, Lorenzkapelle) let the structure of the body show under the folds of the drapery, the latter being no longer just purely ornamental. Multscher's finest work was the main altar for the Frauenkirche in Sterzing, 1456–1459. Unfortunately this work, too, has been tampered with. The shrine figures, however, are still in place. They differ from the Rottweil figures in that they look immensely lively, almost passionate, in movement and rendering of drapery, reaching almost a Baroque richness. The panels are closely related to those at Wurzach in terms of motif, but suggest the hand of a younger master.
*Illustration:*
143    Resurrection, 1437

## MUNCH Edvard
1863 Løten (Hedmark) – 1944 Ekely (near Oslo)
Munch came from a family of famous artists and scientists. Tragic family events mark his œuvre. In 1868 his mother died, in 1877 his favourite sister

Sophie died, and his father began to suffer from melancholia. In 1881 Munch began to study at the royal drawing school in Oslo, and under Krohg painted light-flooded, naturalist landscapes and studies of people. In 1885 he visited Paris for the first time. During this period he developed a personal style, using colour and form as vehicles to express atmosphere. In 1889 he had his first one-man exhibition, which brought him a state scholarship. Returning to Paris, 1889–1892, he took drawing lessons from Bonnat and studied the old masters and Impressionism. He visited Berlin in 1892 and exhibited his work at the Verein der bildenden Künstler which caused a scandal and had to be closed. This was followed by the foundation of the Berlin Secession. From 1894 he used many graphic media, publishing a large number of famous illustrations around 1900. In the 1890s he lived mostly in France, Italy and Germany. From 1896 to 1898 he showed his work at the Salon des Indépendants in Paris. In 1902 he exhibited his "Frieze of Life", a series of pictures begun in 1893, at the Berlin Secession of which he became a member in 1904. After a mental breakdown he returned to Norway in 1908, settling in the small fishing town of Kragerø. In 1916 he completed three large murals for Oslo University. From 1916 he lived in Ekely, near Oslo. In 1921/22 he decorated the dining hall at the Freia chocolate factory in Oslo. His eyesight began to fail in the 1930s.
*Illustrations:*
560    Puberty, 1895
560    Girls on the Bridge, 1901

## MURILLO Bartolomé Esteban
c. 1617/18 Seville – 1682 Seville
Murillo was the youngest of fourteen children of a doctor in Seville, where he probably remained all his life, a visit to Madrid in 1642 being unsubstantiated. Being orphaned at the age of ten, he was apprenticed early to a painter by the name of Castillo. He gained sudden fame with the cycle of paintings he did for the cloisters of the the Franciscan monastery in Seville (1645/46). While his earliest works show him working in a tenebrist style derived from Zurbarán and then in the style of Ribera with a preference for cool colours, he soon developed his characteristic style of soft forms and warm colours, which owed something to the works of van Dyck, Rubens and Raphael which he had studied in local collections. Today considered somewhat sentimental, his genre scenes nevertheless represent a new way of perception ("Grape and Melon Eaters", Munich, Alte Pinakothek; "Little Fruit-Seller", ill. p. 267). When Hegel said about Murillo's beggar children that they sat on the ground "contented and blissful almost like Olympian gods", he cleared them of pathos, and so brought out the sensitisation for simple objects and feelings which would first find full expression in the 18th century. Murillo's many devotional pictures, particularly of the Madonna, reflect a piety which was sensitive and close to the people. Apart from this new approach he commanded a brilliant painterly technique, which made him the head of the Seville school. He also founded the Academy of Seville and became its president.
*Illustrations:*
223    The Pie Eater, c. 1662–1672
265    Annunciation, c. 1660–1665
266    La Immaculada, undated
266    The Toilette, c. 1670–1675
267    The Little Fruit-Seller, c. 1670–1675

## NATTIER Jean-Marc the Younger
1685 Paris – 1766 Paris
Nattier received early training from his father Jean-Marc the Elder and then probably was the pupil of

Jouvenet. He studied the older masters in the Galerie du Luxembourg, particularly Rubens. At the early age of fifteen he received an Academy prize for a drawing after Rubens, which pleased Louis XIV so much that he had an engraving made of it. The Russian ambassador sent the young Nattier to Amsterdam to paint members of the Tsar's family who were staying there. Nattier's achievement was to translate the traditional type of mythological portraiture into the language of the Rococo (e.g. "Mademoiselle de Lambesc as Minerva", Paris, Louvre, 1737; "Madame Bouret as Diana", Lugano-Castagnola, Thyssen-Bornemisza Collection, 1745). These paintings, which were not meant to turn the sitters into mythological figures but merely give them their attributes, created a vogue amongst the court ladies and favourites of Louis XV. As such, they form a significant aspect of Louis Quinze painting. Nattier's works are noted for their mother-of-pearl-like lustre, in contrast to High Baroque coloration.
*Illustration:*
353    Madame Henriette as Flora, 1742

## NAY Ernst Wilhelm
1902 Berlin – 1968 Cologne
Nay began to teach himself, but in 1925 attended the Berlin art academy for three years, where Carl Hofer trained and encouraged him. In 1931 he was awarded the Rome Prize. He turned increasingly to Surrealist abstraction, first in his compositions resembling still lifes, then in his large-figured pictures. His art was branded as "degenerate" under the Nazi regime. He often visited the Lofoten islands off Norway to seek in the bleak landscape inspiration for his abstractions. After the war he lived at Hofheim/Taunus, and moved to Cologne in 1951. His exploration of the abstract lasted well into the 1950s. Around 1955 his first round disc compositions were produced, which were of a decorative and sometimes nervous, strong coloration. In the 1960s he adopted elements of the Informel, and noticeably so from 1963 in his series of "Eye Pictures".
*Illustration:*
639    Yellow Chromatic, 1960

## NEWMAN Barnett
1905 New York – 1970 New York
Newman came from a family of Polish Jews. From 1922 to 1930 he studied philosophy and ornithology as well as art at the Art Students' League. In about 1930 he became acquainted with Still, Pollock, Adolph Gottlieb and Milton Avery. He destroyed his early work, but allowed his writings to be published. His theoretical essays *The First Man was an Artist*, 1947, and *The Sublime is Now*, 1948, appeared in the journal *Tiger's Eye*, of which he was co-editor. He did not develop a personal style until the age of 43, when he began to paint "mystical abstractions", variations on the theme of thin vertical colour lines against a monochrome background. With these works he became one of the most important representatives of minimalist colour surface painting. After a first one-man exhibition in 1950, which engendered much hostile criticism, he retired from the world of art for eight years, but subsequently gained wide recognition with the picture series "Stations of the Cross".
*Illustration:*
650    Vir Heroicus Sublimus, 1950/51

## NICHOLSON Ben
1894 Denham (Buckinghamshire) – 1982 London
Nicholson's parents were both painters, but he himself studied only briefly at the Gresham School in Holt and at the Slade School of Art in London.

When in Paris in 1921, he became greatly inspired by the works of Braque, Matisse and Picasso. In exploring Cubism, Nicholson developed his own idiom in that he transferred three-dimensional natural phenomena to the two-dimensional canvas, turning the picture into an autonomous object. In the early 1930s he made his first purely abstract reliefs: cut-out geometrical forms in varying colours arranged in several layers. During this period Nicholson became a member of the Abstraction-Création group to which he belonged until 1937. In 1940 he moved with his second wife, the sculptress Barbara Hepworth, to Cornwall where, together with the sculptor Naum Gabo, the abstract group Painters of St Ives was formed. After 1945 objective elements returned to his work. Besides strictly geometrical abstractions, he produced still lifes and landscapes reduced to a sketch-like structure. His late work was again marked by its geometric harmony. Nicholson was the major representative of concrete art in England.
*Illustration:*
614    Still Life, 1947

## NOLAND Kenneth
born 1924 Asheville (North Carolina)
Noland studied from 1946 to 1948 at the Black Mountain College in New York and in 1948/49 with Ossip Zadkine in Paris. He then taught until 1956 at various institutions in Washington. Together with Louis he developed colour surface painting with diluted paints. Noland is also a hard-edge painter and minimalist artist. Painters of minimalist art deliberately reduce all elements in their work. Noland worked first with disc-like colour fields, then turned to horizontally arranged colour bands in soft, harmonious colours. In the mid-1980s Noland discovered computer art. In collaboration with the architect I.M. Pei, he designed buildings for the Massachusetts Institute of Technology.
*Illustration:*
651    Ember, 1960

## NOLDE Emil
(Emil Hansen)
1867 Nolde (near Tondern) – 1956 Seebüll (near Neukirchen)
Nolde began his career by learning to carve in Flensburg, and then worked as a craft teacher in St Gallen from 1892 to 1898 before further studies in Munich, Paris and Copenhagen. In 1901 he joined the Berlin Secession group, and in 1905 he was briefly associated with the Dresden *Brücke* group, leaving it in 1907. As a pugnacious loner, he agitated against the art policies of Liebermann, president of the Berlin Secession, and was expelled from the group in 1911. From then on he only spent the winter months in Berlin, painting on the island of Alsen in the summer. In 1913/14 he went on an expedition which took him through Russia, China and Japan, and as far as Polynesia. From 1940 he lived permanently in Seebüll, Schleswig-Holstein. Nolde's work belongs in subject matter and style to the more emotional branch of Expressionism. His pictures are marked by the dissolution of forms and glowing intensity of colour. His renderings of nature are usually very dramatic and often seem threatening in their combination of bilious, dark colours. From about 1910 he began painting religious subjects. To express what the inner eye saw he used distortion, ugliness and elements of primitive art. His generally positive attitude to National Socialism did not prevent his being denounced as "degenerate" in 1933.
*Illustrations:*
582    Christ among the Children, 1910
582    Nordermühle, 1932

## OEHLEN Albert
born 1954 Krefeld
Oehlen was trained in the book-trade. From 1978 to 1981 he studied at the art college in Hamburg. He first painted large-scale pictures which expressed his critical attitude to society. In 1984 he exhibited at "Wahrheit ist Arbeit" (Truth is Work) at the Folkwang Museum in Essen (with Werner Büttner, Georg Herold and Kippenberger). International exhibitions followed, including 1984 "Von hier aus" (Point of departure), Düsseldorf; 1988 "Deutsche/Amerikanische Kunst der späten 8oer Jahre" (German/American art of the late 80s), Düsseldorf and Boston; 1989 "Bilderstreit" (Iconographic controversy), Cologne; 1991 "Metropolis", Berlin. His first abstract paintings were produced towards the end of the 1980s. In 1991 he paid his first visit to Los Angeles (overpainting of representational subjects). Computer pictures were produced and also abstract oil-paintings. Further exhibitions: 1993 "Der zerbrochene Spiegel" (The cracked mirror), Vienna and Hamburg; 1995 Wexner Center, Columbus (Ohio); 1994 retrospective at the Deichtorhallen, Hamburg. Oehlen lives in La Palma, Spain.
*Illustration:*
677    Untitled, 1983

## ORLEY Bernaert van
c. 1488 Brussels – 1542 Brussels
Orley holds an important position in Flemish painting at the transition from Early to High Renaissance. Trained to follow the example of the great "old" Flemish masters, as his early works demonstrate ("Lamentation of Christ" from the triptych of Philippe de Hanetou, Brussels, Musées Royaux, c. 1515), he increasingly adopted the classical form language of the Italians ("Last Judgment Altar", Antwerp, Koninklijk Museum voor Schone Kunsten, 1525). It is not known whether he had ever been to Italy, but he met Dürer on his visit to Holland in 1521, and this could have had a mediating influence. Noted both for his great altarpieces and fine portraits, Orley enjoyed early high esteem in his native town and was appointed painter to Margaret of Austria, the governess of the Netherlands.
*Illustration:*
202    Holy Family, 1522

## OSTADE Adriaen van
(Adriaen Hendricx)
1610 Haarlem – 1685 Haarlem
The father, Jan Hendricx, came from Ostade near Eindhoven, and his sons Adriaen and Isaac adopted this name as painters. In 1627 Adriaen was a pupil of Frans Hals in Haarlem (as probably was the somewhat older Brouwer), where he joined the Lukas Guild in 1634. He was one of the most popular Dutch painters, specialising from the start in genre painting of peasant life. Initially he painted small pictures showing humble interiors and shabby inns with peasants in dim lighting carousing or brawling. Later the tones became warmer, the interiors more pleasant, and open-air scenes were added, including genre portraits of organ-grinders and pedlars. From about 1650 this tendency continued, the work showing greater accuracy and lighter colouring. One could say that the development ran from Rembrandtesque chiaroscuro towards Delft genre painting. The exaggerated manner of his early work had little to do with Dutch peasant life but was meant to make the town-dweller laugh. Ostade's most important pupils were his younger brother Isaac, and Steen.
*Illustration:*
319    Peasants Carousing in a Tavern,
       c. 1635

733

## OUDRY Jean-Baptiste

1686 Paris – 1755 Beauvais

Oudry was a pupil at the Académie de St.-Luc, where his father was principal. He received further training under Michel Serre, who introduced him to 17th century Dutch painting which was then experiencing a revival. He then became a pupil of Largillière, under whom the same influences were reinforced. Oudry's thematic spectrum is particularly wide. He is noted for his animal and still life pictures, but he also painted landscapes and was a successful portrait painter. He made a name for himself as a religious painter, too, and for this reason was accepted by the Academy in 1719. From 1726 Oudry made designs of hunting-scenes on a commission from the King for the Gobelin tapestry works in Beauvais, becoming its director in 1734. One of his most famous designs was Les Chasses de Louis XV consisting of a series of eight large tapestries. His landscapes show Ruisdael and Berchem as the source of inspiration, while the still lifes are of extreme refinement and elegance, as for example the one depicting a white duck (ill. p.352) which is painted entirely in variations of white and silver tones.

*Illustration:*

352   Still Life with White Duck, 1753

## OVERBECK Johann Friedrich

1789 Lübeck – 1869 Rome

Overbeck, from an upper-class Lübeck family, can be regarded as the founder of German Romantic art. His study of Italian and German late medieval and Renaissance art made him a dissatisfied student at the Vienna Academy, where he enrolled in 1806. In 1809 he formed with his like-minded friend Franz Pforr the Lukasbund (after St Luke, the patron saint of painters), the first modern association of artists. Art was to go back to religion and to the honest craftsmanship of the Middle Ages. The Protestant members of this group, including Overbeck, converted to Catholicism. In the same year connections with the Academy were broken off, and the young artists moved to Rome, where they found refuge at the monastery of San Isidoro and could realise their ideas on life and art. They were given the nickname "Nazarenes" by the Italians because of their hair style, and this is how the movement was called. Their first commission came from the Prussian consul Bartholdy to decorate the Casa Zuccaro with frescos. The theme chosen was the Old Testament story of Joseph. The decoration of the Casino Massimo with scenes taken from the "Liberation of Jerusalem" by Torquato Tasso was the next project, completed in 1827. After this the group dissolved, and Overbeck was the only one who remained in Rome.

*Illustration:*

454   Italia and Germania (Sulamith and Mary), 1828

## PACHER Michael

c. 1435 Bruneck (Tyrol) – 1498 Salzburg

Pacher was one of the few 15th century artists equally gifted in painting and wood sculpture. His training and early work are still a matter of conjecture. His altarpiece in the Liebfrauenkirche of Sterzing, completed in 1457/58, may have been inspired by Multscher. Records show that Pacher was active in Bruneck in 1467, where he ran a large workshop. His altarpiece depicting the crowning of Mary in the shrine of the parish church in Gries near Bozen, begun in 1471, was a preliminary step to his masterpiece in St Wolfgang in the Salzkammergut (ill. p.144), a winged altar combining reliefs, statues and panel paintings. For this, the contract was signed in 1471, and Pacher himself had to deliver the work, signed 1481, to St Wolfgang and to install it.

In this work, the crowning of Mary interweaves with the rich forms of the tracery into a unified pattern of lines, and light and shade create the suggestion of unlimited depth. The life-size figures, in particular those of St Wolfgang and St George beside the closed shrine, reveal Pacher as a contemporary of Verrocchio and Pollaiuolo: both north and south of the Alps, efforts were being made to depict the human figure moving in space and seen from different angles. The paintings of the altar wings are reminiscent of the works of Mantegna in their bold treatment of perspective, which Pacher could possibly have studied in Verona, Mantua and Padua. And while Pacher in his capacity of carver introduces elements of this art into painting, the painter in Pacher uses his insight into carving to deal with surface. With the "Church Fathers Altar" (ill. p.144) created in 1483 for the Neustift monastery near Brixen, Pacher reached a point at which the borders between painting and sculpture in the north were no longer clearly distinct.

*Illustrations:*

144   The Resurrection of Lazarus (St Wolfgang Altar), 1471–1481

144   St Augustine and St Gregory (Church Fathers' Altar), c. 1480

## PÄHL ALTAR → Master

## PALADINO Mimmo

born 1948 Paduli (near Benevento)

Paladino studied from 1964 to 1968 at the Liceo Artistico di Benevento. He now lives most of the time in Milan, where he had his first successes, and in his home town of Benevento. Together with Clemente, Chia and Cucchi he is one of a generation of young Italian painters who, supported by critics, reacted to the somewhat tired art scene, and who succeeded in making a name for themselves within a very few years. Paladino's art is individual and less based on style than on inner dictates. His pictures are produced as a kind of psychological projection of archetypes and symbols on to the canvas. He uses objects in his works, which are mostly abstract, and also paints flat pictures giving almost no sense of space but full of objective, symbolic allusions. He has paid several visits to Brazil, the first in 1982. Since then a fascinating combination of African and Catholic cultural elements has entered his work.

*Illustration:*

670   Ronda Notturna (Nightwatch), 1982

## PALMA (IL) VECCHIO

(Jacopo Negretti)

1480 Serina near Bergamo – 1528 Venice

Probably in the 1490s Jacopo was already apprenticed to Francesco di Simone da Santacroce in Venice, and there picked up the basic techniques of painting. But for composition, coloration and the portrayal of the human character, his inspiration came from the somewhat older Giorgione and Titian. In 1513 Palma became a member of the Scuola di S. Marco which commissioned a history painting from him. He enjoyed high esteem in Venice, commanding fees comparable to those of Titian. Many of his commissions came from churches for paintings in the classical Renaissance style in the manner of Giorgione, and in Palma's work this style came to a full flowering, particularly in terms of coloration. His religious themes, of which Mary and the Child surrounded by saints was a subject often repeated, are characteristic in their well-balanced composition and lack of drama. He was particularly noted for his fine portraits.

*Illustration:*

173   Diana discovers Callisto's Misdemeanour, c. 1525

## PARMIGIANINO

(Girolamo Francesco Maria Mazzola)

1503 Parma – 1540 Casalmaggiore (near Parma)

In following the style of Correggio, Parmigianino also became his most significant successor in 16th century painting in the Emilia region. His "Self-Portrait before a Convex Mirror" (Vienna, Kunsthistorisches Museum, 1523), which was to recommend him to the Pope, already shows him at the height of his art. The wealth of imagination and delicacy of approach shown in this work already hint at the dissolution of the ideal of High Renaissance portraiture. During his visit to Rome from 1524 to 1527 he was particularly impressed by Raphael and Giulio Romano. This did not, however, cause him to abandon his Mannerist tendencies. On his return to Emilia he worked predominantly in Parma and surroundings, carrying out many notable religious works and portraits. He also executed several frescos, and in this field he contributed greatly in removing the division between painting and sculpture (Scenes from the story of "Diana and Actaeon", Fontanellato, Kastell, c. 1523; "Virgins carrying Urns", Parma, Santa Maria della Steccata, between 1531 and 1539). Parmigianino was influential both in his native region and in Venice.

*Illustration:*

180   Madonna of the Long Neck, c. 1534–1540

## PATINIR Joachim

(also: Patenier)

c. 1480 Dinant, near Namur (?) – 1524 Antwerp

No records exist about Patinir's training and early work. In 1515 he was elected as master to the Antwerp Lukas Guild. He is noted as one of the earliest painters to make landscape a main element in pictorial composition, developing a so-called "world landscape", a bird's-eye view, with a seemingly endless horizon. This brought him international fame during his lifetime. Thus, three of his paintings were mentioned in 1523 in the records of the Palazzo Grimani in Venice, and Dürer also frequently mentioned him in his notes on his travels in the Netherlands. Patinir had a huge influence on succeeding generations as well as on his contemporaries. About twenty of his signed paintings cannot be regarded as pure landscape. He mostly depicted religious scenes, but his figures seem incidental to his landscapes.

*Illustration:*

201   Landscape with Charon's Bark, c. 1521

## PECHSTEIN Max

1881 Zwickau – 1955 Berlin

After an apprenticeship as a decorative painter, Pechstein studied in 1900 at the College of Applied Arts and 1902–1906 at the Academy in Dresden. In 1906 he met Heckel and joined the group Die Brücke. Initially influenced by Munch and van Gogh, he became interested in the Fauves once he had met van Dongen. He inclined more to the decorative rather than to deformation, and was therefore welcomed to exhibit at the Berlin Secession in 1908 and 1909. Being excluded in 1910, he founded with other artists in this position the Neue Secession. He had contacts with the Neue Künstlervereinigung München (New Artists' Association) and met Marc, Macke and Kandinsky. He left the Brücke in 1912. As an enthusiast of "primitive art" he visited the Palau Islands in the South Seas in 1914. Returning to Germany via Manila, Japan and the USA, he was called up for military service in 1915. After the war he joined the Arbeitsrat für Kunst (Arts Council) and the Novembergruppe. In 1922 he was elected a member of the Prussian Academy of Arts, where he taught until dismissed during the Nazi period when his paintings were condemned as "degenerate".

*Illustration:*
586   Open Air (Moritzburg), 1910

## PENCK A.R.
(Ralph Winkler)
born 1939 Dresden
Penck was taught drawing at the Deutsche Wer-
beagentur, Dresden, but in painting he is self-
taught. From 1965 he began to develop his "system
and world pictures" which were to become his
theme. These are canvases covered over with characters and little figures reminiscent of children's drawings, cave drawings and contemporary logos. From
1968 he was recognised as a painter, although
under the East German regime he was often forced
to carry out other tasks, working as a postman,
stoker, night-watchman and margarine packer.
From 1971 to 1976 he was a member of the Lücke
(gap) group of artists. Repeated invitations to exhibitions in the West caused him to be expatriated
in 1980. After living in the Rhineland, he moved
to London in 1983, then to Dublin and New York.
He has been teaching at Düsseldorf Academy since
1988. He also produces wooden sculpture, casting
them in bronze since 1982.
*Illustration:*
674   The Birth of Mike Hammer, 1974

## PERUGINO Pietro
(Pietro di Cristoforo Vannucci)
c. 1448 Città della Pieve – 1523 Fontignano
Perugino was one of the masters who widened the
scope of the Umbrian school, making Perugia an artistic centre of great excellence and thus paving the
way to the High Renaissance. Today his fame has
been eclipsed by Raphael, who was his greatest
pupil and owed much to him. Perugino probably
studied under Benedetto Bonfigli, but more important was his long stay in Florence from 1472. There
he may have worked in the workshop of Verrocchio
and have been introduced to the new developments
in depicting space and the physical form. But his
lasting influence was Piero della Francesca, who
taught him how to balance surface with space and
to structure large-scale compositions. Perugino became one of the greatest fresco painters of his time
(in 1481 he was one of the artists chosen to embel-
lish the Sistine Chapel; Crucifixion in the chapter
house of Santa Maria Maddalena dei Pazzi, Florence,
1493–1496; frescos in the Collegio del Cambio, Perugia, from 1499). His panel paintings already show
an almost classical balance in their composition.
This harmony is also reflected in the expression,
movement and gestures of his figures and not least
in his landscapes which succeed in heightening the
overall atmosphere.
*Illustrations:*
111   Christ giving the Keys to St Peter,
      c. 1482
111   The Vision of St Bernard, 1489

## PIAZZETTA Giovanni Battista
1683 Venice – 1754 Venice
Piazzetta received early instruction from Antonio
Molinari, but Crespi in Bologna became his real
teacher. To him he owed his loose manner of painting; an earthy, warm palette competing with
whites, and a chiaroscuro used to create an atmosphere rather than the pathos which had been produced until recently by Liss and Loth. When he
left Crespi and returned to Venice in 1711, his art
presented a complete contrast to the prevailing
Venetian style as represented by Ricci, Pellegrini
and Amigoni. It was not until the 1720s that Piazzetta used lighter tones. His scenes from the
Old and New Testaments were painted in the
genre style, and have an almost tactile closeness.

Piazzetta is regarded one of the most important
representatives of 18th century Venetian painting.
*Illustration:*
369   Beggar-Boy, c. 1740 (?)

## PICABIA Francis
1879 Paris – 1953 Paris
Born in Paris of Spanish parents, Picabia attended
various art schools in Paris. Until 1908 he painted
in the Impressionist style, but then came under the
influence of the Fauves and Cubists. In his search
for new experiences he produced his work "India-
Rubber" (Paris, Musée National d'Art Moderne) in
1909 which became a precursor of abstract art. He
continued this trend while staying mostly in the
USA from 1913 until 1915. Out of these sharp-
edged, abstract works developed his "machine" pictures, which raise questions about the value of technical progress. In 1916 he returned to Europe and
the Paris Dadaists. He made collages of buttons,
matches, feathers and other non-artistic materials.
The series of "transparencies" begun in 1927 are regarded as his most individual achievement. In
these, linear representations are superimposed on a
foundation layer.
*Illustration:*
595   Catch as catch can, 1913

## PICASSO Pablo
(Pablo Ruiz y Picasso)
1881 Málaga – 1973 Mougins (near Cannes)
His father was a drawing-master, an artist in his
own right, who promoted his son's early talent. Picasso went to complete his studies in Madrid in
the advanced course at the Academy of San Fernando. In 1899 he went to Barcelona, where he frequented the café of the intellectuals, "El Quatre
Gats". In 1900 he went to Paris for the first time.
During this period he painted music-hall and
circus pictures, now only signing them with "Picasso", his mother's maiden name. His dominant
colour was an almost monochrome blue-green –
his so-called "blue period". In 1904 he settled in
Paris, moving into a studio in the Bateau-Lavoir.
His "blue" period was followed by the "rose"
period. He met Matisse and later Derain, and also
made the acquaintance of Gertrude Stein, his first
patron.
   In 1906 he made an intensive study of
Cézanne's work. An exhibition at the Louvre of pre-
Roman, Iberian sculpture excited a lasting interest. From 1907, before meeting Kahnweiler and
Braque, his style began to take a dramatic, revolutionary direction. His "Demoiselles d'Avignon"
(ill. p. 569) completed the breach with formal and
aesthetic 19th century ideas of painting. This was
the key work leading into Cubism, which at the
end of 1909 entered the initial "analytical" phase
and was further developed by Picasso and Braque
around 1912 as a parallel to "synthetic" Cubism.
In the spring of 1912 he produced his first three-
dimensional "picture", which included sheet metal
and wire, shortly followed by his first collage. His
collaboration with Braque and Derain came to an
end when those two were called up in August
1914.
   Through Jean Cocteau's friendship with Diaghilev, Picasso won commissions for the "Ballets
Russes". In 1917 he visited Rome, Naples and Pompeii. During this time he met Igor Stravinsky and
Erik Satie. Besides abstract works still rooted in
Cubism, he again returned to more classical figurative painting between 1920 and 1924. In the
1930s he continued to move between these two
poles, creating his major works. In 1937 he produced his picture "Guernica" (ill. p. 549) for the
Spanish pavilion at the Paris World Exhibition,
using abstraction, deformation and anatomical dis-

section to express the feeling aroused by the bom-
bardment of the town by the German air force. In
1930 he had begun a series of 100 etchings for the
art dealer Vollard depicting scenes from his workshop in the Boisgeloup castle in Normandy, and
from the Minotaur myth, which included autobiographical elements. The work was published in
1939 under the title "Suite Vollard". During the
Second World War Picasso lived in Paris, painting
deformed, tortured heads of women and severe still
lifes, and he wrote the Surrealist piece "How to
catch desires by their tails". After the liberation of
Paris in 1944 he joined the French Communist
Party, and in 1946 he moved to the Côte d'Azur.
He turned to designing pottery in 1950 and began
exploring the works of older masters, producing
variations on paintings by Velázquez, Delacroix and
Manet. He also produced sculpture and illustrated
books.
*Illustrations:*
402   The Kiss, 1925
544   Portrait of Dora Maar, 1937
549   Guernica, 1937
569   Les Demoiselles d'Avignon, 1907
570   "Ma Jolie", 1914
570   Three Women at the Spring, 1921
571   Girl before a Mirror, 1932

## PIERO DELLA FRANCESCA
(Piero di Benedetto dei Franceschi)
c. 1420 Borgo San Sepolcro (near Arezzo) – 1492
Borgo San Sepolcro
Piero was probably trained in a Sienese-Umbrian
workshop, where he developed his power as a colourist and his interest in landscape painting. Between 1439 and 1445 he explored the new ideas on
space and physical form of the Florentine Early Renaissance, and he experimented with colour while
assisting Domenico Veneziano with the now lost
fresco cycle in San Egidio (now Santa Maria
Nuova). By adding a larger proportion of oil as binder it was possible to achieve atmospheric lighting
effects. As Veneziano's successor, Piero became a
pioneer in this field. After 1452 he created his
most famous fresco works in S. Francesco of Arezzo,
"The Discovery of the Wood of the True Cross"
(ill. p. 100). These show not only Piero's advanced
knowledge of perspective and mastery of colour,
achieving almost luminous effects as never before
in fresco painting, but also his geometric orderli-
ness and skill in pictorial construction. With his innovations he paved the way for the High Renaissance. From 1469 mention was made of him at the
court of the Montefeltre in Urbino, where he came
into contact with Dutch art. Already celebrated in
his life-time, Piero was greatly influential in northern Italian art in the second half of the 15th century. Later, he also set down his theoretical ideas in
writing.
*Illustrations:*
83    Senigalla Madonna, c. 1460–1475
99    The Baptism of Christ, c. 1440–1450
99    Double Portrait of Federigo da Montefeltro
      and his Wife Battista Sforza, c. 1470
100   The Discovery of the Wood of the True Cross
      and The Meeting of Solomon and the Queen
      of Sheba, after 1452

## PIERO DI COSIMO
(Piero di Lorenzo)
1462 Florence – 1521 Florence
Piero came from an artistic family and at the age of
18 entered the workshop of Cosimo Roselli, whose
name he adopted and with whom he travelled to
Rome in 1481/82 to assist in painting the frescos in
the Sistine Chapel at the Vatican. He specialised in
the decoration of Cassoni, heavy chests, whose unusual format he covered with skilled compositions.

His early work was influenced by Filippino Lippi; later he received stimulation from the works of Ghirlandaio and Dutch masters. At the turn of the century he followed Leonardo, who had again returned to Florence, in his treatment of colour. Piero di Cosimo knew how to combine these varied strands, producing atmospheric and dramatic moments occasionally bordering on the grotesque. For this reason his work was highly valued by the Surrealists.

*Illustrations:*
112    Death of Procris, c. 1510
112    Venus and Mars, c. 1498

## PISANELLO
(Antonio di Puccio Pisano)
before 1395 Pisa – 1455 Rome
Pisanello's father came from Pisa, his mother from Verona, both these cities then being under the rule of the Visconti. His training was undertaken in the Lombardy region, though it is not possible to say exactly where. We do know that he worked with Gentile da Fabriano on the decoration of the Doge's Palace in Venice, and earlier he may have been his pupil. It is said that Pisanello participated in the "Adoration of the Magi" at the Uffizi (ill. p. 54), bathing painting the horses and other animals. It is certain that he assisted Fabriano with the frescos in the Lateran Basilica in Rome and completed them after Fabriano's sudden death. A large number of drawings survive of both masters, which in itself is remarkable for the time, but more important are the conclusions to be drawn from these about their work. They show an intense interest in the study of nature, such as animals and plants, and other subjects or observation, whether it be a hanged man or a bathing girl. There is in addition a new preoccupation with Antiquity, which led to copying Roman sarcophagus reliefs and statues. The collection also includes copies made of contemporary works, such as those by Michelino da Besozzo and Altichiero, and by the Tuscan innovators Donatello, Fra Angelico and Luca della Robbia. Pisanello received commissions from most of the northern Italian noble families, including the Gonzaga in Mantua, the Este in Ferrara and the Malatesta in Rimini, and also from King Alfonso of Naples. But he never became dependent on any of these patrons. He was greatly admired for his animal drawings and closeness to nature, and his fame continued even after the new Florentine art had become dominant.

*Illustrations:*
51    The Vision of St Eustace, c. 1435
52    Portrait of Lionello d'Este, 1441 (?)
52    The Virgin and Child with Saints George and Anthony Abbot, c. 1445

## PISSARRO Camille
1830 Charlotte-Amalie (Antilles) – 1903 Paris
As the son of well-to-do parents Pissarro was sent to a school in Passy near Paris from 1842 to 1847. Despite his early promising talent he worked first in his father's business on the island of St Thomas from 1847 to 1852. Finding little fulfilment in the life of a merchant, he left St. Thomas in 1852 and travelled via Caracas to settle in Paris in 1855. There he discovered his great admiration for Corot at the World Exhibition held at that time. From 1859 to 1861 he studied at the Académie Suisse, where he encountered Monet, Guillaumin and Cézanne. This led to a fruitful and life-long friendship with Monet. Like Monet, he escaped the war in France by going to London in 1870/71. There he married Julie. He was particularly impressed with Turner's work. Pissarro was one of the most active members of the Impressionist group, giving his support freely and working together with his

friends. Between 1872 and 1878 he worked at Pontoise, often together with Cézanne, and from 1879 also with Gauguin. He was the only painter who participated in all eight Impressionist Exhibitions between 1874 and 1886. He received some financial support from Murer, a café proprietor, during the years 1876–1879.

From 1882 to 1884 he lived at Osny, and around this time produced a series of pictures of peasant life and began to become interested in Socialism. In 1883 he had his first one-man-exhibition at Durand-Ruel. His son Lucien, a graphic artist and painter, moved to London. In 1884 he settled permanently in Eragny on the river Epte, his political views shifting towards anarchism. In 1886 he exhibited at Durand-Ruel in New York. His sight began to fail in 1888. In 1889 he was represented at the Paris World Exhibition and Les XX in Brussels. In 1890 he visited London, later returning several times. In 1894 he was in danger of being arrested as an anarchist and had to flee to Belgium. In 1896 and 1898 he was in Rouen, painting views of the town and harbour and always remaining loyal to the Impressionist school. Between 1897 and 1903 he produced many impressions of Paris boulevards, and also painted in Dieppe and Le Havre. In 1900 he again showed his work at the Paris World Exhibition, finally gaining universal recognition.

*Illustrations:*
482    Landscape at Chaponval, 1880
496    Red Roofs (Village Corner, Impression of Winter), 1877
496    The Old Marketplace in Rouen and the Rue de l'Epicerie, 1898

## POLIAKOFF Serge
1900 Moscow – 1969 Paris
Poliakoff left Russia in 1918 during the revolution, settling in Paris in 1923, where he studied music and earned his living as a guitarist. He began to study art in Paris in 1929/30, first at the Académie Frochot, then at the Académie Bilbul and the Grande Chaumière. From 1935 until 1937 he studied at the Slade School of Art in London. On his return to Paris he became acquainted with Kandinsky, Sonia and Robert Delauny and Otto Freundlich. He was granted French citizenship in 1962. Poliakoff developed a very personal variant of abstract painting. In the 1940s his handling of colour was discreet and calming. This was followed by a period when he coloured his irregular, adjoining fields with great intensity, provoking a reaction of keen fascination. Initially he had to support himself by working as a textile designer, but from 1950 onwards he found wide recognition as a painter.

*Illustration:*
637    Composition, 1959

## POLKE Sigmar
born 1941 Oels (Lower Silesia)
Polke's family moved to Germany in 1953. He was trained as a stained glass artist, then studied at Düsseldorf Academy with Karl Otto Götz, Gerhard Hoehme and Beuys from 1961 to 1967. Polke's work is concerned with the effects of manipulation by the mass media. He treats the subject ironically, applying the painterly devices of classic modern painting, but also using materials of the sub-culture. He delights in exploring motifs taken from Picabia, side by side with kitsch and advertising. His pictorial world is tending increasingly towards the magical and diabolical, which is further emphasised by his skilled use of chemical agents which cause gradual colour changes due to environmental influences.

*Illustration:*
672    Remingtons Museums-Traum ist des Besuchers Schaum, 1979

## POLLAIUOLO Antonio del
(Antonio di Jacobo d'Antonio Benci)
1432 Florence – 1498 Rome
Trained as a goldsmith, then probably the pupil of Donatello, Pollaiuolo was one of the most versatile talents to exercise influence on the future development of 15th century Florentine art. The moving physical form in space was a subject he explored as a sculptor in bronze, and as a painter, engraver and draughtsman. The aim was no longer to produce a vigorously modelled, polychrome "statue", but sculpture in the round. His small bronzes in particular became desirable objects for collectors, a field which he helped to open up. But his talent for small-format work, applying his early training in the goldsmith's workshop, was an expression of only one aspect of his skill. His artistic development culminated in his two great monuments for St Peter's in Rome (Popes Sixtus IV, completed 1492, and Innocent VIII, completed 1496). While the figures in relief are reminiscent of the northern Schongau school in the handling of contour and drapery, the figure of Innocent, reaching far out into space, does not appear old-fashioned today in the vicinity of Lorenzo Bernini's Baroque monuments. His younger brother Piero (1443–1496) worked alongside Antonio in the Pollaiuolo workshop. From 1460 Antonio also turned to painting, engaging in themes similar to those of his sculpture.

*Illustration:*
103    The Martyrdom of St Sebastian, 1475

## POLLOCK Jackson
1912 Cody (Wyoming) – 1956 Easthampton (New York)
Pollock grew up in California and Arizona. From 1928 to 1930 he studied at the Manual Arts High School in Los Angeles and from 1930 to 1933 in New York. There he met Thomas Hart Benton, the most important representative of American Scene painting, with whom he painted murals. He also took part in the US government programme for wallpainting from 1936 to 1943. In 1939 Pollock received psychiatric treatment for his alcoholism and this led him to study the works of C.G. Jung, and he became particularly interested in his theory of archetypes. In 1942 he met Motherwell, the most important exponent of abstract Expressionism, and the Surrealist painter Matta. He occupied himself with the unconscious in art, and began to write Surrealist poems. His early work was abstract with elements of primitive, mostly Indian, art in stylised form. In 1945 Pollock married the painter Lee Krasner. A year later he began to develop a completely new style. With this he made a name for himself, becoming a key figure in American painting. Long before this his work had shown that he was turning away from the conventional use of brush and easel. This he finally achieved with his "drip painting". The canvas is placed on the floor, and paint is dribbled and splashed over it spontaneously from perforated cans. An inner tension or relaxation, a psychic automatism determines the speed, the rhythm, the action. With this, Pollock achieved the high point of his expressive energy. In 1943 he had his first one-man exhibition in New York. In 1956 he died in a car accident.

*Illustrations:*
619    Painting, 1948
632    Blue Pole, 1953

## PONTORMO
(Jacopo Carrucci da Pontormo)
1494 Pontormo (near Empoli) – 1556 Florence
Pontormo can be regarded as one of the most interesting figures in 16th century Italian art and also as an exponent of Florentine Mannerist paint-

ing. Like Rosso Fiorentino, a pupil of del Sarto, his early work still reflected the High Renaissance, apart from increased movement (fresco of the "Visitation" in the forecourt of Saint Annunziata, Florence, 1514–1516). In subsequent years Pontormo abandoned this style, with its balanced composition, logical construction, idealised figure representation and clear coloration ("Sacra Conversazione", Florence, San Michele in Visdomini, 1518).

Pontormo's fresco cycle in the cloister of Certosa di Galluzzo near Florence, 1530, draws on an intensive study of Dürer's graphic art. Then, in the following period, Pontormo increasingly set out to portray movement in all its forms and directions ("Visitation", Carmignano parish church, near Florence). By distortion of the ideal physical proportions – elongated figures with small heads – exaggerated perspective and use of relatively harsh, vivid colours, he transposed traditional pictorial themes into a new sphere in some respects related to medieval art. His late works, particularly in the rendering of figures, strongly reflect Michelangelo's influence, whom he met around 1530 in Rome. A favourite of the Medici, he carried out much important fresco work, which has, however, not survived. Pontormo's portraits belong to the greatest achievements in this field in Florentine painting.

*Illustrations:*
155    Joseph in Egypt, c. 1515
181    Deposition, c. 1526–1528

## POST Frans
1612 Leiden – 1680 Haarlem
Post is unique amongst Dutch painters in that he depicted almost exclusively Brazilian landscapes, being the first European to paint views of South America. From 1637 to 1644 he accompanied Prince Johann Moritz von Nassau-Siegen, the governor of the region colonised in 1630 by the Dutch West India Company. Post spent most of the time in Pernambuco and the delta region of the Rio São Francisco. On his return to Haarlem, where he became a member of the Lukas Guild in 1646, he painted about a hundred pictures of his impressions of his travels, using his sketches and drawings, and also improvising from memory. These works were exotic views of grey rivers coursing through green, hilly landscapes, with realistic renderings of the flora and fauna, and natives in traditional costume in their villages under palm trees. A bluish-green tone predominated, and he retained the traditional pattern of Dutch view painting.

*Illustration:*
318    Hacienda, 1652

## POTTER Paulus
1625 Enkhuizen – 1654 Amsterdam
Potter was probably trained by his father Pieter, a landscape and still life painter, who had moved from Enkhuizen to Amsterdam. He became a member of the Delft Lukas Guild in 1646, lived sporadically in The Hague, but the last two years of his life again in Amsterdam. Potter is famous for his animal pictures, mostly sheep, goats and cows grazing peacefully and in complete harmony with the landscape. He is regarded as the actual founder of animal painting, in that his animals become the subject rather than playing an incidental role. His lifesize "Bull" (The Hague, Mauritshuis) is still admired today. Although a painter of realism, he also adopted elements of Italianised pastoral landscape, probably attributable to his collaboration with Karel Dujardin.

*Illustration:*
324    Peasant Family with Animals, 1646

## POUSSIN Nicolas
c. 1593/94 Villers-en-Vexin (Eure) – 1665 Rome
The son of an impoverished family, Poussin received some early training from the painter Varin, who was travelling through his town. More thorough training followed in Paris, 1612–1624, as assistant to Champaigne and pupil of the Mannerist Lallemand, reinforced by independent study of predominantly Italian art in the Royal Collections. After several unsuccessful attempts, he finally went to Rome in 1624 with his patron and supporter Marino. The latter was a celebrated poet who introduced Poussin to ancient mythology and Ovid's works. Marino wrote an epic entitled *Adone* (1623) which was illustrated by Poussin. In Rome he worked for some time with Domenichino and developed his own style by exploring and perfecting Annibale Carracci's ideas on classical landscape painting.

Already in his thirties, his palette became lighter and he showed a tendency to poetical and idealised representation of subjects from Antiquity and the Bible ("The Inspiration of the Epic Poet", Paris, Louvre, 1630; "Martyrdom of St Erasmus", Rome, Musei Vaticani, 1629). His knowledge of the literary and pictorial traditions of Antiquity and of the Renaissance, and his contact with contemporary intellectuals, plus his knowledge of history, all combined to turn Poussin into the prototype of a Classical painter. With his Arcadian yearnings, his idealisation of friendship and manly virtues, and his predilection for sentimental resignation, he set a course for the moral and doctrinal tendencies of future generations of painters. During a brief stay in Paris, 1640–1642, he painted the Hercules scenes for the Louvre at the invitation of Richelieu and Louis XIII. Finding the artistic climate unfavourable, he returned to Rome and friends such as Dughet and Lorrain, and never left the city again.

*Illustrations:*
217    Triumph of Neptune and Amphitrite, 1634
245    Midas and Bacchus, c. 1630
245    Landscape with Three Men, c. 1645–1650
246    Echo and Narcissus, c. 1627/28
246    Moses Trampling on Pharaoh's Crown, 1645
247    St Cecilia, c. 1627/28

## PRENDERGAST Maurice Brazil
1859 St. John's (Newfoundland) – 1924 New York
Prendergast initially supported himself by working as an advertisement painter in Boston, attending evening classes at the Star King School. In 1886/87 he visited England, then went to France from 1891 to 1894. In Paris he met Whistler, Manet and Bonnard, who all influenced him greatly. He was also impressed by the Nabis group and, like many contemporary artists, by Japanese woodcuts. Prendergast was one of the first American artists to discover and admire Cézanne. In 1894 he returned to Boston, painting the surrounding scenery. A second visit to Europe from 1898 to 1900 also took him to Italy, where he spent most of his time studying the old masters in Venice. Back in America he often visited New York in search of inspiration, painting in a serene, late Impressionist style. In 1908 he exhibited with The Eight group. In 1909/10 he was again in Paris, and on his return worked during successive summers on the New England coast. In 1913 he participated in the legendary Armory Show in New York, where he finally settled a year later. As a committed Impressionist and Post-Impressionist, Prendergast was one of the painters who pioneered this style in the USA.

*Illustration:*
541    Ponte della Paglia in Venice, 1899

## PRETI Mattia
(called: Il Cavaliere Calabrese)
1613 Taverna (Calabria) – 1699 Valletta (Malta)
Preti joined his brother in Rome in 1630. He probably studied in Modena, Parma, Bologna and Venice until 1641, when he returned to Rome to become a member of the Maltese Order. Initially influenced by the Roman High Baroque, including Lanfranco and Cortona ("Alms-Giving of St Charles Borromeo" for San Carlo ai Cartinari, c. 1640), he developed a vigorous style of his own which reflected the influence of Guercino combined with a Venetian treatment of colour, as shown in his frescos in Sant' Andrea della Valle (1651) and San Biago (Modena, 1653–1656). Between 1656 and 1659 Preti produced votive pictures against the Plague in Naples, using sombre colours which show his great skill at rendering the human figure. "Absalom's Feast" (Naples, Galleria Nazionale, before 1660) and "Belshazzar's Feast" (also Naples, before 1660) typify Preti's complicated method of composition and his startling light effects. Preti spent his last years as a Knight Hospitaller in Malta where he achieved a most touching depiction of human deeds and sufferings with his "Scenes from the Life of St John the Baptist" for San Giovanni (Valletta).

*Illustration:*
237    The Tribute-Money, c. 1640

## PRUD'HON Pierre Paul
1758 Cluny – 1823 Paris
Prud'hon began his career as painter at the Dijon Academy under François Devosge and continued his studies at the Paris Academy. In 1784 he won the Prix de Rome, which took him to Italy from 1785 to 1788. Although this coincided with David's triumphs in Rome, he remained unimpressed by this painter's Neo-Classicism. He became a friend of the sculptor Antonio Canova and studied the art of Antiquity. The masters of the Renaissance, in particular Leonardo and Correggio, were to become his greatest influence. On his return to France he settled in Paris, supporting himself with the sale of his drawings and miniature paintings. His first important commission came in 1798 for a ceiling painting in the palace of Saint-Cloud. This was followed by similar orders with allegorical themes. The Empress Joséphine was his most influential patron, and Prud'hon became the portrait painter of the royal family. Napoleon's second wife, Marie-Louise, also admired him, securing many commissions for him and employing him as her drawing-master. In the prevailing austere Neo-Classical atmosphere he occupied a rather isolated position, yet his sensitive handling of colour and composition helped to usher in Romanticism.

*Illustration:*
423    Empress Joséphine, 1805

## PUCELLE Jean
active between 1319 and 1335 in Paris
This greatest of illuminators at the French court was probably trained in the workshop of Maître Honoré of Amiens, perhaps already working there around 1315. The first written record is a money order from between 1319 and 1324 for the design of a seal of the Brotherhood of the Hospital St. Jacques aux Pélerins in Paris. The master is mentioned in small signatures as well as inventory notes. In the Duc de Berry's inventory Jeanne d'Evreux's book of hours is recorded as *Heures de Pucelle*. In those days, naming the book after the artist was a great honour. Pucelle's style was carried on by his assistants almost until the end of the 14th century, and often copied at the request of King Charles V and also of the Duc de Berry.

The artist must have visited Italy around 1320 judging by his thorough knowledge of Duccio's works and his use of motifs taken from Giotto and other Italian painters.

*Illustration:*

43 The Betrayal of Christ and The Annunciation (from the Book of Hours of Jeanne d'Evreux), between 1325 and 1328

## PUVIS DE CHAVANNES Pierre

1824 Lyon – 1898 Paris

Puvis came from a family of the old gentry. After studying law, he went to Paris where he was trained in the studio of Henri Scheffer, and later under Thomas Couture. Like Moreau, he was influenced by the works of Chassériau. He had his first success at the Salon in 1850, but it took nine further years to have another picture accepted. In 1854/55 he received his first commission for a fresco painting, and decorative, monumental works in this field were to become his speciality. Many of these were not easily accessible, which for a long time prevented proper appreciation of his work. His manner of painting, too, was an obstacle initially. He did not follow the Impressionists, nor did his work come into the category of history painting. His pictures showed a strict linear ordering with simple colour-areas. His choice of subjects allows us to place him as a Symbolist, as he preferred allegorical themes as well as religious and historical subjects with classical figures and poses. In 1887 he had his first large exhibition at Durand-Ruel; in 1890 he became co-founder and in 1891 chairman of the Société Nationale des Beaux-Arts which supported the causes of French artists.

*Illustration:*

509 The Poor Fisherman, 1881

## QUARTON Enguerrand

(also: Charonton, Charton, Charretier)

c. 1410 Diocese of Laon – 1461 or later Avignon (?)

No other work in European painting of the Early Renaissance has presented as many research problems as the large panel painting of the "Pietà" (ill. p. 139). This work came from Villeneuve-lès-Avignon and was rediscovered at the "Les primitifs français" exhibition in Paris in 1904. In an endeavour to place this work, it has been attributed to various artists, including to the Catalan master Bartolomeo Bermejo and the great Portuguese painter Nuño Gonçalves. The painting cannot be compared with any other work from around 1450–1460, with its utter lack of physical effect and the depth of emotion shown in the faces and gestures of the figures, each seemingly isolated in their own grief. It must be assumed that the painter knew Italian art (unity of composition), Catalan painting (ascetic severity of the heads), and also Dutch works (precision of detail). Only in recent times has it been possible to attribute the work to Quarton, a major master of the Avignon school. Records show that he lived in Aix-en-Provence before 1440 and from 1447 to 1466 in Avignon. In collaboration with Pierre Villate he painted the "Madonna with the Mantle" in 1452 (Chantilly, Musée Cluny) and around 1453/54 the "Coronation of the Virgin" (ill. p. 139)

*Illustrations:*

139 Coronation of the Virgin, c. 1453/54

139 Pietà, c. 1460

## RAPHAEL

(Raffaello Santi)

1483 Urbino – 1520 Rome

Raphael's fame as the greatest painter of the Western world will continue despite certain dectracting voice which made themselves heard at the beginning of the 20th century. He began his apprenticeship with his father Giovanni, learning basic manual skills, but would have had greater artistic and educational benefits from the circle surrounding the court of Montefeltre. Fundamental to his development was his training under Perugino, whom he later assisted. Here Raphael learned the art of composition and gained the knowledge which enabled him to merge landscape and figure sensitively, and so develop the dreamy sensitivity of expression so characteristic of his work, particularly of his Madonnas.

His move to Florence in 1504 at the age of 21 marked a decisive period in his stylistic development. There a large field of artistic possibilities open to him, particularly with regard to design and form, which he was capable of assimilating within a few years. Figure and space were at the heart of his learning. Raphael had an extraordinary power of assimilation without falling into the trap of eclecticism. In exploring the works of the past and present he only adopted such elements which served to perfect his own original artistic personality. Already in 1508 his fame began to spread when Pope Julius II called him to Rome for the decoration of apartments at the Vatican. His fellow countryman Donato Bramante, who was engaged in the rebuilding of St Peter's, may have helped to secure this commission. His first large work in the Stanza della Segnatura (1509–1512, ill. p. 172) already shows his personal conception of design and form with figures combining statuesque dignity with freedom of movement. However, with his decoration of the Stanza d'Eliodoro (1512–1514) he achieved further heights in dramatic expression, suggestion of depth and colour modulation (the "Liberation of Peter" is the first large "night picture" of European art). Raphael crossed the border between High Renaissance and Mannerism as demonstrated in the large panel paintings of his late period ("Sistine Madonna", Dresden, Gemäldegalerie, 1512/13; group portrait "Pope Leo X with Cardinals Giulio de' Medici and Luigi de' Rossi", ill. p. 151; "Transfiguration", ill. p. 172).

The large number of commissions for fresco cycles (Loggias at the Vatican, Farnesina) and other works resulted in the organisation of a large workshop. Of great importance for Raphael's work was his contact with Antiquity while in Rome (in 1514 he was appointed prefect of the Roman antiquities). His significance as an architect can now only be traced in outline. In 1514 he became chief architect of St Peter's; in 1515/16 he built the Palazzo Madama in Rome and designed the Palazzo Vidoni-Caffarelli, also in Rome (1515) as well as that of the Pandolfini in Florence (1517–1520). In just two decades of creativity Raphael's work made unique, influential history, outgrowing the 15th century, leading the High Renaissance to its peak and finally paving the way for Mannerism, often leaping ahead to the Baroque.

*Illustrations:*

151 Pope Leo X with Cardinals Giulio de' Medici and Luigi de' Rossi, 1518/19

170 Madonna of the Meadows, 1505/06

171 Marriage of the Virgin (Sposalizio della Vergine), 1504

171 Madonna di Foligno, c. 1512

172 The Transfiguration, c. 1517–1520

172 The School of Athens, 1511/12

## RAIGERN ROAD TO CALVARY → Master

## RAINER Arnulf

born 1929 Baden (near Vienna)

Rainer studied from 1947 to 1949 in Villach at the Staatsgewerbeschule. In 1950, after one day's attendance, he left the College of Applied Arts in Vienna, and after only three days Vienna Academy. His early work was inspired by Surrealism. From 1951 he gave up figurative representation, after exploring Expressionism and Tachism. During the next two years he produced his "atomisations", which dissolved surface and form, and "blind drawings". From 1953 he developed his "overpaintings" which came to form the basis of his work. Around 1964 he painted pictures after experimenting with hallucinogenic drugs. Rainer also visited psychiatric clinics for inspiration, his aim being to fathom the depths of his personality through art. Since 1969 he has been using photographs of himself for his overpaintings. Subsequently he used prints of old masters, and since 1977 pictures of death-masks and faces. In the 1980s he returned to religious subjects and produced a series of crucifixions and pictures of martyrs, angels and of catastrophies.

*Illustration:*

667 Zünglein ohne Waage (Tongue that tips no scales), 1975

## RATGEB Jörg

c. 1480 Schwäbisch Gmünd – 1526 Pforzheim

Nothing is known about Ratgeb's early life and training. He was one of the most unconventional artists during the Dürer period and was evidently inspired by Grünewald. As a journeyman he went to Flanders and northern Italy, as shown by the handling of colour and composition of his first authenticated work (Catherine Altar in the parish church of Schwaigern, 1510). From 1514 to 1517 Ratgeb painted in the cloisters and refectory of the Carmelite monastery in Frankfurt/M one of the most important fresco cycles of the time, with scenes from salvation history (severely damaged in 1944). Ratgeb's predilection for foreshortening and for exaggerated figure movement is most marked in the Herrenberg Altar (ill. p. 198). During the Peasants' Revolt he vigorously supported the side of the peasants and was executed in 1526.

*Illustration:*

198 The Flagellation of Christ, 1518/19

## RAUSCHENBERG Robert

born 1925 Port Arthur (Texas)

Rauschenberg had a thorough education and was trained in Kansas City, in Paris, and from 1948 to 1949 by Albers at the Black Mountain College, where he himself taught in 1952. There he organised "happenings" with John Cage, Merce Cunningham and David Tudor. Motherwell, Kline and Jack Tworkov also taught at the College. A likeminded artist friend was Jasper Johns, their studios were in the same building from 1955 to 1960. After producing a series of black and white pictures, he began in 1953 to make his "combined paintings" which incorporated pictorial elements, whole and fragmented objects. He also produced collages and material assemblages. The pictorial parts are Action paintings, but the realistic objects lead away from the abstract. Rauschenberg has been one of the major influences on American Pop Art. From about 1970 he has been working with cardboard with which he entered the field of Minimal Art. In the 1980s he produced sculpture from scrap metal and pictures etched with acid on metal plates. In 1966 he founded with the engineer Billy Klüver the company "Experiments in Art and Technology" (E.A.T.). Since 1984 he has been working on the project entitled "Rauschenberg, Overseas Cultural Interchange" (ROCI), which provides work for artists worldwide. He also travels with dance and theatre groups for whom he produces sets.

*Illustrations:*

657 Charlene, 1954

657 Trophy I, 1959

## RAY Man
(Michael Radnitzky ?)
1890 Philadelphia – 1976 Paris
As one of the most imaginative exponents of Dadaism, Ray was a man of many talents: sculpture, photography, film, literature, architecture. He frequented the *avant garde* circles in New York, in particular the Gallery Stieglitz. After meeting Duchamp and Picabia in 1915, he devoted himself to Dadaism, taking part in the manifestations and exhibitions in New York from 1916 to 1921 and the publications "391" and New York Dada. He followed Duchamp to Paris in 1921, joining the circle around Tristan Tzara, Breton and Picabia. He experimented in the fields of photography and film, and produced collages and other artefacts. Later he joined the Surrealists, becoming their "official" photographer, and also returned to painting. From 1940 to1951 he worked in Hollywood. He then returned to Paris.
*Illustration:*
595    The Rope Dancer Accompanies Herself with her Shadows, 1916

## RAYSKI Ferdinand von
(Louis Ferdinand von Rayski)
1806 Pegau (near Leipzig) – 1890 Dresden
Rayski was the son of an aristocratic cavalry officer and received a corresponding education. From 1823 he attended the Dresden Academy. A visit to Paris in 1834/35, where he became most enthusiastic about the works of Géricault, was decisive for his development. Subsequently he devoted himself to painting equestrian subjects and battle scenes in a free, pasto manner. He also painted portraits of the Saxon and Prussian landed gentry on whose estates he was a frequent visitor. From the 1850s Rayski was the first German portrait painter to use colour as a determining device rather like the early Impressionists, subordinating form and giving preference to tones of grey, black and brown. He is noted for his sensitive portrait studies.
*Illustration:*
460    Portrait of a Young Girl, c. 1840

## REDON Odilon
(Bertrand-Jean Redon)
1840 Bordeaux – 1916 Paris
Until the war of 1870/71 Redon lived in Bordeaux. The son of a well-to-do explorer and a Creole mother, he was delicate, sensitive and introverted. As a child he loved drawing and reading. The botanist Armand Clavaud, whom he met when he was fifteen, introduced him to contemporary art and biology. He became strongly influenced by Rembrandt and made his first etchings, of which he sent a sample to the Salon in Paris in 1867. After 1870 he lived mostly in Paris, where he met Corot and Courbet and he greatly admired Delacroix. He often went to the Louvre with Fantin-Latour to copy works. Through Fantin-Latour he developed an interest in lithography, and in 1879 his first series of lithographs, entitled "Dreaming", appeared. The fantastic and dream-like was to become the theme of his work, which was strongly rooted in Symbolism. The writer Joris-Karl Huysmans greatly admired Redon's art and described his graphic works and those of Moreau in his controversial *fin-de-siècle* novel *A Rebours*. Durand-Ruel showed Redon's work in his gallery, and in 1884 Redon became a co-founder of the Salon des Indépendants, contributing to its first exhibition. In 1886 he took part in the eighth Impressionist exhibition and also exhibited with Les XX in Brussels. He was on friendly terms with the Nabis group and with Gauguin, as well as with the writers Mallarmé, Gide and Valéry. Having until then published mainly lithographs, he

started in the 1890s to produce paintings. He worked a great deal in pastels, and his pictures display a colouring which is delicately muted but nevertheless intensive. From 1900 until his death he lived quietly in Bièvres near Paris.
*Illustration:*
513    Still Life (Flowers), c. 1910

## REINHARDT Ad
1913 Buffalo (New York) – 1967 New York
After studying art history at Columbia University in New York under Meyer Schapiro from 1931 until 1937, Reinhardt attended for two years the National Academy of Design. From 1937 to 1947 he was a member of the American Abstract Artists group. During the war he worked as an art critic on a New York paper and served as a marine photographer. After the war he continued his studies of art history, specialising in Far Eastern art. From 1947 he taught at Brooklyn College and numerous other American educational institutions. He travelled widely in the 1950s and 1960s, visiting Europe and Asia. As an extension to Mondrian's abstract art, he attempted to achieve a purely self-sufficient art with a minimum of devices, terminating in his pictures of black squares in which slight shading can only be detected after prolonged observation. As both an artist and critic of contemporary art and a writer on the *avant-garde*, Reinhardt exercised considerable influence on many artists of the 1960s and 1970s.
*Illustration:*
648    Red Abstract, 1952

## REMBRANDT
(Rembrandt Harmensz van Rijn)
1606 Leiden – 1669 Amsterdam
Rembrandt, the son of a miller and a baker's daughter, was originally intended to become a scholar. He went to Latin School and then enrolled at the University of Leiden. After only a year he left to become apprenticed from 1622 to 1624 to a mediocre Leiden painter, Jacob van Swanenburgh. More important for his artistic development, however, was the short period of about six months that he spent training under Pieter Lastman in Amsterdam. In 1625 he began a working association with his friend Jan Lievens in Leiden, finally moving to Amsterdam in 1631/32. In the history of Dutch painting this date represents an important milestone, as Rembrandt was to become the incomparable representative of Amsterdam art. He soon established himself in Amsterdam, received many commissions and opened a large workshop. In 1634 he married Saskia, a lawyer's daughter, who brought a considerable dowry into the marriage. In 1639 he bought a large house, never quite paid for, which he filled with works of art and curios. Soon his passion for collecting exceeded his finances. In 1642, the year he painted "The Night Watch" (ill. p. 313), Saskia died, and from 1649 he lived with Hendrickje Stoffels whom he could not marry without losing Saskia's legacy to their son Titus. In 1656 he went bankrupt, and his house and all possessions were put up for compulsory auction. Rembrandt spent his final years in poverty and isolation in rooms on the outskirts of Amsterdam, his powers of creation undiminished.
   Rembrandt was the most universal artist of his time and he influenced painting for half a century, irrespective of schools or regional style. From his many fields of activity his pupils developed their own specialities, ranging from *trompe l'œil* painting to the very detailed Leiden style. Unlike most Dutch painters of the time, who worked in fairly narrow fields, Rembrandt depicted almost every type of subject. Although Amsterdam's leading portraitist for a decade ("Jan Six", Amsterdam,

Foundation Six), also doing group portraits ("The Staalmeesters", ill. p. 316), he was a painter of numerous biblical scenes ("The Sacrifice of Isaac", St Petersburgh, Hermitage), of mythological works ("Philemon and Baucis", Washington, National Gallery) and landscapes ("Landscape in Thunderstorm", Brunswik, Herzog-Ulrich-Museum) as well as still lifes ("The Slaughtered Ox", ill. p. 315). In his work, branches of painting often overlapped, as for example in the group portrait "The Night Watch", where he took liberties with a number of rules.
   Rembrandt's fame rests on his continual development of pictorial devices and unvarying excellence of execution (unlike the works of Rubens, many of which were left in part to workshop routine), as well as on his brilliant handling of light and shade and his ability to suggest states of mind through facial expression.
   Apart from his greatness as a painter he was a powerful draughtsman and etcher. About 300 of his etchings survive. In this field he extended the technical and artistic possibilities, for example introducing the chiaroscuro effect, raising it to an art form in its own right. Amongst his approximately 1500 drawings, the landscape scenes are particularly captivating in their serenity and harmony despite the spontaneous handling of line.
*Illustrations:*
276    Self-Portrait with Stick, 1658
312    The Artist in his Studio, c. 1626–1628
312    The Anatomy Lesson of Dr. Nicolaes Tulp, 1632
313    The Night Watch, 1642
314    Self-Portrait aged 63, 1669
315    The Descent from the Cross, 1633
315    The Slaughtered Ox, 1655
316    The Syndics of the Amsterdam Clothmakers' Guild, 1662
316    Aristotle Contemplating the Bust of Homer, 1653

## RENI Guido
1575 Calvenzano – 1642 Bologna
The son of a musician, Reni was also musically gifted, but began his training as a painter at the age of nine in the workshop of Calvaert, then at thirteen in that of the Carracci brothers. In 1598 he was already involved in the façade decoration of the Palazzo Pubblico in Bologna. He went to Rome with Albani in 1602; he returned to Bologna and again left for Rome in 1605, where he was to spend many years. His patron Cardinal Caffarelli-Borghese secured innumerable commissions for him, causing him to employ assistants. Later, he went in for mass production to pay for his passion for gambling.
   In 1622 he returned to Bologna and became the leader of the Bolognese school on the death of Lodovio Carracci. In early works, such as the "Coronation of Mary, with Saints" (Bologna, Pinacoteca Nazionale, 1595), Reni combined Mannerist and also northern elements with those of the Roman High Renaissance, that had been revived by the Carracci. The "Crucifixion of St Peter" (Rome, Pinacoteca Vaticana, 1603) may be seen as an example of his Caravaggist period, which was followed by the development of a personal style around 1608 (Samson frescos, Vatican). His most celebrated work, "Aurora", a ceiling fresco in the Palazzo Rospigliosi, 1612–1614, combines a clear palette and harmonious composition with masterly figure representation. His Madonna pictures (e.g. "Madonna del Rosario", Bologna, Pinacoteca Nazionale), to which Reni owed his fame in his lifetime and until the 19th century, no longer appeal today with their grand and monumental perfection.
*Illustrations:*
232    The Massacre of the Innocents, 1611
232    The Baptism of Christ, c. 1623

## RENOIR Pierre-Auguste

1841 Limoges – 1919 Cagnes-sur-Mer (near Nice)
The son of an impecunious tailor, he moved with his family to Paris in 1844. He was apprenticed as a painter to a Paris porcelain-maker, 1854–1858, and then painted fans and blinds. From 1860 to 1864 he studied painting under Gleyre and at the Academy, where he met Bazille, Monet and Sisley who became life-long friends. The young painters worked together, copied the old masters in the Louvre, or painted at Barbizon in the open. Renoir exhibited at the Salon in 1864 and 1865, but was rejected by the Salon in 1866 and 1867. Together with Monet he stayed in 1867 with Bazille, with whom he shared a studio between 1868 and 1870, frequented the Café Guerbois and met Manet. When living in Bougival in 1869, he developed with Monet the Impressionist manner of painting. Subsequently he went to paint with Monet in Argenteuil and took part in the first three Impressionist Exhibitions, 1874–1877, and showed his work at the Salon, 1878–1881.

In 1880 he met his future wife, Aline Charigot. He broke his right arm and painted with his left hand. In 1881 he visited Algeria, and later went to Italy. In 1882 he painted a portrait of Richard Wagner in Palermo and visited Cézanne in L'Estaque. Visits to Jersey, Guernsey and the Côte d'Azur followed. His work was now sometimes characterised by firmly outlined, rounded figures. In 1886 he exhibited with the Les XX group in Brussels, also in New York through Durand-Ruel, and at G. Petit in Paris, but refused to show his work at the Paris World Exhibition in 1889. He married Aline in 1890, with whom he was to have three sons. During this period he returned to painting in intense colours and loose brushwork, producing mainly nudes and landscapes. For the first time in 1892 the French nation bought one of his pictures, in a transaction arranged by Mallarmé. Visits to Spain and Brittany (Pont-Aven) followed. In 1894 Renoir was executor of Caillebotte's will in which he left his collection of Impressionist paintings to the nation. During a visit to Germany he visited Bayreuth and Dresden in 1896. He again broke his arm when he fell off his bicycle in 1897. In 1898 he visited Holland. He began to suffer from rheumatism, and after 1899 spent much of his time in southern France. In 1900 he was represented in the centenary exhibition of French art at the Paris World Exhibition, and was made a Knight of the Grand Cross of the Legion of Honour. His work was also increasingly shown abroad. During this time his health deteriorated further, his hands becoming crippled with gout. In 1904 he bought the house "Les Colettes" in Cagnes. A retrospective of his work was held at the 9th Biennale in Venice in 1910. During that year he visited Munich. In 1911 he was made an Officer of the Legion of Honour. In collaboration with R. Guino he began to produce sculpture in 1913. In 1919 he became Commander of the Legion of Honour and one of his paintings was hung in the Louvre.

Like Monet, Renoir delighted in painting family scenes and depicting life in the city and the country. Pure landscapes were unusual for Renoir; his main interest was in people, and women held a special fascination for him. He also produced still lifes and portraits. Although he adopted the broken brushwork of the Impressionists, his works had a character of their own, distinguishing themselves from those of Monet, Sisley and Pissarro though their gaiety and brilliance of colour.
*Illustrations:*
477   The Swing, 1876
484   Two Girls, c. 1881
502   The Painter Sisley and his Wife), 1868
502   Bal au Moulin de la Galette, 1876
503   La Première Sortie (The First Outing), c. 1876/77
504   On the Terrace, 1881
504   Bather with Long Blonde Hair, 1895

## REPIN Ilya Yefimovich

1844 Tschuguev (Ukraine) – 1930 Kuokkala (Finland)
Repin was trained as an icon painter. In 1863 he came to St Petersburg where he studied at the Academy of Fine Arts for six years, gaining the Grand Gold Medal. In 1873 his picture "Volga Tower" was shown in Vienna at the World Exhibition. With a scholarship he travelled in Italy and France, 1873–1876, and then lived in Moscow from 1877 to 1882 before returning to St Petersburg, where he met Tolstoy. In 1894 he accepted a professorship at the Academy, and became rector in 1898/99. From 1878 to 1891, and again from 1897, he was a member of the "Wanderers" whose aim was to take art to the outlying regions of Russia. Repin specialised in genre pictures and portraits, the former having an overtone of social criticism. After his West European tour with Stassov in 1883 he adopted Impressionistic elements. In 1887 he visited Italy and Germany, and the Paris World Exhibition in 1889. Further travels took him to England, Germany and Switzerland, later to Constantinople and Jerusalem. He bought a house in Kuokkala; there were signs of paralysis in his right side. In 1900 he was again in Paris, acting as juror at the Paris World Exhibition and becoming a member of the Legion of Honour. In 1917 he retired to Kuokkala, which had by then become part of Finland. Repin was noted for his portraits; he painted many of the distinguished Russian personalities of his time. The inspiration received from Courbet and the Impressionists did not find entry into his work until late in his life.
*Illustrations:*
542   Zaporozhian Cossacks (sketch), c. 1878
542   Portrait of Vera Alekseevna Repin, 1882

## REYNOLDS Joshua

1732 Plympton (Devon) – 1792 London
Reynolds was the son of a clergyman and was sent at the age of seventeen to study under the popular portrait painter Thomas Hudson in London. For some years he worked in his teacher's somewhat dry style in Plymouth, London and Devonport. His meeting with William Gandy (Gandy of Exeter) inspired him to adopt a new technique and a more fluid style, probably influenced by his study of Rembrandt. He went to Rome via Lisbon and Algeria with his patron Admiral Keppel, where he was particularly impressed by the works of Raphael and Michelangelo. Here he produced his famous "Caricaturas", portraits of English visitors to Rome. He returned by way of Florence, Parma, Venice and Paris to London, where he settled in 1753. Here he painted a portrait of Keppel depicted in the pose of the Apollo of Belvedere after a shipwreck (Greenwich, National Maritime Museum). Through the use of such citations and dramatic events Reynolds attempted to elevate portraiture to the level of historical painting. In 1768 he was appointed president of the newly-founded Royal Academy. In his *Discourses*, given annually at the awards ceremony, he presented the theory of the Grand Manner, that art must be more idealistic than realistic. His contact with Gainsborough, who came to live in London in the 1770s, remained tense, probably because of their difference in temperament. His last visit to the Continent in 1781, mainly devoted to the study of Rubens' works, also took him to Antwerp and Düsseldorf, amongst other places. Reynolds, who was knighted in 1769, was one of the great British painters of the 18th century and influenced generations of portrait painters.
*Illustrations:*
346   Portrait of Susanna Beckford, 1756
383   Sarah Siddons as the Tragic Muse, 1784
383   The Infant Samuel, 1776

## RIBERA Jusepe de

(also: José de Ribera; called: Lo Spagnoletto)
1591 Játiba (near Valencia) – 1652 Naples
In Valencia Ribera was trained by Ribalta, who introduced him to his tenebrism, a technique of painting in a dark, low key, characterised by contrasting use of light and shade. On his travels to Parma, Padua and Rome, Ribera became acquainted with the works of Raphael, Correggio, Titian and Veronese. In 1616 he settled in Naples and developed a style which owed much to Caravaggio. There he became painter to the Spanish Viceroy and later to his successor, the Duke of Monterrey, who procured for him commissions from the Augustine monastery in Salamanca ("Nativity", "Pietà", "The Virgin with Saints Antony and Augustine", 1631–1635). He subsequently abandoned the dark and sombre style, finding new ways of treating light and using brilliant colours (12 pictures of the prophets, Naples, Museo Nazionale di San Martino, 1637/38). His "Boy with a Clubfoot" (ill. p. 259) is typical of his more mature style, both thematically and in terms of pictorial composition. During this period of realism he had a leaning towards harrowing subjects, the crippled and malformed. Italian, Spanish and Flemish painters were engaged in his workshop, and while Ribera was of particular importance to Neapolitan art, great painters, such as Rembrandt and Velázquez, also found him an inspiration.
*Illustrations:*
259   The Boy with a Clubfoot, 1642
260   Archimedes, 1630
260   Martyrdom of St Bartholomew, 1630
261   St Christopher, 1637

## RICHTER Gerhard

born 1932 Waltersdorf (Oberlausnitz)
Richter worked initially as a painter of stage sets and posters in Zittau before attending the Dresden Academy, 1952–1955. On moving to West Germany he took up further studies for three years, from 1961, under Karl Otto Götz at the Düsseldorf Academy. Together with Konrad Fischer-Lueg and Sigmar Polke he arranged an "Action" in a furniture store in 1963, proclaiming capitalist realism in the manner of a parody. In 1964 he produced his first works with snapshots and magazine photographs. Richter often copied these in smudged tones of grey in enlarged form, retaining their context. He collected the originals, his own photographs and other pieces used to form an atlas, which has been displayed at exhibitions since 1972. Apart from these works occupying a place between Photo-Realism and Pop Art, he has produced coloured landscapes and cloud pictures, candle still lifes, and also roughly painted aerial views and paintings of RAL colour sample cards. From about 1968 he began to paint mostly large-scale "abstract pictures" based on structural studies, which impress with their colour intensity. He has been teaching at the Düsseldorf Academy since 1971.
*Illustrations:*
627   Ema – Akt auf einer Treppe (Ema – Nude descending a staircase), 1966
673   Untitled, 1984
673   Mountains (Himalaya), 1968

**RICHTER Ludwig**
(Adrian Ludwig Richter)
1803 Dresden – 1884 Dresden
The son of a copper engraver, Richter made a name for himself with his woodcut illustrations for books of fairytales, folklore and traditional songs. He began to work in this field in 1838 and retained an interest in it until the end of his life. Initially he wanted to become a landscape painter. This wish was granted in 1823, when he received a scholarship for a visit to Rome offered by the Dresden bookseller Arnold. In Rome he met Koch and the Nazarene group of painters, and produced idyllic Italian landscapes. On his return to Dresden, where he was appointed professor of landscape painting at the Academy in 1836, he continued with this subject, but lack of funds for another visit to Italy caused him to change direction. In search of new themes, he took his students on walking tours along the Elbe valley and through parts of Bohemia, using the studies made on these tours as a basis for his compositions. It appears that here he found what he had expressed in his Italian pictures: a harmonious relationship between man and nature. His last oil-painting dates from 1847.
*Illustration:*
457   Church at Graupen in Bohemia, 1836

**RIGAUD Hyacinthe**
(Jacinto Rigau y Ros)
1659 Perpignan – 1743 Paris
Rigaud's surviving business records reveal that he had an extensive workshop and employed speciality painters for flower decorations, textiles and background battle scenes and landscapes. After his early training in Montpellier and Lyon, Rigaud came to Paris in 1681, where already in 1682 he aroused Le Brun's interest with his historical painting "Cain building the City of Enoch". Le Brun urged him to take up portrait painting, and Rigaud soon became popular, and also known in court circles, where his van Dyck-inspired manner was met with approval under the absolutist monarchy of Louis XIV. Despite the fact that he used assistants, Rigaud proved to be an acute reader of character, as is evident in his portraits of "King Philip V" (Madrid, Prado, 1701) and that of "Elisabeth Charlotte, Duchess of Orléans" (Brunswik, Herzog-Anton-Ulrich-Museum, 1713). In his famous portraits of the "Sun King", however, he showed his mastery as a colourist and ability to satisfy ceremonial demands in pose and expression.
*Illustration:*
253   Portrait of Louis XIV, 1701

**RIVERA Diego**
1886 Guanajuato (Mexico) – 1957 Mexico City
Rivera was already studying at the S. Carlos Academy in Mexico City at the age of ten. A scholarship enabled him to visit Europe in 1907 and continue his studies in Madrid and Paris. The works of Cézanne and Picasso inspired him to adopt the Cubist manner. However, a visit to Italy in 1920/21, where he spent several months studying Renaissance fresco painting, caused him to change direction. On his return to Mexico he received commissions to produce large-scale wall paintings. His cycle in the Ministry of Education in Mexico City, 1923–1928, already showed his personal style. His monumental compositions narrate the story of the life of ordinary Mexican people. In 1927/28 he travelled to the USSR, but later he was expelled from the Communist Party because of his Trotskyist tendencies. From 1929 to 1935 he decorated the Mexican National Palace, taking as his theme the history of Mexico from the time of the ancient civilisations to the modern age.

He received various commissions from the USA, but because of ideological differences his work in the Rockefeller Center in New York in 1933 was not completed. Until late in life he received more work than he could cope with, mostly murals of Mexican history. Rivera, who was married to Frida Kahlo, is regarded as one of the three great Mexican mural painters, in company with Orozco and Siquieros.
*Illustration:*
604   The History of Mexico: Huastec Civilization, 1930–1932

**ROBERT Hubert**
1733 Paris – 1808 Paris
Robert's father was *valet de chambre* to the Marquis de Stainville, later to be Duc de Choiseul, who promoted the boy's talent. Robert accompanied the Marquis to Rome, where he attended the French Academy. Under the influence of Pannini's work and the etchings of Piranesi he painted pictures of ruins from Antiquity. In 1760 he visited with the Abbé de Saint-Non the recently discovered ruins of Pompeii and Herculaneum. Robert combined in his work representations of real and imaginary ruins, even depicting ruin versions of existing buildings. After spending eleven years in Italy, he returned to Paris in 1765, where he became a member of the Academy a year later. In 1784 he was appointed as the King's garden designer and curator of his art collection. He produced plans for redesigning the park at the Palace of Versailles along the lines of an English garden. During the Revolution he belonged to the commission, which also included Fragonard, that was to turn the Louvre into a museum. His best-known works are depictions of actual events, such as "The Conflagration at the Paris Opera" and "The Razing of the Bastille" (both Paris, Musée Carnevalet), and "Demolition of the Houses on the Pont du Change" (Munich, Alte Pinakothek).
*Illustration:*
367   The Porta Octavia in Rome, undated

**ROHAN BOOK OF HOURS** → Master

**ROMNEY George**
1734 Dalton-in-Furness (Lancashire) – 1802 Kendal (Westmorland)
The son of a cabinet-maker, Romney worked first in his father's workshop before being apprenticed to Christopher Steele, a portrait painter and former pupil of Carle van Loos. Romney set himself up in London in 1762 and aroused public attention with his painting "The Death of General Wolfe". His travels to France and Italy between 1764 and 1775 introduced him to French Neo-Classicism, Antiquity and the masters of the Roman High Renaissance. On his return to London he worked as a portrait painter and developed an interest in literary themes, making many drawings. His most famous sitter was Emma Harte, later Lady Hamilton, whom he presented in many mythological and literary roles. Bad health compelled him to retire to Kendal in 1795. Romney is considered one of the most important British portrait painters of the 18th century, along with Gainsborough and Reynolds.
*Illustration:*
388   The Leigh Family, c. 1767–1769

**ROSA Salvator**
1615 Arenella (near Naples) – 1673 Rome
Rosa was one of the most versatile talents of his period, working as painter, poet, etcher, actor-musician and composer. After an apprenticeship with

his uncle and brother-in-law he studied under Falcone, in whose style he later painted the wild battlepieces which made him famous ("Battle Scene", Florence, Palazzo Pitti, c. 1640). In his bizarre scenes of witchcraft and dramatic landscapes he showed an emotional and personal world which was the antithesis of the Classical stereotype. In the second half of the 1640s Rosa began to paint allegories of death, which have only now found due recognition (*L'umana fragilità*, Cambridge, Fitzwilliam Museum, 1651/52). He left Rome for Florence in 1640, where he lived for nine years and founded the Accademia dei Percossi, where he gathered a circle including painters of all kinds. Rosa was highly educated, and his intellectualism found expression in his philosophically condensed art and in the complex thoughts found in many of his pictures.
*Illustration:*
237   Democritus in Meditation, c. 1650

**ROSENQUIST James**
born 1933 Grand Forks (North Dakota)
Rosenquist studied at the University of Minnesota, 1952–1955, and in New York at the Art Students' League, 1957–1959, under Indiana and Jack Youngerman. In his spare time he worked as a designer and poster painter. Rosenquist, who is considered one of the major representatives of American Pop Art, produces objective motif assemblages. These consist of everyday objects and pictorial advertising material, which are arranged on large canvases. He uses simple, immediately recognisable objects without any attempt at Symbolism, an exception being his vast mural "F III" (3x26m) which aims to depict the interaction between man and technology in contemporary American society. This work went on a world tour from 1965 until 1968. In the 1970s Rosenquist was active in the movement opposing America's role in the Vietnam war, and he supported the democratic rights of artists. He settled in Aripeka, Florida, in 1983.
*Illustration:*
663   Marilyn Monroe I, 1962

**ROSLIN Alexander**
1718 Malmö – 1793 Paris
Roslin was noted for his portrait painting in the 18th century. After studying in Sweden he worked at the margrave's court in Bayreuth, 1745–1747. On his visit to Italy in 1747 he studied the works of Titian, Veronese, Reni and the Carracci. The Duchess of Parma, a daughter of King Louis XV, recommended him to the French court. In 1752 he arrived in Paris, where, apart from brief intervals, he settled for the rest of his life, becoming a close friend of Boucher. His manner of painting appealed to the aristocracy, and by the 1770s he had established himself as the favourite portrait painter of the nobility. His pictures show great skill in rendering texture and in capturing the characteristic essence of his sitters. In 1774 he received a call from the Stockholm court; in 1775 he became court painter in St Petersburg, returning via Warsaw and Vienna to Paris in 1778. His popularity waned as Neo-Classical tendencies became fashionable after the Revolution, but nevertheless Roslin left an enormous number of works.
*Illustration:*
345   Woman with a Veil: Marie Suzanne Roslin, 1768

**ROSSETTI Dante Gabriel**
(Gabriel Charles Rossetti)
1828 London – 1882 Birchington-on-Sea (Kent)
Rossetti's father was a Dante scholar and had to

leave his native Italy because of his liberal political attitude. In 1843 Rossetti began his training, and from 1846 he studied at the Royal Academy in London. He then worked with Hunt and Ford Madox Brown, and in 1848 was one of the founders of the Pre-Raphaelite Brotherhood. Most of his work was produced in the spirit of this movement, although he soon left it again. Many of his themes were taken from Dante or the *Morte d'Arthur* and have a strong overtone of Symbolism. In his later work he concentrated on single studies of allegorical females.
*Illustration:*
527   The Bride, 1865–1866

## ROSSO FIORENTINO
(Giovanni Battista Rossi)
1494 Florence – 1540 Paris
Rosso was one of the few Italian painters of the 16th century who refused to work within the rules of the High Renaissance. His tendency to distortion, to breaking up the human body into geometrical areas, and his unconventional treatment of colour, meant that due recognition was withheld until the beginning of the 20th century. It was only when art turned away from its traditional aim of creating ideal representations of what we see, that Rosso's work became interesting to such groups as the Expressionists, Cubists, and particularly the Surrealists. However, the modern view of Rosso's work was again based on a misconception. His intention had not been to create an aesthetically pleasing work, but to find a new way of expression that transcended realistic experience. Like Pontormo, to whose early work Rosso's coloration and figure representation have an affinity, Rosso was probably a pupil of del Sarto. Under this master Rosso would have been fully trained in the art of the High Renaissance and its further possibilities. Already in his first work, the fresco of the "Assumption" in the forecourt of Saint Annunziata in Florence (1517), his Mannerist tendencies were detectable, and this development established itself in his great altarpieces of the following years. While in Rome, 1524–1527, he also became strongly influenced by Michelangelo, whose Sistine ceiling he had studied.

In 1530 he received a call from King Francis I to Paris, and during the following decade he was mostly engaged in decorating the Palace of Fontainebleau. His principal contribution was the design of the gallery of Francis I, in which he created a unity of frescos, decorative elements and plasterwork. Together with the Bolognese painter Primaticcio, he founded the Fontainebleau school, which did much to disseminate Renaissance ideas north of the Alps.
*Illustration:*
181   Desposition, 1521

## ROTHKO Mark
(Markus Rothkovitz)
1903 Dvinsk (Lithuania) – 1970 New York
Rothko's family emigrated to Oregon when he was seven years old. He first studied at Yale University, then under Max Weber at the Art Students' League in New York, 1924–1929. Together with Adolph Gottlieb he founded the Expressionist group The Ten in 1935. In about 1938 he began to take an interest in Surrealism and engaged in the study of Greek mythology and metaphysics, Jung's theory of archetypes and primitive art.

He produced his first pictures depicting forms floating in space from 1947. Three years later he had evolved his distinctive manner. In 1949 he founded with William Baziotes, Motherwell and Newman the Subject of the Artist School, which only functioned for a year. He taught until 1955 at its successor, Studio 35. In 1950 he travelled in Eu-

rope, and from 1951–1954 he taught as assistant professor at Brooklyn College. In 1958 he received the lucrative commission of painting a mural in the Seagram Building. After 1960 his palette became noticeably darker and gloomier. In 1964 he decorated a chapel in Houston designed by Philip Johnson for Jean and Dominique De Menil. Rothko committed suicide in 1970. He was one of the most significant representatives of flat area colour painting.
*Illustrations:*
620   Red, Green, Blue, 1955
649   Number 10, 1950

## ROTTMANN Carl
1797 Handschuhsheim (near Heidelberg) – 1850 Munich
Rottmann came from a family of painters and therefore had early contact with other Heidelberg artists. In 1821 he began to study historical painting at Munich Academy and went on nature studies in the Bavarian mountains. A visit to Italy, 1826–1828, and again in 1829, introduced him to the Roman manner of open-air painting. Important for his development was his meeting with the Bavarian Crown Prince, who lived in Rome and was to become King Ludwig I. He commissioned Rottmann to paint the "Italian Cycle" in the Munich Hofgarten Arcades (1830–1833), a series of frescos depicting Italian landscapes, a subject often repeated by Rottmann. Another major work was the "Greek Cycle", for which Rottmann had made nature studies during a visit to Greece in 1834/35 and which were destined for the Neue Pinakotek in Munich. These were encaustic paintings (a technique with hot wax colours that are fused after application), and Rottmann worked on them until his death. In these landscapes, the architectonic structure of strictly classical composition is combined with a dramatic treatment of colour expressed through light and other natural phenomena.
*Illustration:*
455   Sicyon and Corinth, c. 1836–1838

## ROTTMAYR Johann Michael
1654 Laufen (Upper Bavaria) – 1730 Vienna
Trained by his mother, Rottmayr received decisive inspiration from Loth, in whose workshop in Venice he worked from 1675 to 1688. He came through Passau and reached Salzburg in 1689 (mythological ceiling frescos, Archbishop's Palace). During this period he also produced panel paintings which still owed much to the Venetian "tenebrosi", but he soon evolved his own powerful, drastic style with popular appeal. He visited Frain (in Moravia) and Prague, and then moved on to Vienna. While there he succeeded in getting commissions around Austria and southern Germany. Particularly in his fresco painting Rottmayr was successful in freeing himself from the illusionist manner of presenting architecture, as practised by Pozzo, for example, and in discovering illusionist devices in the field of colour and figure composition (Apotheosis in the cupola of the ancestral hall of Vranov castle, Frain, 1696). Like Altomonte, Rottmayr prepared the way to a new form of monumental painting by closing up all ceiling space and introducing a coloration which foreshadowed the Rococo. The finest examples of this are the ceiling frescos of the castle at Pommersfelden (1716–1718), those in the church of Melk monastery (1716–1722), and the Karlskirche in Vienna (1726).
*Illustration:*
258   St Benno, 1702

## ROUAULT Georges
1871 Paris – 1958 Paris
Rouault served his apprenticeship under a painter of stained glass, and it was his task to restore medieval windows. Later he studied with Moreau, under whose influence he remained until 1903. His early works were mostly religious themes treated in Rembrandt's chiaroscuro manner. After Moreau's death, Daumier and Toulouse-Lautrec inspired him to turn to other subjects. His palette was dark and sombre until he came into contact with the Fauves in 1905, when he began to choose colour for expression. His figures – clowns, prostitutes, peasants, labourers, judges – are drawn in wild, powerful brushstrokes against a glowing background, boldly outlined in black. In their iridescent, brilliant coloration they reveal Rouault's early connections with the stained glass art.
*Illustrations:*
561   The Holy Face, 1933
561   The Old King, 1937

## ROUSSEAU Henri
1844 Laval – 1910 Paris
Rousseau, known as "Le Douanier" because he was a customs officer who painted in his spare time, had no artistic training whatsoever and did not devote himself to painting until he took early retirement at the age of 40. He took painting seriously, copying in the Louvre, but allowing his heart and feeling to dictate irrespective of academic rules, examples and theories. The simplicity of his pictures, which were painted in strong, cheerful colours with figures in stiff poses, aroused much derision. Pissarro was one of the first to recognise his talent, and Gauguin also took him seriously. Picasso possessed some of his pictures, which are now in the Louvre. His portraits, still lifes, landscapes and exotic scenes are the first examples of a manner of painting which came to be called "naive". Painters in this field treat the subject in their own visionary way without realistic analysis or intellectual reflection.
*Illustration:*
513   War, 1894

## ROUSSEAU Théodore
(Pierre Etienne Théodore Rousseau)
1812 Paris – 1867 Barbizon
Already as a boy of ten Rousseau made drawings in the open in the Boi de Boulogne. In 1829 he became a pupil of Charles Rémond at the Ecole des Beaux Arts in Paris. In the Louvre he copied the works of Claude Lorrain and the Dutch masters and studied the more recent British artists, including Constable and Bonington. He also painted in the open and was probably the first to work in the woods of Fontainebleau. He became known at first through his nature studies, which he had brought back from the Auvergne, where he stayed in 1830. He travelled extensively to capture French landscapes, visiting Normandy, Brittany, Provence, the Jura region and the Vendée. From 1836 he stayed regularly in Barbizon, a village near Fontainebleau, to paint there, and almost spending all his time there between 1848 and 1863. In 1867 he was chairman of the painting judges at the Paris World Exhibition. Rousseau's enthusiasm was centred on nature: "To hell with the civilised world! Long live nature, the forests and the poetry of old." His determined effort to save the Compiègne forest resulted in the formation of the first nature conservation movement in the world. It follows that he painted predominantly wooded scenery and trees, which he rendered realistically and yet atmospherically in their seasonal and diurnal changes. Long before Monet he captured one and the same motif at different times of the day. For a long time his pictures were rejected by the Salon. It was not until the

1850s that he had some success. Although his friends, the Barbizon painters Jules Dupré and Constant Troyon, gained more public recognition, it was Rousseau who was the spiritual leader of this colony of artists.
*Illustrations:*
439    The Chestnut Avenue, 1837
439    Oak trees near Apremont, 1852


## RUBENS Peter Paul
1577 Siegen (Westphalia) – 1640 Antwerp
His father was a Calvinist and so had to live in exile from Antwerp, so Rubens grew up in Cologne. On his father's death, his mother returned to Antwerp in 1587, where he was brought up and educated in the Catholic faith. At the age of fourteen he entered the household of a Flemish princess as a page, and later studied under Tobias Verhaecht, a landscape painter, then under Adam van Noort, and the last four years until 1600 under Otho Venius. While still working in the latter's workshop he was accepted as master in the Lukas Guild in 1598. In 1600 he visited Italy, and while in Venice attracted the attention of Duke Vincenzo Gonzaga, finally taking up residence at his court in Mantua. Rubens accompanied the duke on his travels to Florence and Rome, and was sent by him with gifts and paintings on a diplomatic mission to Spain in 1603. In Venice, Rome and Genoa, Rubens copied Titian, Tintoretto and Raphael, and also the works of contemporaries, including Caravaggio, the Carracci and Elsheimer. Having already executed several large commissions in Italy, he returned as a successful painter to Antwerp in 1608.

There he was appointed court painter in 1609 to the Regent Albert and Isabella, receiving an annual salary of 500 guilders, and was exempted from the guild's restrictions and taxation. He received permission to establish himself outside the regent's residence, which was in Brussels, and married Isabella Brant, daughter of the town clerk (ill. p. 291). In 1610 he built himself a large house and studio. During his Antwerp period, until 1622, he received a flood of commissions from the church, state and nobility, employing in his large workshop many pupils who later became famous to help with the work. They included van Dyck, Jordaens, Snyders and Cornelis de Vos. The Gobelin factory produced tapestries after his sketches, and engravers used his paintings, disseminating the "Rubens style" all over Europe. His largest commission was for a series of 21 paintings of the life of the Queen Dowager Marie de'Medici for the Palais Luxembourg in Paris, for which he received a fee of 20.000 ducats (ill. p. 292). Between 1623 and 1631 he travelled frequently on diplomatic missions, visiting London and Madrid, where he received peerages from both Charles I of England and Philip IV of Spain. The most important painter of the International Baroque thus became the first artistic aristocrat, whose fame and wealth constantly increased. Isabella Brant died in 1626; a year later he sold his great art collection, which included works by Raphael, Titian, Tintoretto and himself, for 100.000 guilders to the Duke of Buckingham, and in 1630 he married the 16-year-old Helene Fourment, whom he immortalised in many portraits. After the death of Queen Isabella he gradually withdrew from court and bought Steen castle near Mecheln. His last big commission was the decoration of the Spanish king's hunting lodge, Torre de la Parada near Madrid, which he designed but was no longer able to carry out himself.

Rubens, the great Baroque master, successfully brought together in his style northern and Flemish elements of this period with those of Italy. His influence on the painters of his century was enormous, as it was on sculpture and architecture. His

sometimes gigantic "pictorial inventions", which do not always appeal to today's taste, were pioneering in composition, design and the art of colour, taking as subject all major themes of painting: Biblical scenes and lives of the saints, mythology and subjects of Antiquity, and also peasant scenes, landscapes and portraiture. "My talent is such," he wrote, "that no undertaking, however large and varied in theme, has ever gone beyond my self-confidence."
*Illustrations:*
274    Portrait of Susanne Fourment (La chapeau de paille), c. 1625
277    Venus at a Mirror, c. 1615
290    The Four Philosophers, c. 1611
290    Stormy Landscape with Philemon and Baucis, c. 1620
291    Rubens with his first wife Isabella Brant in the Honeysuckle Bower, c. 1609/10
292    The Landing of Marie de' Medici at Marseilles, c. 1622–1625
292    The Rape of the Daughters of Leucippus, c. 1618
293    Hippopotamus and Crocodile Hunt, c. 1615/16
294    The Three Graces, 1639


## RUISDAEL Jacob van
(also: Ruysdael)
c. 1628/29 Haarlem – 1682 Haarlem
Ruisdael's father was a frame-maker and art dealer. He probably studied under his uncle Salomon or the landscape painter Cornelis Vroom. He was already accepted into the Lukas Guild in Haarlem at the age of 20, but also seems to have studied medicine and to have practised it although he did not receive his doctorate until 1676. Ruisdael belonged to the greatest of Dutch landscape painters and was certainly dominant in this field in the second half of the century. During his early period he mostly painted dune landscapes in the surroundings of Haarlem. After 1650 he visited with his friend Berchem the eastern parts of Holland and the wooded, hilly regions of the Rhineland. His range from then on included hilly landscapes traversed by rivers, with mighty, gnarled oaks, picturesque waterfalls and old water mills, often spanned by clouded sky. These works were to have a particularly strong influence on the Romantics. In the 1660s, after Ruisdael had settled in Amsterdam, he also painted panoramic views of cities, winterscapes and vedutas. His most important pupil was Hobbema.
*Illustrations:*
280    The Windmill at Wijk bij Duurstede, c. 1670
327    Two Watermills and an Open Sluice near Singraven, c. 1650–1652


## RUNGE Philipp Otto
1777 Wolgast (Pomerania) – 1810 Hamburg
Runge's father was a grain merchant and ship owner. When still a child, Runge already showed an extraordinary talent at cut-out silhouettes. His brother Daniel helped him greatly in his career, introducing him to artists and supporting him financially through his Hamburg trading company. Runge studied at Copenhagen Academy, 1799–1801, then visited Friedrich at Greifswald and went to Dresden. During this time he became fascinated with the works of the poet and dramatist Ludwig Tieck, whom he visited in Berlin. He fell in love with Pauline Bassenge, a fundamental experience for his artistic as well as his personal life. After marrying her in 1804, he returned with her to Wolgast. Runge often suffered from ill-health, and from 1807 he and his family lived with his brother in Hamburg. In Runge's drawings, etchings and paint-

ings, real objects are mere indications of a world imbued with God's spirit, in which substance and light represent two different levels of an all-embracing spiritual unity, the material and the immaterial. His work on colour theory formed the basis for his metaphysical light and colour treatment, with symbolic elements drawn from Protestant Baroque mysticism.
*Illustrations:*
413    The Hülsenbeck Children, 1805/06
452    Rest on the Flight into Egypt, c. 1805/06
452    The Artist's Parents, 1806
453    Morning (first version), 1808


## RUYSDAEL Salomon van
(also: Ruisdael)
c. 1600–1603 Naarden – 1670 Haarlem
Ruysdael, the uncle of Jacob van Ruisdael, came to Haarlem in 1616, where he probably trained in the workshop of Esaias van de Velde, and became a member of the Lukas Guild in 1623. He must have been highly respected because he was made borough councillor, 1659–1666. His early dune and wood scenes, painted predominantly in yellow-browns and grey-greens, are reminiscent of his teacher and of the works of van Goyen. His best works were produced after 1645: landscapes with wide, peaceful rivers, fringed with trees, on which drift boats or ferries, houses and spires, and a deep blue sky with only a suggestion of cloud formation on the far horizon.
*Illustration:*
310    The Crossing at Nimwegen, 1647


## RYMAN Robert
born 1930 Nashville (Tennessee)
Ryman studied at the Tennessee Polytechnic Institute, 1948/49, and the George Peabody College for Teachers in Nashville, 1949/50. In 1952 he settled in New York where his interest in painting became more pronounced. Until 1960 he worked as an attendant at the Museum of Modern Art, where he met other artists, including Dan Flavin and Sol LeWitt, who were also exponents of Minimal Art like himself. In his first works dating from the early 1950s he explored the evolutionary process of pictures; to this day his work is determined by his interest in these matters. In the late 1950s Ryman opted for the square format, and his more extensive colour scale became later limited to white. His explorations concentrated on how the diverse handling of brushwork was affected by different surfaces and how colour reacted to it, and in this way he produced several sequences of paintings. Since the 1960s he has also investigated the visual effects achieved by fastening pictures to the wall, and the fastenings and holders became an integral part of his work. The strict ordering of his work and concentration on the very few features which constitute his pictures, make him an outstanding representative of American conceptual art.
*Illustration:*
678    Summit, 1978


## SAENREDAM Pieter Jansz.
(also: Zaenredam)
1597 Assendelft – 1665 Haarlem
The son of a famous engraver, Saenredam worked for ten years in the workshop of Frans Pietersz Grebber before becoming independent in 1623. He specialised in architectural views and especially in church interiors, establishing this theme as a branch of painting in its own right in Dutch art. He minutely prepared each work with sketches and drawings, and with his accurate representation of perspective and proportion, and skilled handling of light effects, achieved a wonderful suggestion of

lightness and spaciousness with only a few colour tones. He also produced exterior views, faithful representations of actual buildings, whose main attraction lies in their sparse linearity.
*Illustration:*
310 Church Interior in Utrecht, 1642

## SÁNCHEZ COTÁN → Cotán

## SANDRART Joachim von
1609 Frankfurt/Main – 1688 Nuremberg
Today Sandrart is less known for his painting than for his theoretical work *Teutsche Academie der edlen Bau-, Bild- und Mahlerey-Künste* [German Academy of the Fine Arts and Architecture] (Nuremberg, 1675–1679), a historically arranged compendium of great significance to German art history writings. In Strasbourg (training under Stoßkopf), Prague (assistant to Sadeler), Utrecht (working with Honthorst), London, Bologna, Venice and Rome, Sandrart had met the most famous artists of his time, including Rembrandt, Rubens and Liss. From today's point of view he seems to have had little originality, yet his contemporaries regarded him as the best German painter of his generation. His large repertoire included portraits, altarpieces, mythological and allegorical scenes as well as historical paintings.
*Illustration:*
257 November, 1643

## SARGENT John Singer
1856 Florence, – 1925 London
The son of an emigrant American doctor, Sargent studied at the Accademia delle Belle Arti in Florence, 1870–1874, and worked in the studio of Carolus-Duran in Paris in 1874. In 1879 he visited Spain, where he saw the works of Velásquez. From 1880 to 1882 he stayed in Holland, studying Frans Hals. His painting "Madame Gautreau" created a scandal at the Salon in 1884. He left for London, making friends with Whistler, whose studio he took over in 1885. In 1886 he became a co-founder of the Impressionist association The New English Art Club. From 1888 he began to gain attention with his portraits, working exclusively as a portrait painter in England and America between 1893 and 1906. In their characteristic realism, but also pleasing representation, his portraits were aimed at meeting upper-middle-class taste. In 1890 he became a member of the Legion of Honour, in 1894 a member of the National Academy of Design in New York, and in 1897 a member of the Royal Academy, London. In 1907 he turned to landscape painting, mostly in water-colour, and in 1914 went to the Continent to paint in the open. Among his most notable works are his mural decorations at Boston Public Library, 1890–1916. He produced war scenes in northern France in 1918. In the 1920s he painted wall decorations in the Boston Museum of Fine Arts and the Widener Library at Harvard University.
*Illustration:*
540 The Daughters of Edward Darley Boit, 1882

## SARTO Andrea del
1486 Florence – 1530 Florence
The son of a tailor (hence the nickname del "Sarto"), he was trained by Piero di Cosimo in the late 15th century tradition, but after studying the works of Leonardo, Raphael and Michelangelo, he developed around 1505 his own style which made him a major representative of the Florentine High Renaissance. From about 1517 he began to break through these conventions ("Madonna delle Arpie", Florence, Uf-

fizi), moving towards Mannerism ("Sacrifice of Isaac", Dresden, Gemäldegalerie, c. 1527). Equally brilliant in drawing as in painterly techniques, he exercised a strong influence on Rosso and Pontormo, who, in turn, inspired his own late work. The range of his development becomes apparent by a comparison of frescos of the life of San Filippo Benizzi (Florence, forecourt of Saint Annunziata, 1508–1510), which seem to consist of many small parts, and those of the life of St John the Baptist in the Chiostro dello Scalzo in Florence (1514–1526), which are monochrome and give an impression of overall unity.
*Illustration:*
166 Pietà, c. 1519/20

## SASSETTA
(Stefano di Giovanni)
c. 1392 Siena (?) – 1450 Siena
The first record of Sassetta dates from 1423. Nothing is known about his origins and training. His work shows that he orientated himself towards the art of Simone Martini and also of Lorenzetti, without becoming an imitator, as did some of the painters of the Sienese school. In opposition to the local trend he also received inspiration from the schools of Lombardy and Florence, as shown in his handling of space. In terms of theme and form he went beyond all Sienese painters of the 15th century. His contemporaries placed him next to the great masters of the Trecento, and he had so many imitators, that many of their works were long regarded as carried out by this master's own hand.
*Illustrations:*
55 The Mystic Marriage of St Francis, 1437–1444
55 The Procession of the Magi, c. 1432–1436

## SAVERY Roelant
(also: Ruelandt Savery)
1576 Kortrijk – 1639 Utrecht
In 1590 Savery came with his parents to Holland, living first in Haarlem, then in Amsterdam. This is reflected in his work, which shows Dutch and Flemish influences. He worked for the Emperor Rudolf II in Prague, 1604–1612, and in 1615/16 went to the court of the Emperor Mathew in Vienna. He then lived at Utrecht, becoming a member of the Lukas Guild in 1619. He delighted in late Mannerist extremes, taking as starting point the wild, romantic landscapes of van Coninxloo and Jan Brueghel's love of detail. Typical of his work are landscapes which are often dotted with ancient ruins or with a Noah's ark in the background, with all kinds of beasts romping about, both native and exotic. Despite their faithfulness in observation and detail, these pictures suggest in their bold coloration a paradisiacal, fairy-tale world.
*Illustration:*
299 Landscape with Birds, 1628

## SCHICK Gottlieb
1776 Stuttgart – 1812 Stuttgart
Schick was the son of a publican and tailor, and was sent for early training to the Stuttgart Karlsschule, where he received a broad education in the humanities. He then became a pupil of David in Paris and subsequently went to Rome for further studies, as was usual at the time. His most noted works were created in 1802 in Stuttgart, before he went to Rome, "Heinrike Dannecker" (Stuttgart, Staatsgalerie), the portrait of the wife of his teacher and friend, the sculptor Johann Heinrich Danecker, and the portrait of "Wilhelmine von Cotta" (ill. p. 451), the wife of the famous Tübingen publisher. In these pictures Schick succeeded in combining Classicist form with uncon-

ventional liveliness of expression. In Rome, Schick was introduced by Wilhelm von Humboldt to the circle of German intellectuals gathered there, including Ludwig Tieck, the Schlegel brothers and the philosopher Schelling. His portraits of members of the Humboldt family count as some of his best works, although he also aspired at rendering mythological and allegorical themes as well as those from Roman history ("Apollo amongst the Shepherds", Stuttgart, Staatsgalerie).
*Illustration:*
451 Wilhelmine von Cotta, 1802

## SCHIELE Egon
1890 Tulln (Austria) – 1918 Vienna
Although Schiele's brief period of creativity took place during the era of the Vienna Jugendstil, which he actively supported, he nevertheless followed his own personal inclinations, developing a style which contained Art Nouveau elements but already pointed towards Expressionism. He attended the Vienna Academy of Fine Arts, 1906–1909, was involved in the foundation of the Neukunstgruppe in 1909, and worked for the Wiener Werkstätten, an arts and crafts establishment. He admired van Gogh and Toulouse-Lautrec and was influenced by Munch and Hodler. His friendship with Klimt brought with it a reciprocal artistic influence which proved to be fruitful to both. Although his early work took into account major ideas of the Vienna Jugendstil, Schiele soon converted these into his own idiom of flat and ornamental representation, choosing as subjects the human figure and landscape. His colours were lively, almost glowing, because he accorded colour the highest place in the scale of expressiveness. He exaggerated and distorted his subjects, using bold perspectival angles and feverish colour accents. Drawings make up the greater part of his work, and his oil paintings always followed the concept of prior drawings. Schiele died in 1918 of the Spanish influenza, as did Klimt.
*Illustrations:*
537 Female Model in Bright Red Jacket an Pants, 1914
537 Krumau Landscape (Town and River), 1915/16

## SCHLEMMER Oskar
1888 Stuttgart – 1943 Baden-Baden
After completing his apprenticeship in a workshop specialising in marquetry, Schlemmer went to the School of Applied Arts and then studied at the Academy in Stuttgart, 1905–1909. In 1910 he paid an extended visit to Berlin, and in 1912 he became a pupil in the class of Adolf Hoelzel in Stuttgart. Walter Gropius invited him to the Weimar Bauhaus in 1920, where he became first the head of mural painting, then took over the workshop of wood and stone sculpture. He became widely known when his Triadic Ballet was first performed in Stuttgart in 1922, which involved model figures clad in stereometric costumes to act as "people in space". His aspirations in this field found their culmination when appointed head of the theatrical set workshop at the Dessau Bauhaus, where he was able to establish an experimental stage. His exploration of the relationships between and the effects of space, form, colour, tone, movement and light found pictorial expression in his mural paintings and various pictures. In 1929 he accepted an invitation to the Breslau Academy, then going to the Vereinigte Staatsschulen in Berlin in 1932, before being dismissed from his teaching position by the National Socialists in 1933.
*Illustration:*
600 Bauhaus Stairway, 1932

## SCHMIDT-ROTTLUFF Karl

1884 Rottluff (near Chemnitz) – 1976 Berlin
In 1905 Karl Schmidt followed his schoolfriend Heckel to Dresden to study architecture. There they founded with Kirchner and Fritz Bleyl the Brücke group. As a self-taught painter Schmidt's early work was under the influence of Neo-Impressionism. In approaching Fauvism his colour fields became broader and more brilliant. Schmidt painted landscapes, still lifes and nudes as well as portraits. He also produced a great number of graphic works, particularly woodcuts. By 1910 he had abandoned Impressionist coloration in favour of clear colours, and his now more simplified forms resulted in a tighter pictorial structure. In 1911 he moved with the other Brücke members to Berlin. Elements of Cubism and traces of African sculpture now entered his figurative representations. His bodies appeared heavy, large, block-like and primitive, and were framed by curving and angular black outlines. A similar tendency is detectable in his landscapes. In the mid-1920s his pictures became more relaxed, more scenic, and showed greater spatial depth. Under the repressive working conditions in the Third Reich – he had been banned from painting since 1941 – his pictures had an air of melancholy and depression.
*Illustration:*
583   Gap in the Dyke, 1910

## SCHNABEL Julian

born 1951 New York
Schnabel's family moved in 1965 from New York to Texas, where Julian studied at the University of Houston, 1969–1972. In the following two years Schnabel attended the Independent Study Programme of the New York Whitney Museum, supporting himself by casual labour. Like his fellow artist David Salle, who had made his name in the early 1980s, Schnabel entered the art scene in 1979 with his one-man exhibition at Mary Boone's gallery in New York. His mainly large-scale works combine unusual backgrounds, such as velvet and carpet, with objects, such as porcelain fragments or deer antlers, while fragmented lettering is worked wildly into the picture. From the mid-1980s Schnabel also began to produce collages, etchings and bronze sculpture.
*Illustration:*
680   L'Heroïne, 1987

## SCHÖNFELD Johann Heinrich

1609 Biberach an der Riß – 1682 Augsburg
After an apprenticeship in Memmingen, Schönfeld went via Basle, where he studied Callot's works and the Dutch Mannerists, to Rome and Naples for further studies in 1633. In 1652 he settled in Augsburg, where he lived until the end of his life. He began to apply all he had seen and learned: the serene, classical landscapes of Nicolas Poussin in Rome, the multi-figured, lively compositions of Salvator Rosa in Naples, the fine coloration of the Venetian masters. From being a painter of small-figured, mythological and Biblical scenes in broad atmospheric landscapes, Schönfeld developed under the Italian influence, and particularly the Neapolitan example, into an imaginative, original and versatile artist whose themes included mythology, triumphal processions, historical subjects, battle-pieces, genre scenes and imaginary landscapes. He also took up new subjects ("The Treasure-Hunters", Stuttgart, Staatsgalerie, 1662), developed a finely-graded, light coloration and had many followers in southern Germany. He was regarded as the most important German painter between 1630 and 1680.
*Illustration:*
257   Il Tempo (Chronos), c. 1645

## SCHONGAUER Martin

c. 1450 Colmar – 1491 Colmar
His name probably derives from the town of Schongau, although the family are recorded among the gentry of Augsburg since 1329. Schongauer's father Caspar, evidently a well-known goldsmith, moved from Augsburg to Colmar in 1445. Martin was first sent to study at the University of Leipzig, then learned engraving and drawing in his father's workshop before being trained as a painter, probably under Caspar Isenmann in Colmar. Schongauer is the most outstanding engraver and draughtsman in German art before Dürer. So far 115 engravings and 52 drawings by him have been authenticated, and added to these innumerable copies after his works have survived. He was a master of fine detail and most imaginative in his handling of line. In this he followed the general tendency of European art in the 1470s and 1480s – comparable, perhaps, to the somewhat older Botticelli in Italy. Major elements in his figurative and landscape painting make it reasonable to assume that he visited the Netherlands, where he might have gained particular inspiration from van der Weyden and his followers.
*Illustration:*
143   Madonna of the Rose Bower, 1473

## SCHOOL OF FONTAINEBLEAU

c. 1530 – c. 1570
This name is given to the group of artists, predominantly from Italy, who were involved in the decoration of the palace of Fontainebleau, begun in 1528 under Francis I. They brought Mannerist style elements to France and contributed greatly to their introduction north of the Alps. With the arrival of Rosso Fiorentino in 1530, Primaticcio in 1531, and Niccolò dell'Abbate in 1552, Fontainebleau became the centre of exchange between Italian and French art. Notable works combining various artistic branches are the galleries of Francis I (Rosso) and Henry II (Primaticcio).

During the so-called second school of Fontainebleau (from 1590) a decorative style was developed under the leadership of the Antwerp artist Ambroise Dubois and two French painters, Toussaint Debreuil and Martin Fréminet, which through printed copies became widely distributed all over Europe. It is not always possible to determine the relative degree to which Italian, French and Dutch masters contributed.
*Illustrations:*
150   Gabrielle d'Estrées and One of her Sisters in the Bath, c. 1594–1599
209   Diana the Huntress, c. 1550
209   Landscape with Threshers, c. 1555–1565

## SCHUMACHER Emil

born 1912 Hagen (Westphalia)
From 1932 to 1935 Schumacher attended the School of Applied Arts in Dortmund where, following his parents' wishes, he studied commercial art. Initially he worked as a painter and lithographer before being called up for compulsory service as an engineering draughtsman in the armaments industry, 1939–1945. Under the influence of the works of Christian Rohlfs, he began to paint Cubist landscapes after the war, but through a visit to Paris in 1951 and acquaintance with the German painter Wols he found his own pictorial idiom, closely related to the Informel. In his now entirely abstract works he uses colour as a pure substance, achieving depth by building it up, occasionally to almost relief-like thickness. From 1958 to 1960 Schumacher was professor at the Hamburg College of Fine Arts, and from 1966 to 1977 he taught at the Karlsruhe Academy. During this period he developed a style between painting and relief by in-troducing materials such as lead, asphalt, sisal and paper which are hammered into the surface. In recent years Schumacher's style has become more serene.
*Illustration:*
643   Spatial Division, 1955

## SCHWIND Moritz von

1804 Vienna – 1871 Munich
Schwind was the son of a senior civil servant and was educated at a public school and university in Vienna. His painting was concerned with the visual representation of Romantic literature and music, and was influenced by his friendship with poets and musicians, including Franz Grillparzer, Nikolaus Lenau and Franz Schubert. The foundations of his idealistic style had been laid by his teachers at the Vienna Academy, and later by Cornelius, whom he met in Munich in 1828. He worked in Karlsruhe and Frankfurt am Main before being appointed professor at the Munich Academy in 1847. Schwind delighted in the chronological depiction of a story, as was possible in fresco painting (Wartburg, Vienna Hofoper), or in painting a picture which unites a number of small scenes, a kind of panel painting invented by him in analogy to poetry and music ("The Symphony", 1852, Munich, Neue Pinakothek). He produced many small pictures with romantic scenes from his own memories or from literature, most of which are now at the Munich Schack-Galerie ("Morning Hour", "The Honeymoon").
*Illustration:*
457   Fairy Dance in the Alder Grove, c. 1844

## SCHWITTERS Kurt

1887 Hanover – 1948 Ambleside (Westmorland)
Schwitters studied art in Hanover, Dresden and Berlin, 1909–1914, then returned to Hanover. There he wrote a poem in the style of the Expressionist writer August Stramm. In 1918 he showed his first series of abstract paintings at the Berlin Sturm, the gallery of Herwarth Walden. During this time he had his first contacts with the Dadaists in Zurich and Berlin, including Hans Arp, Raoul Hausmann and Hannah Höch. In exploring new pictorial and sculptural forms of expression he developed the idea of the Merz picture. In 1919 he produced his first Merz assemblage consisting of a variety of pasted-on objects, and published his first collection of poems, Anna Blume, which are constructed according to the same principles. In 1922 he attended the Weimar Dada congress and helped van Doesburg in bringing Dadaism to Holland. From 1920 he used the title Merz for all his works, in particular his "total sculpture", the Merzbau in his house in Hanover, and also for the magazine which he published between 1923 and 1932. In 1932 he became a member of Abstraction-Création.
*Illustration:*
609   Merz 25 A. The Constellation, 1920

## SCOREL Jan van

1495 Schoorl (near Alkmaar) – 1562 Utrecht
After an apprenticeship with Jacob Cornelisz in Amsterdam, Scorel went south on an extended tour, visiting Dürer in Nuremberg, painting his first representative work in Obervellach in Austria ("Sippenaltar", 1520), then travelling via Venice to Rome. Here Pope Adrian VI, a native of Utrecht, appointed him painter to the Vatican and successor to Raphael as Keeper of the Belvedere. From Rome he went on a pilgrimage to the Holy Land. In 1524 he settled in Utrecht and as the leading Netherlandish "Romanist" developed a brilliant career as a painter and teacher. Highly educated, equally endowed

with intellect and spontaneity, he created a wealth of altarpieces and portraits in which Italian art merged with native tradition.
*Illustration:*
203   Mary Magdalene, 1529

## SEBASTIANO DEL PIOMBO
(Sebastiano Luciani)
c. 1485 Venice – 1547 Rome
Sebastiano was trained in the workshop of Giovanni Bellini and under Giovanni Battista Cima. He had close contacts with Giorgione, after whose death he went to Rome in 1511 to carry out fresco decorations of mythological themes for the banker Agostino Chigi in the hall of the Villa Farnesina. In Rome he met Raphael, whose style is reflected in some of Sebastiano's portraits. Their friendship turned into enmity in 1515, and Sebastiano turned to Michelangelo, whose formal ideas he expressed in some of his religious works. After a visit to Venice he returned to Rome in 1528/29, where in 1531 he became keeper of the papal leaden seal, hence his name. Sebastiano became famous as a portrait painter; his mythological and religious paintings showed too often a dependence on the works of his two famous friends.
*Illustration:*
173   Cardinal Carondelet and his Secretary,
      c. 1512–1515

## SEGANTINI Giovanni
1858 Arco (Lake Garda) – 1899 near Pontresina (Engadine)
Segantini grew up in poor circumstances and was apprenticed to a decorative painter. He attended evening classes at the Brera Academy in Milan, 1875–1879, received a contract from the art dealer Grubica, and went for five years to Puisano to make nature studies. During this period he was fascinated by Swiss mountain scenery and peasant life. He usually chose the large format, painting in light, brilliant colours, using broken brushstrokes and dazzling lighting. In 1886 he settled in Savognin, and from 1894 he lived in Maloja in the Upper Engadine. From 1890 he devoted himself increasingly to allegorical themes with Symbolist influences ("Cross Mothers", Vienna, Kunsthistorisches Museum). In 1898 he became a member of the Vienna Secession. In 1909 the Segantini Museum in St Moritz was opened. His work is regarded as belonging both to Symbolism and to the Jugendstil.
*Illustration:*
530   The Hay Harvest, 1899

## SEURAT Georges
1859 Paris – 1891 Paris
Seurat, the son of a bailiff, took drawing lessons from 1875 and later copied works in museums. In 1878/79 he studied at the Academy and read works on colour theory. After military service in 1880 he settled in Paris. In 1883 a large drawing was accepted by the Salon, and he began a large painting, an open-air scene, in the pointillist, or divisionist manner. In 1884 he met Signac and, with other likeminded artists, the Society of Independent Artists was founded to hold its own exhibitions. In 1885 he worked on the Paris Seine island Grand Jatte and in Grancamp on the coast of Normandy. He met Pissarro, who followed his style. In 1886 Seurat aroused great attention at the VIII Impressionist Exhibition with his picture "Sunday Afternoon on the Island la Grande Jatte" (ill. p.507). He began to show his work alongside that of Pissarro and Signac; he met the art theorist C. Henry, and was in contact with Symbolists and anarchists. In 1887 he exhibited at Les XX in Brussels, attending the opening. In 1888

he painted in Port-en-Bessin, in 1889 on the coast of Crotoy, and again showed his work at Les XX in Brussels. In 1890 he painted in Gravelines and laid down his theories in writing. His arrogance contributed to the disintegration of the Neo-Impressionist movement. In 1891 he was once again represented at Les XX, and he died of diptheria.

Seurat belonged to the generation of painters who could build on the inventions of early Impressionism and develop them further. Impressed by the colour experiments of his precursors, which, however, still owed much to intuition or chance and therefore still left room for individual artistic expression, Seurat began to study scientifically developed theories of colour, starting with those of Chevreul and Blanc. These studies enabled him to construct his paintings in accordance with the principle of optical mixture, or broken colour, which made him the initiator and leading representative of pointillism. From then on Seurat's works were based entirely on theoretical considerations; nothing was left to chance, each dot of colour had its appointed place. Each painting involved drawn-out preparation, working out the optical effect to be achieved. After Seurat's early death, his friend Signac took on the task of expounding his theories and gathering followers to find recognition for Seurat's endeavours. Seurat influenced many artists of the 20th century with his attempt at basing painting on a scientific footing and his adherence to strict forms.
*Illustrations:*
506   Model, Front View (study for "Les Poseuses")
      1887
506   Bathing at Asnières, c. 1883/84
507   Sunday Afternoon on the Island of La Grande
      Jatte, 1884–1886

## SEVERINI Gino
1883 Cortona – 1966 Paris
Severini went to Rome in 1899, where he attended evening courses at the Villa Medici. His meeting with Balla and Boccioni became decisive for his artistic career. He began to paint pictures influenced by divisionism. From 1906 he lived in Paris, where he discovered the works of Seurat and met Modigliani, and signed the *Manifesto of Futurist Painting* of 11 February, 1910. From this period date his first cabaret and dancing girl scenes. Severini kept the Milan Futurists in touch with Paris, and also organised their 1912 exhibition in Paris. During this period he produced his best work. Apart from an increasing interest in movement and light, there were other features, such as the superimposition of chronologically separated events brought together by memory.
*Illustration:*
577   Spheric Expansion of Light (Centrifugal),
      1914

## SIBERECHTS Jan
1627 Antwerp – c. 1700–1703 London
Siberechts joined the Antwerp Lukas Guild around 1648/49. Before that he had probably visited Italy, as his early works bear a resemblance to the Italian landscapes painted by the Dutch painters Both, Berchem and Dujardin. In the 1660s his Flemish landscapes usually concentrated on a limited view, such as a meadow, a ford or a roadside embankment, with carts, animals, peasants or servant girls in greygreen or bluish coloration and silvery light. In 1672 he went to London, where he carried out commissions for the Duke of Buckingham. In England he painted actual views of country estates. His landscapes, now in warm brown tones, began to open outwards.
*Illustration:*
328   Landscape with Rainbow, Henley-on-
      Thames, c. 1690

## SIGNAC Paul
1863 Paris – 1935 Paris
The son of a saddler, Signac abandoned plans of becoming an architect and began to paint in 1880. He attended the Academy of Bing in 1883 and became interested in Monet and Guillaumin. In 1884 he was a co-founder of the Independents. He became friendly with Seurat, whose divisionist-pointillist manner he adopted in his cityscapes, river scenes and figure painting. In 1886 he took part in the VIII Impressionist Exhibition. Durand-Ruel began to show his work in New York, and it was also shown in Nantes, together with Seurat's and Picasso's works. During this period Signac was much involved in organising exhibitions and writing reviews.

In 1887 he went with Seurat to Brussels and for the first time visited the Mediterranean (Collioure). In 1888 he exhibited for the first time with Les XX in Brussels. In 1889 he visited van Gogh at Arles, illustrated theoretical works of C. Henry and joined the anarchists. In 1890 he made the first of several visits to Italy and became the first foreign member of Les XX. In 1892 he married Berthe Roblès, a relation of Pissarro, and sailed from Brittany to Marseilles. He remained keen on sailing for the rest of his life. He painted many landscapes and seascapes, both in oil and water-colour, using mosaic-like blocks of pure colour. In 1893 he bought a house in Saint-Tropez, which was then becoming a popular seaside resort and a meeting place for modern painters. In 1896 he made his first visit to Holland. In 1899 he published his theoretical aims for Neo-Impressionism *D'Eugène Delacroix au Néo-Impressionisme*. In 1907 he visited Constantinople, and in 1908 became the president of the Independents. Like his friend Seurat, Signac was an important representative and leader of Neo-Impressionism. After his initial leaning towards Monet's style, he became a whole-hearted follower of Seurat's technique and theories.
*Illustrations:*
483   Riverbank, Petit-Andely, 1886
508   Two Milliners, Rue du Caire, c. 1885/86
508   The Port of Saint Tropez, 1907

## SIGNORELLI Luca
(Luca d'Egidio di Maestro Ventura de' Signorelli)
c. 1450 Cortona – 1523 Cortona
Born in the borderland between Tuscany and Umbria, it is likely that Signorelli received his artistically formative training in Florence, where he would have come under the influence of Florentine sculpture, particularly bronze casts. He probably studied under Pollaiuolo and Verrocchio for some years. Signorelli's special interest was the human figure in action. One of the main concerns of Florentine painting of the early 15th century had been the plastic, convincing rendering of the human body on the flat canvas, and this theme was taken up again by Signorelli; no longer, however, in an endeavour to depict three-dimensional forms, but rather to record exact details. His religious and secular subjects demonstrate his mastery in this field. Already in 1481 he was one of the artists chosen to participate in the fresco cycle below the window area in the Sistine Chapel (amongst others, Botticelli, Ghirlandaio and Perugino were engaged in this work). Piero della Francesca's influence on Signorelli should not be over-emphasised. Although his tendency to abstract composition ("Virgin and Saints", Perugia, Domopera, 1484) and his handling of lighting effects may have been influenced by Piero, Signorelli's intention was not to create an atmosphere flooded with light, but to use strong light and deep shadow to model the forms of the body. Signorelli reached the height of his development with his frescos depicting the Last Judgement in Orvieto cathedral (1499–1504, ill. p.110).

*Illustrations:*
110 Portrait of a Lawyer, c. 1490–1500
110 The Damned Cast into Hell (detail), 1499–1503

## SIMONE MARTINI
(Simone di Martino)
c. 1280–1285 Siena – 1344 Avignon
The assumed date of birth is based on a 16th century source but it is probably correct, even though Simone's first signed work, the fresco of the Maestà in the Palazzo Pubblico in Siena, dates from 1316. His versatility of talent has made it impossible so far to reconstruct his life chronologically. The Maestà in Siena, the devotional pictures for Cardinal Orsini and the altarpieces, such as those for Pisa and Orvieto, all show some affinity. But there is evidence in all his works that he had studied Duccio with the same intensity as he had Giotto, and French art, plus the field of sculpture and in particular Giovanni Pisano. This diversity of influences is still clearly detectable in the Orsini polyptych. It is certain, however, that around 1315 Simone must already have been a famous master to have received the commission in Siena and to be mentioned in the records of 1317 as being employed as an ennobled artist by Robert d'Anjou at an astonishingly high salary. During this period the Neapolitan kings of Anjou and their circle were his major patrons. His large workshop also produced works for the city of Siena and other parts of central Italy.

Simone introduced some of the most significant innovations, especially in the field of devotional picture painting, such as the so-called Madonna dell'Umiltá (Mary kneeling and suckling the child). From 1339 he is mentioned in Avignon, where he worked for Cardinal Stefaneschi and other senior clerics. He left a school of followers of his style, both in Siena and Avignon. Some of his inventions became almost common property in the 14th century. Already celebrated in his lifetime – praised even by Petrarch, for whom he executed several works – his fame continued not only in Siena, where in the early 15th century he was considered the greatest Sienese painter of all, but also north of the Alps.
*Illustrations:*
18 Maestà, 1315/16
35 Guido Riccio da Fogliano, c. 1328
35 Musicians. Detail from: St Martin is dubbed a Knight, between 1317 and 1319
36 The Road to Calvary (part of the Orsini Polyptych), c. 1315 (or later)
36 The Desposition (part of the Orsini Polyptych), c. 1315 (or later)

## SISLEY Alfred
1839 Paris – 1899 Moret-sur-Loing (near Paris)
Sisley came from a middle-class English background and was intended to become a merchant. He started drawing between 1857 and 1862. Then he studied in the studio of Gleyre in Paris, where he met Monet, Renoir and Bazille. In 1863 he began to paint in the open with his friends in Chailly-en-Bière near Barbizon. In 1865 he worked with Renoir, Monet and Pissarro in Marlotte and also with Monet on his boat on the Seine. In 1866 he showed his work for the first time at the Salon. He married Marie Lescouezec, with whom he had two children. He was rejected by the Salon in 1867 and became a co-founder of the "Salon des Refusés". He began to paint in Honfleur, and in 1868 went with Renoir to Chailly and showed his work at the Salon. He was again turned down by the Salon in 1869, and began to frequent the Café Guerbois in Paris. In 1870 he was represented at the Salon with his Impressionist work. He stayed in Voisins-Louveciennes during the Commune in 1871. Durand-Ruel showed one of his pictures in London and began to buy his work regularly from 1872. In the following years he painted mostly in Argenteuil, Bougival and Louveciennes, producing Impressionist village and river scenes and snowscapes. In 1874 he took part in the first Impressionist exhibition, and the singer and art collector J.B. Faure financed his visit to England. From 1875 to 1877 he lived in Mary-le-Roi. In 1875 an auction was held at the Hôtel Drouot to sell his pictures and those of other Impressionists, with little success.

In 1876 and 1877 he showed his work at the second and third Impressionist exhibitions, and a further auction was held. He moved to Sèvres, where he was aided financially by the inn-keeper Murer and the publisher Charpentier. In 1878/79 Duret helped him out of his financial difficulties by finding some buyers. From 1880 to 1882 he lived in Veneux-Nadon near Moret and had a one-man exhibition at Charpentier's publishing house, which printed the journal *La Vie moderne*. In 1882 he participated in the seventh Impressionist exhibition. Durand-Ruel showed his work in Paris in 1883, without success, but nevertheless arranged to show it in London, Boston, Rotterdam and Berlin in 1885. Together with Renoir and Pissarro, he again exhibited at Durand-Ruel in 1888. In 1889 he had a one-man show at Durand-Ruel in New York. Sisley now settled permanently at Moret and continued to paint Impressionist landscapes until the end. He reached the height of his career with his series of paintings from 1893/94, which followed Monet's manner. In 1894 he worked in Normandy as the guest of the collectors Murer and Depeaux. In 1897 a large retrospective took place at G. Petit without any success with critics and buyers. During that year he painted on the English coast. In 1898 it was diagnosed that he suffered from cancer. His lack of funds prevented him from becoming a French citizen. When his estate was auctioned in 1899, his paintings rapidly rose in value. He was the first of the Impressionists for whom a small memorial was erected, in Moret in 1911.
*Illustrations:*
497 The Bark during the Flood, Port Marly, 1876
497 The Bridge of Moret, 1893

## SLEVOGT Max
1868 Landshut (Bavaria) – 1932 Neukastel (Palatinate)
Slevogt studied at the Academy of Fine Arts in Munich, 1884–1890, where he was influenced by Leibl and Trübner. In 1889 he went to Paris to study at the Académie Julian, and the following year continued his studies in Italy. In 1893 he became a member of the Munich Secession and the Freie Vereinigung. From 1896 he worked for the magazine *Simplizissimus*, and Leistikow put him into contact with the Berlin Secession. In 1900 he visited the Paris World Exhibition and in 1901 he went to Frankfurt am Main, where his famous, brilliantly-coloured zoo pictures were produced. He then lived in Berlin, working mostly on portraits and teaching a class at the Academy. In 1914 he went to Egypt and painted landscapes flooded with sunlight. He became a member of the Academy of Fine Arts in Berlin, and in 1915 went to Belgium to paint war scenes. After 1918 he settled in Neukastel, where he produced his graphic cycles, over 500 illustrations of Goethe's *Faust*. His murals in the concert hall in Neukastel date from 1924, and he carried out further fresco commissions in Berlin, Bremen (1927), and the Friedenskirche in Ludwigshafen (1932). In 1924 he created the sets for *Don Giovanni* for the Dresden Opera.
*Illustration:*
535 The Alster at Hamburg, 1905

## SNYDERS Frans
(also: Snijders)
1579 Antwerp – 1657 Antwerp
Snyders' parents kept an inn well-known for good food, which many artists frequented. In about 1592/93 he studied under the younger Pieter Brueghel, then Hendrik van Balen. In 1602 he joined the Lukas Guild, then travelled in Italy for a time, returning in 1609. In 1611 he married a sister of the painter Cornelis de Vos. Apart from his domestic scenes, which showed the Mannerist influence, Snyders created two new categories of painting: the hunting still life and the "larder" picture. He excelled as a painter of still lifes, often magnificent, tastefully arranged banqueting scenes in intensive colours, showing game, poultry, fruit and all kinds of tableware fit for a palace, which he sometimes further enlivened by adding living, jumping animals. Snyder transformed the still life into a lively scene, and also produced minutely observed, dramatic hunting scenes. He was one of Rubens' assistants, who employed him as specialist for animals, fruit and flowers.
*Illustration:*
299 Still Life, 1614

## SOEST → Konrad of Soest

## SOULAGES Pierre
born 1919 Rodez (Aveyron)
Soulage's studies at the College of Graphic Arts in Montpellier were cut short by the war. During the German occupation he worked in the vineyards, then set up a studio in Paris in 1946. Here he met Picabia, Hartung and Léger, amongst others. On a visit to the USA he met American artists and museum staff, including J.J. Sweeney, the director of the Museum of Modern Art in New York. Soulage's Tachisme compositions soon became recognised, and his work was shown world-wide at one-man and group exhibitions. In 1987 he designed a monumental wall tapestry for the newly-built Finance Ministry in Paris. In 1995 he completed a series of stained glass windows for the Abbey of Conques.
*Illustration:*
636 Painting 21. 6. 53, 1953

## SOUTINE Chaïm
1893 Smilovitchi (near Minsk) – 1943 Paris
As the tenth of eleven children of a poor Jewish tailor, Soutine had a hard childhood. However, after working in an art school at Vilna, he made his way to Paris in 1913. In 1916 he moved into one of those ramshackle ateliers, known as La Ruche, where Chagall also lived. Modigliani introduced him to the art dealer Léopold Zborovsky, who encouraged him in 1919 to attempt landscape painting at Céret. The following three years were his most important period, during which he produced a great number of landscapes in impasto, using intensely brilliant colours. The overall effect was one of tortured disquiet. On his return to Paris in 1923 the American collector Albert Barnes bought all the pictures kept in his studio. This new prosperity tempered Soutine's vehemence, but he succeeded in reaching another height with a series of "battle scenes", with which he paid homage to Rembrandt. Figures in uniform were another of his favourite subjects.
*Illustration:*
605 Page at Maxim's, c. 1925

## SPITZWEG Carl
1808 Munich – 1885 Munich
Spitzweg is still regarded as one of the most popu-

lar 19th century painters. By profession he was an apothecary, and began to teach himself painting in the 1820s. Most of his pictures have a humorous side which he achieved by depicting the yearnings for higher things of people with rather limited horizons, both intellectually and materially. Thus the aspiring poet in his leaky garret, or the portly, elderly widower ogling a passing young girl. In 1851 Spitzweg travelled with his Munich painting friends to Paris and then London, where he was particularly impressed by the works of the Barbizon painters and the works of Constable. This experience led him increasingly to landscape painting, in which he explored the open brushwork technique of the Barbizon school. From then on his figures became incidental, mere witty asides, rather than the main focus of his pictures.
*Illustration:*
460　The Poor Poet, 1839

### STAËL, Nicolas de
1914 St Petersburg – 1955 Antibes
When only two years old, Staël was made a page at the St Petersburg court. After the Revolution in 1919 his family emigrated first to Poland and then to Brussels, where he studied at the Academy of Fine Arts from 1933 to 1936. He first worked as a painter of theatrical sets. From 1938 he lived in Paris. He began his career by painting portraits and still lifes, but he destroyed most of his early works, in particular his water-colour landscapes. His friends included Braque and Léger. After experimenting for some time in the field of Tachisme, de Staël developed an original form of abstract painting in which the suggestion of figure, landscape or still life is implicit, using the palette knife to create large, flat areas of colour. From the early 1950s, the representational element became increasingly evident in his pictures. He committed suicide in 1955.
*Illustration:*
638　Figure on the Beach, 1952

### STEEN Jan
c. 1625/26 Leiden – 1679 Leiden
Steen and Ostade were the two most popular and versatile of the Dutch genre painters. Steen led an unsettled life, often moving home, but he cannot have been an undisciplined drunkard, as has often been suggested, because he produced around 800 paintings. Steen was the son of a Leiden brewer, and there he was introduced to the very detailed style of painting developed in Leiden which was to become important in his later career. He enrolled briefly at the university in 1646, probably to avoid military service. In 1648 he was one of the founding members of the guild. He probably received his training in Utrecht and worked in the workshops of Ostade and van Goyen. In 1649 he married a daughter of van Goyen in The Hague, where he remained until 1654. He then took over a brewery in Delft, which soon failed, and then moved to Warmond near Leiden. From 1661 to 1670 he was in Haarlem, and finally settled for the last ten years of his life again in Leiden where he obtained a licence to operate a tavern. In his portrayal of merry or riotous drinking scenes, weddings, fairs and other themes drawn from popular life, he proved himself a most acute observer of this particular milieu, whose study his life and occupation had given him ample opportunity. But he was also at home with the depiction of refined society and modish interiors. His style was never fixed, tending sometimes towards Ostade and Brouwer, then again towards de Hooch, Terborch or Vermeer. He treated human follies and weaknesses with humour and wit, revealing the hidden moral and "truth" as Molière did in his comedies.

*Illustrations:*
278　Rhetoricians at a Window, c. 1662–1666
325　The Lovesick Woman, c. 1660
325　The World Upside Down, c. 1660

### STEFANO DI GIOVANNI
(Stefano da Verona, Stefano da Zevio)
c. 1374/75 – after 1438
More recent research has changed the received image of this important artist of northern Italy. It has also brought to light his new name: Stefano di Giovanni or da Francia (from France). His father was the painter Giovanni d'Arbois (in the Franche Comté), who had been invited by the Duke of Burgundy to leave Lombardy and become his court painter. Unfortunately nothing of his work remains; it would have thrown some light on how he combined early Burgundian painting with that of Lombardy. His son Stefano must have had a good knowledge of French art, though it is not known whether he went to France. What can be substantiated is an extensive visit to Padua, 1396–1414, and an earlier visit to Treviso. His activity in Verona is first recorded in 1425. If his "Virgin of the Rose Garden" had actually been painted for the nunnery of San Domenico in Verona before finding its way to the museum, then it must have been produced in 1425 or later. His surviving work includes some important drawings, mostly still in Verona and the surrounding area, as well as many frescos. Important for his stylistic development was the somewhat older Michelino da Besozzo.
*Illustration:*
49　The Virgin of the Rose Garden, c. 1425

### STELLA Frank
born 1936 Malden (near Boston)
From 1954 to 1958 Stella studied history and art under Steven Greene and William C. Seitz at Princeton University. While staying in New York in 1959 he developed his general concept: broad black lines in a symmetrical, horizontal-vertical arrangement. These deliberately impersonal pictures were produced with almost mechanical precision. In exploring flat area colour painting he attempted to achieve a total lack of effect by eradicating painterly devices almost completely. He chose paint and utensils used in house decoration for painting his symmetrical, regular patterns. Towards 1966 he produced a series of works whose compact inner form stood in contrast to the frame, and he also began to produce work in copper and aluminium paint. His first "shaped canvas" was created, a canvas cut to suit the painted form. From about 1975 his work became more relaxed, and he produced montages made of multi-coloured, bent aluminium strips. In 1983 he was visiting professor at Harvard University. In 1990 his first three-dimensional plastic works were produced, and in 1992 his first architectural designs were executed, including that for a museum of modern art in Dresden.
*Illustration:*
653　Guadalupe Island, Caracara, 1979

### STILL Clyfford
1904 Grandin (North Dakota) – 1980 New York
From 1931 to 1933 Still studied at Spokane University (Washington), where he subsequently taught art. There followed many other teaching assignments at colleges and universities in California, Virginia and New York, where many of the painters of Abstract Expressionism held positions, including Tobey and Rothko. In the 1930s and 1940s he concentrated on abstracting figure and landscape painting, taking Cézanne and van Gogh as his starting point. Then under the influence of Surrealism he turned to representations of the unconscious and

mythological themes. From about 1947 his mature style evolved: large-scale canvases covered in black, framed by strong, contrasting colours, which channelled his manner of painting into a serene, meditative direction.
*Illustration:*
630　Untitled, 1954

### STROZZI Bernardo
(called: Il Cappuccino)
1581 Genoa – 1644 Venice
Strozzi received his early training under the Sienese painter Sorri, who introduced him to Tuscan traditions and the works of Barocci. Further influences on his development came from Lombardian artists, notably Crespi. But it was Rubens, who came to Genoa in 1607, and the works of van Dyck who were to become the inspiration of his work in the first decade of the 17th century. This was most noticeable in his handling of colour and the amplitude of the female figure, as shown in his picture "Woman playing the Gamba" (Dresden, Gemäldegalerie). Strozzi, who had entered the Capuchin Order at the age of 17, executed fresco paintings only in his early youth. His knowledge of the works of Caravaggio and his followers found expression in his genre scenes, which also reveal Flemish inspiration. With his move to Venice in 1630 he entered a new creative phase which led to a simplification of composition and greater serenity ("St Sebastian", Venice, Museo Correr), during which he gradually approached the personal, free character of his mature work.
*Illustration:*
234　Vanitas Allegory, c. 1635

### STUART Gilbert
1755 North Kingston (Rhode Island) – 1828 Boston
Stuart grew up in ordinary, small-town circumstances. In 1769 he was apprenticed to the travelling artist Cosmo Alexander, who took him with him to Scotland. After his teacher's death Stuart set up a studio in Newport, Rhode Island, in 1773 and began to specialise in portraits. In 1775 he went to England and two years later became a pupil of Benjamin West. Here he remained until 1782, studying Continental and in particular English traditions in portraiture, such as those of Reynolds and Gainsborough. His popularity as a portrait painter enabled him to live the life of a successful artist in London and Dublin. In 1792/93 he returned to America where he became the leading portraitist of his time. He moved to Philadelphia, which was then the capital city, where he lived until 1795. He portrayed many distinguished Americans, including George Washington, of whose portrait he made many copies to be sold. He also painted all subsequent Presidents and in this way became the pictorial chronicler of the young republic. In 1805 he settled in Boston, and there spent his last years beset by debts and his addiction to drink.
*Illustration:*
391　Portrait of Don José de Jaudenes y Nebot, 1794

### STUBBS George
1724 Liverpool – 1806 London
Stubbs was an illustrator of scientific anatomical works before becoming a painter, particularly of animals. His illustrations for a work on obstetrics date from 1751, and in 1766 he published *The Anatomy of the Horse*, illustrated by his own engravings. Another large work was *A Comparative Anatomical Exposition of the Structure of the Human Body with that of a Tiger and a Common Fowl*, 1817. He travelled to Rome and then Morocco, where he observed a horse

being attacked by a lion, and this experience was to become important for his development. He later repeatedly depicted scenes of animals fighting ("Horse frightened by a Lion", Liverpool, Walker Art Gallery). Together with Ben Marshall, Stubbs is the most important representative of animal portraiture, a genre that captures British fondness and enthusiasm for animals. He experimented in working in enamel on copper, and also on china plaques provided by the Wedgwood potteries, working jointly with Josiah Wedgwood. Apart from his devotion to animal subjects, he also painted scenes of traditional English rural life. However, with his concern for anatomical accuracy and remarkable control of line and shape, Stubbs exercised an enduring influence on the European tradition of animal painting.
*Illustration:*
387   "Molly Longlegs" with Jockey, c. 1761/62

## STUCK Franz von
1863 Tettenweis (near Passau) – 1928 Munich
Von Stuck was, with Lenbach, one of the great Munich painters. After three years at art school and college he studied at Munich Academy, where he came under the influence of Wilhelm von Diez, Böcklin and Lenbach. He was a co-founder of the Munich Secession and was appointed professor in 1895. He was an inspiring, tolerant teacher and always intent on promoting the talent of his students. During his lifetime his works were well represented at the Salons and exhibitions. His style was influenced by the Jugendstil, and he painted pictures of a Symbolist and allegorical nature.
*Illustration:*
533   The Dinner Party, 1913

## SUTHERLAND Graham
1903 London – 1980 London
Sutherland studied graphic art at Goldsmiths' School of Art, London. From 1921 to 1926 he worked as a book illustrator and poster designer, then taught at the Chelsea School of Art. In the mid-1930s he turned to painting and under the influence of Surrealism produced landscape forms charged with mystery and drama. From 1941 to 1945 he was an official war artist, painting pictures of bombed buildings in London and southern England. After the war he produced a number of religious paintings. While the original source of inspiration for his gloomy, imaginative pictures had been the austere scenery of western Wales, his palette lightened under the influence of regular visits to the Côte d'Azur, though his vegetal subjects remained as disturbing as ever. In the late 1950s Sutherland's work became more abstract. During this period Sutherland portrayed many distinguished personalities, including Winston Churchill and Konrad Adenauer.
*Illustration:*
614   The Bridle Path, 1939

## TAAFFE Philip
born 1955 Elizabeth (New Jersey)
He studied at the Cooper Union, New York (BFA, 1977). In the early 1980s he explored the works of Op Art artists, such as Bridget Riley, translating them into new pictorial constructions. Besides his interest in Op Art techniques Taaffe also experimented with Newman's work. From 1988 to 1992 he stayed in Naples. During this period he studied ornamental forms of various cultural fields. In the late 1950s he produced acrylic pictures based on diverse printing techniques with elements of collage, which he subsequently gradually reduced further. From 1982 his work was shown regularly at galleries in Europe and America. He was represented at the following exhibitions: "German and American Art of the Late 1980s", Düsseldorf and Boston (1988); "Post Abstract Abstraction", Aldrich (1987); "Doubletake", Vienna and London (1992) and "ARS 95", Helsinki (1995). Taaffe was also invited to the "Whitney Biennale" in New York in 1987, 1991, 1995. He lives in New York.
*Illustration:*
680   Conflagration, 1991

## TANGUY Yves
1900 Paris – 1955 Woodbury (Connecticut)
Tanguy spent much of his childhood in Brittany and came to love the scenery. He first joined the French merchant navy, and while working on a cargo ship visited England, Spain, Portugal and South America between 1918 and 1920. After military service he turned to painting in 1923, having been much impressed by a picture by de Chirico displayed in the window of the Paul Guillaume gallery in Paris. Tanguy was entirely self-taught. In his pictures de Chirico's spatial limitations are turned into long perspectives, and architectural elements and figures are eliminated. This process led Tanguy to a subject which was to become a never-ending source of inspiration to him: the boundlessness of the sea. In 1925 he met Breton and other Surrealist painters and began to take part in their exhibitions with his imagined landscapes, abstract and sculptural works. Like many Surrealists he emigrated to America in 1939.
*Illustrations:*
557   The Five Strangers, 1941
610   The Palace of the Window Cliffs, 1942

## TÀPIES Antoni
born 1923 Barcelona
Tàpies studied law in Barcelona from 1943 to 1946, at the same time attending the Academy for two months. In 1948 he was a co-founder of the group Dau al Set and the magazine of the same name. His starting point was the Surrealists, and he came under the influence of Picasso, Miró and Klee. But he soon began to produce collages for which an extended range of materials was available, and in this field he continued to work. His interest in mythology and philosophy was transferred to his work in the form of symbols and runes carved into the surface or perhaps appearing as pictorial symbols. To Tàpies, these have a magic and cosmic significance, as does colour.
*Illustrations:*
642   Relief in Brick Red, 1963
642   Armchair, 1982/83

## TENIERS David the Younger
1610 Antwerp – 1690 Brussels
While his father David Tenier the Elder, from whom he received his principal instruction, had been unsuccessful and was even put into the debtors' prison, Teniers the Younger became known all over Europe and amassed a considerable fortune. In 1633 he became a master in the Antwerp Guild, and in 1637 he married a daughter of "Velvet Brueghel", who brought a large dowry into the marriage. In 1645 he was elected deacon of the Lukas Guild, and in 1651 he was appointed court painter to Archduke Leopold Wilhelm and keeper of his pictures in Brussels. He painted still lifes, landscapes and portraits, but was happiest in his scenes of popular Flemish life depicting rustic interiors with card-players, village fêtes, taverns and other themes, in which he was much influenced by Brouwer. Of particular note are his gallery pictures, in which he showed the works contained in the Archduke's collection as in a photograph. He also made small-scale copies of 246 pictures in this collection, another record which helped to retrace the fate of several Titians, Giorgiones and Veroneses.
*Illustration:*
319   Twelfth Night (The King drinks),
       c. 1634–1640

## TERBORCH Gerard
(also: Gerard or Gerrit ter Borch)
1617 Zwolle – 1681 Deventer
Terborch studied drawing under his father, then was apprenticed to Pieter de Molyn in Haarlem. In 1635 he started on his five-year-travels, visiting England, Italy and France, later also Spain. On his return he worked in Haarlem, Amsterdam and Münster, where he painted "The Treaty of Westphalia" (Peace Treaty of Münster) which marked the end of the Thirty Years' War, before settling at Deventer in 1654. In his predominantly small-scale interiors and conversation pieces and in his masterly portraits, Terborch depicts the life of refined society, limiting himself to one or only a few figures and presenting sparsely furnished interiors. His pictures have an air of stillness and restraint and are characterised by a beautiful, cool tonality and an exquisite ability to render the texture of rich materials, features which point to Metsu, de Hooch and Vermeer.
*Illustrations:*
281   A Concert, c. 1675
321   The Card-Players, c. 1650
321   The Letter, c. 1655

## TERBRUGGHEN Hendrik
(also: Hendrick ter Brugghen)
c. 1588 near Deventer – 1629 Utrecht
Terbrugghen grew up in Utrecht, where he received instruction from the late Mannerist painter Bloemaert. In 1604 he went to Italy for ten years. There he may have been in direct contact with Caravaggio, either in Rome or Naples, and also met his followers, including Gentileschi and Saraceni, whose influence became decisive. With Baburen and Honthorst he brought the chiaroscuro technique to Utrecht, where he became a member of the Lukas Guild in 1616. His religious, half-length figure pictures probably met with little enthusiasm, for he increasingly turned to genre painting, choosing as subjectmatter drinking, card-playing and musical scenes. He was the most vital and uncompromising member of the Utrecht school. The soft lighting developed by him anticipated the Delft school.
*Illustration:*
301   The Duo, 1628

## THEODERICH → Master

## THORN-PRIKKER Jan
1868 The Hague – 1932 Cologne
After studying in The Hague, Thorn-Prikker was professor at the Munich school of applied arts, 1920–1923, then taught in Düsseldorf and later at the school of applied arts in Cologne. He was one of the most prominent representatives of the Dutch Jugendstil, but also incorporated elements of pointillism and Symbolism. His major concern was with the applied arts, which he led to new heights. His most important work in this field was his stained glass with which he found many followers in Germany. He also produced ceramic and batik works. His paintings follow the ornamental principles of the Jugendstil with themes of a mostly symbolist, allegorical content. With his geometrical stylisation he often came close to abstract art.
*Illustration:*
525   Madonna among the Tulips, 1893

## TIEPOLO Giovanni Battista
(also: Gian Battista Tiepolo)
1696 Venice – 1770 Madrid

Tiepolo was the son of a ship-broker. His teachers were Lazzarini and the old masters, amongst whom he studied Titian and Tintoretto and in particular Veronese, to whose style he owed much. In 1719 he married a sister of the painter Guardi. His eldest son was Giovanni Domenico, who later became his assistant and successor. Tiepolo's early work still showed the influence of Piazzetta, Bencovich and Ricci. A high point in his early career were the frescos in the archbishop's palace in Udine (ill. p.376), which anticipated his mature style. The sombre 17th century tonality was giving way to a light, transparent palette. This new lightness also determined the coloration of his many panel paintings. In the 1740s his son became his most faithful assistant in dealing with the large number of often extensive commissions flowing in from Venice, Milan, Bergamo and Vicenza. His finest achievement and largest of undertakings abroad was the commission by the Prince-Bishop of Würzburg to decorate the ceiling of the Kaisersaal and the huge staircase of his nearly completed residence at Würzburg with historical and allegorical scenes glorifying the bishopric and the noble family to which the Prince-Bishop belonged. A further period of eight years filled with a wealth of commissions in and around Venice went by before a second call from abroad arrived. In 1762 Tiepolo and his son travelled to Spain, partly on a diplomatic mission, but mainly to follow an invitation by Charles III to decorate the royal palace in Madrid. Tiepolo never returned to Italy but died in Madrid, where his art was to be replaced by Neo-Classicism as expounded by Winckelmann who had an influential follower in Mengs.

Tiepolo's son Giovanni Domenico (1727–1804), besides acting as assistant to his father on large commissions, was an original painter of religious and secular works in his own right. He brought his father's enigmatic imagination into the bizarre world of the *commedia dell'arte*, the fun-fair and carnival genre, in which his cool tonality became increasingly rationalised. Like his father he was also a master of drawing and of the graphic arts.

*Illustrations:*
339   St Charles Borromeo, c. 1767–1769
375   Rinaldo and Armida, 1753
376   Rachel concealing the Images of the Gods, 1726–1728
376   Sarah and the Archangel, 1726–1728
377   Hagar and Ismael in the Wilderness, c. 1732

## TINTORETTO
(Jacopo Robusti)
1518 Venice – 1594 Venice

In the great triad of 16th century Venetian art, Tintoretto upheld Mannerist principles more rigorously than either Titian or Veronese. Jacopo Robusti, called Il Tintoretto because his father was a dyer by trade, was trained in the workshop of Titian. He was first mentioned as master in 1539. Between 1548 and 1563 he painted several large-scale pictures of the "Miracle of St Mark". They stand out in their vehement dynamism achieved by bold foreshortening and exaggerated gestures. This was new in Venetian painting, as was the plastic modelling of the forms which went beyond Michelangelo's inventions. Also, the overall unity of the composition was disturbed by flickering light. It is not known whether Tintoretto ever went to Rome, but he is said to have made studies of copies of Michelangelo's and Giambologna's paintings and of ancient art, even for his later works, when light became the determinant factor in his art. According to Marco Boschini, Tintoretto used to set up a scene with small wax figures equivalent to the painting he had in mind, and then experimented with light sources. From 1564 to 1587 he was engaged in the decoration of the Scuola di San Rocco; the comprehensive scope of this work demonstrates the quality and range of his talents. Alongside works of the highest order stood those in which the virtuoso effect gained the upper hand. But it has to be taken into account that Tintoretto had a large workshop and inexhaustible energy which made any commission welcome.

*Illustrations:*
155   The Origin of the Milky Way, c. 1575–1580 (?)
182   St George and the Dragon, c. 1550–1560
182   Christ with Mary and Martha, c. 1580
183   Vulcan surprises Venus and Mars, c. 1555
183   Susanna at her Bath, c. 1565

## TISCHBEIN Johann Heinrich Wilhelm
1751 Haina (Hesse) – 1829 Eutin

Tischbein belonged to an artistic family branching out in all directions, and in whose circle he received early instruction. After studying under his uncle Johann Heinrich Tischbein the Elder at Kassel, another uncle, Johann Jacob Tischbein, took over, with whom he worked in Hamburg and Holland. From 1777 to 1779 he worked as a portrait painter in Bremen and Berlin. He then went to Italy, remaining there for almost twenty years. His friendship with Goethe produced the well-known portrait "Goethe in the Roman Campagna" (ill. p.395), which he completed in Rome in 1787. In 1789 he was appointed director of the Accademia di Belle Arti in Naples. After returning home and settling in Hamburg in 1801, he was called seven years later to the court of the Duke of Oldenburg, at whose court in Eutin he worked until his death.

*Illustration:*
395   Goethe in the Roman Campagna, 1787

## TITIAN
(Tiziano Vecelli)
between 1473 and 1490 Pieve di Cadore (Venetia) – 1576 Venice

Titian was the most outstanding painter of the 16th century. At a time when Mannerist tendencies became prevalent, he took over the heritage of the High Renaissance and carried it further. Although the standards of "classical art" of about 1500 were his guideline, he endowed them with a new dynamism for greater effect. He played a unique role in the history of colour and found ways of achieving unprecedented freedom in pictorial composition, making him not only the most important precursor of European Baroque (Rubens), but also a lasting influence on painters until the late 19th century. Manet, for example, studied and copied his work in the Louvre.

Titian's training under Giovanni Bellini was decisive for his career. In his workshop he probably also worked with Giorgione, his senior by ten years. The artistic temperament of these two young painters was obviously closely related, because to this day their contributions are inseparable in some pictures. Titian's "Assumption of the Virgin" altarpiece in Santa Maria dei Frari in Venice (1516–1518) represented an important innovatory development in Venetian painting, both in composition and handling of colour. With this work, he had created an entirely new type of altarpiece which was to set a standard for the future, also in terms of dimension and the way it merged with the space of the building. It ushered in a "proto-Baroque" phase in Titian's development. His "Madonna with Saints and members of the Pesaro family" (1519–1528, also in Frari) represented a similar milestone in the "Sacra Conversazione" field. Apart from altarpieces Titian painted religious pictures, mythological, poetical and allegorical subjects, and excelled as a portrait painter. The constant refinement of his painterly devices made the canvas his ideal medium, according the fresco a background role.

Already in 1530 Titian had become of European eminence. In 1533 the Emperor Charles V called him to his court and made him a Count Palatine. But Titian never left Venice for very long. In his late work colour achieved an almost "Impressionistic" effect ("Annunciation", Venice, San Salvatore, 1565; "Christ Crowned with Thorns", ill. p.178). By abandoning all outlines, he contrived to let air, light and colours unify the scene, so transcending earthly experience.

*Illustrations:*
154   Portrait of a Bearded Man ("Ariosto"), c. 1512
176   Venus of Urbino, c. 1538
176   Bacchanalia (The Andrians), c. 1519/20
177   La Bella, c. 1536
178   Christ Crowned with Thorns, c. 1576
178   Pietà, c. 1573–1576

## TOBEY Mark
1890 Centerville (Wisconsin) – 1976 Basle

Tobey began his career as a fashion designer. In 1922 he took up the study of Chinese calligraphy and the teachings of Eastern philosophy, specialising in the Baha'i religion. He travelled extensively in Europe and the Middle and Far East, also spending periods in a Zen monastery in Japan. His "white writings", a network of fine, calligraphically modelled patterns, initially showed slight representational elements, but became increasingly abstract, being an expression of his meditative-contemplative approach to life. Tobey settled at Basle in 1960, where the humanist tradition appealed to him, but he also spent periods in Seattle, Chicago and New York.

*Illustration:*
635   North-west current, 1958

## TOMMASO DA MODENA
c. 1325/26 Modena – before 16.7. 1379

Tommaso was the son of a painter called Barisino dei Barisini, and his own son Bonifacio also became a painter. Tommaso was probably trained in Bologna. By the mid-14th century the Bolognese School with masters like Vitale da Bologna had eclipsed Tuscan art. Tommaso obviously also had knowledge of Sienese art, including the works of Simone Martini. He probably produced miniatures as well as panel paintings. He lived and worked in Modena, but carried out commissions all over northern Italy. Most notable were his frescos in Mantua and Trento as well as those in Treviso. The Emperor Charles VI commissioned him to paint panel pictures for Karlstein castle. His most famous work, however, is the series of portraits of Dominican theologians of 1352 which he painted for the chapter hall in the Dominican church of Treviso, which showed him to be a shrewd reader of character. The heads of these "famous men" of the order are beautifully drawn, sitting in their little studies, and arranged in order of their clerical importance. Tommaso seemed to be happiest in rendering the figure or groups of figures, without much interest in spatial problems.

*Illustration:*
46   The Departure of St Ursula, c. 1355–1358

## TOOROP Jan
1858 Poerworedio (Java) – 1928 The Hague

The son of a Dutch government official stationed at Java, Toorop studied at the Technical College in

Delft, 1876–1878, at the Reichsakademie in Amsterdam, 1878–1880, and finally at Brussels Academy, 1880–1882. He was influenced by Gustave Courbet and James Ensor. In 1884 he met Whistler in London and became a member of the Belgian group of artists Les XX, where he showed his work regularly.

On a visit to Paris in 1885 he discovered Seurat and began to paint in the pointillist manner. In 1886 he moved to The Hague, and in 1892 he organised the first large van Gogh exhibition in Holland. In the 1890s he adopted Symbolist elements and became the most important representative of Dutch luminism, a technique in which adjoining broad colour dots achieve the appearance of a mosaic. In 1911 he became president of the Moderne Kunstkring. After converting to Catholicism in 1905 he began to concentrate on religious and mythical subjects.
*Illustration:*
525   The Three Brides, c. 1892/93

## TOULOUSE-LAUTREC Henri de
1864 Albi – 1901 Château Malromé (Gironde)
Toulouse-Lautrec was the descendant of an old French noble family. He broke both legs in childhood and this prevented their normal growth. Though saved by the family fortune from any financial worries, he resolved on taking up painting as a profession, studying under Cormon from 1882–1886. There he met Bernard and van Gogh, amongst others, and began to paint in light colours in an Impressionistic manner. His subject matter became intimately connected with the life he led. He frequented theatres, cabarets, circuses, bars, dance-halls and brothels, rendering these scenes realistically but as seen through the lens of his genius. He showed his work on Montmartre. He spent every summer by the sea. In 1886 he had a brief relationship with the model Suzanne Valadon, who was also a painter, and during this year his first drawings were published in magazines. In 1888 he showed his work at the Les XX exhibition in Brussels, and Théo van Gogh bought one of his pictures for the Goupil gallery. In 1889 he exhibited for the first time at the Salon des Indépendants and became a regular at the newly-opened Moulin Rouge. In 1890 he went with Signac to the Les XX exhibition in Brussels, then visited Spain. In 1891 he joined the Impressionists and Symbolists at their exhibition in the gallery Le Barc de Boutteville and began to produce posters in a novel, stylised manner for bars, music-halls and book publishers. His poster of the singer Aristide Bruant made him famous overnight. In 1892 he visited Brussels and London.

In 1893 he had his first one-man exhibition at Goupil and contributed to other exhibitions. From time to time he lived in brothels to draw and paint there. Between 1894 and 1897 he travelled in France and Belgium, Holland, Spain, London and Lisbon. He exhibited at the Salon Libre Esthétique in Brussels, had contact with the Nabis group of artists and the journal *La Revue Blanche*, and became increasingly dependent on alcohol. He collapsed in 1899 and was taken to mental hospital in Neuilly, against which his friends protested, but he continued to drink. In 1901 he suffered a partial paralysis and died at his mother's château. Toulouse-Lautrec painted with verve and excelled in graphic art. His lithographs and posters are still being copied today. Only lightly touched by Impressionism, his work had a stamp of its own, characterised by his handling of line and the dynamic use of colour.
*Illustrations:*
487   Jane Avril Dancing, 1892
516   Two Women Dancing at the Moulin Rouge, 1892
517   Henry Samary, 1889

517   The Clownesse Cha-U-Kao, 1895
518   The Toilette, 1896
518   Interior in the Rue des Moulins, c. 1894

## TROGER Paul
1698 Welsberg near Zell (Tyrol) – 1762 Vienna
Little is known about Troger's beginnings. He went to Italy, visiting Venice, Rome and Naples. There he became influenced by the works of Pittoni and Solimena. His first great work was the cupola fresco in the Kajetanerkirche in Salzburg, 1727. In his development as a fresco painter he soon abandoned the sombre, dark tonality of his early work in favour of a more colourful palette which, inspired by Rottmayr, achieved an increasing lightness in his late work (Maria Dreieichen, 1752). In his panel paintings he never achieved this but continued to present his religious scenes in dark contrasts of light and shade. In his frescos he skilfully adapted his handling of colour and his composition to the architecture and the spatial conditions. His spontaneous, often even sketchy approach became a source of inspiration to many significant fresco painters, including Bergl and Maulbertsch, Knoller and Zeiller.
*Illustration:*
393   St Sebastian and the Women, c. 1746

## TRÜBNER Wilhelm
1851 Heidelberg – 1917 Karlsruhe
Trübner studied at the Karlsruhe Academy under K.F. Schick in 1867/68 and at the Munich Academy under A. von Wagner in 1868. At the International Art Exhibition in Paris he became acquainted with the works of the Impressionists. In 1869 he received private tuition in Stuttgart, and in 1870 he took up his studies again at the Munich Academy. He met Leibl in 1871, who advised him to leave the Academy, and in the same year he joined the Munich association of realist painters. In 1872/73 he went with Carl Schuch to Italy, in 1873 to Brussels and then to the Chiemsee where, from 1890, he spent many summers. From 1875 to 1884 he again lived in Munich, and in 1876 he painted with Schuch in Weßling and Bernried. In 1879 he visited Paris, and in 1884 London. In the 1890s he began to abandon his dark tonality and gradually adopted the light colouring of the Impressionist manner. With his friends Corinth and Slevogt he joined the Munich Secession in 1894. From 1896 he taught at the Städelsche Kunstinstitut in Frankfurt am Main, then was appointed professor at the Karlsruhe Academy in 1903, where he worked until 1907.
*Illustration:*
532   Landscape with Flagpole, 1891

## TÜBKE Werner
born 1929 Schönebeck (near Magdeburg)
After an apprenticeship as a decorator and training at a craft school in Magdeburg, Tübke went to Leipzig to study at the College of Graphic Arts. This was followed by further studies at Greifswald University, where his subjects were art history and psychology. From 1954 he worked as a painter in Leipzig. He began to lecture at the Leipzig Academy in 1964, was appointed professor in 1972, and held the post of rector for some years. In 1984 he taught at the Salzburg summer academy. In the early 1970s came his first opportunity to visit Italy, and the direct contact with the Italian masters became important for his work. His sometimes monumental historical paintings and murals show undeniable traces of the old masters. As an official artist Tübke participated in the documenta 3 (1964), the documenta 6 (1977) and showed his work at many other exhibitions abroad. In 1973 he

was made rector of the Leipzig College of Graphic Arts. Between 1983 and 1989 he painted with the help of assistants the panorama of the Peasants' War in Bad Frankenhausen, which measures 1722 square metres and is the largest work in oil in the world.
*Illustration:*
669   Portrait of the Libvestock Brigadier Bodlenkov, 1962

## TURA Cosmè
(Cosimo)
c. 1430 Ferrara – 1495 Ferrara
About the middle of the 15th century Ferrara developed under the rule of Borso d'Este into a cultural centre of the first order, particularly in the field of painting. Here an independent school evolved which stood in sharp contrast to those in Tuscany, Lombardy and Venice. Of this, Tura was the leading master and oldest representative. Being of about the same age as Mantegna, he had, as Mantegna, studied under Francesco Squarcione in Padua, where he had obviously taken a great interest in the works of Donatello. On his return to Ferrara in 1456 he was appointed court painter to Borso d'Este. Unfortunately details on his manifold activities are scanty, but his surviving panel paintings give a glimpse of his artistic personality. Architectural elements inspired by Antiquity (organ wing depicting the Annunciation, in the cathedral museum, Ferrara, 1469), fantastic landscapes, sharply outlined almost like etchings, and brilliant perspectival constructions which defy logical spatial unity, add up to a style which in varying degrees characterised the artists of the Ferrara School (Francesco del Cossa, Ercole de'Roberti). Tura's Roverella Altarpiece, dating from before 1474 (only the central panel with the Madonna Enthroned survived, now in London, National Gallery), exemplifies his style in its abstract spatial composition and ornamental grouping of figures reminiscent of heraldic principles. Between 1460 and 1470 Tura collaborated with Cossa in painting the Pictures of the Months in the Palazzo Schifanoia; their respective contributions cannot always be separated (ill. p. 113).
*Illustration:*
113   St George and the Dragon and The Princess, c. 1470

## TURNER J.M.W.
(Joseph Mallord William Turner)
1775 London – 1851 London
Turner was only fourteen years old when he was admitted to the Royal Academy. He started his career by painting water-colours and producing mezzotints which were strongly influenced by John Robert Cozen's work. He started painting in oil from 1796 in the Classicist manner of Wilson and Poussin, and these paintings found general approval. Turner, who was one of the most prolific painters of his time, made extensive travels in many parts of England, Scotland and Ireland, and also on the Continent (France, Belgium, Holland, Germany, Italy).

In 1802 he made his first visit to Paris, studying the old masters in the Louvre, giving particular attention to Dutch seascapes and Claude Lorrain, which greatly influenced his work. In 1804 he had his first private exhibition in his own house. During this period his style was beginning to evolve; atmospheric light effects were gaining in importance. His visits to Italy in 1819 and 1829 completed this process.

Like the works of Constable, his seemingly effortless water-colours and oil-sketches were drawn from nature, as for example his series of landscapes painted from a boat on the Thames in 1807. But his way of seeing the world differed vastly from

Constable's view. Turner's pictures transcend the ordinary world; they are visions conveying the power of nature. In his atmospheric depictions of shipwrecks and natural disasters, perhaps inspired by such works as the "Battle of Trafalgar" by Loutherbourg, who lived in Turner's neighbourhood, reality and fantasy merge, and colour becomes a metaphor for the power of natural forces. By abandoning form or showing it only in shadowy outline, Turner endowed colour with a power of its own. This development was to be especially influential on the art of the 20th century.

*Illustrations:*

419    Rome from Mount Aventine, 1836
468    Snow Storm. Hannibal and his Army crossing the Alps), ca. 1810–1812
468    Peace – Burial at Sea, 1842
469    The "Fighting Téméraire" Tugged to her Last Berth to be Broken Up, 1838
470    Rain, Steam and Speed – The Great Western Railway, 1844
470    Snow Storm – Steam-Boat off a Harbour's Mouth making Signals in Shallow Water, and going by the Lead. The Author was in this Storm on the Night the Ariel Left Harwich, 1842

## TWOMBLY Cy

born 1929 Lexington (Virginia)
In 1948/49 Twombly studied at the Boston School of Fine Art, and in 1950/51 at the Art Students' League, then at the Black Mountain College. The next few years he lived partly in Europe, partly in America, until settling in Rome in 1960. He usually produces a series of pictures, bringing them together in cycles. From abstract Expressionism he developed his own, strongly calligraphic idiom. His pictures have a strongly modelled background with rhythmically interwoven, blurred lines in delicate colouring.

*Illustration:*

678    Pan (part four), 1980

## UCCELLO Paolo

c. 1397 Pratovecchio (near Arezzo) – 1475 Florence
Uccello was one of the most versatile founders of the Italian Early Renaissance, although his later reputation did not reflect his true significance. His first formative experience came from working with Ghiberti, whom he assisted with the decoration of the paradise doors of the Florence baptistry. Nothing survives of his contribution to the mosaics of San Marco in Venice, but his frescos of the Genesis in the Chiostro Verde of Santa Maria Novella in Florence (c. 1430) show that he was a follower of Ghiberti and that he was firmly rooted in the International Gothic style (Gentile da Fabriano, Pisanello). It comes therefore as a great surprise to note his change of direction in the 1430s. Developing an intense interest in perspective under the influence of Masaccio's and Donatello's works, he became engrossed in the problem of rendering figures that would stand out in space and appear solid and real. His first great achievement was the equestrian picture of John Hawkwood (ill. p. 96), followed by the Noah scenes in the Chiostro Verde in Santa Maria Novella (c. 1450), which anticipate Mannerist pictorial construction, such as the spatial "crater" in the Flood scene with its effect of compelling the eye to travel down into the depth. Proof of Uccello's obsession with perspective are his drawings in the Uffizi of objects which he made look transparent in order to be able to show them in their stereometric complexity. Unfortunately he outlived his own time: after painting his three battlepieces of "Battle of San Romano" (ill. p. 97), commissions dwindled away as general taste changed and demanded courtly refinement.

*Illustrations:*

96    Equestrian Portrait of Sir John Hawkwood, 1436
96    St George and the Dragon, c. 1456
97    Battle of San Romano (left panel), c. 1456
97    Battle of San Romano (centre panel), c. 1456
97    Battle of San Romano (right panel), c. 1456

## UHDE Fritz von

1848 Wolkenburg (Saxony) – 1911 Munich
Uhde's talent was recognised and supported by his parents. After passing his school-leaving examinations, he enrolled in 1866 at the Dresden Academy. He left after only a few months to pursue a military career, c. 1867–1871, advancing to cavalry captain. He studied painting in his spare time. In 1876 he visited Hans Makart in Vienna, whose dark, dramatic style influenced him. Makart refused him as pupil, and after a stay in Paris, in 1879 Uhde also tried in vain to be accepted by the Academy in Munich. He settled in Munich in 1880, where he met Liebermann who introduced him to painting in the open and encouraged him to visit Holland in 1882. In 1892 Uhde became a co-founder of the Munich Secession. He developed a manner of painting reminiscent of Impressionism, but his approach was realistic. His subjects were mostly of a religious nature, Biblical scenes presented in modern dress.

*Illustration:*

534    In the Garden (The Artist's Daughters), 1906

## UTRILLO Maurice

(Maurice Valadon)
1883 Paris – 1955 Dax (Landes)
Utrillo was the illegitimate child of the painter Suzanne Valadon. He lived an unsettled life and developed a dependency on alcohol. In 1902 his mother was advised by a doctor to encourage him to paint. This did not cure him of his addiction, but proved that he had an astonishing natural talent. His output was large, although his work was repeatedly interrupted by periods of treatment in clinics. His main theme was the streets of Montmartre, and he had no problem selling these pictures. From 1909 he rarely painted from nature, using picture postcards as his model. After a suicide attempt in 1924 he retired to his mother's home, the Castel St.-Bertin (Ain). There he returned to producing graphic works at the encouragement of his publisher Frapier. It was not until the 1930s that Utrillo was able to free himself of his addiction. He married, and organised many exhibitions. His success with his street scenes probably caused him to look no further for other subjects.

*Illustrations:*

562    Impasse Cottin, 1911

## VALDÉS LEAL Juan de

1622 Seville – 1690 Seville
Valdés Leal, who was trained by Castillo y Saavedra in Córdoba, developed a very personal, unusual style which he retained all his life. Already in the pictures painted for the Clares of Carmona in 1653/54 ("Saracens Attacking the Monastery of St Francis") he showed a high degree of exaltedness in form and expression which was to mark the entire work of this last great exponent of Andalusian Baroque. Within his style he employed two diverse ways of treating colour side by side, one being marked by a palette of delicate, fine pinks and grey tones of lucid quality, and the other by deep, often sombre shades of green, violet and deep reds. While he employed the first method for a series of pictures of the St Jerome cycle for the monastery of San Jeronimo

in Seville (1657/58), he chose the second technique for greater effect in his two large Vanitas Allegories for the hospital de la Caridad, also in Seville (1672).

*Illustration:*

268    Allegory of Death, 1672

## VALENTIN DE BOULOGNE

(also: Jean de Boullongne)
1594 Coulommiers – 1632 Rome
As the most important representative of the French Caravaggists, Valentin de Boulogne came to Rome in 1612, where he was introduced to Caravaggio's work by Vouet and Manfredi. Valentin subsequently developed geometrical rules to deal with chiaroscuro, working out a system for light and shade effects. In Rome he belonged to a group of Scandinavian and German artists who called themselves "Bentvögel" and had chosen the motto "Bacco, Tabacco e Venere" (To Bacchus, tobacco and Venus). Through this group he came into contact with thieves, drunks, prostitutes, receivers of stolen goods and other members of an underworld which he vividly portrayed. Apart from scenes of popular and soldiering life ("Disputing Card-Players", Tours, Musée des Beaux-Arts; "Musicians and Soldiers", Strasbourg, Musée des Beaux-Arts), he also produced religious works, preferably scenes from the Old Testament ("Judgment of Solomon", Paris, Louvre; "Judith and Holofernes", Valletta, Nationalmuseum).

*Illustration:*

244    The Concert, c. 1622–1625

## VALLOTTON Félix

1865 Lausanne – 1925 Paris
Vallotton came to Paris at the age of 17 to study at the Académie Julian. There he became impressed by the works of van Gogh, Gauguin and the Symbolists. It became his maxim never to aim at painting anything as it can be seen in nature. In his work he combined Symbolist and Art Noveau tendencies, and it is marked either by a dream-like aestheticism or a cold, revealing realism. He painted landscapes, portraits and genre scenes and also perfected the art of the woodcut, producing many single works and also some series. His realist pictures influenced the artists of the Neue Sachlichkeit.

*Illustration:*

528    Sandbanks on the Loire, 1923

## VARIN Quentin

c. 1570 Beauvais – 1634 Paris
Today his name is usually mentioned in connection with Poussin, whose first teacher he was. Varin himself was trained in Beauvais by François Gaget, then worked as a journeyman in the workshop of Duplan in Avignon (1597–1600). Maria de'Medici became his patroness in Paris, where he also assisted in decorating the Luxembourg and became "peintre du Roi" in 1623. He adopted some formal elements of the Fontainebleau school by emulating them at a somewhat superficial level, and painted his figures in strangely elongated proportions on his oversized canvases.

*Illustration:*

240    Presentation of Christ in the Temple, c. 1618–1620

## VASARÉLY Victor de

(Győző Vásárhelyi)
1908 Pécs (Hungary) – 1997 Paris
From 1928 to 1930 Vasarély studied under Sándor Bortnyik who introduced him to the works of the Russian Constructivists, an influence that was to remain with him. In 1930 he settled in Paris, where he worked as a graphic artist. From 1944 he

devoted himself again to painting and produced works which were the result of the systematic observation of optical stimuli generated by graphic means. Art was to do away with conventional means and to utilise modern media and techniques, thus becoming part of everyday life. By playing with variations on geometrical abstractions he arrived at his dazzling optical patterns, which he patented. Geometric forms in brilliant colours or in black and white are arranged within a grid in such a way that a fluctuating movement is achieved. Vasarély is the most creative representative of Op Art. His first kinetic pictures date from 1951. From 1955 he designed wall pictures made of metal and ceramics, mainly for buildings in France. He has been living in Annet sur Marne since 1961. In 1970 a museum dedicated to him was opened in Gardes (Vaucluse), apart from those in Pécs and Budapest. In 1976 he set up the Vasarély foundation in Aix-en-Provence.

*Illustration:*
655 Arcturus II, 1966

## VELÁZQUEZ Diego
(Diego Rodríguez de Silva y Velázquez)
1599 Seville – 1660 Madrid

Velázquez' father was the descendant of a noble Portuguese family, which was to become a significant factor in his career at the Spanish royal court. He studied briefly under Herrera the Elder, then was apprenticed to Francisco Pacheco whose daughter Juana he married in 1618. During that year his first dated painting was produced. In 1622/23 he travelled with his father-in-law to Madrid, to be introduced at the court. There he was appointed "pintor del Rey", but, as was the custom of the day, without a fixed income. Thanks to Pacheco many valuable details of Velázquez' early career have been handed down. For example he recorded that his son-in-law took samples of his art to present at the court, and these consisted of "bodegones", interior scenes with a strong still life element, such as "The Water Seller of Seville" (London, Wellington Museum, c.1619/20) and "Christ in the House of Martha and Mary" (ill. p.269). Pacheco remarked that this kind of painting was still new in Spanish art and that he generally disapproved of it unless "painted as Velázquez painted it".

Velázquez' estimation at court rose rapidly. After a painting competition in 1627 he was appointed court door-keeper and later, in 1652, court marshall. Important was his meeting with Rubens, who visited the Spanish court on a diplomatic mission in 1628. Perhaps this inspired him to visit Italy, where he met Ribera in Naples. After having been appointed painter to the royal chamber in 1643, he had another opportunity to visit Italy five years later in order to buy pictures for the royal collection. In Rome he was honoured by being made a member of the Accademia di San Luca after having exhibited one of his pictures publicly. Two years before his death he was made a knight of the Order of Santiago. This was due to the King's mediation, as it required proof of never having earned his living by working with his hands. As one of the foremost artists of the 17th century, he owed something to the School of Seville, but achieved a style which was entirely his own. Although open to the innovations of Titian, Caravaggio and Rubens, he transformed any inspirations he received in his own inimitable manner.

*Illustrations:*
222 Portrait of Philip IV of Spain in Brown and Silver, c. 1631
269 Christ in the House of Martha and Mary, c. 1619/20
269 Los Borrachos (The Drinkers), 1628/29
270 The Surrender of Breda, 1635
270 Prince Baltasar Carlos, Equestrian, c. 1634/35

271 A Dwarf Sitting on the Floor (Don Sebastían de Morra), c. 1645
272 Venus at her Mirror (The Rokeby Venus), c. 1644–1648
272 Las Meninas (The Maids of Honour), 1656/57

## VELDE Willem van de, the Younger
1633 Leiden – 1707 London

With his father, also a marine painter, Willem came to Amsterdam in 1636. Here his brother Adriaen was born, who became a landscape and animal painter. Willem received early instruction from his father, then was apprenticed to Simon de Vlieger, who specialised in seascapes. In 1652 he was made an independent master in Amsterdam, and in 1672 King Charles II called him to England, where he was made court painter. Together with Capelle he introduced a new type of marine painting, giving his ships individuality as in a portrait and presenting sea-faring as a dramatic event. His sea-battles and ships at sea, usually in calm or only slightly choppy waters, are notable for their precision of detail and fine colour and for the light effects which skilfully convey mood and atmosphere.

*Illustration:*
326 The Cannon Shot, undated

## VENEZIANO → Domenico Veneziano

## VERMEER Jan
(Jan van der Meer, Jan Vermeer van Delft)
1632 Delft – 1675 Delft

Although Vermeer was one of the greatest of Dutch genre painters, with Frans Hals and Rembrandt, and his work is unique in the history of art, very little is known about his life. He was the son of a weaver in silk and satin, who later became an art dealer and inn-keeper. Vermeer was probably a pupil of Fabritius. In 1653 he married Catharina Bolens, whom he often portrayed in his pictures, and became a member of the Delft Lukas Guild. He worked slowly and therefore his output was small, and insufficient to keep a large family, although he achieved fairly high prices. He tried to supplement his income by acting as an art dealer, but this also failed. Only one of his 36 surviving paintings is dated ("The Procuress", Dresden, Gemäldegalerie, 1656).

"Diana and her Companions" (The Hague, Mauritshuis) and "Christ in the House of Martha and Mary" (Edinburgh, National Gallery) probably date from about 1655, a period when he explored Italian art and came to terms with the Utrecht Caravaggists. These were followed by genre scenes, conversation pieces, in which detail and gestures are still somewhat over-emphasised. The pictures with which Vermeer's name is now mostly associated were painted shortly before and after 1660 , including "Girl Reading a Letter at an Open Window", "The Milkmaid", "Woman Holding a Balance" (ill. p.332) and "The Artist's Studio" or "Allegory of Painting" (ill. p.334). In these intimate scenes, light itself seems to have become the subject of the picture; a moment of stillness captured on canvas. Vermeer stands apart from his contemporary genre painters through his superb draughtsmanship and skill in perspective, his colour harmonies, in which cool blue and a brilliant yellow predominate, and his incomparable ability in setting enamel-like highlights which impart a glow to surfaces. In his late work his treatment of light lost some of its poetry, his drawing became less fluid, and the interiors less simple. On his death his pictures were auctioned off and he was forgotten, and it was not until towards the end of the 19th century that his true significance was recognised.

*Illustrations:*
285 Street in Delft ("Het Straatje"), c. 1657/58
332 The Lacemaker, c. 1665
332 Woman Holding a Balance, c. 1665
333 View of Delft, c. 1658–1660
334 Allegory of Painting (The Artist's Studio), c. 1666
334 Young Woman Seated at a Virginal, c. 1675

## VERONESE Paolo
(Paolo Caliari)
1528 Verona – 1588 Venice

Veronese studied under Antonio Badile in Verona from 1541, but his true masters were the Venetian painters Titian and Tintoretto as well the painters of the Emilia region, including Parmigianino. In 1553 he went to Venice, where he was called Veronese after his place of birth. Veronese was the opposite of Tintoretto: while the latter moved into Mannerism, Veronese's art was securely rooted in the Italian High Renaissance. His works not only reflect the religious and political unrest of his time, but also the love of pomp and worldly splendour of Venetian life. In so far as content often seems to have been subordinated to form in his works, he was also a typical representative of 16th century art. This is why three centuries later Cézanne saw him as the precursor of pure form.

His first large commission was the decoration of the sacristy and ceiling in San Sebastiano, Venice, in 1555/56. For this he executed a great many pictures on canvas with bold perspectival views and foreshortening of figures. During a visit to Rome in 1560 he studied in particular Michelangelo's work in the Sistine Chapel. In subsequent works the impressions he received there found application in the plastic modelling of figures in movement and the further development of illusionistic spatial depth. A major example of this period are his frescos in the Villa Barbaro in Maser executed in the early 1560s (ill. p.184). Veronese's influence reached far beyond his time. The virtuosity of his composition not only played an important part in the works of Rubens and Tiepolo, but also had many followers amongst the European painters of the Baroque; and his handling of colour remained of importance in French art until the 19th century.

*Illustrations:*
156 Allegory of Vice and Virtue (The Choice of Hercules), c. 1580
184 Giustiana Barbaro and her Nurse, c. 1561/62
184 Allegory of Love: Unfaithfulness, c. 1575–1580
185 The Finding of Moses, c. 1570–1575

## VERROCCHIO Andrea del
(Andrea di Michele Cione)
c. 1435 Florence – 1488 Venice

Verrocchio was a goldsmith, sculptor, carver and painter, but it was in the field of sculpture that he excelled in the second half of the 15th century. After his training under the goldsmith Giuliano del Verrocchio, whose name he adopted, he schooled himself in the works of Donatello, not in a pupil-teacher relationship, however, but in a spirit of idealised rivalry which seeks completely new solutions for one and the same task (statue in bronze of David, c. 1476; equestrian statue of Colleoni in Venice, 1480–1488). While Donatello's approach conveyed a closed, solid strength, Verrocchio excelled in expressing an almost nervous, concentrated energy. And instead of a fixed aspect, he presented his subject from nearly all aspects, and later even all aspects, anticipating the 16th century Mannerist approach.

Little is known about his early work. It was not until 1472 that he made his mark as a leading mas-

ter of his generation with his sepulchral monument for Piero and Giovanni de'Medici (San Lorenzo, Old Sacristy). The culmination of his achievement was the bronze group "The Incredulity of St Thomas" (1464–1482) at Or San Michele. From about 1475 Verocchio's workshop became a kind of academy of arts comparable to that of Lorenzo Ghiberti in the second quarter of the century. It is difficult to separate Verrocchio's works in the field of painting from that of his pupils: a number of important painters were trained at his workshop, Leonardo da Vinci being the most famous of them, and they remained in his workshop longer than was required. Other painters who emerged from this workshop include Lorenzo di Credi, Perugino and Signorelli. Verrocchio's paintings "The Baptism of Christ" (ill. p. 109) and the "Sacra Conversazione" in Pistoia cathedral (1478) are the finest representations of these subjects in Early Renaissance Florentine art, alongside those of Domenico Veneziano.
*Illustration:*
109    The Baptism of Christ, c. 1475

### VIEIRA DA SILVA Maria Elena
1908 Lisbon – 1992 Paris
Vieira da Silva is one of the key figures of the Ecole de Paris. Initially she intended to become a sculptor and received training in Paris from Emile Bourdelle and Charles Despiau, but then changed to painting. In 1928/29 she worked with Orthon Friesz and Léger and was drawn into the circle of young *avant-garde* painters, but she was also inspired by the works of Bonnard, the late medieval Sienese masters and the Cubists. She began her career by working as an industrial designer and illustrator of books and magazines. From 1940 to 1947 she lived in Portugal and Brazil, then returned to Paris. Her work is often categorised as belonging to the Informel, but she has always remained true to the principle of her own pictorial aesthetic. Typical for her pictures are spatial, architectonic and urban compositions drawn in fine lines and beautiful tonal harmonies which in her later work give place to more abstract, lyrical arrangements.
*Illustration:*
638    The Library, 1949

### VIGÉE-LEBRUN Elisabeth
(Marie Louise Elisabeth Vigée-Lebrun)
1755 Paris – 1842 Paris
Vigée-Lebrun received early training from her father, a painter in pastels. Other teachers and those helpful in her career were Doyen, Vernet, Davesne and Briard. She also copied the old masters, particularly Dutch art. She soon became a celebrated portrait painter and was appointed court painter to Marie-Antoinette. She became a member of the Academy in 1783. She had to leave France in 1789 because of her court connections. From that time she travelled widely, visiting Vienna, Dresden, Berlin, London, St Petersburg and Switzerland, and was inundated with academic honours and commissions. Her emotional, idealising portraits of women and children, which were often criticised for their sentimental touches, were representative of an international style of portraiture already in transition; the characteristics come out more fully in her many self-portraits.
*Illustration:*
367    Portrait of Madame de Staël as Corinne, c. 1807/08

### VLAMINCK Maurice de
1876 Paris – 1958 Reuil-la-Gadelière
As a young man Vlaminck supported himself as a violinist in a suburban orchestra. He was an enthusiastic cyclist and took part in many races. Around

1900 he began to paint with Derain in Chatou in the vicinity of Paris. After a visit to the van Gogh exhibition in 1901 he became intoxicated with colour. Until 1907 he painted pictures in violent brushstrokes and unmixed colours which in their boldness outstripped all other Fauves. In 1908 the Fauvist movement began to split, and Vlaminck temporarily turned to Cézanne and the Cubists for inspiration until he adopted a type of "romantic realism", following Derain's example. His work became darkly dramatic. From 1918 he lived quietly in the country.
*Illustration:*
564    Les Bateux-Lavoirs, 1906

### VOS Cornelis de
c. 1584 Hulst (Zeeland) – 1651 Antwerp
Vos was the brother-in-law of Snyder and was accepted as a master in the Antwerp Guild in 1608, but worked as an art dealer for a time. In 1635 he worked with Jordaens as assistant to Rubens on the decorations for the reception of Cardinal Ferdinand. From 1636 to 1638 he worked with Rubens on the decoration of the hunting-lodge Dorre de la Parada near Madrid. Vos was primarily a portrait painter of Antwerp society and of family groups. In their restrained elegance and fine observation of character his portraits approach those of van Dyck. Among his best works were those of children ("The Painter's Daughters", Berlin, Gemäldegalerie), which stand out for their freshness, naturalness, and alertness of expression and fine colouring.
*Illustration:*
300    The Family of the Artist, c. 1630–1635

### VOUET Simon
1590 Paris – 1649 Paris
Vouet received only basic training from his father, a sign painter, but his talent developed rapidly; he is said to have been called to England at the age of fourteen to paint portraits. After visiting Constantinople and Venice, he came to Rome, where he became influenced by Caravaggism in the manner of Valentin ("The Birth of Mary", San Francesco a Ripa, c. 1622). Reni's monumentality, the classical serenity of Domenichino's work and the ideas of Lanfranco and Guercino were also to have a lasting effect. In Genoa, where he met Strozzi, he produced one of his major works, the Crucifixion for San Ambrogio (1622). Louis XIII recalled him to France as "peintre du Roi" (1627) where Vouet – always intent on furthering his career and never turning down a commission – produced works of great beauty and loftiness. Apart from painting altarpieces and portraits he also designed tapestries in his richly decorative style. He worked in the royal residence St Germain, the Palais du Luxembourg, Fontainebleau and the Louvre. His most important paintings include "Lot and his Daughters" (Strasbourg, Musée des Beaux-Arts, 1633) and the "Allegory of the Victor" (Paris, Louvre, 1630). In his studio many of the great decorative painters of the age were trained, including Le Brun, Mignard and Le Sueur.
*Illustrations:*
221    The Toilet of Venus, c. 1628–1639
240    Saturn, conquered by Amor, Venus and Hope, c. 1645/46

### VUILLARD Édouard
1868 Cuiseaux (Saône) – 1940 La Baule (Loire-Atlantique)
Vuillard was a life-long friend of Bonnard, with whom he shared a studio, and with whom his work offers a parallel. In 1888 he came to Paris to study at the Académie Julian, and a year later was already participating in founding the Nabis group. Despite

his friendship with Gauguin, Maurice Denis and Paul Sérusier, he never adopted Symbolist or pointillist elements. His work shows his interest in Japanese art, and there are also traces of the Art Nouveau style. He is noted for his intimate paintings of domestic interiors and he also painted still lifes, portraits and street scenes in fresh, delicate colours in the Impressionist manner. For *Revue Blanche* he produced illustrations and designed posters and interiors.
*Illustration:*
519    Portrait of Toulouse-Lautrec, 1898

### WALDMÜLLER Ferdinand Georg
1793 Vienna – 1865 Hinterbrühl (near Vienna)
Waldmüller was the most important Viennese representative of the Biedermeier style. His main subjects were portraiture and the landscape, and he later added genre scenes. From 1807 he studied at Vienna Academy, at whose gallery he became curator in 1829 and also professor at the Academy. In the full knowledge of the difficulties of an artist's life – so far his wife, an actress, had provided for both of them – he risked again in the 1840s the financial security that the Academy gave him. As a dedicated Realist he attacked in two polemical papers of 1846 and 1849 the idealist doctrines expounded by his colleagues at the Academy. This led to a cut-back in salary and pension, and Waldmüller lived in rather restricted circumstances in later years. Although finding recognition outside Austria, he was not rehabilitated until 1864. Like his friend Franz Steinfeld, he was interested in colour as seen in daylight. In his landscapes he developed a realism akin to photography and explored particularly the effects of extreme sunlight.
*Illustration:*
455    The Last Calf, 1857

### WARHOL Andy
(Andrej Warhola)
1928 Pittsburgh – 1987 New York
From 1945 to 1949 Warhol studied at the Carnegie Institute of Technology in Pittsburgh. He then went to New York where he became one of the key figures of Pop Art. While working as an illustrator and graphic artist he developed his technique of the "blotted line", the first step to the reproduction process which was to become the basis of his pictorial work. From 1960 he produced pictures after comic-strips, then motifs from the world of American consumerism, such as Coca-Cola bottles, dollar notes and Campbell soup cans. He also used subjects found in newspapers and magazines, such as snapshots of road accidents. In his New York Factory, which was set up in 1962, he produced his portraits of famous personalities, photographic works, films and music, often in team-work. He also published the magazine *Interview* and organised TV shows and multi-media concerts with the pop group Velvet Underground. For his later works he chose more conventional subjects, such as old master paintings (e.g. Leonardo's "Last Supper") or Schloss Neuschwanstein built by King Ludwig II of Bavaria.
*Illustrations:*
658    200 Campbell's Soup Cans, 1962
658    Do it Yourself – Landscape, 1962
659    Marilyn, 1964

### WATTEAU Jean-Antoine
1684 Valenciennes – 1721 Nogent-sur-Marne
As the son of a craftsman Watteau was apprenticed to a decorative painter at the age of eleven. About five years later he left for Paris and joined the Flemish artists' colony in St Germain-des-Prés. His master Claude Gilot introduced him to the world of the theatre and elegant society. After a dispute with

Gilot he painted for the art dealer Sirois scenes from military life in 1709/10. In 1712 he was accepted by the Academy, and five years later he became a member with his "Pilgrimage to Cythera" (ill. p. 349). As this picture did not fit into any of the existing categories, a new one was created, and Watteau became a "peintre des fêtes galantes". In this way Watteau's own creation, the elegant party group, achieved respectability in academic circles. From then on, Watteau's work became dominated by the poetical representation of love. The theatre, music, the conversation piece and mythical scenes, all enter the realm of love. His extremely fine palette reveals Flemish influences, particularly that of Rubens, and his draughtsmanship was superb. His patron Crozat's collection of graphic works by Renaissance masters gave him ample scope for study in this field. Apart from elegant party scenes, Watteau excelled in the portrayal of scenes from Italian comedy. In the last two years of his life he suffered from tuberculosis. He went to London for treatment and on his return retired to Nogent-sur-Marne, where he died, not yet aged forty.
*Illustrations:*

342   Scale of Love (La gamme d'amour), c. 1717–1719
349   L'Indifférent, 1717
349   Pilgrimage to Cythera, c. 1718/19
350   Gilles (Pierrot), 1721
350   The Indiscretion, 1717
351   Fêtes Vénetiennes, 1719

**WENCESLAS BIBLE** → Workshop

**WESSELMANN Tom**
born 1931 Cincinnati
From 1951 to 1955 Wesselmann studied psychology at the University of Cincinnati, then attended the Academy of Arts and went for further studies to the Cooper Union in New York, where he settled. Wesselmann is an important representative of American Pop Art. He began his career with collages while under the influence of Matisse and de Kooning – two opposing examples to follow. He then turned to painting interiors, colourful and poster-like, often with female nude figures – a subject he was to return to repeatedly. At the same time he produced collages of food illustrations, sometimes presented in relief form. He is noted for his series "Great American Nudes" dating from the early 1960s. In the 1970s he produced pictures on freestanding canvases which are an attempt at eliminating the boundaries between painting and sculpture. From about 1983 he has been concentrating on drawings which are transferred to aluminium or steel and then cut out.
*Illustration:*
661   Bathtub 3, 1963

**WEST Benjamin**
1738 Springfield (Pennsylvania) – 1820 London
West began his career as a portrait painter in Philadelphia and New York. One of his sitters persuaded him to try his hand at history painting, and the result was the "Death of Socrates" (Nazareth, Pennsylvania, Stites Collection), his first attempt in this field. Patrons enabled him to visit Rome by granting him a scholarship, the first American artist to be helped in this way. There he found a new patron in Cardinal Albani. He joined the circle of leading artists gathered in Rome and became friendly with Mengs and Johann Joachim Winckelmann. He was appointed as a member of the Academy, both in Florence and Parma. On his intended return journey to America he stopped off in London in 1763 and remained there for the rest of his life. He had a brilliant career, becoming a founding member of the Royal Academy in 1768 and historical painter

to the royal court in 1772. West was also a respected teacher, especially of fellow American artists in London, including Copley, Trumbull, Sully, Stuart and Pratt.
*Illustration:*
391   Colonel Guy Johnson, c. 1775/76

**WEYDEN Rogier van der**
c. 1400 Tournai – 1464 Brussels
Rogier was the leading Dutch painter to follow in the tradition of the brothers Jan and Hubert van Eyck. Unlike any other painter of the 15th century outside Italy, he extended Dutch art in respect of both composition and figure development, and his innovations became widespread in northern art. His influence spread as far as Italy, particularly with respect to his painting techniques, and he was much respected there. Surprisingly late, in 1427, he became a pupil of Campin. To identify his early work as that of his master, as has been attempted, is not tenable. In 1432 he became an independent master, and in 1436 official painter to Brussels city. A visit to Rome in the Holy Year of 1449/50 brought about the most fruitful exchange between northern and Italian art in the 15th century. Rogier continued what Campin and also Jan van Eyck had begun, perfecting anatomical considerations and the perspectival representation of interior space and landscapes. Direct references to the older masters, such as in his various representations of St Luke painting the Madonna, which hark back to van Eyck's Rolin Madonna (ill. p. 123), became far less frequent from about 1440 as he strove to find an artistic balance between space and picture plane. The figures are more sparsely proportioned, interiors and drapery become more elegant, and the realistic depiction of detail gains in importance in the overall design.
*Illustrations:*

88    Crucifixion in a Church, c. 1445
127   Madonna with Four Saints (Medici Madonna), c. 1450
127   Descent from the Cross, c. 1435–1440
128   Adoration of the Magi (Columba Altar), c. 1455
129   Mary Magdalene, c. 1452
129   Entombment, c. 1450

**WHISTLER James Abbot McNeill**
1834 Lowell (Massachusetts) – 1903 London
Whistler grew up in New England. In 1843 the family moved to Russia, where he received his first drawing lessons at the St Petersburg Academy in 1845. On the death of his father in 1849 the family returned to America. In 1851 he became a cadet at the military college at West Point, but decided to follow art as a profession. In 1855 he went to Paris, entering the studio of Gleyre in 1856. Important for his artistic development was his meeting with Fantin-Latour and Courbet; other friends included Manet, Monet and Degas. On his rejection by the Salon in 1859 he left Paris for London. His work during this period showed the Japanese influence. In 1866 he visited Chile. Around 1870 his first "nocturnes" were produced, an exquisite series of Thames etchings, intended to capture the poetic mood of pictorial and musical harmony. This theme was to hold his attention for nearly a decade. From the 1870s he increasingly turned to painting portraits, which formed his major source of income until the 1890s. In 1878 he sued Ruskin for libel. Despite winning a moral victory, Whistler was driven into bankruptcy by the cost of the action. From 1886 to 1888 he was the president of the Society of British Artists In 1892 the Goupil Gallery in London arranged a successful one-man-exhibition of his work. Whistler's aesthetic approach found expression in the subtle effect of delicate colours and

tone values. His portraits, landscapes and interiors exercise great charm. His manner of painting owes less to the analytical technique of Impressionism, but rather more to the colour impressionism developed in the 17th century.
*Illustrations:*
538   Rose and Silver: La Princesse du Pays de la Porcelaine, 1864
538   Caprice in Purple and Gold, No 2: The Golden Screen, 1864

**WILKIE David**
1785 Cults (Fife) – 1841 at sea, near Gibraltar
Wilkie studied art in Edinburgh and from 1805 at the Royal Academy in London, of which he became a member in 1811. He began his career by painting portraits, but after a great success in 1806 at an exhibition of his genre pictures, he devoted himself for the next two decades almost exclusively to this branch of painting, for which he became famous. His pictures of popular life, often endearing and sometimes with an overtone of caricature, were painted in the manner of the 17th century Dutch genre picture and reminiscent particularly of Ostade and Teniers. They met the taste of the new, rich middle-classes of a country which was poised to become the richest in the world. Between 1825 and 1828 he travelled on the Continent and on his return began to take up history painting. His deep and glowing coloration and generous design show an interest in Correggio, Velázquez and Murillo. In 1840 he embarked on travels in the Near East, visiting Constantinople, Jerusalem and Alexandria. He died at sea during his return to England.
*Illustration:*
467   Reading the Will, 1820

**WILSON Richard**
1714 Penegoes (Wales) – 1782 Colommendy (Wales)
Wilson was a pupil of Thomas Wright in London and, like his master, specialised in portrait painting to begin with. His visit to Italy (1750–1758) took him first to Venice, then to Rome. While in Italy he decided to abandon portrait painting for landscape, later becoming the first great British landscape painter. The principal sources of his inspiration were Poussin, Lorrain and Vernet, and he also owed something to Dutch landscape painting of the late 17th century. Among his finest works are his English landscape and Welsh mountain scenes, which are executed with topographical accuracy and show great skill in composition and a finely graded palette in the way they convey the expanse and peace of the lakes and hills.
*Illustration:*
387   View of Snowdon from Llyn Nantlle, c. 1766

**WILTON DIPTYCH** → Master

**WITTE Emanuel de**
c. 1617 Alkmaar – 1692 Amsterdam
Witte, who became a member of the Lukas Guild in 1636, initially painted mythological and religious scenes as well as portraits. When he settled in Delft around 1640, he began to specialise in scenes of church interiors, perhaps having been inspired by Fabritius' perspective art. From 1651, when he moved to Amsterdam, until his death by suicide, he concentrated almost exclusively on architectural painting. But unlike Saenredam, whose main concern was accuracy of representation, Witte also painted imaginary buildings or mixed features of several churches. He chose unusual interior sections, in which architectural elements often appear askew,

and used light effects in the typical Delft manner, so that the atmosphere thus created seems to become the actual subject of the picture. His large airy compositions are often relieved by dark figure groups in the foreground, perhaps in conversation or listening to a sermon, and often accompanied by dogs.
*Illustration:*
320    Church Interior, c. 1660

**WITTINGAU → Master**

**WITZ Konrad**
c. 1400 Rottweil – 1445 Basle or Geneva
Witz was the most versatile of Germanic artists in the first half of the 15th century. In various respects his significance was comparable to that of Masaccio and Jan van Eyck. His birthplace Rottweil was an important trading centre lying outside the boundaries of feudal or ecclesiastical rule, which might have played a part in Witz's artistic approach to life, although little is known about his early training. Historical records give only a few clues about his life and work. In 1434 he was accepted by the Basle Guild as "Meister Konrad von Rotwil", and in the same year was granted citizenship by the city. His signature and the date 1444 on his painting "Miraculous Draught of Fishes" (ill. p. 142) on the Geneva altarpiece represent the last news of his life and work. Witz was as much concerned with the plastic modelling of figures as with perspectival problems. With his rendering of the polychrome "statue" ("Mirror of Salvation" altarpiece) Witz went far beyond the inventions of both Masaccio and van Eyck. It has been mooted that he might also have worked at woodcarving, but of this no proof exists. The handling of perspective in his interiors ("Annunciation" in Nuremberg; "Mary and Catharine in Church", Strasbourg) may just be based on experience and judgment, but the resulting suggestion of depth is remarkable. In his landscapes and renderings of architecture he always aimed at giving a true and accurate picture of what he saw. It is certain that he had knowledge of Dutch art and possibly also of Italian painting.
*Illustrations:*
142    Sabobai and Benaiah, c. 1435
142    The Miraculous Draught of Fishes, 1444

**WOLS**
(Alfred Otto Wolfgang Schulze)
1913 Berlin – 1951 Paris
Schulze, who called himself Wols from 1937, moved with his family to Dresden in 1919. In 1932 he went to Berlin to apply for training at the Bauhaus. However, on the advice of Moholy-Nagy he went to Paris where he painted, wrote, and worked as a portrait photographer. He met Max Ernst, Léger, César Domela, Arp and Amédée Ozenfant. In 1937 he was the official photographer of the Paris World Exhibition. On the outbreak of war in 1939 he was interned, and after his flight in 1940 he lived in hiding in Cassis near Marseilles, where he made drawings and water-colours. In 1942 he sought refuge in Montélimar. There he met the writer Henri-Pierre Roché, who became his supporter. His first exhibition of water-colours at the Drouin gallery in 1945 was not successful. A year later he returned to Paris, and an exhibition of his work at the same gallery in 1947 became a sensation. He met Sartre and Simone de Beauvoir, who helped him in his further career. He shared his artistic interests with Giacometti and Mathieu. His drawings, water-colours and paintings were at first influenced by the psychic automatism of the Surrealists and produced under the influence of drugs and alcohol. Later he became more interested in

combining vehement brushwork with a structure approaching the relief.
*Illustration:*
641    Le Bateau ivre, 1945

**WOOD Grant**
1892 Anamosa (Iowa) – 1942 Iowa City
Wood studied at the Minneapolis School of Design and Handicraft (1910/11), then worked as a designer, and from 1914 to 1916 had a silversmith's workshop in Chicago with Christopher Haga. In 1920 he visited Paris, where he attended the Académie Julian in 1923/24. While his early landscapes and portraits were painted in the Impressionist manner, he later adopted a hard, precise realism influenced by German Renaissance art and the Neue Sachlichkeit, with which he had come into contact on his visit to Germany in 1928. On his return to America he founded the Stone City Colony and Art School (Iowa) in 1932 and taught at the University of Iowa from 1934 until 1941. His uncompromising portraits of the farmers and townspeople of the American Mid-West, plus his landscapes, make him an important representative of American Realism.
*Illustration:*
601    American Gothic, 1930

**WORKSHOP OF THE GERONA MARTYROLOGY**
active about 1405–1425
This work combined a number of different styles in manuscript illumination, although a convincing differentiation has yet to be made. The so-called Joshua master of the Antwerp Bible was involved; also the school of the martyrology in the Diocesan museum of Gerona, and of the illuminations taken from the book of John of Mandeville in the British Library. This group of illuminators already dominated the direction taken by Prague miniaturist painters in the first decade of the 15th century and carried on well into the second decade. Stylistically their work combined Western influences with those from northern Italy, and a close connection to panel painting is also detectable because techniques were used normally only to be found in panel painting. To the combined effect of these examples, the workshop added a stricter pictorial composition.
*Illustration:*
72    The Story of Creation, c. 1415

**WORKSHOP OF THE INGEBORG PSALTER**
First quarter of the 13th century
Entitled after the psalter of Queen Ingeborg of France, second wife of King Philippe Auguste. She came from Denmark, but her husband expelled her from court. A reconciliation took place in 1213, and the psalter was probably given to her on that occasion. It was produced in a workshop in Paris, which employed two principal painters and several assistants. The work of the two miniature artists is of equal standard, and they produced further illuminated manuscripts, both in collaboration and separately, mainly for the French court. A good knowledge of Byzantine art and close contact with contemporary northern French and English masters of illumination can be assumed, as with the works of the Meuse goldsmith Nikolaus von Verdun. The miniatures appear as a complete series of pictures before the text, and without reference to the text, with two double pages of illuminations followed by two blank pages.
*Illustration:*
27    Embalming of the Body of Christ and The Three Marys at the Empty Tomb. From the Psalter of Queen Ingeborg of Denmark, c. 1213

**WORKSHOP OF THE LOUIS PSALTER**
Third quarter of the 13th century
This royal workshop operating in Paris is referred to by its most important production, the Psalter produced for King Louis IX of France, commonly called Saint Louis. Another magnificent psalter, now in Cambridge, probably belonged to Louis' sister, the Abbess Isabella. The dating of these works can only be estimated by reference to other recorded events and stylistic considerations (after 1258, the year in which one of the King's daughters married the Count of Champagne, but before 1270, the year of the King's death). The workshop was well organised, and there are indications that the master had formerly worked on the illuminations of manuscripts for the royal library of Sainte Chapelle in Paris. Although the work was executed by at least six contributors, the hands are difficult to separate, a sign that the master had impressed his style on his assistants. The uniformity of decoration and pictorial conception point at the mid-13th-century, a period of transition when the first tendencies towards a standardisation of this art become apparent. The basic principles were established, and only the level of refinement and lavish use of rich materials then served as distinguishing features.
*Illustration:*
27    Joshua Stops the Sun and Moon. From the Psalter of Louis IX of France, c. 1258–1270

**WORKSHOP OF THE WENCESLAS BIBLE**
active about 1390–1410 in Prague
This was actually a loose connection of several workshops led by various masters, some of whom are known to us by name because of their signatures, others having been given tentative names with reference to their work. It is nevertheless acceptable to regard these artists as belonging to the "Workshop of the Wenceslas Bible". As most of their commissions came from royal courts, they must have been conversant with esoteric Symbolism and trends in taste. This meant that some of them must have had close connections to persons in court circles who understood the meaning of the private Symbolism at court and so could invent witty references between the principal picture and the bordering miniatures. The artists took as their starting point the older Bohemian and Italian, particularly Bolognese, art of illumination. At the end of the royal patronage around 1405 – the Wenceslaus Bible, for example, remained unfinished – the workshop was dissolved.
*Illustration:*
70    Title illustration to Ptolemy's "Quadripartitus", c. 1395–1400

**WRIGHT OF DERBY Joseph**
1734 Derby – 1797 Derby
Wright studied under Thomas Hudson in London. In 1771 he became a member of the Society of Art and in 1784 of the Royal Academy. A visit to Italy, 1773–1775, gave him the opportunity to study the old masters. Caravaggio and his followers seem to have fascinated him particularly, as shown in his later work with its dramatic light contrasts. On his return to England he tried briefly to set up a portrait practice in Bath, but then went back to Derby, where he remained. Although primarily a portraitist, he also worked on his discovery of the "scientific genre painting". He developed an understanding of how to refine the effect of lighting in order to bring emotion into an apparently objective atmosphere. In landscapes, too, he was innovative in his use of light sources.
*Illustration:*
382    Experiment with an Airpump, 1768

**ZICK Januarius**
(also: Johann Rasso Januarius Zickh)
1730 Munich – 1797 Ehrenbreitstein
Zick received early instruction from his father, the painter Johann Zick, who was an exponent of the Rococo "Rembrandt manner" in easel painting, but in fresco painting followed the tradition of Asam and Bergmüller. In 1757 Zick went to Rome to complete his training under Mengs. Nevertheless he remained true to the Bavarian Rococo manner even though some classical elements entered his work. His first important commission was the decoration of the Watteau room in Schloß Bruchsal (1759), and his greatest work in fresco is in the Klosterkirche of Wiblingen (1778–1780). Zick also produced fine panel paintings, etchings and architectural designs. His work is representative of the critical transitional period leading from the Rococo to Neo-Classicism.
*Illustration:*
395 Gottfried Peter de Requilé with his two sons and Mercury, 1771

**ZIMMERMANN Johann Baptist**
1680 Gaispoint (near Wessobrunn) – 1758 Munich
Zimmermann grew up in the arts and crafts milieu of Wessobrunn which is famous for its school of stucco-work. He received his training as a painter in Augsburg. It appears that he worked as a stuc-coer until 1720. As a fresco painter he often collaborated with his brother Dominikus, an architect (e.g. church at Steinhausen, 1730/31). While in other European countries fresco-painting was already in decline in the first half of the 18th century, it still flourished in southern Germany. Belonging to the same generation as Asam, Zimmermann (with his brother) was the leading master of the early Bavarian Rococo. In his ceiling decorations he abandoned the illusionist element and introduced terrestrial zones around the edges so that the open vault of heaven is framed by bucolic or idyllic landscape scenes (Hofkirche St Michael in Berg am Laim, Munich, 1739; Great Hall in Schloss Nymphenburg, Munich, 1757). Architectural elements, ornament and picture merge along the borders. The high point of his art is the decoration of the Wieskirche, one of his brother's late works, where Zimmermann achieved an overall perfection in his handling of colour and design.
*Illustration:*
392 The Nymph as Symbol of Nymphenburg (Ceiling fresco), 1757

**ZURBARÁN Francisco de**
1598 Fuente de Cantos (Estremadura) – 1664 Madrid
Zurbarán was trained in Seville in 1616/17 by an unknown painter and settled in 1617 near his birthplace to paint a large number of religious pictures for the monasteries of Seville. His work included many pictures of saints at prayer and devotional still lifes in the spirit of the Counter-Reformation. His tenebrist style, reminiscent of Herrera the Elder, with its massively simple figures and objects, clear, sober colours and deep solemnity of feeling expressed in thickly applied paint, made him the ideal painter of the austere religion of Spain. In Seville, where he settled in 1629, he became the leading artist. There he produced many altarpieces and decorated a number of monasteries with extensive fresco cycles. His fortunes fell with Murillo's rise. Having been appointed "pintor del rey" in 1634, he was compelled to supplement his income by acting as an art dealer only a decade later. In 1658 he moved to Madrid, where he entered the Santiago Oder. Caravaggio, Velázquez, El Greco, Cotán, Dürer, Raphael, Titian – all these left traces in his work, which is nevertheless of great originality.
*Illustrations:*
262 The Death of St Bonaventura, 1629
262 St Hugo of Grenoble in the Carthusian Refectory, c. 1633
263 St Margaret, c. 1630–1635
264 The Ecstasy of St Francis, c. 1660
264 Still Life with Lemons, Oranges and Rose, 1633

# Acknowledgements

The editor and publisher wish to express their gratitude to the museums, public collections, galleries and private collectors, the archivists and photographers, and all those involved in this work. The editor and publisher have at all times endeavoured to observe the legal regulations on the copyright of artists, their heirs or their representatives, and also to obtain permission to reproduce photographic works and reimburse the copyright holder accordingly. Given the great number of artists involved, this may have resulted in a few oversights despite intensive research. In such a case the copyright owner or representative should make an application to the publisher.

The copyright of all works shown is the property of the artists, unless stated otherwise, or of their heirs, or representatives, or legal successors: Albers: © VG Bild-Kunst, Bonn 1995. – Appel: © De Tulp Pers, Hilversum. – Bacon: © Marlborough Fine Art, Londres. – Balla: Héritiers Giacomo Balla. – Balthus: © VG Bild-Kunst, Bonn, 1995. – Baselitz: © Galerie Michael Werner, Cologne and New York. – Basquiat: © VG Bild-Kunst, Bonn, 1995. – Baumeister: © VG Bild-Kunst, Bonn, 1995. – Beckmann: © VG Bild-Kunst, Bonn, 1995. – Beuys: © VG Bild-Kunst, Bonn, 1995. – Blake: Waddington Galleries Ltd, Londres. – Bonnard: © VG Bild-Kunst, Bonn, 1995. – Botero: © Fernando Botero. – Braque: © VG Bild-Kunst, Bonn, 1995. – Brauner: © VG Bild-Kunst, Bonn, 1995. – Burri: © Héritiers Alberto Burri. – Carrà: © VG Bild-Kunst, Bonn, 1995. – Chagall: © VG Bild-Kunst, Bonn, 1995. – Chirico: © VG Bild-Kunst, Bonn, 1995. – Clemente: © Francesco Clemente, New York. – Close: © Chuck Close, New York. – Cucchi: © Enzo Cucchi. – Dalí: © VGBild-Kunst, Bonn, 1995/Demart pro arte B.V. – Delaunay: © VG Bild-Kunst, Bonn, 1995. – Delvaux: © VG Bild-Kunst, Bonn, 1995. – Denis: © VG Bild-Kunst, Bonn, 1995. – Derain: © VG Bild-Kunst, Bonn, 1995. – Dine: © Pace Gallery, New York. – Dix: © VG Bild-Kunst, Bonn, 1995. – Doesburg: © VG Bild-Kunst, Bonn, 1995. Dongen: © VG Bild-Kunst, Bonn, 1995. – Dubuffet: © VG Bild-Kunst, Bonn, 1995. – Duchamp: © VGBild-Kunst, Bonn, 1995. – Dufy: © VG Bild-Kunst, Bonn, 1995. – Ensor: © VG Bild-Kunst, Bonn, 1995. – Ernst: © VG Bild-Kunst, Bonn, 1995. – Estes: © VG Bild-Kunst, Bonn, 1995. – Fautrier: © VG Bild-Kunst, Bonn, 1995. – Feininger: © VG Bild-Kunst, Bonn, 1995. – Fontana: © Archivio Lucio Fontana, Milano. – Francis: © VG Bild-Kunst, Bonn, 1995. – Freud: © Lucian Freud, Londres. – Gertsch: © Franz Gertsch, Rüschegg-Heubach. – Giacometti: © VG Bild-Kunst, Bonn, 1995. – Gorky: © VG Bild-Kunst, Bonn, 1995. – Gris: © VG Bild-Kunst, Bonn, 1995. – Grosz: © VG Bild-Kunst, Bonn, 1995. – Guttuso: © Archivi Guttuso. – Hamilton: © VG Bild-Kunst, Bonn, 1995. – Haring: © Keith Haring Etsate, New York. – Hartung: © VG Bild-Kunst, Bonn, 1995. – Heckel: © Succession Erich Heckel, Gaienhofen. – Heisig: © VG Bild-Kunst, Bonn, 1995. – Hockney: © Tradhart Ltd., Slough, Berkshire. – Hofmann: © Hans et Maria Hofmann Memorial Galleries, Berkeley. – Hetertwasser: © Jeram Harel Management, Vienne. – Indiana: © Star of Hope, Vinalhaven. – Jawlensky: © VG Bild-Kunst, Bonn, 1995. – Johns: © VG Bild-Kunst, Bonn, 1995. – Jones: © Allen Jones, Londres. – Jorn: © Jon Palle Buhl, Copenhague. – Kahlo: © Instituto Nacional de Bellas Artes, Mexico City. – Kandinsky: © VG Bild-Kunst, Bonn, 1995. – Kelly: © Elsworth Kelly, Spencertown. – Kiefer: © Anselm Kiefer, La Ribante. – Kippenberger: © Martin Kippenberger, Cologne. – Kirchner: © Galerie Henze & Ketterer AG, Wichtrach/Berne. – Kitaj: © Ronald B. Kitaj. – Klapheck: © Konrad Klapheck, Düsseldorf. – Klee: © VG Bild-Kunst, Bonn, 1995. – Klein: © VG Bild-Kunst, Bonn, 1995. – Kline: © VAGA Inc., New York. – Kokoschka: © VG Bild-Kunst, Bonn, 1995. – Kooning: © VG Bild-Kunst, Bonn, 1995. – Kupka: © VG Bild-Kunst, Bonn, 1995. – Lam: © VG Bild-Kunst, Bonn, 1995. – Léger: © VG Bild-Kunst, Bonn, 1995. – Lichtenstein: © VG Bild-Kunst, Bonn, 1995. – Liebermann: © Marianne Feilchenfeldt, Zurich. – Lindner: © VG Bild-Kunst, Bonn, 1995. – Lissitzky: © VG Bild-Kunst, Bonn, 1995. – Louis: © Garfinkle & Associates, Washington. – Lüpertz: © Galerie Michael Werner, Cologne et New York. – Magritte: © VG Bild-Kunst, Bonn, 1995. – Marquet: © VG Bild-Kunst, Bonn, 1995. – Masson: © VG Bild-Kunst, Bonn, 1995. – Mathieu: © Georges Mathieu, Paris. – Matisse: © VG Bild-Kunst, Bonn, 1995/Succession Matisse. – Matta: © VG Bild-Kunst, Bonn, 1995. – Mirò: © VG Bild-Kunst, Bonn, 1995. – Moholy-Nagy: © VG Bild-Kunst, Bonn, 1995. – Mondrian: © 1995 ABC/Mondrian Estate/Holzmann Trust. – Morandi: © VG Bild-Kunst, Bonn, 1995. – Motherwell: © VG Bild-Kunst, Bonn, 1995. – Mueller: © VG Bild-Kunst, Bonn, 1995. – Munch: © The Munch Museet/The Munch Ellingsen Group/VG Bild-Kunst, Bonn, 1995. – Nay: © Elisabeth Scheibler-Nay, Cologne. – Newman: © Barnett Newman Estate, New York. – Nicholson: © VG Bild-Kunst, Bonn, 1995. – Noland: © VG Bild-Kunst, Bonn, 1995. – Nolde: © Donation Seebüll Ada et Emil Nolde, Neukirchen-Seebüll. – Oehlen: © Albert Oehlen, Hambourg. – Paladino: © Mimmo Paladino, Milano. – Pechstein: © Max Pechstein Communauté d'auteurs, Hambourg. – Penck: © Galerie Michael Werner, Cologne et New York. – Picabia: © VG Bild-Kunst, Bonn, 1995. – Picasso: © VG Bild-Kunst, Bonn, 1995. – Poliakoff: © VG Bild-Kunst, Bonn, 1995. – Polke: © Sigmar Polke, Cologne. – Pollock: © VG Bild-Kunst, Bonn, 1995. – Rainer: © Atelier Arnulf Rainer, Vienne.– Rauschenberg: © VG Bild-Kunst, Bonn, 1995. – Ray: © VG Bild-Kunst, Bonn, 1995. – Reinhardt: © VG Bild-Kunst, Bonn, 1995. – Richter: © Gerhard Richter, Cologne. – Rivera: © Kettenmann de Doniz, Mexico City. – Rosenquist: © VG Bild-Kunst, Bonn, 1995. – Rothko: © VG Bild-Kunst, Bonn, 1995. – Rouault: © VG Bild-Kunst, Bonn, 1995. – Ryman: © John Weber Gallery, New York. – Schlemmer: © Property of the family of Osker Schlemmer. – Schmidt-Rottluff: © VG Bild-Kunst, Bonn, 1995. – Schnabel: © Julian Schnabel, New York. – Schumacher: © VG Bild-Kunst, Bonn, 1995. – Schwitters: © VG Bild-Kunst, Bonn, 1995. – Severini: © VG Bild-Kunst, Bonn, 1995. – Signac: © VG Bild-Kunst, Bonn, 1995. – Slevogt: © VG Bild-Kunst, Bonn, 1995. – Soulages: © VG Bild-Kunst, Bonn, 1995. – Staël: © VG Bild-Kunst, Bonn, 1995. – Stella: © VG Bild-Kunst, Bonn, 1995. – Still: © Clifford Still, New Windsor. – Stuck: © Eva Heilmann, Baldham. – Sutherland: © VG Bild-Kunst, Bonn, 1995. – Taaffe: © Philip Taaffe, New York. – Tanguy: © VG Bild-Kunst, Bonn, 1995. – Tàpies: © VG Bild-Kunst, Bonn, 1995. – Thorn-Prikker: © Heirs of the artist – Tobey: © VG Bild-Kunst, Bonn, 1995. – Toorop: © Heirs of the artist – Tübke: © VG Bild-Kunst, Bonn, 1995. – Twombly: © Cy Twombly, Rom. – Utrillo: © VG Bild-Kunst, Bonn, 1995. – Vasarely: © VG Bild-Kunst, Bonn, 1995. – Vieira da Silva: © VG Bild-Kunst, Bonn, 1995. – Vlaminck: © VG Bild-Kunst, Bonn, 1995. – Vuillard: © Bild-kunst, Bonn, 1995. – Warhol: © VG Bild-Kunst, Bonn, 1995. – Wesselmann: © VG Bild-Kunst, Bonn, 1995. – Wood: © VG Bild-Kunst, Bonn, 1995. – Wols: © VG Bild-Kunst, Bonn, 1995.

The locations and the names of owners of the works are given in the captions to the illustrations unless otherwise requested or unknown to the publisher. Below is a list of archives and copyright-holders who have given us their support. Information on any missing or erroneous details will be welcomed by the publisher. The numbers given refer to the pages of the book, the abbreviations a = above, b = below.

Antella (Firenze), Scala Istituto Grafico Editoriale S.p.A.: 40. – Basle, Öffentliche Kunstsammlung Basel, Kunstmuseum: 599a. – Berlin, Archiv für Kunst and Geschichte: 36b, 39, 44b, 54, 78, 118.f., 122, 144a, 203b, 204, 246a, 533a. – Bottrop, Dr. U. Schumacher: 643b. – Città del Vaticano, Monumenti Musei e Gallerie Pontificie (Photo: A. Bracchetti/ P. Zigrossi): 168f. – Ecublens, Archiv André Held: 242a, 243, 305a, 315a, 320b, 321a, 322a, 324a, 332a, 332b, 349b, 355, 365b, 423a, 424b, 437, 442b, 443a, 444f., 449, 495, 501b, 502b, 509b, 510, 517a, 521b, 523, 524a, 572a, 602b, 638a. – Florence, Raffaello Bencini: 94f. – Graz, Akademische Druck- et Verlagsanstalt: 27a, 27b. – Cologne, Galerie Michael Werner: 674a. – Copenhague, Petersen: 461a, 461b. – London, Tate Gallery: 465, 466a. – Lucerne, Faksimile Verlag Lucerne: 62b, 63, 64a, 64b. – Milano, Gruppo Editoriale Fabbri: 29, 50f., 100f., 108a, 110b, 113b, 115, 117a, 117b, 133, 161b, 164a, 166a, 166b, 171a, 171b, 183b, 184a, 196a, 197a, 200a, 202a, 202b, 225a, 226b, 231b, 233b, 235a, 238a, 239a, 239b, 241b, 246b, 248a, 252b, 253b, 262b, 265a, 290a, 295a, 298a, 299b, 306a, 316a, 333, 351, 354a, 354b, 359, 360a, 364, 365a, 367a, 367b, 368b, 370a, 370b, 373a, 374b, 376a, 376b, 378b, 388a, 391a, 426, 427b, 434a, 443a, 454b, 462b, 463a, 463b, 530a, 530b, 532a, 538a, 538b, 641b. – Munich, Archiv Alexander Koch: 58b, 76a, 103a, 104f., 106b, 112a, 114a, 116a, 123a, 126a, 126b, 127b, 131b, 136, 137, 138b, 140b, 142a, 144b, 178a, 179a, 183a, 184b, 187b, 188a, 189a, 189b, 190a, 192a, 192b, 193, 194, 195a, 195b, 196b, 198a, 201a, 245a, 245b, 247, 249, 254a, 255b, 256a, 260a, 260b, 261, 263, 264a, 265b, 266a, 266b, 269a, 269b, 270b, 271, 272a, 272b, 287a, 288a, 288b, 289, 291, 293, 297, 298b, 300a, 300b, 301a, 301b, 302b, 303, 304a, 304b, 307a, 308a, 308b, 309, 310a, 311b, 314, 317a, 317b, 319a, 319b, 320a, 321b, 323a, 324b, 325a, 326a, 328a, 329a, 329b, 330a, 330b, 331, 334b, 353b, 356, 357a, 363a, 363b, 371, 373b, 374a, 375, 378a, 379a, 379b, 380a, 381, 383b, 384a, 384b, 385, 389a, 389b, 392a, 394a, 395a, 396b, 397a, 397b, 398b, 399, 400, 431, 434b, 440b, 441a, 450b, 451a, 451b, 453, 455a, 455b, 456b, 457a, 457b, 458b, 460a, 464b, 469, 492a, 493, 496a, 499, 500a, 502a, 503, 504b, 506b, 508b, 511a, 512a, 513a, 513b, 515, 516, 517b, 518a, 519a, 526b, 527a, 527b, 529a, 529b, 531a, 531b, 532b, 533b, 534b, 535b, 536a, 536b, 537a, 537b, 542a, 542b, 576b, 578b, 579a, 581b, 583a, 583b, 585b, 586a, 588a, 589a, 589b, 591, 598, 607, 609a, 641a. – Munich, Bayerisches Nationalmuseum: 70b. – New York, Pace Gallery: 660a, 666b. – Paris, Musée Picasso: 402, 544. – Peißenberg, Artothek: 2, 74b, 77, 127a, 143b, 182b, 185, 186, 191, 197b, 256b, 267, 305b, 310b, 323b, 372, 429, 459, 528a. – Prague, Národni Galerii: 45b. – Tokyo, Archiv Kodansha: 227, 559a, 559b. – Venise, Osvaldo Böhm: 120a, 120b, 377. – Weert, Smeets: 313. – Vienna, Kunsthistorisches Museum: 238b. – Vienna, Österreichische Galerie, Belvedere: (Photo: Fotostudio Otto, Vienna): 393a. – Zurich, Thomas Ammann Fine Art: 616, 659. –
The remaining illustrations used belong to the collections mentioned in the captions or to the editor's archive, the archive of the former Walther & Walther Verlag, Alling, the former archive of KML, Munich, and the archive of Benedikt Taschen Verlag, Cologne.

## Authors

INGO F. WALTHER, studied medieval studies, literary history and the history of art at Frankfurt am Main and Munich. Publications on the history of art and literature from the Middle Ages to the 20th century, including *Gotische Buchmalerei* (1978); *Sämtliche Miniaturen der Manesse-Liederhandschrift* (1981); *Codex Manesse* (1988). Editor of German versions of many international exhibition catalogues, including *Paris – Berlin* (1979); *Salvador Dalí* (1980); *Pablo Picasso* (1980); *Paris – Paris* (1981). Works published by Benedikt Taschen Verlag include the monographs on *Vincent van Gogh* (1986); *Pablo Picasso* (1985); *Paul Gauguin* (1988) and *Marc Chagall* (with Rainer Metzger, 1987); the catalogue of works *Vincent van Gogh. The Complete Paintings* (with Rainer Metzger, 1990), as well as the extensive monographs edited by him – *Pablo Picasso* (1992) and *Impressionisme* (1992). Walther is the editor of *Masterpieces of Western Art*.

HERMANN BAUER, doctorate 1955 with thesis on Rocaille. 1969–1973 Ordinarius for history of art at Salzburg University, from 1973–1994 in same capacity at Munich University. Co-editor and author of *Corpus der barocken Deckenmalerei in Deutschland*. Book publications include *Der Himmel im Rokoko* (1965); *Kunst und Utopie* (1965); *Kunsthistorik* (1976); *Rubens* (1977); *Holländische Malerei im 17. Jahrhundert* (1979); *Johann Baptist und Dominikus Zimmermann* (with Anna Bauer, 1985); *Kunst in Bayern* (1985); *Klöster in Bayern* (with Anna Bauer, 1985); *Barock* (1992). Contributed the chapter on the *Baroque in the Netherlands*.

EVA GESINE BAUR studied Germanistik, history of art, musicology and psychology in Munich. Post-doctoral collaboration in a DFG project at Munich University, then work as journalist. Editor and editor-in-chief of various journals. As a freelance journalist since 1989 she works for television and writes books on psychological subjects and art (*Meisterwerke der erotischen Kunst*, 1995). Contributed the chapter on the *Rococo and Neoclassicism*.

BARBARA ESCHENBURG, doctorate 1970 on the sculptor Christian Daniel Rauch; collaboration on catalogues of the Neue Pinakothek in Munich. 1980–1989 worked for Munich Stadtmuseum, since 1989 at Lenbachhaus, Munich. Publications include *Spätromantik und Realismus* (inventory catalogue of Neue Pinakothek, 1984); *Landschaft in der deutschen Malerei vom Spätmittelalter bis heute* (1987); *Der Kampf der Geschlechter. Der neue Mythos in der Kunst 1850–1930* (exhibition catalogue, Lenbachhaus, Munich, 1995), as well as essays on landscape painting and 19th century German art. In collaboration with Ingeborg Güssow contributed the chapter on *Romanticism and Realism*.

VOLKMAR ESSERS, doctorate 1972 with a thesis on the sculptor Drake. Since 1975 curator at the Kunstsammlung Nordrhein-Westfalen in Düsseldorf. Collaboration on educational exhibitions about Klee, Picasso, Max Ernst and Kandinsky. Book publications include *Johann Friedrich Drake* (1976); *Paul Klee* (1992); *Julius Bissier* (1993). Monographs on Pierre Bonnard, René Magritte, Max Ernst, Oskar Schlemmer, and others. Benedikt Taschen Verlag published Essers' *Henri Matisse* (1986). Contributed the chapter on *Classical Modernism*.

INGEBORG GÜSSOW, doctorate 1971, then various positions including one with the Bayerische Staatsgemäldesammlungen and the Haus der Bayerischen Geschichte in Munich. Publications on medieval goldsmith's art and museum pedagogy; exhibition catalogue *Kunst und Technik der 20er Jahre* (1980). In collaboration with Barbara Eschenburg contributed the chapter on *Romanticism and Realism*.

CHRISTA VON LENGERKE, doctorate 1980 with a thesis on the history of object representation from Antiquity to the present times. Works as a journalist and art critic; collaboration on books, catalogues and exhibitions. Since 1980 teaches history of art at Munich University. Contributed the chapters on *Impressionism, Art Nouveau and Jugendstil* and on *Contemporary Painting*.

ANDREAS R. PRATER, doctorate 1974 on Michelangelo's *Cappella Medicea*; postdoctoral work 1984 on *Licht und Farbe bei Caravaggio*. Since 1994 professor of the history of art at Freiburg University. Contributed the chapter on the *Baroque*.

ROBERT SUCKALE, studied at Berlin, Bonn, Paris and Munich. Since 1980 professor of the history of art at Bamberg University, since 1990 at the TU Berlin. Publications include *Die gotische Architektur in Frankreich 1140–1270* (with Dieter Kimpel, 1985); *Die Hofkunst Kaiser Ludwigs des Bayern* (1993). Has published a great number of works on European art and architecture between 1100 and 1530. Contributed the chapter on the *Gothic*.

MANFRED WUNDRAM, doctorate 1952 with a thesis on Lorenzo Ghiberti. 1955–1957 research at the Institute of Art History, Florence. 1967/68 member of the Harvard University Center for Renaissance Studies in Florence. 1970–1989 professor of the history of art at Bochum University. Publications include *Donatello und Nanni di Banco* (1969); *Frührenaissance* (1970); *Europäische Baukunst: Renaissance* (1972); *Raffael* (1977); *Renaissance und Manierismus* (1985); *Florenz* (1993). *Palladio* (with Thomas Pape, 1988) published by the Benedikt Taschen Verlag. Contributed the chapters on the *Early Renaissance* and on *Renaissance and Mannerism*.